OLD HOUSES MADE NEW

OLD HOUSES MADE NEW

teNeues

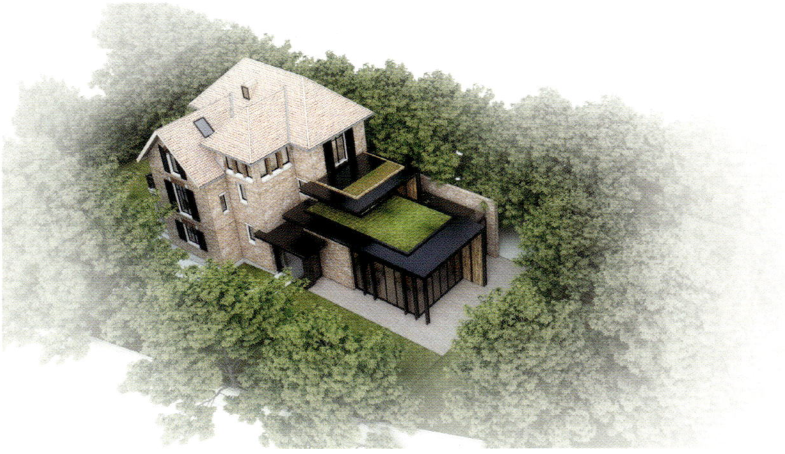

There are many reasons accounting for the increased awareness in recent times of the importance of rehabilitating buildings and residences.

First, the trend of protecting the cultural and artistic heritage of cities has extended to include the preservation of urban centers and buildings that constitute part of the identity of those who live there. We currently place a value on conserving our surroundings, and we increasingly understand that it is possible for the past and present to coexist if proper measures are taken. Many historic buildings that have been lost through disuse can be revived by adapting and repurposing them to meet the needs and standards of the present day—not only highlighting the new architecture but also reclaiming the significance of the original structure, as the old is born again in the new. On the other hand, the shortage of available building space in major cities makes rehabilitation an ideal solution.

Another important reason for undertaking a rehabilitation project is the desire to upgrade the residence's comfort and livability by adapting the space to our new way of living. This goes together with the quest for energy efficiency, since many of the measures employed to save energy—like thermal insulation, improved use of natural light, or natural ventilation—enhance residents' quality of life while representing cost savings and building updates. Qualities that clearly help in the recovery of one's investment.

In other cases, beyond the renovation of a residence, a project may seek to expand usable areas, sometimes by taking advantage of patio, yard, or even rooftop space, at other times by adding a new upper story or developing a basement. Such actions require considerable ingenuity and design sense on the part of the architect to produce a harmonious blend of old and new.

In the pages of this book, we will travel to different cities throughout the world where widely ranging rehabilitation projects have been carried out, from a functional urban apartment to a log cabin hidden away in a meadow to a building in the historic district of an urban core. A great variety of creative and ingenious solutions sharing as their common thread the opening of spaces and the attempt to achieve maximum exploitation of natural light. In all these structures, the architects' exacting work has succeeded in meeting or even surpassing the owners' expectations stated at the start of each respective project.

Es gibt viele Gründe dafür, dass in letzter Zeit die Renovierung von Häusern und Wohnungen eine neue Wertschätzung erfährt.

Zum einen erstreckt sich das Bestreben, das kulturelle und künstlerische Erbe der Städte zu erhalten, nun auch auf urbane Zentren und Gebäude, die wichtig für die Identität ihrer Bewohner sind. Wir legen derzeit besonderen Wert auf den Erhalt unserer Umgebung und darauf, dass Vergangenheit und Gegenwart in Balance gehalten werden können, sofern wir mit Augenmaß vorgehen. Viele historische Gebäude, die durch Vernachlässigung oder Umbauten verunstaltet wurden, können durch die Anpassung an heutige Bedürfnisse und Standards wiedererweckt werden. Wenn nicht nur die neuen architektonischen Elemente betont werden, sondern auch die ursprüngliche Bausubstanz wieder sichtbar gemacht wird, kann das Alte im Neuen fortleben. Zugleich bieten sich Renovierungen als ideale Lösung in Großstädten an, in denen ein Mangel an bebaubaren Flächen herrscht.

Ein weiterer wichtiger Grund für Renovierungen ist es, Komfort und Lebensqualität von Häusern und Wohnungen zu steigern, indem sie heutigen Wohnbedürfnissen angepasst werden. Dies geht vielfach einher mit dem Wunsch nach höherer Energieeffizienz: Viele Maßnahmen, durch die sich Energie sparen lässt - wie Wärmedämmung oder bessere Ausnutzung natürlichen Lichts und natürlicher Belüftung - verbessern die Lebensqualität und führen gleichzeitig zu Kosteneinsparungen und einer Wertsteigerung der Immobilie und sorgen so dafür, dass sich die Investitionen rasch amortisieren.

In anderen Fällen geht es bei der Renovierung der Häuser oder Wohnungen auch darum, die nutzbaren Wohnflächen zu vergrößern, indem Innenhöfe, Gärten und Dachflächen einbezogen oder Dach- oder Kellergeschosse ausgebaut werden. Die Maßnahmen fordern vom Architekten Einfallsreichtum und Gestaltungswille, damit alt und neu harmonisch ineinander übergehen.

Auf den Seiten dieses Buches reisen wir zu verschiedenen Orten dieser Welt, in denen vielseitige Renovierungsprojekte durchgeführt wurden - von einer funktionalen urbanen Wohnung über ein abgelegenes Holzhaus bis zum Baudenkmal in einem historischen Stadtkern. Den unterschiedlichsten kreativen und genialen Lösungen ist gemein, dass sie Räume öffnen und natürliches Licht hineinlassen wollen. Bei all diesen Projekten gelang es den Architekten, die zu Beginn des Projektes von den Bauherren geäußerten Erwartungen nicht nur zu erfüllen, sondern noch zu übertreffen.

La prise de conscience de l'importance de la réhabilitation des bâtiments et des habitats s'est accrue au cours de ces dernières années pour plusieurs raisons.

Tout d'abord, la tendance à préserver le patrimoine culturel et artistique des villes s'est étendue à la conservation des centres-villes et bâtiments, représentant l'identité de la population. Aujourd'hui, la préservation de l'environnement est valorisée en soulignant chaque fois davantage que la cohabitation du passé et du présent est possible si elle se fait de manière appropriée. De nombreux bâtiments historiques, tombés en désuétude, ont été réhabilités et adaptés aux besoins du client et aux normes actuelles. Leur nouvel usage a mis en relief non seulement la nouvelle architecture, mais aussi la valeur de leur structure d'origine, supposant une renaissance de l'ancien. Par ailleurs, la rareté des superficies disponibles dans les grandes villes fait de la réhabilitation une solution idéale.

La volonté d'améliorer les conditions d'habitabilité et de confort de l'habitat afin de les adapter au nouveau mode de vie est une autre raison d'aborder un projet de réhabilitation. Ceci est dû à la recherche de l'optimisation énergétique, car de nombreux travaux réalisés dans le but de gagner de l'énergie, tels que l'isolation thermique, le meilleur profit de la lumière naturelle ou encore la ventilation naturelle, améliorent la qualité de vie des personnes qui l'habitent et résultent également d'une économie et d'une revalorisation de l'habitat, supposant en fin de compte un retour sur investissement.

Dans d'autres situations, il a fallu, en plus de rénover l'habitat, augmenter la surface utile, quelques fois en tirant profit de l'espace d'une cour, d'un jardin, voire d'un plafond, et parfois, en ajoutant un nouvel étage à la partie supérieure ou en agrandissant un sous-sol. L'architecte a dû réaliser un travail d'inventivité et de conception conséquent pour réunir de manière harmonieuse l'ancien et le nouveau.

Au fil des pages de ce livre, le lecteur voyage dans les différentes villes du monde où ont été réalisés des projets de réhabilitation très variés, d'un appartement fonctionnel en ville à une cabane en bois, perdue dans la prairie, en passant par un édifice dans le centre historique d'une ville. Une grande diversité de solutions créatives et ingénieuses, avec comme lien commun : l'ouverture des espaces et la recherche du meilleur profit de la lumière naturelle. Le travail irréprochable des architectes a permis dans chacune d'elles de respecter, voire de surpasser les attentes des propriétaires au moment d'aborder le projet.

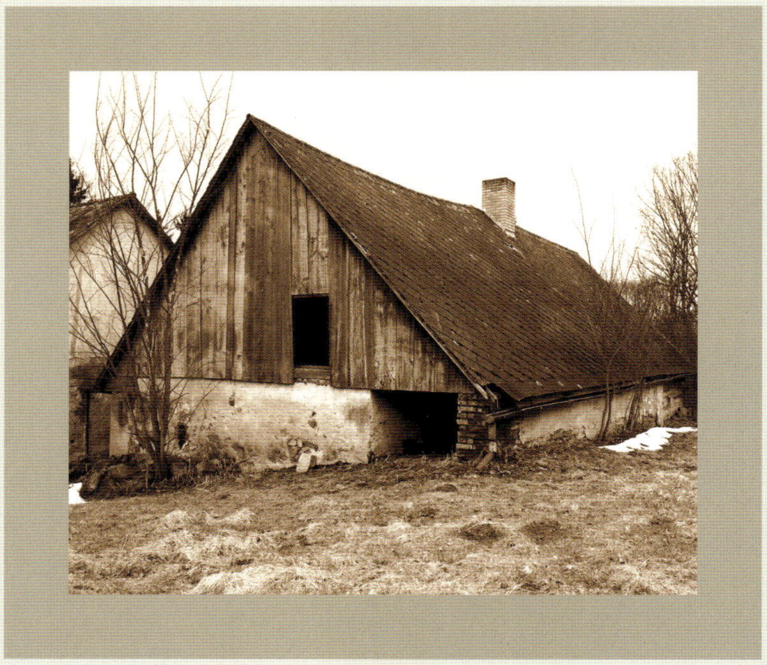

TWO HOUSES, DEERS, AND TREES

LENKA MÍKOVÁ

365 m^2 | 3,930 sq. ft.

South Bohemia, Czech Republic

Photos © **BoysPlayNice**

> Convert a log cabin and stone barn into two dwellings: a residence for the owners and a guest house

> Offer a high level of comfort without losing the original character of both structures

> Use building techniques and traditional materials

> Eine Holzhütte und eine Steinscheune in zwei Häuser verwandeln: eines für die Eigentümer und eines für Gäste

> Ein hohes Maß an Komfort bieten, ohne den ursprünglichen Charakter des Gebäudes aufzugeben

> Traditionelle Bautechniken und Materialien einsetzen

> Transformer une cabane en bois et une grange en pierre en deux maisons : l'une pour les propriétaires et l'autre pour les invités

> Apporter un niveau élevé de confort sans toutefois perdre l'essence originelle du bâtiment

> Utiliser des techniques de construction et des matériaux traditionnels

This rural dwelling, which originally consisted of a log cabin and barn arranged in L formation, lies secluded in a remote meadow. To preserve a harmonious connection to the natural surroundings, a decision was taken to make minimal exterior modifications, with major changes taking place exclusively inside the structures. This project was developed in a manner that relied on the logic and traditional building methods of the original constructions. The objective was to achieve a natural feeling rather than attempt to produce a perfect formal imitation.
The duality of the two structures serves to unify the entire project; their differing characters and original functions are reflected in the construction's repurposing and comprehensive approach. The cabin, designed as the owner's family residence, is more traditionally conceived. The barn has been executed as a secondary house: it serves as either a summer retreat or a guest house. Its general feeling is one of greater openness and lightness, and the architectural interventions are more daring.
The habitable space of both dwellings extends to the roof boards to highlight in each building an original specific feature: for the cabin, the sculptural volume of its traditional kitchen; and for the barn, the view through its doors. There is also a new addition in each of the houses, a simulated black "fireplace"—dominant in the barn, discreet in the house—that contains bathroom facilities.

Auf einer abgelegenen Wiese steht dieses Landhaus, das ursprünglich aus einer Holzhütte und einer Steinscheune bestand und ein L bildete. Um die harmonische Beziehung zu der es umgebenden Naturkulisse zu bewahren, wurde beschlossen, nur minimale Eingriffe im Außenbereich und somit die wichtigsten Veränderungen im Innenbereich vorzunehmen. Bei der Umsetzung dieses Projekts griff man auf die ursprüngliche Logik beim Bauen und traditionelle Bautechniken zurück. Ziel war, ein natürliches Gefühl anstatt einer formal perfekten Imitation zu schaffen.
Die Dualität der beiden Häuser vereint das gesamte Projekt; sein unterschiedlicher Charakter und seine ursprüngliche Funktion spiegeln sich in der neuen Nutzung und dem globalen Ansatz des Umbaus wider. Die Holzhütte wurde als Haus der Besitzerfamilie entworfen und traditioneller konzipiert. Die Scheune wurde als zusätzliches Haus konzipiert, das als Sommer-Lounge und Gästehaus dient. Das allgemeine Gefühl ist offener und leichter, die Eingriffe sind gewagter.
Beide Häuser besitzen einen Wohnbereich, der zum Dach hin offen ist, um eine ursprüngliche Besonderheit jedes einzelnen zu betonen – das skulpturale Volumen der traditionellen Küche in der Holzhütte und der Blick durch die Scheunentore. Zudem gibt es einen neuen Einbau in beiden Häusern, der einem schwarzen „Schornstein" ähnelt und in dem die Sanitäranlagen untergebracht sind, der in der Scheune dominant und im Haus diskret erscheint.

Perdue dans une prairie lointaine, cette maison rurale était initialement composée d'une cabane en bois et d'une grange en pierre en forme de L. Un minimum de travaux a dû être réalisé à l'extérieur afin de conserver la relation harmonieuse existante avec son cadre naturel, concentrant les changements majeurs sur l'intérieur. Pour réaliser ce projet, on a fait appel à la logique constructive d'origine et aux techniques de construction traditionnelles. L'objectif était de ressentir une sensation naturelle dans un lieu d'une imitation formelle parfaite.
La dualité des deux maisons allie tout le projet ; leur caractère différent et fonction d'origine se reflètent dans le nouvel usage et l'approche globale de la reconstruction. La cabane en bois est conçue comme une résidence de la famille propriétaire et se conçoit de manière plus traditionnelle. La grange a été conçue comme une maison supplémentaire : elle sert à la fois de salon d'été et de maison d'invités. La sensation générale qui s'en dégage est plus ouverte et légère, les travaux réalisés apportent plus d'audace.
Les deux maisons disposent d'un espace de vie ouvert jusqu'au plafond afin de mettre en lumière une caractéristique spécifique d'origine de chacune d'elles : l'impressionnant volume de la cuisine traditionnelle dans la cabane et la vue traversant les portes de la grange. Un nouvel élément a été ajouté dans les deux maisons, ressemblant à une « cheminée » noire dans laquelle se trouvent les sanitaires, dominante dans la grange et discrète dans la maison.

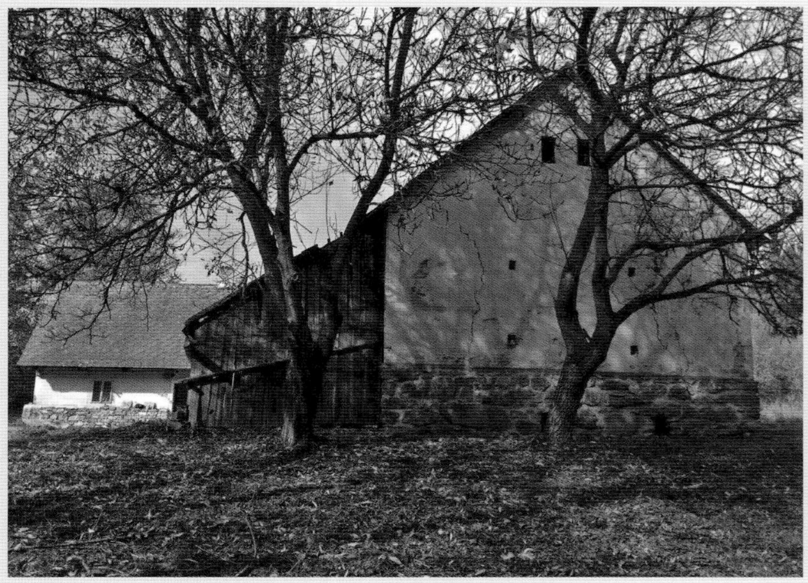
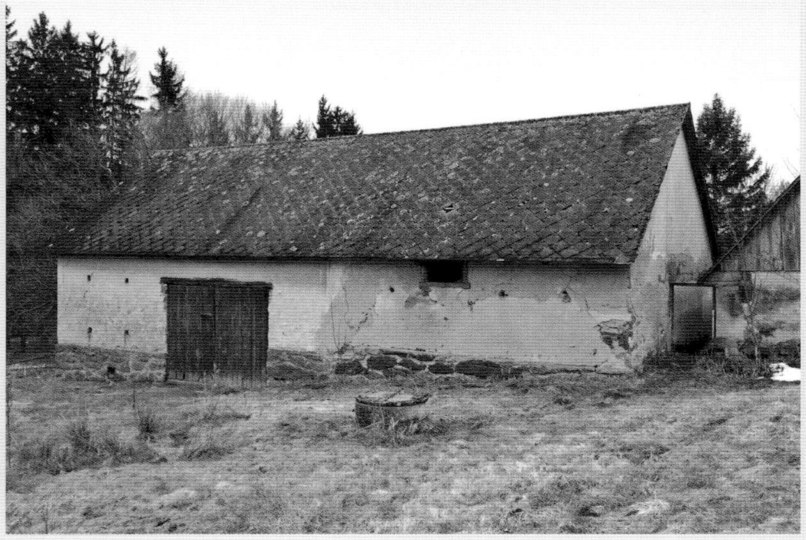
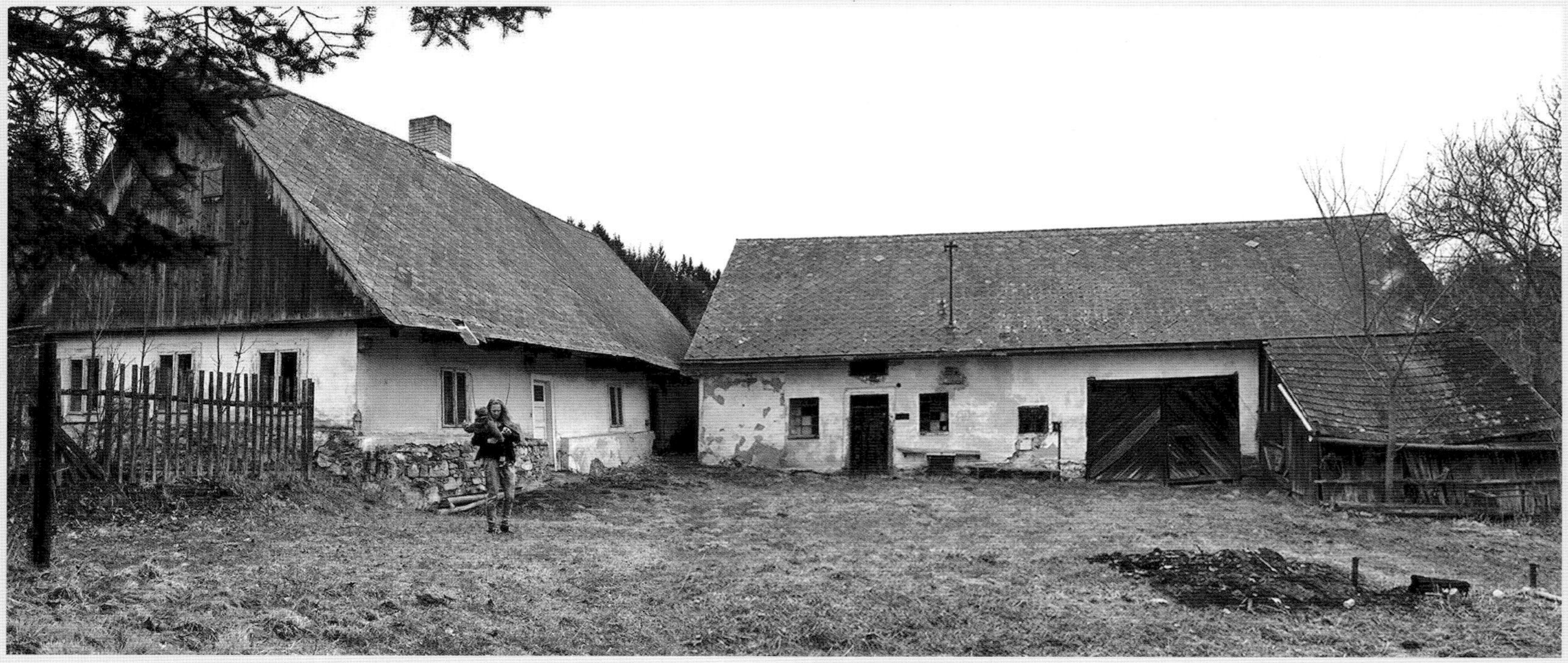
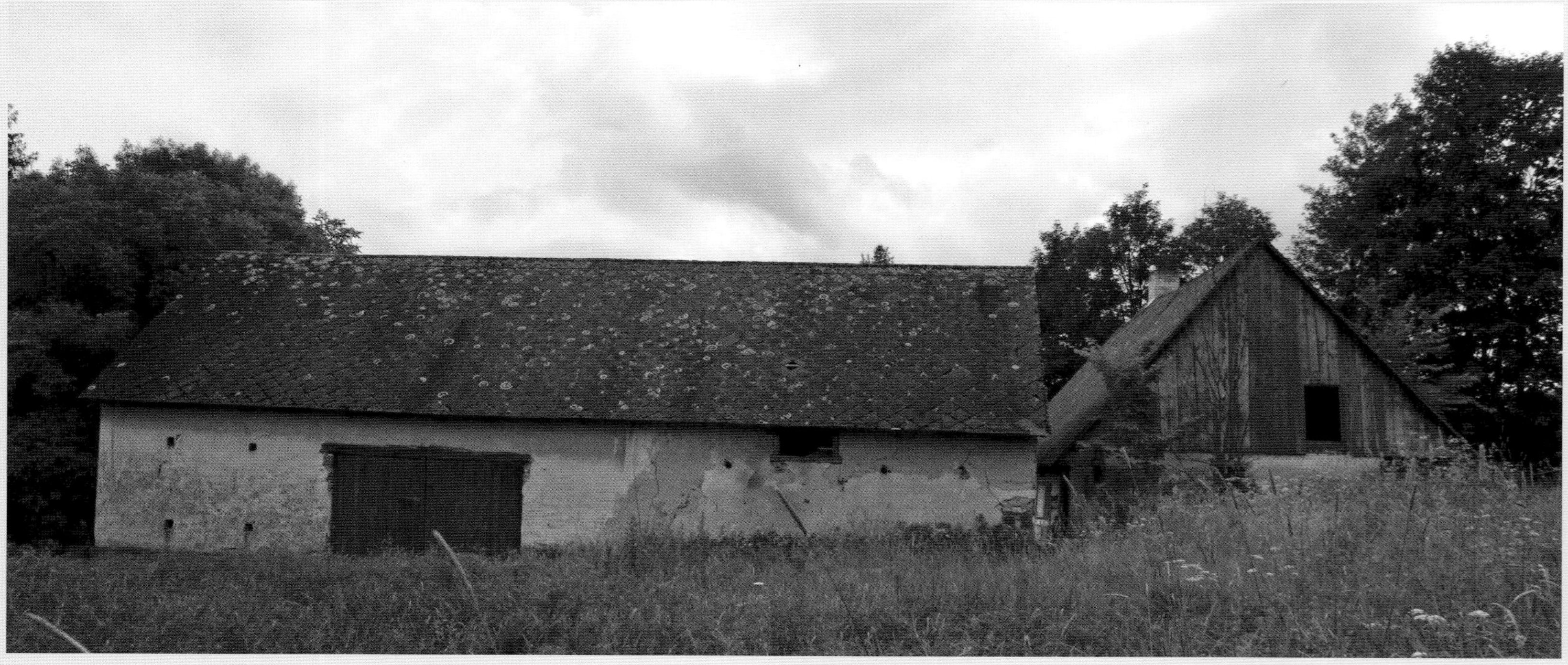

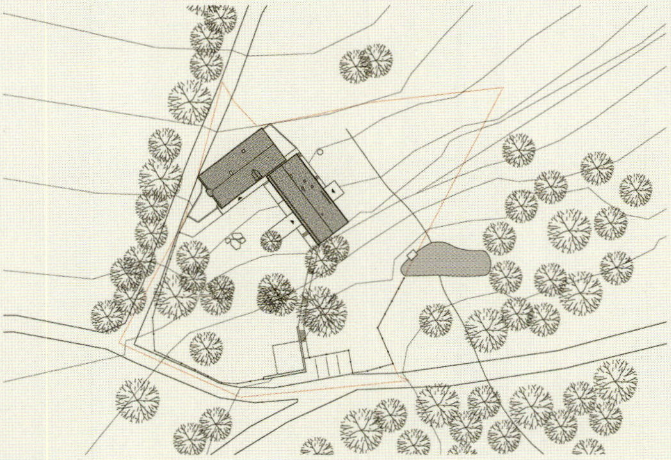

Site plan

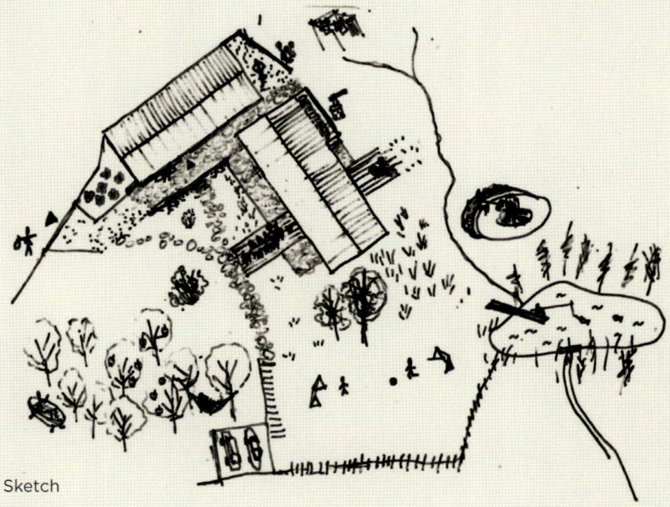

Sketch

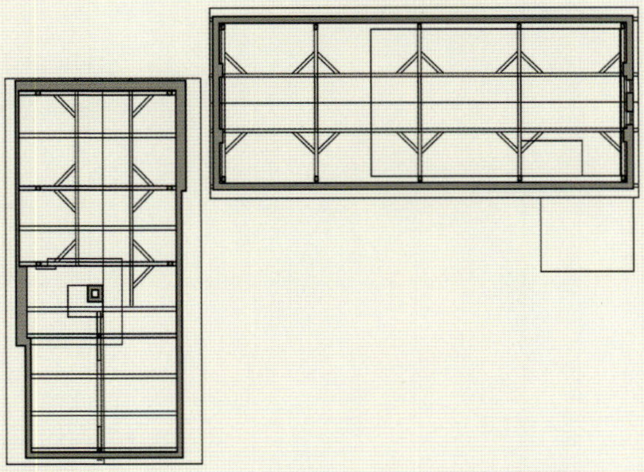

Existing first floor plan

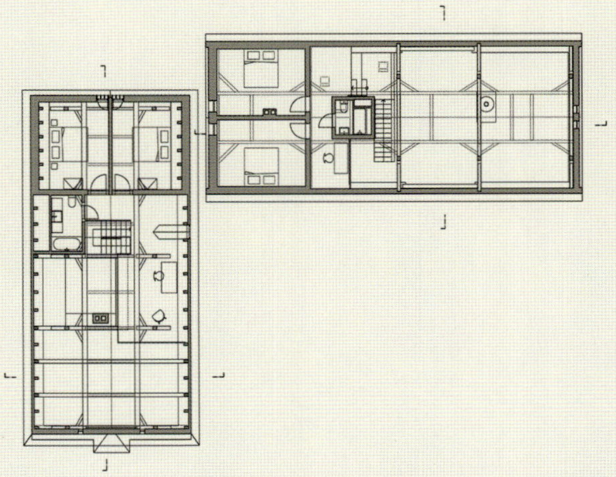

New first floor plan

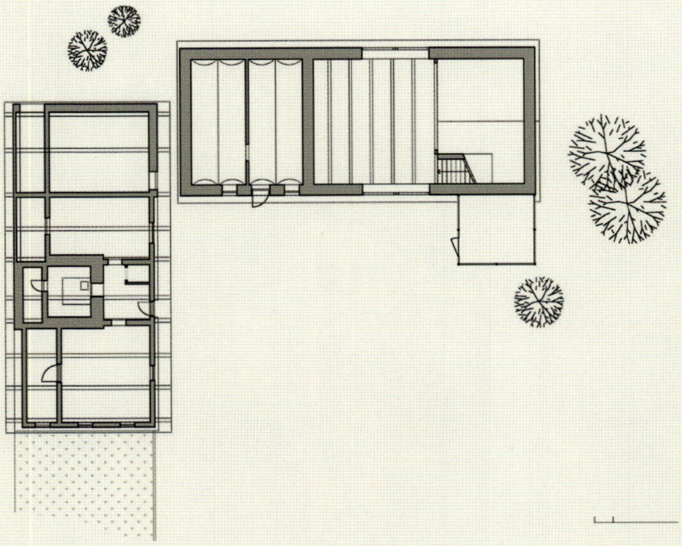

Existing ground floor plan

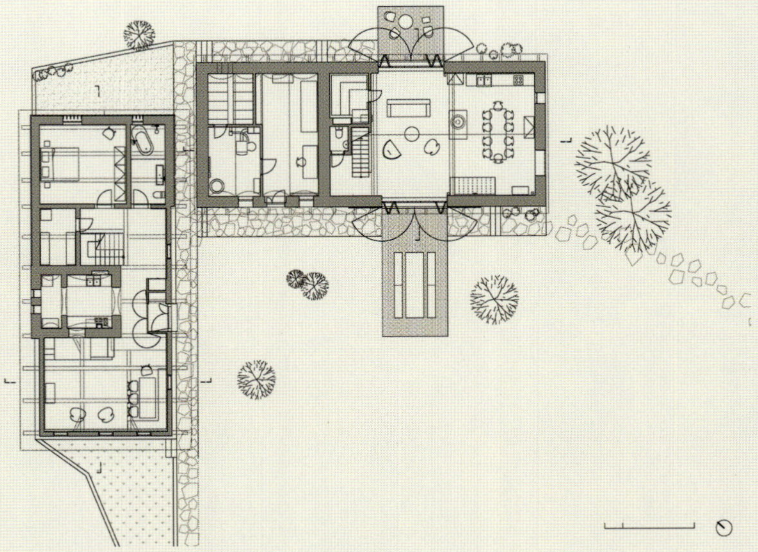

New ground floor plan

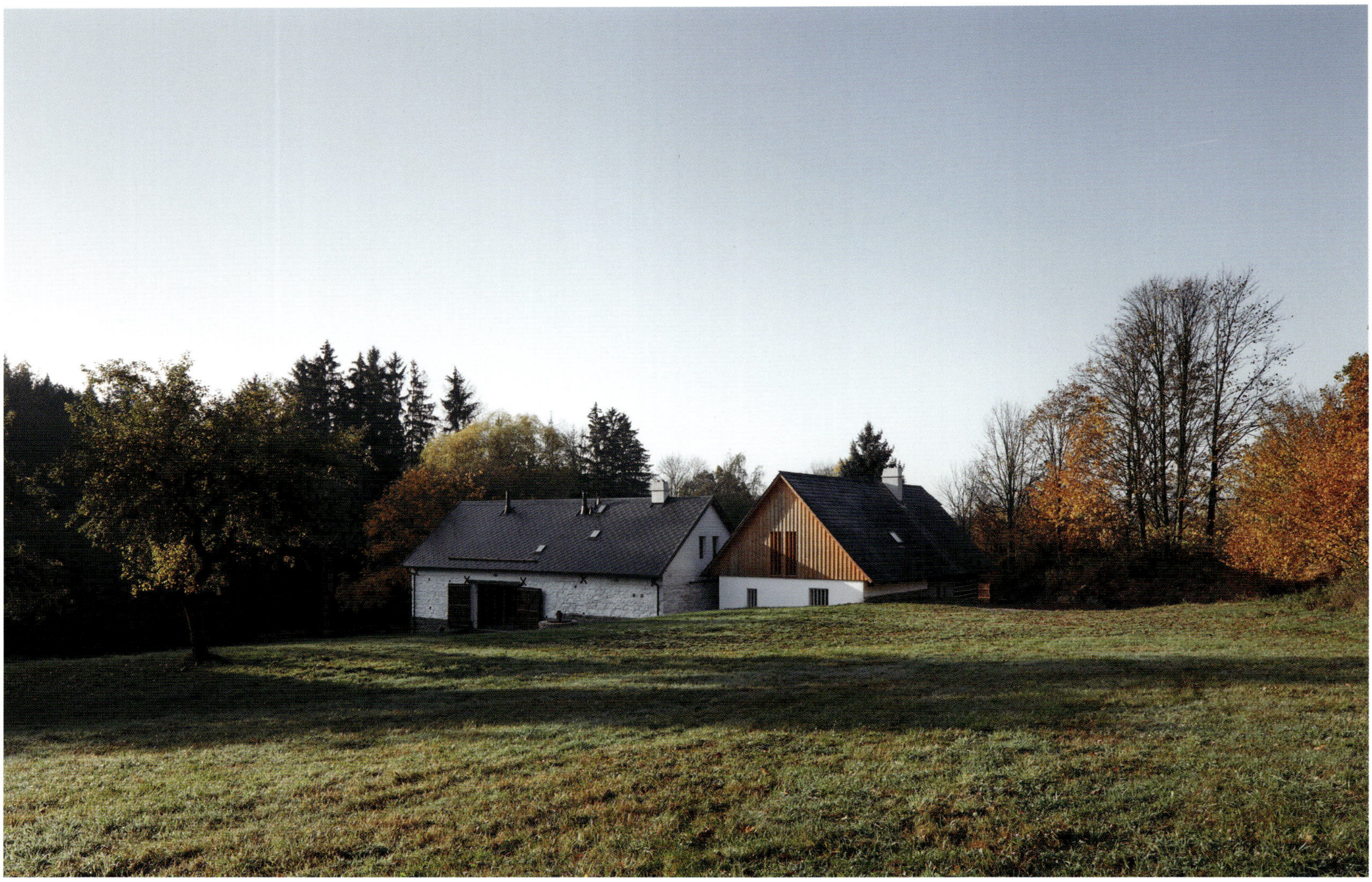

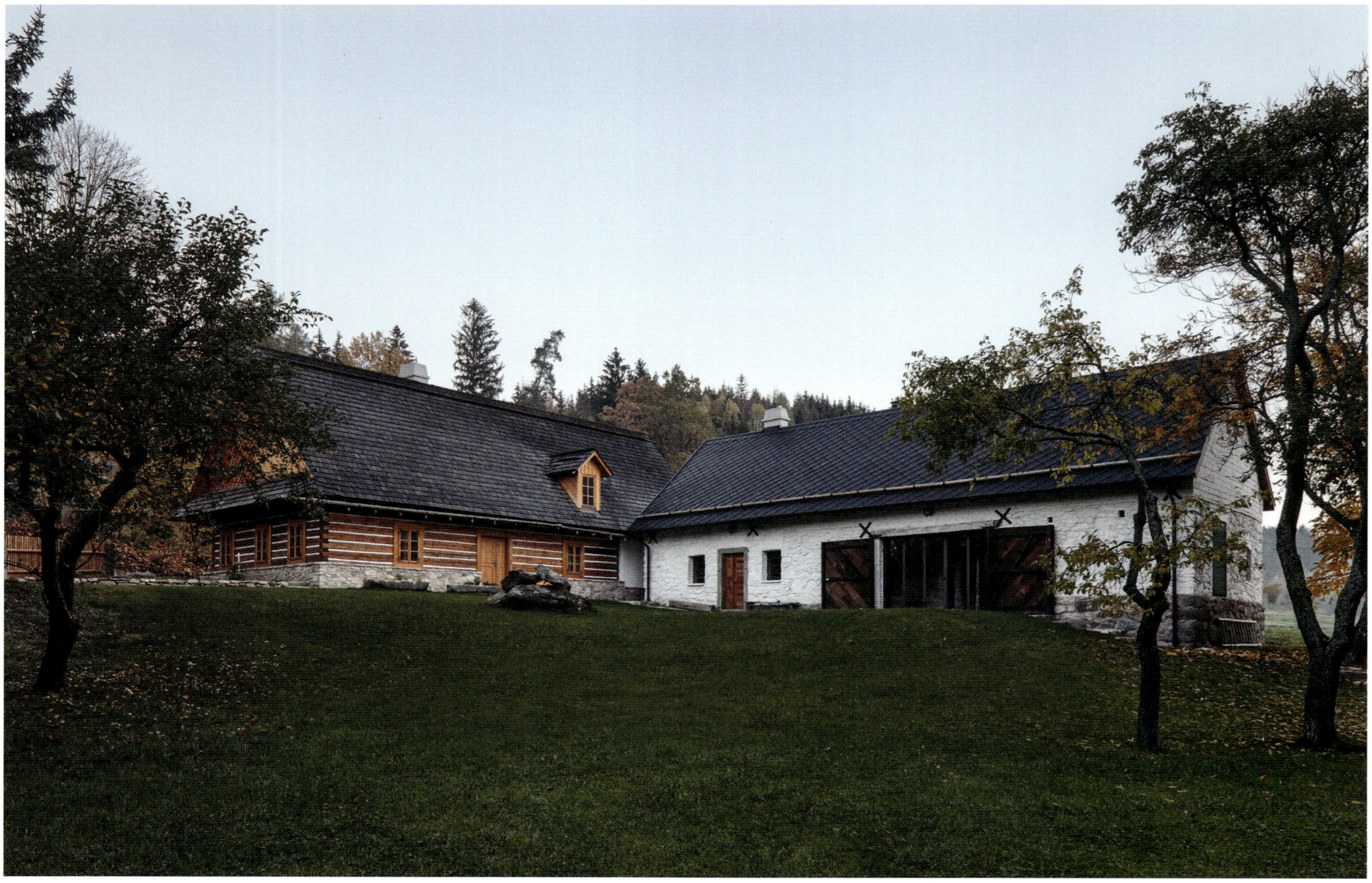

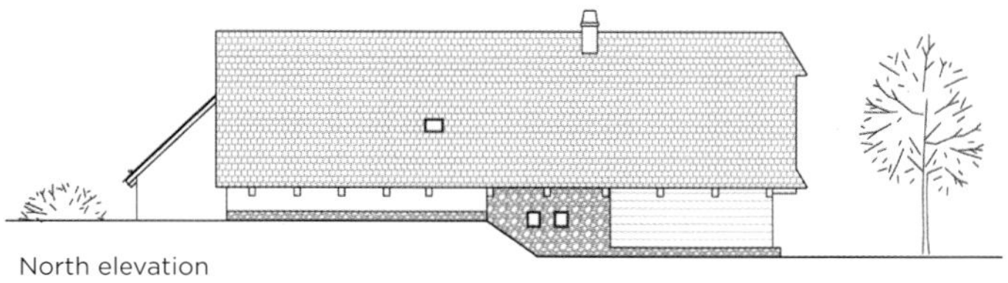

North elevation

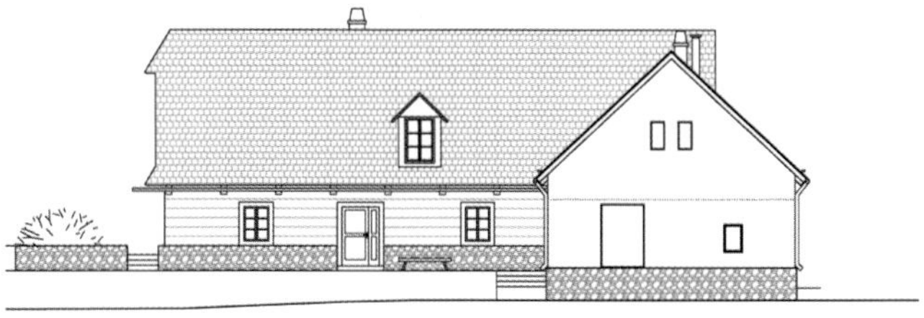

South elevation

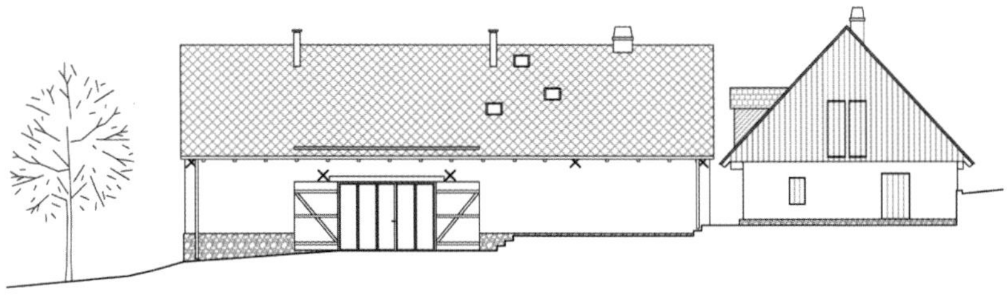

East elevation

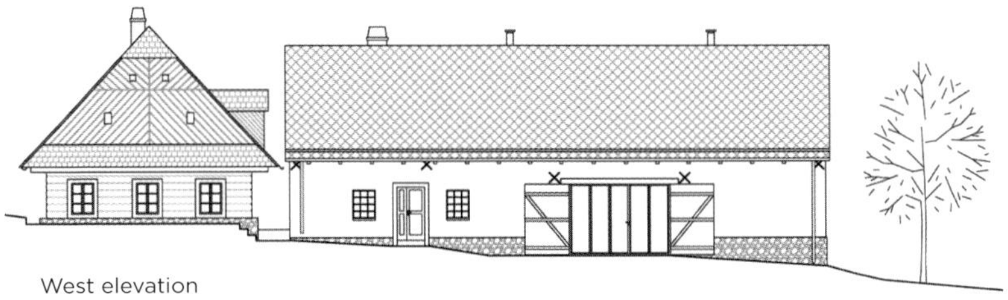

West elevation

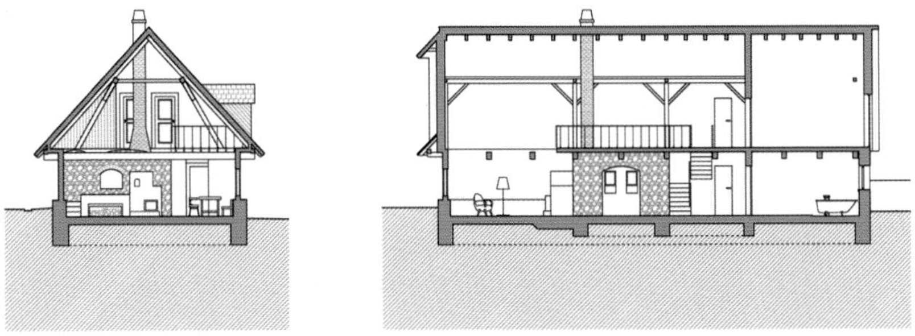

Cottage sections

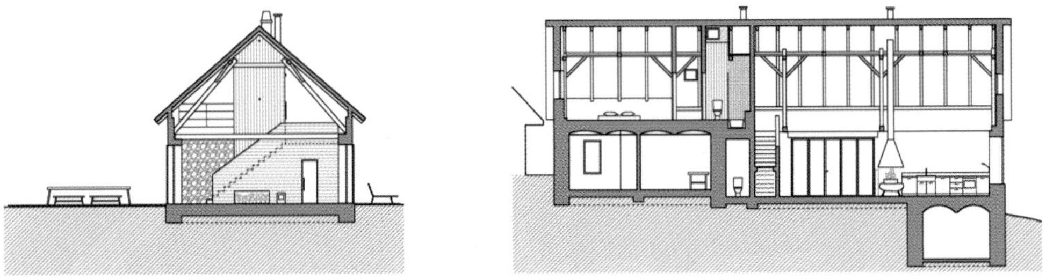

Barn sections

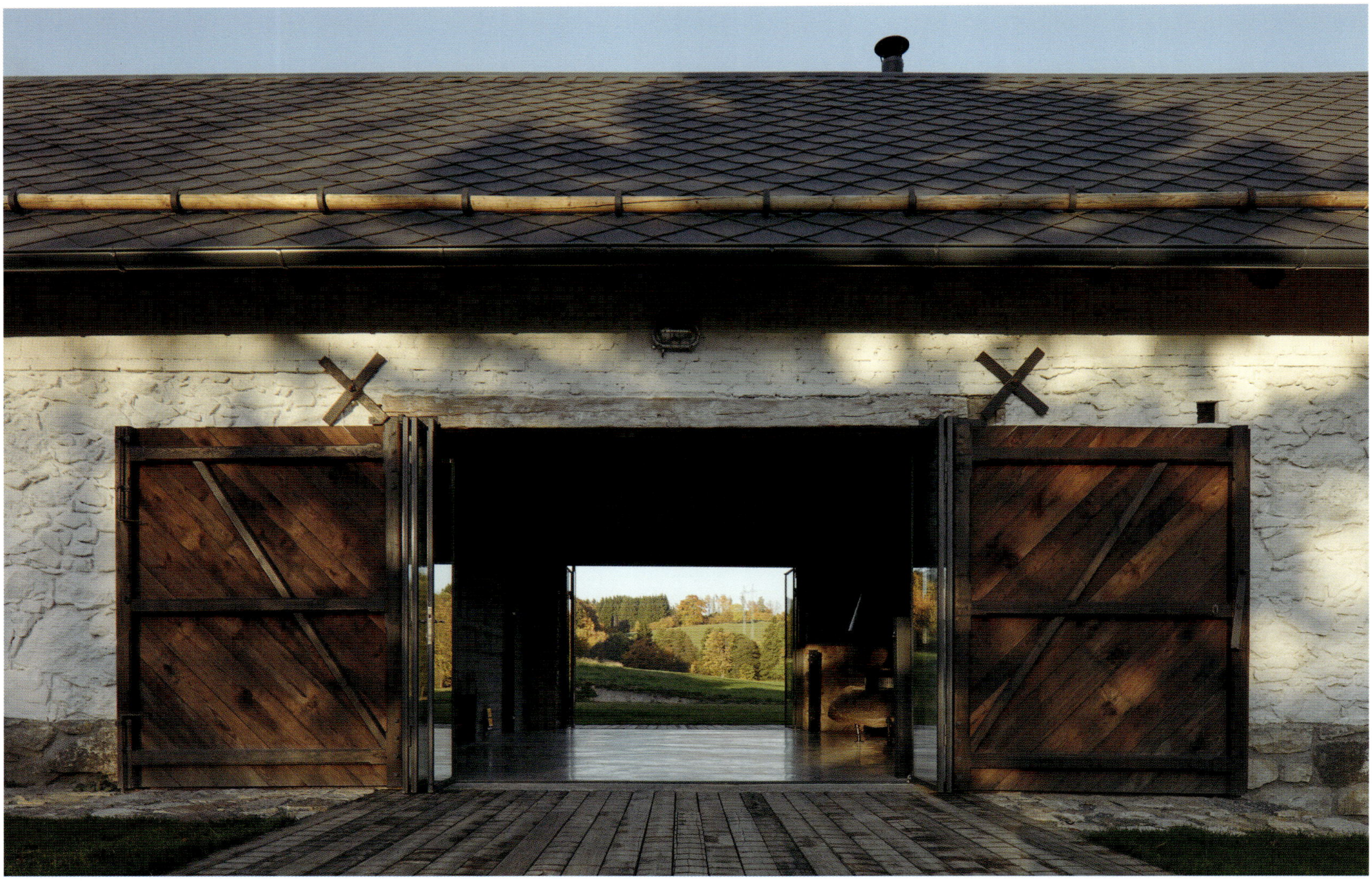

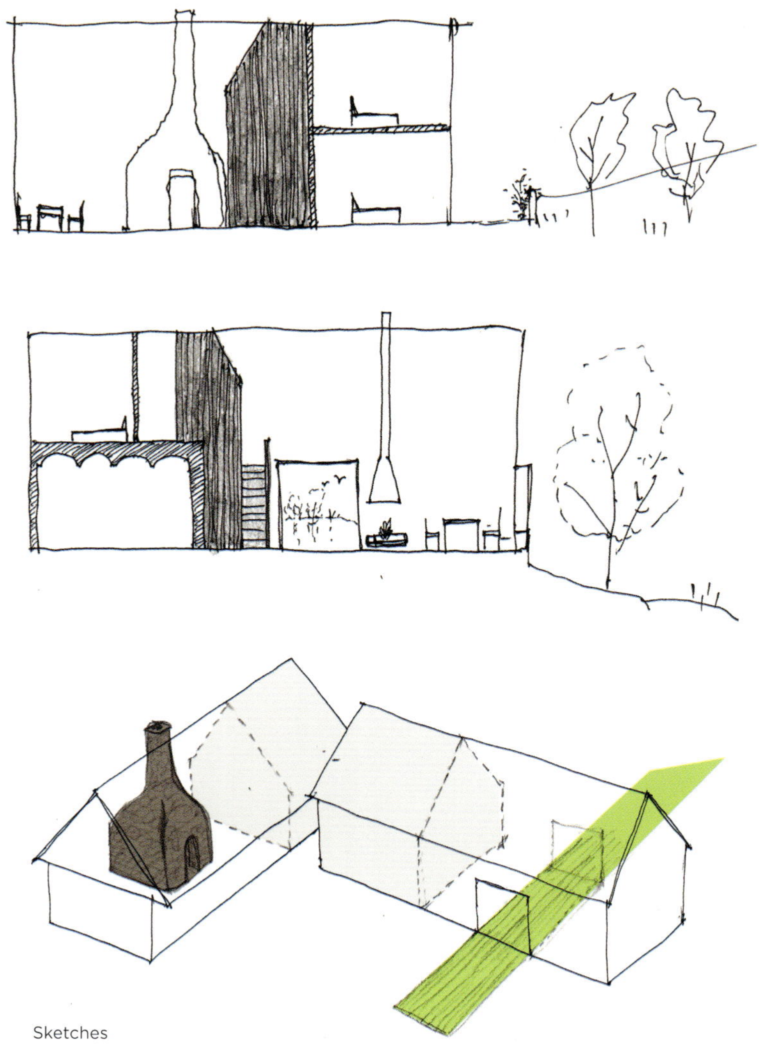

Sketches

The main habitable space extends to the terraces through folding glass doors, opening as well toward the trees by means of an enclosed patio. The space's new focus is the open fireplace created from an enormous rock quarried locally.

Der Hauptwohnraum dehnt sich durch Faltglastüren zu den Terrassen hinaus und öffnet sich zudem durch eine große, feste Umzäunung zu den Bäumen hin. Das neue Herzstück des Raumes ist der offene Kamin, der aus einem riesigen, massiven Stein von einem nahe gelegenen Hügel geschaffen wurde.

L'espace de vie principal donne sur les terrasses, accessibles par des portes vitrées pliantes et sur les arbres par une clôture fixe. La cheminée ouverte créée avec une énorme pierre massive provenant d'une colline proche est le nouveau cœur de l'espace.

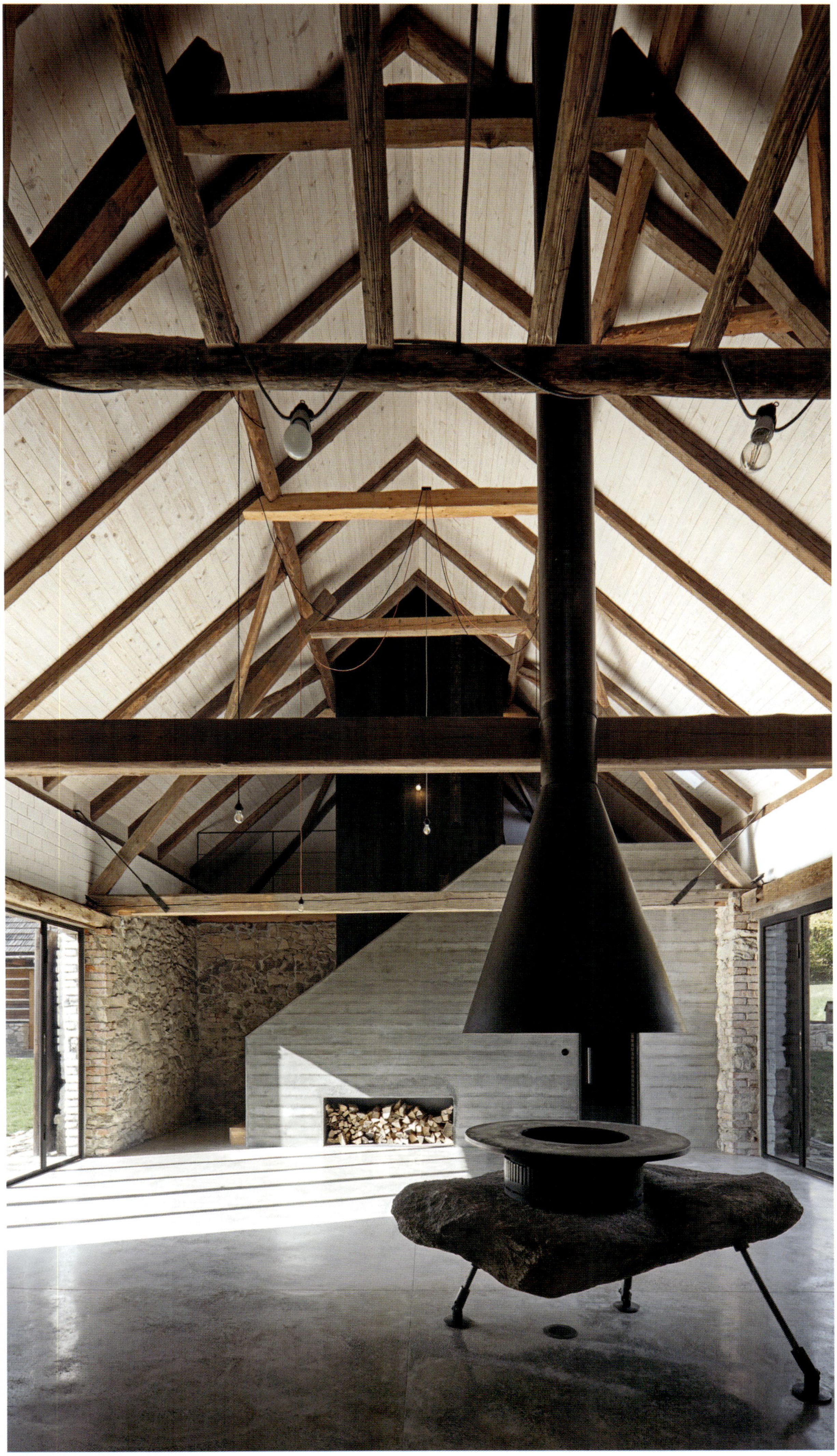

The original stone walls are complemented by a new concrete wall obscuring a staircase and a sauna. Above these walls, all interior surfaces are painted white, unifying the space and highlighting the original wooden ceiling.

Die ursprünglichen Steinmauern wurden durch eine neue Betonmauer ergänzt, die eine Treppe und eine Sauna verbirgt. Oberhalb dieser Wände sind alle Oberflächen in Weiß gehalten, um die ursprüngliche Dachkonstruktion aus Holz zu betonen.

Les murs de pierre d'origine sont complétés par un nouveau mur de béton qui dissimule un escalier et un sauna. Les murs de toutes ces surfaces intérieures sont recouverts de peinture blanche afin de relever le cadre originel de la boiserie du plafond.

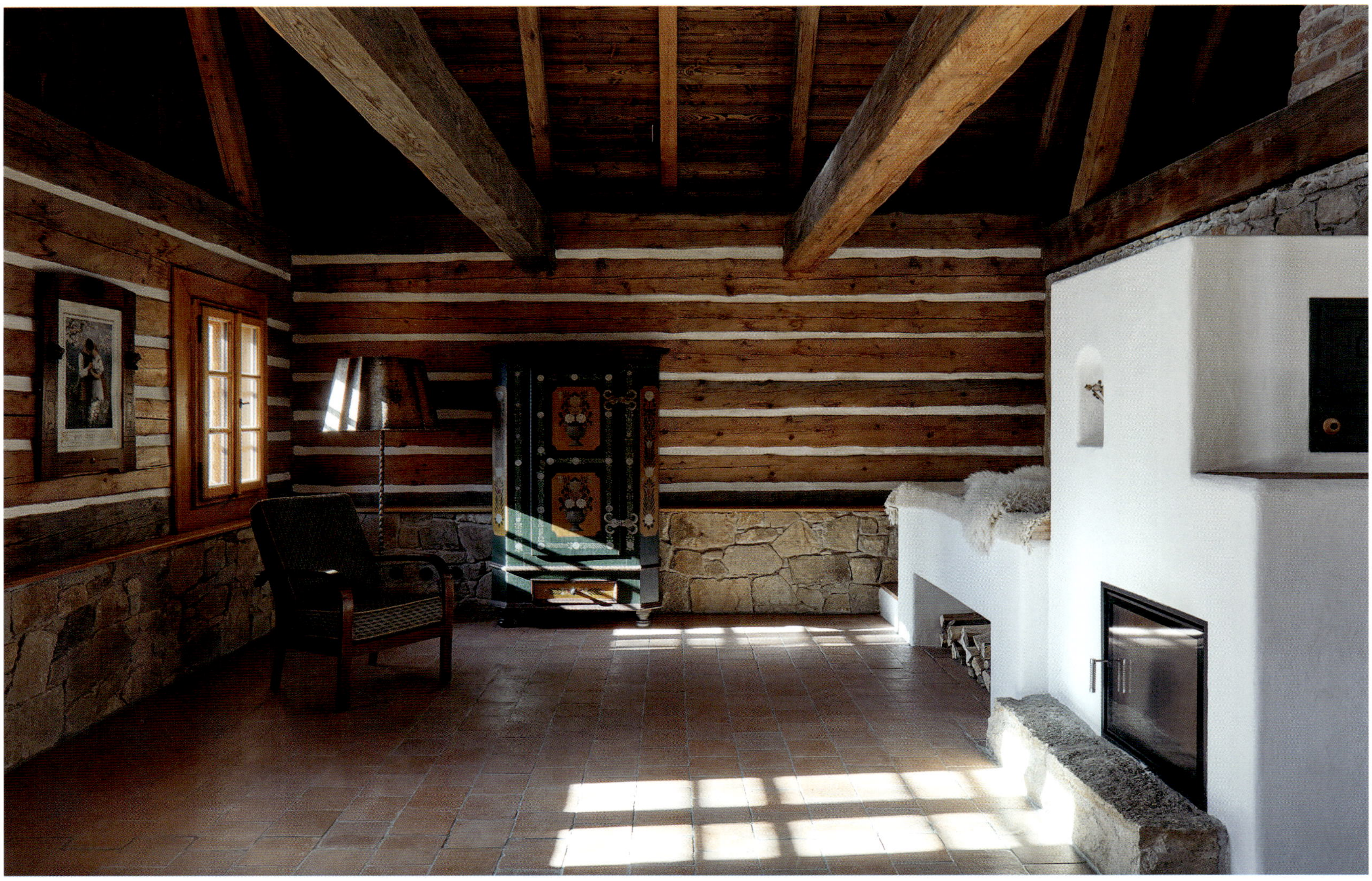

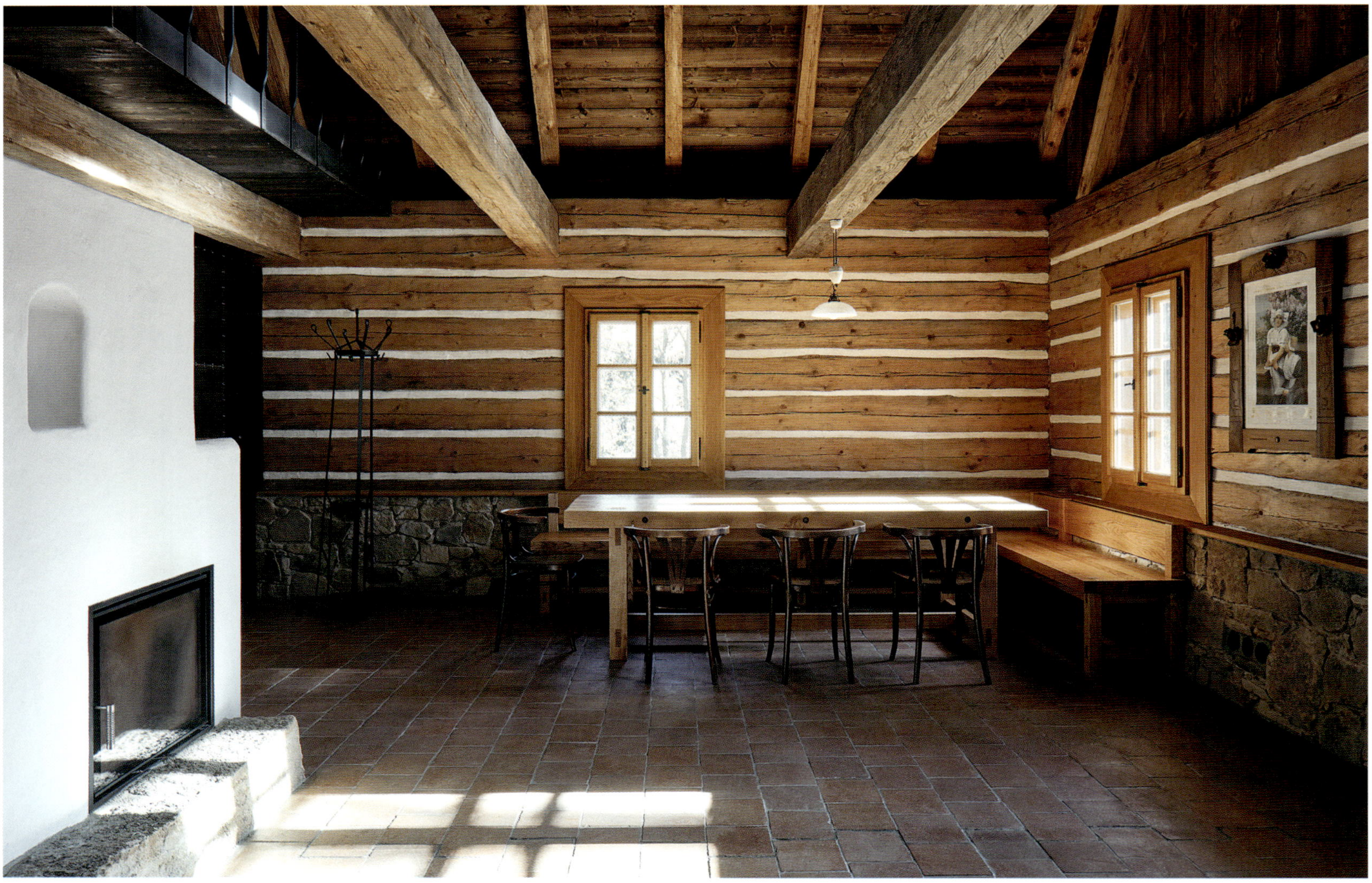

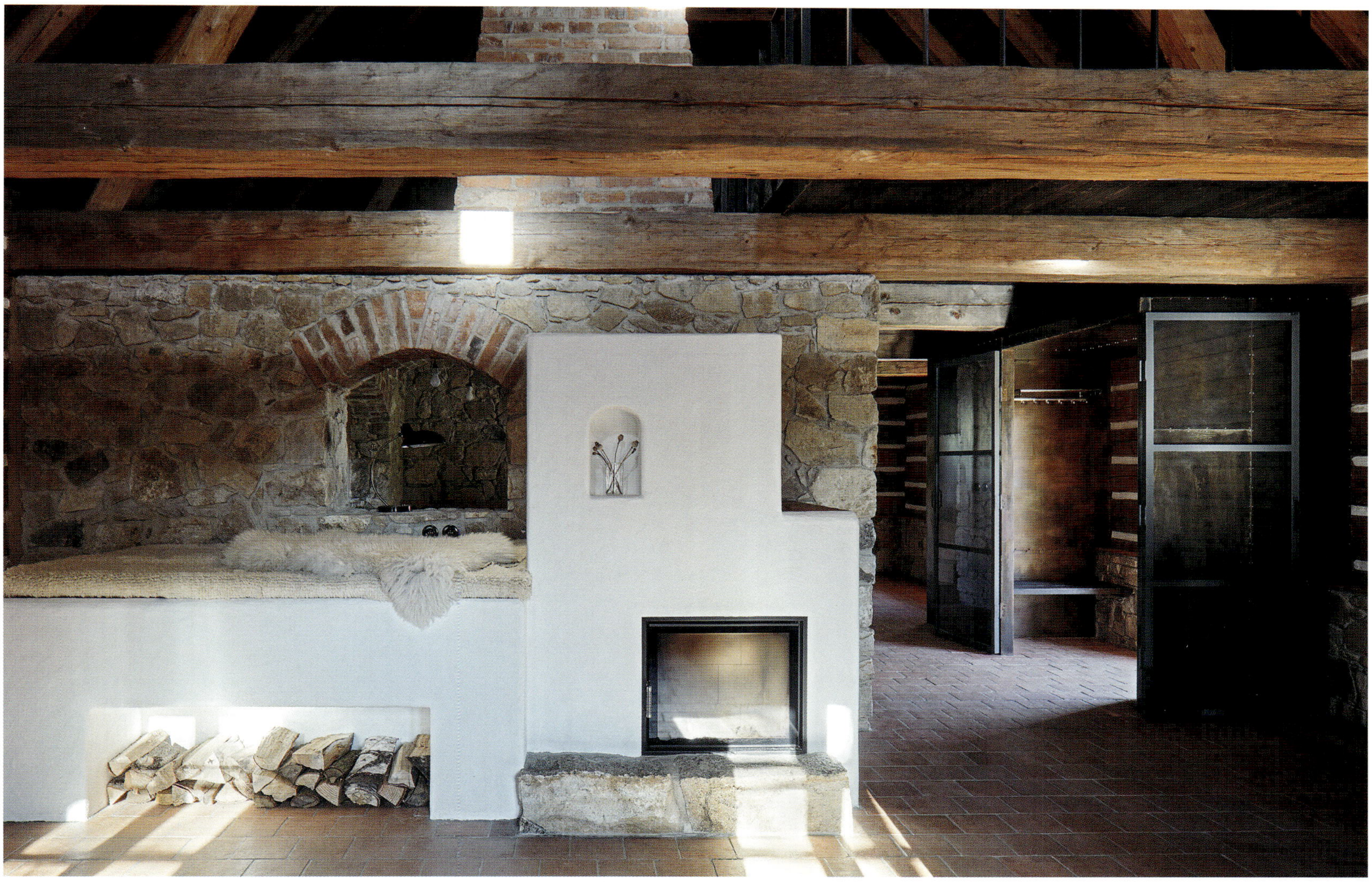

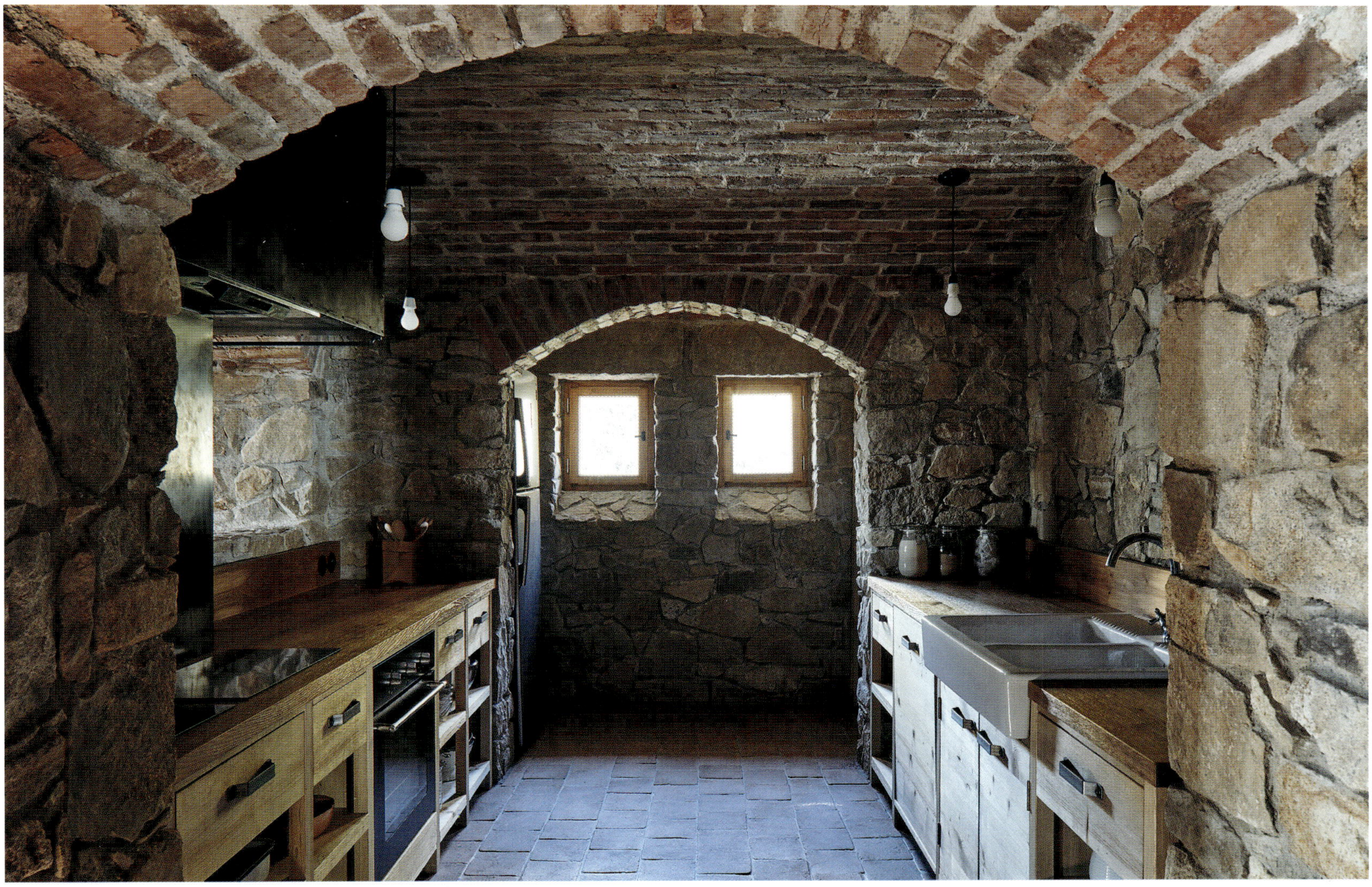

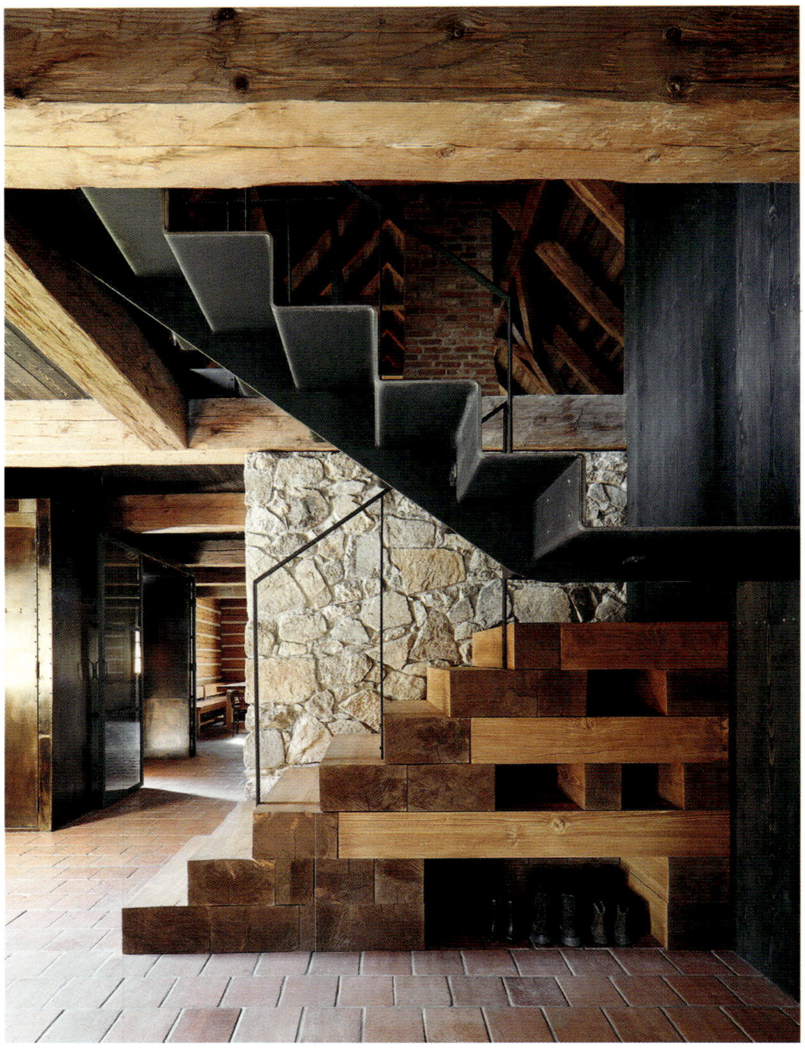

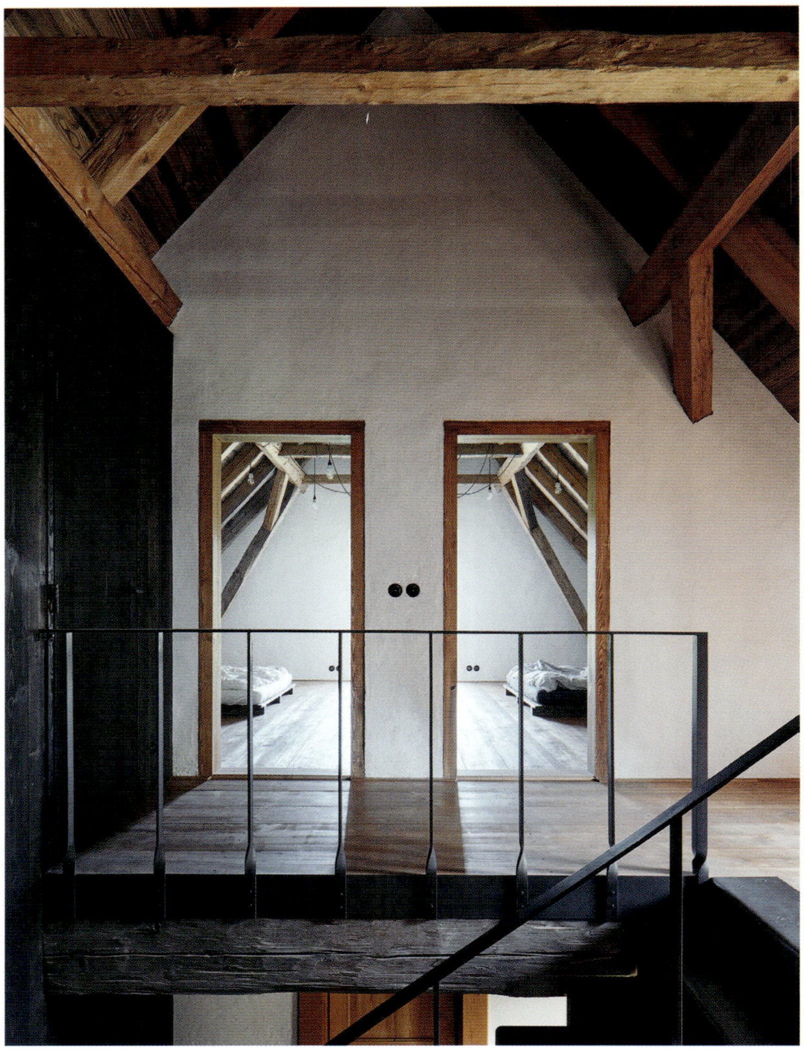

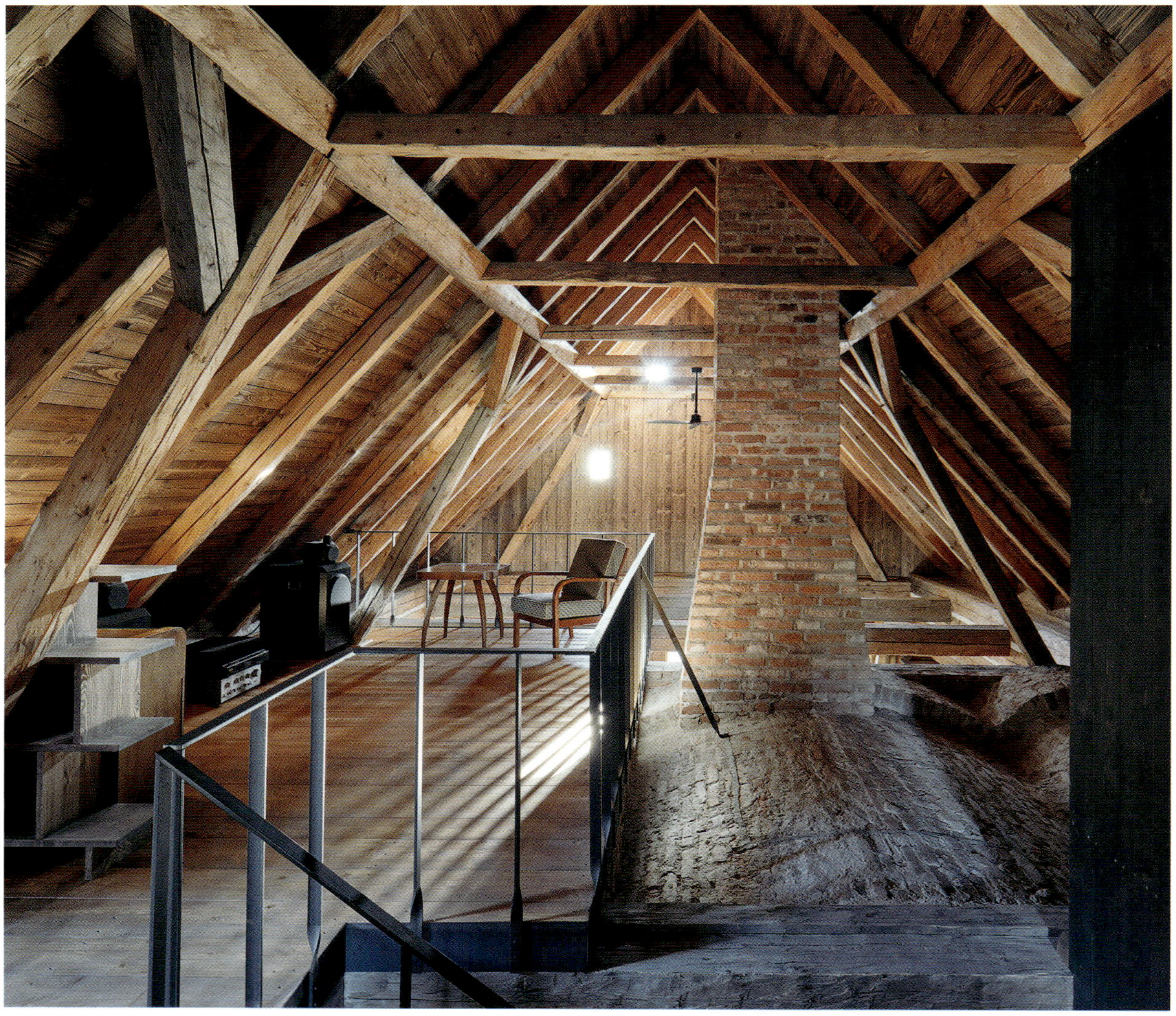

As in typical traditional houses, the interior remains quite dark, closed off, and intimate. Natural and handcrafted materials like wood and stone project an innate imperfection that becomes the project's main feature, kept in focus from the beginning of the design process.

Wie in den typischen Häusern der Gegend wirkt das Innere recht dunkel, verschlossen und intim. Von Hand bearbeitete Naturmaterialien wie Holz und Stein bestechen durch eine ursprüngliche Unvollkommenheit, die von Beginn des Designprozesses an den Hauptaspekt des Projekts darstellte.

Tout comme dans les maisons typiques vernaculaires, l'intérieur reste assez sombre, fermé et intime. Des matériaux naturels et artisanaux tels que le bois et la pierre confèrent une imperfection naturelle qui en font l'aspect principal du projet, pris en compte dès le début de la conception.

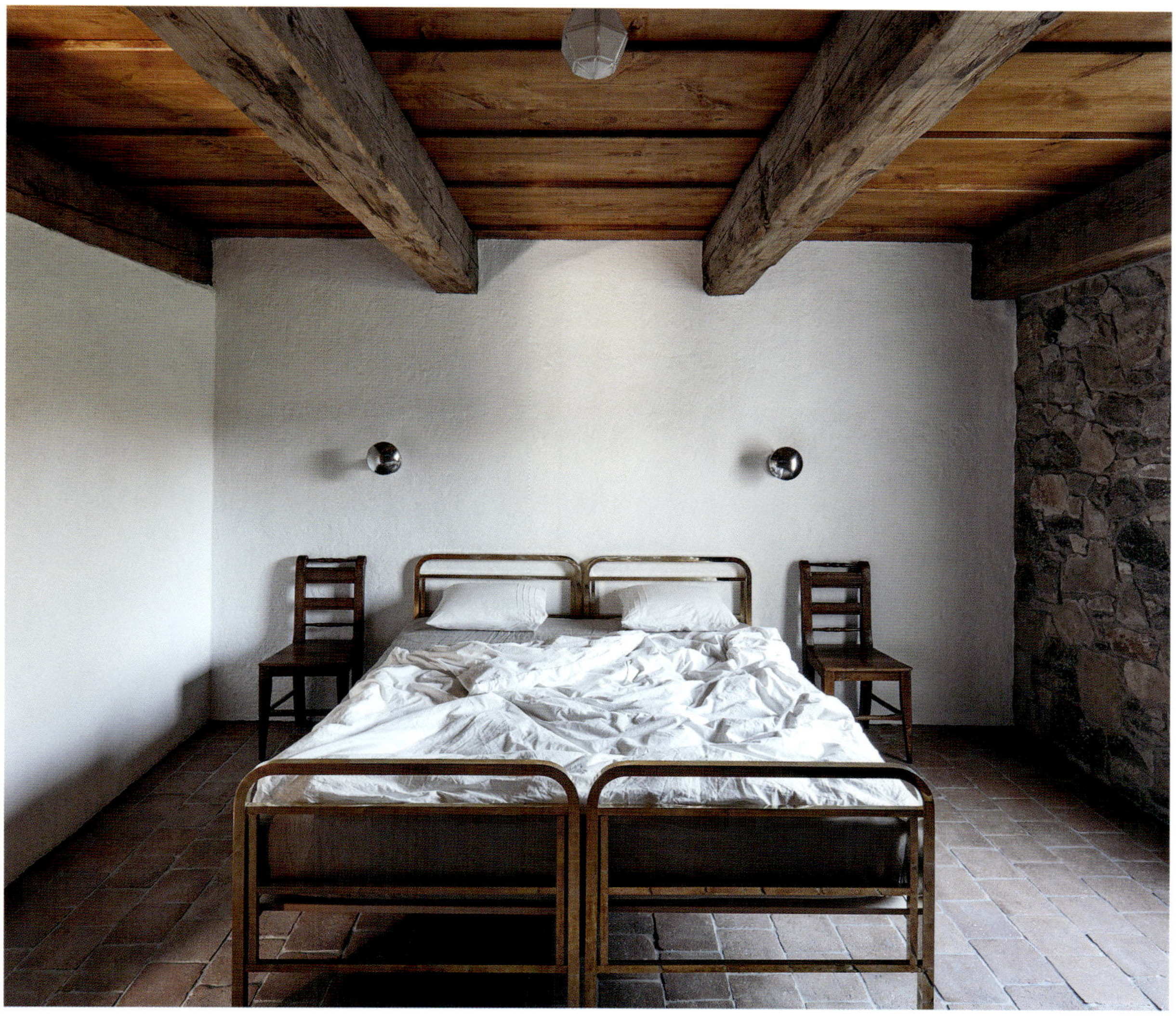

The bedrooms and bathrooms are minimally decorated and free of excess ornamentation, lending even more importance to the residence's structure and building materials.

Die Zimmer sowie die Bäder sind minimalistisch und ohne überflüssige Accessoires eingerichtet, wodurch Struktur und Baumaterialien des Hauses noch mehr an Bedeutung gewinnen.

Les chambres et les salles de bains ont une décoration sobre sans accessoire superflu, ce qui rehausse et donne plus de cachet à la structure et aux matériaux de construction de la maison.

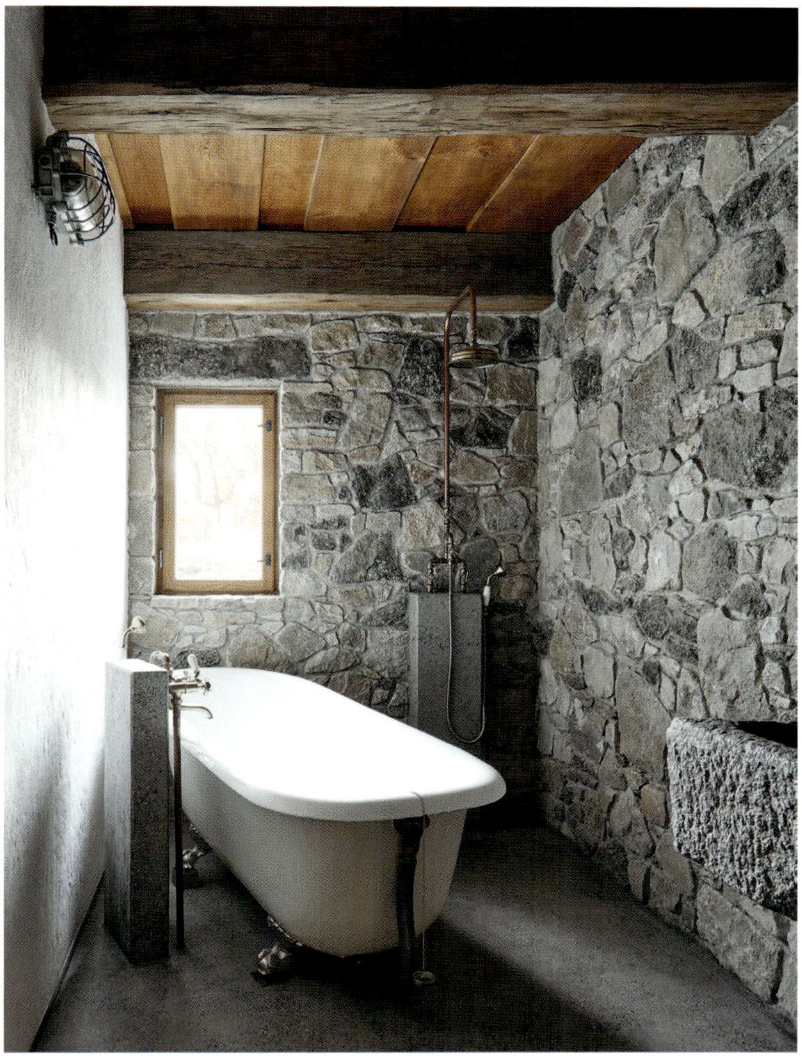

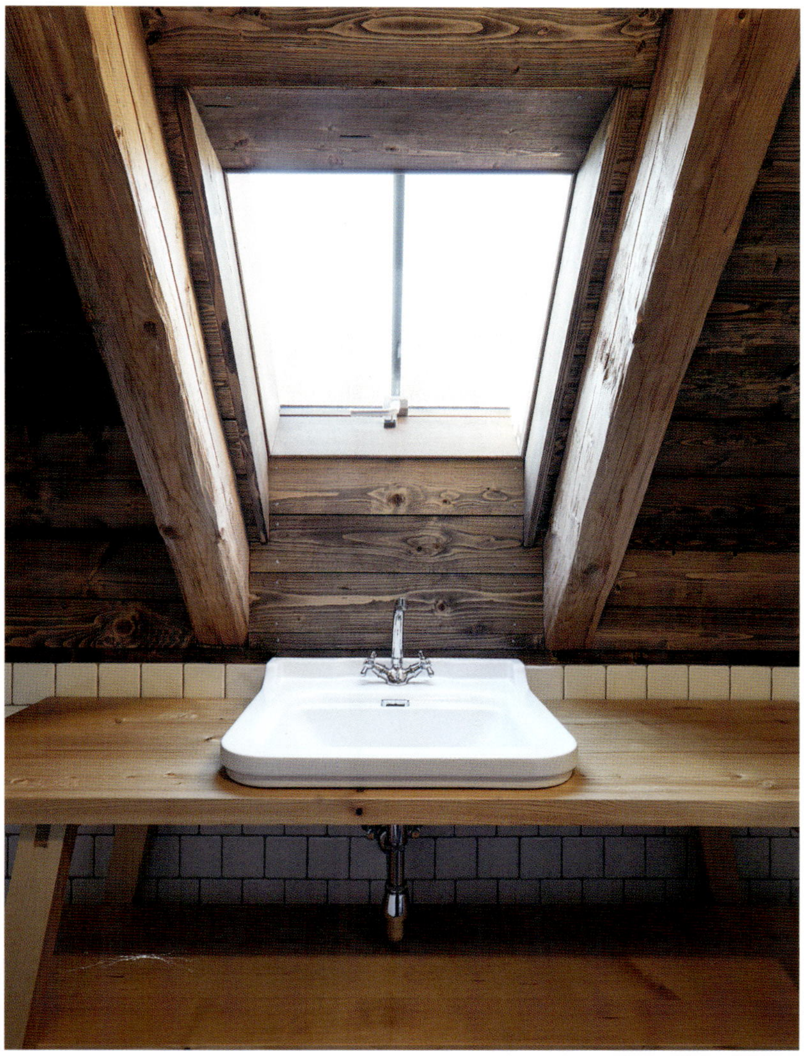

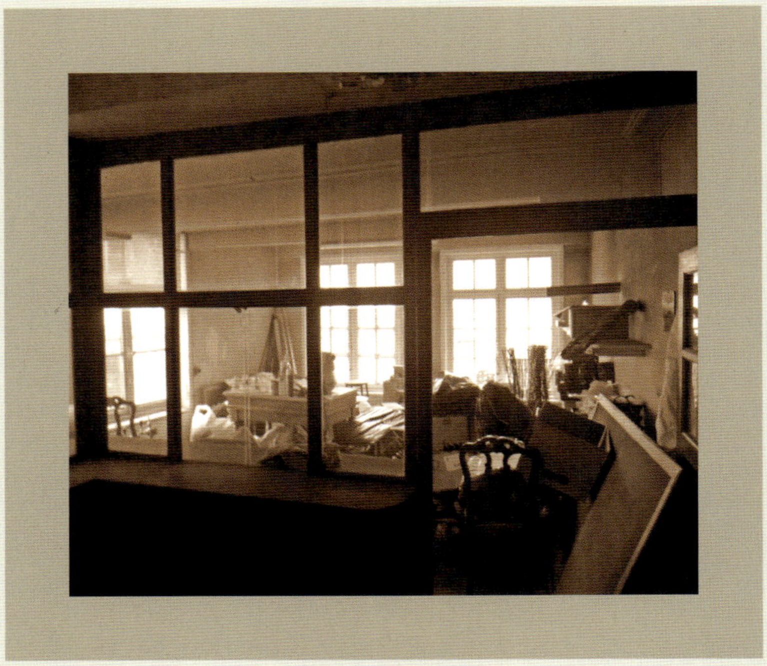

PROTECTED 17TH-CENTURY HOUSES

ATELIER TOM VANHEE

323 m^2 | 3,477 sq. ft.

Bruges, Belgium

Photos © **Filip Dujardin**

> Convert two protected houses dating to the 17th century from their previous brewery function into a residence

> Preserve or reconstruct original features to prevent their character from being lost

> Expand the structure by exploiting attics and between-rooftops space

> Develop well-lit spaces

> Zwei denkmalgeschützte Häuser aus dem 17. Jahrhundert, die eine Brauerei beherbergten, wieder aufbauen und in ein Wohnhaus verwandeln

> Die ursprünglichen Elemente bewahren oder wiederherstellen, um den Charakter der Häuser zu erhalten

> Den Wohnraum durch Ausbau und Verbinden der Dachböden vergrößern

> Helle Räume schaffen

> Reconstruire deux maisons protégées du XVIIe siècle qui comprenaient autrefois une brasserie pour en faire une maison

> Conserver ou reconstruire les éléments d'origine afin de ne pas perdre l'essence de leur origine

> Agrandir la maison en se servant du dernier étage et des espaces entre les toitures

> Obtenir des espaces lumineux

Two abandoned 17th-century houses, a protected part of a brewery in the central part of Bruges, were repurposed as a family residence with commercial areas and a warehouse dating back to the origins of the property. The design picks up from changes already made to the structure, adding a new layer. The historical and authentic portions are preserved or reconstructed and, where necessary, structurally enhanced. These elements—doors, fireplaces, beams, and staircases—remain visible as they go hand in hand with new elements. A patio and sloped roof boards beneath the gabled tiles transform the attic into a completely usable space and capture the space between the existing rooftops.
The existing spatial format of the facade is maintained and adapted to the house's most closed-off functions. In this way, the interventions are unseen from the busy brewery courtyard beyond the building facade. This renovation project repurposes a historically significant building and ensures its existence for generations to come.

In einer Brauerei im Zentrum von Brügge wurden zwei denkmalgeschützte und nicht mehr genutzte Häuser aus dem 17. Jahrhundert zu einem Familienheim mit bereits existierenden Geschäften und Läden umgebaut. Der Entwurf geht von den Änderungen aus, die das Gebäude durchlaufen hat, und fügt ihnen eine neue Ebene hinzu. Die historischen und authentischen Teile werden bewahrt oder rekonstruiert und bei Bedarf strukturell verbessert. Diese Elemente – Türen, Kamine, Balken und Treppen – gehen Hand in Hand mit den neuen Elementen und bleiben erkennbar. Eine Terrasse und ein Schrägdach zwischen den ursprünglichen Giebeldächern verwandeln den Dachboden in eine voll nutzbare Fläche und verleihen dem zwischen den Dächern verbleibenden Raum neues Leben.
Die Struktur der Fassade bleibt von der Änderung der Funktion unberührt, die Eingriffe sind vom belebten öffentlichen Platz aus nicht zu sehen. So erfährt dieses historisch bedeutsame Gebäude durch die Renovierung eine Nutzungsänderung, durch die es für künftige Generationen erhalten wird.

Dans une brasserie du centre de Bruges ont été reconstruites deux maisons protégées du XVIIe siècle tombées en désuétude afin de les transformer en une maison familiale, avec des locaux commerciaux et un magasin qui existaient déjà à l'époque. La conception est partie des modifications subies par le bâtiment et l'ajout d'un nouvel étage. Les parties historiques et authentiques ont été conservées ou reconstruites et, si nécessaire, améliorées de manière structurelle. Ces éléments – les portes, cheminées, poutres et escaliers – vont de pair avec les nouveaux éléments et restent apparents. Une cour et une toiture inclinée entre les toits à deux pans d'origine transforment le dernier étage en une superficie totalement exploitable et donnent vie à l'espace habitable entre les toitures.
L'espace existant de la façade a été conservé et adapté aux fonctions les plus personnelles de la maison. Ainsi, les interventions sont invisibles depuis la place publique animée de la façade du bâtiment. Ce projet de rénovation a permis de redonner à un bâtiment sa valeur historique et garantir son existence pour les générations à venir.

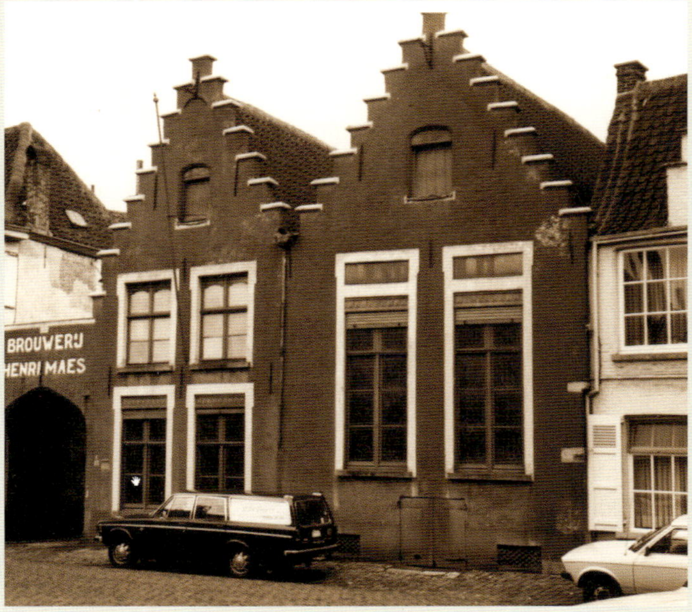
BROUWERIJ
HENRI MAES

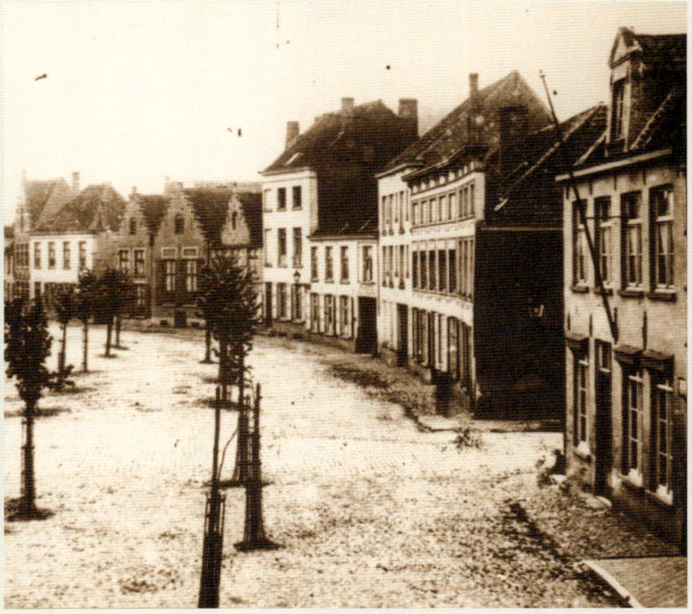

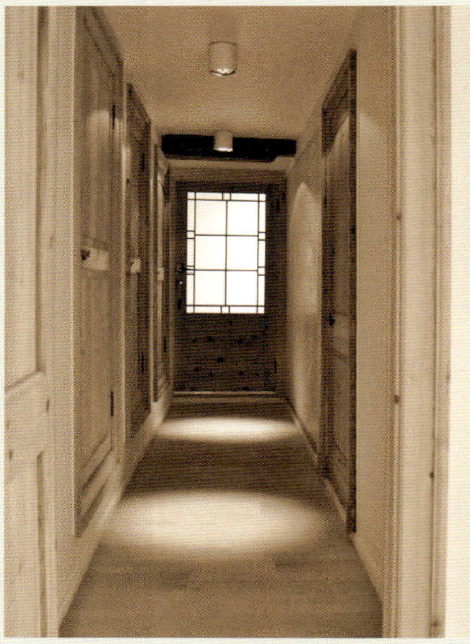

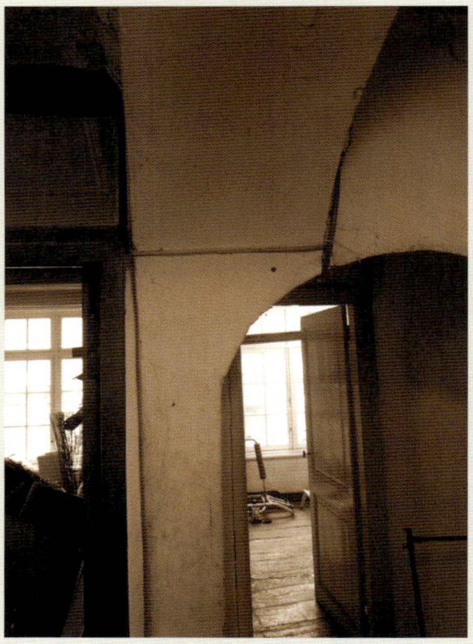

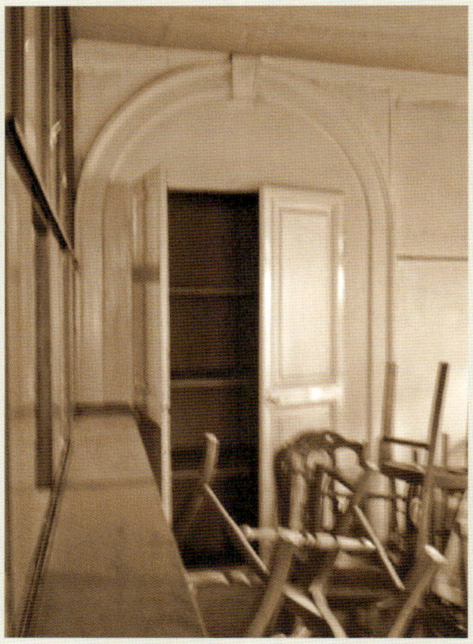

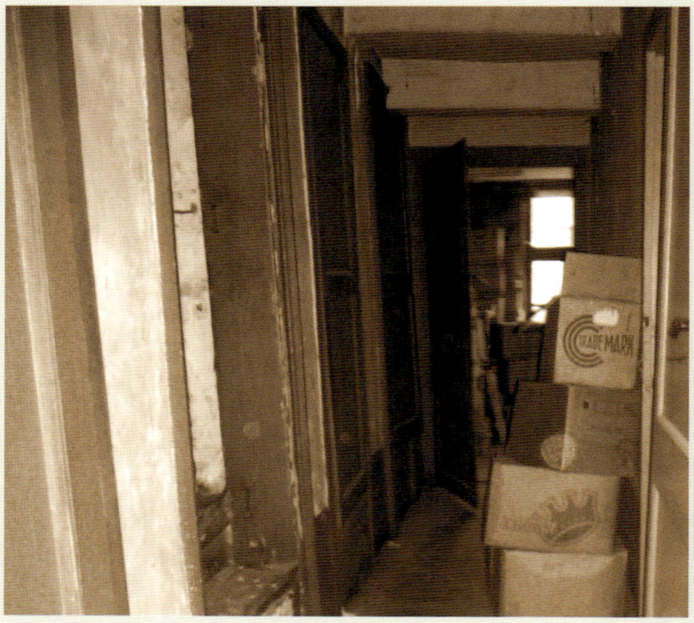

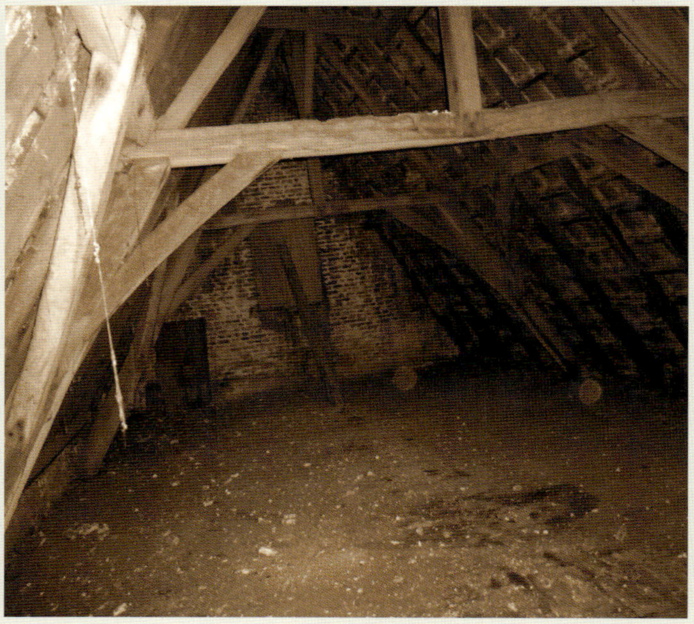

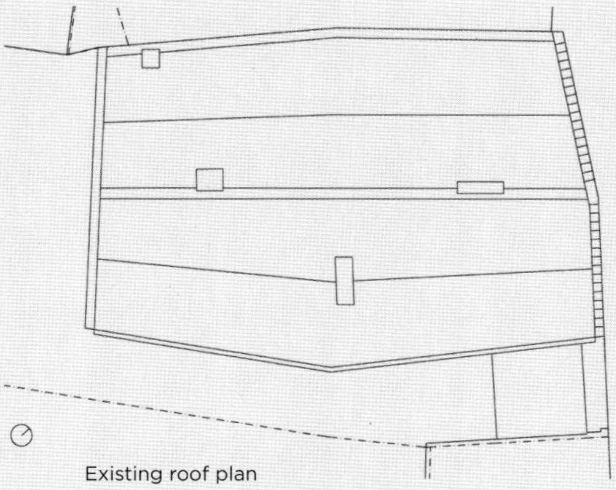

Existing roof plan

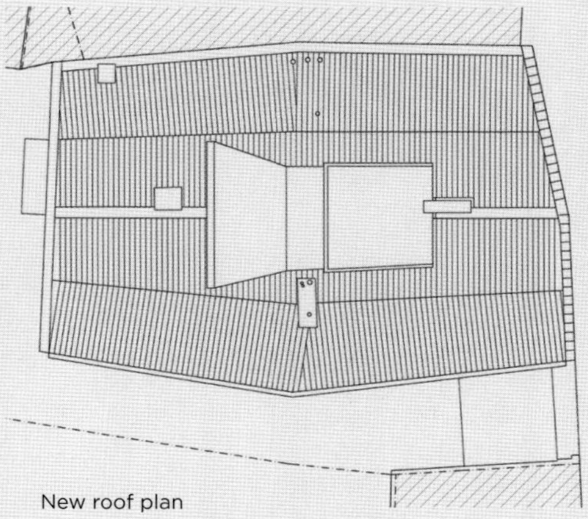

New roof plan

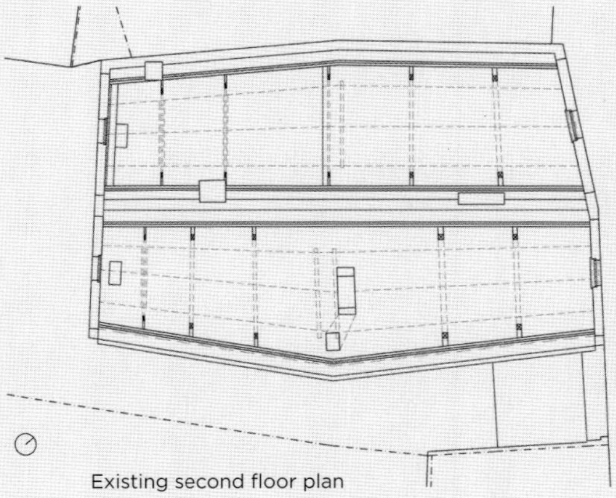

Existing second floor plan

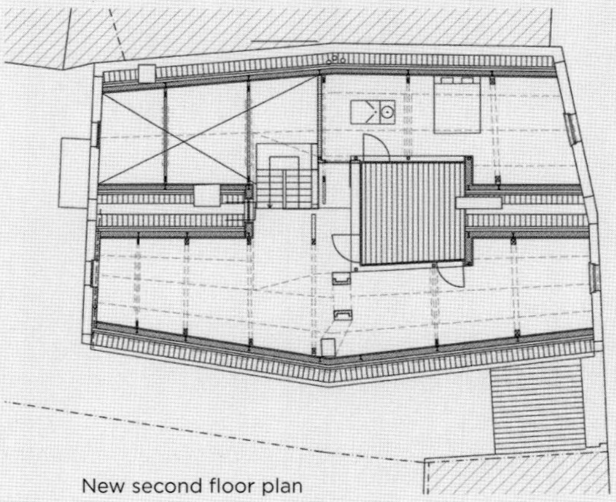

New second floor plan

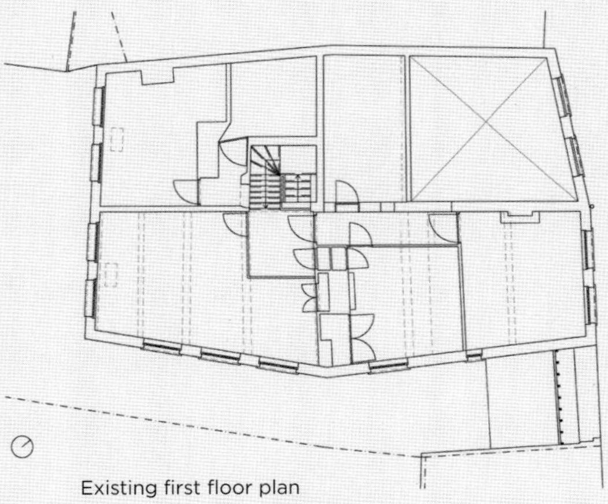

Existing first floor plan

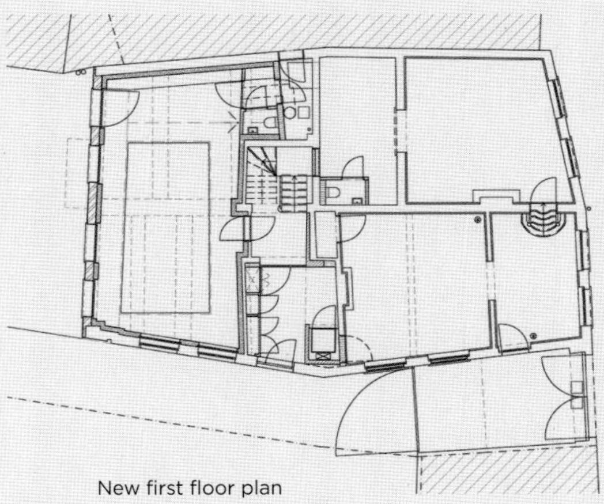

New first floor plan

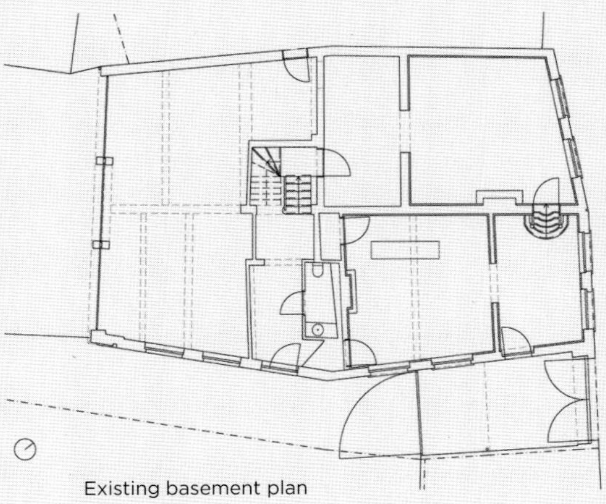

Existing basement plan

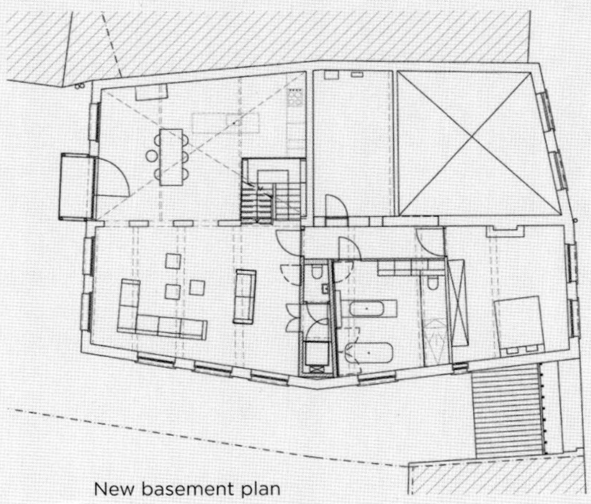

New basement plan

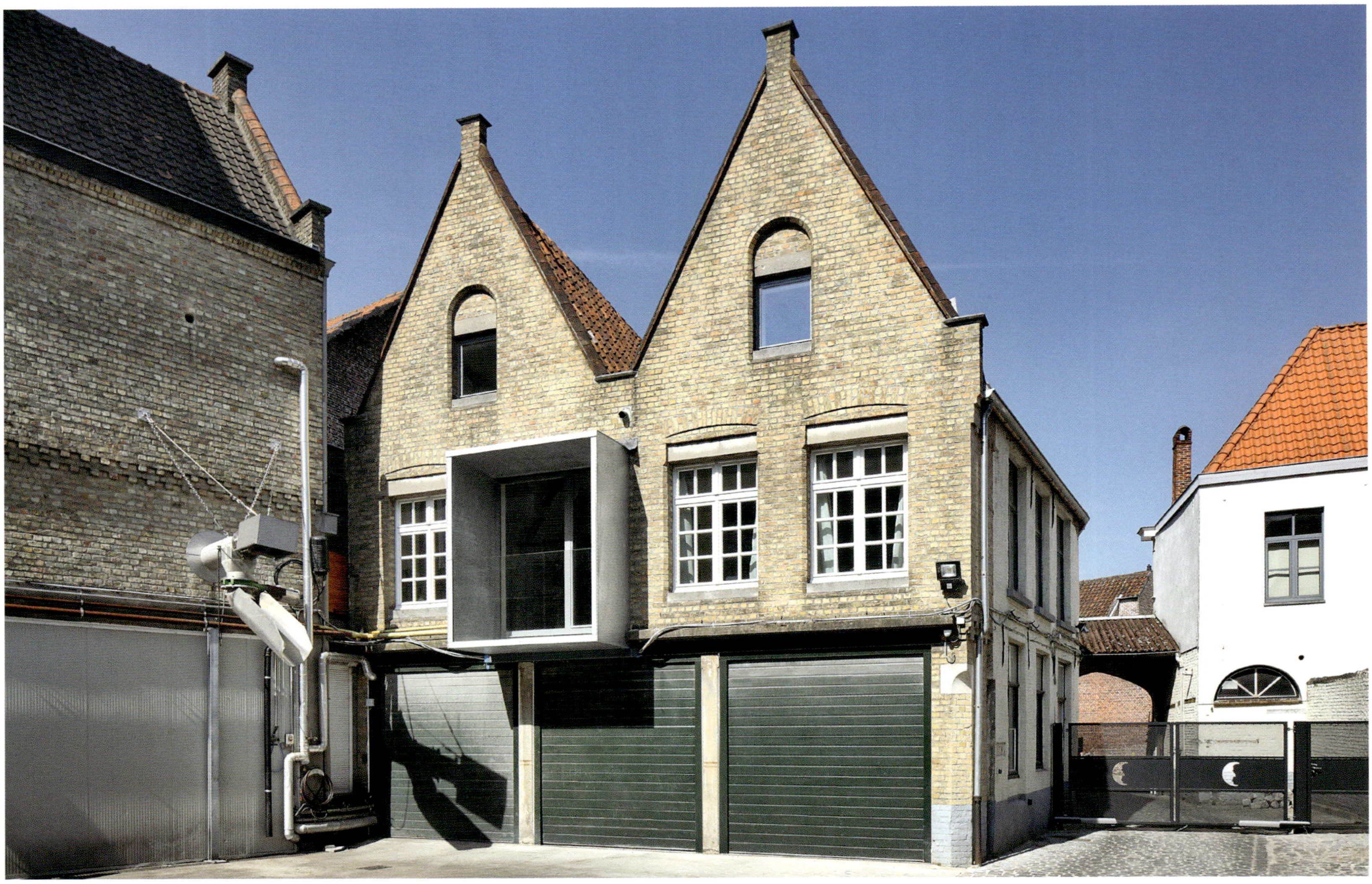

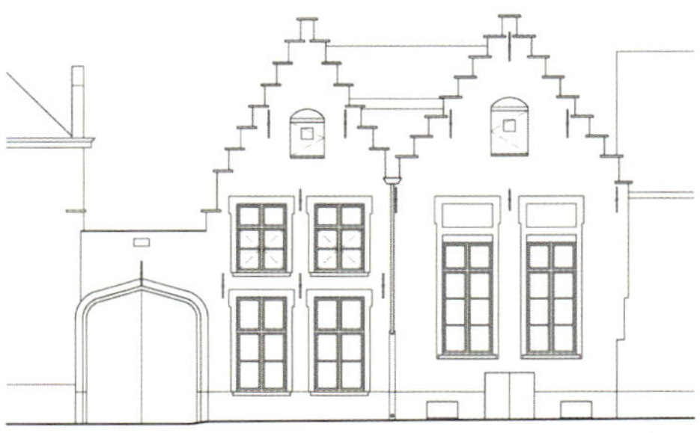

Front elevation

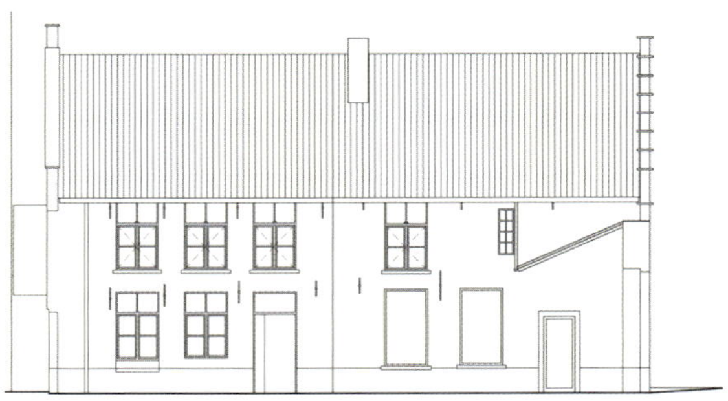

Side elevation

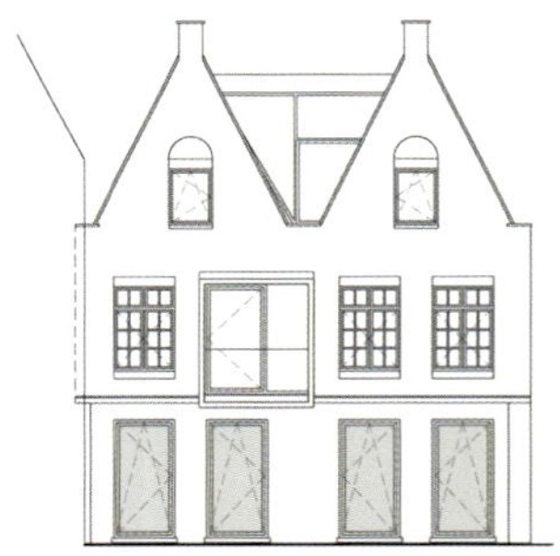

Rear elevation

The different window types and added rear facade are evidence of a series of modifications over time. The windows, stairs, and balconies are given a steel cladding. The old wooden windows are refurbished with wood, fitting the original profile.

Die verschiedenen Fensterarten und die hinzugefügte hintere Fassade zeugen von den vielfachen Umbauten im Laufe der Zeit. Die neuen Fenster, Treppen und Balkone sind aus Stahl gefertigt. Die alten Holzfenster wurden in Holz mit dem gleichen ursprünglichen Profil wiederhergestellt.

Les différents types de fenêtres et la façade arrière ajoutée sont les preuves des transformations successives survenues au fil du temps. Les nouvelles fenêtres, l'escalier et les balcons sont en acier, tandis que les anciennes fenêtres en bois ont été refaites en bois au profil identique à celui de l'époque.

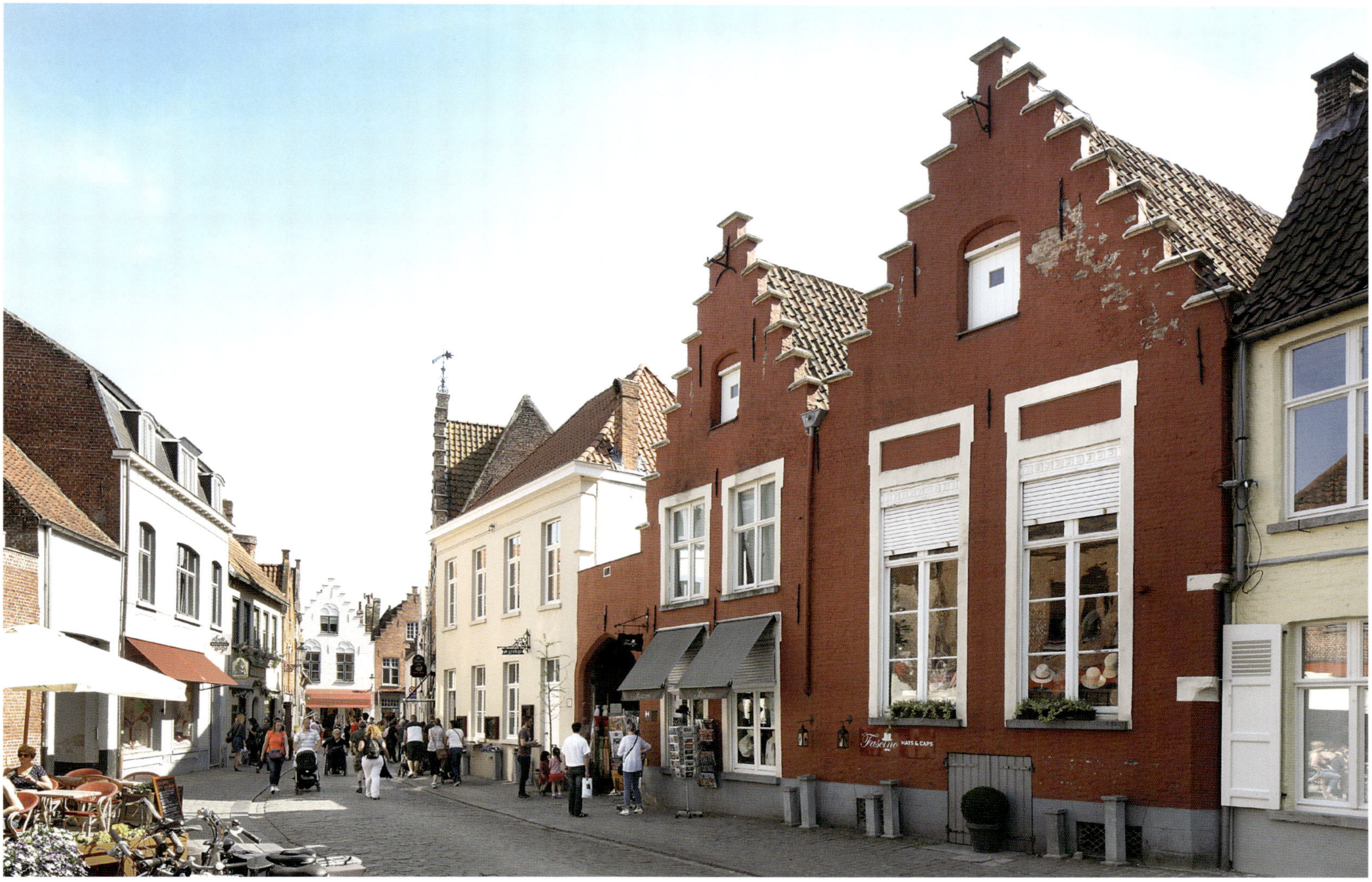

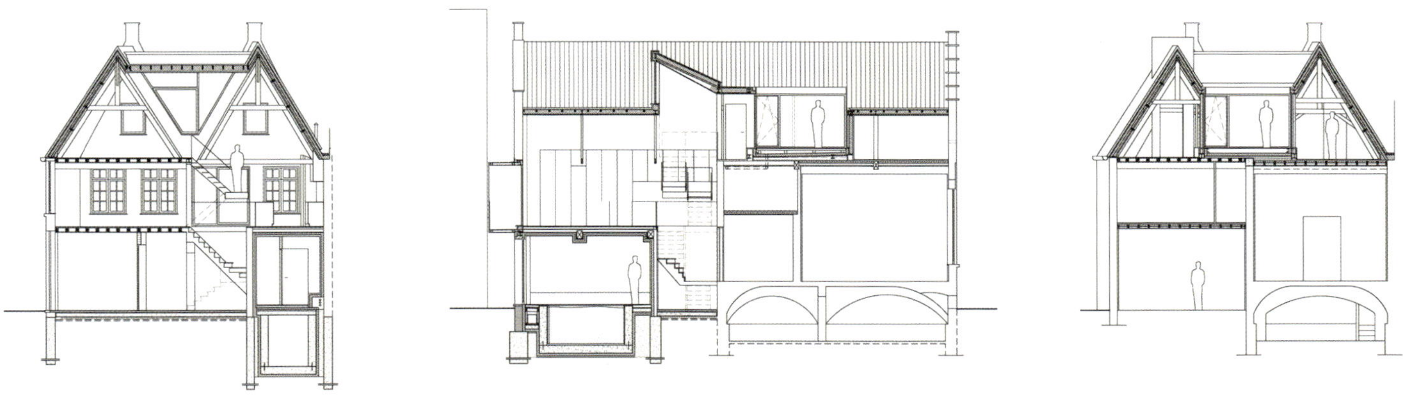

Sections

The darker space represented by the dining room opens toward the apex of the sloped ceiling. This area provides a panorama of activities in the brewery's interior courtyard from an industrial-looking balcony.
The old brick fireplace, wooden beams, trusses, and interior woodworking reveal the building's storied past.

Der dunkelste Raum, der Essbereich, öffnet sich bis zum Dachfirst. Durch einen industriell anmutenden Balkon bietet dieser Bereich einen Blick auf die Aktivitäten der Brauerei auf dem Innenplatz.
Der alte gemauerte Schornstein, die Holzbalken, der Dachstuhl und die Holzarbeiten im Innenraum weisen auf die historische Vergangenheit des Hauses hin.

L'espace le plus sombre, la salle à manger, est ouvert jusqu'à la crête du toit. Cet espace a une vue sur les activités de la brasserie de la place intérieure grâce à un balcon à l'aspect industriel.
L'ancienne cheminée de brique, les poutres en bois, les cintres et la menuiserie intérieure dévoilent le passé historique de la maison.

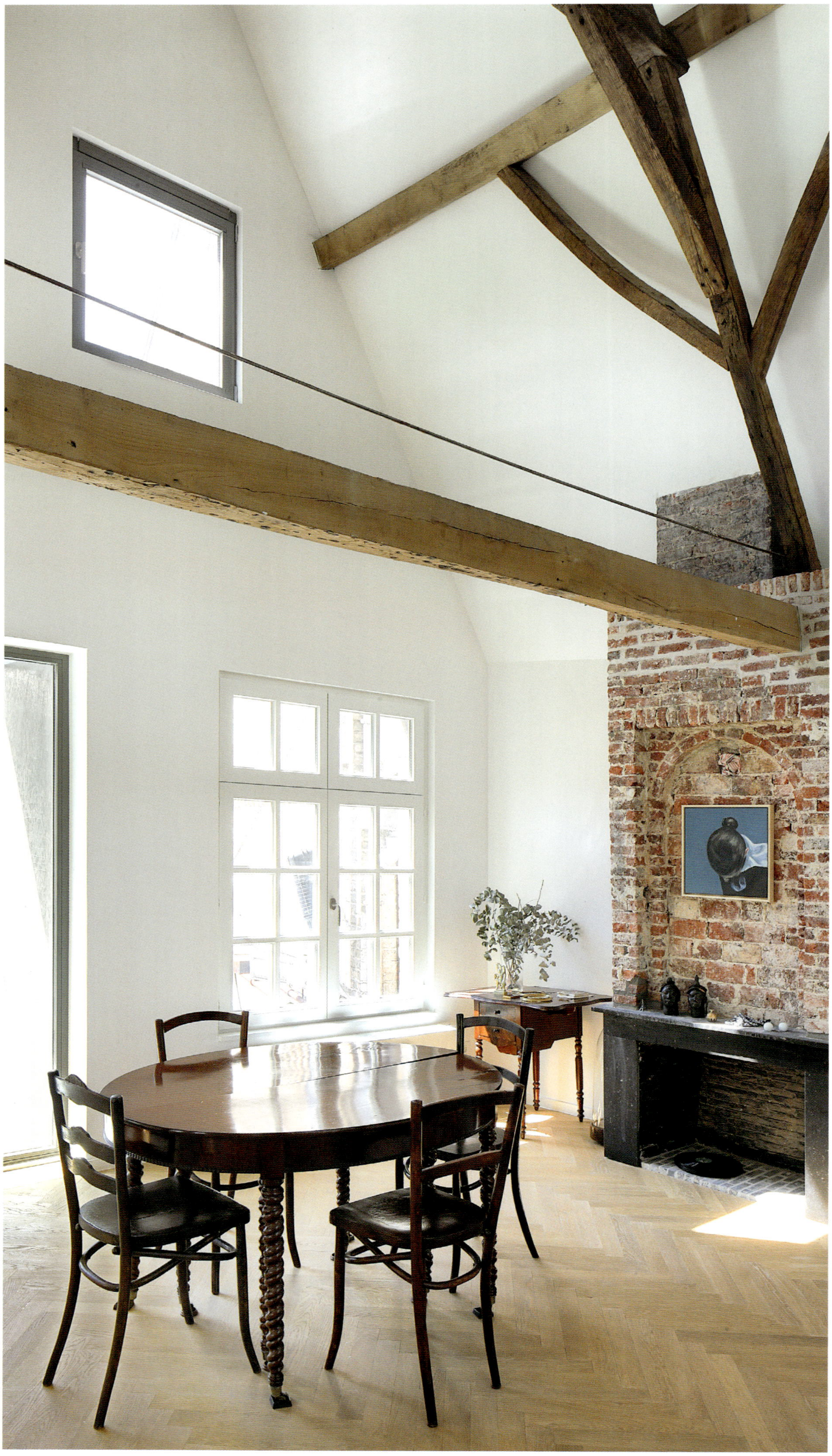

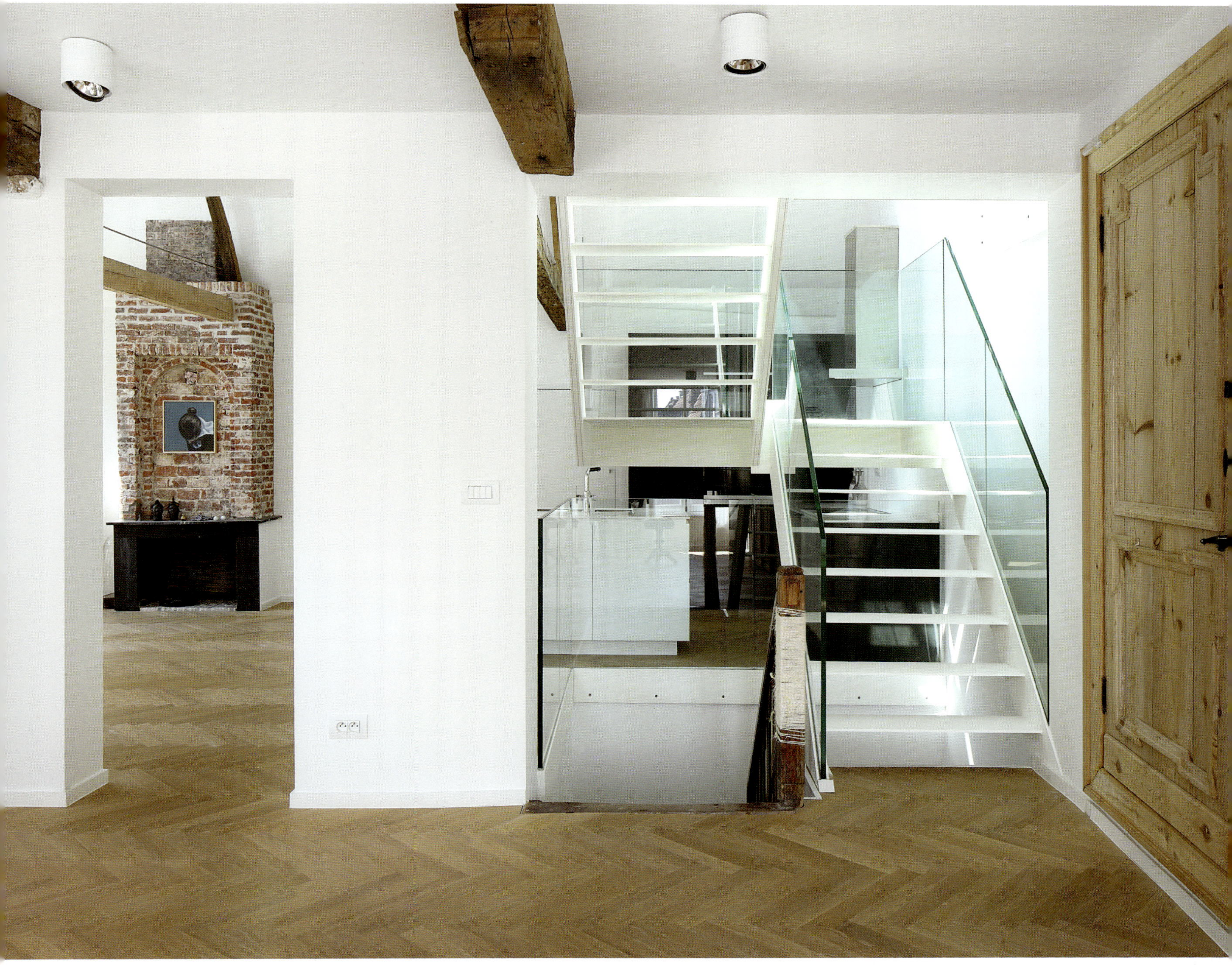

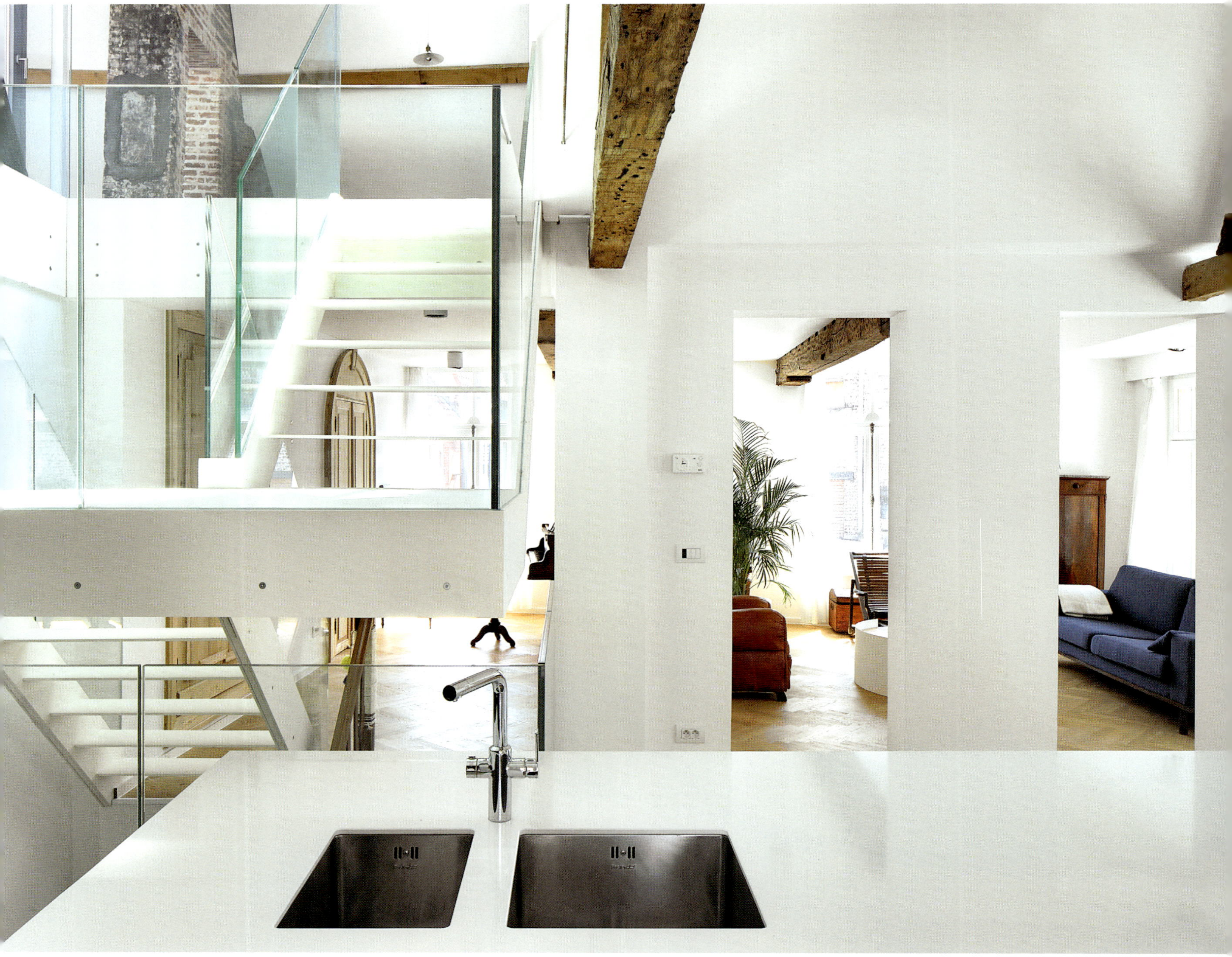

The doorless transitions between rooms, the open design of the staircase with its glass handrails, and the multiple windows allow light to stream into the entire residence, imbuing it with an unequivocal sensation of fullness and spatial flow.

Das Fehlen von Türen in den Durchgängen zwischen den verschiedenen Wohnräumen, die Gestaltung der offenen Treppe und deren Ausführung mit Glasgeländern und verschiedene Fenster lassen das Licht durch das gesamte Haus fluten und geben ihm ein unbestreitbares Gefühl von Großzügigkeit und räumlicher Fluidität.

L'absence de portes dans les couloirs entre les différentes pièces, la conception de l'escalier ouvert et une rampe en verre, ainsi que les diverses fenêtres inondent toute la maison de lumière lui conférant une sensation indéniable de grandeur et de fluidité spatiale.

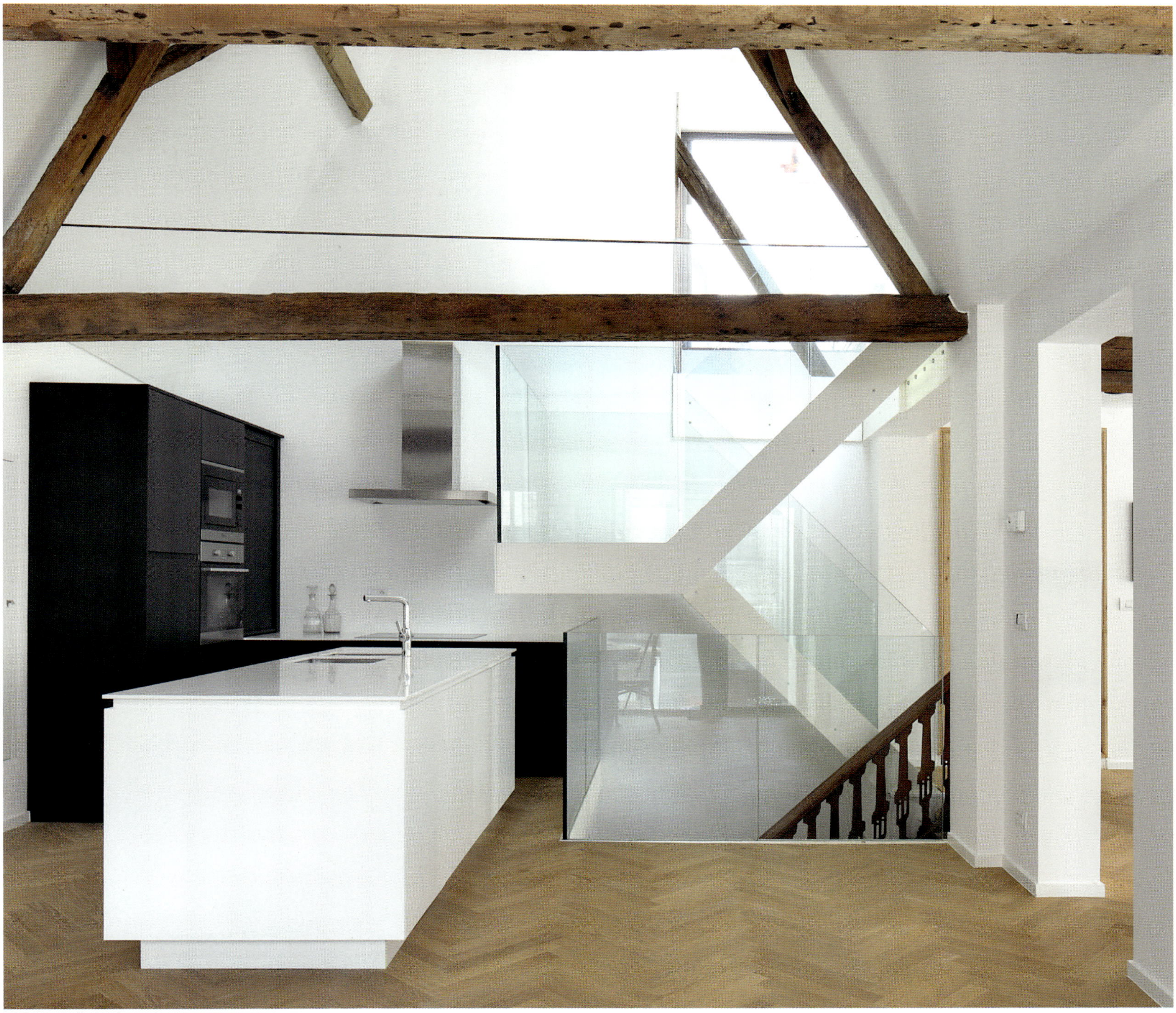

A double space connects each level with the other and carries the light from the patio and the attic's trapezoidal window into the heart of the residence.

Ein Raum mit doppelter Höhe verbindet die verschiedenen Etagen miteinander und bringt das Licht vom Innenhof und dem trapezförmigen Dachfenster ins Herz des Hauses.

Les divers niveaux sont reliés entre eux par un double espace qui emmène la lumière de la cour et de la fenêtre trapézoïdale du dernier étage au cœur de la maison.

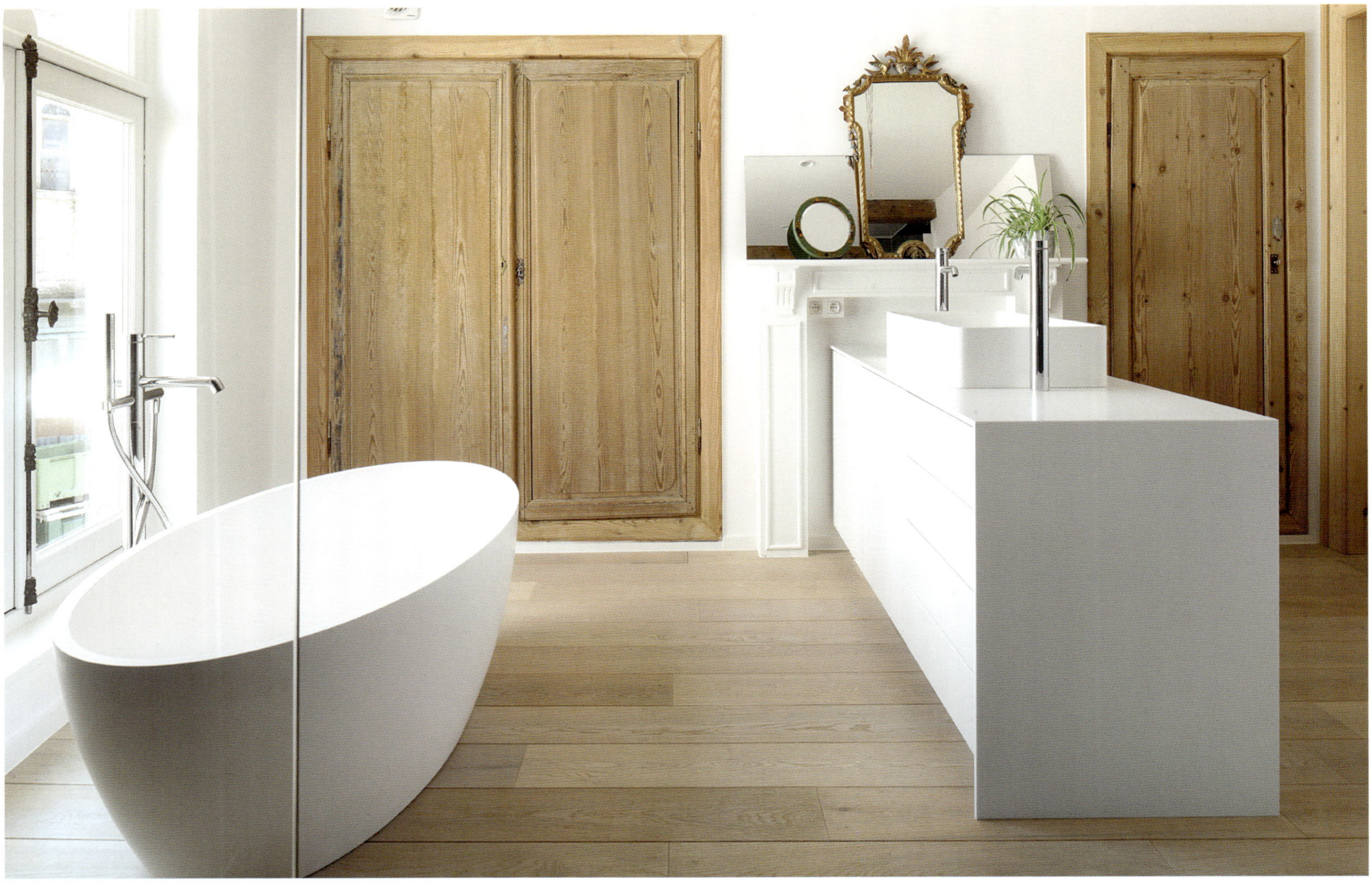

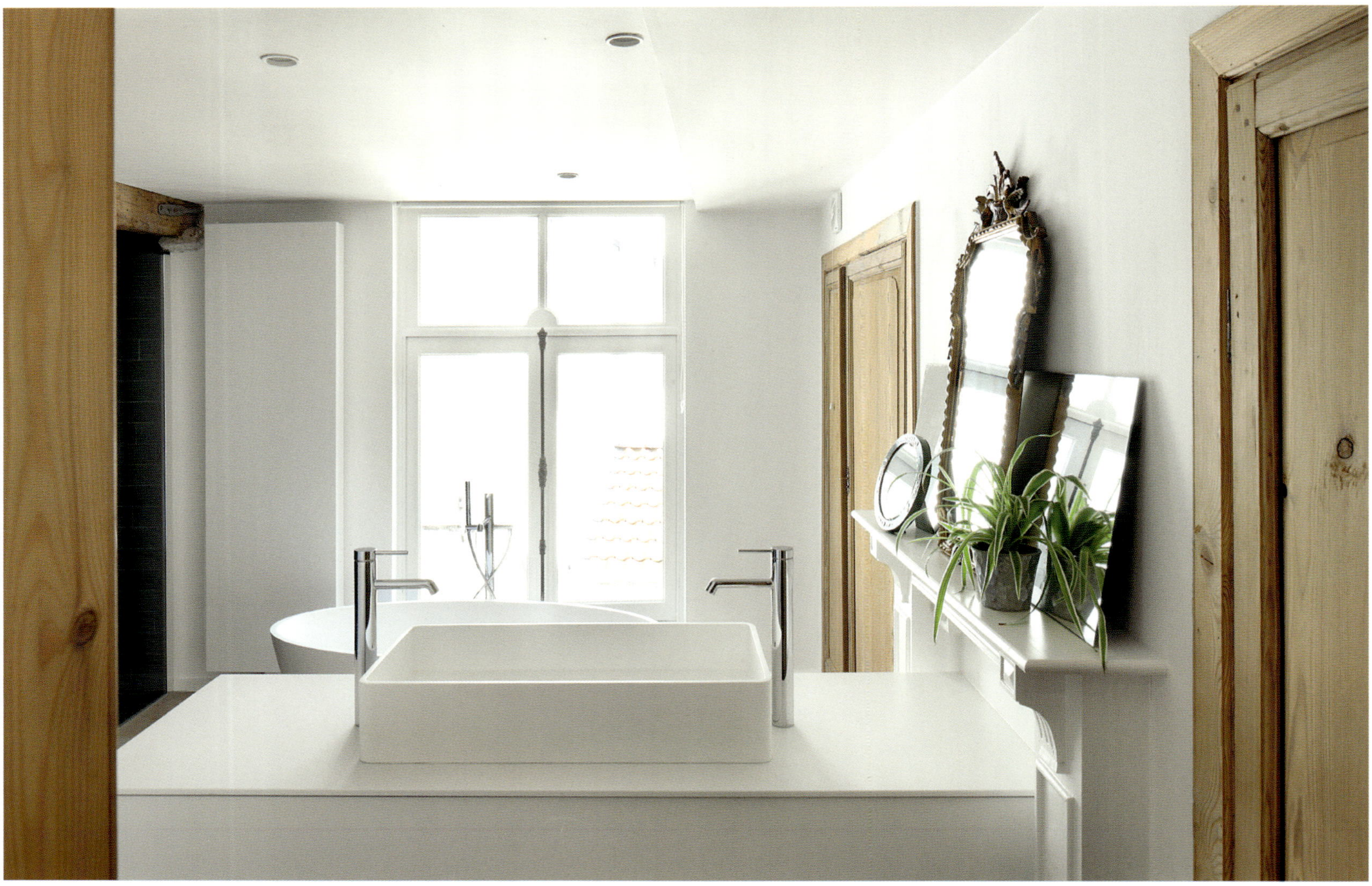

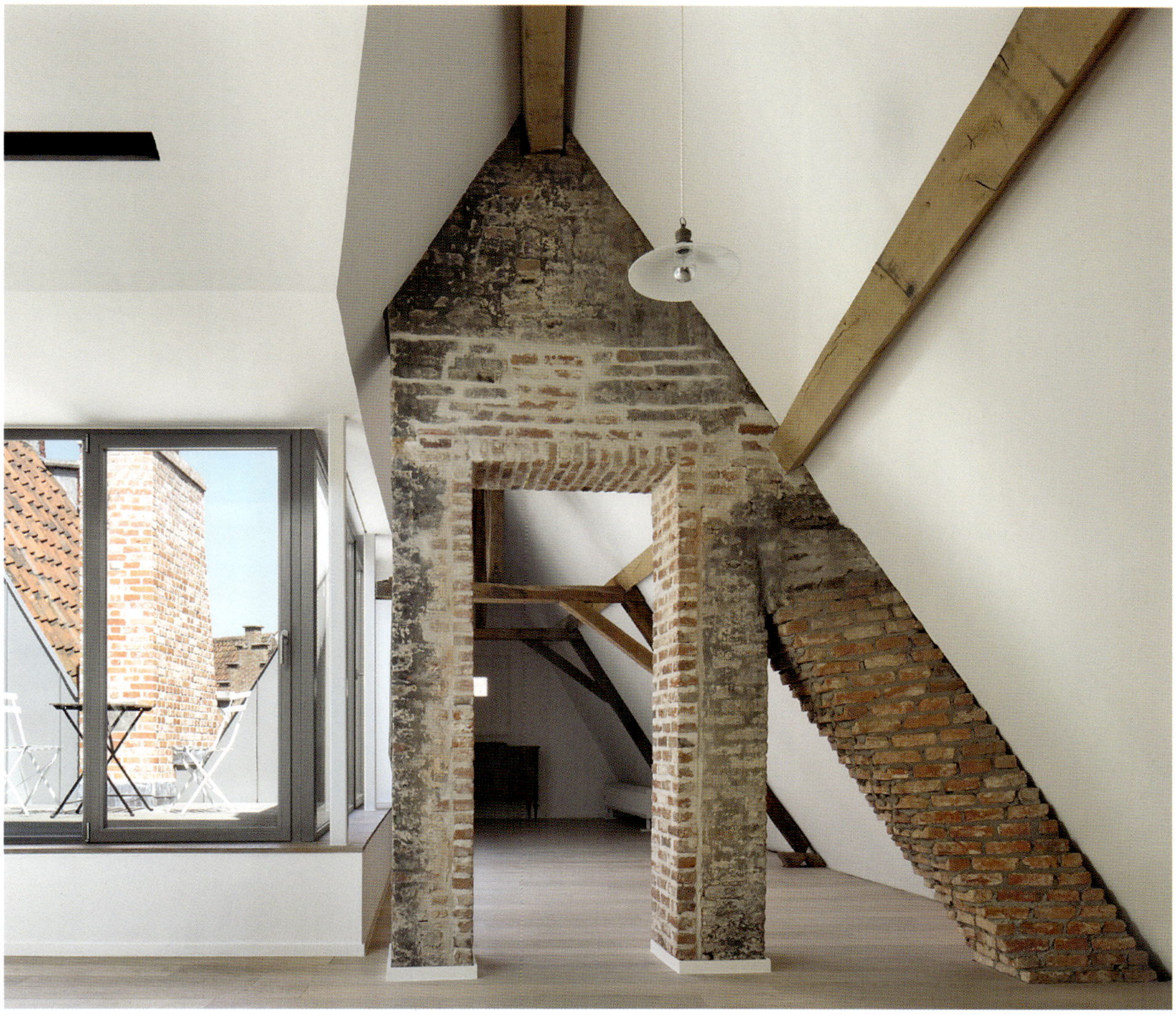

A new stairway above the existing one provides access to the previously unused attics and corresponds to the directive to extend the house. The new terrace enables residents to enjoy the outdoors in privacy.

Eine neue Treppe über der bestehenden Treppe ermöglicht den Zugang zu den Dachböden, die bisher nicht genutzt wurden, und entspricht dem Wunsch nach einem Ausbau des Hauses. Dank der neuen Terrasse können Bewohner und Gäste ungestörte Momente unter freiem Himmel genießen.

Un nouvel escalier, au-dessus de celui existant, permet d'accéder au grenier qui n'était pas utilisé autrefois et répond à la demande d'agrandissement de la maison. La nouvelle terrasse permet de profiter, en toute intimité, de moments agréables en plein air.

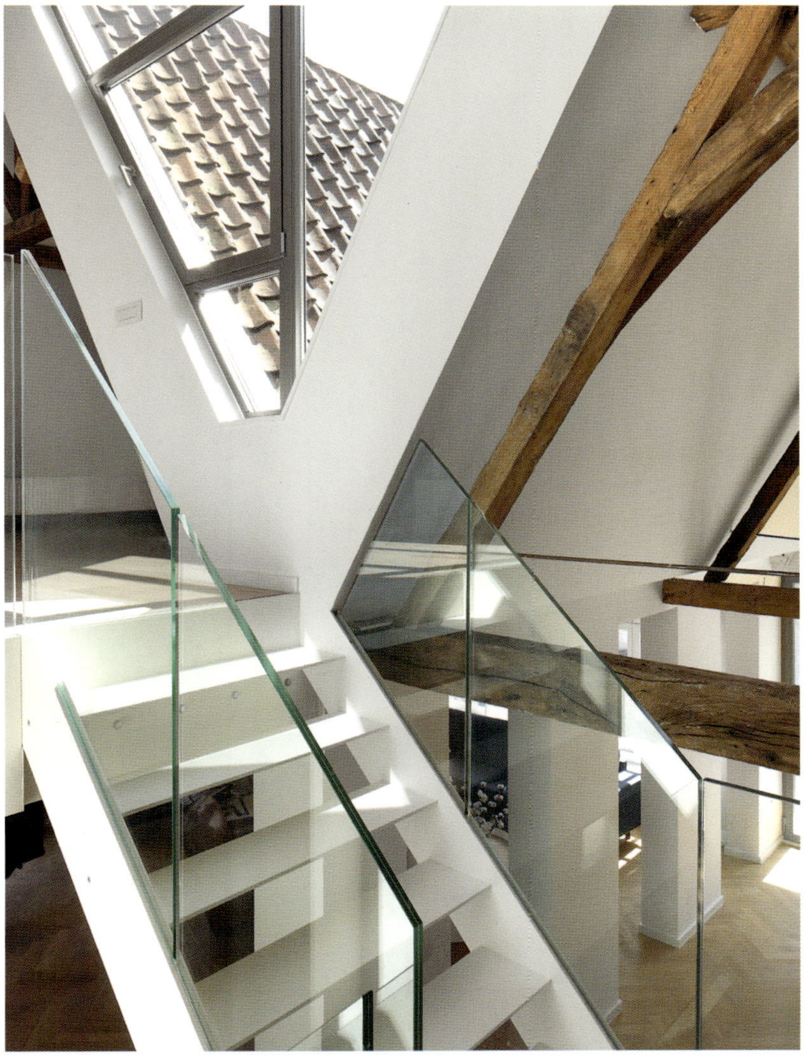

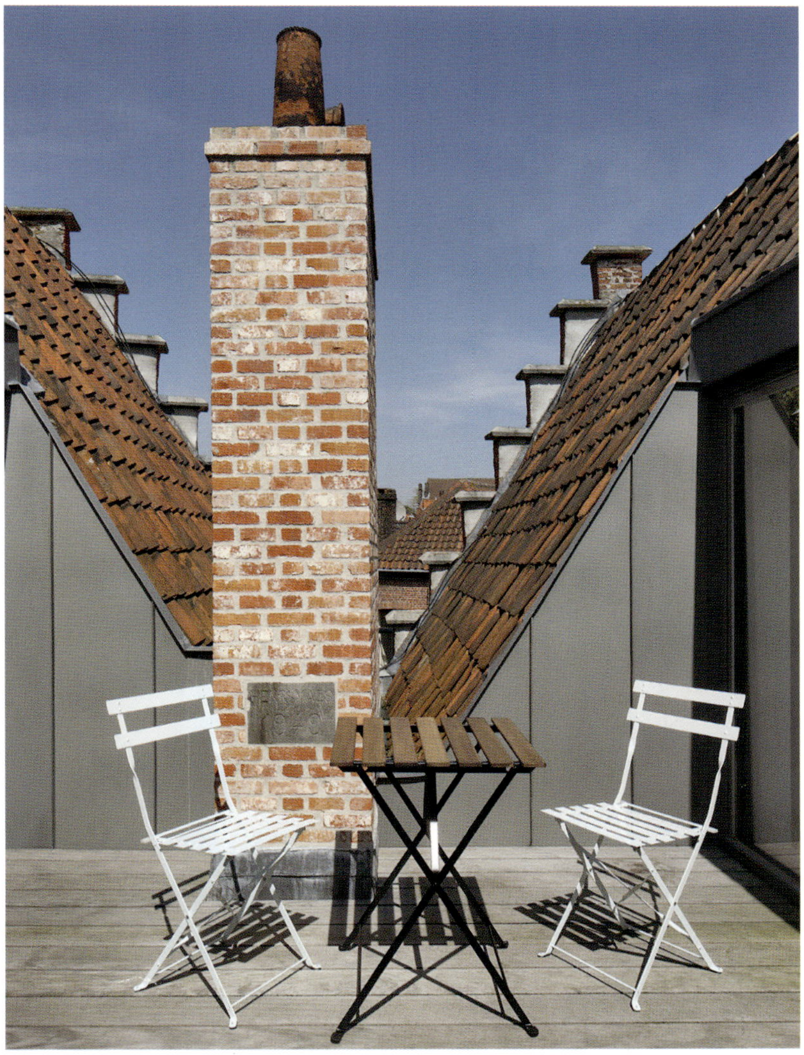

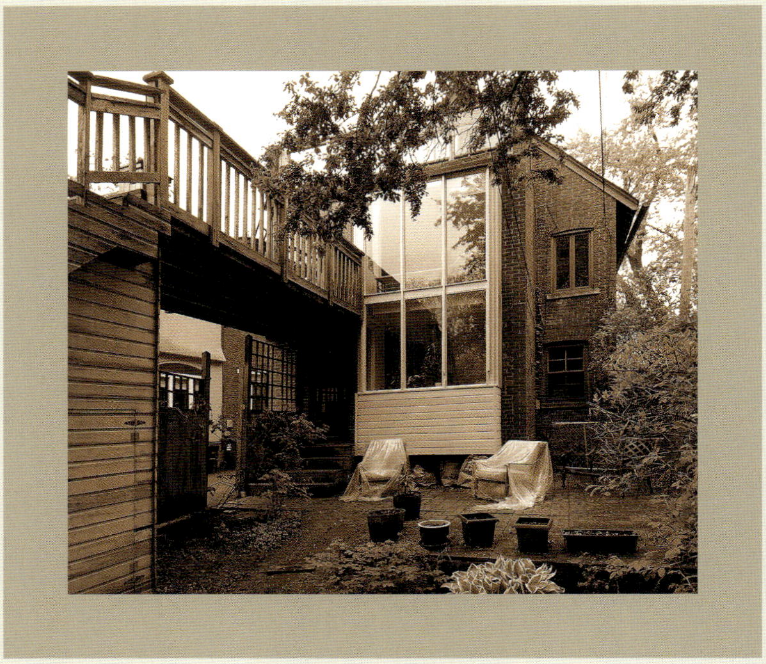

SKYGARDEN HOUSE

DUBBELDAM ARCHITECTURE + DESIGN

225 m² | 2,420 sq. ft.

Toronto, Ontario, Canada

Photos © **Shai Gil**

> Open up house interior to outdoor spaces on all levels

> Den Innenbereich des Hauses auf allen Ebenen zum Außenbereich hin öffnen

> Ouverture de l'intérieur de la maison sur les espaces extérieurs à tous les niveaux

The house provides outdoor living spaces on multiple levels to address the owners' desire for a better connection with the natural surroundings. Most of the rooms open up to a series of outdoor spaces, each with its own unique character and varying level of privacy. Even the existing porch at the front of the house is turned into a private outdoor dining area enclosed by a five-foot-high wooden screen. This expansion beyond the interior spaces makes the house feel larger than it actually is.
On the second floor, two significant outdoor spaces provide green respite. At the front of the house, half of the master bedroom is given over to an intimate exterior space with a recessed planter. Intimately connected to the master suite, this "skygarden" functions as a unique outdoor room, open to the sun, wind, and stars. At the back of the house, an exposed roof-deck has views over the neighborhood and into the extensive green canopy surrounding the house.

Da sich die Bewohner eine engere Verbindung mit der Natur wünschten, verfügt dieses Haus über Außenwohnbereiche auf mehreren Ebenen. Die meisten Räume öffnen sich hin zu einer Reihe von Außenbereichen, die alle über ihren eigenen Charakter und ein unterschiedliches Maß an Privatsphäre verfügen. Selbst die Veranda ist ein privater Essbereich, der von einer 1,5 Meter hohen Holzwand umgeben ist; durch diese Einbeziehung des Außenraums wirkt das Haus größer als es eigentlich ist.
Im zweiten Stock sorgen zwei große Außenbereiche für grüne Auflockerungen. Die Hälfte des Hauptschlafzimmers an der vorderen Hausseite geht in einen intimen Außenbereich mit eingelassenem Blumenkübel über. Dieser, auf diskrete Weise mit dem Hauptschlafzimmer verbundene „Skygarden" ist ein einzigartiger Außenbereich zur Entspannung unter Sonne, Wind und Sternen. Vom Dachbereich an der Hausrückseite blickt man über die Nachbarschaft und die großen Grünflächen rund um das Haus.

Cette maison offre des espaces à vivre extérieurs sur plusieurs niveaux pour répondre au désir du propriétaire de se rapprocher davantage de la nature environnante. La plupart des pièces s'ouvrent sur une série d'espaces extérieurs, chacun ayant son propre caractère et offrant des degrés d'intimité variables. Même le porche d'origine de la façade a été transformé en espace privé pour se restaurer dehors entouré par un panneau en bois haut de 1,5 metre. Cette expansion au-delà des espaces intérieurs donne l'impression que l'habitation est plus grande qu'elle ne l'est en réalité.
Au deuxième étage, deux espaces extérieurs imposants offrent une parenthèse de verdure. À l'avant de la maison, la moitié de la chambre principale est dédiée à un espace extérieur intime doté d'une jardinière encastrée. Intimement relié à la suite parentale, ce « jardin sur ciel » fonctionne comme une pièce extérieure unique, ouverte au soleil, au vent, et aux étoiles. À l'arrière de la maison, un toit-terrasse découvert offre des vues sur le quartier et vers les imposantes frondaisons vertes qui entourent la maison.

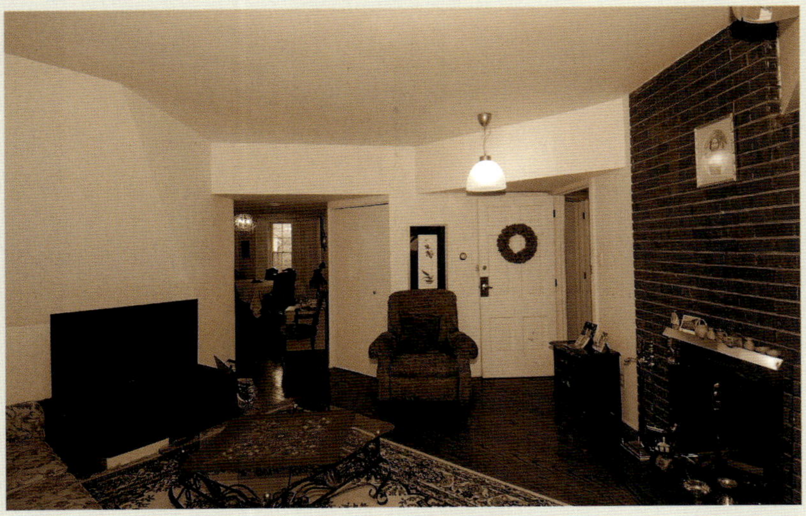

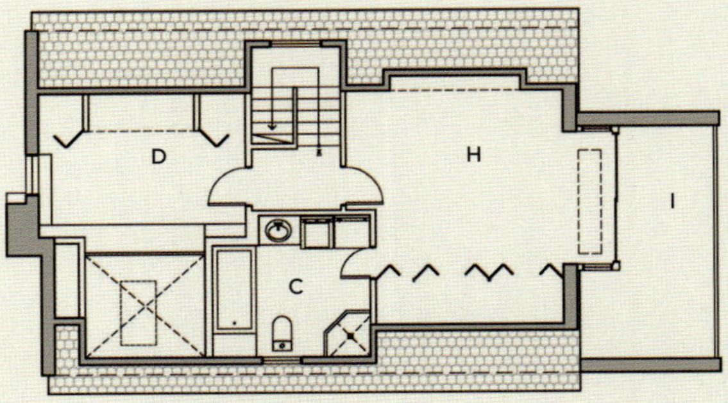

Existing second floor plan

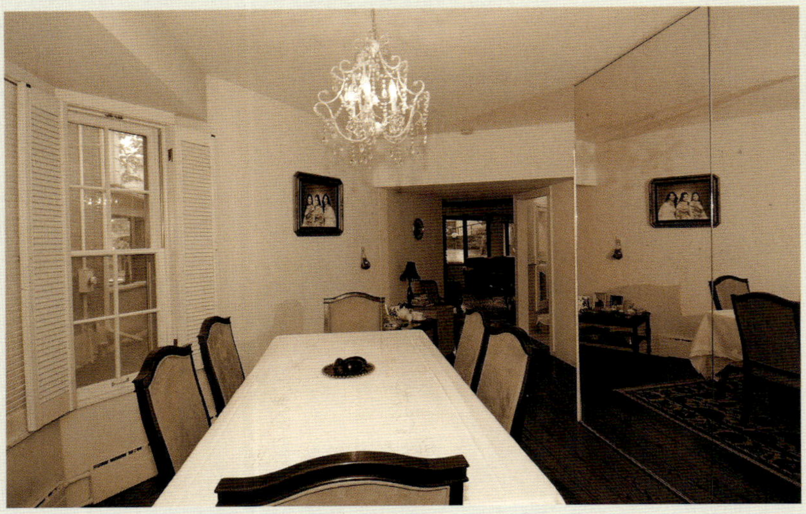

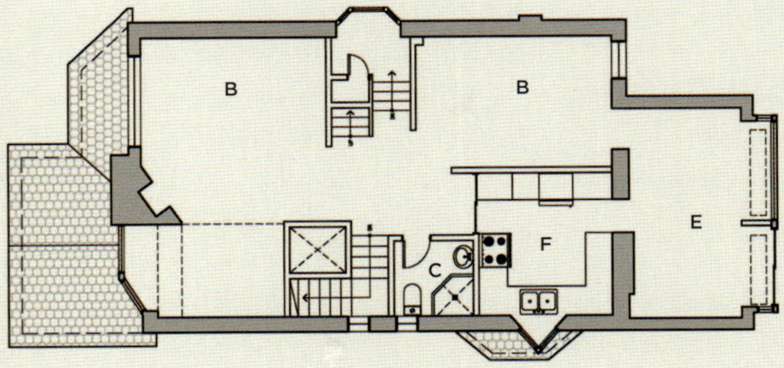

Existing first floor plan

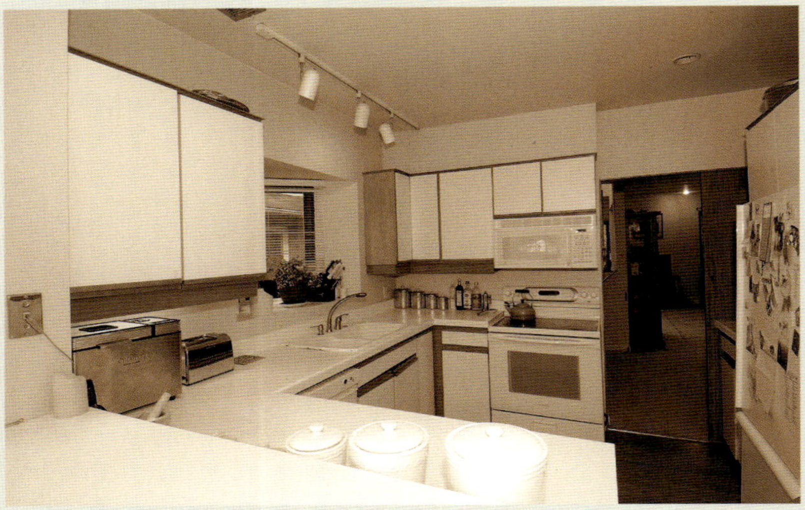

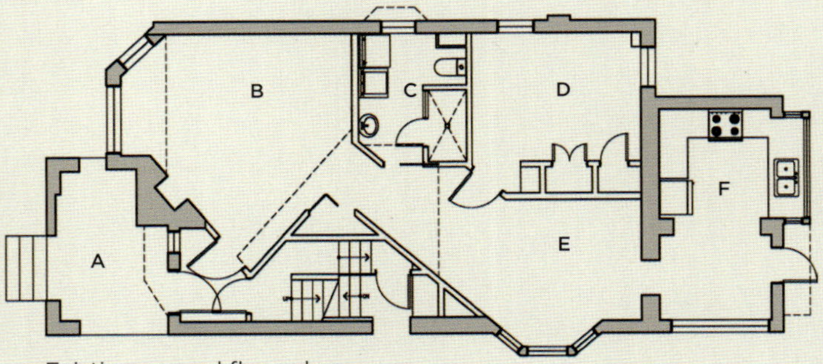

Existing ground floor plan

A. Vestibule
B. Living room
C. Bathroom
D. Bedroom
E. Dining room / sunroom
F. Kitchen
G. Sunroom
H. Master bedroom
I. Roof-deck

Working with the existing footprint of a century-old detached house in the city's midtown neighborhood, only the two exterior sidewalls were retained. The interior was completely gutted. With no obstacles, the new layout is fluid and the connection between rooms is optimized.

Bei der Arbeit an einem Jahrhunderte alten freistehenden Haus inmitten des städtischen Geschäftsviertels blieben nur zwei der ursprünglichen Seitenwände erhalten. Der Innenbereich wurde komplett abgerissen. Somit konnte ohne Hindernisse eine fließende Raumaufteilung mit optimaler Verbindung zwischen den einzelnen Räumen entworfen werden.

Composant avec la superficie existante d'une maison centenaire dans le centre de la ville, seuls les murs extérieurs ont été conservés. L'intérieur a été complètement évidé. Sans un seul obstacle, le nouveau plan est fluide et la liaison entre les pièces optimisée.

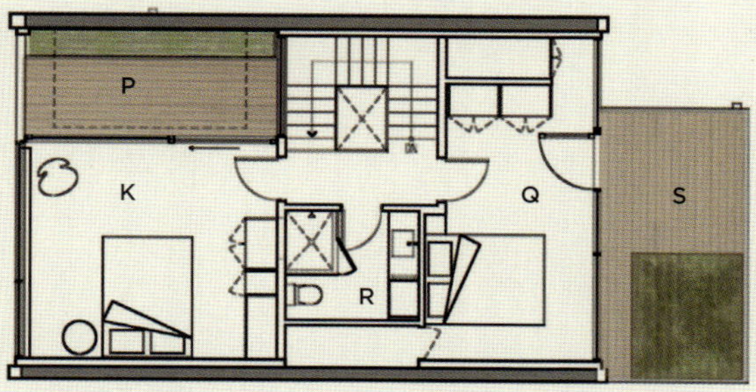

New second floor plan

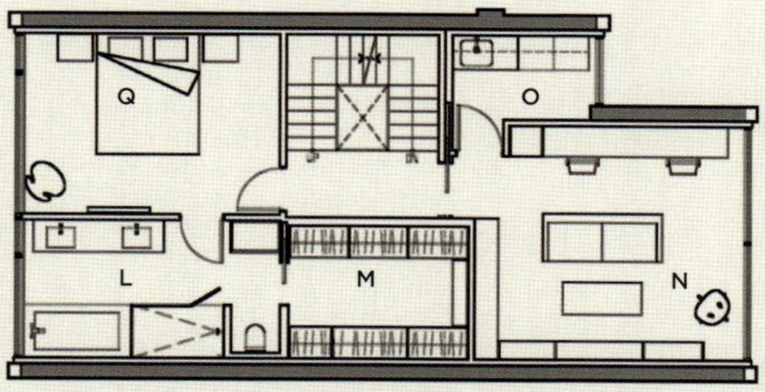

New first floor plan

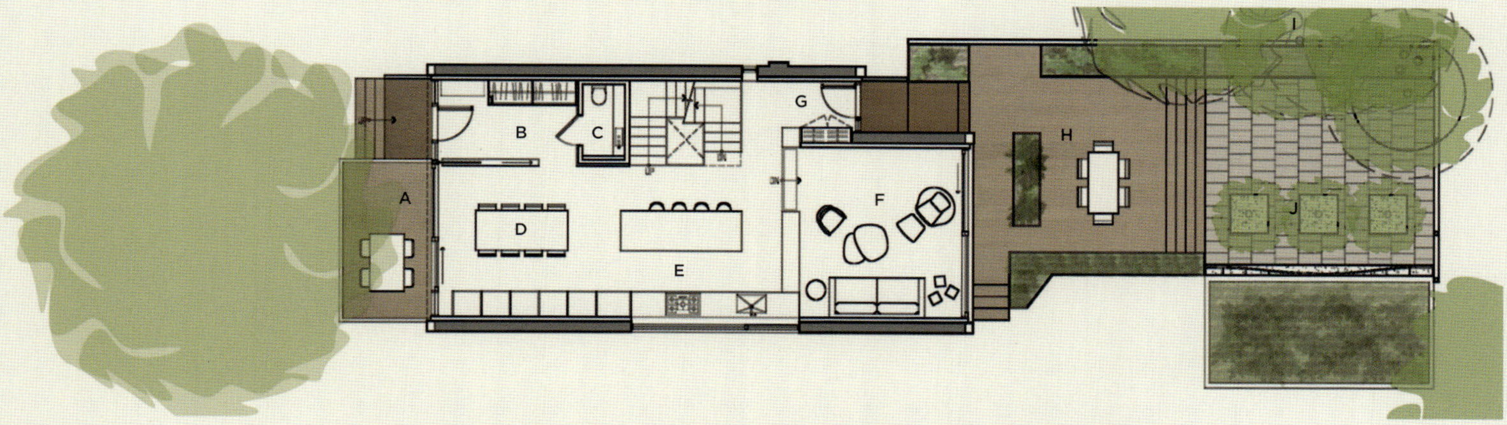

New ground floor plan

A. Outdoor dining area
B. Vestibule
C. Powder room
D. Dining area
E. Kitchen
F. Living area
G. Rear entrance
H. Rear deck
I. Patio
J. Garage
K. Master bedroom
L. En suite bathroom
M. Walk-in closet
N. Study
O. Laundry room
P. Skygarden
Q. Bedroom
R. Bathroom
S. Roof-deck

The landscaped rear yard features an ash wood deck off the living area for outdoor dining when the weather allows it. A few steps down, another zone, defined by granite pavers, is planted with a row of honey locust trees that offer dappled light and shade in summer to make the most of the sizable backyard.

Im mit Eschenholz beplankten Hinterhof können die Bewohner bei schönem Wetter im Freien essen. Über ein paar Stufen gelangt man hinunter zu einer großzügigen Granitterrasse, wo man im Sommer im Schatten Amerikanischen Honigdorns sitzen kann.

L'arrière-cour paysagée est équipée d'une terrasse en frêne devant le coin repas pour pouvoir prendre les repas dehors quand le temps le permet. En descendant quelques marches, une autre zone, définie par des pavés de granit, est plantée d'une allée de féviers d'Amérique qui procurent une lumière mouchetée et de l'ombre en été pour profiter de cette cour aux proportions généreuses.

Skygarden House offers a graphic interpretation of the traditional pitched roof, referencing the domestic scale and form of the neighboring houses.

Das Skygarden House zeigt eine grafische Neuinterpretation des traditionellen Satteldachs, passend zu Form und Art der Nachbarhäuser.

La Skygarden House propose une interprétation graphique du toit traditionnel à deux versants, renvoyant à la petite échelle et à la forme des maisons environnantes.

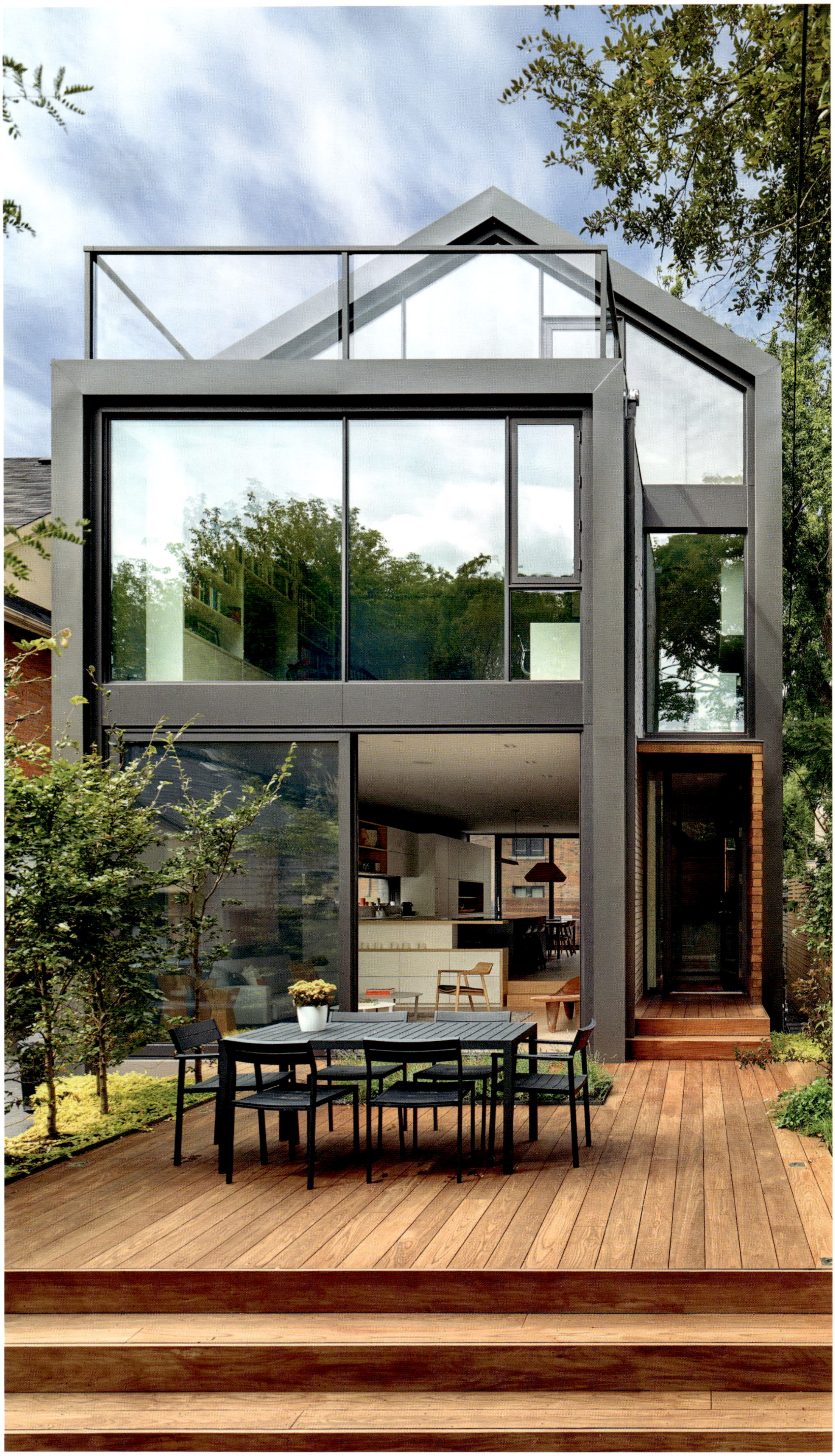

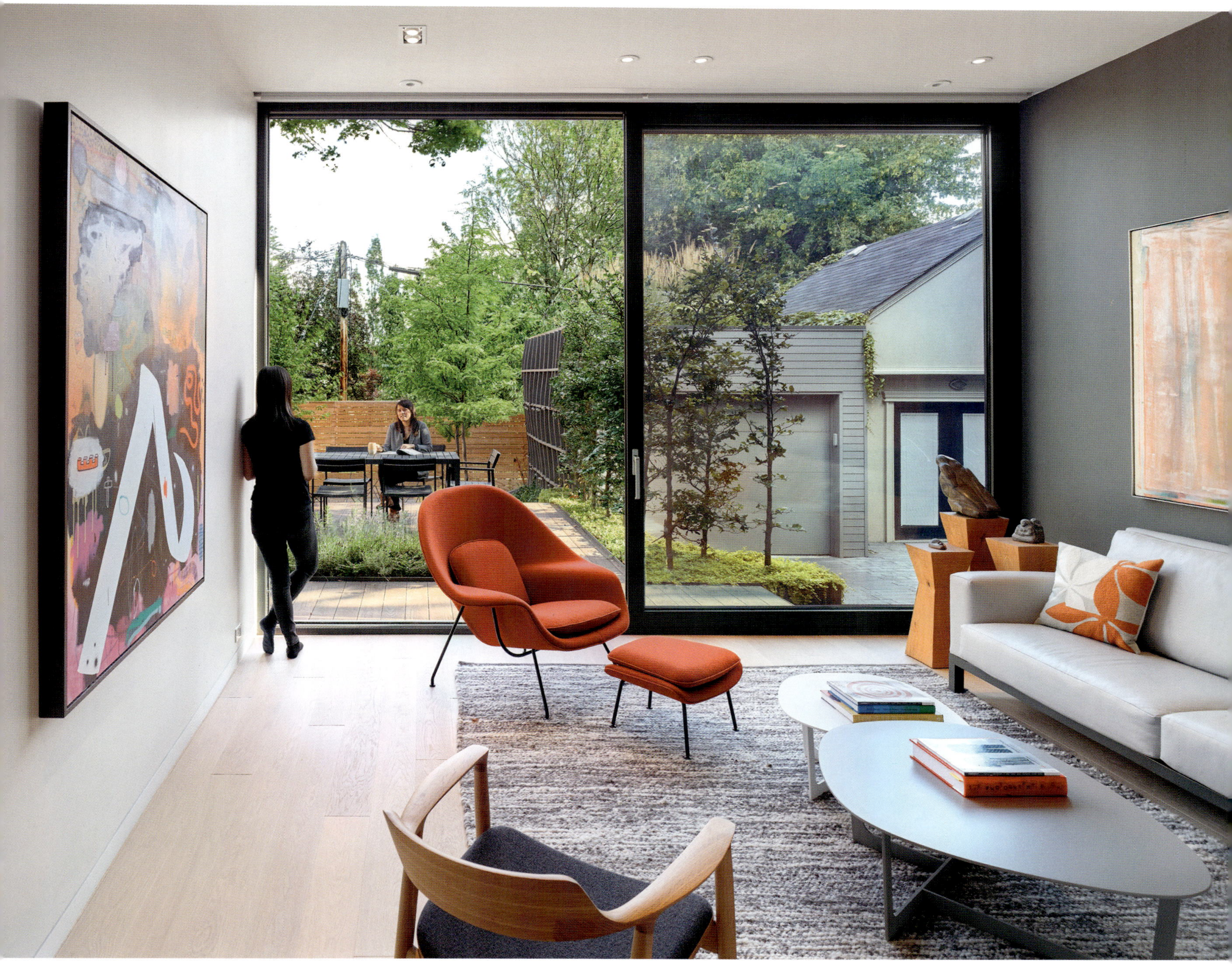

Floor-to-ceiling glass walls made of a combination of windows, doors, and spandrel panels frame views of the outdoors and bring natural light and the changing seasons into the interior.

Raumhohe Glaswände mit Fenstern, Türen und Brüstungen erlauben nicht nur Ausblicke nach draußen, sondern lassen auch natürliches Licht ins Innere und machen den Wechsel der Jahreszeiten erlebbar.

Des cloisons vitrées toute hauteur faites d'un assortiment de fenêtres, de portes, et de panneaux d'allège encadrent les vues sur l'extérieur et font entrer la lumière naturelle et les différentes saisons à l'intérieur.

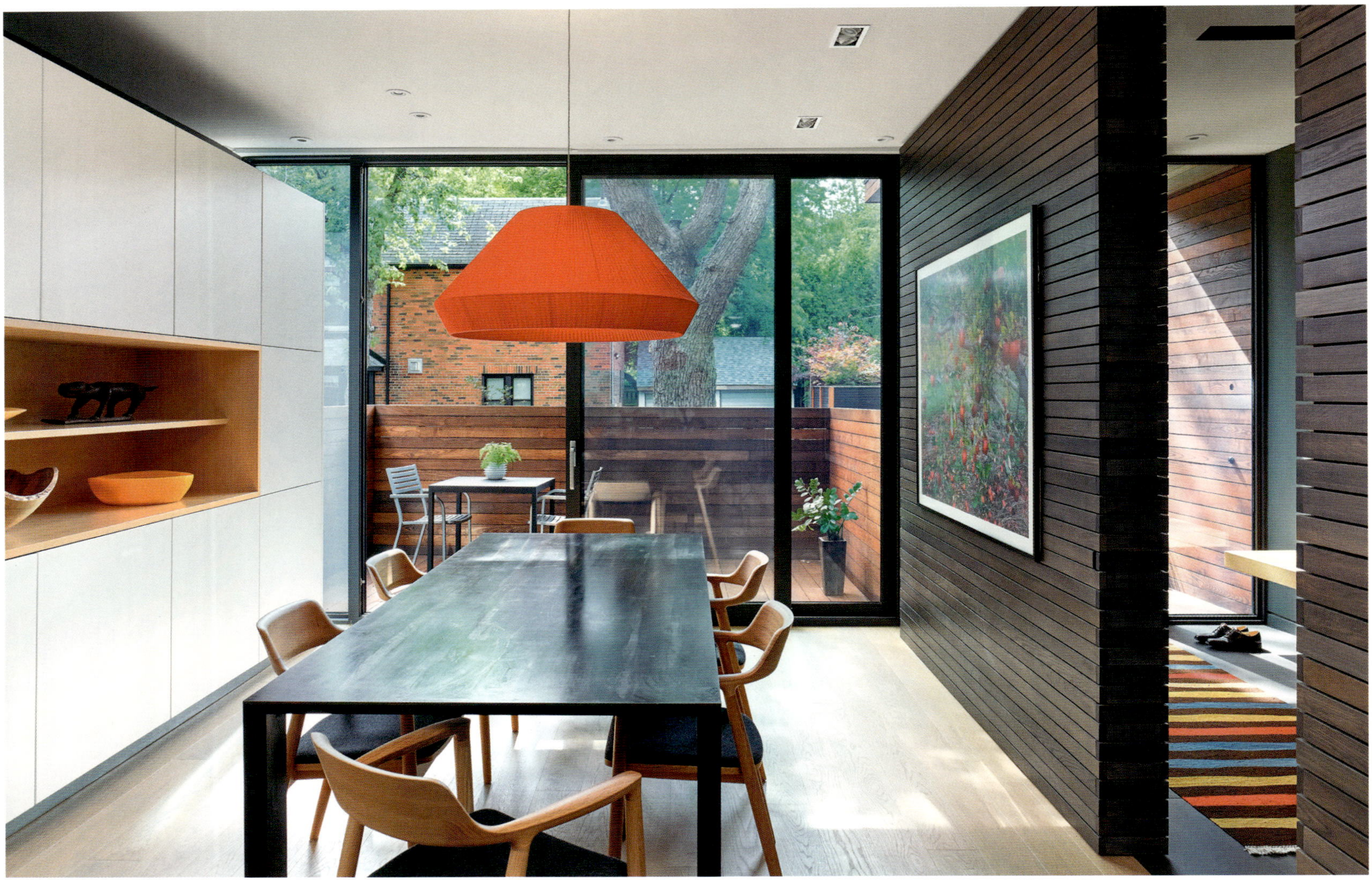

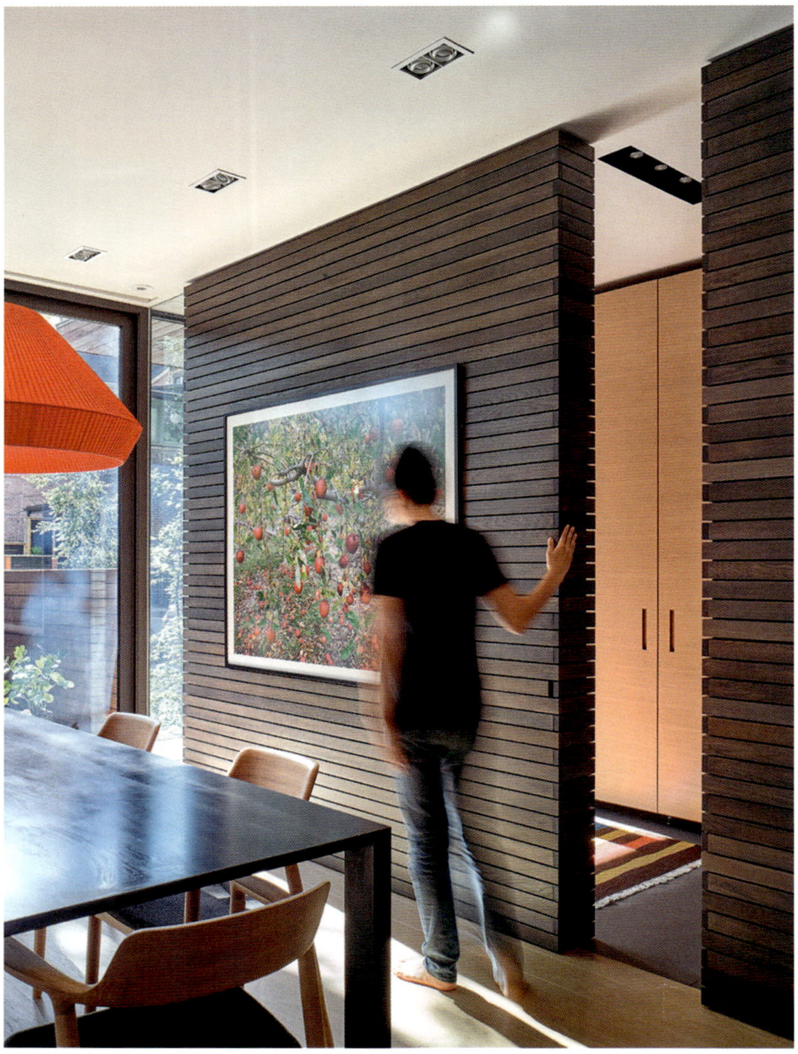

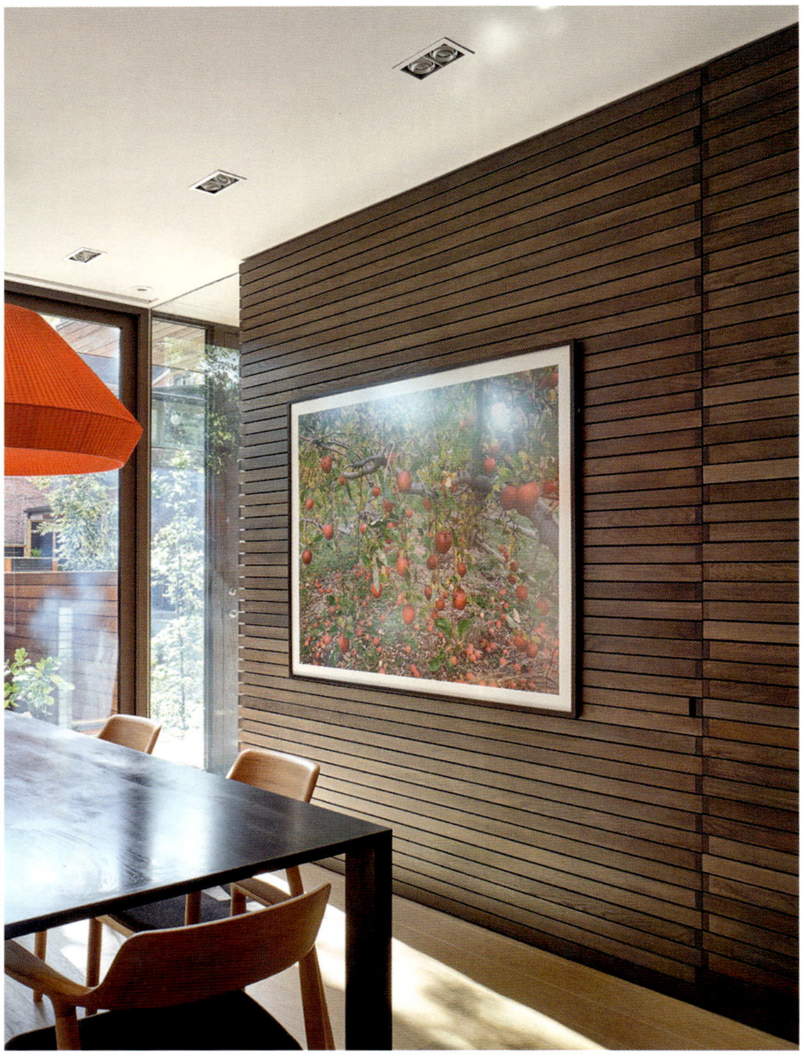

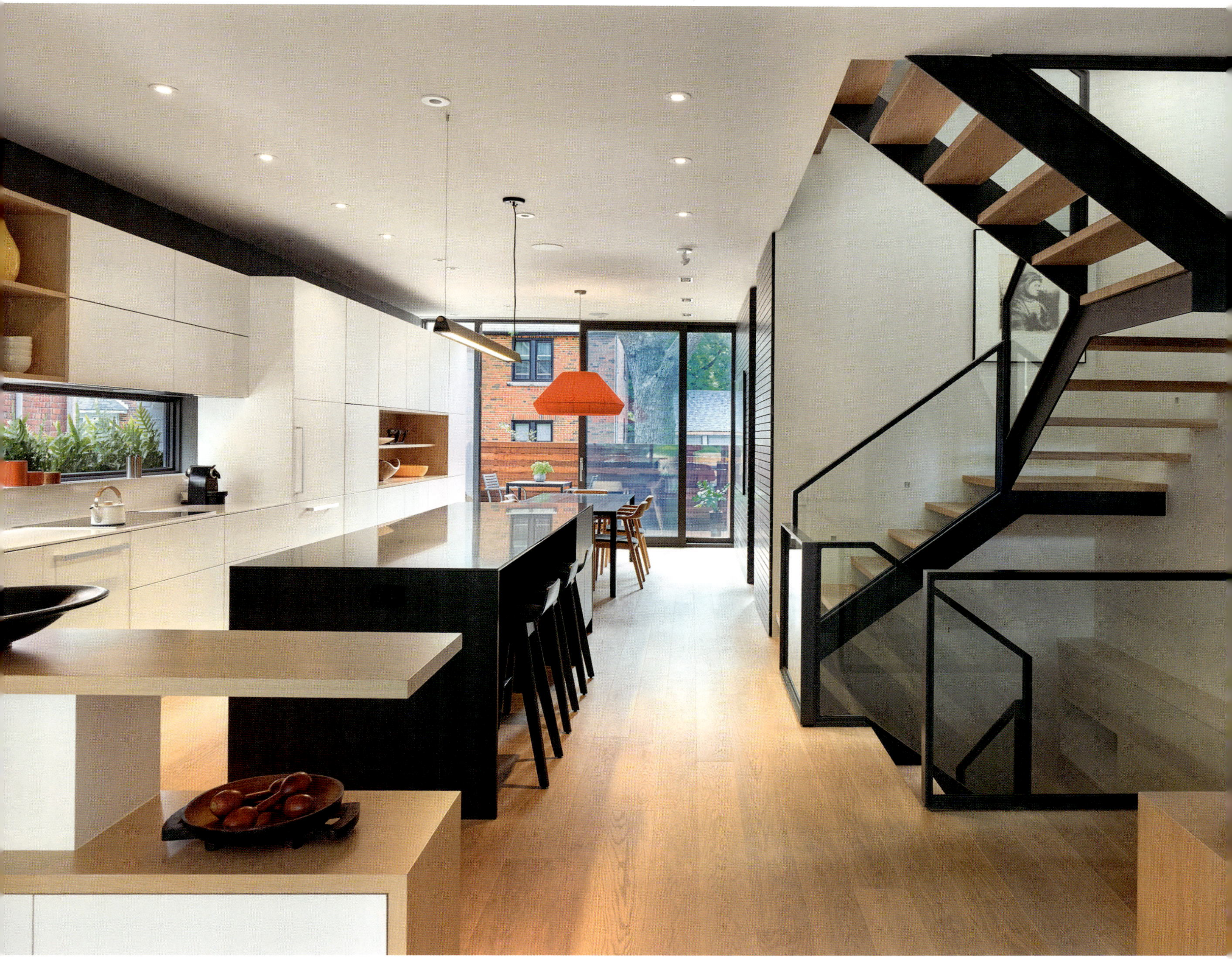

The expansive, crisp white surfaces of the kitchen cabinetry contrast with different elements within, such as the dark-stained oak slats of the movable vestibule screen and wall, the generous kitchen island with a charcoal Silestone countertop, and the white oak shelving dedicated to the display of the owner's collected belongings.

Die strahlend weißen Küchenmöbel stehen im Kontrast zu den übrigen Elementen wie den dunkel gefleckten Eichenleisten des beweglichen Wandschirms und der Wand im Vorraum, der großzügigen Kücheninsel mit der Carbon-Silestone-Arbeitsplatte und den weißen Eichenregalen für die Sammlerstücke der Bewohner.

Les grandes surfaces blanches et lisses des éléments de cuisine contrastent avec les lattes de chêne foncé teintes du paravent mobile du vestibule et avec le mur, l'îlot central opulent et son plan de travail Silestone couleur charbon, ainsi qu'avec les étagères de chêne blanc dédiées à l'exposition de la collection du propriétaire.

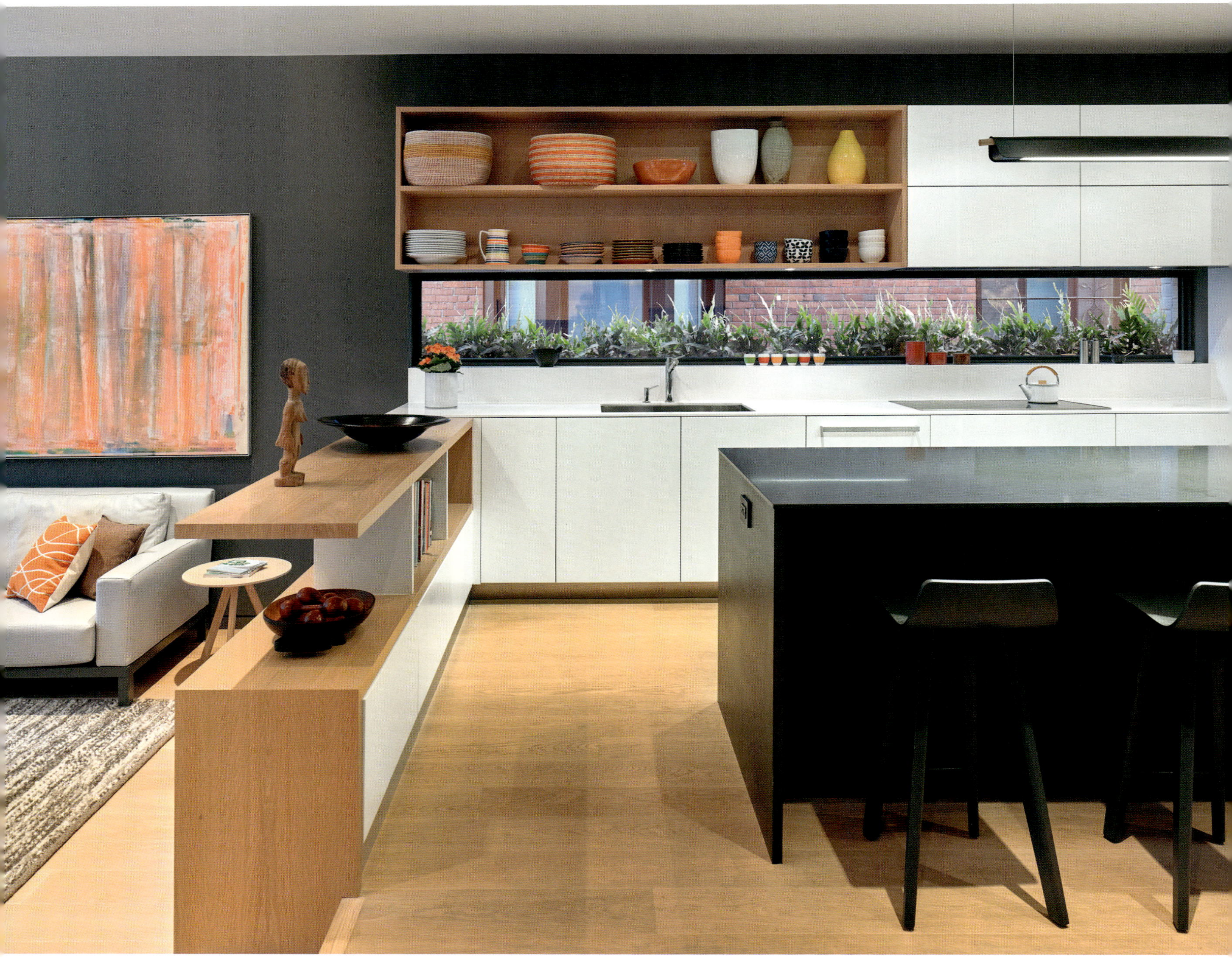

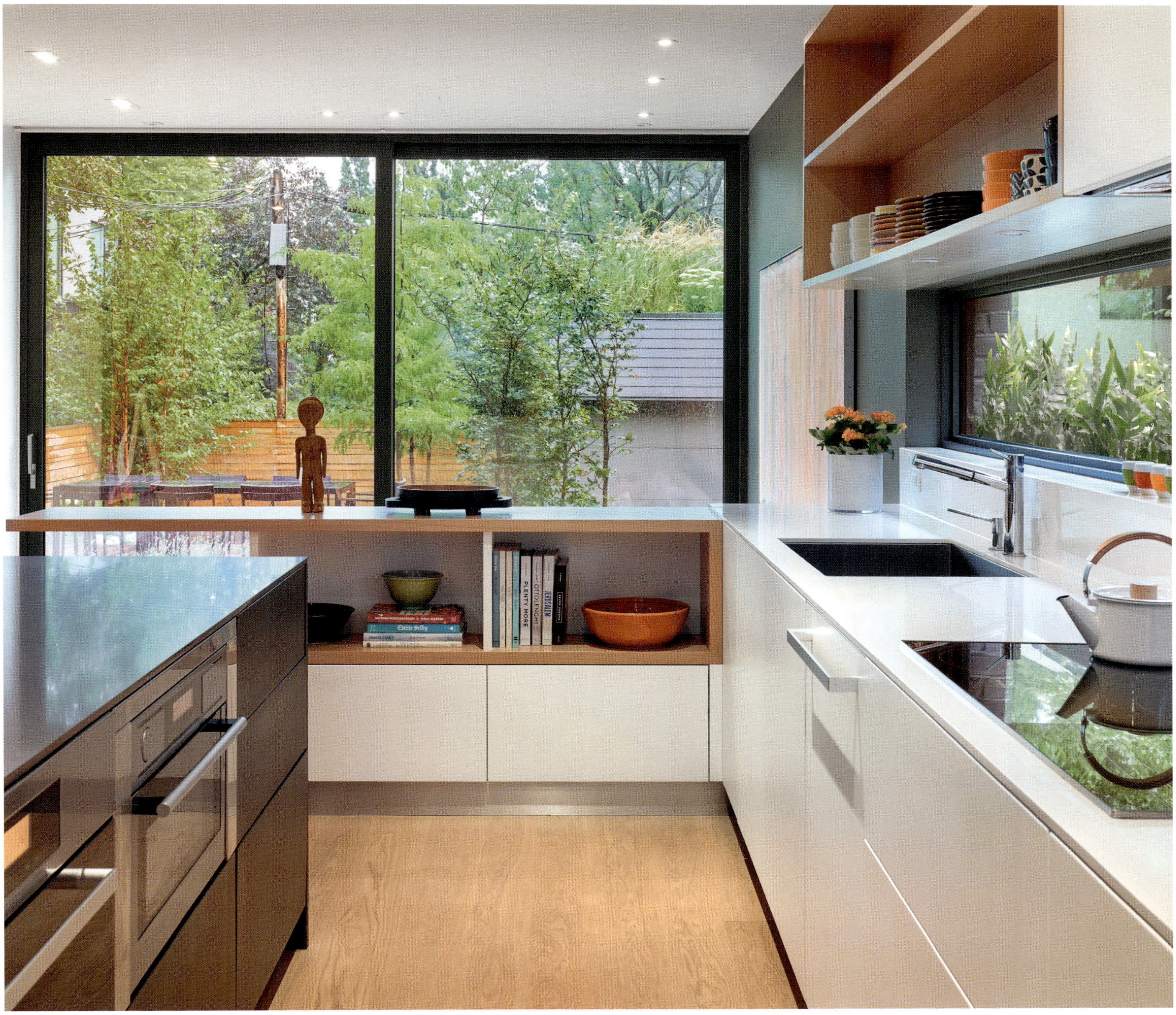
PLENTY MORE
OTTOLENGHI
JERUSALEM

The "skygarden" acts as an extension of the master bedroom. The warm ash cladding gives this outdoor space an intimate feel, while an opening carved into the roof allows for natural light, access to rainwater, and ample views of green.

Der „Skygarden" ist eine Erweiterung des Hauptschlafzimmers. Die warme Eschenauskleidung verleiht dem Außenbereich ein intimes Flair. Eine Dachöffnung lässt natürliches Licht einfallen, bietet Zugang zu Regenwasser und einen tollen Ausblick ins Grüne.

Le *skygarden* sert d'extension à la chambre principale. Le bardage chaleureux en frêne confère à cet espace extérieur un sentiment d'intimité, tandis qu'une ouverture pratiquée dans le toit permet l'entrée de lumière naturelle, l'accès à l'eau de pluie, et des vues panoramiques sur la verdure.

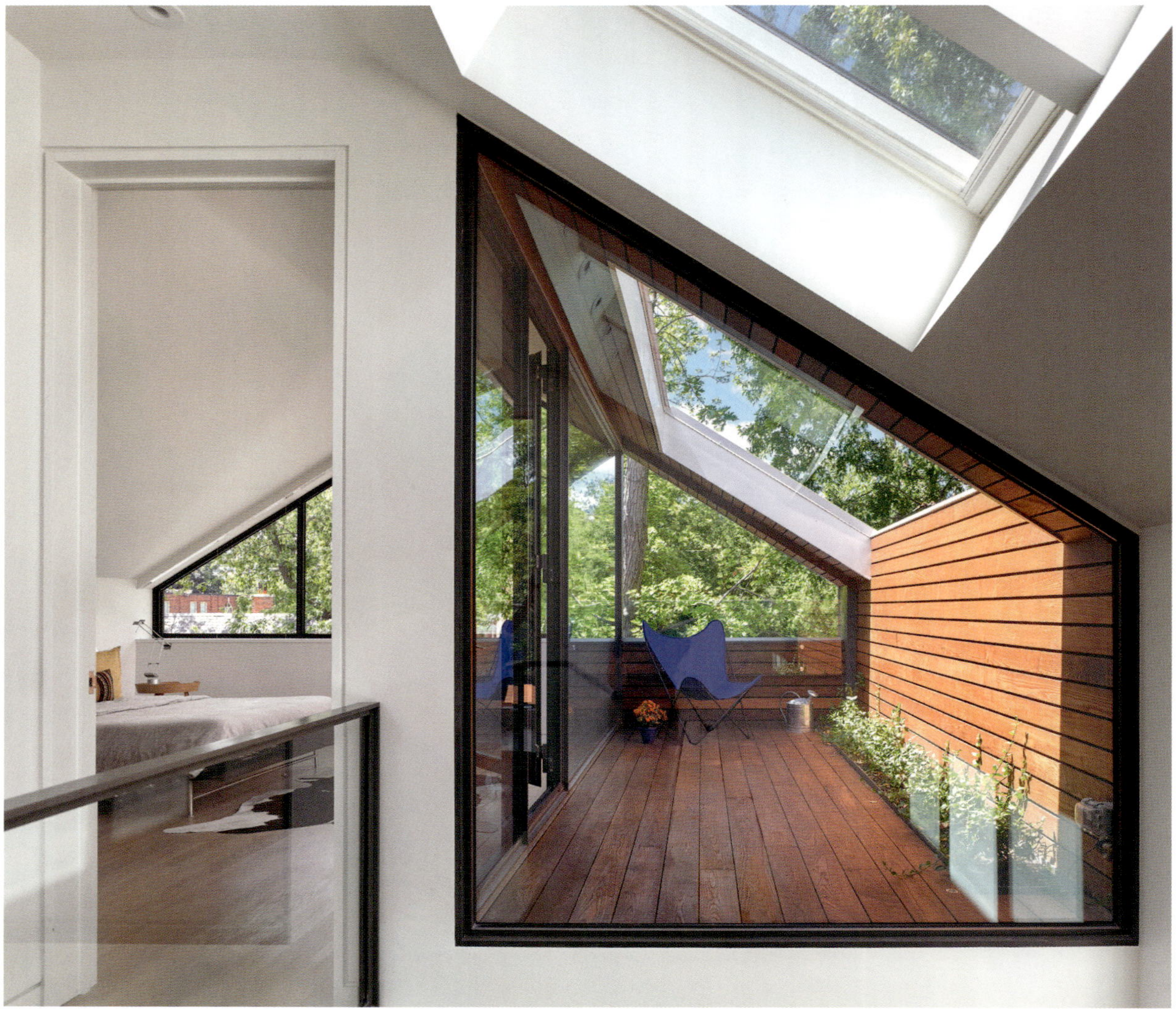

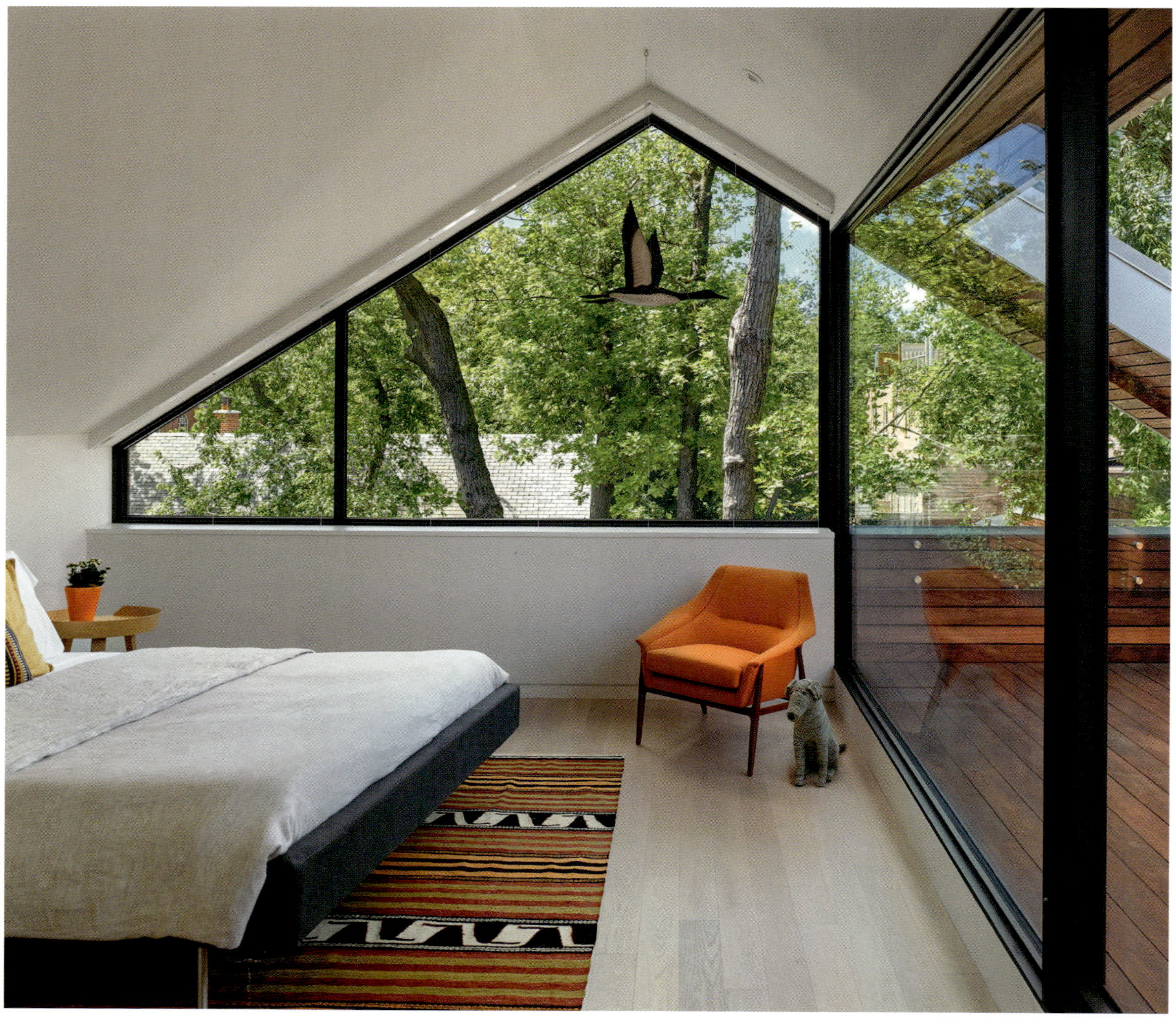

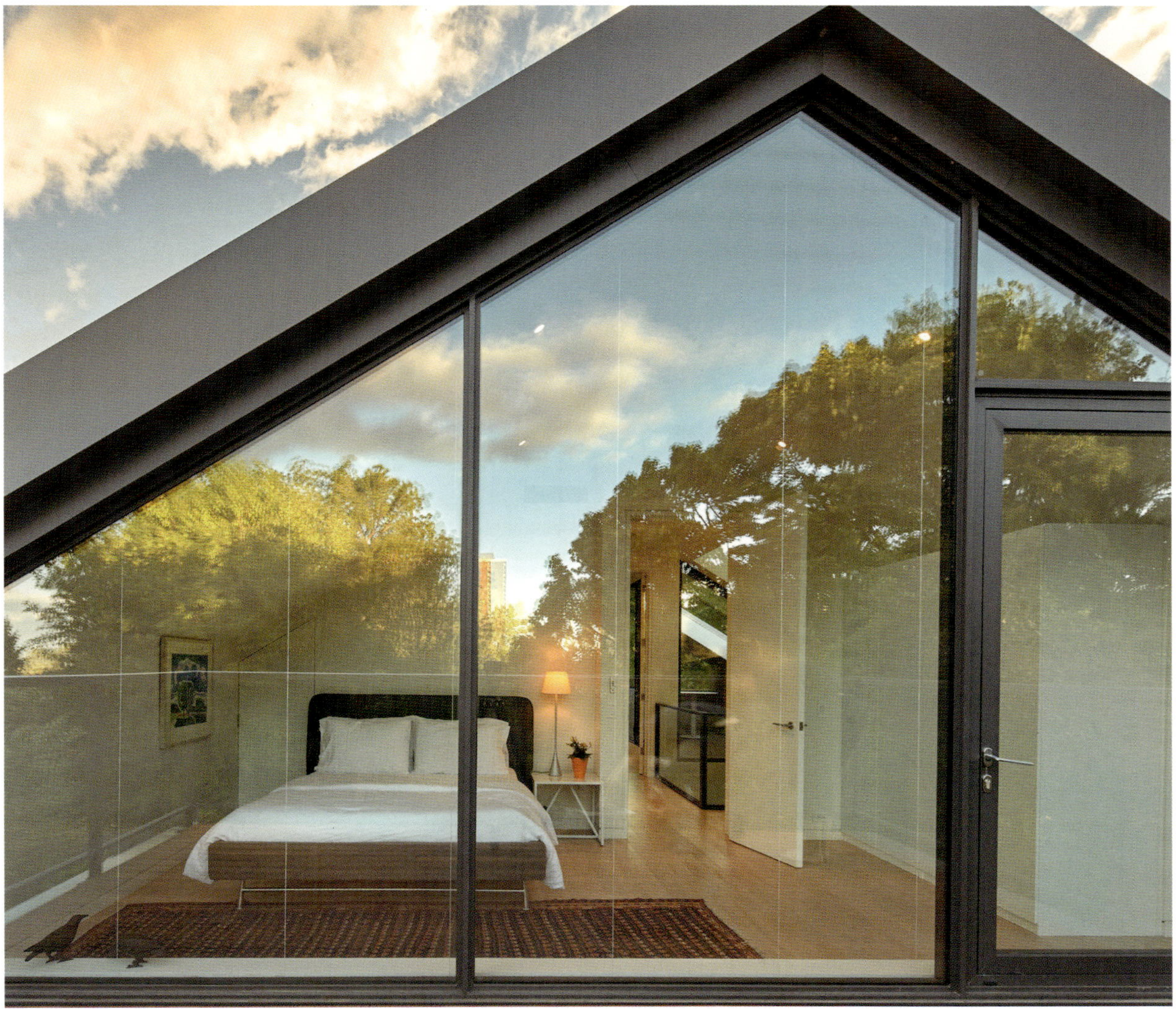

The new roof pitch was made less steep. In the attic, this allowed for taller ceiling height at the eaves, and therefore better use of the space. It made for one of the most appealing spaces in the house.

Das neue Satteldach ist weniger steil. Dies ließ im Dachgeschoss höhere Dachvorsprünge und damit eine bessere Raumnutzung zu. Der Dachboden wurde so zu einem der ansprechendsten Räume des Hauses.

Le nouveau toit a été construit moins pentu. Dans les combles, cela a permis des hauteurs de plafond plus élevées près des bords, et ainsi une meilleure utilisation de la surface, générant l'un des espaces les plus attirants de la maison.

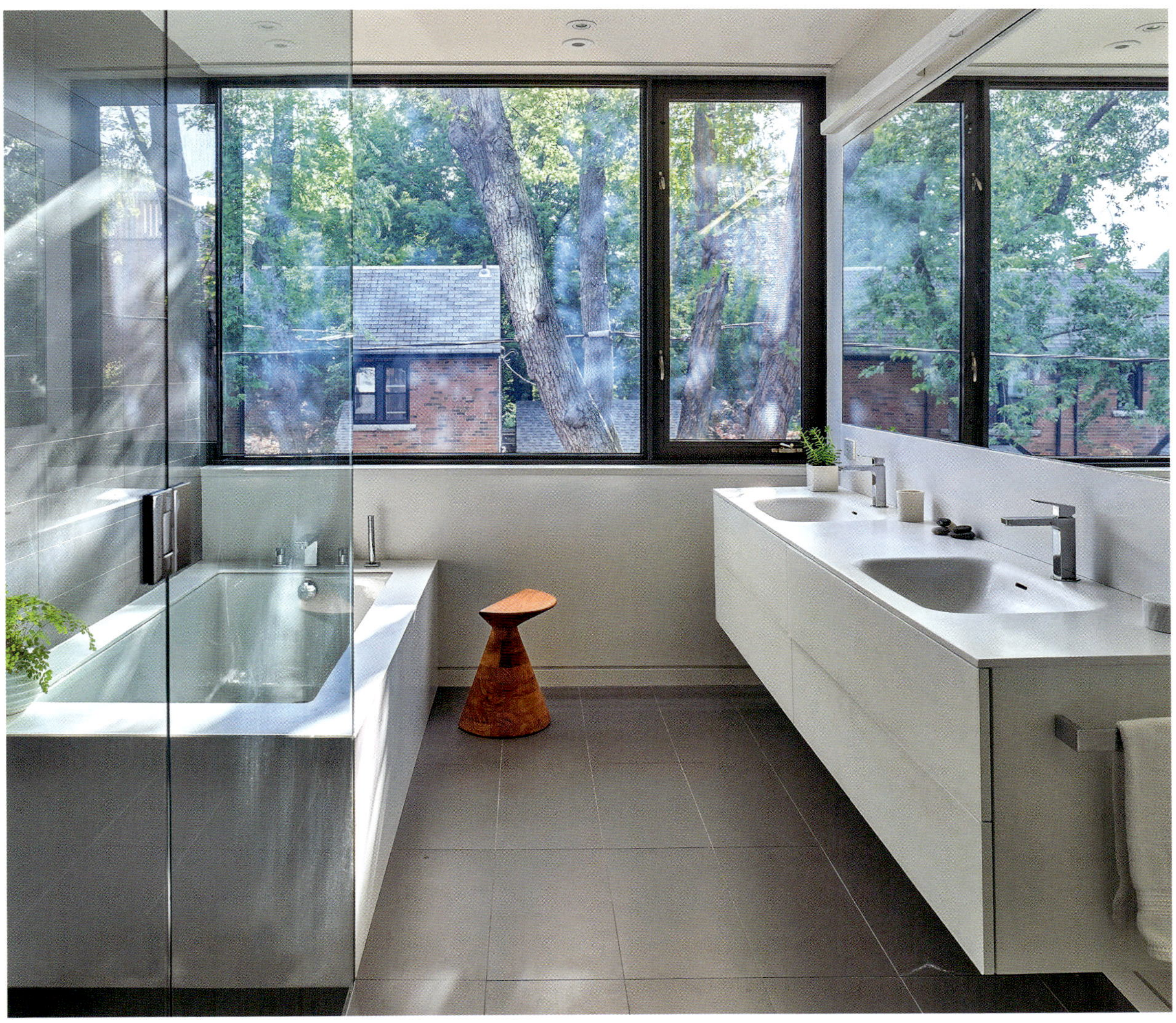

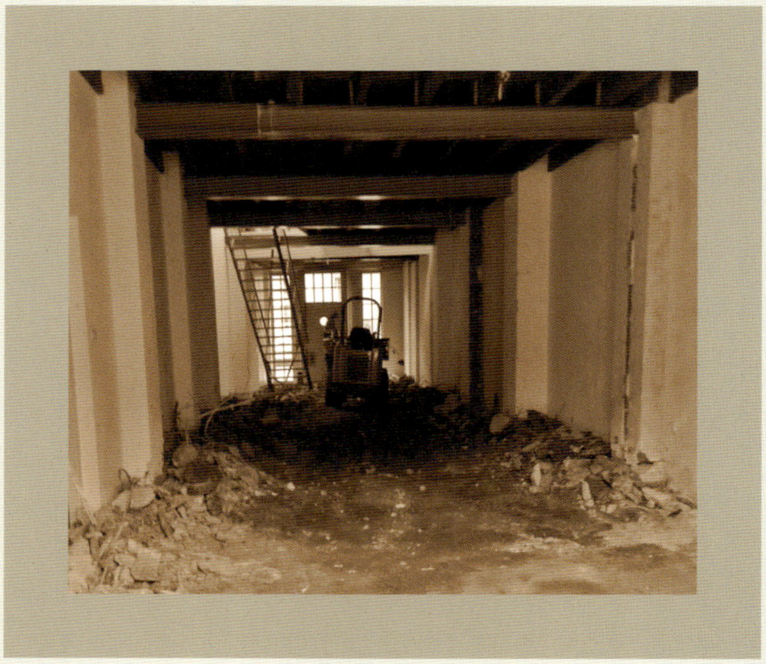

LOFT 64

EVA

200 m² | 2,150 sq. ft.

’s-Hertogenbosch, The Netherlands

Photos © **Sebastian van Damme, EVA architects**

> Create a residence from a building used initially as a workshop and later for offices

> Improve the lighting of the space

> Produce an ambiance that recalls New York City industrial warehouses

> Create a cozy space despite its large dimensions

> Ein Gebäude, das zunächst als Werkstatt und dann als Büros genutzt wurde, in ein Wohnhaus umwandeln

> Natürliches Licht in die Räume lassen

> Eine Stimmung schaffen, die an New Yorker Lofts erinnert

> Trotz seiner Größe einen gemütlichen Raum schaffen

> Transformer cet édifice qui servait initialement d'atelier, puis de bureaux, en un lieu de résidence

> Obtenir un espace plus lumineux

> Créer une ambiance semblable aux entrepôts industriels new-yorkais

> Créer un espace accueillant malgré ses grandes dimensions

This building was constructed as a workshop around 1880 but used as an office building in the last decade. It was refurbished several times over the years. To execute the restoration project, it was necessary to clear out the entire interior space, which dated to the 1990s, and to design a new distribution for the open space.
As the design developed, the architects were confronted with two major challenges: first, the lack of natural light, which only entered via the front and rear of the building. Second, adapting the necessary space—for example, the structure had only one bedroom—within the 2,150-square-feet interior to ensure that the different areas would continue to be warm and manageable. Moreover, since the client held a fascination for New York City, the typical New York warehouse was used as the metaphor. To achieve this, a large wooden element was placed at the center of the house, separating the space but retaining the perception of the space. Three skylights were added to permit daylight to stream into the house, reaching as far as the lower level. With all challenges overcome, the result could not be better: a light-filled residence with the feel of a New York City loft, where spaces flow into one another and invite the beholder to stay.

Dieses Gebäude wurde um 1880 als Werkstatt erbaut, diente im letzten Jahrzehnt jedoch als Büros. Im Laufe der Jahre wurde es verschiedenen Renovierungen unterzogen. Bei der Umsetzung des Sanierungsprojekts wurden alle in den 1990er Jahren eingezogene Innenwände abgerissen, um einen neuen, offenen Grundriss zu schaffen.
Bei der Entwicklung des Entwurfs standen die Architekten vor zwei großen Herausforderungen: erstens dem Mangel an Tageslicht, das nur durch Vorder- und Rückseite eindrang, und zweitens die Räume so auf den 200 m² zu verteilen – es gibt zum Beispiel nur ein Schlafzimmer –, dass die verschiedenen Bereiche gemütlich und überschaubar bleiben. Auf der anderen Seite wurde, da der Kunde New York liebt, beschlossen, das typische New Yorker Loft als Metapher zu nehmen. Als Antwort darauf wurde ein Holzvolumen in der Mitte des Hauses platziert. So wird der Raum getrennt, die Raumerfahrung bleibt jedoch weiterhin erhalten. Mit den drei Oberlichtern kann das Tageslicht selbst bis ins Erdgeschoss des Hauses gelangen. Nachdem alle Herausforderungen gemeistert wurden, ist das Ergebnis unschlagbar: eine helle Wohnung mit der Ästhetik eines New Yorker Lofts, in dem die Räume fließend ineinander übergehen und zum Verweilen einladen.

Ce bâtiment a été construit comme un atelier vers 1880, mais utilisé comme bureau au cours de ces dernières décennies. Il a connu différentes rénovations au fil des années. Pour mener à bien le projet de réhabilitation, tout l'intérieur construit dans les années 90 a été détruit afin de partir d'un espace ouvert et concevoir sa nouvelle répartition.
Pendant la phase de conception, les architectes ont dû faire face à deux grands défis : tout d'abord, le manque de lumière naturelle qui entrait uniquement par les façades avant et arrière ; ensuite, adapter les espaces nécessaires, par exemple, le fait qu'il n'y ait qu'une seule chambre sur une superficie totale de 200 m² de sorte que les différents espaces restent chaleureux et maniables. Par ailleurs, comme le client adorait New-York, il a décidé de choisir un entrepôt typique new-yorkais comme métaphore. En réponse à cela, un volume en bois a été placé au cœur de la maison, séparant ainsi l'espace tout en conservant son expérience. Des verrières ont été ajoutées afin que la lumière du jour puisse pénétrer la maison, y compris au rez-de-chaussée. Après avoir surmonté ces défis, le résultat est parfait : une maison lumineuse, à l'esthétique d'un *loft* New-Yorkais dans lequel les espaces s'échappent et invitent à rester.

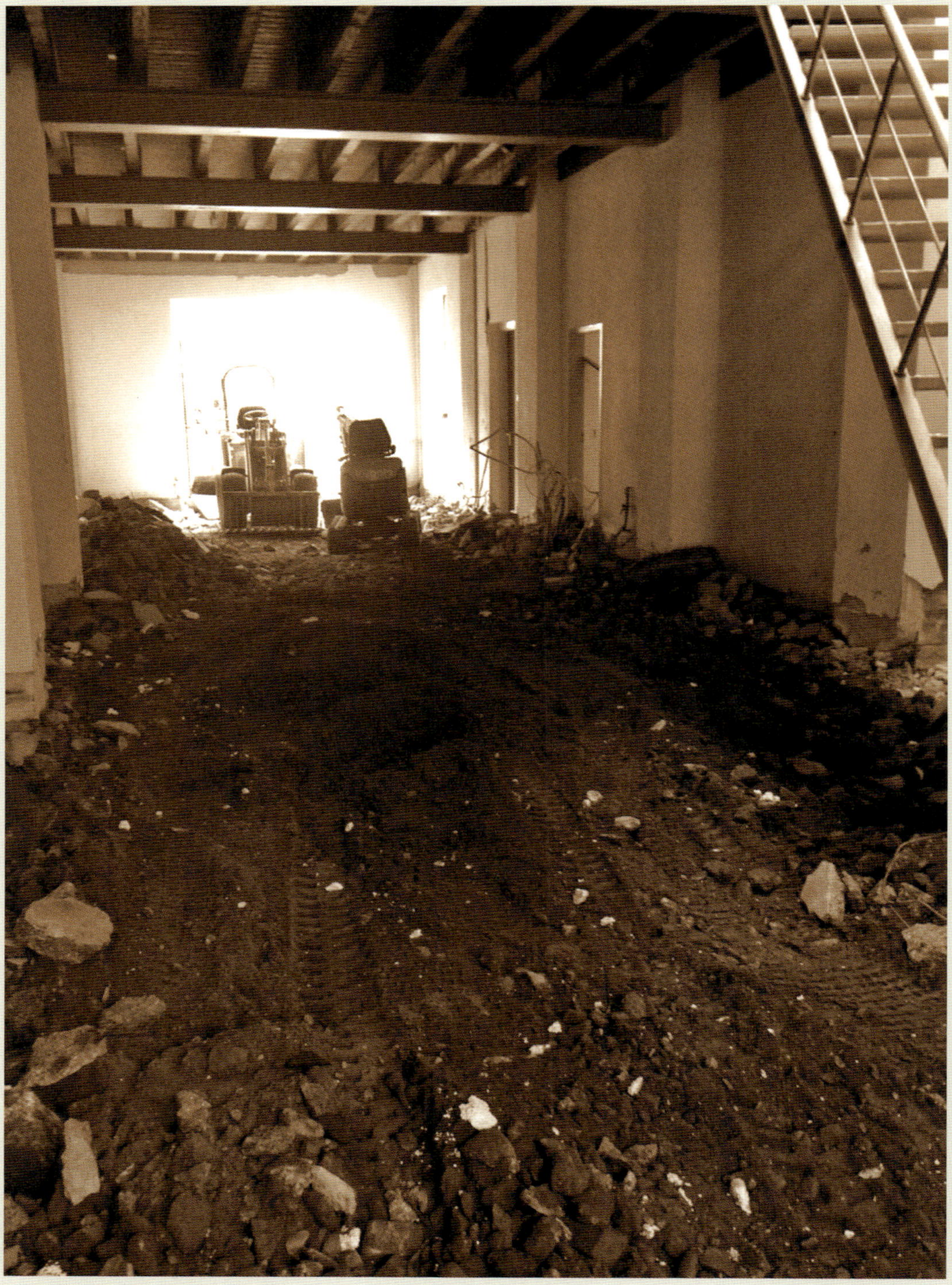

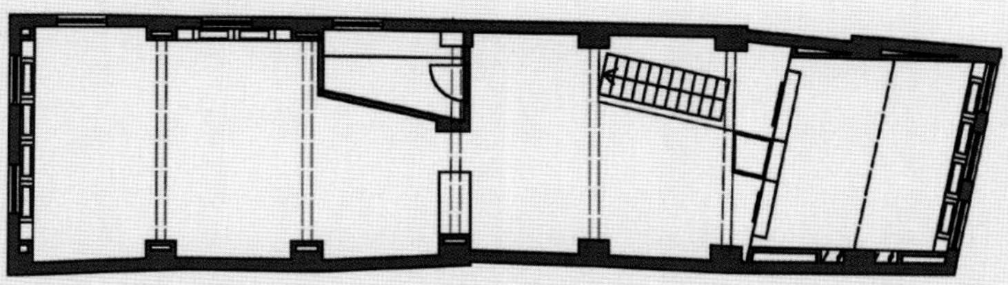

Existing first floor plan

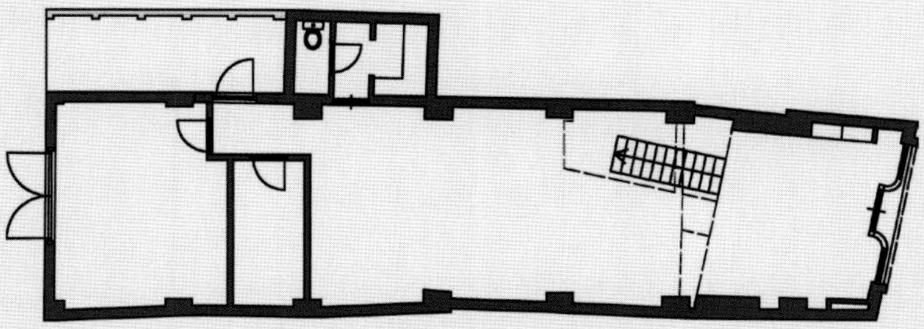

Existing ground floor plan

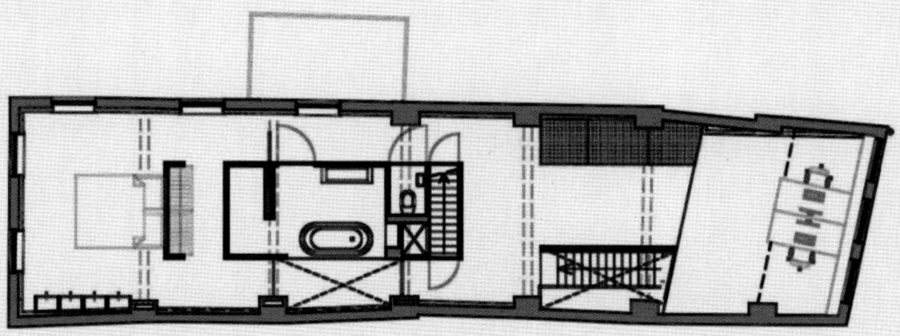

New first floor plan

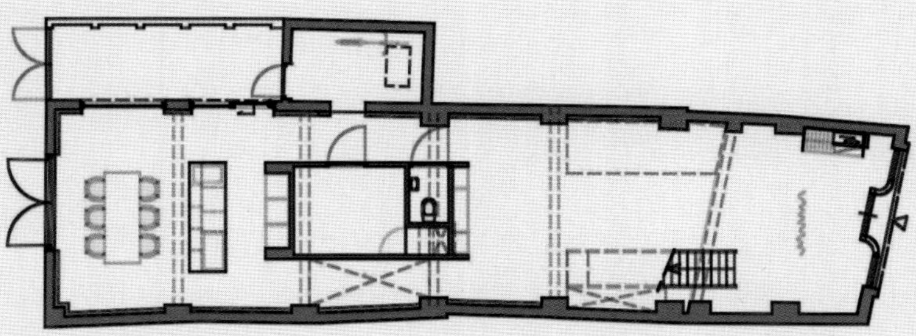

New ground floor plan

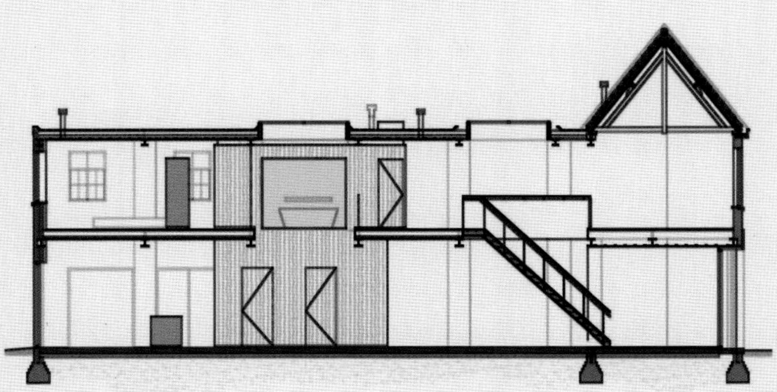

Longitudinal section

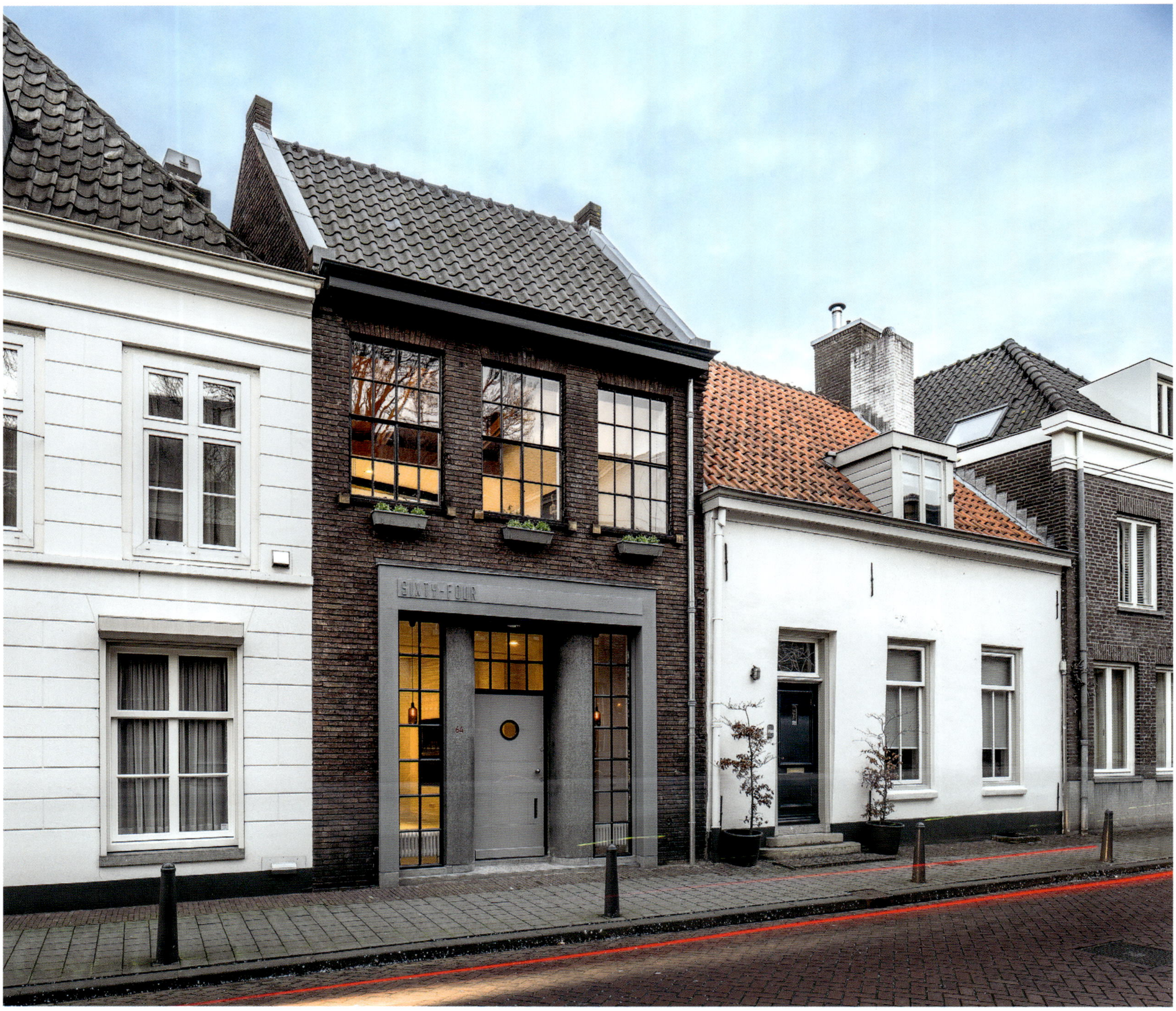

In the restoration, great importance was given to the facade in an effort to produce stylistic coherence between the interior and exterior of the residence. The iron-framed windows and door design suggest what lies hidden behind the walls.

Bei der Sanierung wurde großer Wert auf die Fassade gelegt und ein stilistischer Zusammenhang zwischen dem Inneren und Äußeren des Hauses angestrebt. Fenster mit Eisenprofilen und die Gestaltung der Eingangstür spiegeln wider, was sich hinter den Mauern verbirgt.

Les travaux de réhabilitation se sont focalisés sur la façade à la recherche d'une cohérence stylistique entre l'intérieur et l'extérieur de la maison. Les fenêtres en fer forgé et le design de la porte d'entrée sont le reflet de ce qui se cache derrière les murs.

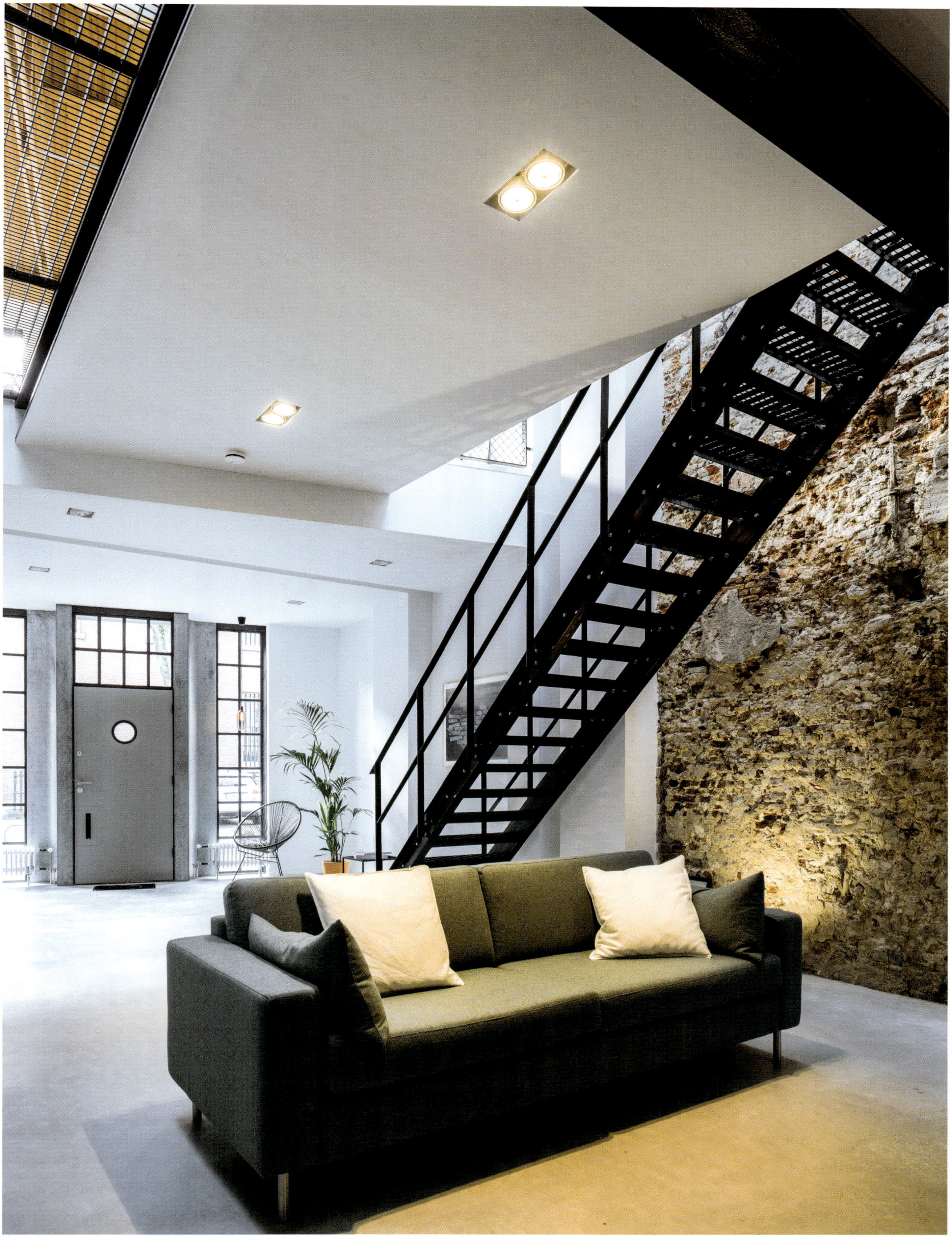

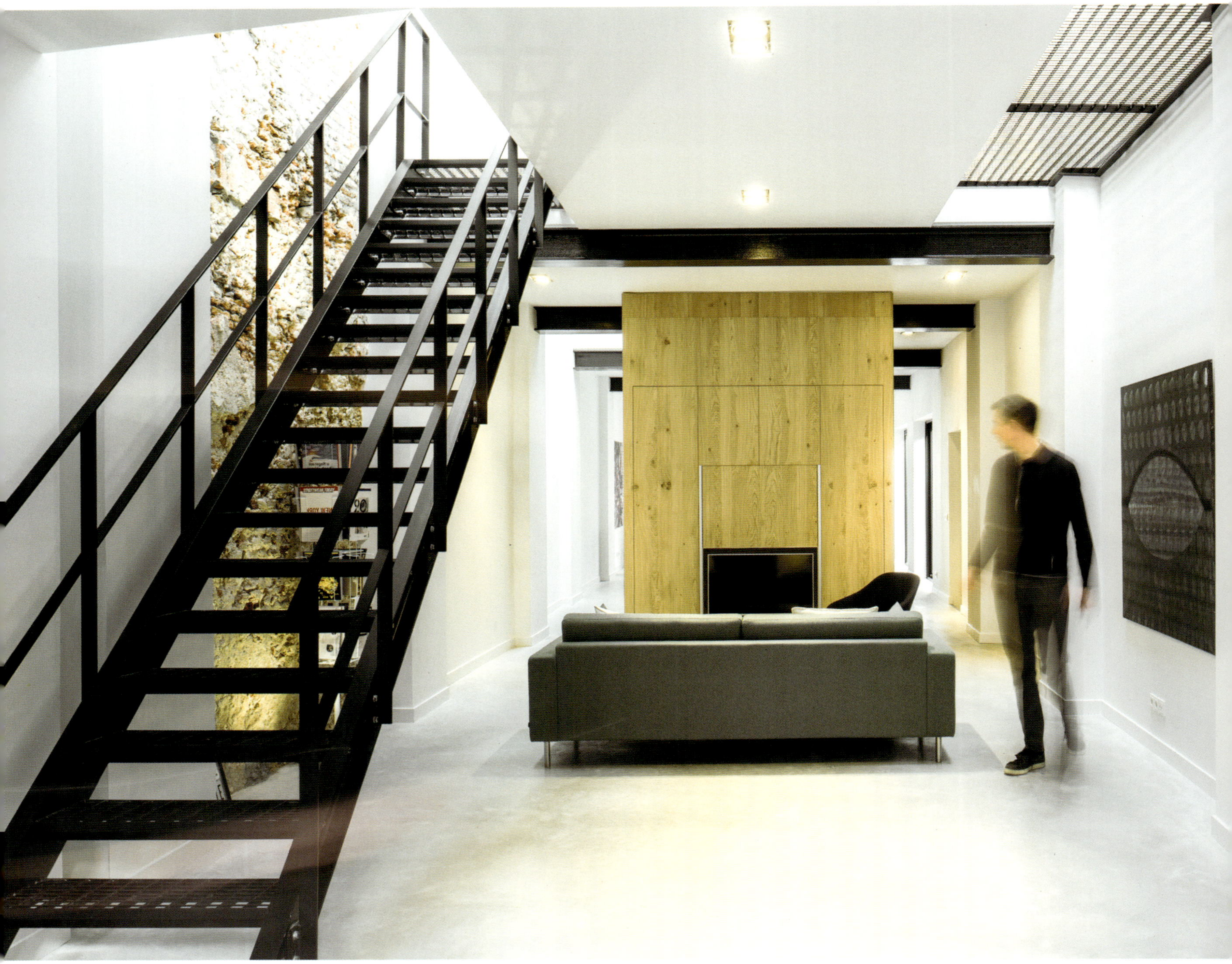

High ceilings, polished cement floor, concrete, neutral colors, structural purity. These are elements that correspond to an industrial feeling that extends throughout the entire residence.

Hohe Decken, polierter Zementboden, Eisen, Beton, neutrale Farben und strukturelle Reinheit sind Elemente, die einer industriellen Ästhetik entsprechen, die sich auf das ganze Haus erstreckt.

Hauts plafonds, sol en béton poli, fer forgé, béton, couleurs neutres, pureté structurelle ... tels sont les éléments qui répondent à une esthétique industrielle à profusion dans toute la maison.

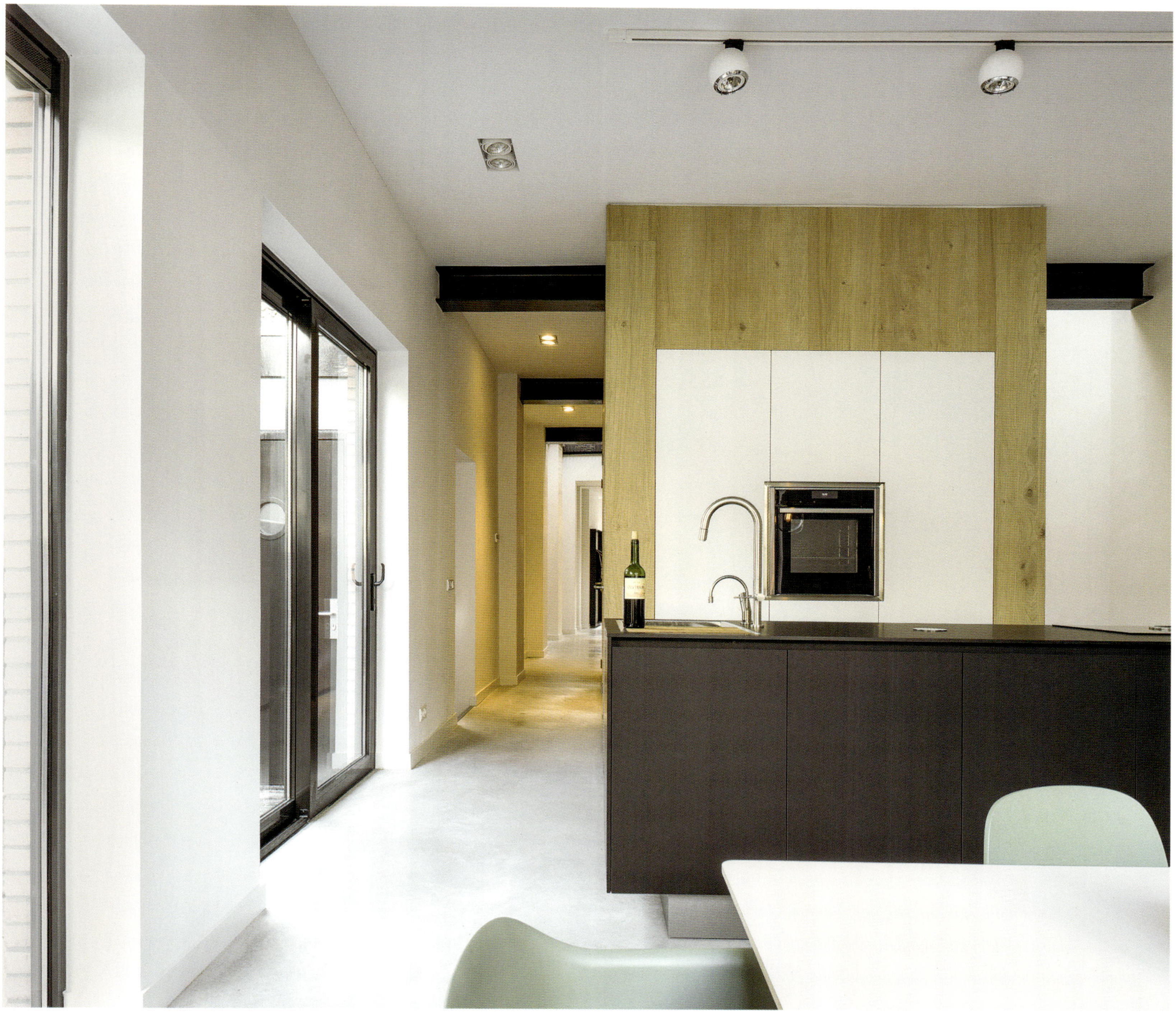

Because the space is the main element, colors and elements were employed that respect but do not invade it. Besides containing storage facilities and a bathroom, the brushed oak element also demarcates the space without the use of screens or dividers.

Raum ist das Hauptelement, daher werden Materialien, Farben und Elemente eingesetzt, die ihn respektieren und nicht verdecken. Das Kernstück aus gebürstetem Eichenholz, in dem ein Lagerraum und eine Toilette untergebracht sind, teilt den Raum und vermeidet so den Einsatz von Trenn- bzw. Zwischenwänden.

L'espace est le principal élément d'où l'utilisation de matériaux, couleurs et éléments qui le respectent et ne l'envahissent pas. Le centre en bois de chêne raboté, en plus d'accueillir un espace de rangement et des toilettes, divise l'espace évitant ainsi l'utilisation de divisions ou de cloisons.

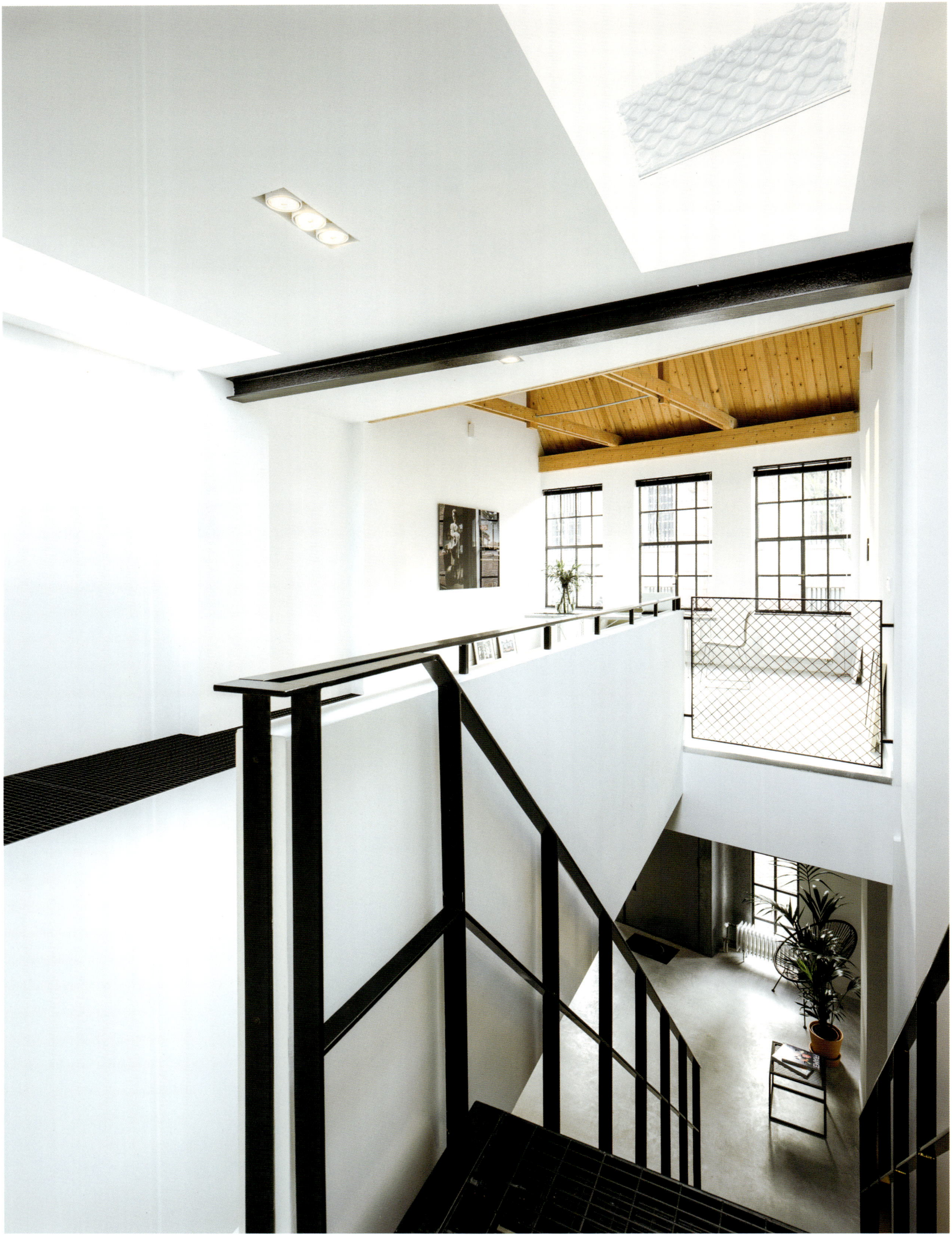

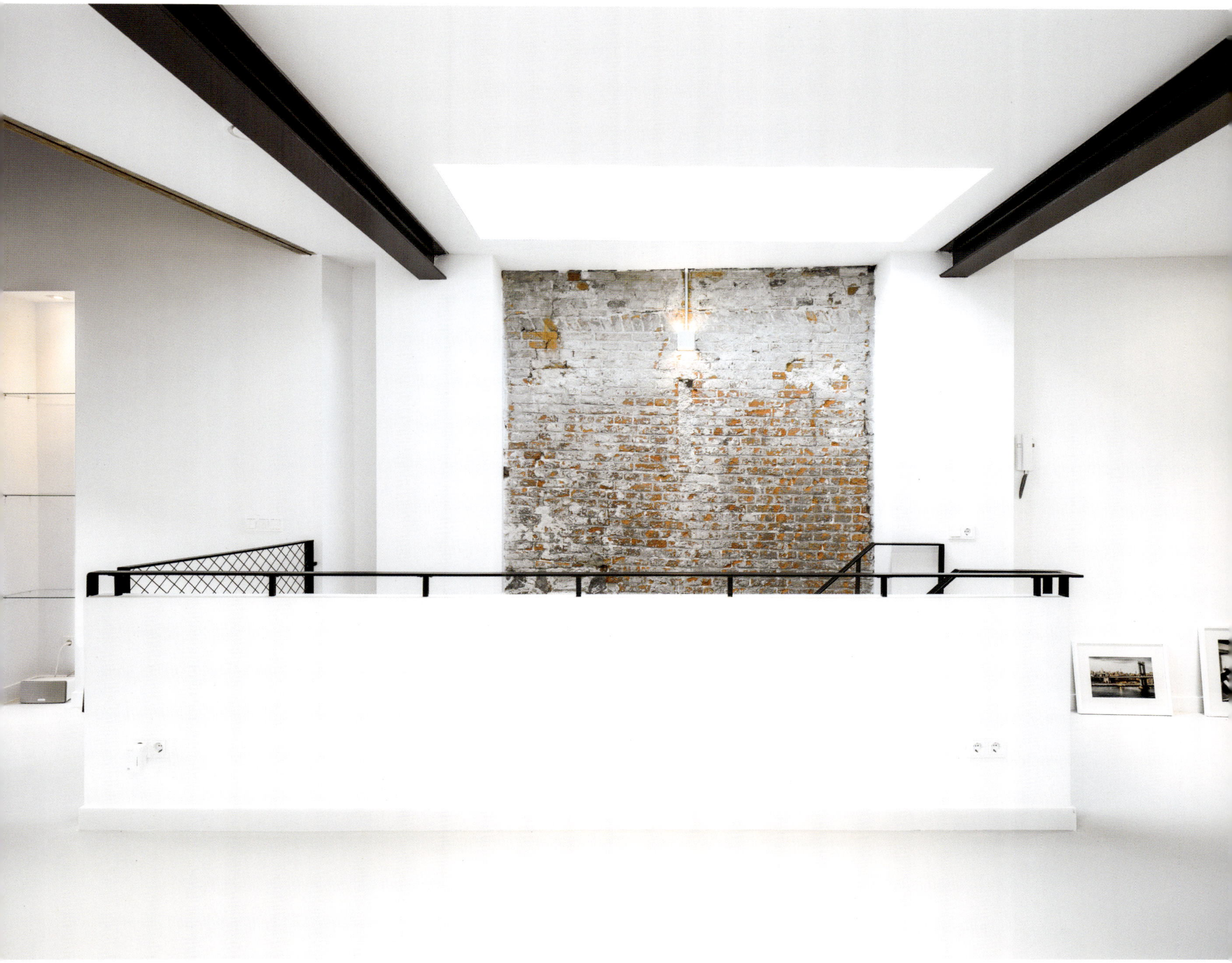

Original elements that illuminate the building's past have been left open to view. Juxtaposed against the predominantly white and smooth surfaces, the restored brick wall creates an engaging contrast of shade and texture, while adding character and personality to the residence.

Ursprüngliche Elemente, welche die historische Vergangenheit des Gebäudes offenbaren, wurden sichtbar belassen. Die restaurierte Backsteinmauer schafft einen interessanten Farb- und Texturkontrast zu den vorherrschenden weißen und glatten Flächen und verleiht dem Haus dadurch Charakter und Persönlichkeit.

Des éléments d'origine ont été laissés apparents révélant ainsi le passé historique du bâtiment. Le mur de brique récupéré offre un intéressant contraste chromatique et de texture avec les superficies blanches et lisses prédominantes, en plus de conférer du caractère et de la personnalité à l'habitation.

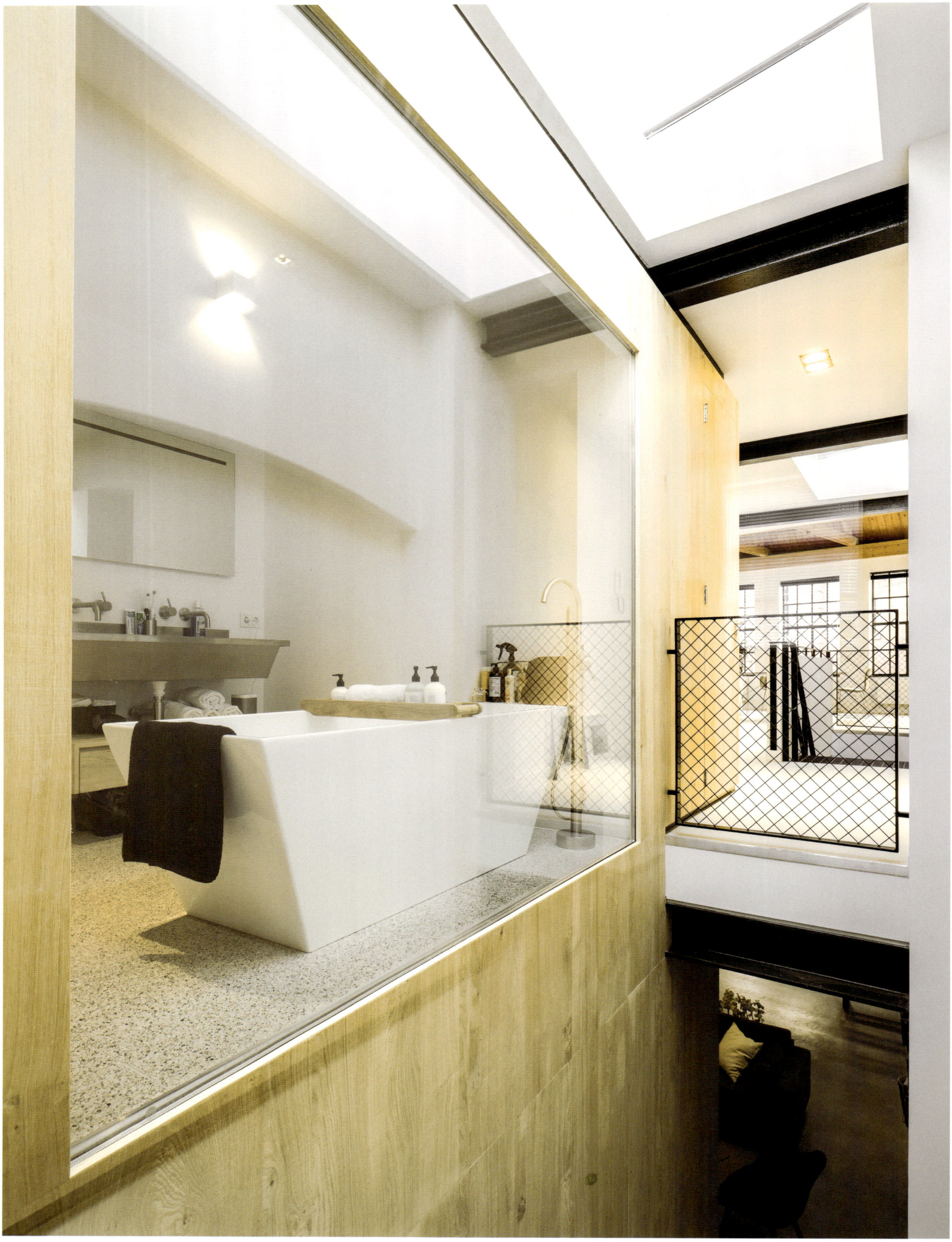

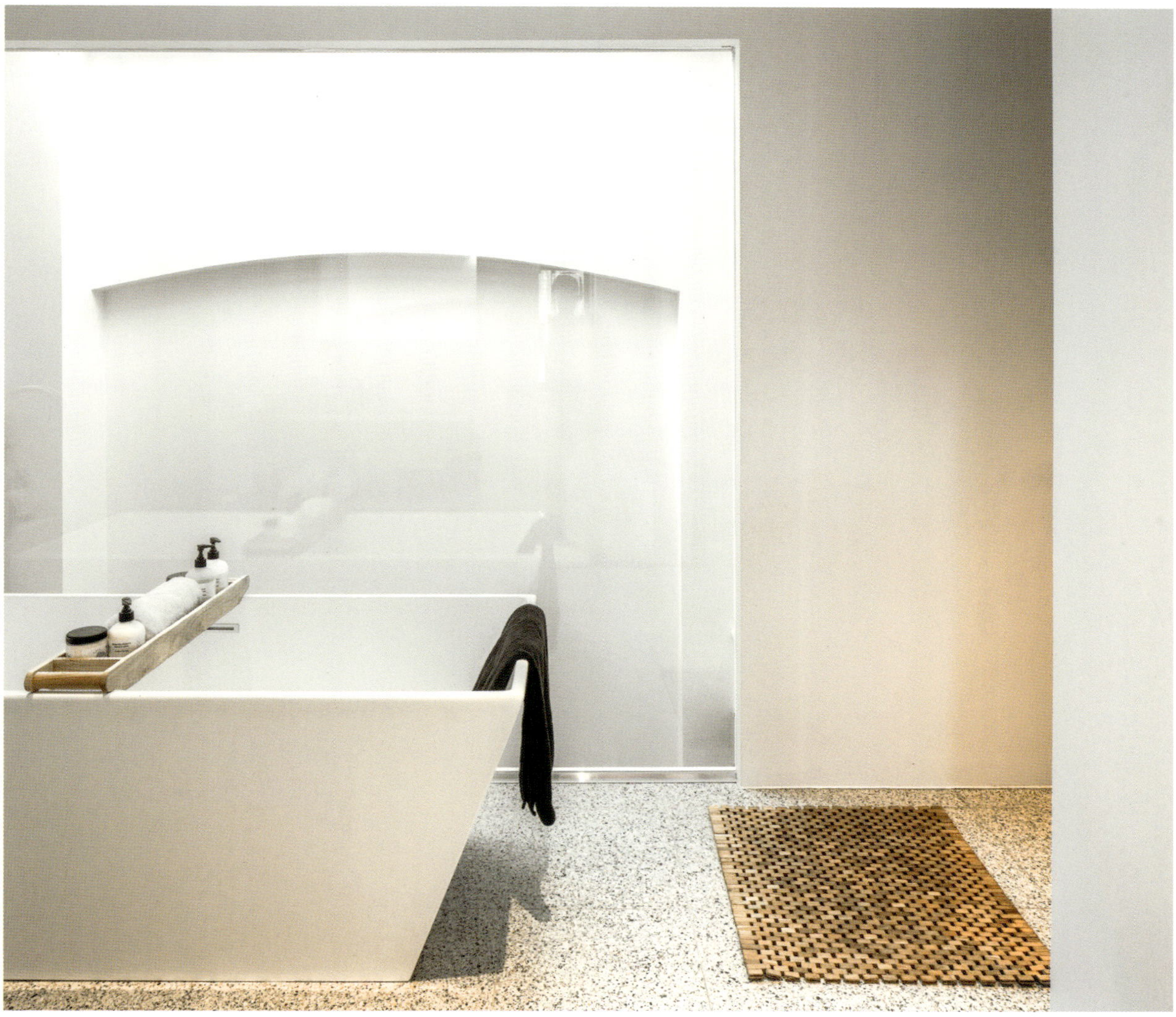

The new skylights and the double space beneath them allow the light to penetrate to the ground floor. The extensive use of white and neutral colors enhances this lighting effect and communicates a feeling of relaxation and utmost tidiness.

Die neuen Oberlichter und der darunterliegende doppelt hohe Raum lassen das Licht bis in das Erdgeschoss vordringen. Der umfangreiche Einsatz von Weiß und neutralen Farben verstärkt diese Leuchtkraft und vermittelt gleichzeitig ein Gefühl von Entspannung und extremer Sauberkeit.

Les nouvelles verrières et le double espace en dessous de celles-ci permettent à la lumière de pénétrer jusqu'au rez-de-chaussée. Cette luminosité est favorisée par l'utilisation intensive du blanc et des couleurs neutres qui procurent une sensation de relaxation et d'extrême attention.

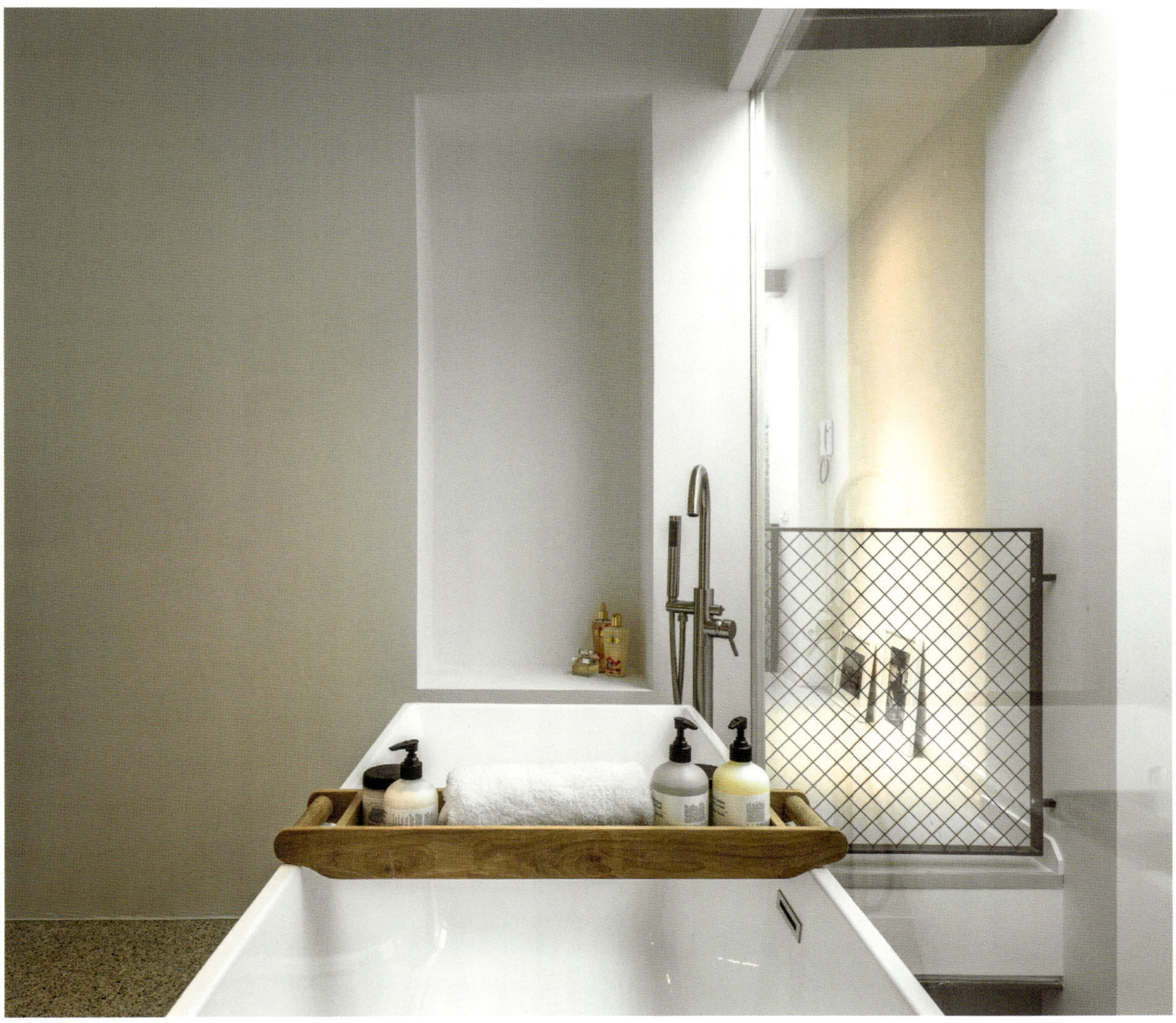

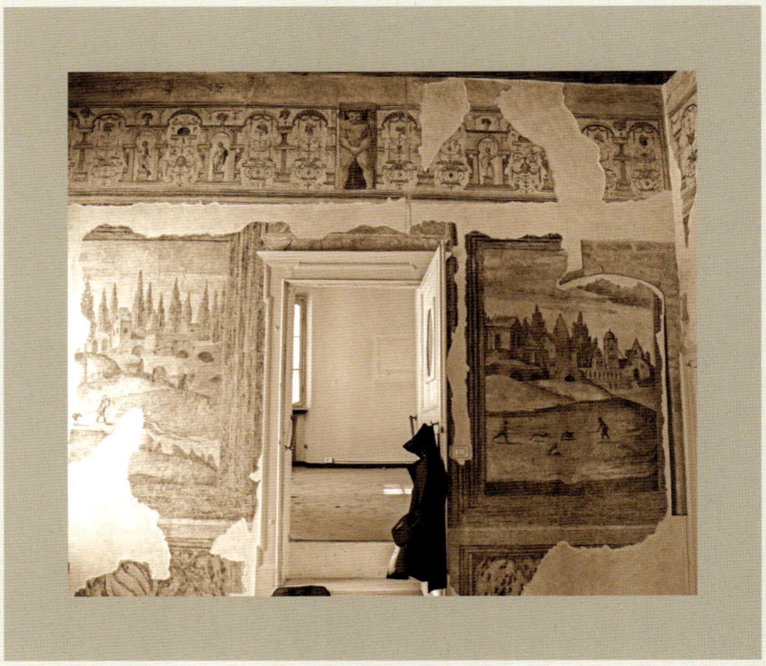

BROLETTO UNO

ARCHIPLAN STUDIO

84 m² | 904 sq. ft.

Mantua, Italy

Photos © **Davide Galli Atelier**

> Restore a small apartment to use as a tourist rental

> Combine old and new worlds without sacrificing the identity of either

> Restaurierung einer kleinen Wohnung als Ferienwohnung

> Vereinigung zweier Welten (alt und neu), ohne dass die Identität beider verloren geht

> Restaurer un petit appartement pour lui apporter un usage touristique

> Réunir deux mondes, l'ancien et le nouveau, sans pour autant perdre leur cachet

The project to reconstruct this apartment located in Mantua's historic center to be rented out to tourists fits into a long line of design research growing out of interventions to heritage buildings.
The architect's original concept was to try to keep together two worlds—old and new—achieving a balance that would assure both identities. The project particularly emphasizes the uniqueness and heterogeneity of the individual spaces, allowing ambiguity and contradiction to prevail over stylistic unity. It preserves traces of the contributions and esthetic intentions left by those who lived in earlier epochs, while the new traits overlap harmoniously.
This rehabilitation process has created a contemporary, comfortable, and welcoming space where history, far from going unnoticed, is constantly present.

Das Renovierungsprojekt für diese Wohnung, die im historischen Zentrum von Mantua liegt und für die Nutzung als Ferienwohnung bestimmt ist, gibt nach aufwändiger Recherchen eine Antwort darauf, wie man in historische Bausubstanz eingreift.
Die Grundprämisse des Architekten bestand darin, zwei Welten, d.h. die des Alten und die des Neuen, zu erhalten und sie in ein Gleichgewicht zu bringen, wodurch die Identität beider garantiert wird. Das Projekt betont insbesondere die Unterschiede und Heterogenitäten der einzelnen Zimmer und gibt Doppeldeutigkeit und Widerspruch Vorrang vor der stilistischen Einheit. Die von der Zeit, der menschlichen Arbeit und den ästhetischen Absichten der verschiedenen Epochen hinterlassenen Zeichen bleiben erhalten, während sich neue Zeichen harmonisch dazugesellen.
Dieser Sanierungsprozess hat einen modernen, bequemen und gemütlichen Raum erschaffen, dessen Geschichte - weit davon entfernt zu verschwinden - in jedem Moment präsent ist.

Le projet de reconstruction de cet appartement situé dans le centre historique de Mantua, destiné à un usage touristique, répond à un énorme travail de recherche de conception, qui survient au cours de plusieurs interventions que le bien a subies.
L'architecte avait pour principe initial de tenter de conserver les deux mondes ensemble, l'ancien et le nouveau, dans un équilibre qui pourrait garantir l'identité des deux. Le projet se focalise en particulier sur les différences et hétérogénéités des espaces individuels, dans lesquels l'ambiguïté et la contradiction priment sur l'unité stylistique. Les signes laissés par le temps, les travaux des ouvriers et l'intention esthétique des diverses époques subsistent, tandis que les nouveaux signes se superposent en harmonie.
Ces travaux de réhabilitation ont donné lieu à un espace contemporain, pratique et accueillant dont l'histoire, loin de passer inaperçue, reste présente à tout moment.

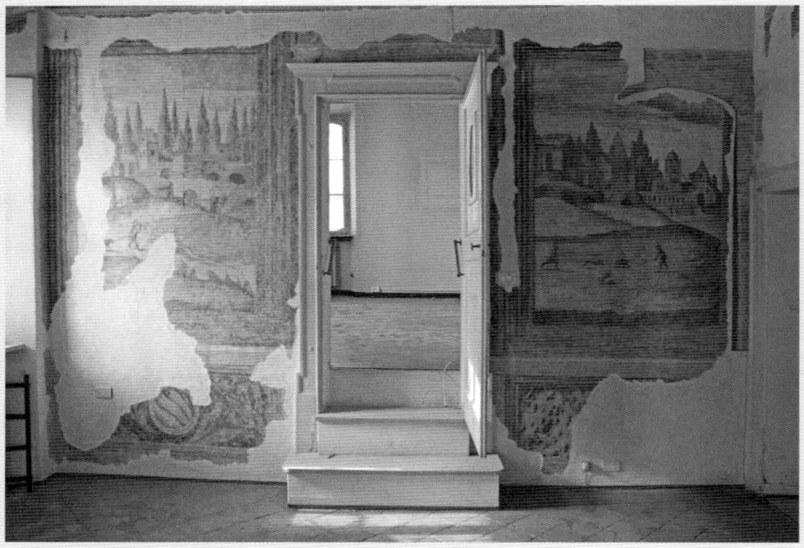
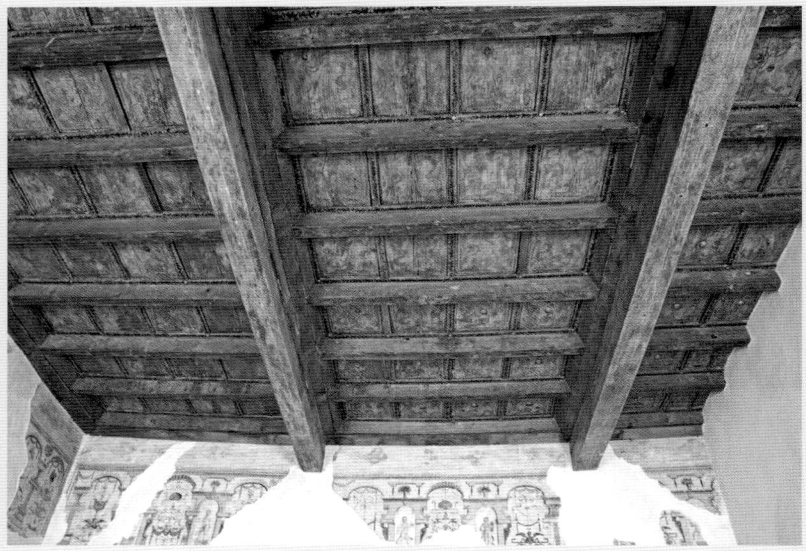
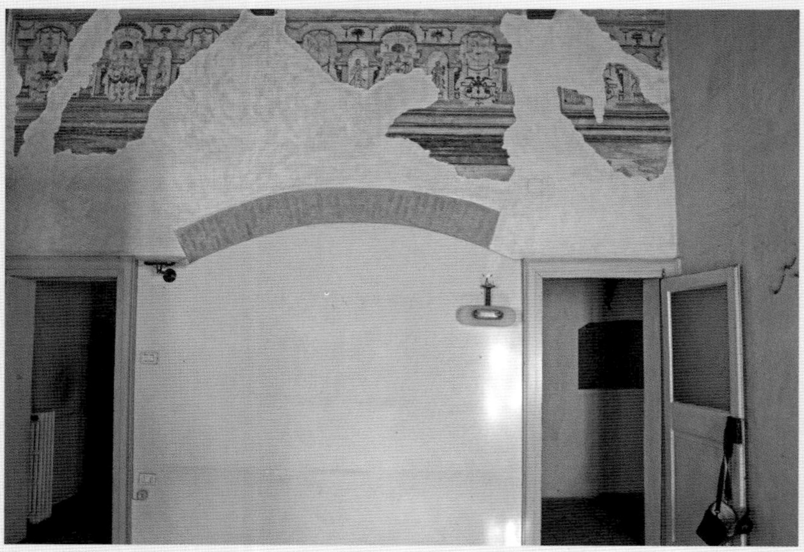
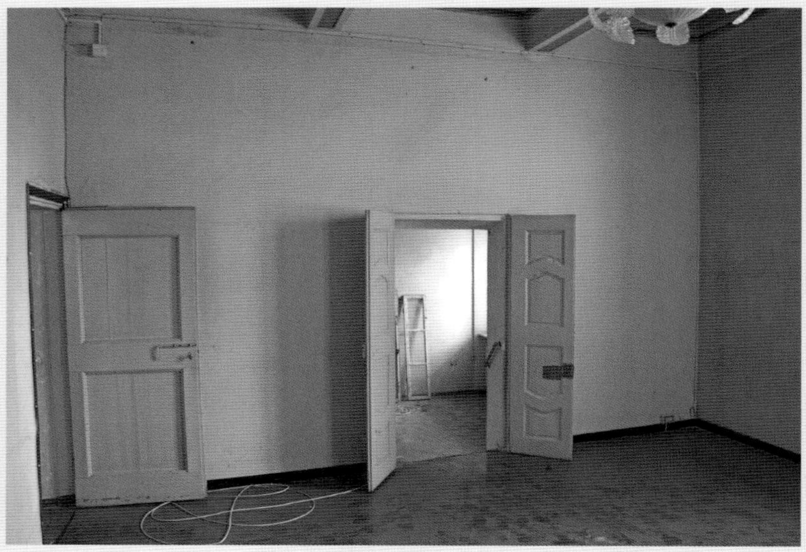
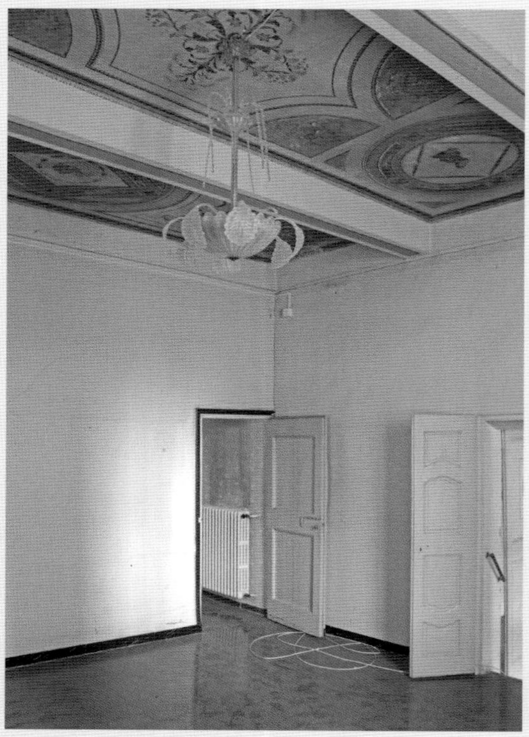
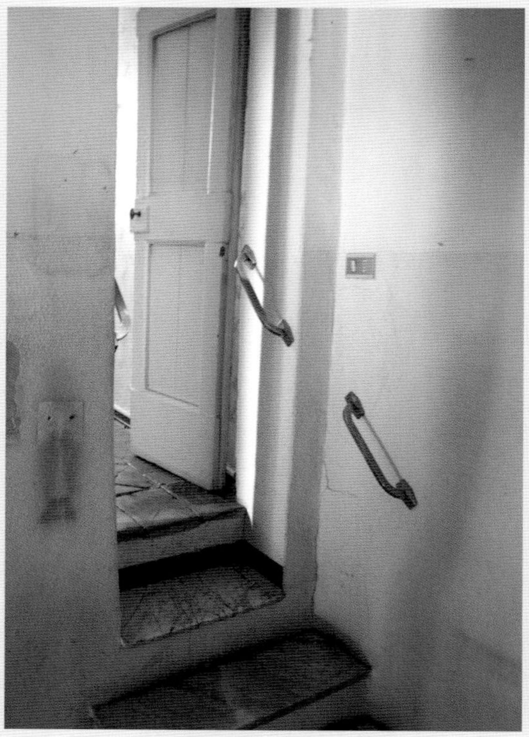
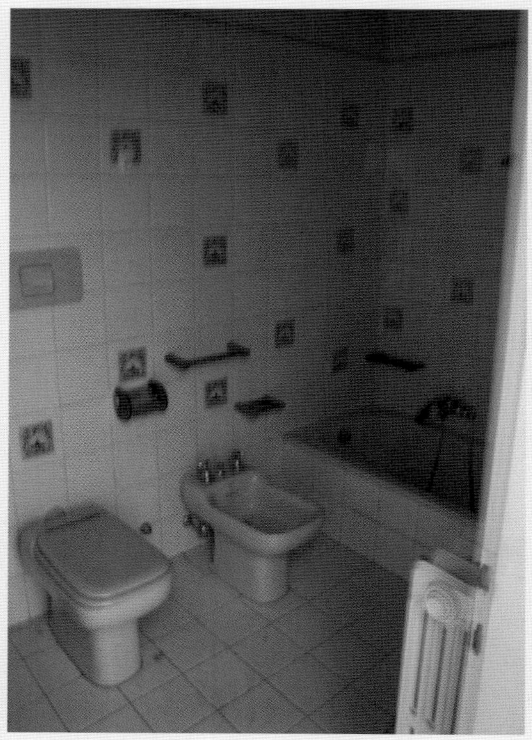

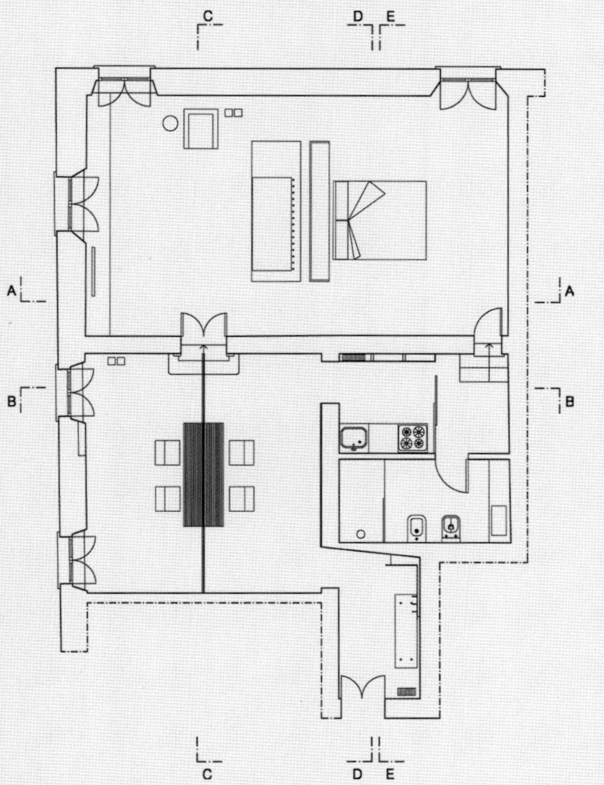

New plan

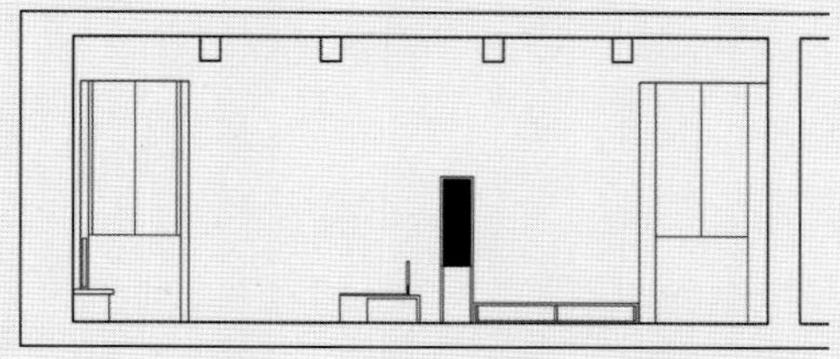

Section A-A

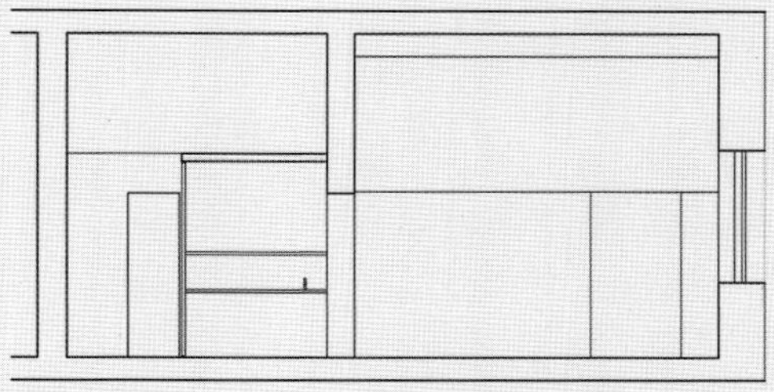

Section B-B

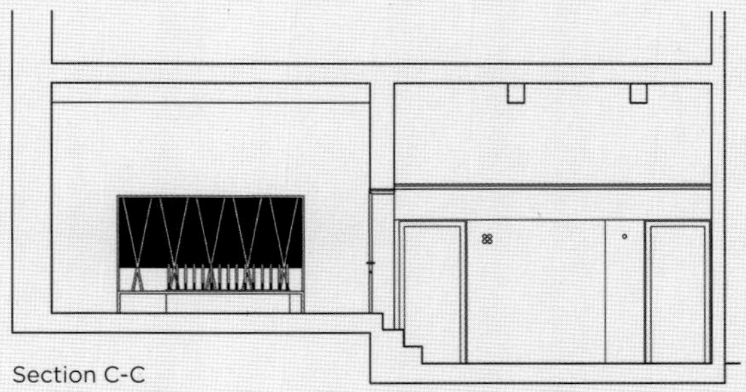

Section C-C

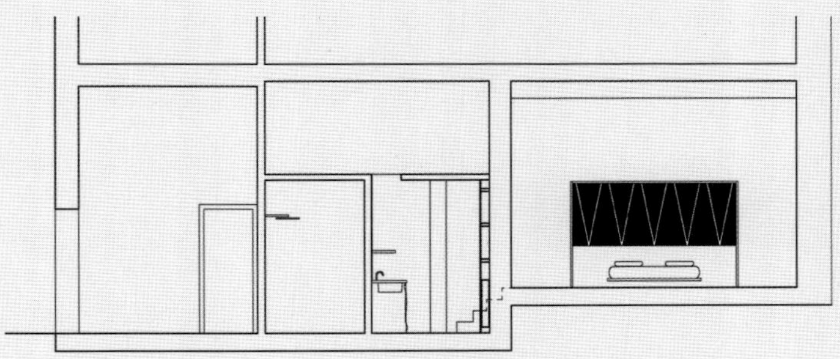

Section D-D

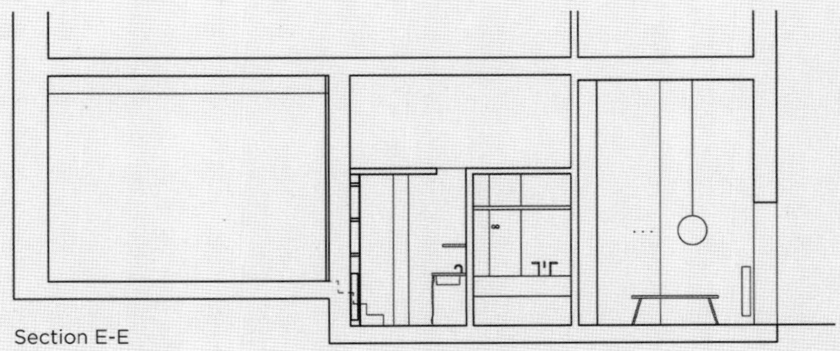

Section E-E

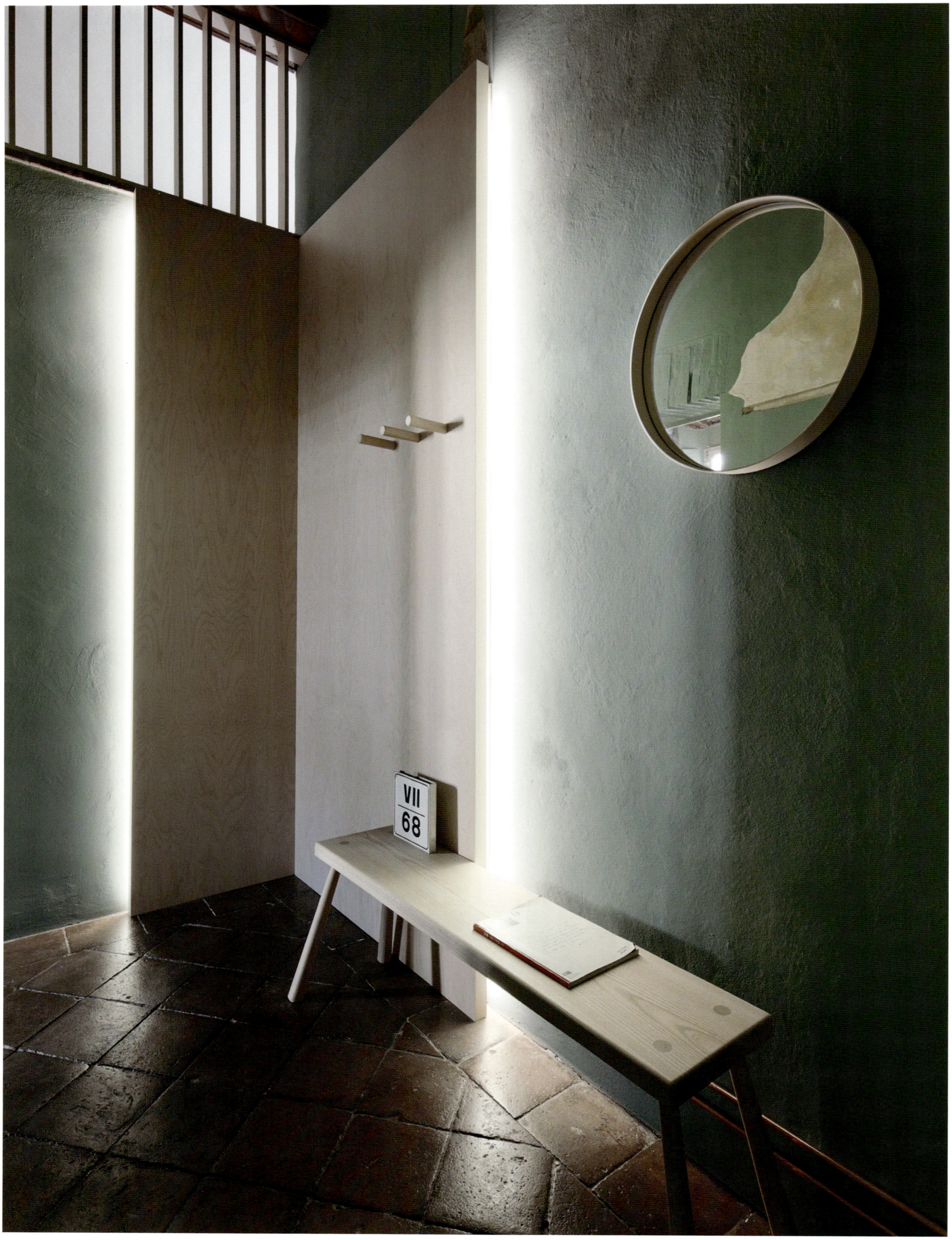
VII
68

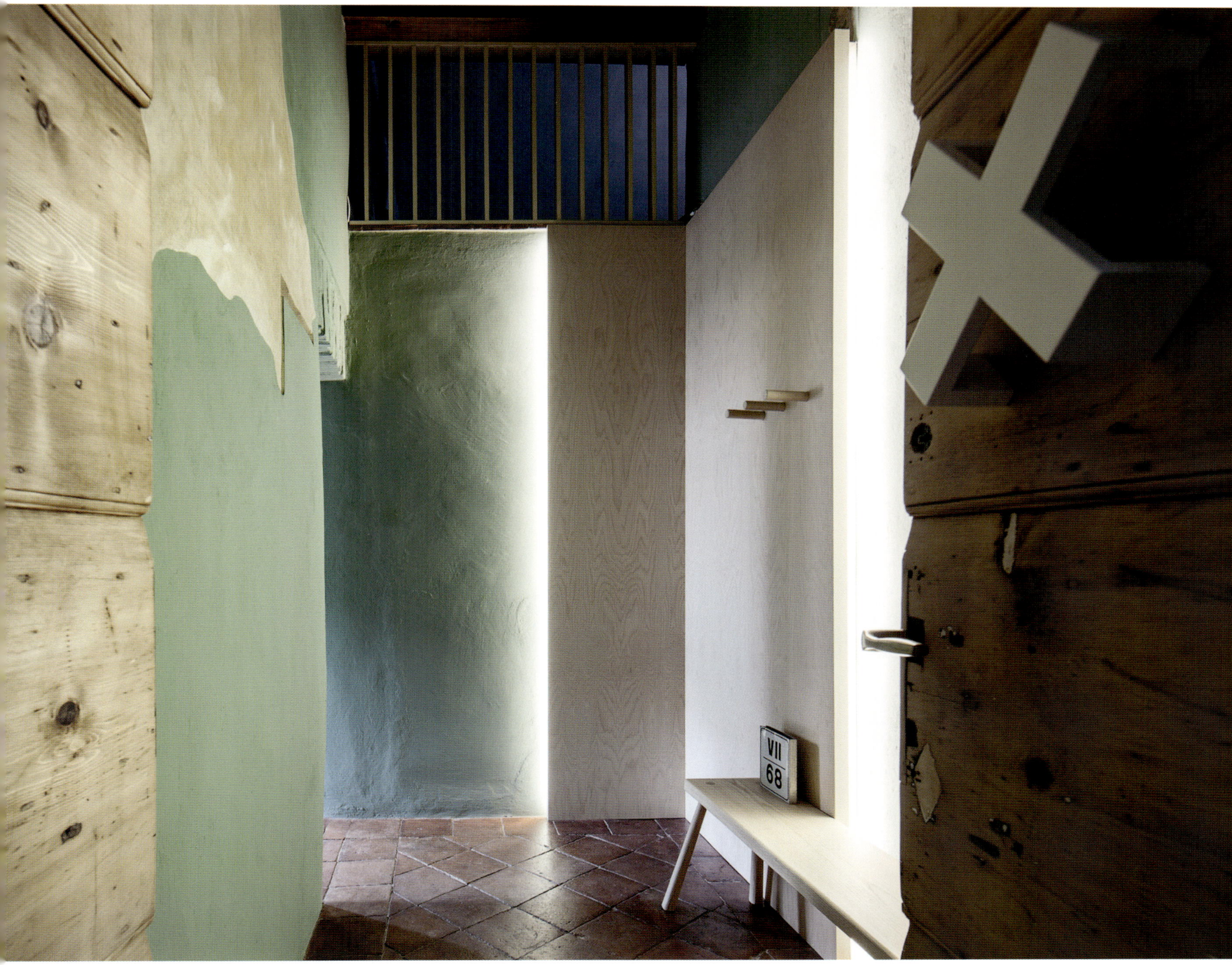

Entering the apartment, one senses a determination to hold opposites together: force and fragility, perfect and imperfect, the luster of a newly made object and the unpredictability of materials that have suffered from neglect.

Sobald man die Wohnung betritt, bemerkt man das Bestreben, die Gegensätze zu vereinen – Stärke und Zerbrechlichkeit, Perfektion und Unvollkommenheit, der Glanz eines kürzlich angefertigten Möbelstücks und die Launenhaftigkeit der schon leicht zerfallenen Materialien.

L'engagement de maintenir réunis les opposés tels que la force et la fragilité, parfaite et imparfaite, la brillance d'un produit récent élaboré et l'imprévisibilité des matériaux tombés en désuétude, se perçoit dès l'entrée dans l'appartement.

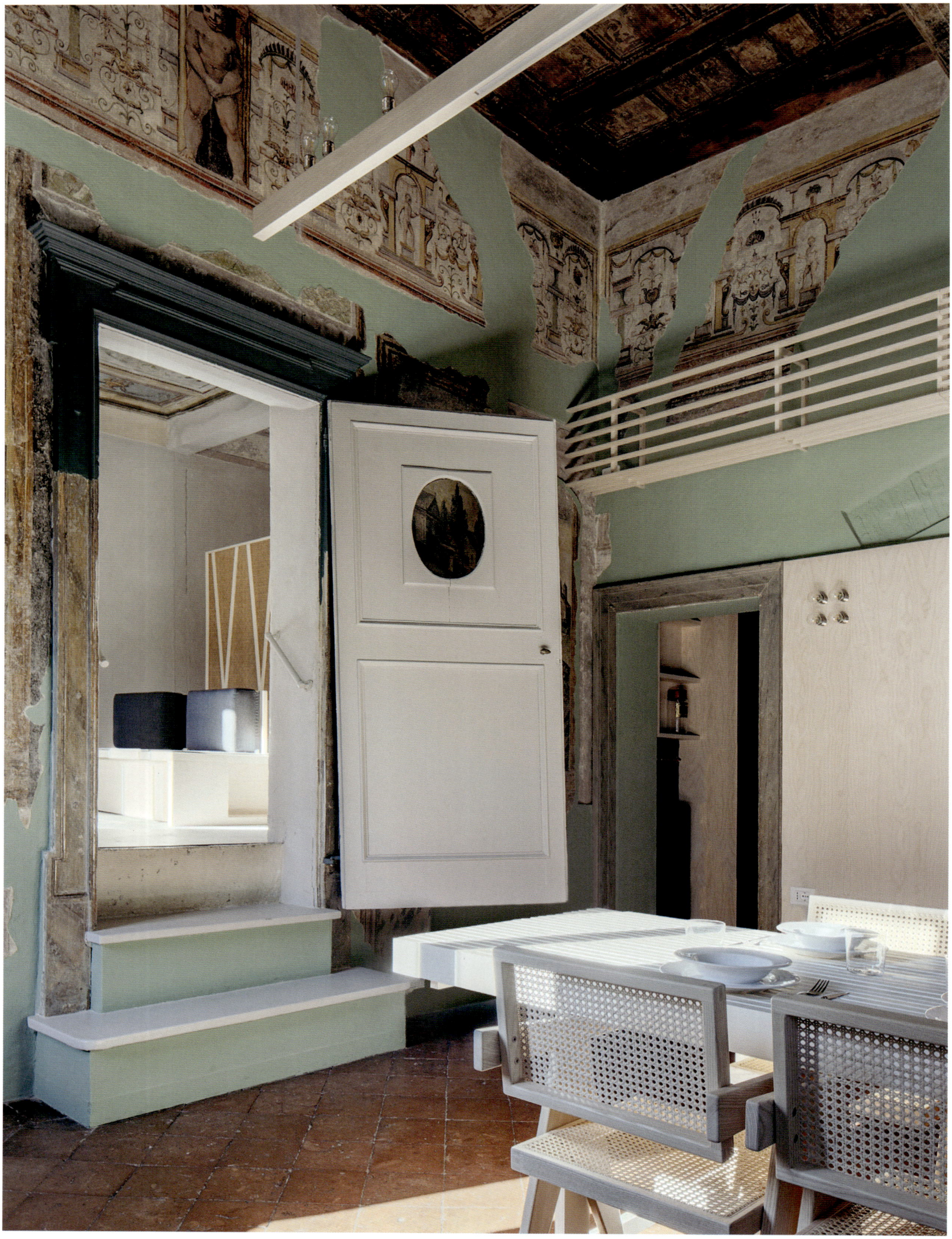

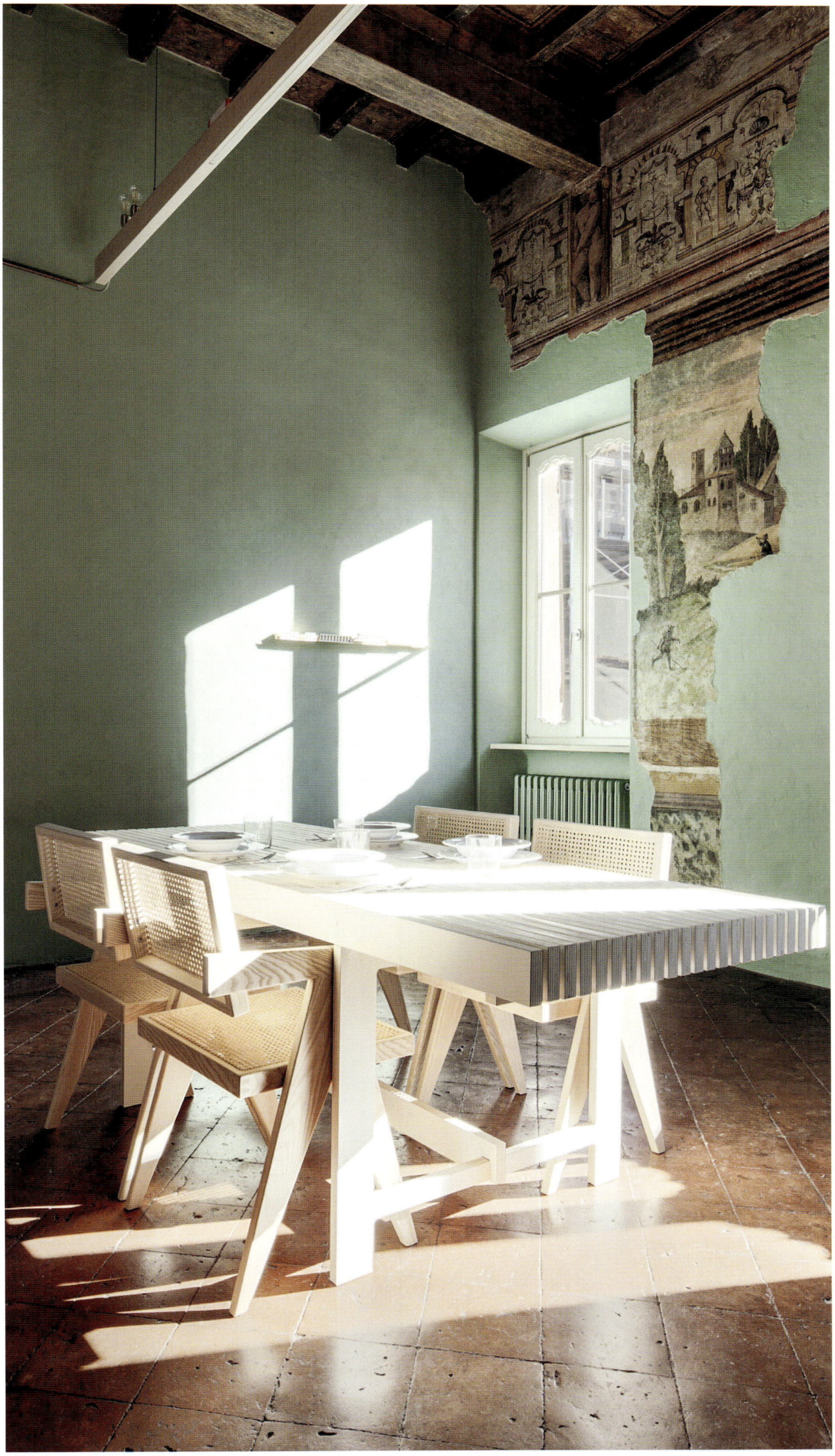

The precision of the designed furnishings, at once coarse and refined, lives in perfect harmony with the imperfection of materials that the forces of time have imbued with a unique energy.

Die Präzision der eigens angefertigten Möbel, die zugleich rau und elegant erscheinen, vereint sich hier in perfekter Harmonie mit der Unvollkommenheit der Materialien, denen der Wandel der Zeiten eine einzigartige Energie verliehen haben.

La précision des éléments conçus du mobilier, à la fois rustiques et raffinés, cohabite en parfaite harmonie avec l'imperfection de l'élément matériel auquel le fil du temps a conféré une énergie unique.

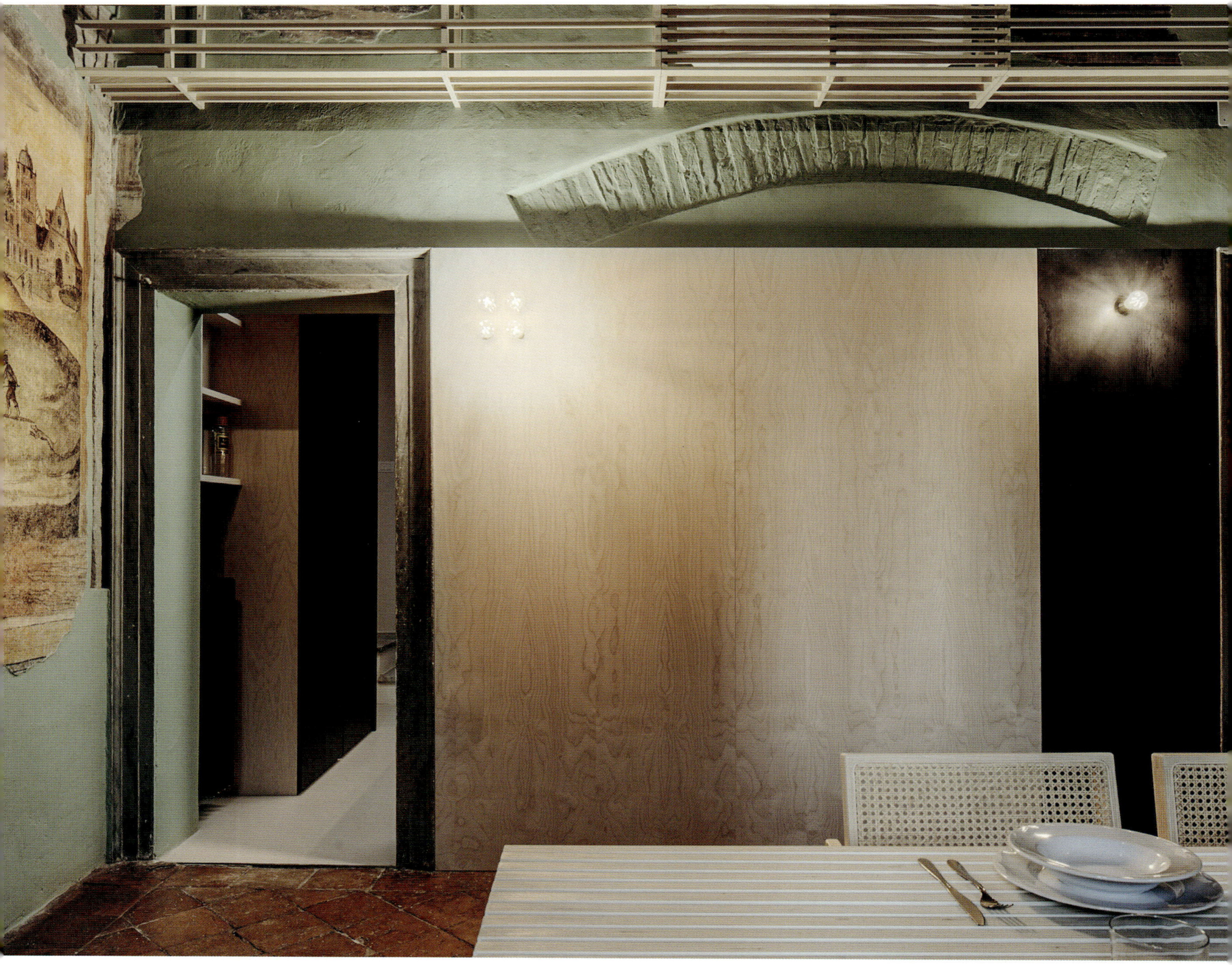

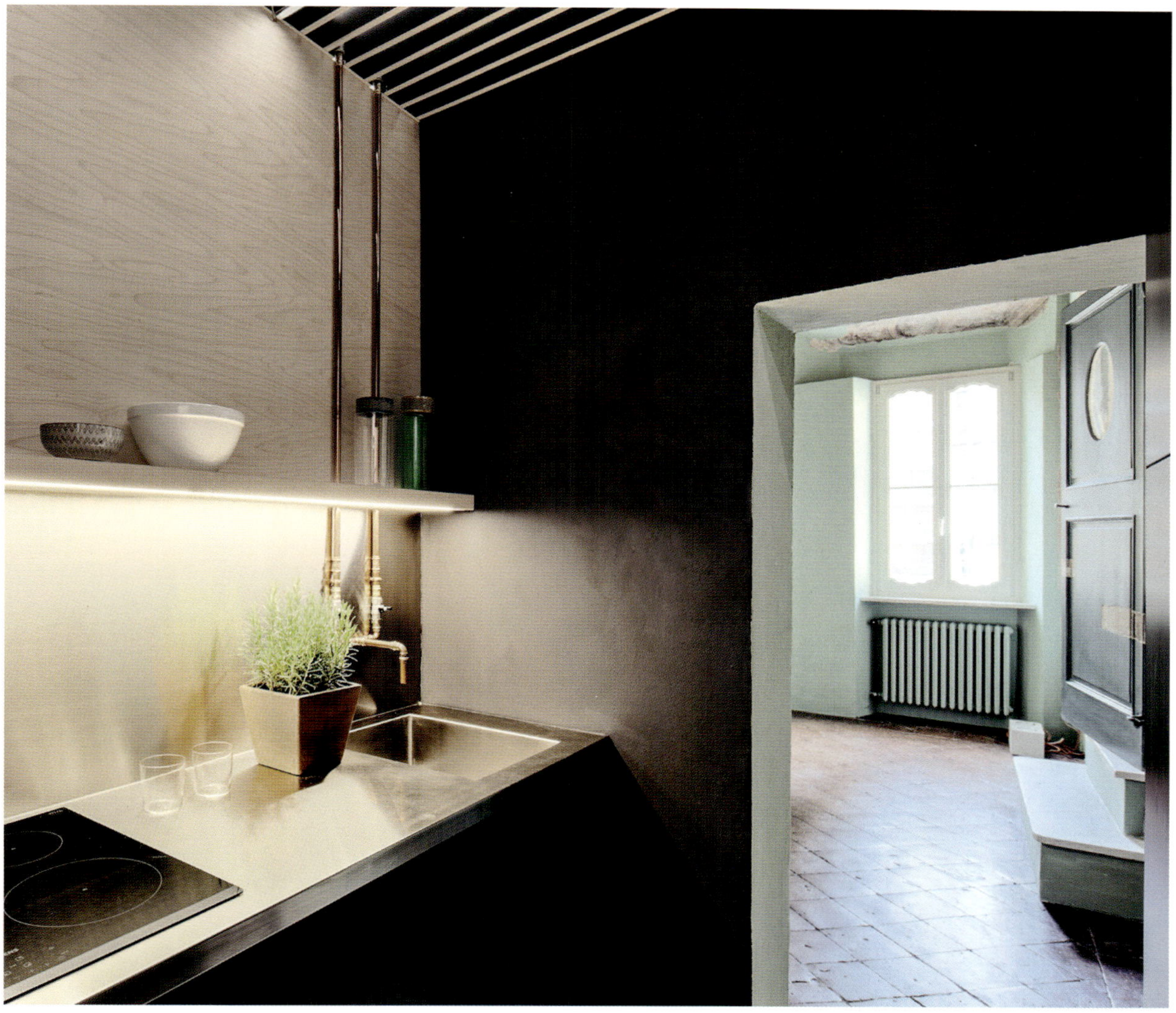

The kitchen was designed to be contemporary, simple, and functional. The color contrast and indirect lighting create a fascinating shadow play that adds excitement to the space.

Das Design der Küche ist modern, schlicht und funktional. Der chromatische Kontrast wie auch die indirekte Beleuchtung sorgen für ein interessantes Spiel mit den Schatten, wodurch dieser Raum einen besonderen Reiz erhält.

Le design de la cuisine est contemporain, simple et fonctionnel. Le contraste chromatique, ainsi que l'éclairage indirect offrent un jeu intéressant d'ombres conférant un intérêt supplémentaire à l'espace.

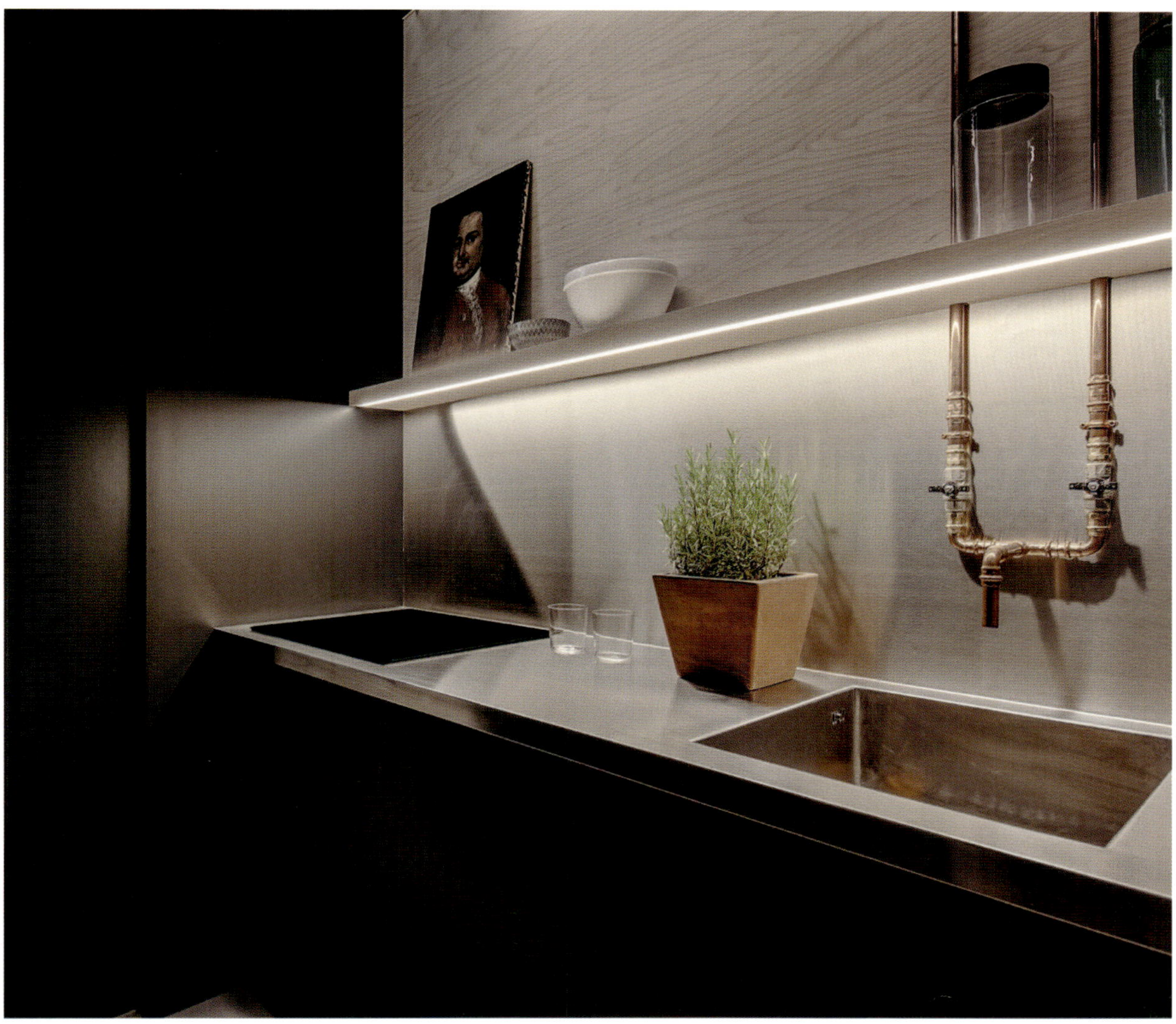

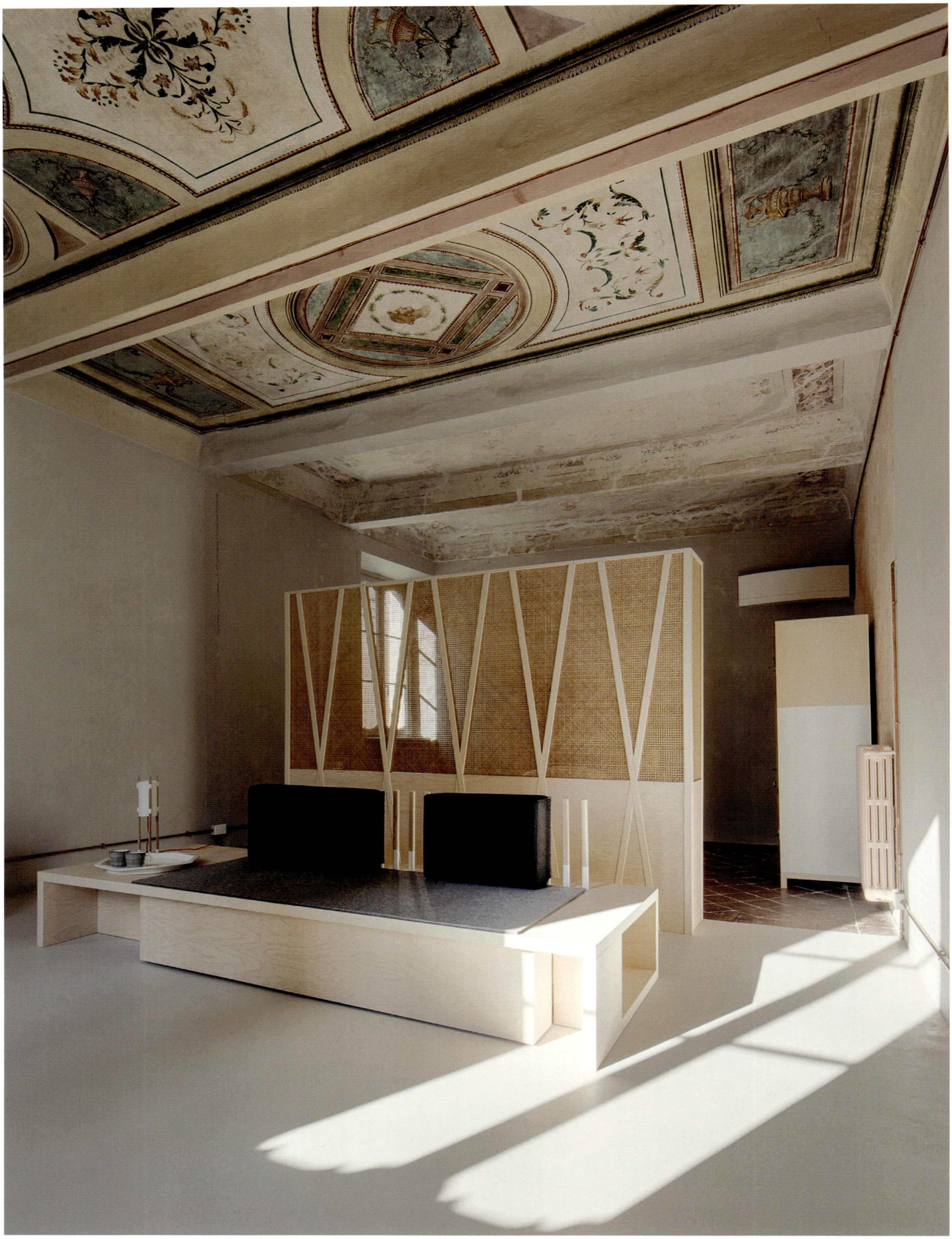

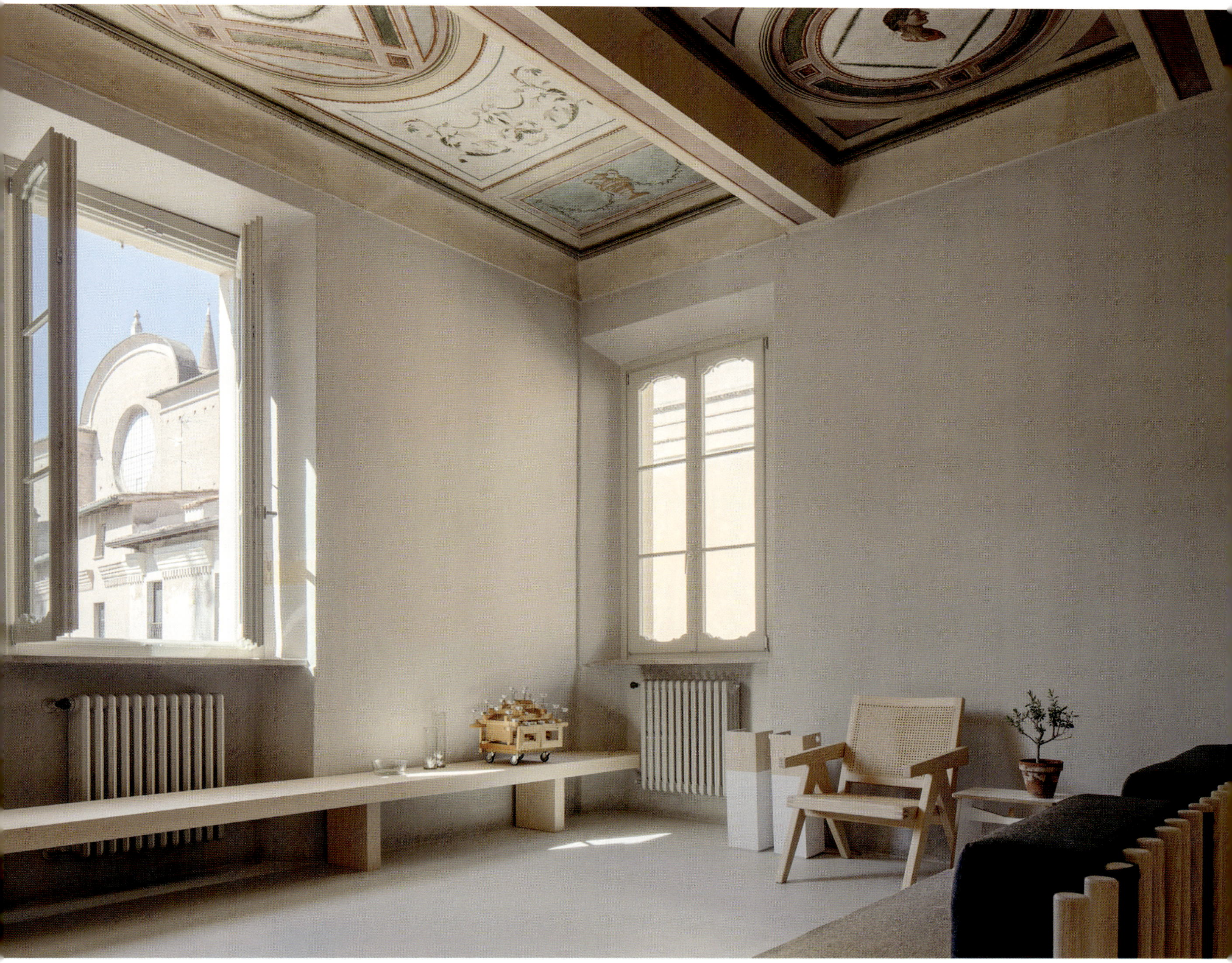

The living room furniture has been arranged facing a large picture window that floods the room with light and offers a panorama of the city. By not reaching the ceiling, the dividing wall allows light to flow freely through a space that seems continuous.

Das Mobiliar des Wohnzimmers wurde so angeordnet, dass man auf das große Panoramafenster schaut, durch das dieser Raum mit Licht erfüllt wird und man den Blick auf die Stadt genießen kann. Der Raumteiler reicht nicht ganz bis an die Decke, wodurch das Licht sich ungehindert ausbreiten kann und man den Raum dahinter als eine Art Fortführung wahrnimmt.

Le mobilier du séjour a été disposé vers la grande baie vitrée qui inonde de lumière la pièce et permet de jouir de la vue sur la ville. Le panneau de séparation, sans pour autant arriver jusqu'en haut, permet à la lumière de traverser librement un espace qui semble être continu.

A customized ash wood structure incorporates the head board and night stands while separating the sleeping area from the living room. The lighting has been carefully positioned to enhance the architectural details of the space.

Es wurde eine originelle Konstruktion aus Eschenholz entworfen, in der das Kopfteil und die Nachttische integriert sind und die außerdem dazu dient, das Schlaf- vom Wohnzimmer zu trennen. Die indirekte Beleuchtung hebt die architektonischen Details des Raumes hervor.

Une structure originale en bois de frêne, incluant la tête de lit et les tables de nuit, a été conçue de sorte à servir de séparation entre la chambre et le séjour. L'éclairage, soigneusement placé, réhausse les détails architecturaux de l'espace.

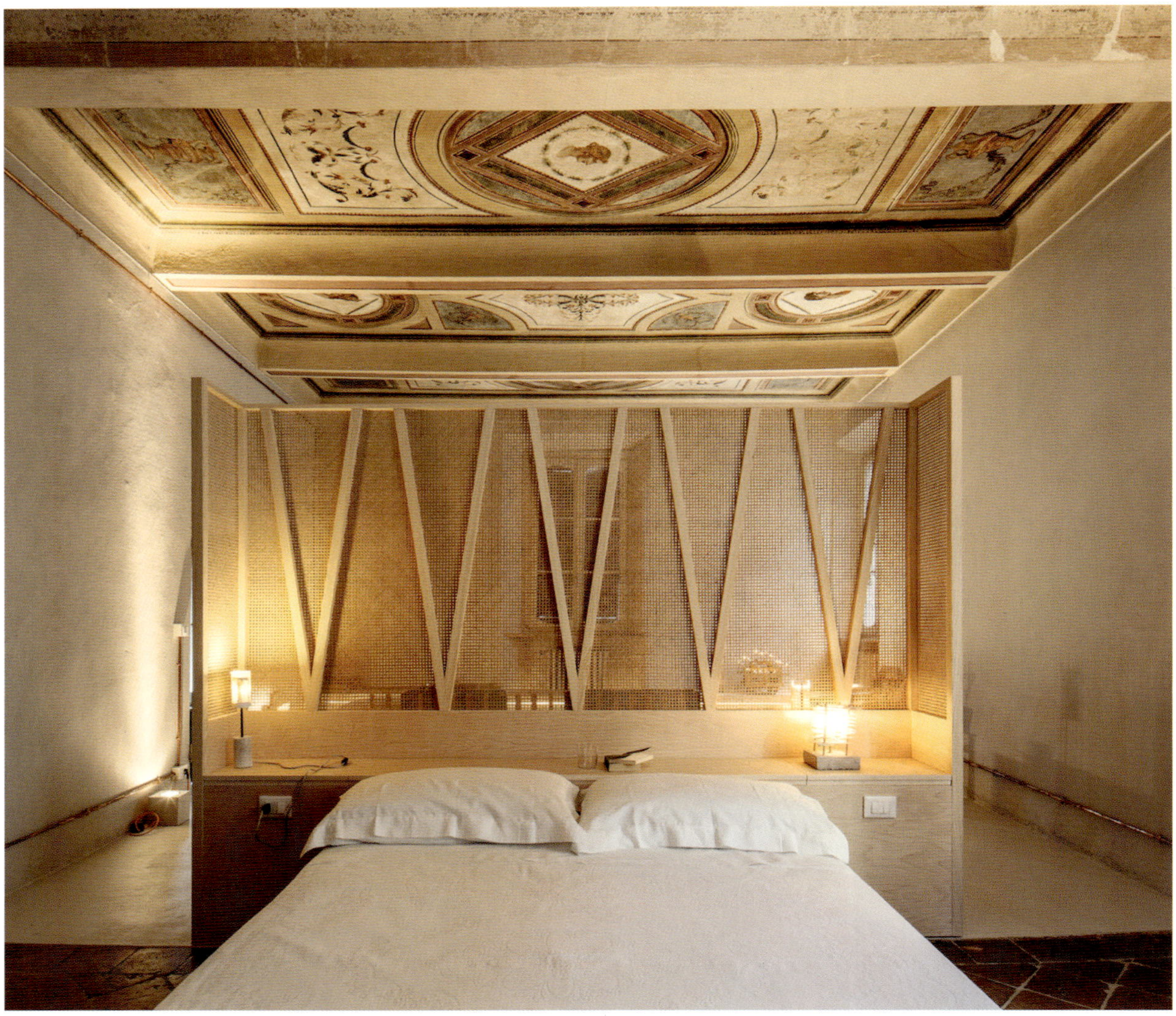

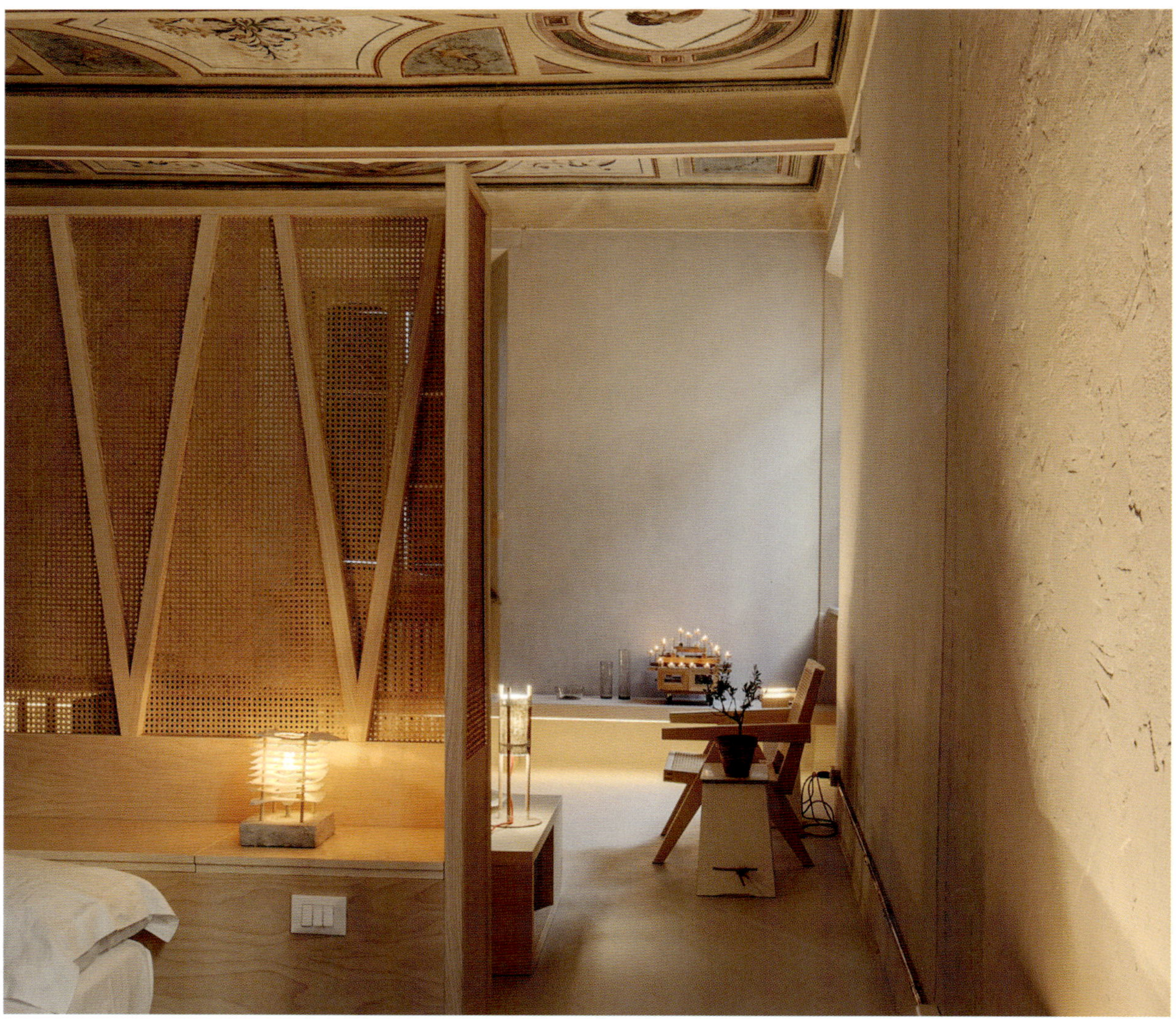

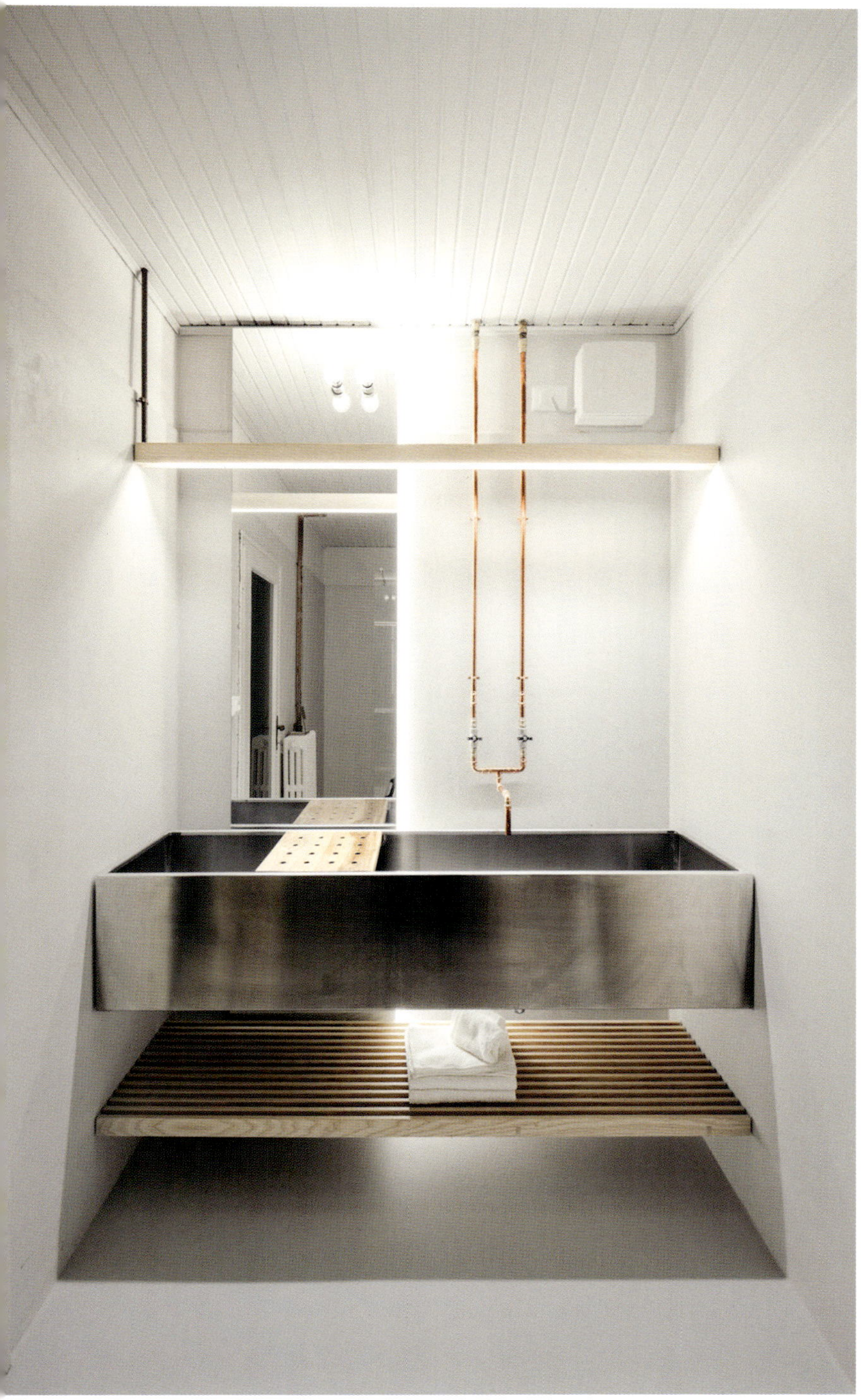 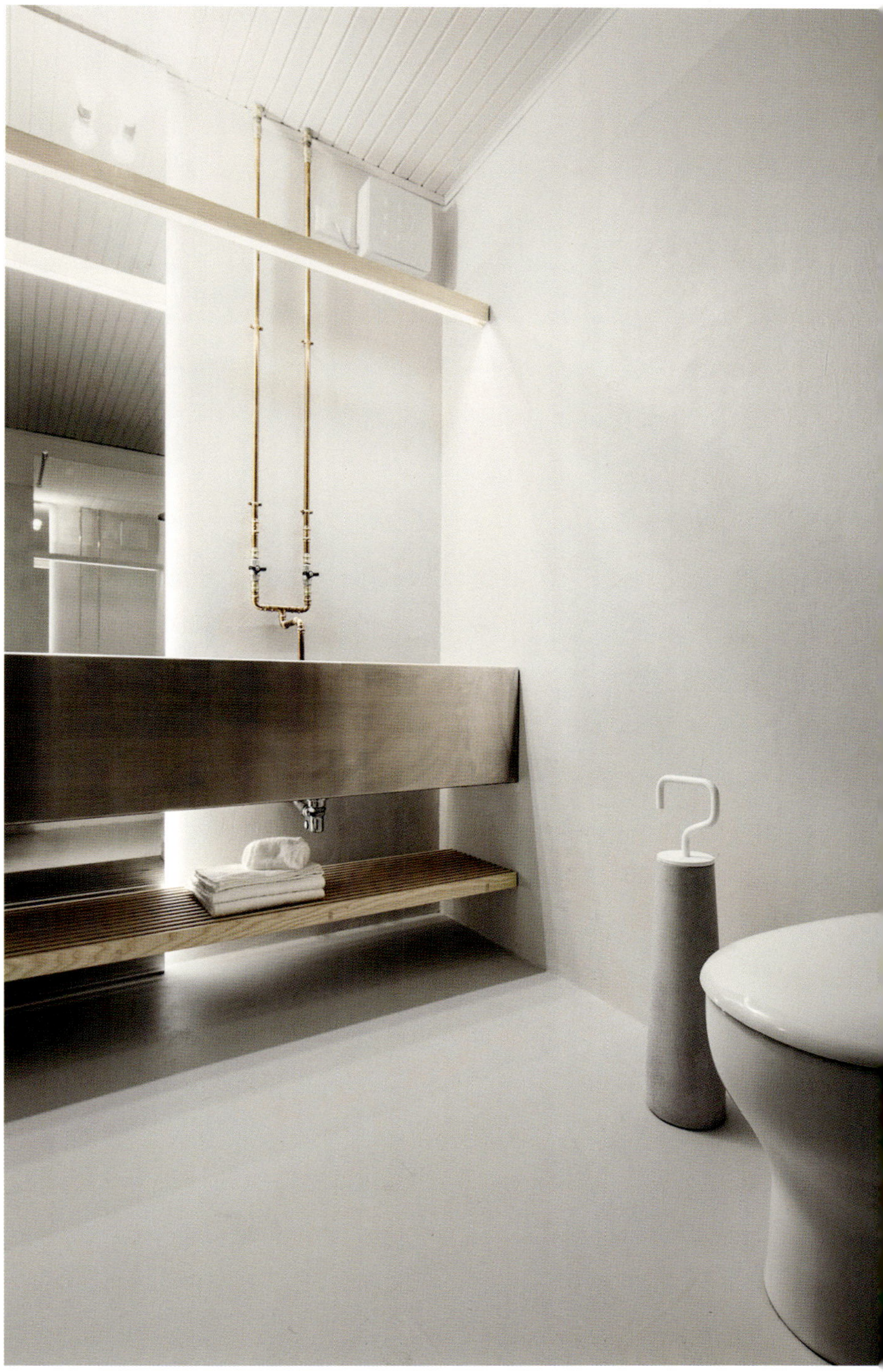

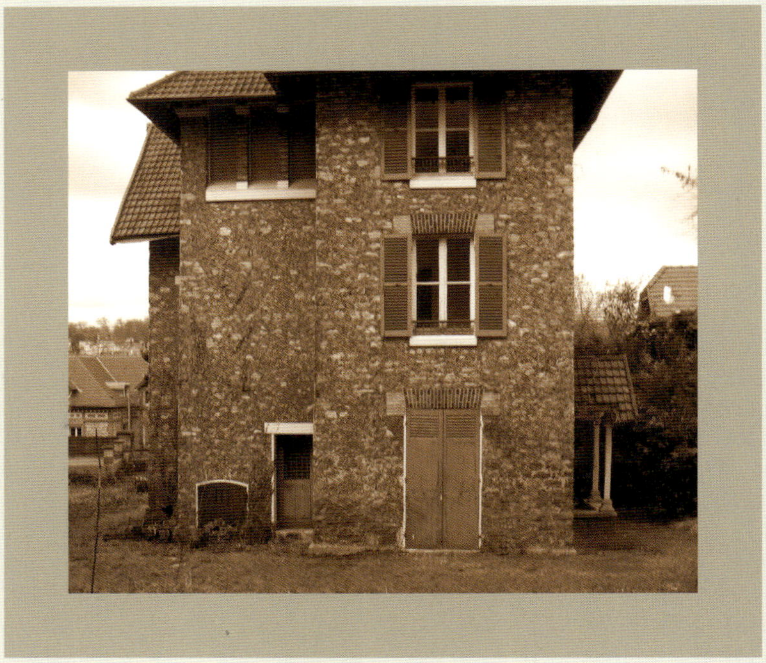

SINGLE HOUSE IN HAUTS-DE-SEINE

ATELIER LAME ARCHITECTS

400 m^2 | 4,305 sq. ft.

Hauts-de-Seine, France

Photos © **Lionel Macor Photography**

> Renovate a house, preserving its original architecture

> Expand the living area by constructing an extension

> Ein Haus unter Beibehaltung seiner ursprünglichen Architektur renovieren

> Den Wohnbereich durch einen Anbau vergrößern

> Rénover une maison tout en préservant son architecture d'origine

> Agrandir le séjour pour lequel est construite une extension

This project was executed in a tranquil neighborhood on the inner periphery of Paris in Île-de-France. It involved renovating and expanding a traditional stone house that was perfectly situated on a large green lot along a quiet street. Since the house had sat empty for several years, the main objective was to renovate the existing structure, preserving its original architectural features. Spurred by the directive to expand the ground-floor living area, the architects added an extension that would respect both the existing building and its surroundings.
The ground level consists of two living rooms respectively in the north and south ends of the home, a hallway displaying a collection of CDs and vinyl records, and the kitchen as the residence's central feature. The floor above accommodates a portion of the bedrooms. There is a guest room in the expanded portion, featuring a spacious terrace opening to a relaxing lawn. On the north side is the master bedroom, with walk-in closet, private bathroom and generous views of the terrace and the distant landscape. The topmost floors are devoted to the children. Each bedroom has sleeping and play areas.
By combining sandstone, a material common to the region, with a modern architectural language incorporating steel and glass, the house becomes a unique architectural ensemble.

Dieses Projekt wurde in einer ruhigen Randgegend in der Nähe von Paris in der Île-de-France umgesetzt. Es handelte sich um die Renovierung und Erweiterung eines traditionellen Steinhauses, ideal gelegen in einer ruhigen Straße und mit einem großen grünen Grundstück. Hauptziel war es, das bestehende Haus unter Beibehaltung der ursprünglichen architektonischen Merkmale zu renovieren. Getrieben von dem Wunsch, den Wohnbereich des Erdgeschosses zu erweitern, wurde ein Anbau hinzugefügt, der sowohl das bestehende Gebäude als auch das Umfeld respektieren sollte.
Im Erdgeschoss befinden sich zwei Wohnzimmer – eines an der Nord- und eines an der Südseite –, ein Korridor mit einer CD- und Plattensammlung und die Küche als zentrales Element des Hauses. Der erste Stock beherbergt einen Teil der Schlafzimmer. Auf der Seite des Anbaus liegt das Gästezimmer mit einer großen Terrasse, die auf den ruhigen und entspannenden Garten hinausblickt. An der Nordseite befindet sich das Hauptschlafzimmer mit offenem Ankleidezimmer, eigenem Bad und großen Fenstern zur Terrasse und der fernen Landschaft hin. Die oberen Stockwerke sind den Kindern gewidmet. Jedes Zimmer hat einen eigenen Schlaf- und Spielbereich.
Die Kombination einer modernen Architektursprache, die sich Materialien wie Stahl und Glas bedient, mit dem für die Region typischen Sandstein machen es zu einem einzigartigen architektonischen Ensemble.

Ce projet a été réalisé dans un quartier tranquille de la périphérie de Paris, en Île-de-France. Il s'agit de la rénovation et de l'agrandissement d'une maison de pierre traditionnelle, idéalement située dans une rue tranquille et qui jouit d'un grand espace vert. Inhabitée pendant plusieurs années, le principal objectif a été de rénover la maison existante tout en conservant ses caractéristiques architecturales d'origine. Poussés par l'envie d'agrandir le séjour du rez-de-chaussée, les propriétaires ont souhaité ajouter une extension qui devait respecter la construction existante, ainsi que l'environnement.
Le rez-de-chaussée comprend deux salons orientés nord et sud, un couloir dans lequel se trouve une collection de CD et vinyles et la cuisine, élément central de la maison. Le premier étage est dédié à une partie des chambres. Dans l'extension se trouve la chambre d'amis avec une grande terrasse qui donne sur un jardin tranquille et relaxant. Du côté nord, la chambre parentale avec son dressing ouvert, sa salle de bains privative et de grandes baies vitrées donnant sur la terrasse et le paysage lointain. Les étages supérieurs sont réservés aux enfants. Chaque chambre dispose d'un espace pour dormir et un autre pour les jeux.
La combinaison de grès, typique de la région, avec une architecture au langage moderne tel que l'acier et le verre en font un ensemble architectural unique.

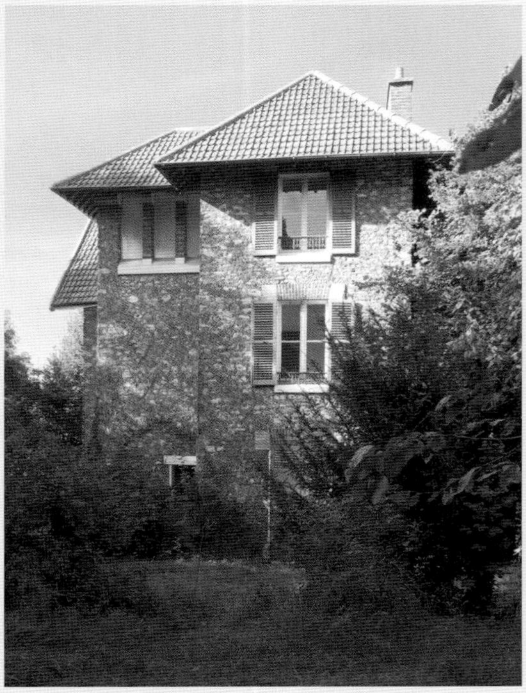
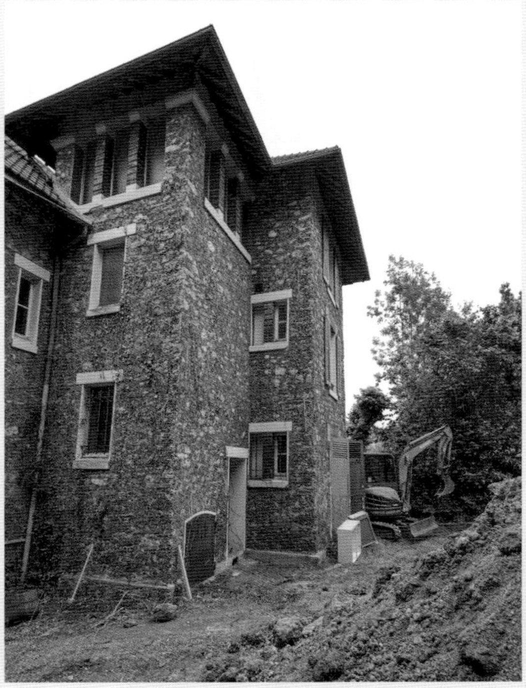
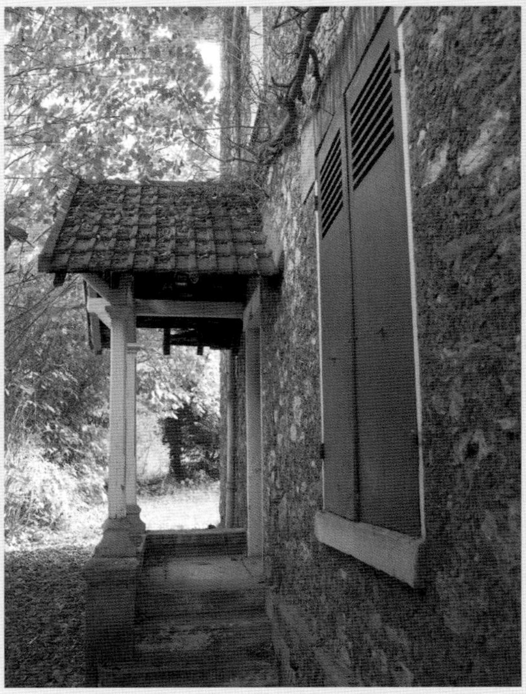
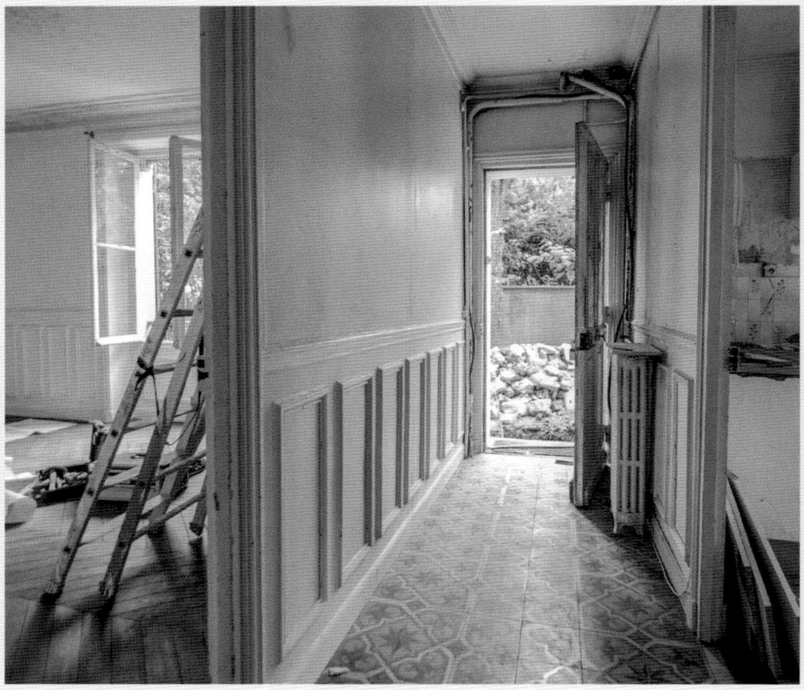
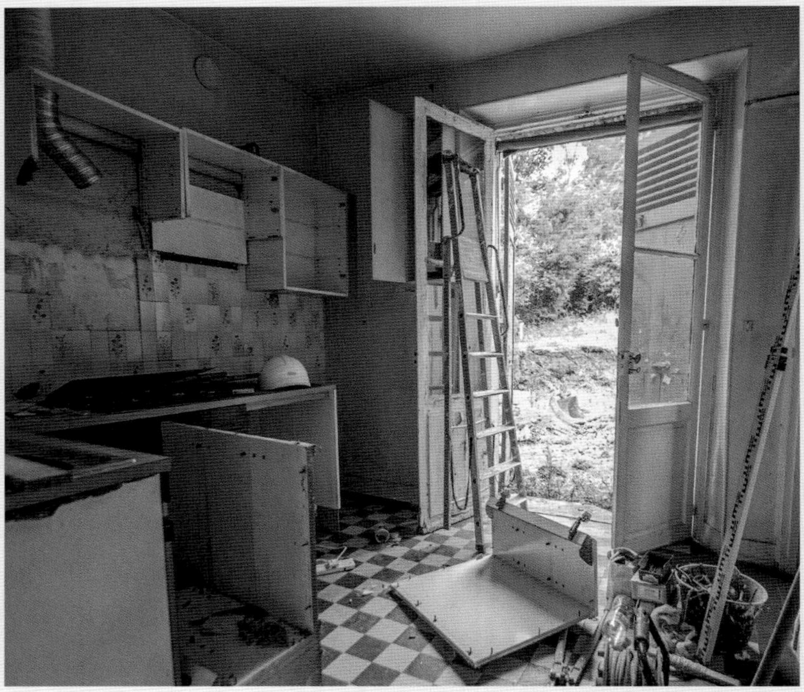
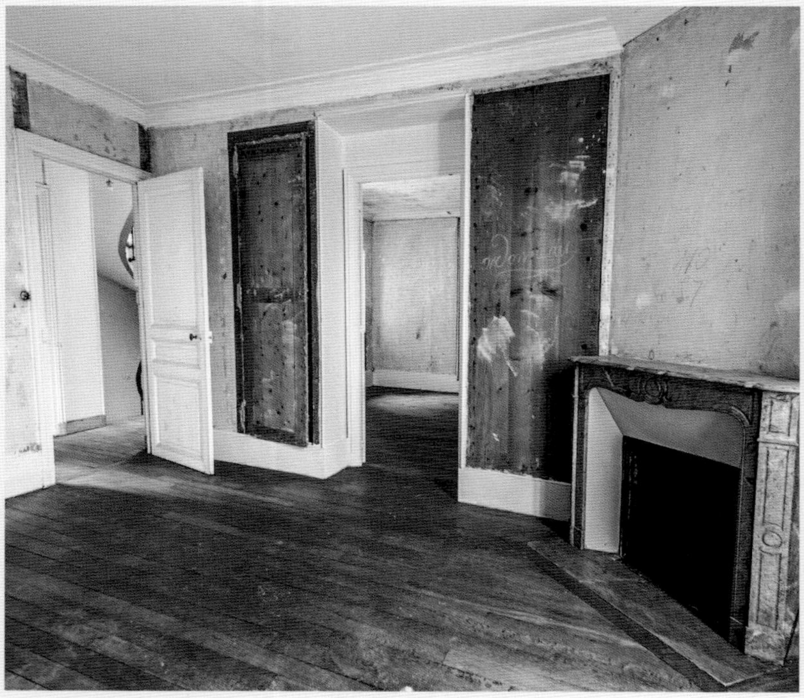
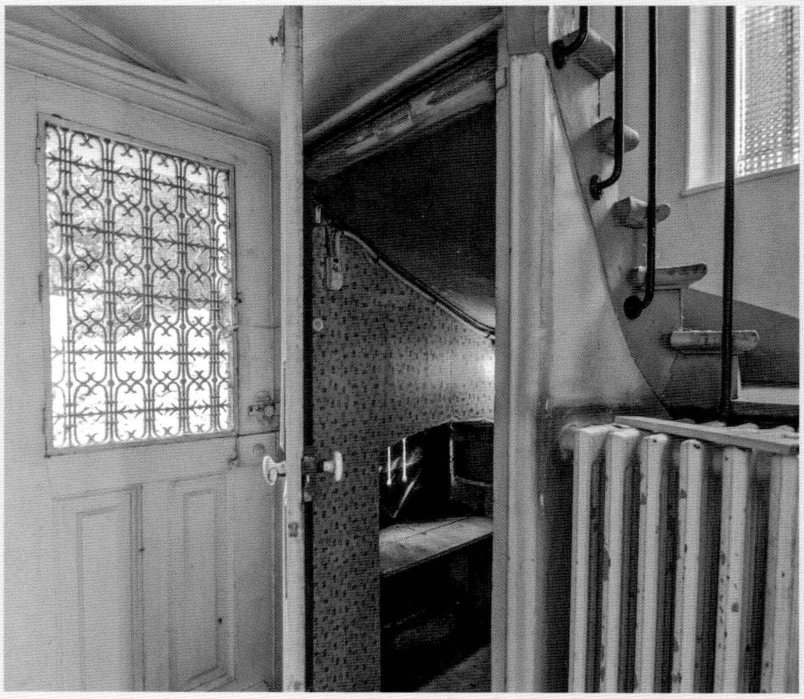

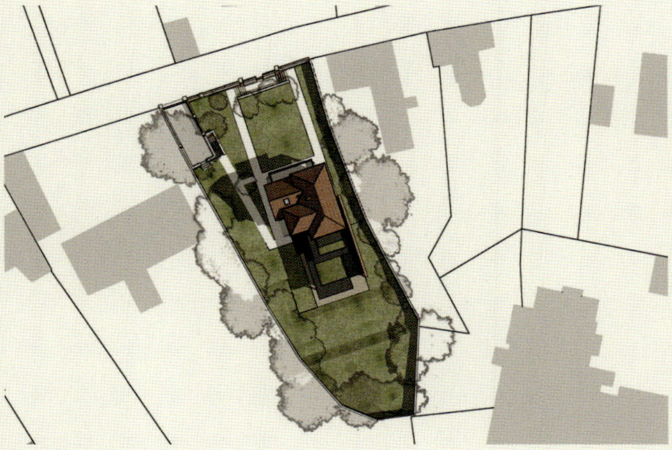

Site plan

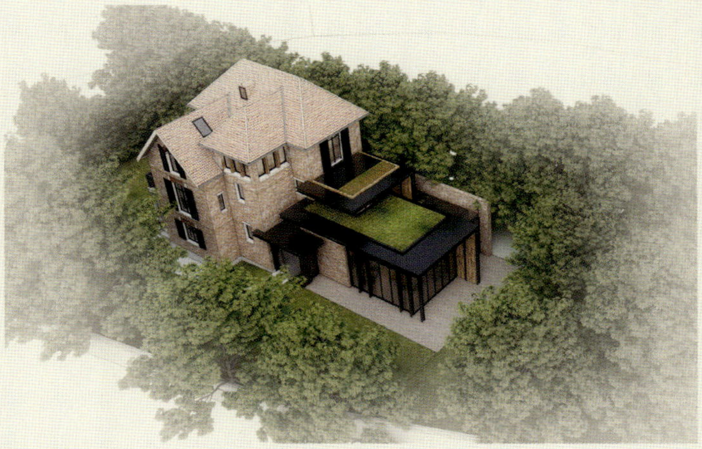

Axonometric view

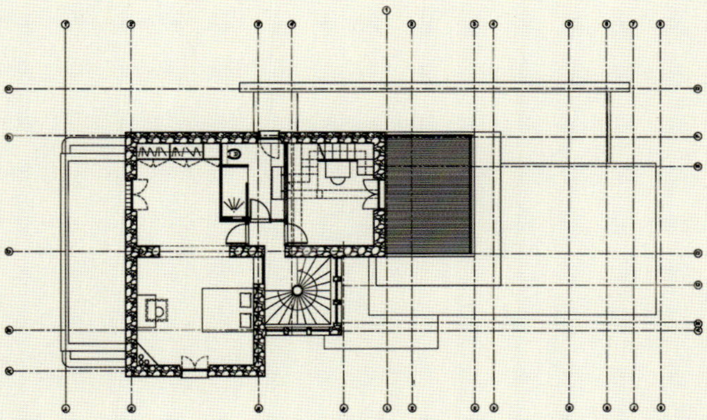

Second floor plan

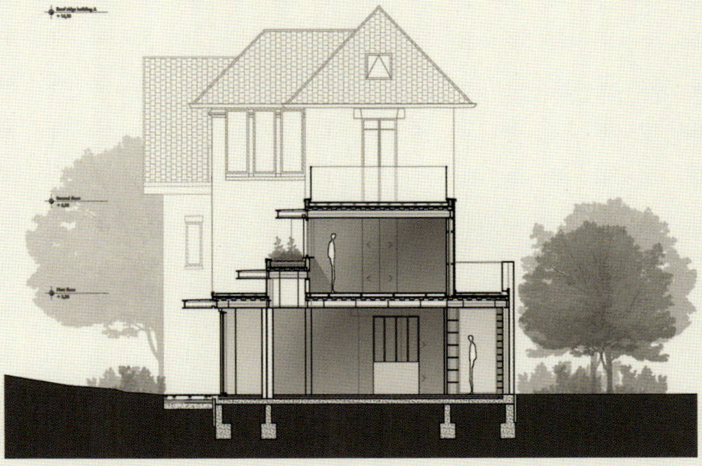

Cross section

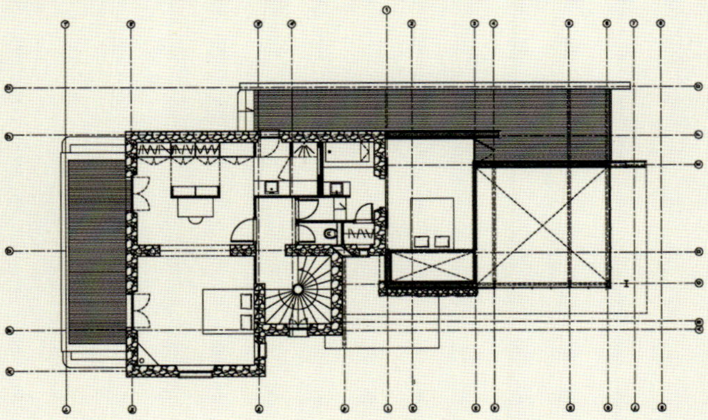

First floor plan

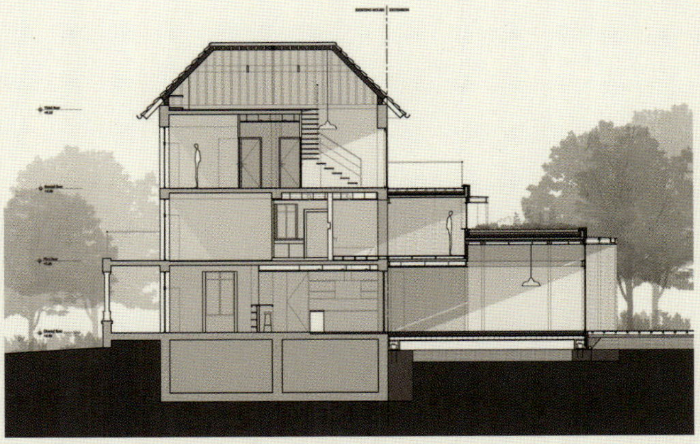

Longitudinal section

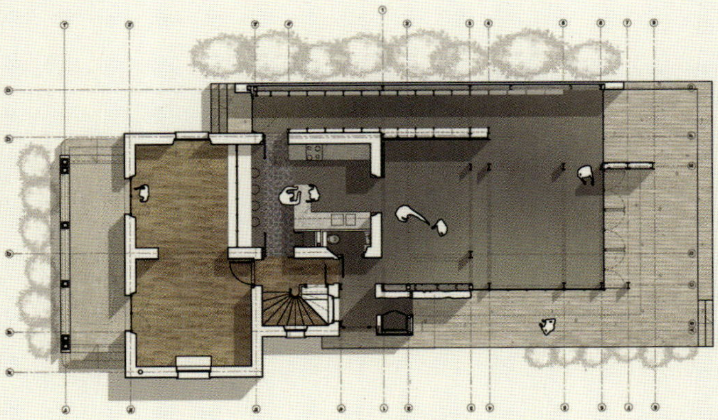

Ground floor plan

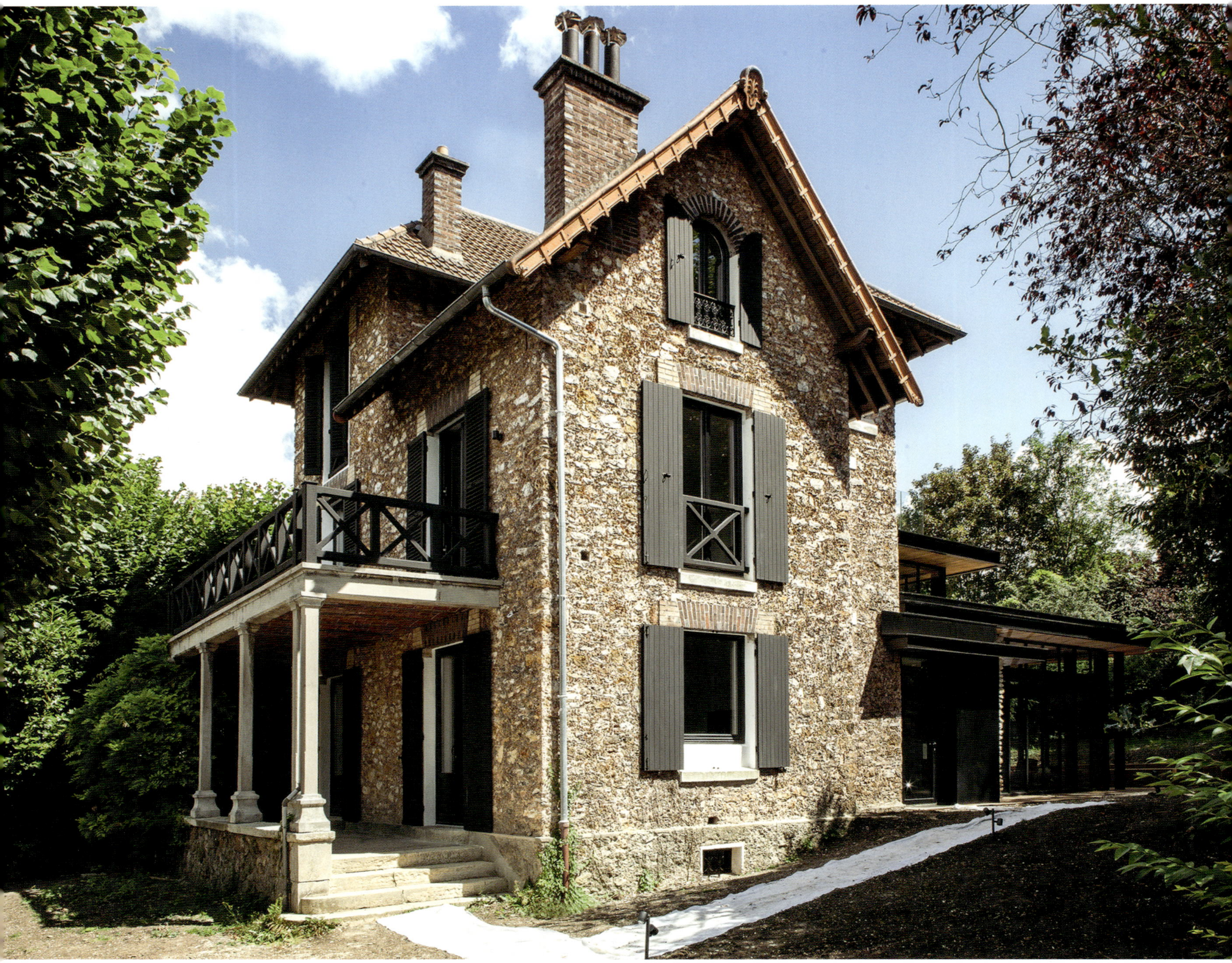

The extensive use of glass in the extension blurs the boundaries between interior and exterior sections. The house's integration with its natural surroundings makes the landscape seem to invade the residence. On the top floor, the unpatterned glass railing facilitates unimpeded views.

Die umfangreiche Verwendung von Glas beim Anbau lässt die Grenzen zwischen innen und außen verschwimmen. Durch die Einbindung in die Natur scheint die Landschaft das Haus zu durchdringen. Im Obergeschoss ermöglicht das profilfreie Glasgeländer, die Aussicht ohne Hindernisse zu genießen.

L'utilisation à profusion de baies vitrées dans l'extension efface les limites entre l'intérieur et l'extérieur. L'intégration à la nature est telle que le paysage semble pénétrer dans la maison. À l'étage supérieur, le garde-corps vitré, sans profilé, permet de profiter des vues sans aucun obstacle.

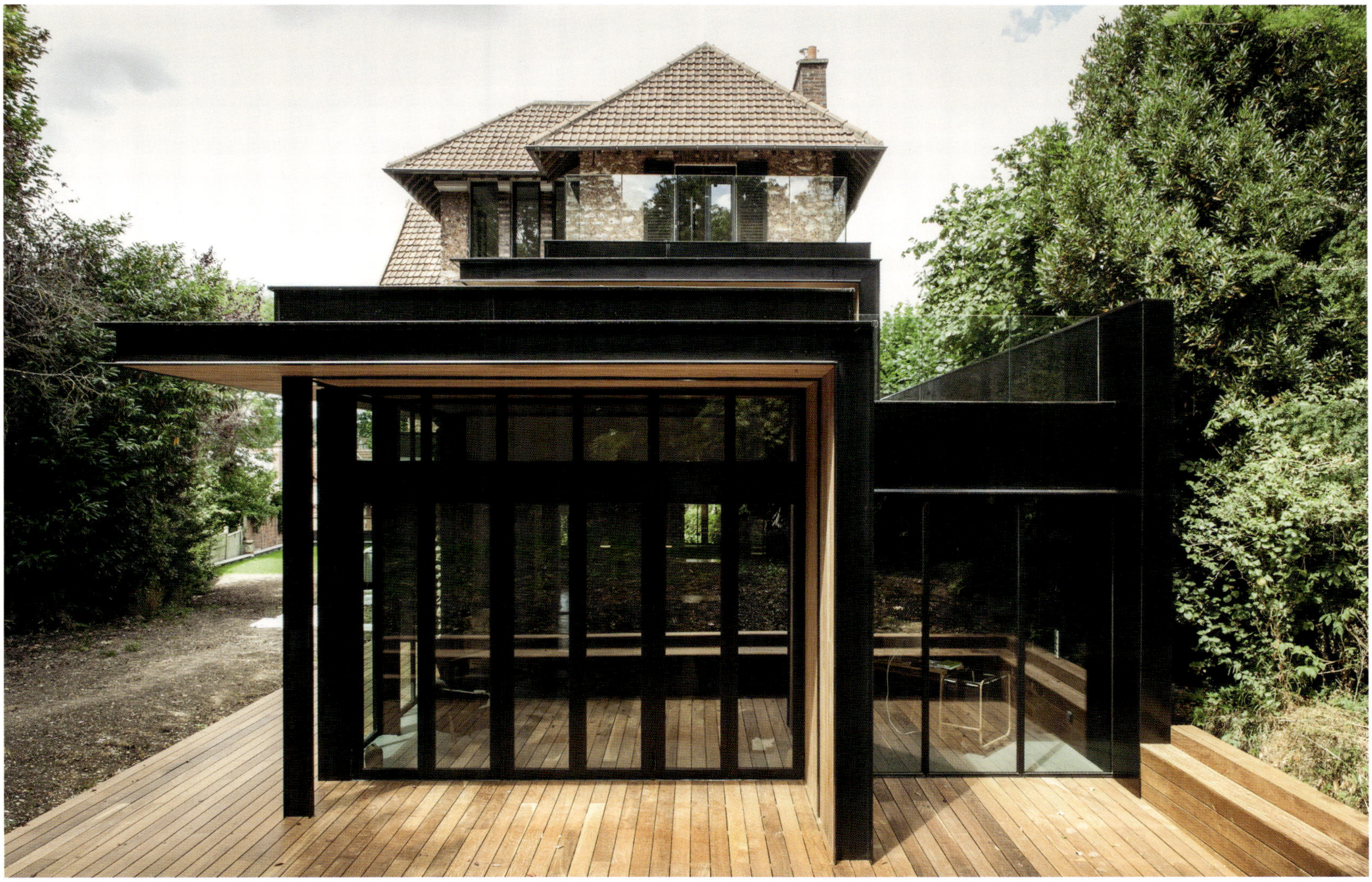

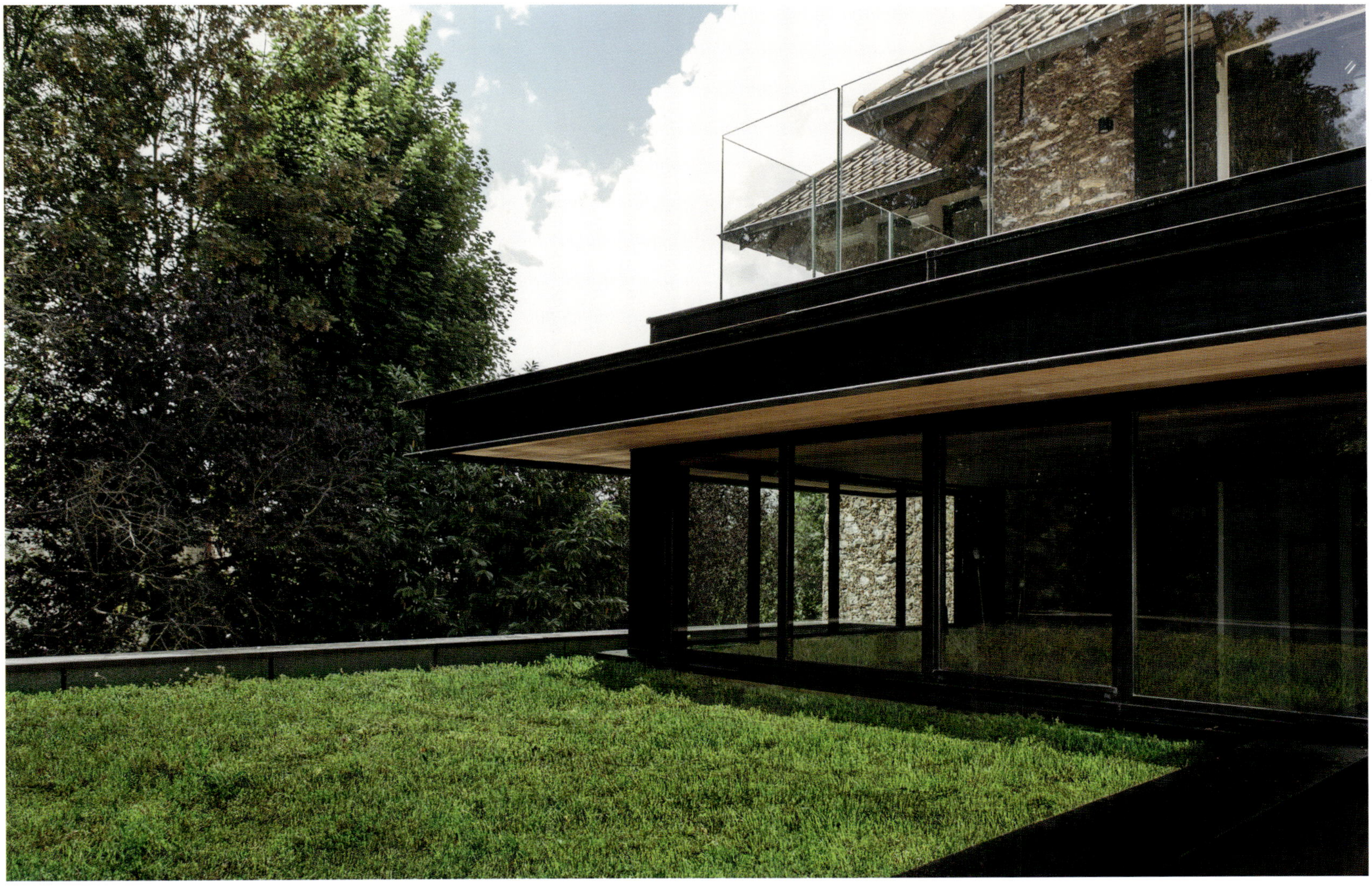

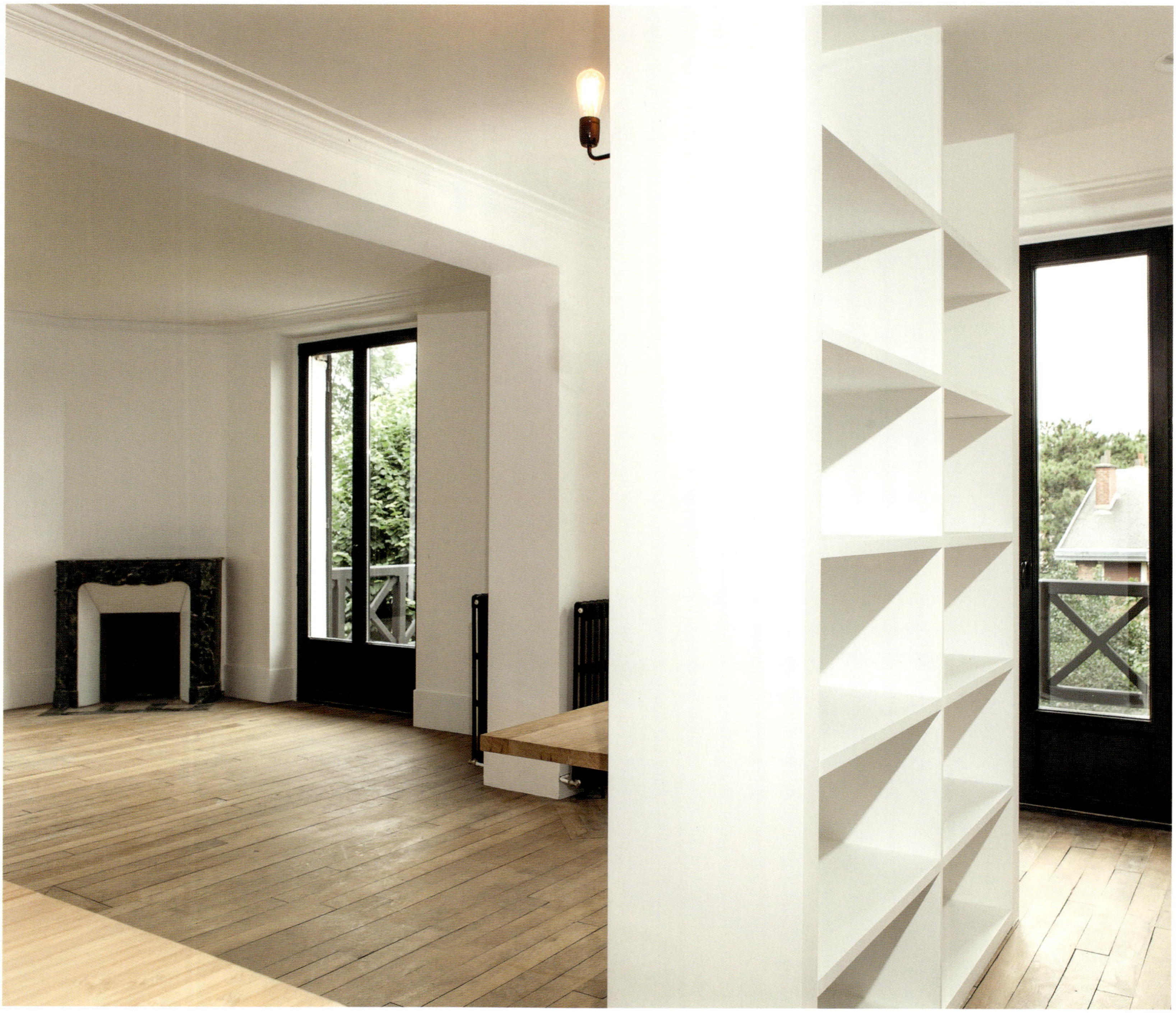

Elements like the ceiling moldings and fireplace along with the narrow windows reveal the building's past and form a perfect complement to the clean, straight-line design of the renovation.

Elemente wie die Deckenleisten und der Schornstein sowie die schmalen Fensteröffnungen lassen die Vergangenheit des Hauses erkennen und ergänzen perfekt das geradlinige und klare Design des neuen Teils.

Des éléments tels que les moulures du plafond et la cheminée, ainsi que les étroites ouvertures révèlent le passé de la maison et se combinent parfaitement avec la conception des lignes droites et pures de la nouvelle partie.

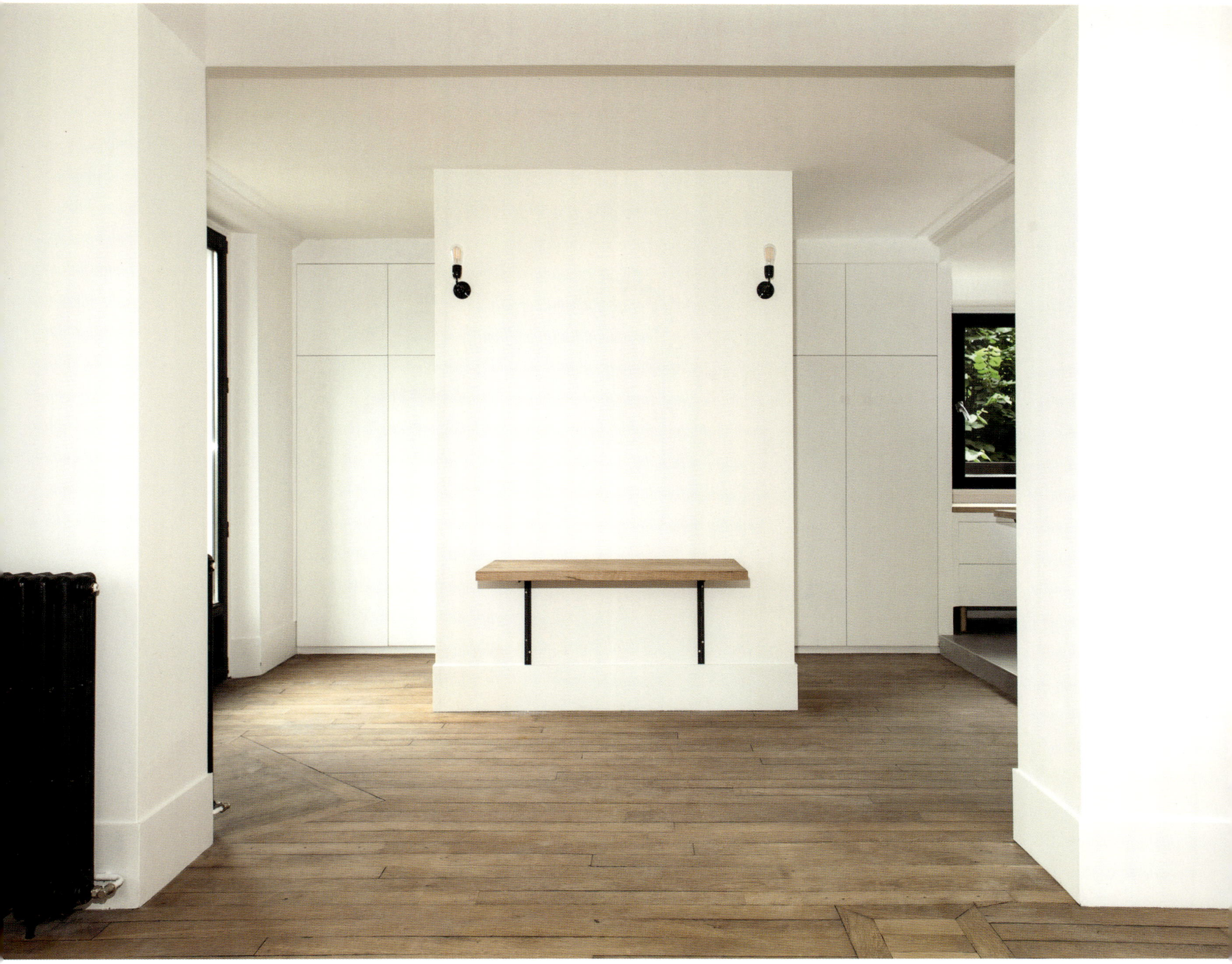

The freestanding wall fulfills a dual function: in addition to separating the settings without breaking the sensation of openness and fluidity, it also features a bookcase built into one side.

Die freie Wand erfüllt eine Doppelfunktion: Neben der Trennung von Bereichen, ohne das Gefühl von Offenheit und räumlicher Fluidität zu zerstören, beherbergt sie an einer Seite ein Buchregal.

Le mur nu a une double fonction : diviser les espaces sans pour autant briser la sensation d'ouverture et de fluidité spatiale et accueillir une bibliothèque sur un de ses pans.

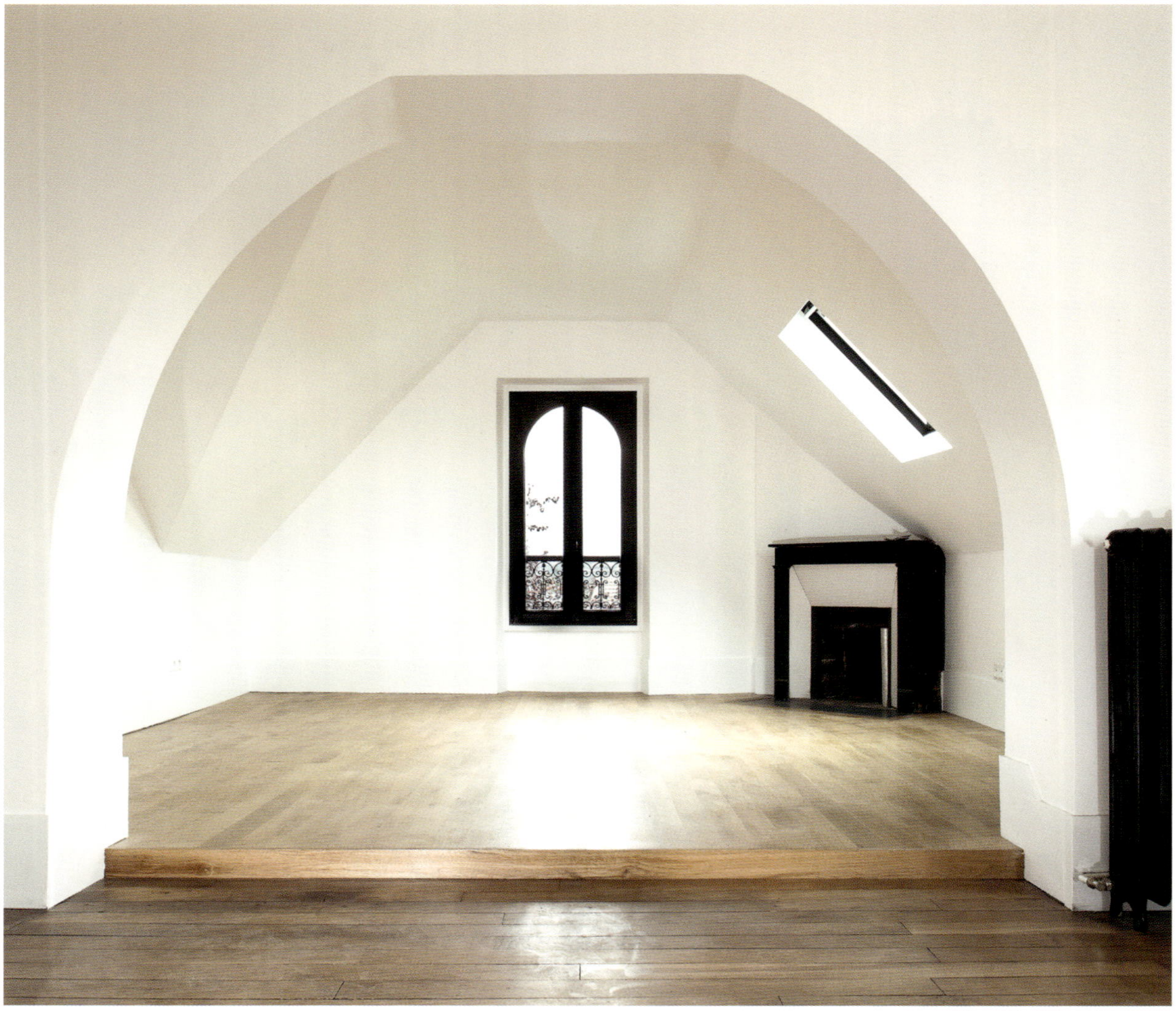

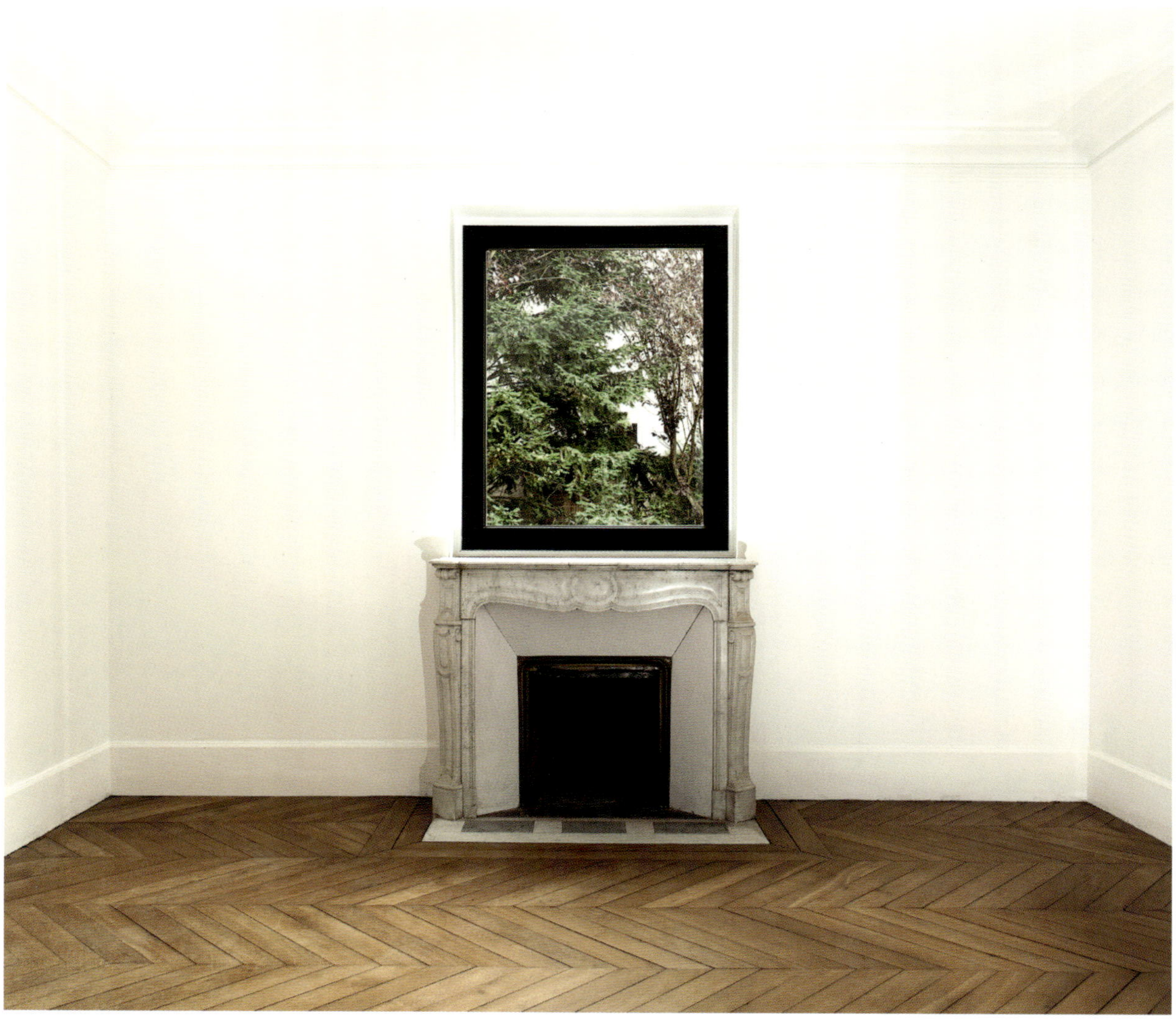

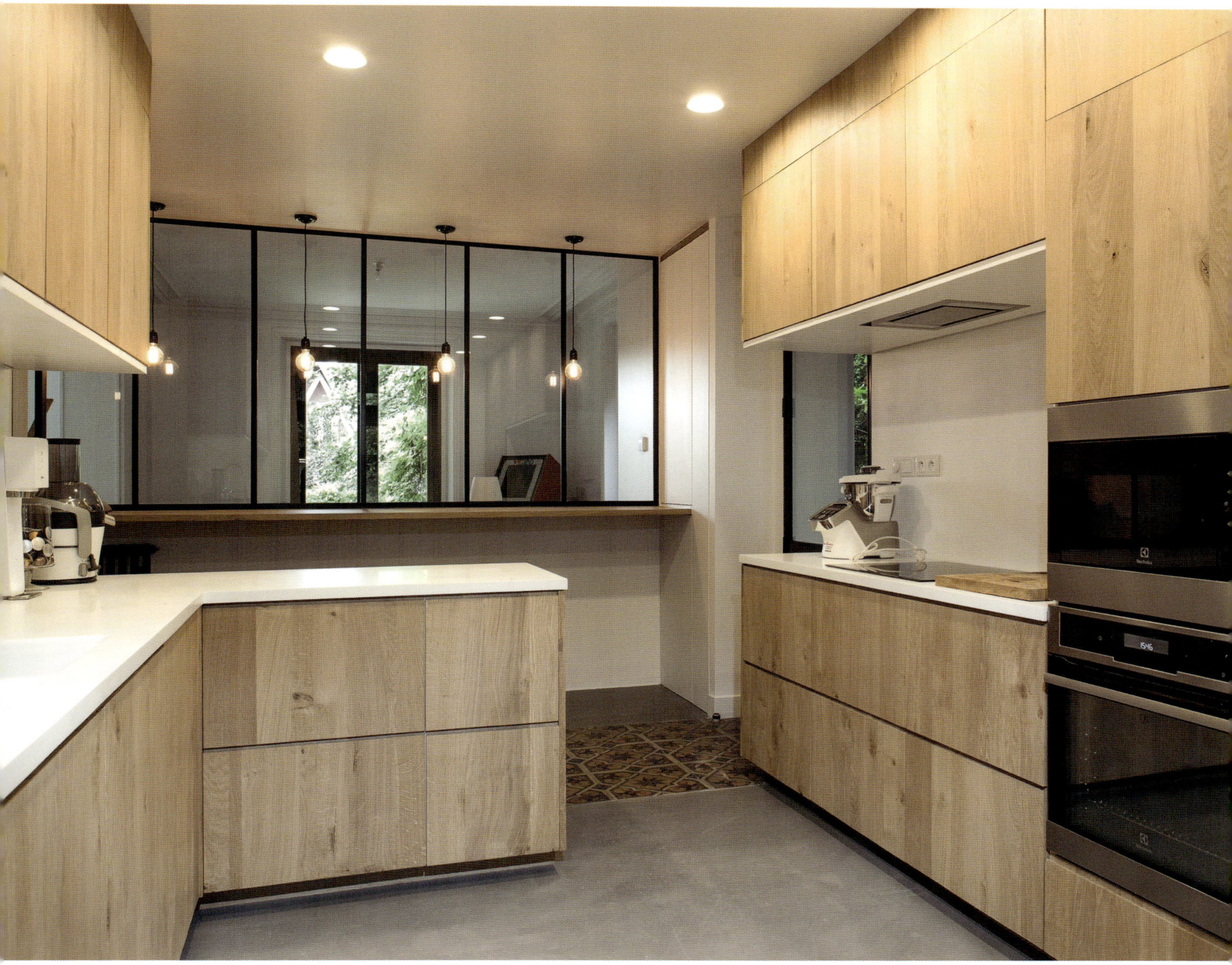

The band of hydraulic tiles along the kitchen floor defies the uniformity of the color palette, and materials extend throughout the interior and exterior of the house. The interior window permits light to penetrate the kitchen, which forms the heart of the residence while also providing a visual connection to one of the living areas.

Der Streifen der Zementfliesen des Küchenbodens bricht mit der Gleichförmigkeit bei der Palette von Farben und Materialien, die im ganzen Haus sowohl innen als auch außen umfangreich eingesetzt wird. Durch das Innenfenster gelangt das Licht in die Küche, die sich im Herzen des Hauses befindet, und gleichzeitig entsteht eine visuelle Verbindung zu einem der Wohnbereiche.

La frange de dalles hydrauliques du sol de la cuisine rompt avec l'uniformité de la palette de couleurs et matériaux intensive dans la maison tant à l'intérieur qu'à l'extérieur. La fenêtre intérieure permet à la lumière de pénétrer dans la cuisine, située au cœur de la maison tout en offrant une connexion visuelle avec un des séjours.

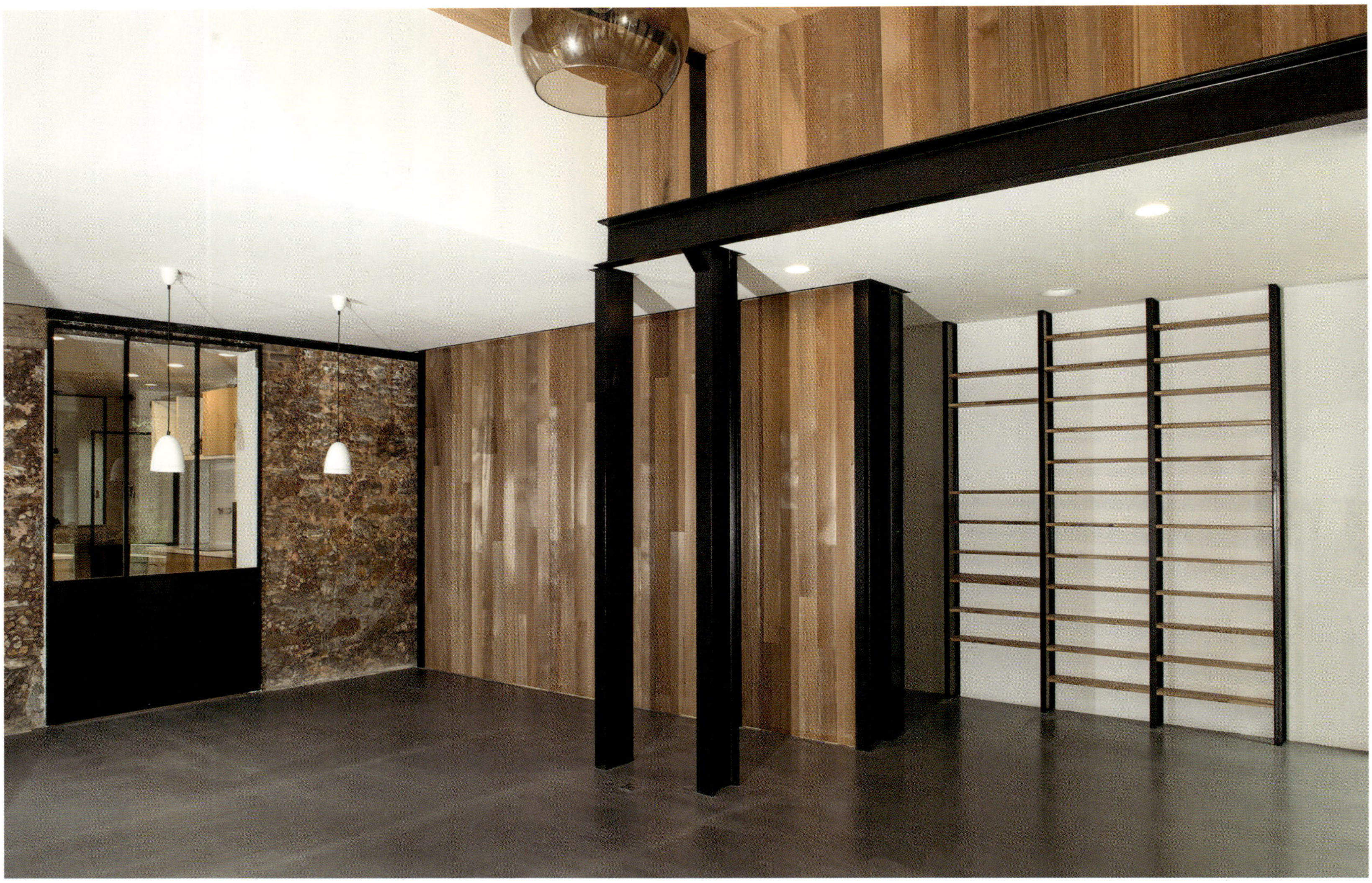

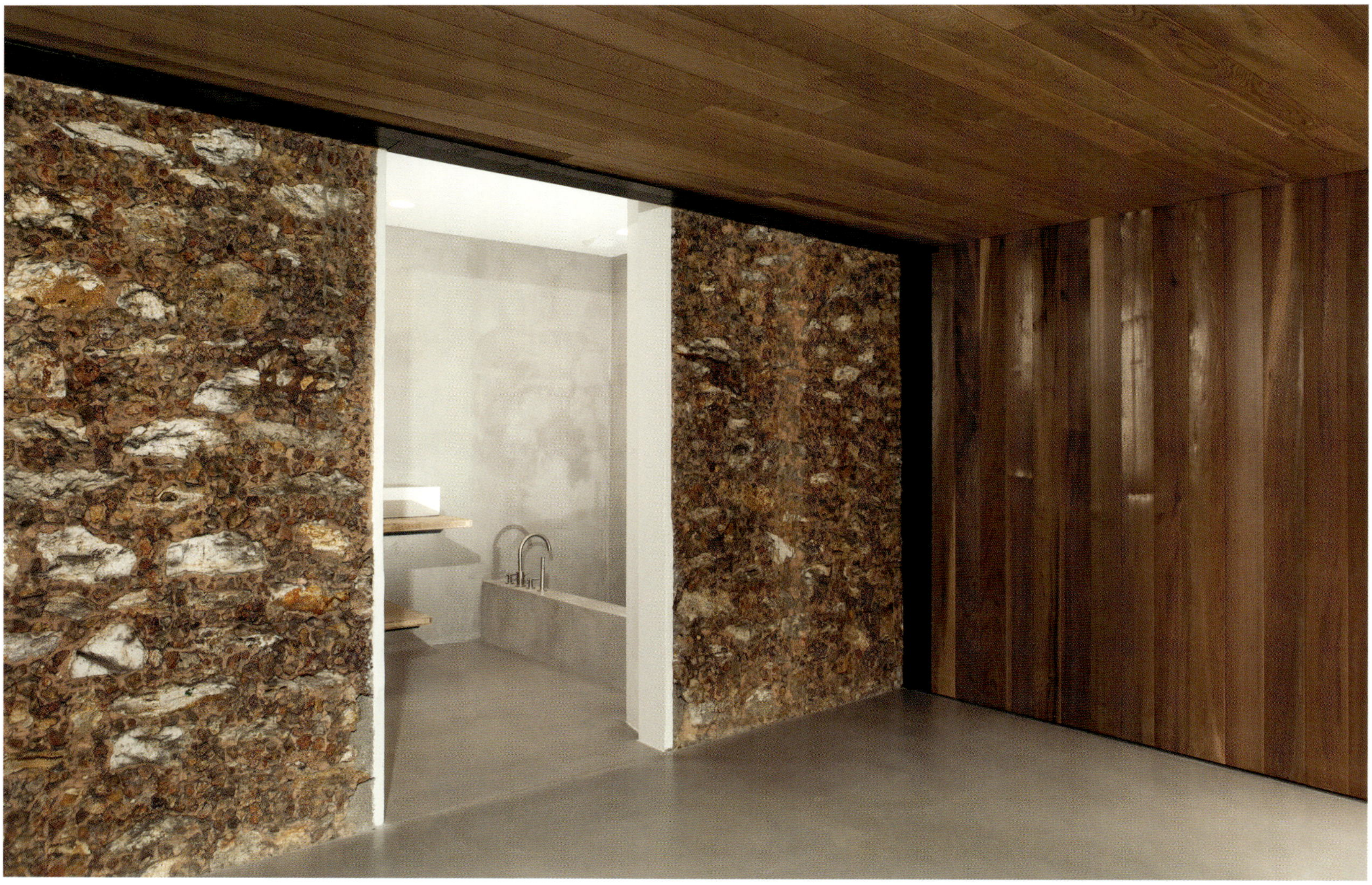

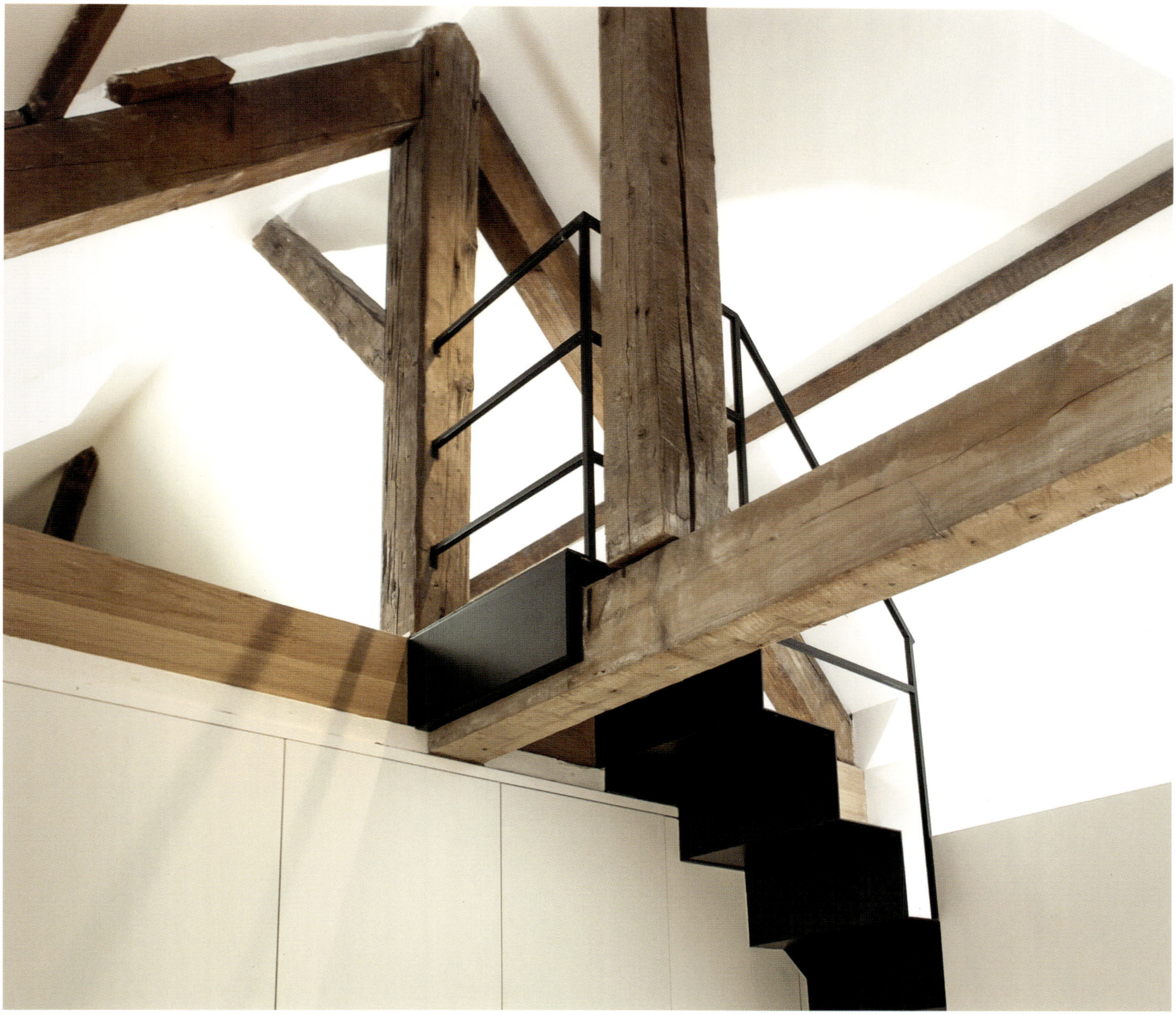

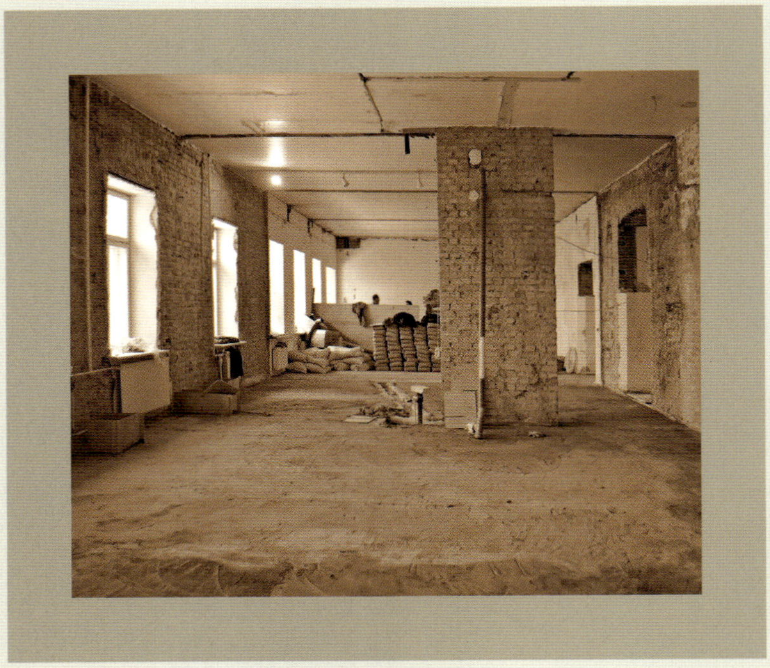

INTERIOR KG

INT2 ARCHITECTURE

215 m² | 2,314 sq. ft.

Saint Petersburg, Russia

Photos © **INT2 architecture**

> Create a functional space for short-term stays by 4–5 individuals

> Design a simple composition featuring interplay of color and textures

> Einen funktionellen Raum für Kurzaufenthalte für 4–5 Personen schaffen

> Eine einfache Komposition entwerfen, die mit Farben und Texturen spielt

> Créer un espace fonctionnel pour de courts séjours de 4-5 personnes

> Concevoir une composition simple en jouant sur la couleur et les textures

This apartment occupies the top floor of an old house constructed in the early 19th century in the central section of St. Petersburg. The house was built in an eclectic style, and several architects contributed to its rebuilding over the years.
The main objective in carrying out the renovation was to create a functional space to accommodate four to five persons for short-term stays. The result was a design for a comfortable two-bedroom apartment with two main bathrooms, living room, kitchen, study, laundry room, guest toilet, and steam bath.
The project's driving concept is to utilize the simple methods of working with space through color and texture: selection of deep colors for the walls and ceilings, combination of various textures of wood with tiles of cement and ceramic granite.

Dieses Apartment befindet sich in der obersten Etage eines Gebäudes, das zu Beginn des 19. Jahrhunderts im Zentrum von Sankt Petersburg entstand. Das Haus wurde im eklektischen Stil errichtet und im Laufe der Jahre von mehreren Architekten umgebaut.
Hauptziel des Umbaus war die Schaffung eines funktionalen Raums für Kurzzeitaufenthalte von vier bis fünf Personen. Als Ergebnis wurde eine komfortable Wohnung mit zwei Schlafzimmern, zwei Hauptbädern, Wohnzimmer, Küche, Arbeitszimmer, Waschküche, Gäste-WC und Dampfbad entworfen.
Farbe und Texturen sind die Kernelemente des einfachen Umbaukonzepts: dunkle Farben finden sich an Wänden und Decken, verschiedene Holzstrukturen werden mit Zementfliesen und Feinsteinzeug kombiniert.

Cet appartement occupe le dernier étage d'une ancienne maison construite au début du XIXe siècle, au cœur de la ville de Saint-Pétersbourg. La maison a été construite dans un style éclectique, puis reconstruite par divers architectes au fil des années.
Au moment de réaliser les travaux, le principal objectif a été de créer un espace fonctionnel pour des séjours temporaires de courte durée pour quatre à cinq personnes. Le résultat en est la conception d'un appartement pratique de deux chambres avec deux salles de bains principales, un salon, une cuisine, un bureau, une buanderie, des toilettes pour invités et un sauna.
Le principal concept du projet est le recours aux méthodes simples de travail avec l'espace grâce à la couleur et la texture : utilisation de couleurs profondes sur les murs et plafonds, combinaison de diverses textures de bois, carreaux de ciment et granit céramique.

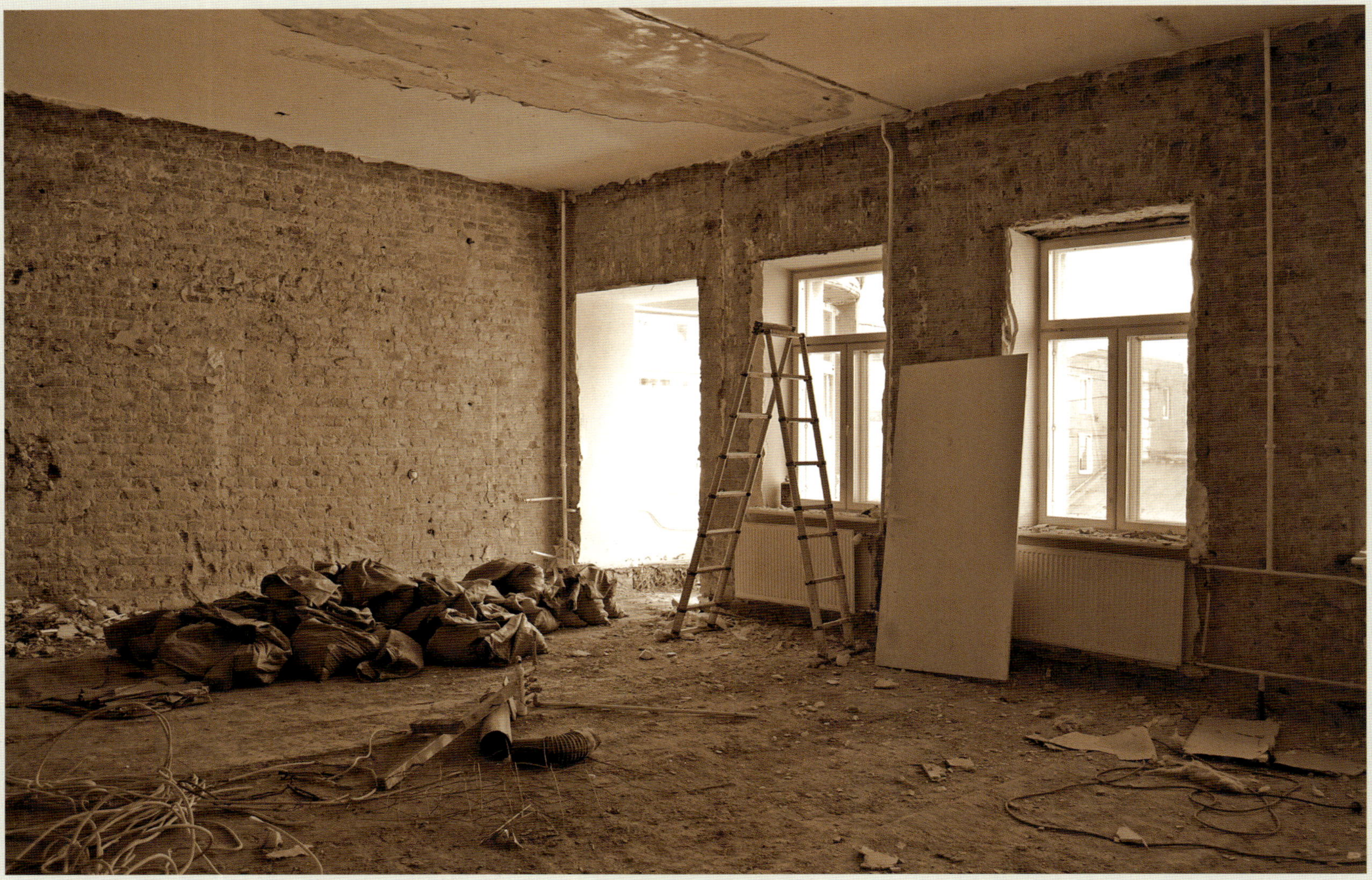

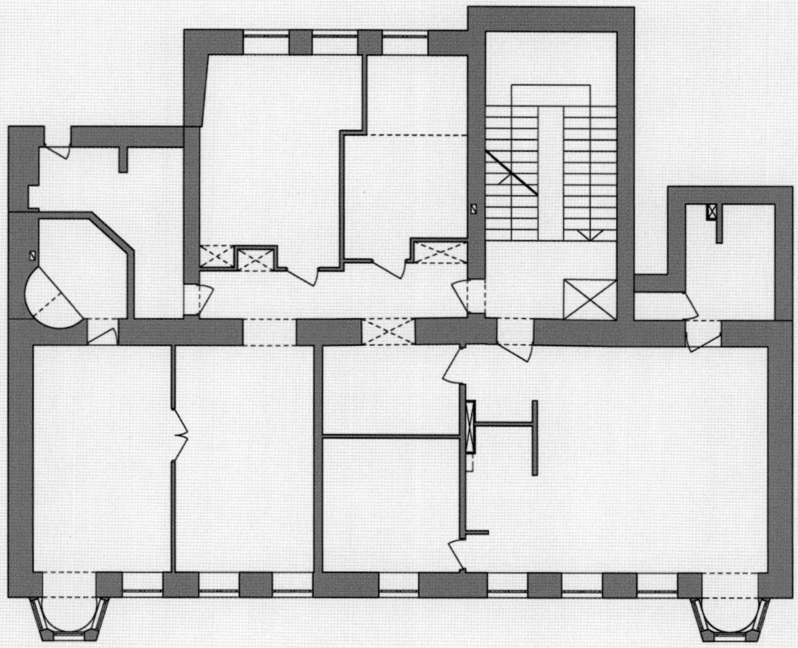

Existing plan

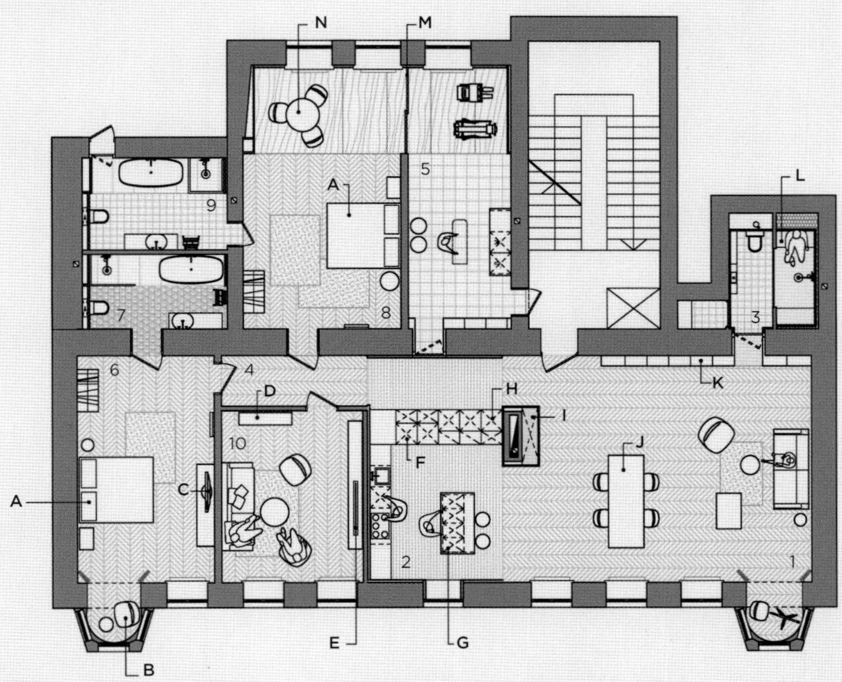

New plan

1. Living / dining room
2. Kitchen
3. Guest bathroom
4. Hall
5. Laundry room
6. Bedroom 1
7. Bathroom 1
8. Bedroom 2
9. Bathroom 2
10. Study

A. Bed
B. Lounge zone
C. TV
D. Sideboard
E. Ethanol fireplace
F. Refrigerator
G. Kitchen island
H. Wardrobe
I. Fireplace
J. Dining table
K. Shelving
L. Steam room
M. Sliding door
N. Breakfast table

The living room is visually separated from the kitchen by the walnut parquet flooring. The fireplace, custom-made in Italy and finished on-site with laminated birch wood, becomes the room's main focus and creates a homey atmosphere.

Durch das Walnussparkett ist das Wohnzimmer optisch von der Küche getrennt. Der in Italien nach Maß gefertigte Kamin wurde vor Ort mit beschichtetem Birkenholz verkleidet. Er wird zum Mittelpunkt des Raumes und schafft eine wohnliche Atmosphäre.

Le séjour est visuellement séparé de la cuisine par le parquet en noyer. La cheminée, faite sur mesure en Italie et finie sur place avec du contreplaqué de bouleau, devient le centre du salon et crée une atmosphère familiale.

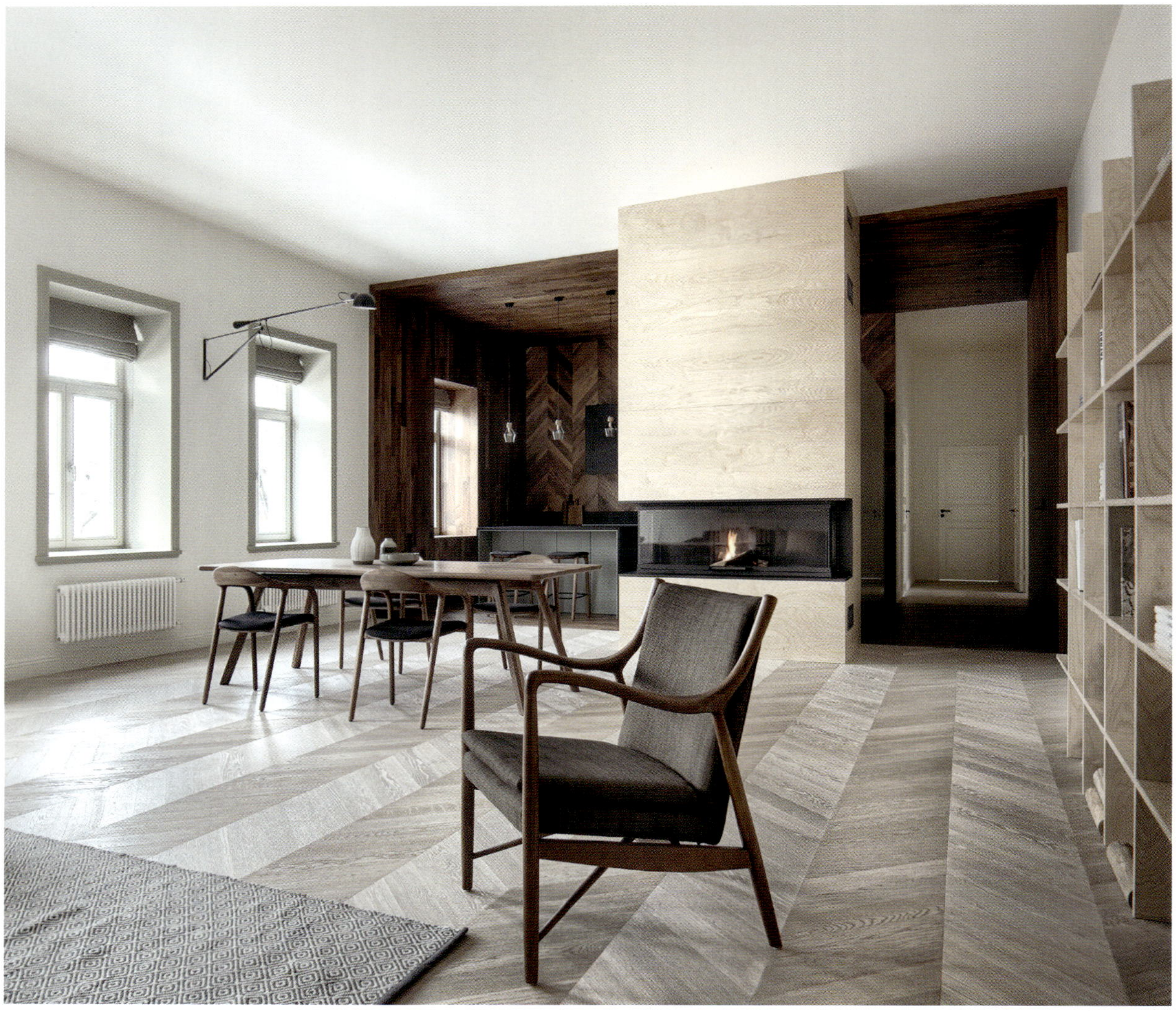

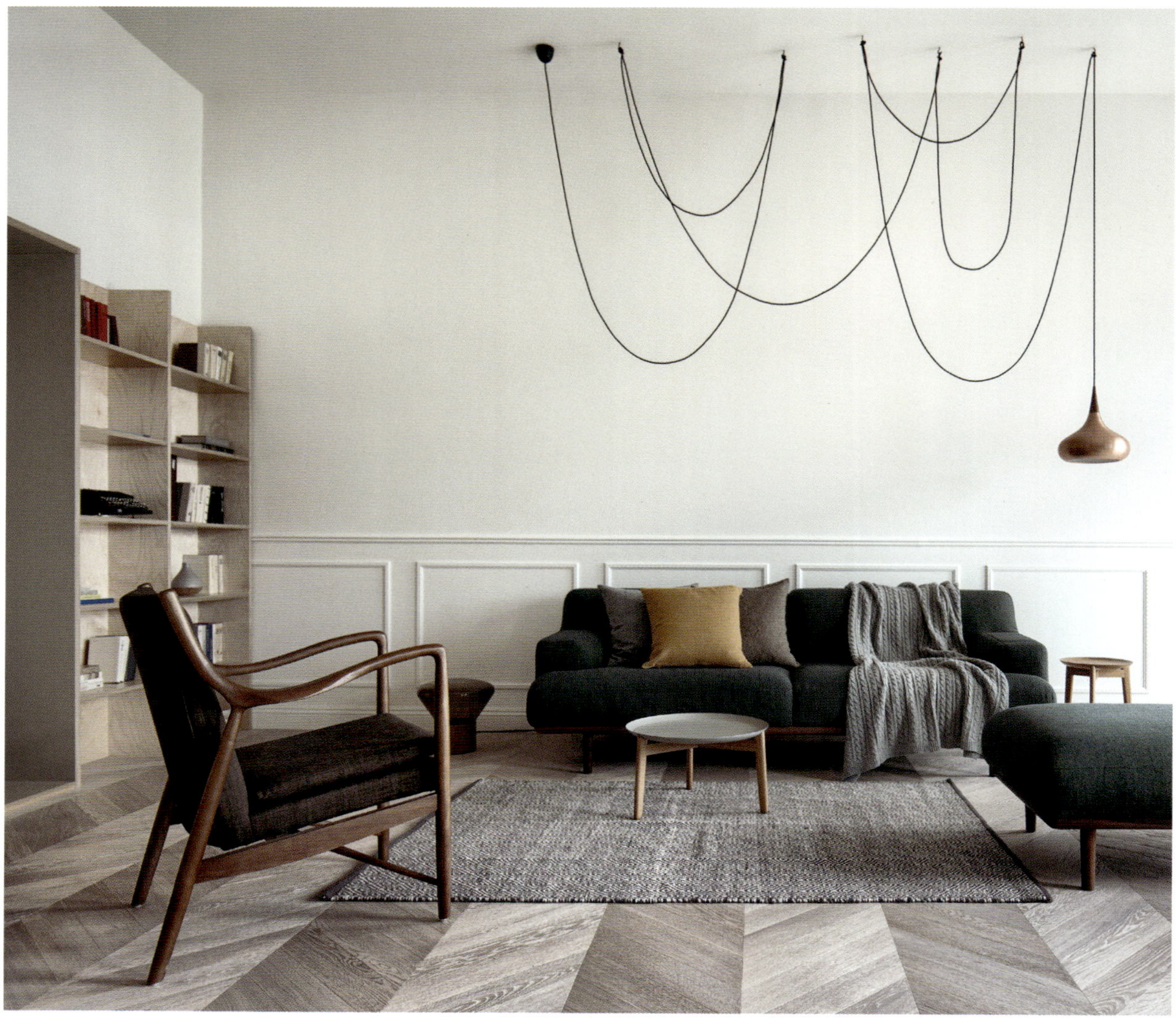

The green rugs and cushions lend a note of color and vitality to a room clearly dominated by neutral shades. Laminated wooden shelving for books, decorative pieces and souvenirs obscures the door to the steam bath.

Das Grün der Polsterung und der Kissen verleiht einem Raum Farbe und Lebendigkeit, wobei neutrale Farben eindeutig dominieren. Regale aus beschichtetem Holz mit Büchern, Dekorationselementen und Erinnerungsstücken verbergen den Eingang zum Dampfbad.

La couleur verte du papier peint et celui des coussins apportent une touche de couleur et de vie à une salle avec une prédominance claire des couleurs neutres. L'entrée du sauna est masquée par des étagères en contreplaqué remplies de livres, d'éléments de décoration et de souvenirs.

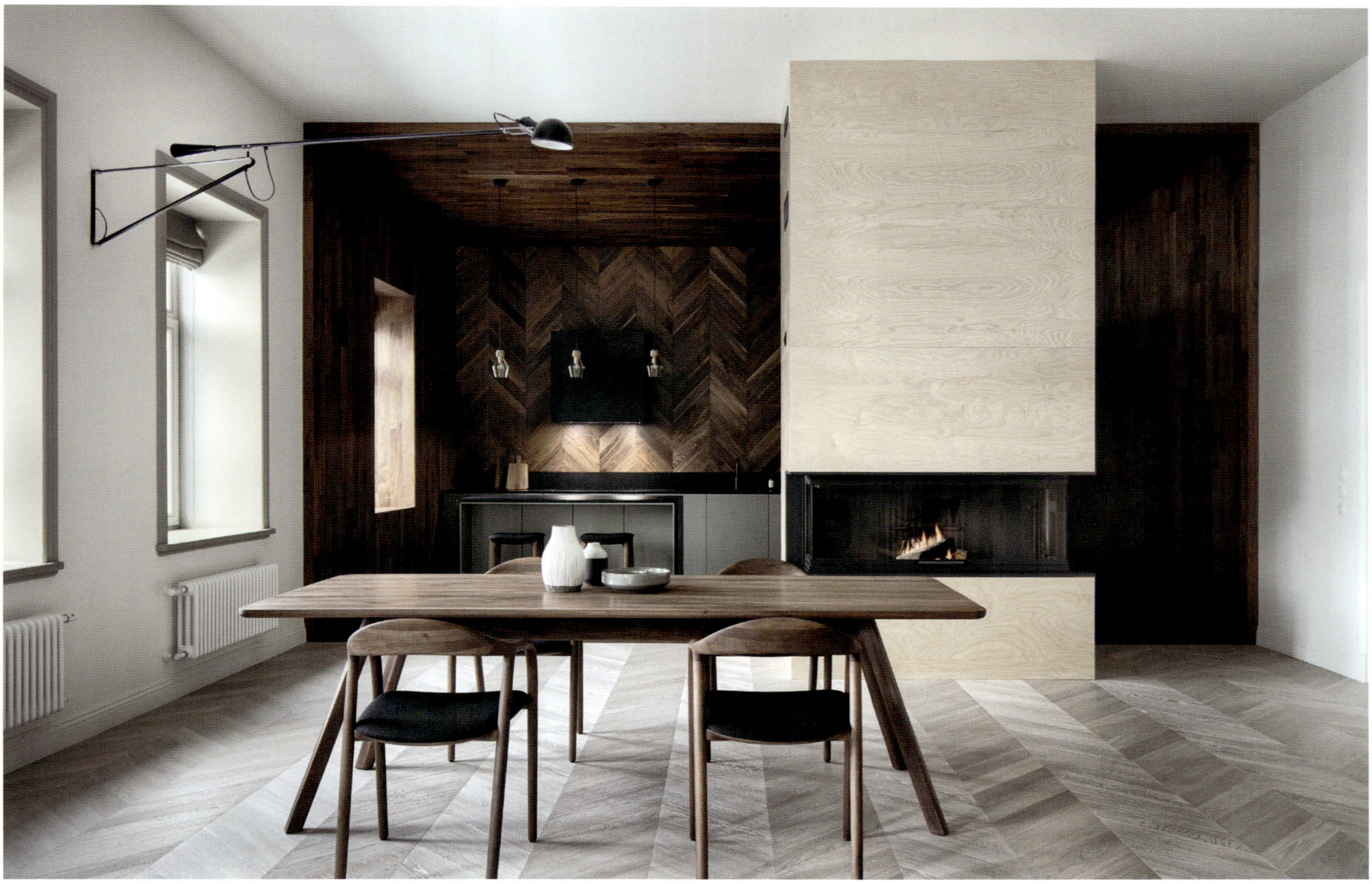

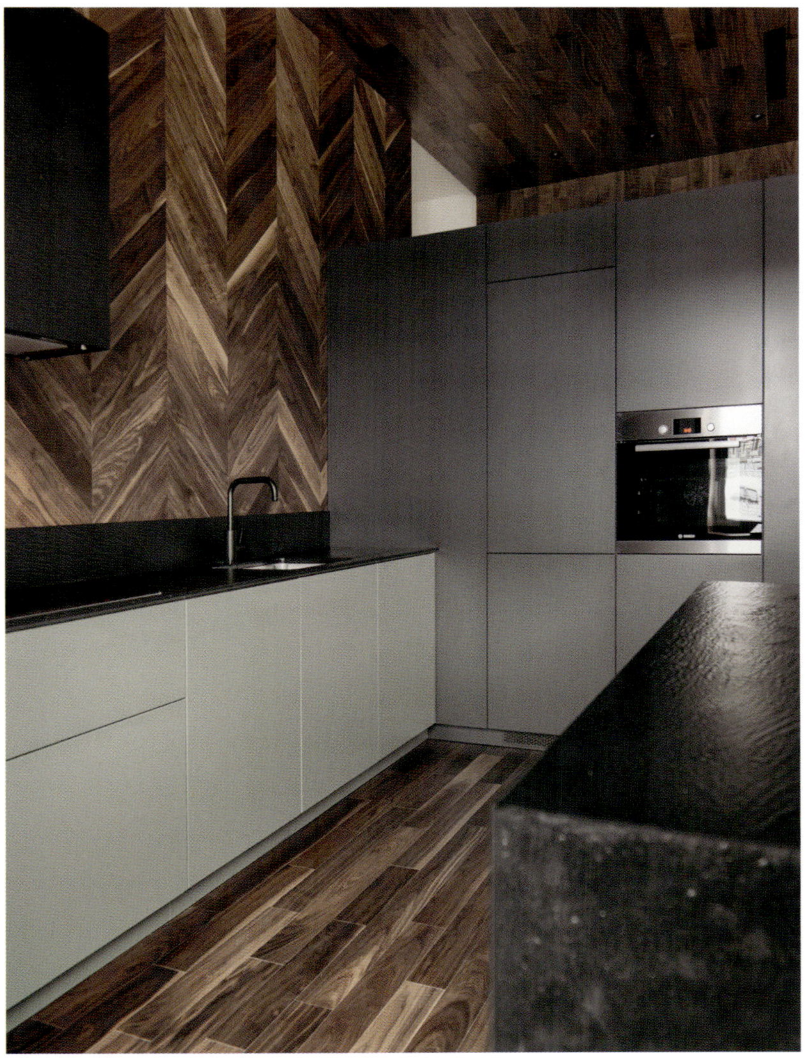

The kitchen is separated from the entrance by double-sided shelves that stop short of the ceiling to permit natural light to stream into the vestibule. In the kitchen, the island and other counters are topped with quartz, as is the range hood cover.

Die Küche ist vom Eingang durch doppelseitige Schränke getrennt, die nicht bis zur Decke reichen und somit Tageslicht in den Flur dringen lassen. Die Arbeitsplatte der Kücheninsel und die übrige Küche sowie die Verkleidung der Abzugshaube sind aus Quarzstein.

La cuisine est séparée de l'entrée par des armoires biface qui ne montent pas jusqu'au plafond laissant ainsi pénétrer la lumière naturelle dans le hall. Le plan de travail de l'îlot et du reste de la cuisine et du châssis de la hotte sont faits en pierre de quartz.

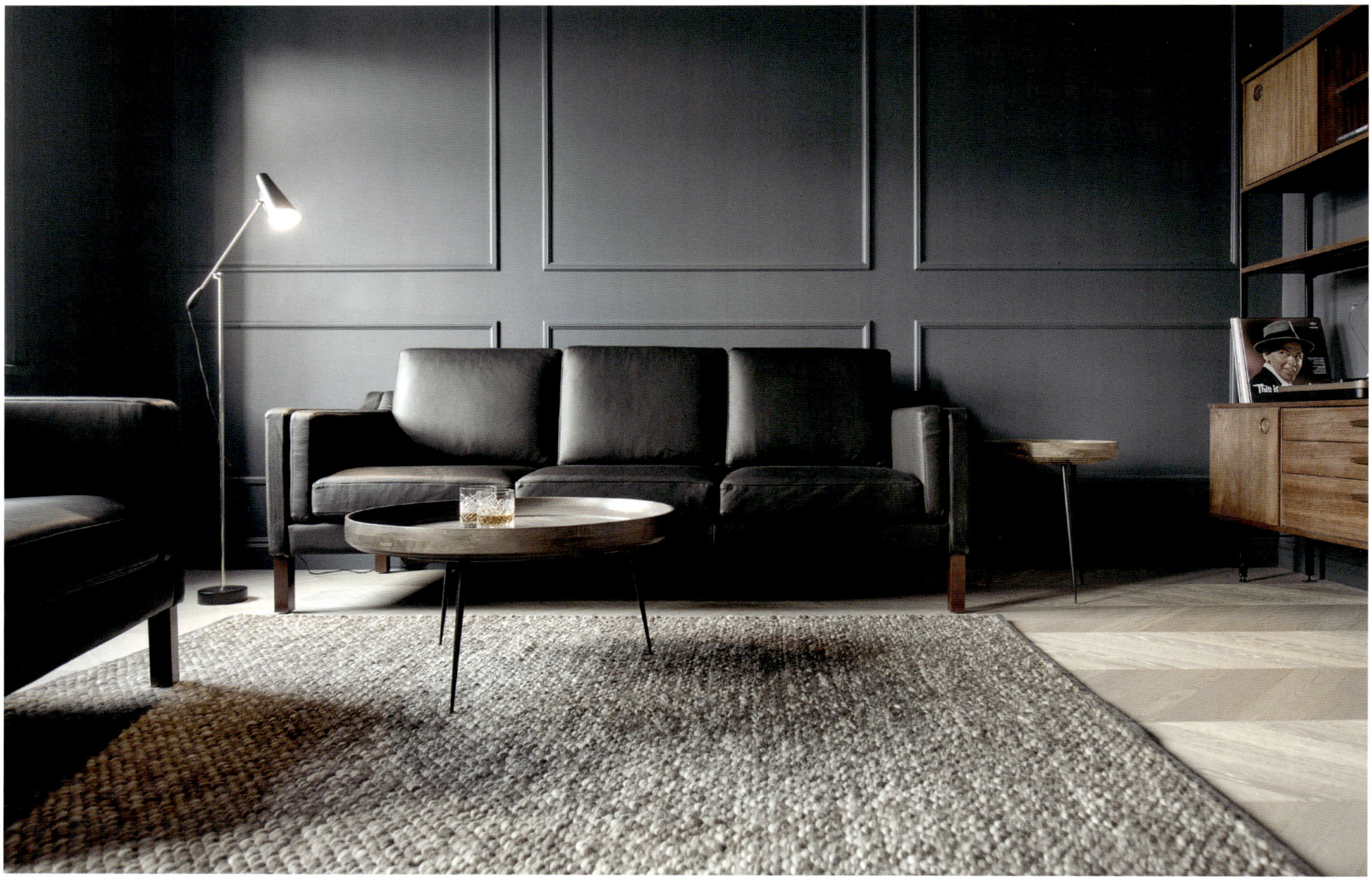

The dark bluish gray of the walls, extensive wood use and the environmental fireplace combine to create a cozy ambiance that invites relaxation. The ceiling, painted in a much lighter shade of gray, appears to be higher, producing a sensation of spaciousness that complements the room's enhanced brightness.

Das dunkle Graublau der Wände, die ausgiebige Verwendung von Holz und der Kamin schaffen eine gemütliche Atmosphäre, die zum Entspannen einlädt. Die in einem viel helleren Grauton gestrichene Decke scheint höher zu sein, was ein Gefühl von Geräumigkeit und Helligkeit im Wohnraum vermittelt.

La couleur gris bleuté foncé des murs, l'utilisation à profusion du bois et la cheminée écologique créent une ambiance conviviale qui invite à la détente. Le plafond peint dans un ton gris beaucoup plus clair semble être plus haut, procurant une sensation de grandeur en plus de donner davantage de luminosité à la pièce.

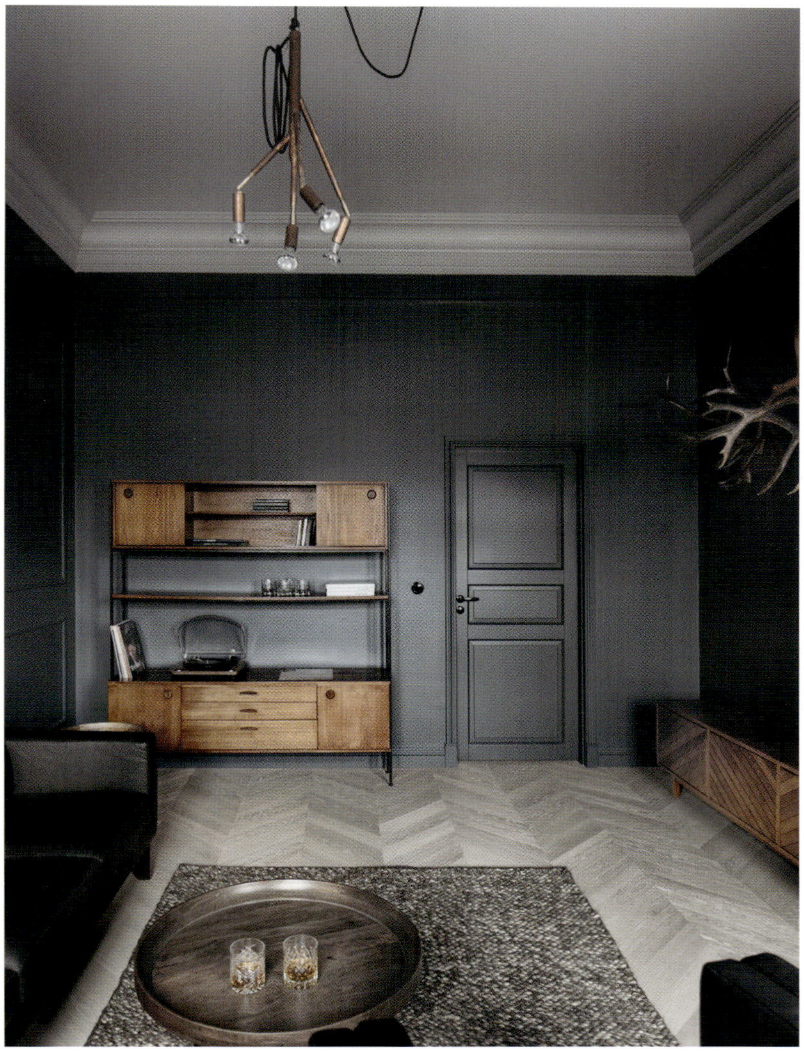
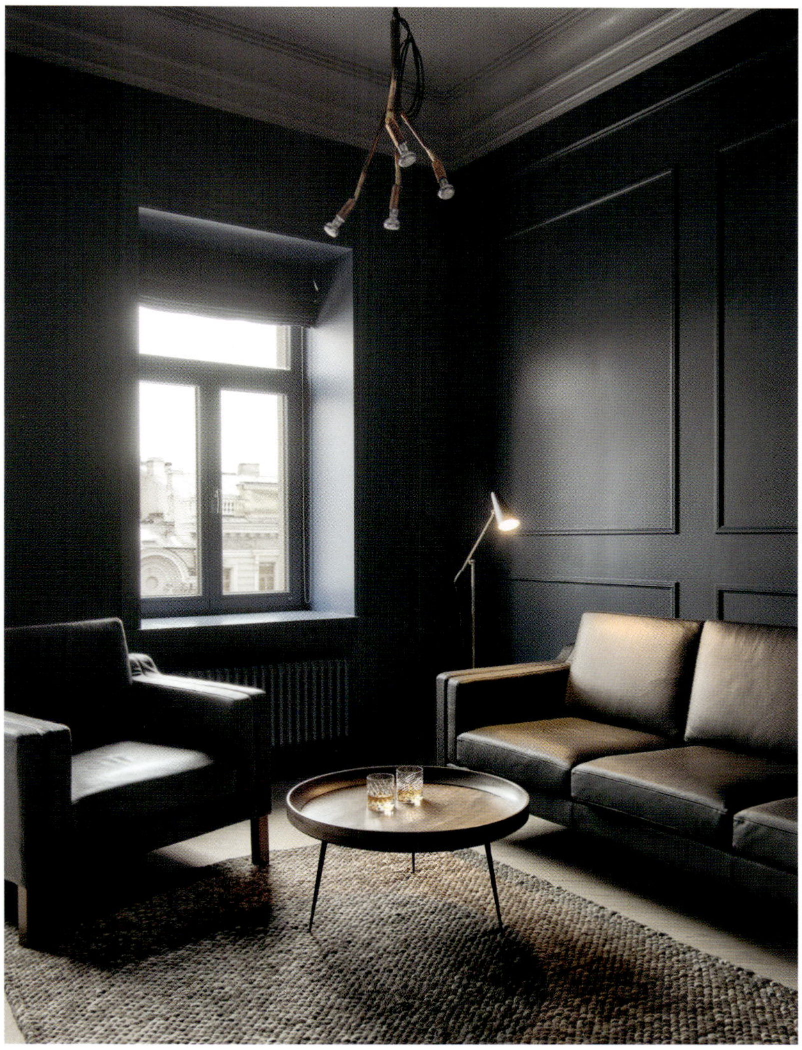
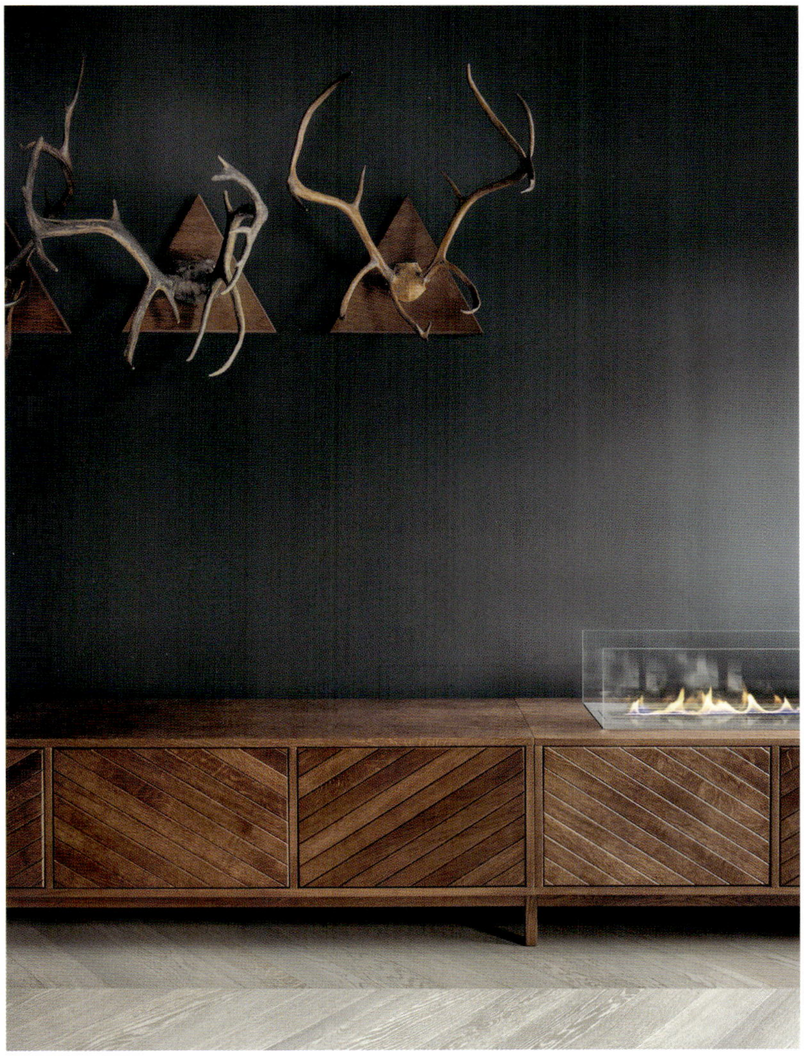
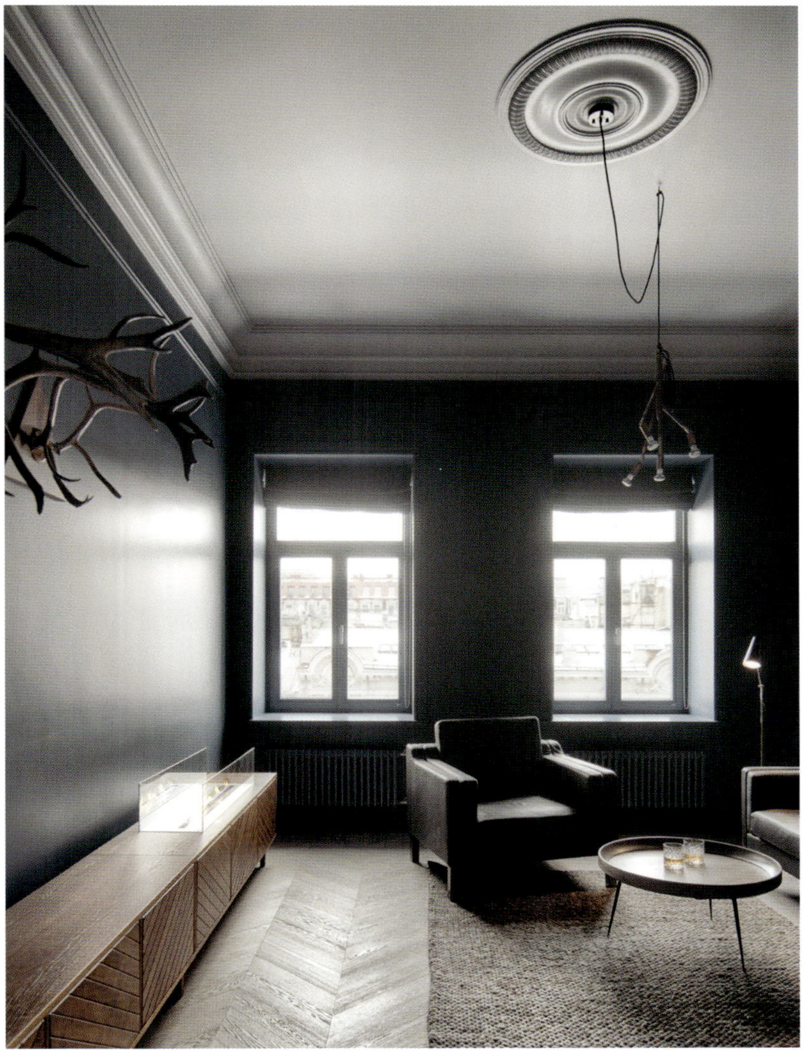

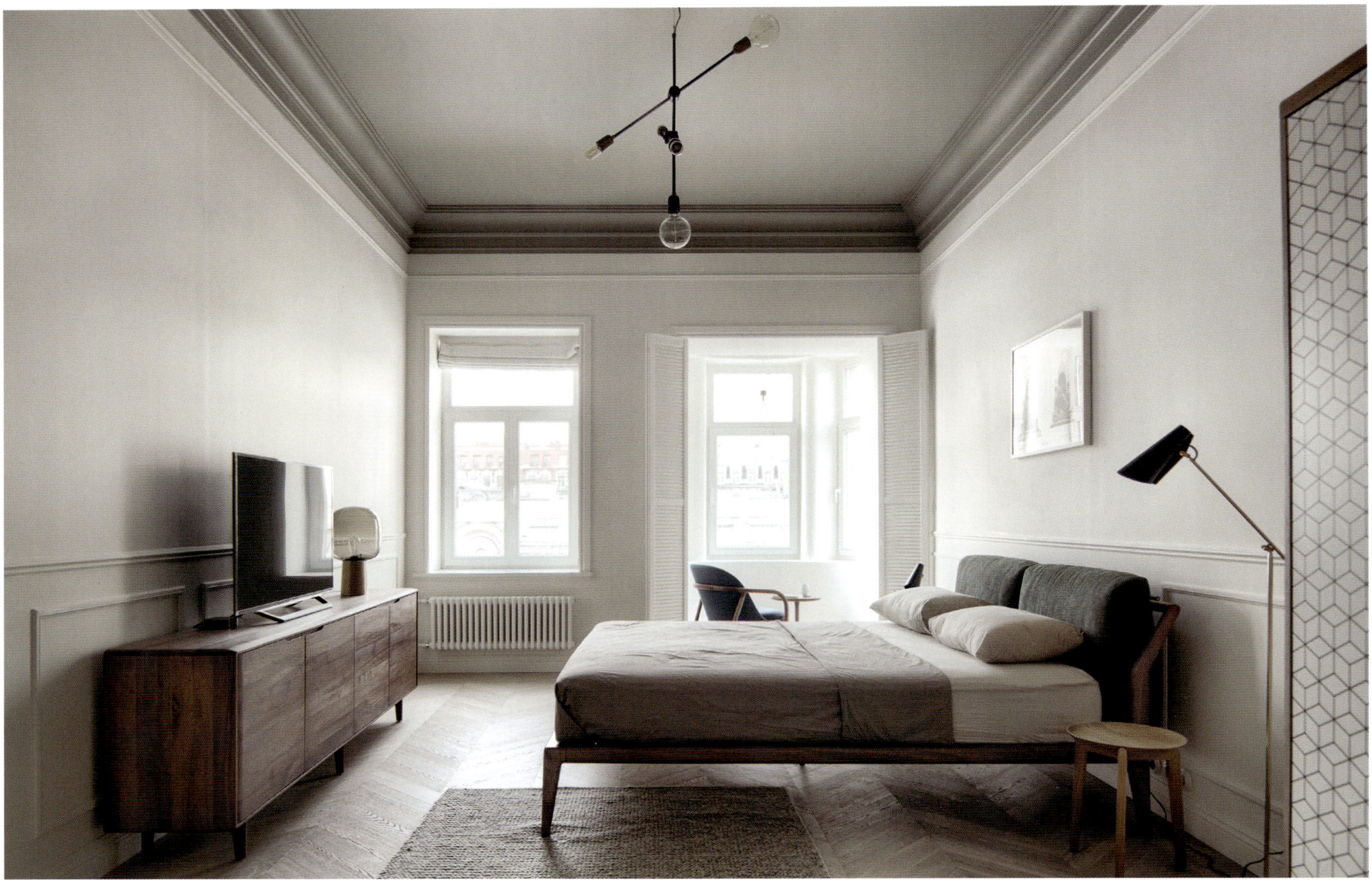

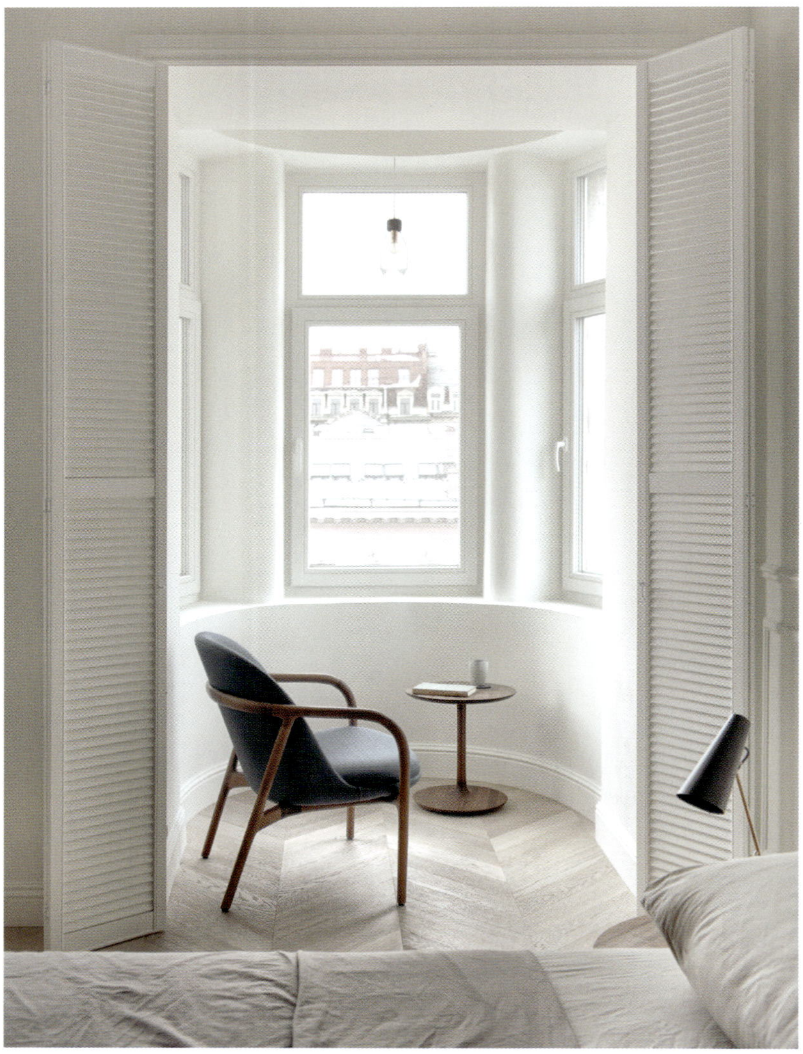

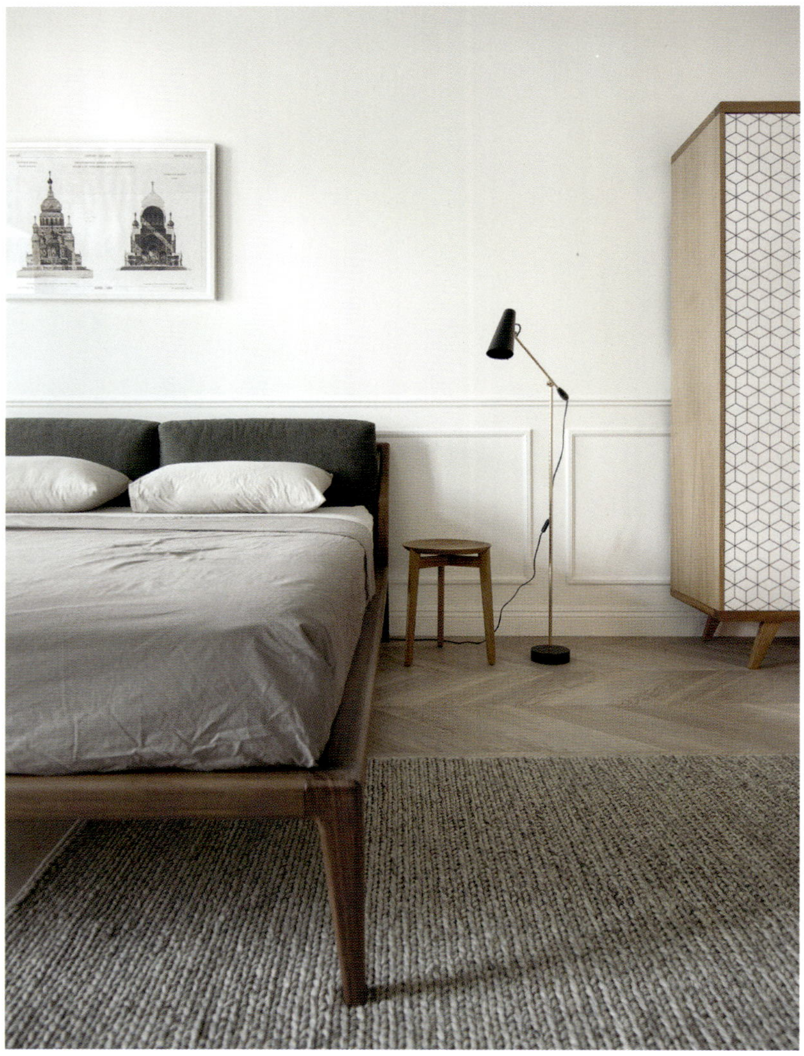

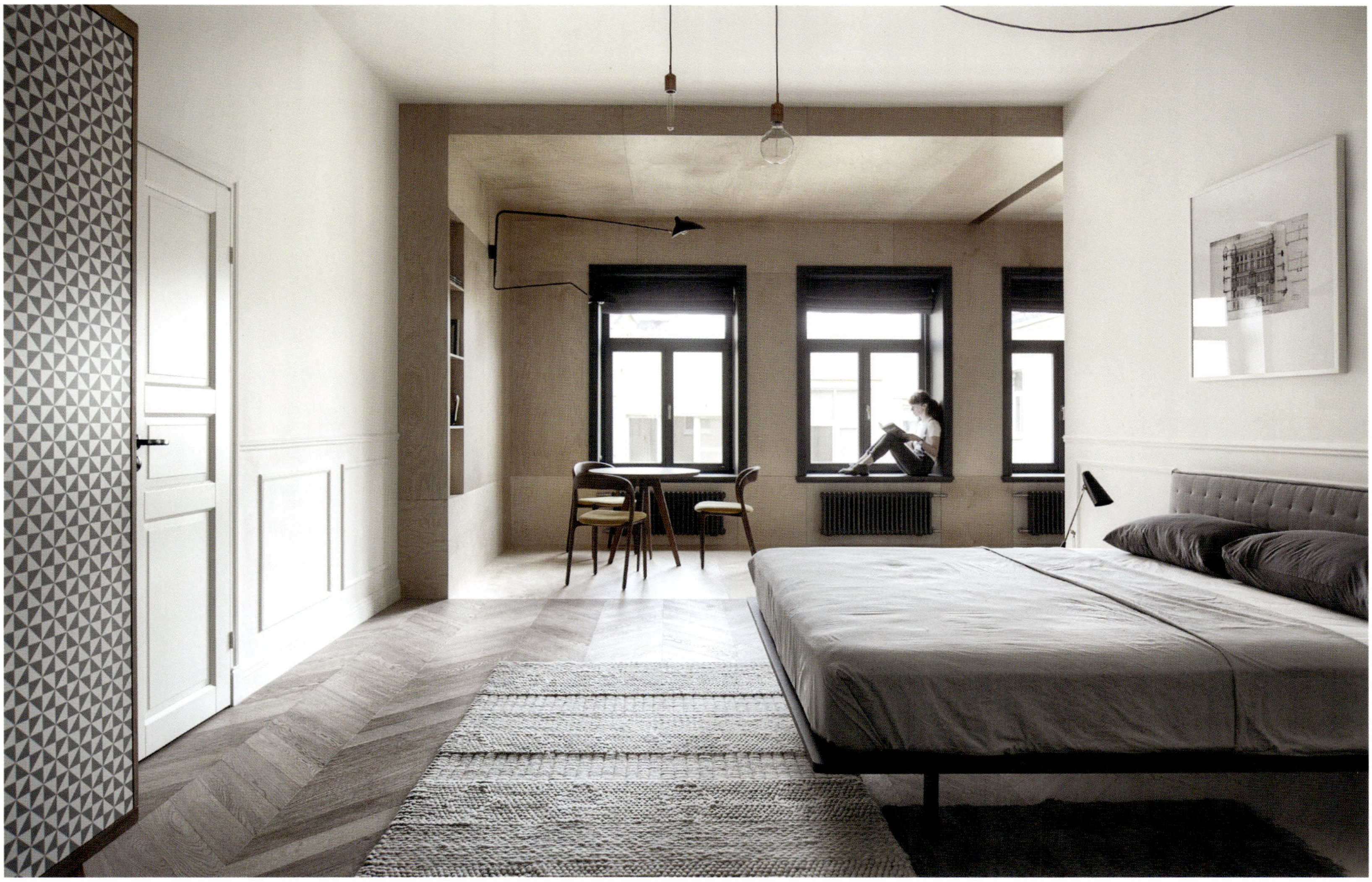

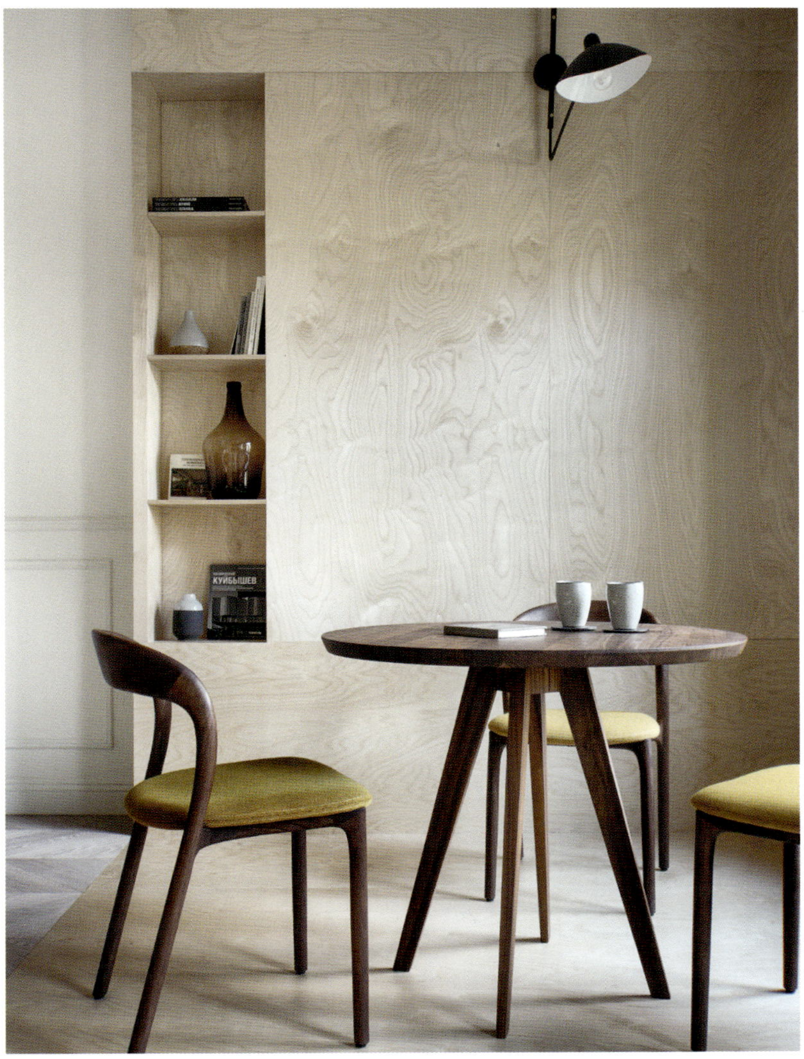

The laquered wooden wall paneling of the breakfast and fitness area separates it from the lounge area. In the absence of partitions or dividers, natural light from the adjoining windows floods the entire apartment.

Der Frühstücks- und Fitnessbereich entlang der Fenster ist durch Wandverkleidungen aus lackiertem Holz vom Loungebereich abgegrenzt. Da es keine Trenn- oder Zwischenwände gibt, kann das Tageslicht den gesamten Raum durchströmen.

Le coin petit-déjeuner et la salle de gym ont été séparés – le long des fenêtres – de l'espace de détente revêtu de bois laqué. La lumière naturelle entre dans toute la maison en absence de cloison ou de panneau de séparation.

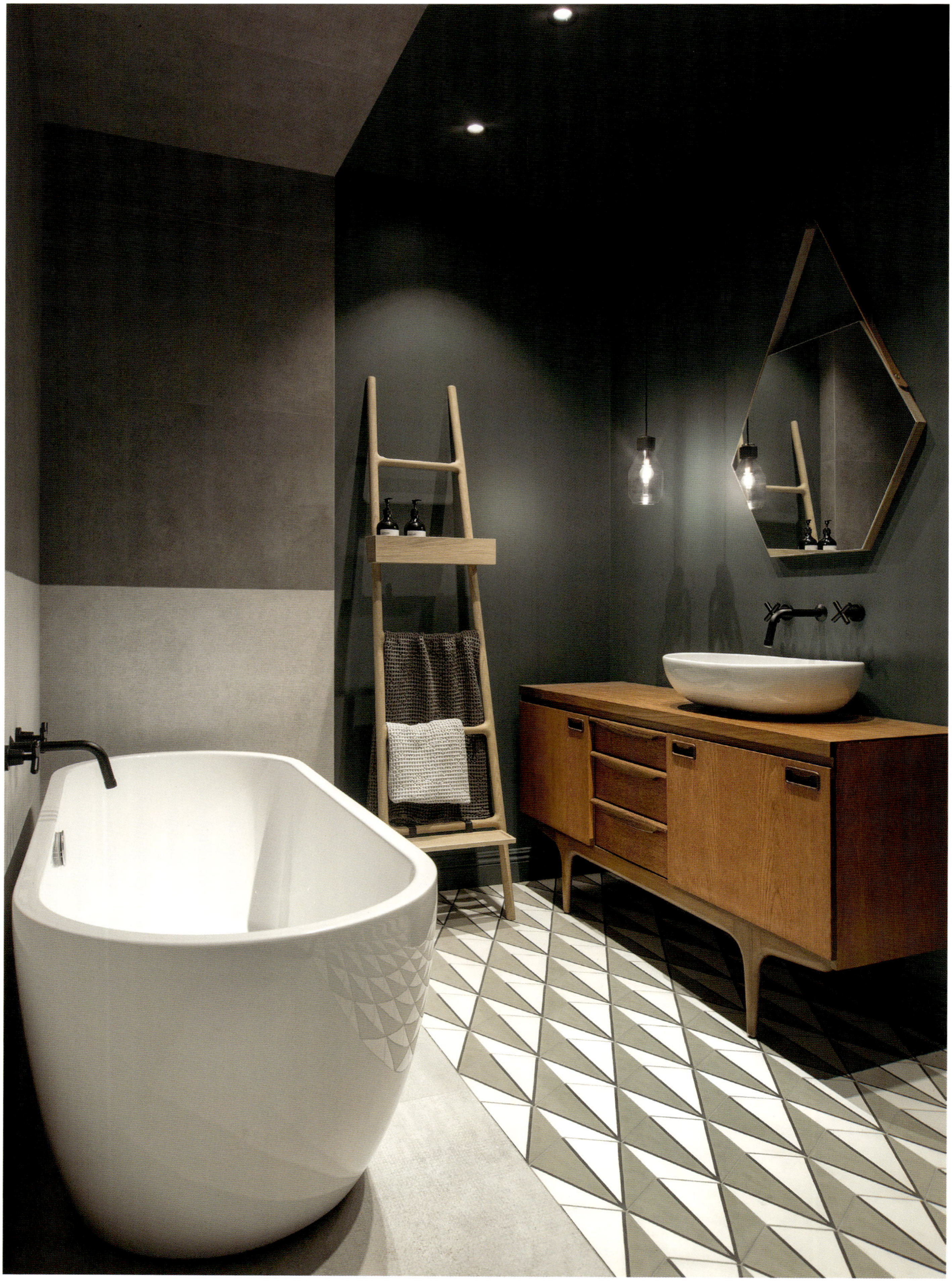

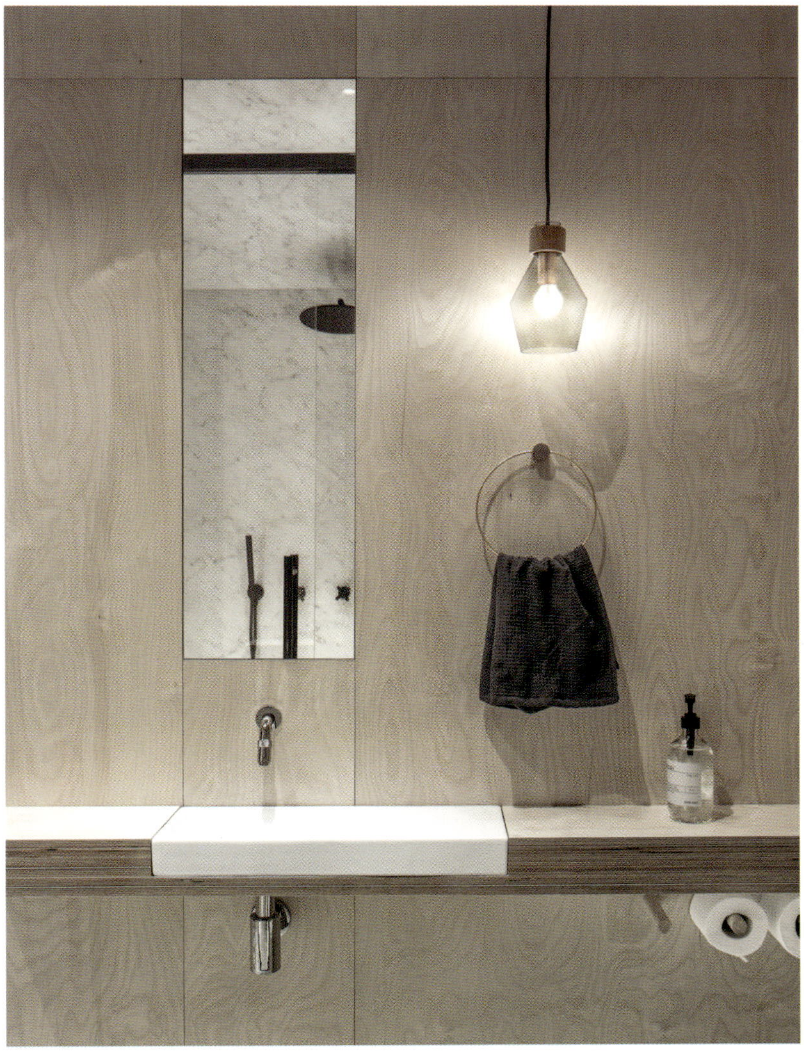

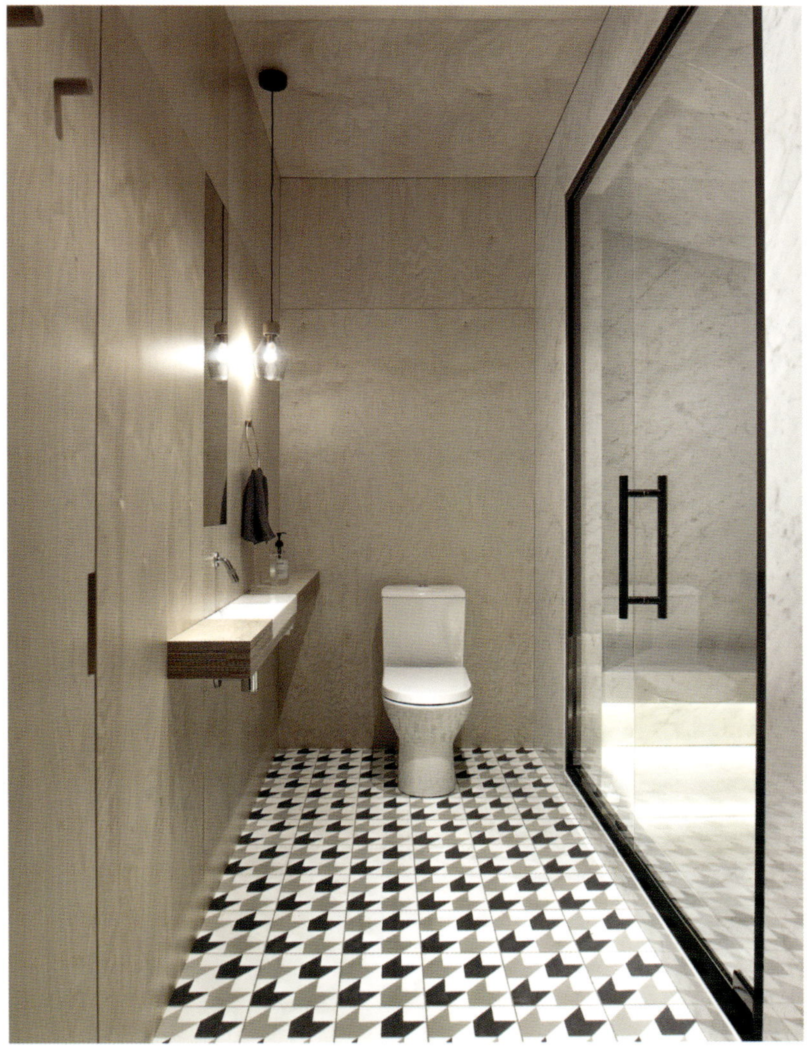

The bathrooms are divided linearly into a "humid" area surfaced in ceramic granite and a painted "dry" area. The design of the guest bathroom is based on the same principle. The shower in the steam room is finished with marble slabs and its "dry" area with lacquered birch wood.

Die Hauptbadezimmer sind linear unterteilt in den „nassen" Bereich, der mit Feinsteinzug verkleidet ist, und den „trockenen" Bereich, der gestrichen ist. Das Gästebad ist nach dem gleichen Prinzip gestaltet. Die Dusche im Dampfbad ist mit Marmorplatten und einem „trockenen" Bereich mit lackiertem Birkenholz verkleidet.

Les principales salles de bains sont réparties de manière linéaire dans la zone « humide », revêtue de granit céramique et, la zone « sèche », quant à elle, est peinte. La salle de bains destinée aux invités a été conçue sur la base du même principe. La douche du sauna est revêtue de dalles en marbre, avec une zone « sèche » en bois de bouleau laqué.

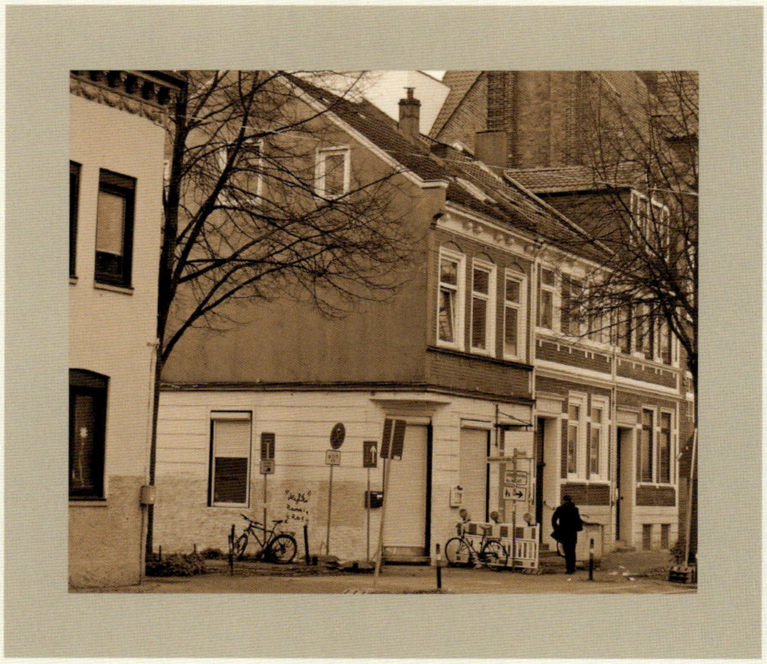

HOUSE CHAPEAU

WIRTH ARCHITEKTEN

235 m^2 | 2,530 sq. ft.

Bremen, Germany

Photos © **Christian Burmester**

> Expand the house to accommodate kitchen, living room, and dining room in a single space

> Achieve balance and harmony between the old house and the extension

> Open up the house to receive maximum light

> Das Haus ausbauen, um Küche, Wohn- und Esszimmer im selben Raum unterbringen zu können

> Balance und Harmonie zwischen der Struktur des ehemaligen Hauses und des Anbaus erzielen

> Ein Höchstmaß an Licht in das ganze Haus bringen

> Agrandir la maison pour faire coexister une cuisine, un salon et une salle à manger dans un même espace

> Obtenir un équilibre et une harmonie entre la structure de l'ancienne maison et celle de l'extension

> Apporter le maximum de lumière dans toute la maison

For this project to renovate a traditional terraced house in Bremen owned by a young family, the point of departure was the wish to create an open living area. The structure's existing rooms were not large enough, however, to accommodate the kitchen, dining room and living room in a single space. The solution was to add a new floor to the original building, giving it a new "hat"—hence the name.
The extension alludes to the original structure by matching the existing roof angles with its own while providing passers-by a new appreciation of the building, offering a dialog between the interior and exterior and between old and new. This remarkable dwelling with its subtle transition between the original space and the addition has become a reference point for the entire neighborhood.

Ausgangspunkt des Sanierungsprojekts dieses traditionsreichen Bürgerhauses in Bremen, das einer jungen Familie gehört, war der Wunsch, einen offenen Wohnbereich zu schaffen. Allerdings waren die vorhandenen Räume nicht groß genug, um Küche, Wohn- und Esszimmer unterzubringen. Die Lösung bestand darin, dem ursprünglichen Gebäude eine neue Etage hinzuzufügen, das einen neuen „Hut" erhielt, daher der Name.
Der Aufbau spielt mit dem alten Gebäude, indem er die Linie der Dachgiebel aufnimmt, aber Passanten eine neue Interpretation des Gebäudes ermöglicht – einen Dialog zwischen innen und außen sowie zwischen alt und neu. Dieses einzigartige Wohngebäude mit seinem subtilen Wechselspiel von Ursprungsbau und Aufbau ist zu einem Bezugspunkt für das gesamte Stadtviertel geworden.

Le point de départ du projet de rénovation de cette traditionnelle maison mitoyenne de Bremen, propriété d'une jeune famille, fut le désir de créer un séjour ouvert. Mais avec la structure d'origine, les pièces existantes n'étaient pas suffisamment grandes pour accueillir la cuisine, la salle à manger et le salon dans un seul et même espace. La solution a été d'ajouter un nouvel étage au bâtiment d'origine qui acquit ainsi un nouveau « chapeau », d'où son nom.
L'extension fait un clin d'œil à la structure historique encastrant les coins du plafond entre eux tout en offrant aux personnes de passage une nouvelle interprétation du bâtiment : un dialogue entre l'intérieur et l'extérieur, entre l'ancien et le nouveau. Cette singulière maison, avec une douce transition du volume initial à celui ajouté, est devenue une référence pour tout le quartier.

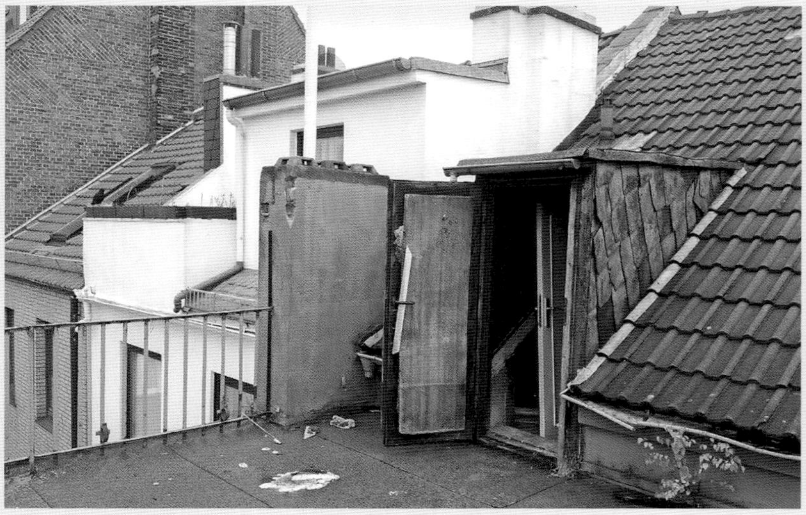
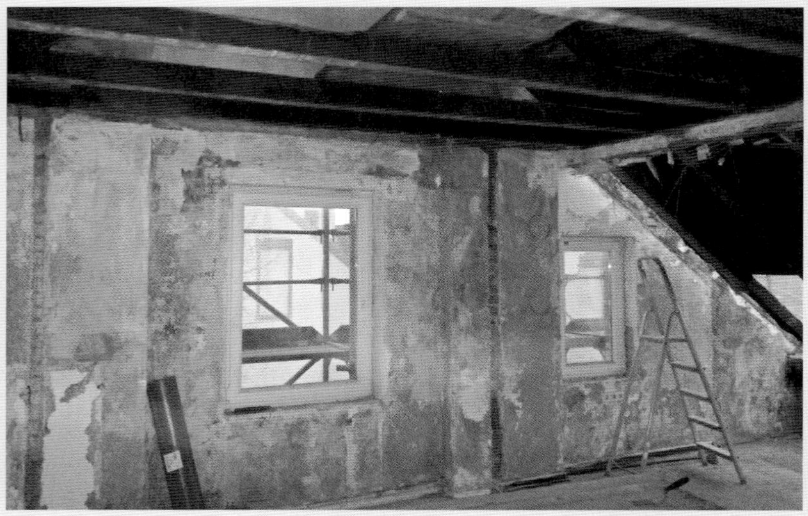
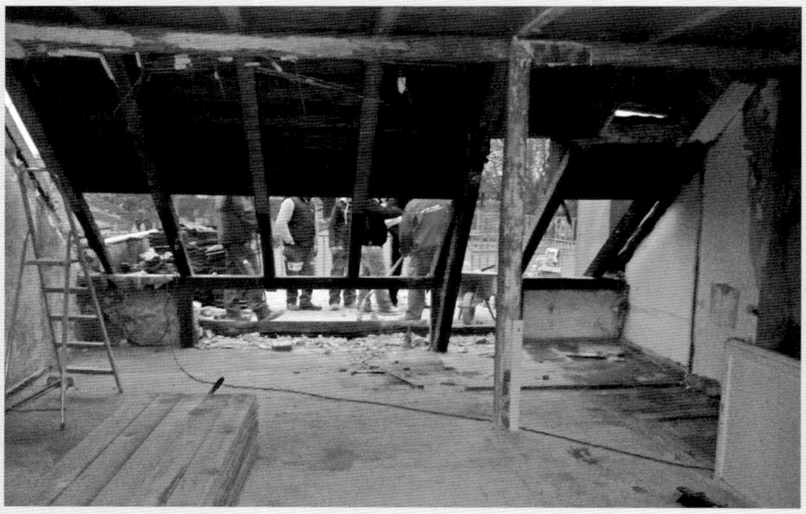
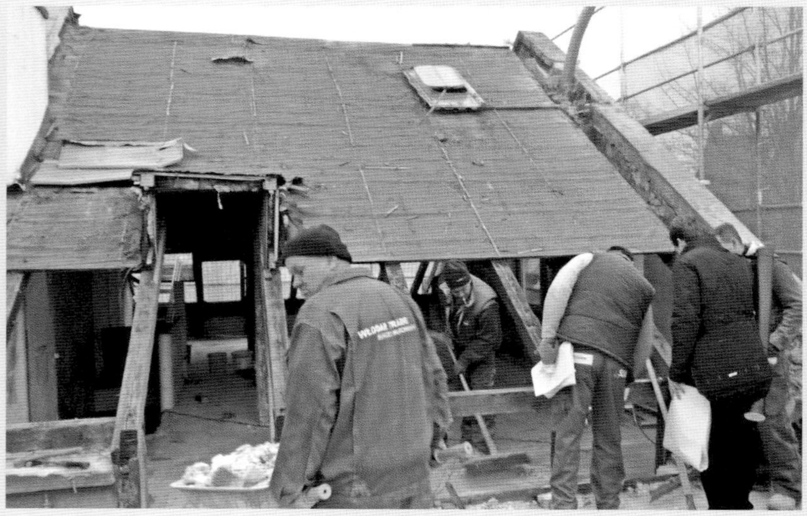
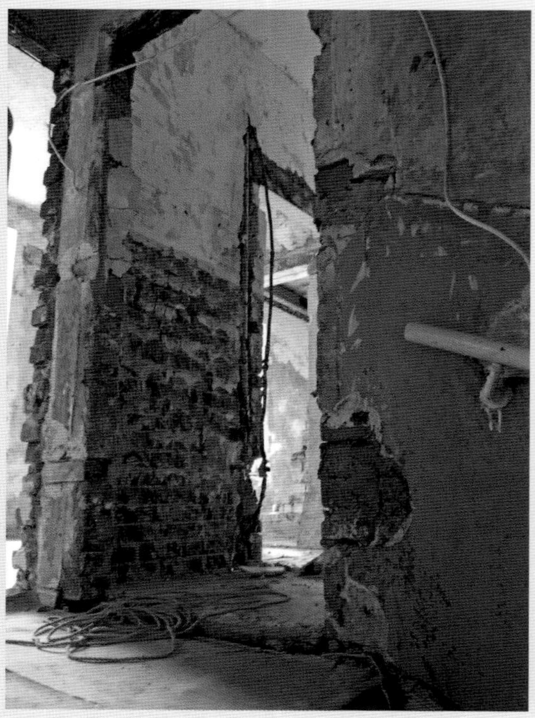
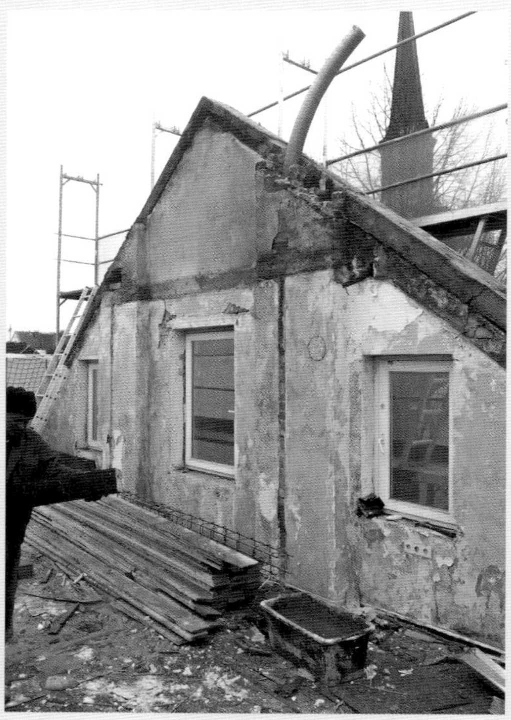
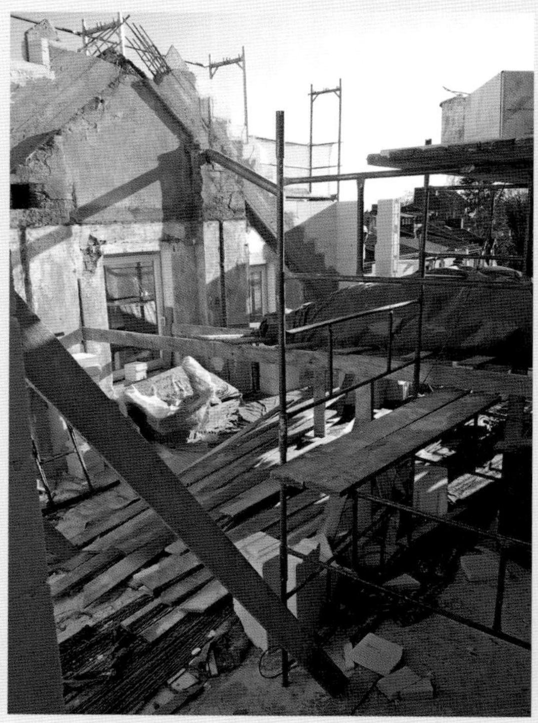

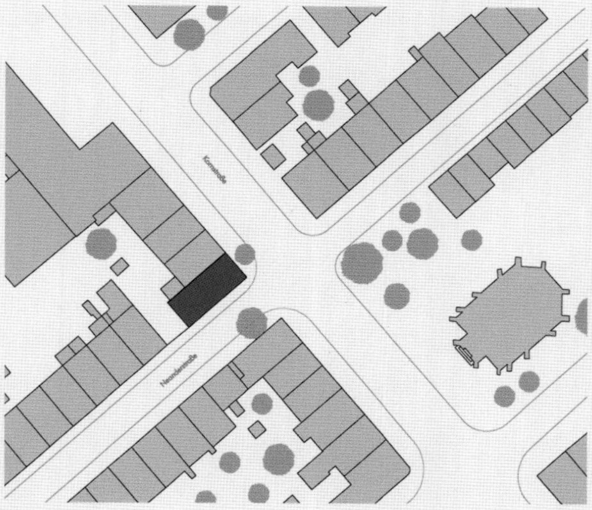

Site plan

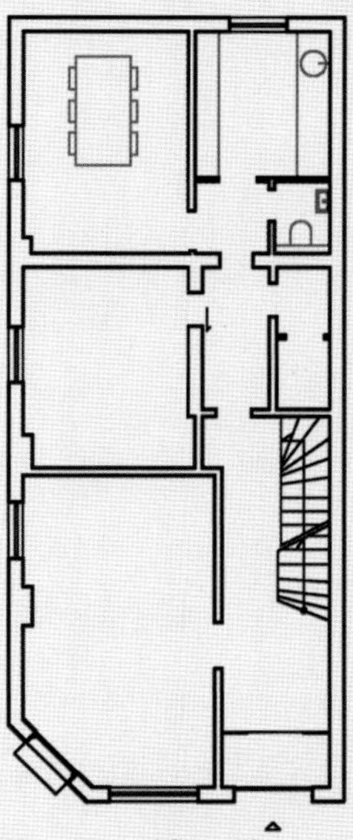

New ground floor plan

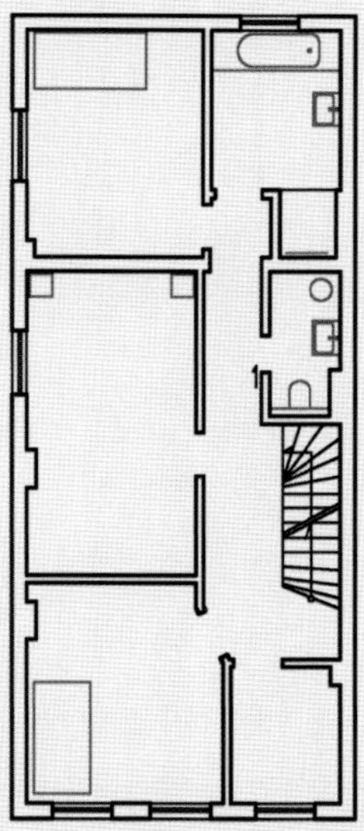

New first floor plan

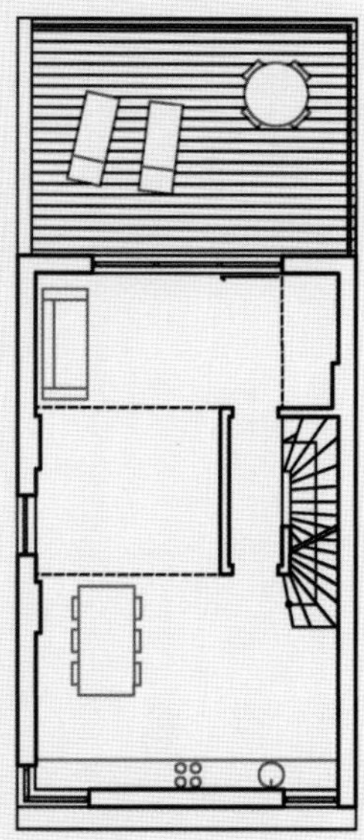

New second floor plan

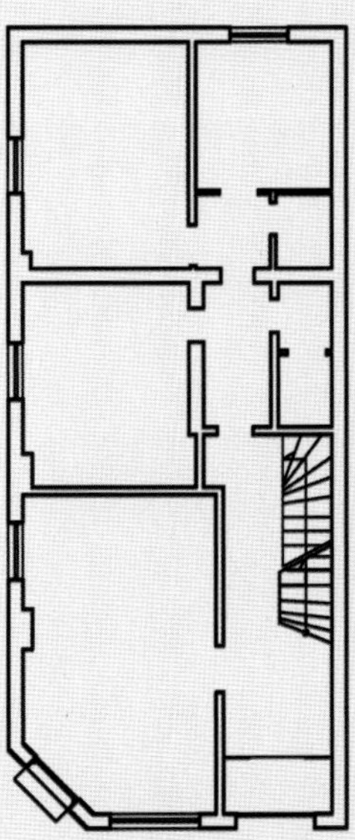

Existing ground floor plan

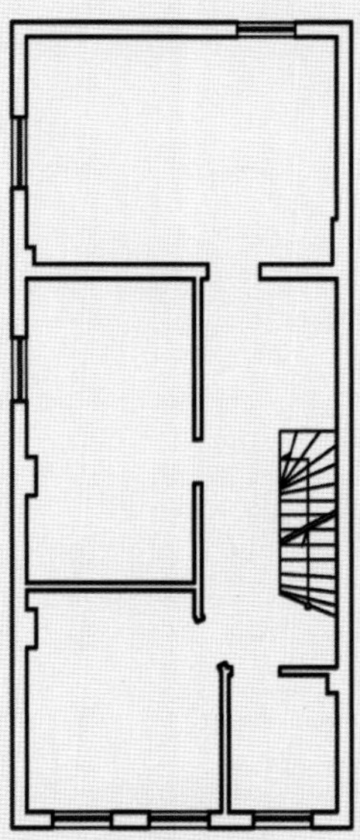

Existing first floor plan

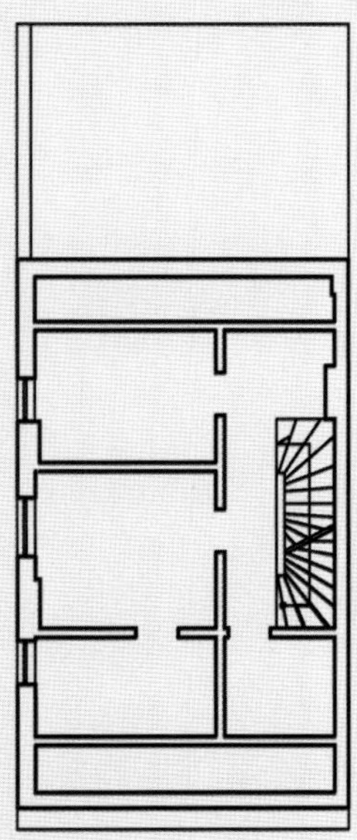

Existing second floor plan

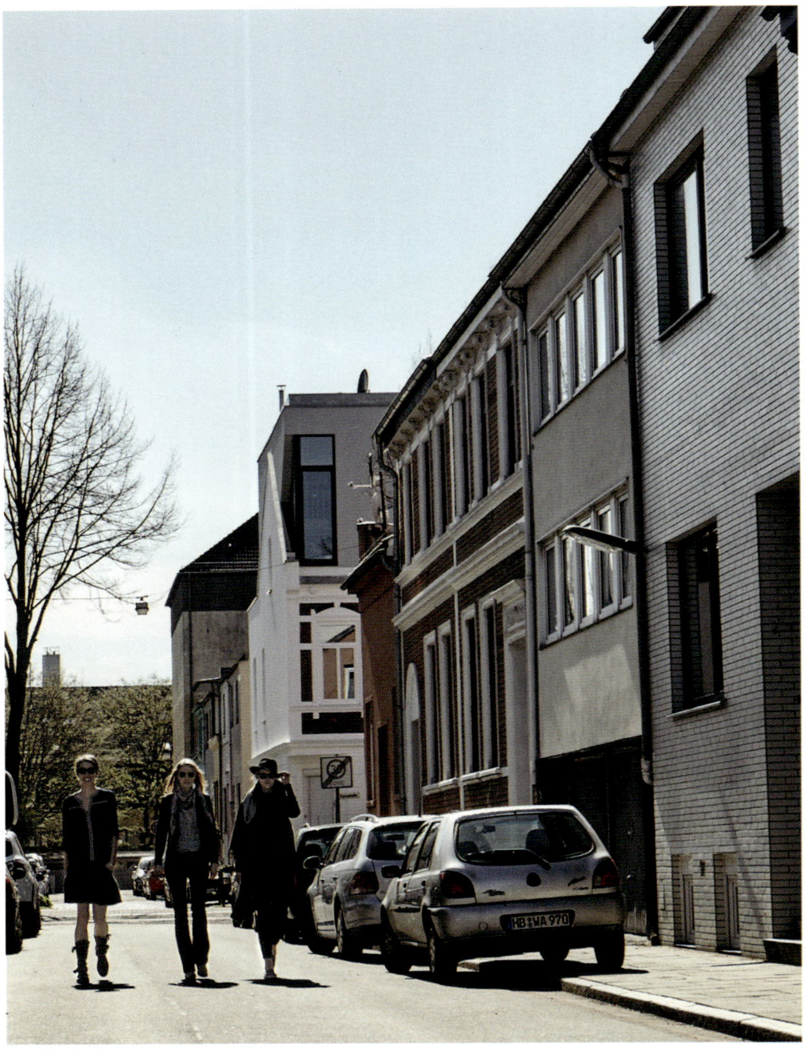

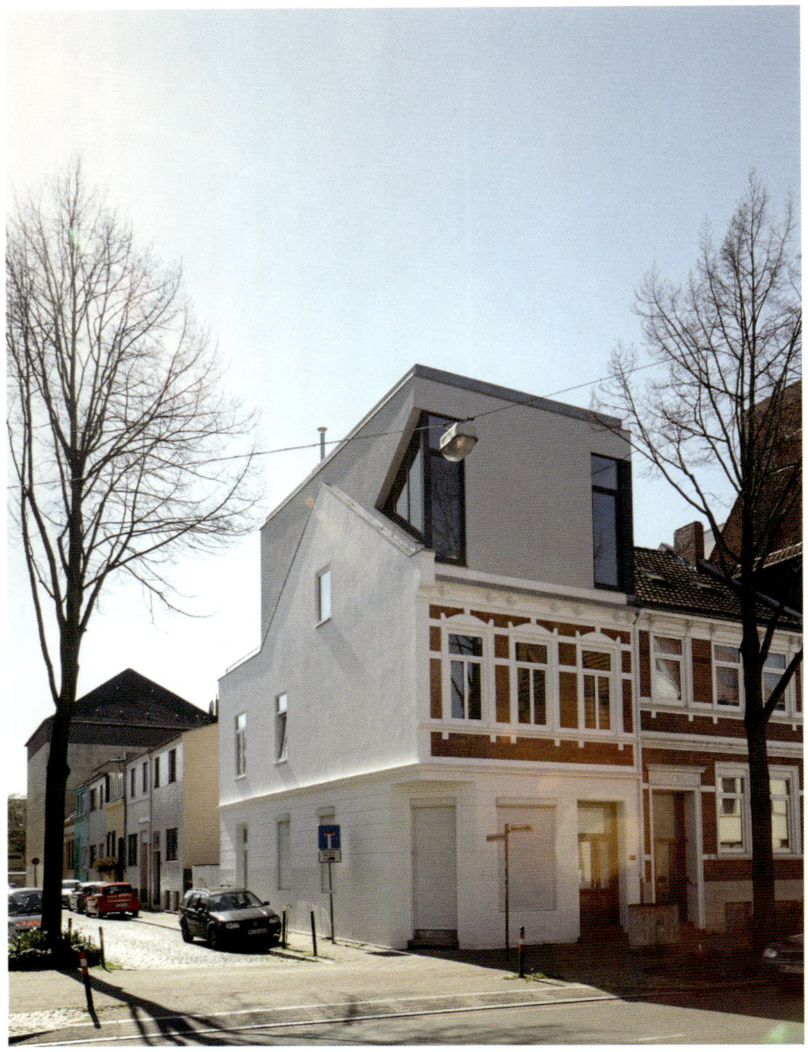

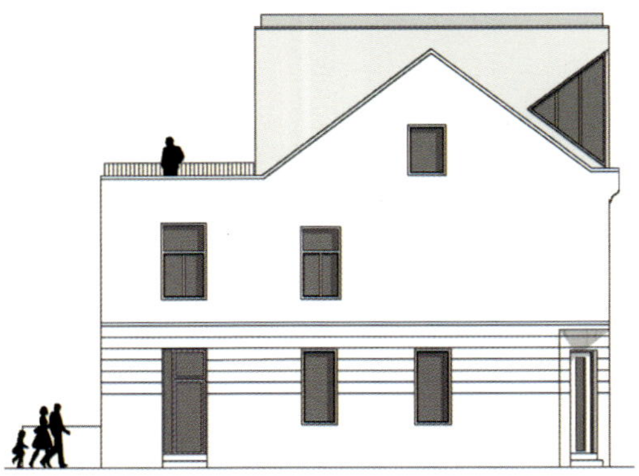

South elevation

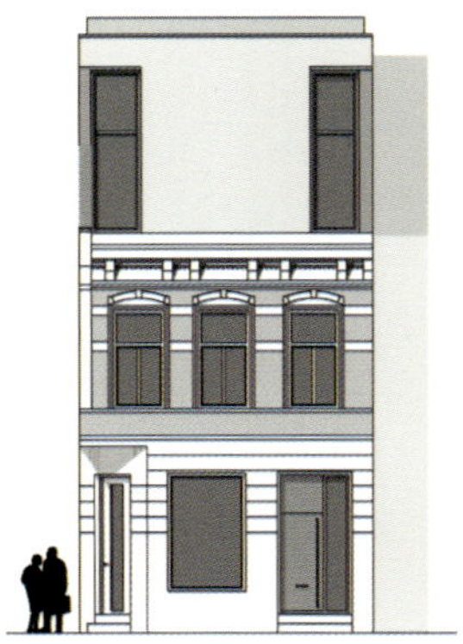

East elevation

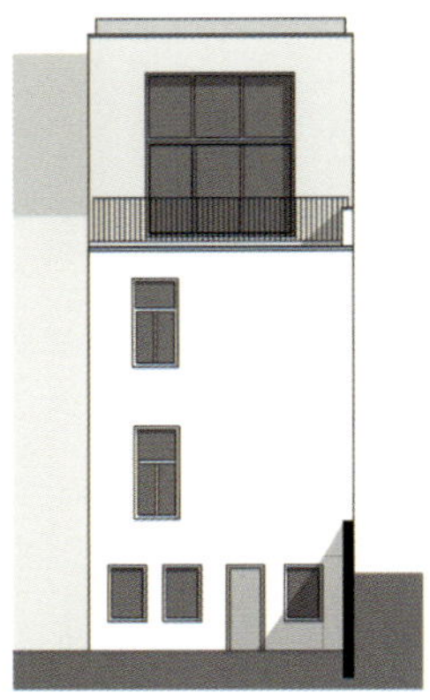

West elevation

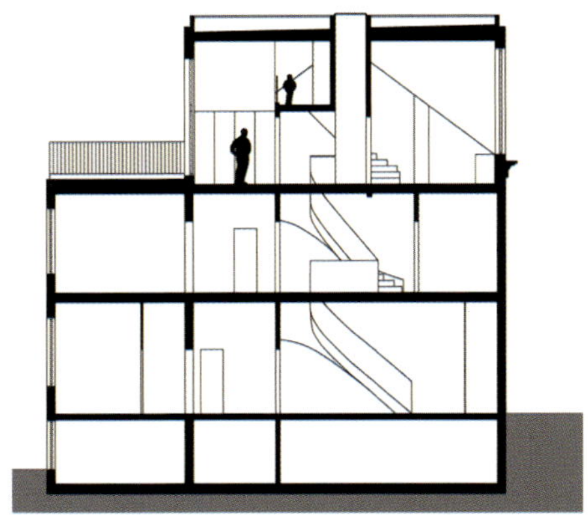

Section

The windows of this new section were positioned to facilitate views of the church situated directly opposite the house.

Die Fenster des neuen Aufbaus wurden so angeordnet, dass sie einen Ausblick auf die gegenüberliegende Kirche bieten.

Les fenêtres de ce nouveau volume ont été disposées de telle sorte à jouir des vues de l'église située juste en face de la maison.

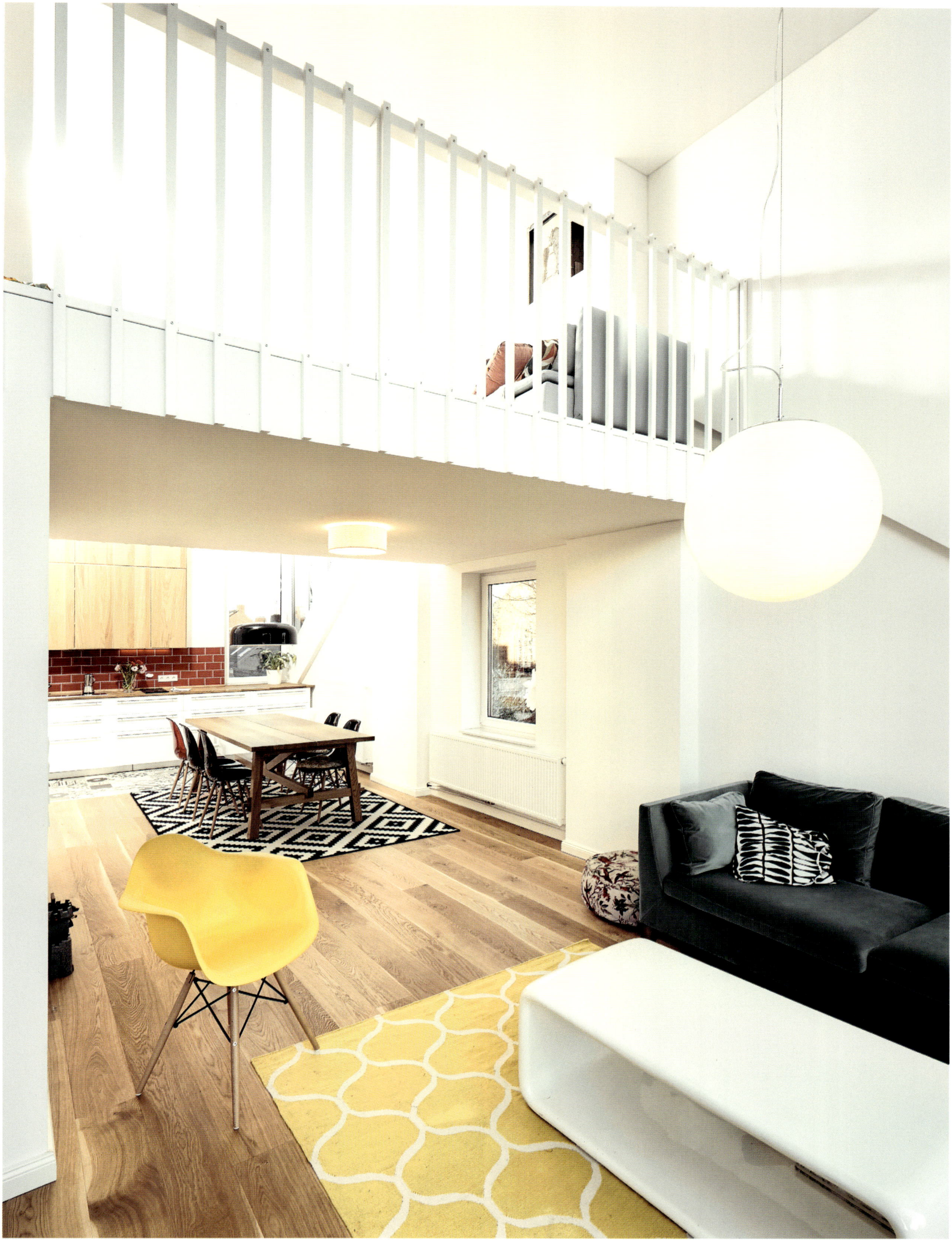

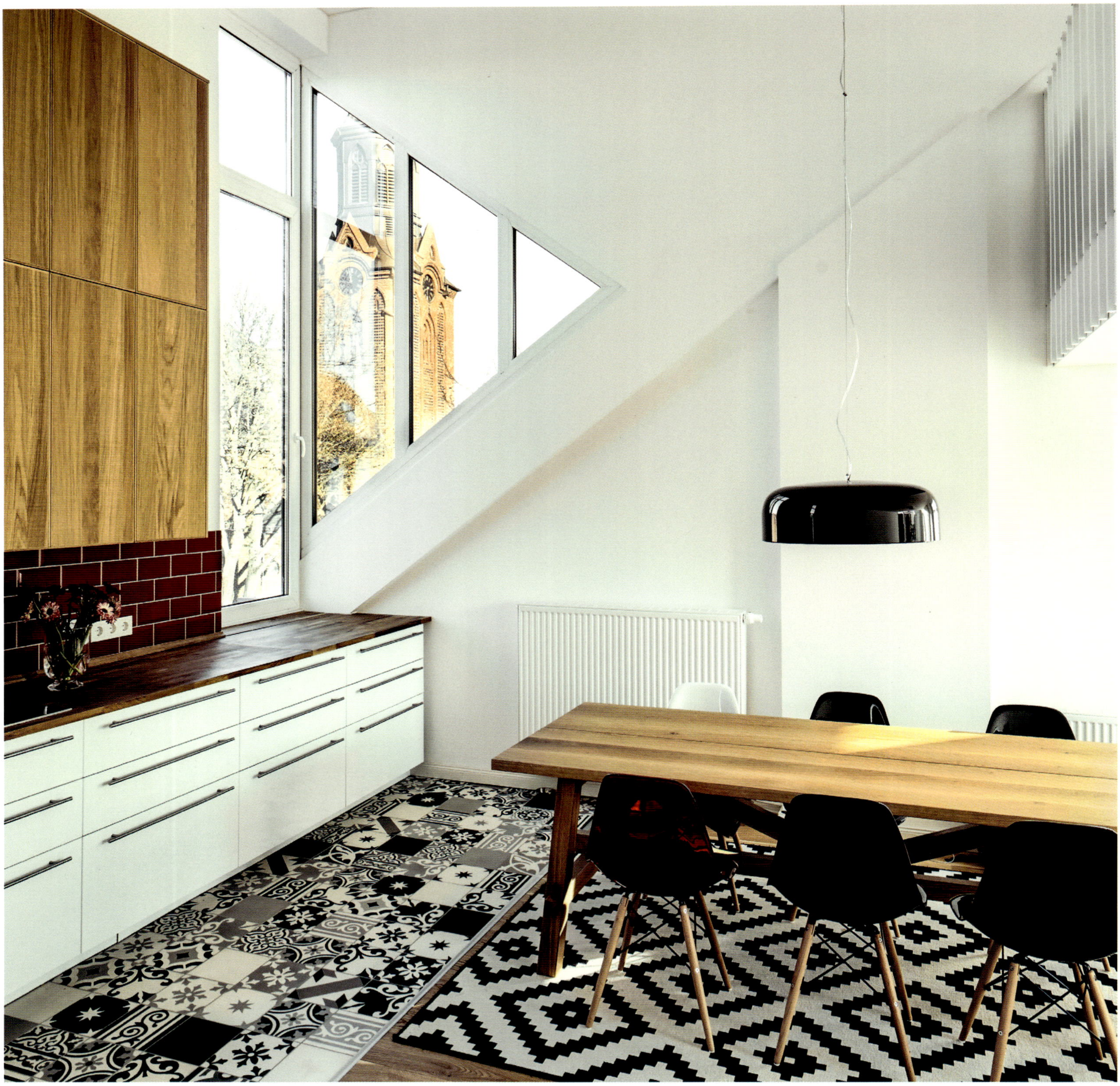

The renovation has achieved three settings within a single well-lit and open space, each of these clearly defined: the kitchen by the floor tiles, the dining and living rooms with rugs, obviating the need for partitions or dividing panels.

Durch die Renovierung entstand ein einziger heller und offener Raum, jedoch mit drei Bereichen, die durch die Bodenfliesen der Küche und die Teppiche des Wohn- und Esszimmers klar definiert sind, ohne dass Trenn- oder Zwischenwände erforderlich wären.

Les travaux de rénovation ont permis d'obtenir un espace unique, lumineux et ouvert avec trois ambiances clairement définies par le carrelage de la cuisine et les tapis de la salle à manger et du séjour, sans nécessité de cloison ni de panneau de séparation.

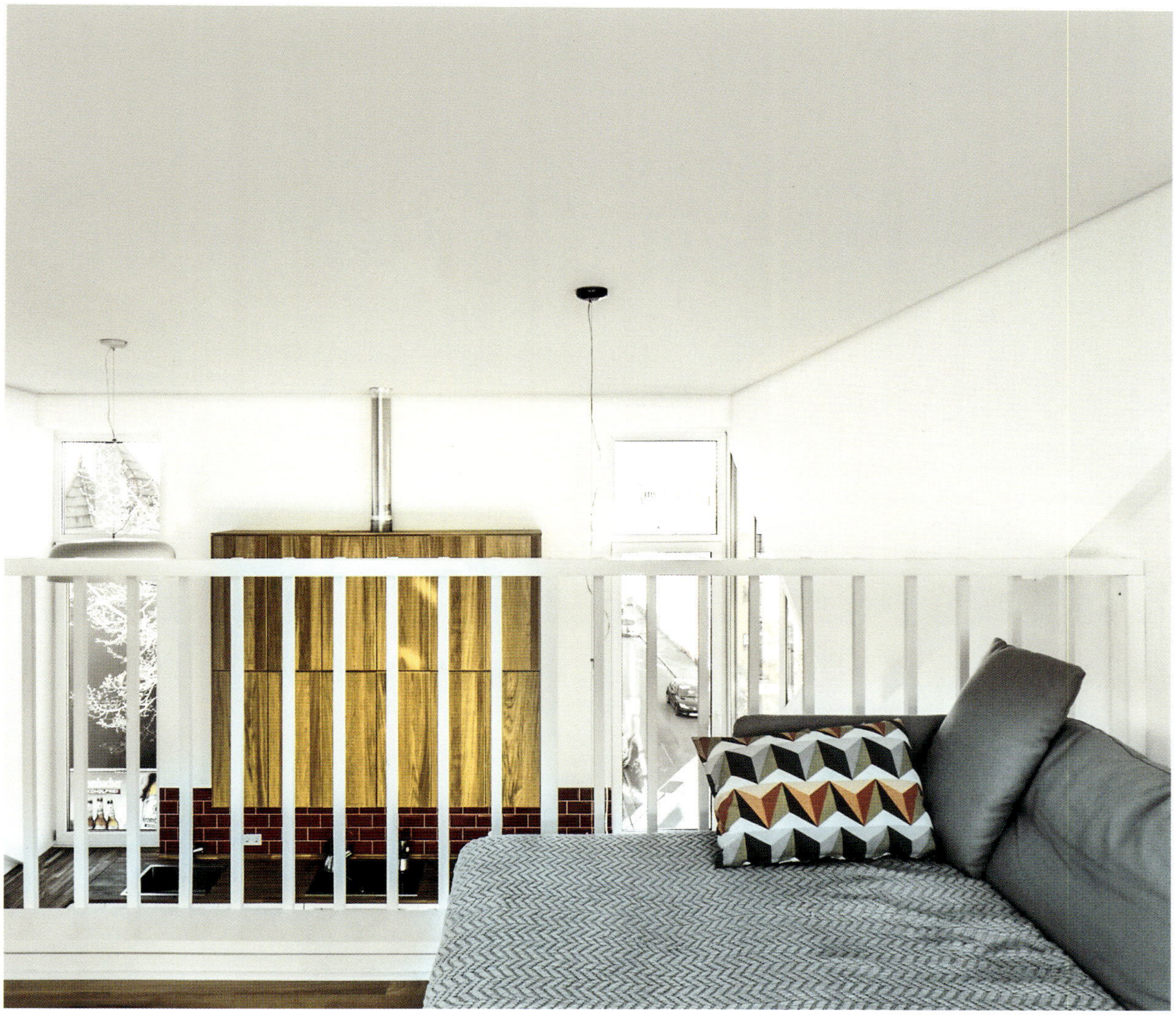

The new level not only increased usable space but also improved the structure's spatial experience, creating compelling visual relationships across the levels.

Die neue Etage vergrößerte nicht nur die Nutzfläche, sondern verbesserte auch das räumliche Erlebnis der Wohnung und schuf interessante visuelle Beziehungen zwischen den Ebenen.

Le nouvel étage a non seulement augmenté la superficie utile, mais a aussi amélioré l'espace de la maison, créant ainsi d'intéressantes relations visuelles entre les niveaux.

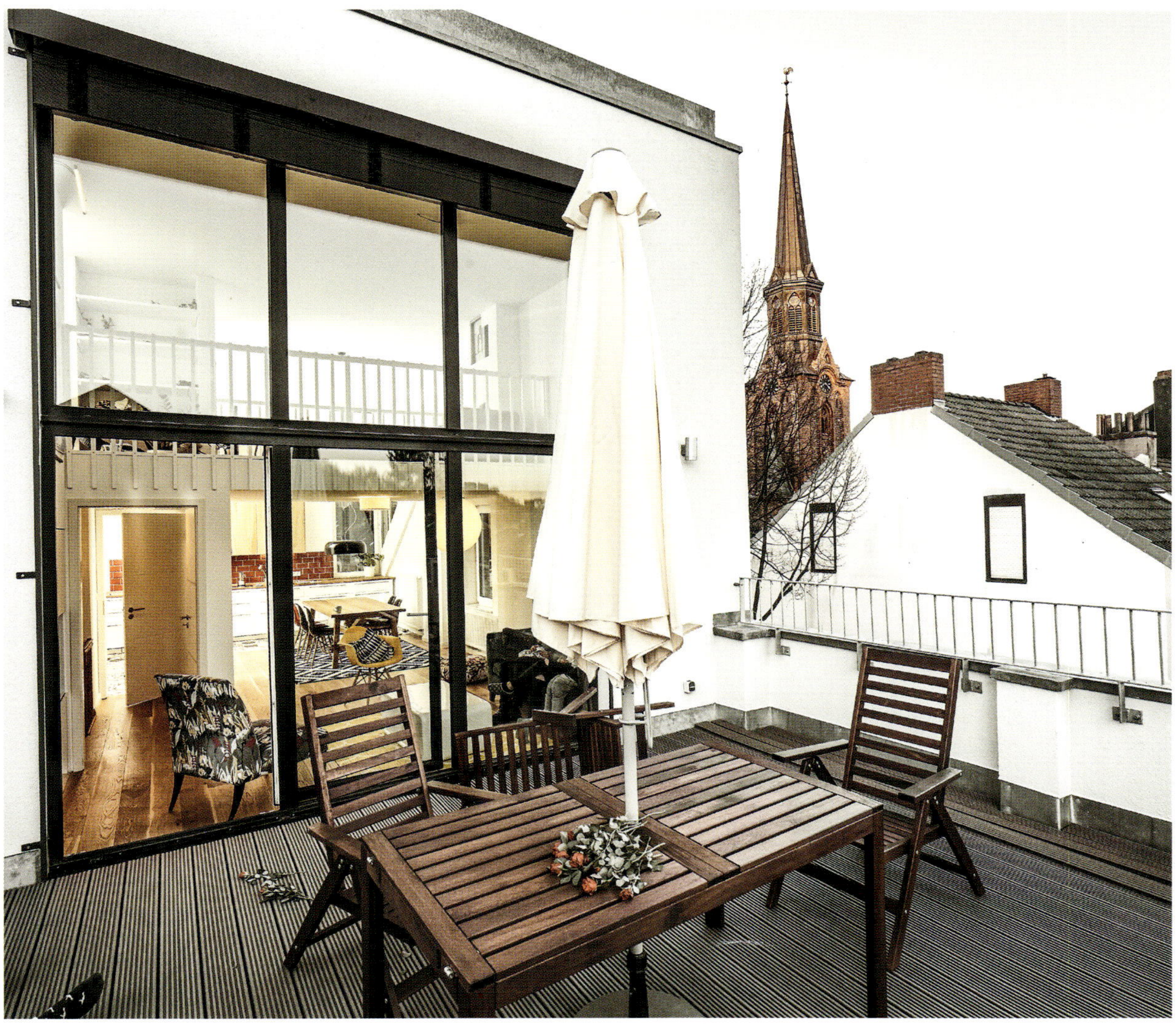

The extensive utilization of glass permits light to reach all corners of the house and lends an air of spaciousness. In addition, it succeeds in fully connecting the interior and the new terrace, which becomes a summer dining and living space.

Der umfangreiche Einsatz von Glas sorgt dafür, dass Tageslicht alle Ecken des Hauses erreicht und vermittelt ein Gefühl von Geräumigkeit. Darüber hinaus schafft er eine enge Verbindung zwischen dem Innenbereich und der neuen Terrasse, die in der Sommersaison zu Essbereich und Sitzecke wird.

La profusion des vitrages permet à la lumière de pénétrer dans tous les recoins de la maison en donnant une sensation de grandeur. Par ailleurs, il y a une totale connexion entre l'intérieur et la nouvelle terrasse extérieure qui se transforme en été en un espace salle à manger-séjour.

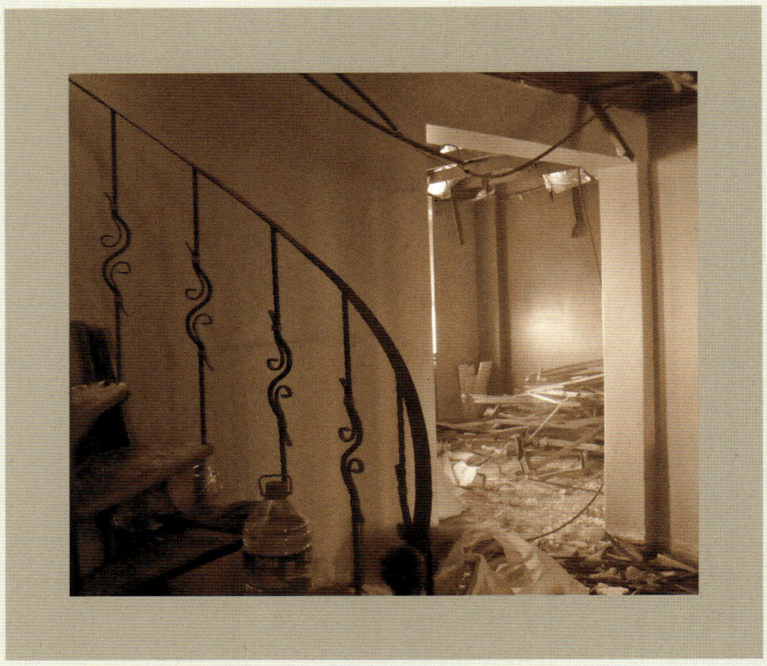

WHITE HOUSE

OFIST

130 m² | 1,400 sq. ft.

Istanbul, Turkey

Photos © **Ali Bekman**

> Transform the old apartment into an open and light-filled space

> Take maximum advantage of the Bosphorus panorama

> Remove any barrier that blocks the views

> Die alte Wohnung in einen offenen und hellen Raum verwandeln

> Die Aussicht auf den Bosporus bestmöglich ausnutzen

> Alle Hindernisse beseitigen, welche die Sicht verstellen

> Transformer l'ancien appartement en un espace ouvert et lumineux

> Profiter au maximum des vues sur le Bosphore

> Évincer tout obstacle qui interfèrerait la vue

This penthouse apartment occupies a top-floor extension to a hundred-year-old historical building in the central part of Istanbul. The expansion was added approximately 40 years ago, yielding a result characterized by mediocrity and bad taste compared to the building itself. The deep traces of the neighborhood's history were absent from this apartment. Despite its low ceilings, undistinguished spatial distribution, and poor-quality workmanship, the apartment boasted a panoramic view of the Bosphorus and the old city. Enamored of the views, the owner determined to create a lovely, light-filled home there.
The primary objective was to design a radiant, open, fresh, and cozy space amid the urban commotion. For this reason, an "all-white" color scheme was employed to create unity, fluidity, and spaciousness, with even the ceiling paneled in white-painted wooden strips. Oiled oak parquet flooring was laid through the entire apartment except for the main bathroom, generating the sense of warmth throughout the space that the owner had requested. At the entrance, a custom-designed spiral staircase, leading up to a terrace which affords the beholder incomparable views, endows the space with personality and singularity.

Als Ausbau nimmt diese Dachwohnung die oberste Etage eines hundert Jahre alten historischen Gebäudes im Zentrum von Istanbul ein. Im Vergleich zum Gebäude selbst wurde der Ausbau vor etwa 40 Jahren eher gewöhnlich und geschmacklos umgesetzt. Die tiefgreifenden Spuren der Geschichte der Gegend gab es in dieser Wohnung nicht. Ziemlich niedrige Decken, eine Standardaufteilung und schlechte Bauausführung wurden jedoch von einem großartigen Blick auf den Bosporus und die Altstadt aufgewogen. Die Besitzerin verliebte sich in die Aussicht und beschloss, ein schönes Zuhause voller Licht zu schaffen.
Hauptziel war, in der Hektik der Stadt einen hellen, offenen, kühlen und einladenden Raum zu kreieren. Um Einheitlichkeit, Fluidität und räumliche Weite zu erreichen, wurde ein komplett weißes Farbschema eingesetzt – sogar die Decke ist mit weiß gestrichenen Holzlamellen verkleidet – und geöltes Eichenparkett in der gesamten Wohnung – außer im Hauptbadezimmer – verwendet, was dem Raum die von der Besitzerin gewünschte Wärme gibt. Beim Betreten stößt man auf eine Wendeltreppe in einem originellen Design, die zu einer Terrasse hinaufführt, von der man eine unvergleichliche Aussicht genießen kann, die dem Raum Persönlichkeit verleiht und ihn einzigartig macht.

Ce penthouse occupe le dernier étage comme une extension d'un édifice historique centenaire au cœur d'Istanbul. L'extension a été construite il y a près de 40 ans de façon ordinaire et de mauvais goût par rapport à l'édifice lui-même. Cet appartement n'existait pas dans les profondes empreintes de l'histoire du quartier. Plafonds assez bas, avec une répartition standard et un travail peu soigné, mais avec une vue magnifique sur le Bosphore et la vieille ville. Sa propriétaire est tombée amoureuse des vues et, pour cette raison, elle a décidé d'y créer un cocon rempli de lumière.
Le principal objectif était de créer un espace lumineux, ouvert, frais et accueillant au cœur de l'agitation de la grande ville. Pour cette raison, un panel de couleur « tout blanc » a été utilisé afin d'obtenir unité, fluidité et amplitude spatiale. Quant au plafond, il est recouvert de planches de bois peintes en blanc. Le parquet de chêne de toute la maison est huilé, à l'exception de la salle de bains principale qui apporte également à l'espace la chaleur souhaitée par sa propriétaire. À l'entrée, un escalier en colimaçon au design original qui mène à une terrasse depuis laquelle on peut profiter des vues incomparables, donnant du cachet à l'espace et le rendant unique.

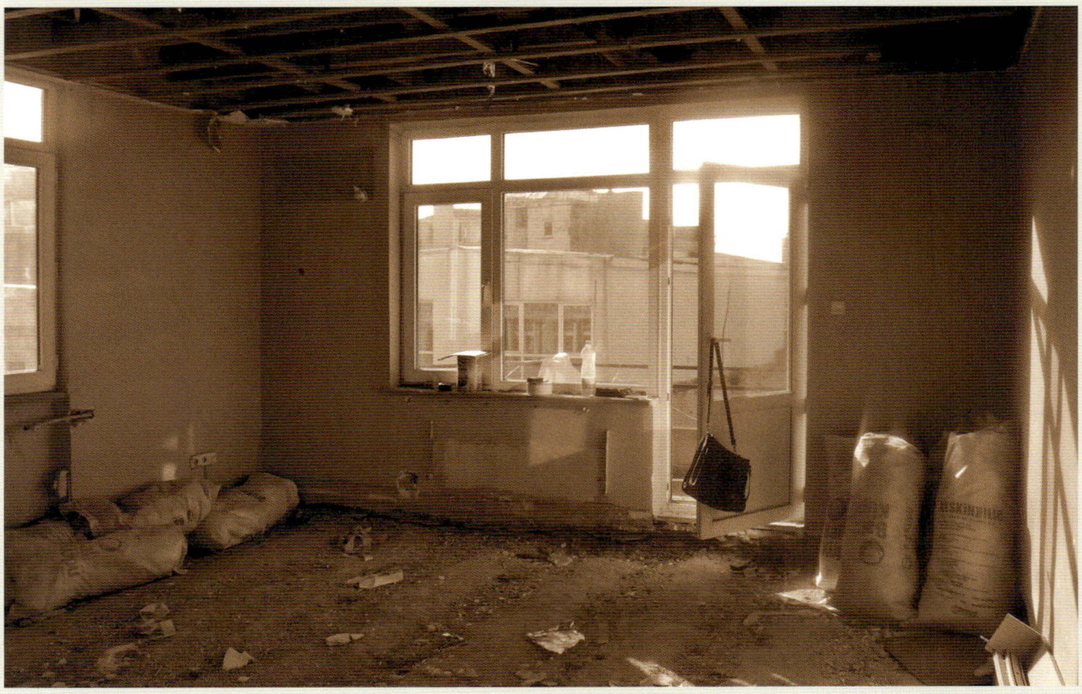

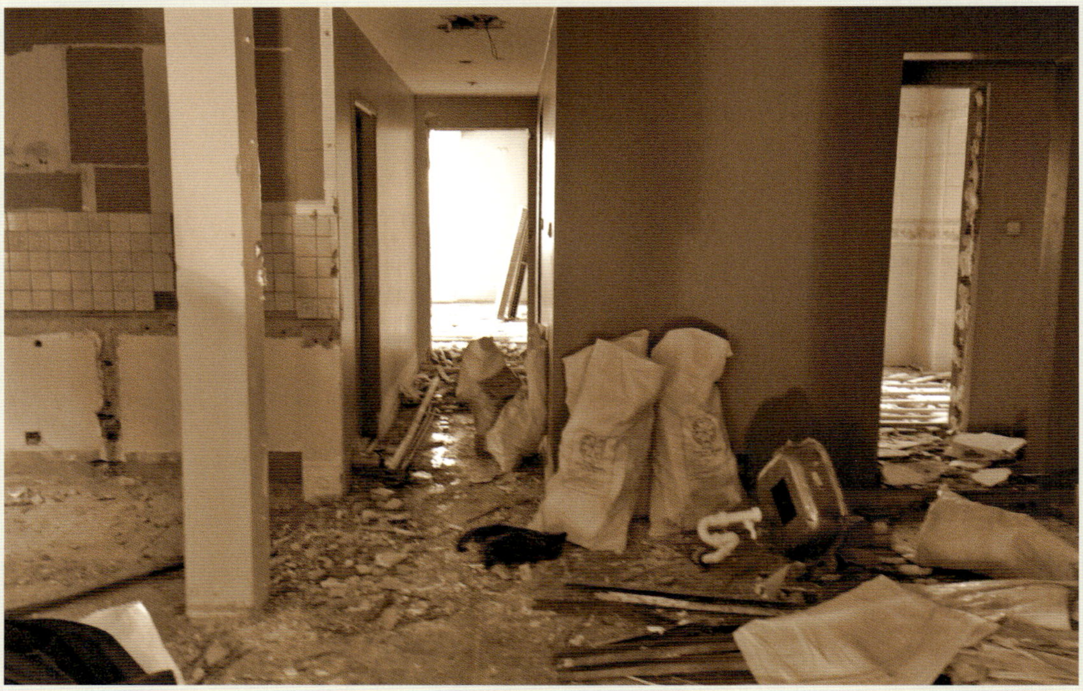

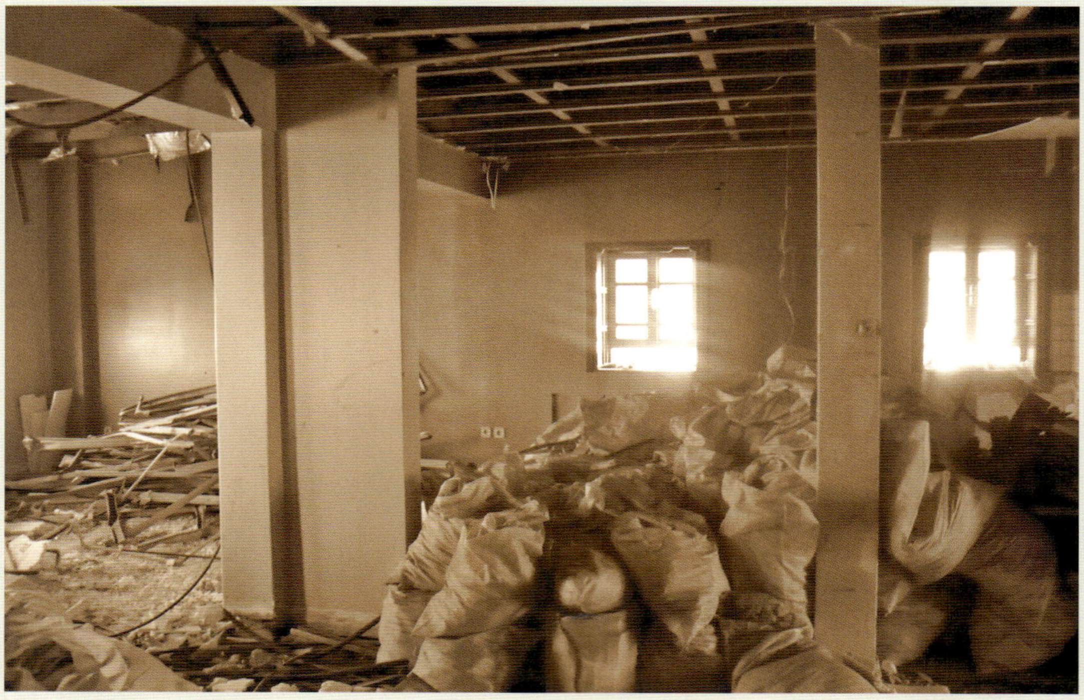

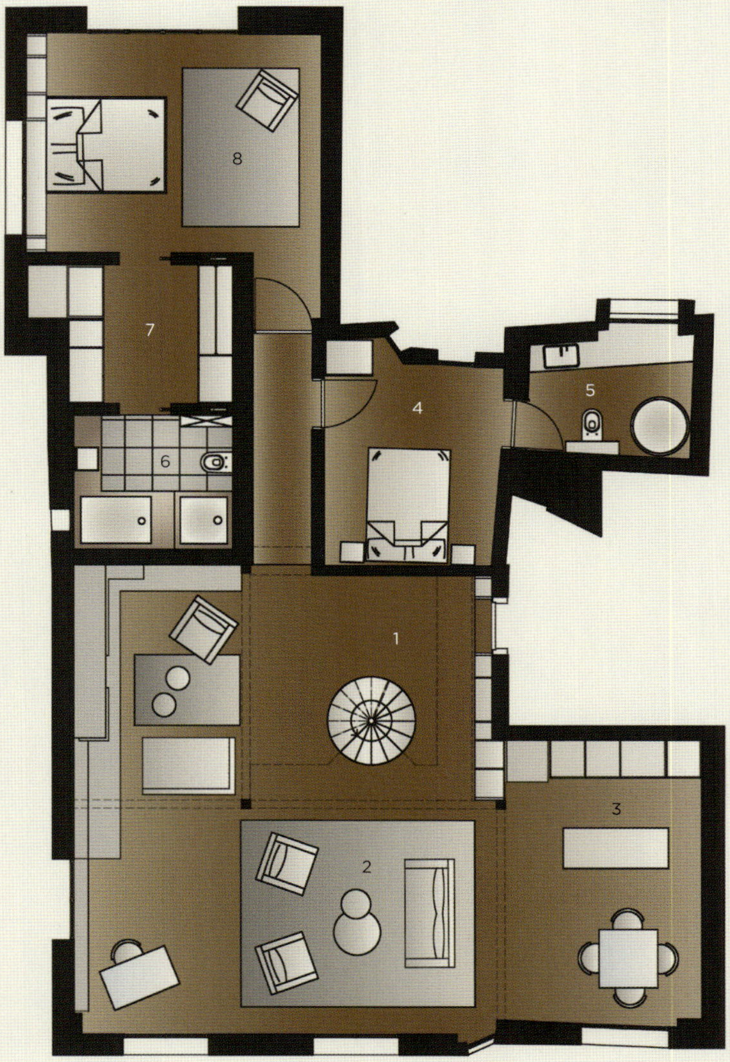

1. Entrance
2. Living room
3. Kitchen
4. Guest bedroom
5. Guest bathroom
6. Master bathroom
7. Dressing room
8. Master bedroom

New plan

Ceilings and unnecessary divisions were removed to achieve a new spatial distribution, resulting in a light-filled apartment with a spacious, high-ceilinged entryway, two bedrooms with bathrooms en suite, a large living room, and a rooftop terrace with spectacular views.

Nach dem Abriss unnötiger Decken und Trennwände wurde die neue Aufteilung beschlossen, was eine helle Wohnung mit einem geräumigen Eingang mit hoher Decke, zwei Schlafzimmern mit eigenem Badezimmer, einem großen Wohnzimmer und einer Dachterrasse mit spektakulärer Aussicht ergab.

Après avoir démoli les plafonds et divisions inutiles, la nouvelle répartition a donné lieu à un appartement lumineux avec une entrée spacieuse au plafond haut, deux chambres avec salle de bains, un grand séjour et une terrasse sur le toit avec des vues spectaculaires.

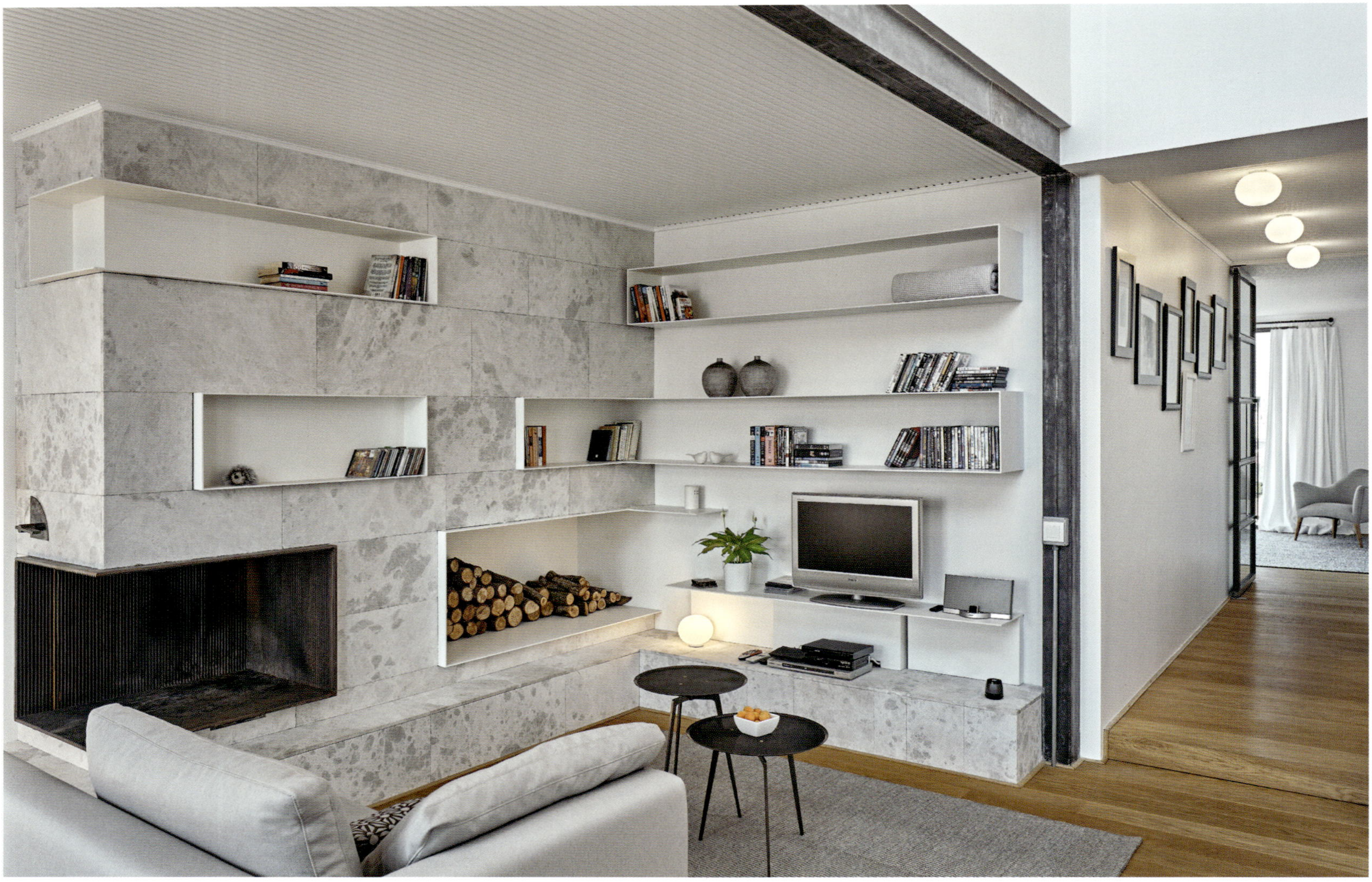

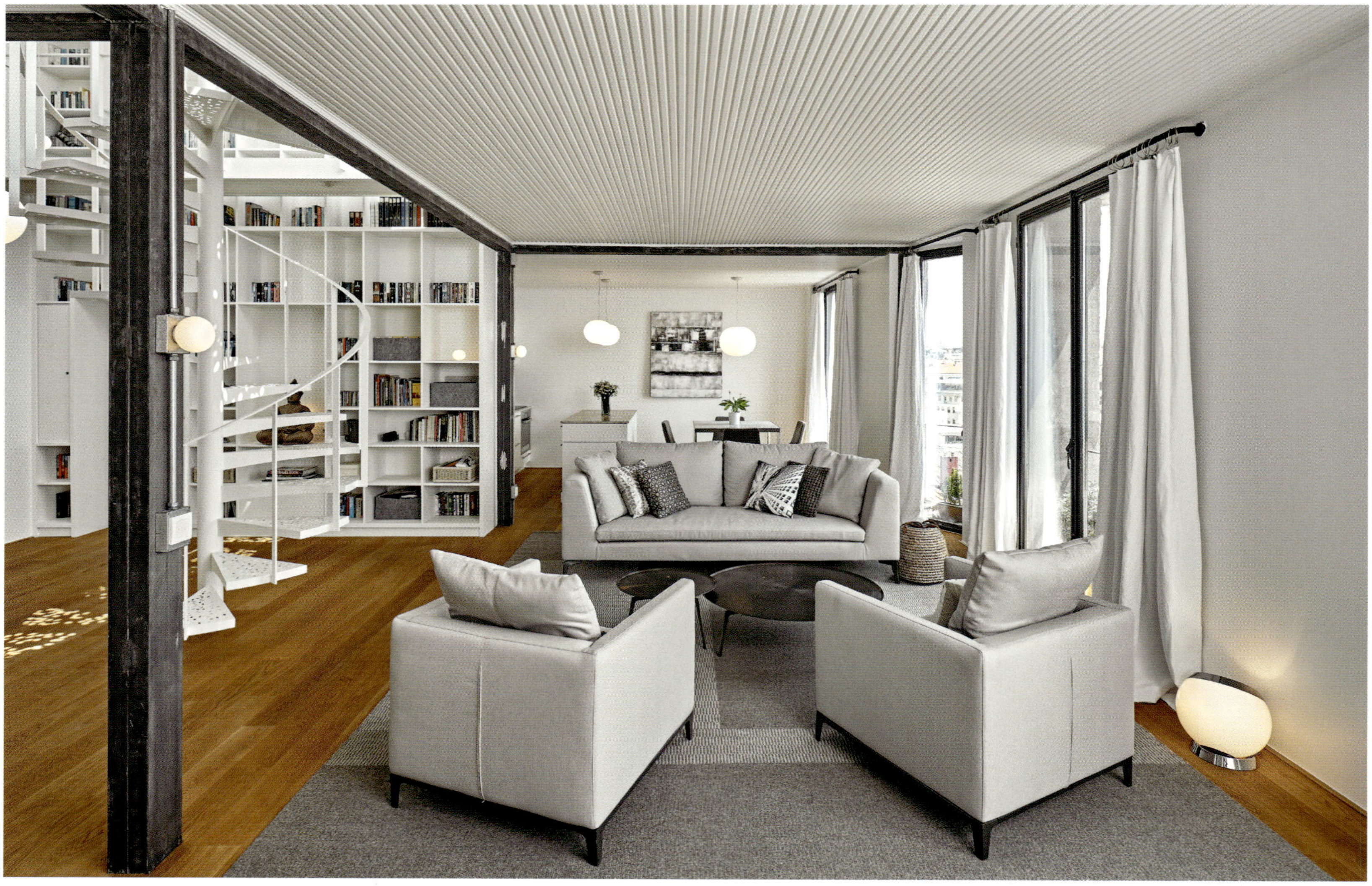

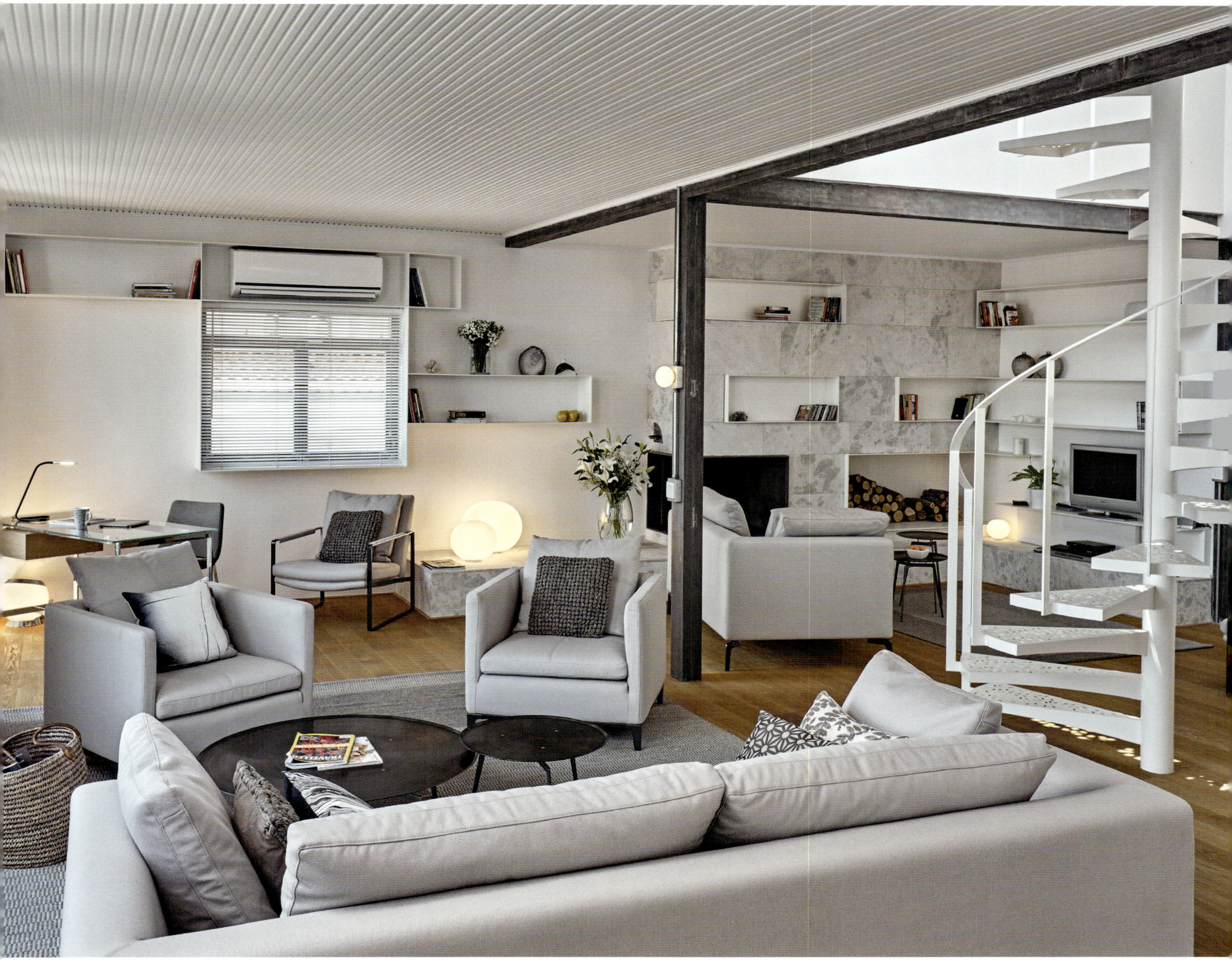

An intimate and cozy reading/ entertainment nook is positioned at one end of the spacious living room next to a wall featuring a cast iron fireplace framed in gray-streaked white marble.

An einem Ende des geräumigen Wohnzimmers, neben einer Wand aus weißem Marmor mit grauen Adern, die einen gusseisernen Kamin beherbergt, entstand eine gemütliche, intime Ecke, wo die Bewohner bequem lesen oder einen Film genießen können.

À une extrémité du séjour spacieux, avec un mur revêtu de marbre blanc aux veines grises qui abrite une cheminée en fer forgé, le client a souhaité créer un coin accueillant plus intime où il serait possible de lire un livre ou de regarder un film en tout confort.

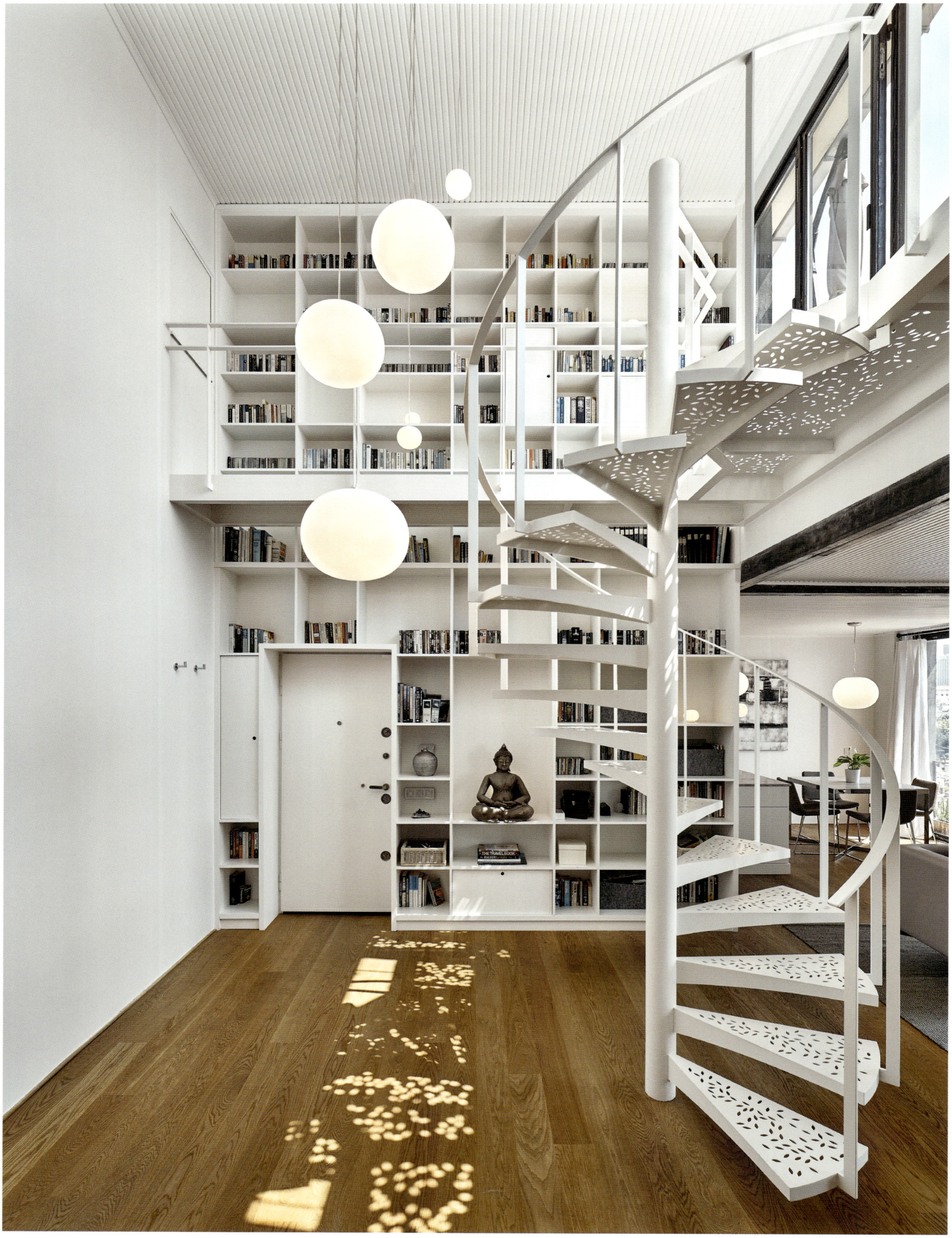

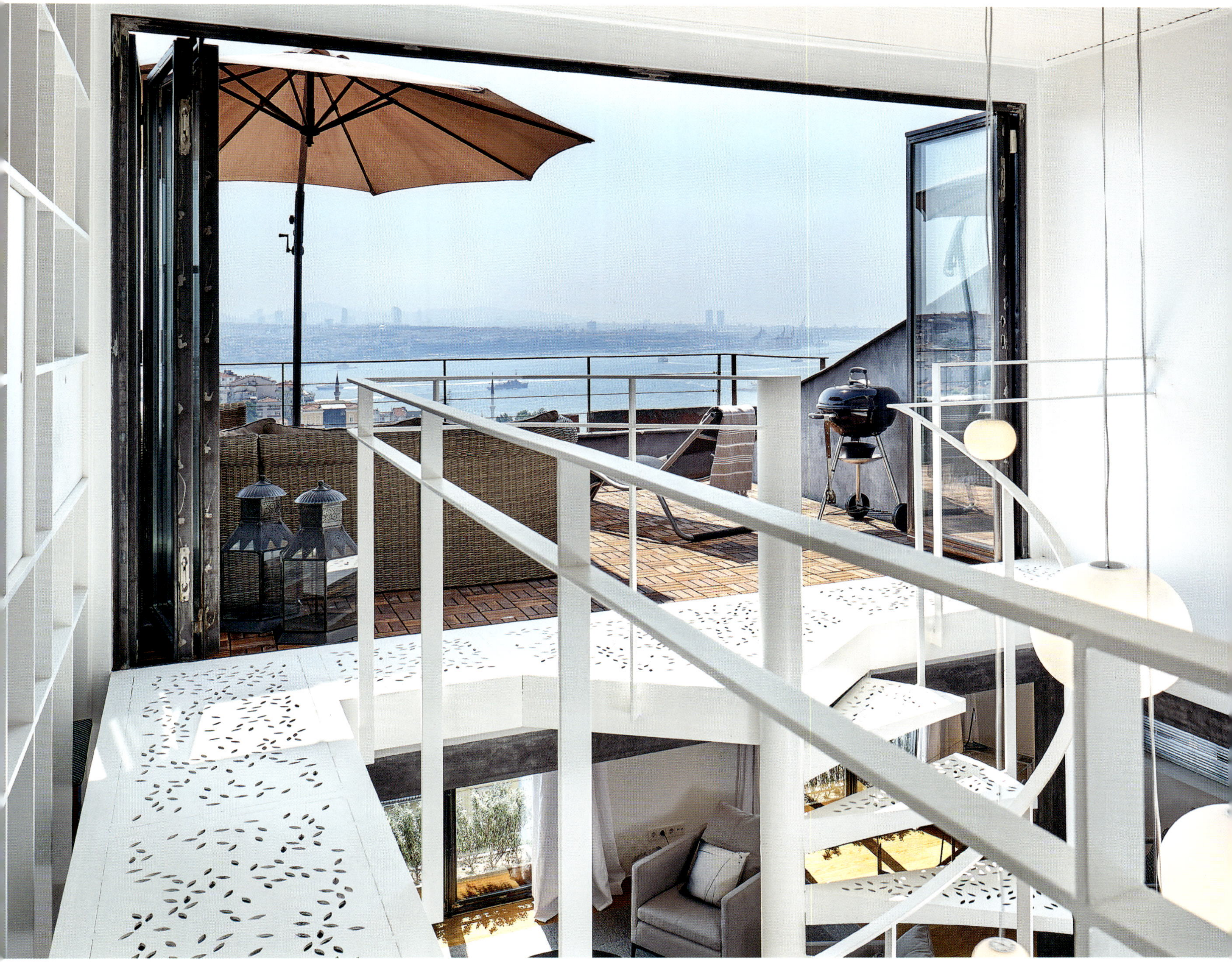

The spiral metal staircase leads to the rooftop terrace, continuing as a bridge to the library's upper shelves. Its surface is perforated by small shapes representing the leaves of trees felled in Gezi Park, an event occurring contemporaneously with the restoration over the protests of environmental groups. These tiny holes produce delightful light and shadow effects.

Die metallene Wendeltreppe führt zur Dachterrasse hinauf und setzt sich wie ein Steg zu den oberen Regalen der Bibliothek fort. Ihre Oberfläche ist durchbrochen von kleinen Formen, welche die Blätter der Bäume des Gezi-Parks darstellen, die zur Zeit des Umbaus gefällt wurden – begleitet von Protesten von Umweltgruppen. Diese kleinen Löcher erzeugen interessante Licht-Schatten-Effekte.

L'escalier en colimaçon métallique s'élève jusqu'à la terrasse du toit et se poursuit comme une passerelle jusqu'aux étagères supérieures de la bibliothèque. Sa superficie est perforée de petites formes qui représentent les feuilles des arbres coupés du parc Gezi qui, sans tenir compte des revendications des groupes écologiques, l'ont été simultanément aux travaux de la maison. Ces petites fentes créent d'intéressants effets du soleil et de l'ombre.

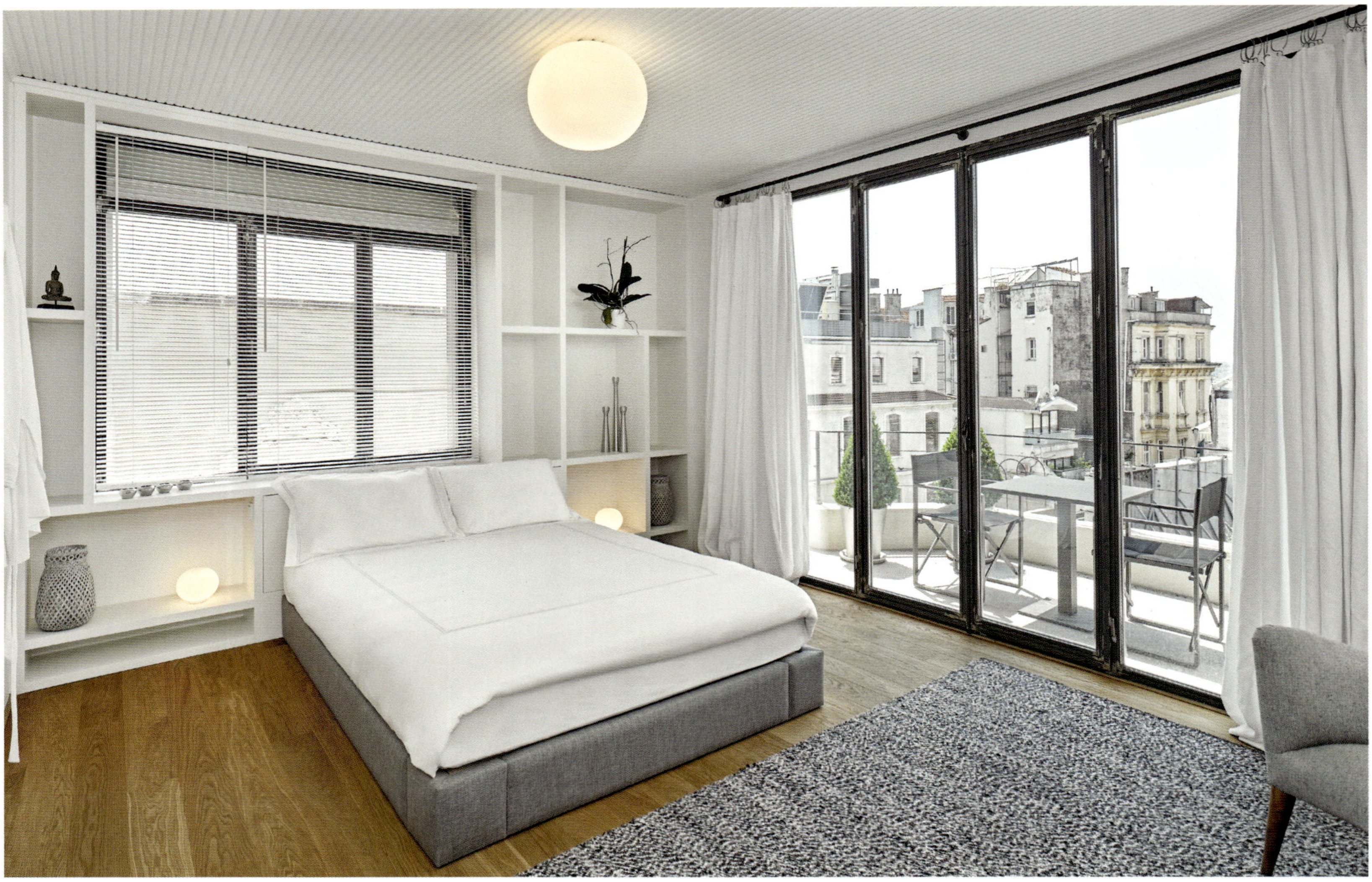

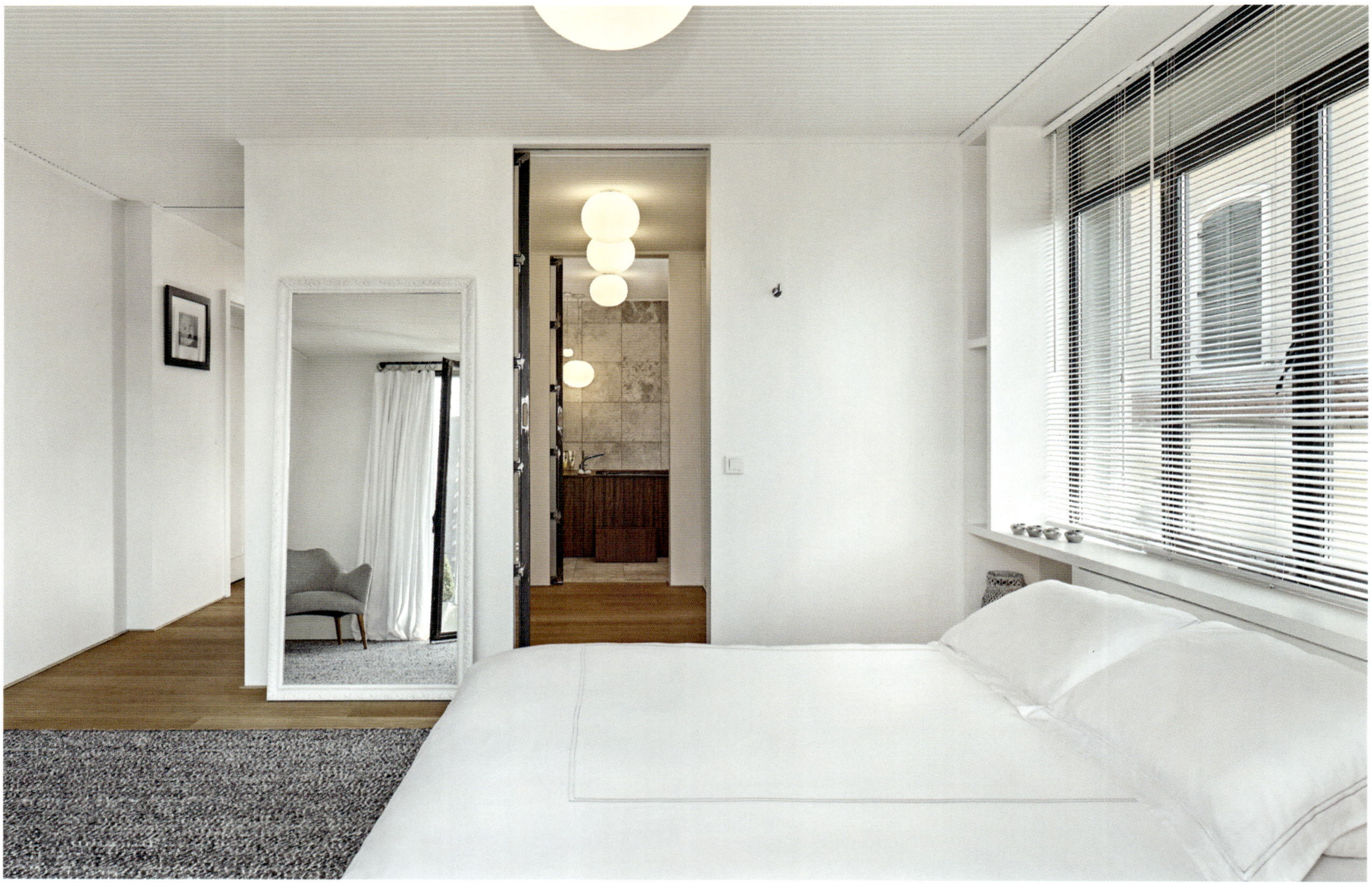

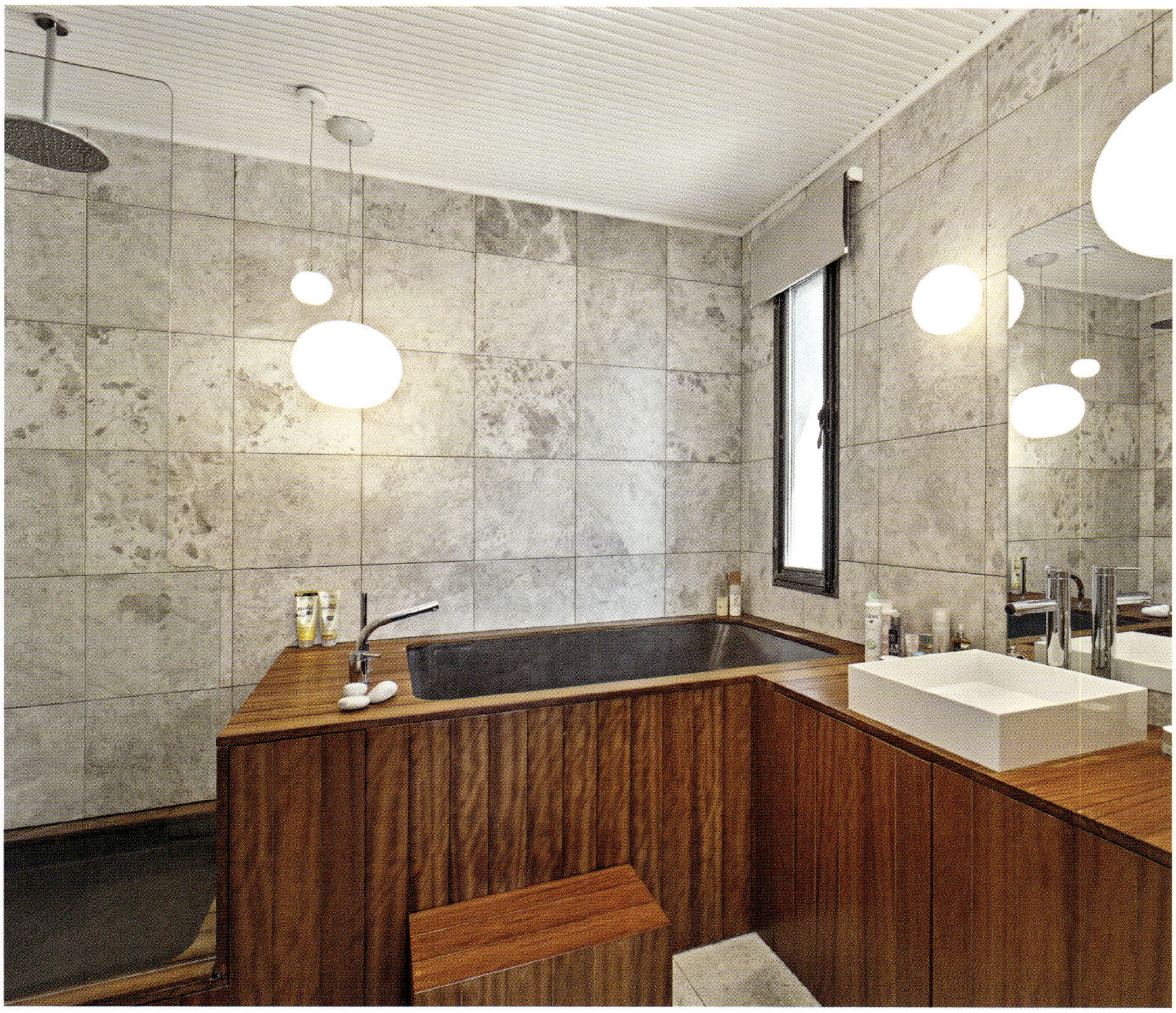

The tub and shower were custom-made from Ytong so that both could fit into the limited space of the main bathroom. These were surrounded by iroko wood, which was also used for the cabinets and counters to create a continuous and fluid surface that contrasts in both color and texture with the marble walls and floor.

Badewanne und Dusche wurden mit Ytong maßgefertigt, um beide in das kleine Hauptbadezimmer zu integrieren. Rundum wurde Iroco-Holz platziert und auch für die Schränke und Arbeitsplatte eingesetzt. Dies schuf eine kontinuierliche und fließende Fläche, die in Farbe und Textur mit dem Marmor der Wand und dem Fußboden kontrastiert.

La baignoire et la douche ont été faites sur mesure avec Ytong afin de les intégrer à la salle de bains principale qui était petite. Elles sont entourées de bois d'Iroko, également utilisé pour les armoires et le plan de travail, créant ainsi une surface continue et fluide qui contraste en termes de couleurs et textures avec le marbre du mur et du sol.

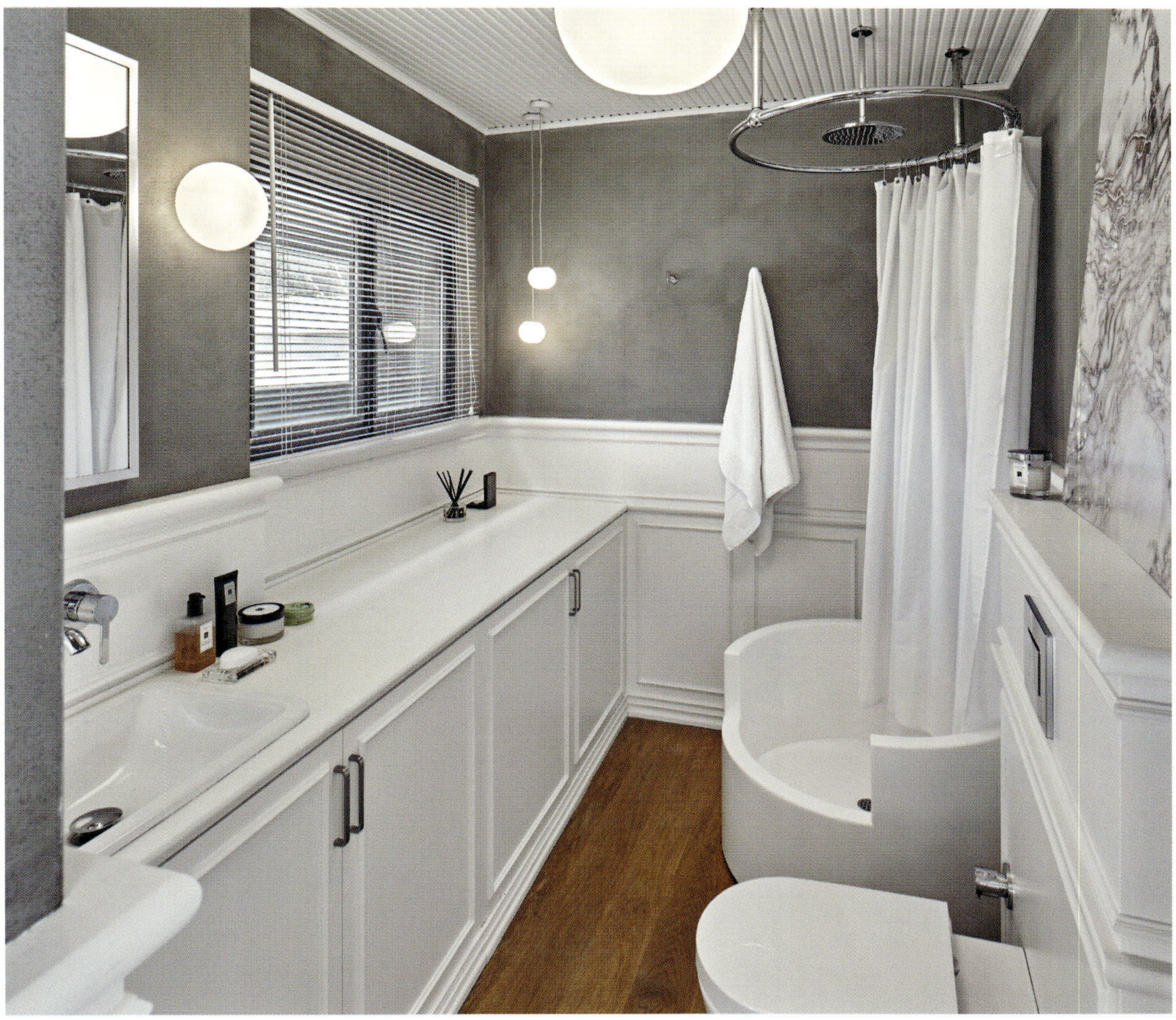

The design of the guest bathroom is more traditional. White-painted cabinets conceal the washer and dryer. A custom-made Corian shower, detached from the wall, becomes the focal point of the space.

Die Gestaltung des Gästebads ist traditioneller. Weiß gestrichene Schränke verbergen Waschmaschine und Trockner. Eine nach Maß angefertigte Corian-Duschwanne, die von der Wand abgerückt ist, wird zum Mittelpunkt des Raumes.

Le design de la salle de bains des invités est plus traditionnel. Les armoires peintes en blanc dissimulent le lavabo et le séchoir mural. Une douche-baignoire en Corian faite sur mesure, séparée du mur, devient le centre de la pièce.

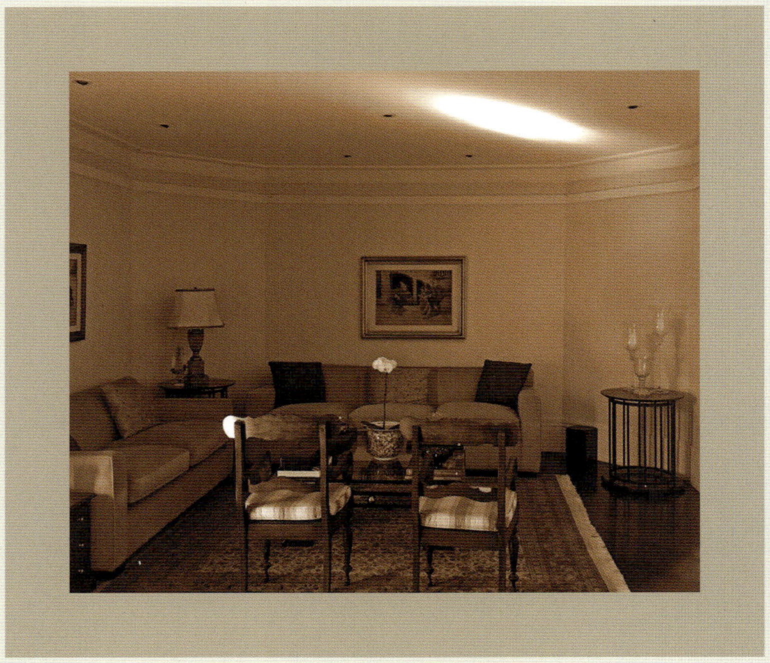

BORDÔ APARTMENT

DIEGO REVOLLO

260 m² | 2,800 sq. ft.

São Paulo, Brazil

Photos © **Alain Brugier**

> Create an in-home movie theater in a burgundy hue

> Illuminate a previously dark and compartmentalized space

> Einrichtung eines Kinoraums im Haus in Burgunderrot

> Verbesserter und vermehrter Lichteinfall in einen vorher dunklen und aufgeteilten Raum

> Créer une salle de cinéma dans une maison dans les tons bordeaux

> Remplir de lumière un espace alors sombre et partagé

The intense color of burgundy was the jumping-off point for the creation of this project, since, when the client contacted the architect, he made it clear that he wanted that color for an in-home movie theater. Responding to the client's behest, the architect lined the wall with a Shantung Bordô screen that became the apartment's distinguishing feature.
What had been a dark and compartmentalized space became much brighter when the spaces were integrated. For this new space with its abundant light and fluid design, a rich color palette was combined with a harmonious mix of furniture and decorative objects. The blend of styles is the high point of the decoration, apparent in the furniture—an easy chair in French style, a sofa from the 1960s, shades of gold that transport us to the 1970s, and contemporary pieces such as the sofas in the living room and in-house movie theater—and in the decorative elements, with textures and finishes ranging from the traditional to the contemporary, featuring objects made of Murano glass, colored glass, ceramic, and metals like brass and silver, creating in this way a refined union of styles and periods. This apartment demonstrates that luxury is primarily about comfort.

Das intensive Burgunderrot war der Ausgangspunkt für die Entwicklung dieses Projekts, da von Anfang an, als der Kunde sich mit dem Architekten in Verbindung setzte, klar war, dass es in diesem Haus einen Kinoraum in dieser Farbe geben sollte. Um diesem Wunsch des Kunden gerecht zu werden, verkleidete der Architekt eine Wand des Wohnzimmers mit einem Shantung-Bordô-Stoff, die sich so in das hervorstechende Kennzeichen dieser Wohnung verwandelte.
Was vorher ein dunkler und unterteilter Raum war, wurde durch den Umbau zu verschiedenen Bereichen mit weitaus mehr Lichteinfall. Für diesen neuen Bereich mit viel Licht und einem fließenden Design wurde eine vielseitige Farbpalette ausgewählt und diese dann mit einer harmonischen Mischung aus Möbeln und dekorativen Stücken kombiniert. Die Mischung der Stilrichtungen ist der Höhepunkt der Dekoration, was sowohl durch das Mobiliar - ein Sessel im französischen Stil, ein Sofa aus den 1960er Jahren, Goldtöne, die uns zurück in die 1970er Jahre versetzen und moderne Stücke, wie die Sofas des Wohnzimmers und des Kinoraums - als auch durch die übrigen dekorativen Elemente mit Texturen und Finishs, die von traditionell bis modern reichen, deutlich wird. Zum Einsatz kamen ebenso Stücke aus Murano, buntes Glas, Keramik und verschiedene Metalle wie Messing und Silber, wodurch eine elegante Mischung von Stilen und Epochen entstand. Diese Wohnung beweist, dass Luxus vor allem Komfort ist.

L'intense couleur bordeaux a été le point de départ pour la création de ce projet, car lorsque le client a contacté l'architecte il souhaitait avoir une salle de cinéma à la maison dans ce ton. Par conséquent, l'architecte, pour satisfaire le souhait du client, a recouvert le mur de la pièce d'une toile Shantung Bordô, devenue la caractéristique distinctive de l'appartement.
L'espace alors sombre et divisé s'est transformé en un autre plus lumineux grâce à l'intégration d'espaces. Une riche palette de couleur a été choisie pour ce nouvel espace avec de la lumière abondante et un design fluide, combinée à un mélange harmonieux de meubles et d'éléments de décoration. Le mélange des styles est au cœur de la décoration qui ressort clairement tant dans le mobilier, un fauteuil au style français, un canapé des années 60, des tons dorés qui nous transportent dans les années 70 et des pièces contemporaines telles que les canapés du séjour et de la salle de cinéma à la maison, que le reste des éléments de décoration, avec des textures et finitions qui vont du traditionnel au contemporain, en utilisant des pièces de Murano, du verre teinté, de la céramique et divers tons métalliques tels que le laiton et l'argent, créant ainsi un mélange raffiné des styles et des époques. Cet appartement fait ressortir que le luxe est surtout du confort.

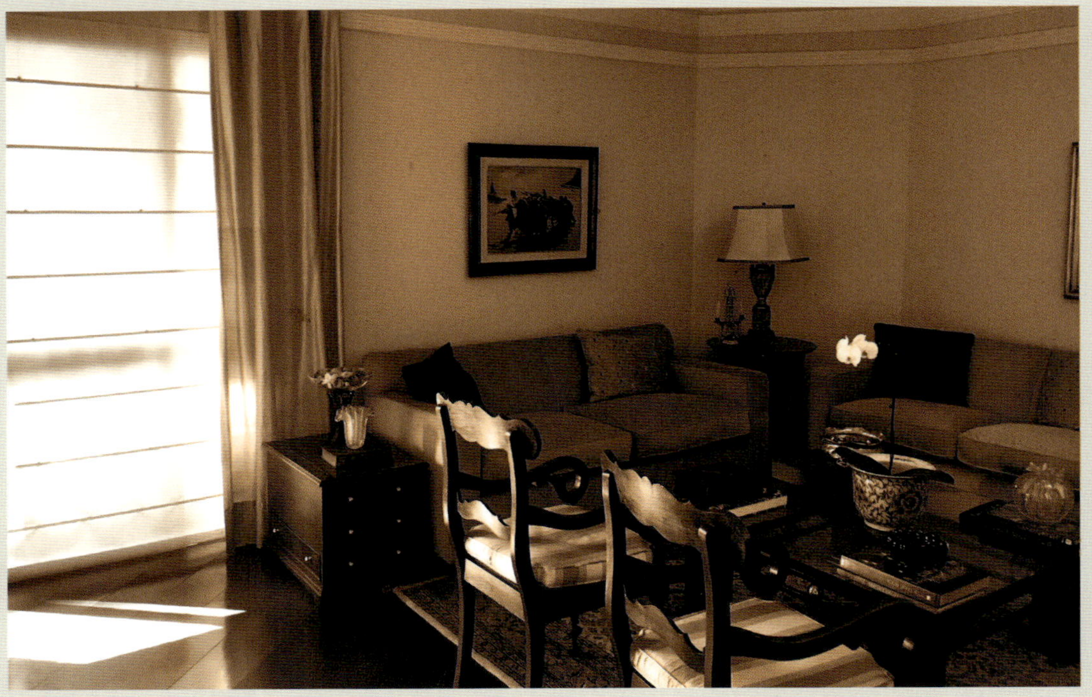
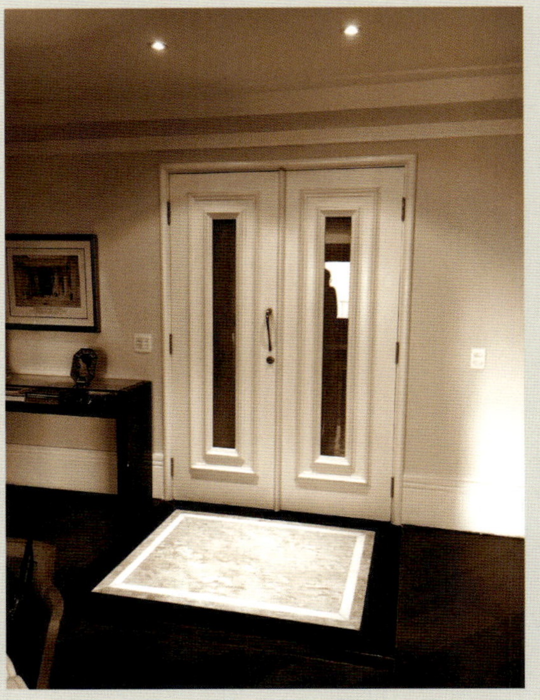
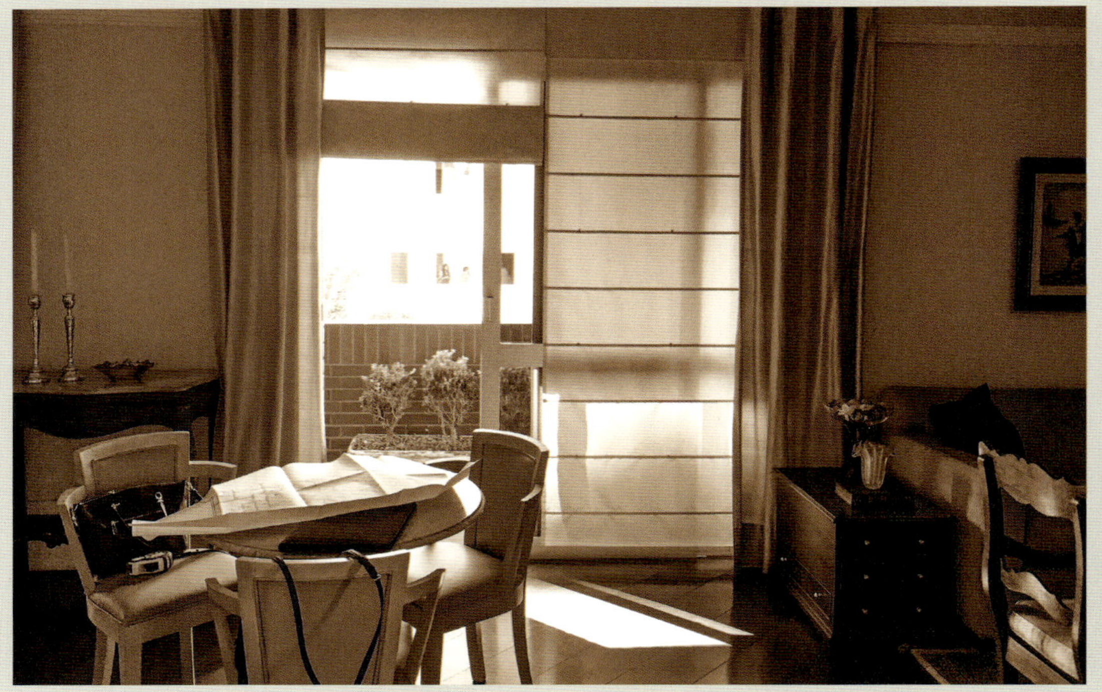
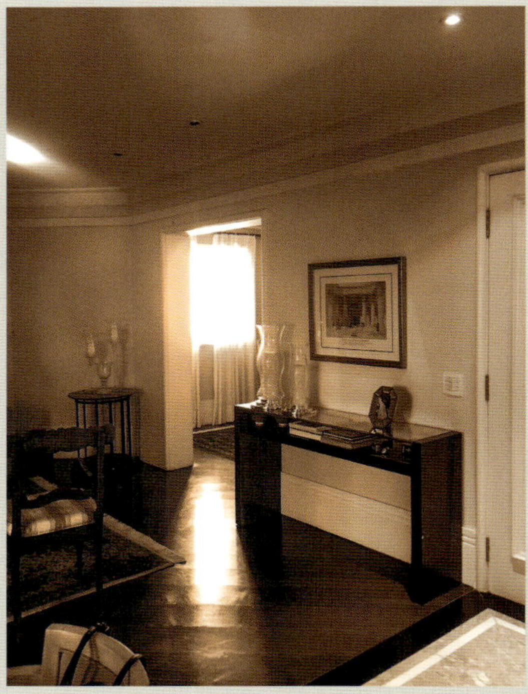
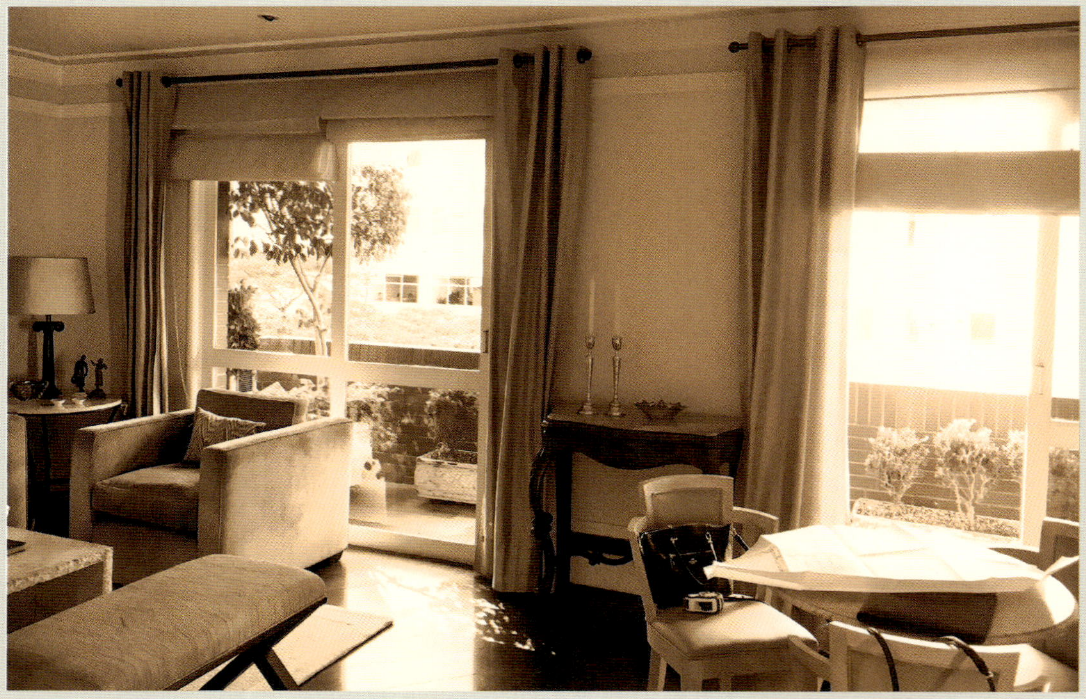
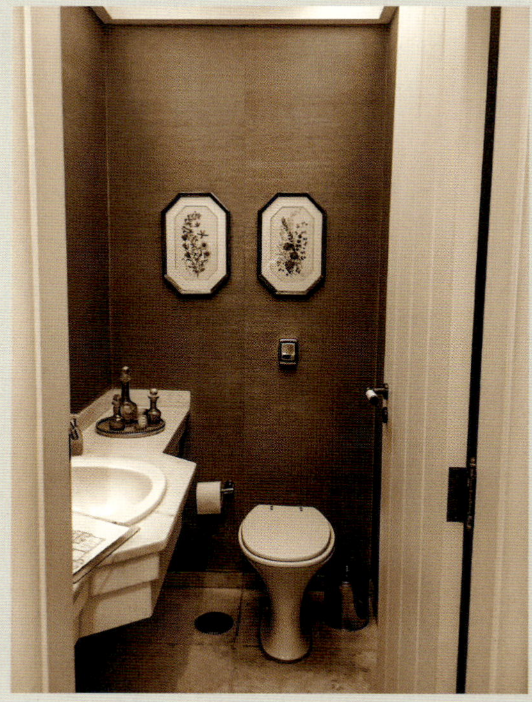

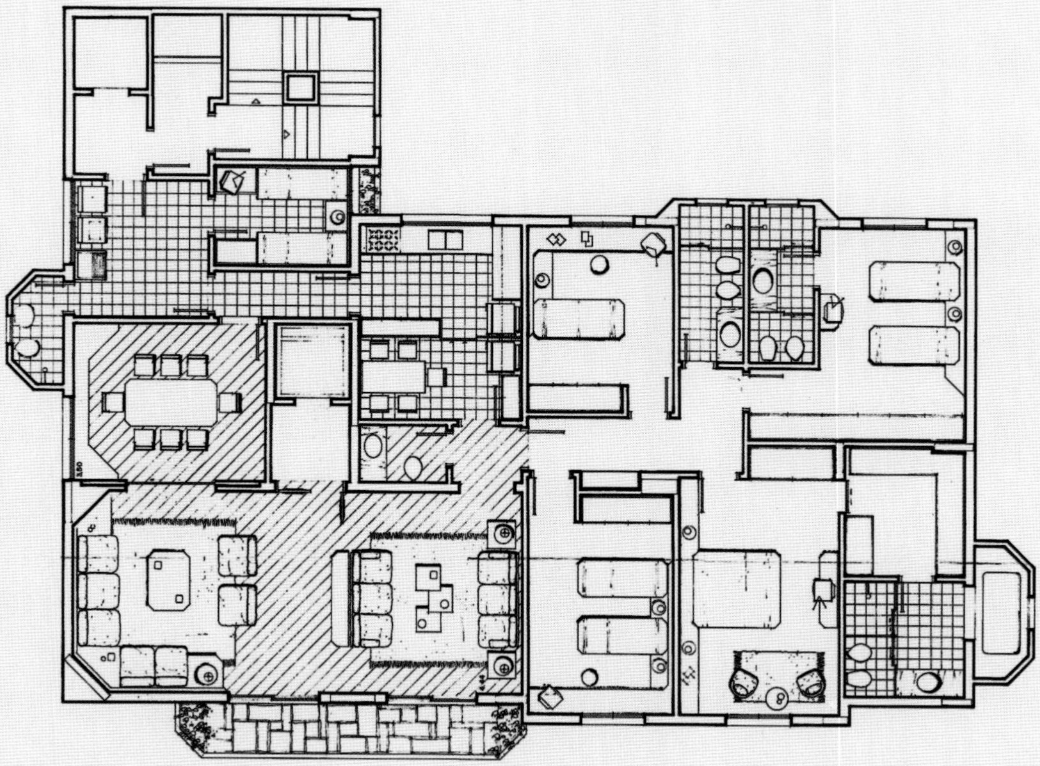

Existing plan

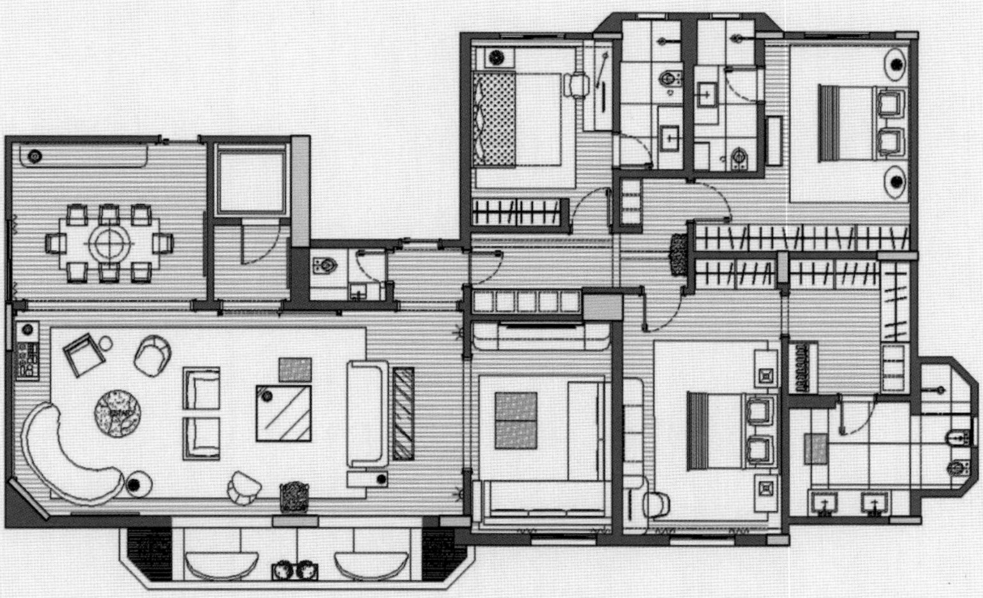

New plan

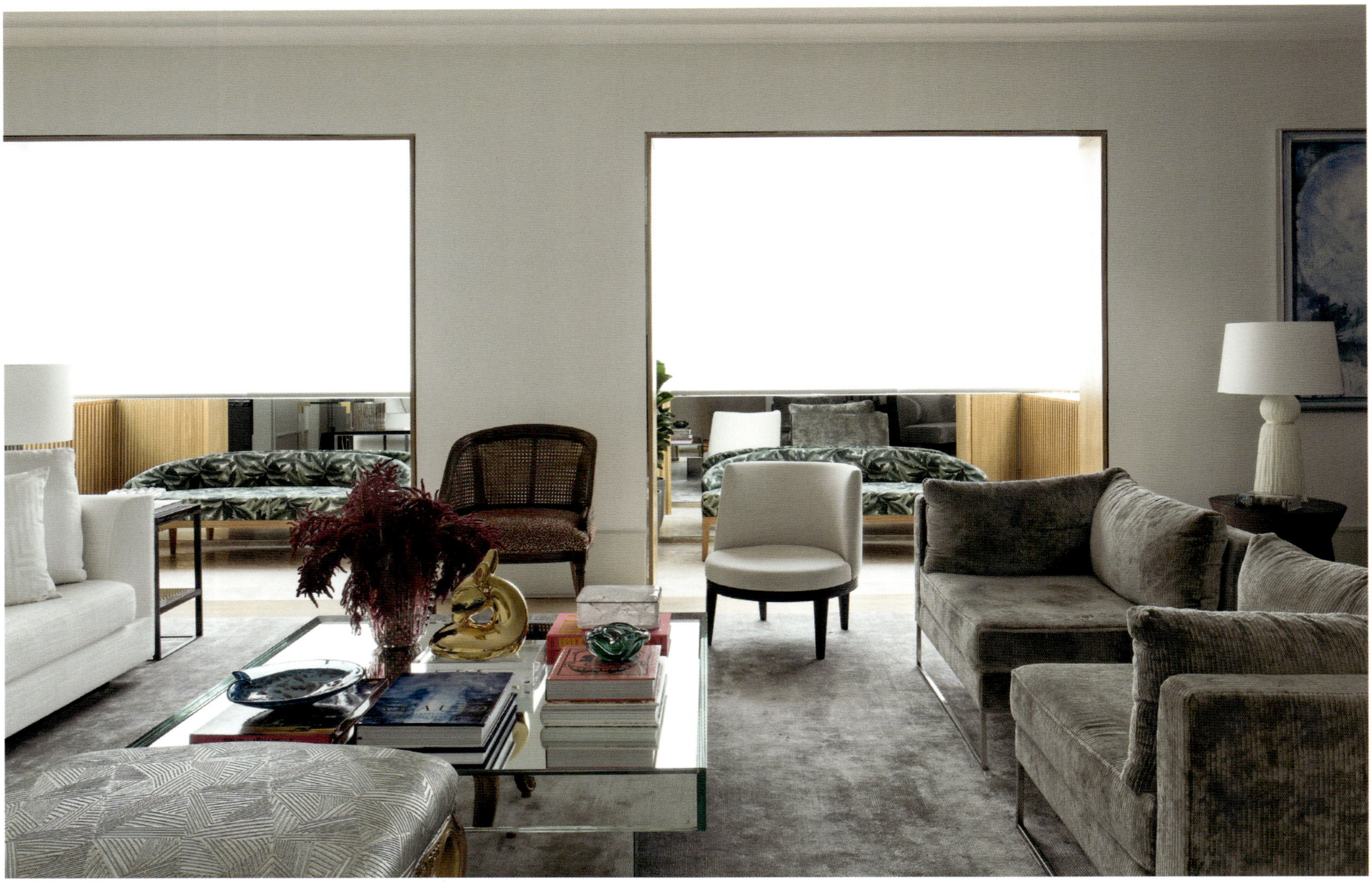

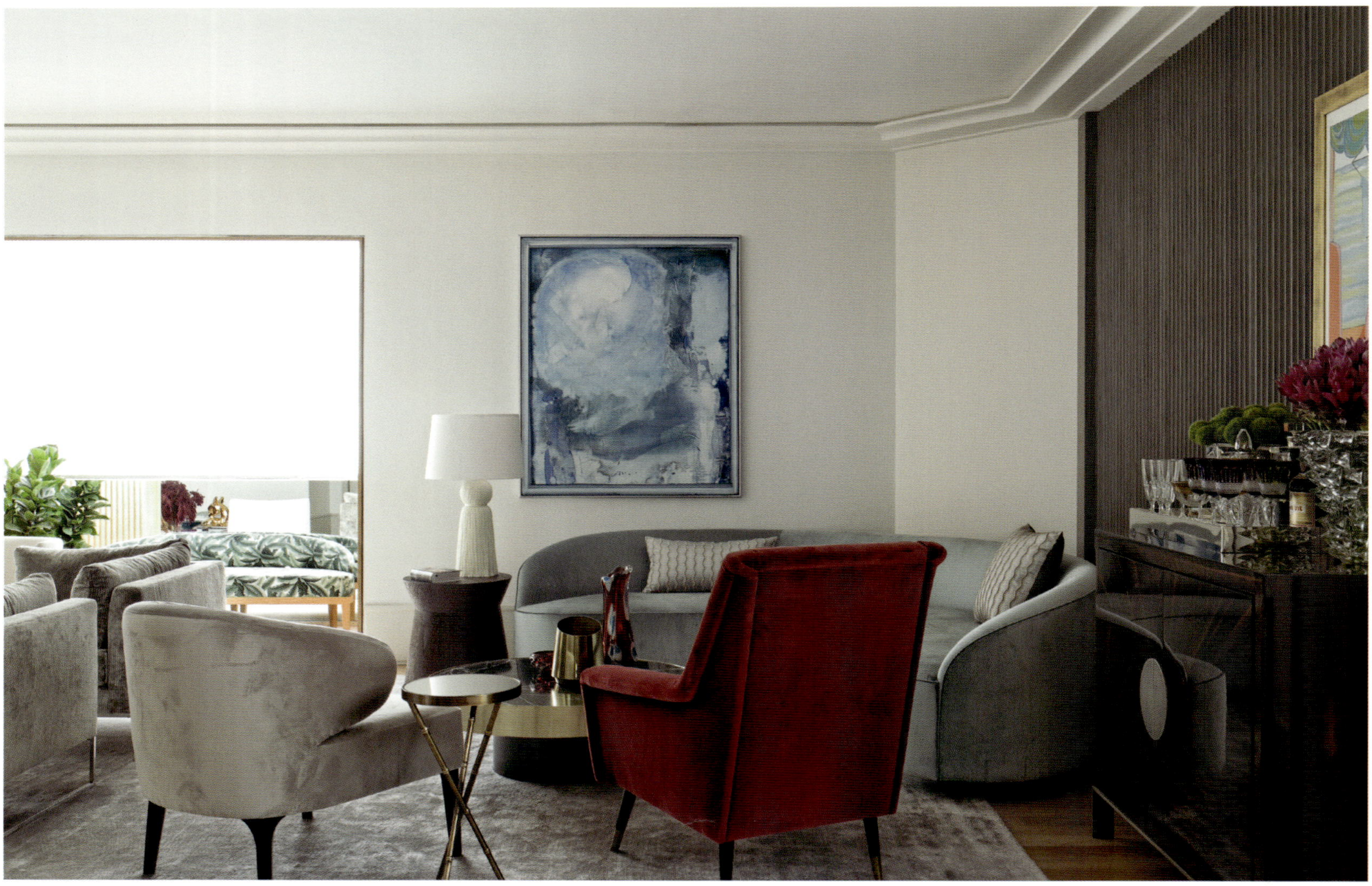

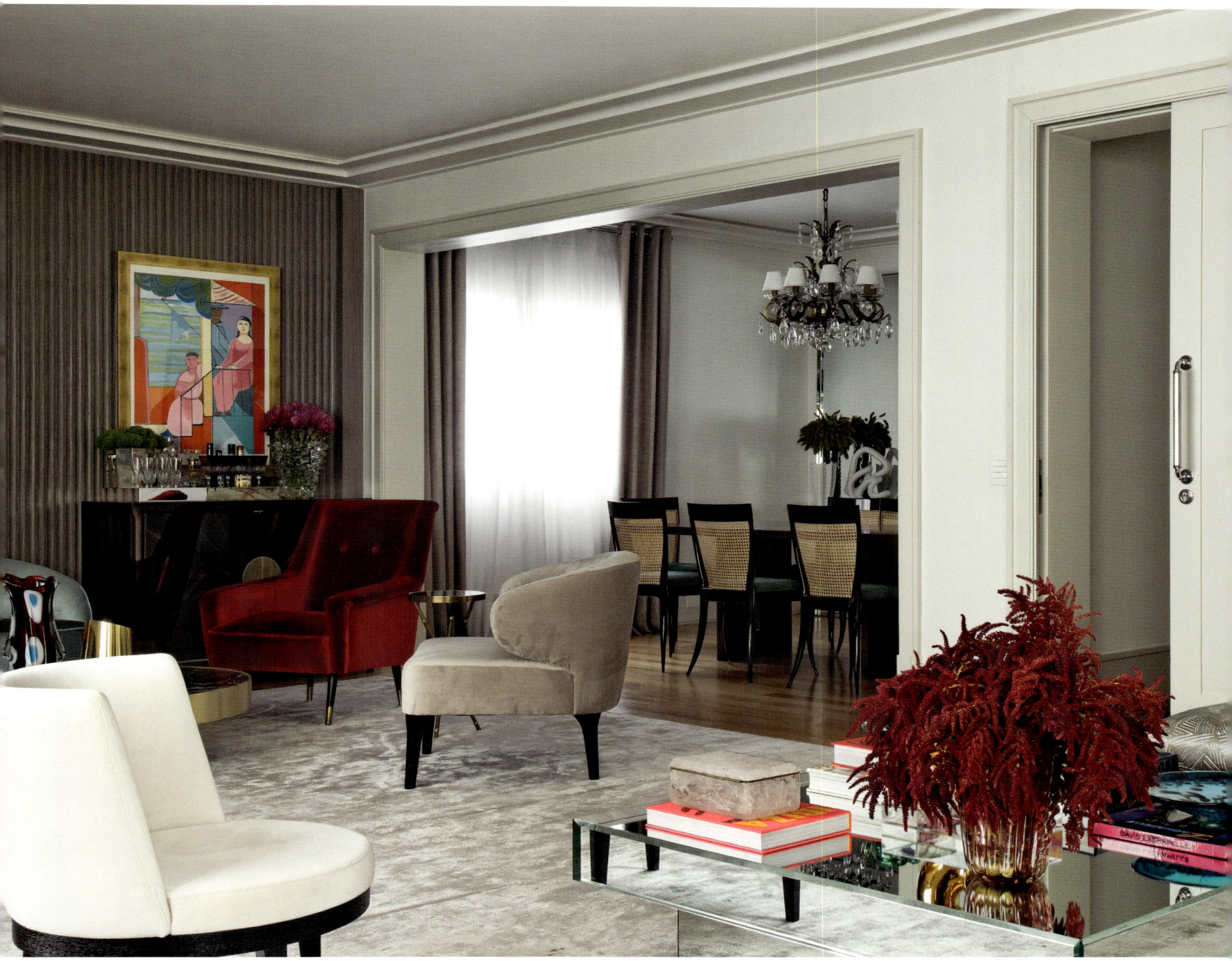

Wood of various shades is present throughout the apartment: the light-colored floors of Tauarí wood, the terrace's honey oak surface, the gray-shaded Grigio wood and dark Macassar ebony of the bar in the salon.

In der ganzen Wohnung wurde Holz in verschiedenen Tönen verwendet: Die hellen Böden bestehen aus Tauari-Holz, die Terrasse wurde aus honigfarbenem Eichenholz entworfen, für die Holzwand wurde graues Grigio-Holz verbaut und die Bar des Wohnzimmers besteht aus dunklem Ebenholz.

Le bois est présent dans tout l'appartement dans divers tons : les sols clairs en bois de Tauarí, le bois de chêne miel de la terrasse, le panneau de bois gris Grigio et le bois d'ébène foncé de Macassar du meuble du bar du salon.

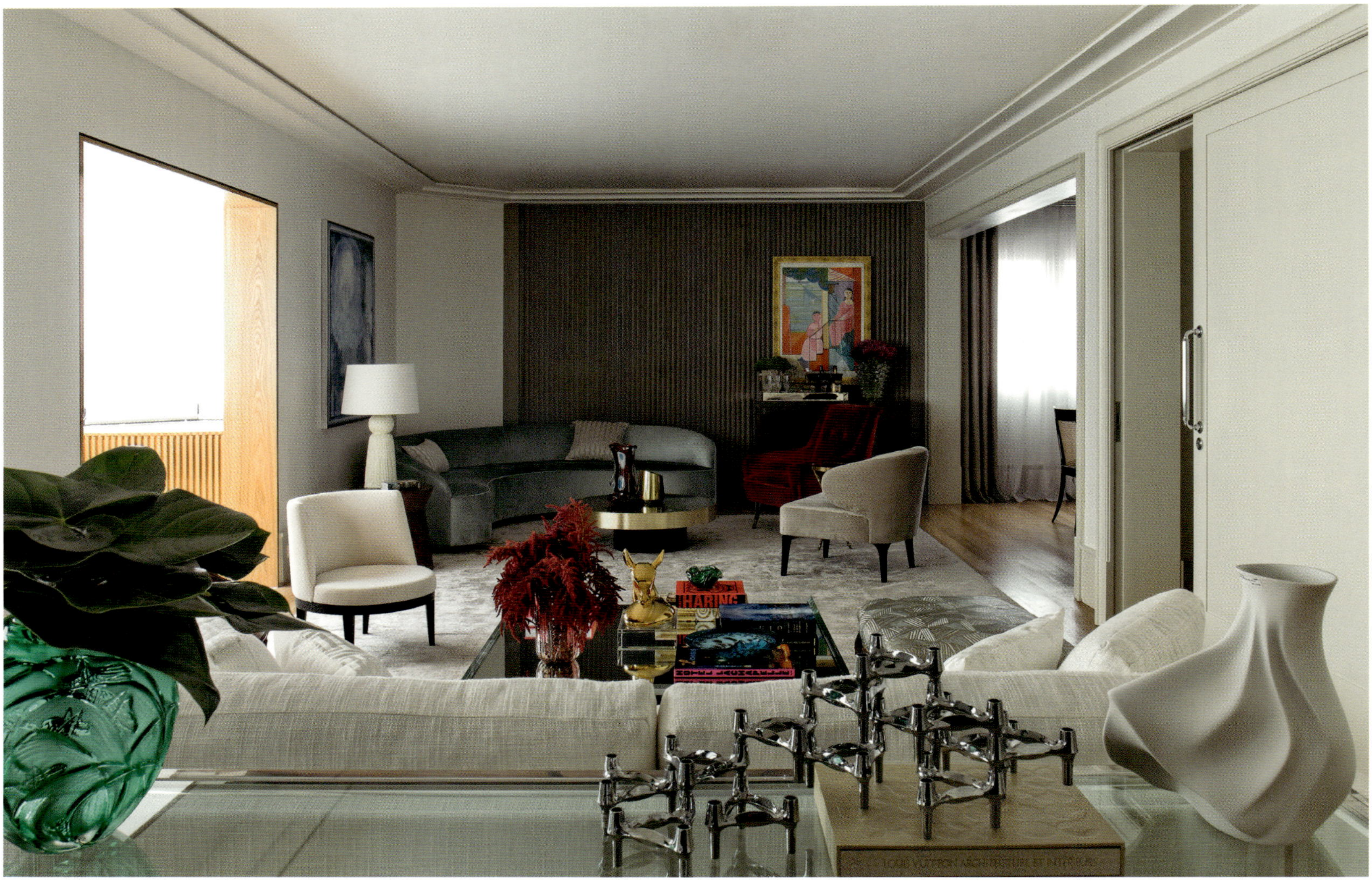

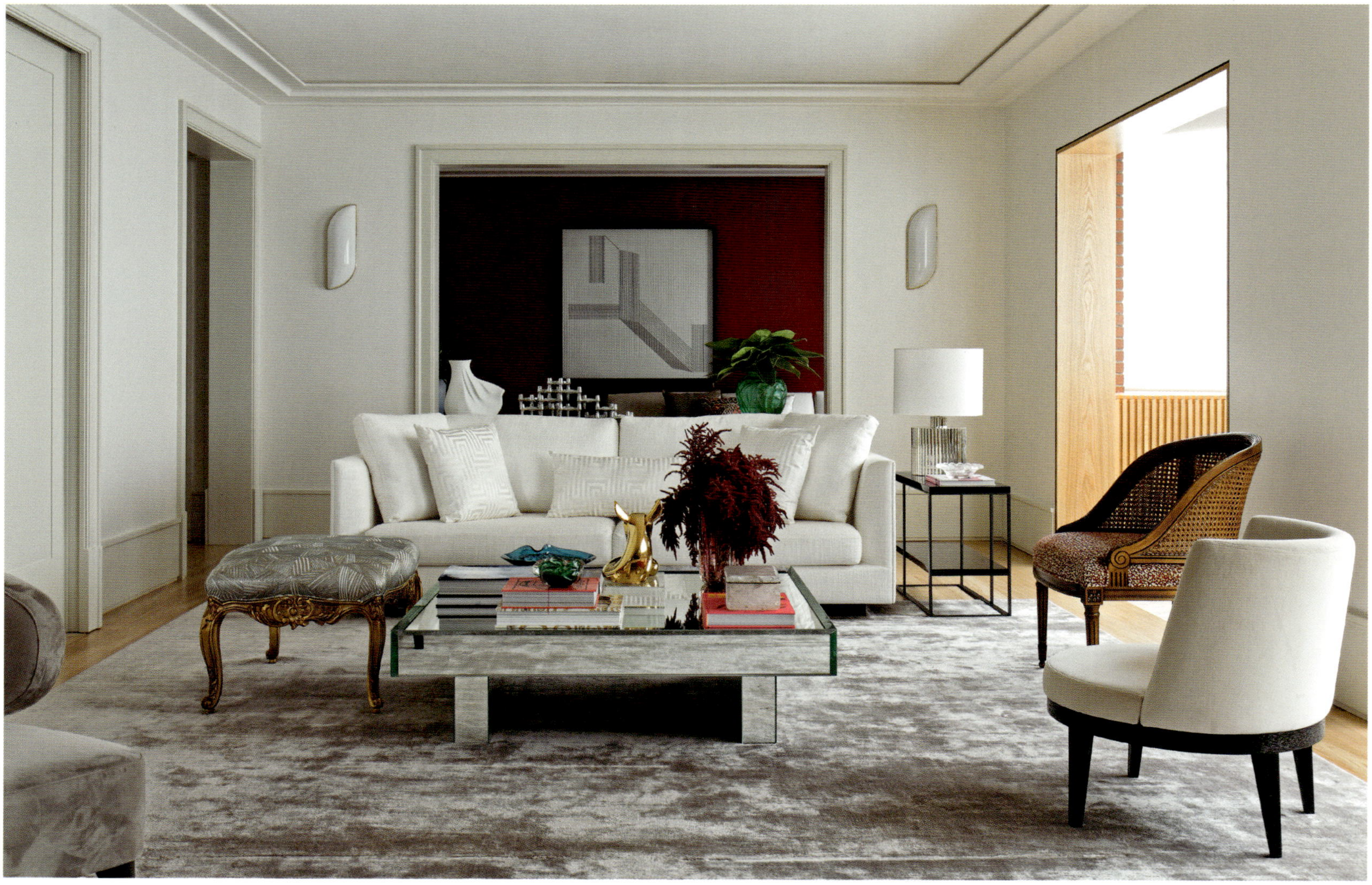

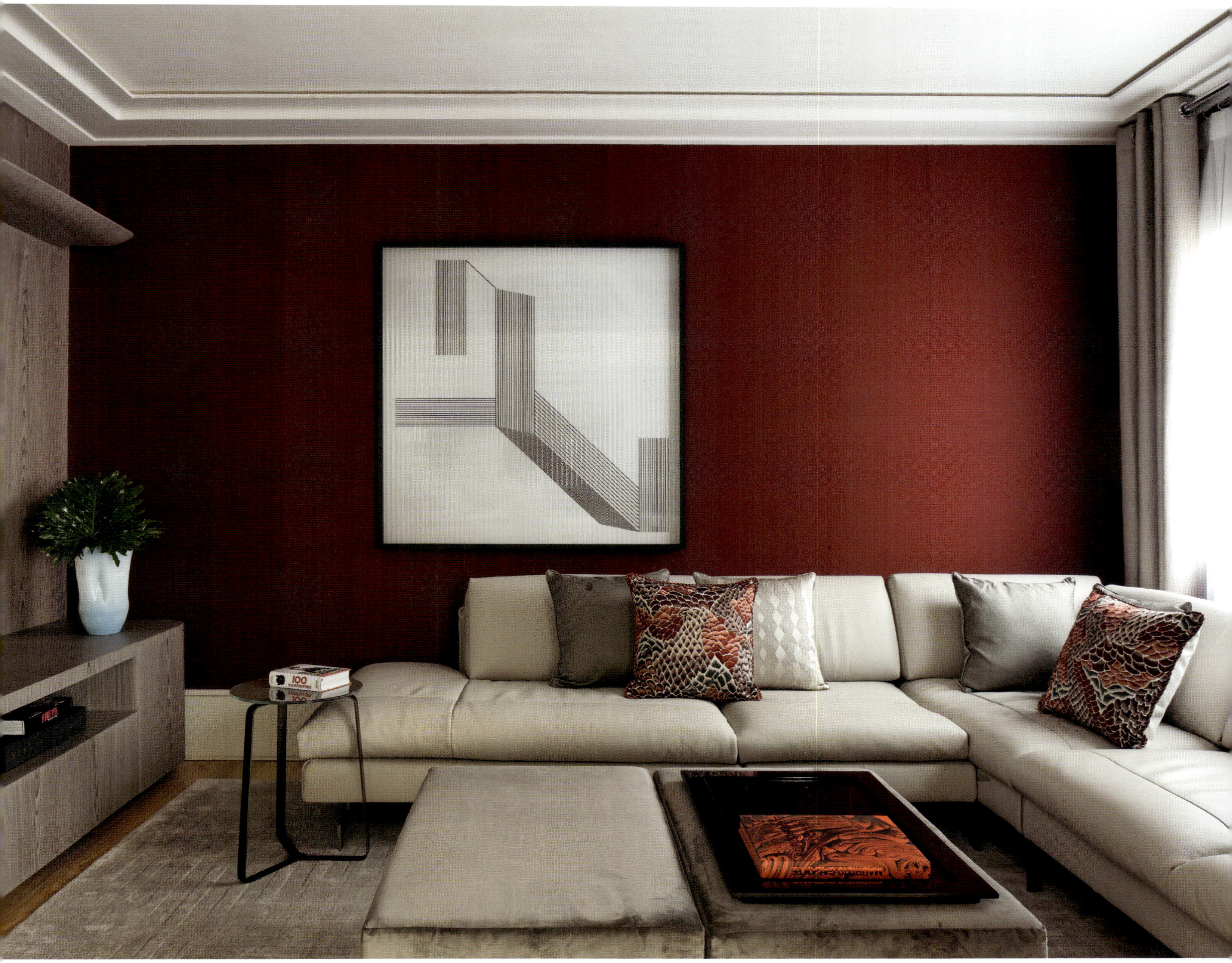

To highlight the apartment's brightness, a completely white sofa was chosen for the living room, perfectly complementing the burgundy backdrop.

Um die Helligkeit der Wohnung zu betonen, wählte man für das Wohnzimmer ein komplett weißes Sofa aus, das außerdem perfekt zum burgunderfarbenen Hintergrund passt.

Un canapé a été choisi dans le séjour entièrement blanc afin d'accentuer la luminosité de l'appartement. De même, il s'intègre parfaitement au fond de couleur bordeaux.

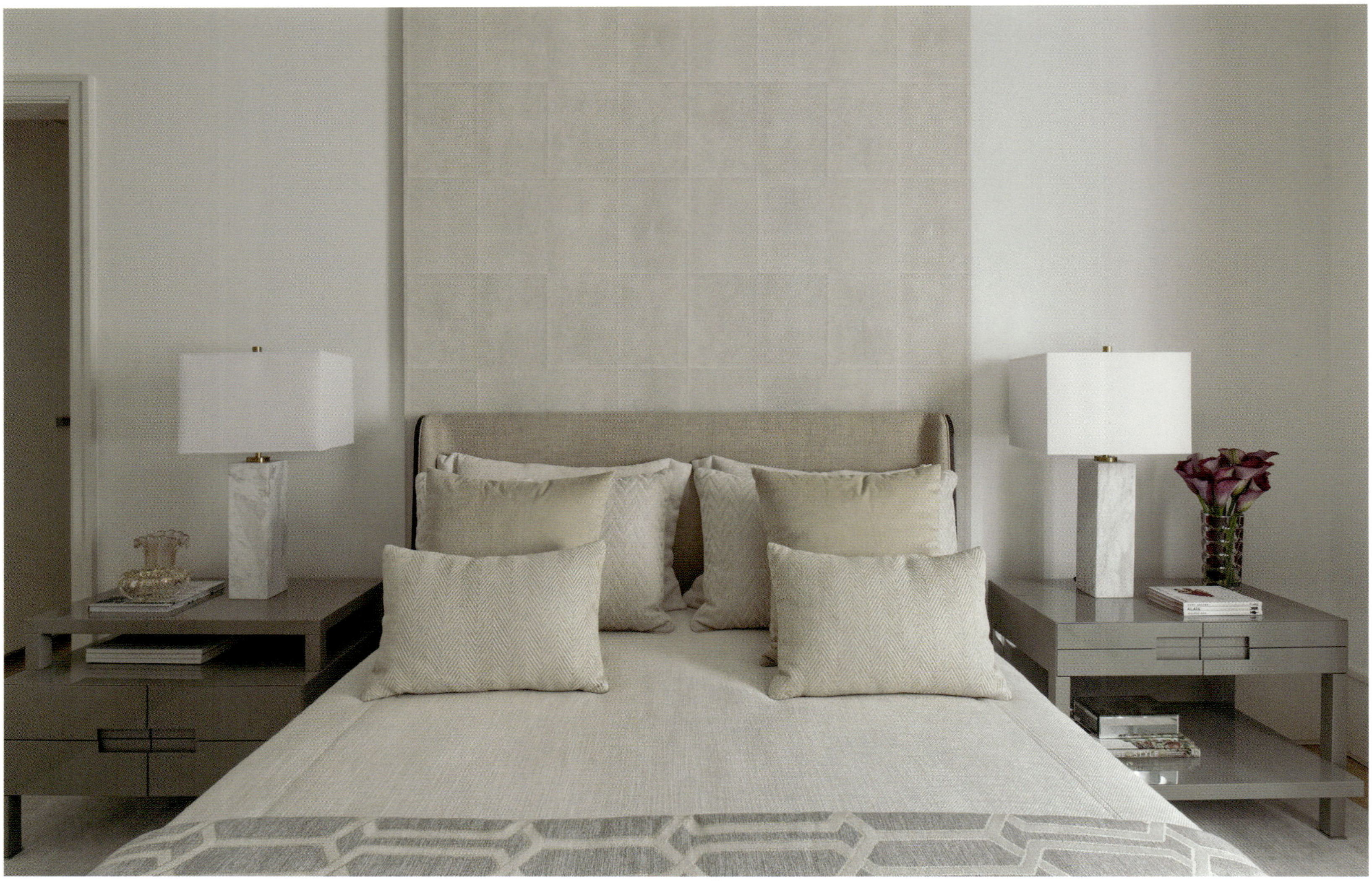

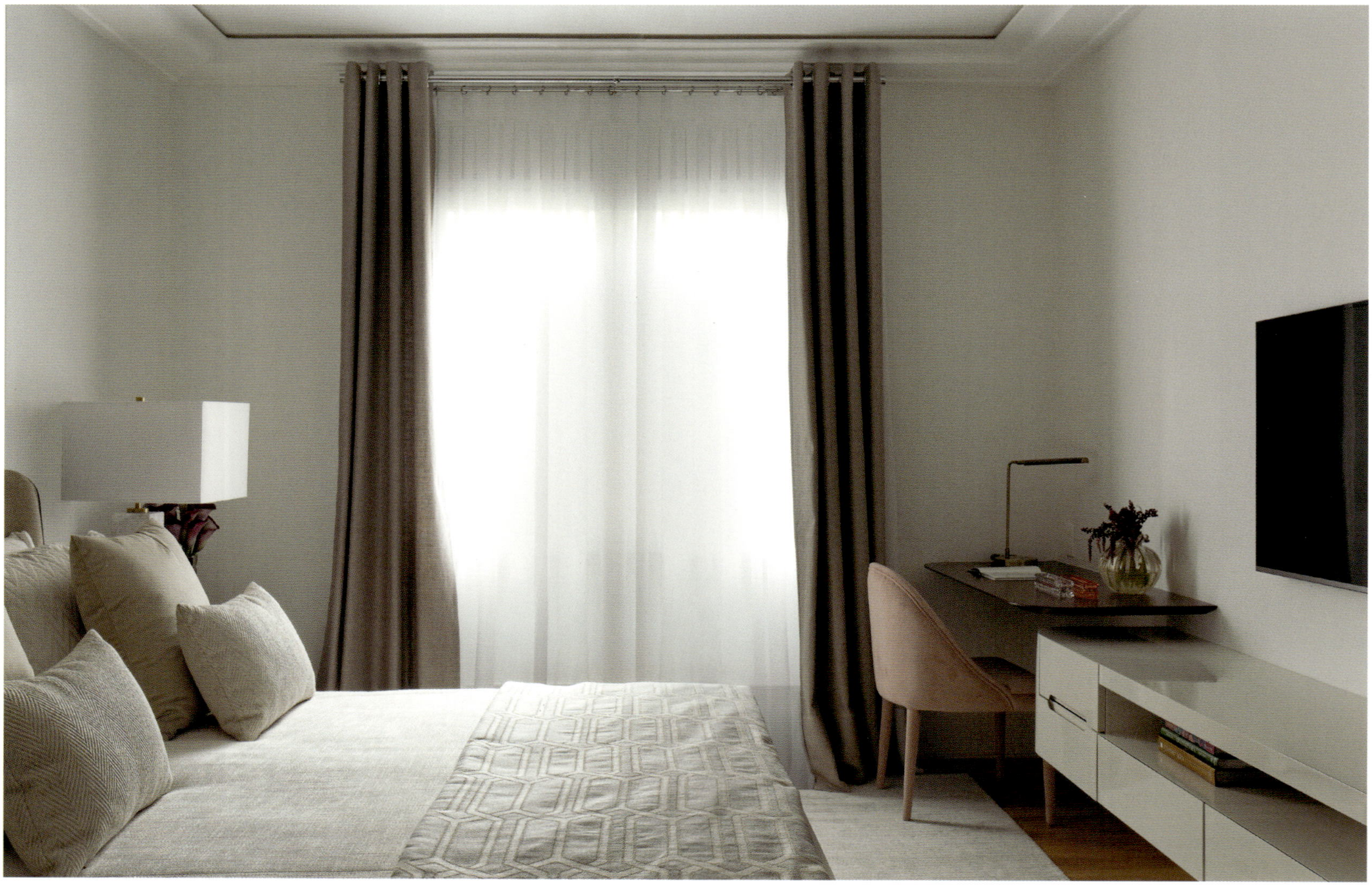

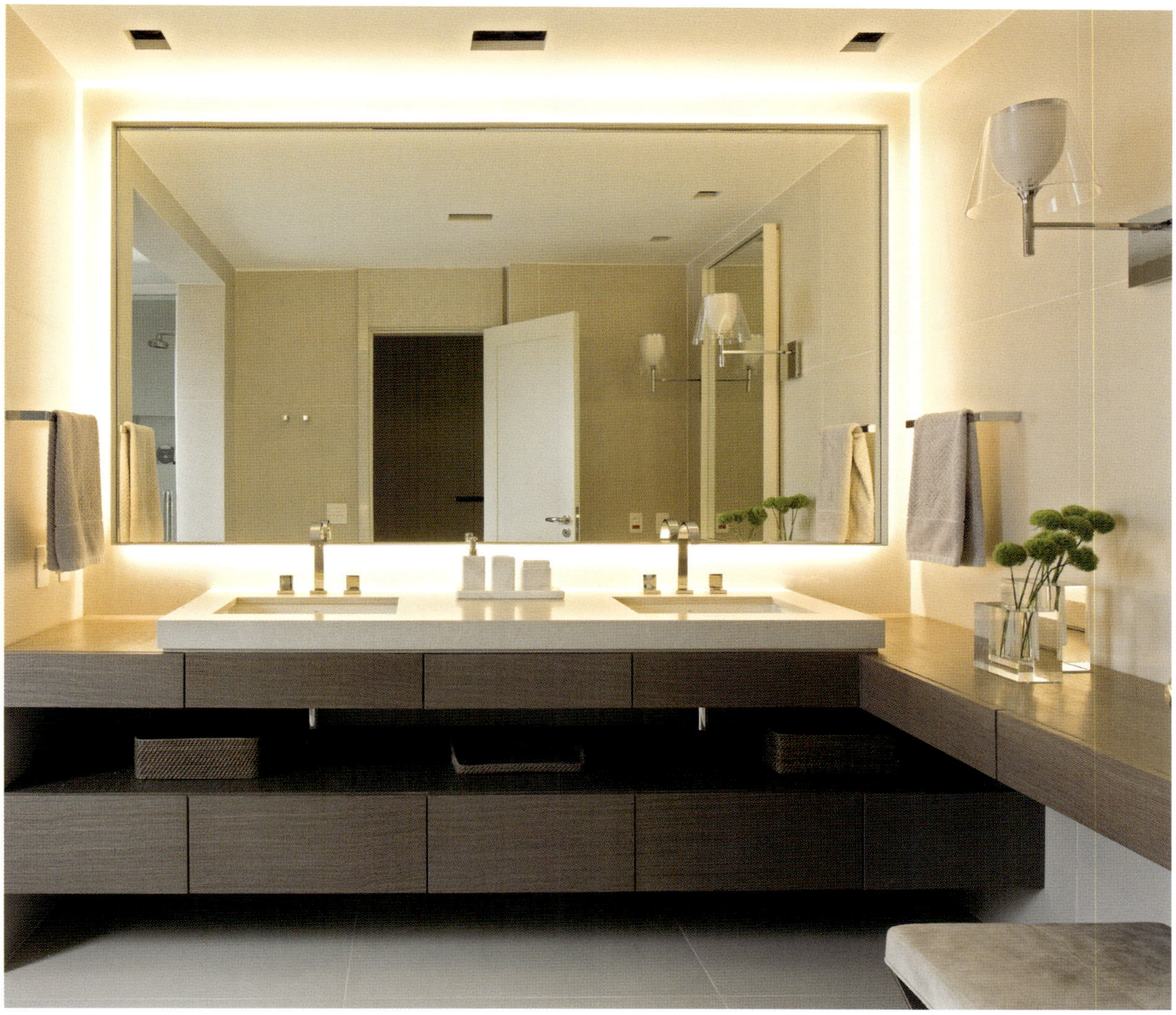

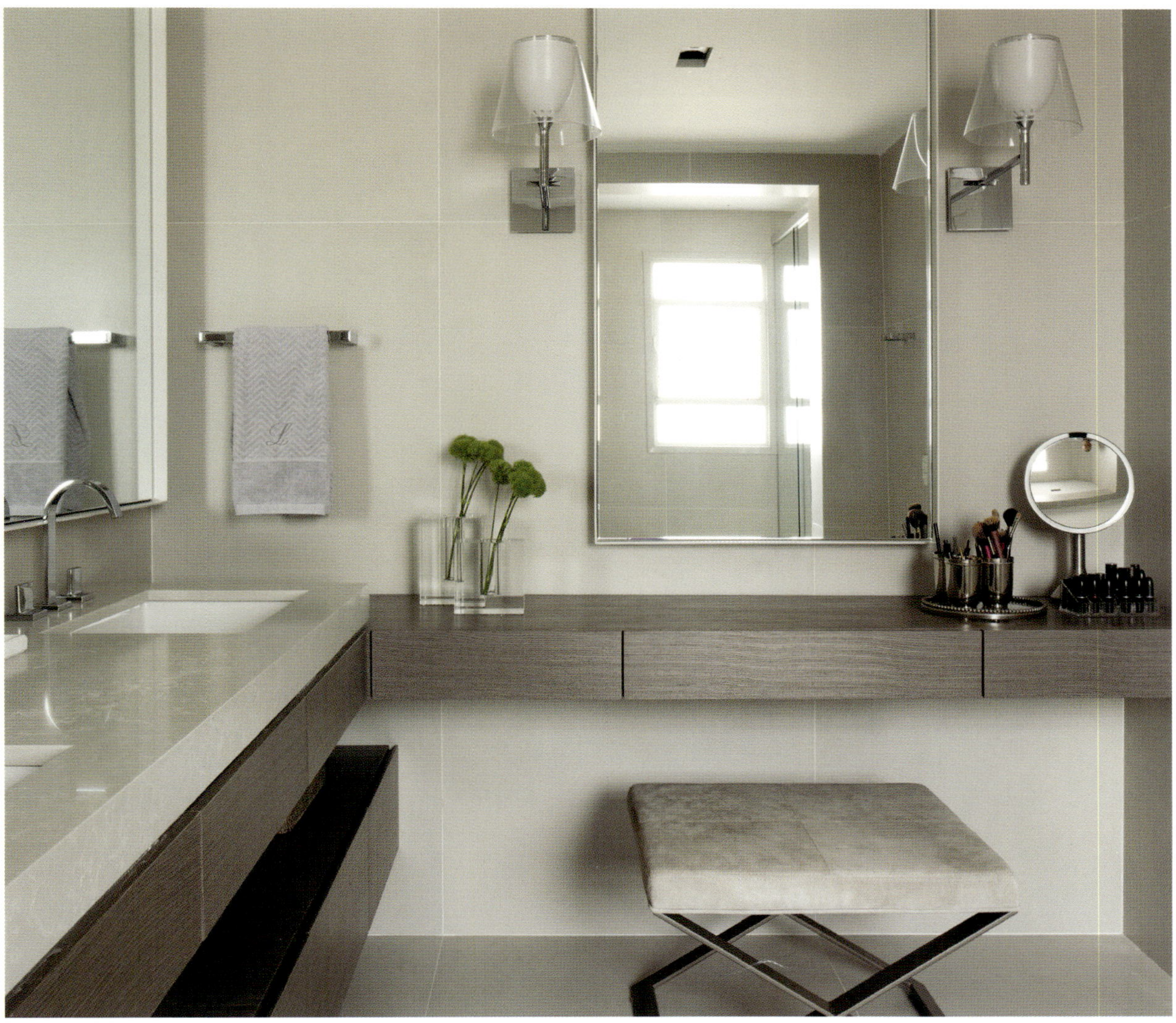

The wood selections, combined with the neutral shades that extend to the most private parts of the apartment, contribute balance and warmth.

Das ausgewählte Holz in Verbindung mit den neutralen Farbtönen, die vielfach in den Privaträumen der Wohnung zum Einsatz kamen, sorgt für Wärme und eine gewisse Ausgewogenheit.

Le choix du bois combiné aux tons neutres agrandit les espaces les plus privés de l'appartement et apporte de l'équilibre et de la chaleur.

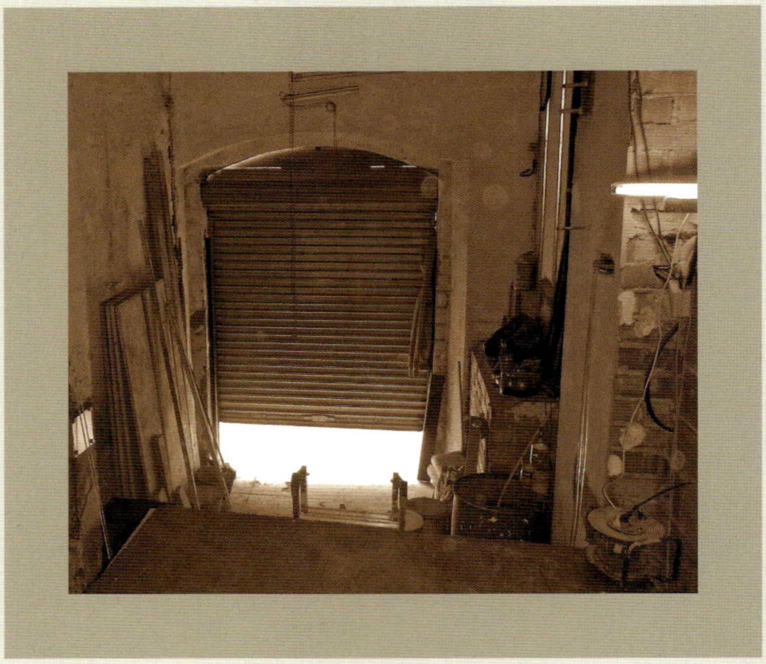

LOFT CIUTAT VELLA

ESTUDIO ATMOSFERA

65 m² | 670 sq. ft.

Barcelona, Spain

Photos © **Nicolás Fotografía**

- Repurpose the space to be used as medium-stay apartments
- Design a practical interior
- Restore original elements to preserve the character of the original structure

- Den Bau so sanieren, dass er als Ferienwohnungen genutzt werden kann
- Einen praktisches Innenraum entwerfen
- Die ursprünglichen Elemente erneuern, ohne das Wesen ihrer Herkunft aus den Augen zu verlieren

- Restaurer les espaces pour les utiliser comme des appartements de moyen séjour
- Concevoir un intérieur pratique
- Récupérer des éléments d'origine afin de conserver l'essence de leur origine

This loft occupies the ground floor of an 1893 building situated in the picturesque Raval neighborhood in Barcelona's historic Old Town. This is the city's largest multicultural district. Until recently, the neighborhood was suffering serious deterioration, although a partial recuperation has recently taken place. Affected by these circumstances, the property has gone from being occupied to experiencing total abandonment in the last few years.
In its plan, the rehabilitation project chose the path of retaining the residence's structure and its spatial distribution, which perfectly takes advantage of the natural light. The space was adapted for its future use as a medium-stay apartment. Original elements such as wooden beams, timbrel vaulting, and brick dividing walls have been restored. The design envisioned a practical, minimalist interior with resistant materials that could be inexpensively replaced, matching this approach with careful selection of natural textures, nuanced colors, and a warm, focused lighting plan. The result revealed a space that prioritizes a tempered industrial style and vintage Provençal and Asian touches, recalling both the neighborhood's industrial history and its current cosmopolitism.

Im Erdgeschoss eines Gebäudes aus dem Jahr 1893, im malerischen Stadtteil Raval, in der Altstadt von Barcelona, befindet sich dieses Loft. Raval ist das Stadtviertel mit der größten multikulturellen Bevölkerungsvielfalt in der Stadt. Bis vor kurzem erlebte dieser Bezirk einen erheblichen Verfall, der sich in den letzten Jahren teilweise wieder umkehrte. Daher war das Anwesen in äußerst schlechtem Zustand, da es in den letzten Jahren erst besetzt und dann völlig seinem Schicksal überlassen wurde.
Bei der Planung des Sanierungsprojekts entschieden sich die Architekten dafür, die Struktur des Hauses und die Aufteilung zu bewahren, da dies eine optimale Nutzung des natürlichen Lichts ermöglicht. Die Räume wurden im Hinblick auf ihre künftige Nutzung als Wohnung für mittellange Aufenthalte angepasst. Originalelemente wie Holzbalken, geteilte Gewölbe oder Trennwände aus Backstein wurden gerettet. Ein praktisches, minimalistisches Interieur wurde entworfen. Es besteht aus strapazierfähigen Materialien – nicht übermäßig teuer beim Ersetzen –, kombiniert mit der sorgfältigen Auswahl natürlicher Texturen, nuancierter Farben und einer warmen und fokussierten Beleuchtung. Das Endergebnis ist ein Raum, in dem der Industriestil dominiert, der durch Vintage-, provenzalische und orientalische Akzente aufgelockert wird und an die industrielle Vergangenheit des Stadtviertels und dessen gegenwärtige Weltoffenheit erinnert.

Ce loft se trouve au rez-de-chaussée d'un édifice datant de 1893 du quartier pittoresque du Raval, au cœur de la vieille ville de Barcelone. C'est la zone la plus multiculturelle de la ville. Jusqu'à peu, ce quartier avait connu de fortes dégradations qui ont été partiellement réparées au cours de ces dernières années, c'est pour cette raison que le bien immobilier se trouve en très mauvais état, du fait d'avoir été occupé, puis laissé à l'abandon ces dernières années.
Au moment de réaliser le projet de réhabilitation, les architectes ont préféré conserver la structure de l'habitation et la répartition afin de jouir pleinement de la lumière naturelle. La réutilisation de l'espace s'adapte à son futur usage en tant qu'appartement de moyen séjour. Des éléments d'origine tels que des poutres en bois, voûtes cloisonnées ou encore des murs mitoyens de brique ont été récupérés. L'intérieur est pratique, minimaliste, avec des matériaux résistants, pas excessivement onéreux à replacer, conjuguant ainsi la sélection minutieuse des textures naturelles, des couleurs nuancées et un éclairage chaleureux et ciblé. Le résultat final est un espace dans lequel prime le style industriel adouci avec des touches de *vintage*, provençales et orientales qui évoquent le passé manufacturier du quartier et son actuel cosmopolitisme.

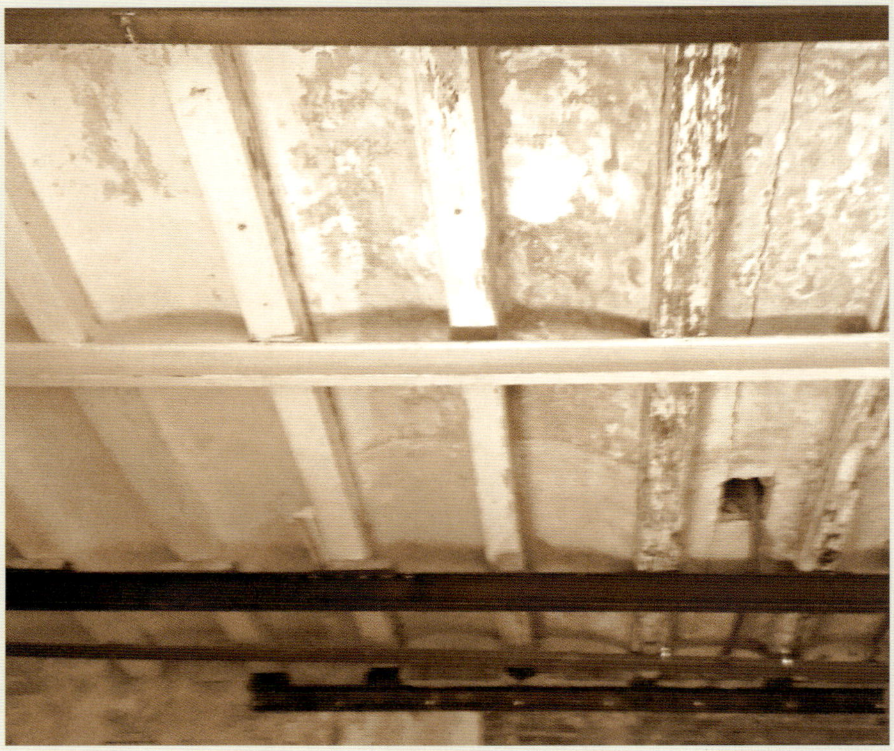

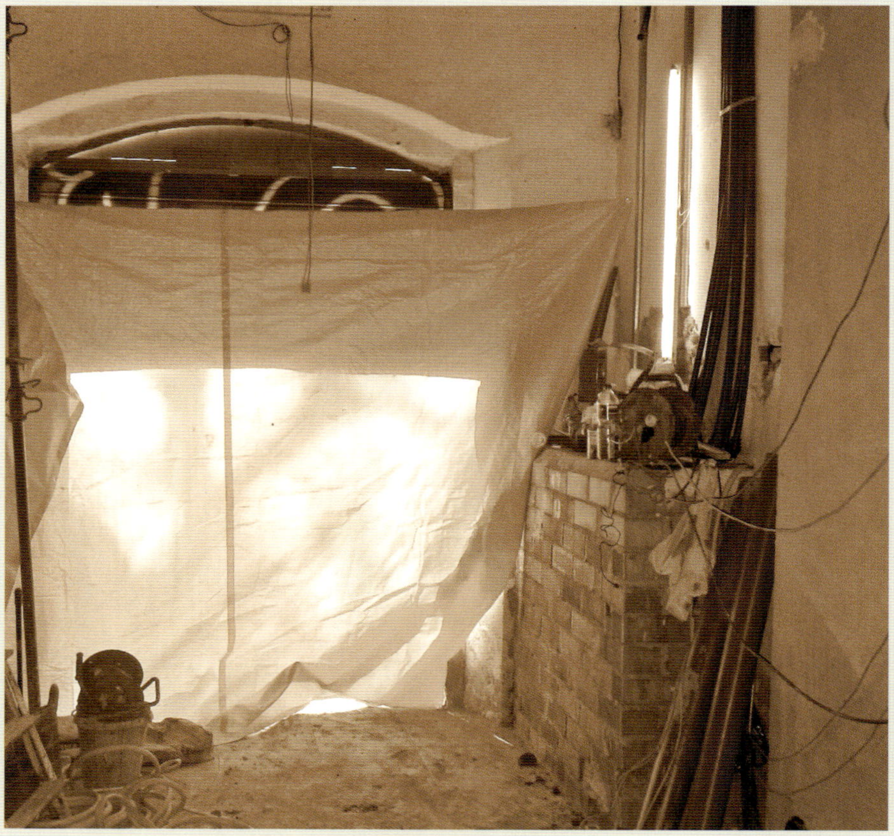

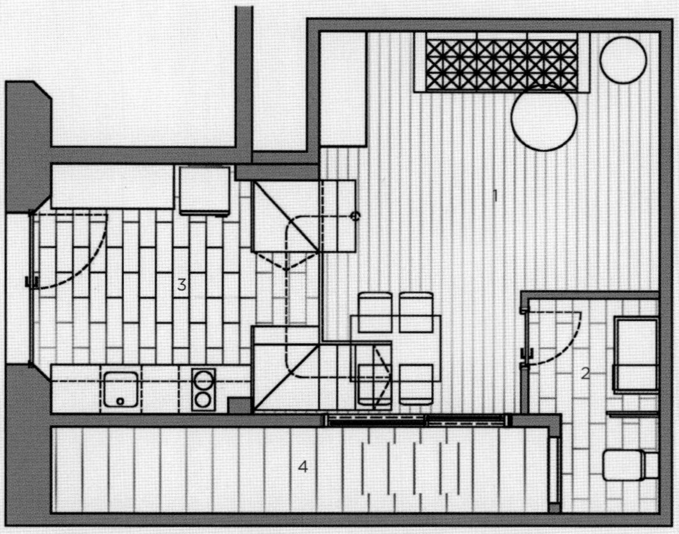

Ground floor plan

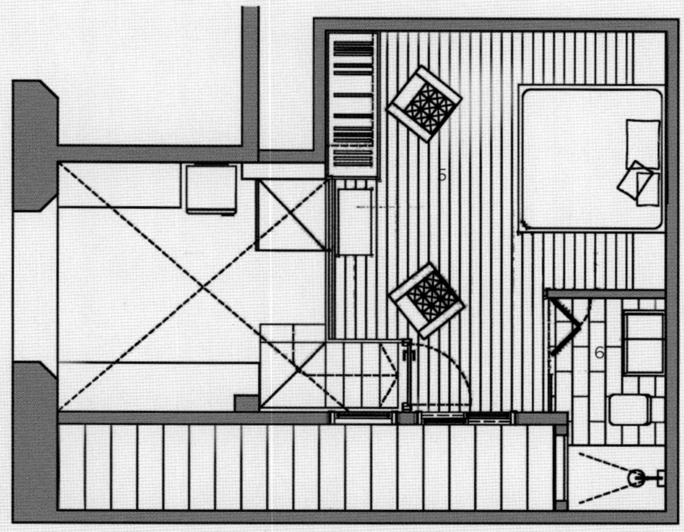

Attic plan

1. Living room
2. Guest bathroom
3. Kitchen
4. Patio
5. Bedroom
6. Bathroom

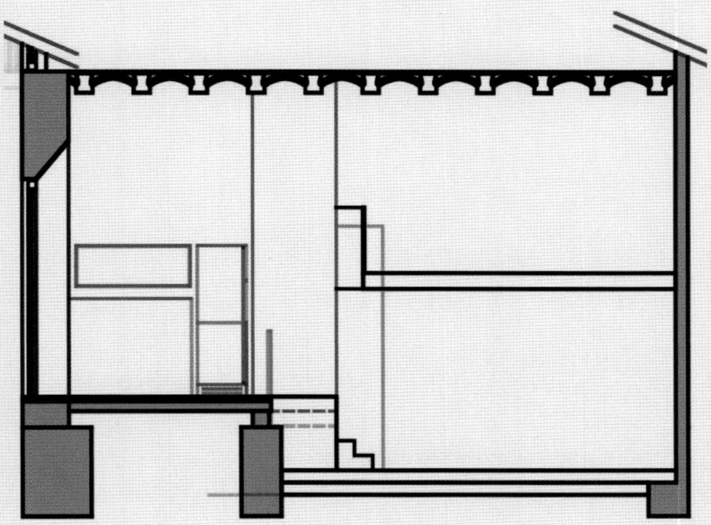

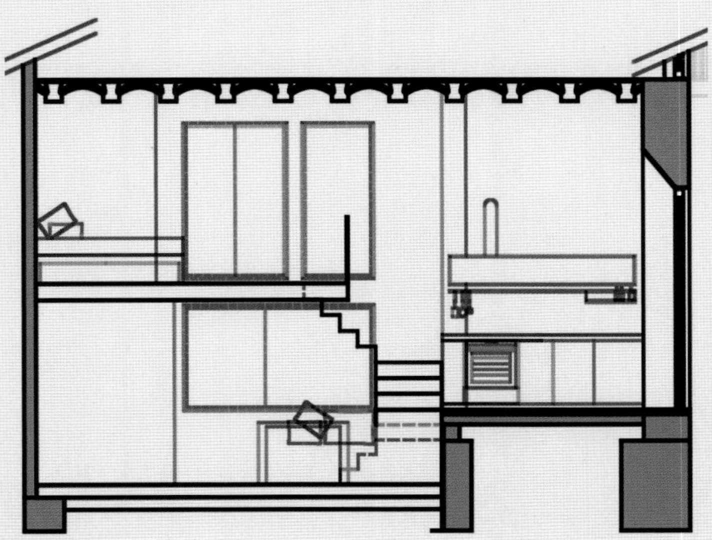

Sections

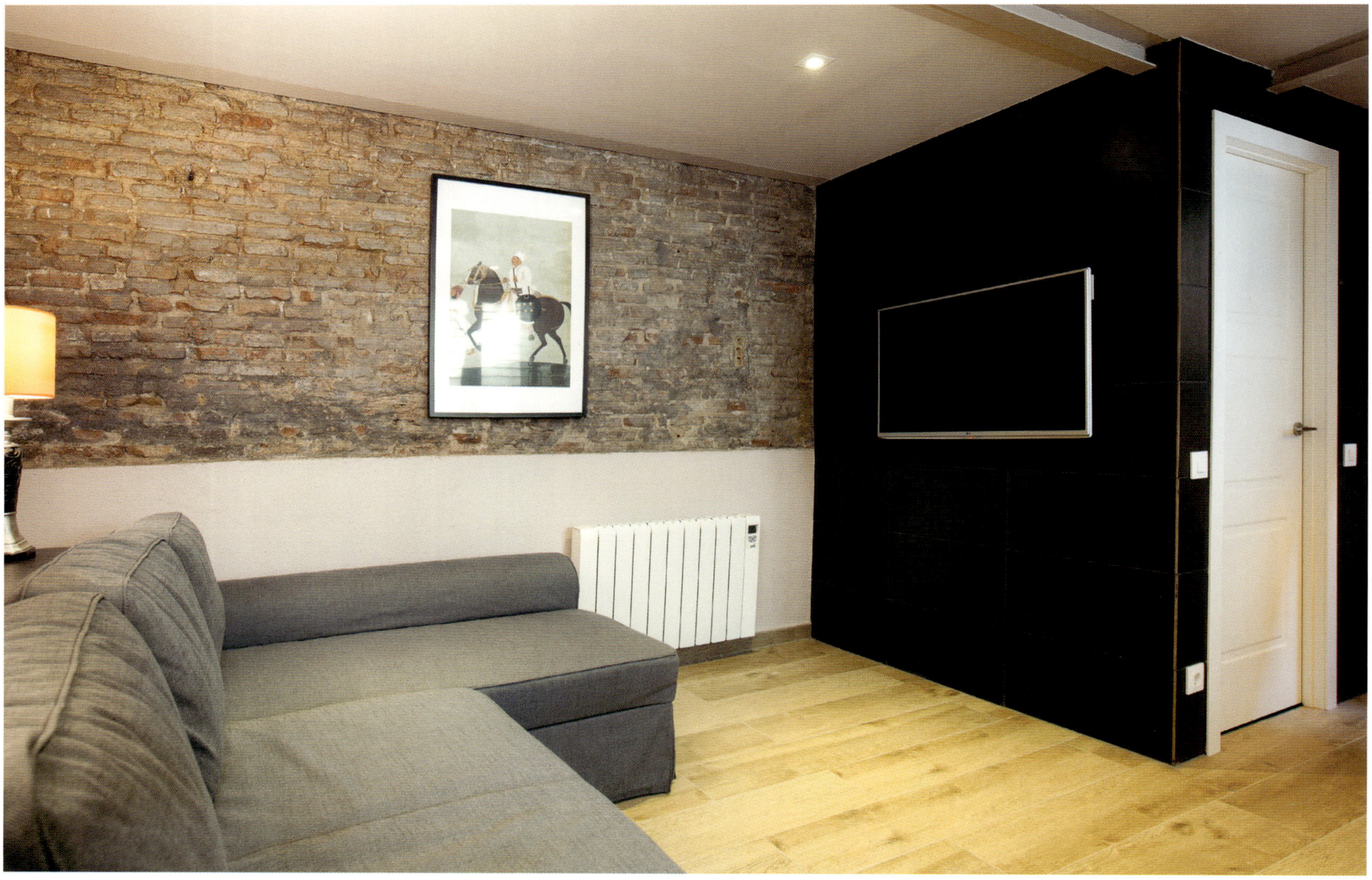

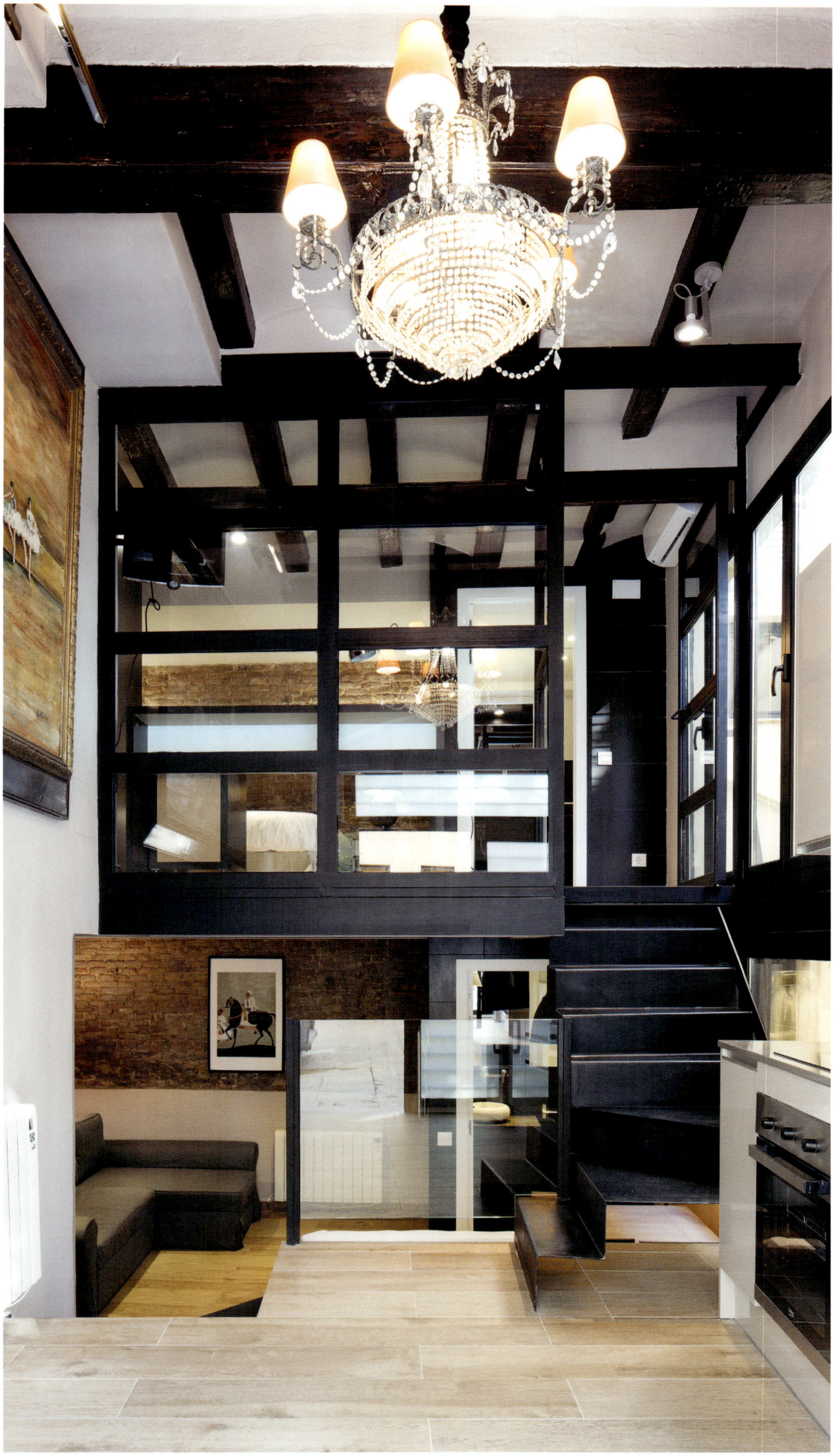

The apartment is divided into three levels, each of a similar surface area. At the lowest level is the living area, which can serve as a bedroom as needed. The dining area and a bathroom also occupy this level.

Die Wohnung ist auf drei Ebenen verteilt, die jeweils eine ähnliche Grundfläche haben. Auf der unteren Ebene befinden sich der Wohnbereich – bei Bedarf kann er auch als Schlafzimmer dienen –, das Esszimmer und ein Bad.

L'appartement est divisé en trois niveaux, chacun d'une surface semblable. À l'étage inférieur, le séjour qui, si nécessaire, peut servir de chambre, la salle à manger et une salle de bains.

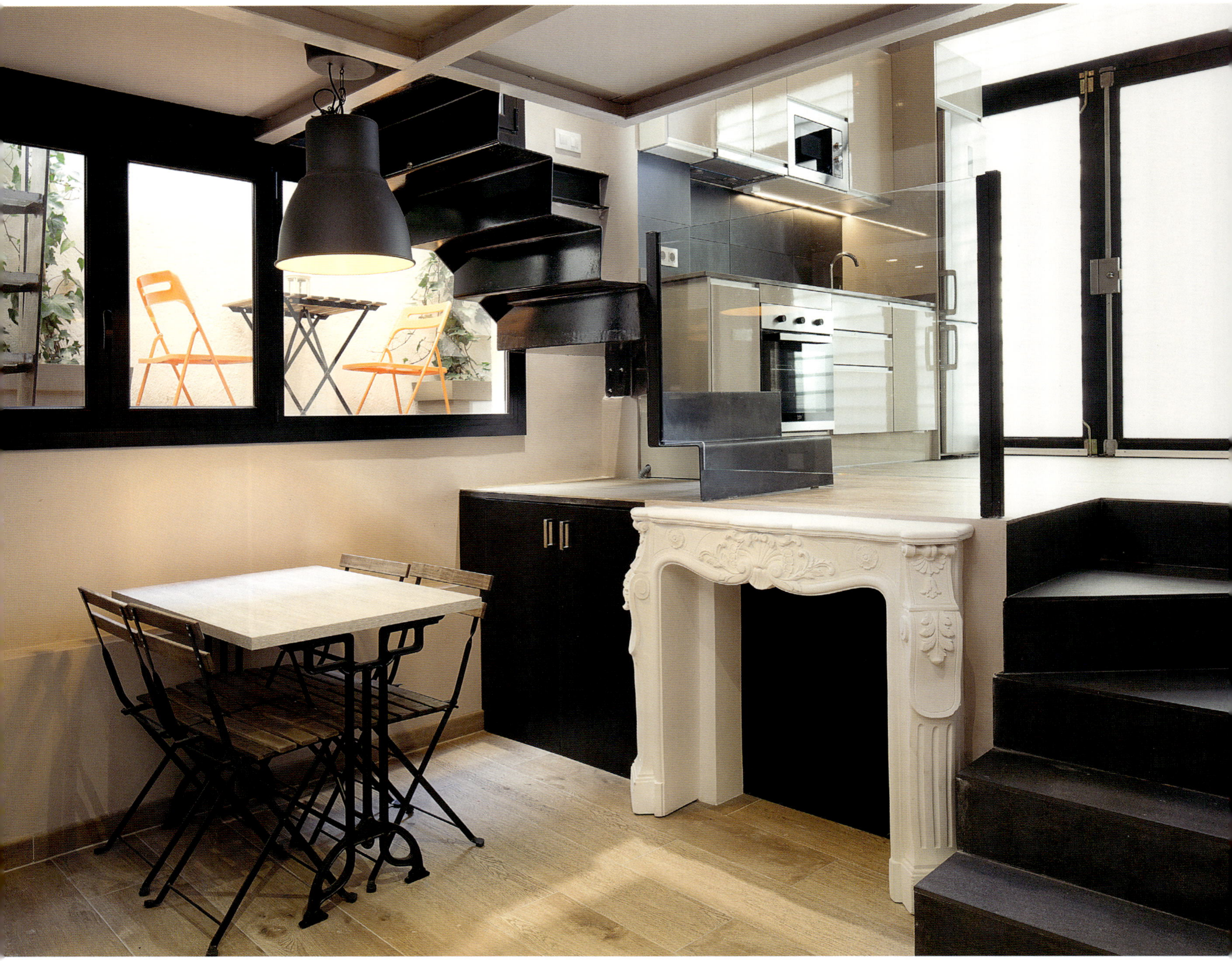

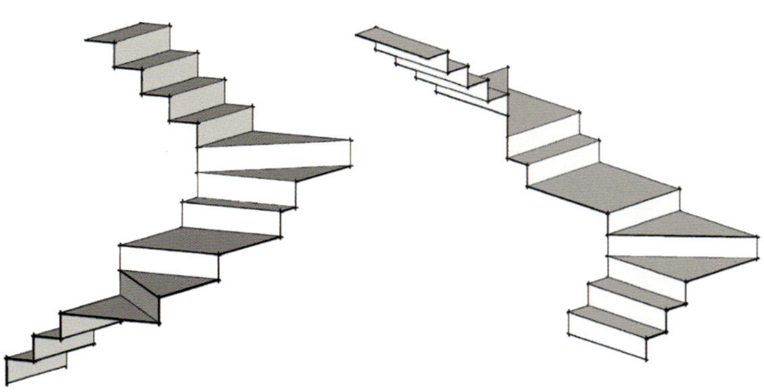

Interior stair sketch

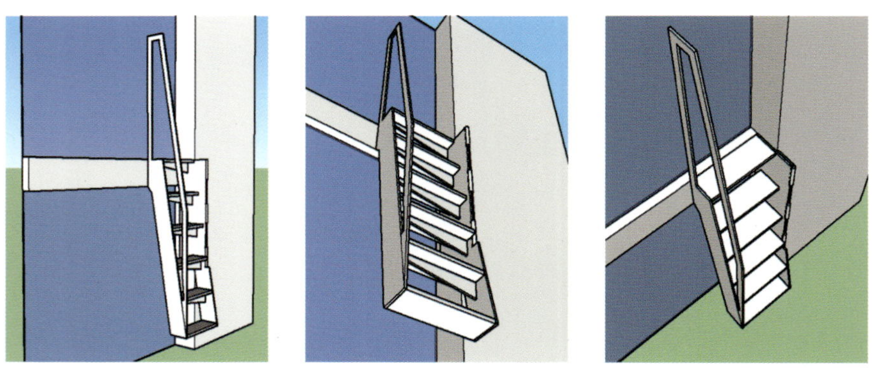

Patio stair sketch

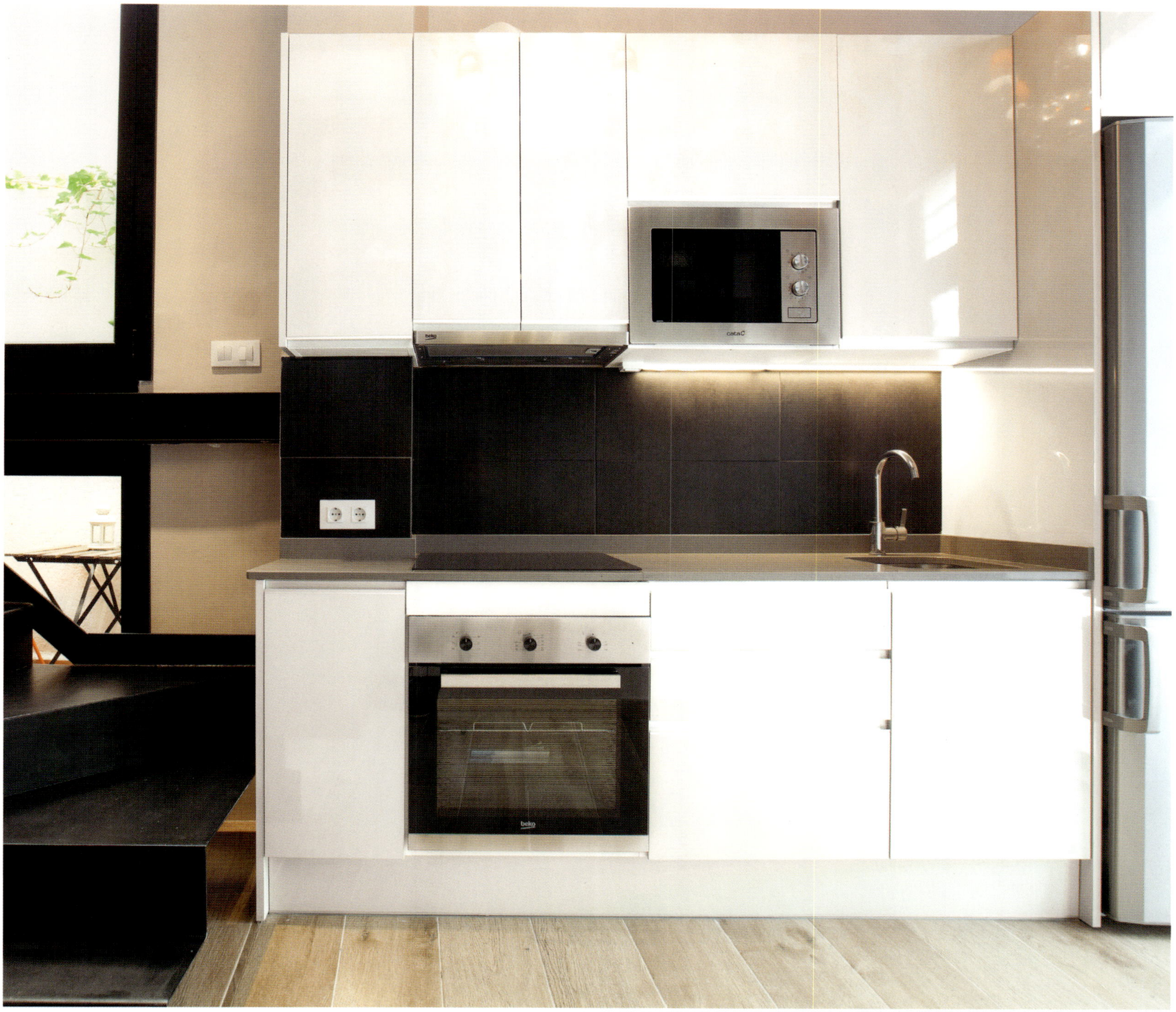

The street entrance, illuminated by a commanding chandelier, leads to the middle level where the kitchen is located. The iron frames of the glass panes are an allusion to the industrial roots of the neighborhood.

Der Zugang von der Straße aus, der von einem imposanten Kronleuchter erhellt wird, befindet sich auf der mittleren Ebene, auf der auch die Küche untergebracht ist. Die Glaseinfassungen mit Eisenprofilen sind eine Anspielung auf die industrielle Vergangenheit des Stadtviertels.

L'accès par la rue, éclairé par un imposant lustre à l'étage intermédiaire, où se trouve également la cuisine. Les cloisons vitrées avec des profilés en fer sont un clin d'œil au passé industriel du quartier.

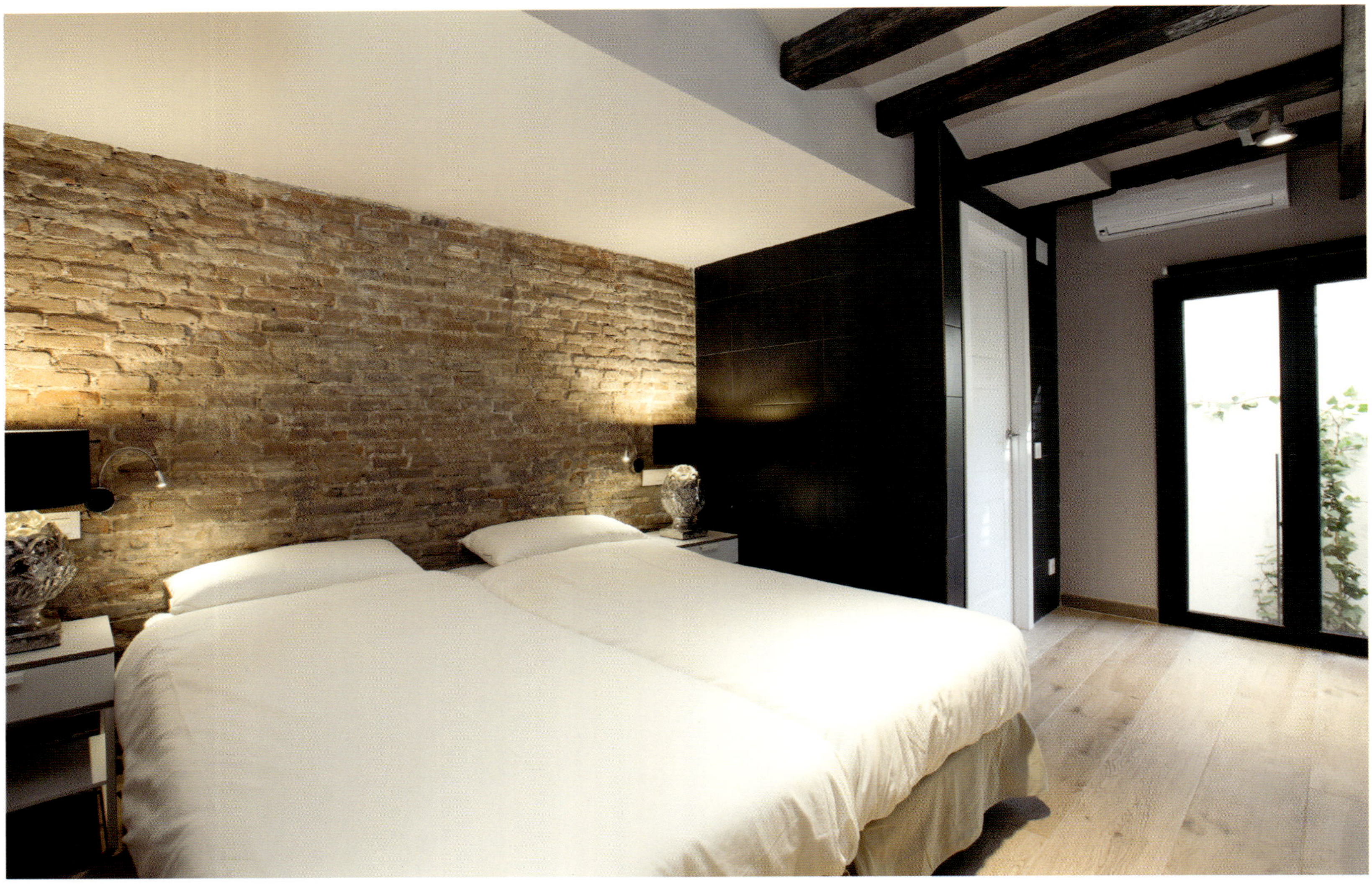

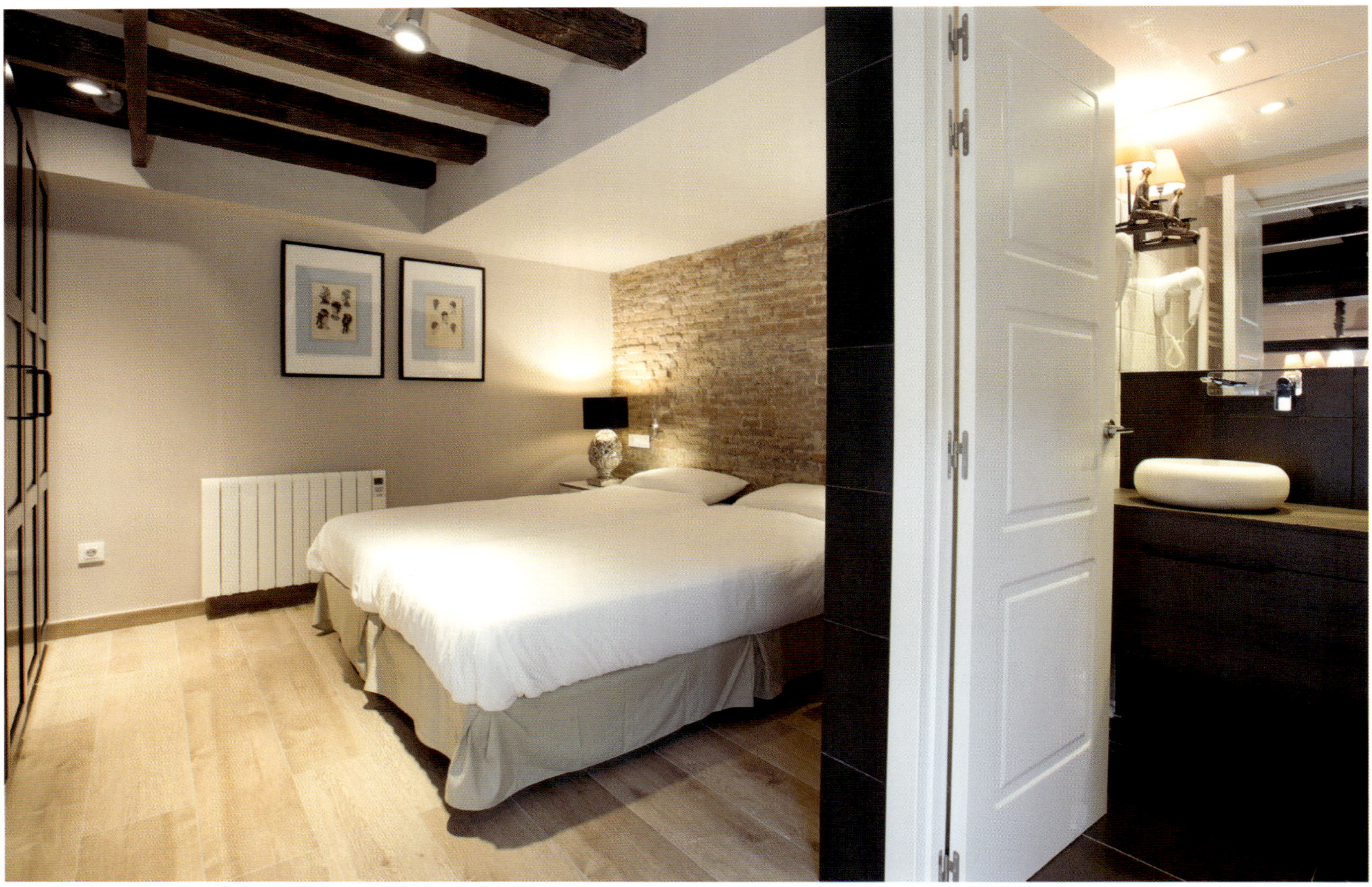

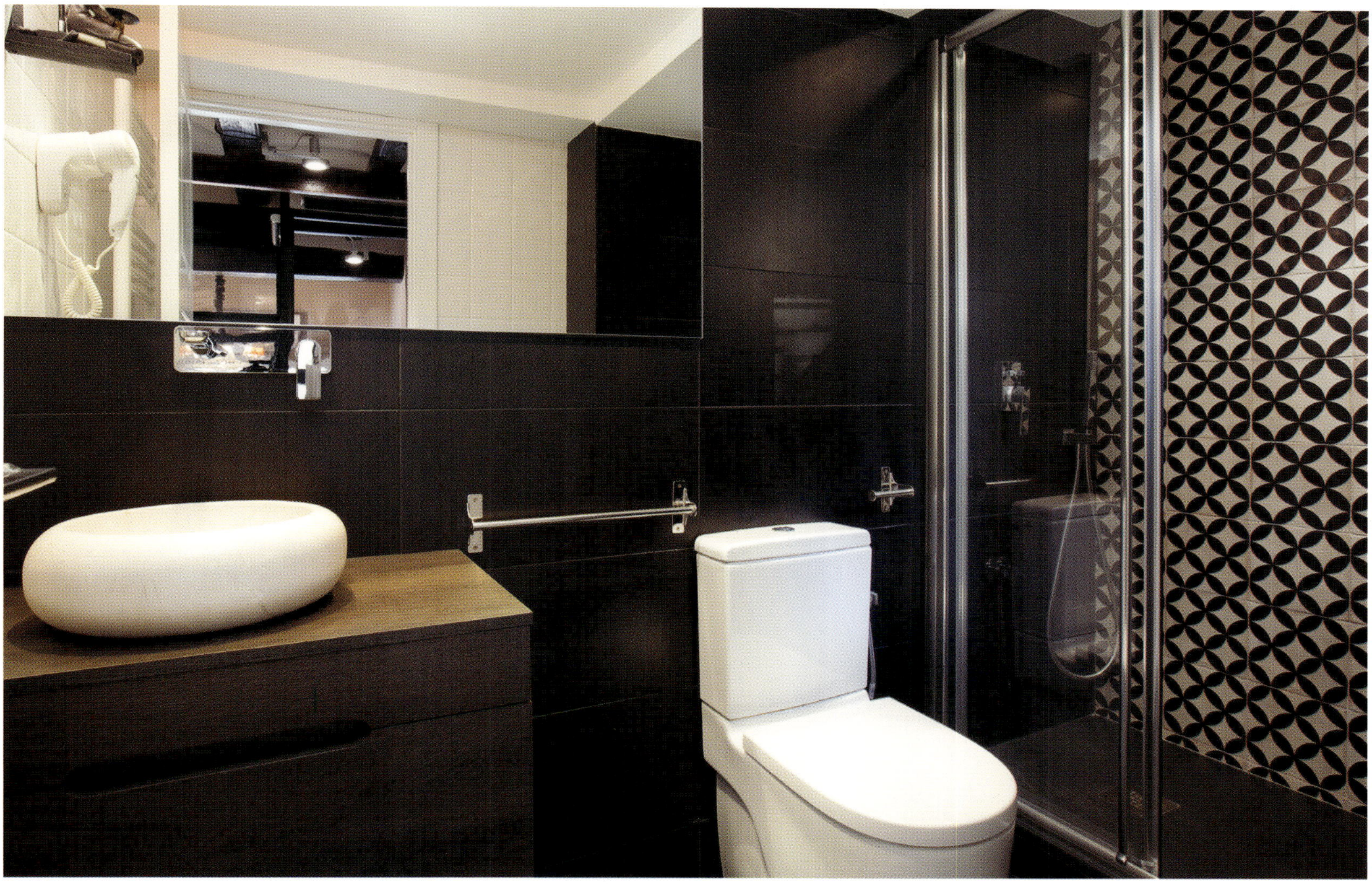

Use of a single color scheme and palette of materials lends a perceived unity to this loft, where spaces flow seamlessly. The patio door expands the bedroom and floods all the rooms with light.

Die Verwendung der gleichen Palette von Materialien sowie das gleiche Farbschema sorgt dafür, dass dieses Loft eine Einheit bildet, in der Räume nahtlos ineinander übergehen. Die Terrassentür erweitert das Schlafzimmer optisch und sorgt für Tageslicht in allen Räumen.

L'utilisation de la même palette de matériaux, ainsi que du même schéma chromatique fait que ce loft est perçu comme une unité où les espaces s'échappent sans fissure. L'ouverture sur la cour offre plus d'espace à la chambre et inonde toutes les pièces de lumière.

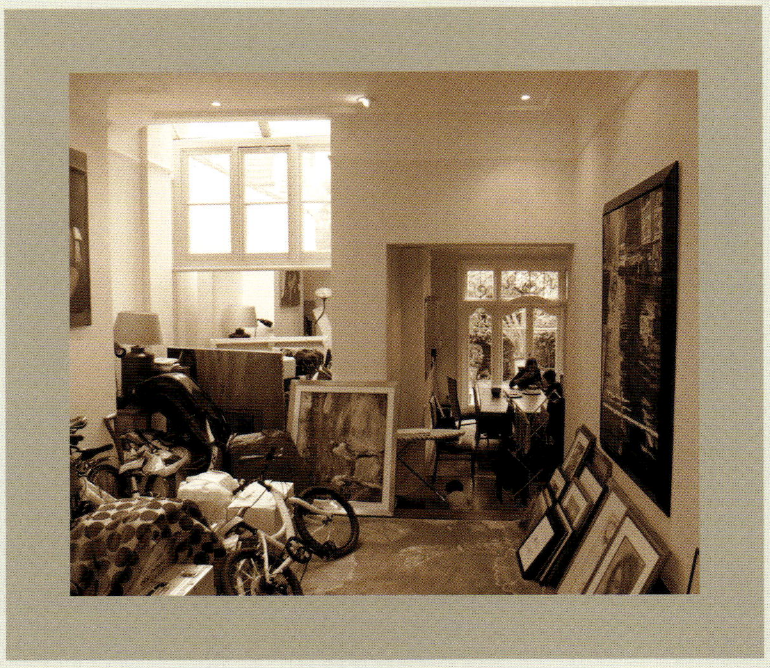

CONTEMPORARY CLASSIC

ROBERT HIRSCHFIELD ARCHITECTS

270 m^2 | 2,900 sq. ft.

London, United Kingdom

Photos © **Matt Clayton**

> Renovate and expand a mid-terraced Victorian house

> Combine classic and modern styles

> Ein viktorianisches Reihenmittelhaus renovieren und ausbauen

> Das Klassische mit dem Modernen verbinden

> Rénover et agrandir une maison mitoyenne victorienne

> Conjuguer le classique et le moderne

This project addresses the wishes of the clients, a young couple expecting a baby, who were eager to start their life as a family in a home that was dearly loved but had needed refurbishing and updating for some time. Situated within a Victorian terrace, the deep footprint meant that the house had spacious areas with various rooms and yet suffered from a lack of natural light in several areas.
The solution was to design an extension at the rear of the residence to accommodate a new kitchen/dining space that would have plenty of room and light. Both the custom woodwork and contemporary furniture have features that are classic and retro at the same time, establishing a dialog with the original Victorian-era sections of the house, demonstrating how modern touches can create a warm and light ambiance instead of the cold sensation that characterizes many of today's home renovations.

Dieses Projekt reagierte auf die Wünsche der Kunden, einer jungen Familie, die ein Kind erwartete und daher bestrebt war, das Familienleben in einem Haus zu beginnen, das sie liebten, das aber schon lange hätte renoviert und modernisiert werden müssen. Angesiedelt in einer viktorianischen Reihenhaussiedlung und aufgrund der Gebäudetiefe verfügte das Haus über eine großzügige Fläche mit mehreren Räumen, doch in einigen Bereichen fehlte es an natürlichem Licht.
Als Lösung wurde ein Anbau am rückwärtigen Teil des Hauses geplant, um einen neuen Essbereich mit einer geräumigen und hellen Küche unterzubringen. Die maßgefertigten Holzeinbauten und die zeitgenössischen Designermöbel bieten klassischen und zugleich Retro-Look und pflegen einen Dialog mit den Originalelementen, die aus der viktorianischen Zeit erhalten blieben. Dies zeigt, wie zeitgenössische Akzente anstelle der kalten Ästhetik, die heute viele der Wohnungsrenovierungen charakterisiert, eine warme und helle Atmosphäre schaffen können.

Ce projet répond aux souhaits des clients, une jeune famille qui, avec l'arrivée imminente d'un bébé, étaient anxieux de commencer la vie de famille dans un foyer très désiré, mais qui nécessitait depuis quelque temps des travaux et une remise au goût du jour. Située sur une « terrasse » victorienne, la profonde empreinte signifiait que la maison avait une généreuse superficie avec plusieurs chambres, mais dont certains espaces manquaient de lumière naturelle.
Comme solution, les clients se sont vu proposer d'agrandir la partie arrière de la maison afin de créer un nouvel espace salle à manger-cuisine, vaste et lumineux. La menuiserie sur mesure et les meubles au design contemporain partagent un aspect à la fois classique et rétro et conservent un lien avec les parties d'origine de l'époque victorienne, soulignant la manière avec laquelle les touches contemporaines peuvent créer une ambiance chaleureuse et légère dans un lieu à l'esthétique froide, caractéristique de nombreuses rénovations résidentielles.

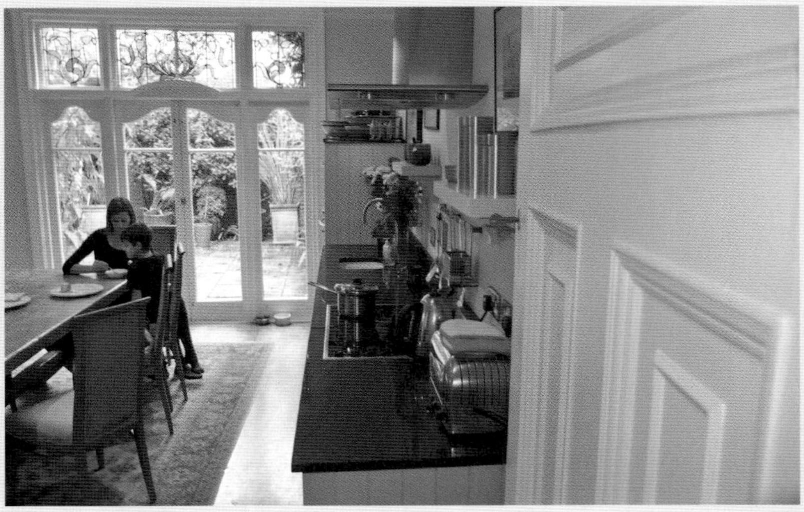
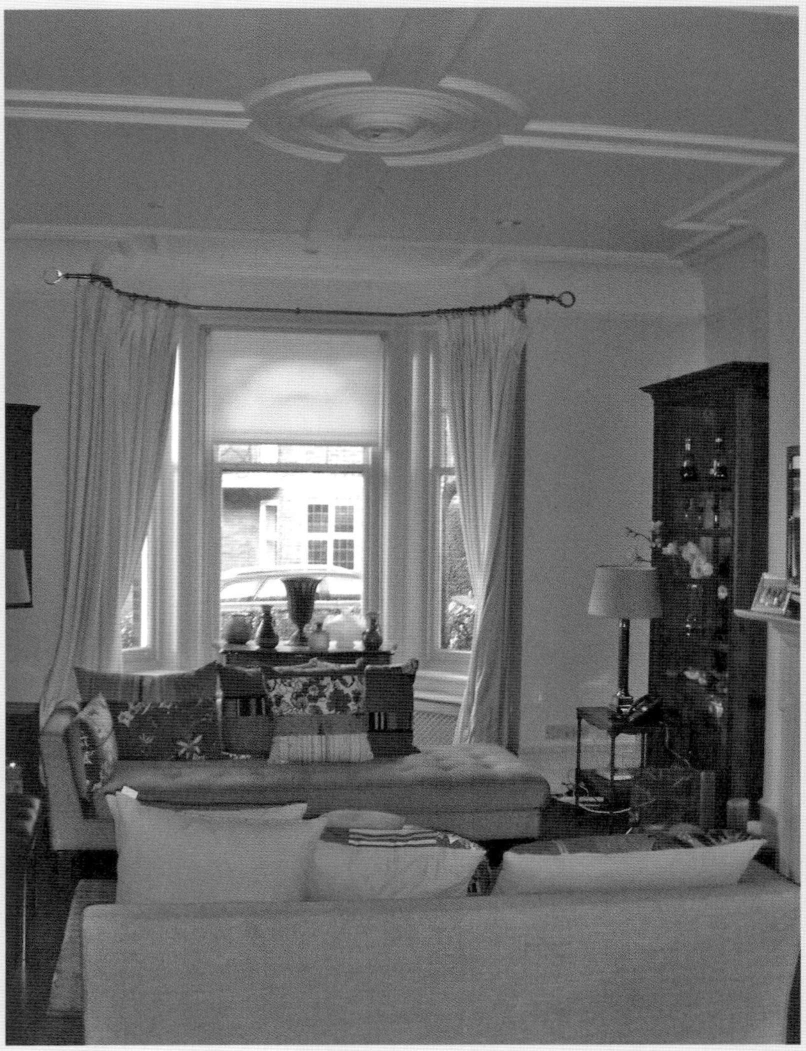
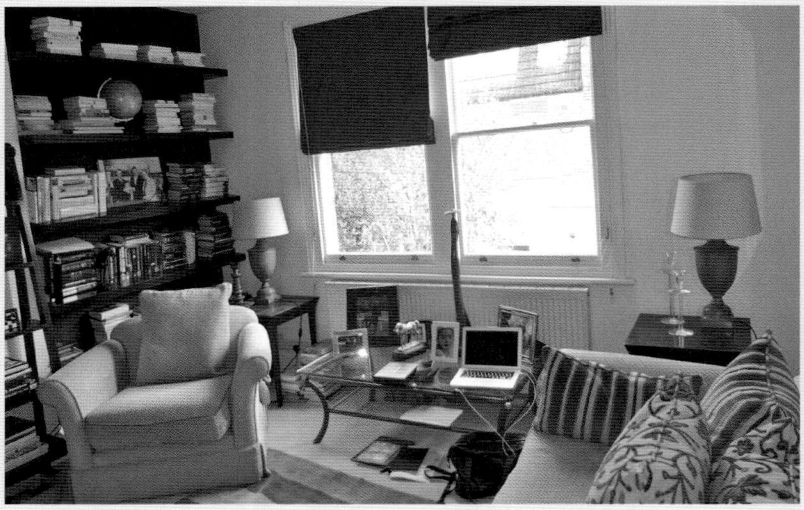
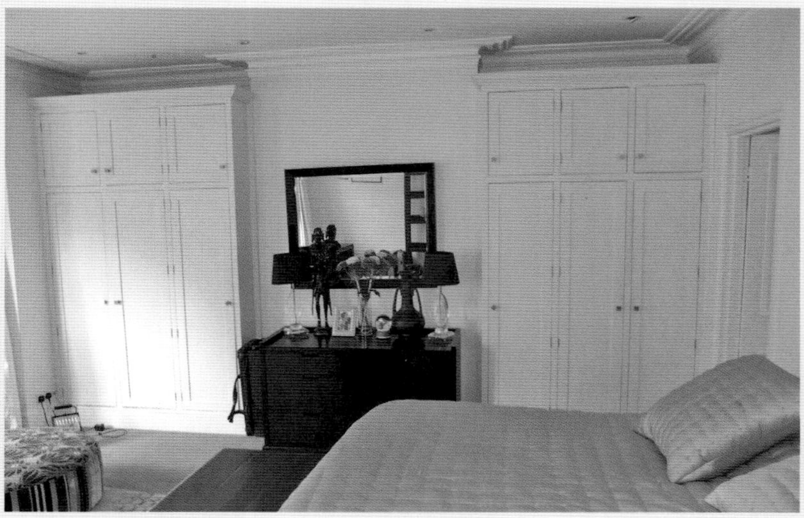
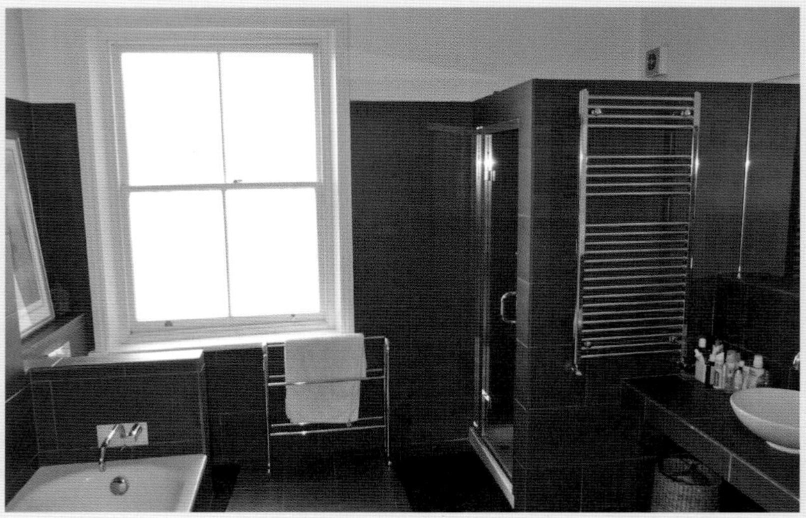

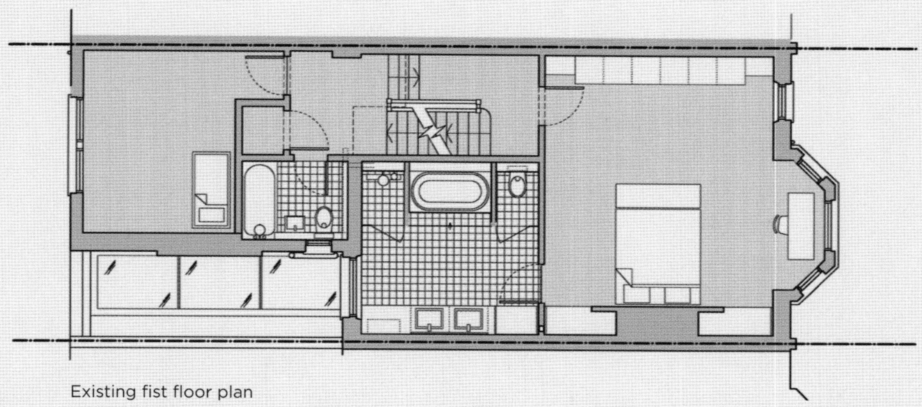

Existing fist floor plan

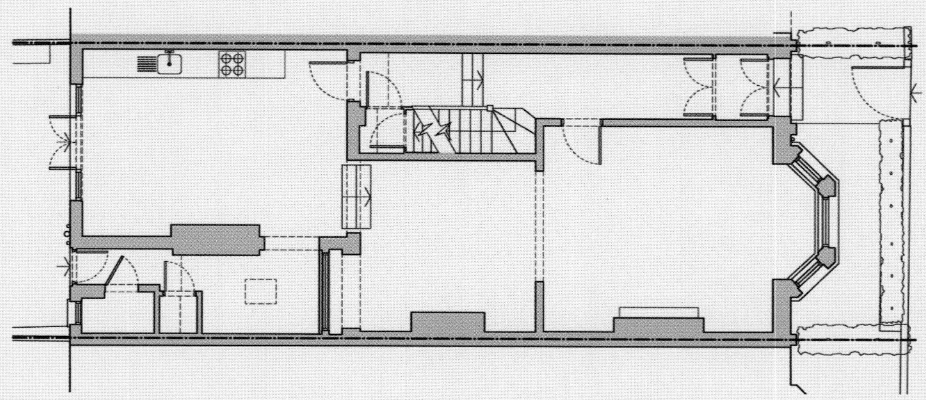

Existing ground floor plan

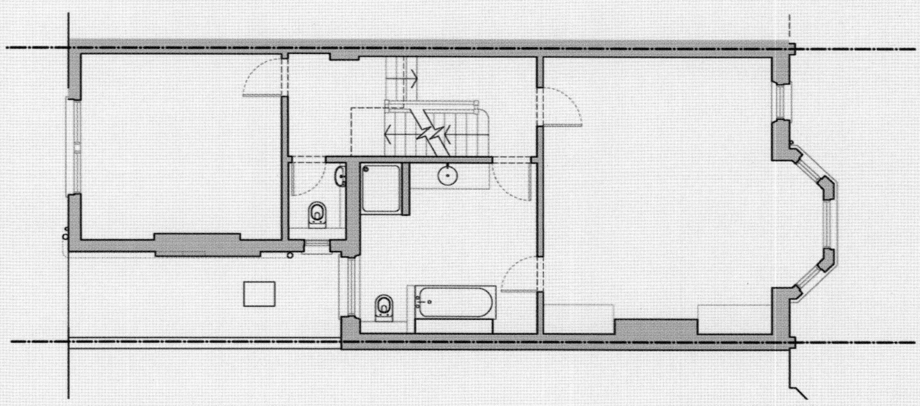

New first floor plan

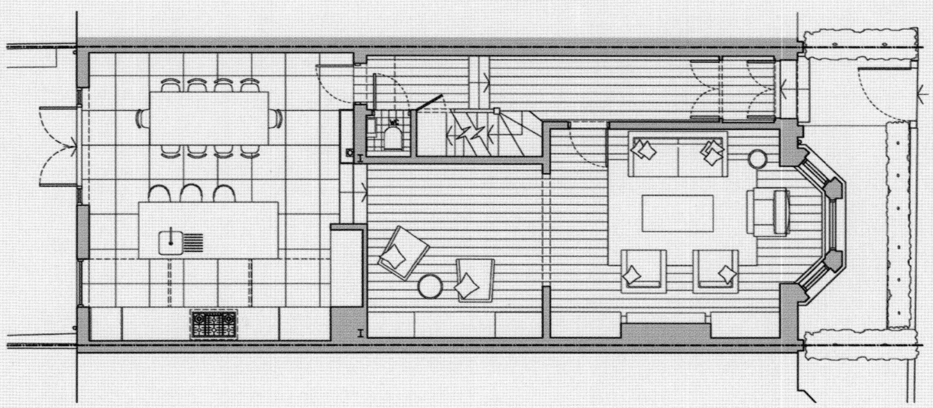

New ground floor plan

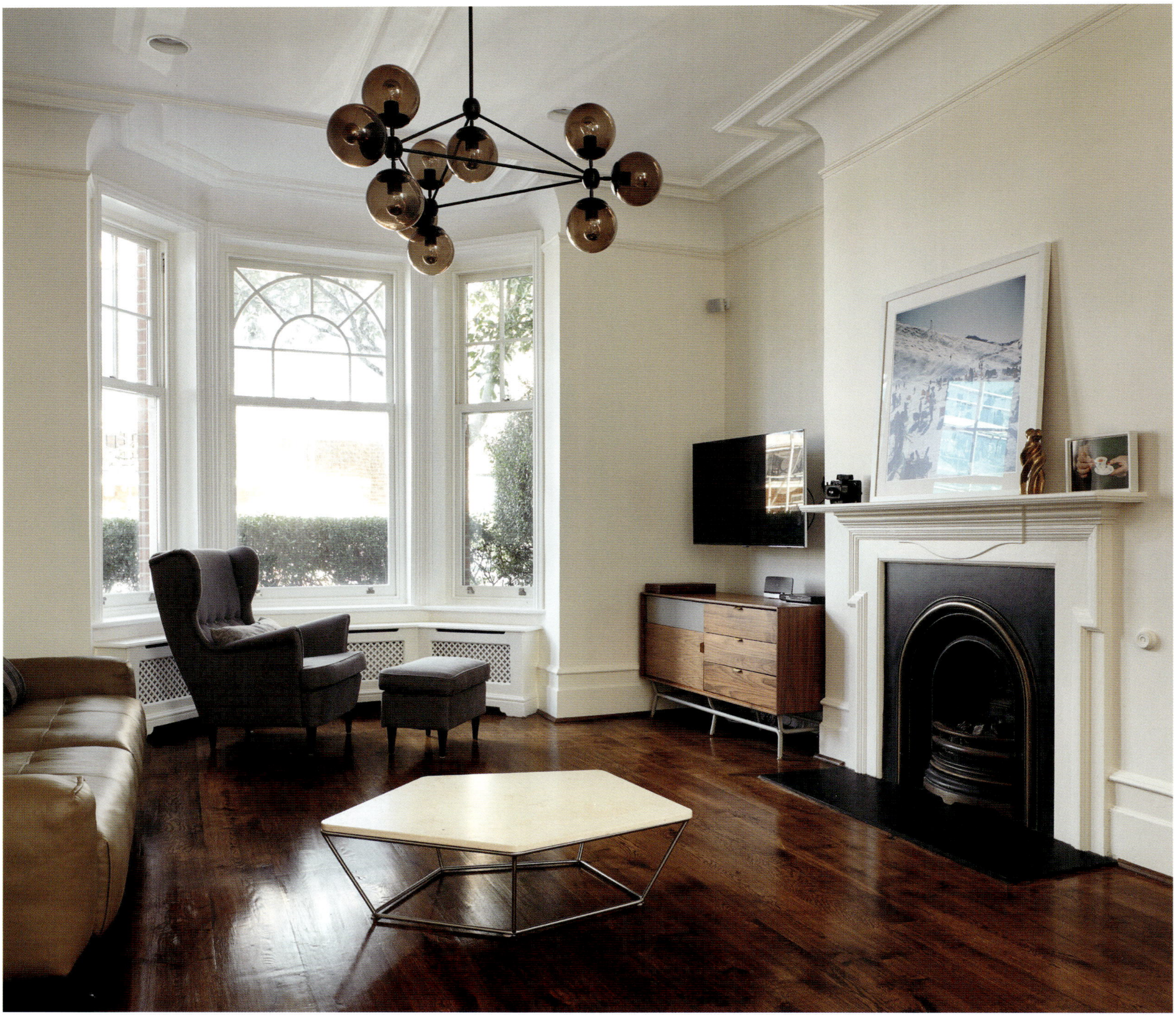

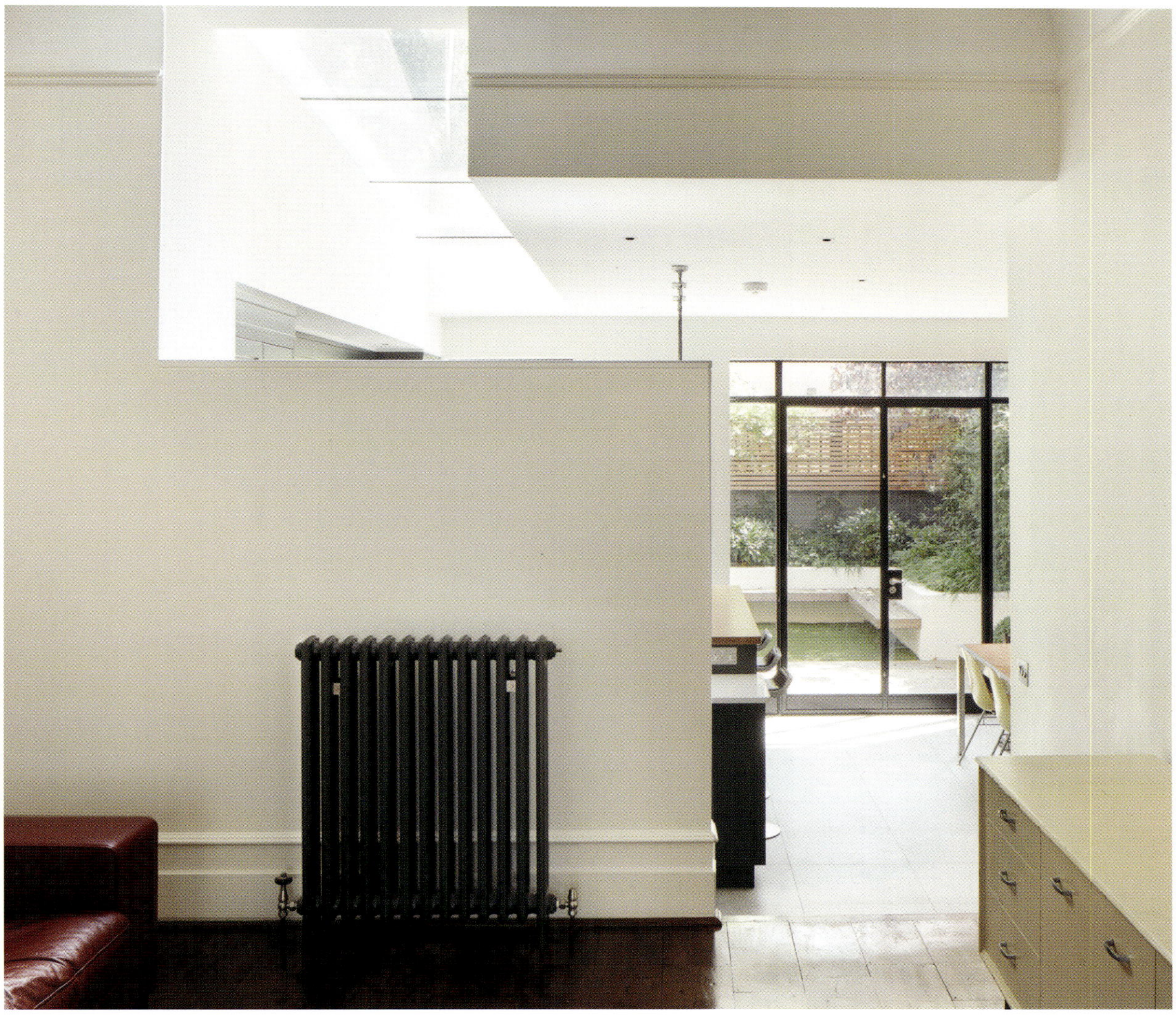

The kitchen island has three functions: work area, storage space, and counter for serving breakfast or an informal meal. Moreover, it acts to separate the kitchen from the dining area and invites social interactions across the two areas.

Die Kücheninsel hat eine dreifache Funktion: Arbeitsbereich, Stauraum und eine Theke, um ein Frühstück oder ein zwangloses Essen zu genießen. Sie dient zudem zur Trennung von Küche und Essbereich und begünstigt die Verbindung und Interaktion zwischen den beiden Räumen.

L'îlot de la cuisine a une triple fonction : espace de travail, rangements et bar pour prendre son petit-déjeuner ou un repas informel. Il sert aussi de séparation entre la cuisine et la salle à manger tout en favorisant la vie sociale et l'interaction entre les deux.

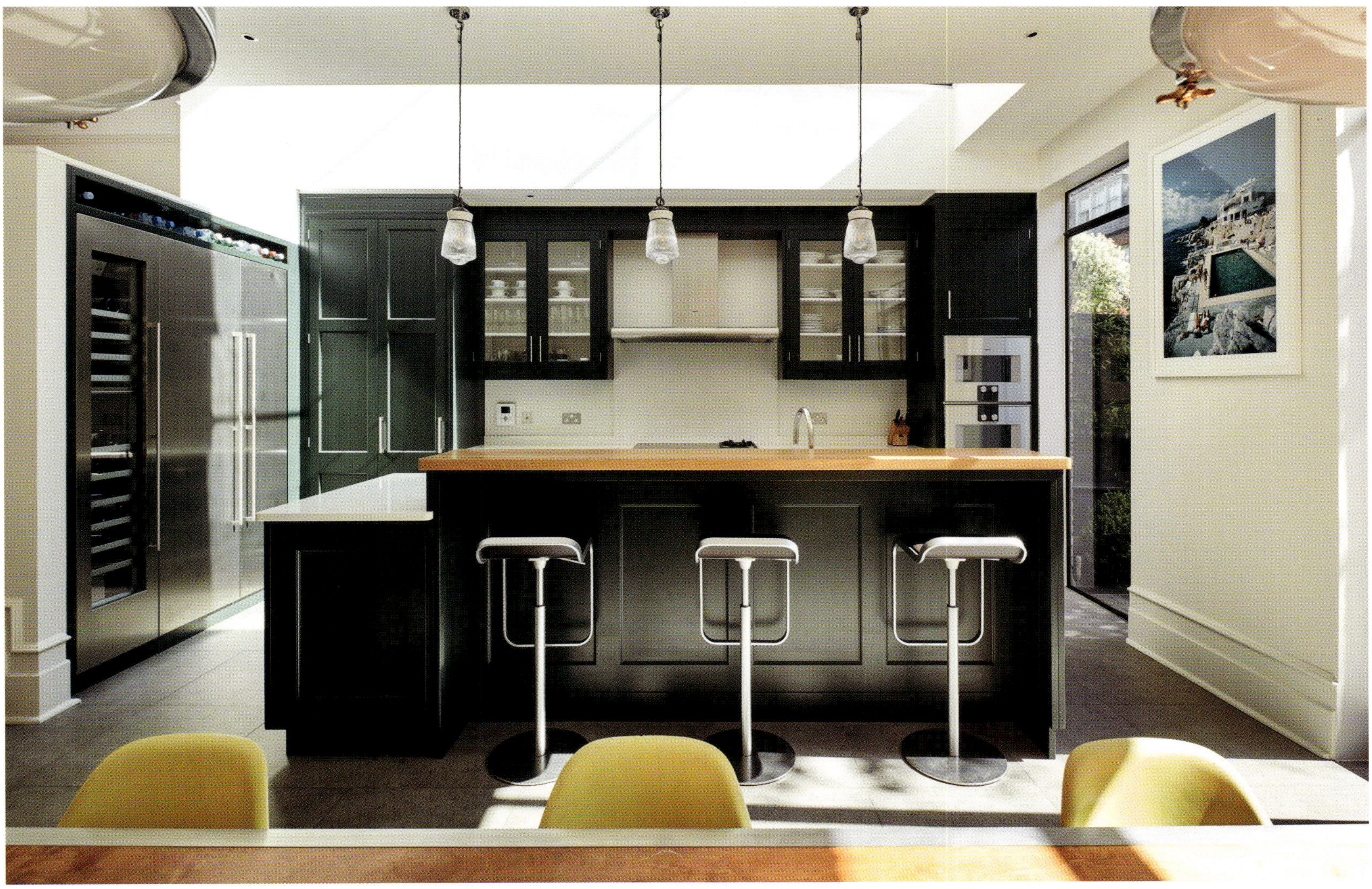

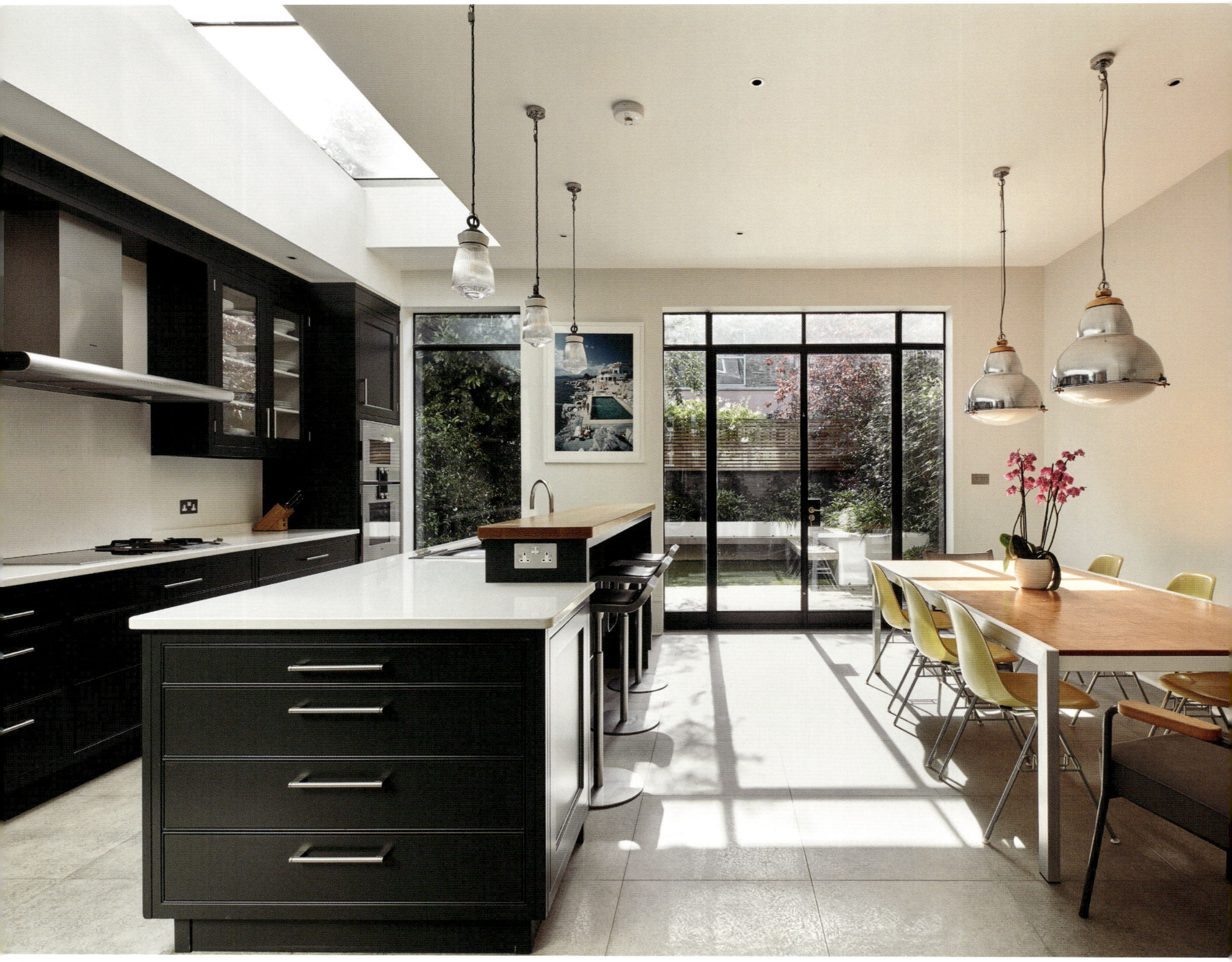

Penetrating the skylight and the glass windows and doors, the light floods the kitchen and dining area and extends to all parts of the ground floor. The skylight has been strategically positioned where it is most needed: in the work area of the kitchen.

Dank des Oberlichts und der Glaswände durchflutet das Licht Küche und Esszimmer sowie alle Räume im Erdgeschoss. Das Oberlicht wurde strategisch sinnvoll im Arbeitsbereich der Küche platziert, wo es am meisten benötigt wird.

La lumière inonde la cuisine et la salle à manger grâce à la verrière et aux cloisons vitrées et s'échappe à travers toutes les pièces du rez-de-chaussée. La verrière a été placée de manière stratégique là où elle sert le plus, dans l'espace de travail de la cuisine.

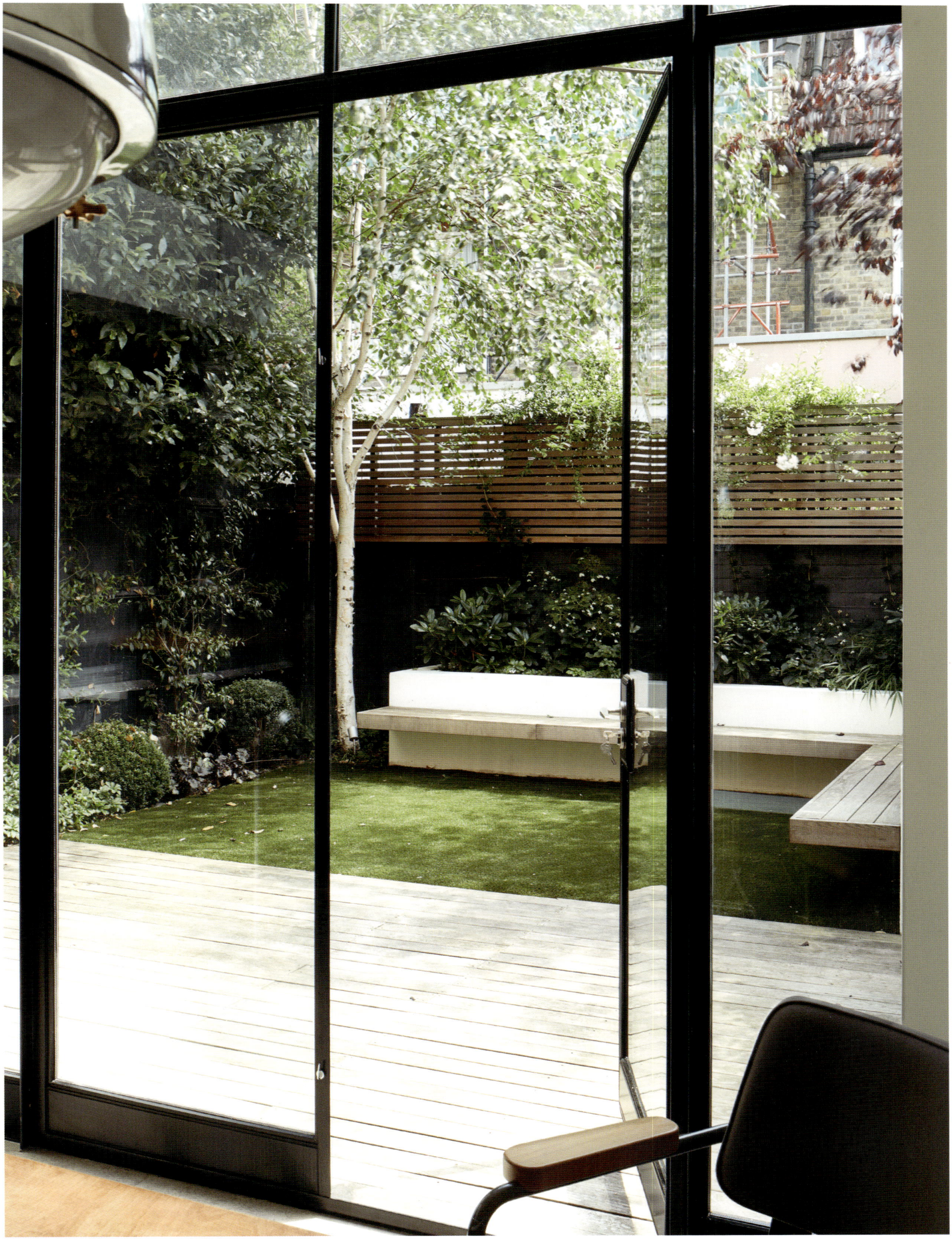

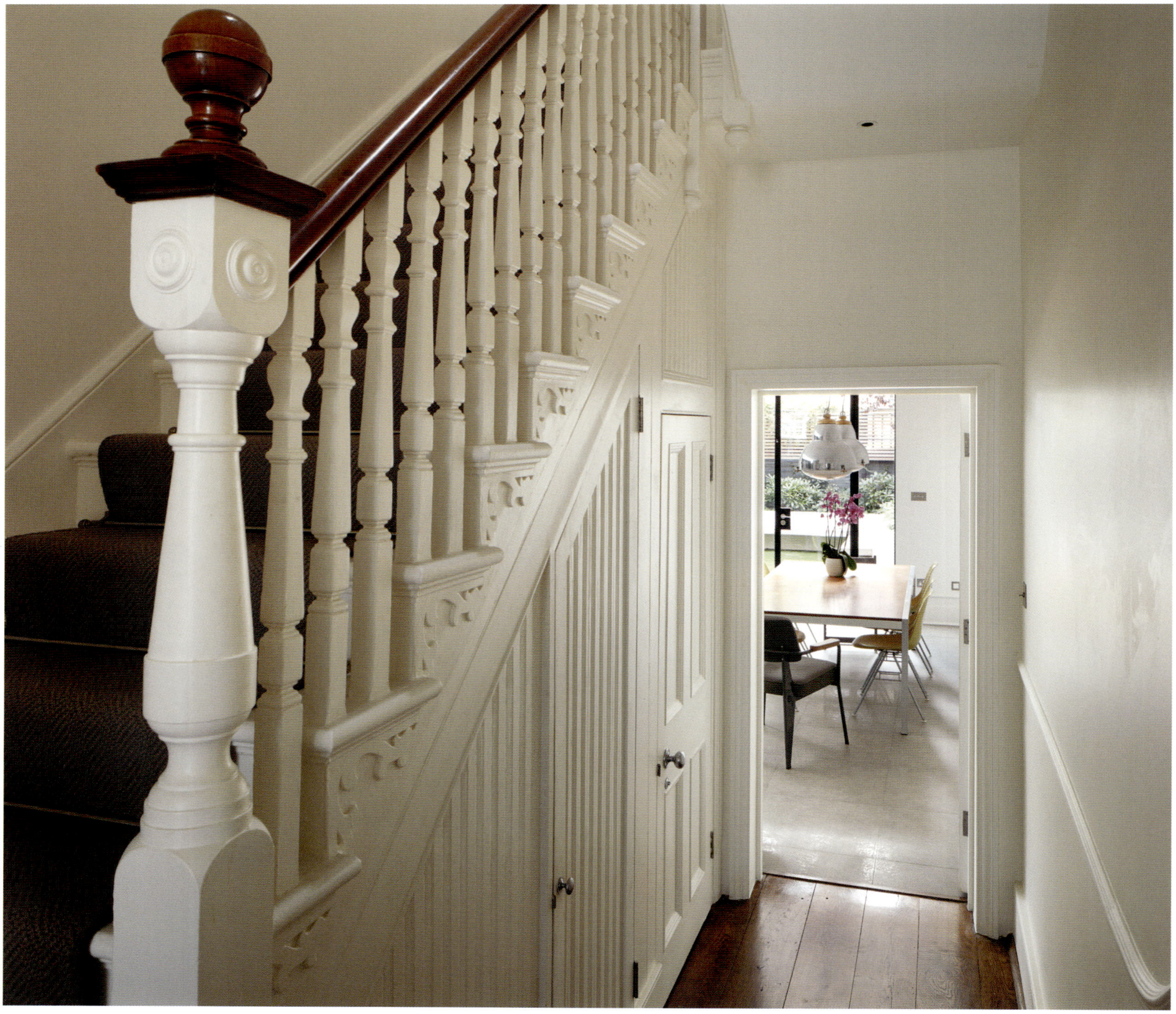

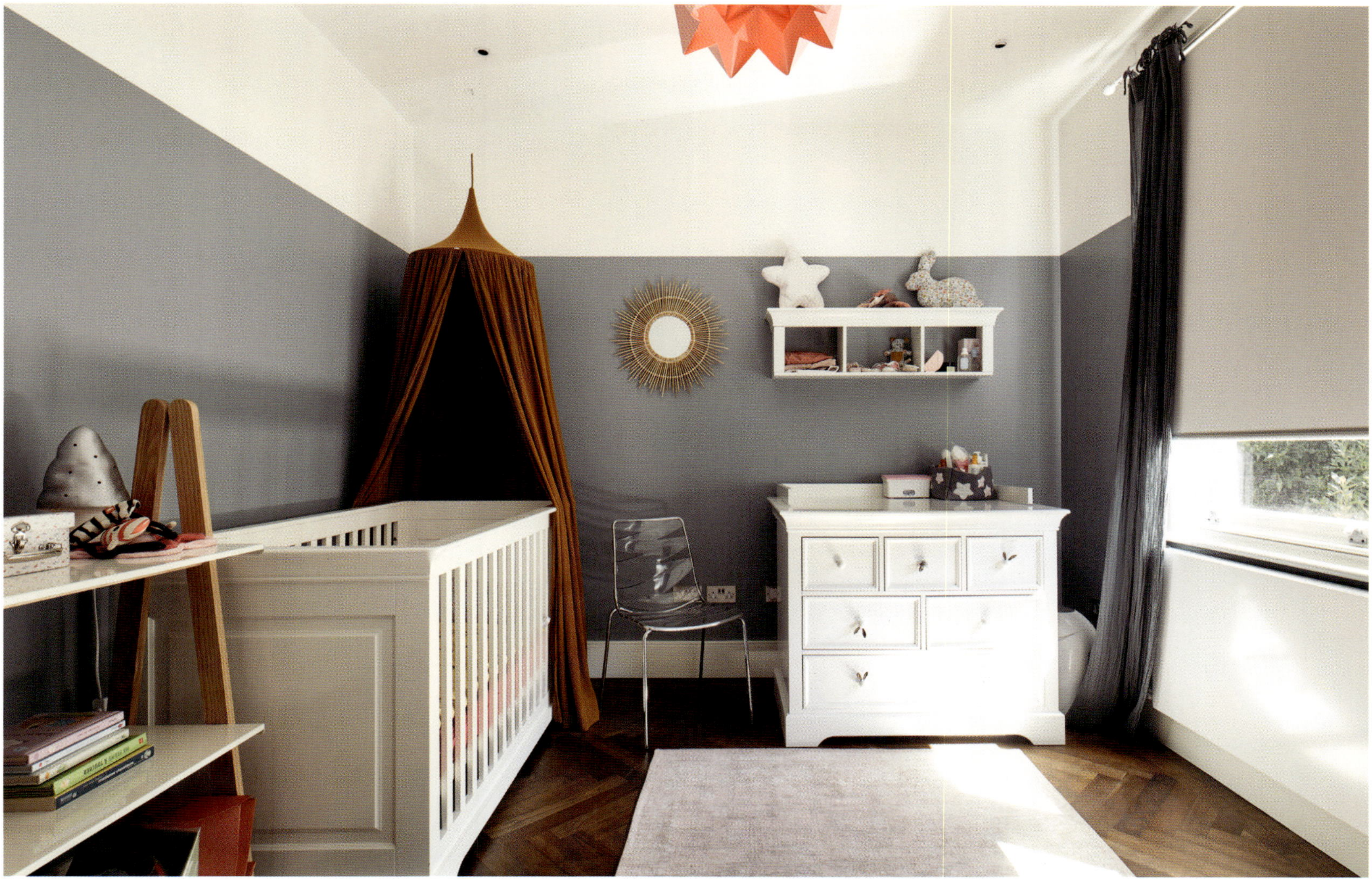

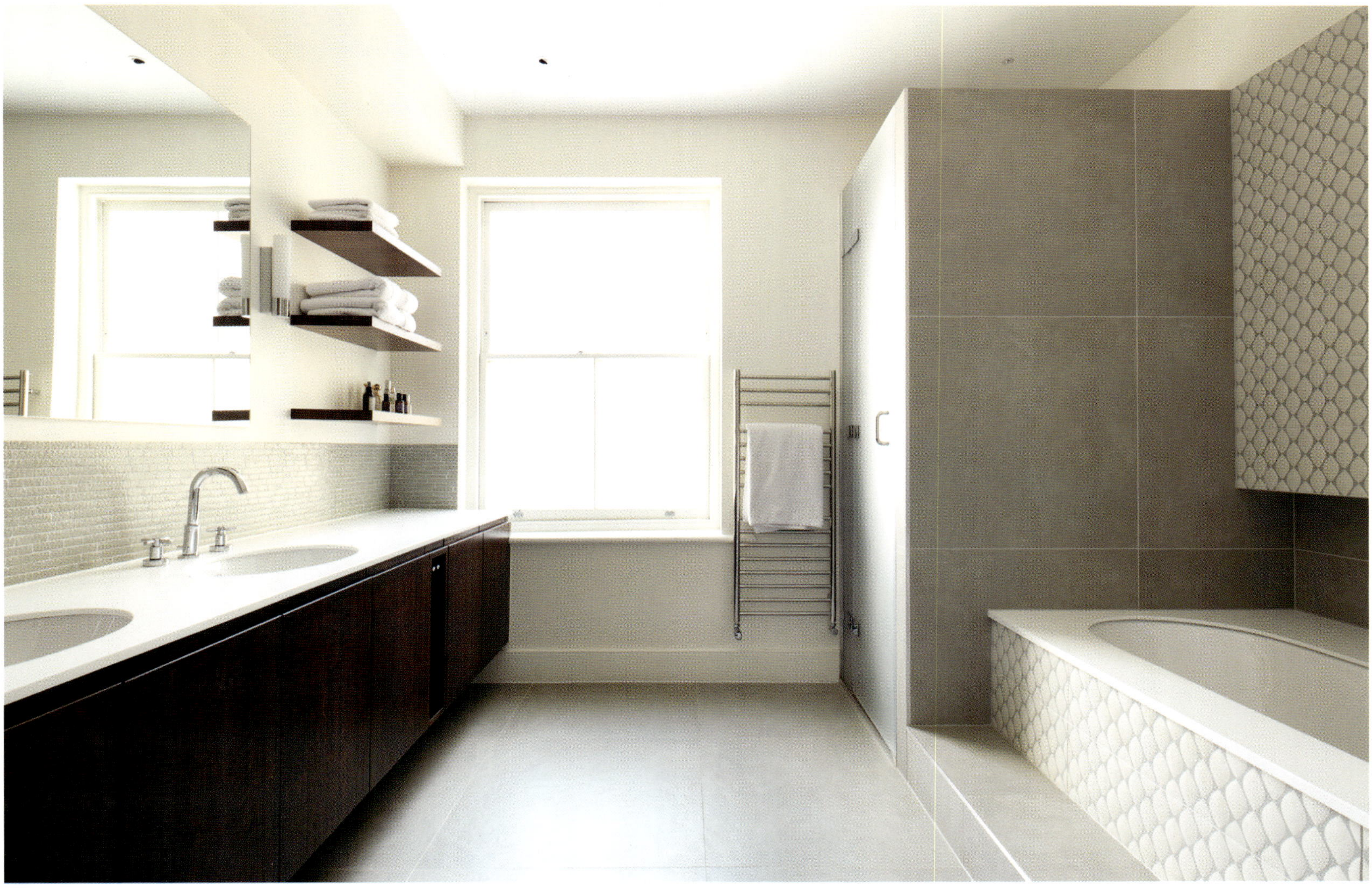

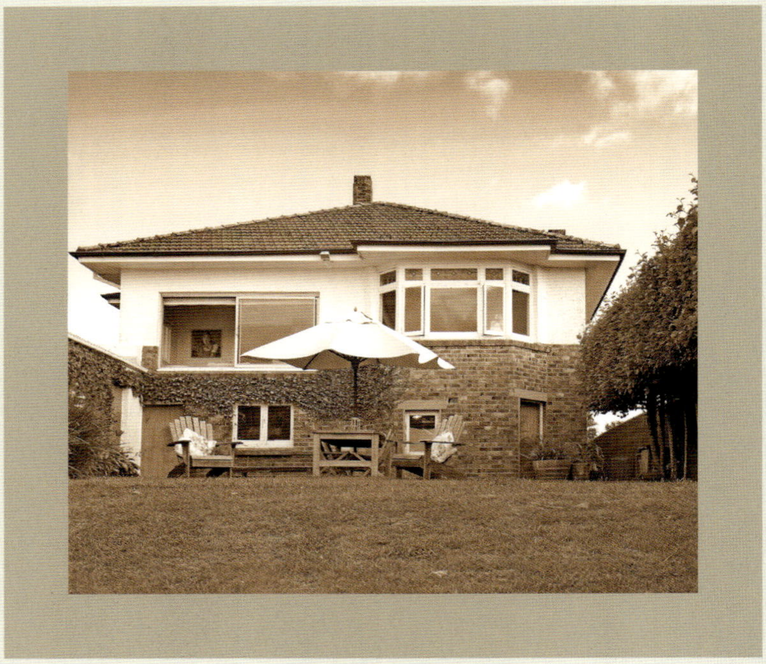

WINSOMERE CRESCENT

DORRINGTON ATCHESON ARCHITECTS

400 m² | 4,305 sq. ft.

Auckland, New Zealand

Photos © **Emma-Jane Hetherington**

> Renovate the residence while preserving as many original elements as possible

> Maximize views

> Renovierung des Hauses unter Beibehaltung möglichst vieler ursprünglicher Elemente

> Maximieren des Ausblicks

> Rénover la maison tout en conservant, dans la mesure du possible, ses éléments d'origine

> Maximiser les vues

This house, situated within an idyllic seaside enclave, combines the enchantment of the original residence with the design of a new addition that permits the enjoyment of impressive views.
The structure was once a double-skin brick bungalow with virtually no beach access and rooms that were small and dark. The new owners liked the traditional feel of the original house but wanted to take full advantage of the sun and views. As they had a philosophical preference for renovation over new construction, the design focused on blending old and new structures.
The house consists formally of two original blocks and two new ones. These are united by the entrance, vestibule, and staircase. The original blocks house two bedrooms, an office, and an original art deco bathroom. One new block contains the zinc-clad living areas, while the other accommodates a master bedroom paneled by a cedar screen. Beneath these spaces is a lower level containing a guest bedroom, bathroom, laundry area, and audio-visual room.

Dieses Haus befindet sich in einem idyllischen Örtchen am Meer und vereint den Charme des ursprünglichen Gebäudes mit dem neu entworfenen Anbau, der eindrucksvolle Ausblicke ermöglicht.
Bei dem ursprünglichen Haus handelte es sich um einen doppelwandigen Bungalow aus Ziegeln mit kleinen, dunklen Zimmern und wenig Verbindungen zum Strand. Den neuen Eigentümern gefiel das traditionelle Aussehen des bestehenden Hauses, sie wollten jedoch den Einfall der Sonne und die Ausblicke so gut wie möglich nutzen. Die Philosophie hinter dem Umbau bestand in einer Renovierung, nicht in einer komplett neuen Konstruktion, und infolgedessen lag der Fokus des Entwurfes auf einer Verschmelzung von alten und neuen Strukturen.
Formal gesehen besteht das Haus aus den zwei ursprünglichen Blöcken und zwei neuen Blöcken, die durch den Eingangsbereich, die Halle und die Treppen geeint werden. In den bestehenden Blöcken liegen zwei Schlafzimmer, ein Büro und das ursprüngliche Bad im Stil des Art déco. Der Anbau beherbergt den Wohnbereich in einem Block, der mit Zink verkleidet ist, und das Hauptschlafzimmer in einem anderen Block, dessen Außenseite mit Zedernholz verschalt wurde. Diese Blöcke sitzen auf einem darunter liegenden Geschoss wie auf einer Art Fundament, in dem ein Zimmer für Gäste, ein Bad, eine Waschküche und ein Medienraum untergebracht wurden.
Durch die Kombination aus Tradition und Moderne erschuf man einen einzigartigen und besonderen Raum, in dem man den Himmel und das Meer betrachten und Sonnenauf- und Sonnenuntergänge genießen kann.

Dans une enclave idyllique face à la mer se trouve cette maison qui allie à la fois l'enchantement de la maison d'origine et le design de la nouvelle extension qui permet de profiter de la magnifique vue.
La maison d'origine était un bungalow en brique à double muret avec des chambres petites et sombres, et peu accessible à la plage. Ce qui a plu aux nouveaux propriétaires, c'est l'air traditionnel de la maison existante dans laquelle ils souhaitaient tirer le meilleur profit du soleil et de la vue. La préférence a été donnée à la rénovation plutôt qu'à une reconstruction. Par conséquent, l'approche de la conception s'est focalisée sur un amalgame des structures, anciennes et nouvelles.
La maison est composée de deux blocs originaux et de deux nouveaux, réunis au niveau de l'entrée, du hall et des escaliers. Les blocs d'origine comprennent deux chambres, un bureau et une salle de bains originale de style Art déco. Les nouveaux blocs comprennent le séjour, dans un bloc recouvert de zinc, et la chambre parentale dans un bloc recouvert d'un pan en cèdre. Ils reposent sur une base inférieure qui accueille une chambre d'amis, une salle de bains, une buanderie et une salle TV.
Le mélange du traditionnel et du moderne a donné lieu à un espace unique et singulier où il est possible d'admirer le ciel et la mer se confondre à l'aube et au coucher de soleil.

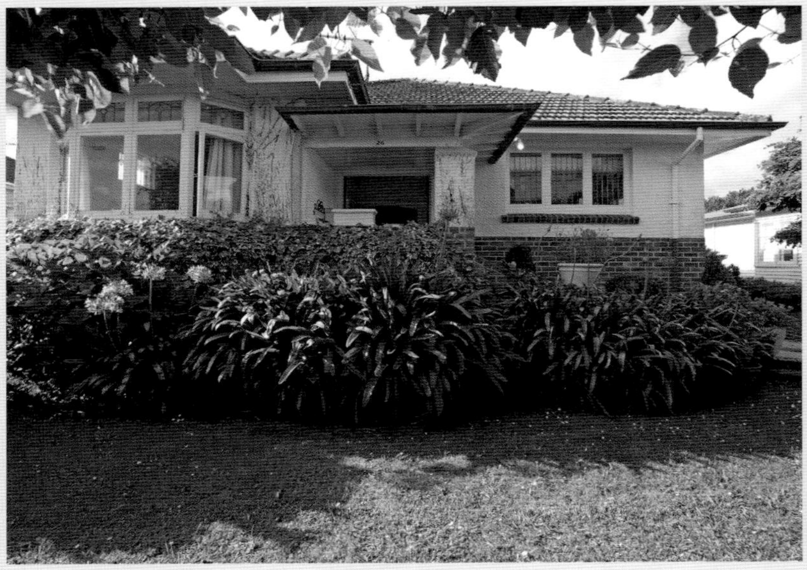
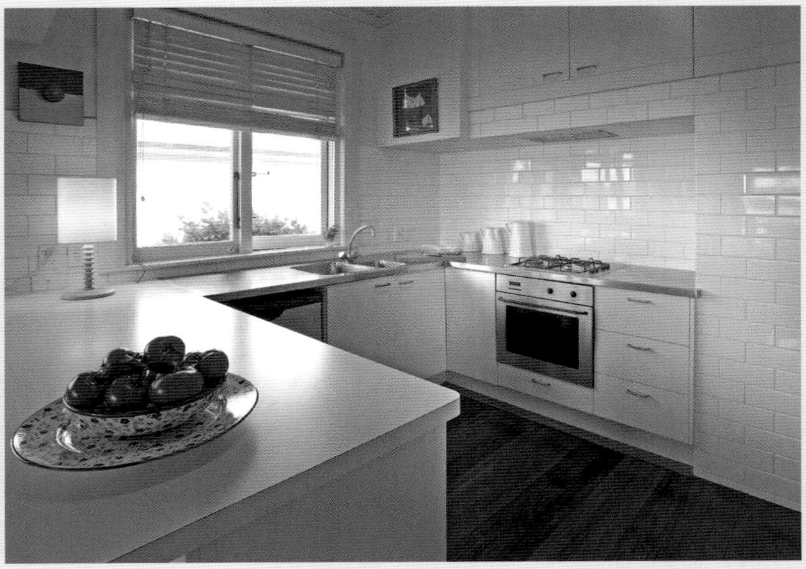
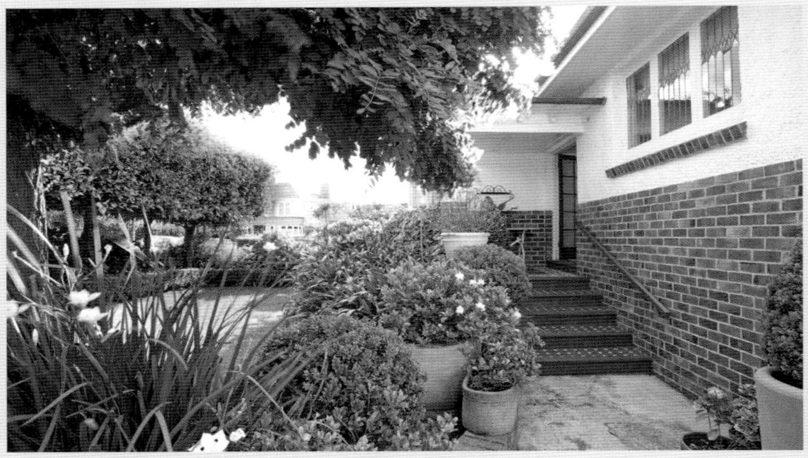
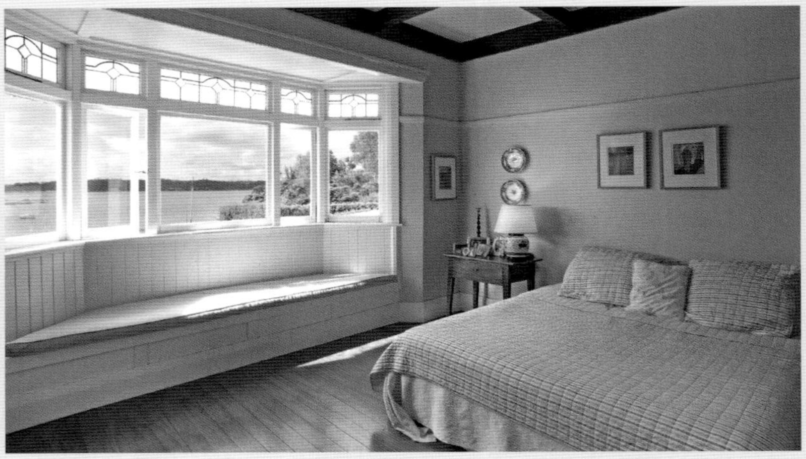
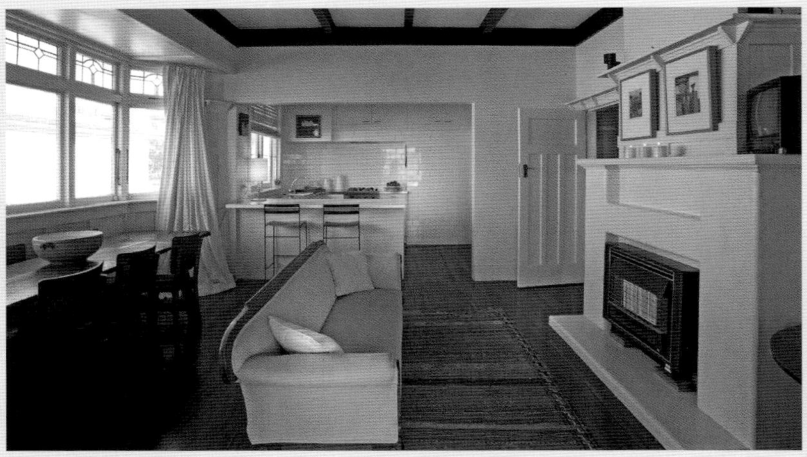
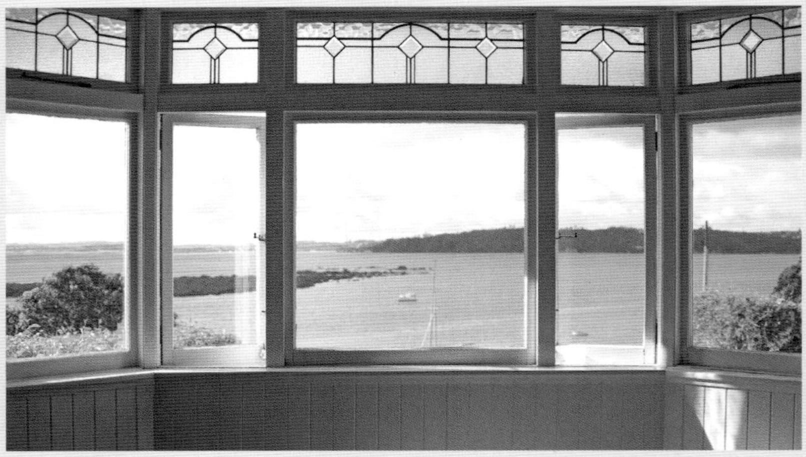
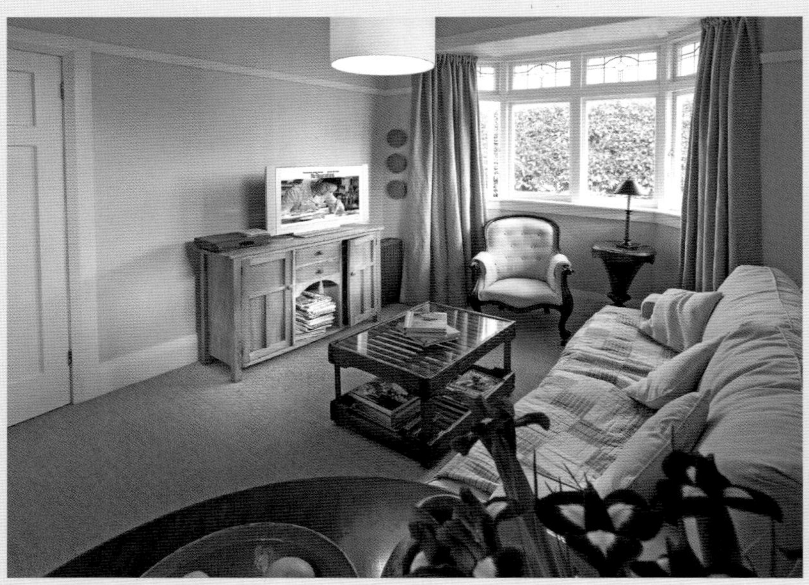
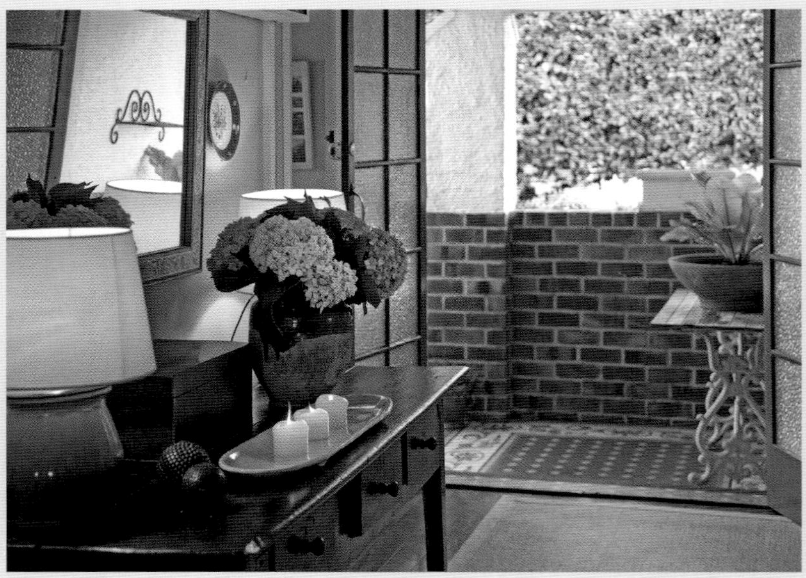

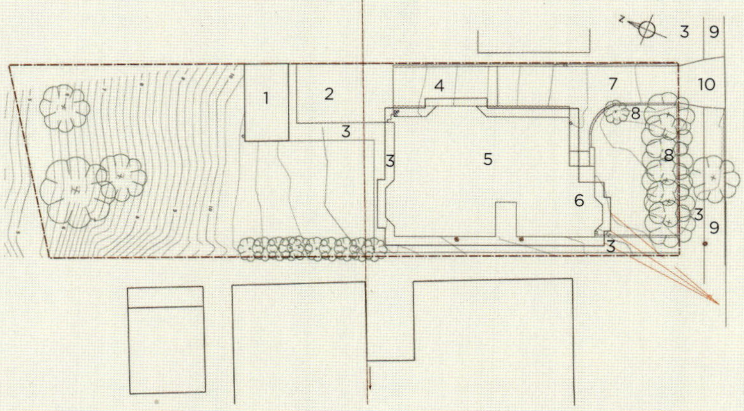

Existing site and roof plan

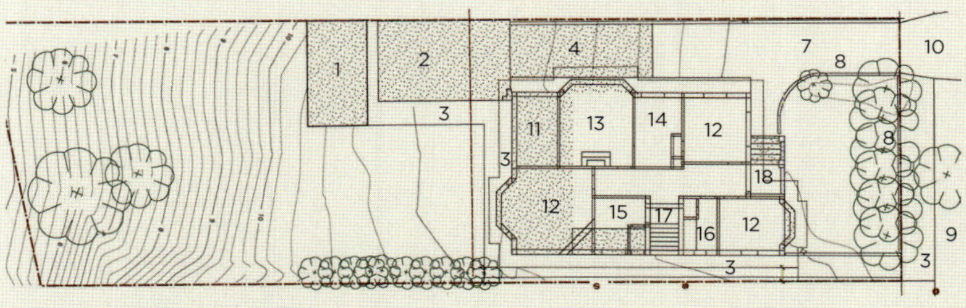

Existing top floor plan

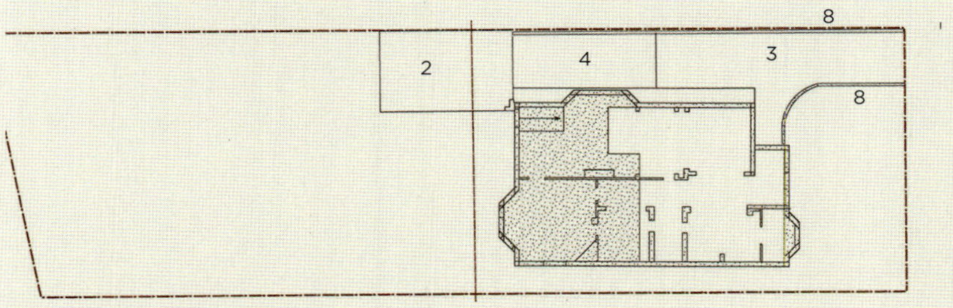

Existing basement floor plan

1. Enclosed veranda
2. Garage
3. Concrete path
4. Carport
5. Existing house
6. Porch
7. Concrete drive
8. Brick wall
9. Grass berm
10. Vehicle crossing
11. Sun room
12. Bedroom
13. Lounge
14. Kitchen
15. Laundry
16. Bathroom
17. Stairs
18. Entry porch

To be removed

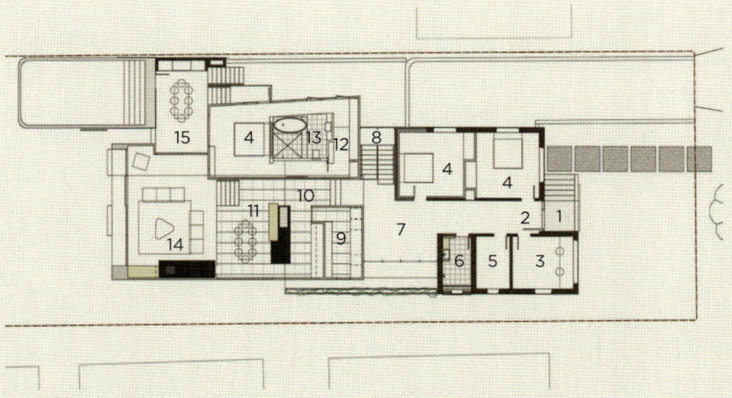

New top floor plan

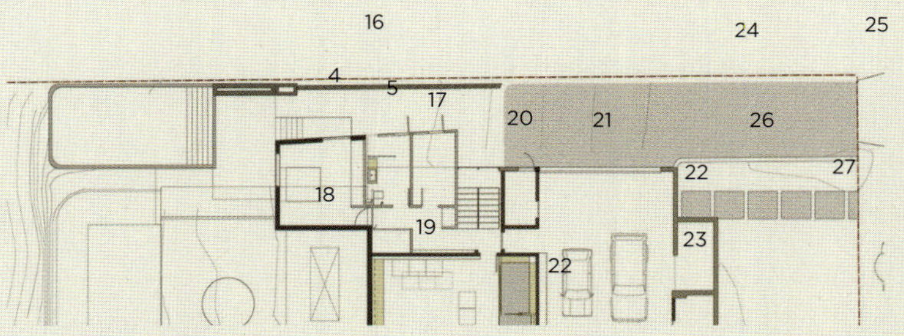

New basement floor plan

1. Porch
2. Entry
3. Bedroom / study
4. Bedroom
5. Bathroom
6. Powder room
7. Light well
8. Stairs
9. Butlers' kitchen
10. Kitchen
11. Dining room
12. Dressing room
13. En suite bathroom
14. Lounge
15. Barbeque / fire / pool deck
16. Service / dog area
17. Laundry
18. Stormwater detention tank
19. Media room
20. Bikes
21. Garage
22. Storage
23. Trash
24. Concrete drive
25. Driveway access
26. Entry path
27. Brick wall

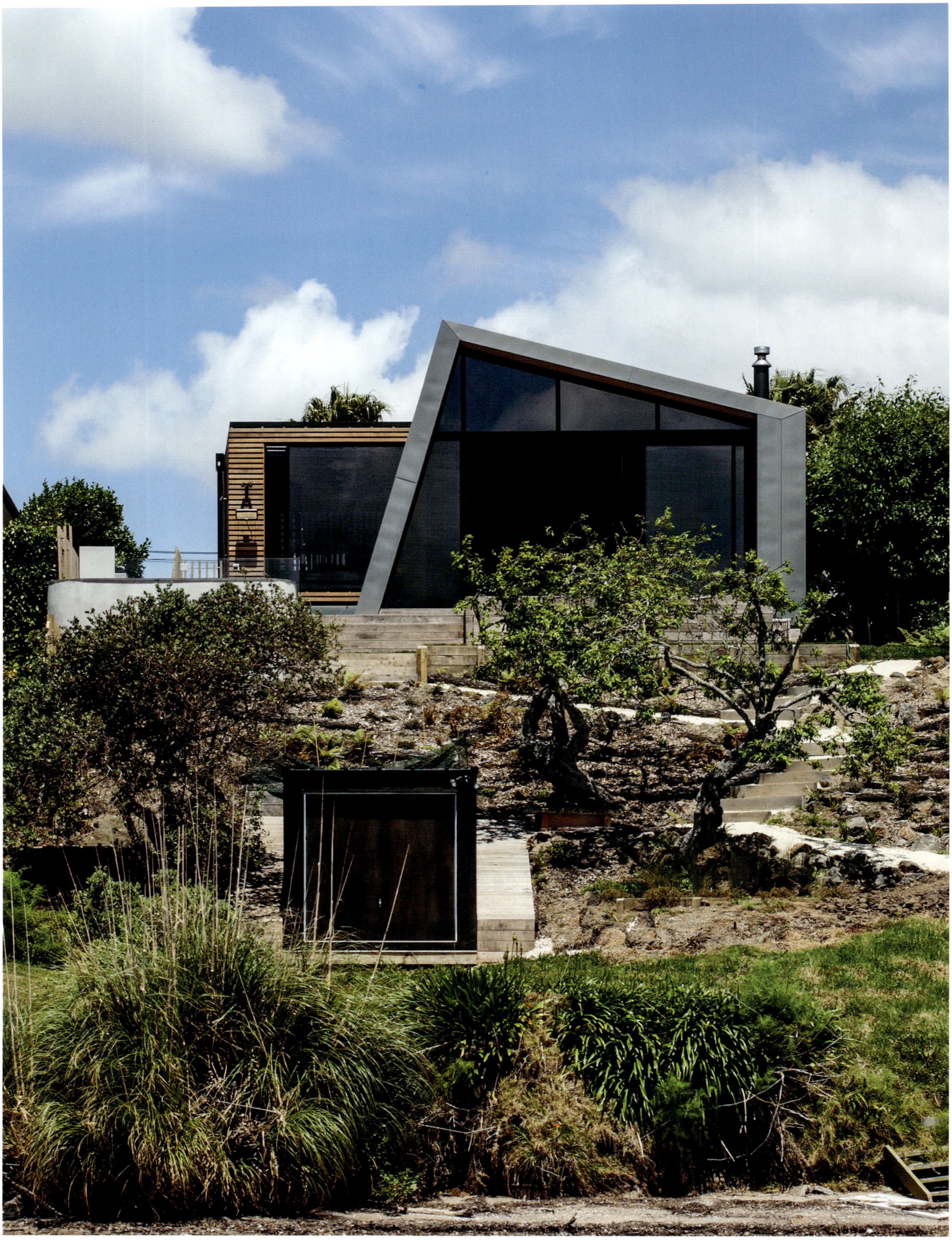

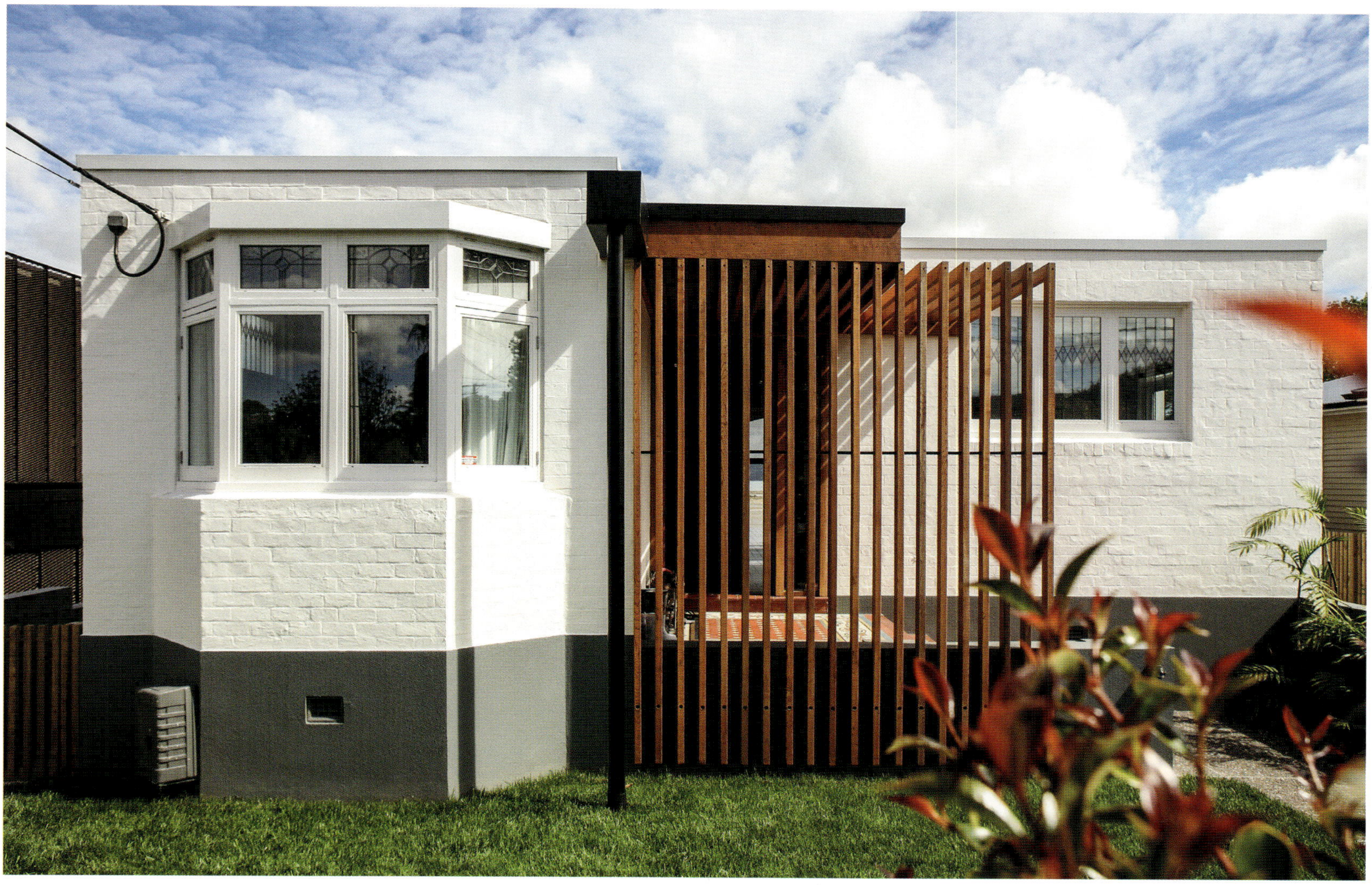

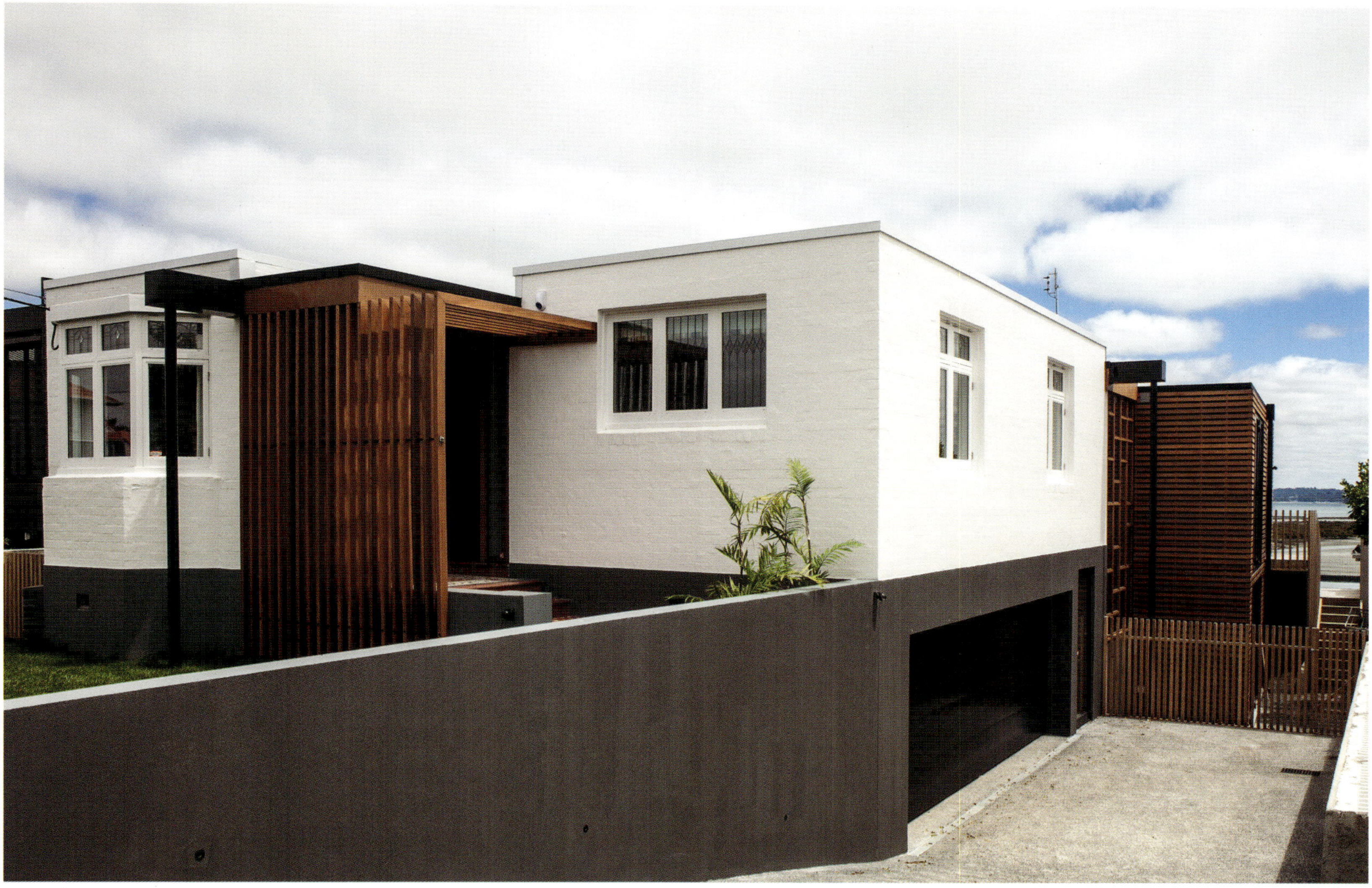

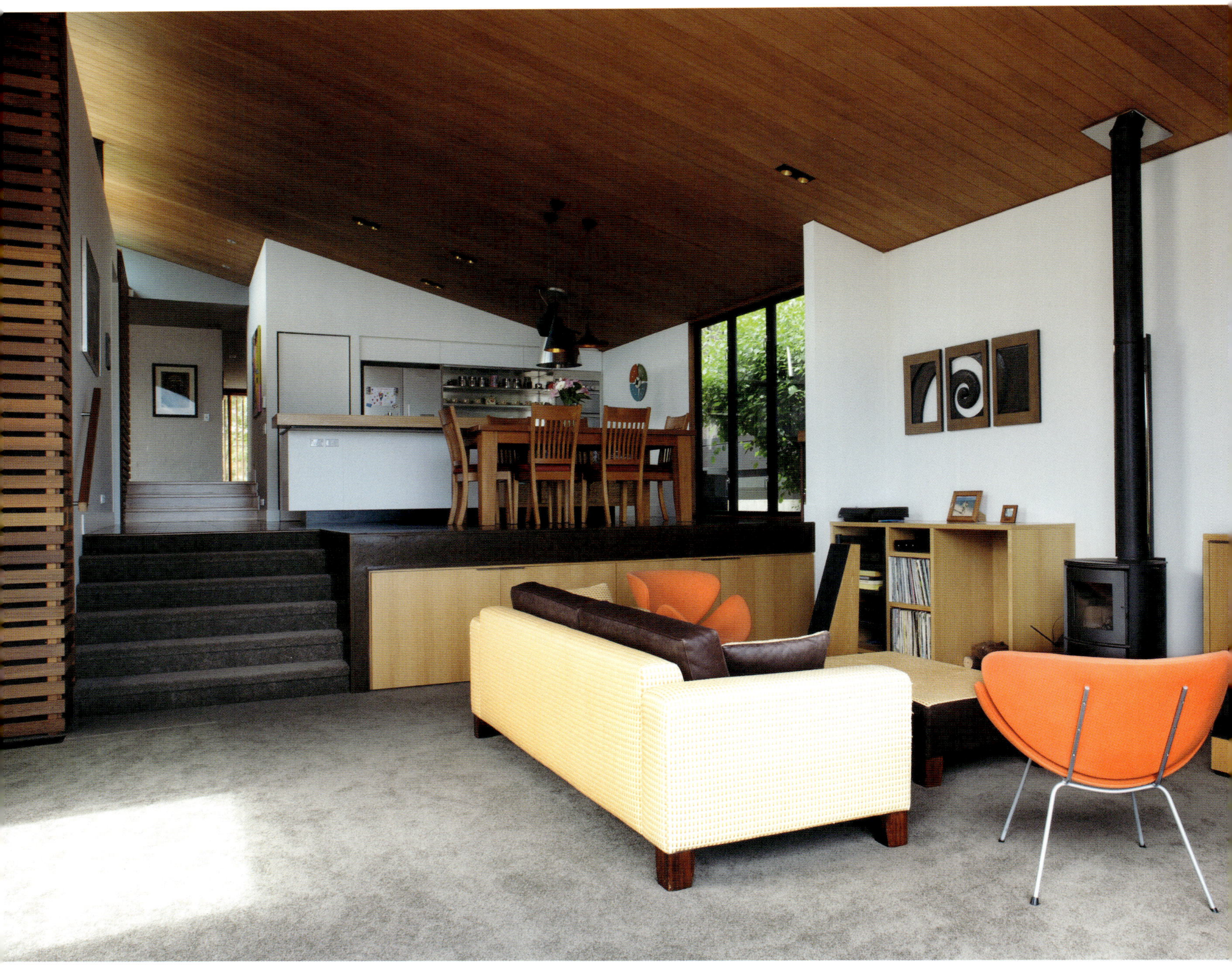

The different levels serve to separate the environments. The living room is separated from the kitchen and dining room without losing either the visual connection between these areas or the sense of openness and spatial continuity.

Der Unterschied in der Höhe der Stockwerke dient als trennendes Element der einzelnen Bereiche. Das Wohnzimmer bleibt getrennt von der Küche und dem Esszimmer, die visuelle Verbindung zwischen beiden Bereichen geht jedoch nicht verloren, und auch der Eindruck von räumlicher Weite und Kontinuität bleibt bestehen.

La différence de niveau permet de séparer les espaces. Le séjour est séparé de la cuisine et de la salle à manger sans pour autant perdre la connexion visuelle entre les deux, ni la sensation de grandeur et de continuité spatiale.

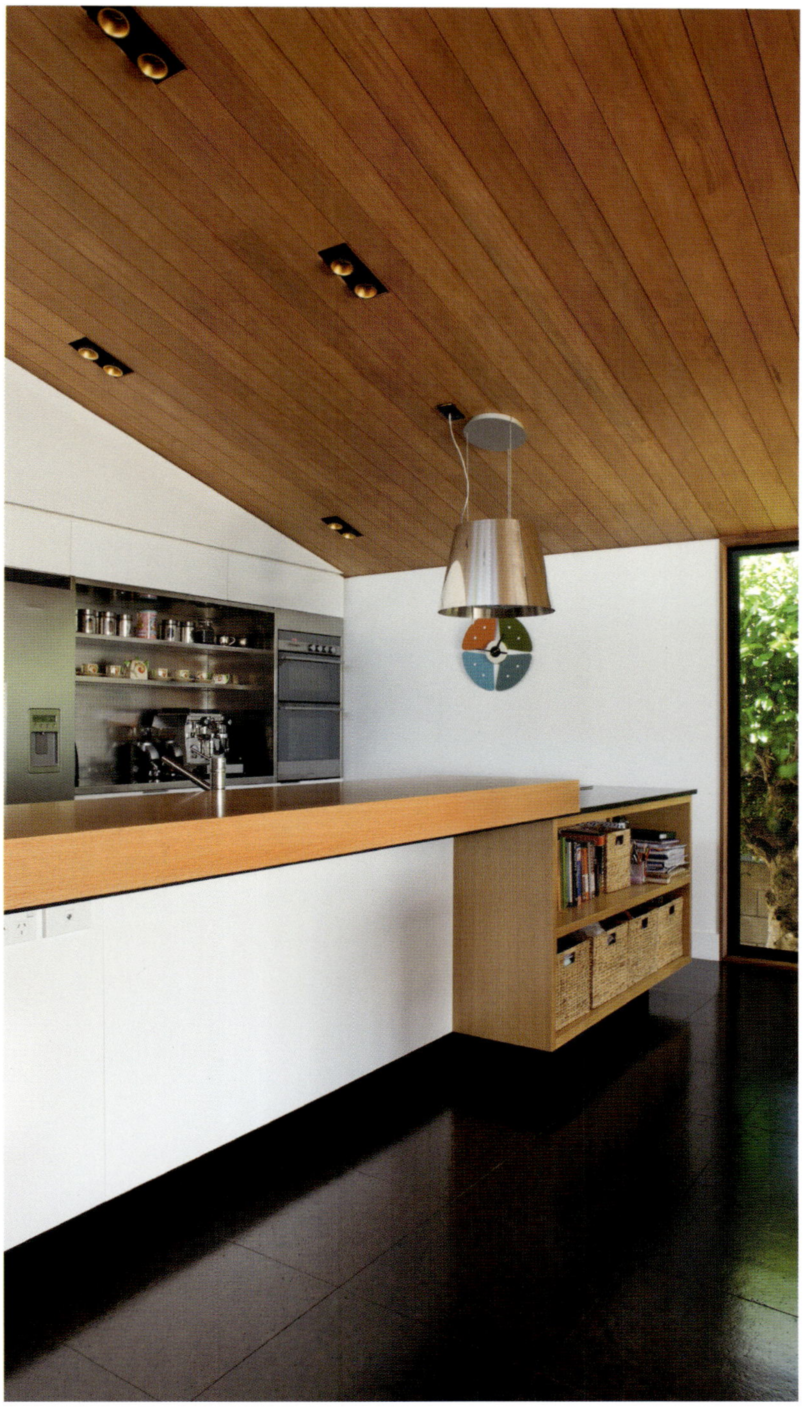

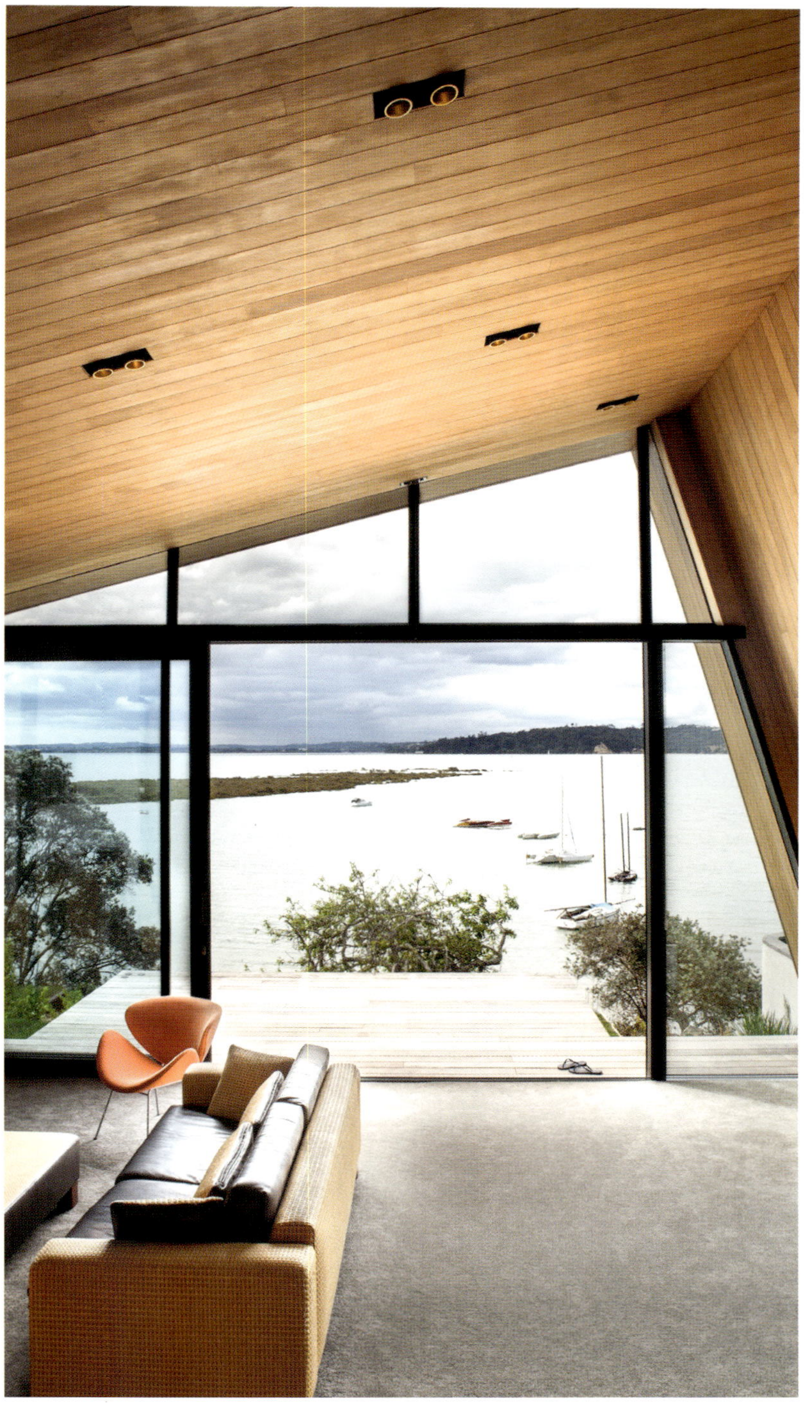

The house is oriented toward the views and arranged in a way that creates a natural progression from the original house to the new sections, starting at the entrance. From the vestibule, the stairway descends to the living areas to reveal the infinite seascape.

Das Haus soll hübsche Ausblicke bieten und ist so ausgerichtet, dass nach dem Betreten des Hauses alter und neuer Teil nahtlos ineinander übergehen. Ab der Eingangshalle führen die Stufen hinunter zum Wohnbereich, von dem aus man die unendlich weite Sicht auf das Meer genießen kann.

La maison offre des vues et est disposée de telle sorte que, selon par où l'on rentre, il existe une progression naturelle de la maison d'origine à la nouvelle. Du hall, les escaliers descendent vers le séjour qui offre des vues à l'infini de la mer.

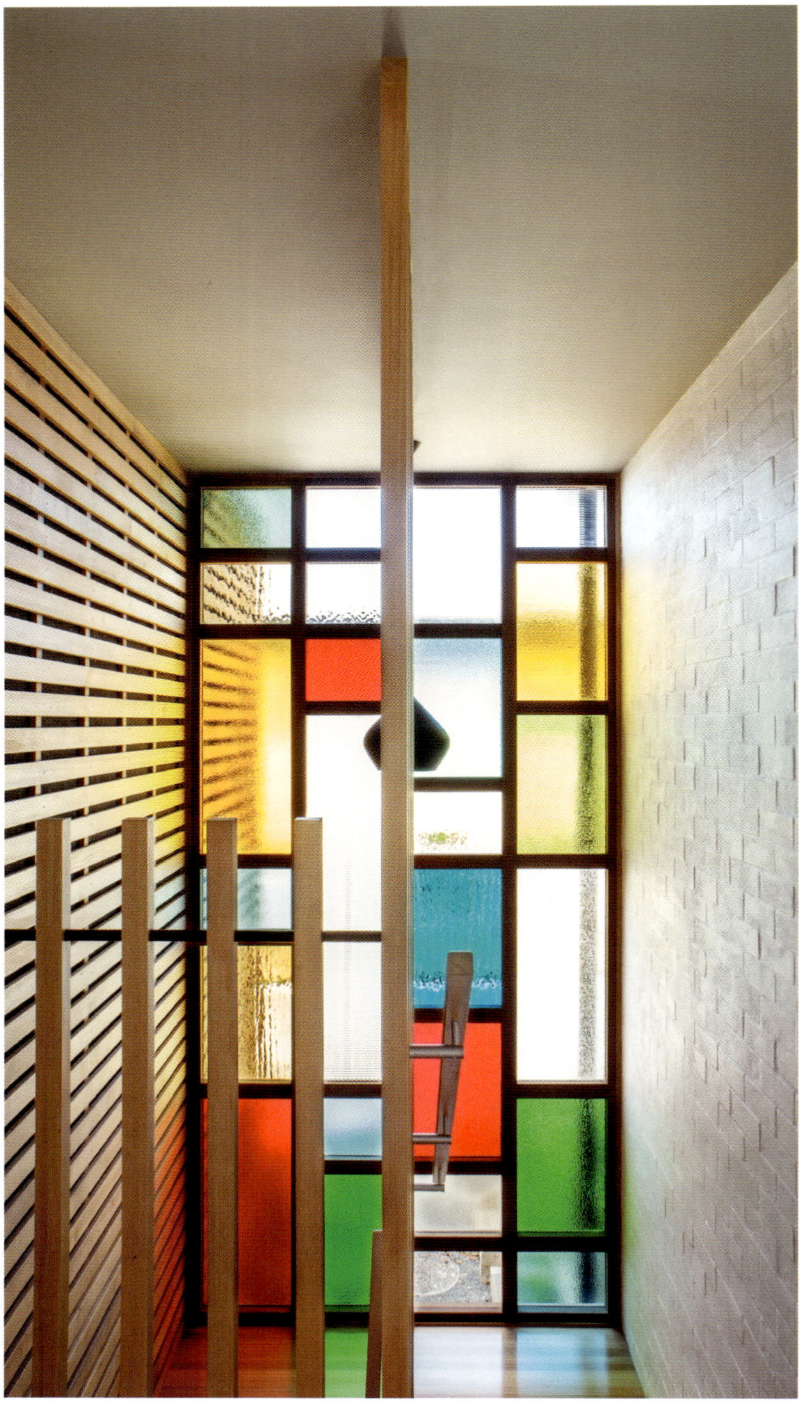

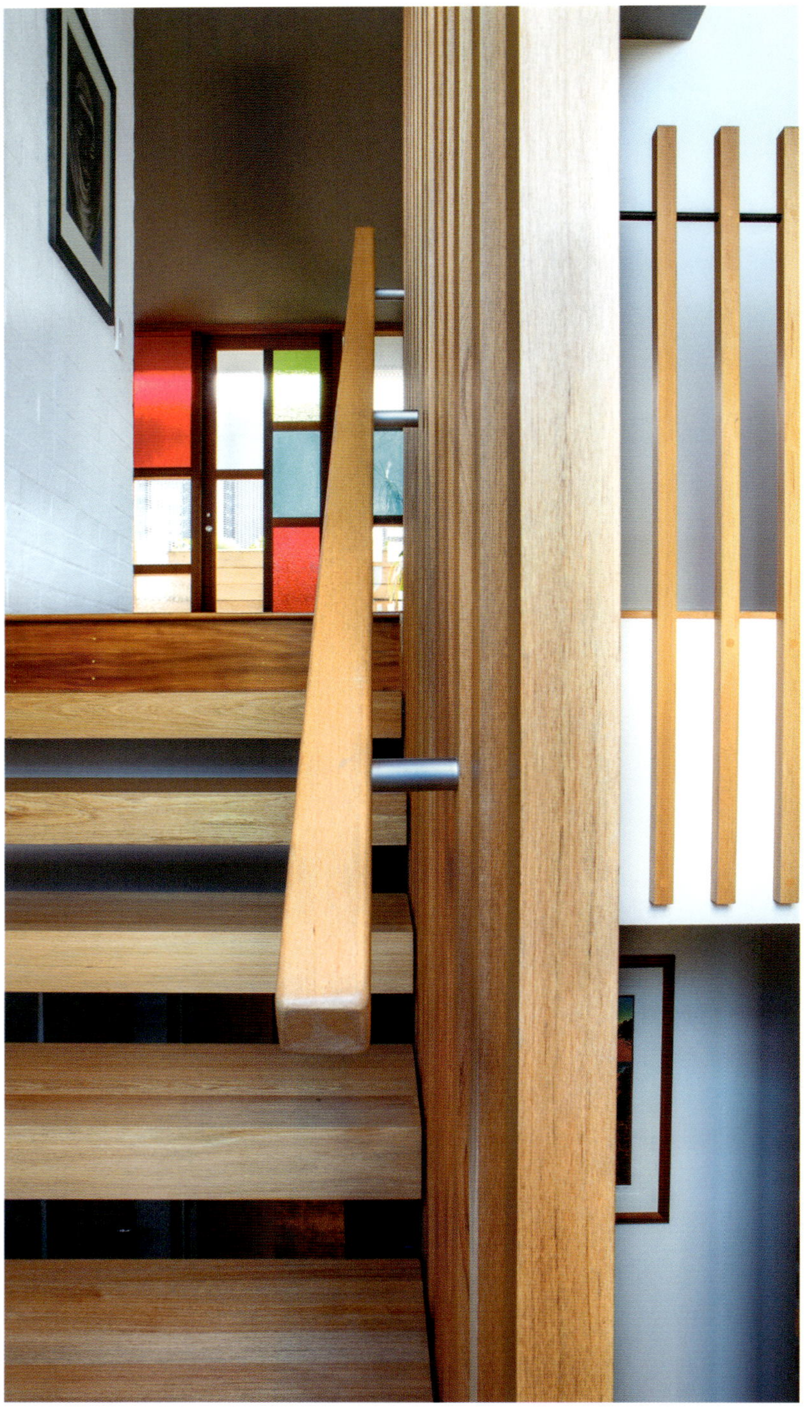

In keeping with the philosophy of preserving key parts of the original residence, some of the woodworking details were retained along with the stained-glass windows that add a note of color to the ensemble.

Aufgrund der Überlegung, einen Teil des Wesens des ursprünglichen Hauses zu bewahren, wurden einige Details aus Holz wie zum Beispiel die Fenster instandgesetzt, wodurch das Gebäude ein bisschen Farbe erhält.

Tout en respectant l'idée de conserver une partie de l'essence de la maison d'origine, certains éléments en bois ont été gardés, ainsi que des vitrages qui donnent une note supplémentaire de couleur à l'ensemble.

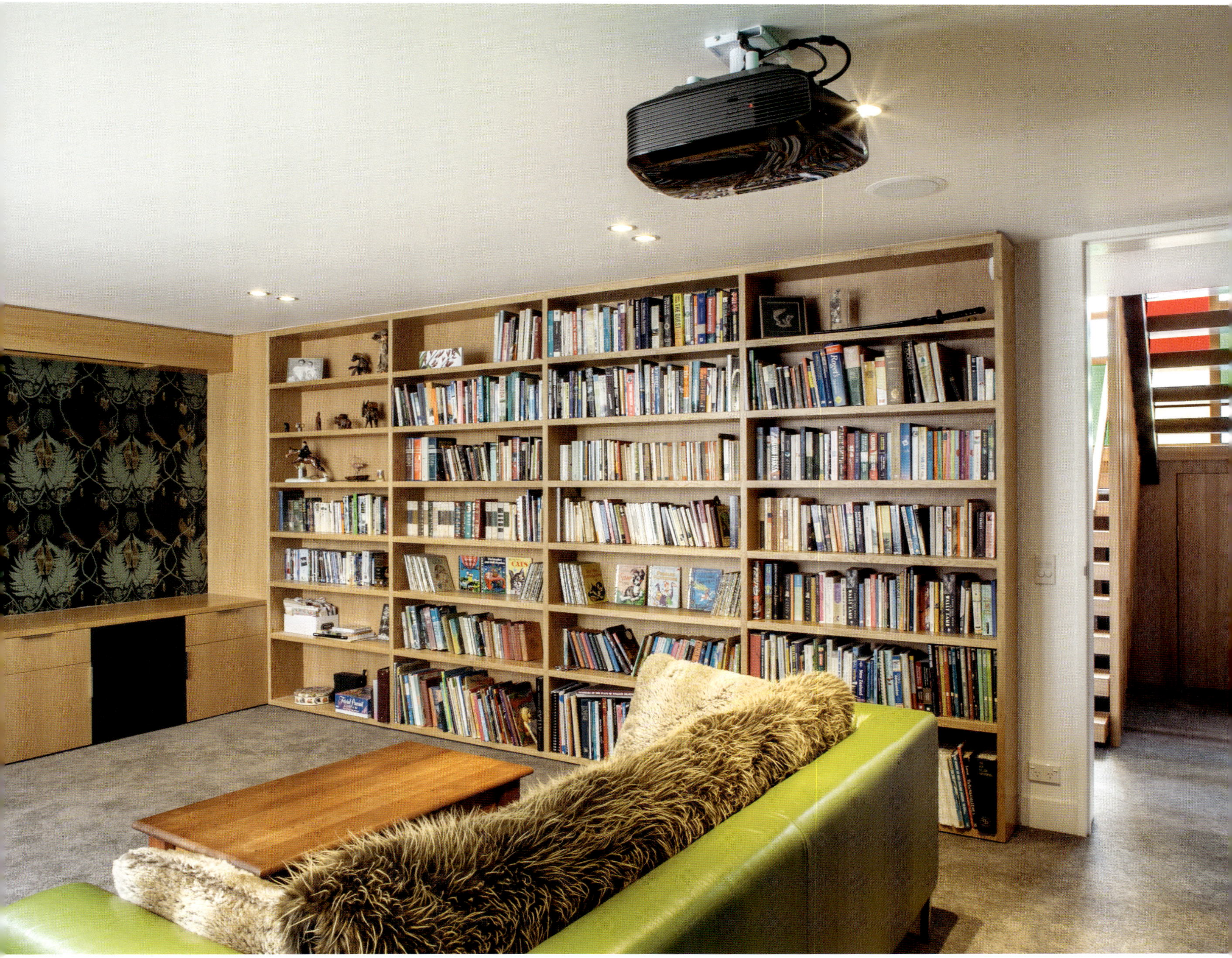

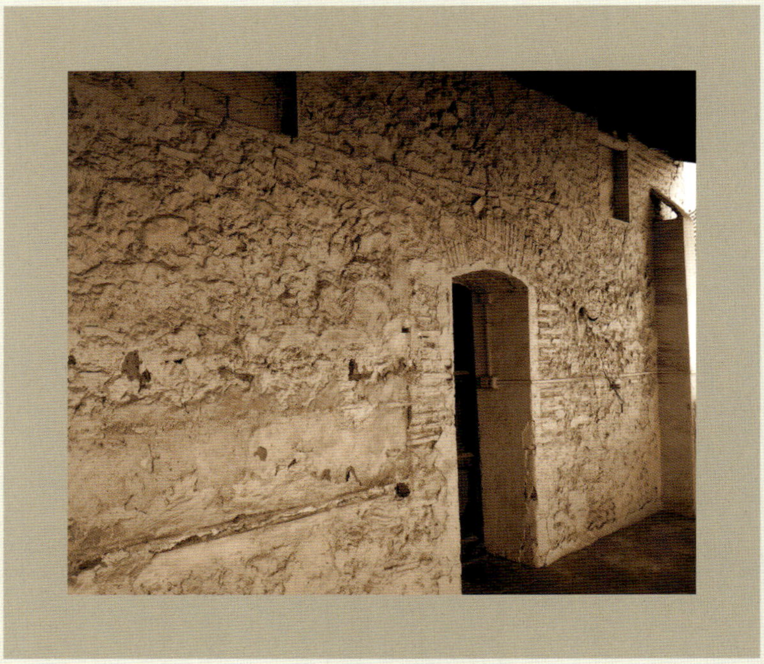

REFURBISHMENT OF A TRADITIONAL RURAL ARCHITECTURE RESIDENCE

STUDIO MONTAÑANA

278 m^2 | 2,207 sq. ft.

Moncada, Valencia, Spain

Photos © **Mayte Piera**

> Bring new life to the structure without losing the essence of its original construction

> Create two independent, yet interconnected residences

> Dem Gebäude neues Leben einhauchen, ohne dass es jedoch seinen ursprünglichen Charakter verliert

> Zwei eigenständige Wohnungen schaffen, die miteinander verbunden sind

> Donner une nouvelle vie au bâtiment, sans toutefois perdre l'essence de son origine

> Créer deux habitations indépendantes tout en étant interconnectées

This house typifies traditional architecture of the 1930s and 1940s, including a gabled roof. Its lower level originally accommodated the living area, while a loft for curing and drying crops occupied the upper story. The client acquired the property for the purpose of creating two residences that could be both interconnected and independent: the lower level for herself, the upper for her son.
In undertaking the restoration process, an effort was made to preserve the identity of a 1940s facade original to the period, retaining all of its features and decorative elements. A fascinating contrast is created between this facade and the new one along the side of the building, which was constructed to meet the requirements of the new project. The latter facade maintains the current beams, imbuing them with a contemporary language. It was resurfaced using lime mortar, a building material common to the architecture of the Mediterranean period.
The project to refurbish this old drying loft was guided by a single objective: to revitalize and unify two different periods, allowing the distinctive character of the roof to harmonize with the architectural elements and new materials deployed throughout the residence, partially exposing the lime-coated original mud brick walls, which were paneled up to a certain height. Without a doubt, this project is an outstanding example of the achievement of perfect harmony between the old and the new.

Dieses Haus ist charakteristisch für die traditionelle Bauweise der 1930er und 1940er Jahre mit Satteldach. Im Erdgeschoss war eine Wohnung untergebracht, und im oberen Teil befand sich ein Trockenboden für die Landwirtschaft. Die Bauherrin erwarb das Haus mit der Idee, zwei miteinander verbundene, aber eigenständige Wohneinheiten zu schaffen: das Erdgeschoss für sie selbst und das Obergeschoss sowie der Dachboden für ihren Sohn.
Bei der Umsetzung des Sanierungsprojektes wurde versucht, die Identität einer aus den 1940er Jahren stammenden Fassade mit all den Spuren und Originalornamenten ihrer Epoche zu erhalten. Diese Fassade und die neue seitliche Fassade, die für die veränderte Nutzung errichtet wurde, bilden nun einen interessanten Kontrast. Bei der neuen seitlichen Fassade werden die gegenwärtigen Öffnungen belassen, was ihr eine zeitgenössische Sprache verleiht. Für die Verkleidung wird ein Kalkmörtel verwendet, wie er in der mediterranen Architektur der Zeit eingesetzt wurde.
Die Sanierung dieses alten Trockenbodens verfolgte das Ziel, zwei verschiedene Epochen zu vereinen, wobei der ausdrucksstarke Charakter des Dachs mit den neuen architektonischen Elementen und Materialien harmoniert, die bei der Aufteilung der Wohnung eingesetzt wurden und den Blick auf einen Teil der gekalkten Lehmziegelwände ermöglichen, die bis auf eine bestimmte Höhe verschalt sind. Zweifellos ist dieses Projekt ein außergewöhnliches Beispiel für das perfekte Zusammenspiel von alt und neu.

Cette maison est caractéristique de l'architecture populaire des années 30-40, avec une toiture à deux pans, qui abritait un logement au rez-de-chaussée, et la chambre de séchage pour les cultures, à l'étage. La cliente a acquis le bien dans l'idée de créer deux habitations à la fois connectées et indépendantes : le rez-de-chaussée pour elle et l'étage supérieur et les combles pour son fils.
Au moment de lancer le projet de rénovation, on a cherché à conserver le cachet de la façade d'origine datant des années 40, avec tous les vestiges et ornements de leur époque. Cela a donné un intéressant contraste entre celle-ci et la nouvelle façade latérale, construite selon les exigences des travaux de rénovation. Les baies actuelles ont été conservées lors de ces derniers, lui donnant une touche contemporaine. Pour son revêtement, on a utilisé du mortier à la chaux, typique des bâtiments de l'époque de l'architecture méditerranéenne.
Le projet de rénovation de cette ancienne chambre de séchage avait pour objectif : redynamiser et homogénéiser les deux époques de sorte que le cachet du plafond cohabite avec les éléments architecturaux et les nouveaux matériaux qui ont été ajoutés pour l'aménagement de la maison, laissant apparents les murs d'origine de brique d'argile recouverte de chaux, avec du revêtement jusqu'à une certaine hauteur. Ce projet est sans aucun doute un exemple exceptionnel de cohabitation de l'ancien et du nouveau, en parfaite harmonie.

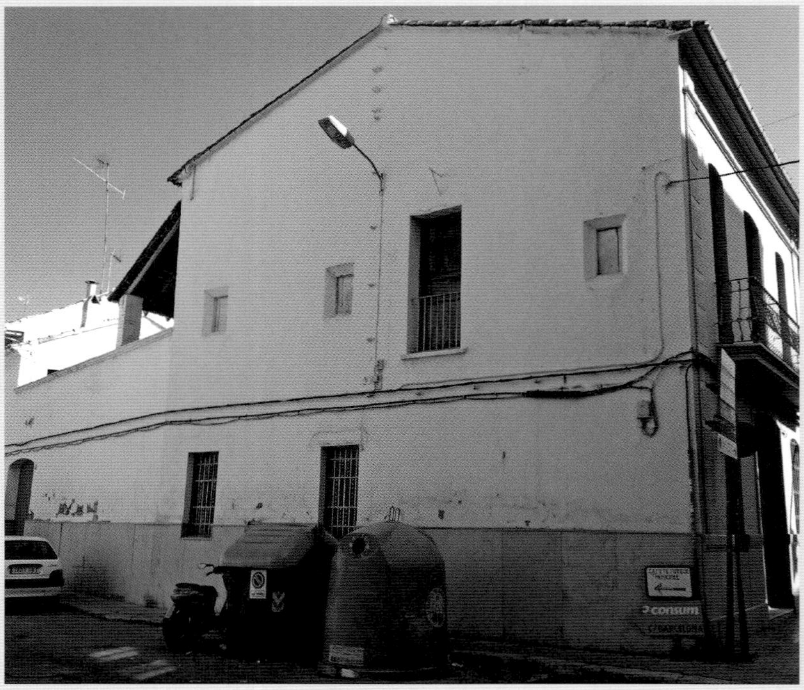
consum
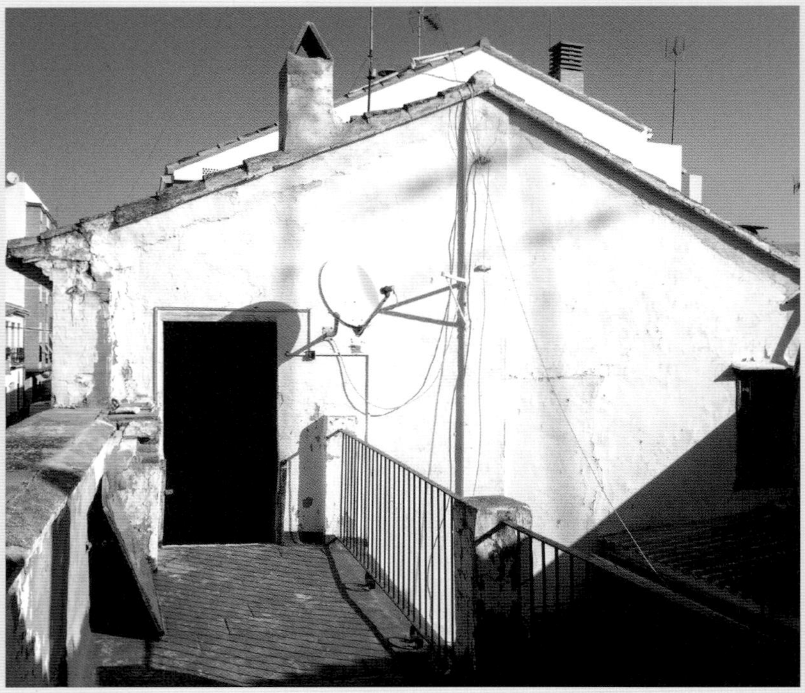
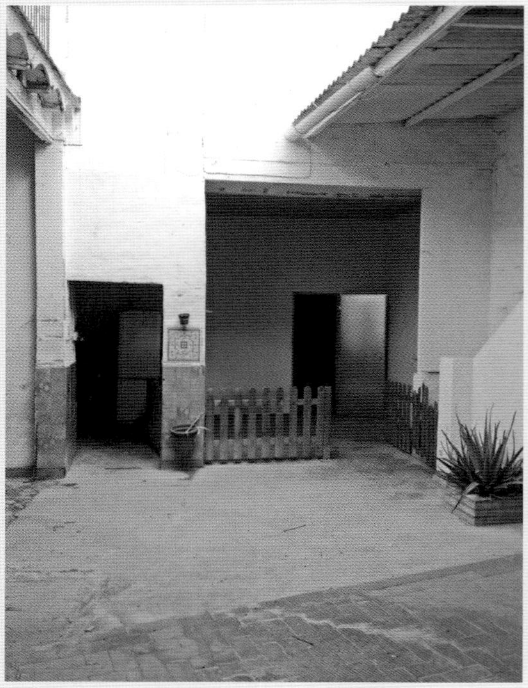
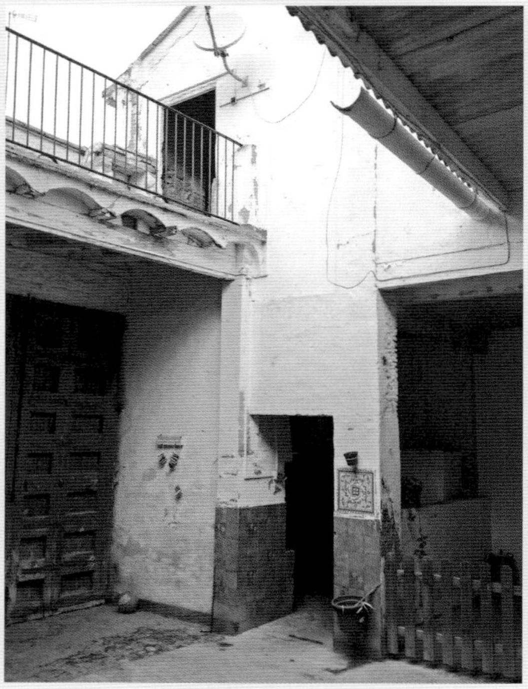
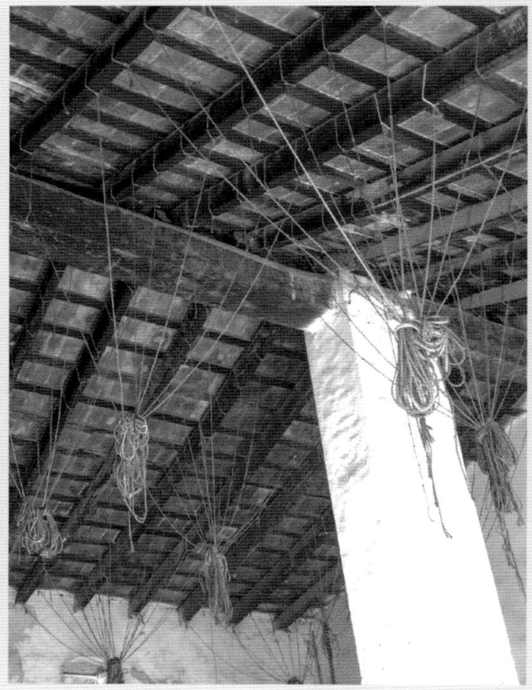
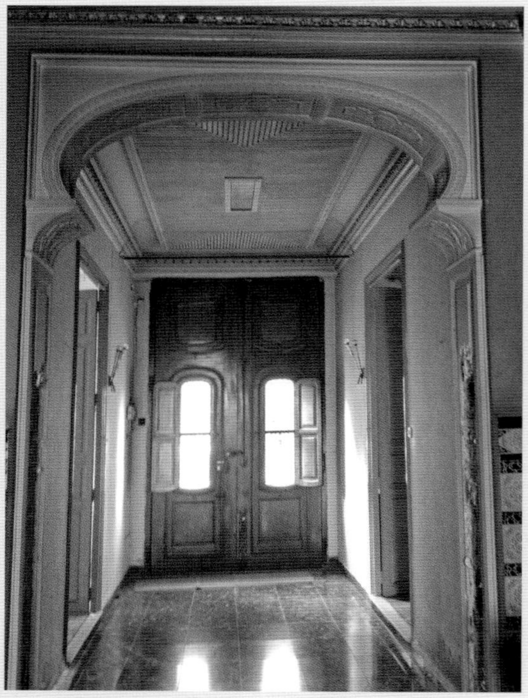
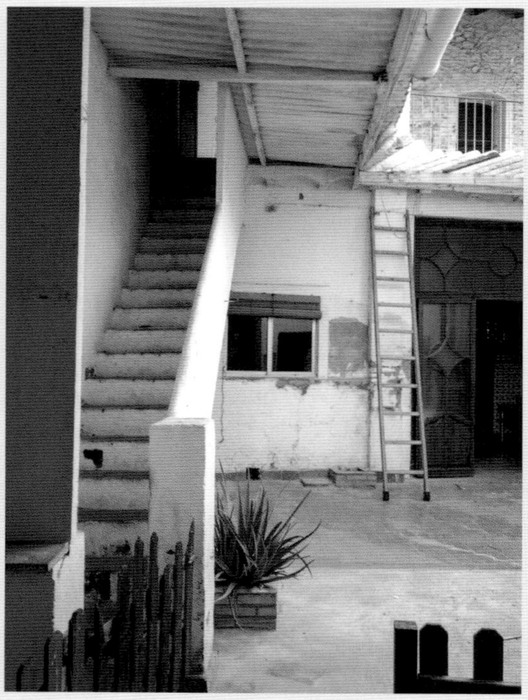
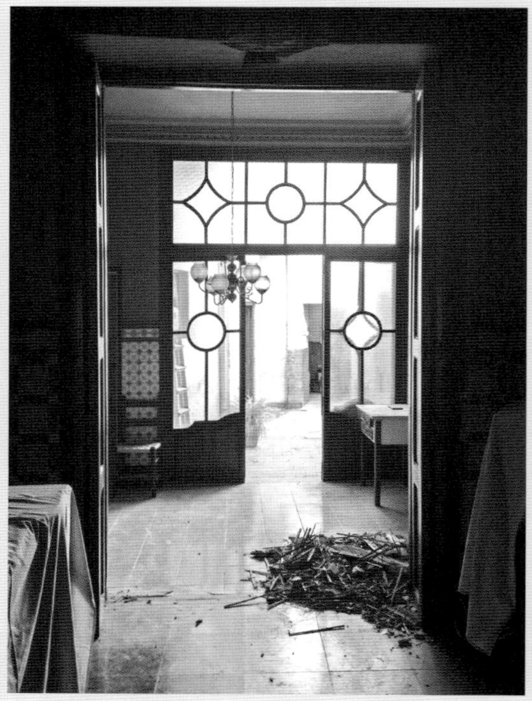

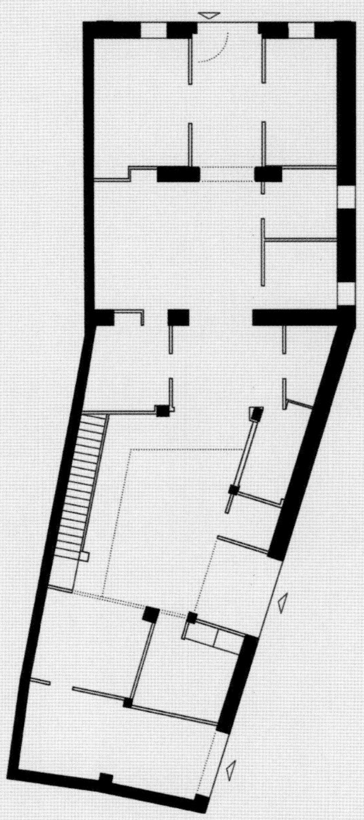

Existing ground floor plan

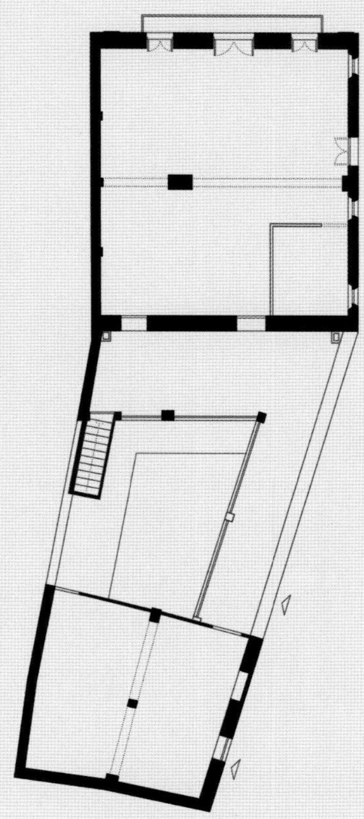

Existing first floor plan

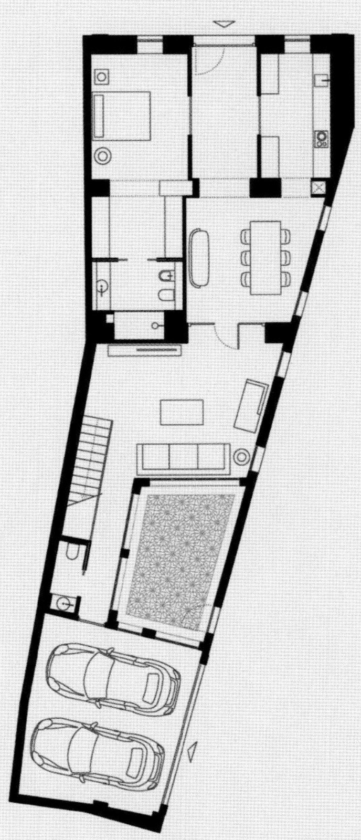

New ground floor plan

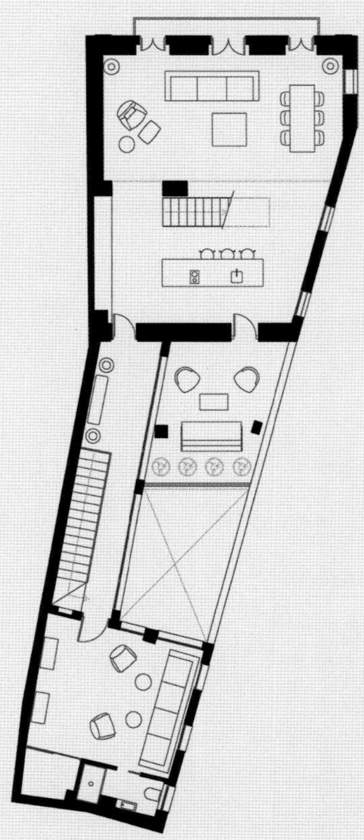

New first floor plan

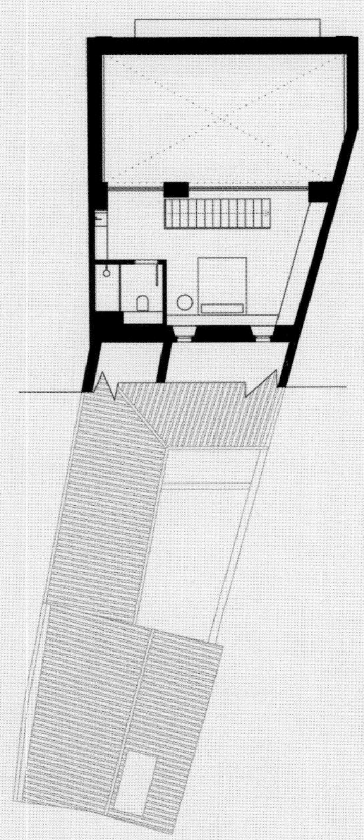

New attic plan

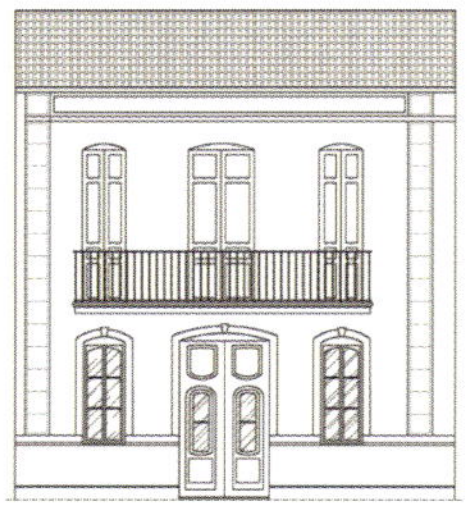

Front elevation

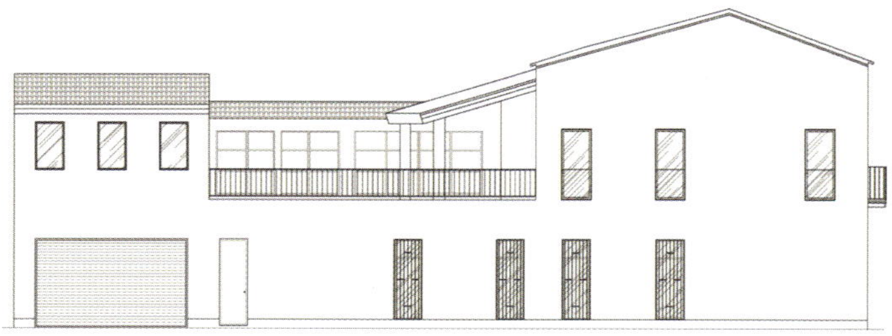

Longitudinal elevation

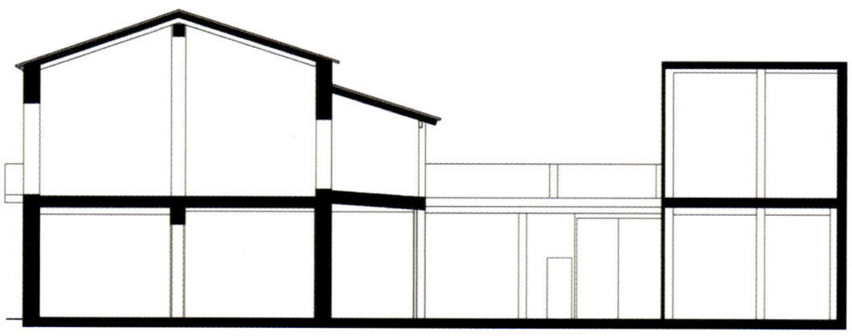

Existing section

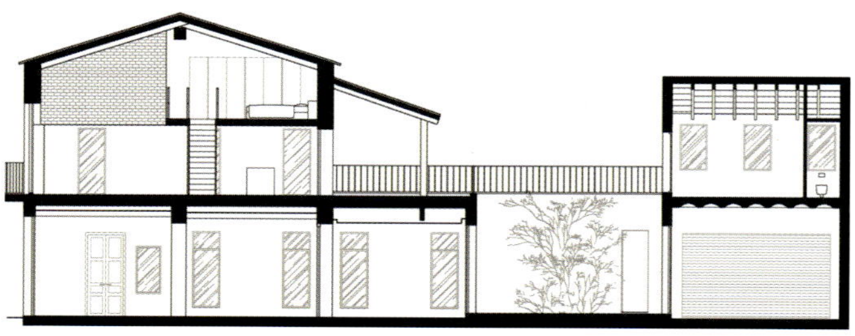

New section 1

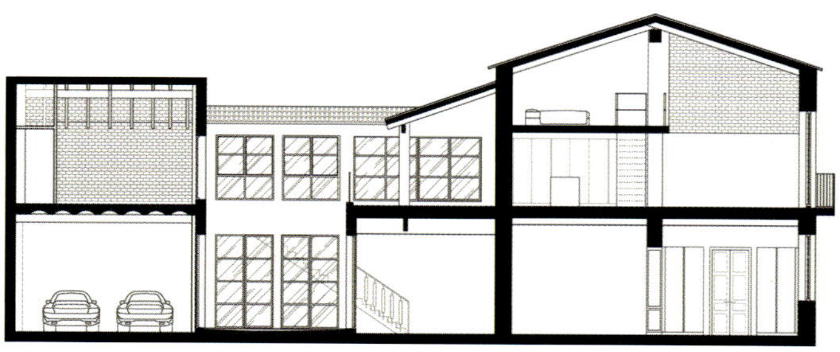

New section 2

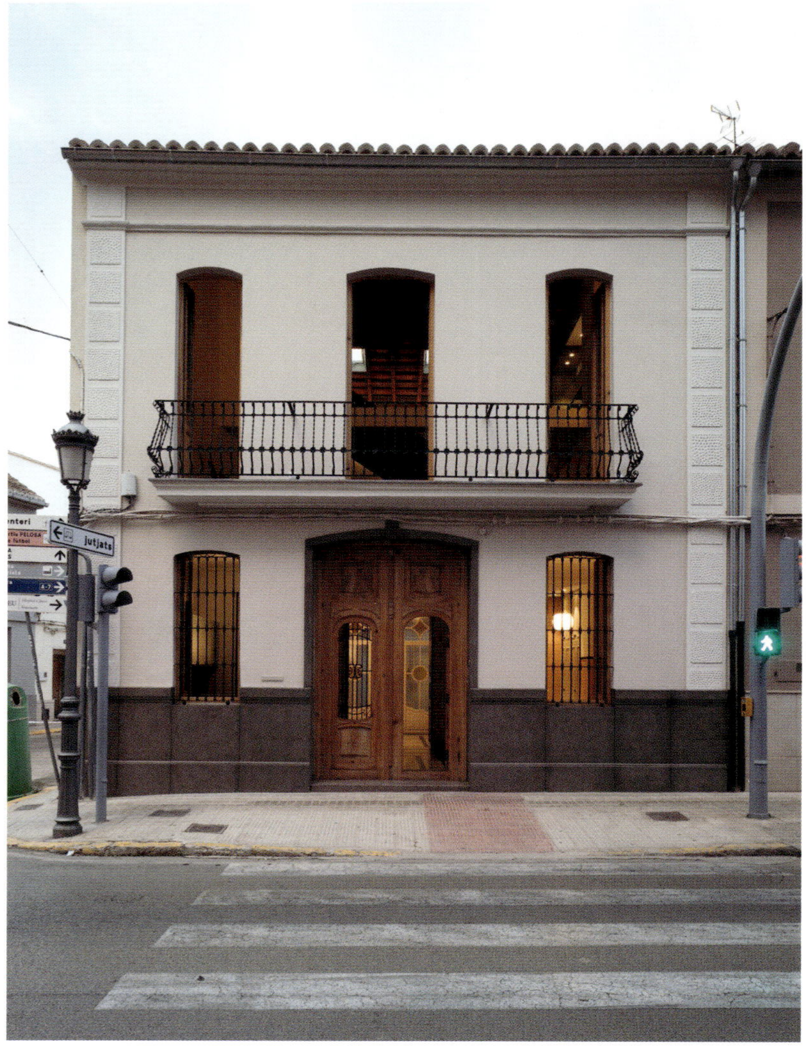

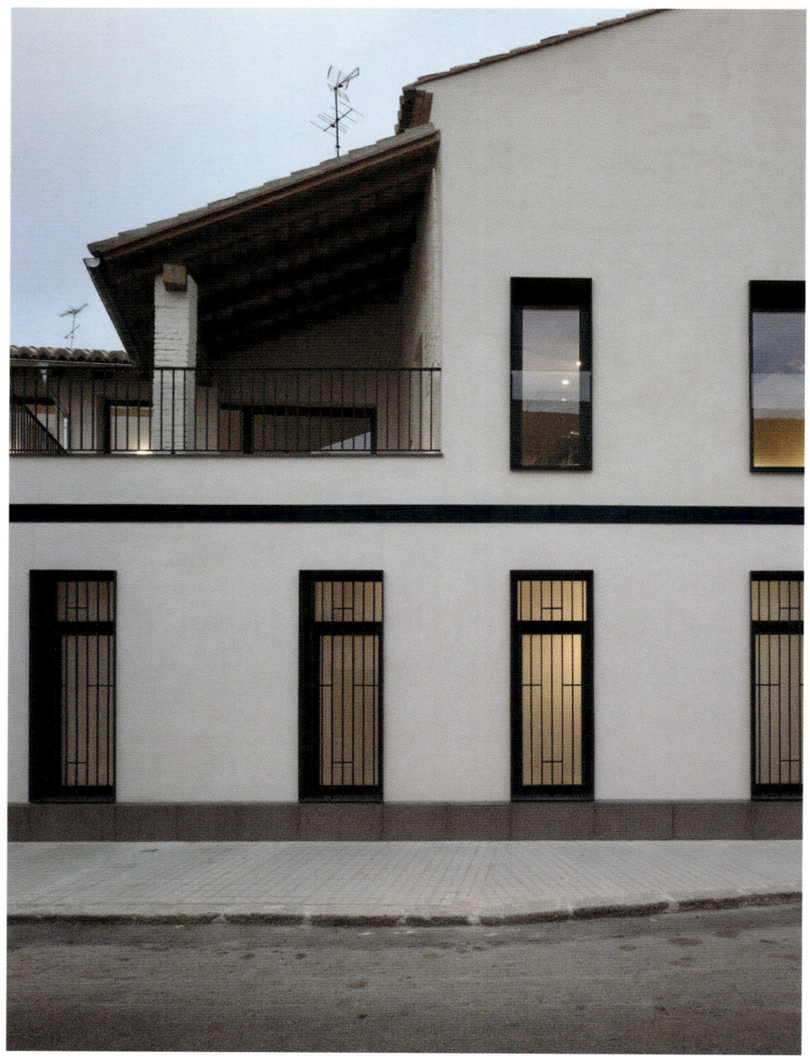

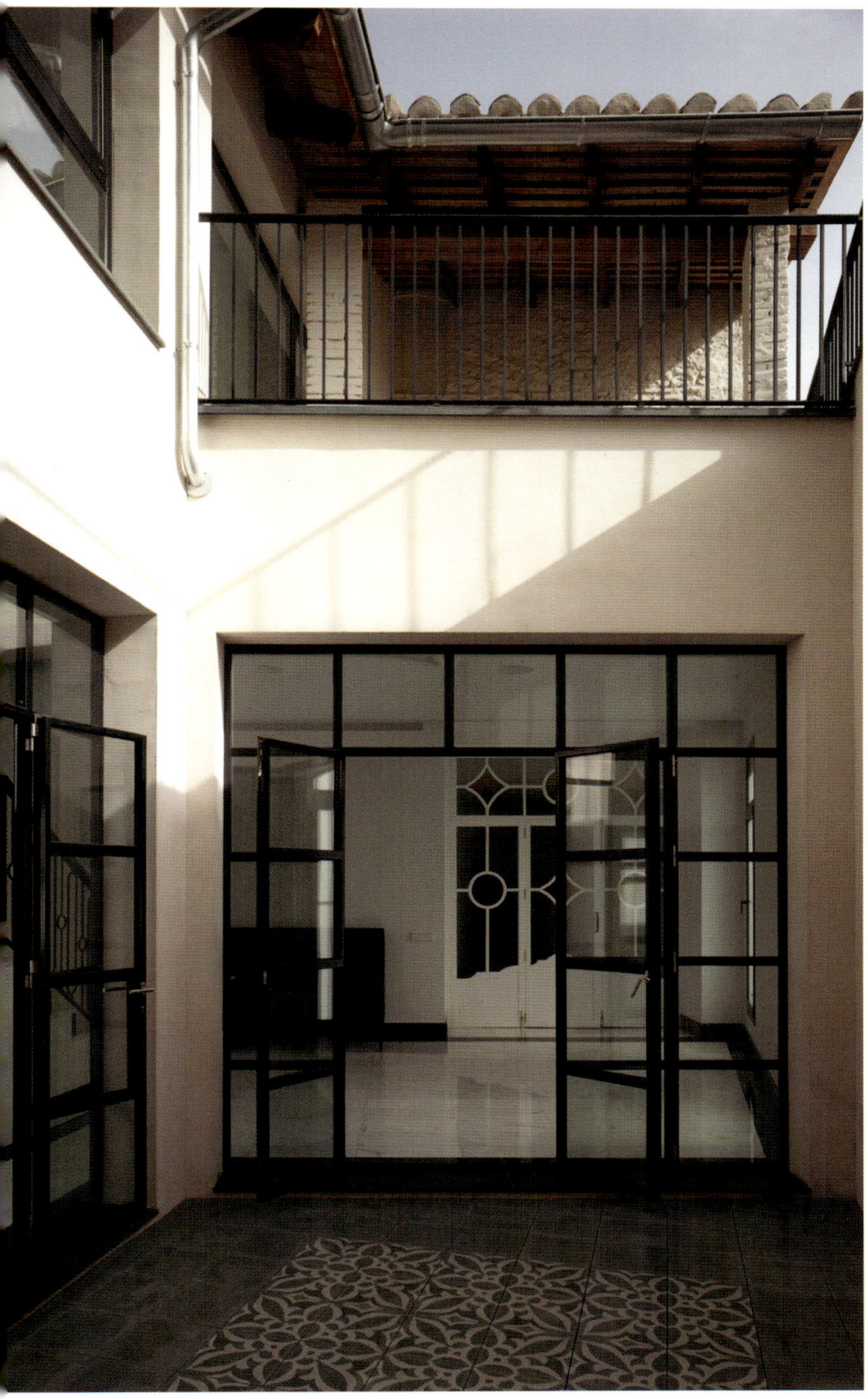

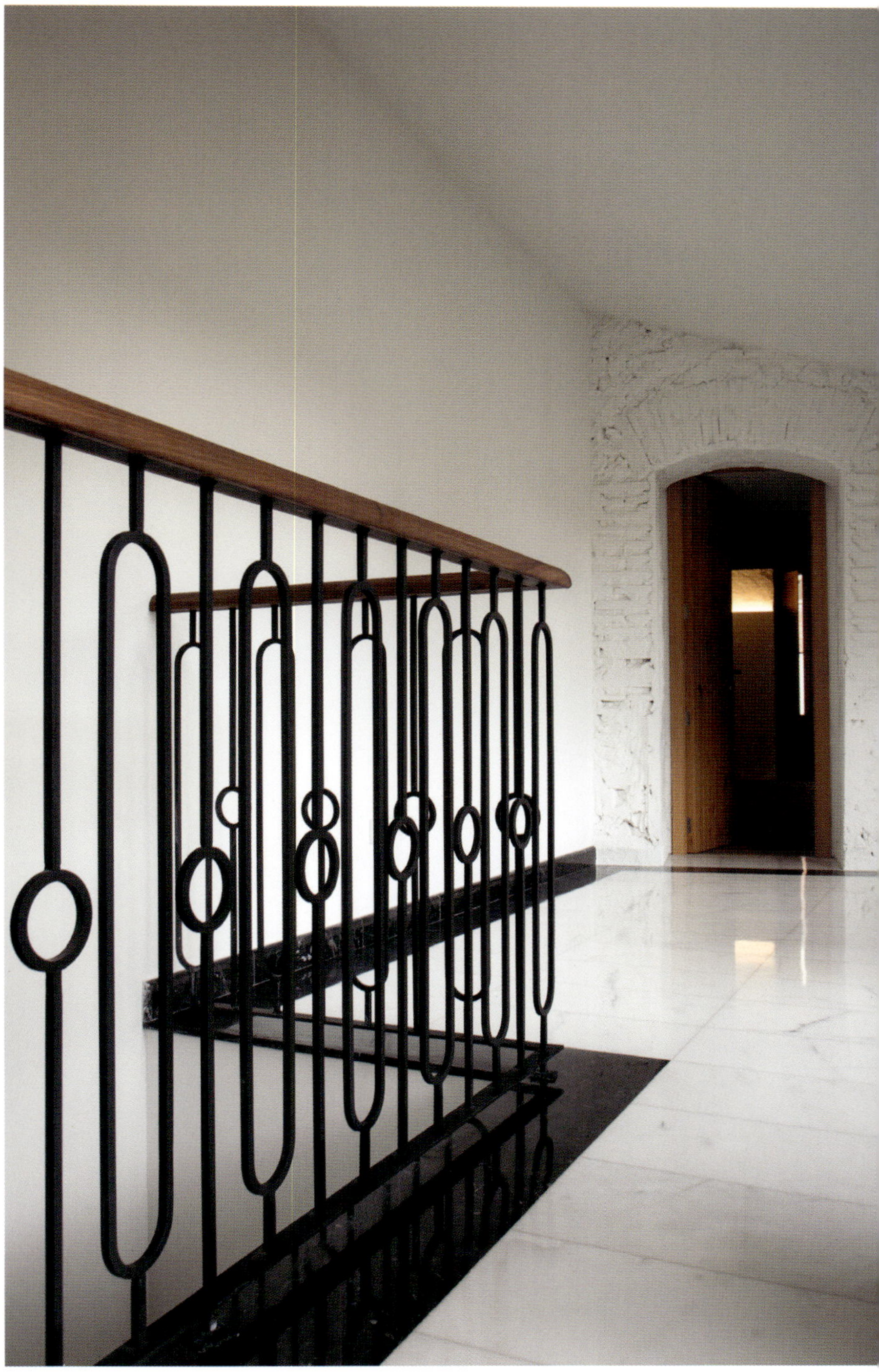

The central patio, retained as the nexus between the two stories, lends a character that recalls Mediterranean dwellings and becomes an essential core of the structure. The original exposed staircase is transformed into an interior stairway that serves as the internal connection between the house's two levels.

Der Innenhof bleibt als Bindeglied zwischen den beiden Etagen erhalten, er verleiht dem Gebäude einen für Mittelmeerhäuser typischen Charakter und ist dessen Kernstück. Die ursprüngliche Außentreppe wurde zur Innentreppe, um eine Verbindung innerhalb des Hauses zu ermöglichen.

La cour centrale a été conservée comme une connexion entre les deux étages, lui conférant un caractère typique des maisons méditerranéennes. Elle devient alors une cellule fondamentale. L'escalier d'origine découvert se transforme en un escalier intérieur qui favorise la communication au sein de la maison.

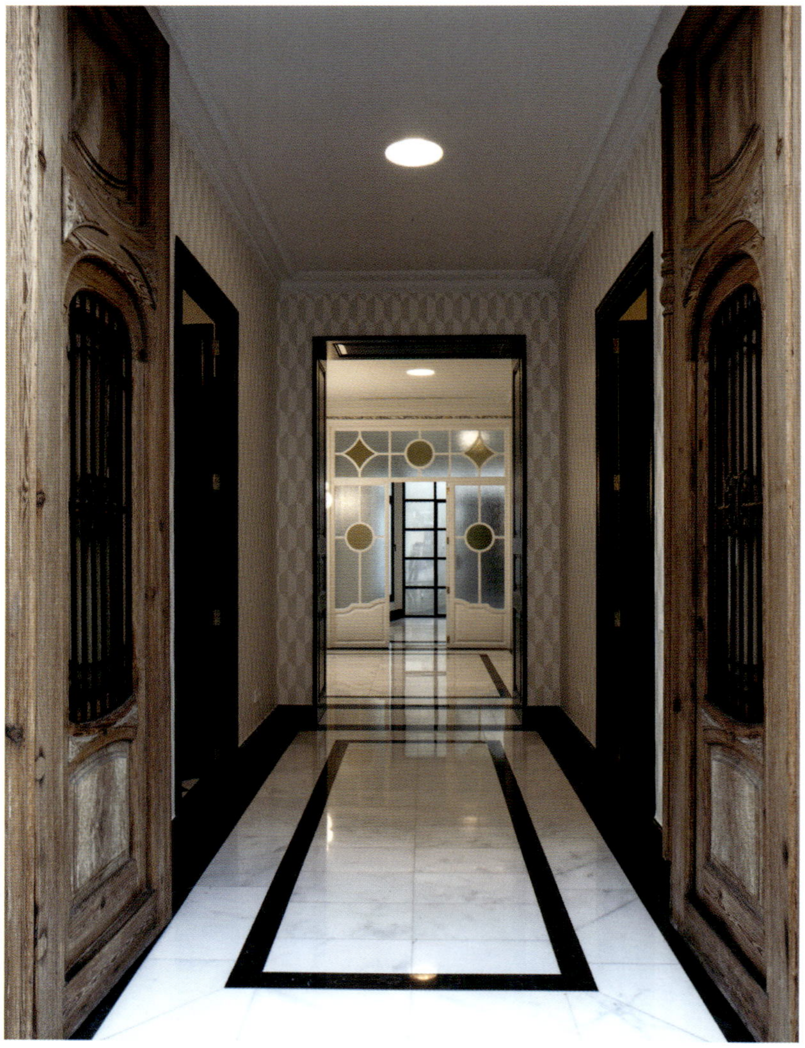

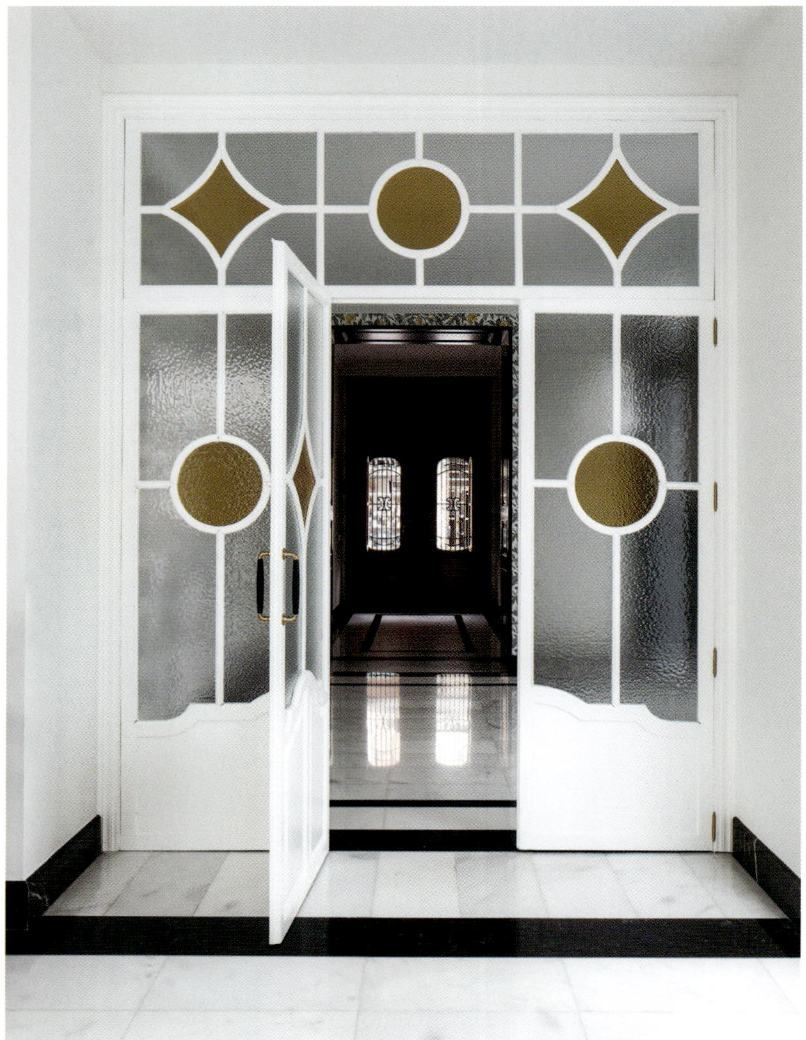

The lower-level restoration preserves key existing elements such as the woodwork, which was refurbished and lacquered to give it a more contemporary appearance.

Bei der Umgestaltung des Erdgeschosses wurden wichtige vorhandene Elemente beibehalten, wie etwa die Schreinerarbeiten, die restauriert und lackiert wurden, was ihnen eine modernere Note gab.

Lors des travaux du rez-de-chaussée, certains éléments importants tels que la menuiserie en bois, ont été restaurés et traités avec des finitions laquées lui donnant ainsi un air plus actuel.

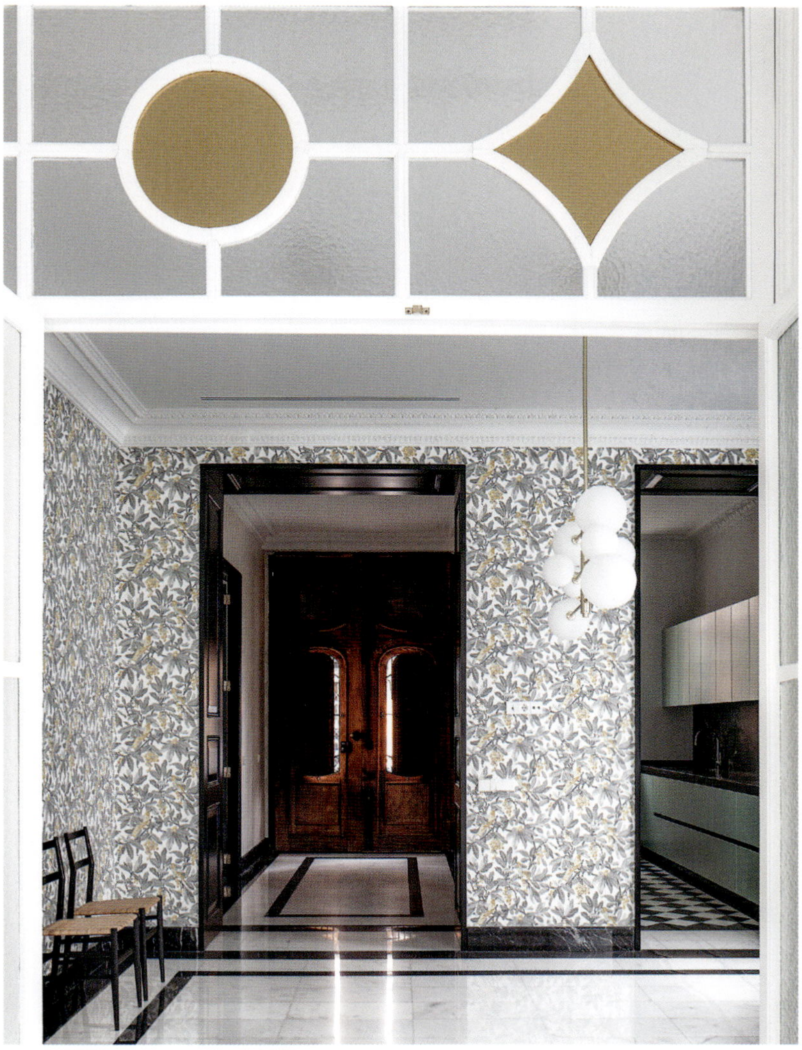

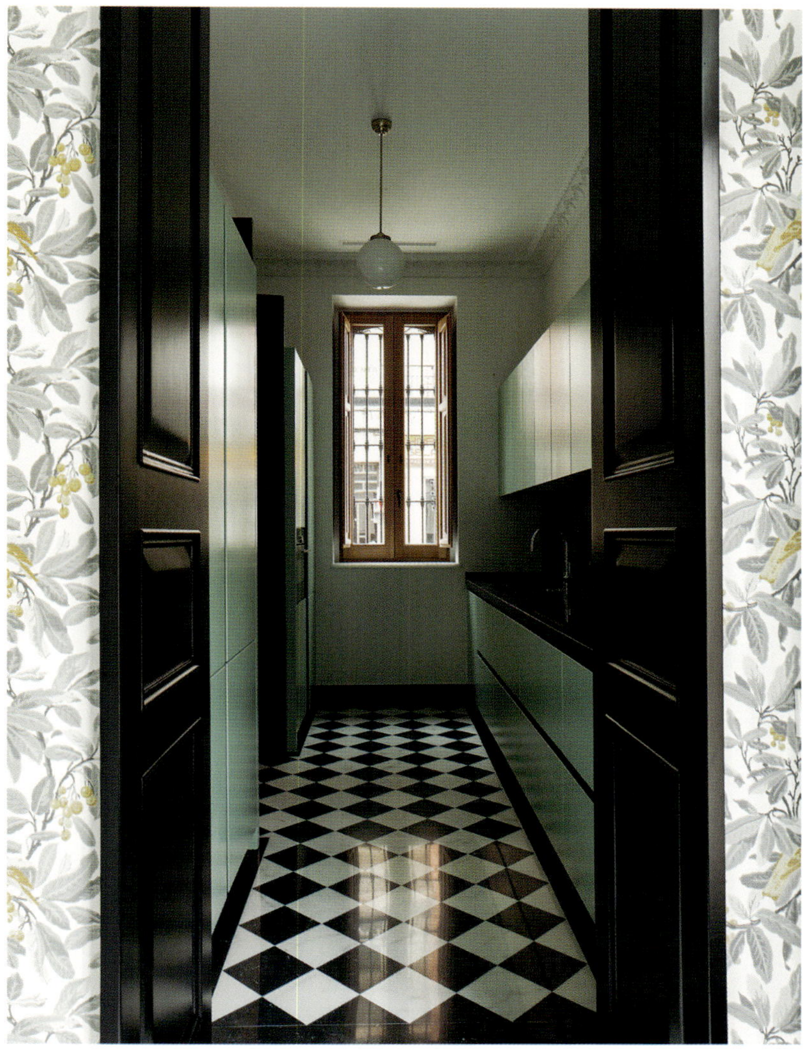

The entire building retains the features that typified the physical arrangement of such residences while consistently seeking out and integrating new materials representative of the art deco style of the period.

Das gesamte Gebäude bewahrt die Merkmale der Aufteilung bei diesem Haustyp und bindet neue Materialien ein, die Anleihen am Art-déco-Stil nehmen.

Tout le bâtiment conserve les caractéristiques propres de la répartition de ce type de maison, intégrant de nouveaux matériaux, toujours recherchés et basés sur le style Art déco de l'époque.

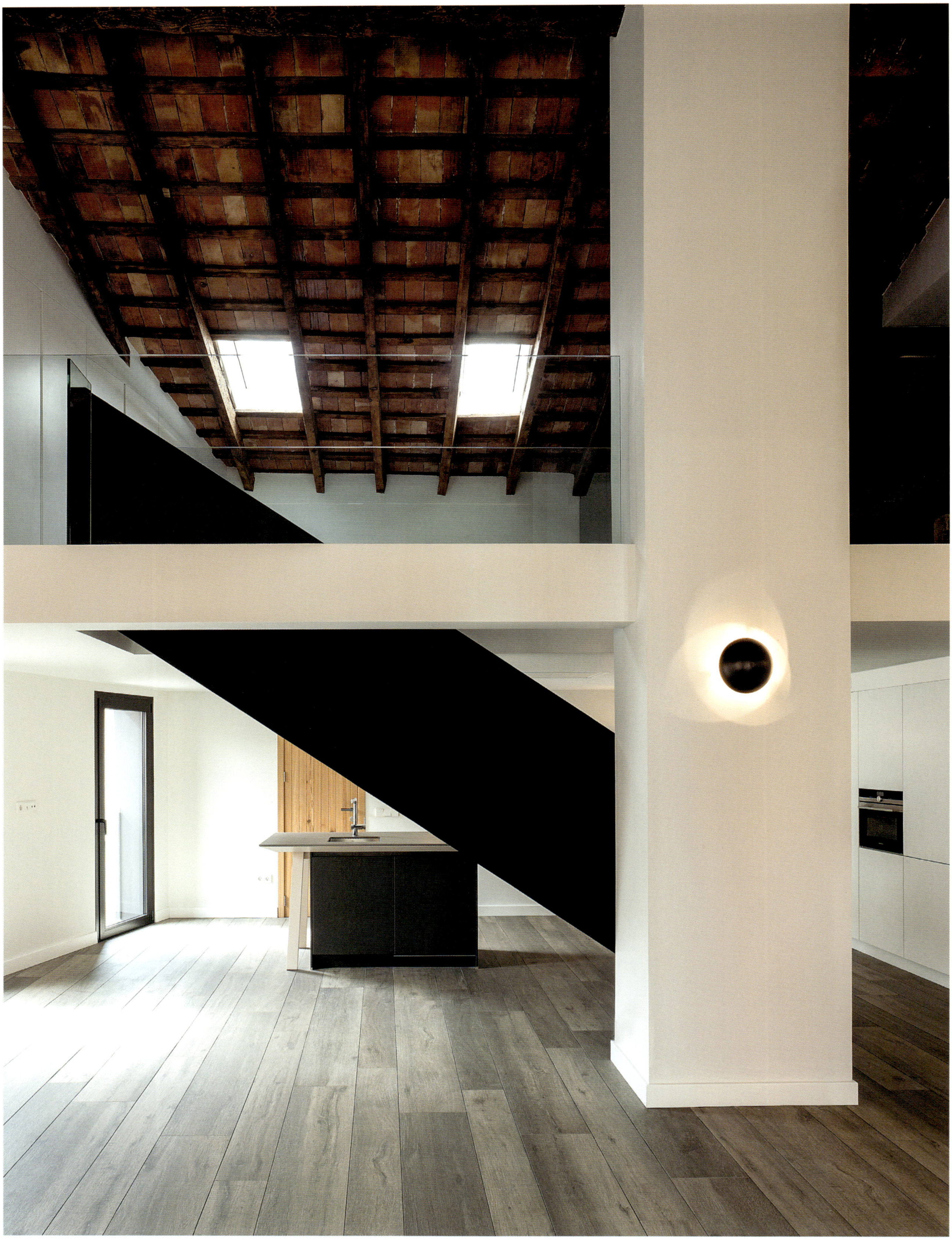

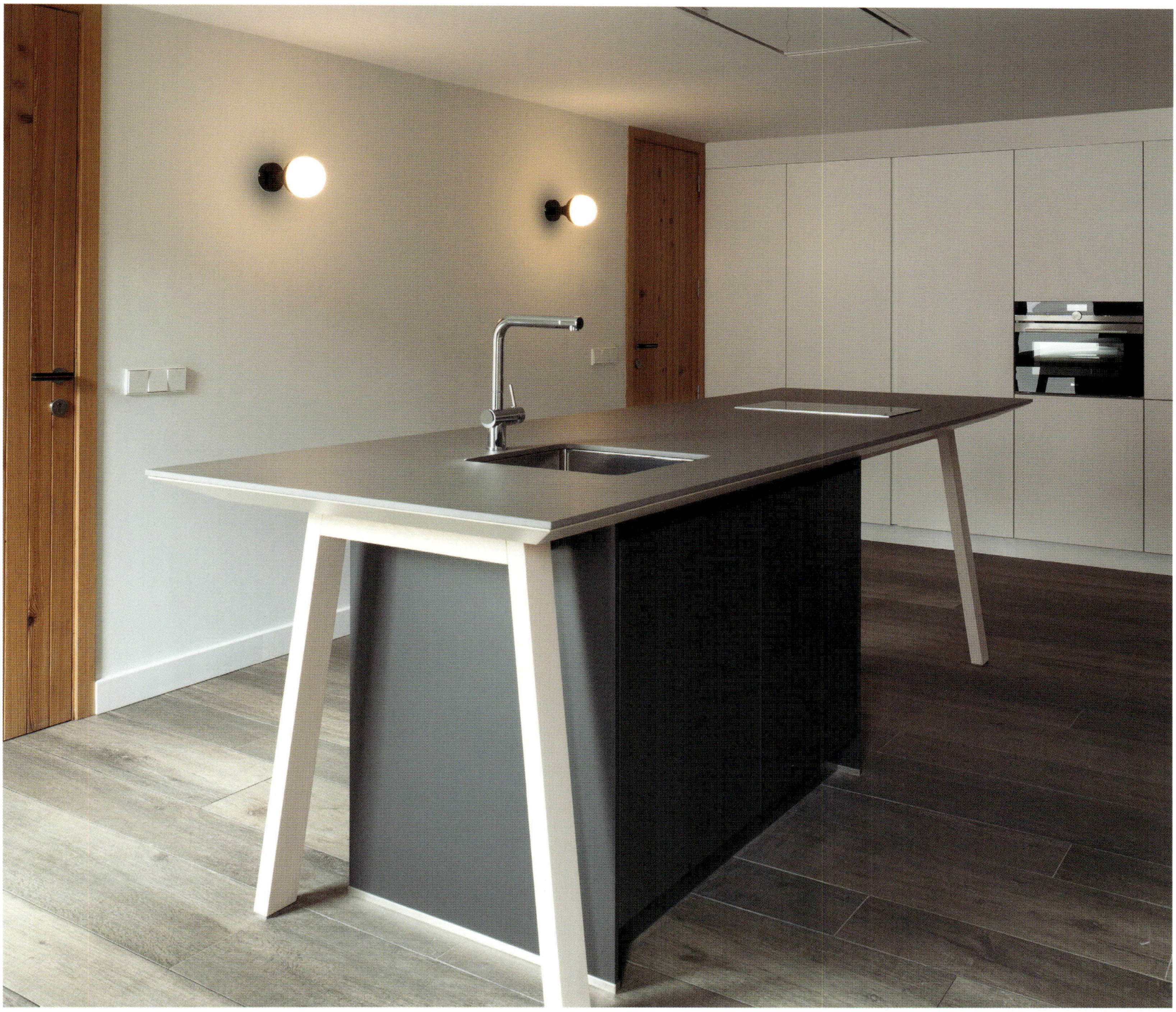

The first floor envisions an open living/dining area, with the stairs and kitchen island serving to distribute the space by separating the kitchen activities from the living and dining area.

Für die erste Etage wurde ein offener Wohn- und Essbereich entworfen, in dem die Treppe und die Kochinsel als Raumteiler fungieren und den Küchenbereich vom Wohn- und Essbereich trennen.

Au premier étage se trouvent un séjour et une salle à manger ouverte où l'escalier et l'îlot de la cuisine jouent le rôle de séparateurs d'espaces, divisant la cuisine du séjour et de la salle à manger.

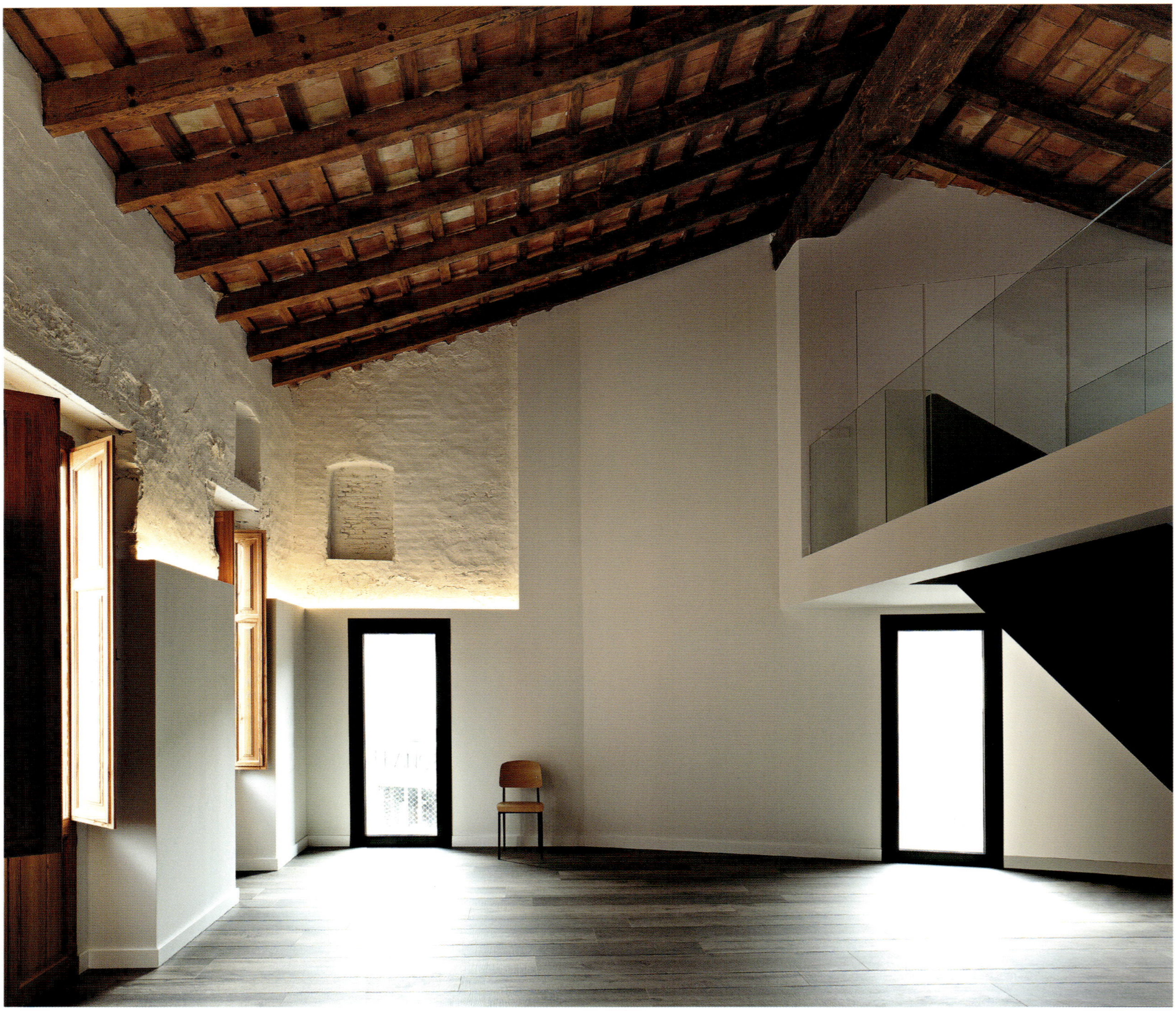

The main restoration work performed on the upper area, formerly the loft where crops were dried/cured, involved cleaning existing elements and incorporating new, but extremely simple materials—in this way, enhancing the profile of the original roofing with its wooden beam supports and mud brick, unquestionably the dominant characteristic of this architectural space.

Der Eingriff im oberen Bereich, dem alten Scheunenboden, bestand vor allem aus einer Reduzierung der Elemente durch neue, extrem einfache Materialien, die das ursprüngliche Dach mit seinen Holzbalken und Lehmziegeln als unbestrittenen Protagonisten des Raumes stärker hervortreten lassen.

Les travaux de l'étage, ancien grenier, consistaient essentiellement à nettoyer des éléments, tout en intégrant de nouveaux matériaux extrêmement simples et donner ainsi plus de relief à la toiture d'origine, posée sur des poutres en bois et des briques d'argile, éléments incontournables de l'espace.

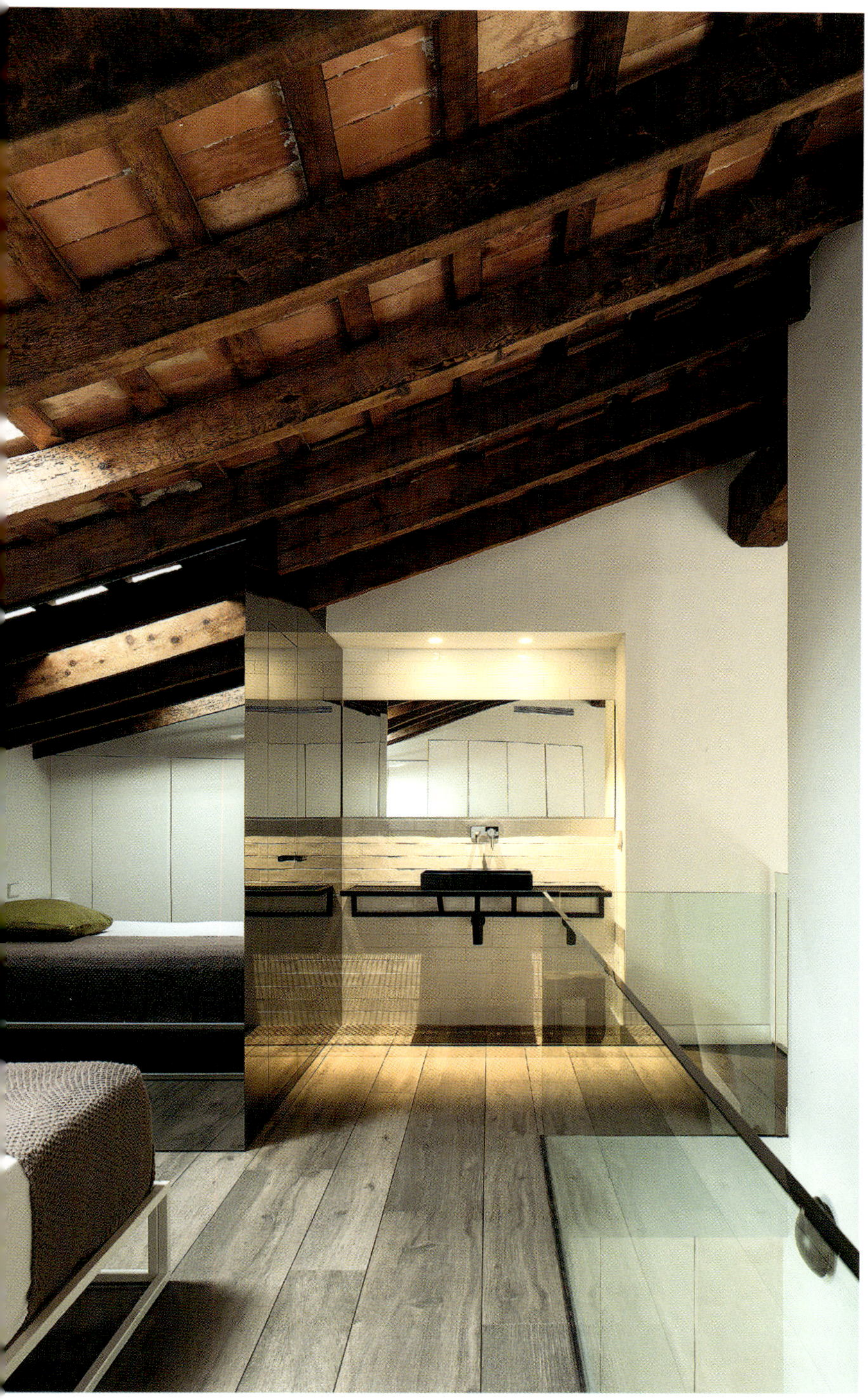

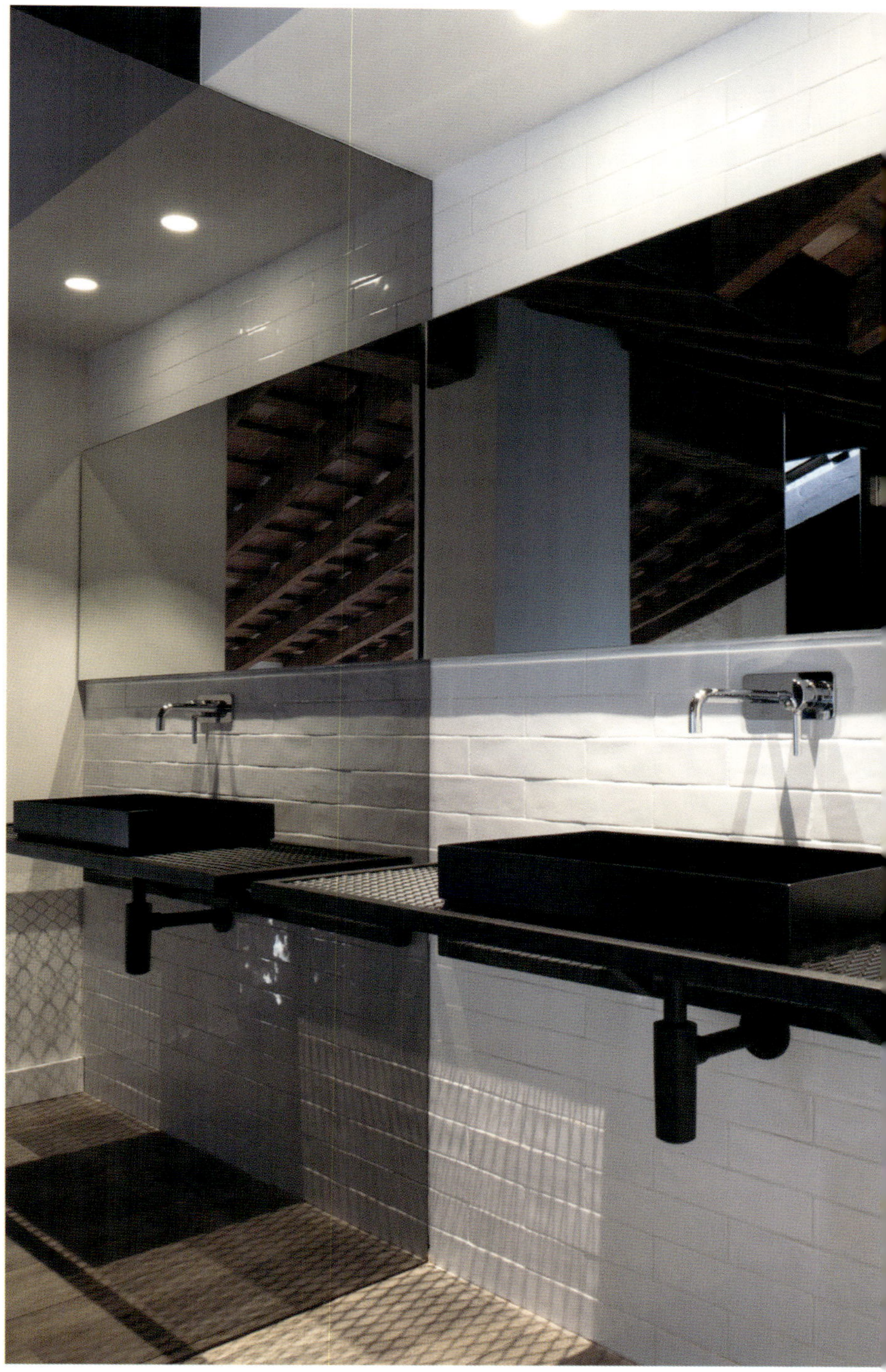

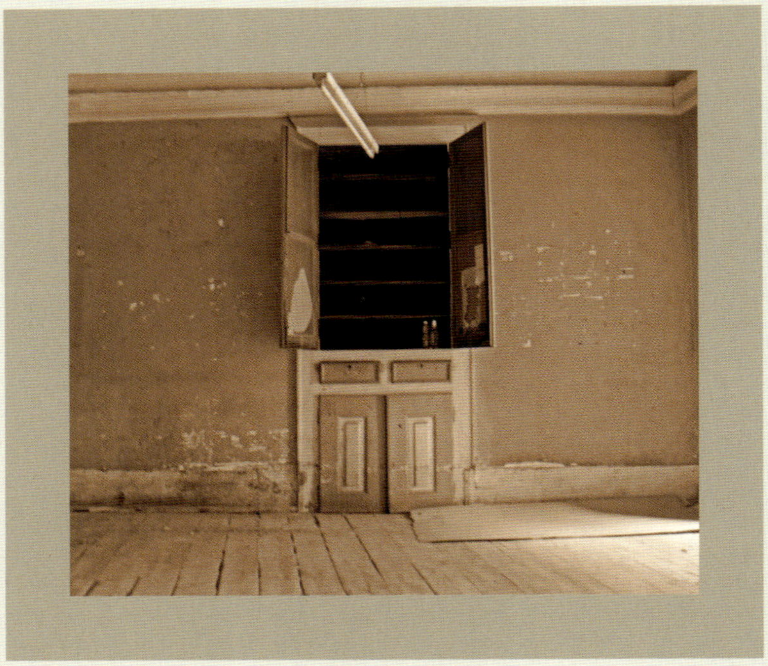

APARTMENT IN CHIADO

RAUL SERRA

130 m² | 1,400 sq. ft.

Lisbon, Portugal

Photos © **EMONTENEGRO Architectural Photography Studio**

- Reconstruct the house, preserving the original details
- Repurpose the original spaces
- Create an artificial lighting design to accentuate all historical details

- Wiederaufbau des Hauses und Bewahrung der ursprünglichen Details
- Neue Nutzungsmöglichkeiten für die alten Räume
- Entwerfen einer künstlichen Beleuchtung zur Betonung aller Details, die Teil der Geschichte des Hauses sind

- Reconstruire la maison tout en conservant les éléments d'origine
- Donner une nouvelle fonction aux espaces d'origine
- Concevoir un éclairage artificiel afin de mettre en valeur les éléments faisant partie de l'histoire de la maison

According to available records, this space dates to 1722 (prior to the Pombaline period), surviving various events in the city's history including the Great Earthquake (1755).
The rehabilitation project was designed around two principles: the architectural program and the strategy to restore and preserve each element that belonged to the site's legacy. Prior to the definition of the spaces, a demolition process was carried out, revealing indelible treasures that helped form the final result: 18th-century tiles along the baseboards, massive brick vaulting, stone blocks from the 14th-century wall built by Fernando I, as well as shutters.
It's a house filled with memories narrated by different spatial areas, with a high vaulted ceiling and a direct and effective connection across these spaces. The new history being built on this site strives to be careful and sparing, based largely on details, materials, and technology that enhance the ways of experiencing these spaces and lingering in them. Without doubt, this is a house that endures over time.

Laut der verfügbaren Aufzeichnungen liegt der Ursprung dieses Gebäudes im Jahr 1722 (vor-pombalinisch), und es überdauerte verschiedene geschichtliche Epochen der Stadt, darunter auch das große Erdbeben (1755).
Das Renovierungsprojekt gründete sich auf zwei Voraussetzungen: Definition der architektonischen Ausrichtung und Erstellung einer Strategie für die Restaurierung und Erhaltung jedes Elements, das zum Erbe dieses alten Gebäudes gehört. Bevor die einzelnen Räume festgelegt wurden, riss man verschiedene Bauelemente ab, wodurch prachtvolle Schätze zum Vorschein kamen, die zum finalen Ergebnis der Arbeiten beitrugen: Kacheln aus dem 18. Jahrhundert an den Sockelleisten, massive Gewölbe aus Ziegelsteinen, Steinquader der alten fernandinischen Mauer sowie Fensterläden.
Es ist ein Haus aus Erinnerungen, das durch die Geschichte der Räume der verschiedenen Bereiche, eine hohe Decke und eine direkte und effektive Verbindung der einzelnen Zimmer zusammengesetzt ist. Die neue Geschichte, die so für diesen Ort erschaffen wurde, wirkt behutsam ausgewählt und essenziell wichtig und gründet sich hauptsächlich auf Einzelheiten, Materialien und Technologien zur Verbesserung der einzelnen Räume. Definitiv also ein Haus, das die Zeit überdauert.

Selon les registres disponibles, cet espace date de 1722 (pre-pombalino) et a résisté à divers événements qu'a connus la ville tels que le grand tremblement de terre de 1755.
Le projet de réhabilitation reposait sur deux principes : la détermination du programme architectural et la stratégie de restauration et préservation de chaque élément et détail appartenant au leg de ce lieu. Avant de définir les espaces, il a fallu démolir pour découvrir des trésors inestimables ayant donné lieu au résultat final : carreaux de faïence du XVIIIe siècle des plinthes, des voûtes imposantes en brique, des blocs de pierre de l'ancienne muraille « Fernandina », des volets, etc.
Il s'agit d'une maison pleine de souvenirs qui raconte l'histoire des divers espaces avec un haut plafond voûté et une connexion directe et efficace entre eux. La nouvelle histoire qui se construit pour ce lieu se veut être soignée et essentielle, principalement basée sur des détails, des matériaux et la technologie afin d'améliorer l'expérience et le séjour dans ses divers espaces. Il s'agit finalement d'une maison qui perdure dans le temps.

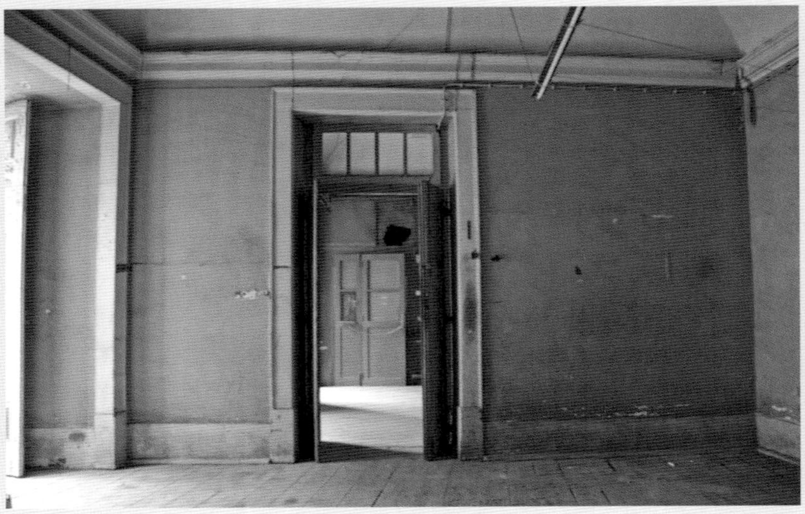
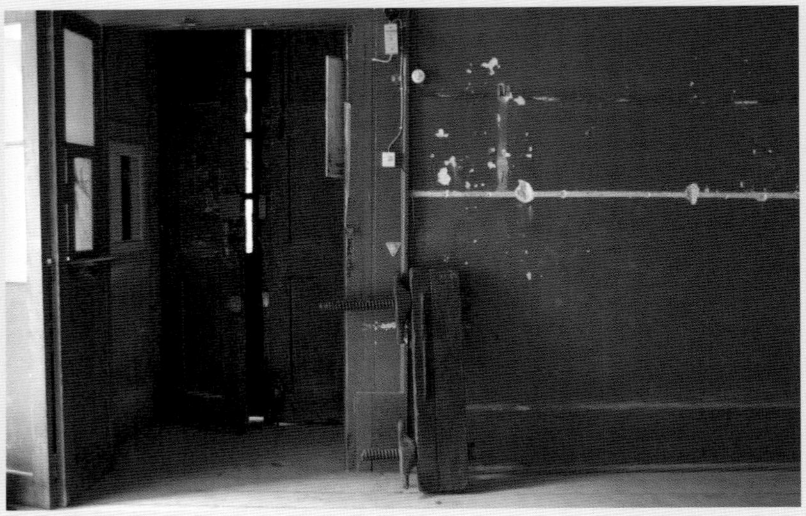
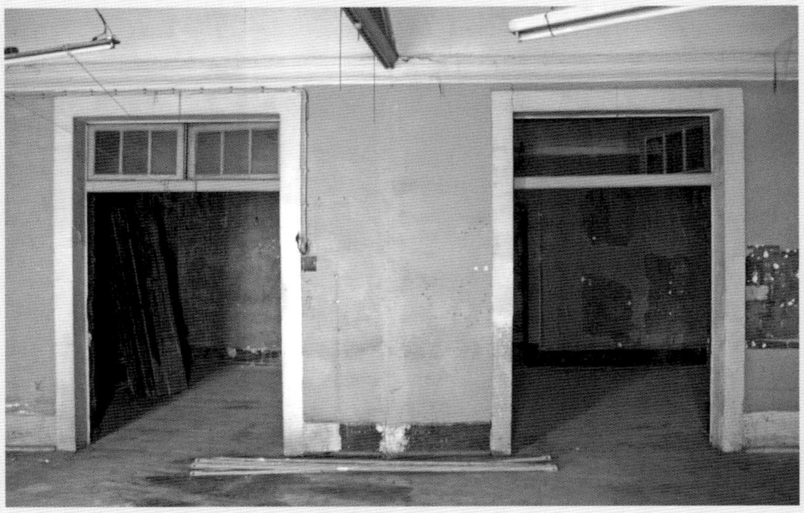
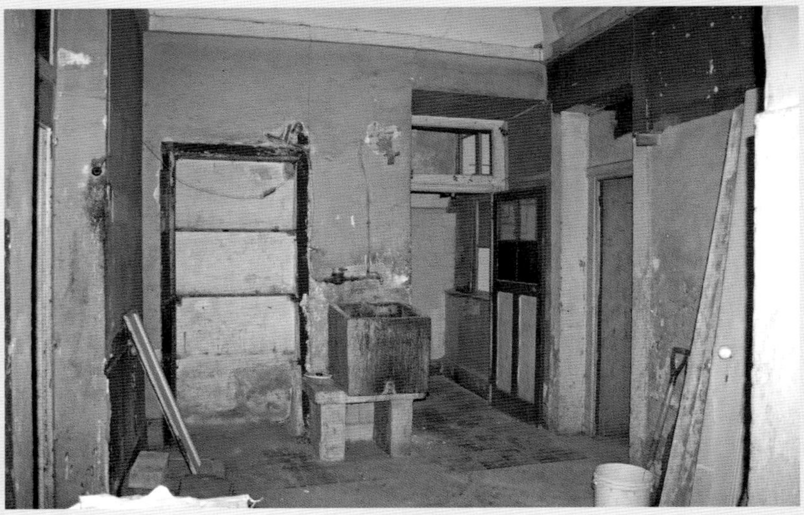
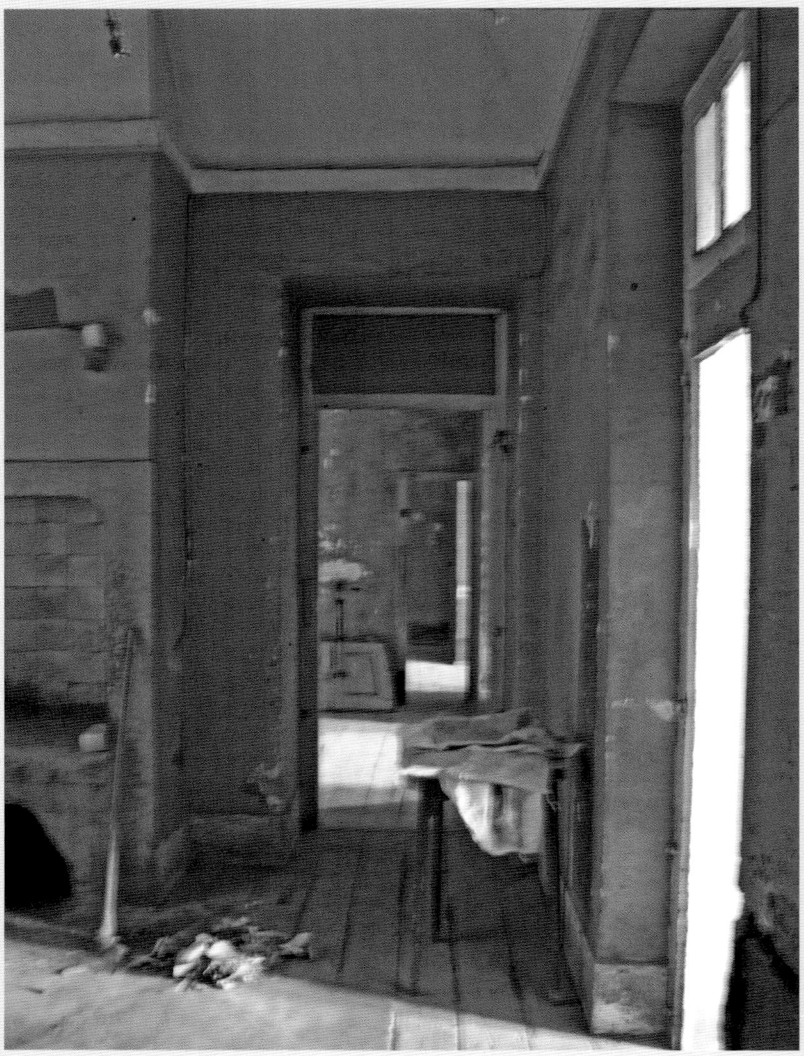
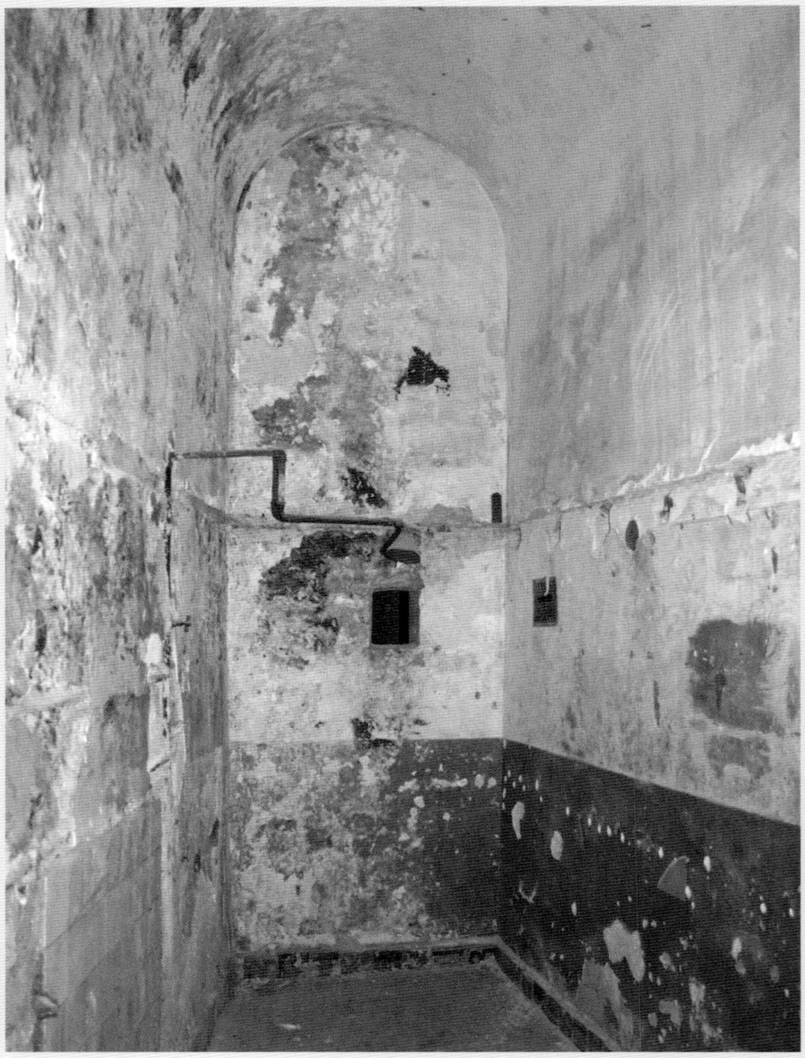

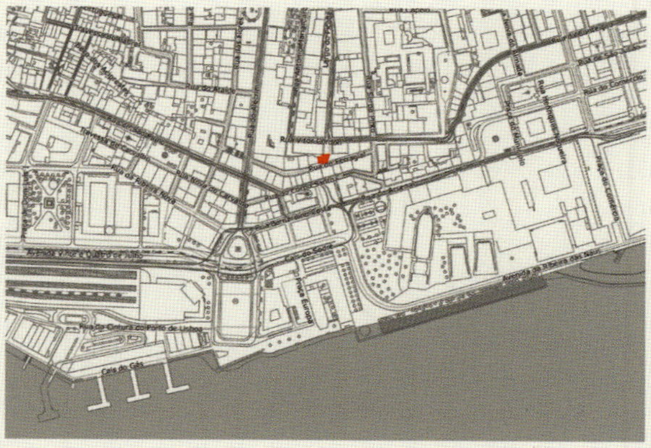

Location plan

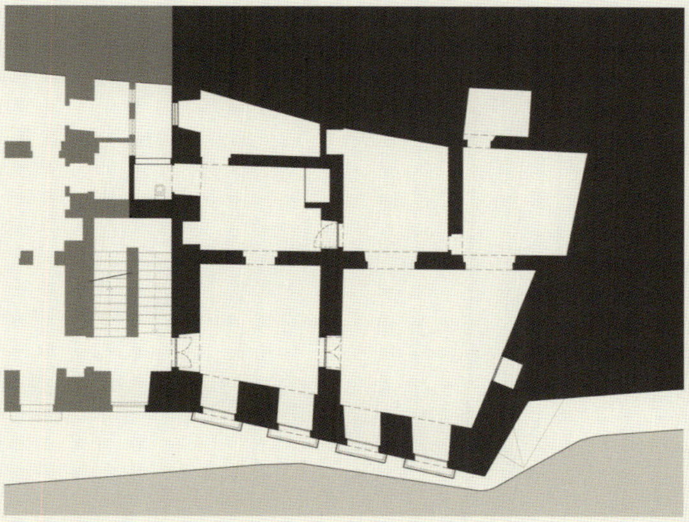

Existing floor plan

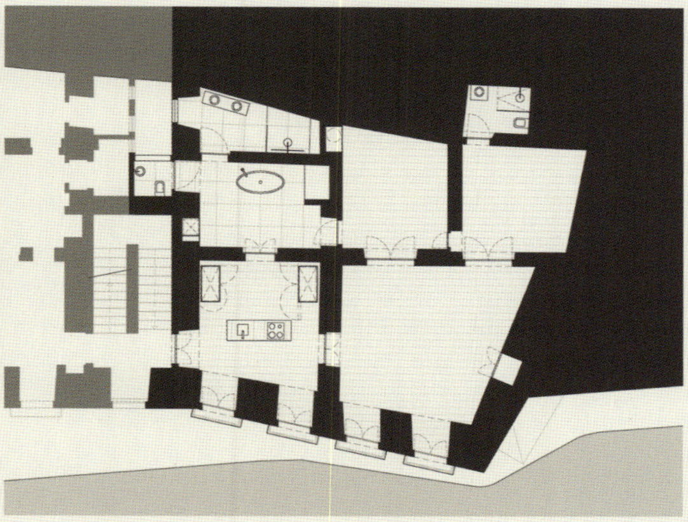

New floor plan

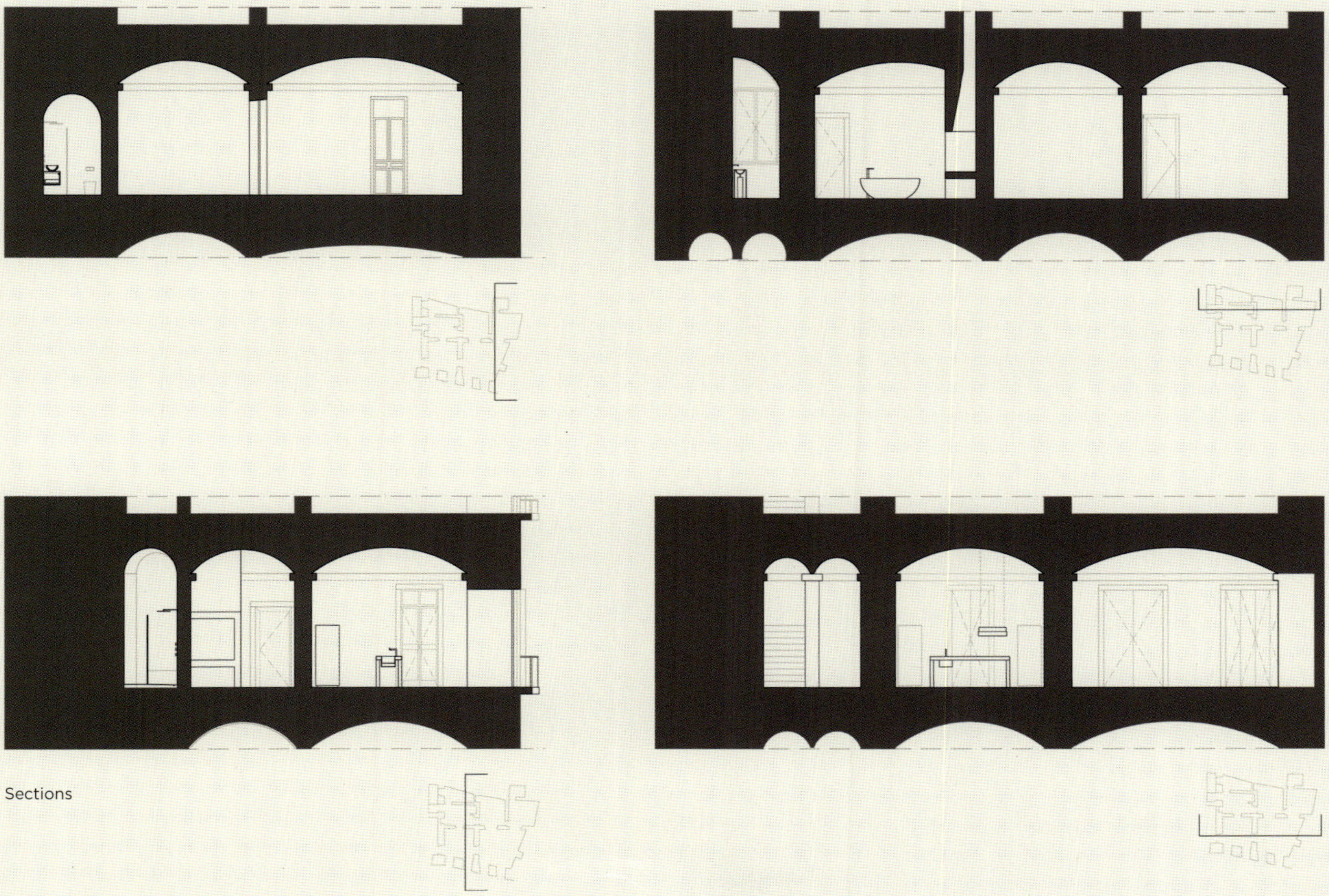

Sections

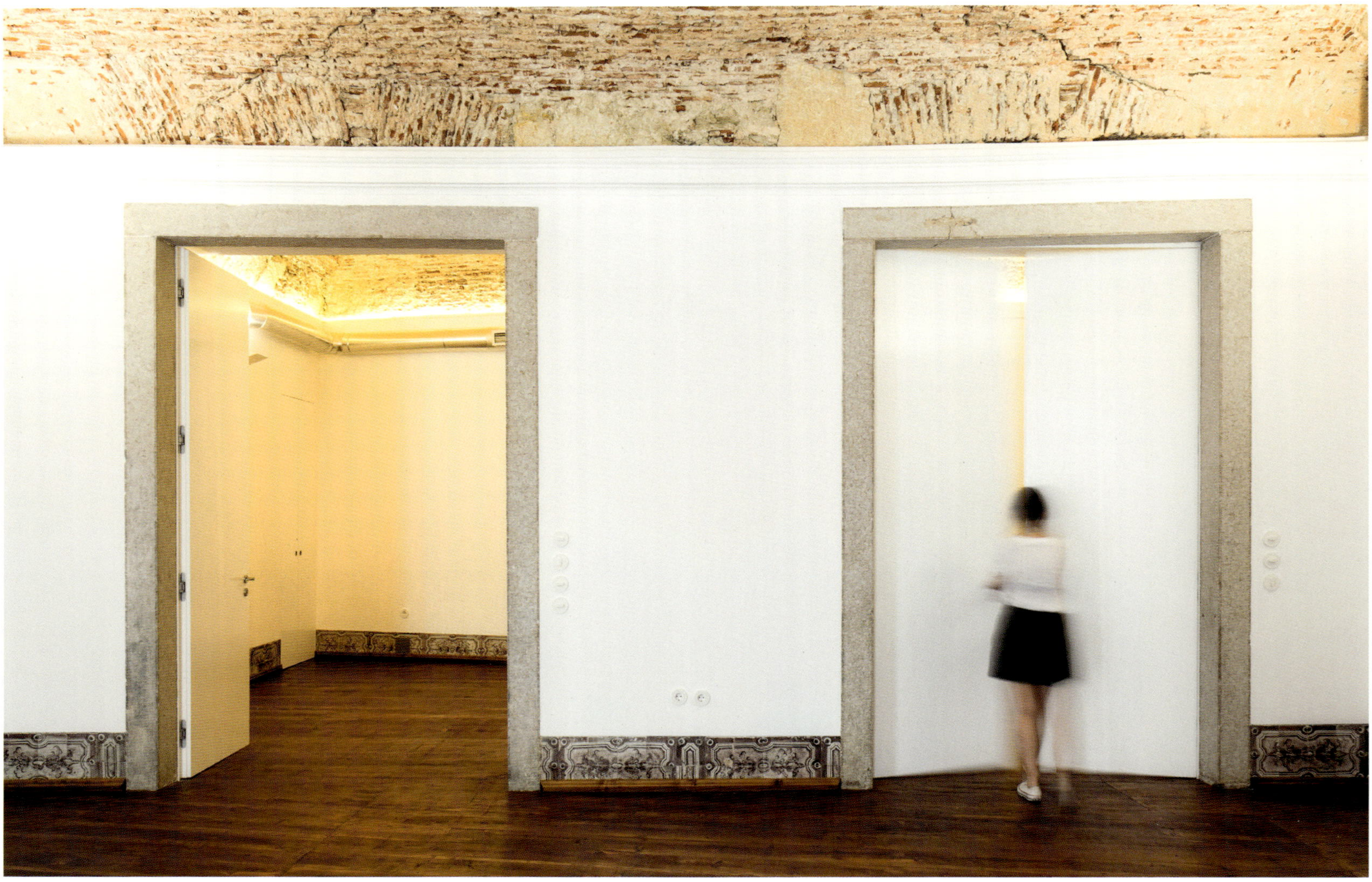

The original interior shutters were restored and remounted. Some of the fittings were adapted or preserved. The wood floor was sanded to remove the many layers of varnish and return it to its original appearance.

Die Original-Fensterläden im Innenbereich restaurierte und montierte man neu. Ein Teil der Beschläge wurde angepasst oder beibehalten. Den Holzboden schliff man ab, um die verschiedenen Schichten Lasur zu entfernen und ihm sein ursprüngliches Aussehen zurückzugeben.

Les volets intérieurs d'origine ont été restaurés et remontés. Une partie des éléments en fer forgé ont été adaptés ou préservés. Le parquet en bois a été poncé afin de retirer les différentes couches de vernis et lui rendre son apparence d'origine.

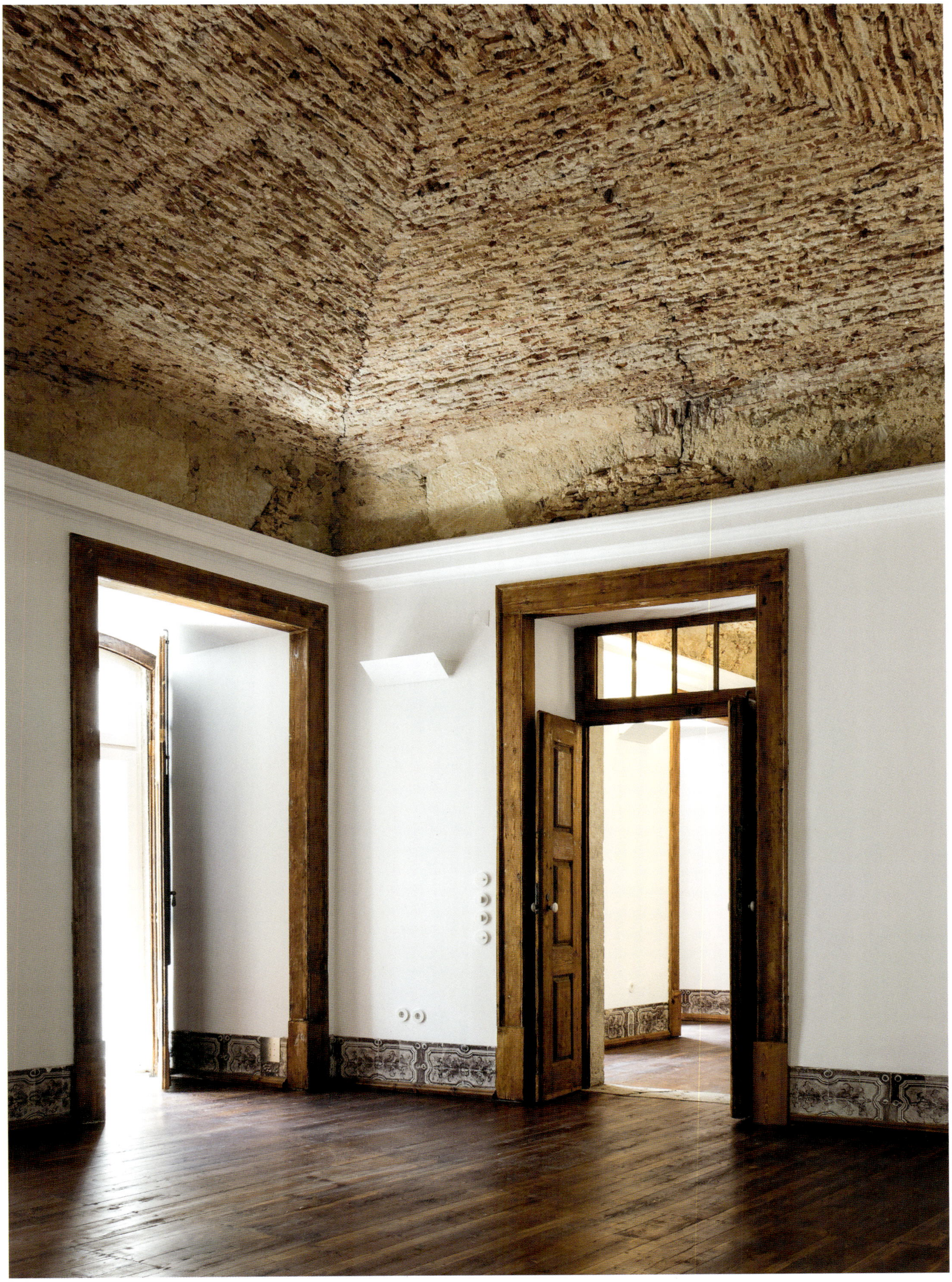

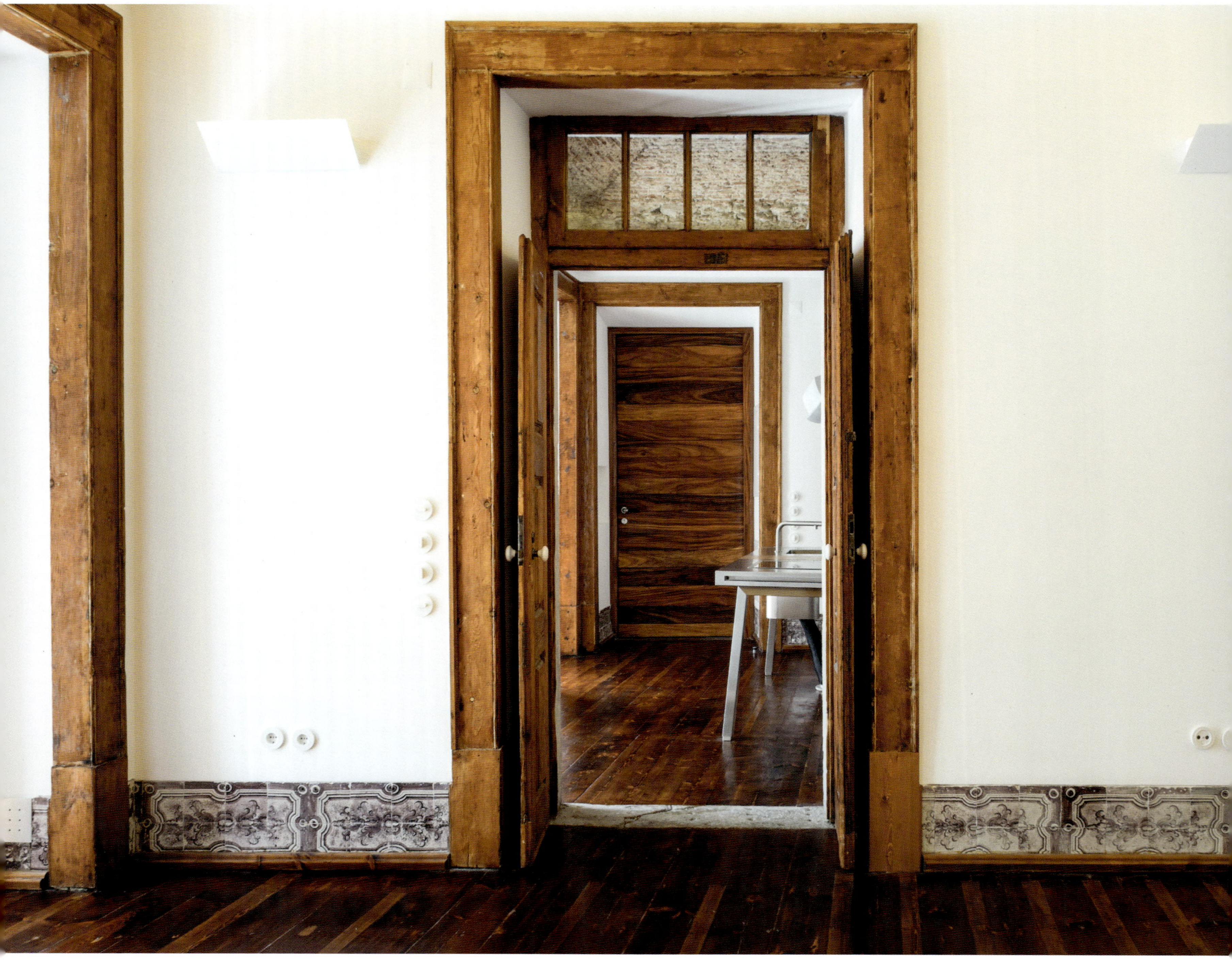

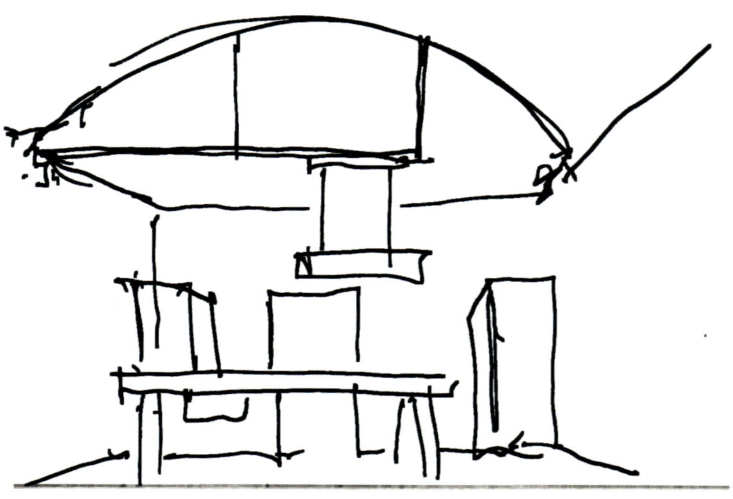

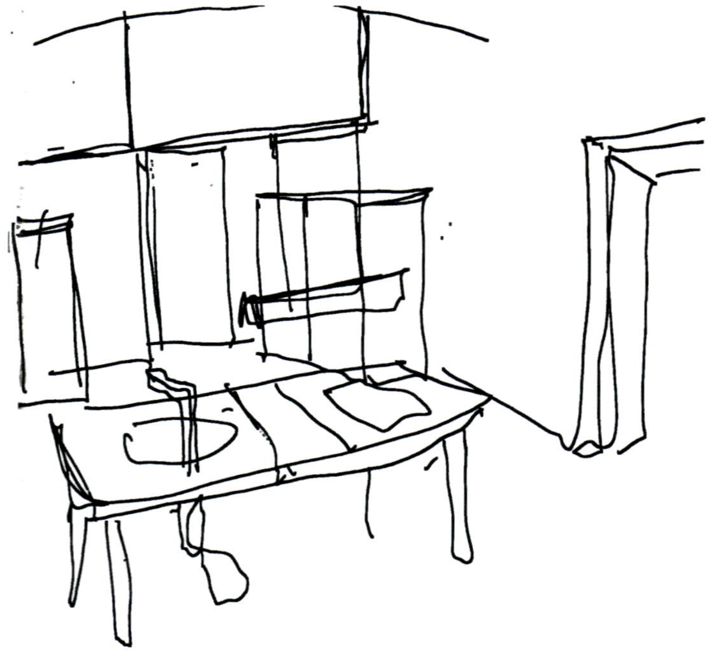

Kitchen sketches

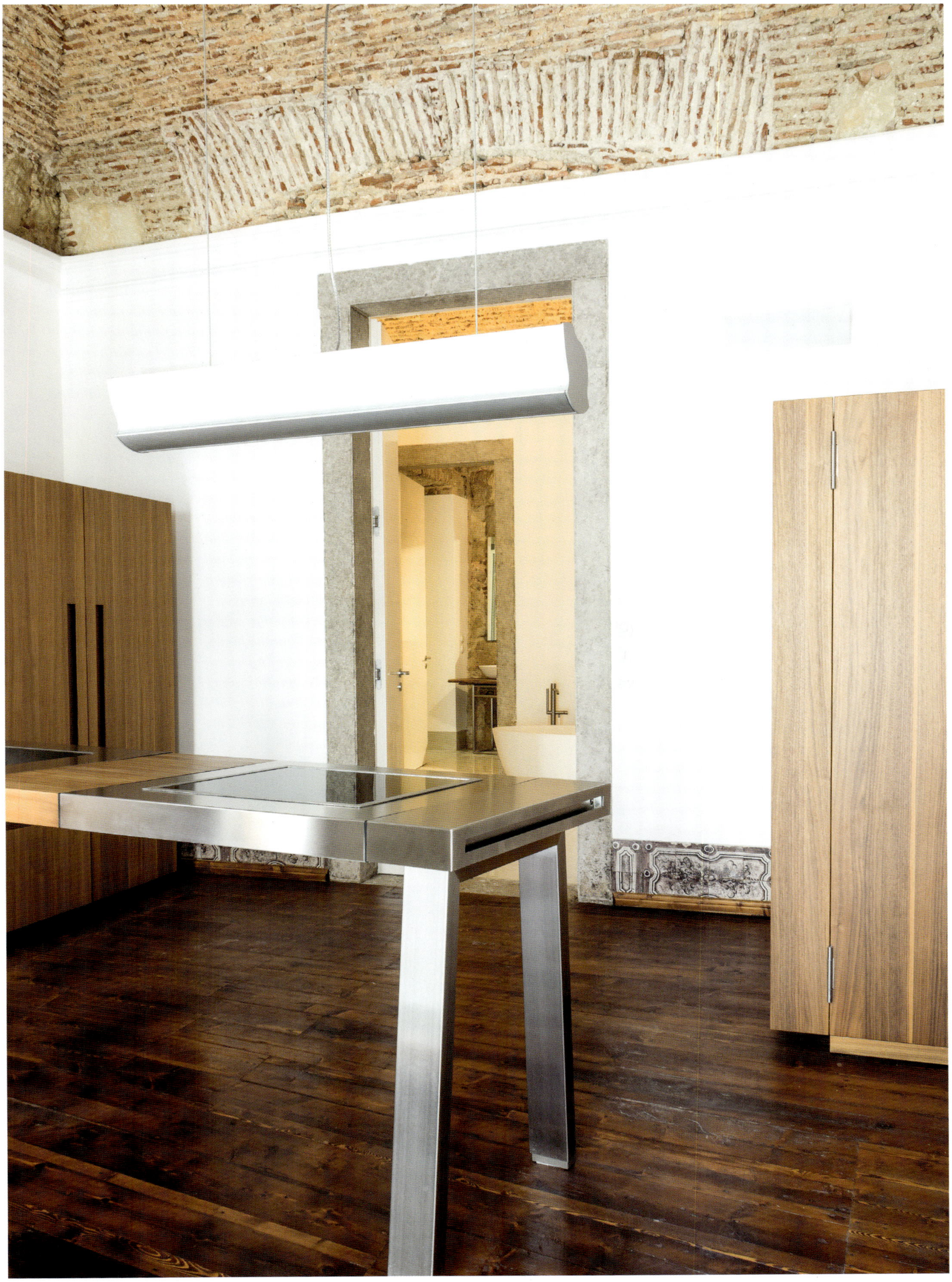

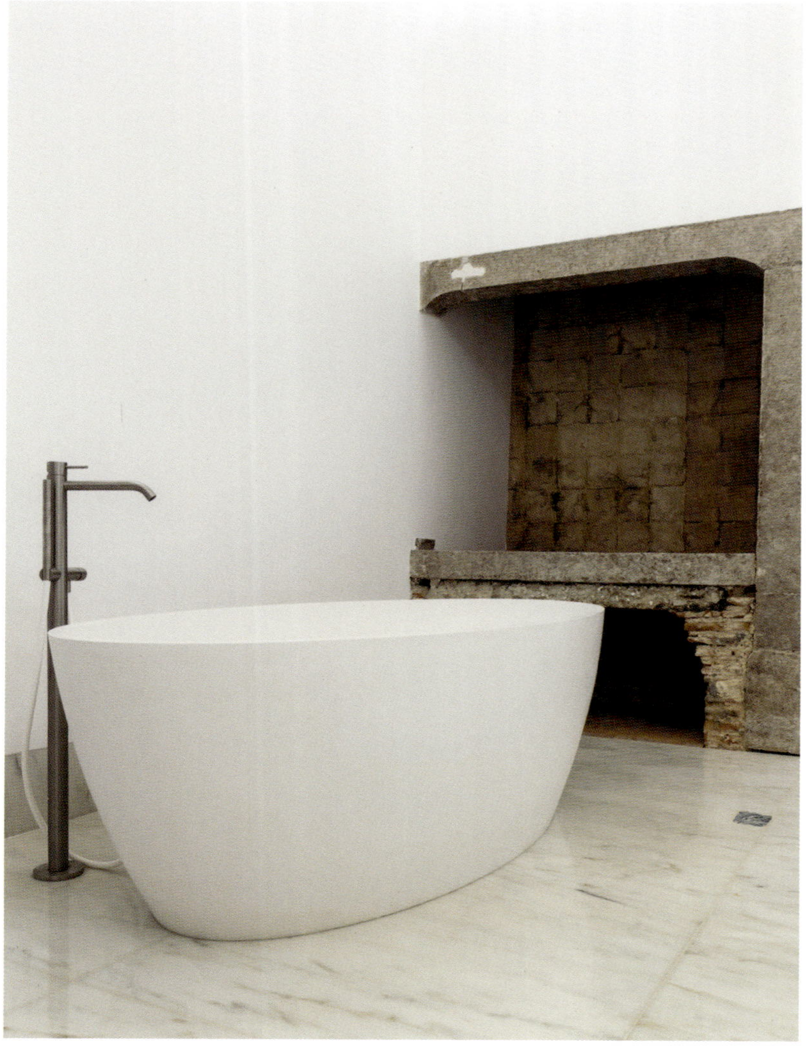

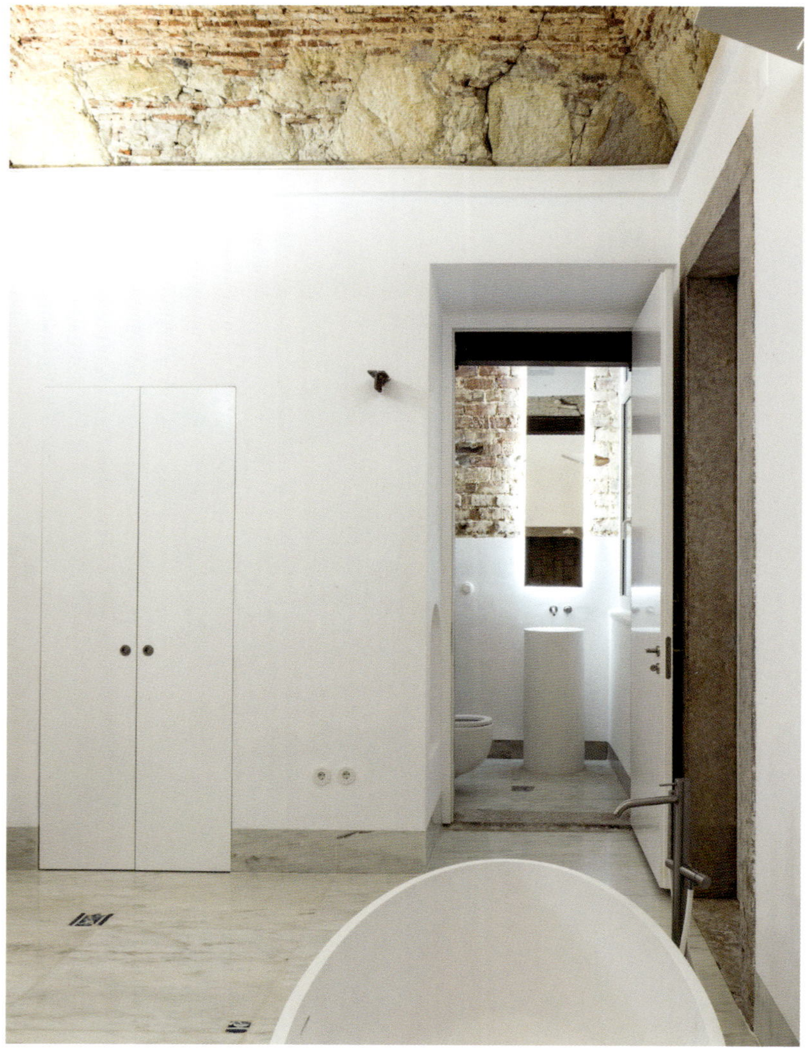

All existing woodwork was thoroughly treated to remove paint and enamel traces, returning it to its natural finish and retaining all the imperfections, scratches, and patches that it had suffered over the centuries. The artificial lighting brings out every preserved detail, and the materials and fixtures are restrained to avoid overpowering the existing space.

Die gesamten vorhandenen Schreinerarbeiten aus Holz wurden umfassend behandelt: Jeder Farb- und Lackrest wurde entfernt und den Objekten so ihr natürliches Aussehen zurückgegeben. Jeder Schönheitsfehler, jede Schramme und jede ausgebesserte Stelle, die sich im Lauf der Zeit angesammelt haben, ist nun wieder sichtbar. Das künstliche Licht betont jedes bewahrte Detail, Materialien und Installationen sind bewusst schlicht gehalten, damit sie den bestehenden Raum nicht zu sehr überfrachten.

Toute la menuiserie existante a été traitée en profondeur, en retirant les résidus de peinture et vernis pour mettre en valeur leur finition naturelle, avec toutes les imperfections, égratignures et rafistolages dont elle a fait l'objet au fil du temps. La lumière artificielle met en relief chaque détail conservé, et les matériaux et accessoires sont sobres sans pour autant empiéter sur l'espace existant.

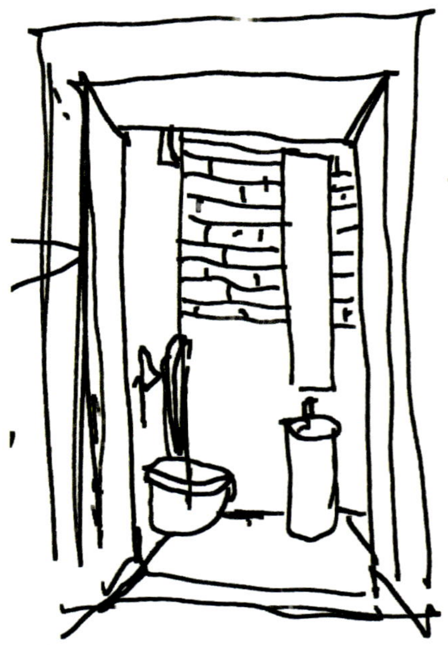

Bathroom sketch

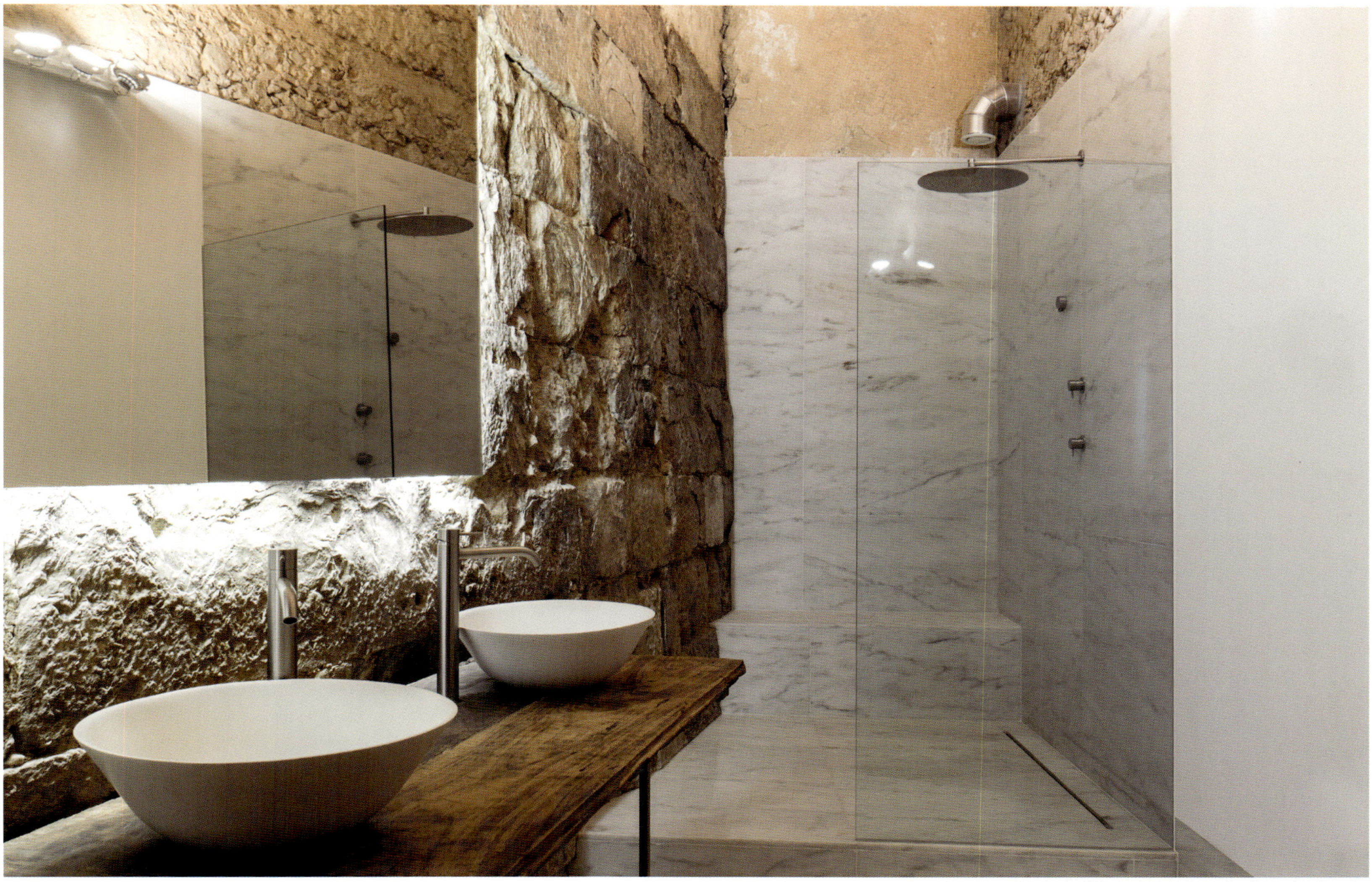

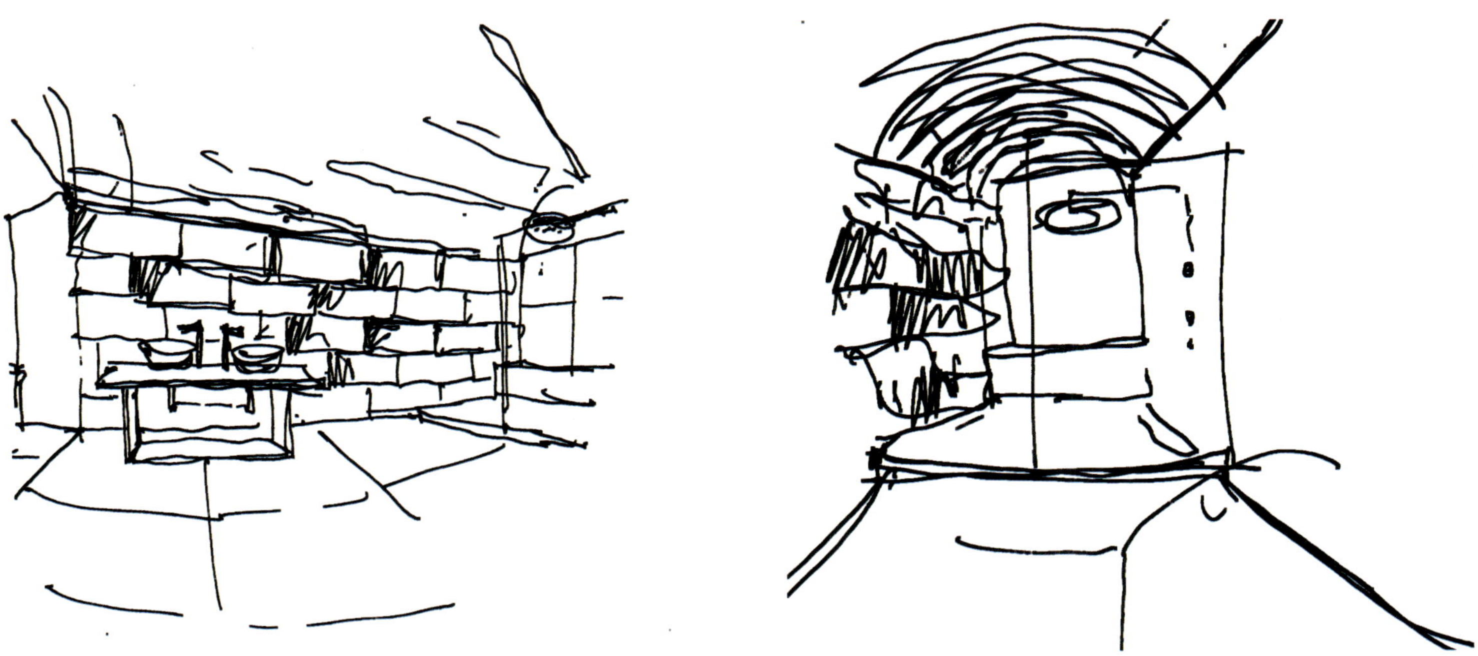

Bathroom sketches

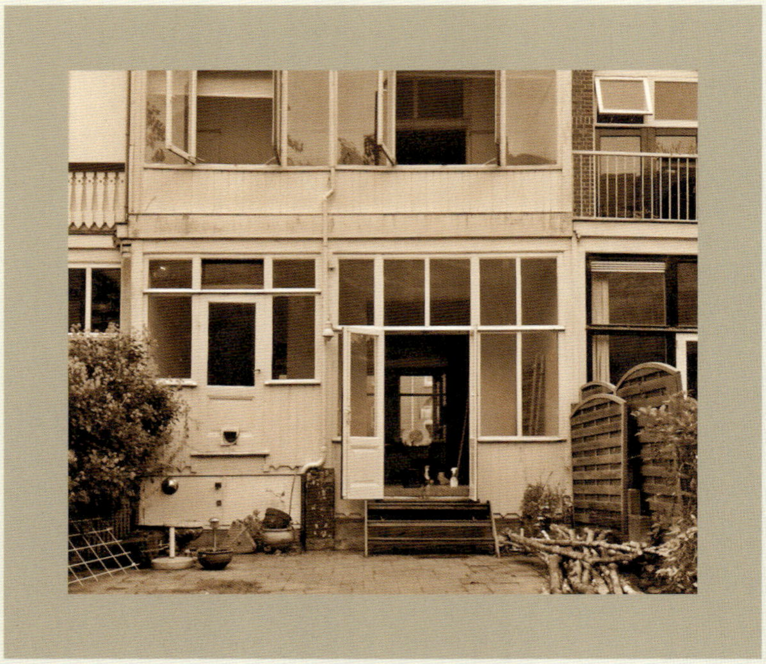

RENOVATION AND EXTENSION OF A 30'S ROW HOUSE

LAB-S

190 m² | 2,045 sq. ft.

Utrecht, The Netherlands

Photos © **Suzanne Paap**

> Build an extension that harmonizes with the original house

> Adapt the design to the lifestyle of a young couple with three children

> Einen Anbau in Harmonie mit dem alten Haus bauen

> Die Gestaltung an das Leben eines jungen Paares mit drei Kindern anpassen

> Construire une extension en harmonie avec l'ancienne maison

> Adapter la conception à la vie d'un jeune couple avec trois enfants

This typical 1930s row house in the city of Utrecht has been renovated to include a modern two-story extension that exists in harmony with the old house. The residence, featuring a new spatial distribution for each floor, was designed for a young couple with three children. In addition, the existing expansion of the house's rear section has been replaced by a new one with identical dimensions. The new facade design was inspired by the old rear facade with its multiplicity of identically-colored steel window frames. It was decided to retain the steel framework in the new expansion and to add new steel window frames of matching color. The result is an extension that is solid yet spare, permitting natural light to flow into the old building.
One can speak of a home of contrasts: light yet robust, with details both traditional and modern.

Dieses für die 1930er Jahre typische Reihenhaus in der Stadt Utrecht wurde renoviert. Ein zeitgenössischer Anbau mit zwei Etagen wurde in Harmonie mit dem alten Haus hinzugefügt. Das Haus ist für eine junge Familie mit drei Kindern gedacht, und für jede Etage wurde eine neue Aufteilung entworfen. Zudem wurde der alte Anbau an der Rückseite des Hauses durch einen neuen in der gleicher Größe ersetzt. Die Gestaltung dieser neuen Fassade ist an die ehemalige hintere Fassade mit mehreren Stahlfensterrahmen angelehnt. Die Architekten beschlossen, die Stahlkonstruktion des neuen Anbaus sichtbar zu belassen und neue Stahlfensterrahmen in der gleichen Farbe hinzuzufügen. Das Ergebnis ist ein robuster und gleichzeitig schlanker Anbau, der den Einfall von Tageslicht in den Altbau ermöglicht.
Es kann als ein Zuhause der Kontraste bezeichnet werden: leicht und robust zugleich; mit alten und modernen Details.

Située dans la ville d'Utrecht, cette maison mitoyenne, typique des années 30, a été rénovée et à laquelle a été ajoutée une extension contemporaine sur deux niveaux en harmonie avec l'ancienne maison. La maison a été pensée pour une jeune famille avec trois enfants. Pour cela, il a fallu concevoir une nouvelle répartition pour chaque étage. En outre, l'ancienne extension de la partie arrière de la maison a été remplacée par une nouvelle de même taille. Le design de cette nouvelle façade s'inspire de l'ancienne façade de derrière, avec de nombreux cadres de fenêtre. La structure en acier de la nouvelle extension apparente a été conservée et de nouveaux cadres de fenêtres en acier dans la même couleur ont été ajoutés. Le résultat est une extension à la fois robuste et svelte laissant entrer la lumière naturelle dans l'ancienne maison.
Elle peut être défini comme un lieu de contrastes : léger et robuste à la fois, avec des détails de l'ancien et du moderne.

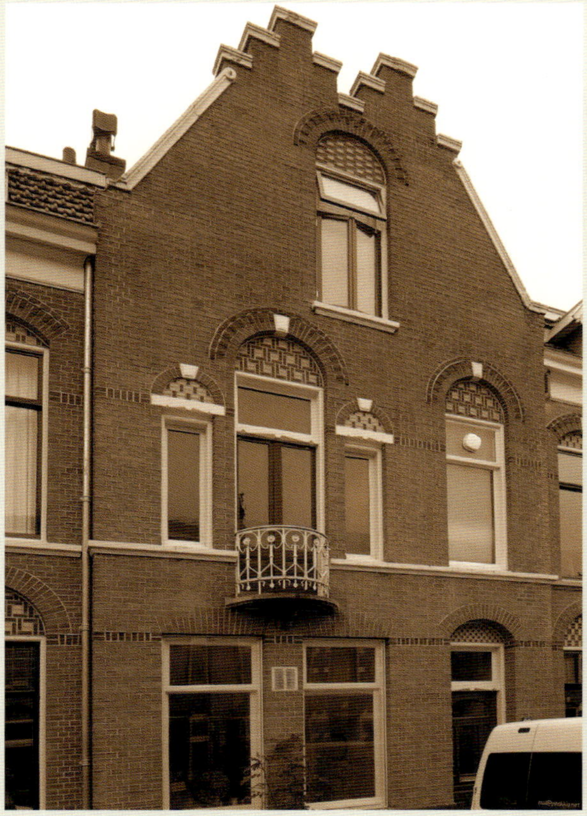

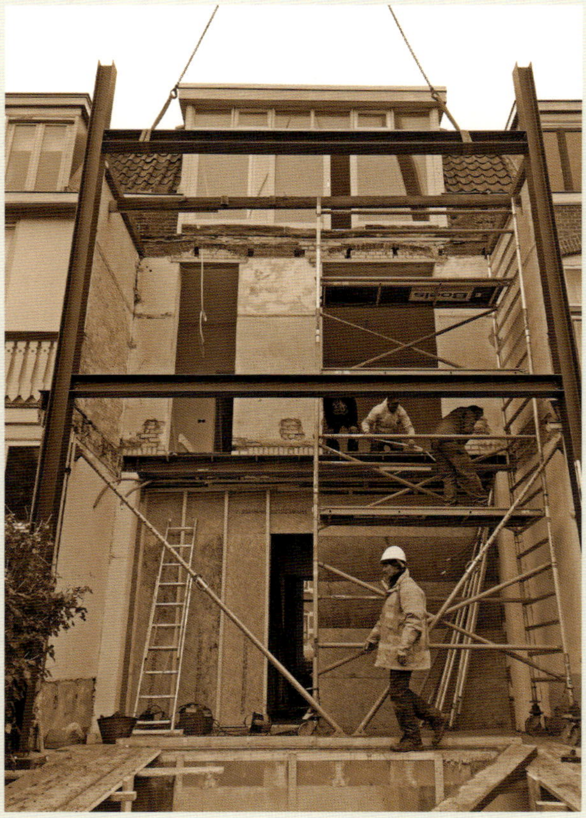

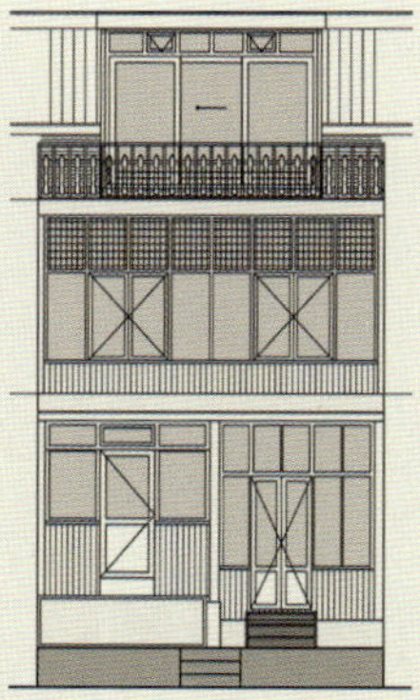

Existing elevation

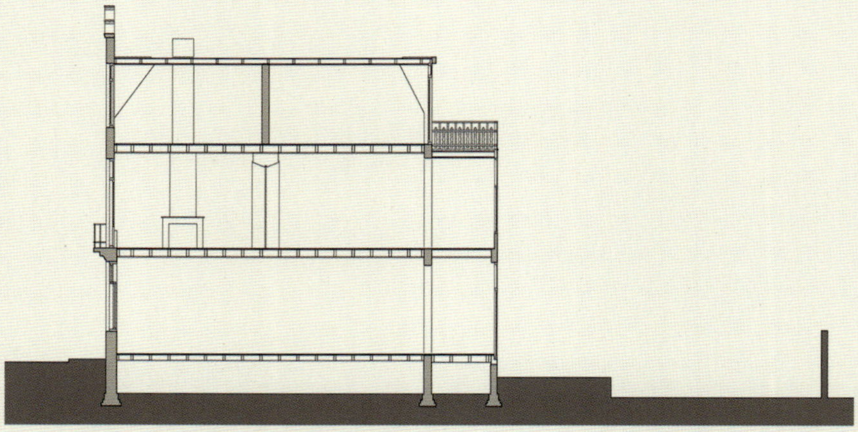

Existing section

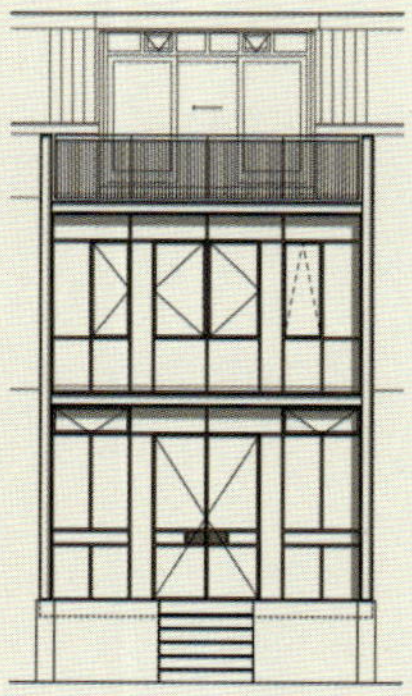

New elevation

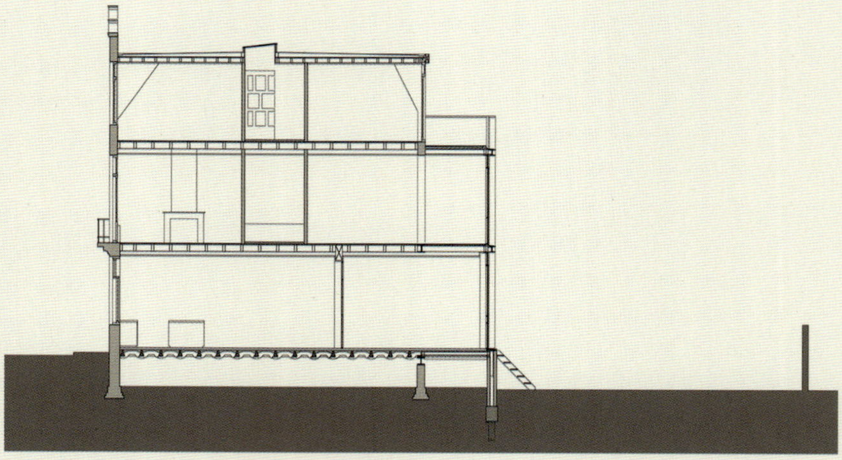

New section

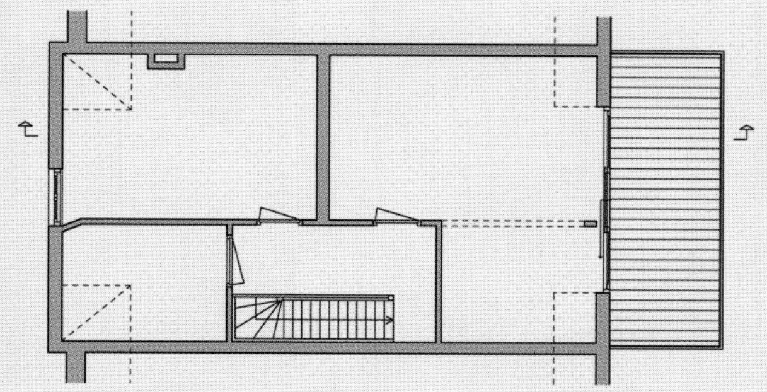

Existing second floor plan

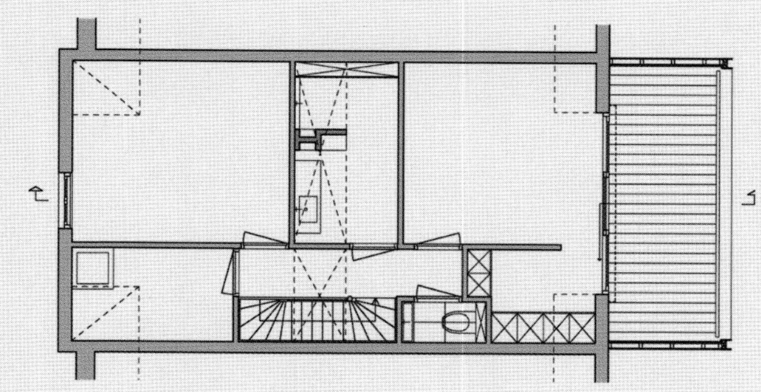

New second floor plan

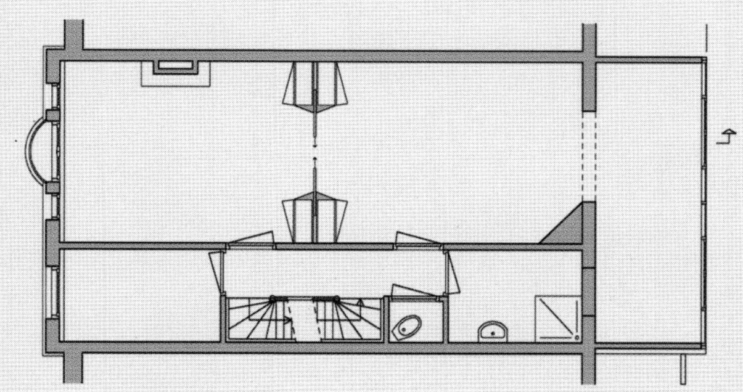

Existing first floor plan

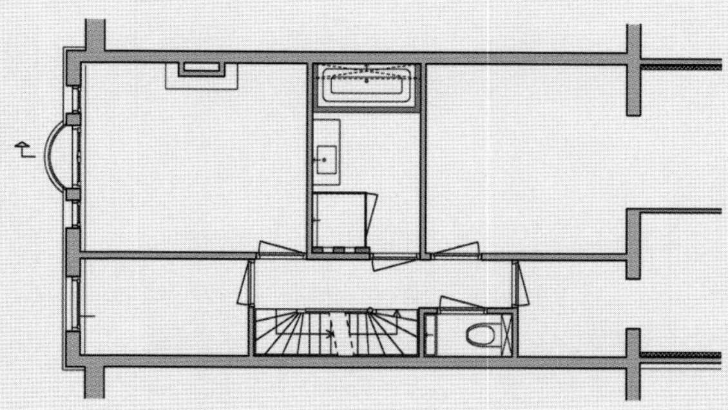

New first floor plan

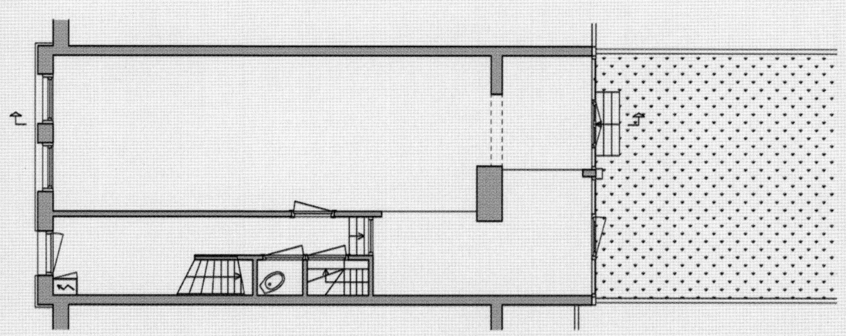

Existing ground floor plan

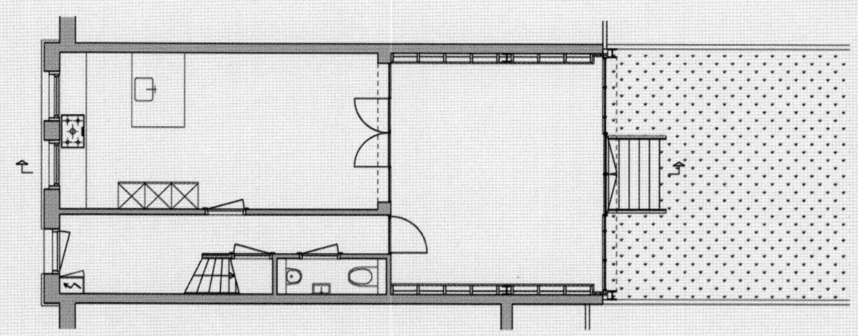

New ground floor plan

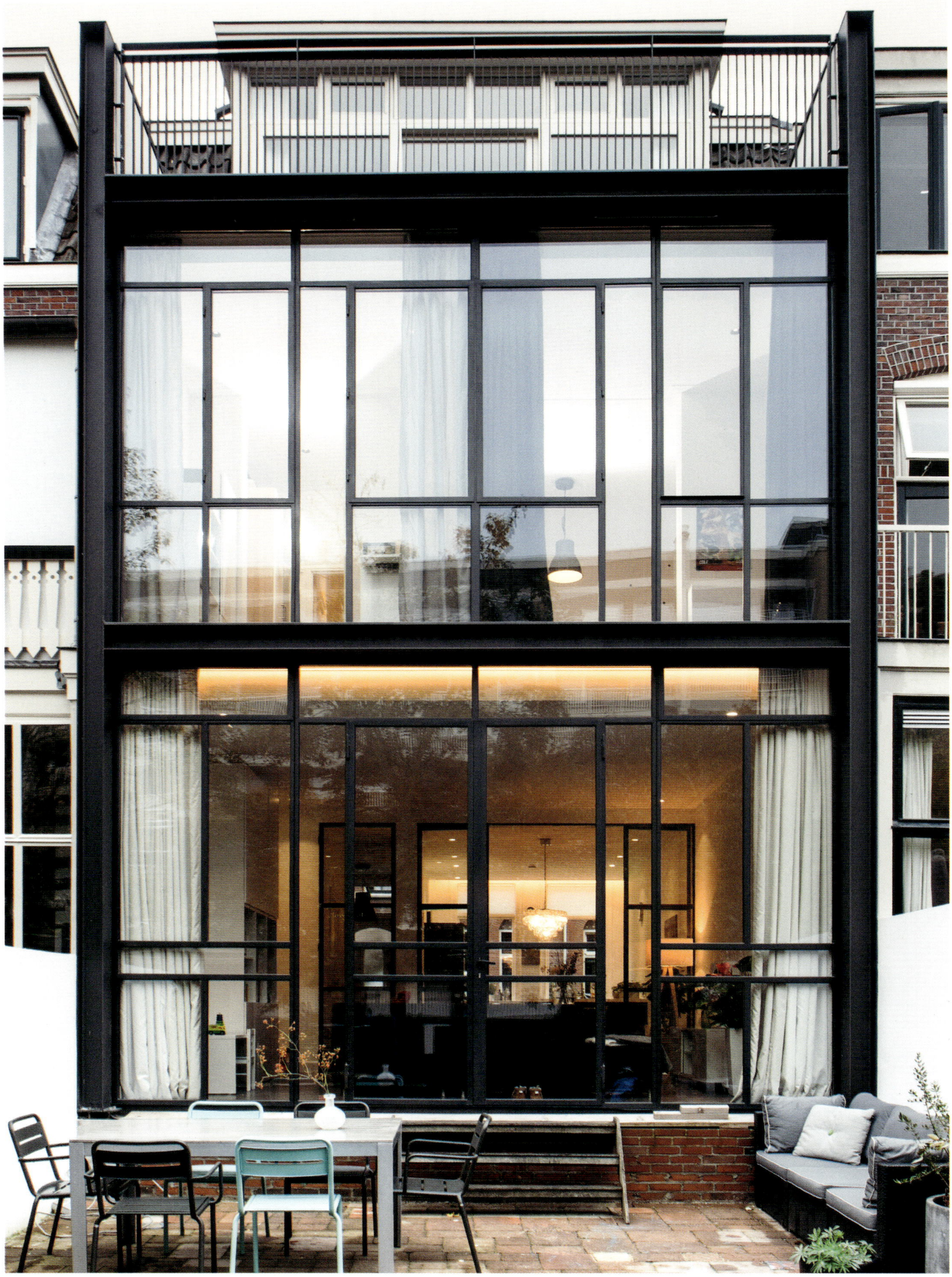

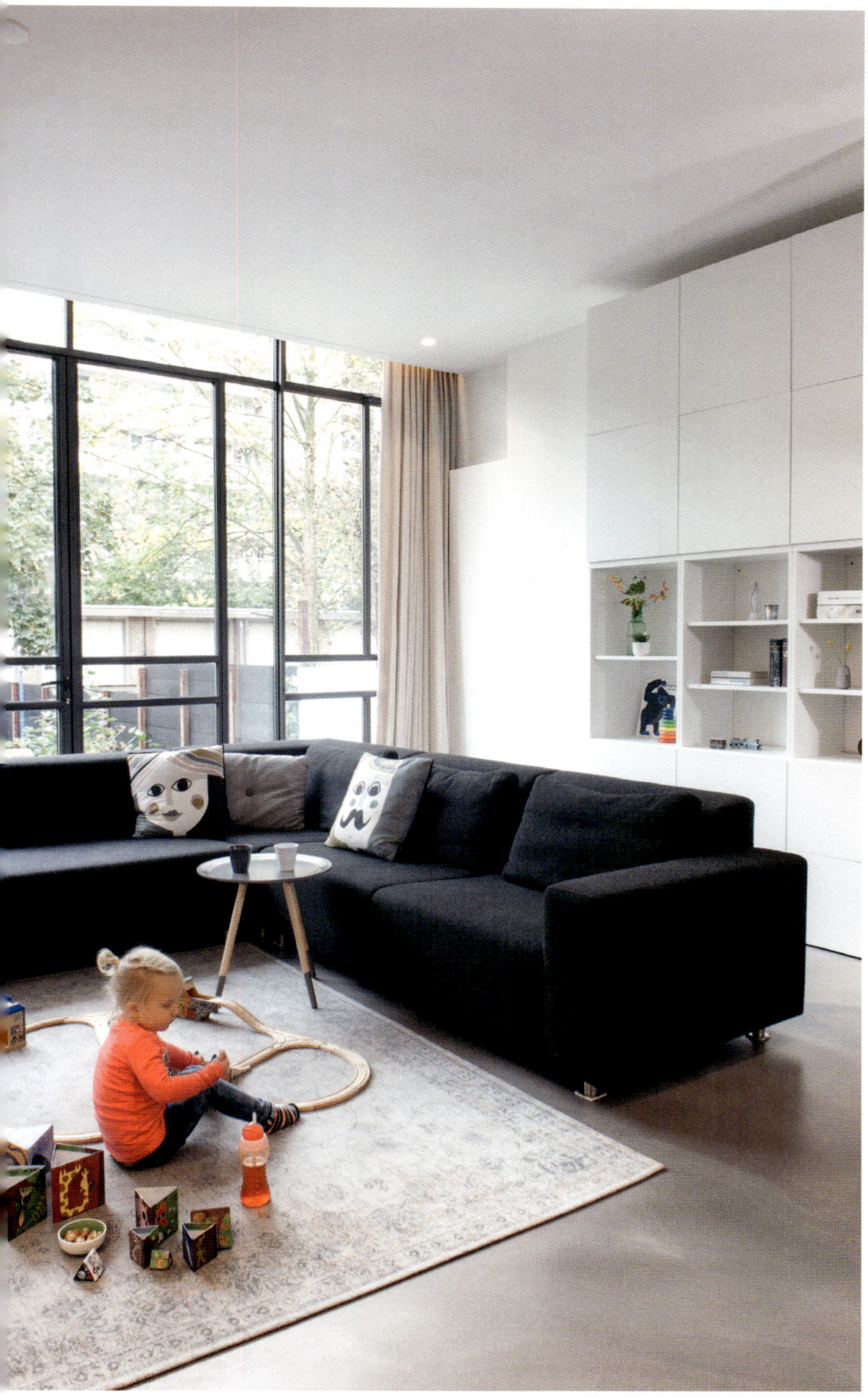 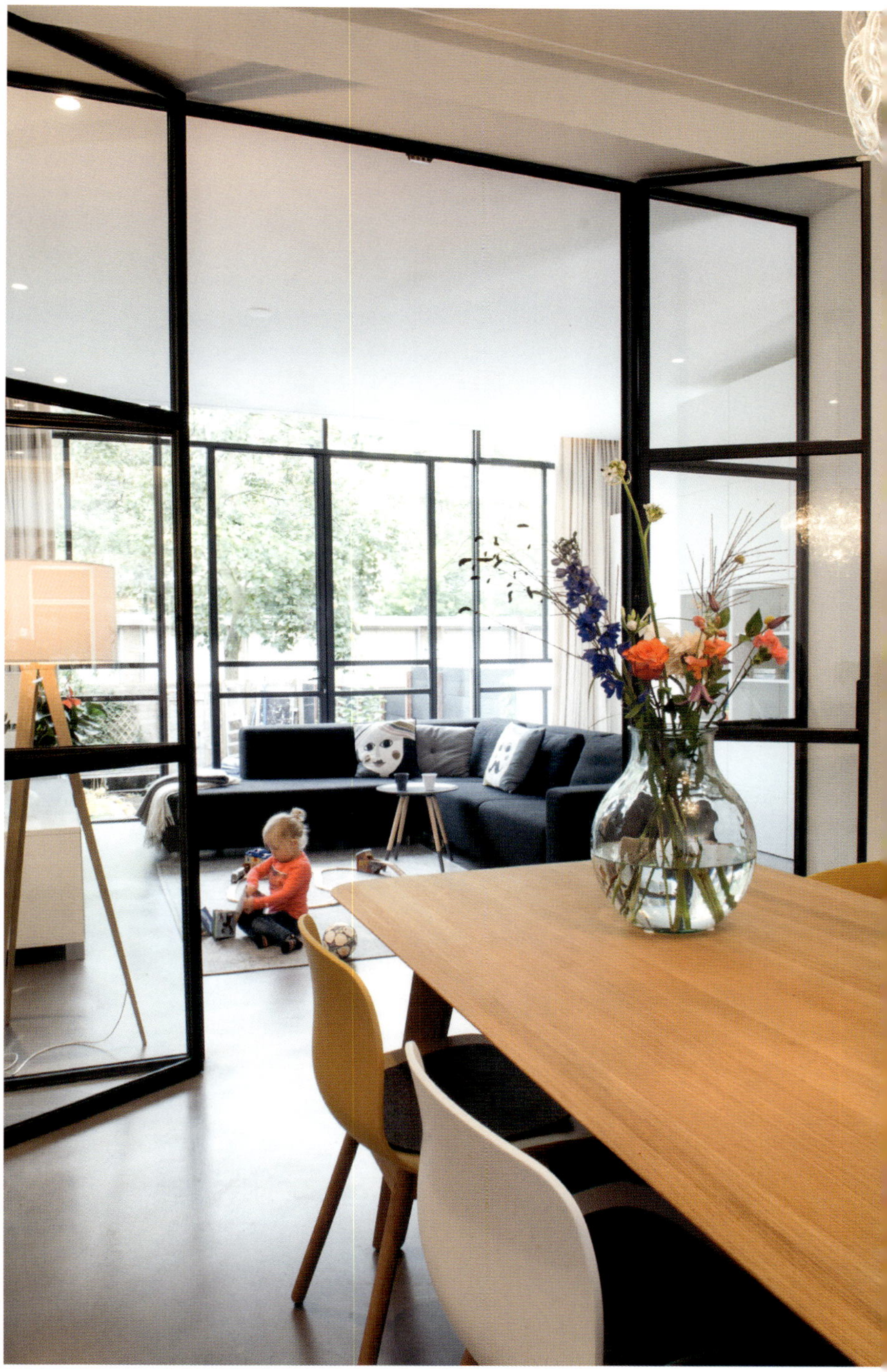

The new ground-floor living room is positioned at the rear of the house near the backyard. This space is separated from the dining area and kitchen by means of high glass-and-steel doors that not only serve to divide the spaces but also become a center of attraction in the living room.

Das neue Wohnzimmer im Erdgeschoss befindet sich auf der Rückseite des Hauses in der Nähe des Gartens. Dieser Raum wird durch hohe Stahlglastüren vom Esszimmer und der Küche getrennt, die nicht nur als Raumteiler, sondern auch als Anziehungspunkt im Wohnzimmer dienen.

Le nouveau séjour au rez-de-chaussée se trouve dans la partie arrière de la maison, à proximité du jardin. Cet espace est séparé de la salle à manger et de la cuisine par de hautes portes en acier vitrées qui servent non seulement de séparation, mais aussi de point d'attraction dans le salon.

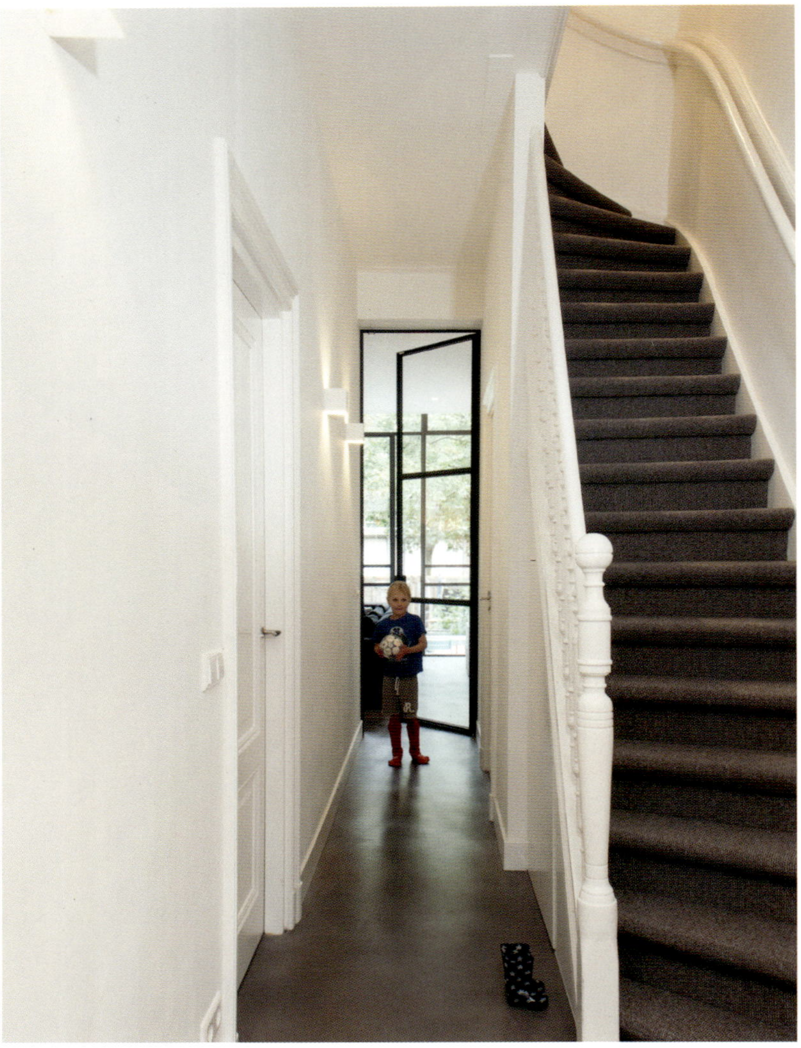

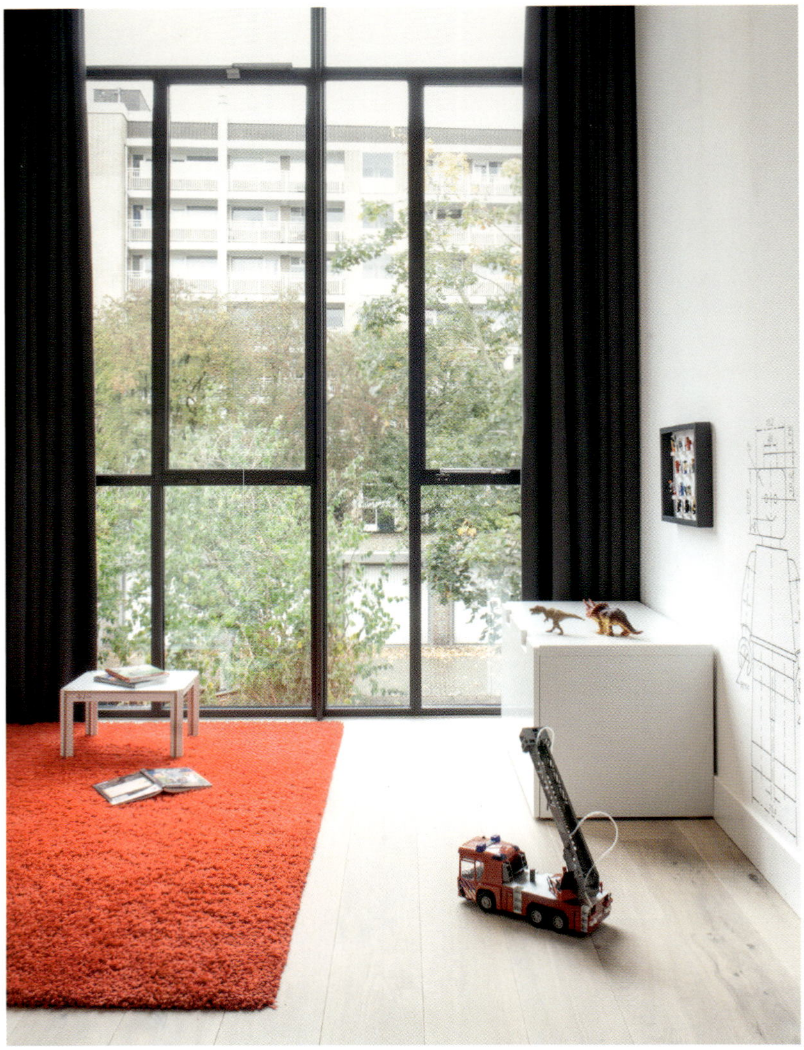

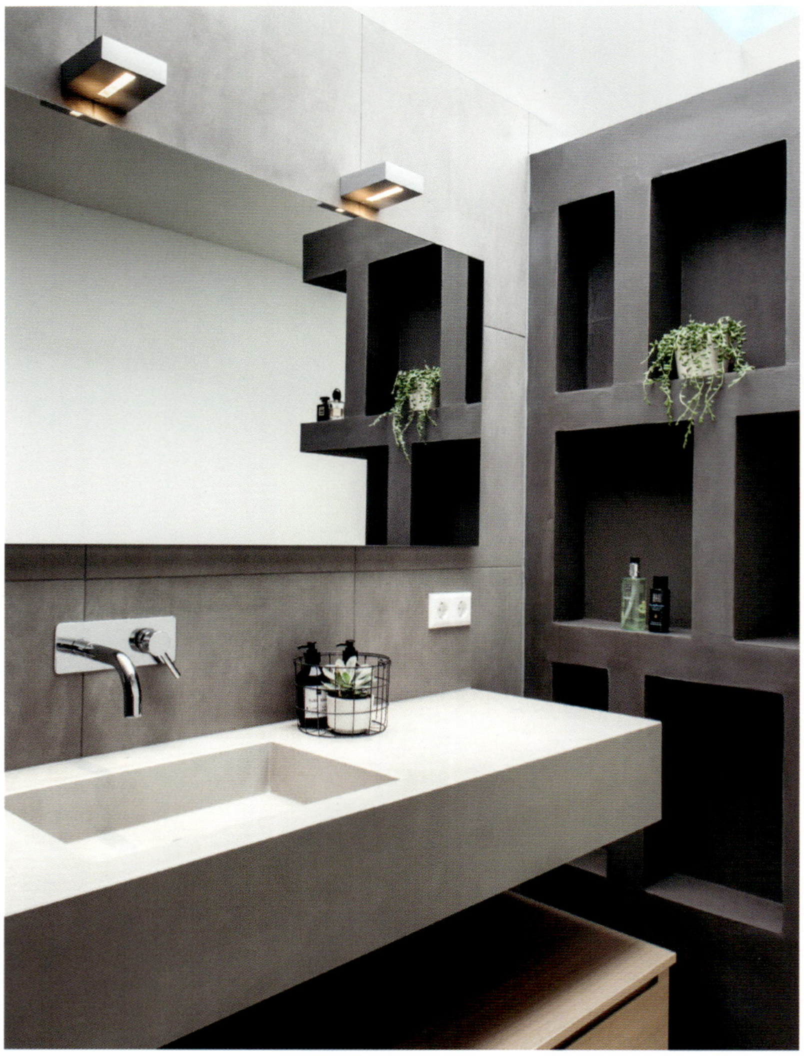

Two new bathrooms are located in the middle of the house, one each on the lower and upper floors. Separated from the outer walls and thus lacking windows, they receive natural light from a large skylight in the middle of the roof. The main bathroom on the upper floor features an aperture that carries daylight to the children's bathroom directly below.

Zwei neue Badezimmer befinden sich im Zentrum des Hauses im ersten und zweiten Stock. Da sich diese Bäder nicht an der Außenwand befinden, wurde in der Mitte des Daches ein großes Oberlicht angebracht, das ihnen Tageslicht schenkt. Eine Öffnung im Boden des Hauptbadezimmers im zweiten Stock lässt Tageslicht in das Kinderbadezimmer auf der unteren Ebene gelangen.

Deux nouvelles salles de bains ont été installées au centre de la maison, aux premier et deuxième étages. Ces deux salles de bains ne sont pas situées du côté de la façade, par conséquent une grande lucarne a été ouverte au centre du plafond afin de leur apporter la lumière naturelle. Une ouverture dans le sol de la salle de bains principale au deuxième étage permet à la lumière du jour d'arriver jusqu'à la salle de bains des enfants au niveau inférieur.

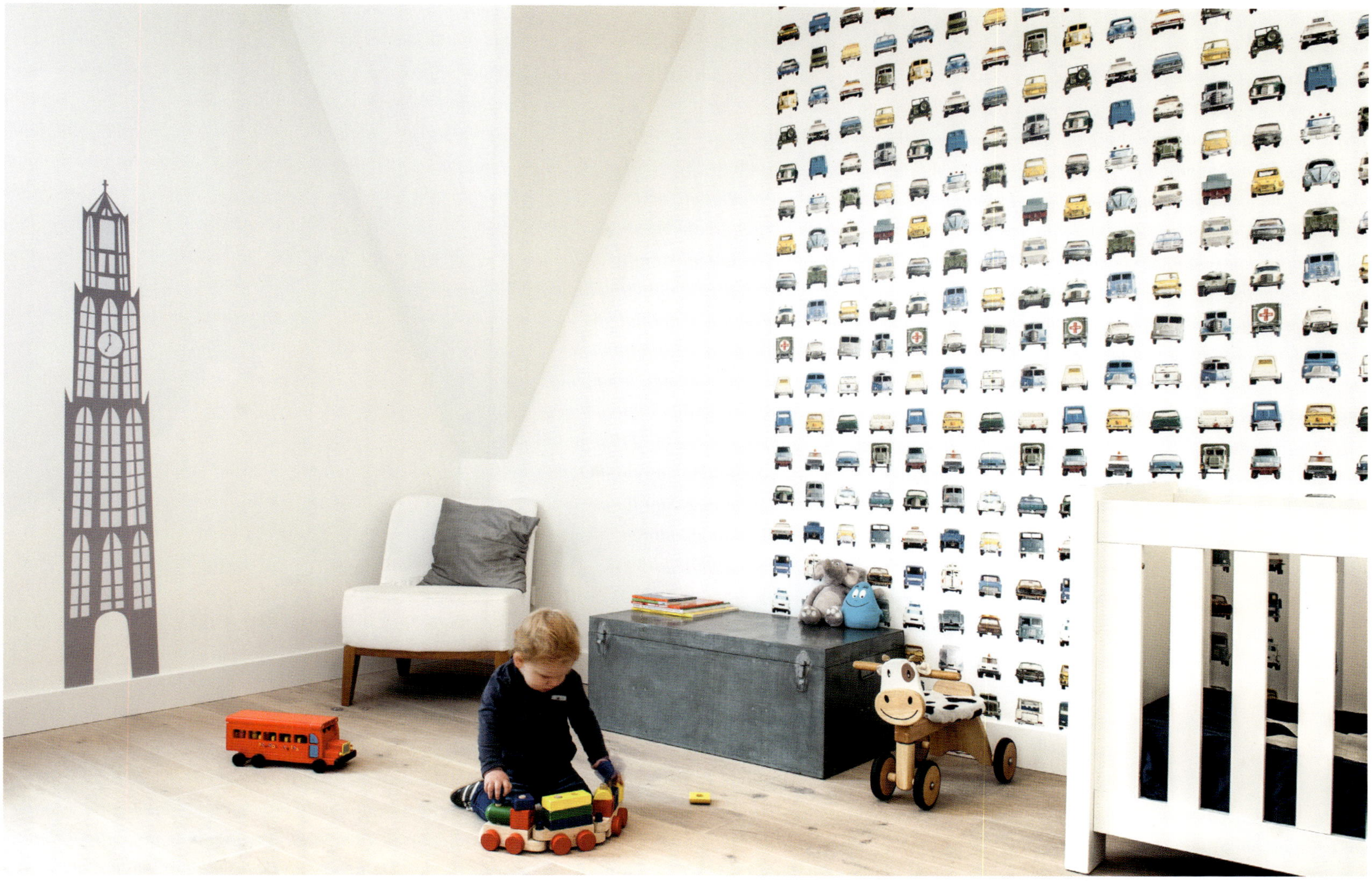

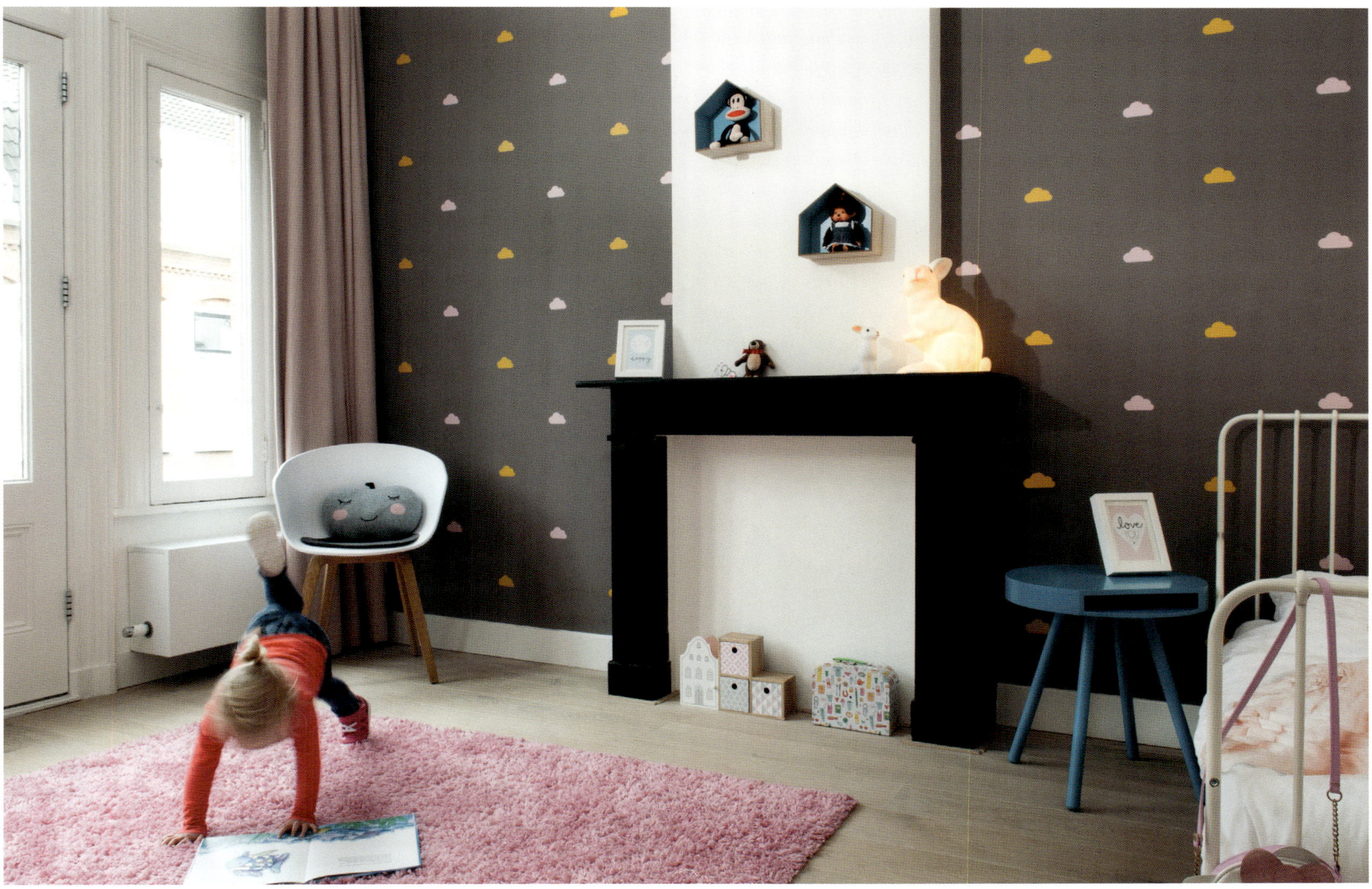

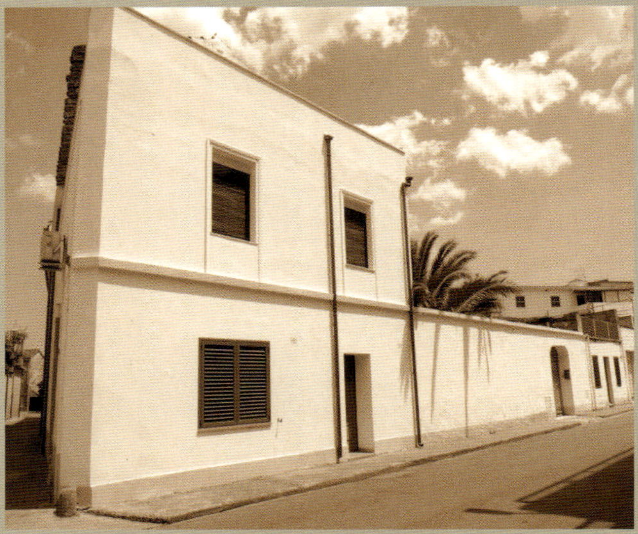

VILLA RENOVATION CC

MATTEO FORESTI

260 m² | 2,800 sq. ft.

San Vito (CA), Sardinia, Italy

Photos © **Atelier XYZ**

> Remove unneeded old structures to reveal the house's origins

> Create new openings to facilitate movement into the patio

> Preserve intimacy

> Entfernen der alten, unnötigen An- und Einbauten, um das Wesen des ursprünglichen Hauses wieder freizulegen

> Schaffen neuer Öffnungen, um den Hof einzubeziehen

> Beibehalten der Privatsphäre

> Retirer les anciennes constructions inutiles pour mettre en valeur les éléments d'origine de la maison

> Créer de nouvelles ouvertures afin d'améliorer la circulation avec la cour

> Préserver la vie privée

This immaculate, secret residence is hidden away behind its white walls under the intense San Vito sun.
From its beginnings as a small house, it grew over the next hundred years, adding two shops, a bathroom, and other rooms that gradually overran the patio. When the rehabilitation project was proposed, the first and most important step was to remove all unnecessary elements to approximate the original structure as much as possible. This served in the end to define the sizes more clearly and reveal the thick stone walls.
The placement of new passageways allows for fluid movement between the public spaces—living room, kitchen, and dining room—and the patio. To preserve intimacy and quiet, the bedrooms are located on the upper floor, which also features a living area that overlooks the patio.
The wholly dominant whiteness, the purity of the design, and the landscaped patio make this residence an authentic and serene oasis that exudes peacefulness and relaxation.

Versteckt hinter den weißen Wänden und unter der hellen Sonne von San Vito liegt dieses makellose Bauwerk.
Ursprünglich war es ein kleines Haus, dessen Anbauten im Laufe eines Jahrhunderts immer mehr wurden: zwei Geschäfte, ein Badezimmer und einige andere Räume drängten sich nach und nach im Hof. Als das Umbauprojekt in Angriff genommen wurde, bestand der erste und wichtigste Schritt darin, alle unnötigen Bauten abzureißen, um so weit wie möglich den Ursprungszustand des Hauses wiederherzustellen. Als Resultat sind die Räume nun klar definiert und die verbliebenen dicken Steinwände sichtbar.
Die Erschaffung neuer Öffnungen sorgt für eine fließende Zirkulation zwischen den für alle zugänglichen Bereichen – Wohnzimmer, Esszimmer und Küche – und dem Hof. Um die Privatsphäre und Ruhe zu bewahren, wurden die Schlafzimmer im ersten Stock untergebracht, in dem auch ein Wohnzimmer liegt, das den Hof überblickt.
Die dominierende weiße Farbe, die Klarheit des Entwurfs und der durchgestaltete Hof machen aus diesem Gebäude eine wahre Oase der Stille, die Frieden ausstrahlt und zum Entspannen einlädt.

Cette magnifique maison, sous l'intense soleil de San Vito, est secrètement cachée derrière ses murs blancs.
À l'origine, il s'agissait d'une petite maison qui a été agrandie au fil d'un siècle : deux magasins, une salle de bains et plusieurs autres pièces ont peu à peu envahi la cour. Lors de l'étude de réhabilitation de la maison, la première étape et la plus importante a été de retirer toutes les constructions inutiles afin de se rapprocher au maximum du schéma original. Cela a donné lieu à des volumes clairement définis et de gros murs de pierre apparents.
La disposition des nouvelles ouvertures facilite la circulation entre les parties communes – le séjour, la cuisine et la salle à manger – et la cour. Pour préserver l'intimité et le silence, les chambres sont situées au premier étage où se trouve également un séjour qui domine la cour.
La prédominance absolue de la couleur blanche, la pureté du design et la cour aménagée font de cette maison une authentique oasis silencieuse qui respire le calme et invite à la détente.

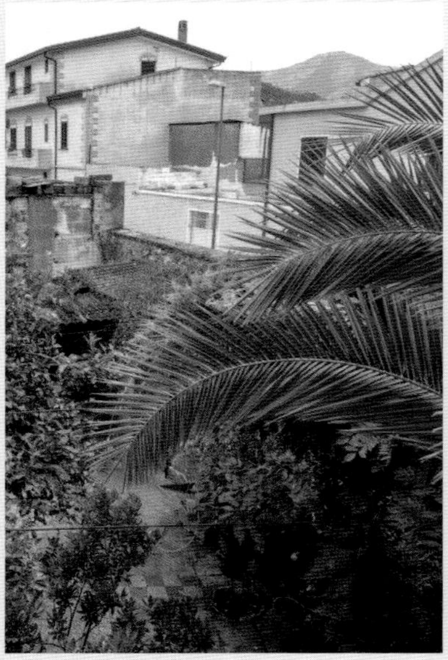
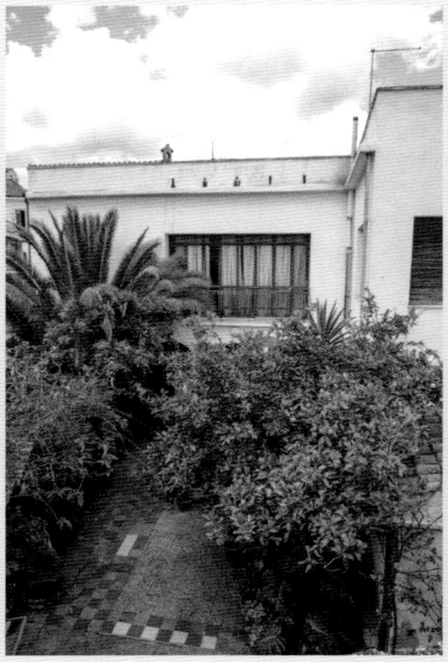
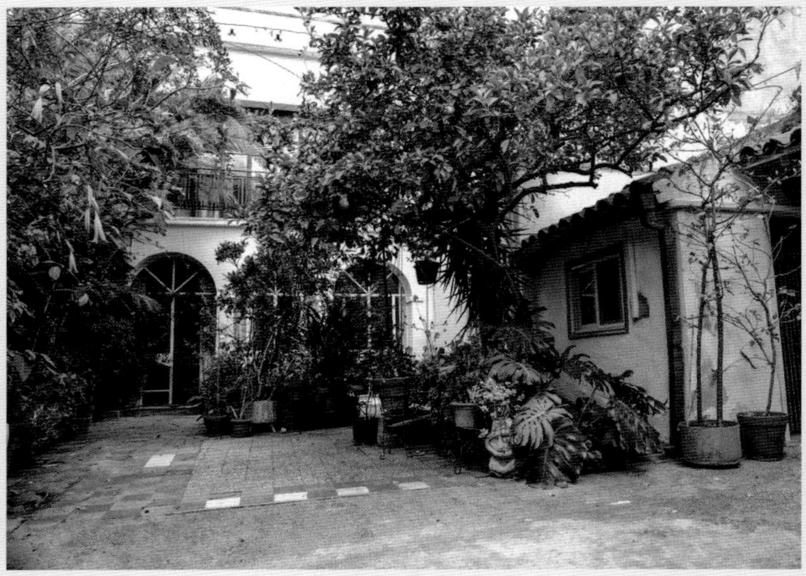
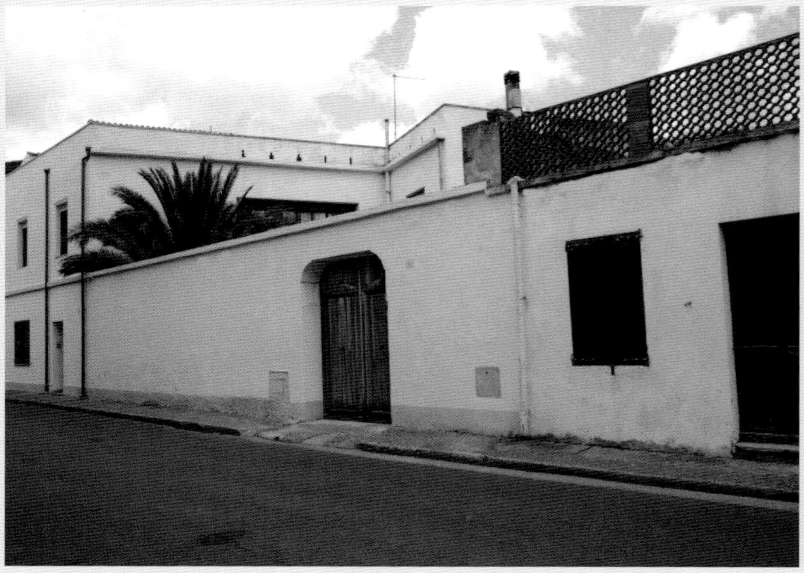
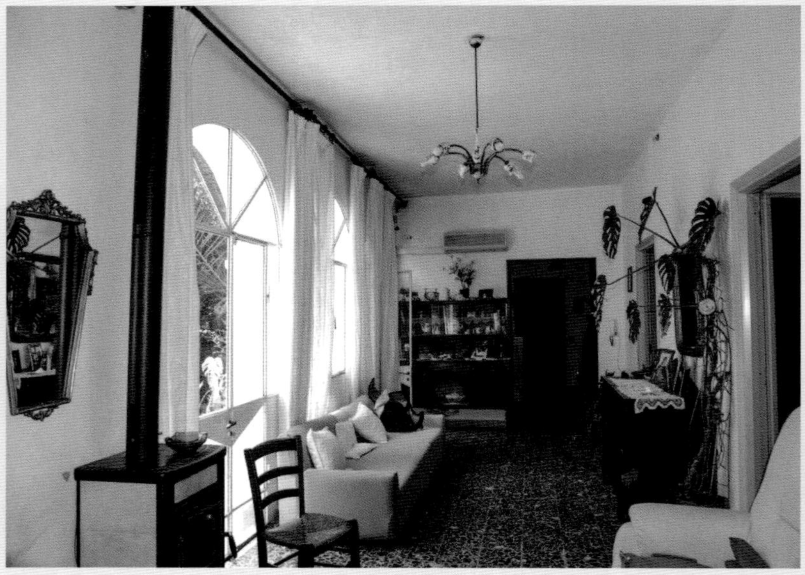
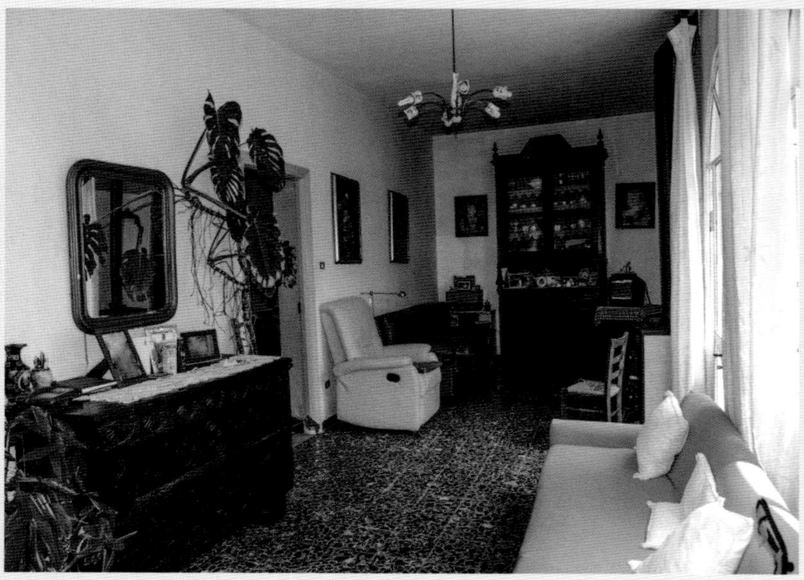
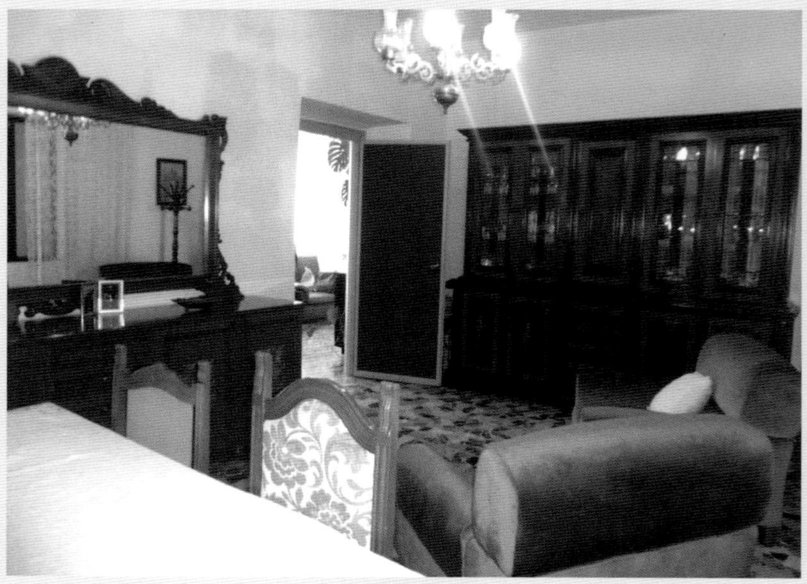

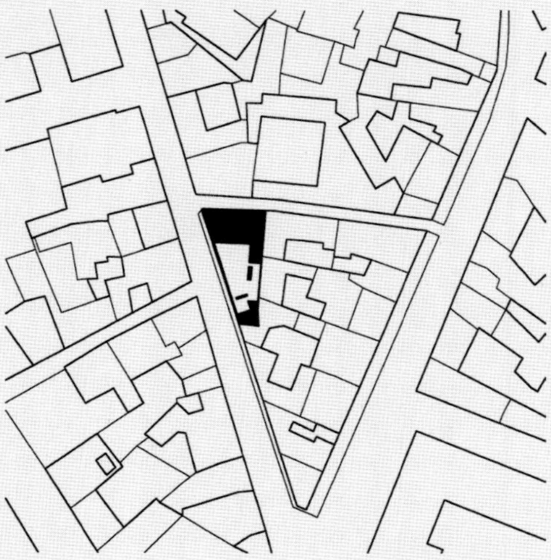

Location plan

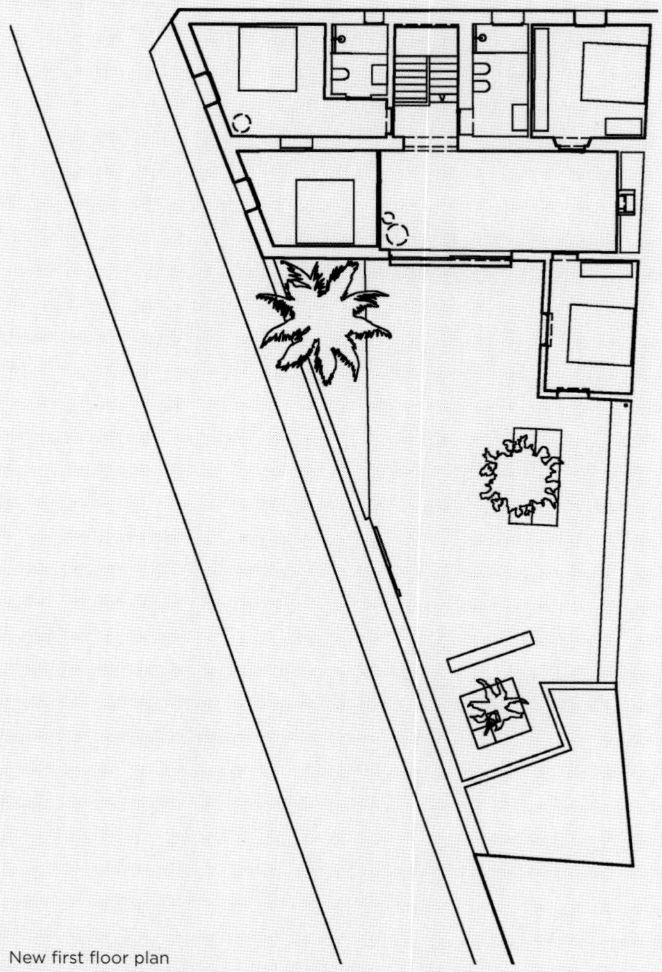

New first floor plan

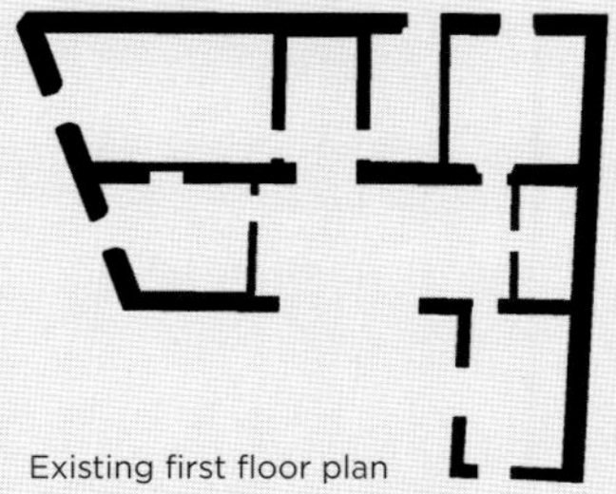

Existing first floor plan

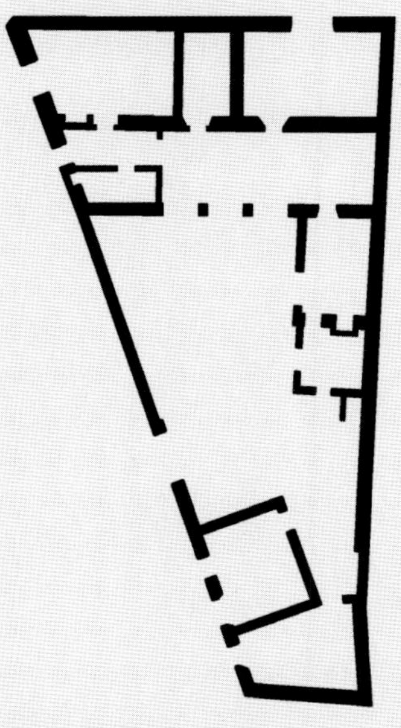

Existing ground floor plan

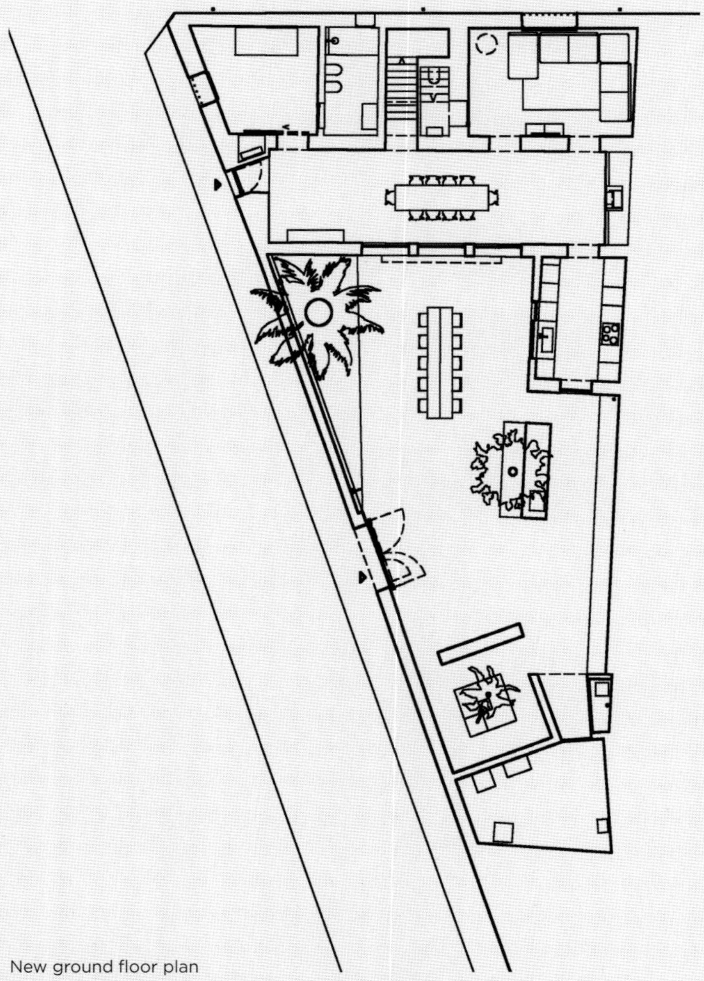

New ground floor plan

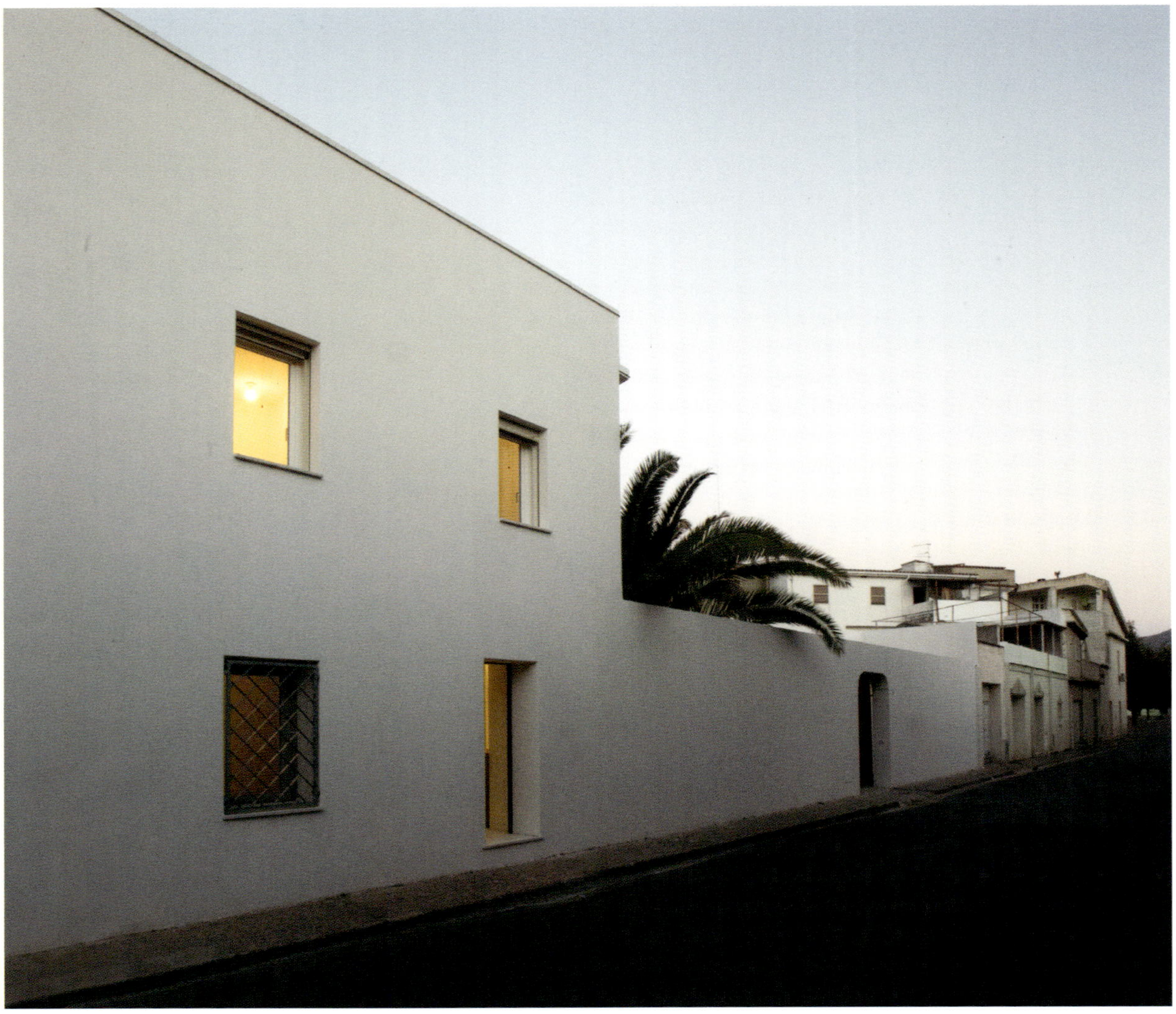

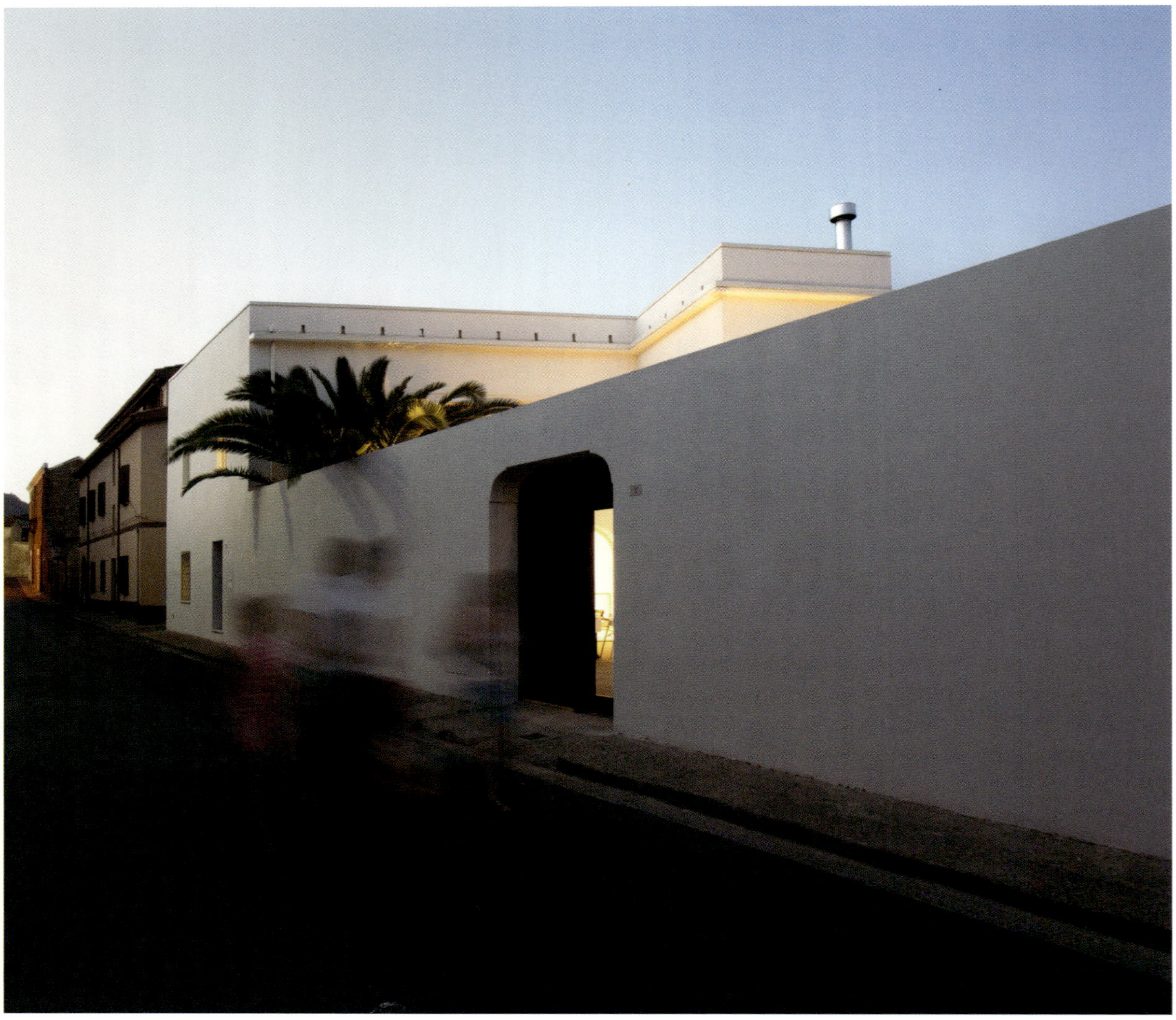

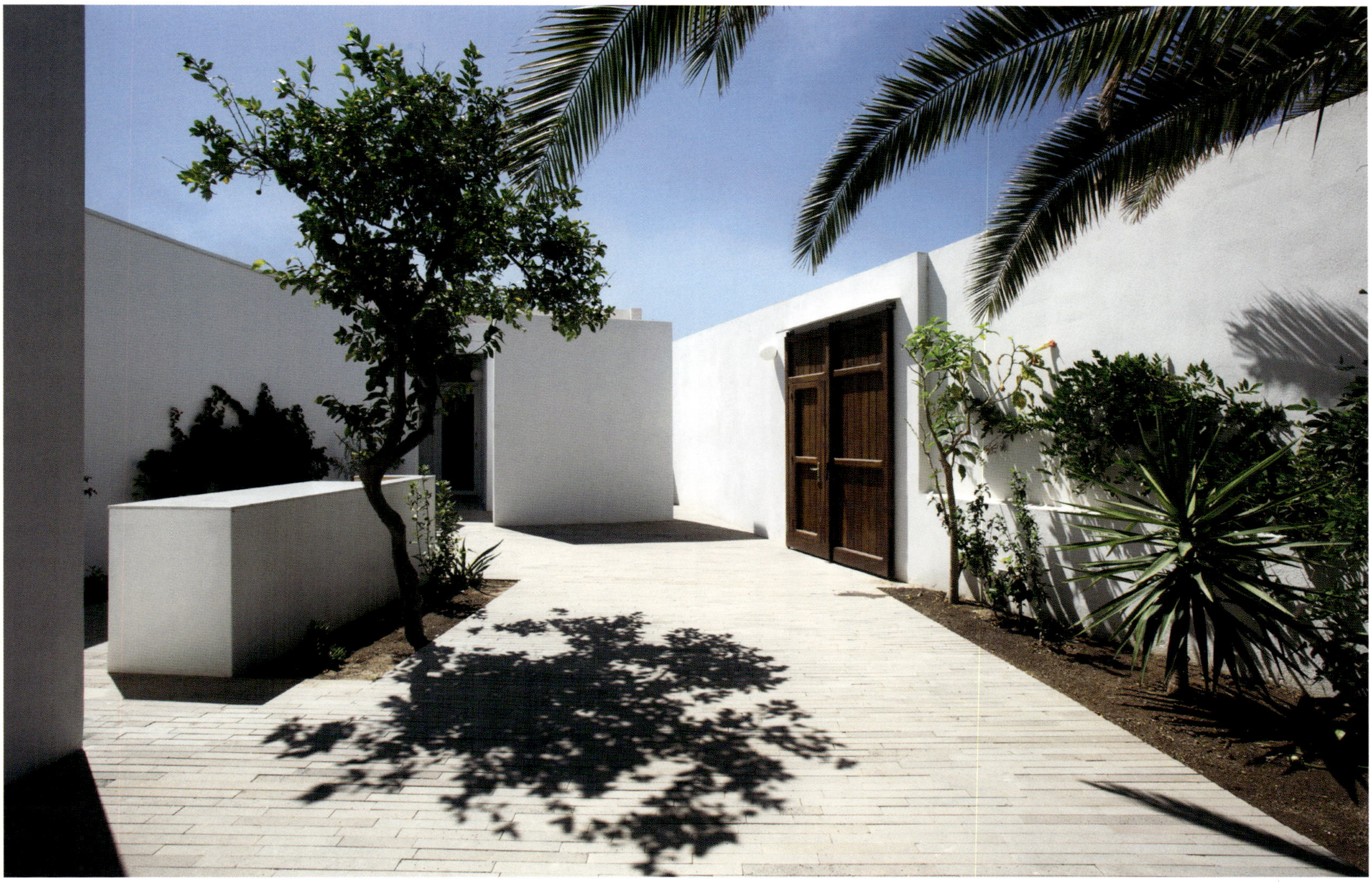

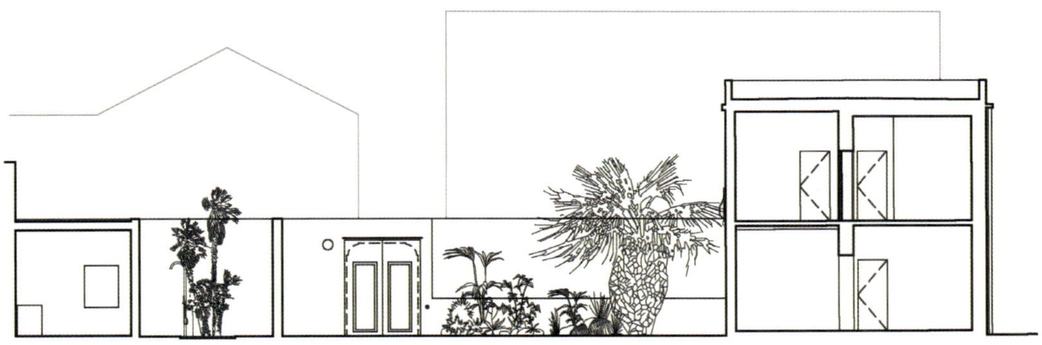

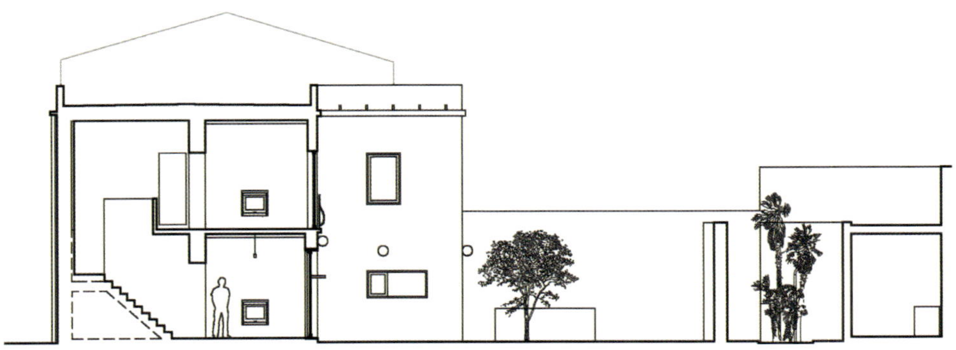

Sections

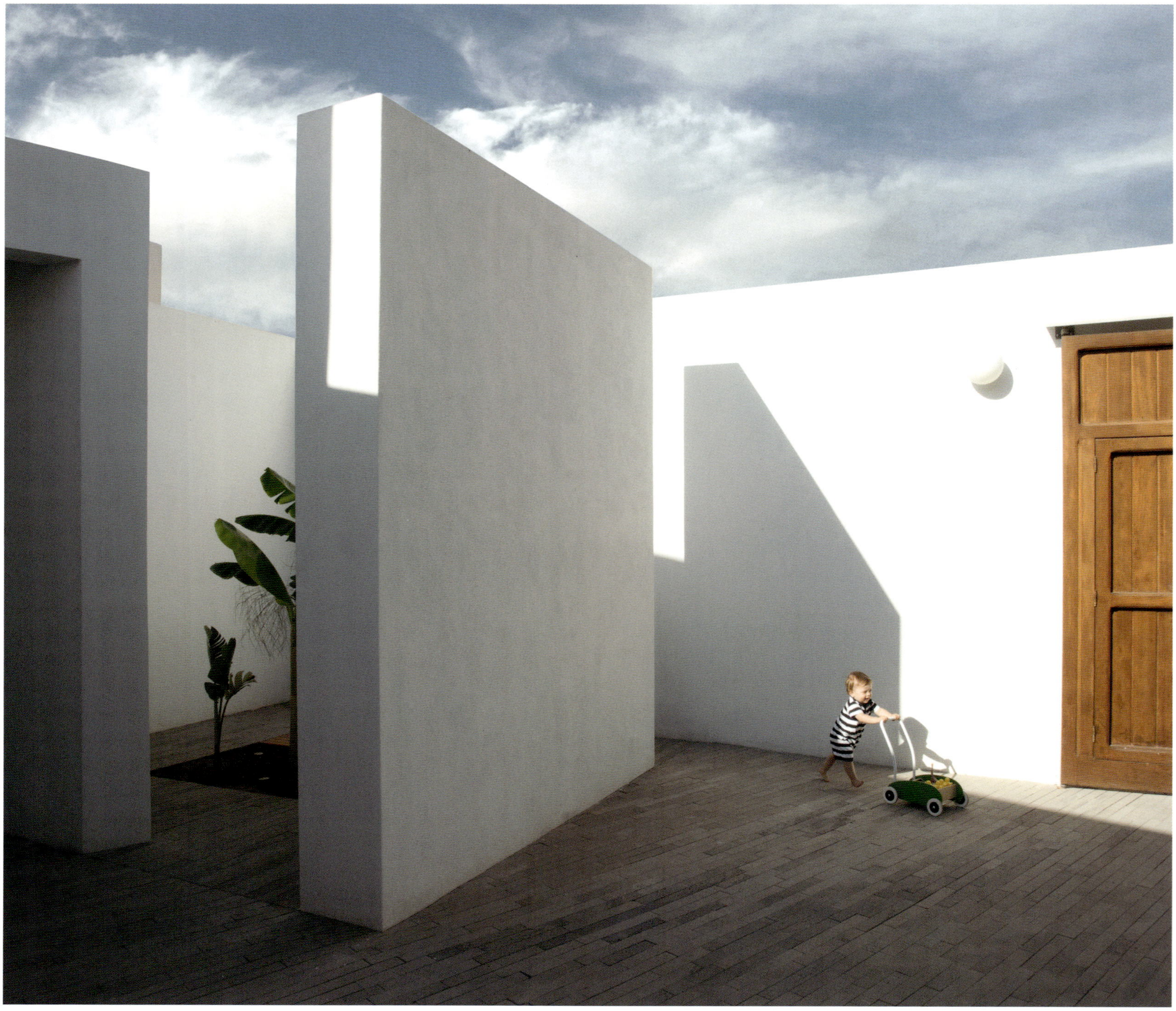

All external walls and partitions are finished in white plaster, matching the residence's interior walls. Gray porphyry, a rock highly resistant to weather changes, was used to surface the exterior walkways.

Alle Wände und Trennwände im Außen- und Innenbereich sind weiß verputzt. Für den Bodenbelag im Außenbereich wurde grauer Porphyr verwendet, der klimatischen Veränderungen einen sehr guten Widerstand entgegensetzt.

Tous les murs et cloisons extérieurs de la maison, ainsi que ceux intérieurs sont finis de la même façon, avec du plâtre blanc. Le revêtement extérieur est, quant à lui, en pierre porphyre gris, très résistant aux changements climatiques.

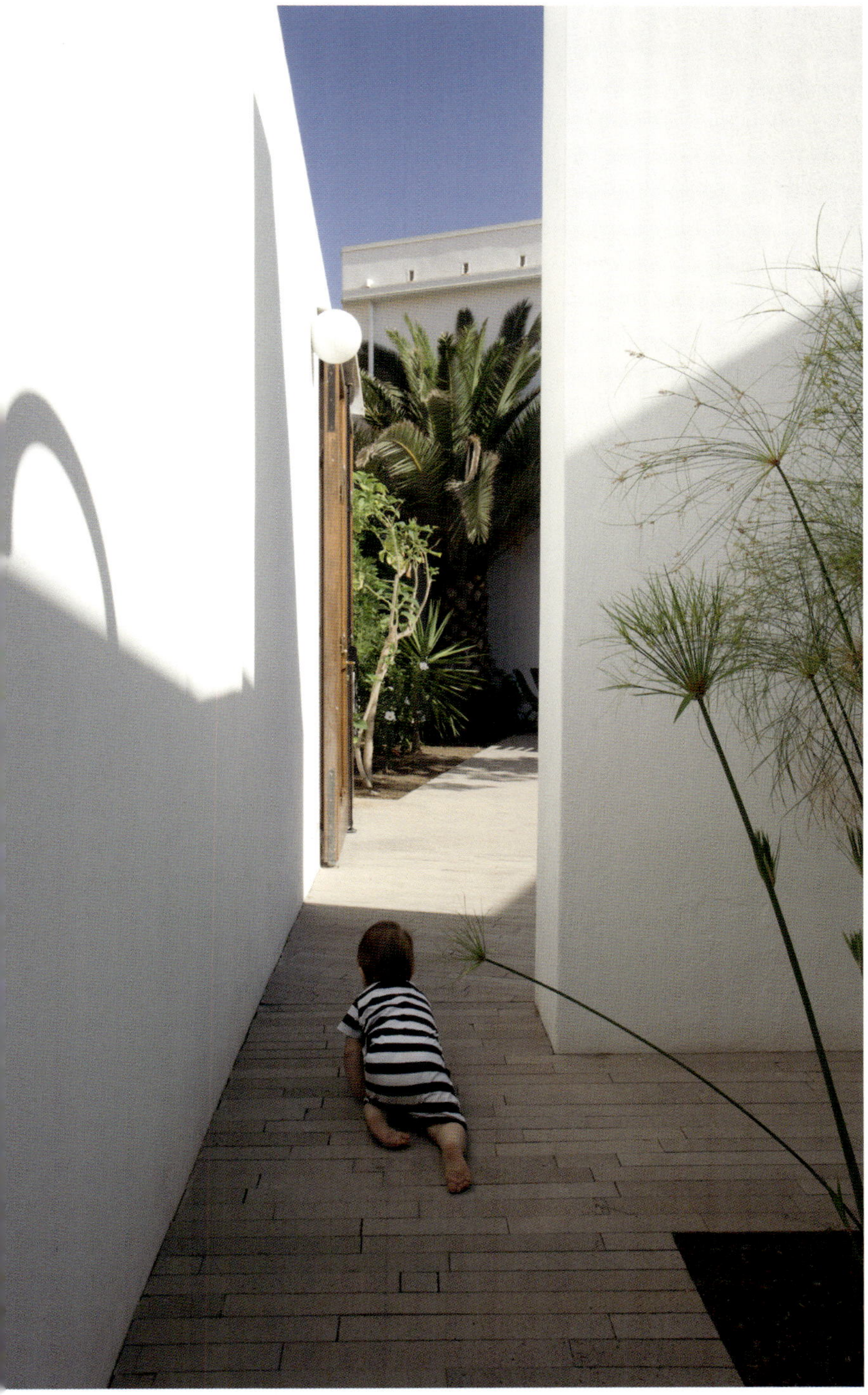

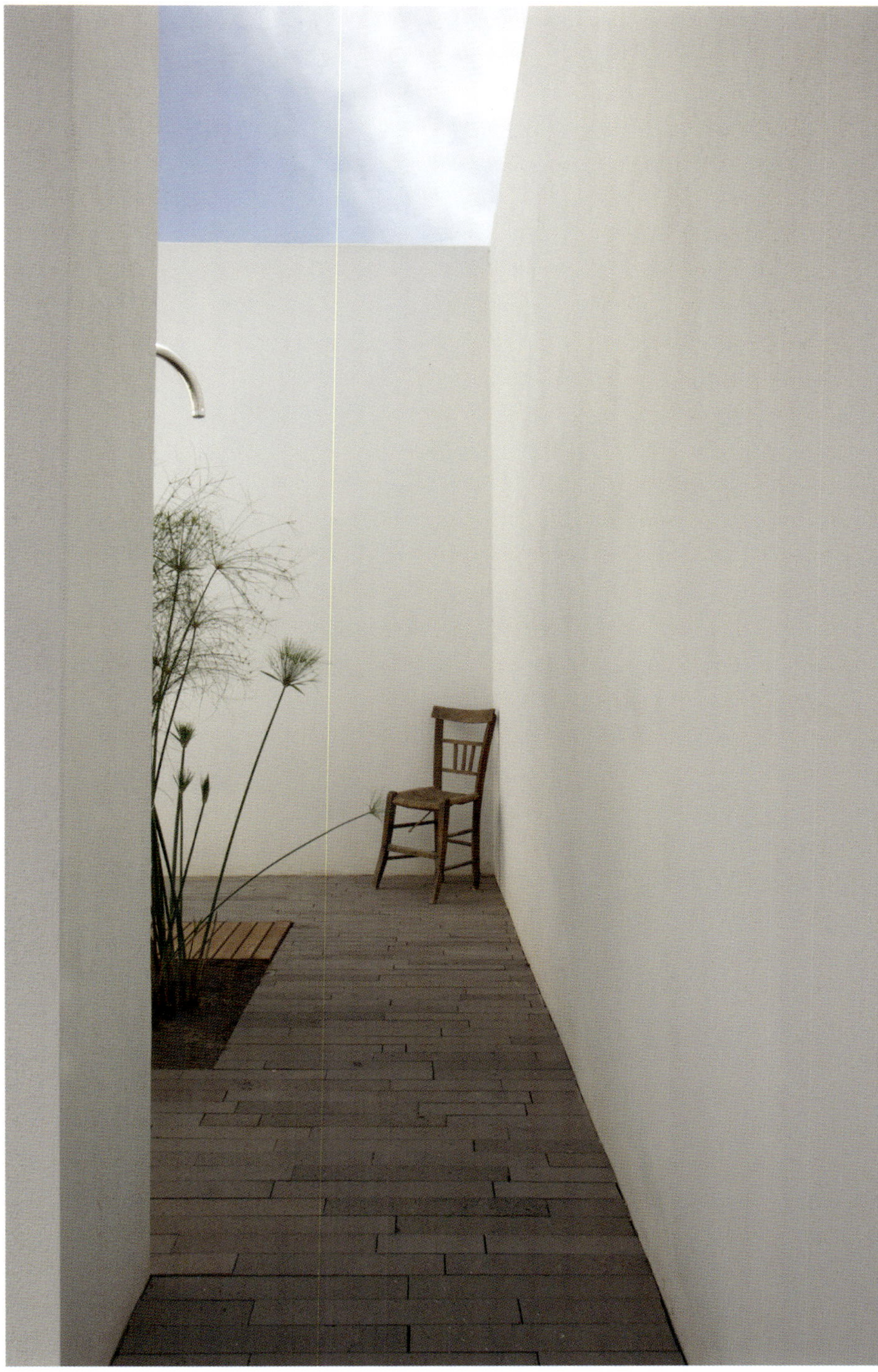

The absence of doors separating the different rooms permits light to reach all corners of the residence. The unbroken white color scheme reinforces the luminous effect.

Aufgrund der fehlenden Zimmertüren kann das Licht in jede Ecke der verschiedenen Räume fallen. Das vollständig in Weiß gehaltene Farbschema verstärkt diesen Helligkeitseffekt noch mehr.

L'absence de porte entre les diverses pièces permet à la lumière de pénétrer chaque recoin de la maison. Le jeu de couleur entièrement blanc renforce l'effet de luminosité.

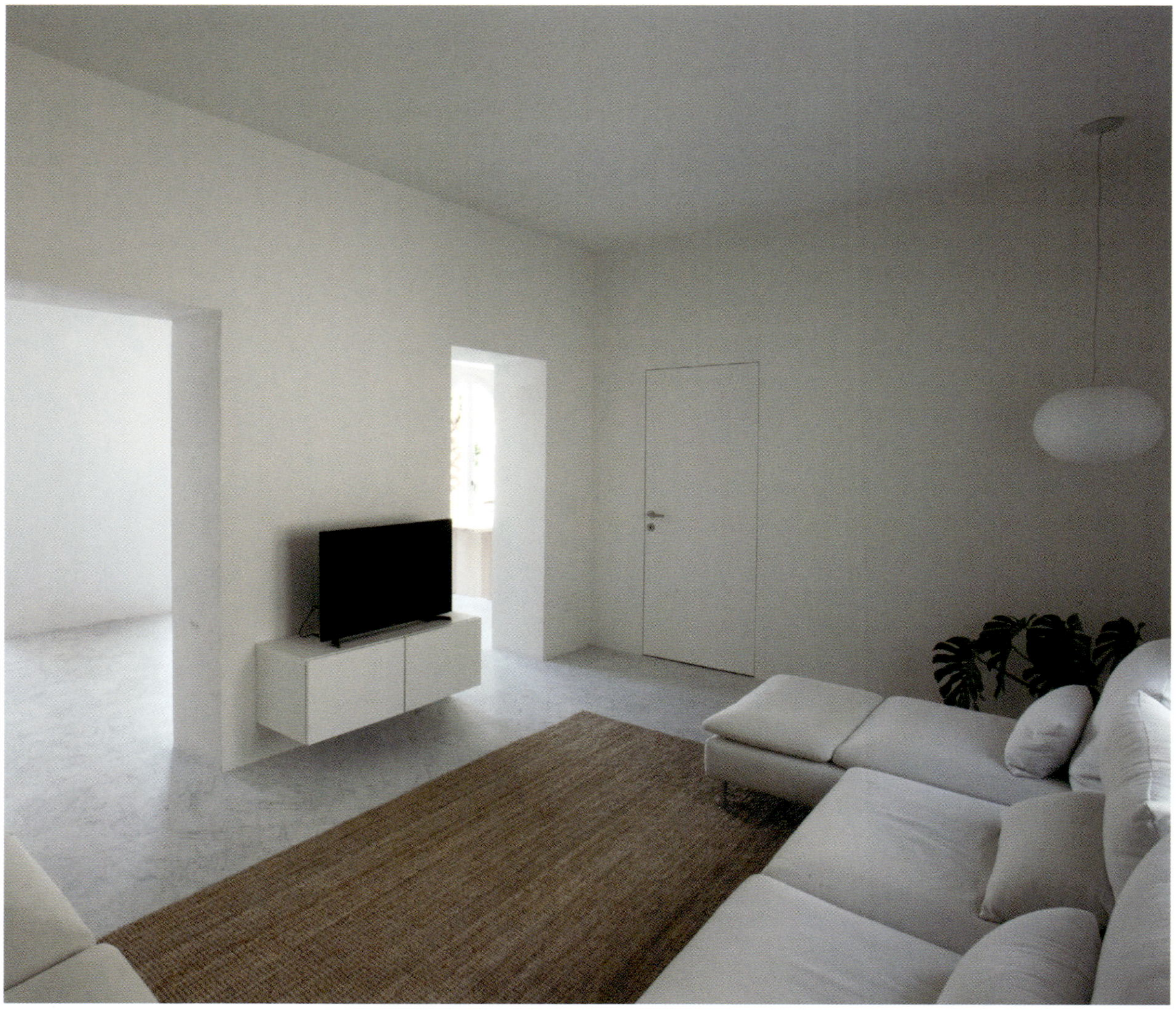

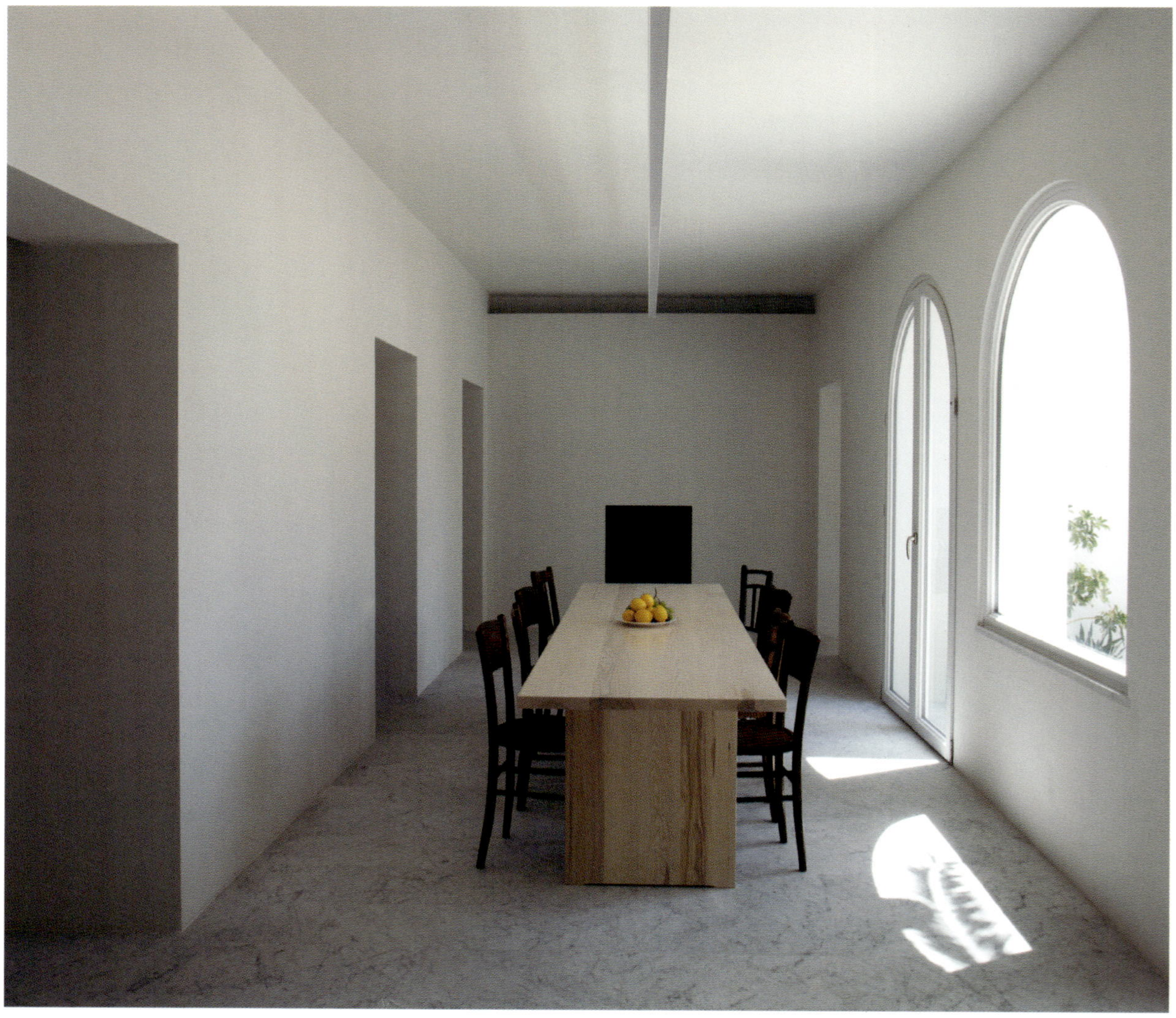

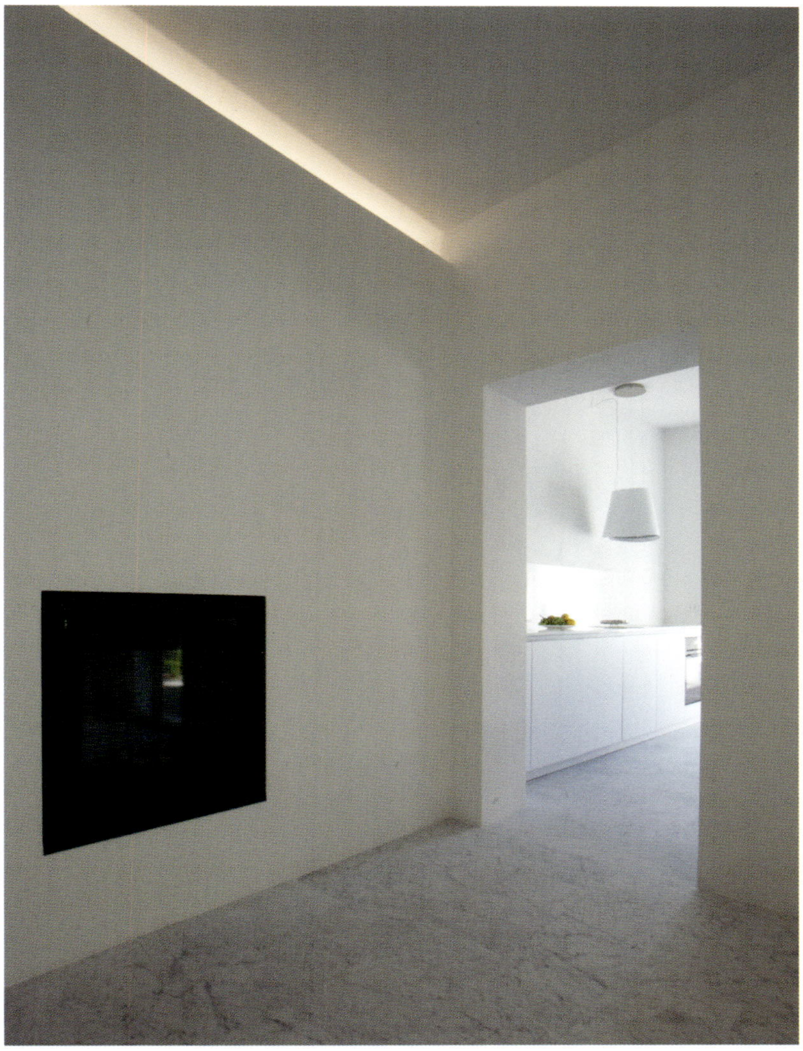

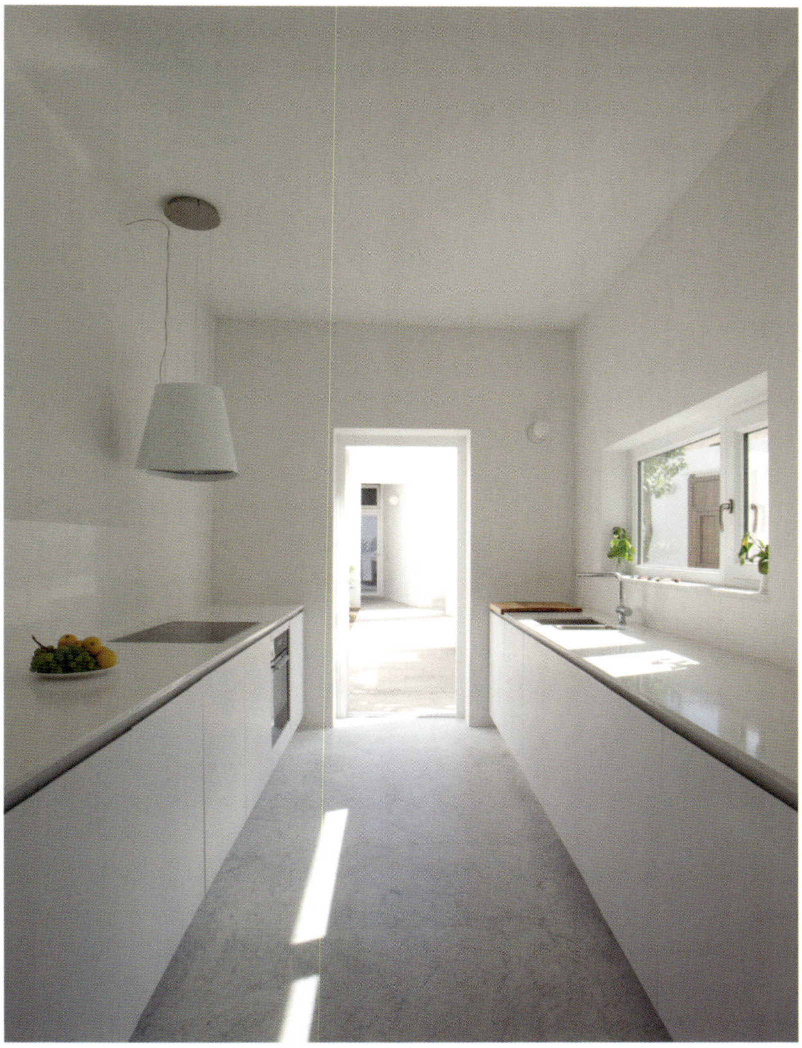

In keeping with the rest of the house, the kitchen features a minimalist design, with clean lines, smooth surfaces, and an absolute preponderance of whiteness. Other materials provide the contrast: the Carrara marble floor, OKITE® countertop, and lacquered furniture.

Wie in allen Räumen ist auch in der Küche das Design minimalistisch, die Linienführung ist klar und die Oberflächen sind glatt. Farblich dominiert hier das Weiß. Für den nötigen Kontrast sorgen die Materialien: Der Boden besteht aus Carrara-Marmor, die Arbeitsplatte ist von OKITE® und die Schränke sind lackiert.

En accord avec toute la maison, la cuisine est minimaliste, avec des lignes épurées, des surfaces lisses, avec une prédominance absolue du blanc. Les divers matériaux apportent un contraste : le sol en marbre de Carrara, le plan de travail d'OKITE® et les meubles laqués.

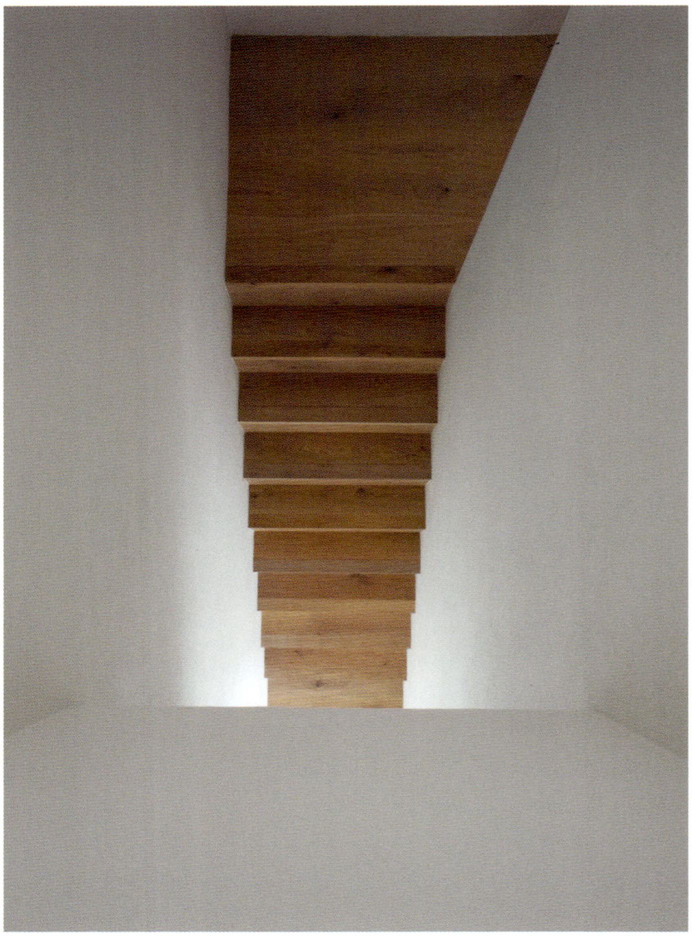

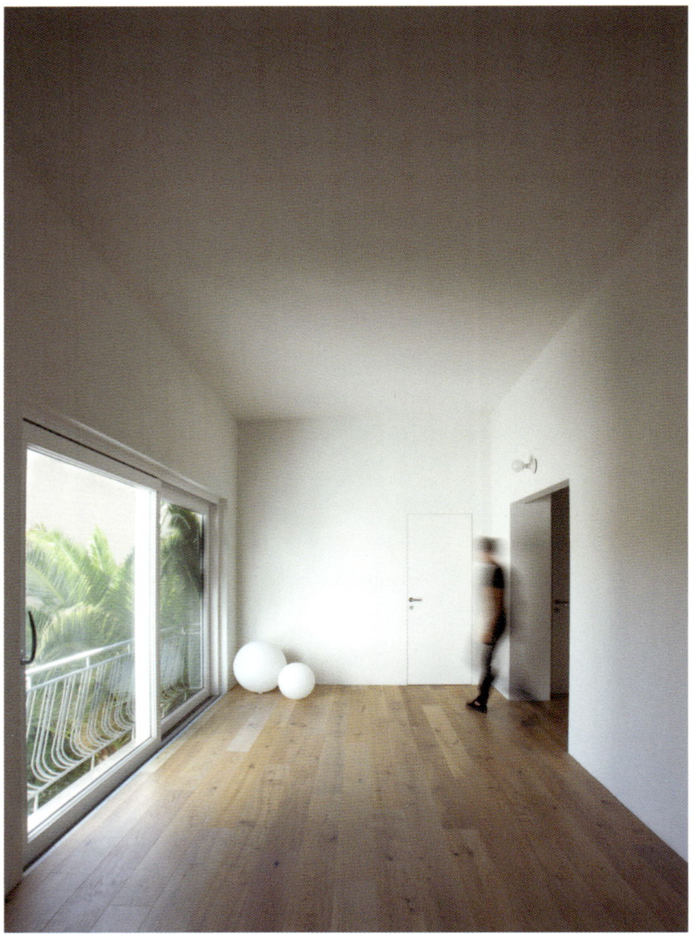

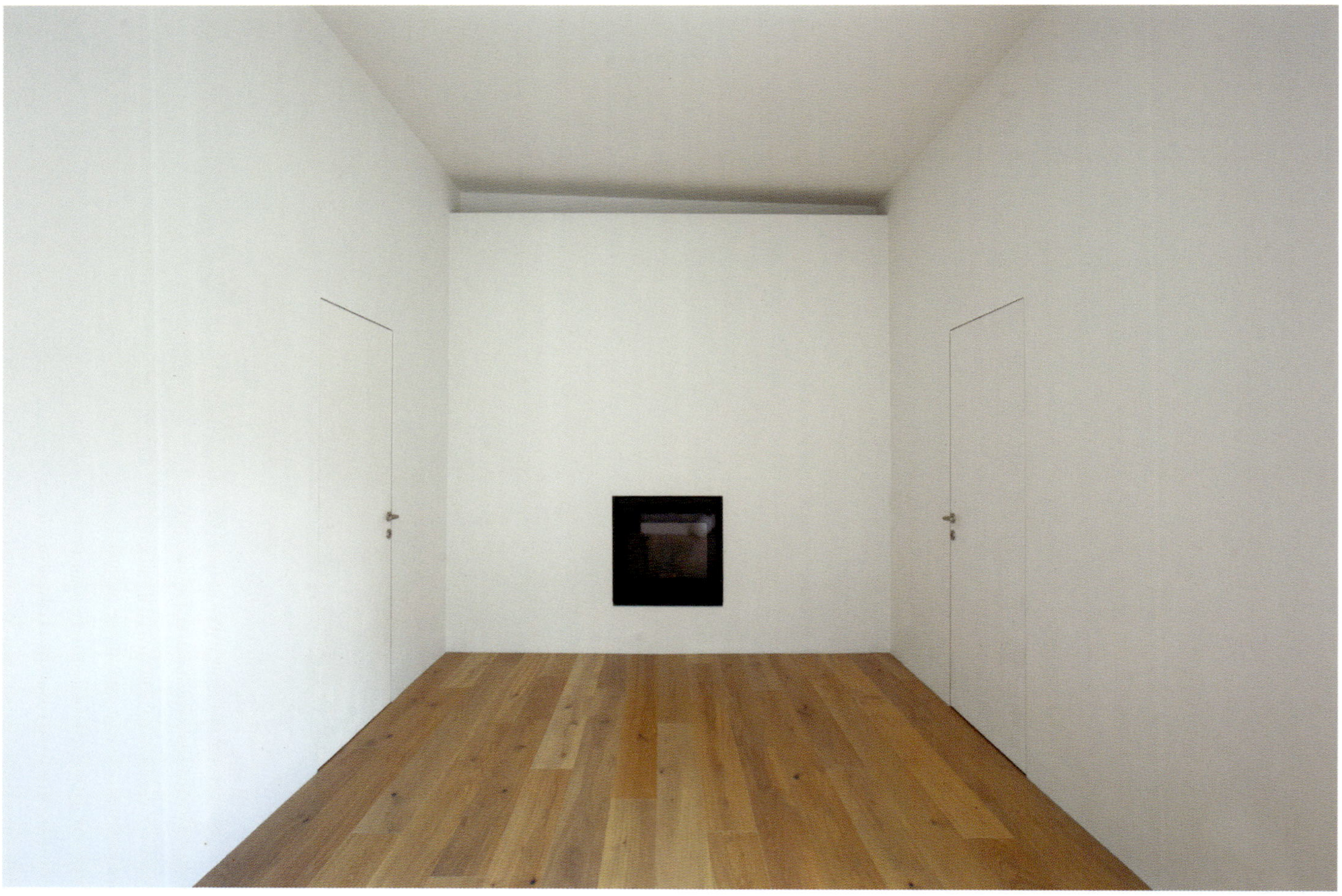

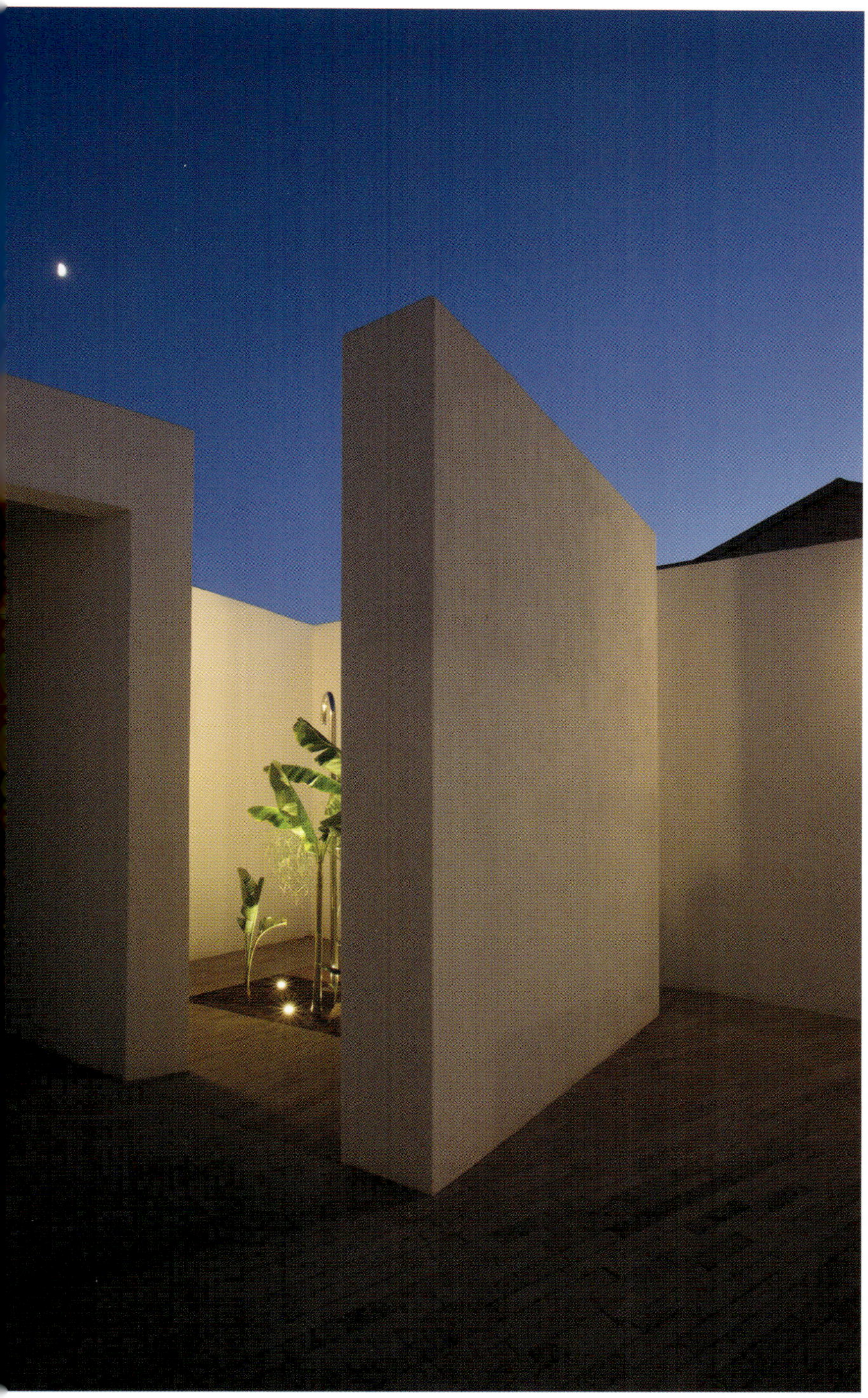

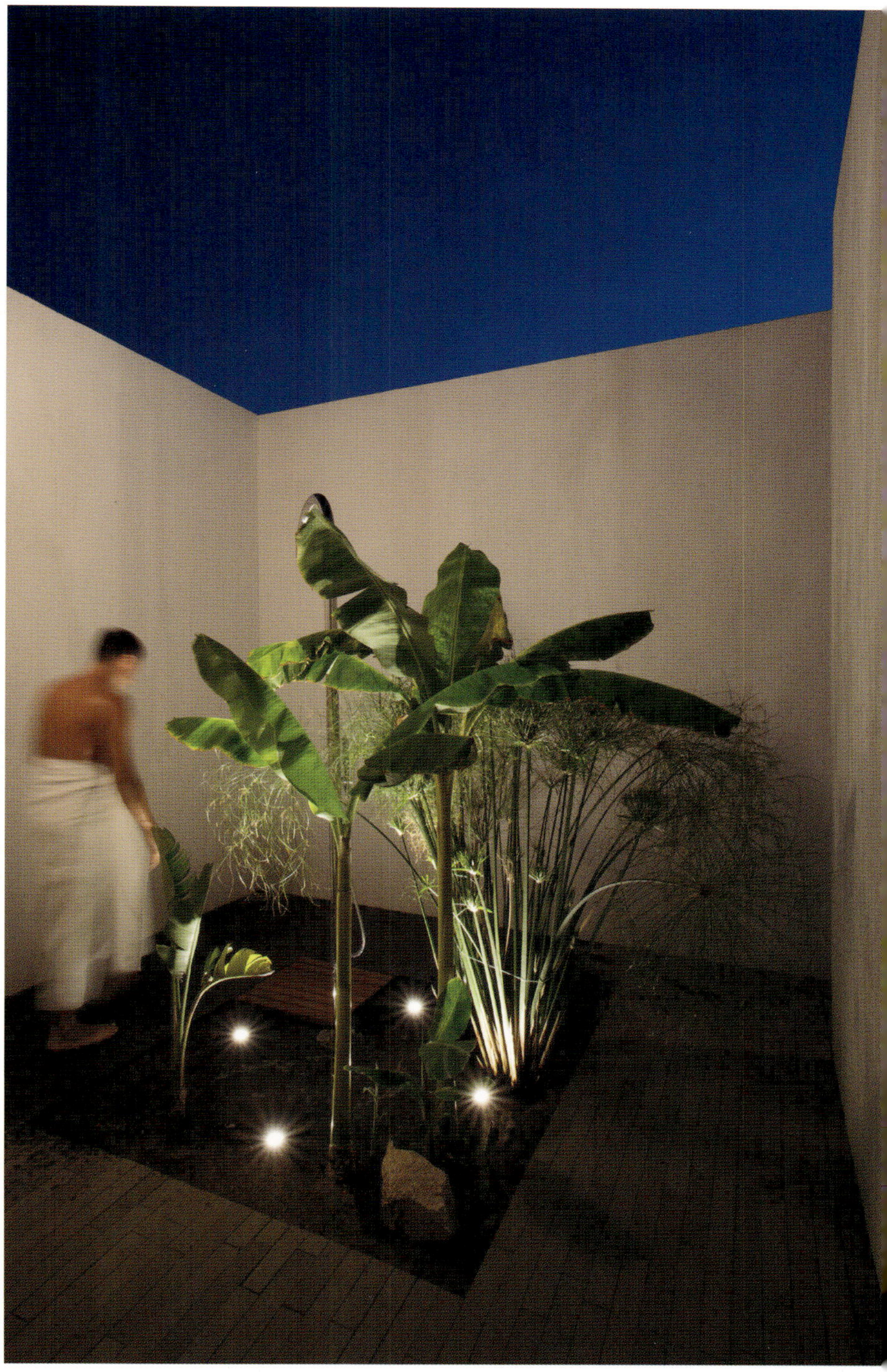

By preserving a wall from one of the former shops and removing the roof, space was created for a "secret garden" with decorative banana trees and a facility for enjoying a shower beneath the sun or stars.

Die Wände des einen Geschäfts blieben stehen, das Dach jedoch wurde zurückgebaut, um einen „versteckten Garten" mit dekorativen Bananenstauden anzulegen. Außerdem gibt es dort nun eine Dusche, in der man sich im Licht der Sonne oder der Sterne erfrischen kann.

Les murs de l'un des magasins ont été conservés, tandis que le toit a été détruit pour laisser place à un « jardin dissimulé » avec de jolis bananiers, une douche à la lumière du soleil ou des étoiles.

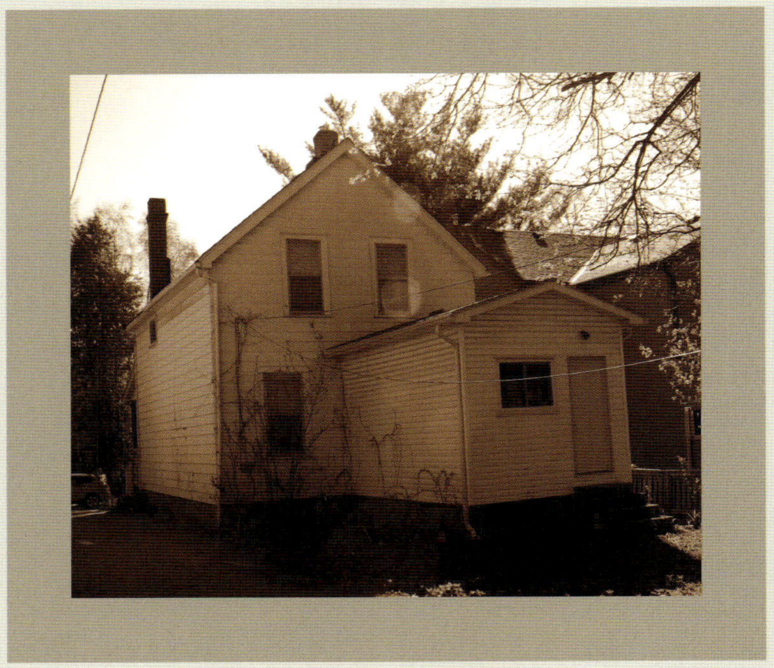

46H

BAUKULTUR/CA

267 m² | 2,880 sq. ft.

Toronto, Ontario, Canada

Photos © **Alex Lukey, Silverhouse**

> Reinvent the existing house and turn it into a bright, modern, and sustainable home with three bedrooms on the first floor, a master retreat on the second floor, and an open main floor with a strong connection to the west-facing backyard

> Die Neuerfindung des bestehenden Hauses und dessen Umgestaltung zu einem hellen, modernen und nachhaltigen Zuhause mit drei Schlafzimmern im ersten Stockwerk, einem Rückzugsraum im zweiten Stockwerk und einem offenen Hauptgeschoss mit enger Verbindung zum westlichen Hof

> Réinventer la maison d'origine et la transformer en habitation claire, moderne, durable, de trois chambres au premier étage, une suite-principale indépendante au deuxième étage, et un rez-de-chaussée ouvert en lien étroit avec l'arrière-cour orientée vers l'ouest

From the first time the architect visited the site, he realized the potential of the property, and within a short time span the first design concepts evolved. Instead of building out into the backyard, he decided to go with the more challenging option to stay within the footprint of the existing building and build upwards to create a compact house. The addition allowed for a more cohesive organization of the rooms, but, most importantly, the architect maintained the proportions of the large backyard, minimally encroached upon by a trellis mediating between interior and exterior spaces.
The building forms found in the vicinity served as a starting point for the design development. The project had to fit in with the surrounding houses. Yet, it was conceived to display a more contemporary architectural language. The front of the house offers a modern interpretation of the existing bay windows and porch configurations found in many of the neighboring houses. It gives the front facade a distinctive look, but is still perfectly in line with the architectural context. In contrast, the back of the house surprises with a copper-clad addition on the ground-floor opening onto the backyard.
The design of the roof was certainly not an easy task and was a hard nut to crack for the engineering team. While the new plan maintains some of the first floor layout, new foundations had to be provided, the existing structure had to be reinforced, and two steel frames had to be integrated to support the unique roof.

Bereits beim ersten Besuch erkannte der Architekt das Potential des Grundstücks, und schon nach kurzer Zeit waren die ersten Entwürfe fertig. Anstand eines Ausbaus zum Hof hin entschied er sich für die schwierigere Möglichkeit, die ursprüngliche Gebäudeform beizubehalten und nach oben auszubauen, um so ein eher kompakteres Haus zu schaffen. Der Ausbau ermöglichte eine zusammenhängende Raumaufteilung, vor allem konnte jedoch der große Hof erhalten bleiben. Die einzige Veränderung in diesem Bereich war ein Spalier als Verbindung zwischen Innen- und Außenbereich.
Als Ausgangspunkt für das Design dienten die Gebäude der Umgebung. Das Gebäude sollte schließlich zu den umliegenden Häusern passen. Andererseits war eine eher zeitgemäße Architektur erforderlich. Die Hausvorderseite ist eine moderne Interpretation der Erkerfenster und Veranden vieler Nachbarhäuser. Dadurch hebt sich die Frontfassade von ihrer Umgebung ab, passt jedoch dennoch in den architektonischen Rahmen. Dagegen überrascht die Hausrückseite mit einem mit Kupfer verkleideten Anbau des Erdgeschosses, der sich zum Hinterhof hin öffnet.
Beim Dachdesign hatte das Ingenieurteam eine harte Nuss zu knacken. Der neue Plan behielt teilweise die Struktur des Erdgeschosses bei. Dennoch bedurfte es neuer Ansätze. Die vorhandene Struktur musste verstärkt werden, weshalb zwei Stahlrahmen für das Hauptdach integriert wurden.

Dès la première visite de l'architecte sur le site, il réalisa le potentiel de la propriété, et peu de temps après les premières idées de design évoluèrent. Au lieu de construire à l'extérieur vers l'arrière-cour, il décida de prendre l'option plus risquée de garder la superficie au sol de la maison d'origine et de construire en hauteur pour créer une maison compacte. Cet apport permit une organisation cohérente des pièces, mais avant tout, l'architecte réussit à conserver les proportions de la vaste arrière-cour, sur laquelle un treillage faisant le lien entre les espaces intérieur et extérieur empiète de façon négligeable.
Les formes de construction présentes dans le voisinage ont servi de point de départ pour le développement du design. Il fallait que ce projet s'inscrive dans le cadre urbain. Cependant, il a été conçu pour exprimer un langage architectural plus contemporain. La partie avant de la maison propose une interprétation moderne des bay-windows et de la configuration du porche d'origine de plusieurs des maisons environnantes. Elle donne à la façade un aspect distinctif, mais s'aligne parfaitement avec le contexte architectural. En contraste, l'arrière de l'habitation surprend par son rajout recouvert de cuivre au rez-de-chaussée, ouvrant sur l'arrière-cour.
Le design du toit n'était certainement pas chose simple et a donné du fil à retordre à l'équipe d'ingénieurs. Alors que la nouvelle configuration conserve une partie du plan du premier étage, de nouvelles fondations ont dû être ajoutées, la structure existante a dû être renforcée, et deux cadres en acier ont dû être intégrés pour soutenir ce toit singulier.

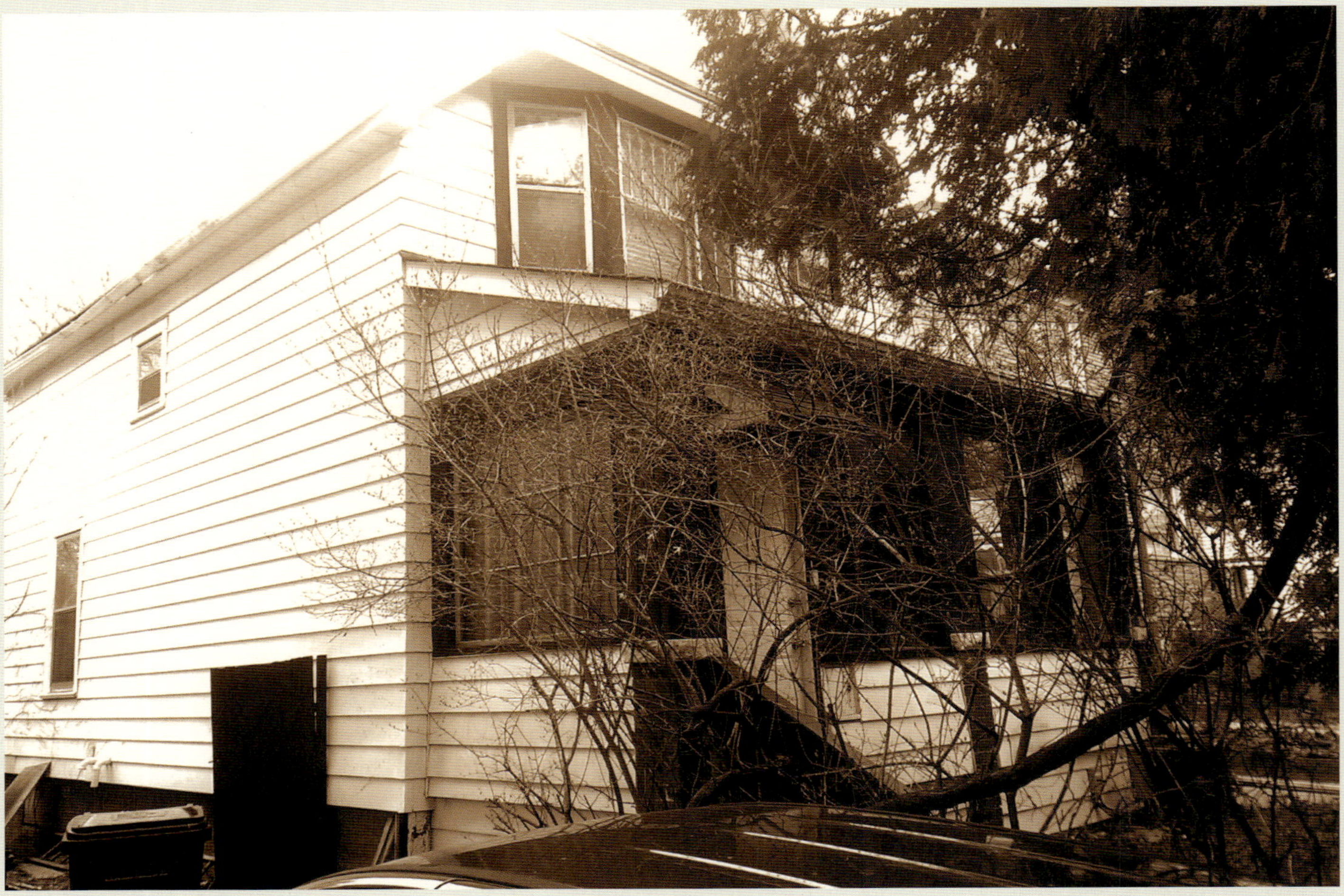

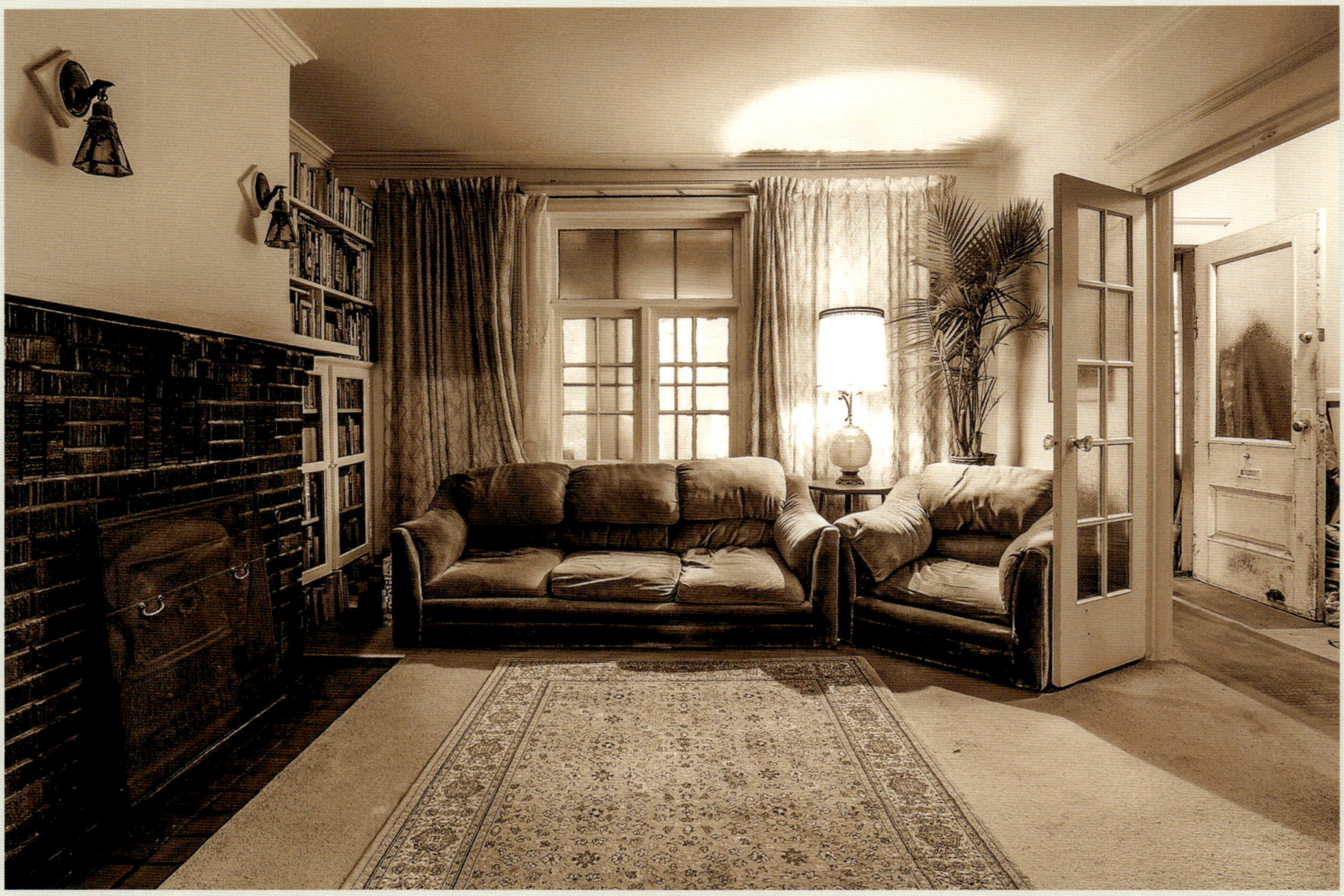

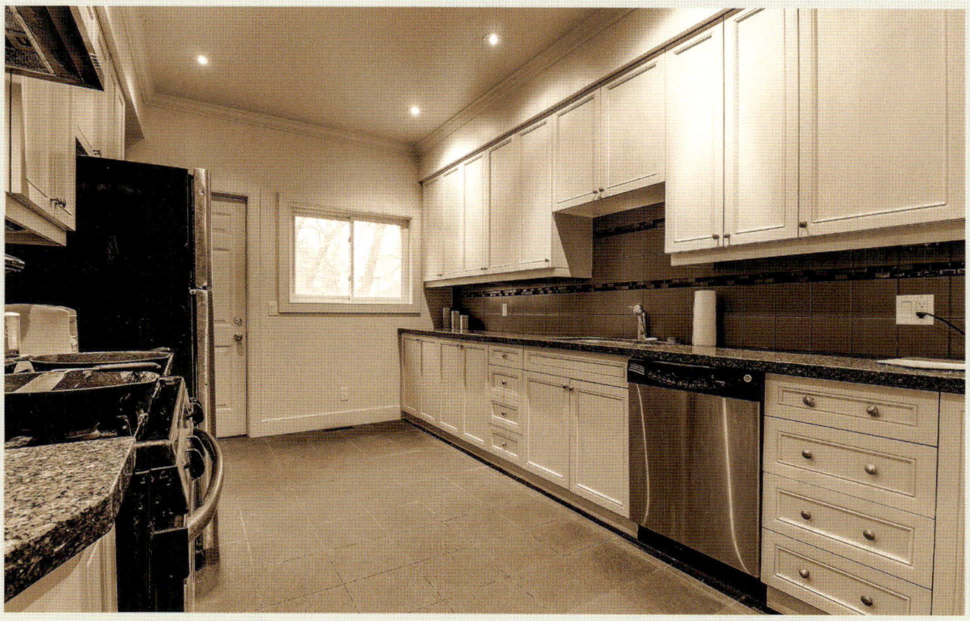

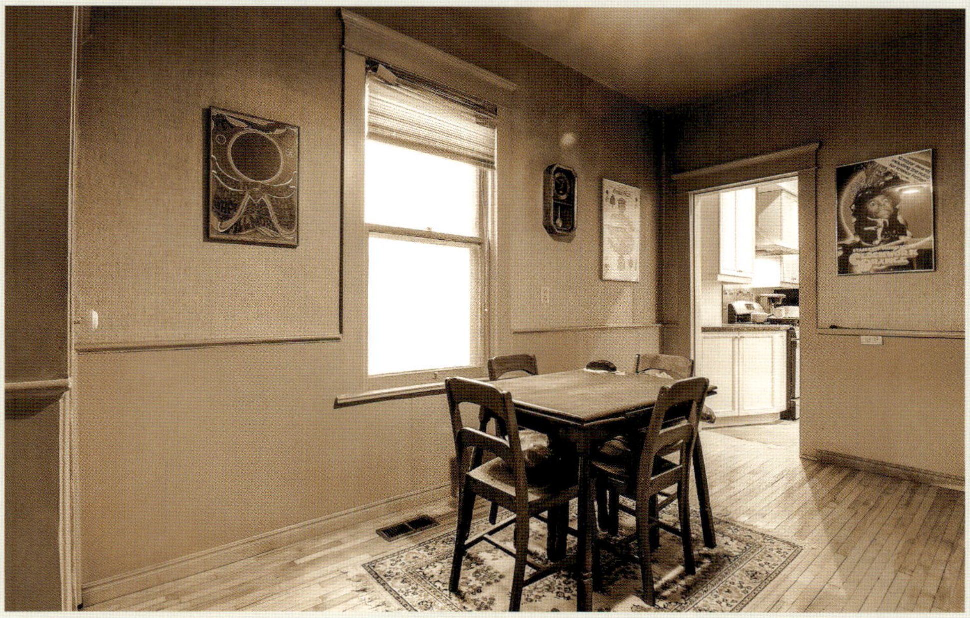

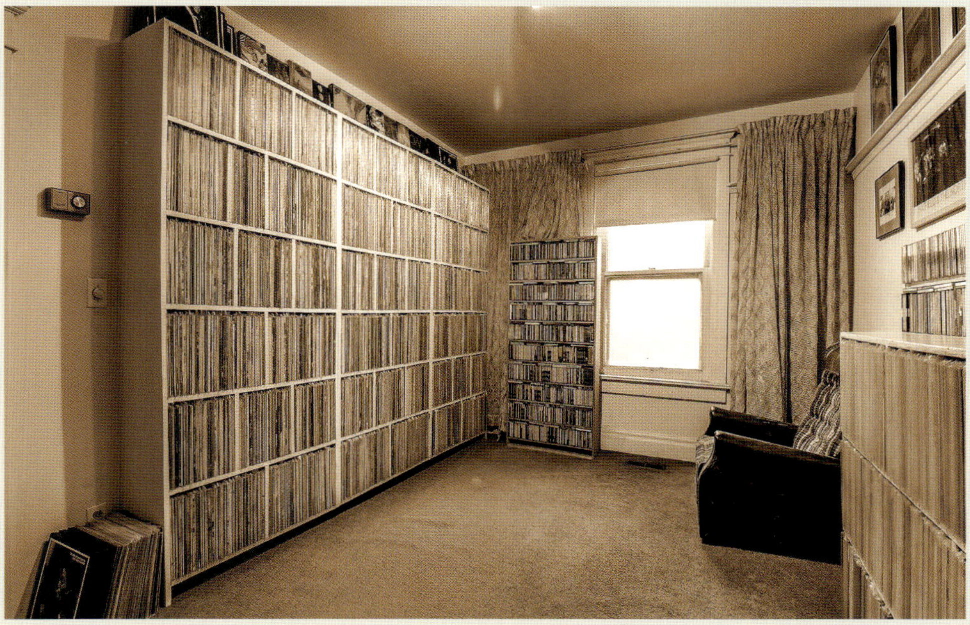

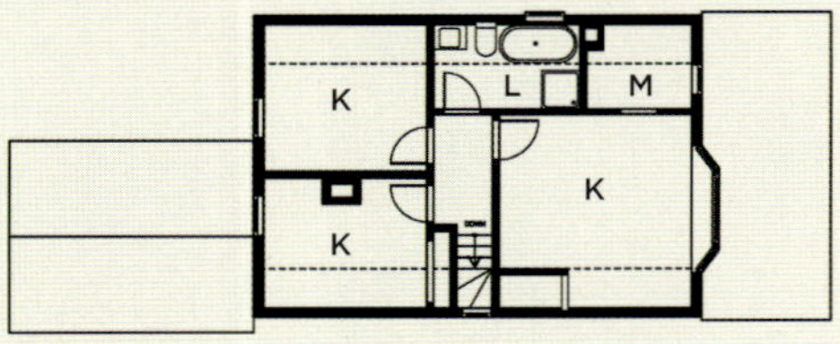

Existing second floor plan

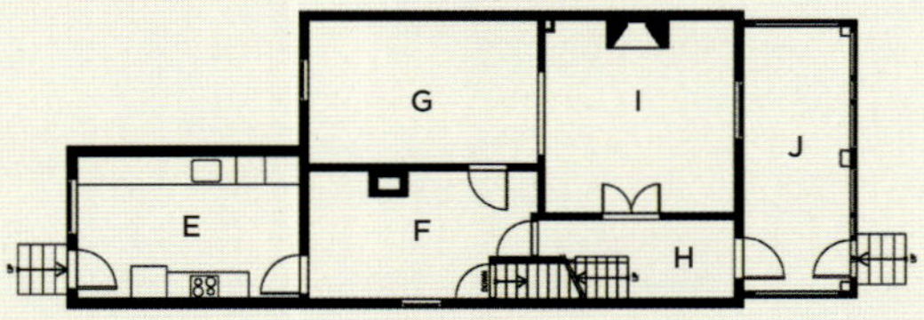

Existing ground floor plan

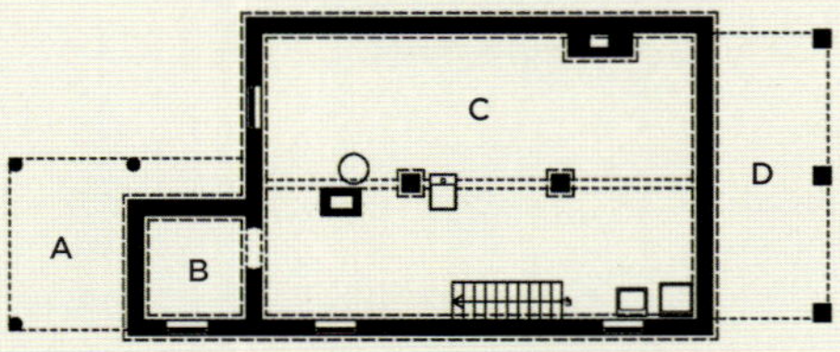

Existing basement floor plan

- A. Existing addition partly excavated
- B. Storage partly finished
- C. Utility room and storage unfinished
- D. Porch unexcavated
- E. Kitchen
- F. Dining room
- G. Family room
- H. Entry
- I. Living room
- J. Enclosed porch
- K. Bedroom
- L. Bathroom
- M. Walk-in closet

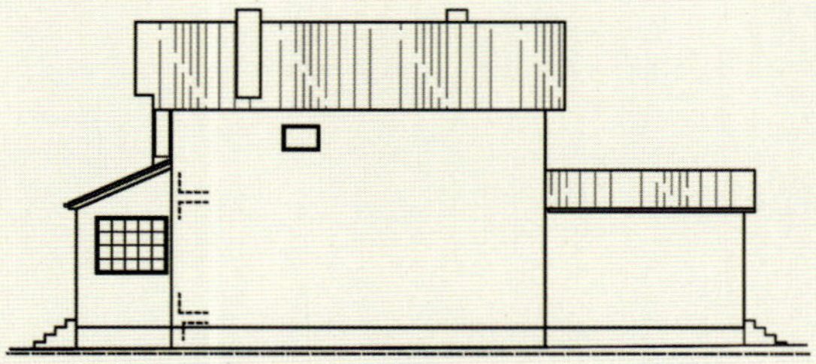

Existing north elevation

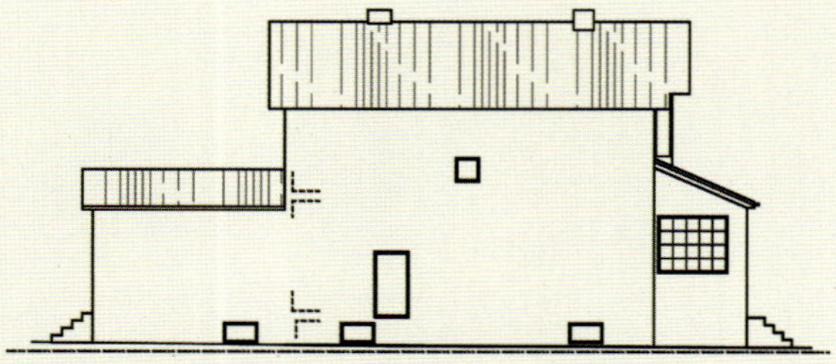

Existing south elevation

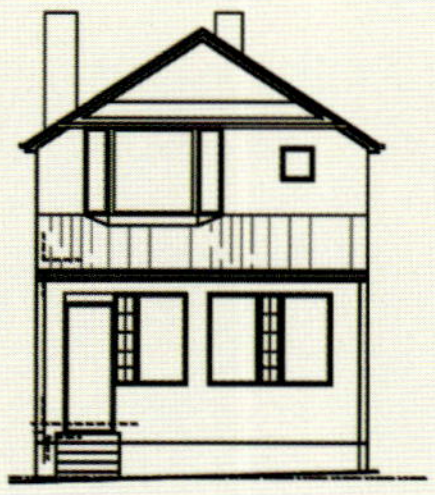

Existing east elevation

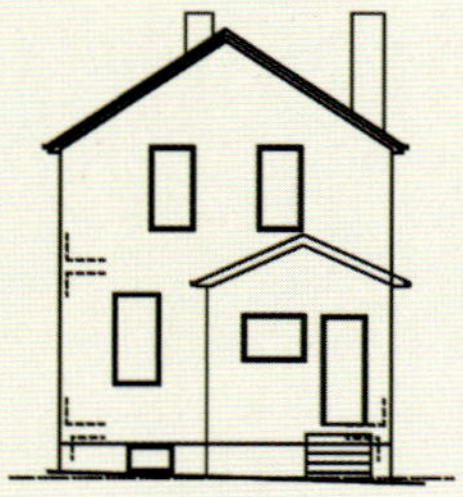

Existing west elevation

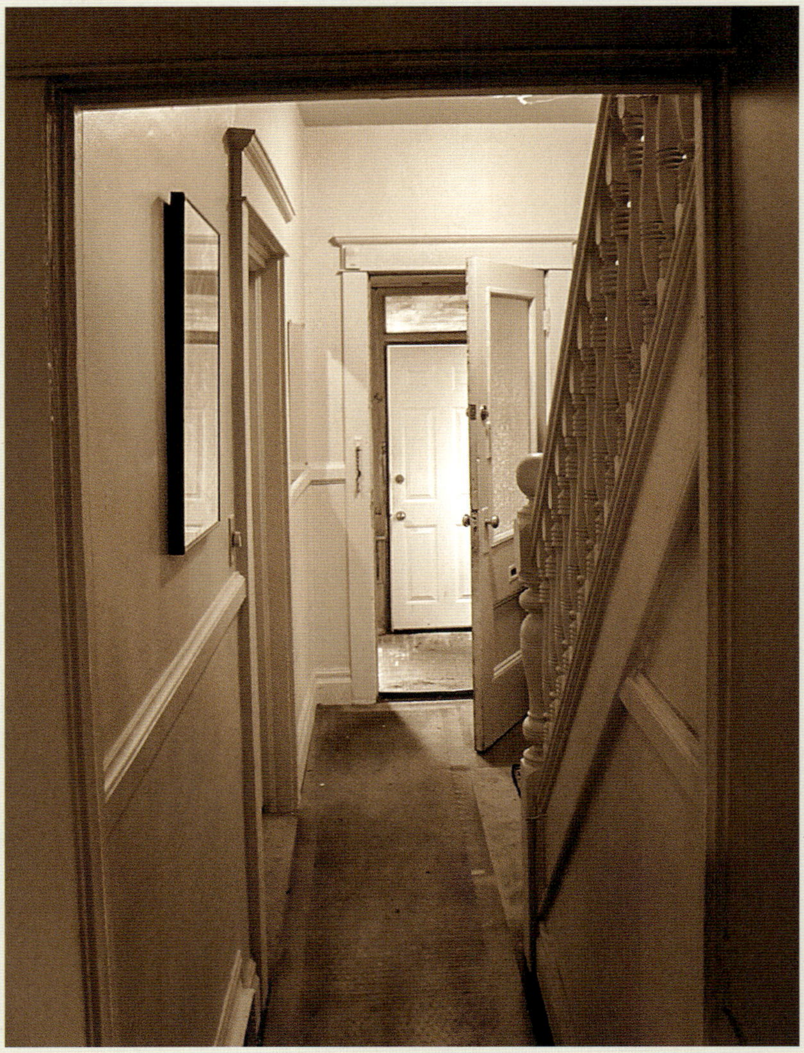

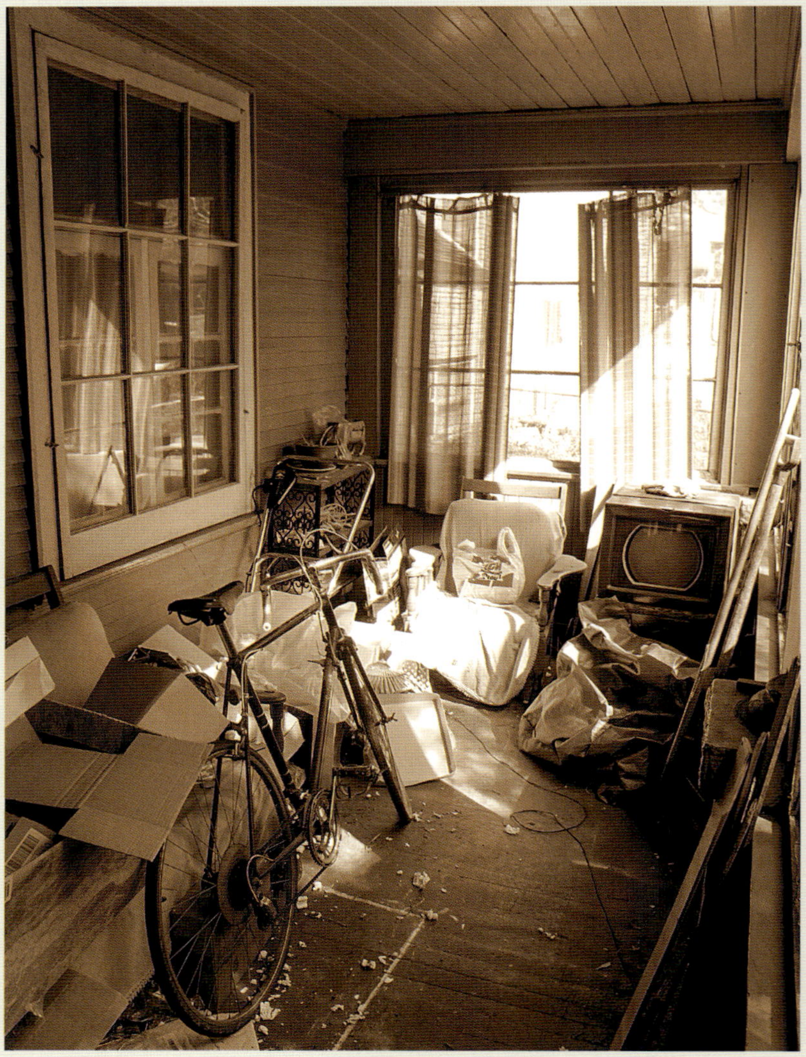

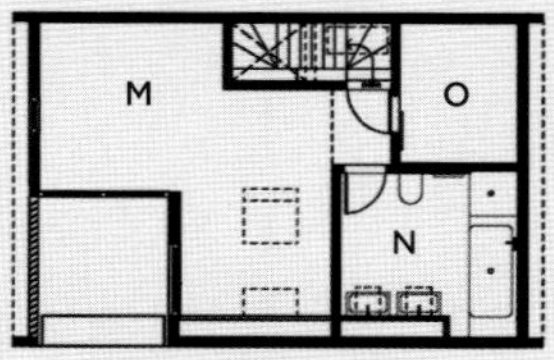

New second-floor-addition floor plan

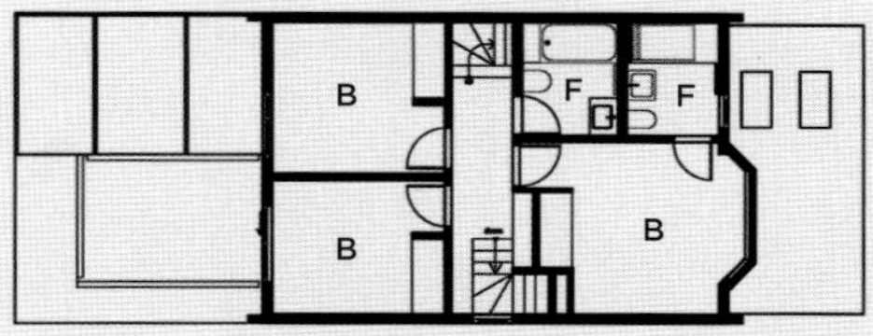

New first floor plan

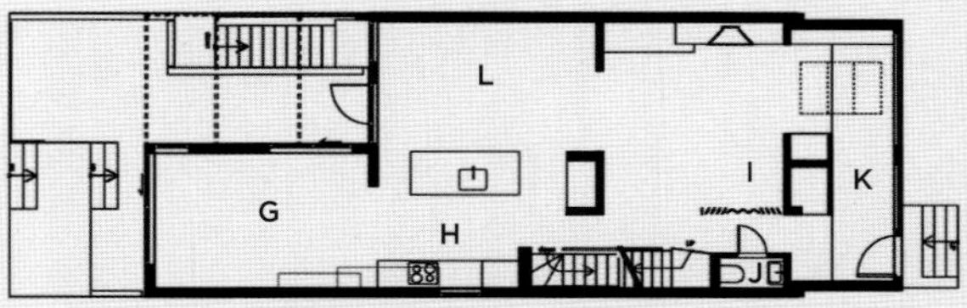

New ground floor plan

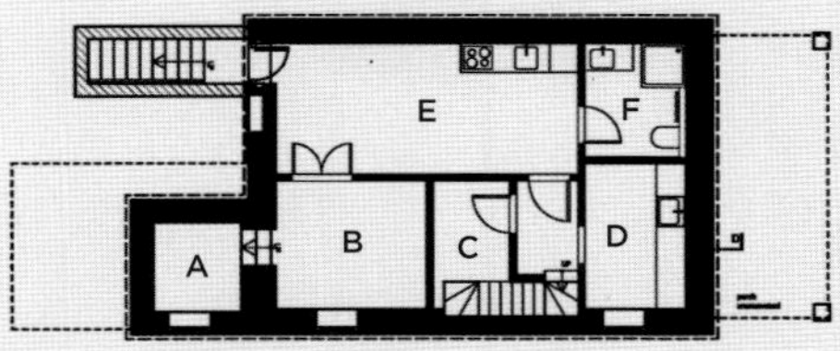

New basement floor plan

A. Walk-in closet
B. Bedroom
C. Mechanical room
D. Laundry room
E. Living / dining / kichenette
F. Bathroom
G. Family room
H. Kitchen
I. Living area
J. Powder room
K. Entry
L. Dining area
M. Master bedroom
N. Master bathroom
O. Master closet

The design started with simple sketches to explore dimensions, volume, and proportions. It then evolved to include blanketing the sidewalls in metal and draping an asymmetrical roof over the house's wood-clad structure.

Die Planung begann damit, anhand einfacher Zeichnungen Maße, Volumen und Proportionen zu untersuchen. Dann wurden Metallabdeckungen für die Seitenwände entworfen und ein asymmetrisches Dach auf der Holzstruktur des Hauses platziert.

Ce design a débuté avec de simples esquisses pour explorer les dimensions, le volume, et les proportions. Il a ensuite évolué pour inclure l'habillage des murs latéraux avec du métal et le drapé du toit asymétrique sur la structure bardée de bois de la maison.

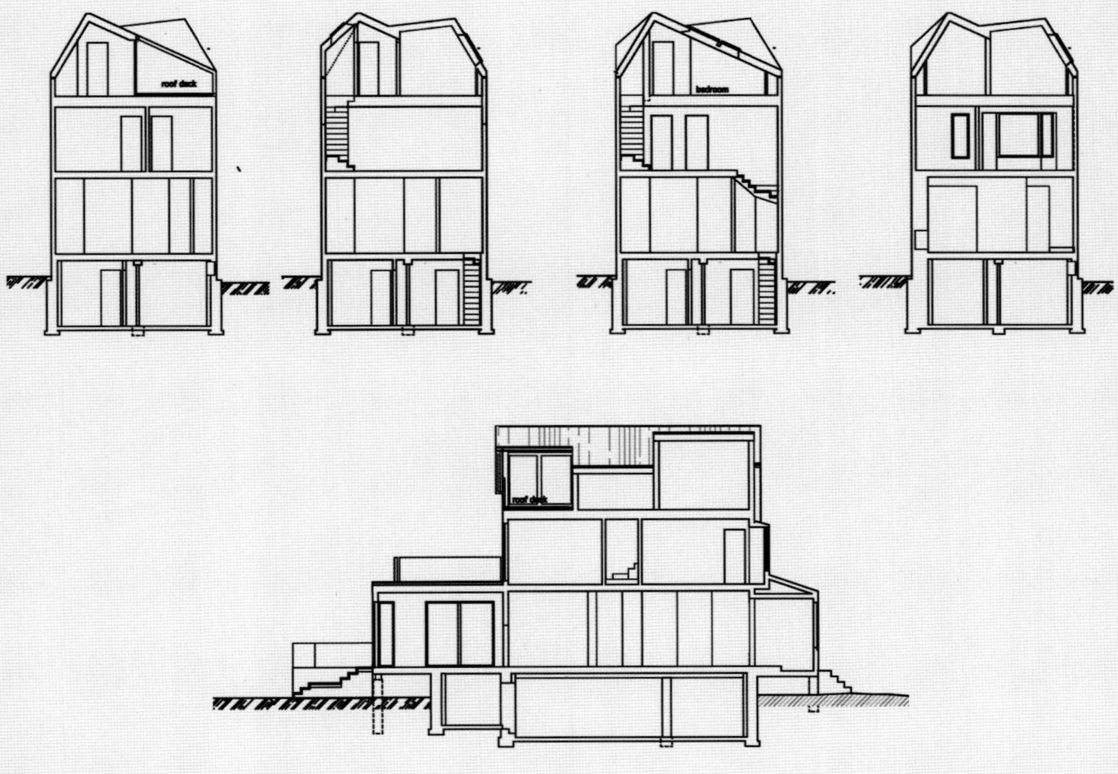

New building sections

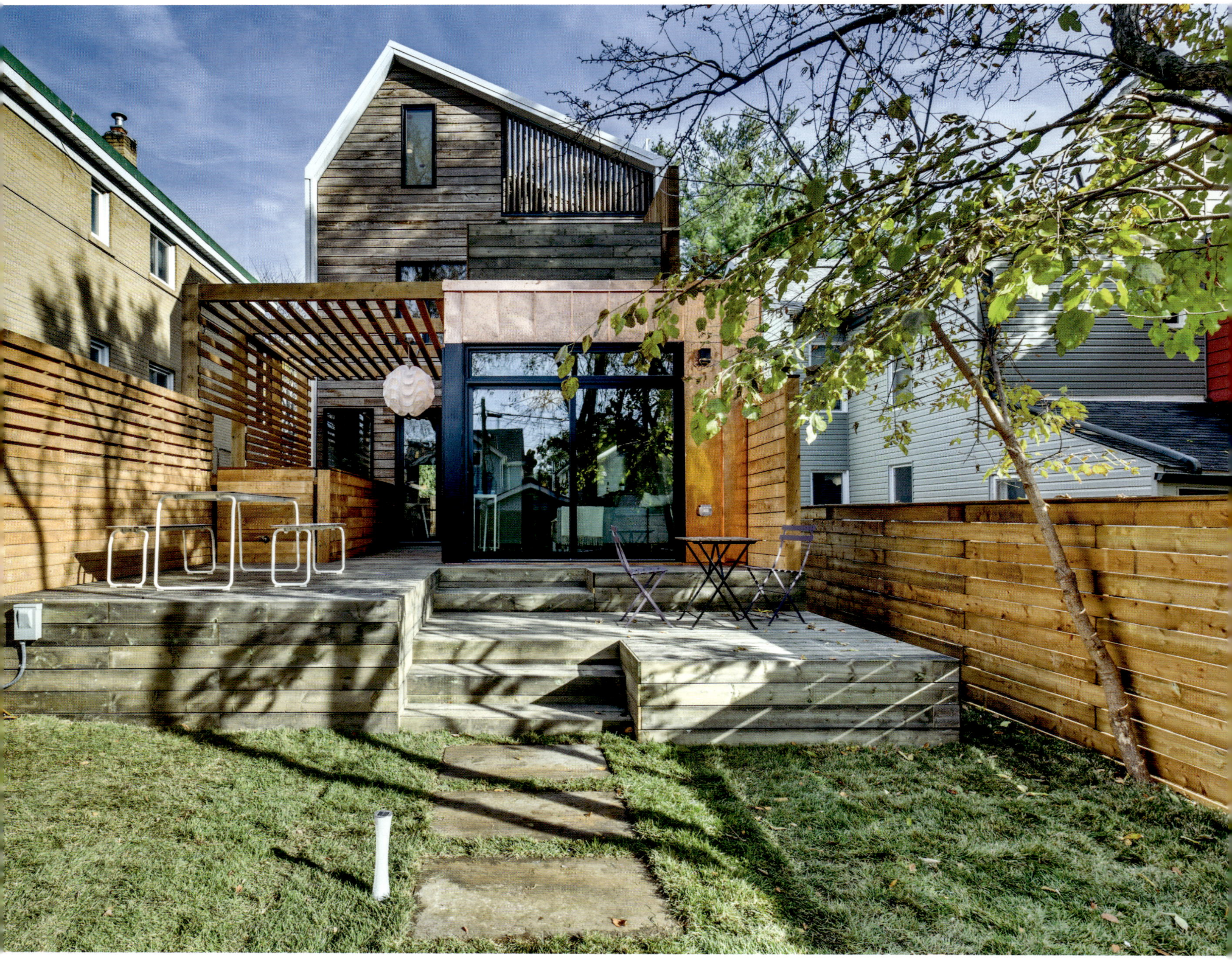

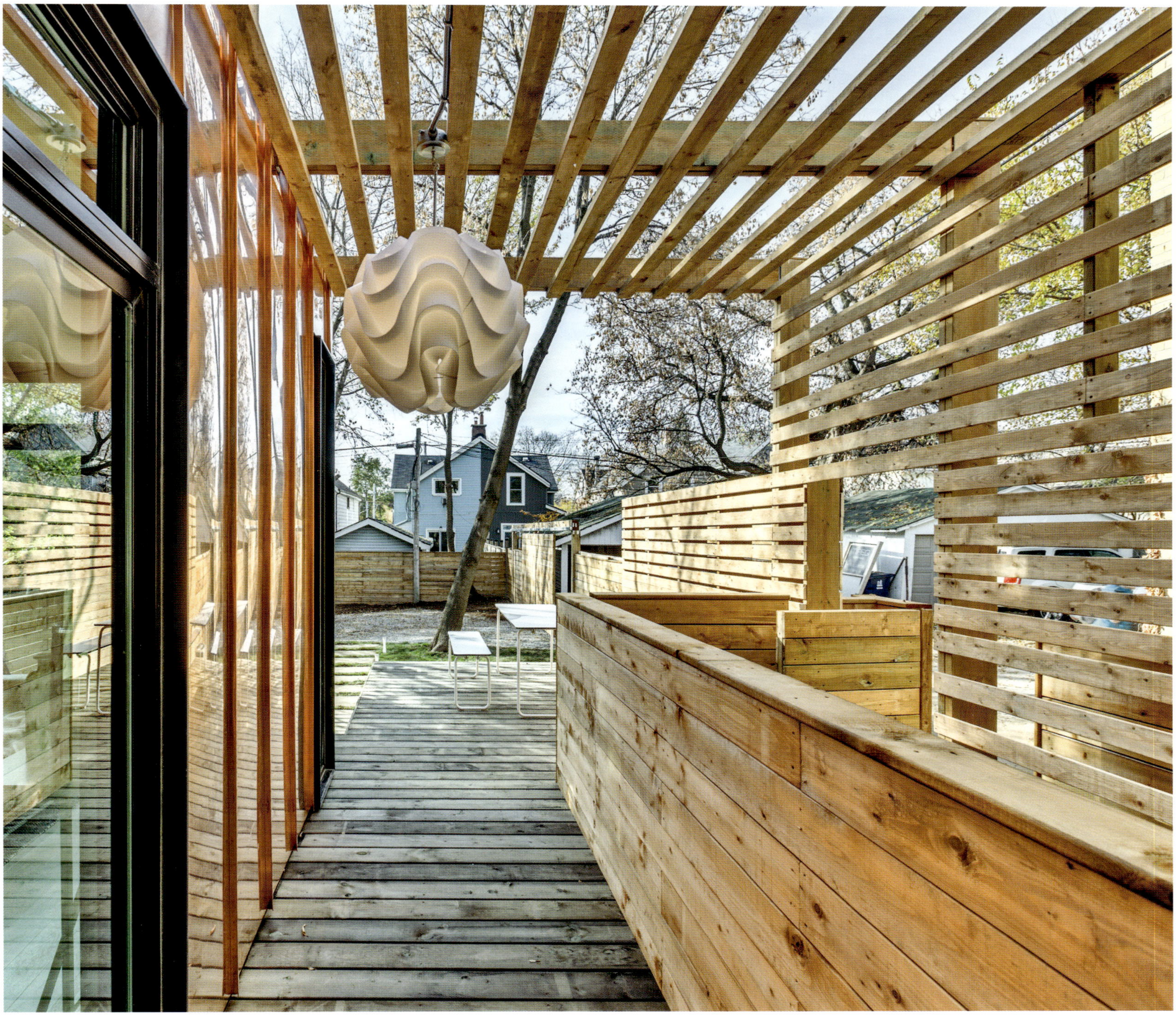

The main floor flows effortlessly from one end of the house to the other, yet this continuous flow does not interfere with the specific function of each of the areas.

Das Hauptgeschoss verläuft ganz einfach fließend von einer Seite des Hauses zur anderen, ohne dabei die jeweilige Funktion der einzelnen Räume zu beeinträchtigen.

L'étage principal est d'une grande fluidité, d'un bout de la maison à l'autre, mais ce flux continu n'interfère pas avec les fonctions spécifiques de chacun des espaces.

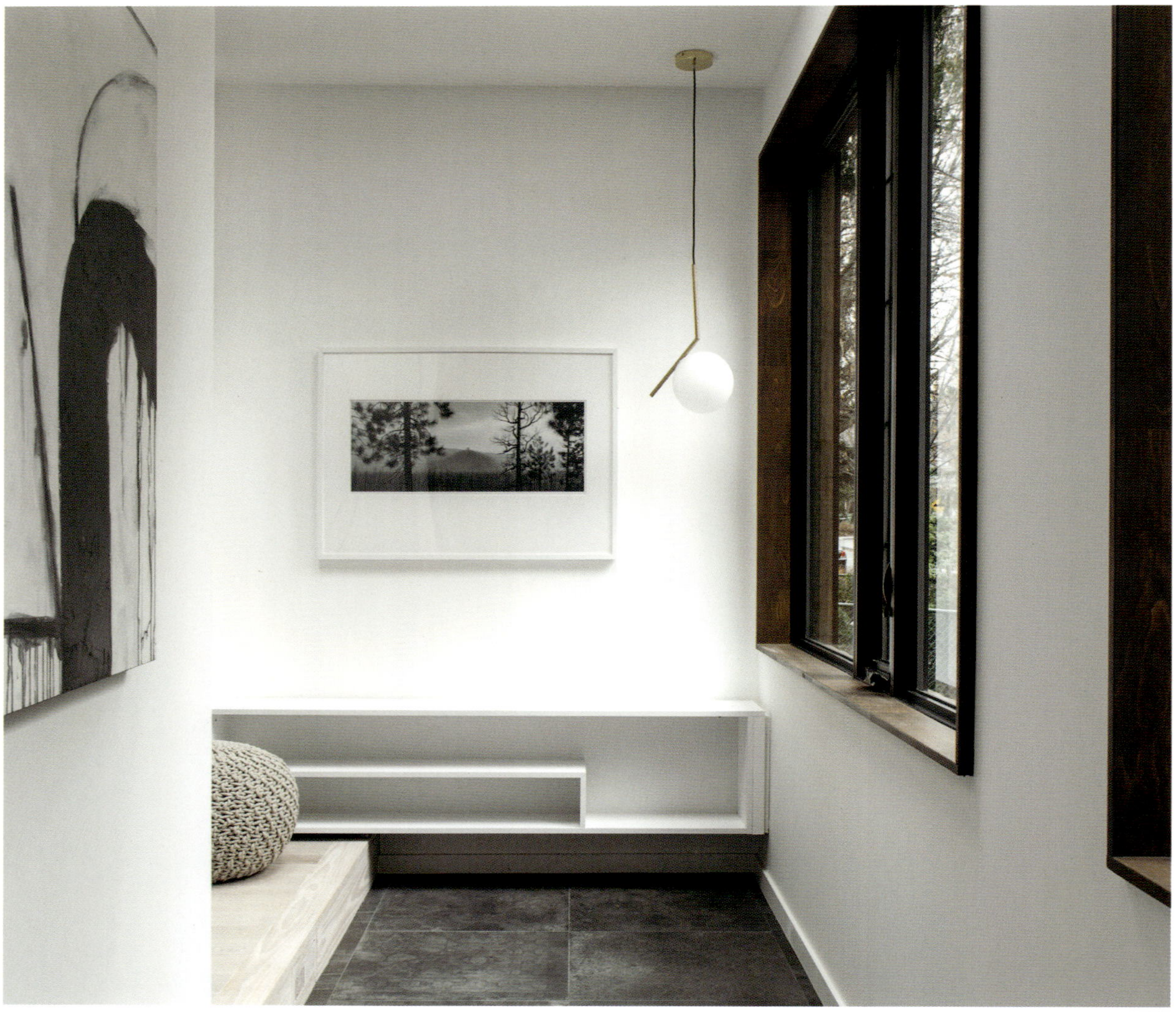

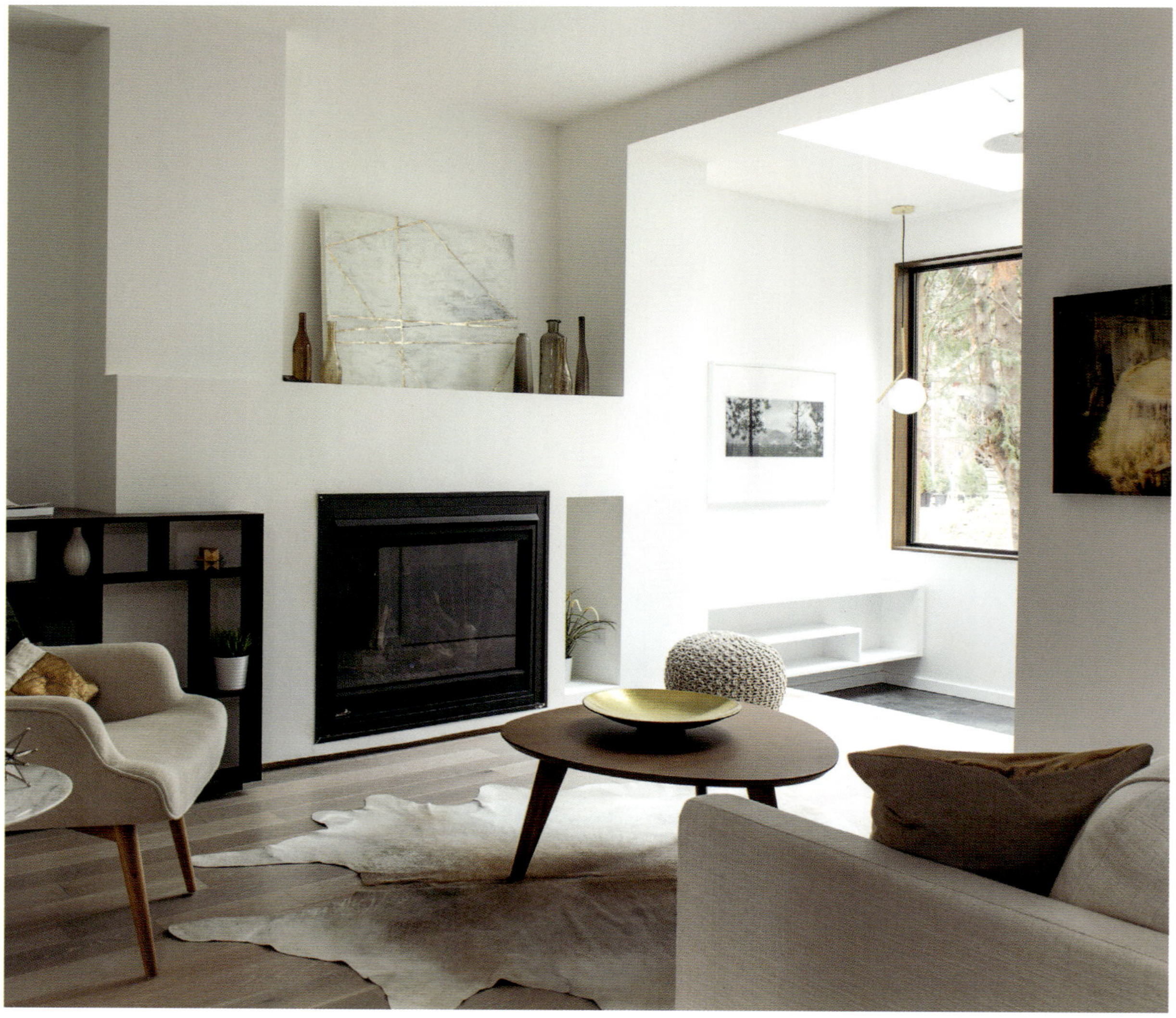

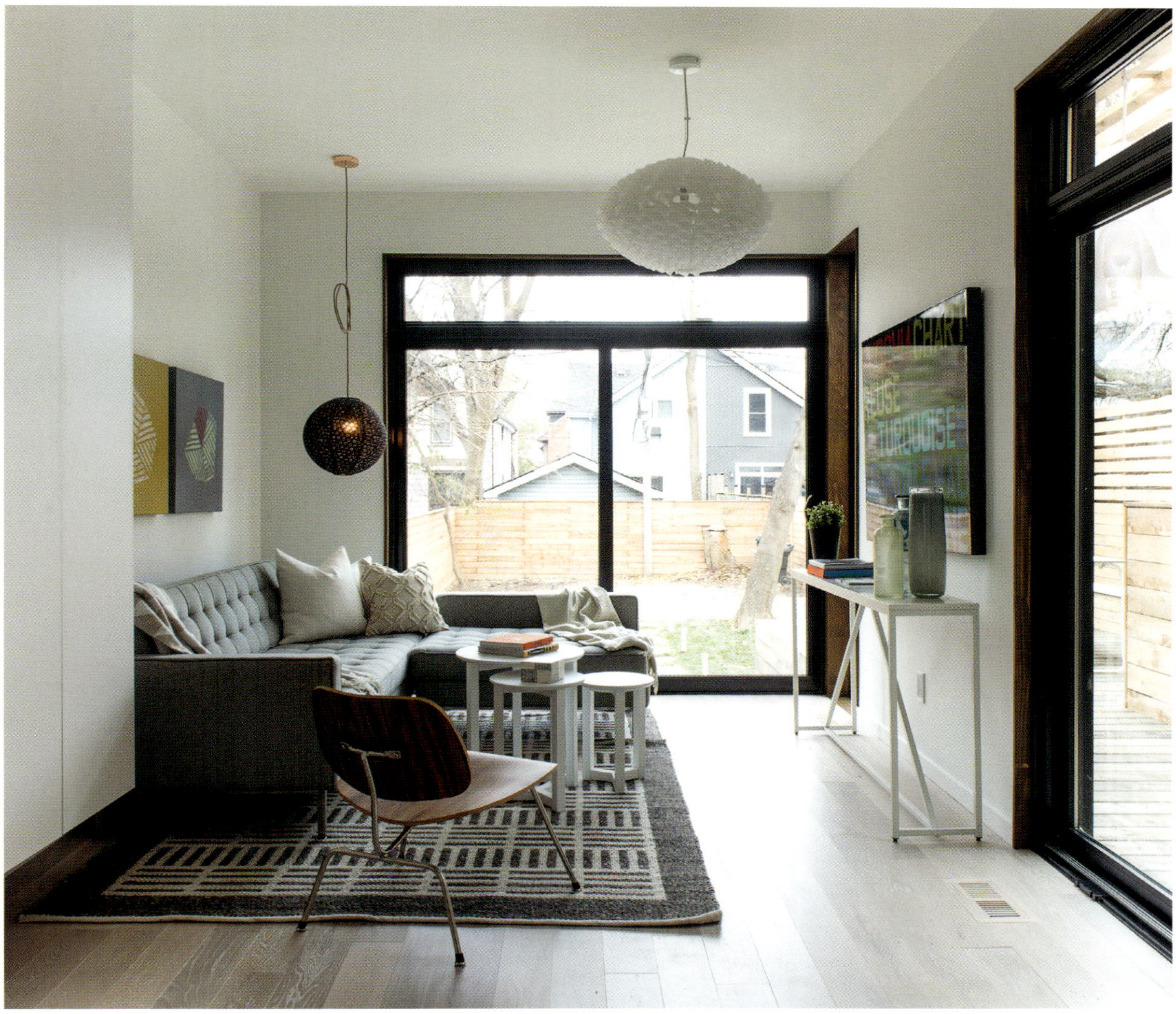

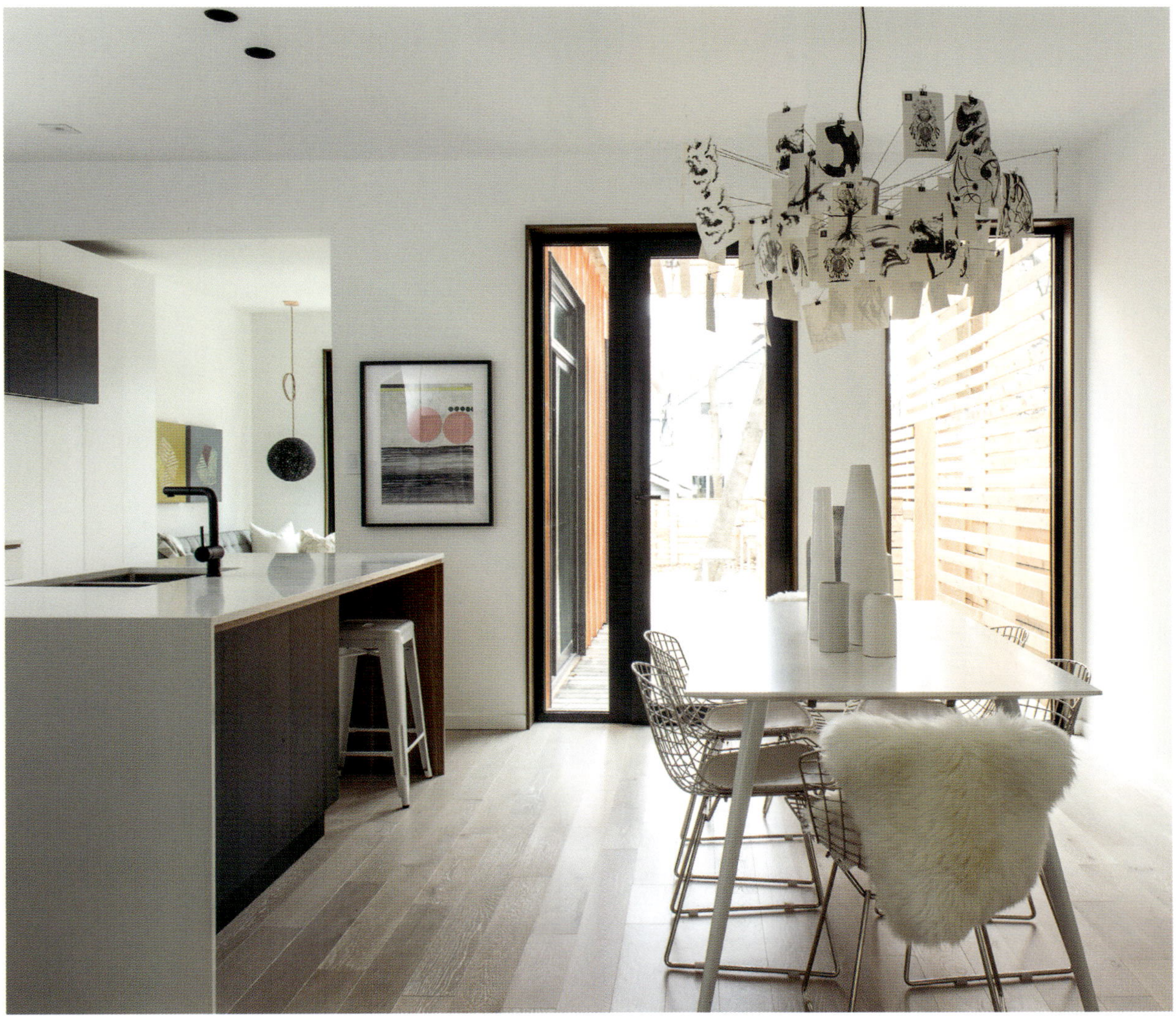

The layout organizes all the daytime areas into one single open space, where each function is connected yet has its own place and identity.

Als Aufenthaltsbereich dient ein großer offener Raum, der dennoch für jede Tätigkeit und Funktion seinen eigenen Bereich hat.

Le plan organise toutes les zones d'habitation de jour en un seul espace ouvert, auquel chaque fonction est reliée tout en ayant sa propre place et sa propre identité.

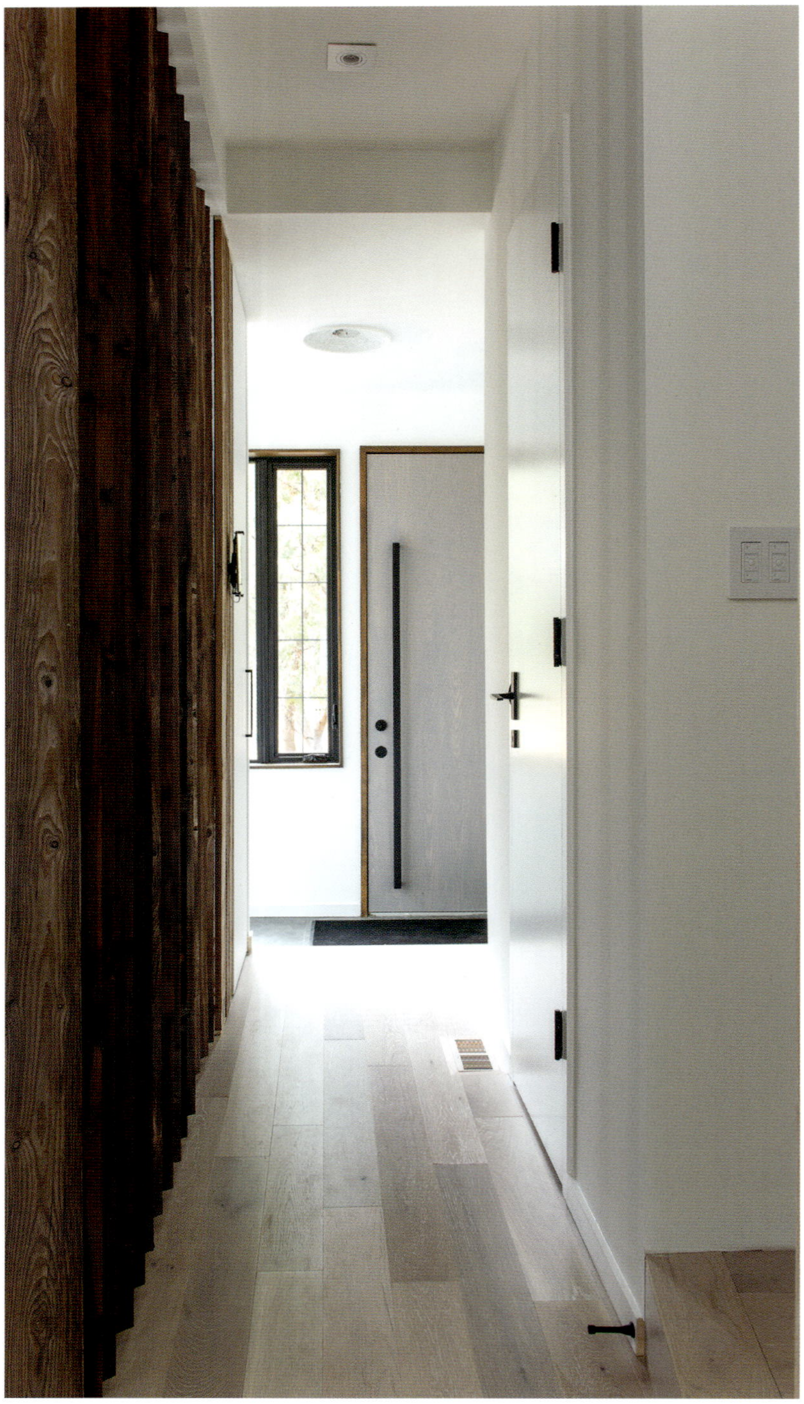

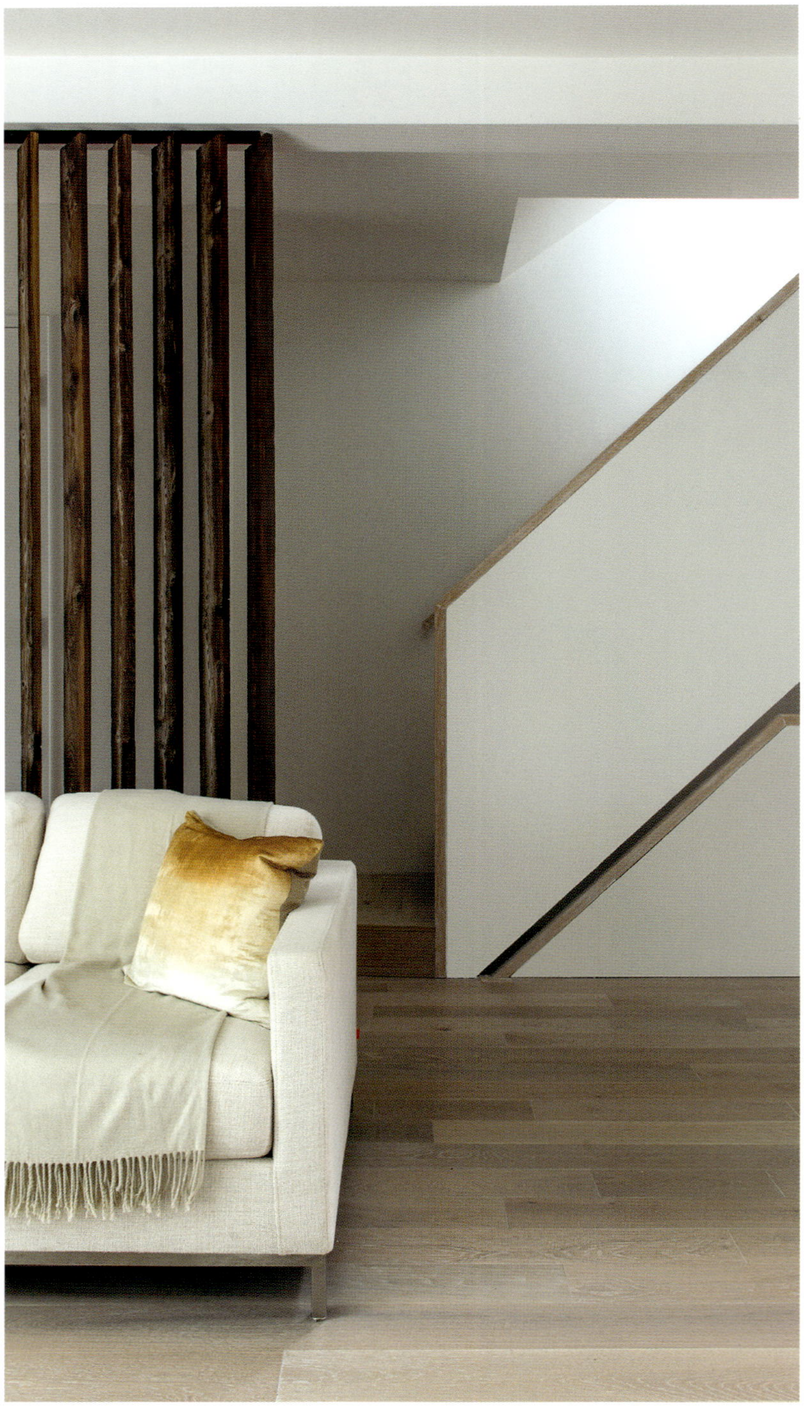

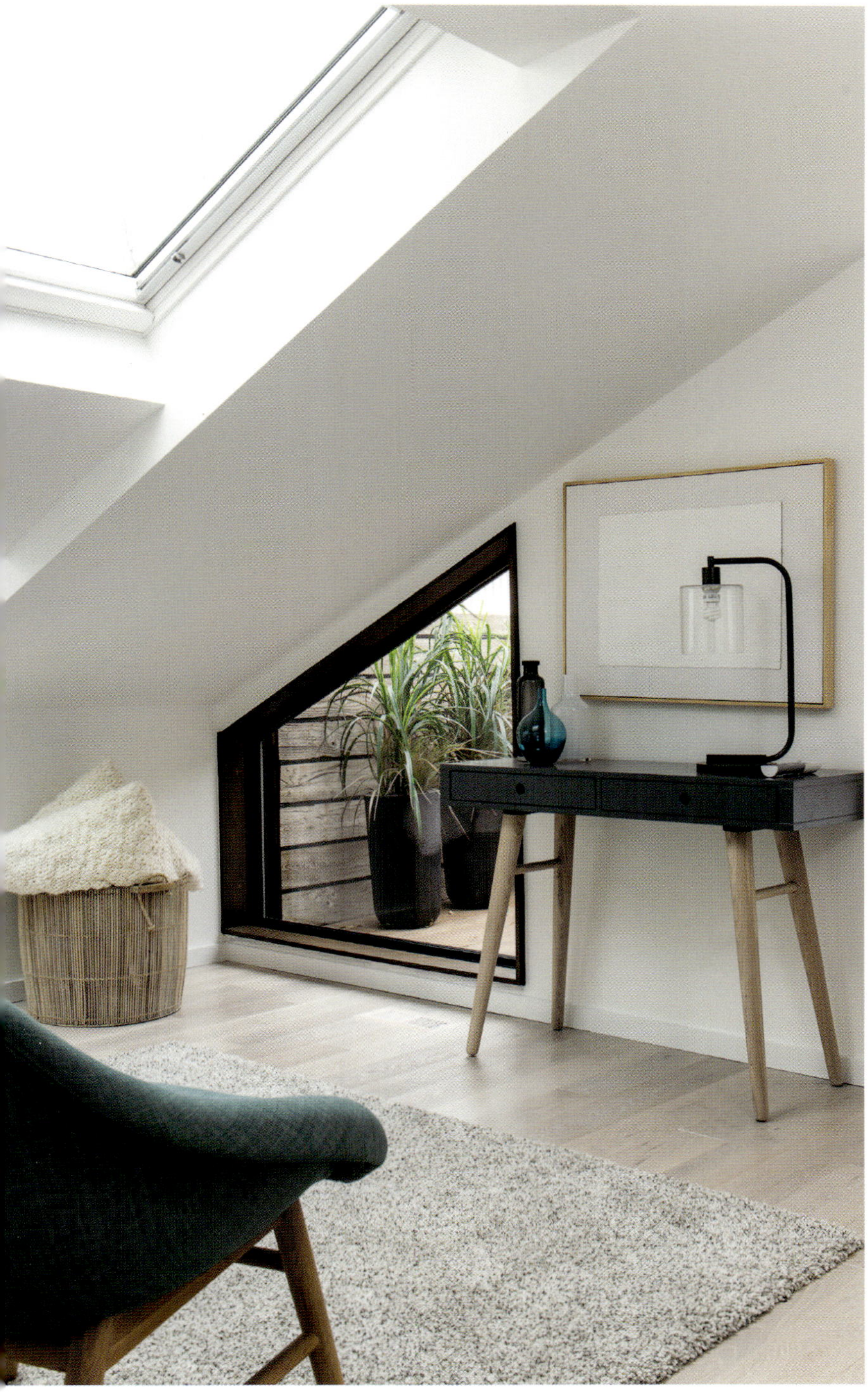

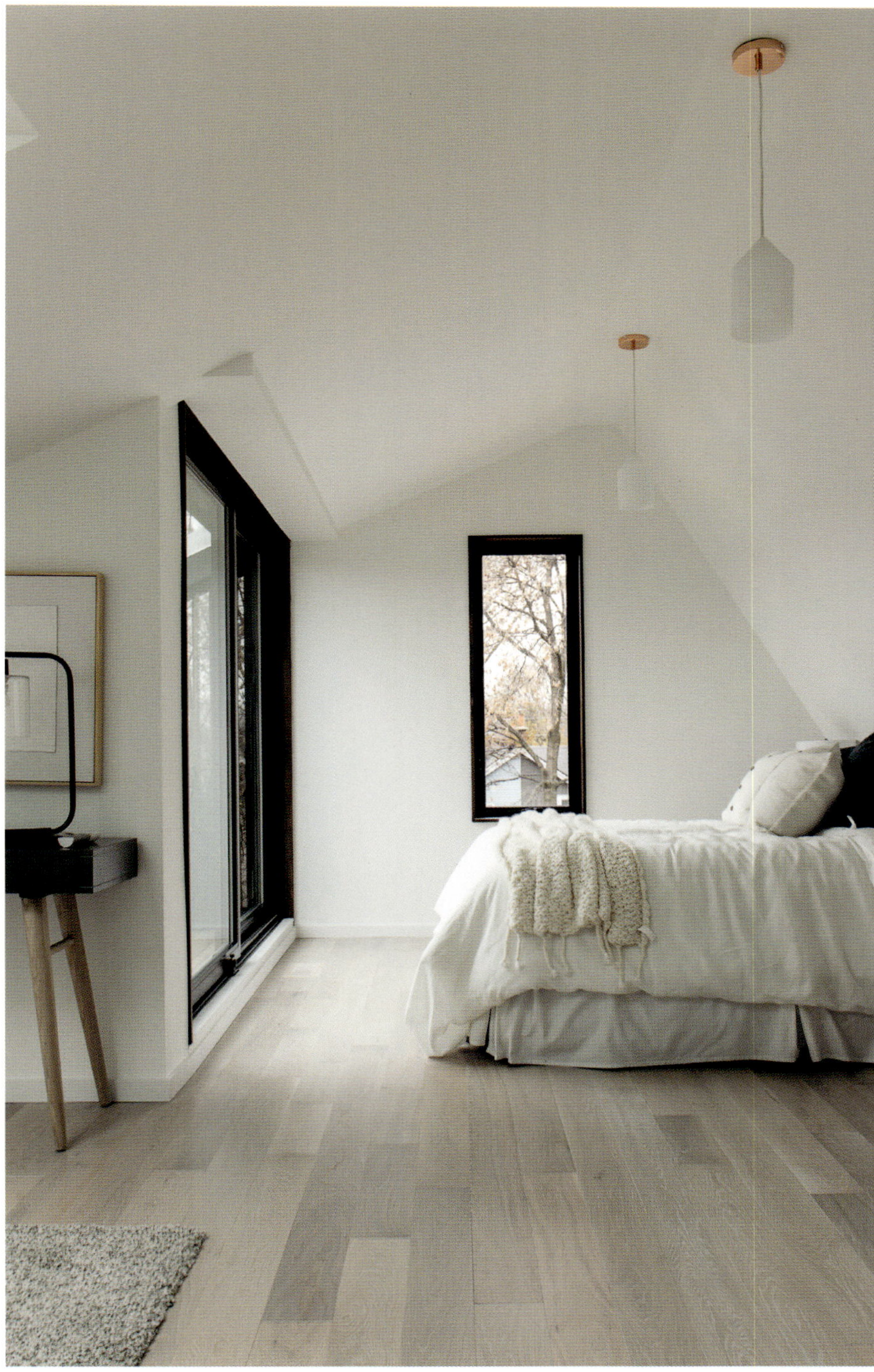

Windows, doors, and skylights encourage the connection between interior spaces and the exterior, while the interior finishes take in and reflect natural light to create a bright and clean living environment.

Fenster, Türen und Dachfenster sorgen für eine Verbindung zwischen Innen- und Außenbereich. Die im Innenbereich verarbeiteten Materialien nehmen natürliches Licht auf und reflektieren es, wodurch eine saubere und helle Wohnumgebung entsteht.

Les fenêtres, les portes, et les fenêtres de toit encouragent le lien entre les espaces intérieurs et extérieurs, tandis que les finitions extérieures absorbent et réfléchissent la lumière naturelle pour créer un environnement de vie lumineux et soigné.

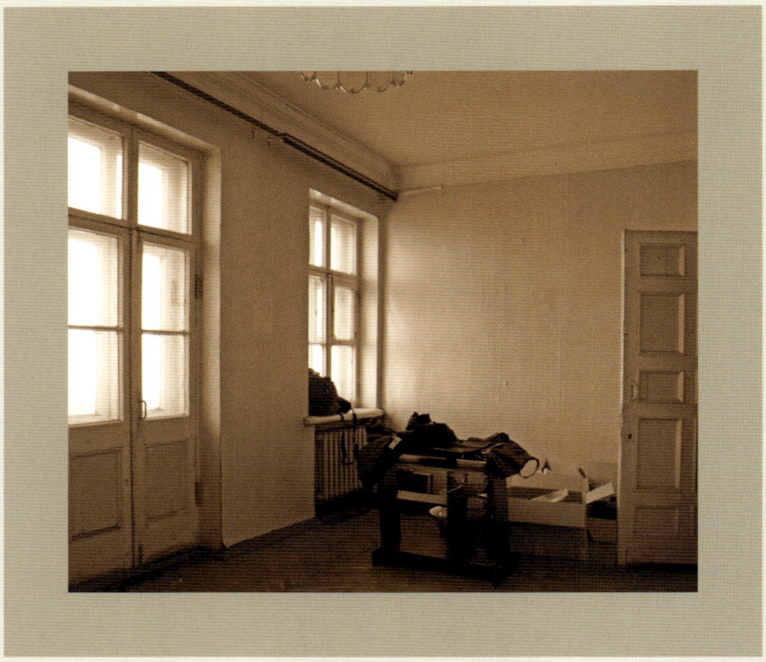

INTERIOR AM

INT2 ARCHITECTURE

56 m^2 | 603 sq. ft.

Moscow, Russia

Photos © **INT2 architecture**

> Renovate a pre-Revolution apartment in central Moscow

> Retain traditional elements to create a contrast between new and old

> Eine Wohnung aus der vorrevolutionären Ära im Zentrum von Moskau renovieren

> Die klassischen Elemente bewahren, um einen Kontrast zwischen alt und neu zu schaffen

> Rénover un appartement de l'époque prérévolutionnaire du centre de Moscou

> Conserver les éléments de style classique afin de créer un contraste entre l'ancien et le nouveau

This apartment is situated in a pre-Revolution building in central Moscow. The "shell" of the apartment is designed with reference to French neo-classicism—white walls, high ceilings, large windows, herringbone parquet floors, plaster cornices, and moldings. The white walls highlight the apartment's proportions and the clarity of its architectural form. These classic elements form the backdrop for a minimalist black box containing all technical spaces: bathroom, water heater, and cabinet. The box is a compositional center, around which the main functional areas are positioned: the kitchen, living room, and bedroom with a small office area.
In their color, material, and style, the modern interior elements contrast with the classic as each period complements the other. In this way, objects take on individuality and create a fresh architectural space.

Diese Wohnung befindet sich in einem vorrevolutionären Gebäude im Zentrum von Moskau. Die „Hülle" der Wohnung nimmt Bezug auf den französischen Neoklassizismus – weiße Wände, hohe Decken, große Fenster, Parkett mit Fischgrätmuster, Stuckgesims und Stuckleisten. Die weißen Wände unterstreichen die Proportionen der Wohnung und die Reinheit der architektonischen Form: Die klassischen Elemente bilden den Hintergrund einer minimalistischen schwarzen Box, in der sich alle technischen Einrichtungen verbergen – Bad, Therme und Garderobe. Diese Box ist ein Kompositionszentrum, um das sich die wichtigsten Funktionsbereiche gruppieren: Küche, Wohnzimmer und das Schlafzimmer mit einem kleinen Bürobereich.
Die modernen Elemente im Innenbereich kontrastieren in Farbe, Material und Stil mit den klassischen und ergänzen diese gleichzeitig. Dadurch erhalten die Objekte Individualität und schaffen einen frischen architektonischen Raum.

Cet appartement se trouve dans un bâtiment prérévolutionnaire au cœur de Moscou. La « carcasse » de l'appartement a été conçue en prenant comme référence le néoclassicisme français – murs blancs, plafonds hauts, grandes fenêtres, parquet en chevrons, corniches en plâtre et moulures. Les murs blancs mettent en valeur les proportions de l'appartement et la pureté de la forme architecturale. Ces éléments classiques sont la toile de fond d'une boîte noire minimaliste dans laquelle se regroupent tous les espaces techniques – salle de bains, chaudière et armoire. Cette boîte est un centre de composition autour duquel se trouvent les principales zones fonctionnelles : la cuisine, le séjour et la chambre avec un coin bureau.
Les éléments intérieurs modernes contrastent en termes de couleurs, matériaux et style avec ceux classiques, se complétant simultanément. Les objets acquièrent ainsi leur personnalité en créant un espace architectural sain.

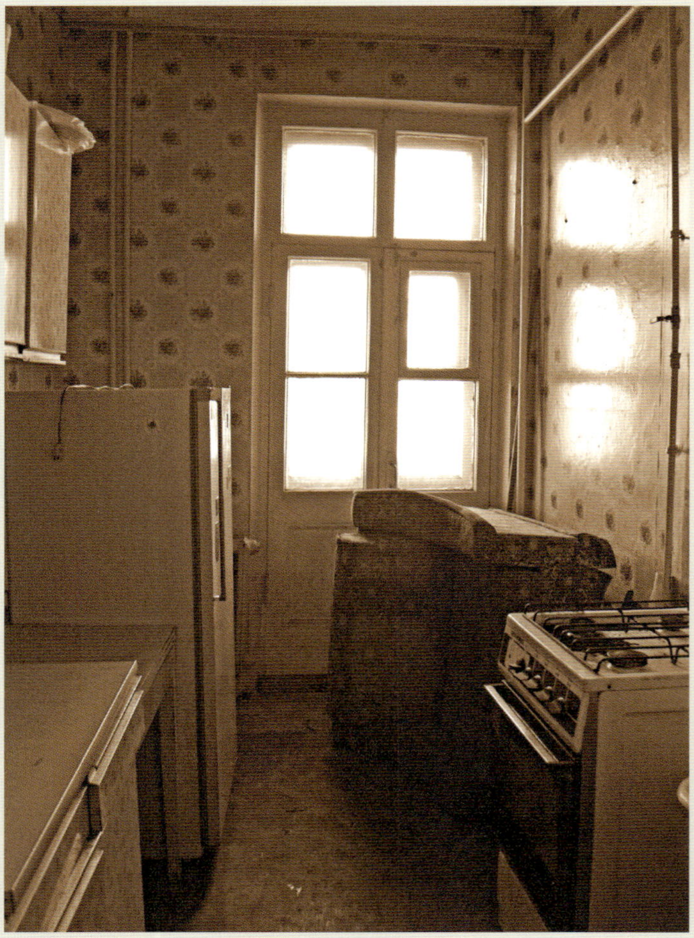

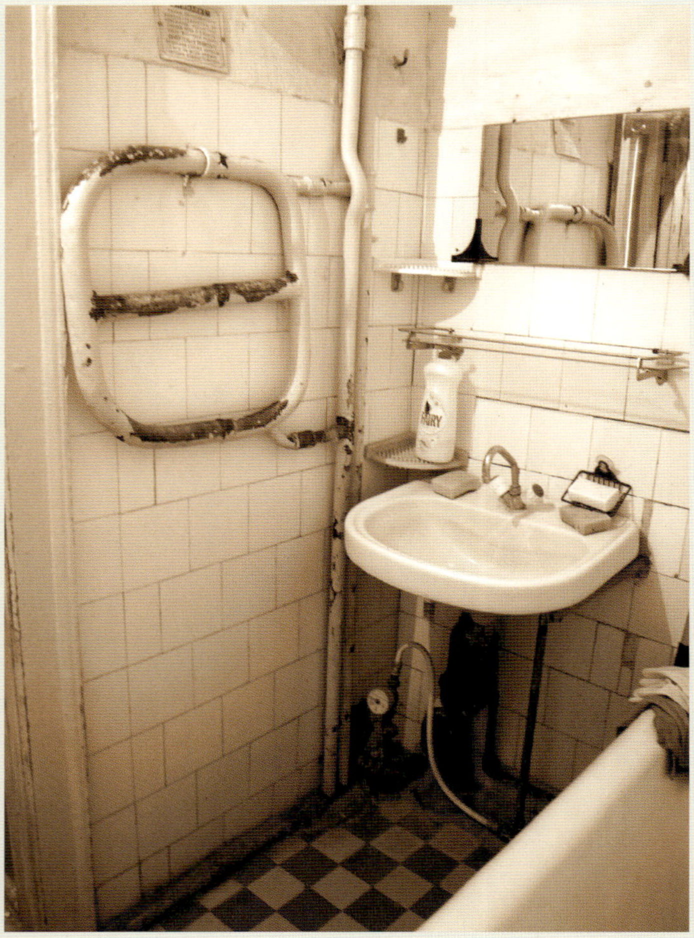

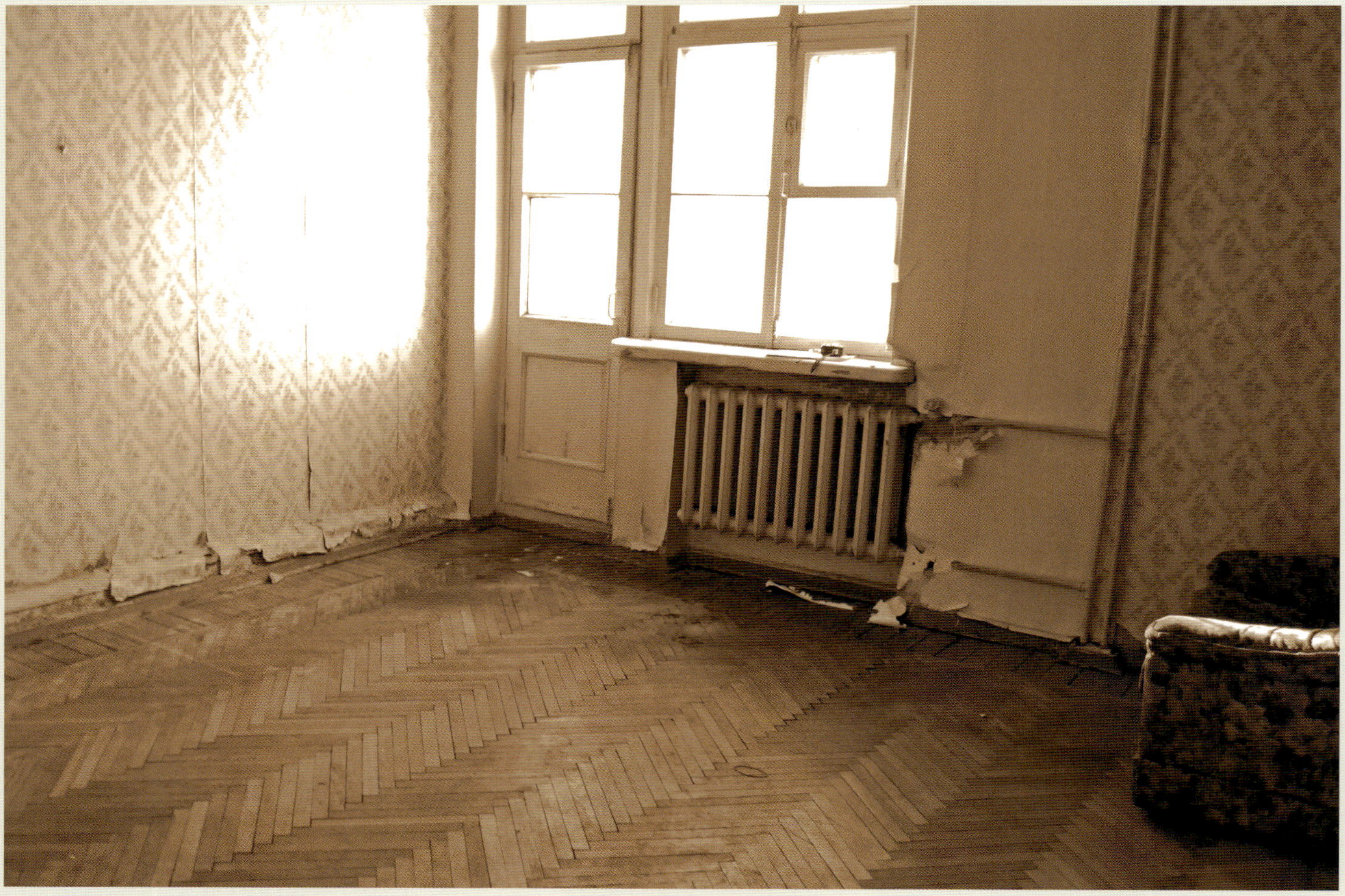

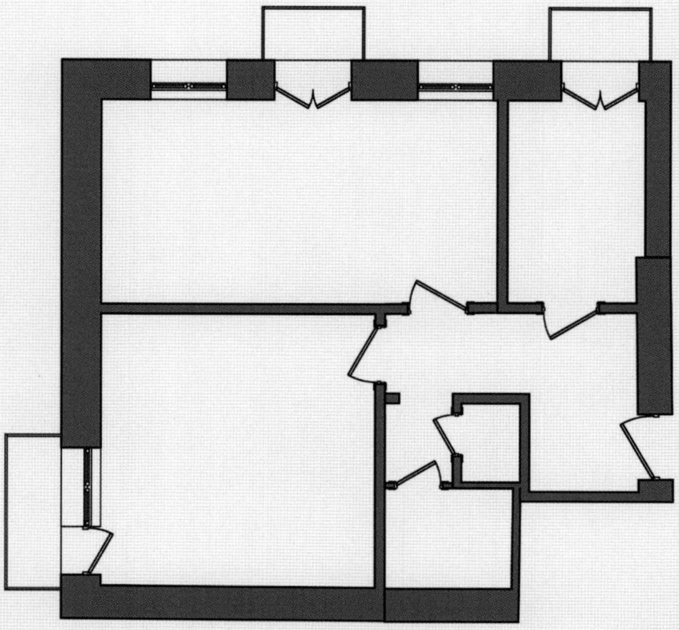

Existing plan

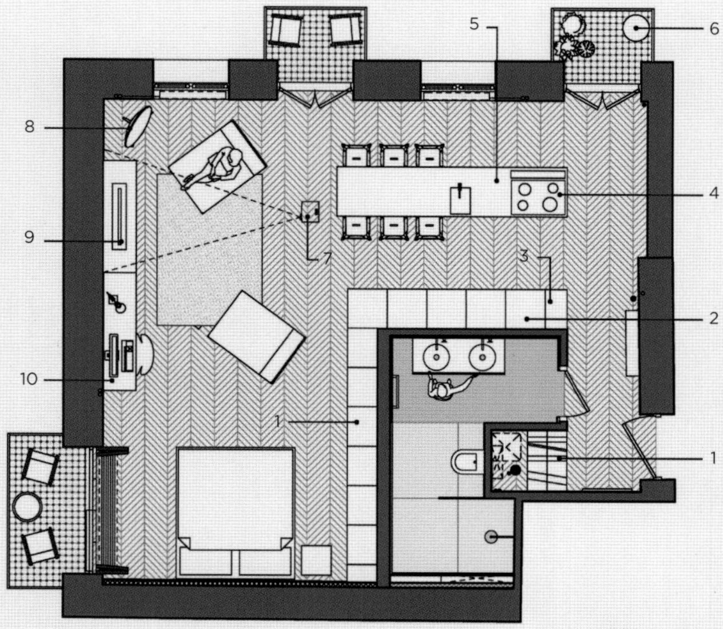

New plan

1. Wardrobe
2. Refrigerator
3. Wine shelf
4. Extendable table / ventilation
5. Dishwasher
6. Barbeque
7. Projector
8. Speaker
9. Ethanol fireplace
10. Desk

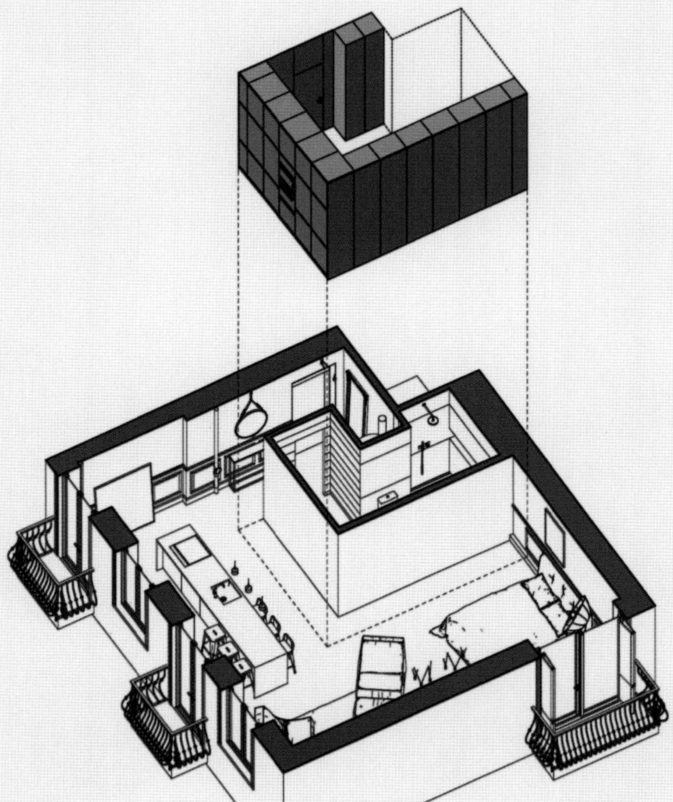

Axonometric view

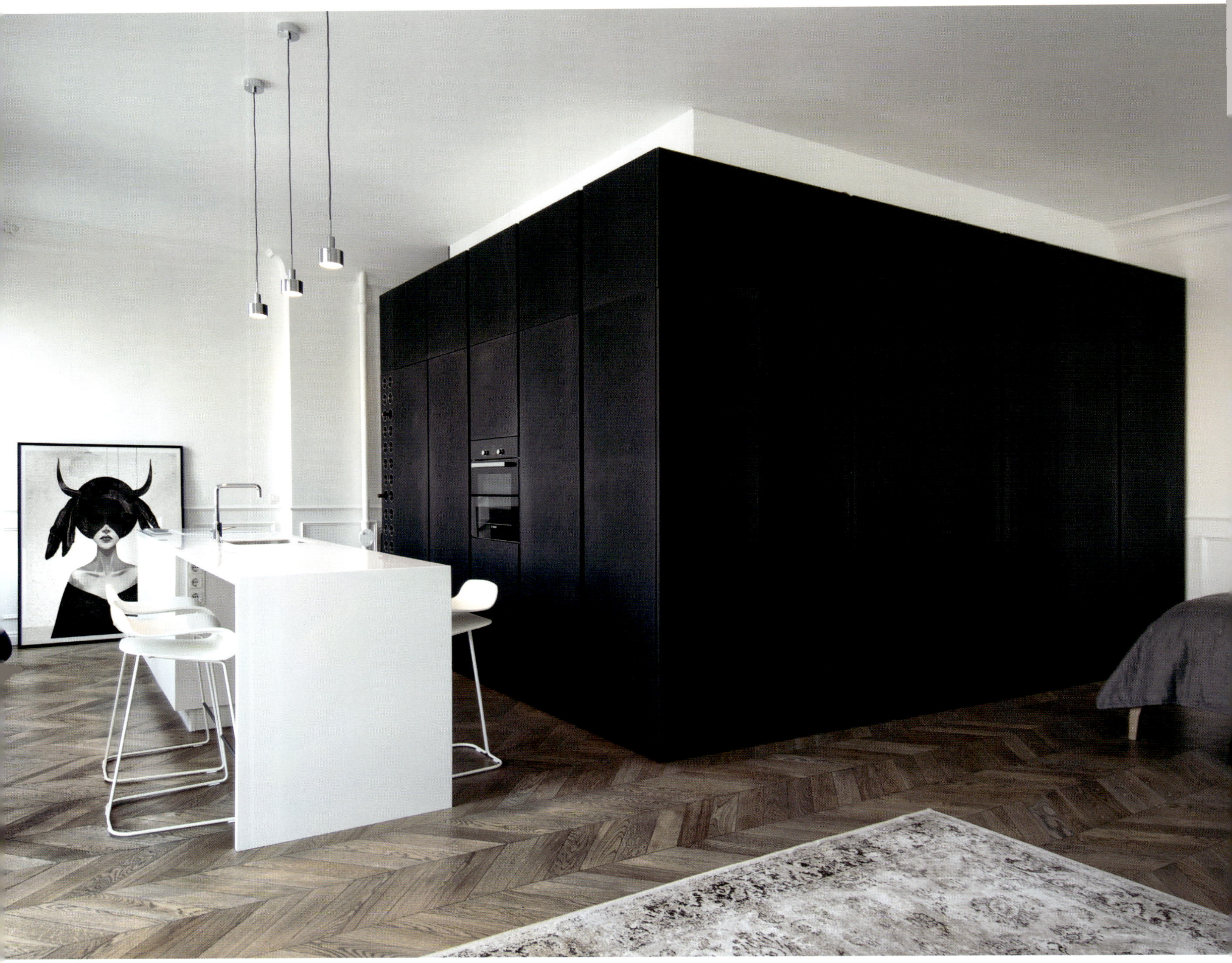

The kitchen island, 13 feet in length, serves as a work space and informal dining area. In the black box, electrical appliances are masked by the appearance of the cabinets, and an original bottle rack is integrated into one end.

Die Kücheninsel mit vier Metern Länge dient als Arbeitsbereich und als zwangloser Essbereich. In der schwarzen Box sind Schränke und Küchengeräte verborgen, und an einem Ende ist ein originelles Flaschenregal integriert.

L'îlot de la cuisine de quatre mètres de long sert à la fois de plan de travail et de salle à manger informelle. Dans la boîte noire, à l'apparence d'armoires, sont dissimulés les appareils électroménagers et à une extrémité, un casier à bouteilles intégré.

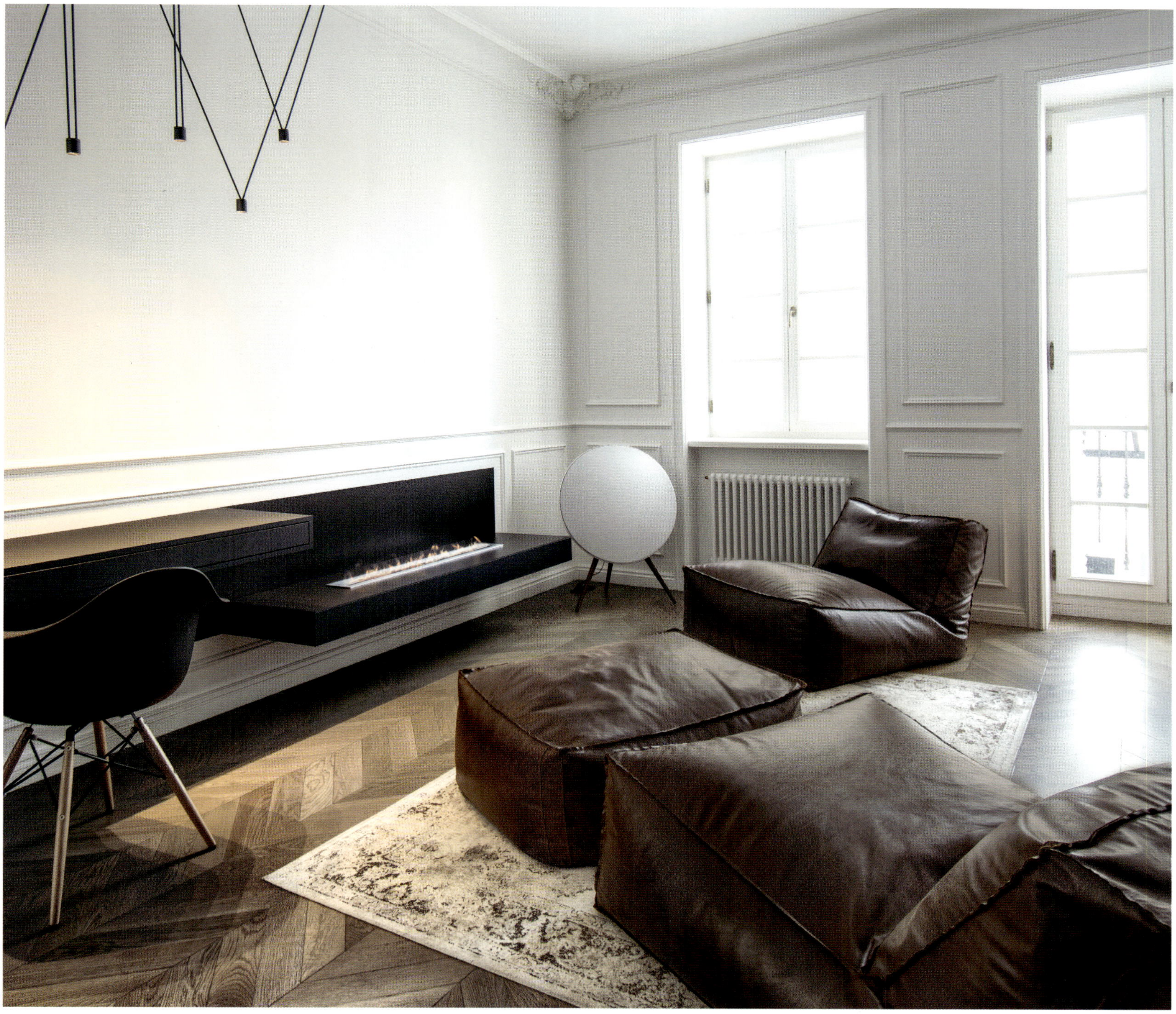

The leather sofas, rug, and hardwood floor lend warmth to the ensemble. The Eames chair and the desk's modern and minimalist design form a fascinating contrast in colors, textures, and styles in which the modern exists in perfect harmony with the classic.

Ledersofas, Teppich und Holzboden verleihen dem Ganzen Wärme. Das moderne und minimalistische Design des Schreibtisches neben dem Eames-Stuhl schafft einen interessanten Kontrast von Farben, Texturen und Stilen, bei dem das Moderne perfekt mit dem Klassischen harmoniert.

Les canapés en cuir, le tapis et le parquet en bois apportent de la chaleur à l'ensemble. Le design moderne et minimaliste du bureau et la chaise Eames créent un contraste intéressant de couleurs, textures et styles où le moderne cohabite à la perfection avec le classique.

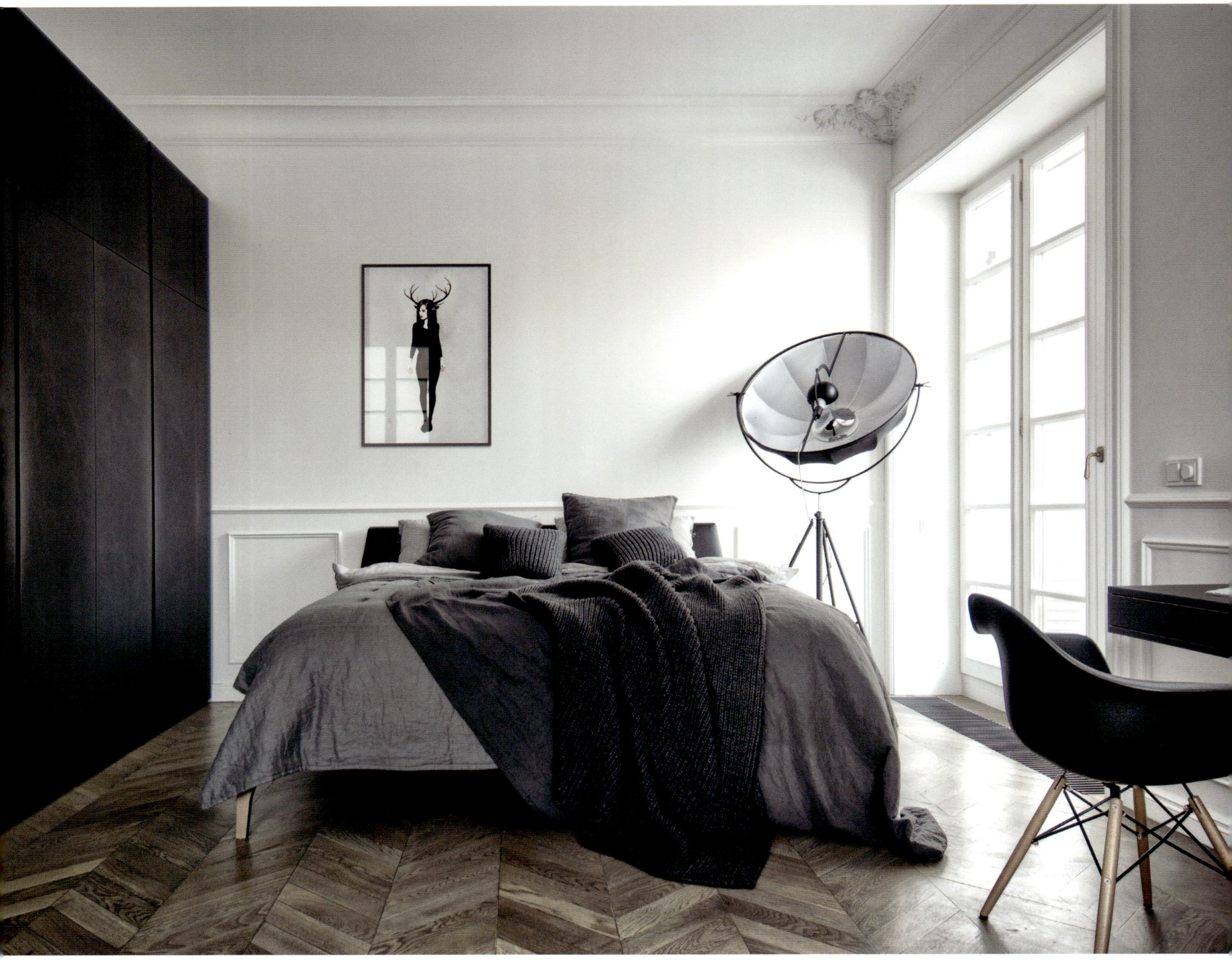

The neutral color palette of the bedroom ranges from white to black and includes all shades of gray. Far from appearing cold, it uses cushions and bed covers to create a warm and cozy mood.

Eine neutrale Farbpalette, die von Weiß über alle Grautöne bis Schwarz reicht, wurde eingesetzt. Dank Kissen und Bettwäsche wirkt das Schlafzimmer überhaupt nicht kalt, sondern gemütlich.

Pour cela, on a eu recours à une palette neutre de couleurs allant du blanc au noir en passant par tous les tons de gris. Grâce aux coussins et à la parure de lit, la chambre, loin de sembler froide, est au contraire accueillante.

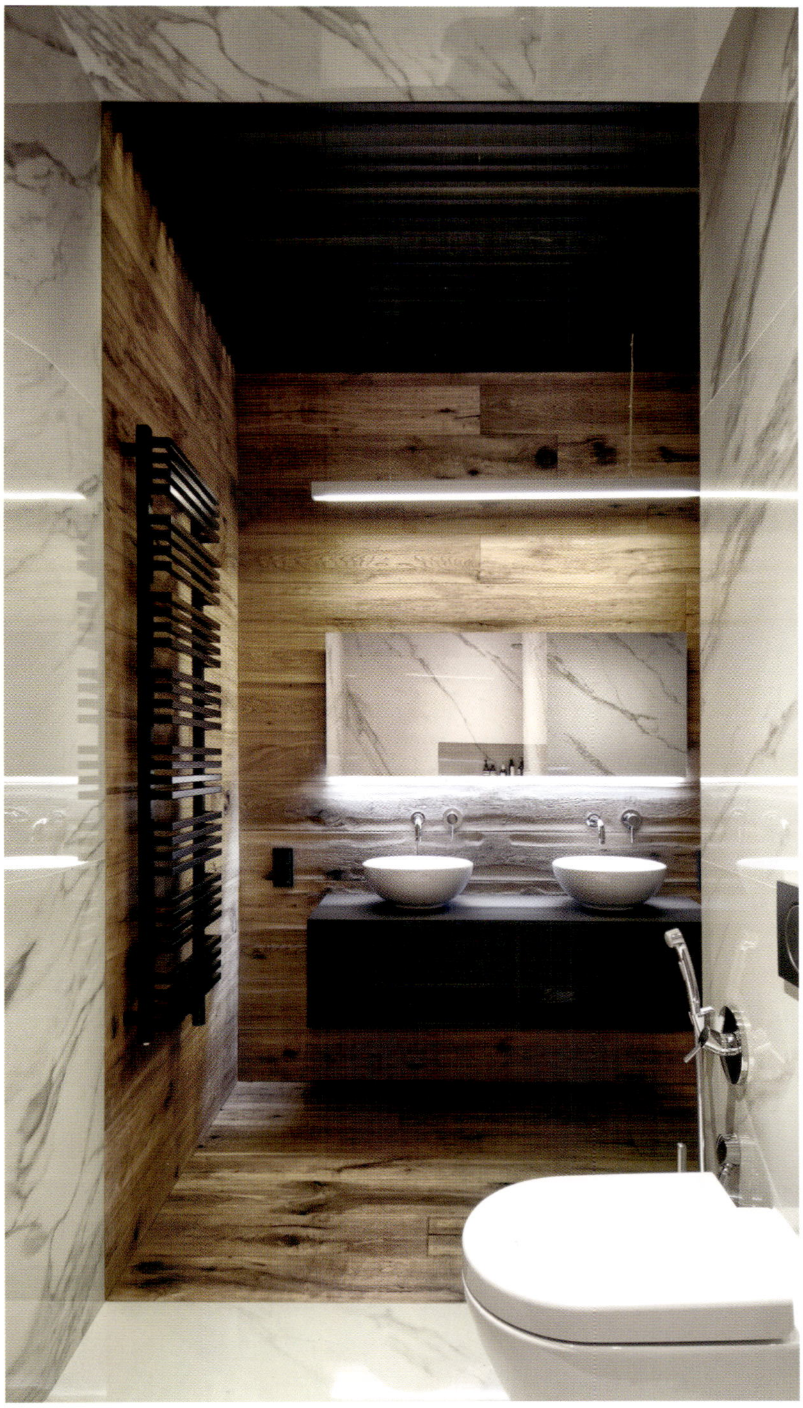

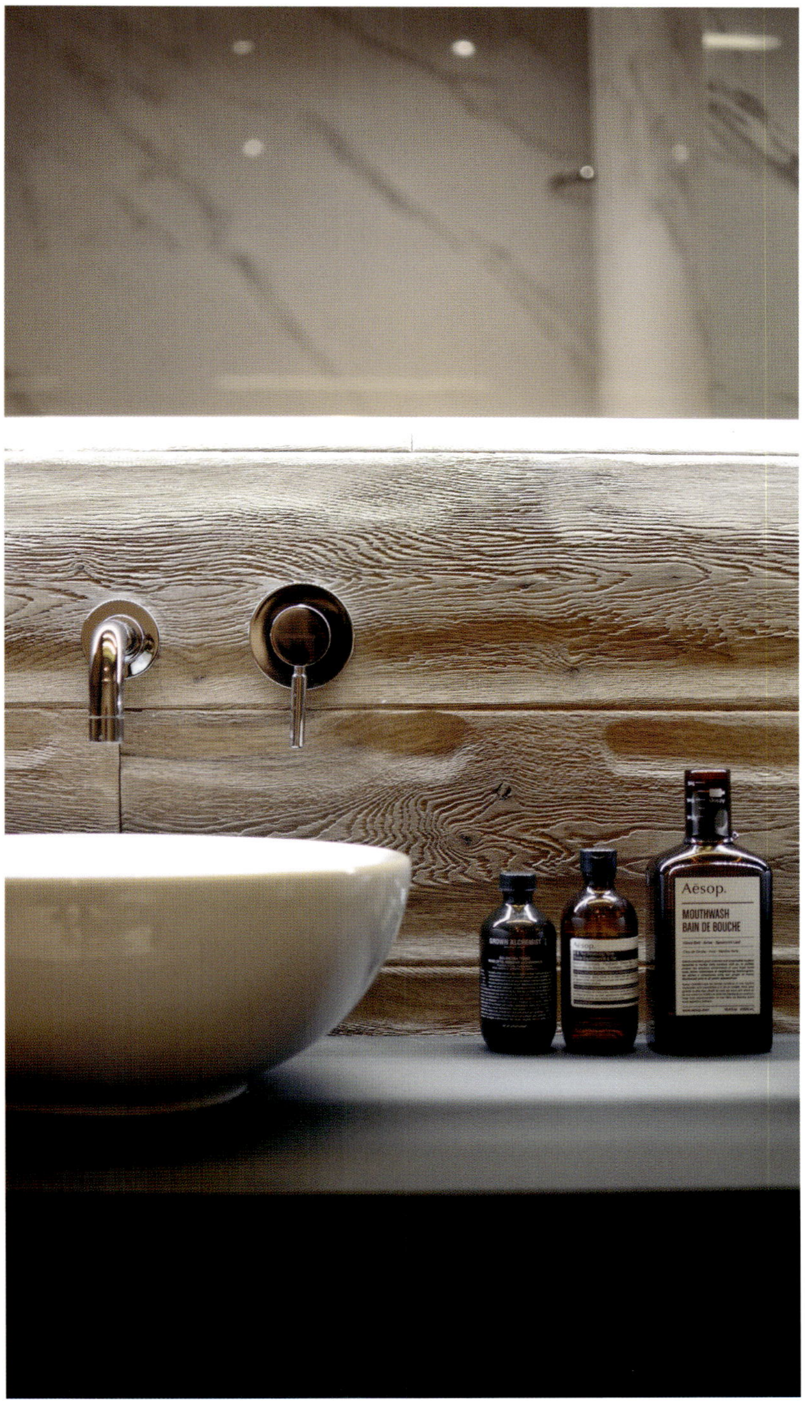

Different materials have been used to demarcate the bathroom areas. In this way, the residence's overall color palette has been retained, while textures are employed as the contrasting element.

Um die Bereiche des Badezimmers voneinander zu unterscheiden, wurden verschiedene Materialien verwendet. Auf diese Weise wurde die Farbpalette des ganzen Hauses beibehalten und die Texturen wurden als Kontrast eingesetzt.

Divers matériaux ont été utilisés pour différencier les zones de la salle de bains. De cette manière, la palette chromatique de toute la maison a été conservée et les textures ont été utilisées comme un élément de contraste.

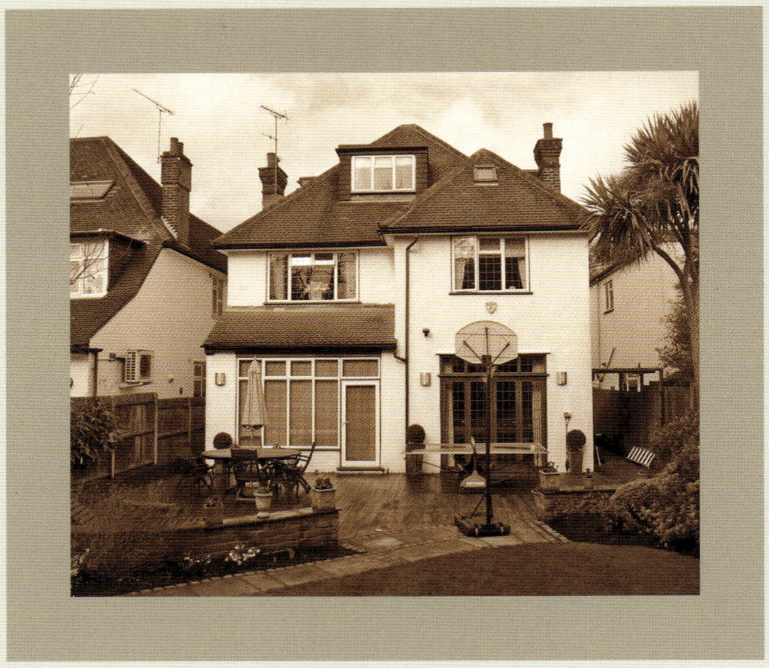

OPEN HOUSE

ROBERT HIRSCHFIELD ARCHITECTS

335 m^2 | 3,605 sq. ft.

London, United Kingdom

Photos © **Matt Clayton**

> Reorganize all spaces

> Expand the house, taking advantage of extensive, but previously unused exterior space

> Forge a greater connection to the outdoors

> Take maximum advantage of an under-utilized upper-story area

> Alle Räume neu anordnen

> Das Haus erweitern, indem der großzügige, zuvor ungenutzte Außenraum genutzt wird

> Eine stärkere Verbindung nach außen hin erzielen

> Den zu wenig genutzten Dachbodenbereich so optimal wie möglich nutzen

> Réorganiser tous les espaces

> Agrandir la maison en profitant du vaste espace en plein air qui était alors inutilisé

> Obtenir une meilleure connexion avec l'extérieur

> Profiter au maximum d'un espace séjour qui était négligé

The starting point in conceptualizing the restoration of this Edwardian residence was the need for a complete reorganization of the space. Common areas were dark and narrow and there was no connection to its ample open-air spaces. Moreover, the house's uppermost area had not been exploited.
The solution involved reconfiguring the layouts of each floor and extending the house to create a spacious living area at the rear of the ground floor, a large, glazed space that frames the newly landscaped garden and terrace. The reconfiguration provided the family with generous sized rooms that offer an appealing interplay of level changes and spatial areas. These are connected by a new helical staircase featuring a ribbon-like handrail that curves as one ascends through the house within the three-story atrium space. The topmost area contains a bedroom with a small private recessed terrace.
The bathrooms, bedrooms, and living areas have built-in customized woodwork, storage areas, and shelving, all of which is fully incorporated into the concept and overall design. Throughout the house, the warmth and texture of the wooden staircase has been accented in the floors and countertops.

Der Ausgangspunkt für die Renovierung dieses Hauses im edwardianischen Stil war die erforderliche komplette Neuordnung der Räume. Die Gemeinschaftsbereiche waren dunkel und eng. Zudem fehlte eine Verbindung zu den großzügigen Außenflächen und dem bisher ungenutzten Dachbodenbereich.
Als Lösung entschied sich der Architekt, die Aufteilung jeder Etage neu zu gestalten und das Haus so auszubauen, dass im hinteren Teil des Erdgeschosses ein geräumiger Wohnbereich mit einer großen verglasten Struktur entstand, die den neuen Garten und die Terrasse umrahmt. Die Umgestaltung der Etagen brachte der Familie große Zimmer mit einem interessanten Spiel mit Höhen- und Volumenänderungen. Diese sind durch eine neue Treppe mit einem bandförmigen Handlauf, die sich im Atrium über drei Etagen in die Höhe windet, miteinander verbunden. Der Dachbodenbereich beherbergt ein Schlafzimmer, das zudem das Privileg genießt, eine kleine private Terrasse zu haben.
Bad, Schlafzimmer und Wohnräume verfügen über maßgefertigte Schreinerarbeiten, Stauräume und Regale, die vollständig in das Gesamtkonzept und Design integriert wurden. Im gesamten Haus wurden die Wärme und Textur der Maserung des Holzes, das für die Treppe verwendet wurde, auf dem Boden und auf den Arbeitsplatten betont.

Au moment de réaliser les travaux de cette de maison de style édouardien, le point de départ était la nécessité d'une réorganisation totale des espaces. Les parties communes étaient sombres et étroites. Il y avait également un manque de connexion avec ses vastes espaces en plein air et les combles qui étaient inutilisées.
Comme solution, il a été proposé de reconfigurer la répartition de chaque étage et d'agrandir la maison afin de créer un séjour spacieux au fonds avec une grande structure vitrée qui entoure le nouveau jardin et la terrasse. La reconfiguration des étages a permis à la famille d'offrir de grandes chambres avec un jeu de changements intéressant de niveau et volumes. Ceux-ci sont reliés par un nouvel escalier hélicoïdal avec une rampe en forme de ruban qui se courbe au fur et à mesure que l'on descend en parallèle au vide central à double hauteur. La zone des combles accueille une chambre qui a le privilège d'avoir une petite terrasse privative.
Les salles de bains, chambres et espaces habitables ont une menuiserie encastrée sur mesure, des espaces de rangement et des étagères, tout ceci est entièrement intégré au concept et design global. La chaleur et la texture des veines du bois utilisé pour l'escalier ont accentué le sol et les plans de travail de toute la maison.

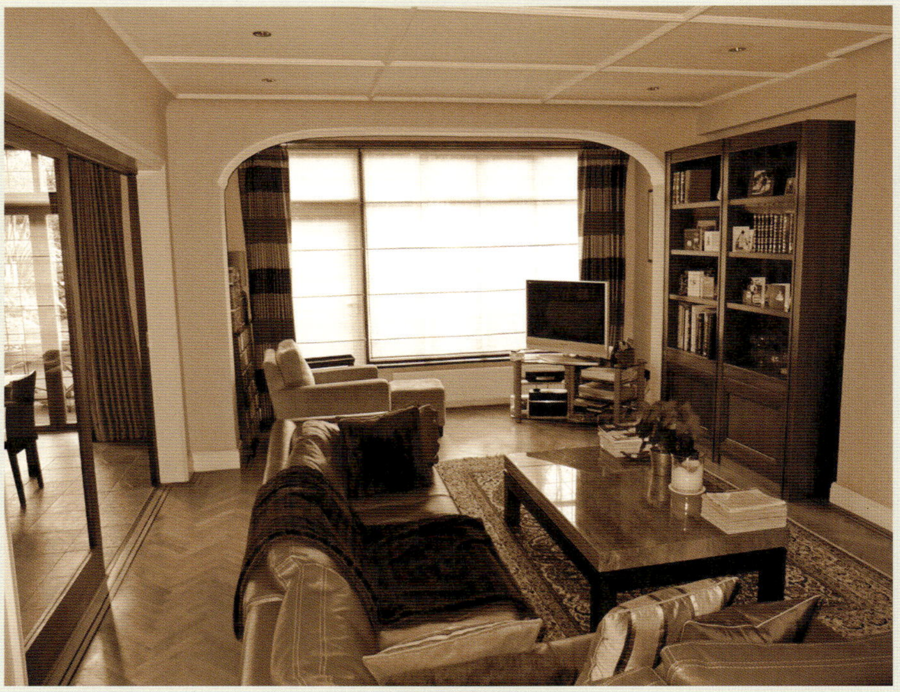

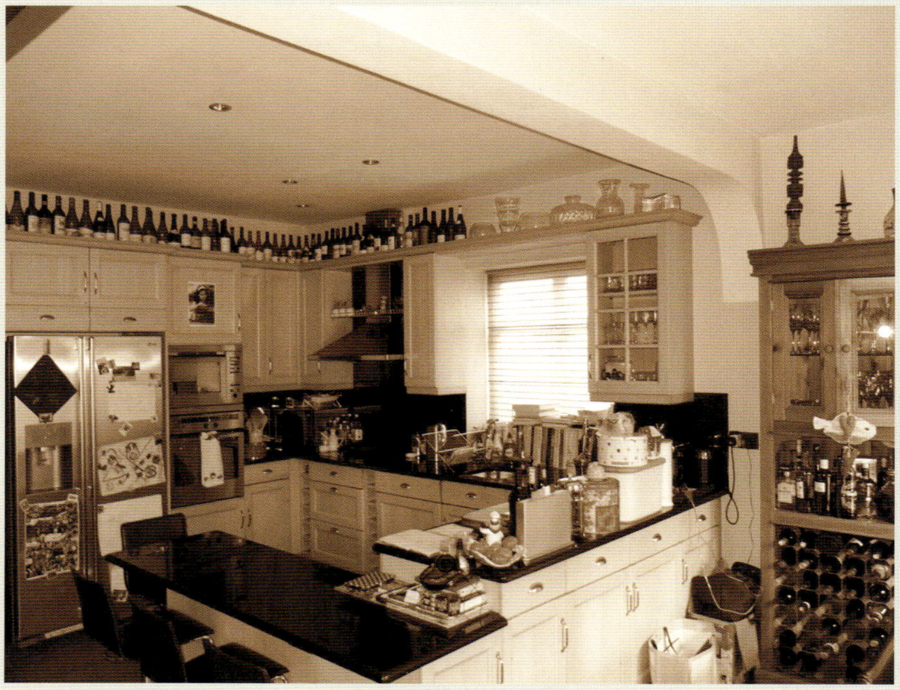

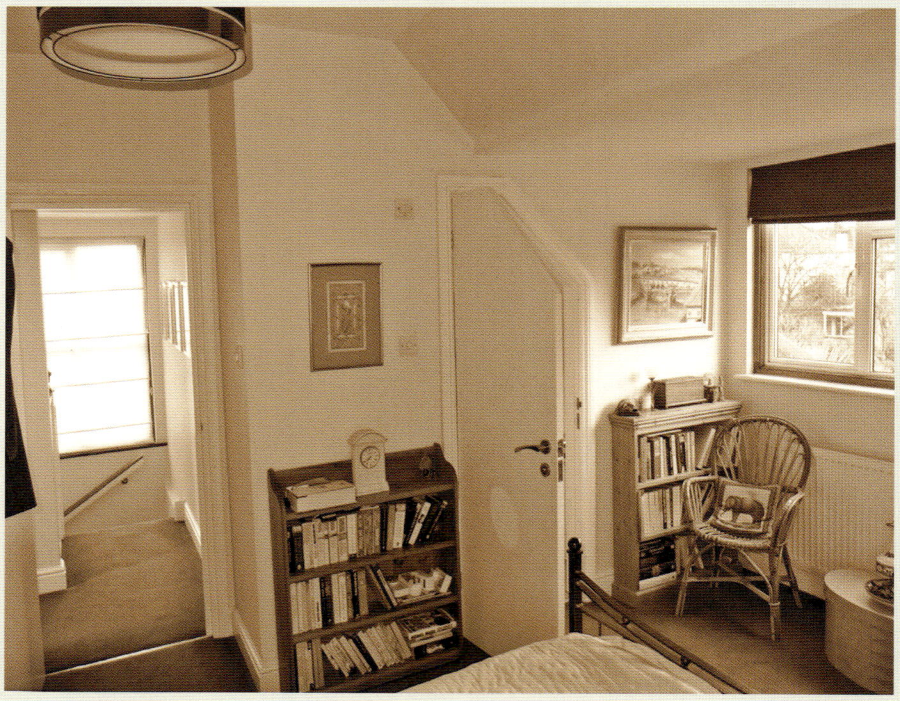

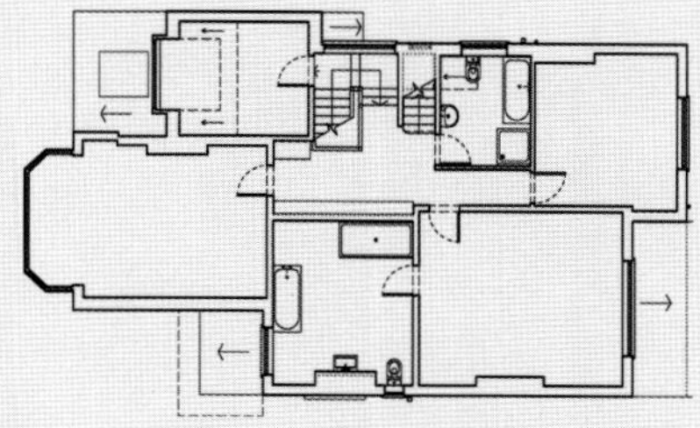

Existing first floor plan

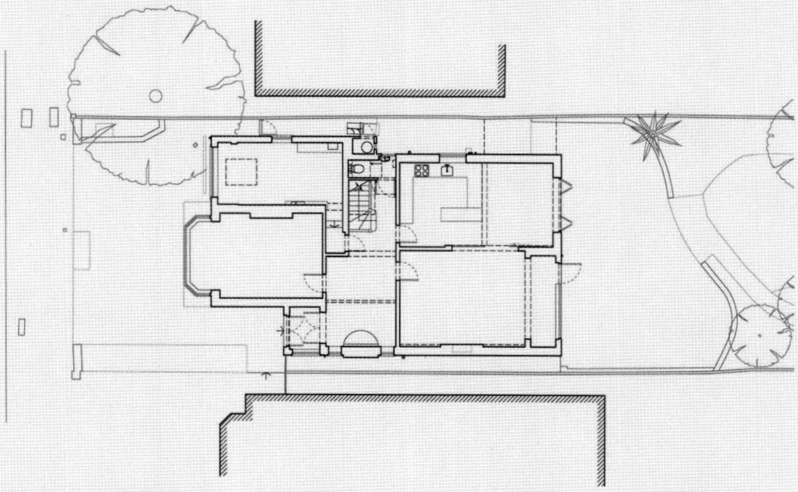

Existing ground floor plan

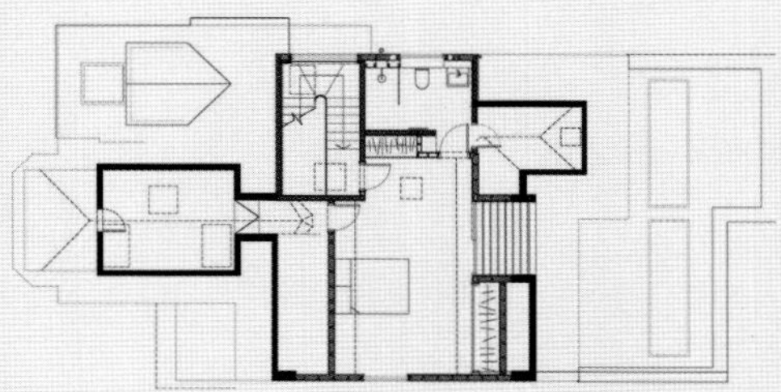

New second floor plan

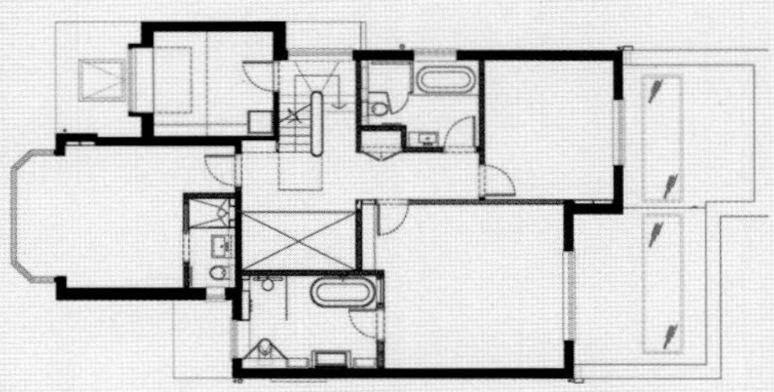

New first floor plan

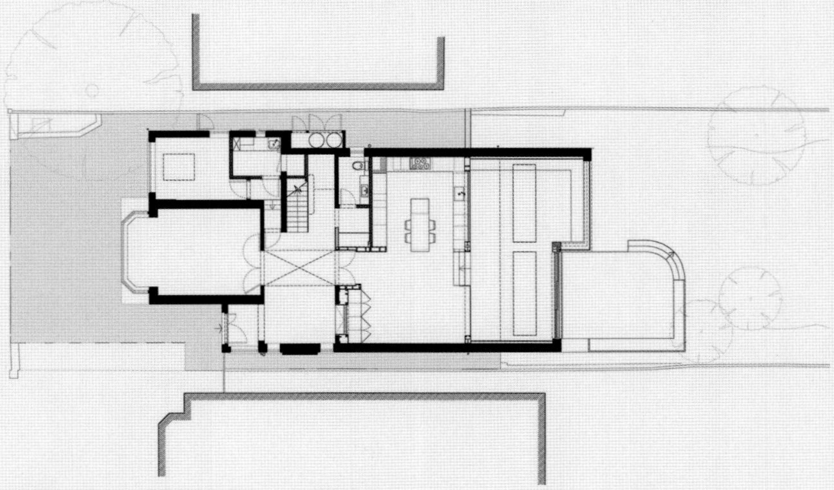

New ground floor plan

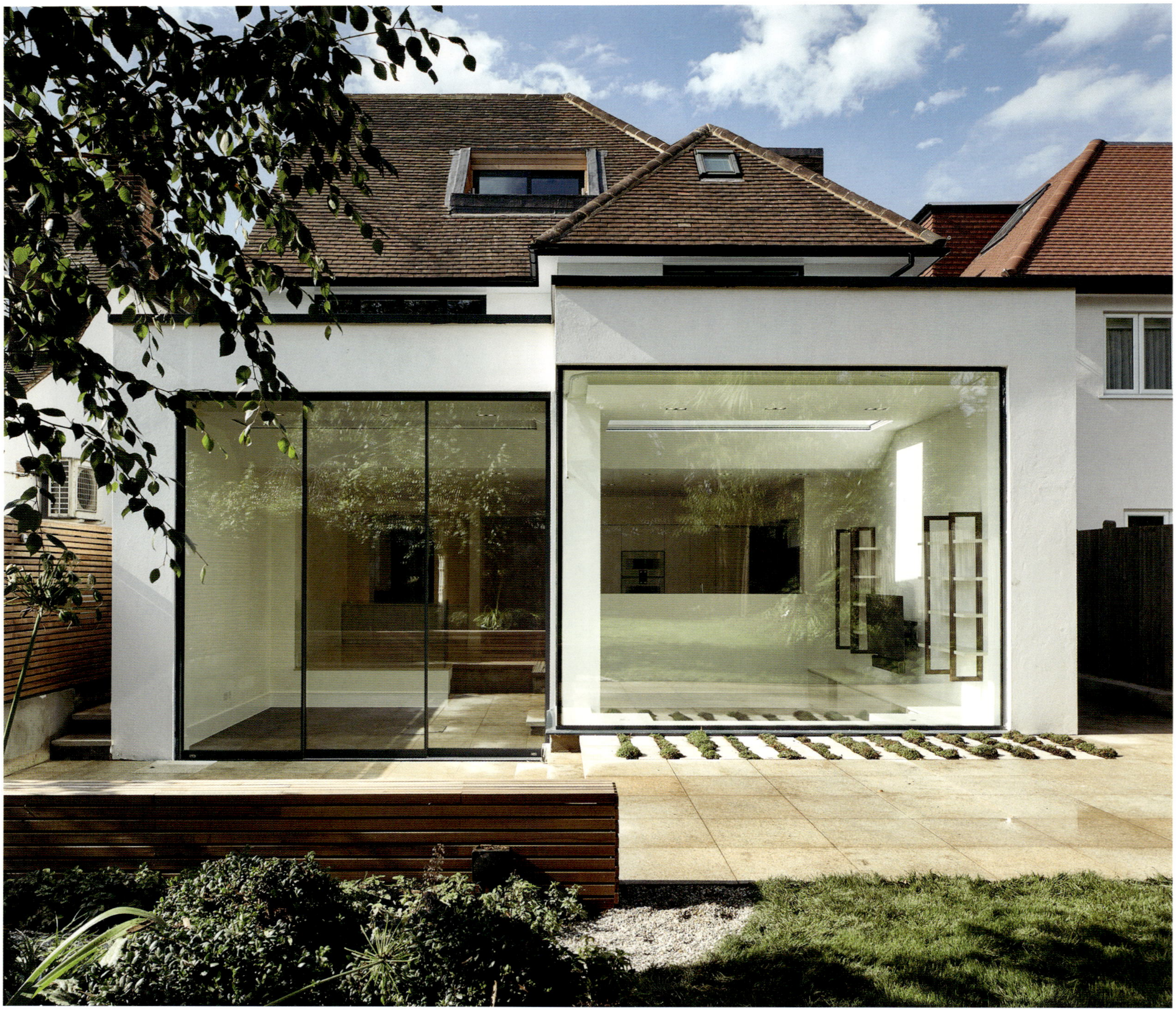

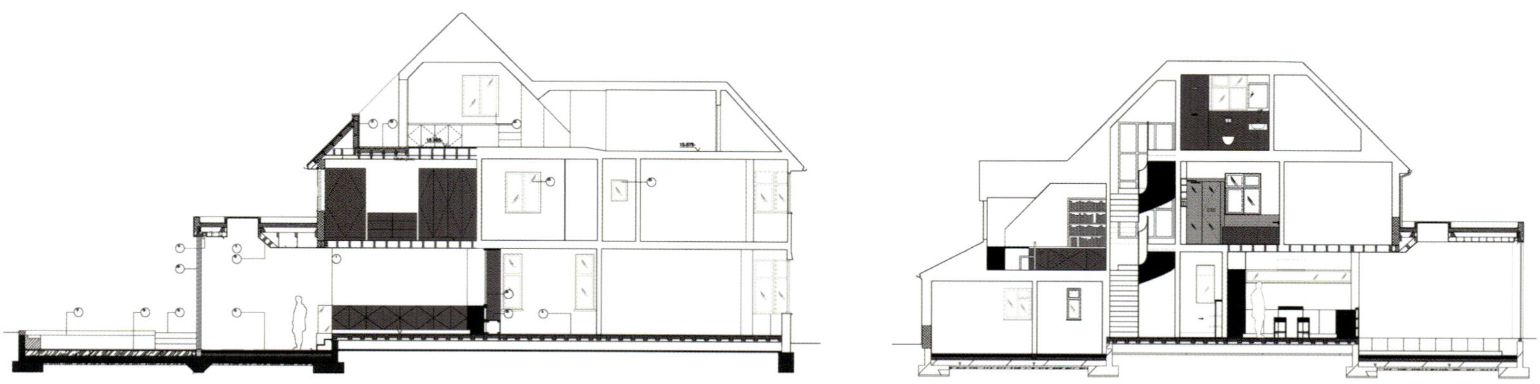

Sections

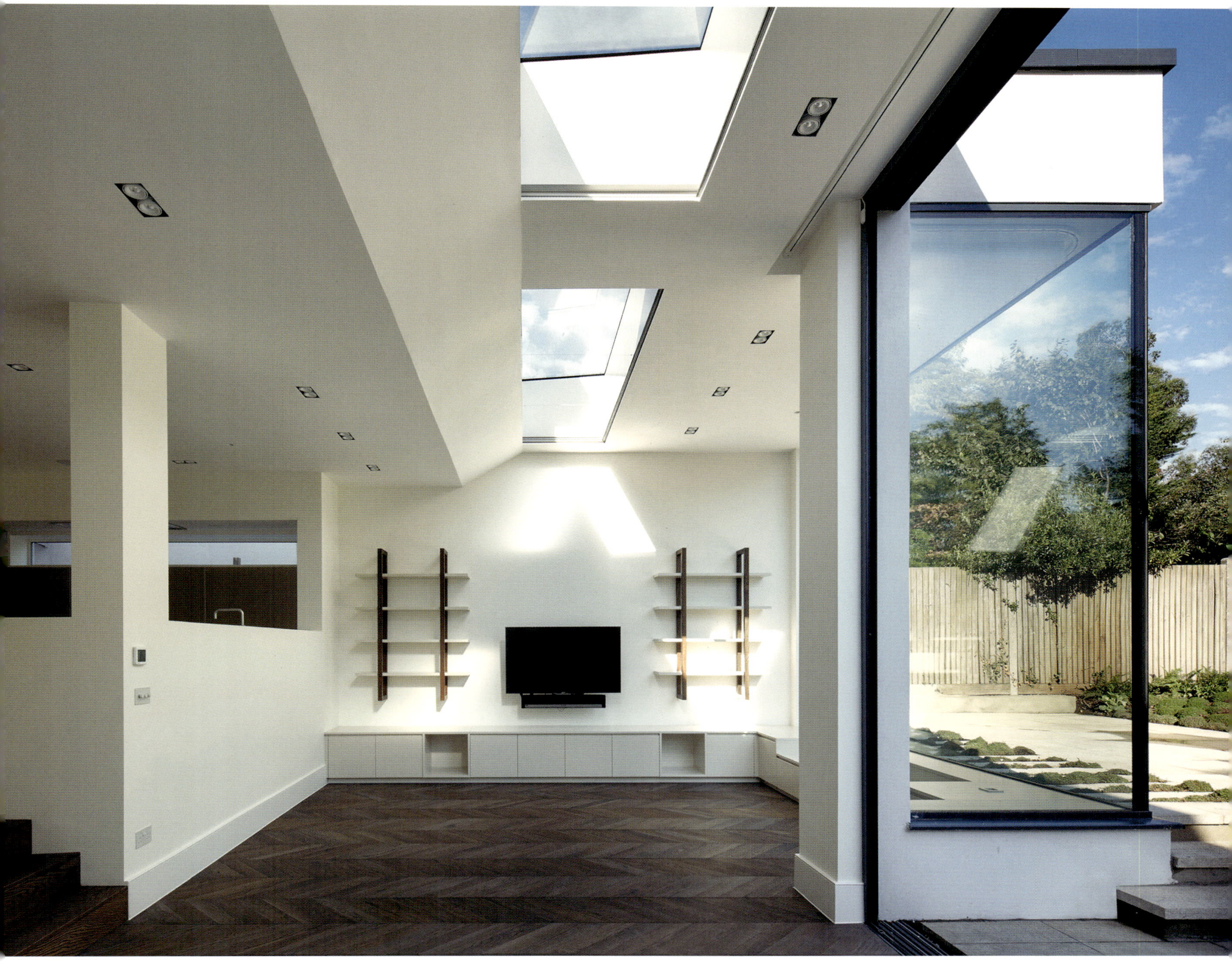

The extension creates a substantial living room that can be enjoyed by the whole family. The widespread use of glass and the two rectangular skylights allow light into the deepest corners of the ground floor and create a solid connection to the outdoors. When the living room's glass doors are opened, the terrace becomes an extension of the living space.

Durch den Ausbau entstand ein großes Wohnzimmer für die ganze Familie. Der umfangreiche Einsatz von Glas sowie die beiden rechteckigen Oberlichter ermöglichen das Eindringen von Licht bis in die hintersten Ecken der Etage sowie eine Verschränkung mit dem Außenbereich. Durch das Öffnen der Türen wird die Terrasse zur Erweiterung des Wohnzimmers.

L'agrandissement donne lieu à un grand séjour qui permet de profiter de moments en famille. La profusion de verre et les deux verrières rectangulaires permettent à la lumière de pénétrer jusque dans les recoins les plus profonds de l'étage, ainsi que de créer une connexion absolue avec l'extérieur. Lorsque les portes sont ouvertes, la terrasse s'intègre au séjour se transformant en une extension de celle-ci.

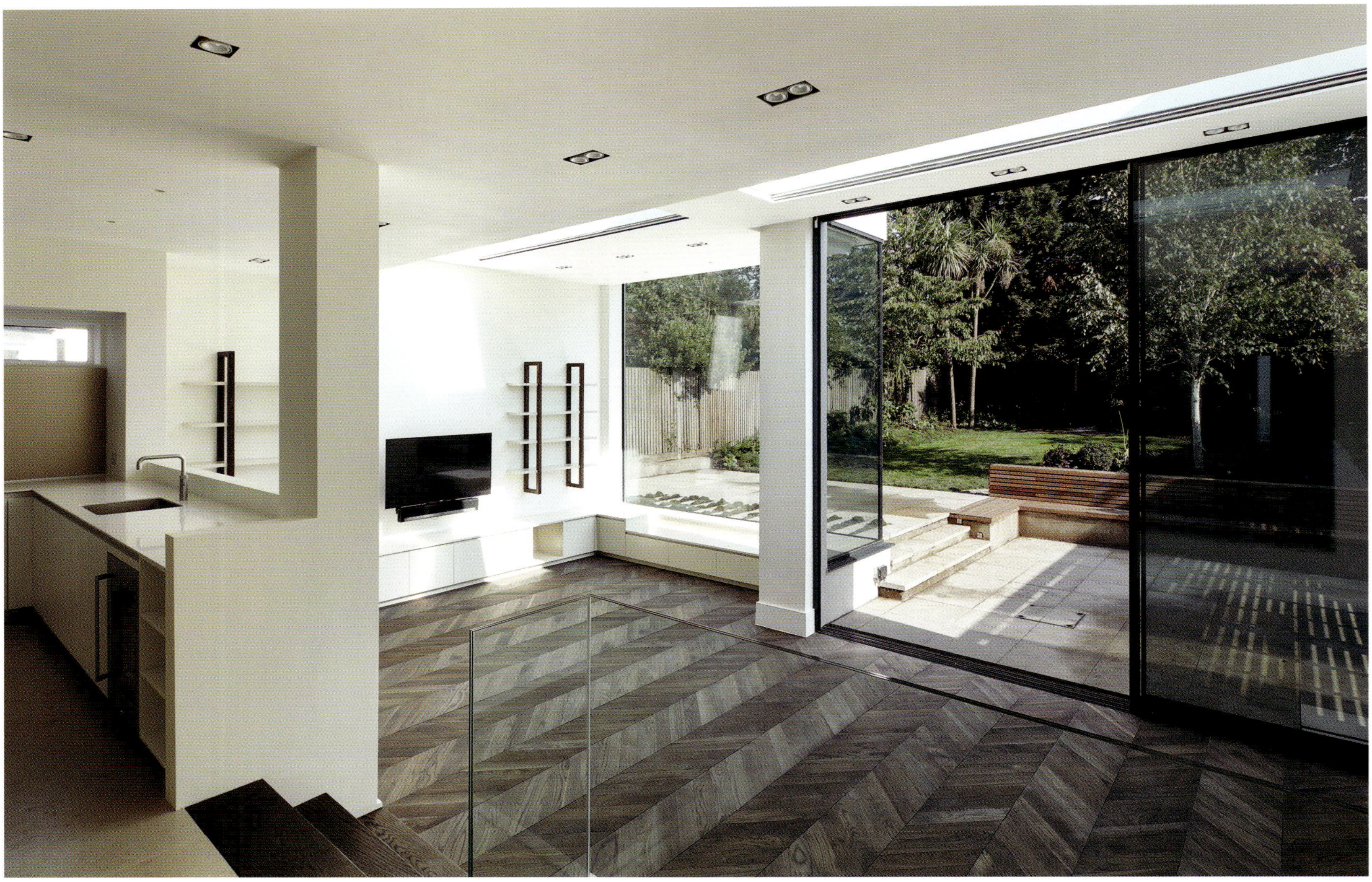

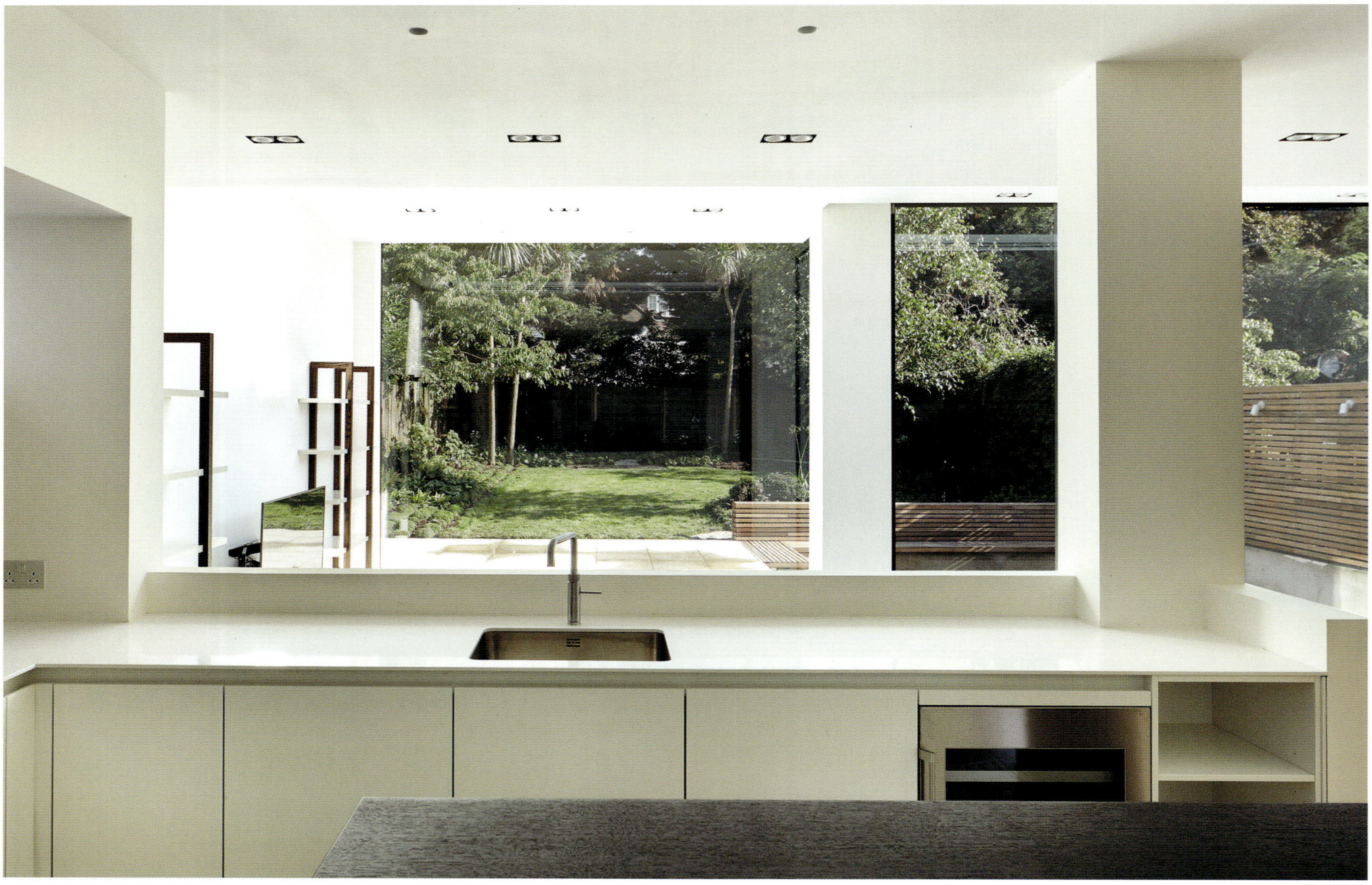

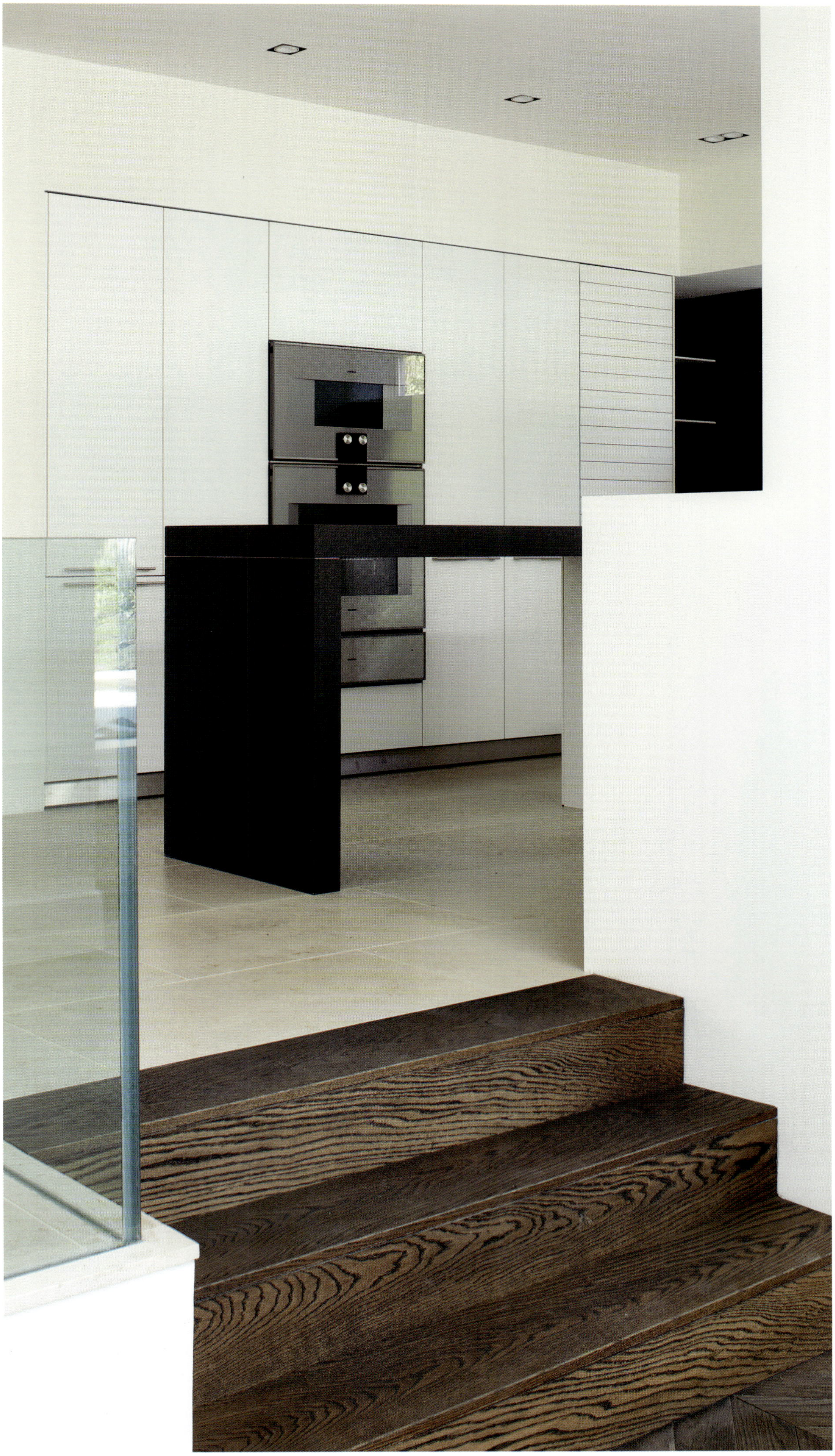

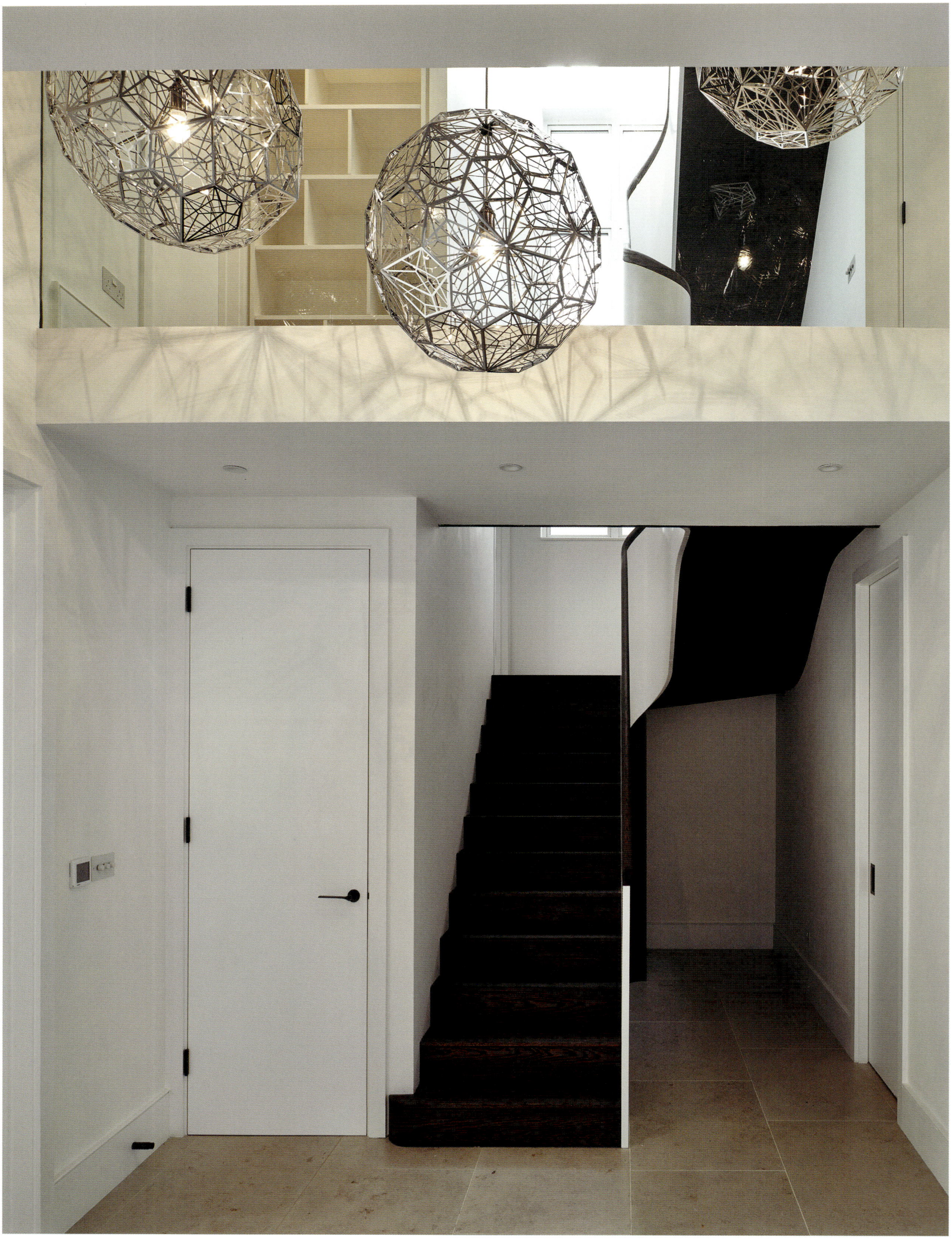

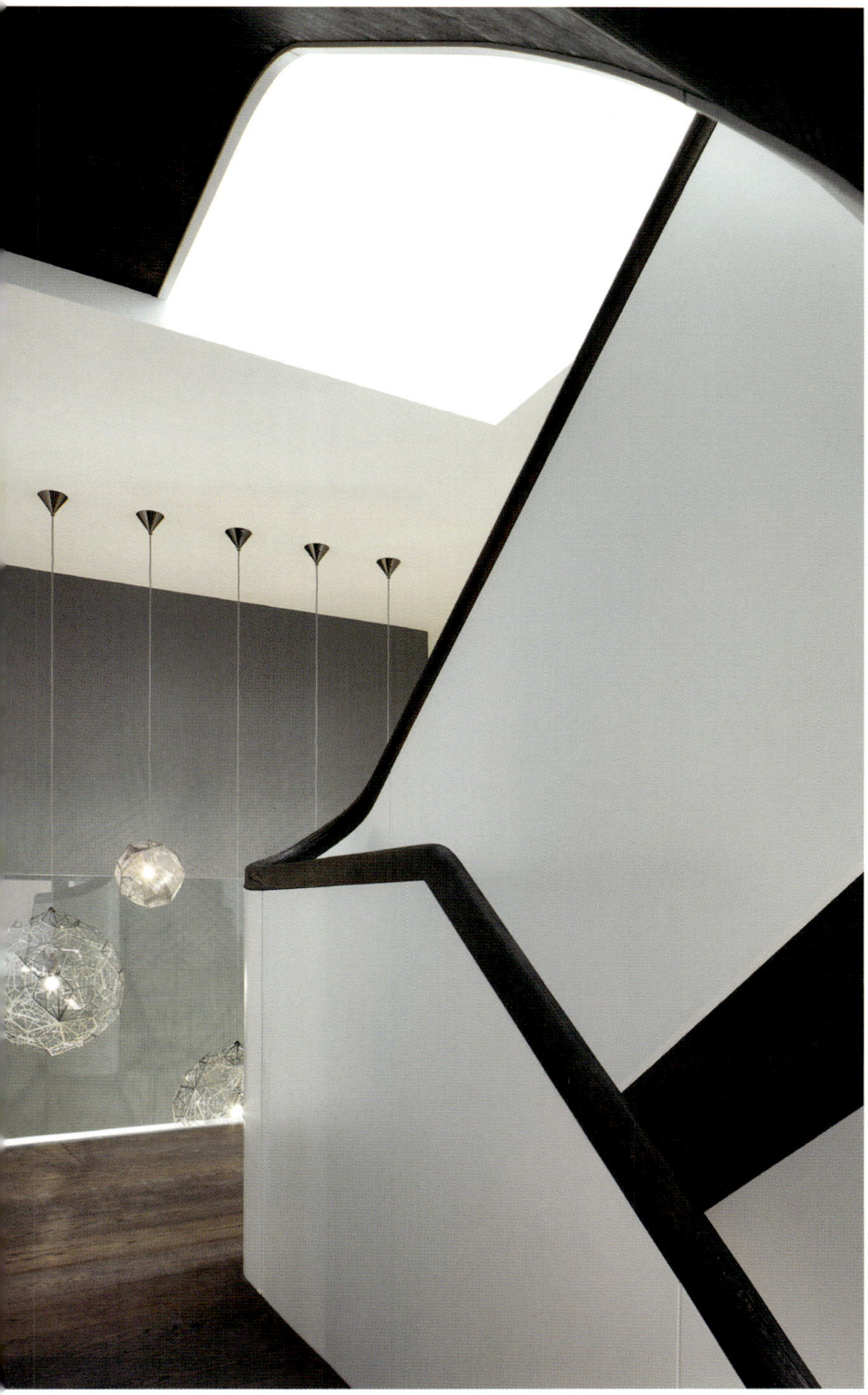 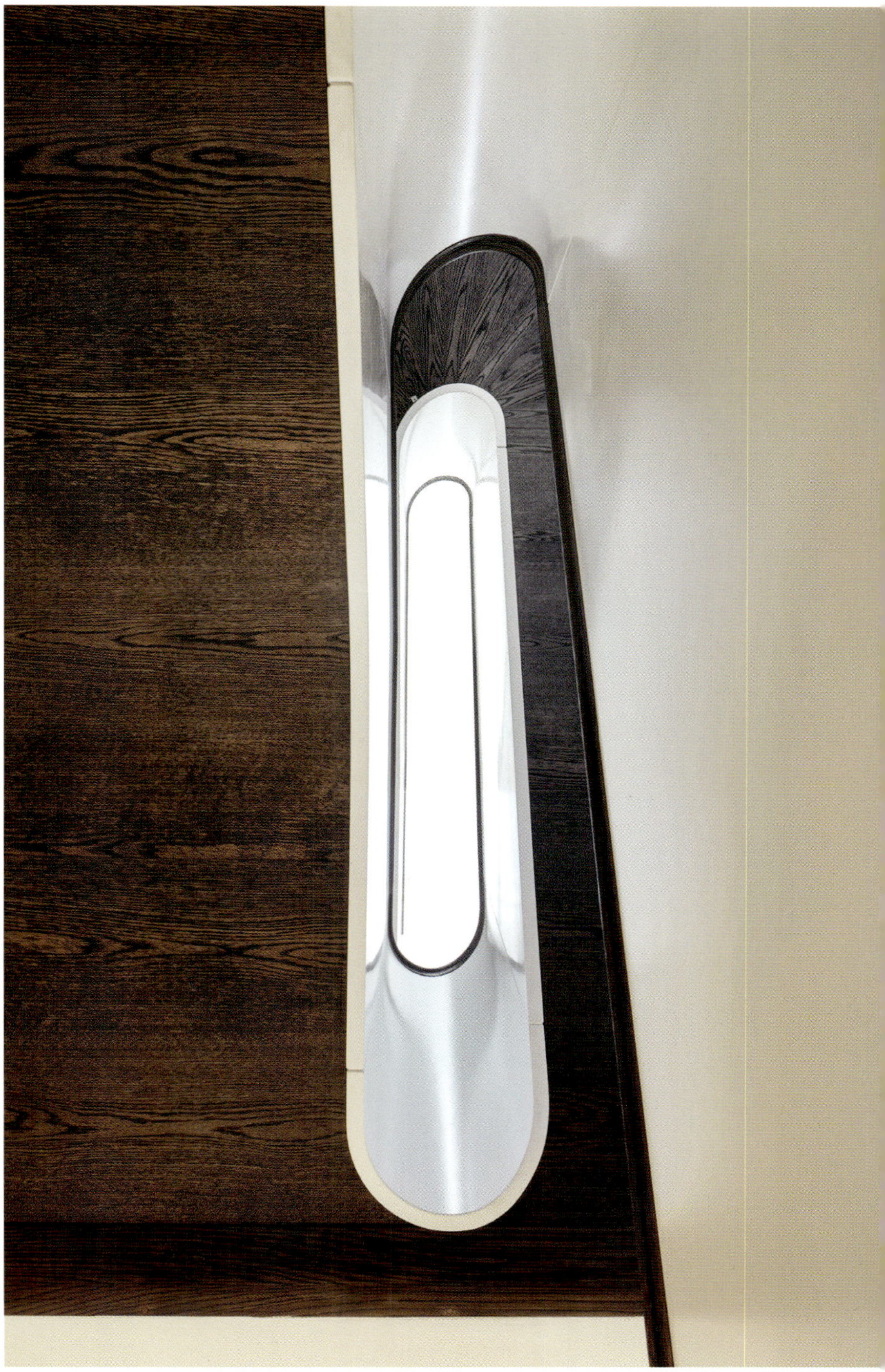

The wooden staircase was designed as a single object extending from the ground floor to the highest area of the house. This central element consists of a solid helical balustrade that is "suspended" within the space and enveloped by the stairs. The elegant lacquered balustrade is topped with a continuous molded handrail, hand-crafted in oak to match the fluid lower section that follows the curves of the staircase.

Die Holztreppe wurde als ein eigenständiges Objekt konzipiert, das sich zwischen Erdgeschoss, erstem und zweitem Stock erstreckt. Die zentrale Form besteht aus einer massiven spiralförmigen Balustrade, die in der Mitte des Hohlraums um die Treppe herum „hängt". Die elegante lackierte Balustrade ist mit einem durchgehenden Handlauf gekrönt, der aus Eiche geschnitzt wurde, um dem fließenden unteren Teil zu entsprechen, der den Rundungen der Treppe folgt.

L'escalier en bois a été conçu comme un seul objet qui va du rez-de-chaussée au deuxième étage en passant par le premier. La forme centrale est composée d'une solide balustrade hélicoïdale qui est « suspendue » dans le vide, entourée de l'escalier. L'élégante balustrade laquée se termine par une rampe moulée continue, sculptée à la main, en chêne, pour s'accorder avec la partie inférieure fluide qui suit les courbes de l'escalier.

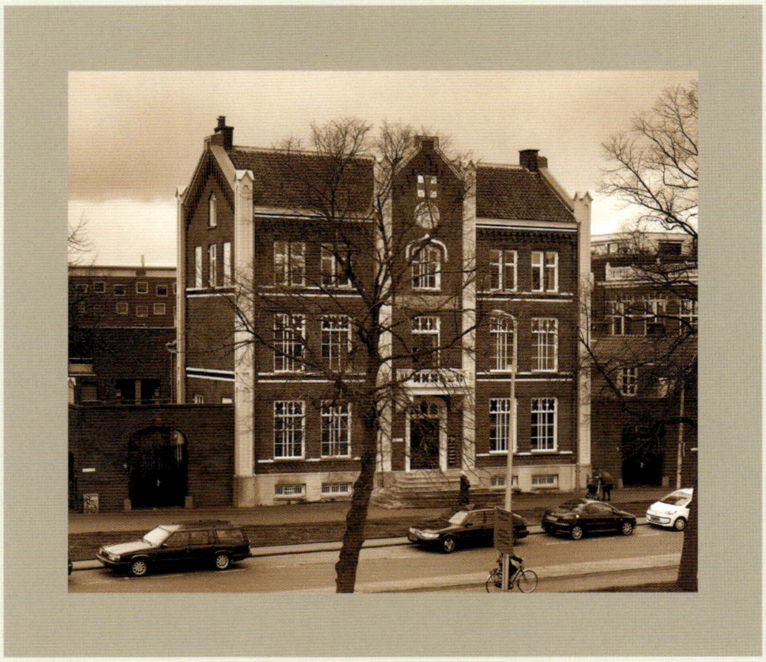

CREATING A NEW HOME IN A NATIONAL MONUMENT IN UTRECHT

LAB-S

212 m² | 2,282 sq. ft.

Utrecht, The Netherlands

Photos © **Wim Hanenberg**

> Design the new space to harmonize with the original building

> Preserve as many of the residence's original elements as possible

> Maintain continuity in the space

> Provide illumination to all rooms

> Den neuen Raum in Harmonie mit dem ursprünglichen Gebäude gestalten

> Die ursprünglichen Elemente des Hauses so gut wie möglich erhalten

> Eine Kontinuität im Raum beibehalten

> Licht in alle Räume bringen

> Concevoir un nouvel espace en harmonie avec le bâtiment d'origine

> Conserver, dans la mesure du possible, les éléments d'origine de la maison

> Maintenir une continuité dans l'espace

> Apporter de la lumière à toutes les pièces

This apartment in a lovely building in Utrecht has been designed in harmony with its original style. The apartment is situated within a complex of buildings constructed in 1873 as a military hospital. It is an excellent example of neo-Gothic architecture.
The residence is located in the main building, one floor above street level, and consists of two parts. The common areas are at the front of the building. These spaces have monumental proportions, with high ceilings and large windows. A circular hallway around the main staircase connects these rooms with the building's rear area. The most private spaces, such as bedrooms and bathrooms, are found there. These are situated on the uppermost floor of the building beneath the roof, where the original wooden beams dominate the interior space.
The result of the conversion is a comfortable home within a distinctive building, a home that achieves the right balance between the old and the new. The new residential use becomes part of the building's history, creating a setting in which the original elements can be fully appreciated.

Diese Wohnung in einem schönen Gebäude in Utrecht wurde im Einklang mit dem ursprünglichen Stil entworfen. Die Wohnung befindet sich in einem Gebäudekomplex, der 1873 als Krankenhaus für verwundete Soldaten errichtet wurde. Er ist ein gutes Beispiel für neugotische Architektur.
Die Wohnung befindet sich im ersten Stock des Hauptgebäudes und besteht aus zwei Teilen. Die Gemeinschaftsbereiche sind im vorderen Teil des Gebäudes untergebracht. Diese Räume haben monumentale Proportionen mit hohen Decken und großen Fenstern. Ein um die Haupttreppe verlaufender Korridor verbindet diese Zimmer mit dem hinteren Teil des Gebäudes. Hier sind auch die privaten Bereiche wie Schlafzimmer und Bad untergebracht. Sie befinden sich im Dachgeschoss, wo die Originalholzbalken den Innenraum dominieren.
Das Ergebnis der Umwandlung ist eine komfortable Wohnung in einem einzigartigen Gebäude mit genau der richtigen Balance zwischen alt und neu. Die neue Wohnnutzung wird Teil der Geschichte des Gebäudes und schafft so ein Umfeld, in dem die Bewohner die ursprünglichen Elemente voll und ganz genießen können.

Situé dans un joli bâtiment de la ville d'Utrecht, cet appartement a été conçu en harmonie avec le style initial. L'appartement se trouve dans un complexe de bâtiments, construit en 1873 comme hôpital pour les soldats blessés. Il s'agit d'un exemple représentatif de l'architecture néo-gothique.
Situé au rez-de-chaussée du bâtiment principal, il est composé de deux parties. Les parties communes se trouvent à l'avant du bâtiment. Ces espaces ont des proportions monumentales avec de hauts plafonds et de grandes baies vitrées. Un couloir autour de l'escalier principal relie ces chambres à la partie arrière du bâtiment. Ce côté comprend les espaces les plus intimes tels que les chambres et salles de bains. Elles se trouvent à l'étage supérieur de la construction du toit où les poutres en bois d'origine dominent l'espace intérieur.
Le résultat de la conversion est une maison confortable dans un bâtiment unique avec le juste équilibre entre l'ancien et le nouveau. Le nouvel usage résidentiel fait partie de l'histoire du bâtiment, créant ainsi un cadre dans lequel il est possible de profiter pleinement des éléments d'origine.

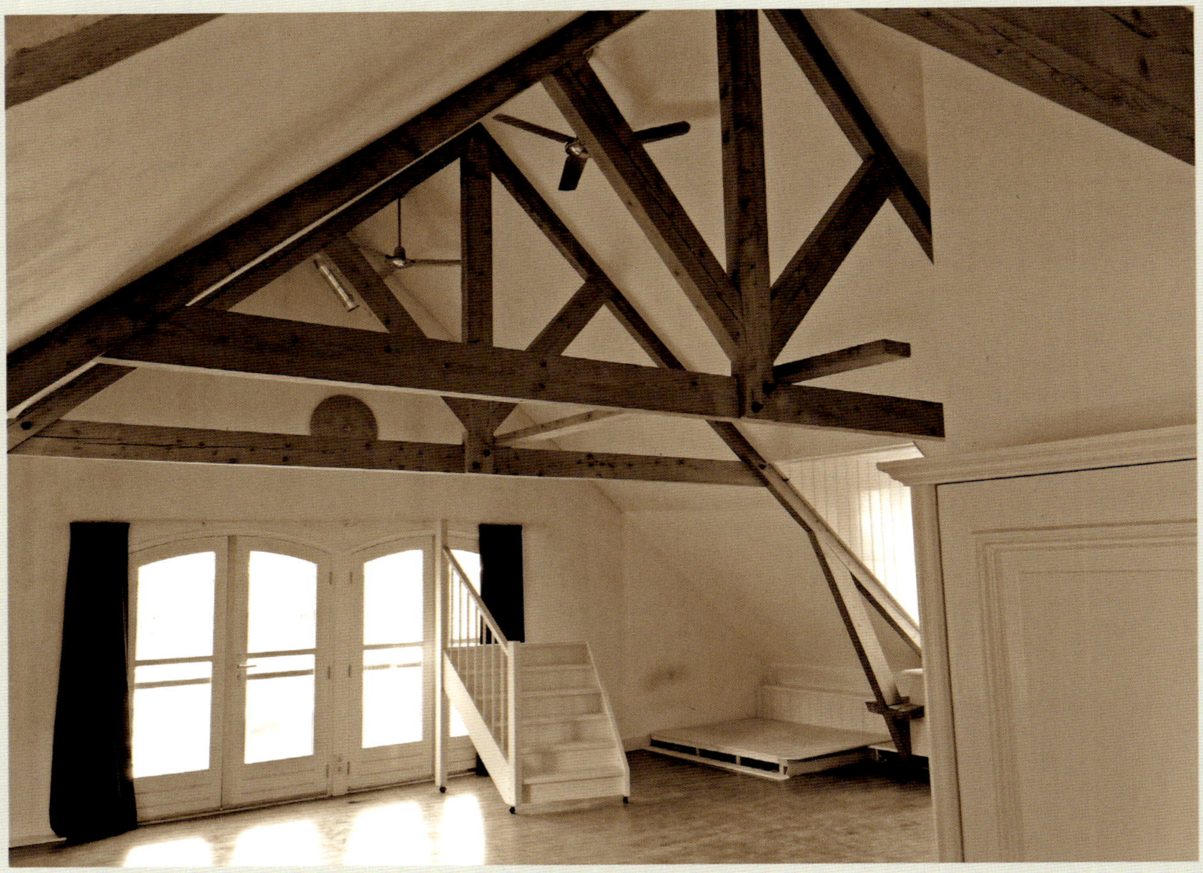

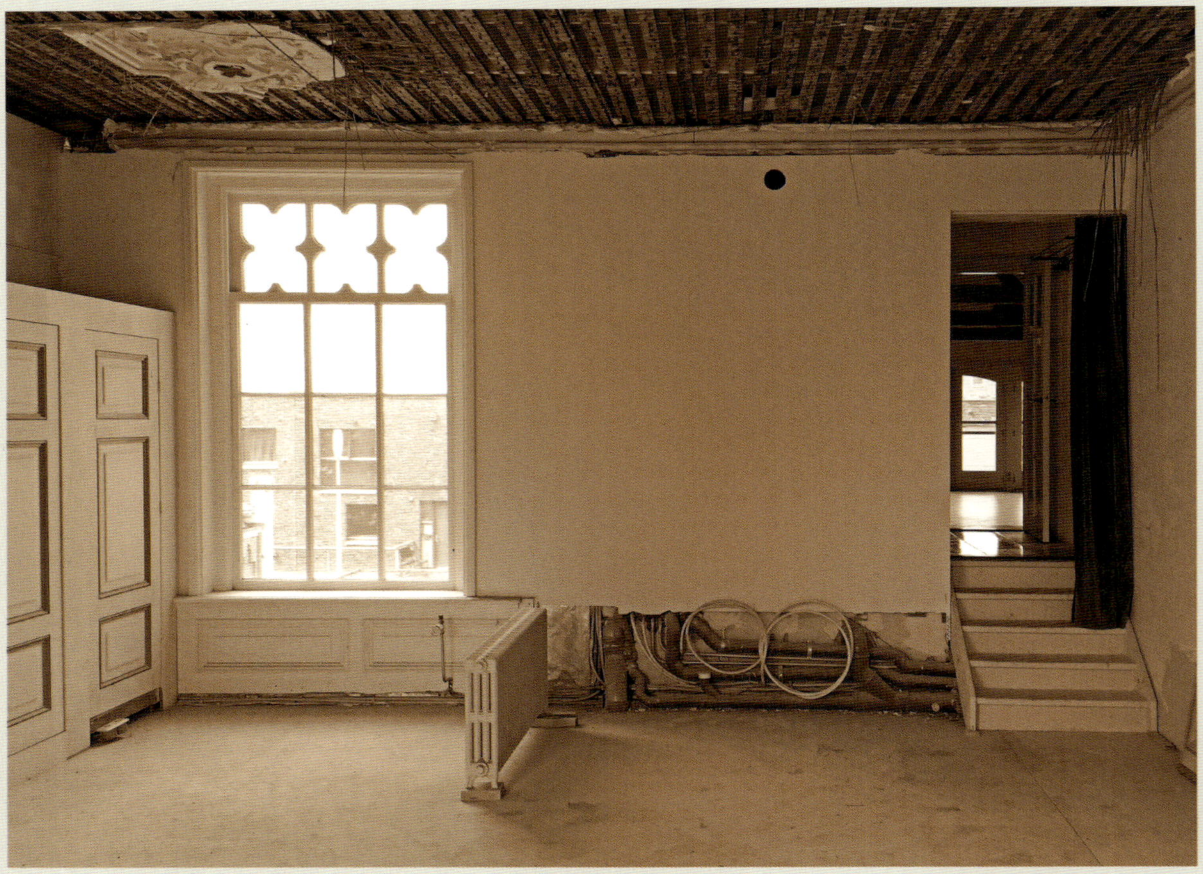

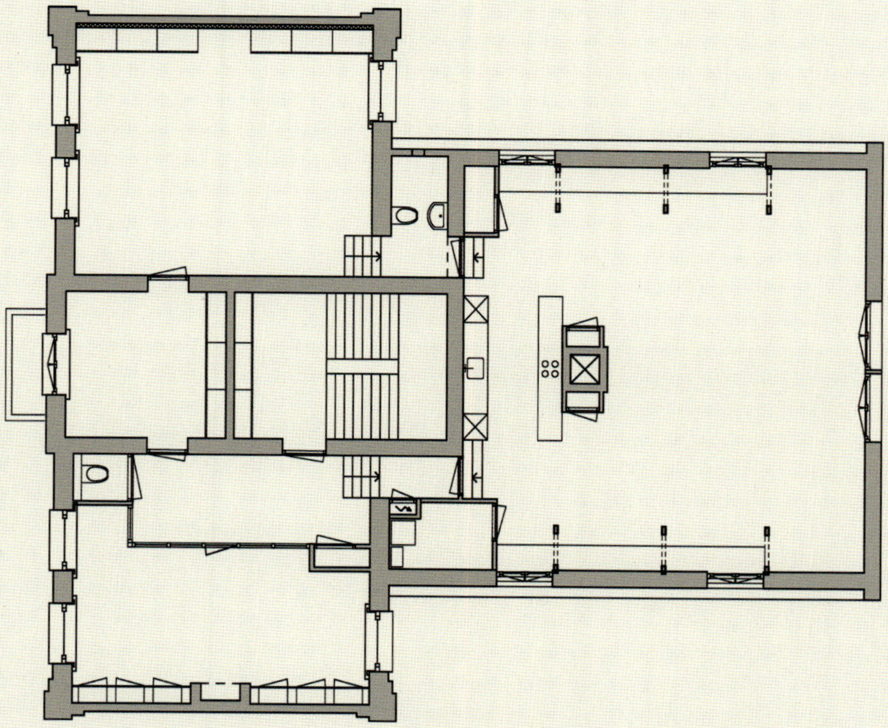

Existing plan

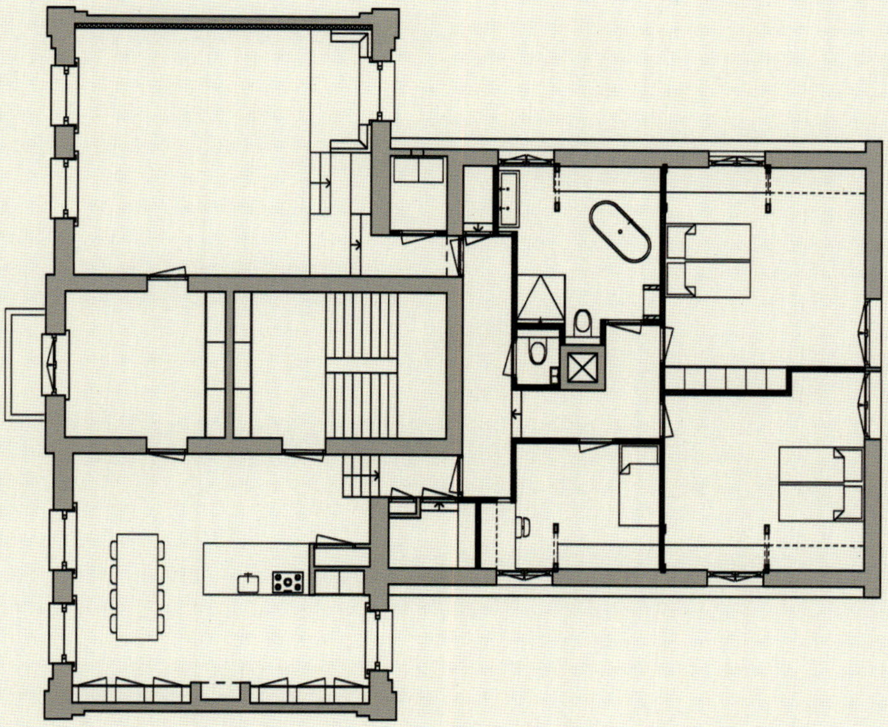

New plan

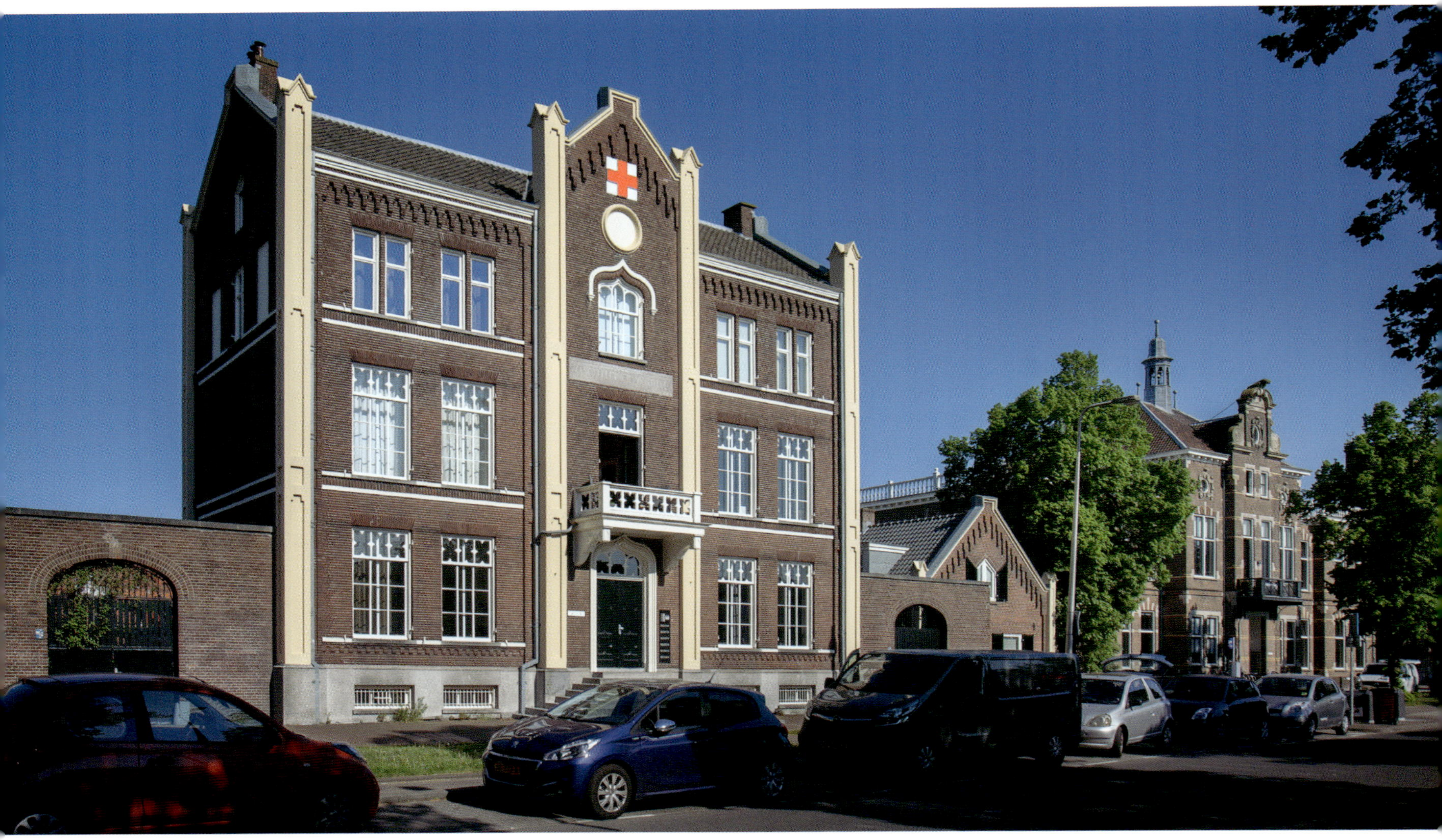

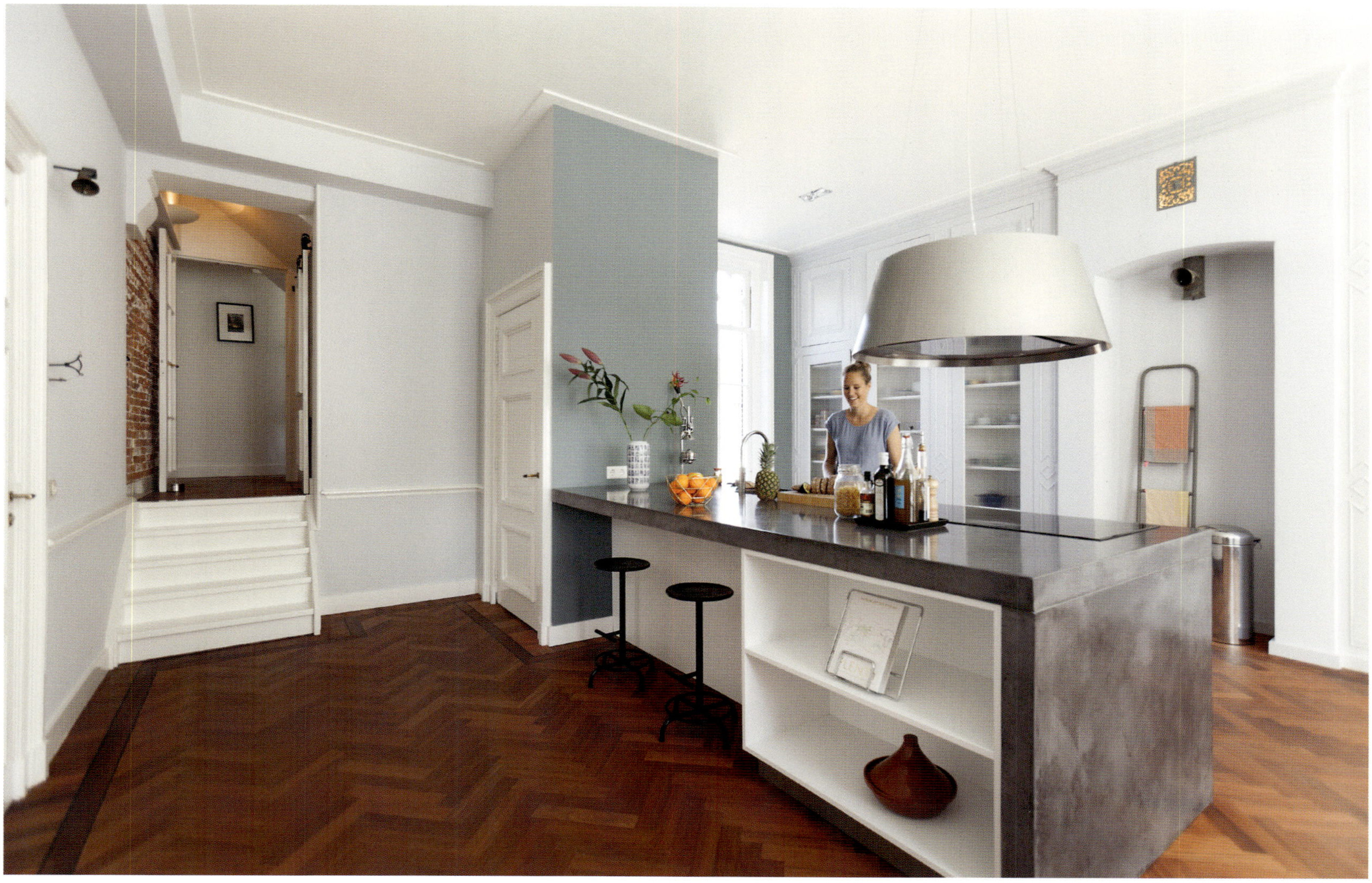

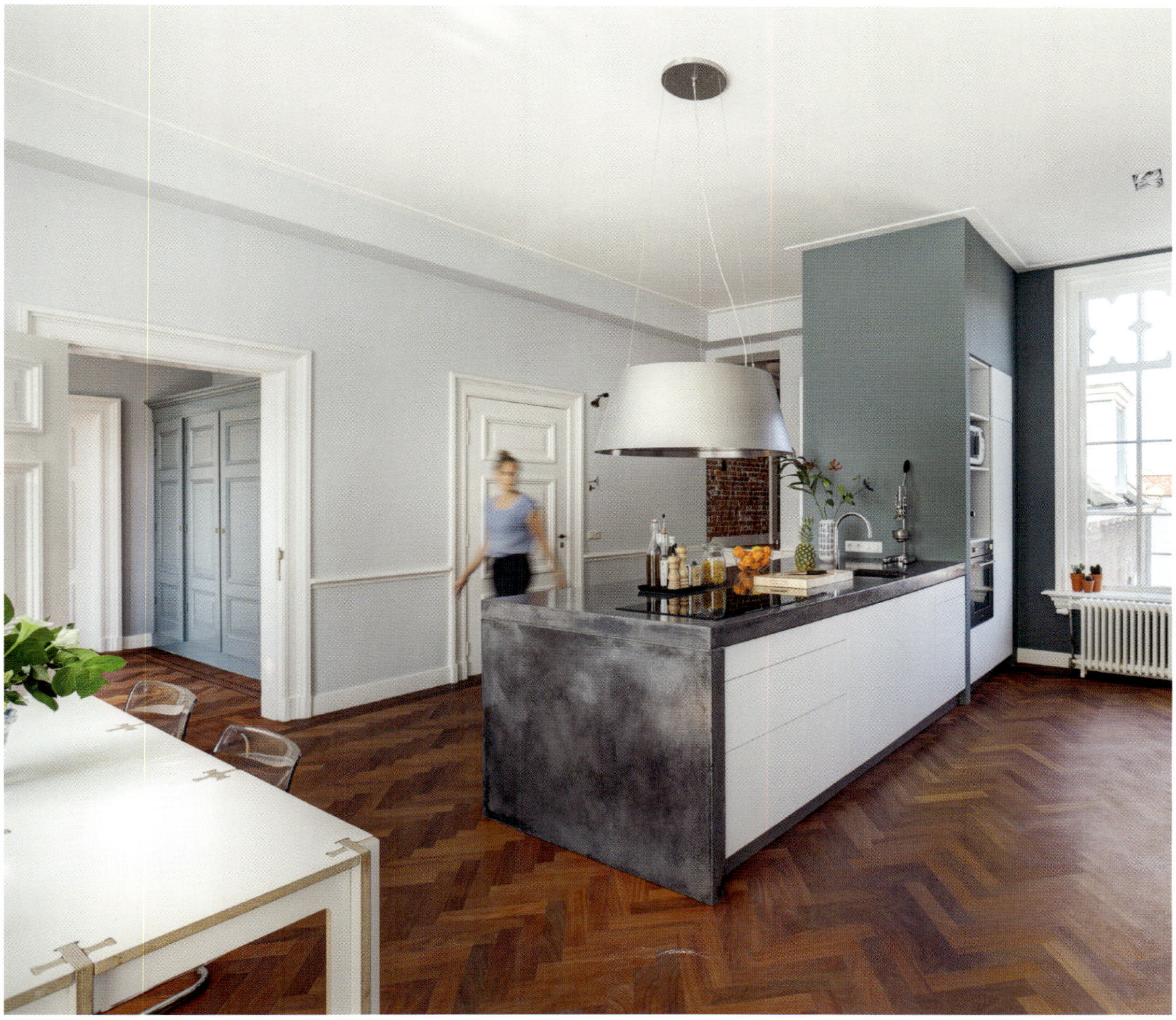

A new, solid kitchen island forms the center of attention in the dining area. In its modern appearance, it is conspicuous without competing with the built-in furnishings. A continuation of the original hardwood floor connects and unifies the separate spaces.

Eine neue massive Kücheninsel steht im Esszimmer im Mittelpunkt. Ihr zeitgemäßes Äußeres lässt sie hervortreten, ohne mit den Schrankeinbauten zu konkurrieren. Die Fortsetzung des ursprünglichen Holzbodens vereint und vereinheitlicht die getrennten Räume.

Le nouvel îlot de la cuisine robuste est le centre d'attention dans la salle à manger. Son aspect contemporain le distingue sans toutefois concurrencer le meuble mural. La continuité du sol en bois d'origine unit et unifie les espaces séparés.

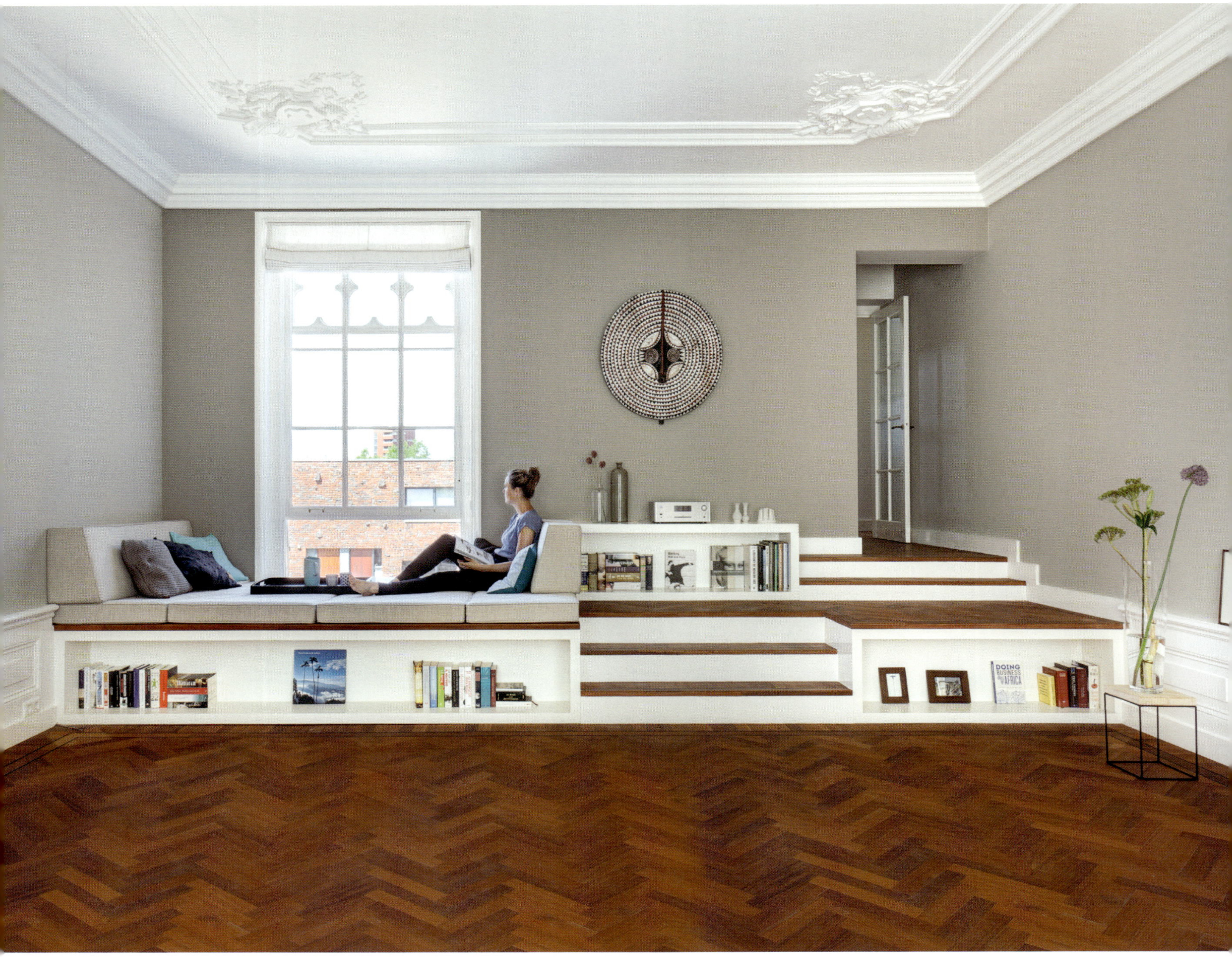

Special attention was paid to restoring original details such as the singular ceiling with moldings and wood paneling. The uneven levels of the living room were ingeniously exploited to create a reading nook and bookshelves.

Besonderes Augenmerk wurde auf die Restaurierung alter Details gelegt. Hierzu gehören die einzigartige Decke mit Zierleisten und die Wandpaneele aus Holz. Der Höhenunterschied im Wohnzimmer wurde auf geniale Weise für eine Leseecke und Buchregale genutzt.

Une attention particulière a été apportée à la restauration de détails de l'époque tels que le plafond singulier avec des moulures et les panneaux en bois du mur. Le dénivellement du salon a été mis à profit de manière ingénieuse comme coin de lecture et bibliothèque.

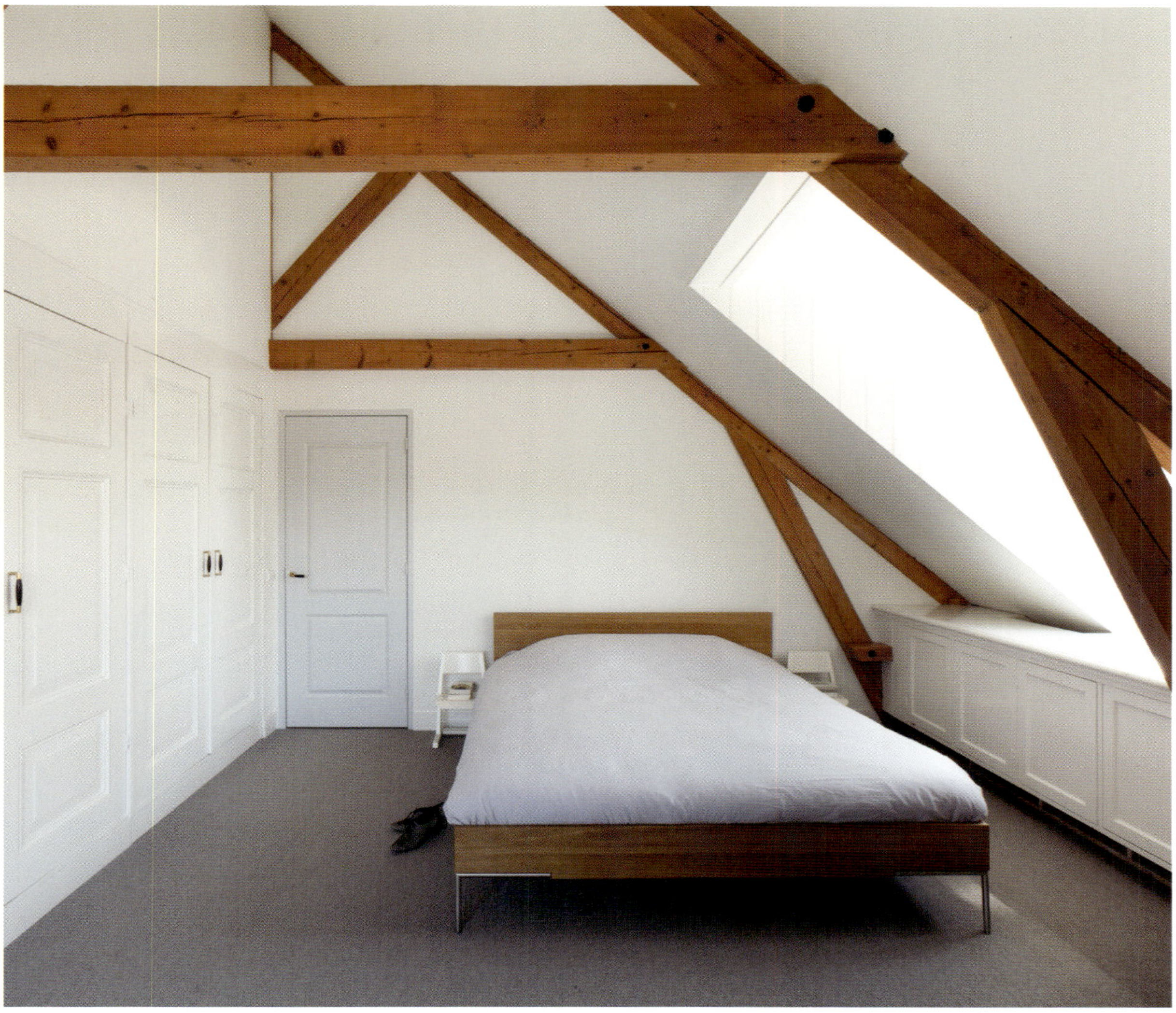

A practical new design that respects the existing wooden features was developed for the rear area. The rooms have a subtle coloration that spotlights the wooden trusses.

Für den hinteren Teil wurde eine funktionale neue Gestaltung gewählt, die das bestehende Holztragwerk hervorhebt. Die Zimmer sind in sanften Farben gehalten, welche die Holzbalken gut zur Geltung bringen.

Pour la partie arrière, un nouveau concept pratique a été conçu respectant les structures en bois existantes. Les chambres sont dans un ton doux qui met en relief les poutres en bois.

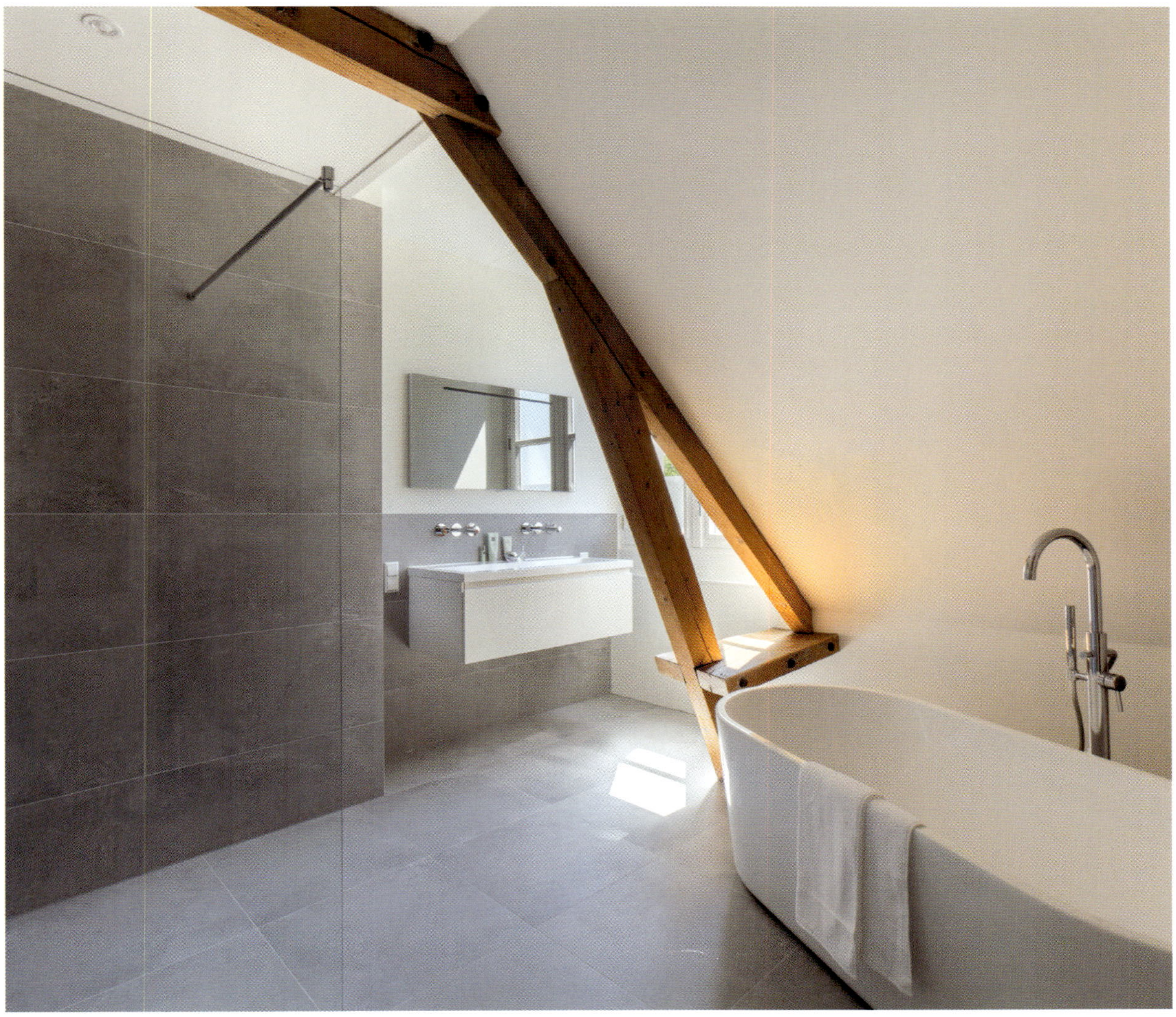

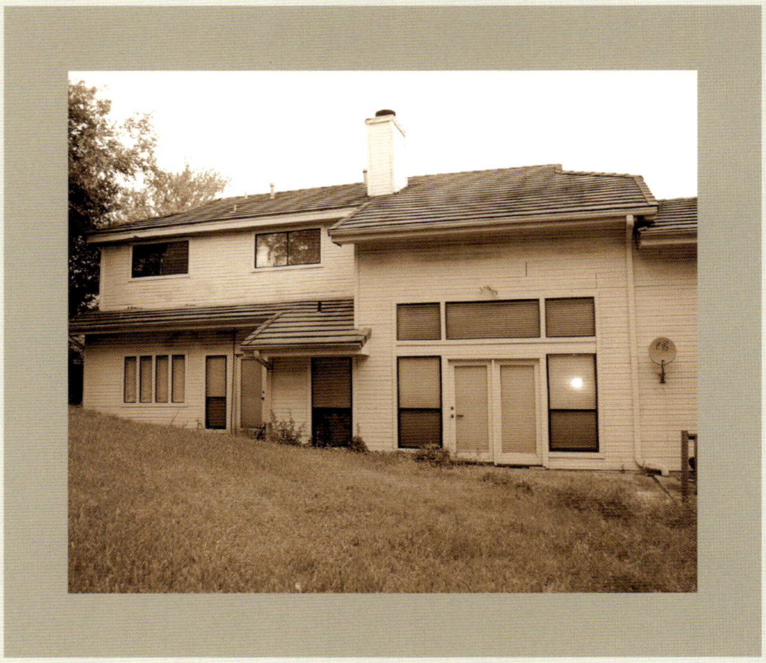

WINTER PARK

ARBIB HUGHEY DESIGN

241 m² | 2,600 sq. ft.

Austin, Texas, United States

Photos © **Whit Preston, Andrea Calo**

> Transform a standard-design house into a unique and modern residence

> Open up the space

> Open the house to the outside, in this way maximizing the natural light

> Design a large kitchen with generous storage capacity

> Verwandeln eines Hauses im Standarddesign in ein einzigartiges und modernes Haus

> Öffnen des Raumes

> Das Haus nach außen öffnen, um möglichst viel Tageslicht hineinzulassen

> Entwerfen einer großen Küche mit entsprechendem Essbereich

> Transformer une maison à la conception standard en une maison unique et moderne

> Ouvrir le plan

> Ouvrir la maison sur l'extérieur et gagner ainsi le maximum de lumière naturelle

> Concevoir une vaste cuisine avec de grands espaces de rangement

The client's objective in reforming this residence was clear: transform a nondescript 1980s standard-design residence into a unique and modern house. In the face of budgetary restrictions that limited remodeling of the existing footprint as well as costly foundation and infrastructure issues, it became necessary to employ several design strategies to engender a powerful transformation while still keeping environmental sustainability factors very much in mind.
Broad eaves sheltering the large new openings create a strong and unifying presence both inside and out. The interior of the small original tower was reconfigured as a round room where the walls seamlessly transition to uninterrupted serpentine cabinets that flow from the room's entrance through the kitchen to the dining room. These not only unify the different spaces but also create a unique sculptural element within the overall area. These cabinets terminate in wide openings that incorporate the outdoor landscape into the home's interior. Three enormous picture windows were added to bathe the interior space in natural light and permit views to the outside from any part of the living area.
The house that was once indistinguishable from the others in the neighborhood now stands proudly, boasting a unique living experience throughout the interior a and exterior of the home.

Das Ziel des Kunden für den Umbau dieses Hauses war eindeutig: Ein unscheinbares Wohngebäude aus den 1980er Jahren, das etwas zwischen den anderen Gebäuden der Nachbarschaft verschwand, sollte in ein einzigartiges und modernes Haus umgebaut werden. Es gab Budget-Vorgaben, die die Umgestaltung der bisherigen Hülle einschränkten, sowie Probleme mit dem Fundament und der Infrastruktur, was einen Großteil des Budgets verschlang. Es waren also verschiedene Strategien für das Design nötig, um eine umfassende Veränderung zu bewirken, bei der außerdem Kriterien der ökologischen Nachhaltigkeit Beachtung fanden.
Auskragende Dächer geben dem Haus ein markantes Aussehen und schützen gleichzeitig die neuen, großzügigen Fensteröffnungen. Das Innere des kleinen Turms des ursprünglichen Hauses wurde in ein kreisrundes Zimmer verwandelt, dessen Wände sich ohne Unterbrechungen in gewundene Schränke verwandeln, die vom Eingangsbereich durch die Küche hin zum Esszimmer zu fließen scheinen. Dieses Element vereint nicht nur die unterschiedlichen Räume, sondern besitzt im Hauptwohnbereich eine skulpturale Qualität. Die Einbauschränke werden durch Fensteröffnungen unterbrochen, die eine Verbindung zur Landschaft schaffen. Außerdem wurden drei riesige Fenster eingebaut, um den Innenbereich mit natürlichem Licht zu fluten und von jedem Punkt des Wohnzimmers aus eine hübsche Sicht zu bieten.
Was also vorher ein Haus war, das oft mit den Nachbarhäusern verwechselt wurde, präsentiert sich nun stolz und strahlt sowohl im Innen- als auch im Außenbereich ein einzigartiges Lebensgefühl aus.

L'objectif clair du client quant aux travaux de cette maison était : transformer une maison des années quatre-vingt, achetée sur plan, qui passait inaperçue dans le voisinage, dans une maison unique et moderne. En raison d'un budget limité pour réorganiser l'organisation existante et résoudre les problèmes de ciments et de l'infrastructure, représentant une partie importante du budget, plusieurs stratégies de conception ont été appliquées pour réaliser une transformation importante tout en prenant en compte les critères de durabilité écologique.
De grands auvents créent une présence imposante et unifiée à la fois à l'intérieur et à l'extérieur protégeant ainsi les nouvelles et généreuses ouvertures. L'intérieur de la petite tour d'origine a été redessiné comme une habitation circulaire dont les murs se transforment sans interruption en armoires sinueuses qui vont de l'entrée à la salle à manger, en passant par la cuisine. Ceci permet non seulement d'unir les divers espaces, mais de créer aussi un élément sculptural unique dans l'espace plus spacieux. Ces armoires se terminent par de vastes ouvertures qui emmènent le paysage extérieur à l'intérieur de la maison. Trois grandes fenêtres ont été également ajoutées afin de baigner l'espace intérieur de lumière naturelle et d'obtenir des vues depuis n'importe quel coin du séjour.
La maison qui se fondait avant dans le paysage des maisons avoisinantes, se dresse dorénavant de manière fière offrant ainsi une expérience unique de vie tant à l'intérieur qu'à l'extérieur.

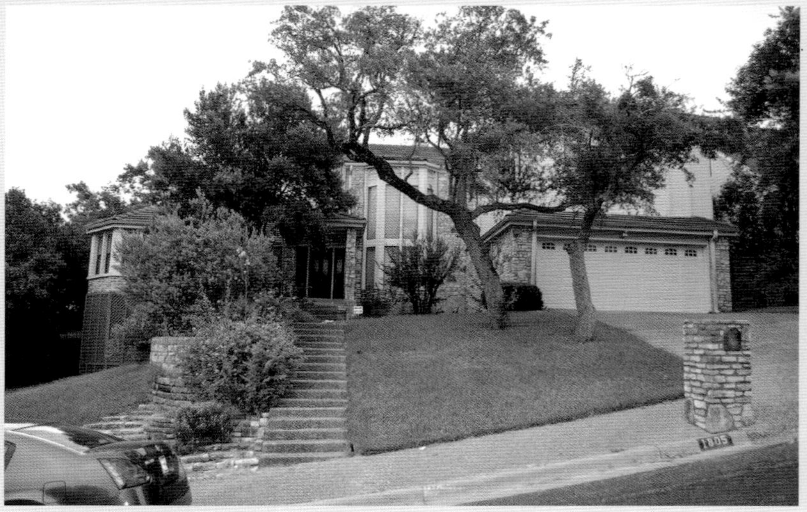
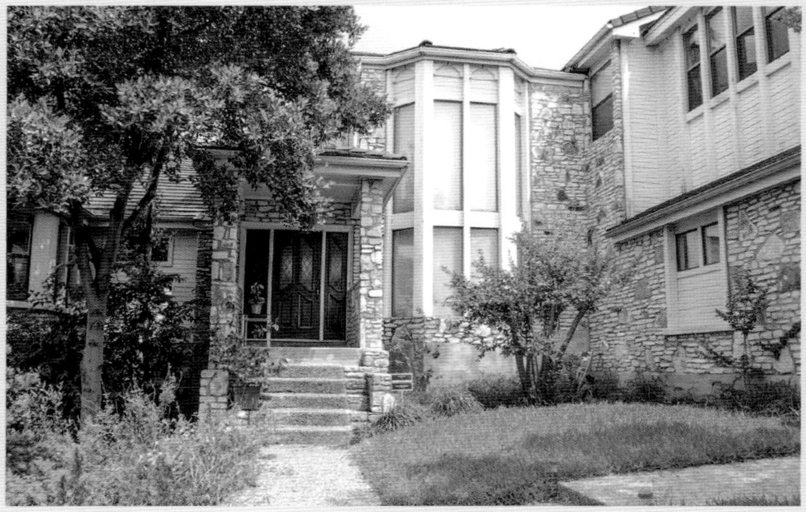
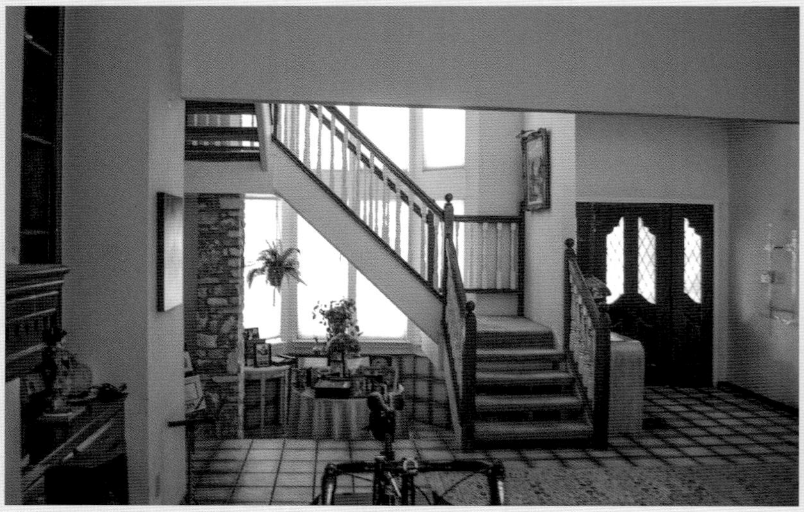
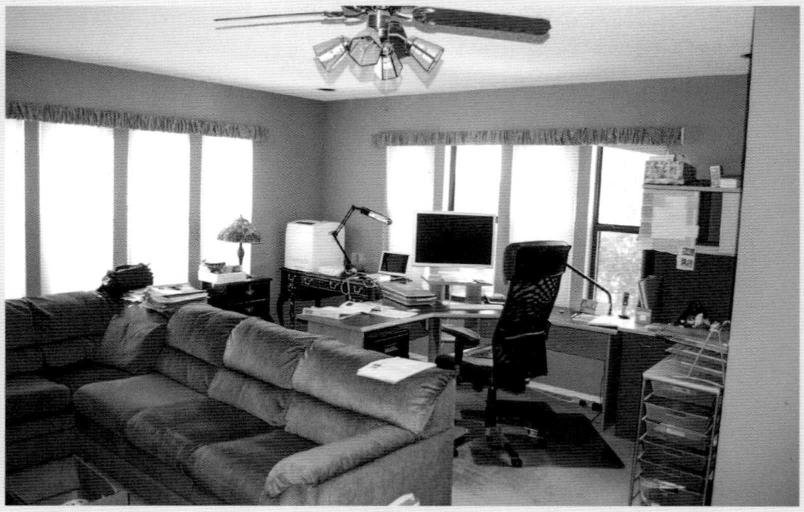
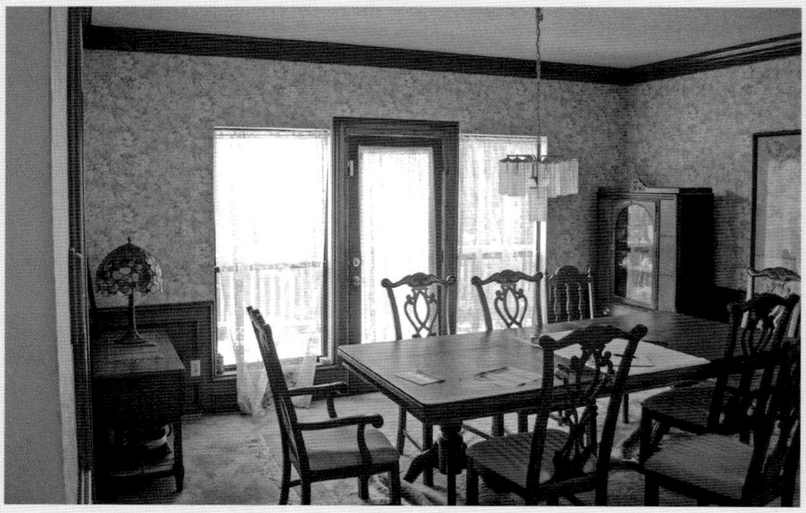
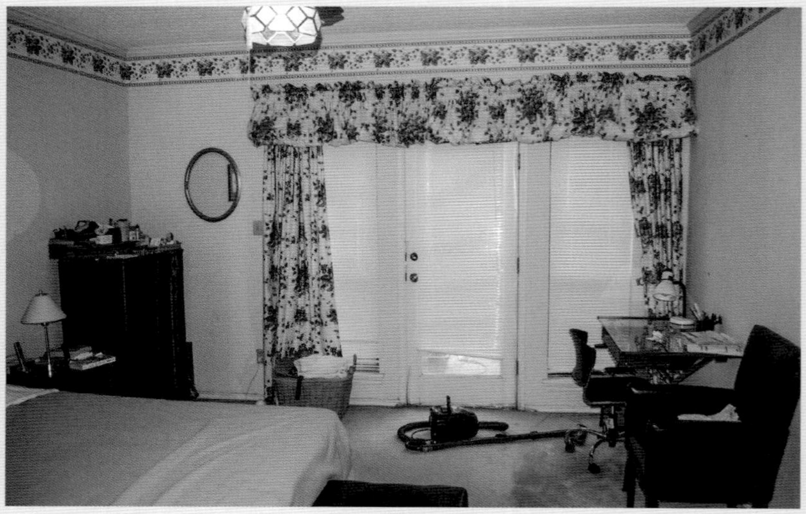
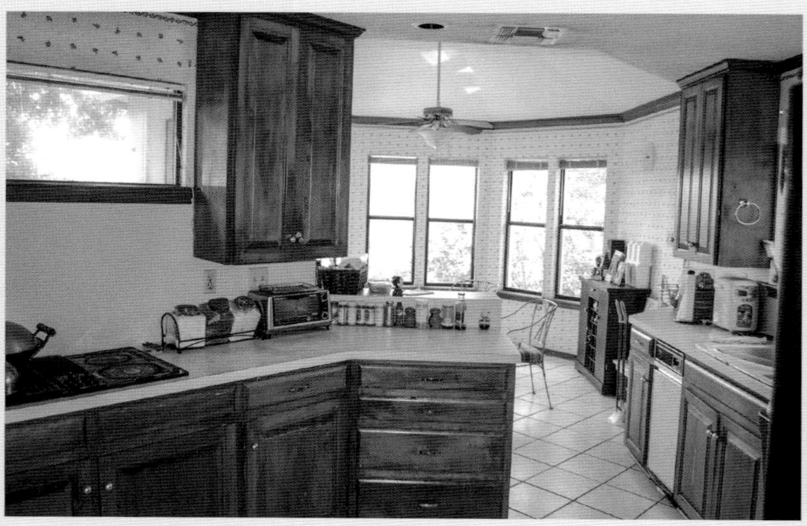
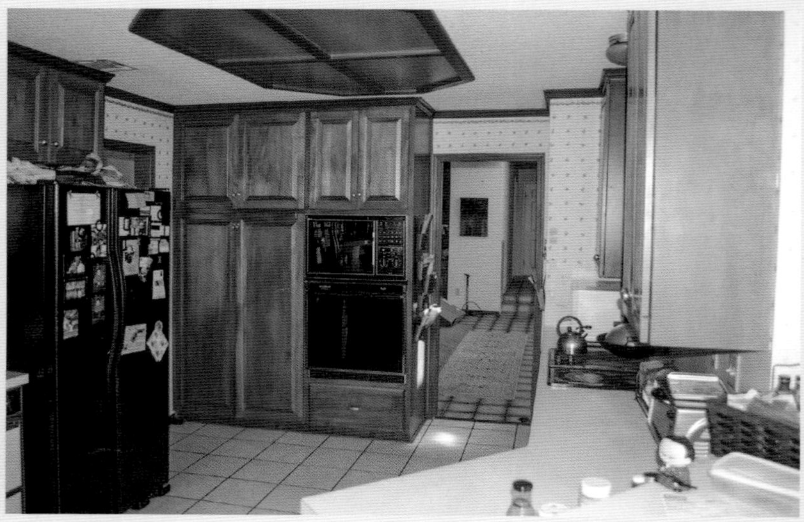

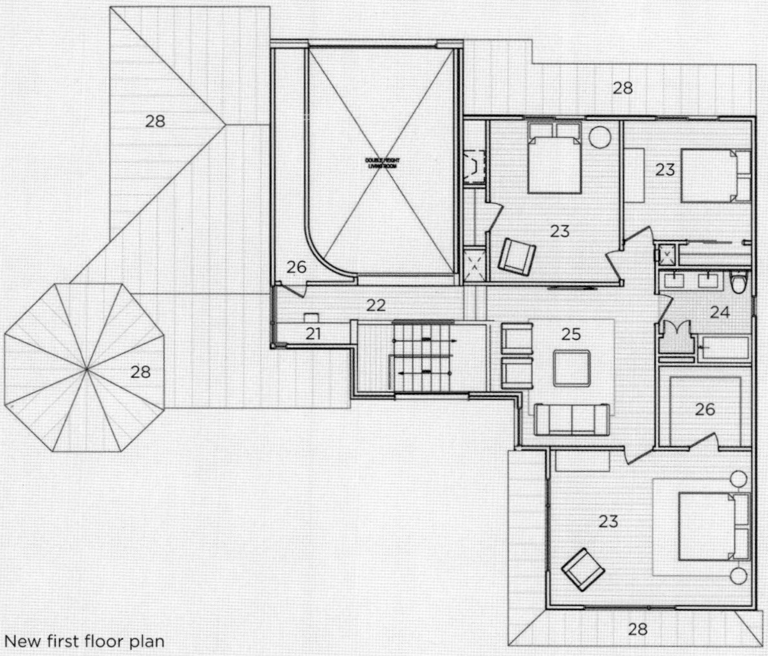

New first floor plan

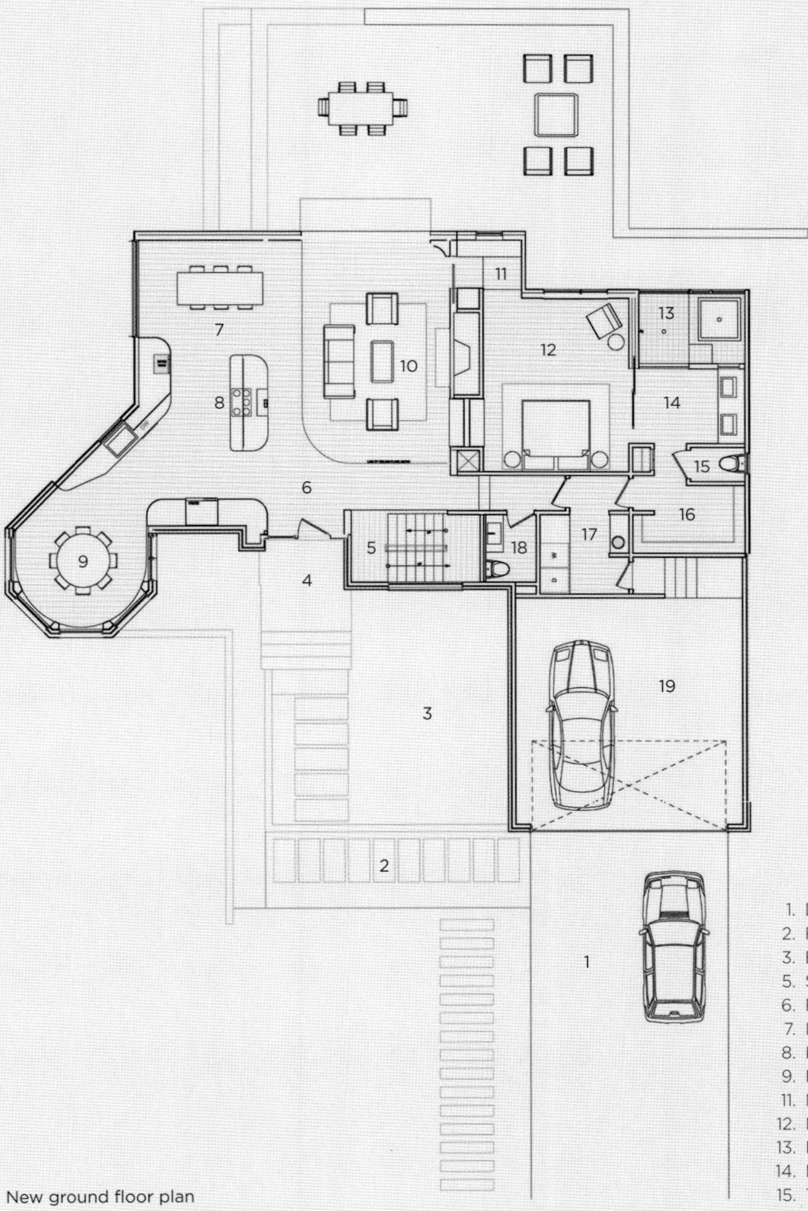

New ground floor plan

1. Driveway
2. Front walk
3. Entry porch
5. Stairwell
6. Foyer
7. Informal dining
8. Kitchen
9. Formal dining
11. Master foyer
12. Master bedroom
13. Master shower
14. Master bathroom
15. Toilet
16. Master closet
17. Laundry
18. Powder
19. Garage
20. Back courtyard
21. Workroom
22. Catwalk
23. Bedroom
24. Bathroom
25. Media room
26. Storage
27. Bedroom / office
28. Roof below

The multileveled terrain results in priceless views. To give the exterior a more modern look, its masonry was replaced by a facing of white hand troweled stucco and dark-shaded Hardie® panels.

Das unterschiedlich hohe Gelände ermöglicht zahlreiche wunderhübsche Ausblicke. Um dem Gebäude ein moderneres Aussehen zu verleihen, wurde das äußere Mauerwerk mit einer weißen Schicht zur besseren Wärmeisolierung und einer Hardie®-Schicht in einem dunklen Ton verkleidet.

Les différentes hauteurs du terrain permettent de profiter de la vue magnifique. Pour conférer un aspect plus moderne à l'extérieur, la maçonnerie extérieure a été remplacée par un revêtement à isolation thermique blanche et revêtement Hardie® dans un ton foncé.

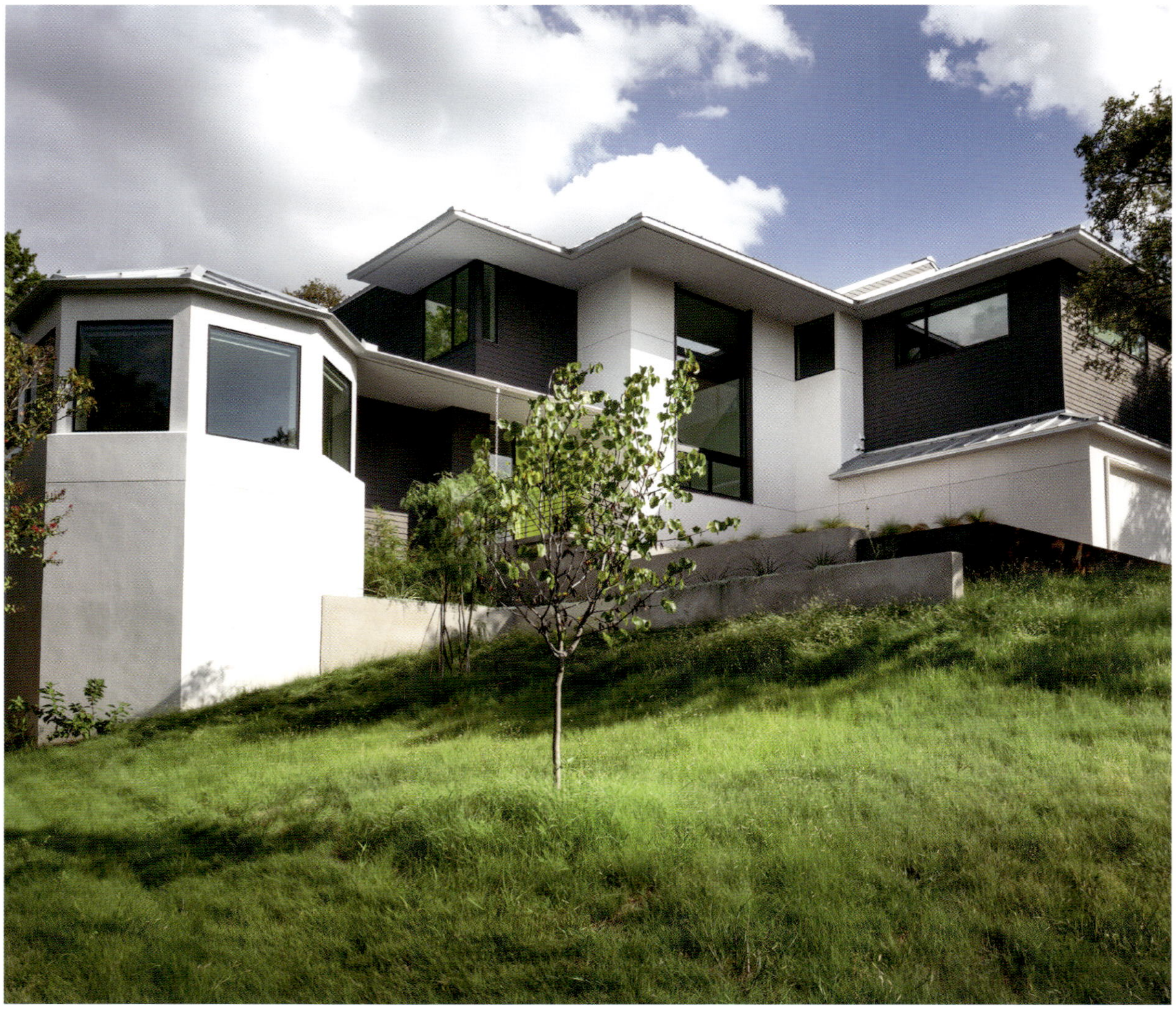

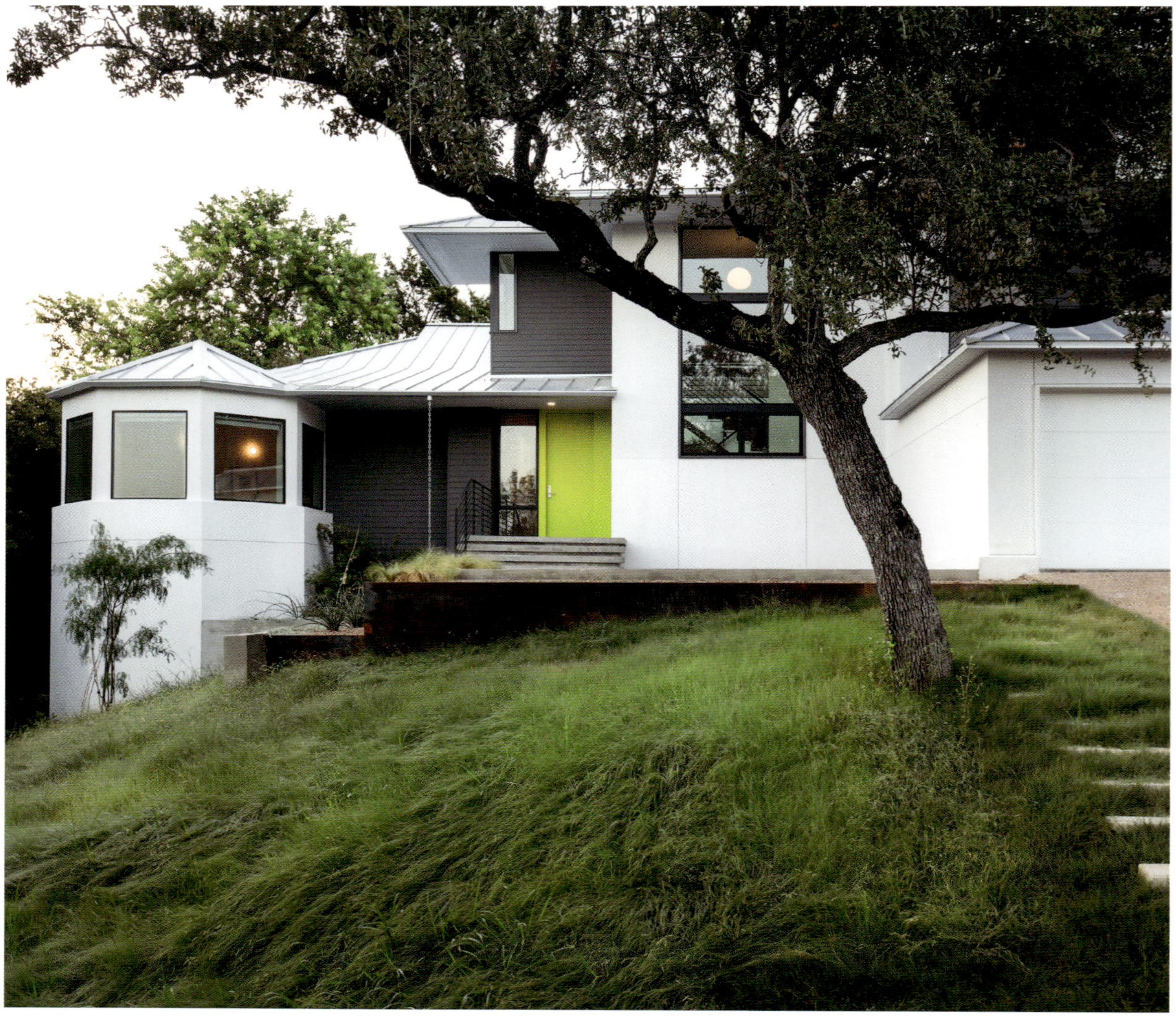

The street access at the front of the structure was redesigned to replace the original steps with natural stone slabs embedded into the lawn, leading to the new terraced patio and main entrance, which features a lime-green door to add a note of color to the residence's overall neutral color palette.

Im vorderen Bereich wurde der Zugang von der Straße aus umgestaltet: Die ursprüngliche Treppe wurde durch Stufen aus Natursteinen ersetzt, die in den Rasen eingelassen wurden und zu einem neuen, terrassenförmig angelegten Hof und zum Haupteingang führen. Die Eingangstür wurde in Gelbgrün gestrichen und fügt der chromatisch neutralen Farbe des gesamten Gebäudes einen bunten Fleck hinzu.

Au niveau de la partie avant de la maison, l'accès donnant sur la rue a été revu en remplaçant l'escalier d'origine par des marches en pierre naturelle imbriquées dans la pelouse. Elles mènent à une nouvelle cour adossée et à l'entrée principale, avec une porte de couleur vert-citron qui ajoute une note de couleur à la palette chromatique neutre de toute la maison.

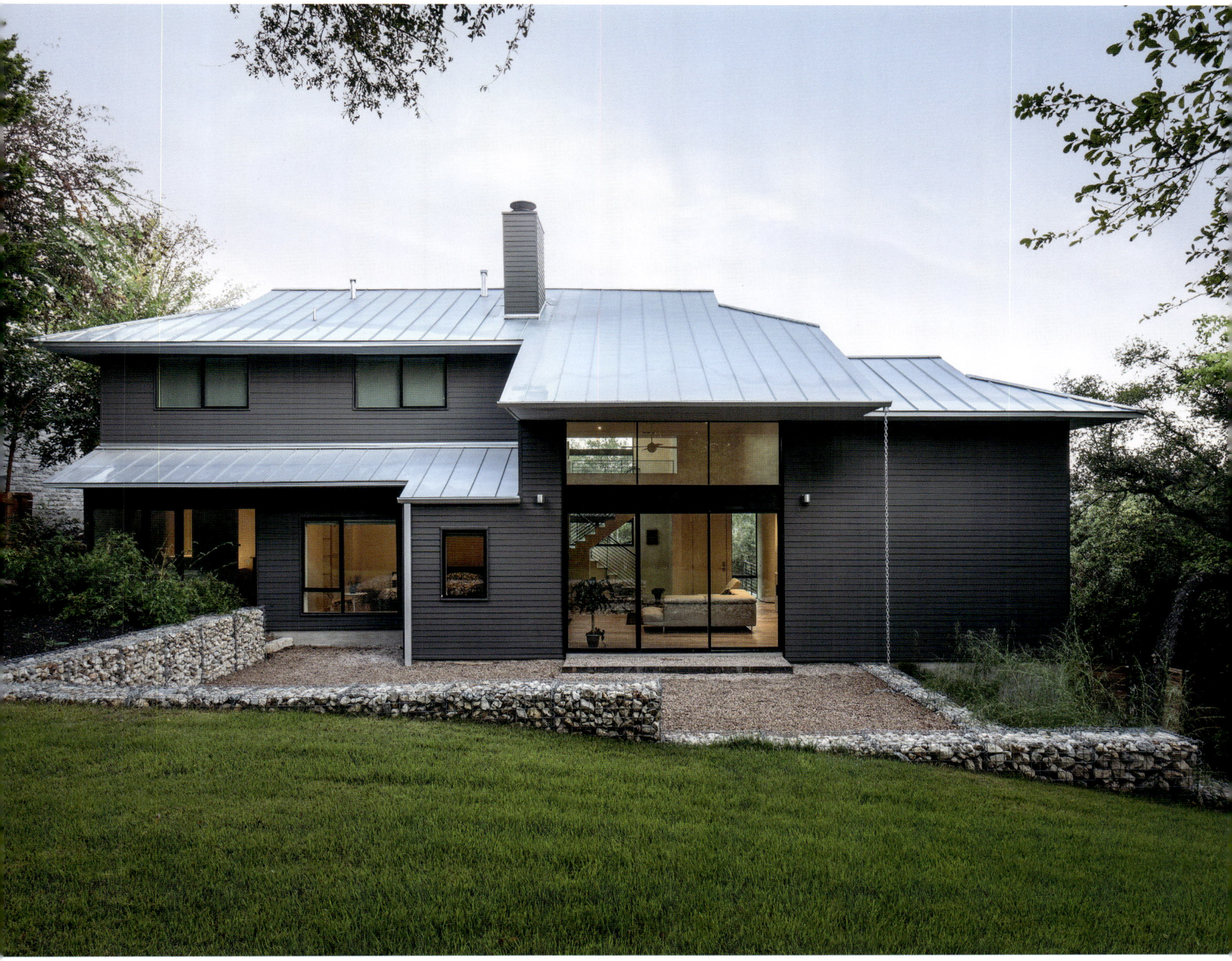

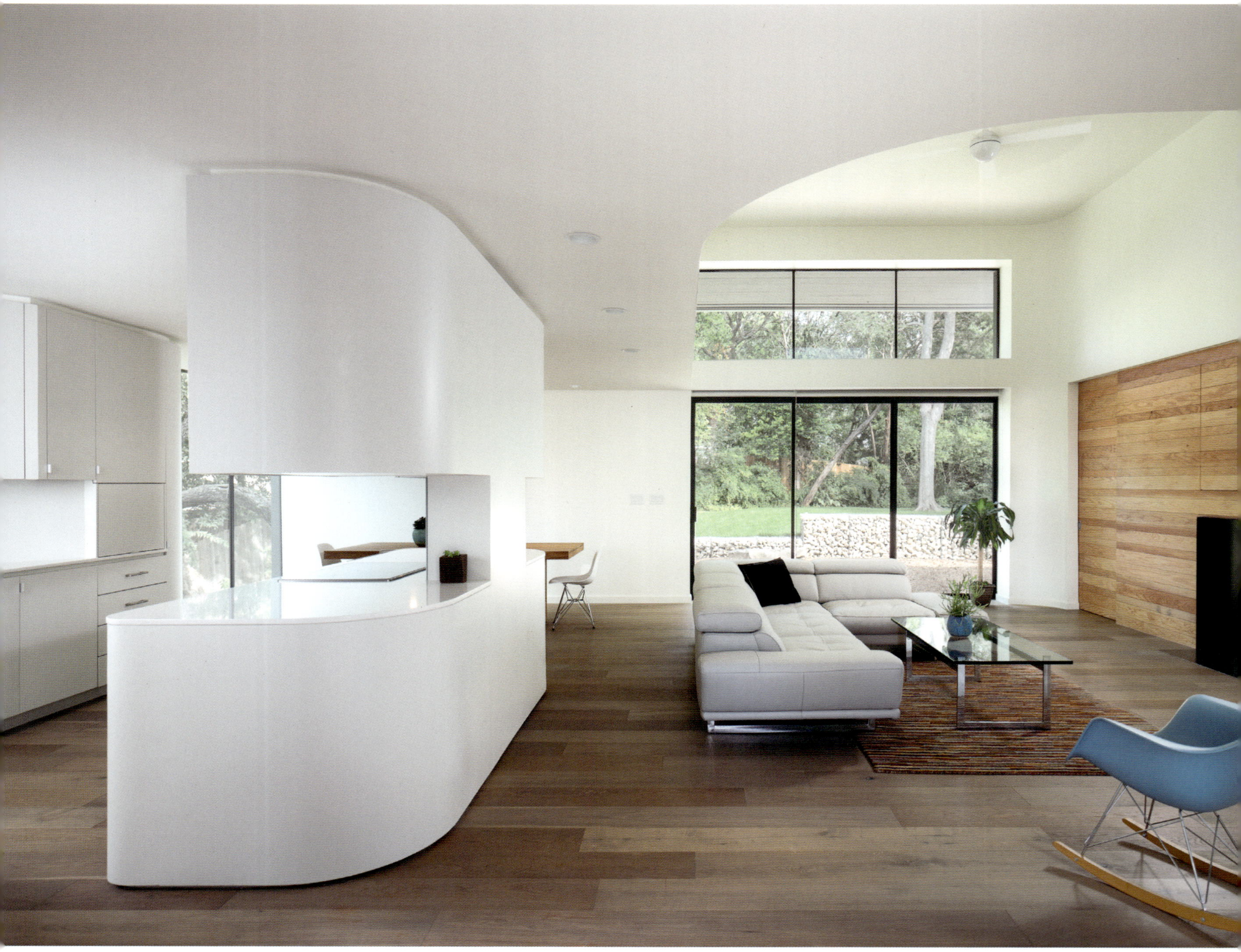

To open the house to the outside, large picture windows were added in the main dining room, living room, and stairwell. These also serve to conduct natural light from all sides of the structure.

Um das Haus nach außen zu öffnen, wurden im Hauptessbereich, dem Wohnzimmer und dem Treppenbereich große Fenster eingebaut. Auf diese Weise fällt weitaus mehr natürliches Licht von allen Seiten ein.

Pour ouvrir la maison sur l'extérieur, de grandes baies vitrées ont été ajoutées dans la salle à manger principale, le séjour et un espace de l'escalier. Ceci a apporté de la lumière naturelle depuis tous les coins.

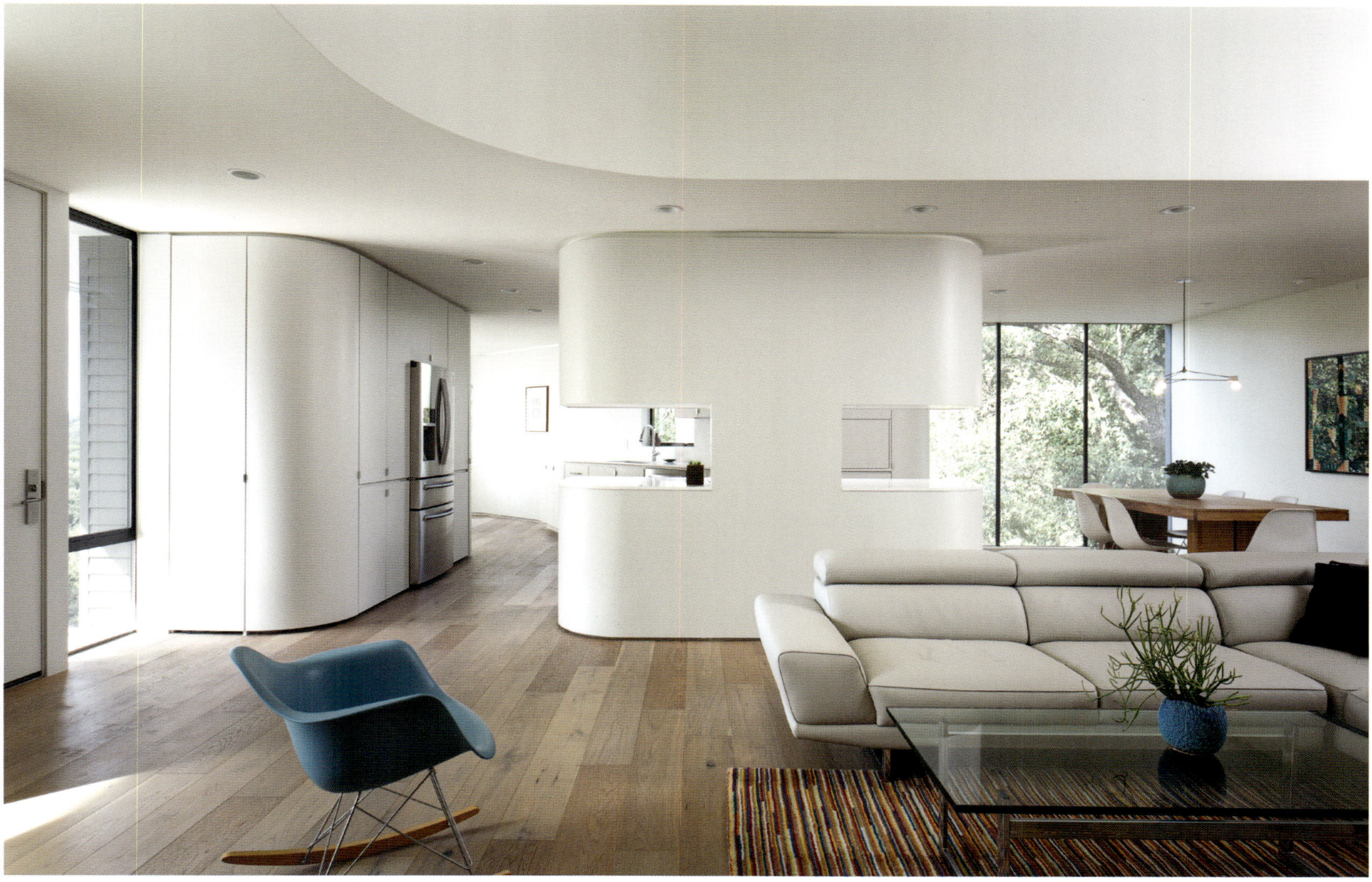

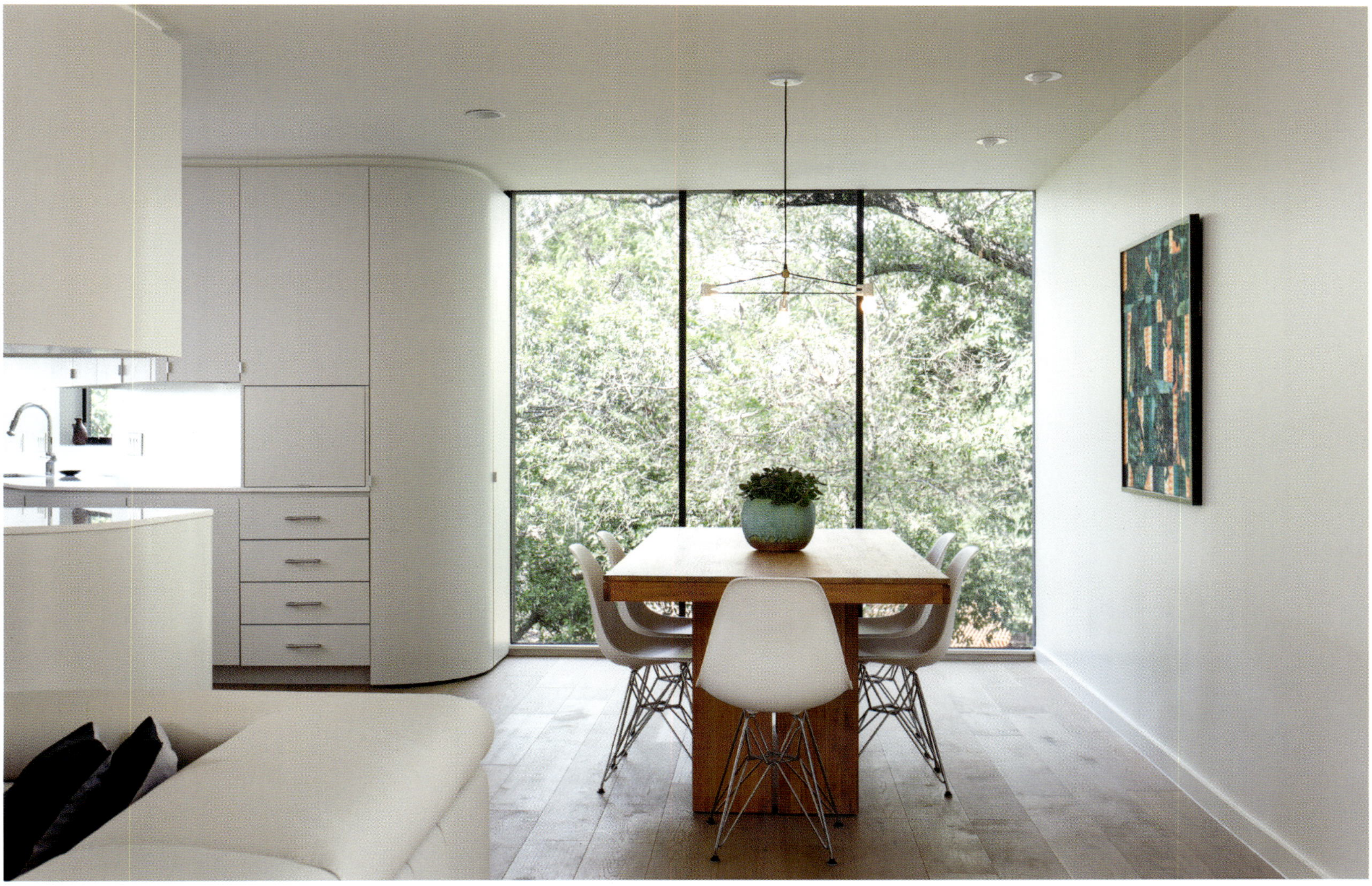

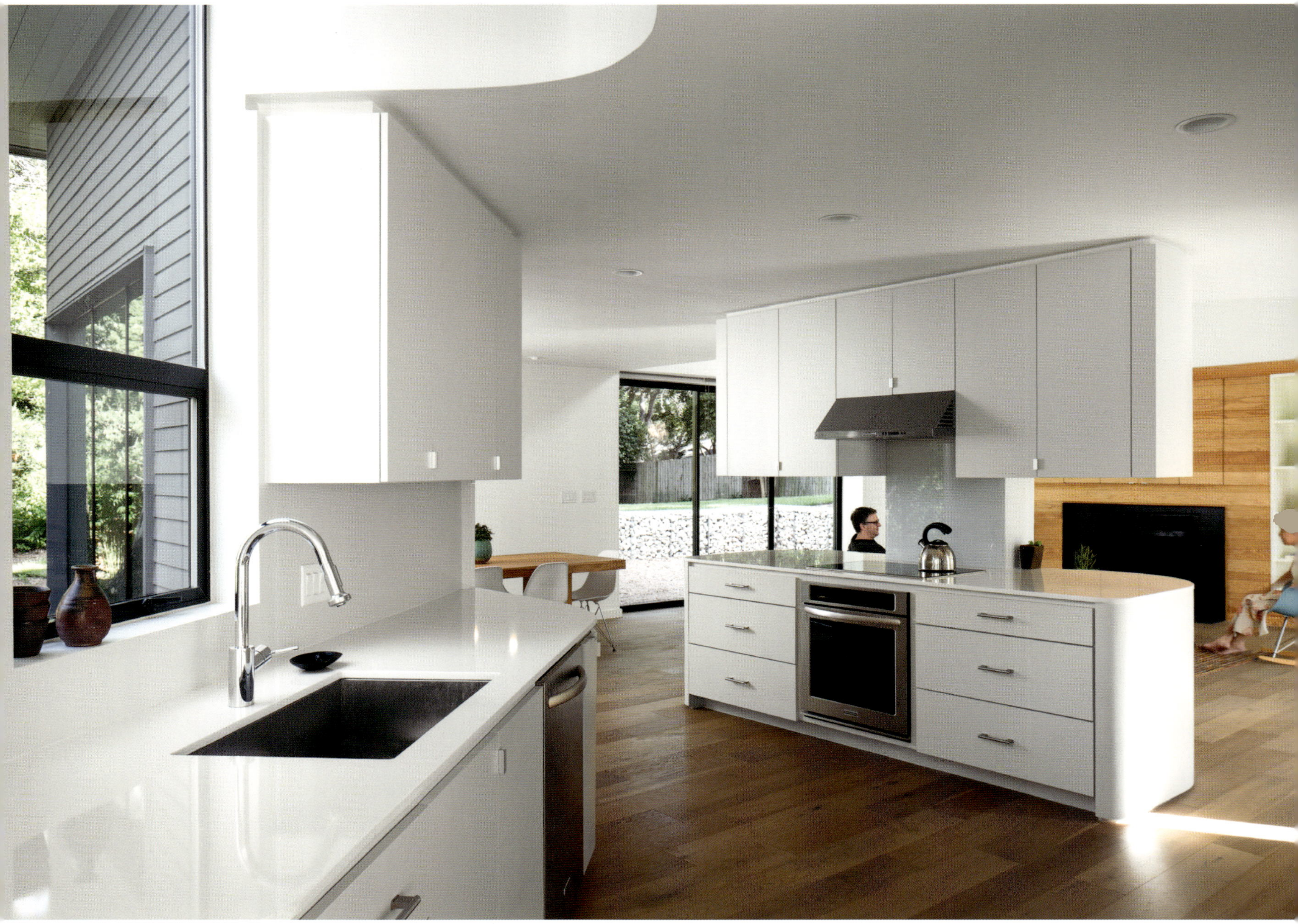

By tearing down the walls separating the dining room, kitchen, and living room, it was possible to create a pleasant open space where the different cabinets define and contextualize the distinct settings.

Nachdem die Wände, die das Esszimmer, die Küche und die Wohnzimmer voneinander trennten, eingerissen wurden, erschuf man einen angenehm offenen Raum, in dem unterschiedliche Schränke die einzelnen Bereiche definieren und zueinander in Beziehung setzen.

Après avoir fait tomber les murs qui séparaient la salle à manger, la cuisine et le séjour, un agréable espace ouvert a été créé, dans lequel les diverses armoires définissent et donnent du cachet aux différentes pièces.

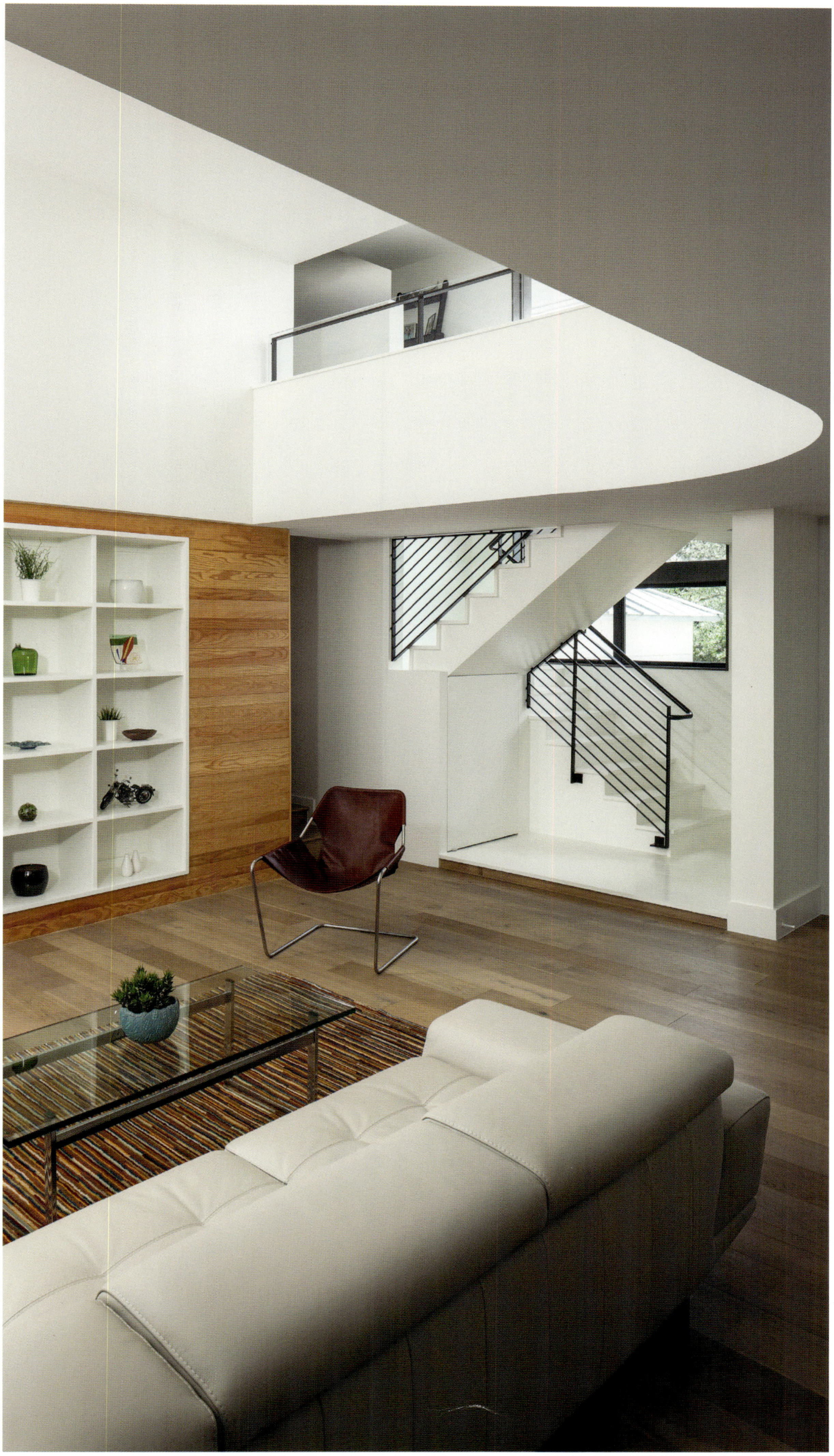

The idea of the curve flowing through the space is replicated in the new raised ceiling above the salon. The added ceiling height creates a visual connection between the two floors and generates a sense of openness and spatial continuity.

Die Idee der Kurve, die sich durch den Raum windet, wird durch die neue Wohnzimmerdecke aufgenommen. Die großzügige Raumhöhe schafft eine visuelle Verbindung zwischen den beiden Stockwerken und eine räumliche Weite und Kontinuität.

L'idée de la courbe qui traverse l'espace a également été utilisée pour le nouveau plafond élevé au-dessus du salon. Cette augmentation de la hauteur de plafond permet une connexion visuelle entre les deux niveaux et une sensation de grandeur et continuité spatiale.

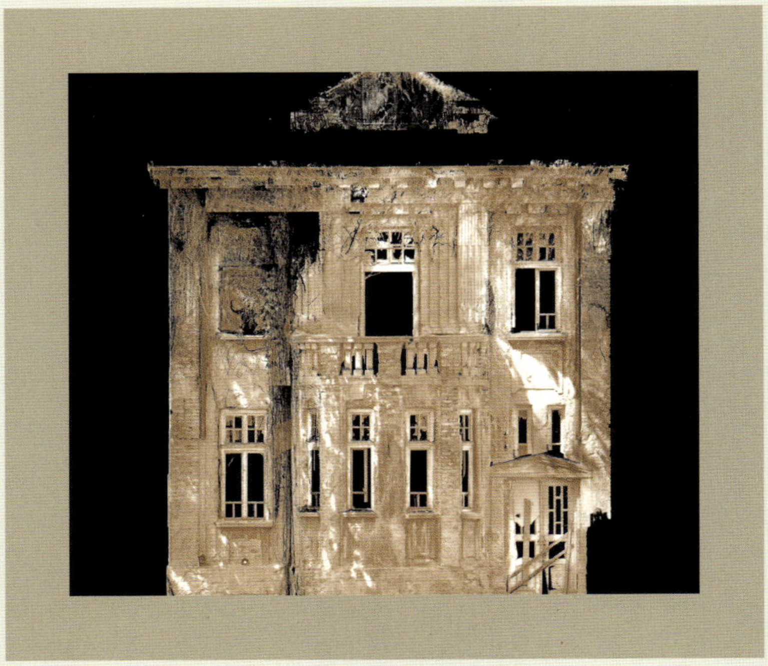

WHITE CONCRETE HOUSE

I/O ARCHITECTS

425 m² | 4,575 sq. ft.

Stara Zagora, Bulgaria

Photos © **Assen Emilov**

> Convert an abandoned house into a modern and up-to-date residence

> Expand the structure by adding new space that exists in harmony with the original structure

> Ein Haus in Trümmern in ein zeitgenössisches Wohnhaus umwandeln

> Das Haus mit einem neuen Volumen ausbauen, das mit dem ursprünglichen Gebäude harmoniert

> Transformer une maison tombée en désuétude en un logement moderne et contemporain

> Agrandir la maison en ajoutant un nouveau volume en harmonie avec sa structure d'origine

Prior to its rebuilding, this house, which had been constructed in the 1920s, was a romantic ruin surrounded by authentic fragments and renovations of the ancient city of Augusta Traiana, clearly separated from the modern city yet located at its center. The intervention continues the interplay between epochs, with the design inspiring a modern interpretation of the innovations from the period when the house was built.
A new application of simple white concrete complements the old house's structure and function. The two distinct entities are brought together by the composition of the openings, the ambiguous elements of the new addition, and the materiality. The space and design of the new stairway, featuring translucent glass steps, draw light to the center of the entire composition. The shiny white concrete slabs integrate and conceal the house's modern technological systems.
No one can remain indifferent to this imposing yet harmonious residence, which reclaims its history while gradually and elegantly yielding to the contemporary age.

Vor dem Umbau war dieses in den 1920er Jahren erbaute Haus eine romantische Ruine, umgeben von authentischen Fragmenten und Neubauten der alten Augusta Traiana, ziemlich isoliert von der heutigen Stadt, doch in deren Zentrum. Der Eingriff spielt mit dem Kontrast und der Balance zwischen alt und neu und macht den Entwurf zu einer zeitgenössischen Interpretation der Avantgarde der Epoche, in der das Haus erbaut wurde.
Ein neues und nüchternes Volumen aus weißem Beton ergänzt die Struktur und das Programm des altehrwürdigen Hauses. Die Anordnung der Öffnungen, die doppeldeutigen Elemente des Anbaus und die Materialität vermischen die beiden unterschiedlichen Einheiten. Der Raum der neuen Treppe und deren Gestaltung mit lichtdurchlässigen Glasstufen bringen Licht ins Zentrum der gesamten Komposition. Die neuen glänzenden weißen Betondecken integrieren und verstecken die gesamte moderne Haustechnik.
Dieses imposante Haus, das jeden beeindruckt, erweckt eine Vergangenheit, die mit eleganter Harmonie der Gegenwart Platz macht.

Avant sa reconstruction, cette maison construite dans les années 20 était une ruine romantique entourée de vestiges authentiques et de nouvelle construction de l'ancienne Augusta Traiana et assez isolée de la ville contemporaine tout en étant au cœur même de celle-ci. Les travaux de rénovation jouent avec le contraste entre l'ancien et le nouveau, amenant la conception à une interprétation contemporaine du modernisme de l'époque à laquelle la maison fut construite.
Un nouveau volume sobre en béton blanc complète la structure et l'aménagement de l'ancienne maison. La composition des ouvertures, les éléments ambigus de l'extension et la matérialité mélangent les deux espaces distincts. L'espace du nouvel escalier et son design, avec des marches en verre transparentes, apportent de la lumière au centre de toute la composition. Les nouvelles dalles de béton ciré blanc intègrent et masquent toute la technologie contemporaine de la maison.
Cette imposante maison qui ne laisse personne indifférent a retrouvé un passé qui fait place à un présent moderne avec une élégante harmonie.

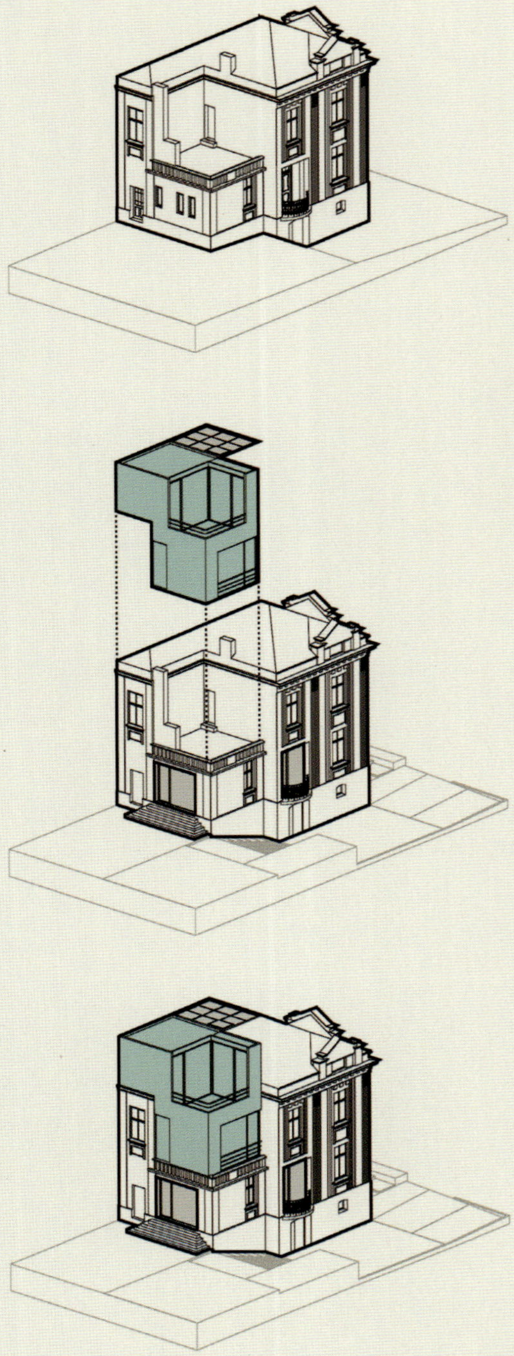

Axonometry

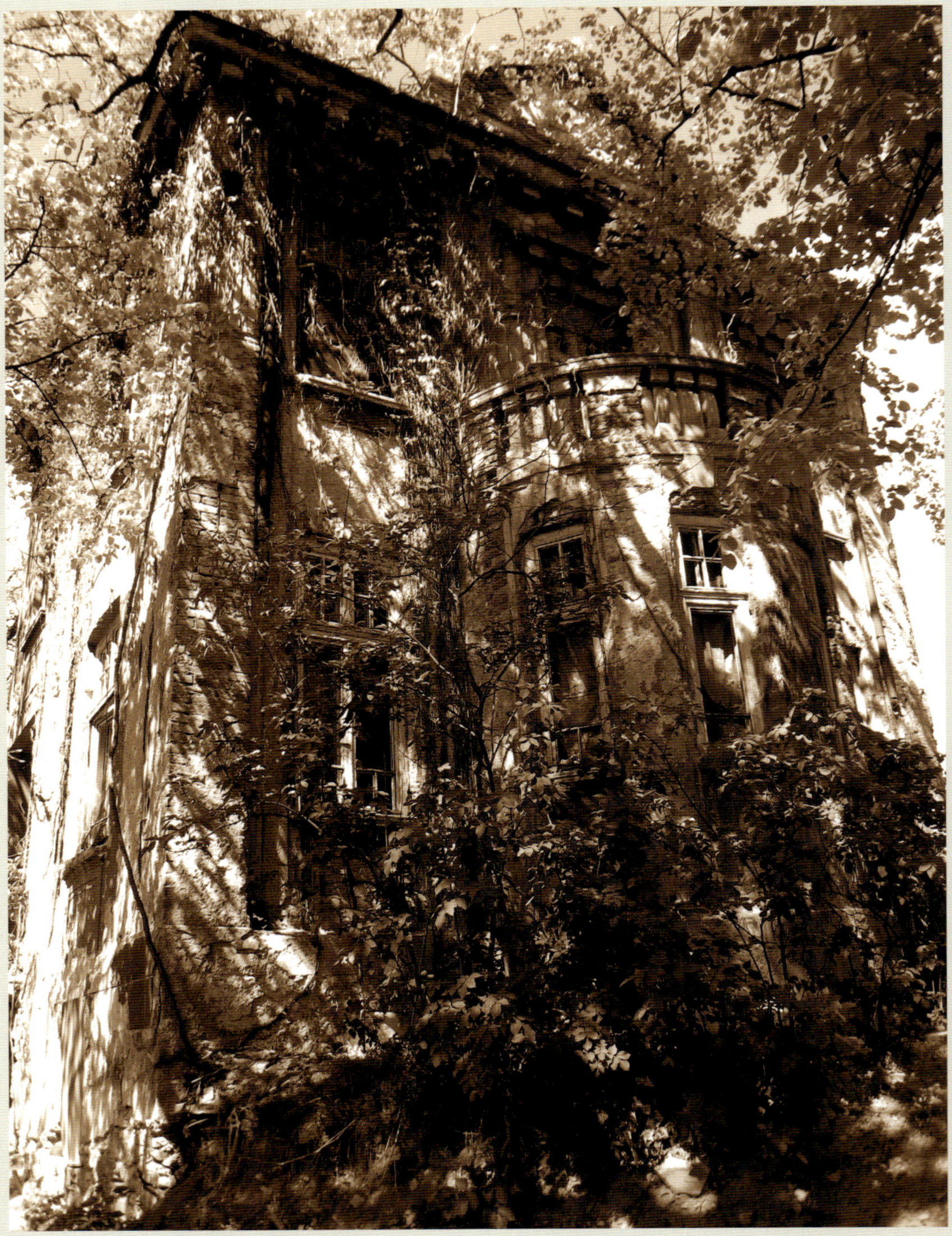

The dwelling has been expanded through the addition of a new space that fits perfectly above the terrace of the original structure. This space contains two bedrooms, one of which features terrace access, a bathroom, and a bi-level mechanical room/storeroom.

Beim Ausbau des Hauses wurde ein neues Volumen hinzugefügt, das sich perfekt auf der Terrasse des ursprünglichen Gehäuses einpasst. Dieses Volumen beherbergt zwei Schlafzimmer, von denen eines Zugang zu einer Terrasse hat, ein Bad, einen Technik- und Abstellraum, der auf zwei Etagen verteilt ist.

La maison a subi des travaux d'extension en ajoutant un nouveau volume qui s'intègre à la perfection sur la terrasse de la maison d'origine. Ce volume comprend deux chambres, dont l'une dispose d'un accès à la terrasse, une salle de bains et une buanderie, répartis sur deux niveaux.

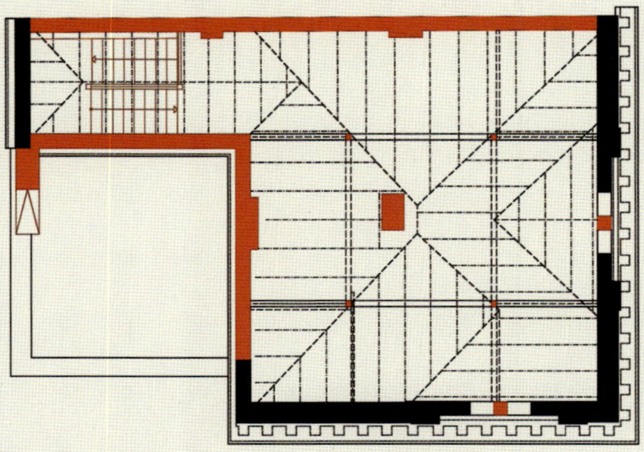

Demolition plan third floor

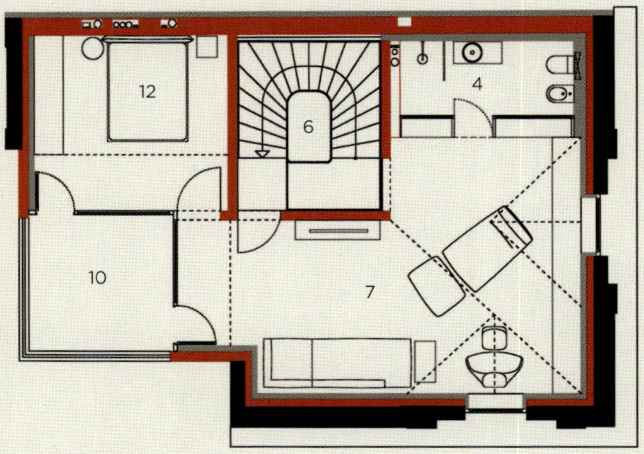

Third floor plan

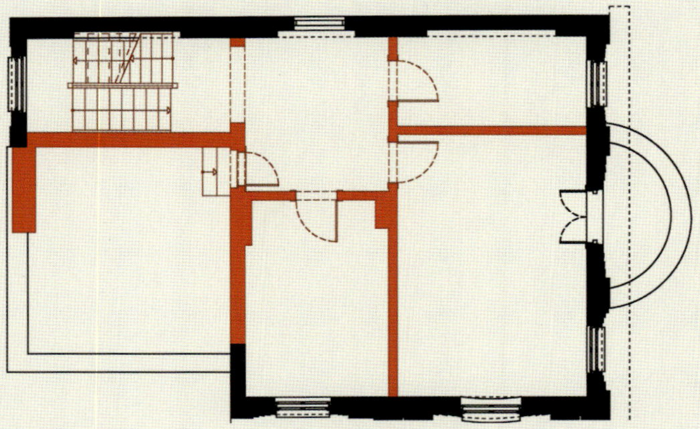

Demolition plan second floor

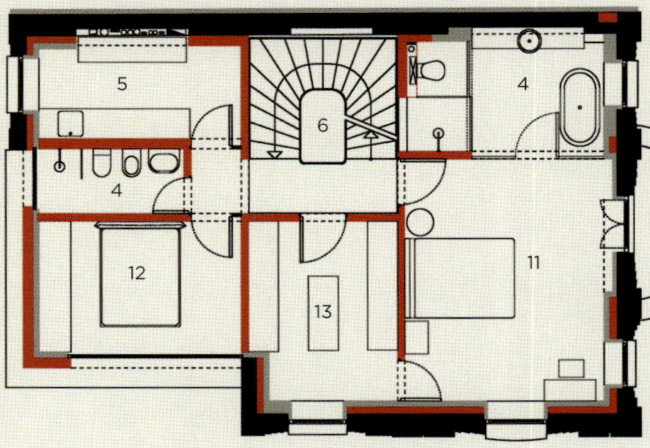

Third floor plan

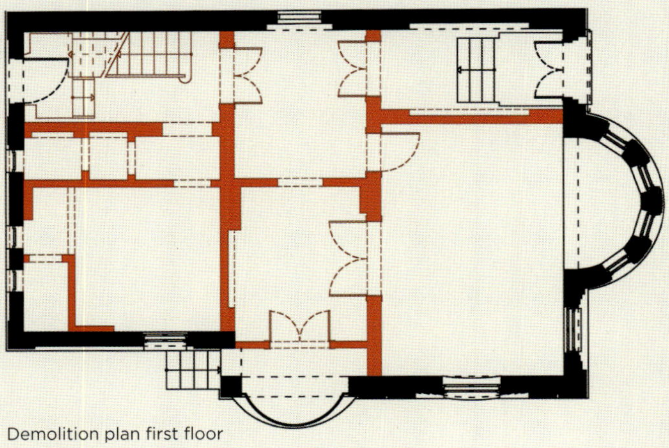

Demolition plan first floor

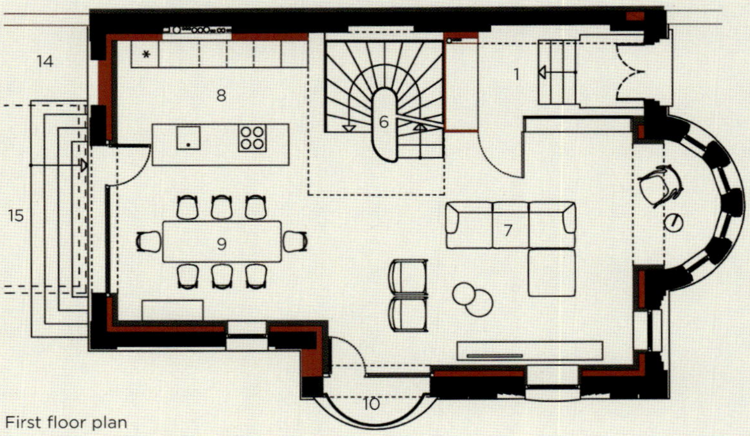

First floor plan

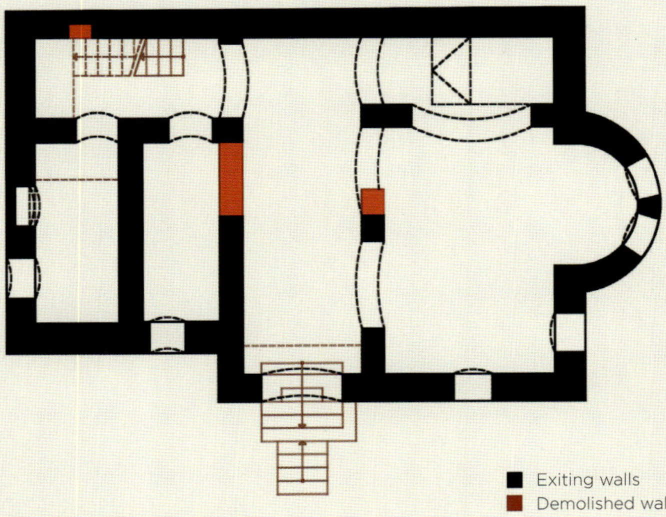

- Exiting walls
- Demolished walls

Demolition plan ground floor

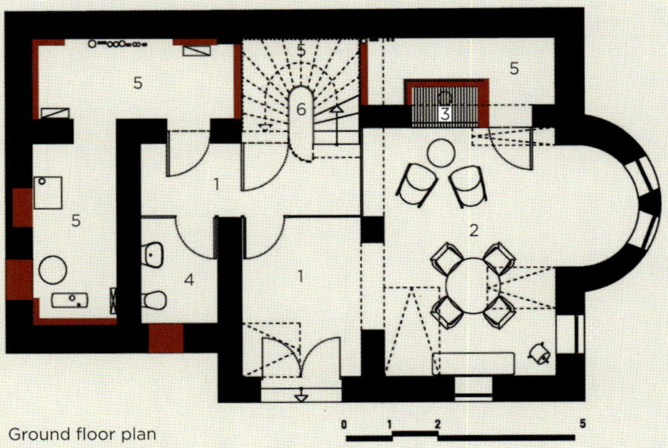

Ground floor plan

1. Entrance / hallway
2. Bridge room
3. Fireplace
4. Bathroom / toilet
5. Storage / technical room
6. Staircase
7. Living area
8. Kitchen
9. Dining area
10. Terrace
11. Master bedroom
12. Bedroom
13. Wardrobe
14. Outdoor kitchen
15. Patio

- Existing walls
- New construction / walls
- Thermal insulation

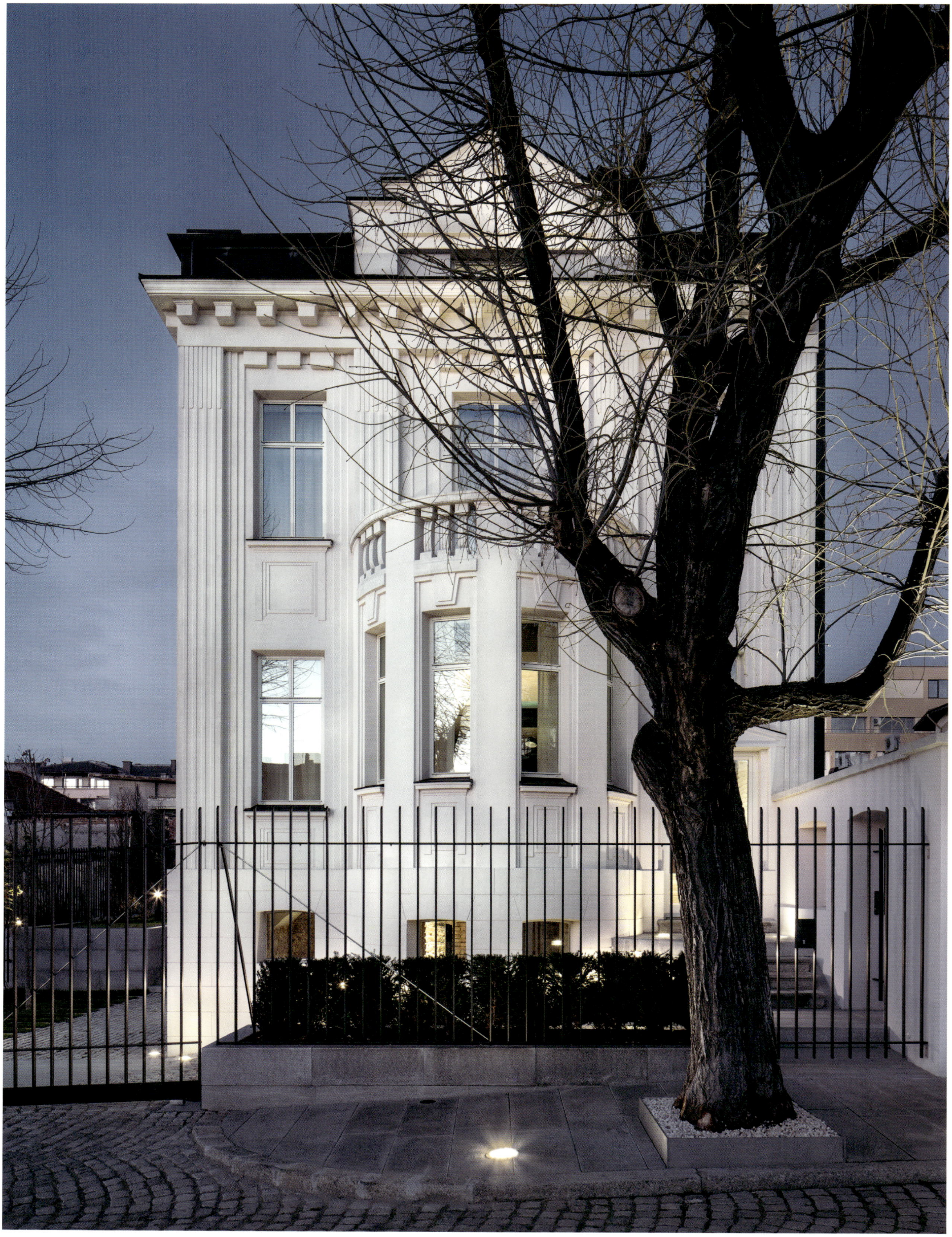

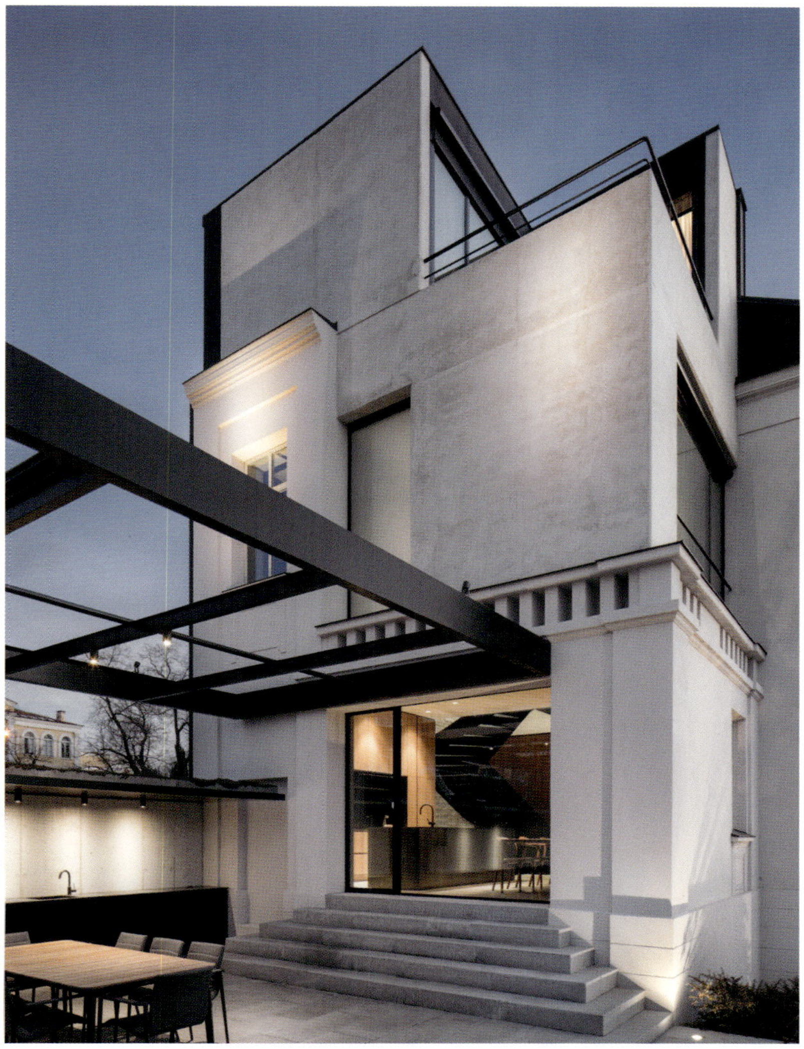

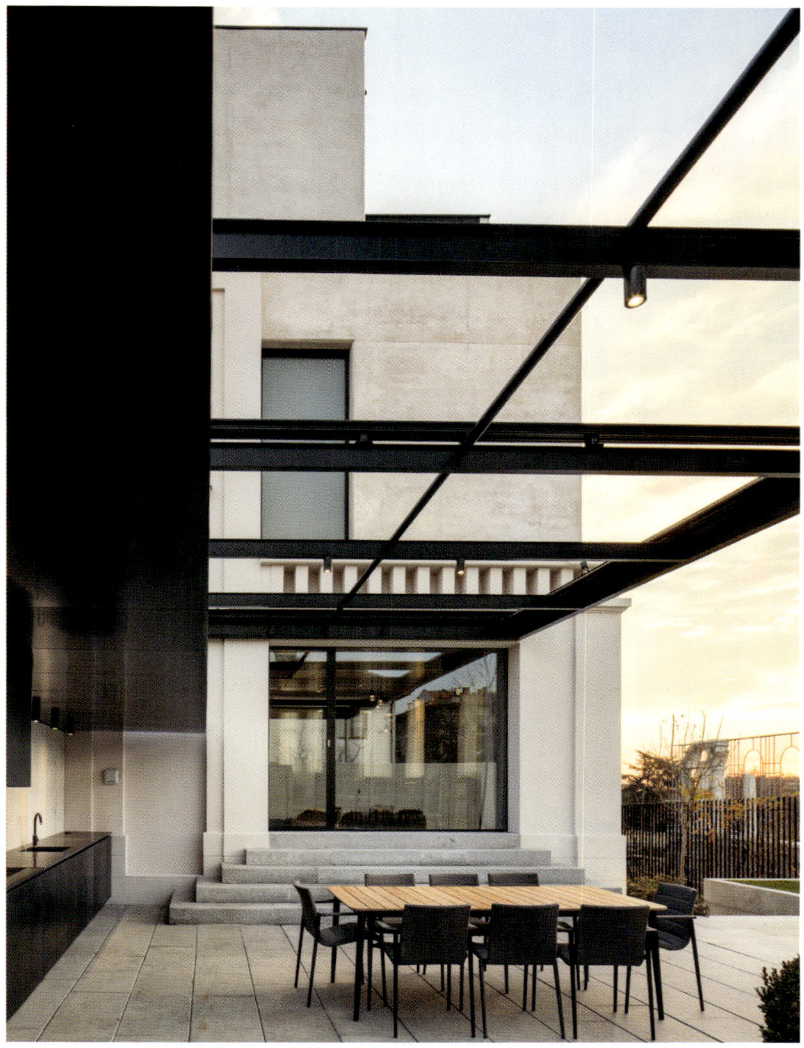

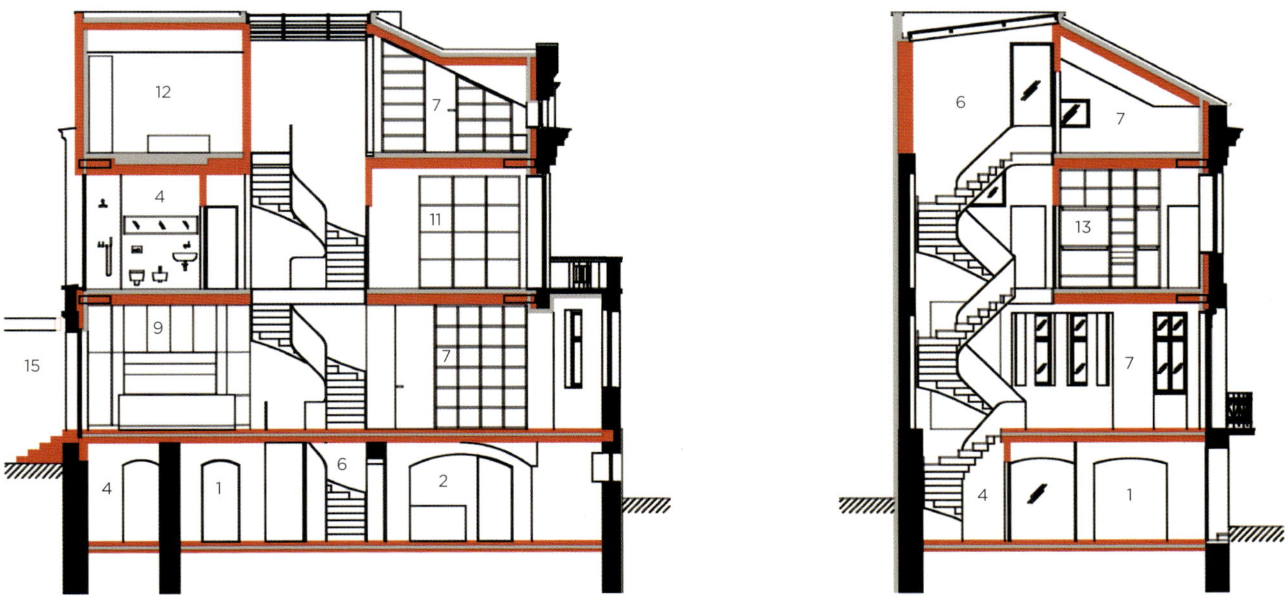

Sections

1. Entrance / hallway
2. Bridge room
3. Fireplace
4. Bathroom / toilet
5. Storage / technical room
6. Staircase
7. Living area
8. Kitchen
9. Dining area
10. Terrace
11. Master bedroom
12. Bedroom
13. Wardrobe
14. Outdoor kitchen
15. Patio

- Existing walls
- New construction walls
- Thermal insulation

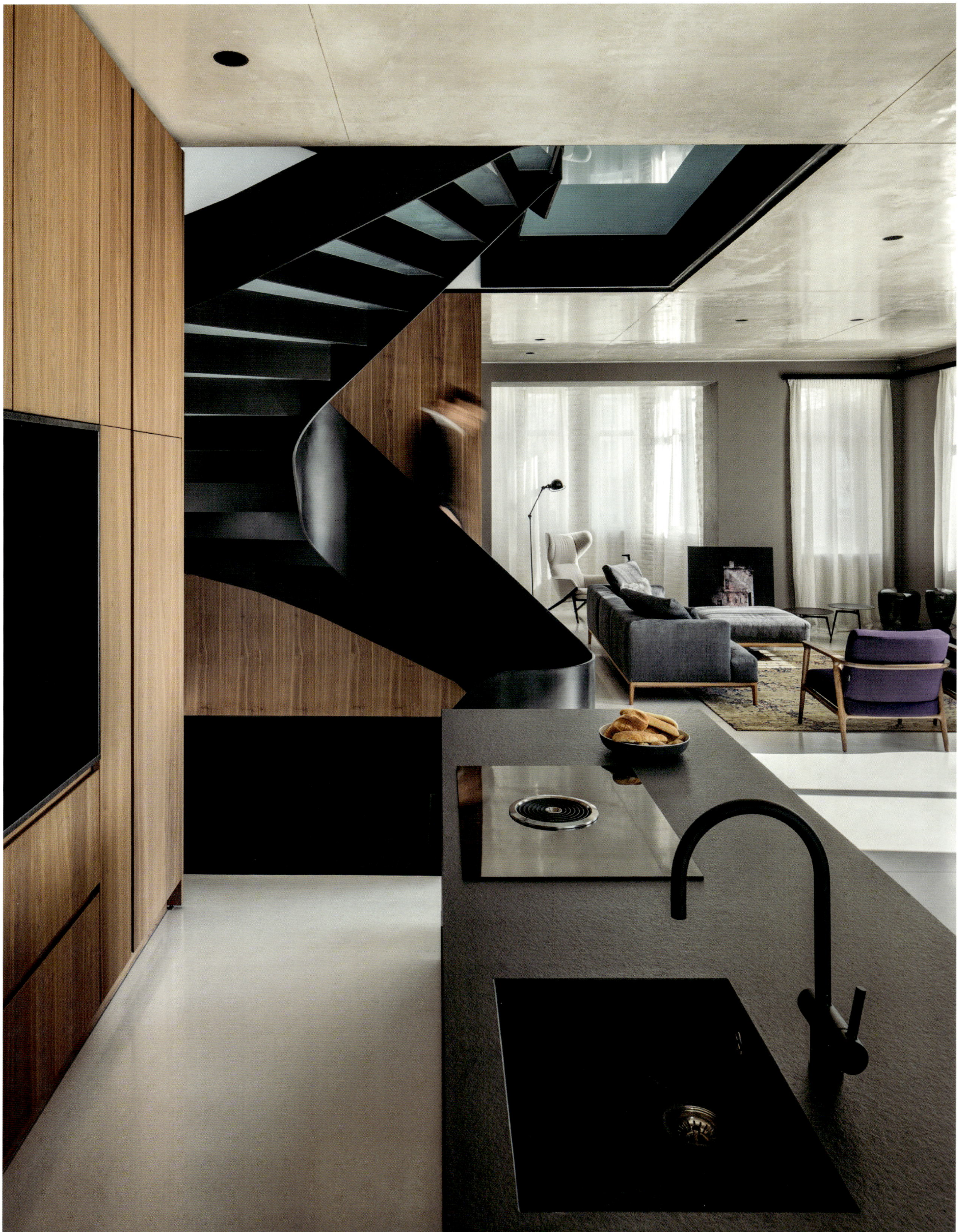

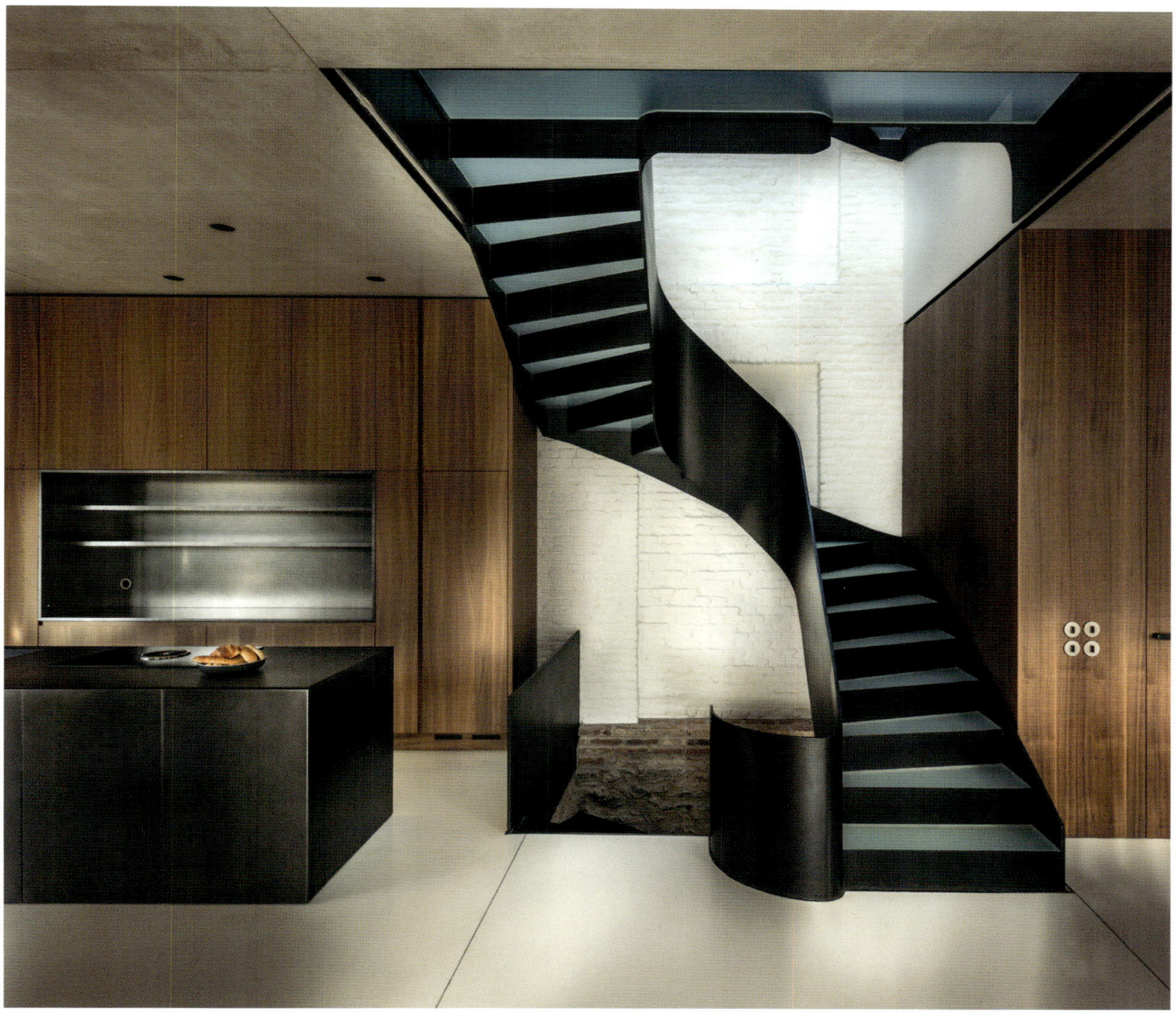

Beyond its main function of articulating the space that connects the two levels, the staircase channels light to the center of the building. Its sculptured design makes it the focal point of this space.

Neben ihrer Hauptfunktion als Artikulator des Raumes, der die verschiedenen Stockwerke verbindet, bringt die Treppe Licht in die Mitte des Hauses. Ihr skulpturales Design macht sie zum Mittelpunkt dieses Raumes.

Outre sa fonction principale d'agent de liaison de l'espace reliant les divers étages, l'escalier apporte de la lumière au cœur de la maison. Son design sculptural en fait le point central de cet espace.

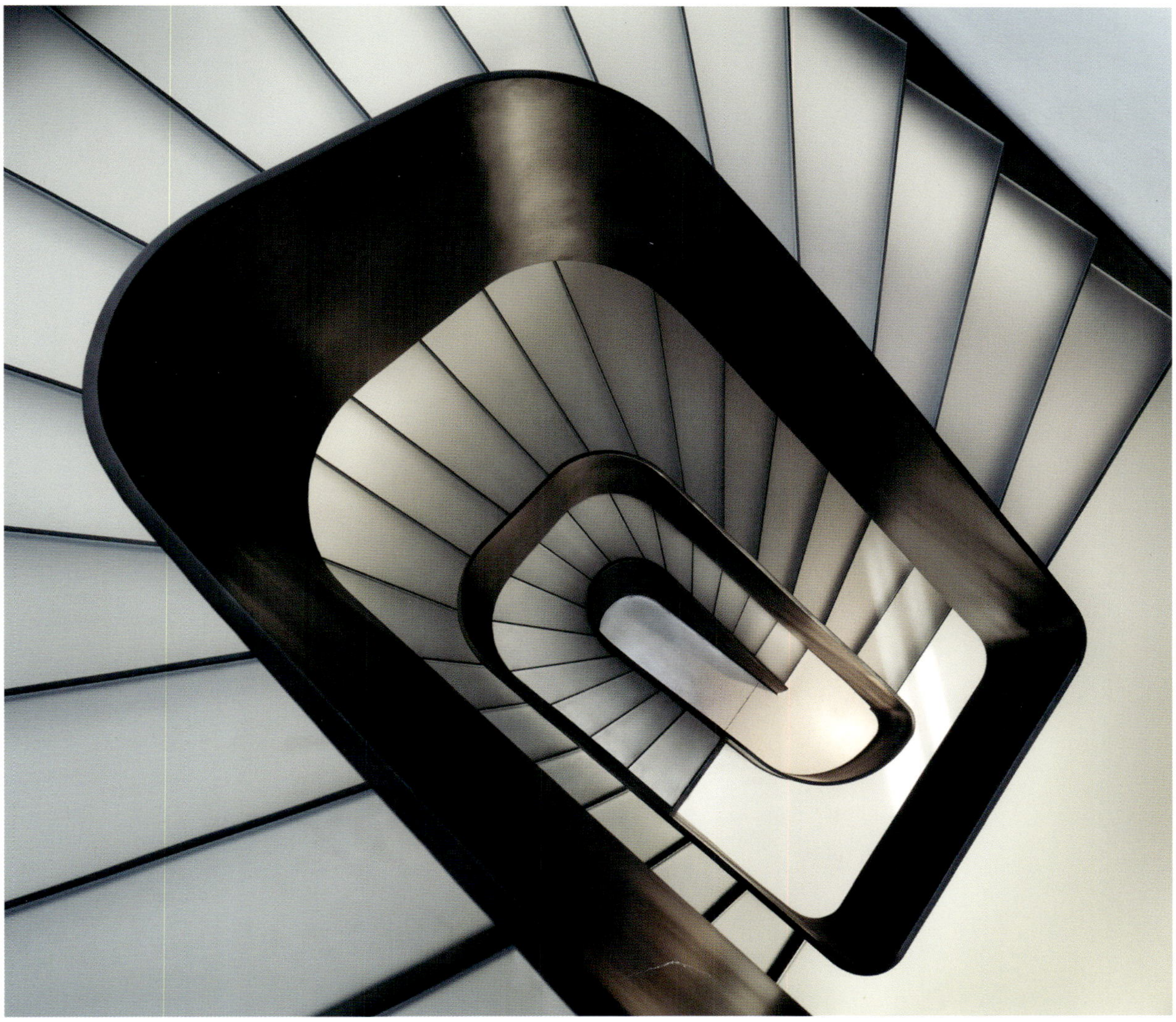

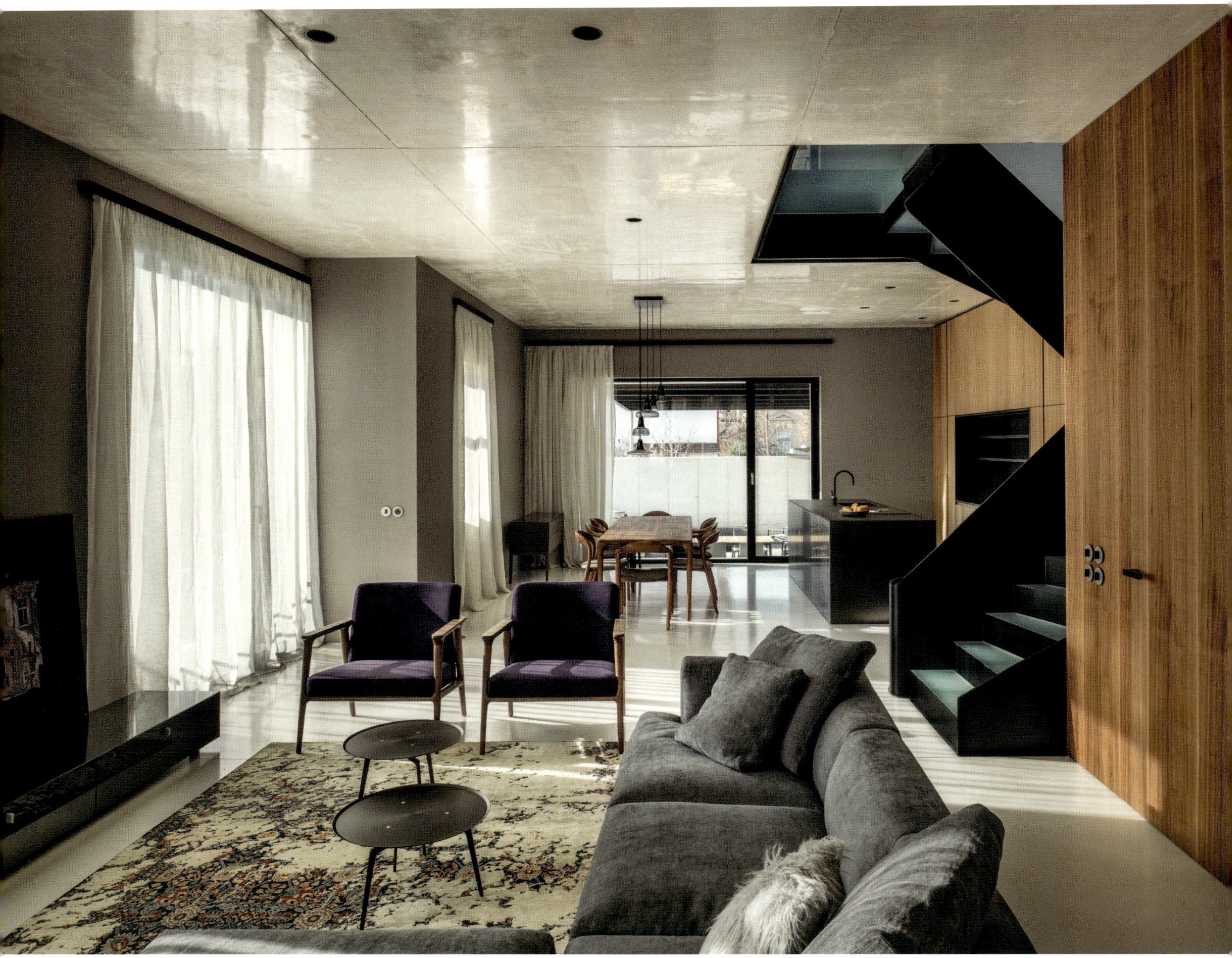

The open, continuous, and dynamic character reveals a modern spatial concept. The kitchen island, in addition to serving as a work area, also separates the settings without resorting to dividers, thus maintaining spatial continuity.

Der offene, durchgängige und dynamische Charakter offenbart eine moderne Raumgestaltung. Kücheninsel und Arbeitsbereich fungieren als Raumteiler, ohne dass Trennwände erforderlich sind, wodurch die räumliche Kontinuität erhalten bleibt.

Le caractère ouvert, continu et dynamique révèle une conception moderne de l'espace. L'îlot de la cuisine, outre sa fonction de plan de travail, sert de séparation des espaces sans nécessité de cloison, conservant ainsi la continuité spatiale.

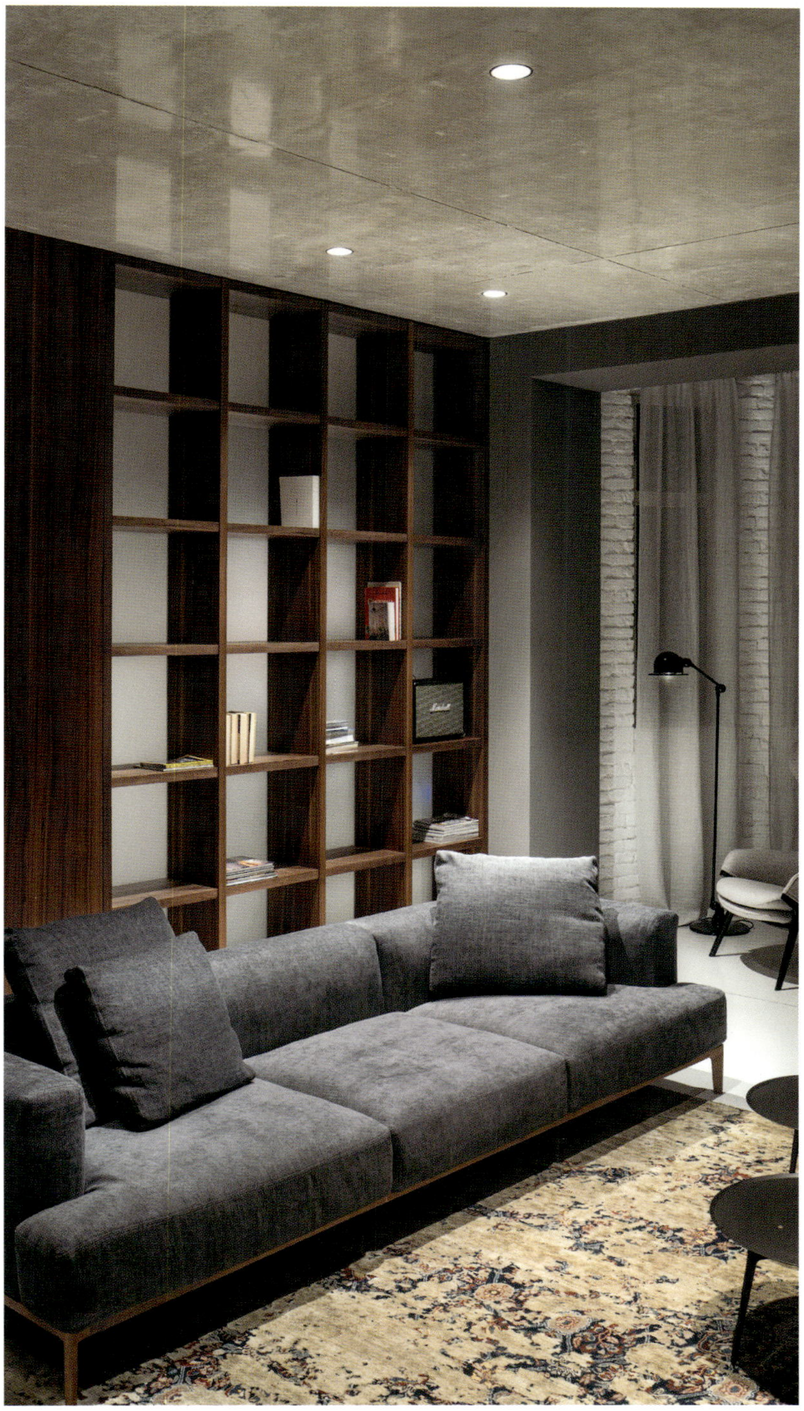

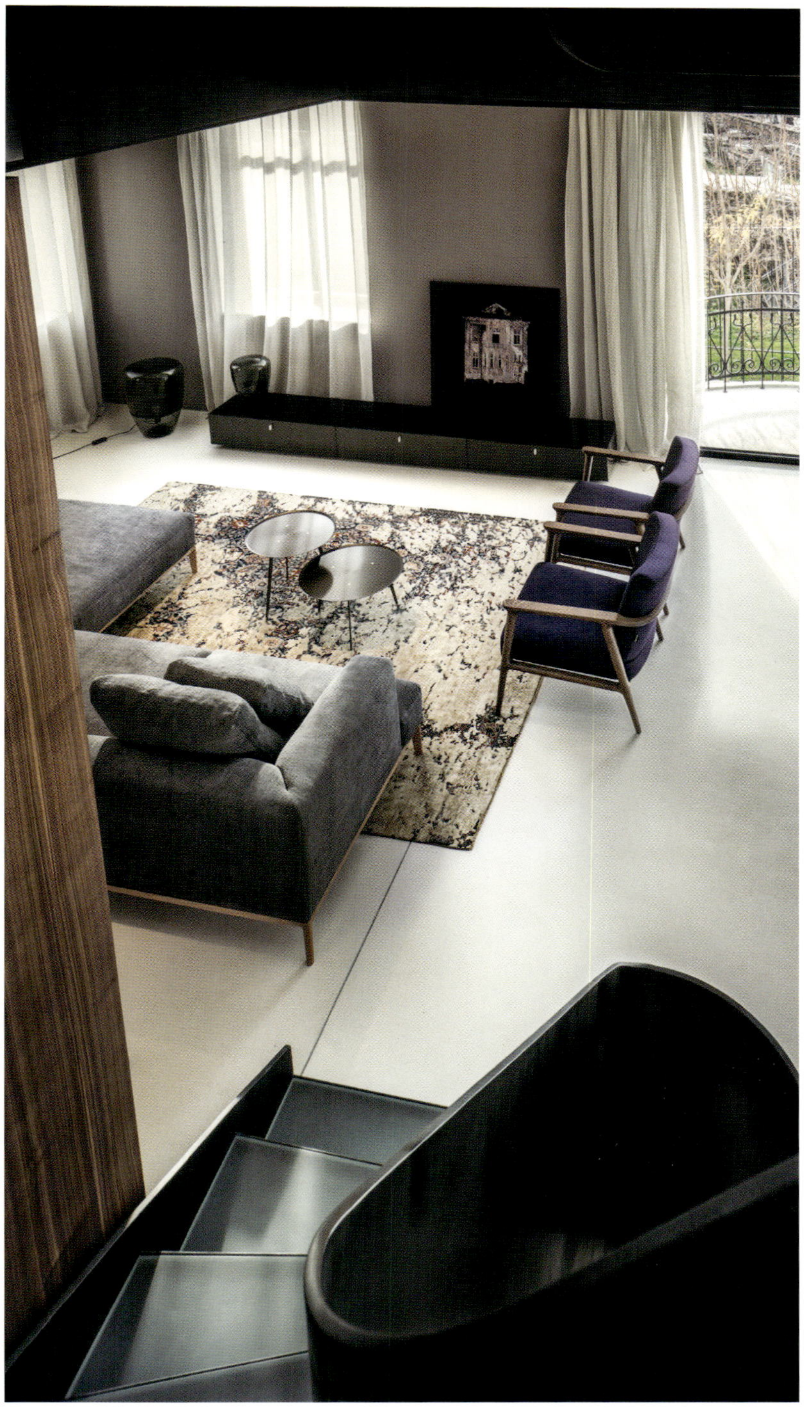

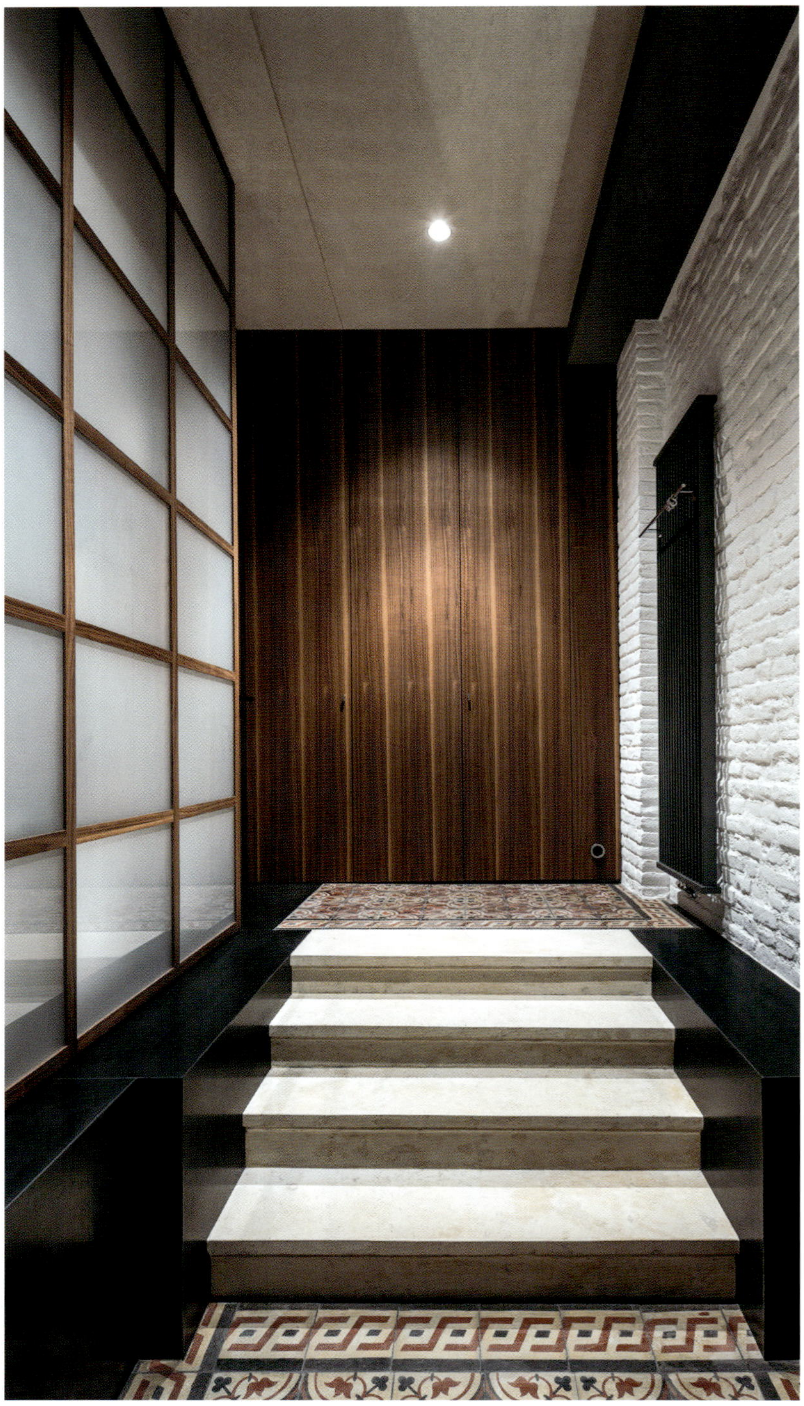

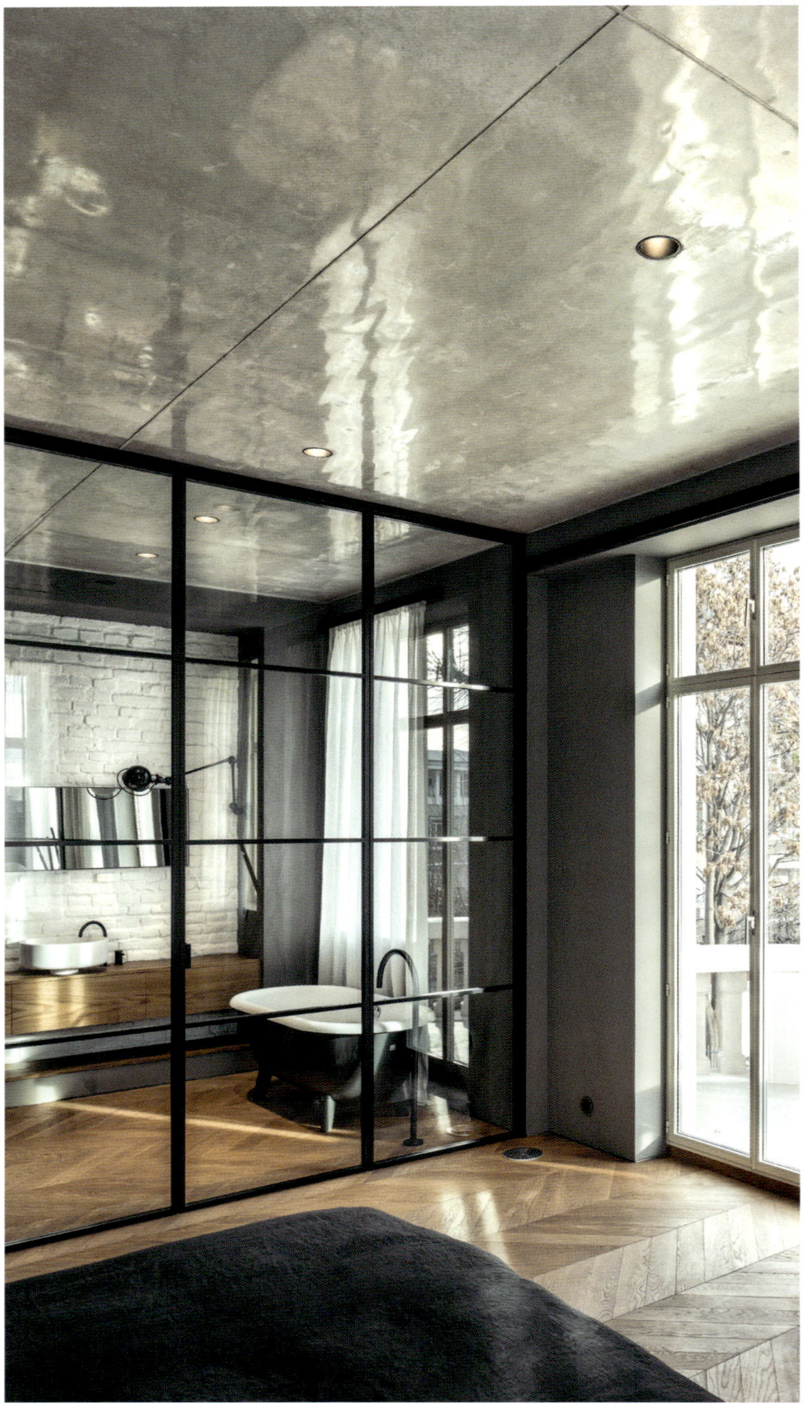

The glass wall separates the two settings without blocking the visual connection between them, making them seem larger than they are. This effect is further enhanced by the continuity provided throughout the space by the hardwood floor.

Die Glaswand trennt die beiden Wohnbereiche, ohne jedoch die visuelle Verbindung zwischen beiden zu verlieren, wodurch sie größer erscheinen. Der durchgehende Holzboden unterstreicht diese Wirkung noch mehr.

Le mur de verre sépare les deux espaces sans toutefois perdre la connexion visuelle entre eux, ce qui donne l'impression qu'ils sont plus vastes. Cet effet est d'autant plus accentué par l'utilisation continue du bois au sol.

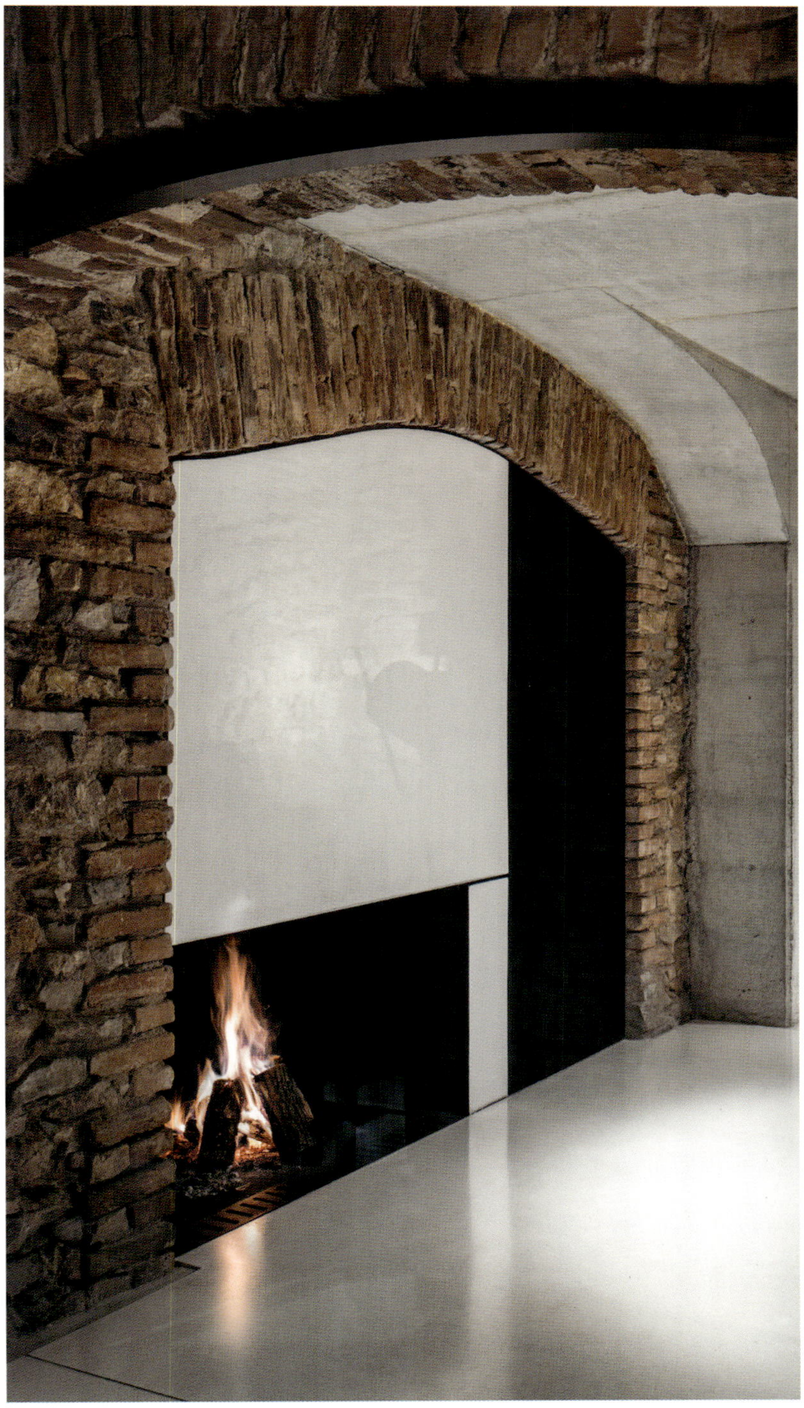

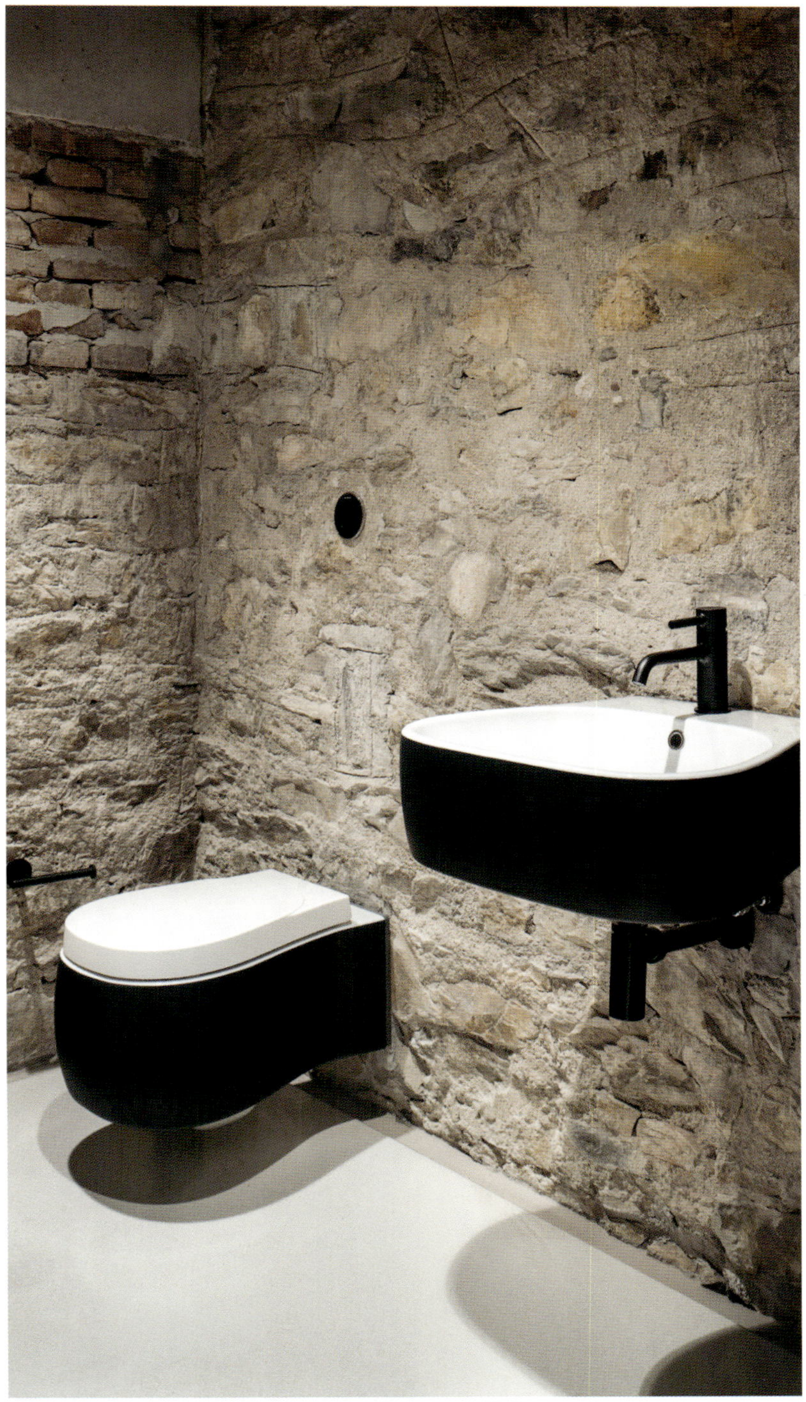

A bathroom filled with contrasts: the sensation of weightless fixtures against the solidity of the wall; textures that juxtapose smooth and polished with coarse and rough; old versus new.

Ein Bad voller Gegensätze: das Gefühl der Schwerelosigkeit der Toiletten kontrastiert mit der Festigkeit der Wand; die glatte, polierte mit der groben, rauen Textur; alt mit neu.

Une salle de bains pleine de contraste : la sensation de légèreté des sanitaires contre la solidité du mur ; la texture lisse et polie contre la texture rustre et rugueuse ; l'ancien contre le nouveau.

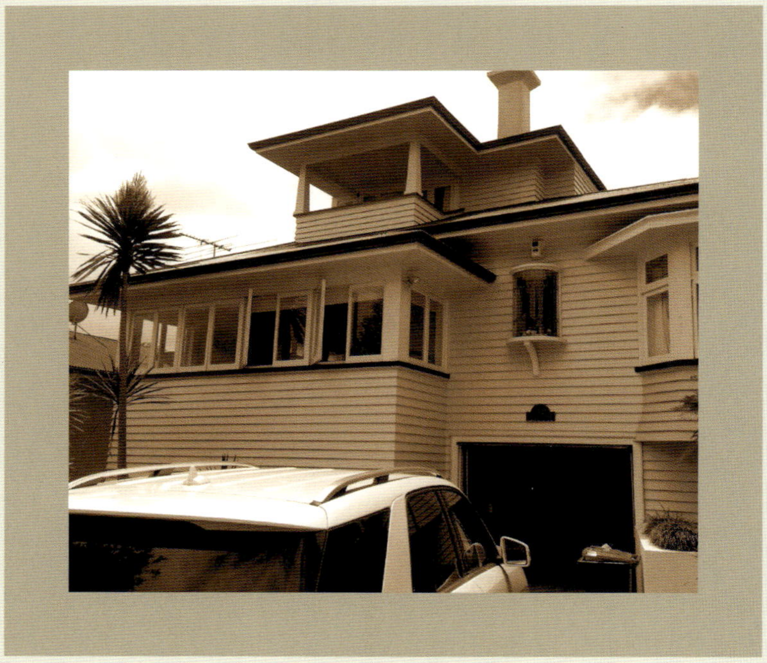

MARINE PARADE 2

DORRINGTON ATCHESON ARCHITECTS

348 m² | 3,746 sq. ft.

Auckland, New Zealand

Photos © **Emma-Jane Hetherington**

> Convert the small rooms into larger spaces

> Provide more light

> Expand the residence by excavating the basement, thus retaining the footprint

> Umwandlung der kleinen Zimmer in größere Räume

> Vermehrter Lichteinfall

> Vergrößern des Haus durch Ausheben des Souterrains bei Beibehaltung des Grundrisses

> Transformer les petites chambres en des espaces plus grands

> Apporter davantage de lumière

> Agrandir la maison en excavant le sous-sol et conserver ainsi son cachet

The renovation of this imposing but antiquated villa called for a spatial redistribution. The smaller rooms of the original structure were expanded to create larger and more coherent spaces. This opening lets in badly needed light and succeeds in taking maximum advantage of the impressive views.
The residence's main area was opened up, both in the direction of the sunlit western side with its swimming pool and sun porch as well as toward the more private greenery of the rear patio.
On the other hand, the entire area beneath the house was excavated, permitting a doubling of its capacity without increasing its apparent size. This new basement accommodates the garage, television room, cellar, laundry room, storage area, and guest suite.
The white-on-white interior color palette stands out against the concrete, glass, and steel elements, while the contemporary black additions subtly combine with the original villa's overall white color scheme.

Der Umbau dieser beeindruckenden, aber bereits älteren Villa erforderte eine Neuanordnung der Räume. Die ursprünglichen Zimmer waren viel kleiner und wurden nun erweitert, um größere und einheitlichere Räume zu erschaffen. Diese Öffnung sorgt für ein Mehr an Licht, und man erreicht außerdem so einen verbesserten Ausblick auf die Umgebung.
Der Hauptbereich des Hauses geht nun ebenso auf eine Veranda und ein Schwimmbad im sonnenbeschienen Westen wie auch auf den begrünten und privaten Abschnitt des rückwärtigen Hofes hinaus.
Zusätzlich wurde die gesamte Fläche des Hauses ausgehoben, wodurch man diese verdoppeln konnte, ohne die sichtbare Größe zu verändern. Dieses neue Souterrain bietet Platz für eine Garage, den Fernsehraum, den Weinkeller, die Waschküche, den Abstellraum und eine Suite für Gäste.
Die im Innenbereich verwendete Farbpalette von Weiß auf Weiß betont in Kombination mit den verwendeten Materialien Beton, Glas und Stahl die subtile Verbindung zwischen den neuen und modern wirkenden eingesetzten Elementen in Schwarz und dem allgemein weißen Farbschema der ursprünglichen Villa.

La rénovation de cette villa, imposante, mais tombée en désuétude, a nécessité la réorganisation de la répartition des espaces. Les pièces d'origine, plus petites, ont été agrandies afin de créer des espaces plus grands et cohérents. Cette ouverture a apporté la lumière indispensable, ce qui a permis de profiter au maximum de ses vues impressionnantes.
L'espace de vie de la maison a été ouvert tant du côté ensoleillé ouest, avec une piscine et un porche, que vers l'espace vert le plus intime de la cour arrière.
Par ailleurs, toute la maison a dû être excavée, permettant ainsi de doubler la superficie sans pour autant augmenter le volume apparent. Ce nouveau sous-sol peut accueillir le garage, la salle de TV, la cave, la buanderie, le débarras et une suite pour les invités.
Une palette intérieure de blanc ton sur ton souligne, avec l'utilisation des matériaux en béton, verre et acier, la subtile combinaison entre les nouvelles insertions contemporaines en noir et le jeu global de couleur blanche de la villa d'origine.

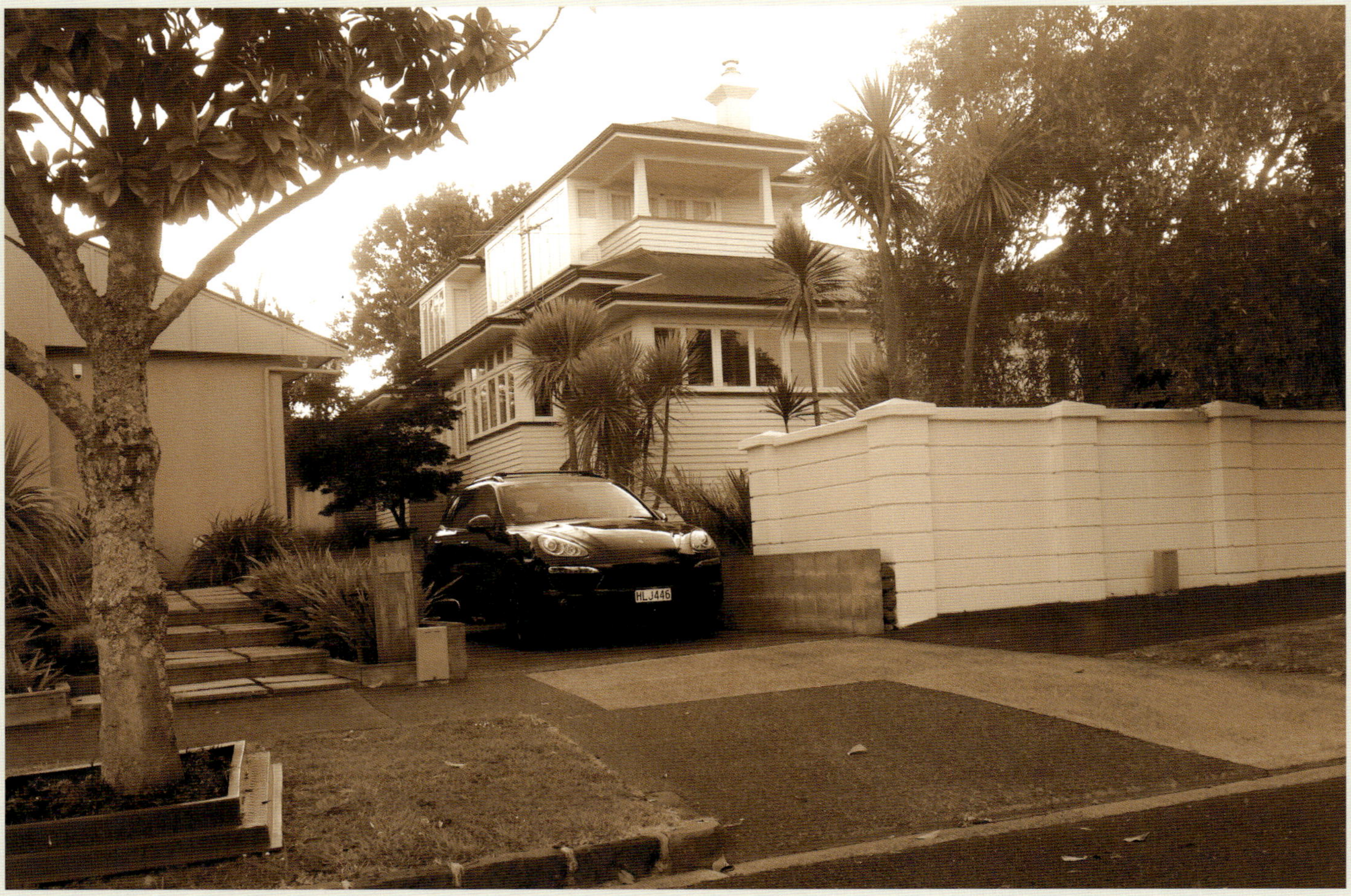
HLJ446

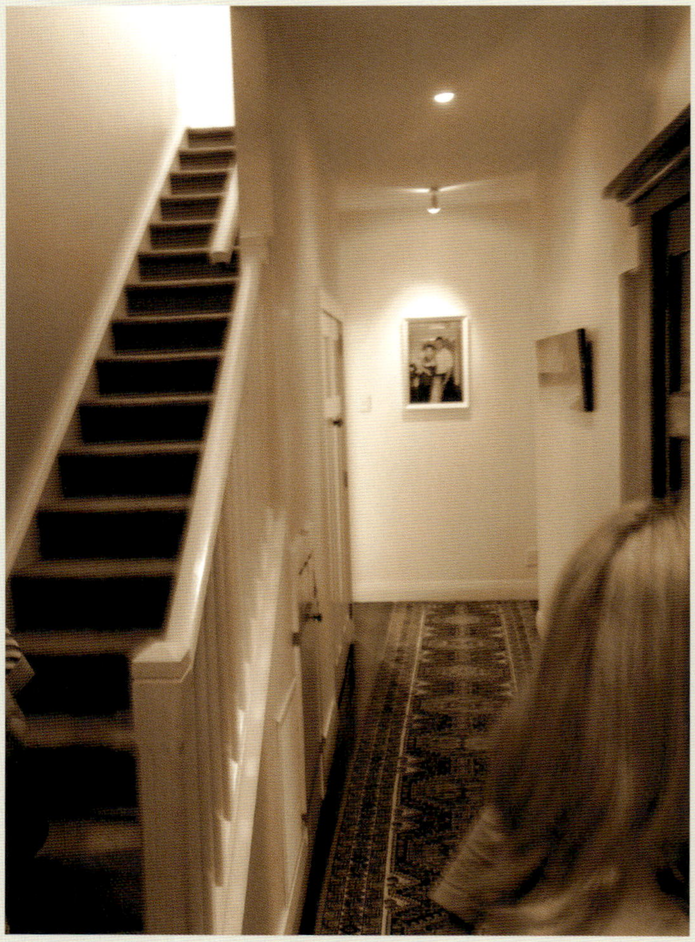

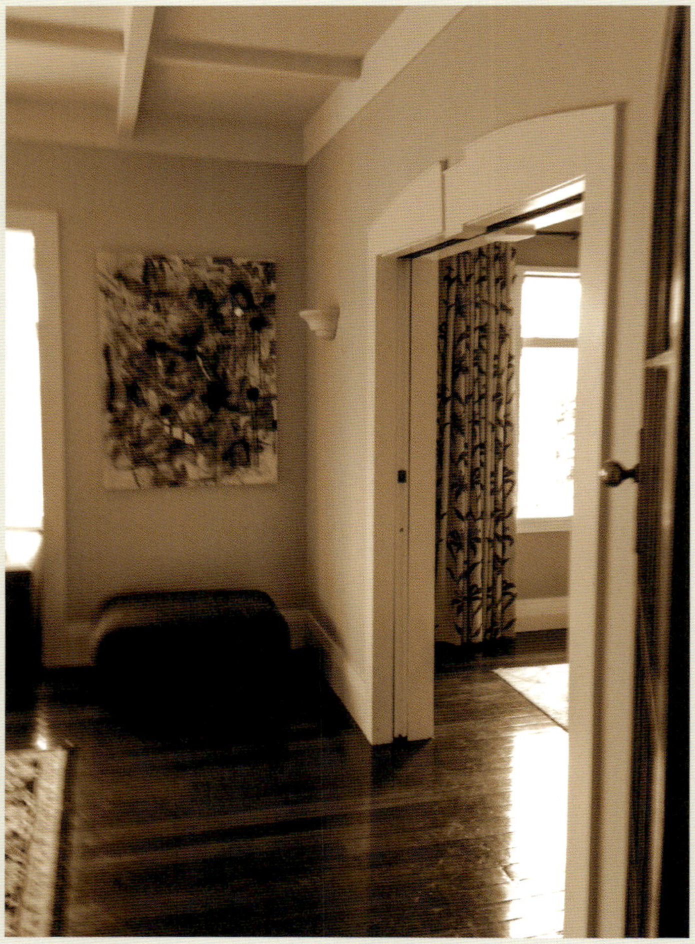

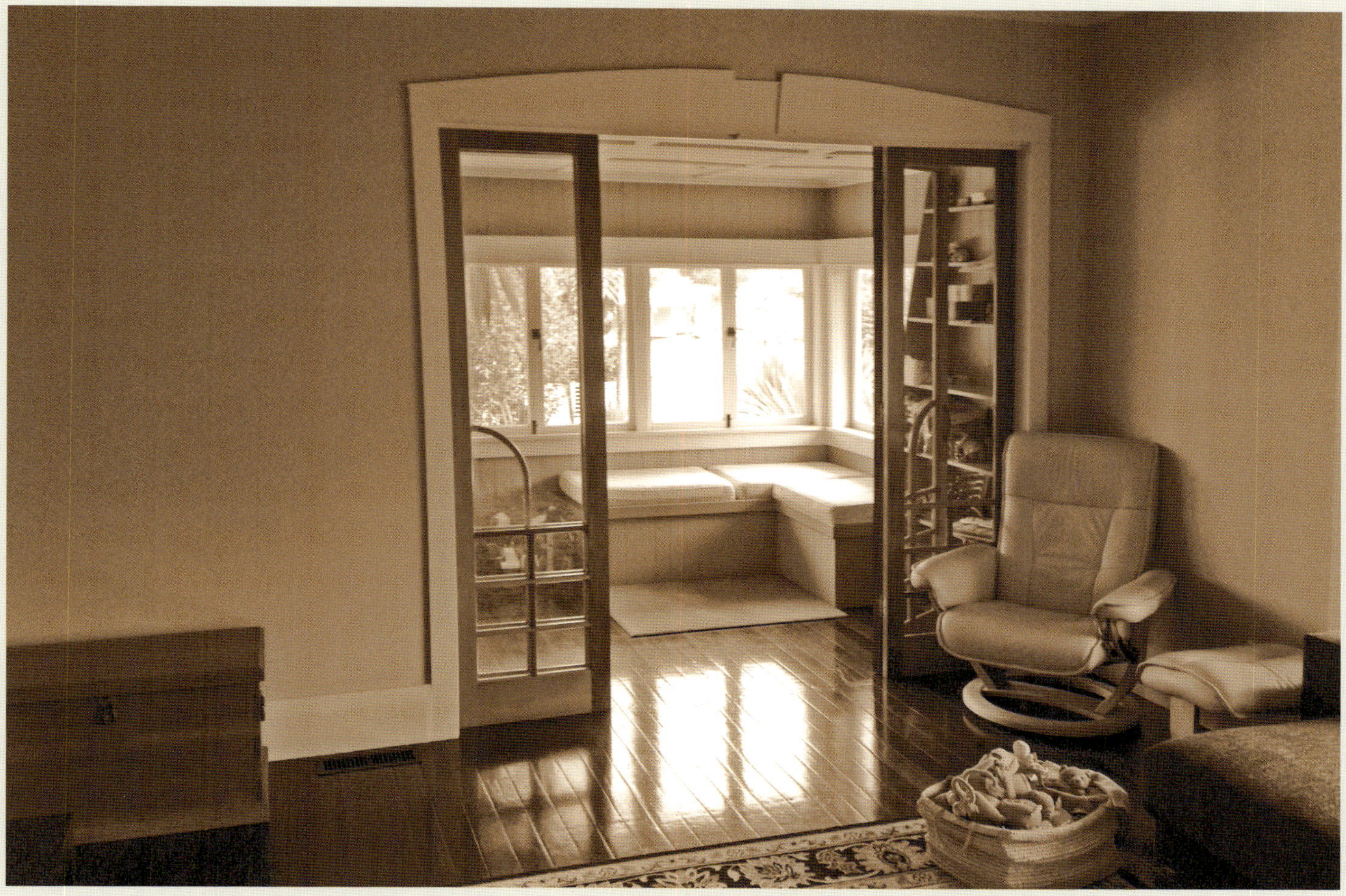

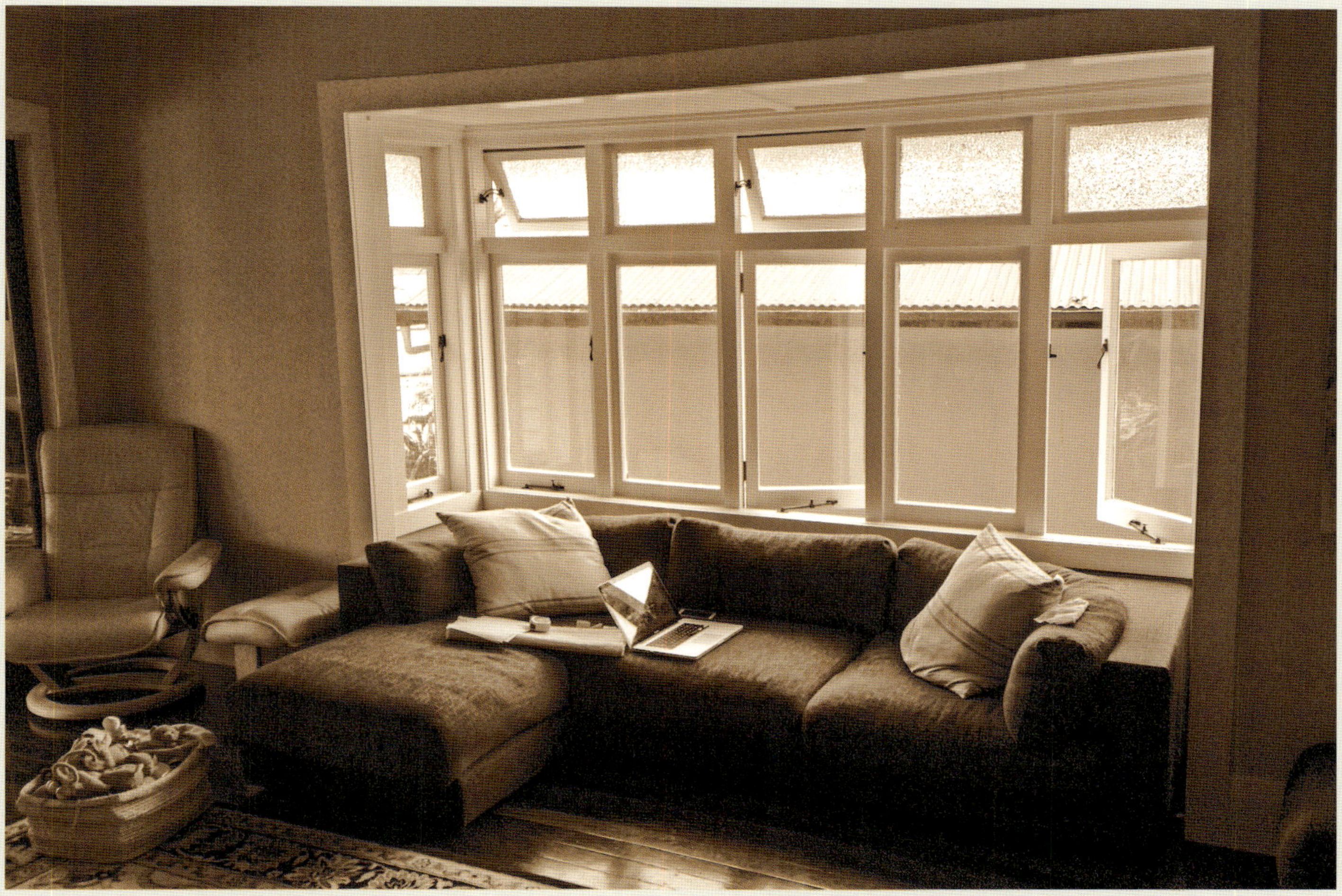

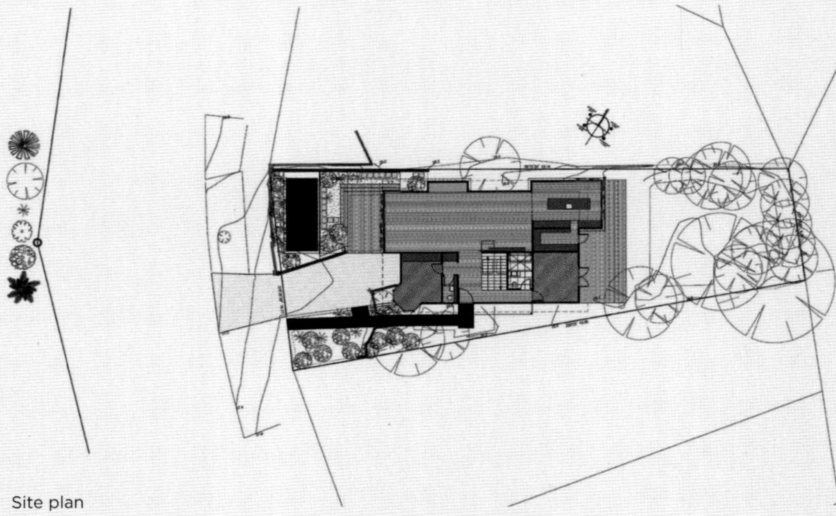

Site plan

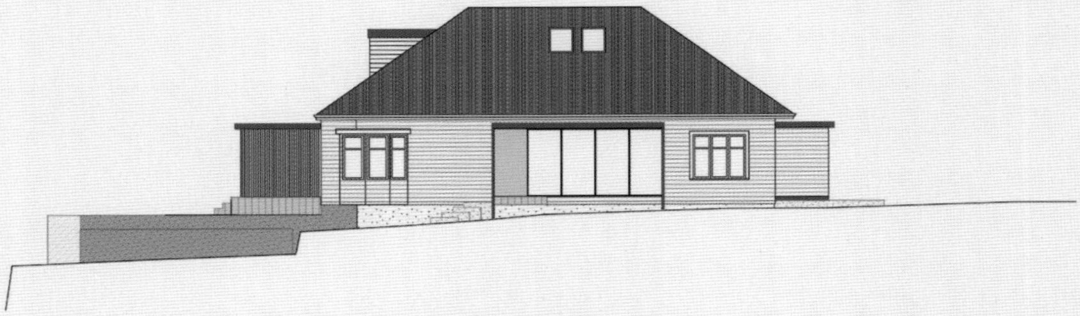

North elevation

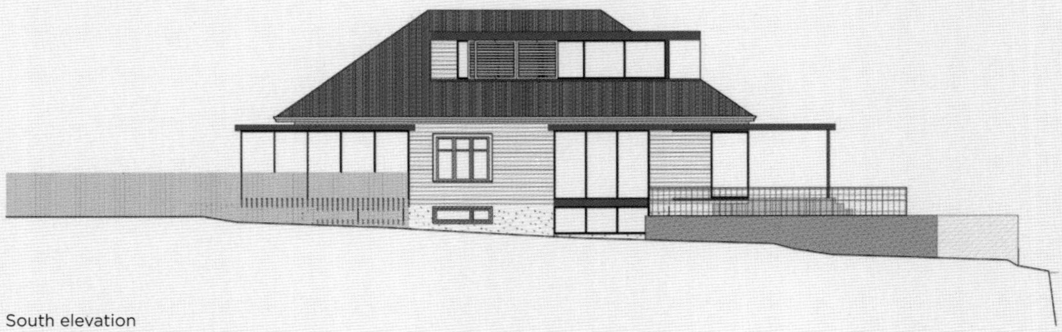

South elevation

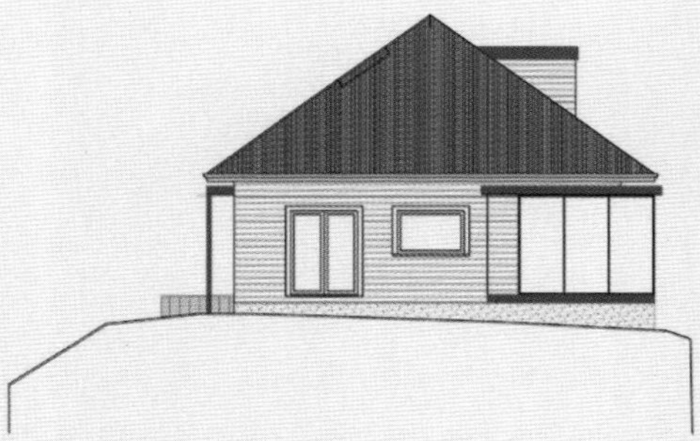

East elevation

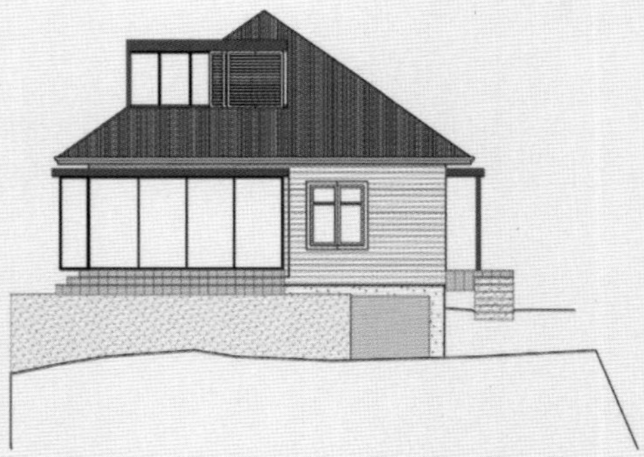

West elevation

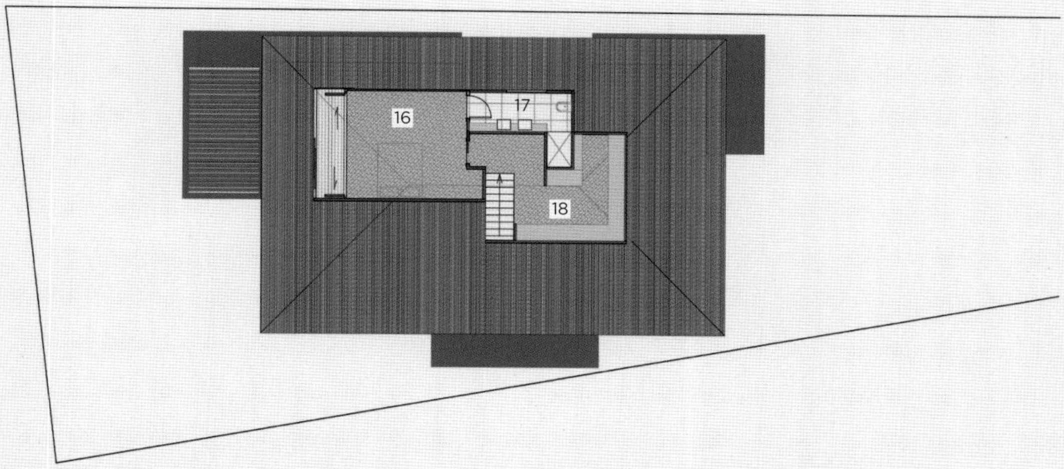

New first floor plan

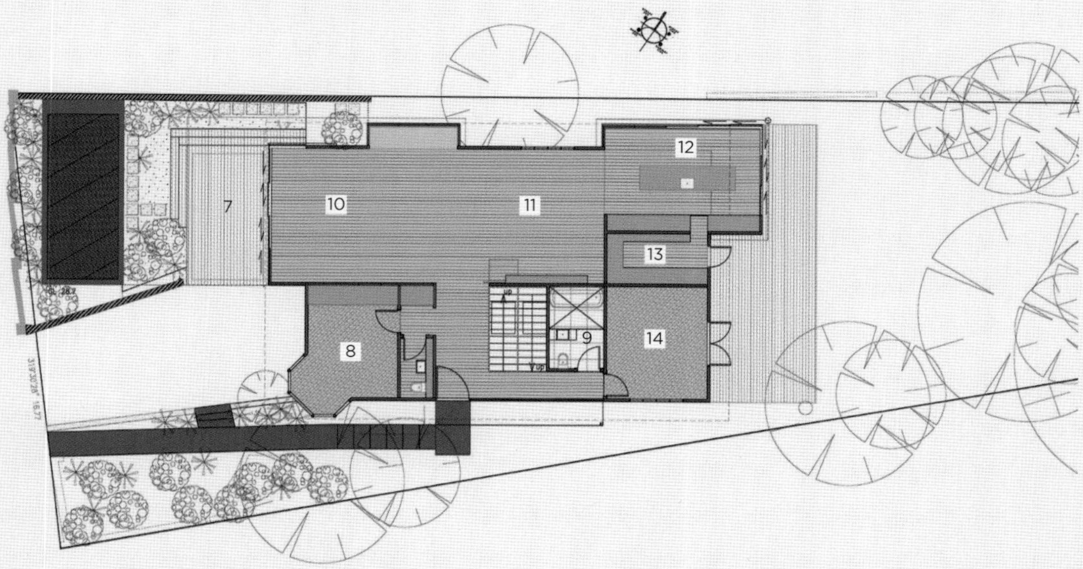

New ground floor plan

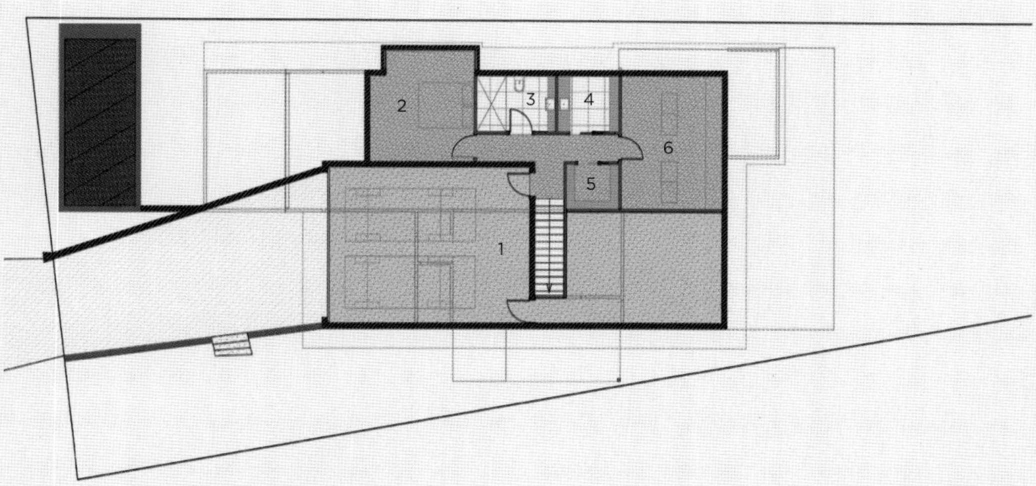

New basement floor plan

1. Garage
2. Bedroom 1
3. Bathroom
4. Laundry
5. Cellar
6. Media room
7. Deck
8. Bedroom 2
9. Powder room
10. Dining
11. Lounge
12. Kitchen
13. Pantry
14. Bedroom 3
15. Bathroom
16. Bedroom 4
17. En suite bathroom
18. Dressing room

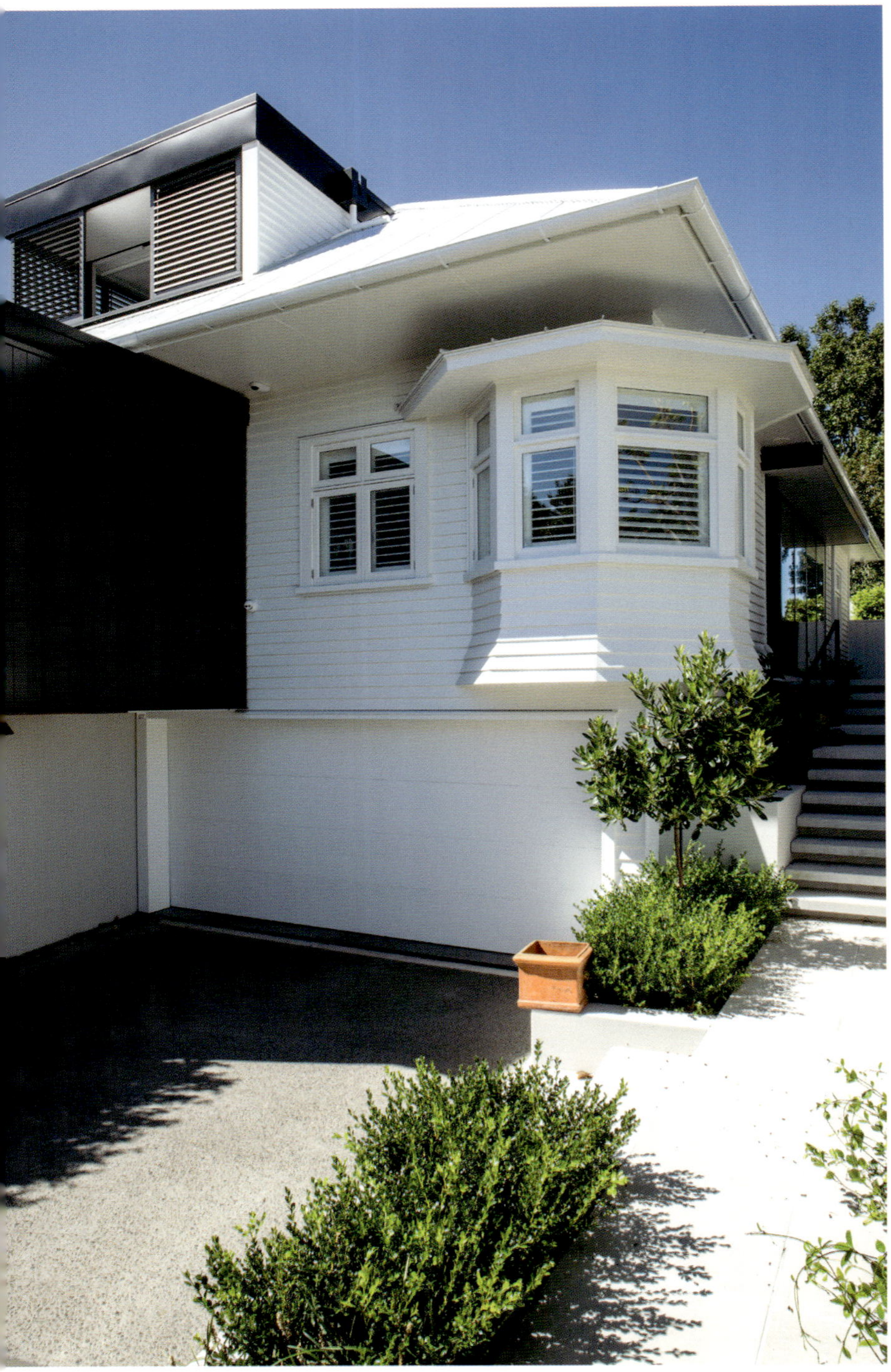

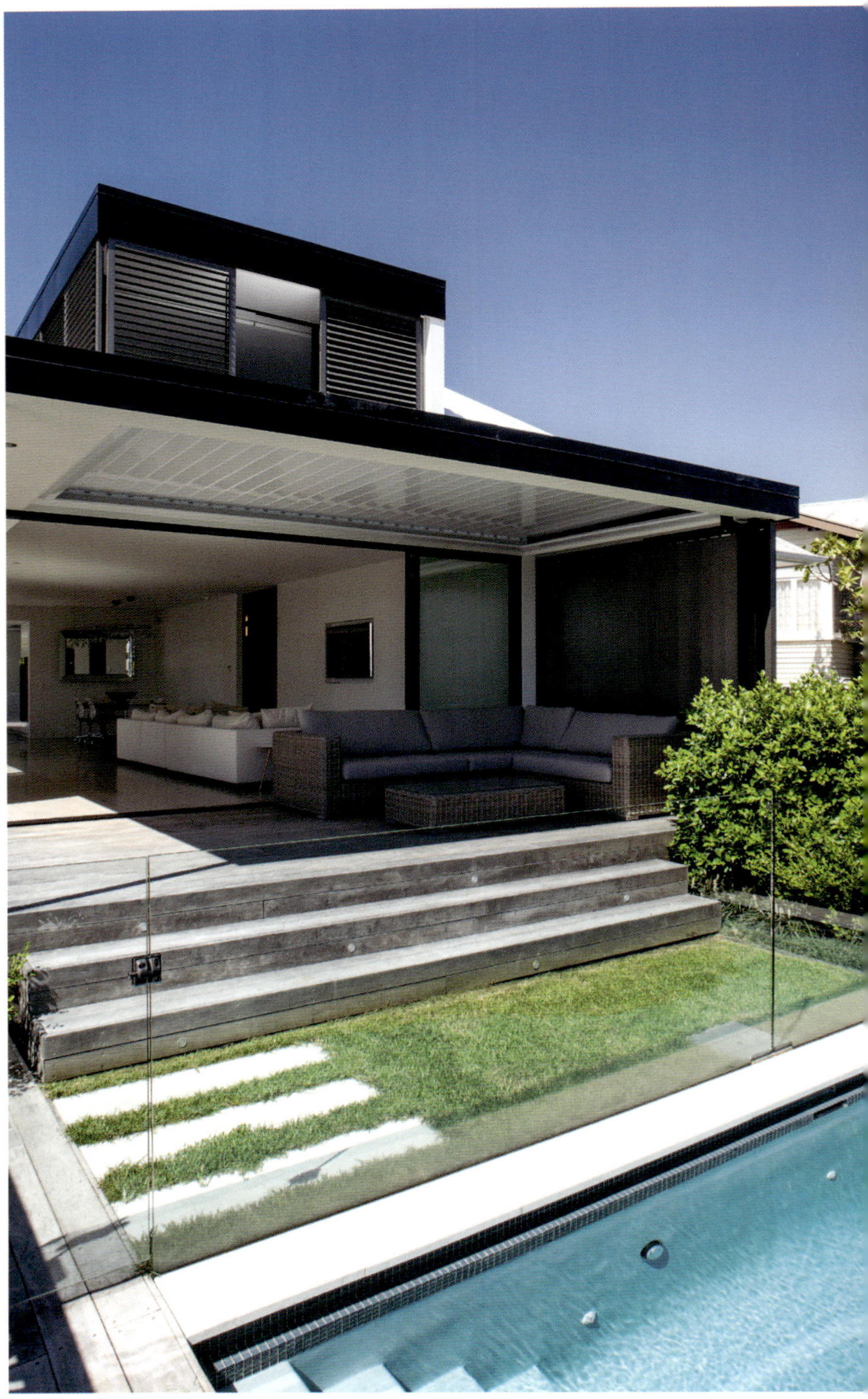

The addition of contemporary facade elements is shown in the black box volumes that work their way around the original white facade. Extensive use of glass produces an unrestricted connection to the outside.

Die hinzugefügten modernen Elemente an der Fassade werden vor allem durch zwei schwarze Anbauten in Kastenform betont, die sich durch die ursprünglich weiße Fassade hindurchzuschieben scheinen. Die großzügige Verwendung von Glas sorgt dafür, dass die Verbindung mit dem Außenbereich vollkommen ist.

Des éléments contemporains ont été mis en évidence sur la façade avec les volumes en forme de boîte noire qui ouvrent le passage au niveau de la façade blanche d'origine. Le recours intensif aux verres offre une connexion totale avec l'extérieur.

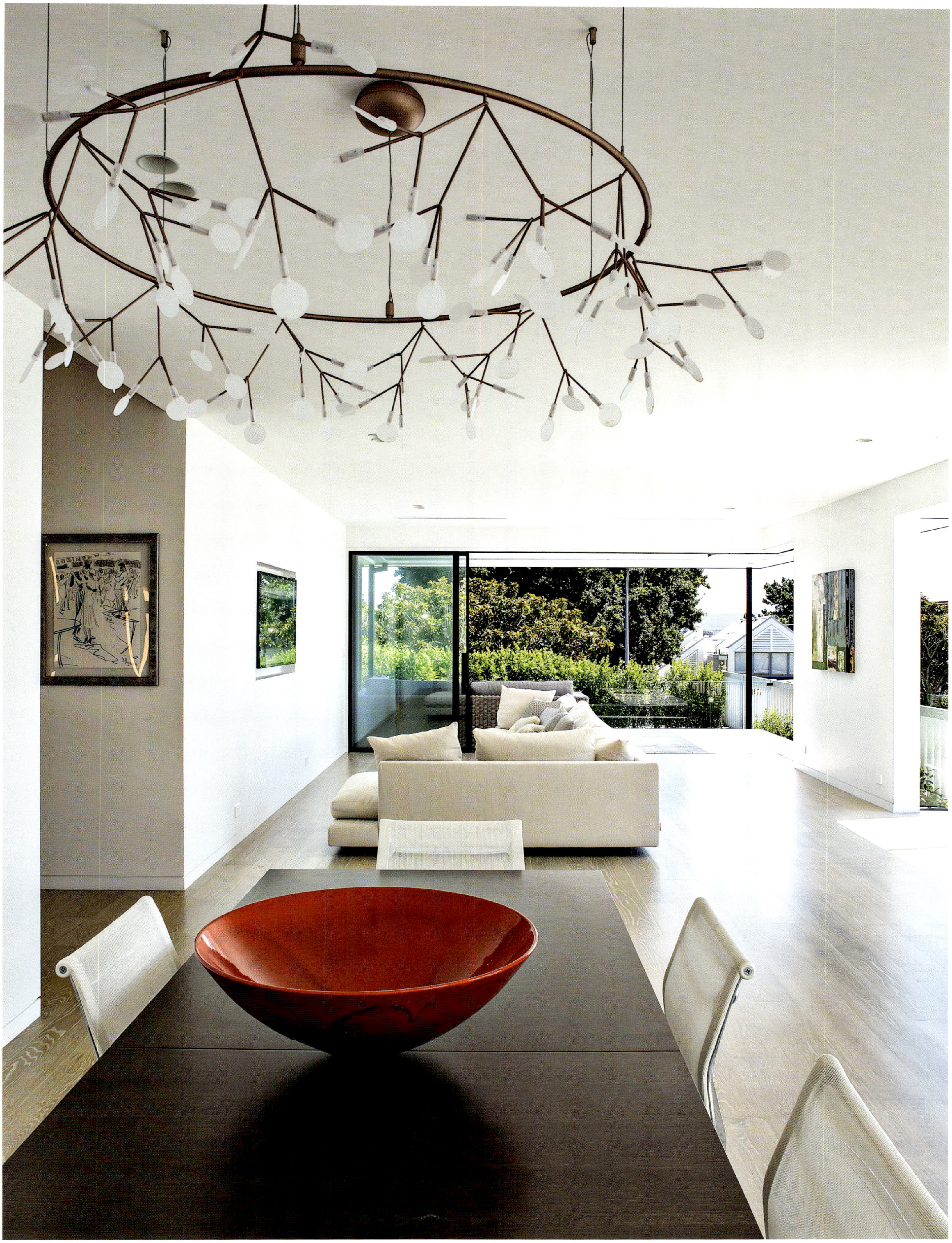

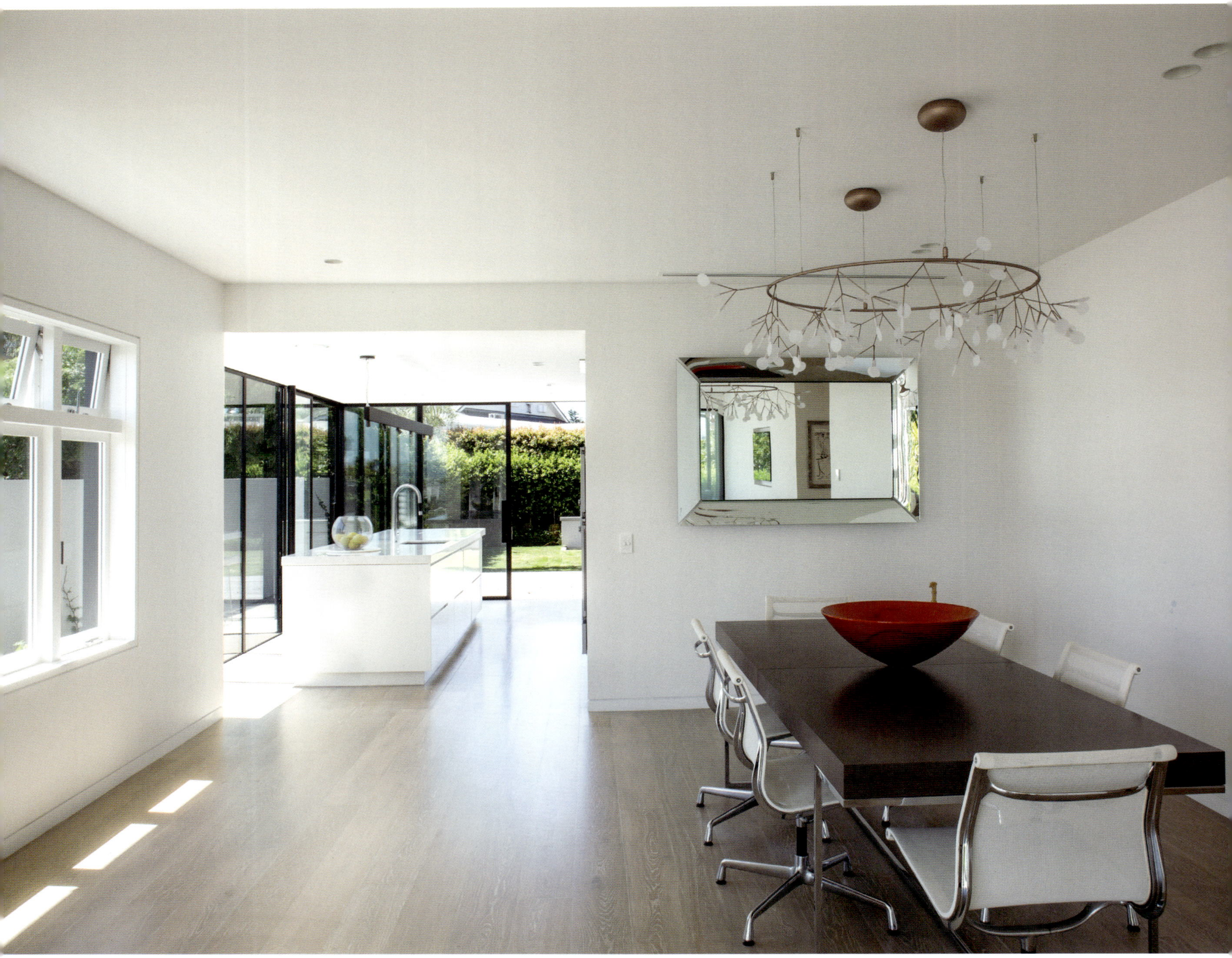

Steelwork has been used in the kitchen and living room to create a contemporary version of the traditional picture window. The contemporary steel details throughout the entire residence compensate for the heavier elements remaining from the original villa.

In der Küche und dem Wohnzimmer wurde mit Stahl gearbeitet, um eine moderne Variante des traditionellen Panoramafensters zu erschaffen. Die modernen Details aus Stahl im gesamten Gebäude gleichen die schwerfälligeren Elemente der ursprünglichen Villa aus.

La menuiserie en acier a été utilisée dans la cuisine et le séjour afin de conférer un aspect contemporain à la baie vitrée traditionnelle. Les détails contemporains en acier dans toute la maison comblent les détails plus pesants de la villa d'origine.

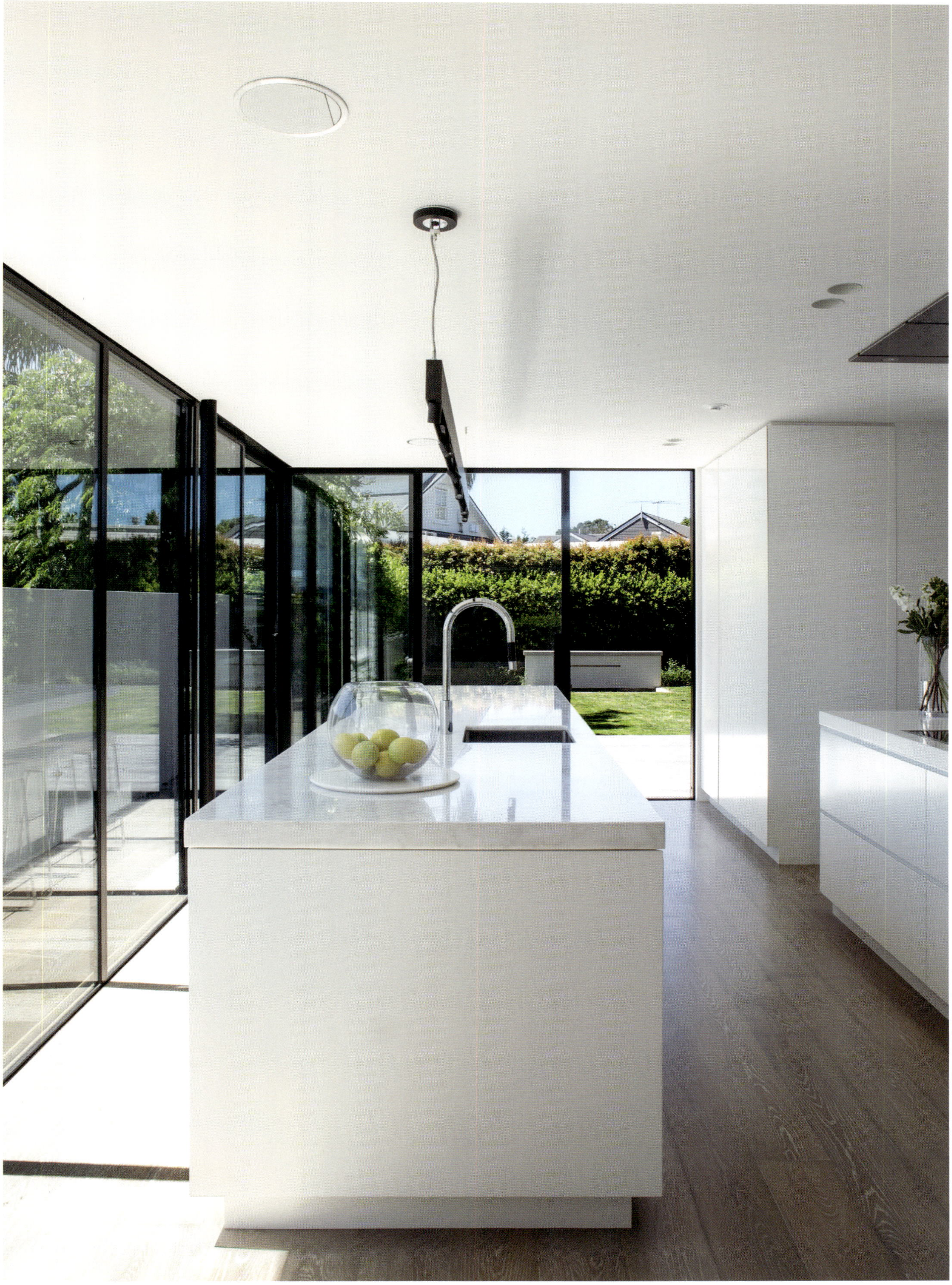

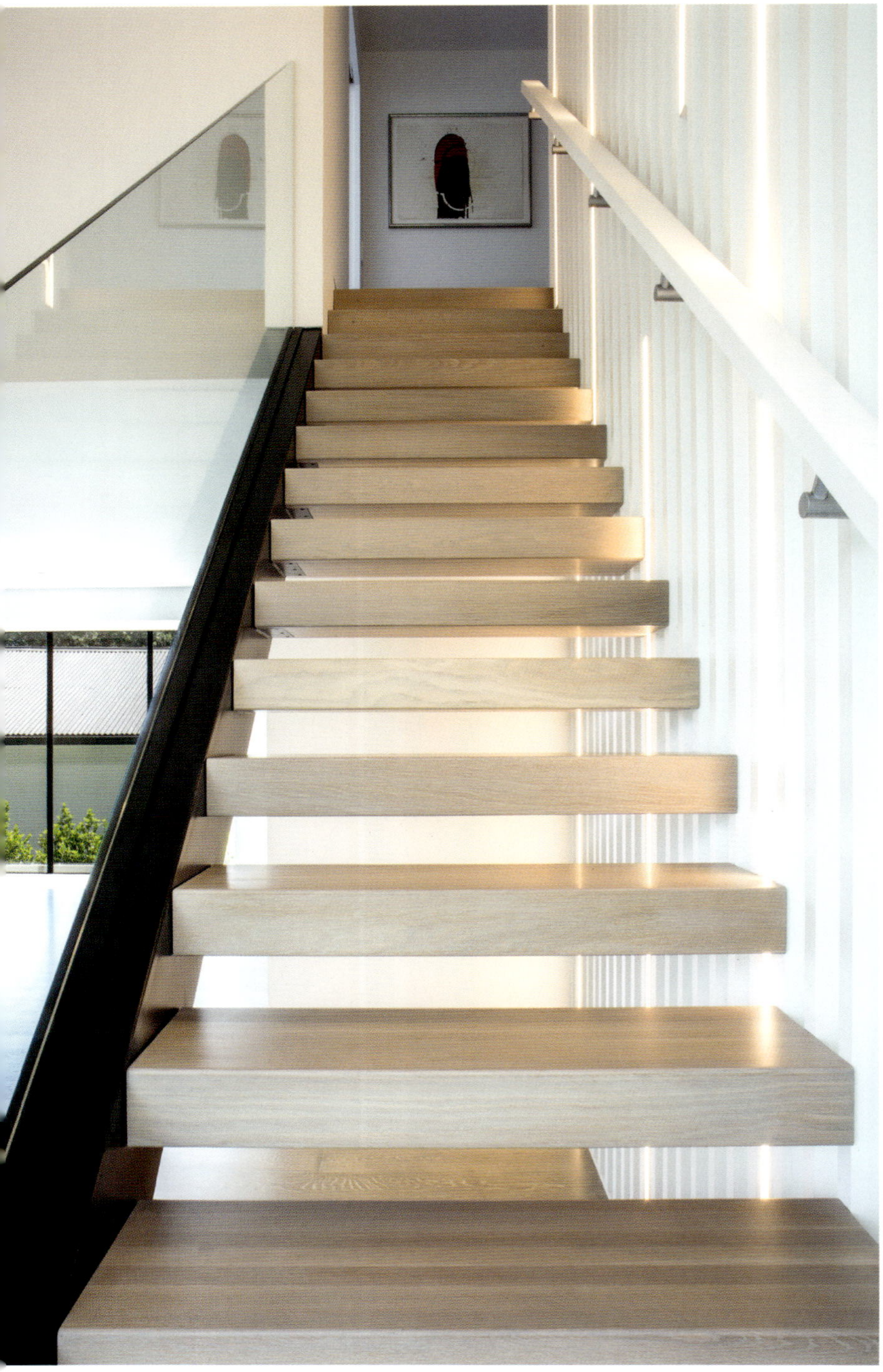

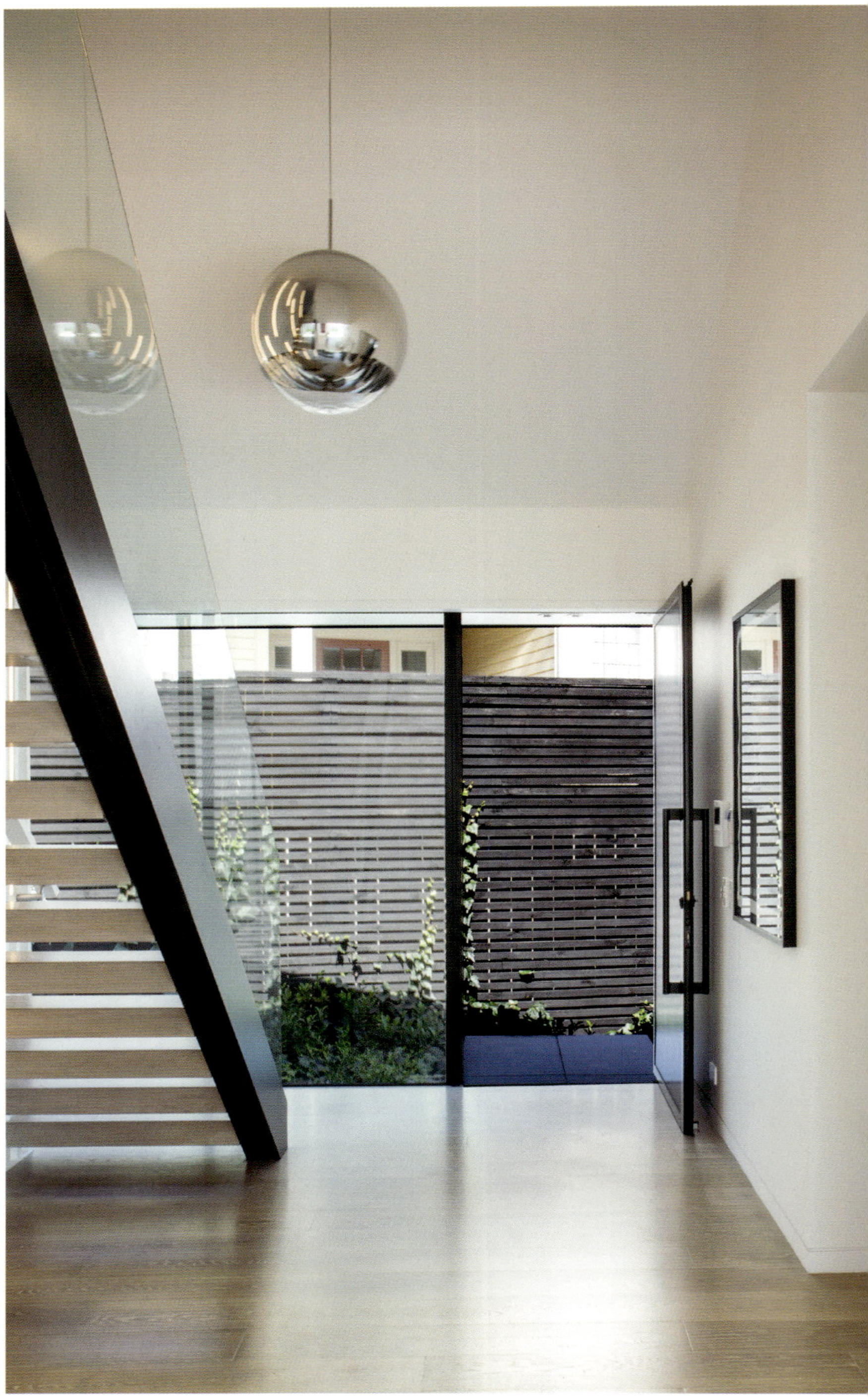

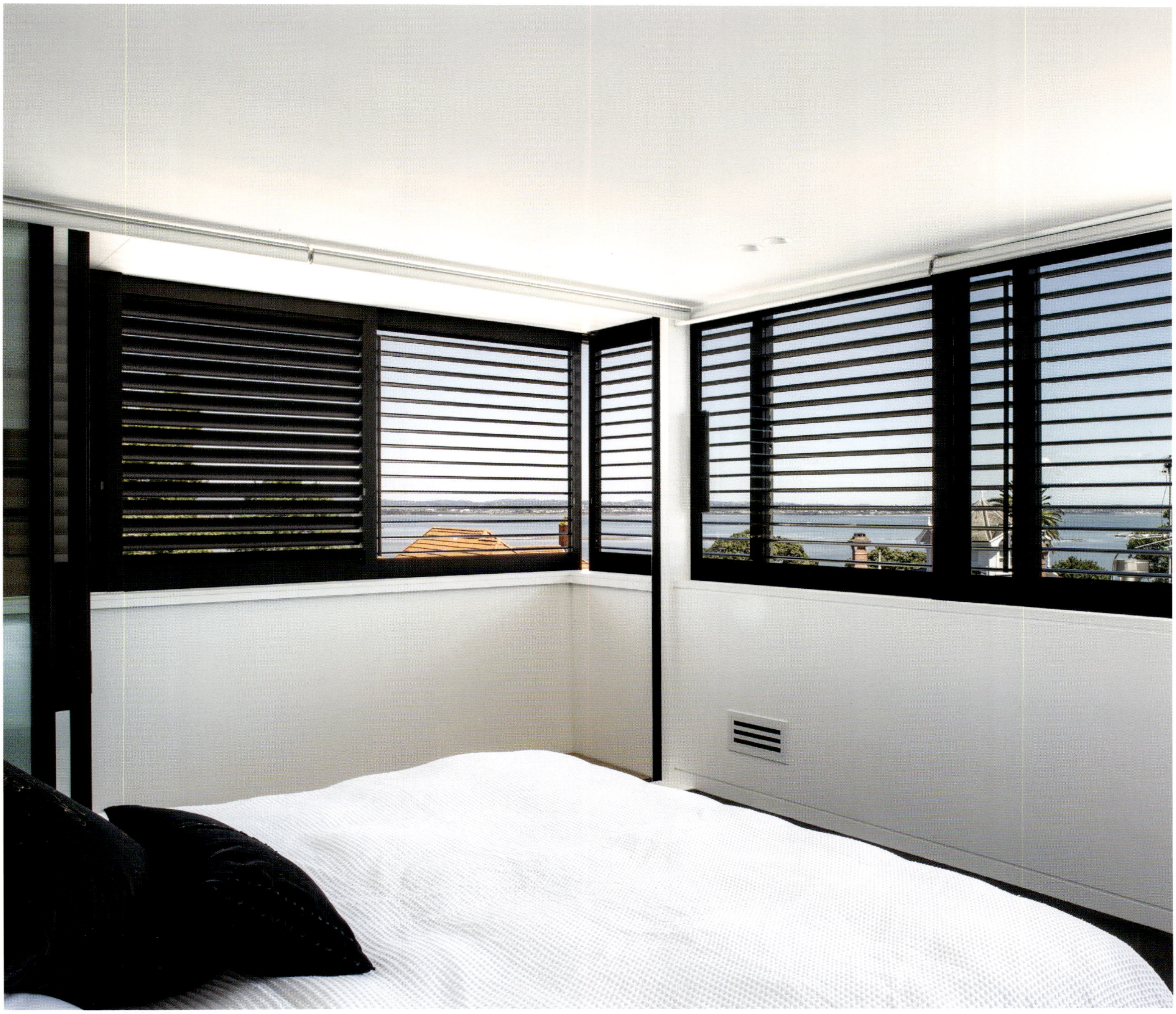

A subtle remodeling of the roofline made it possible to recover additional attic space to accommodate the master bedroom suite, the place for enjoying spectacular views.

Durch die dezente Neugestaltung des Daches wurde ein zusätzlicher Raum im Obergeschoss geschaffen, in dem das Hauptschlafzimmer untergebracht ist, von dem aus man eine spektakuläre Aussicht hat.

La restructuration de la ligne du plafond a permis de gagner un espace supplémentaire au dernier étage où se trouve la suite parentale qui offre une vue magnifique.

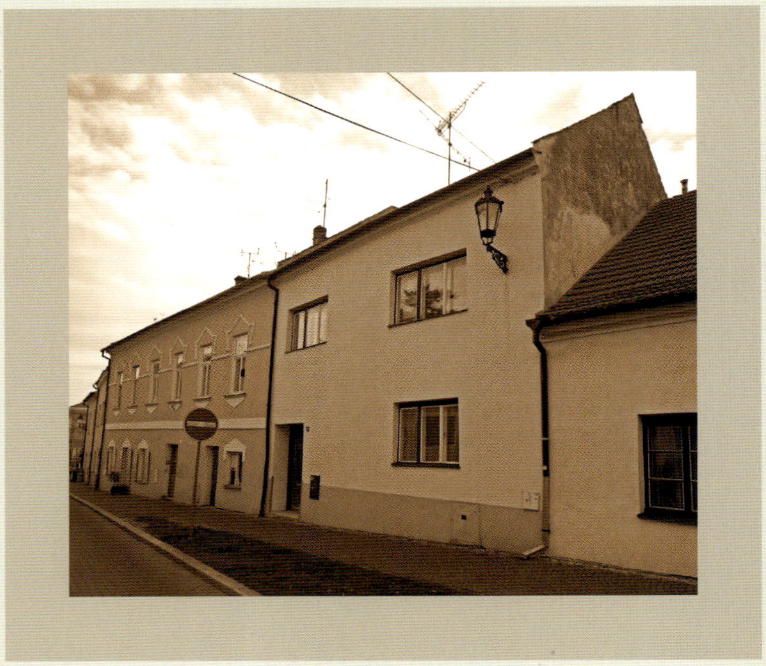

ŠTAJNHAUS

ORA

121 m² | 1,302 sq. ft.

Mikulov, Czech Republic

Photos © **Jakub Skokan, Martin Tůma / BoysPlayNice**

> Convert an old vacant town house into a guesthouse with shared courtyard, kitchen and the wine cellar

> Preserve the house as an organic unit

> Umbau eines alten leerstehenden Stadthauses in ein Gästehaus mit gemeinsamem Innenhof, Küche und Weinkeller

> Das Haus als organische Einheit bewahren

> Transformation d'une ancienne maison de ville vacante en maison d'amis avec cour commune, cuisine et cave à vin.

> Préserver la maison comme unité organique

The Štajnhaus has been a process rather than a project. This house, which is baroque-renaissance at its core, is situated at the foot of a hill dominated by a castle in the ancient Jewish neighborhood of Mikulov. It bears many scars inflicted throughout its existence and has been modified dozens of times. All this has altered the house beyond recognition. Through it all, however, it has remained picturesque, almost medieval.
The architect describes finding a "conglomeration" of stones. As more and more layers, spaces, and surprising details were revealed, more revisions and alterations were required, and these circumstances persisted up to the completion of the work.
The architects' original task was limited to designing the interiors. As work progressed, however, they realized that the structure's interior and exterior could not be addressed separately. This insight becomes manifest when the incredible result is observed: space and form interact, contributing in this way to the creation of an indivisible unity.

Das Štajnhaus war kein Projekt, sondern ein Prozess. Dieses Barock-Renaissance-Haus befindet sich am Fuße der Anhöhe einer Burg im alten jüdischen Viertel Mikulov. Im Laufe seiner Existenz hat es viele Narben erlitten und Dutzende von Umbauten und Operationen durchlaufen. All dies hat das Haus bis zur Unkenntlichkeit verändert. Dennoch hat es seine fast mittelalterliche malerische Schönheit bewahrt.
Wie der Architekt beschreibt, fand sich eine „Anhäufung" aus Steinen. Je mehr überraschende Schichten, Räume und Umstände entdeckt wurden, desto mehr Überarbeitungen und Änderungen mussten vorgenommen werden; und das dauerte tatsächlich bis zum Ende der Umsetzung.
Ursprünglich ging es bei der Arbeit der Architekten nur um die Innenraumgestaltung. Nach und nach stellten sie jedoch fest, dass Innen- und Außenbereich nicht getrennt voneinander betrachtet werden konnten. Dies wird deutlich, wenn man das unglaubliche Ergebnis sieht: Raum und Formen neigen dazu, sich zu vermischen, um eine unteilbare Einheit zu schaffen.

Le Štajnhaus ne fut pas un projet, le Štajnhaus a été un processus. Cette maison avec un cœur de style baroque et de la Renaissance se trouve au pied de la colline d'un château, dans l'ancien quartier juif de Mikulov. Le bâtiment a souffert de nombreuses cicatrices au cours de son existence, subissant des dizaines de reconstructions et de travaux. Tout ceci a altéré la maison au-delà de la reconnaissance. Malgré cela, elle a conservé son caractère pittoresque presque médiéval.
Comme le décrit l'architecte, un « conglomérat » de pierres a été découvert. Plus de couches, d'espaces, de situations surprenantes étaient découverts, plus il fallait réaliser des travaux de vérification et de modification. Ceci a duré, de fait, jusqu'à la fin de la réalisation des travaux.
À l'origine, le travail des architectes consistait uniquement à concevoir la décoration d'intérieur. Mais, au fil du projet, ils se sont rendu compte que l'intérieur et l'extérieur ne pouvaient pas être étudiés séparément. Ceci est devenu évident en voyant l'incroyable résultat : l'espace et les formes tendent à se mélanger pour ne créer qu'une seule et même unité indivisible.

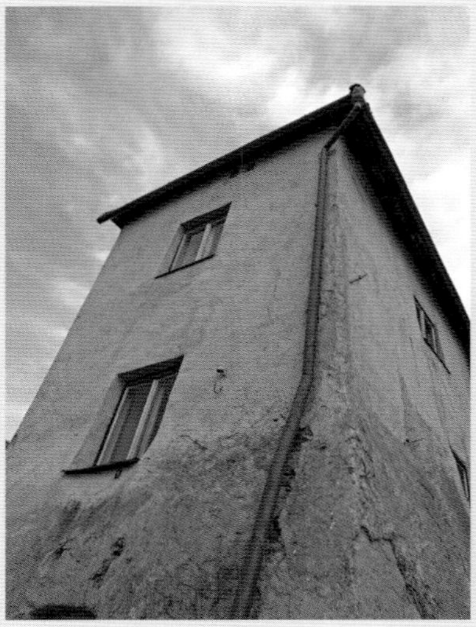
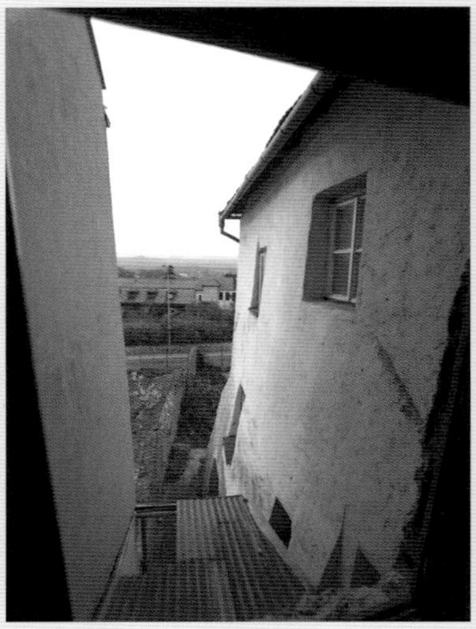
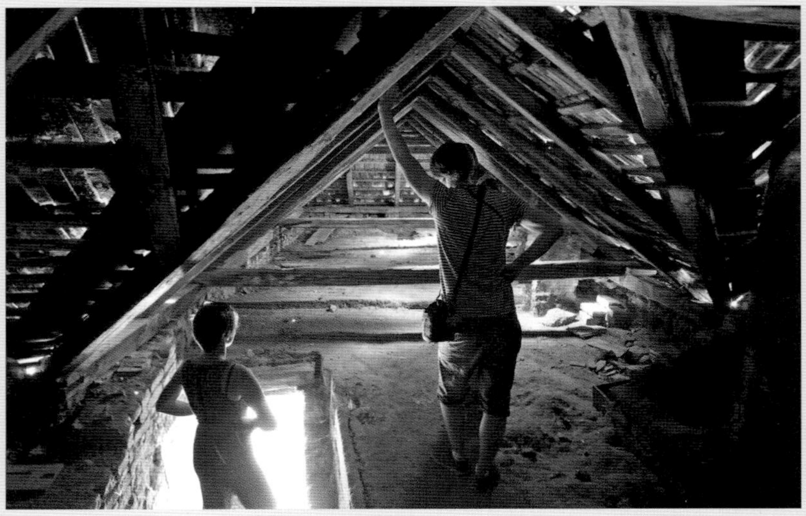
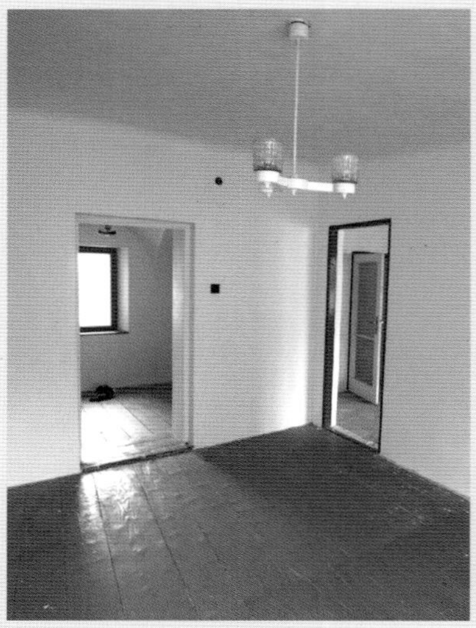
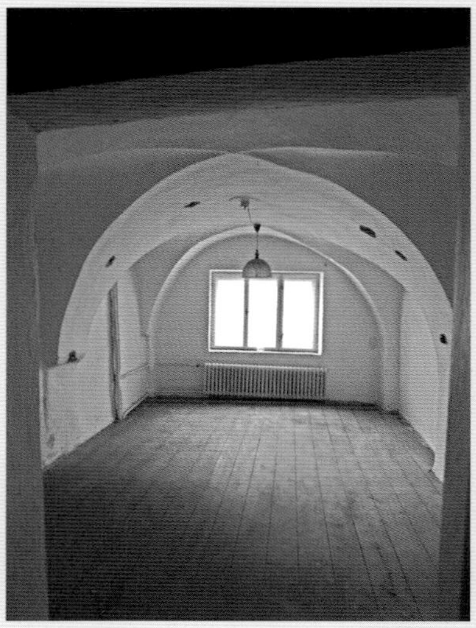
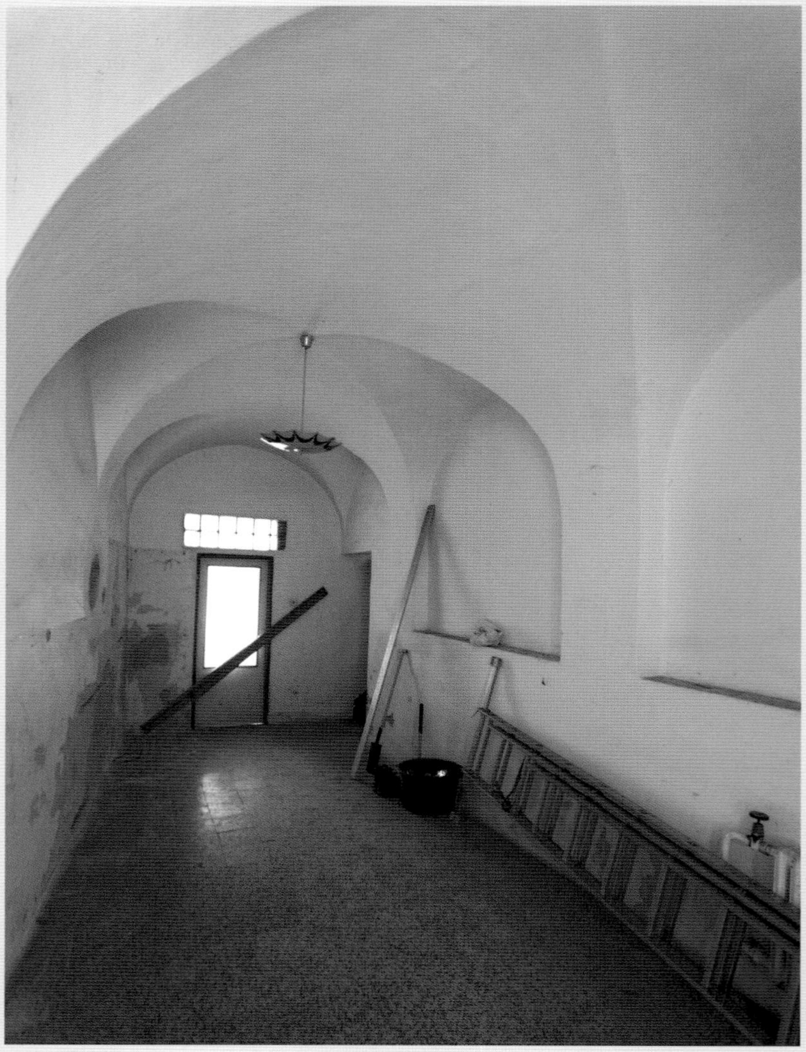
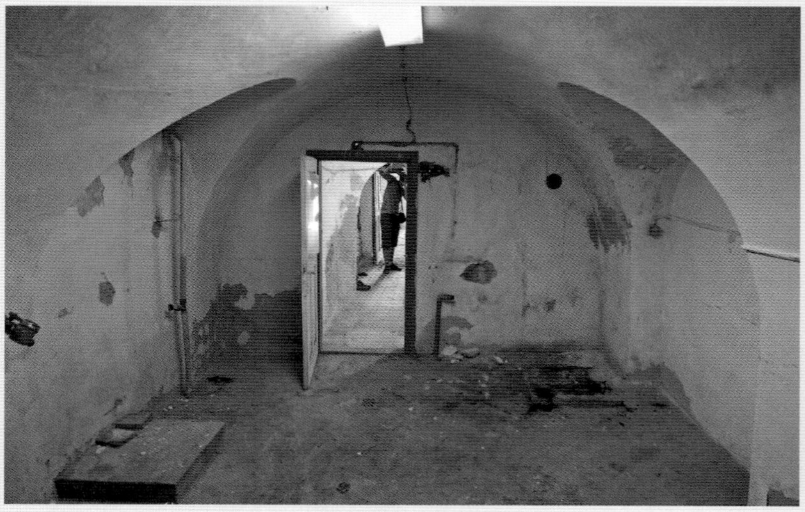
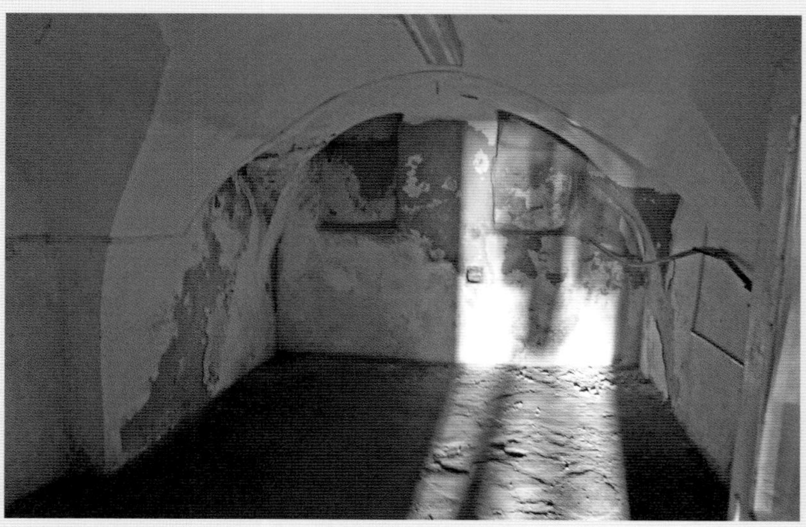
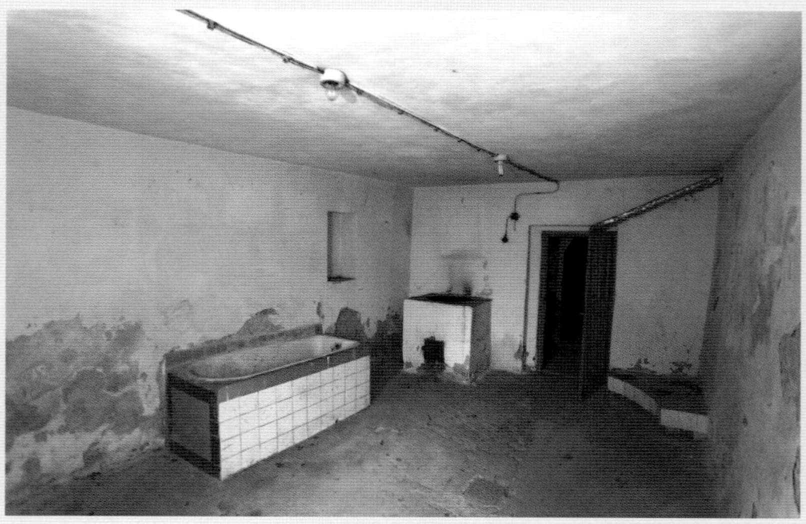

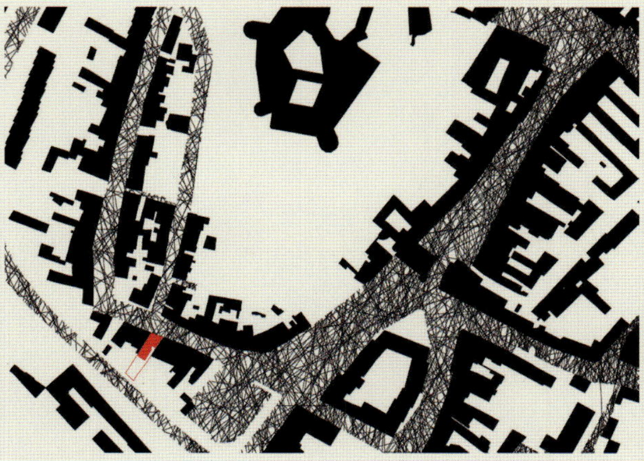

Location plan

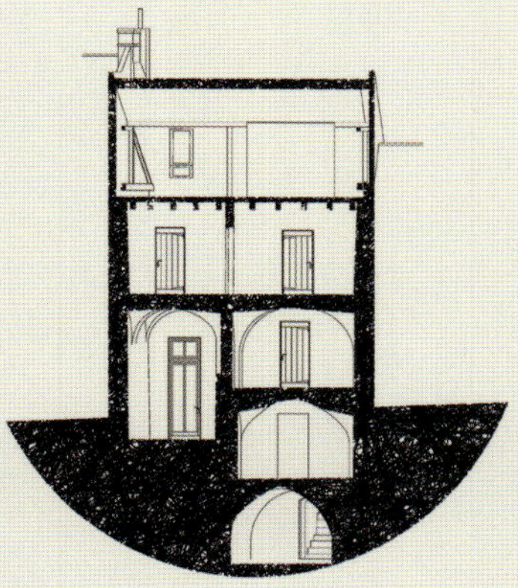

Cross section

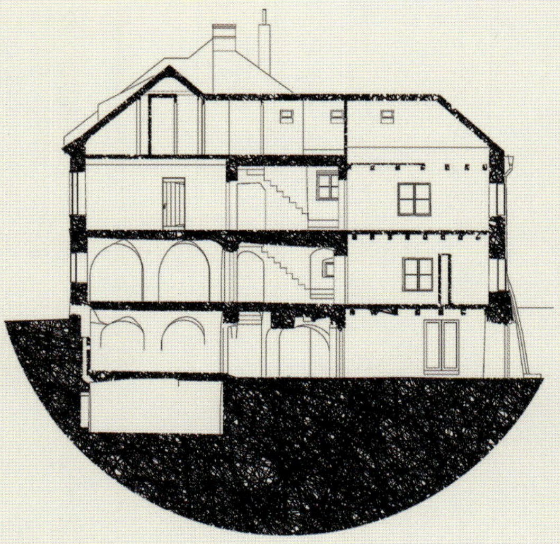

Longitudinal section

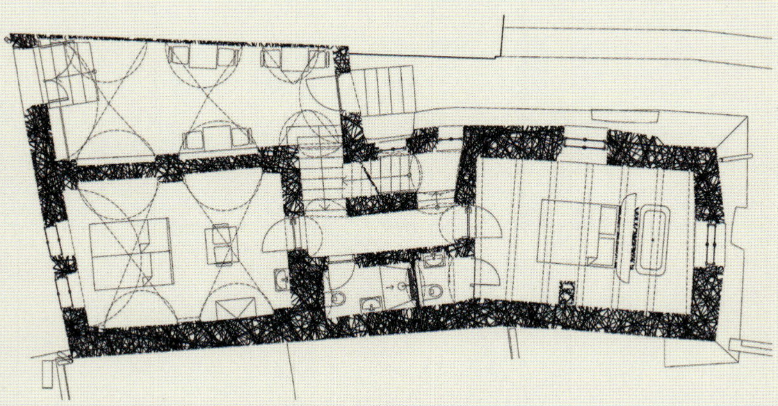

Ground floor plan

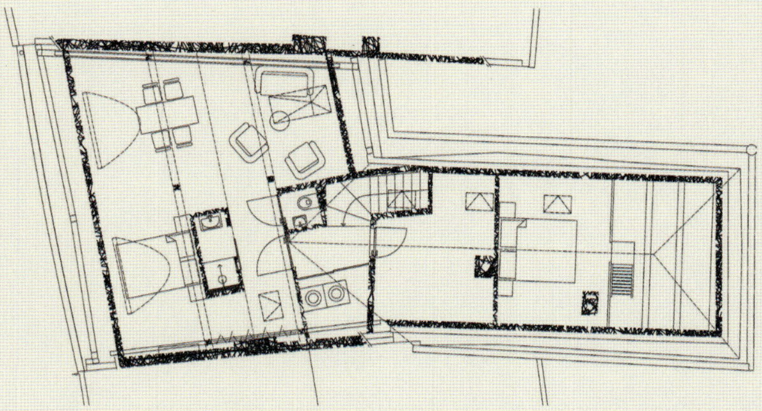

Second floor plan

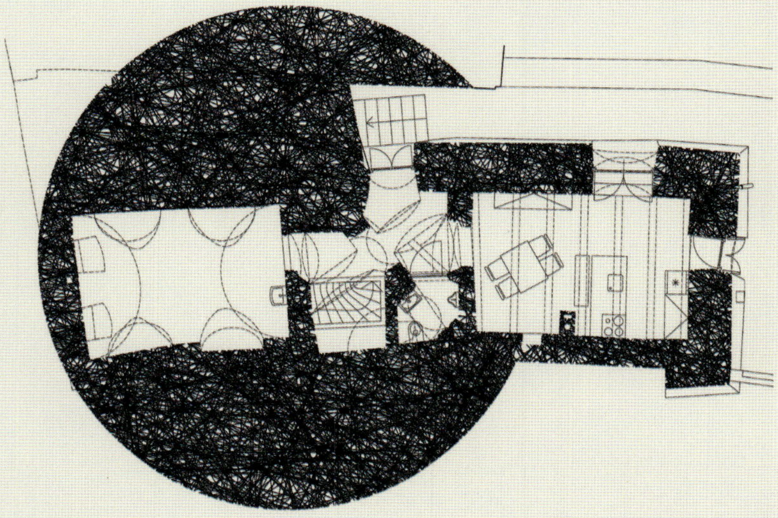

Basement plan

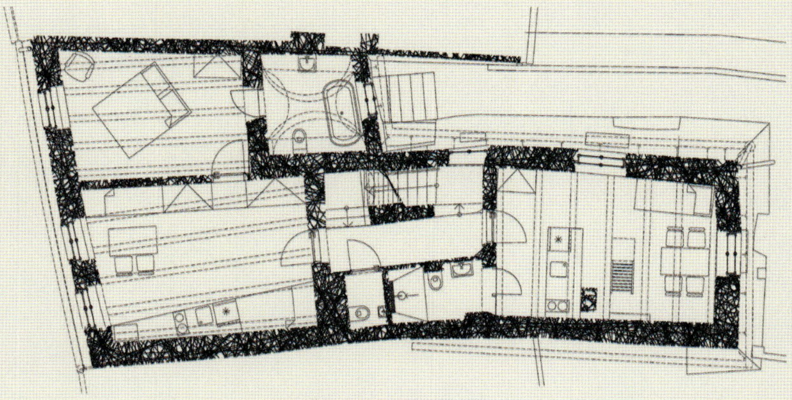

First floor plan

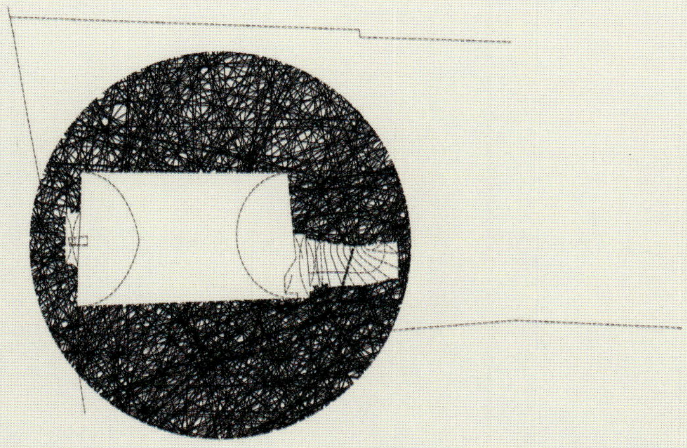

Cellar

Since the building is situated in a historic district, the greatest possible consideration has been shown for its original facade, including walls, roof, and openings, with renovations limited to what was absolutely necessary.

Da das Haus in einem historischen Viertel steht, wurde die ursprüngliche Fassade – Wände, Dach und Fensteröffnungen – bestmöglich geschützt, indem nur die unbedingt notwendigen Verbesserungen vorgenommen wurden.

Comme la maison se trouvait dans un quartier historique, il fallait respecter au maximum sa façade d'origine : des murs, une toiture et des ouvertures, apportant uniquement les améliorations strictement nécessaires.

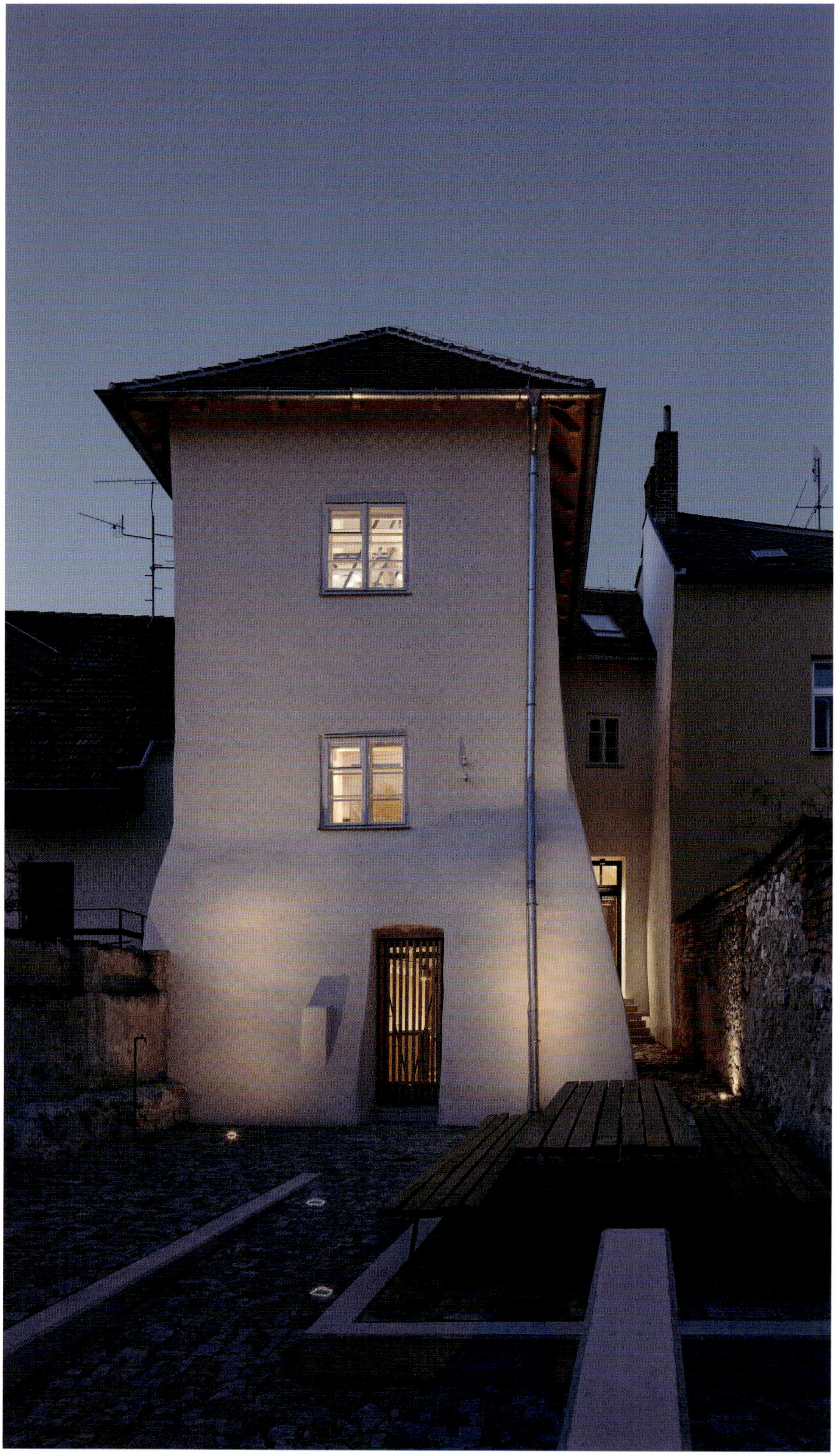

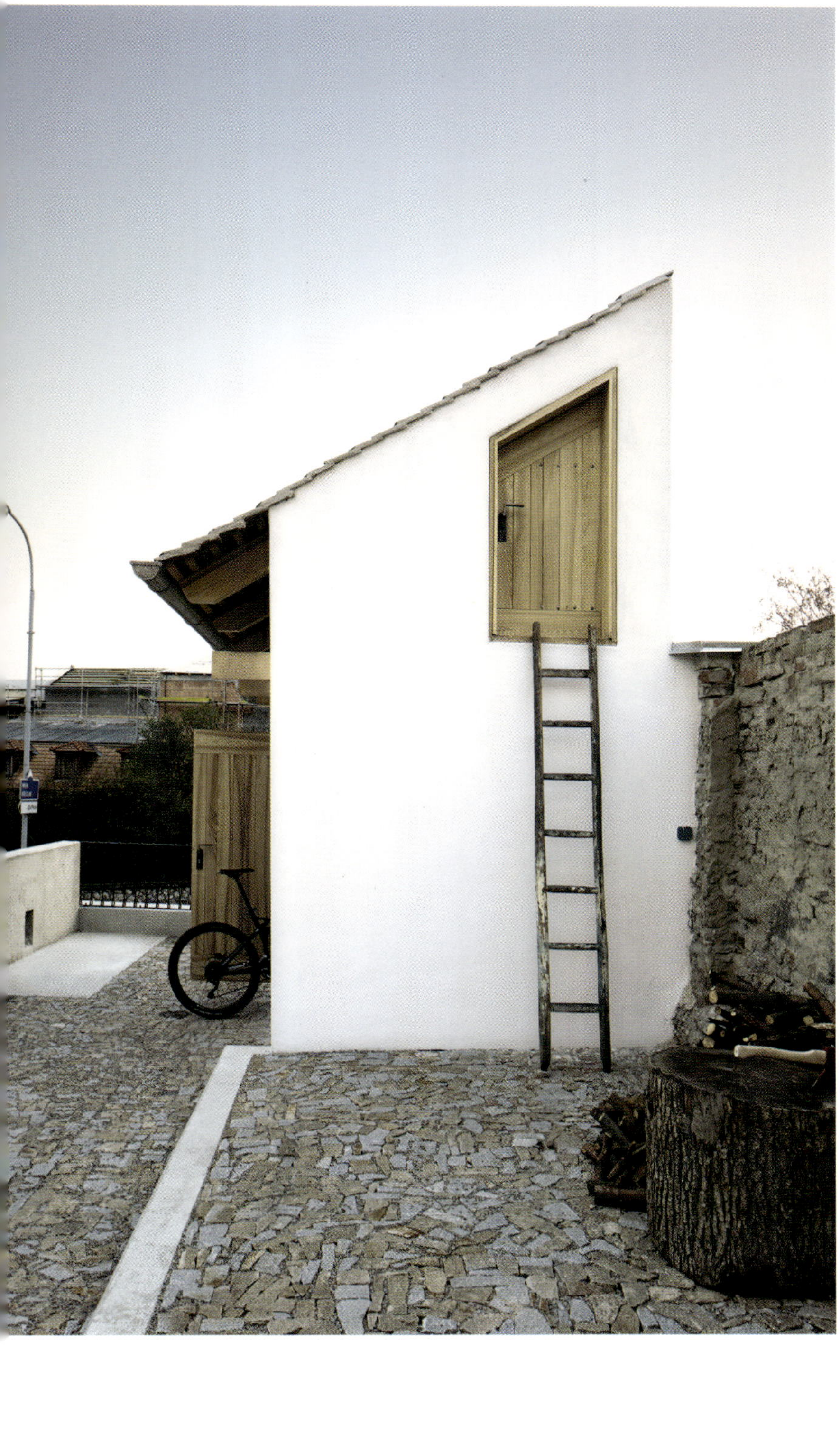

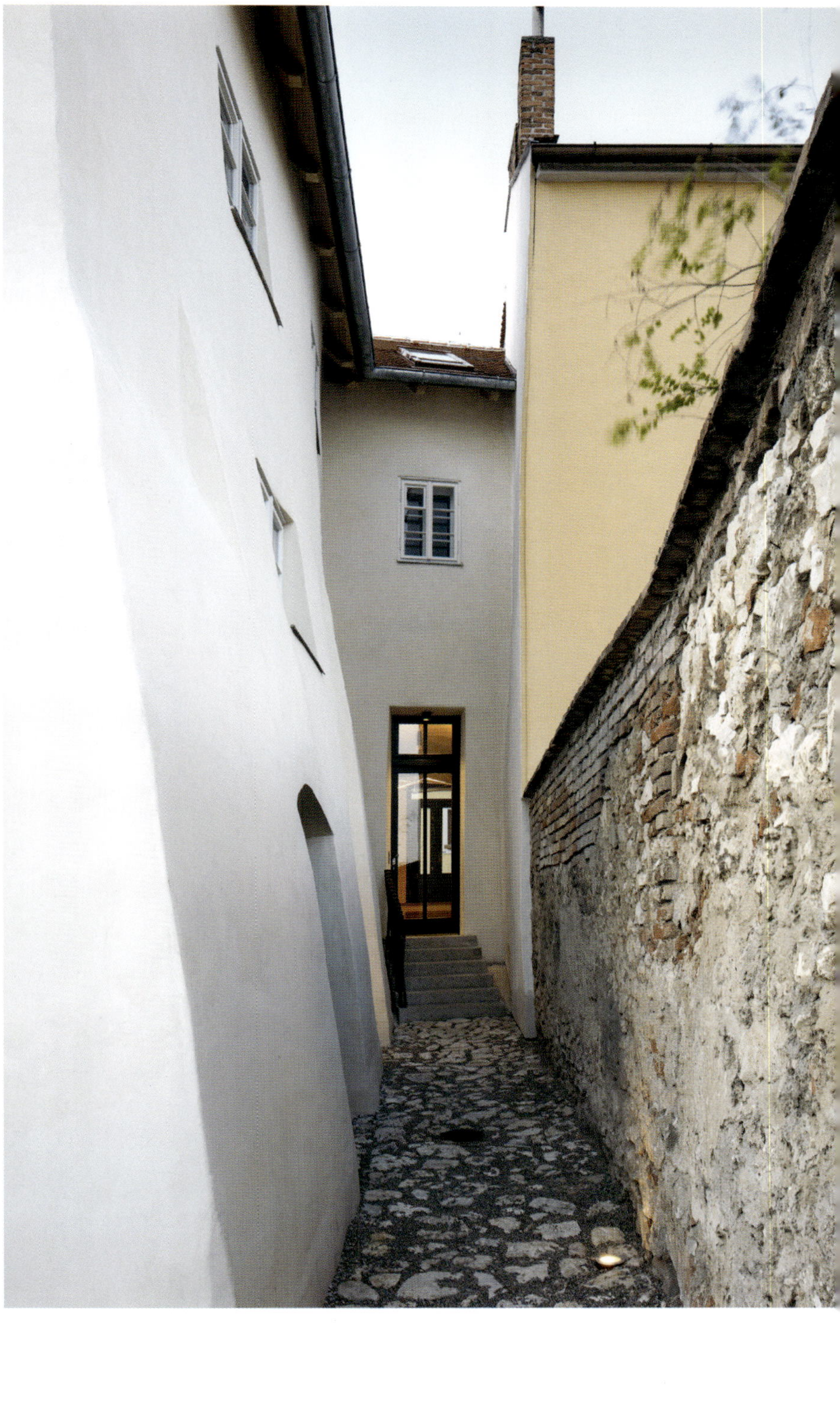

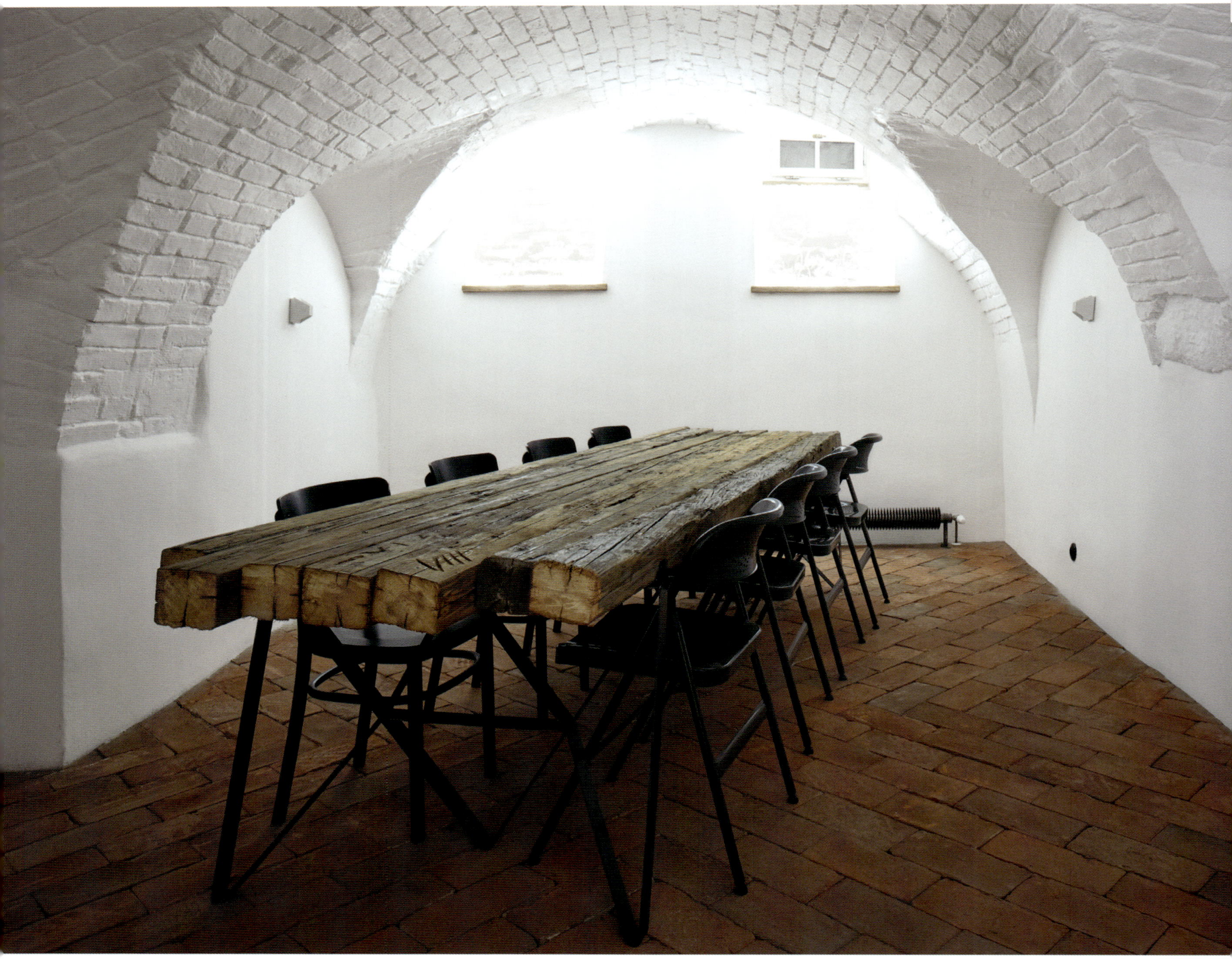

It is difficult to find a straight wall or a rectangular opening in the house. This situation led to a need for customized reinvention and reformation of all its elements to preserve its organic unity.

Im Haus lässt sich nur schwer eine gerade Wand oder eine rechteckige Öffnung finden. Von daher mussten die Architekten im Bemühen, dessen organische Einheit zu bewahren, alle Elemente neu erdenken und nach Maß neu gestalten.

Dans la maison, il est difficile de trouver un mur droit ou une ouverture rectangulaire. À partir de là, il a fallu réinventer et refaire sur mesure tous ses éléments afin de préserver son unité organique.

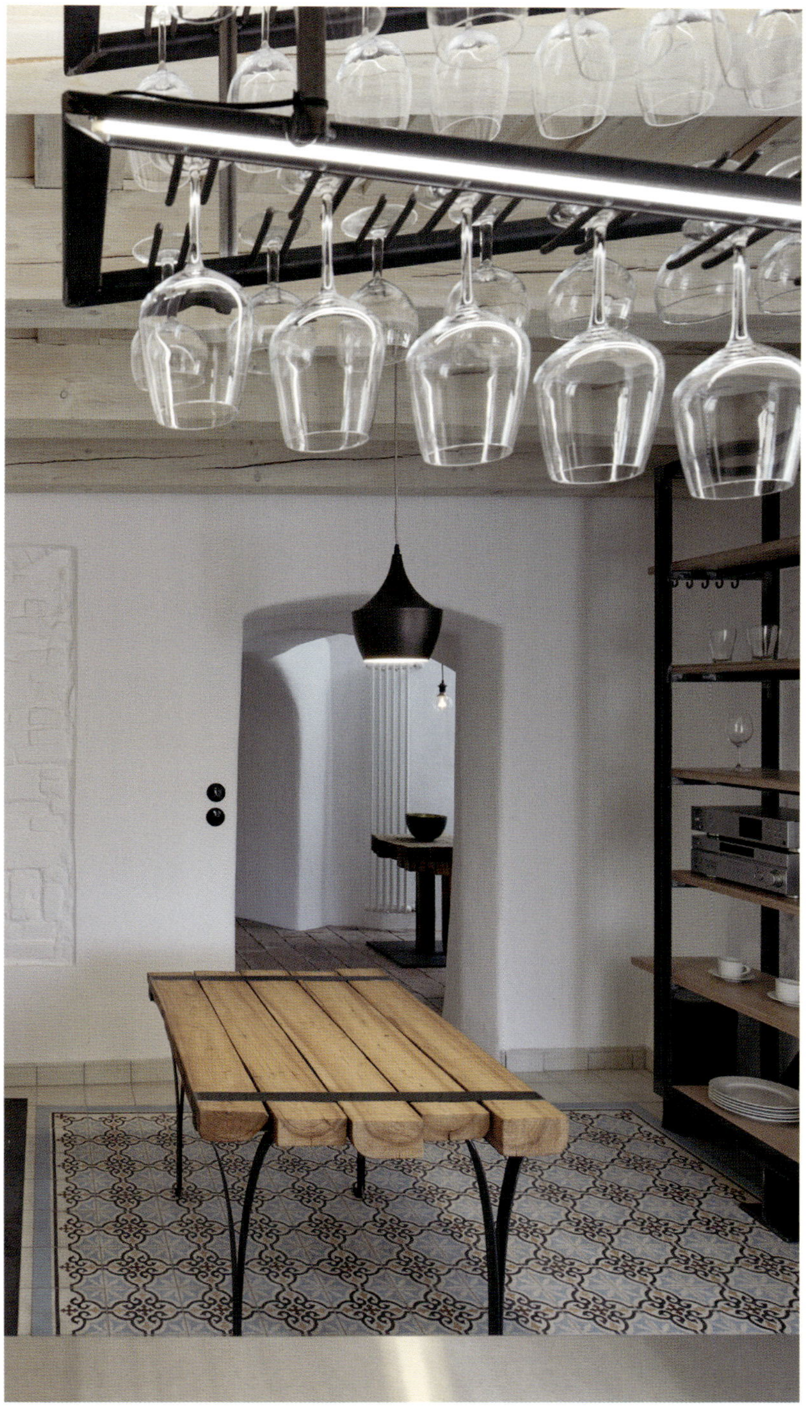

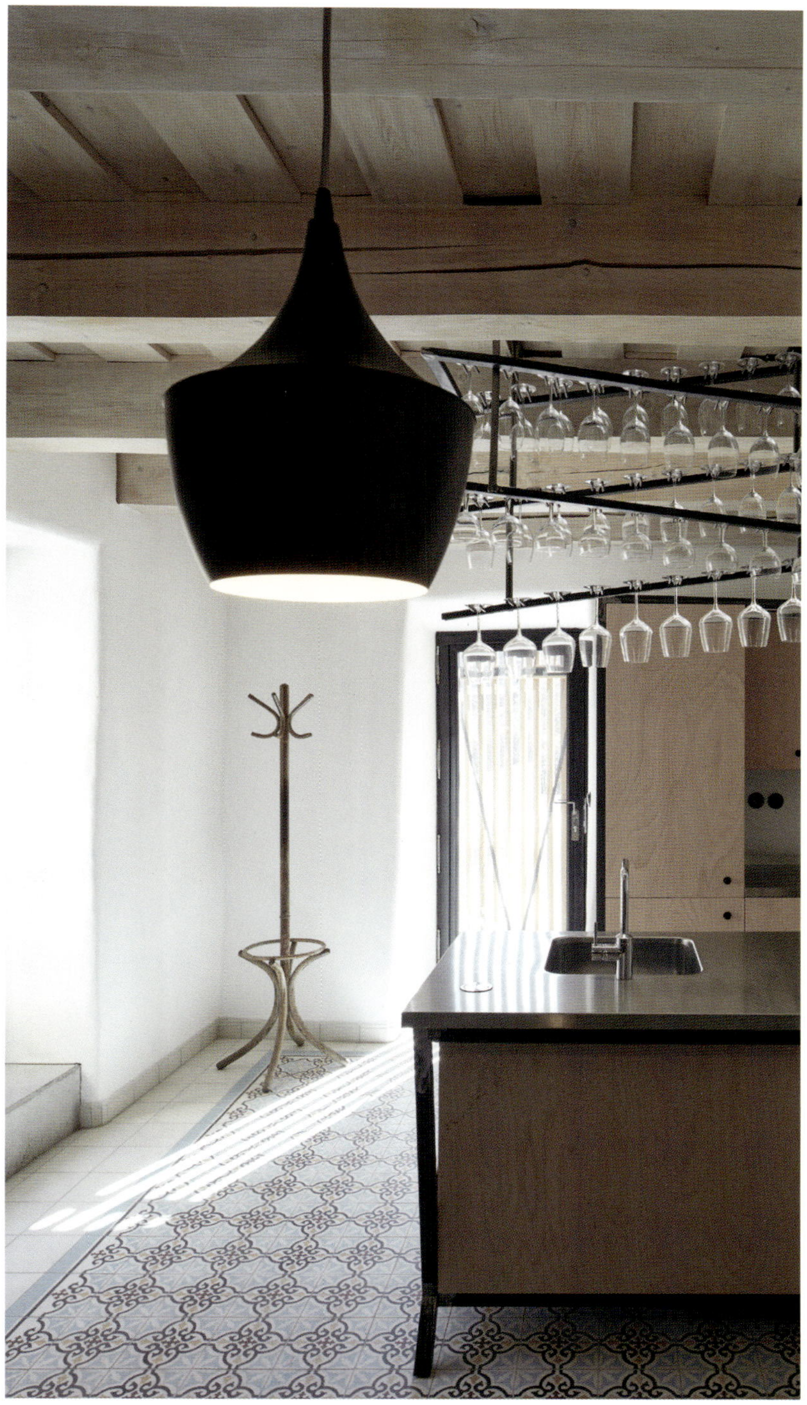

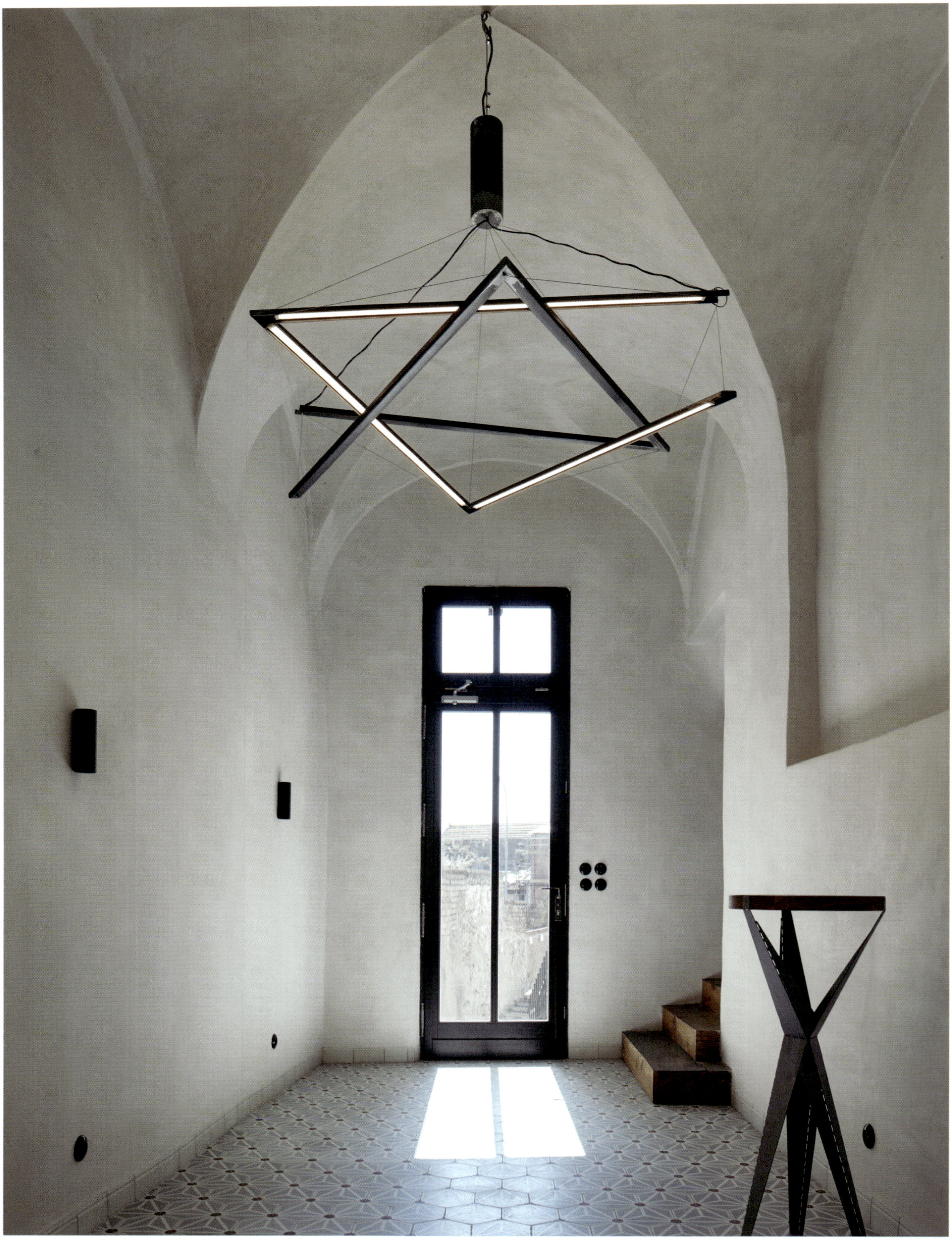

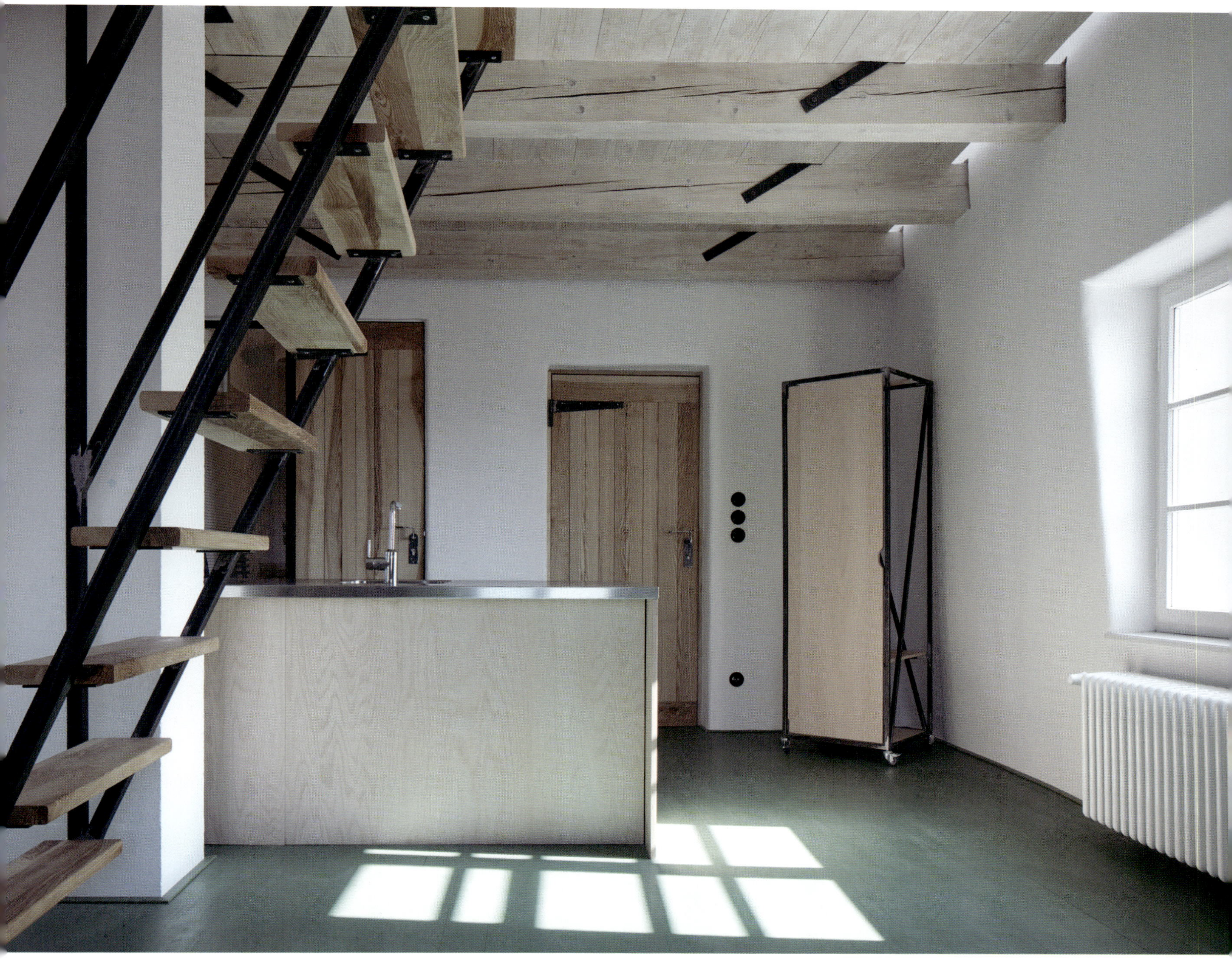

Restraint both in the selection of the range of materials, with a strong predominance of wood and iron, and in the design of furnishings and all decorative and lighting elements is evident throughout the structure, serving as the common theme across the different rooms.

Die Nüchternheit sowohl bei der Wahl der Materialpalette – mit einer klaren Vorherrschaft von Holz und Eisen – als auch bei der Gestaltung der Einrichtung und aller Deko-Accessoires sowie der Beleuchtung ist im ganzen Haus deutlich und fungiert als roter Faden zwischen den verschiedenen Bereichen.

La sobriété tant de la sélection de la palette des matériaux, avec une claire prédominance du bois et du métal, que dans le design du mobilier et de tous les éléments de décoration et d'éclairage, est particulièrement frappante dans toute la maison, servant de fil conducteur entre les différentes pièces.

Since the house has been repurposed to satisfy the requirements of a guest house, each room is unique, having its own ambiance and personality.

Da das Haus für die Anforderungen eines Gästehauses umgebaut wurde, ist jedes Zimmer einzigartig, jedes hat seine eigene Stimmung und Persönlichkeit.

La maison a été construite afin de répondre aux besoins d'une maison d'hôtes, par conséquent chaque chambre est unique, a sa propre ambiance et personnalité.

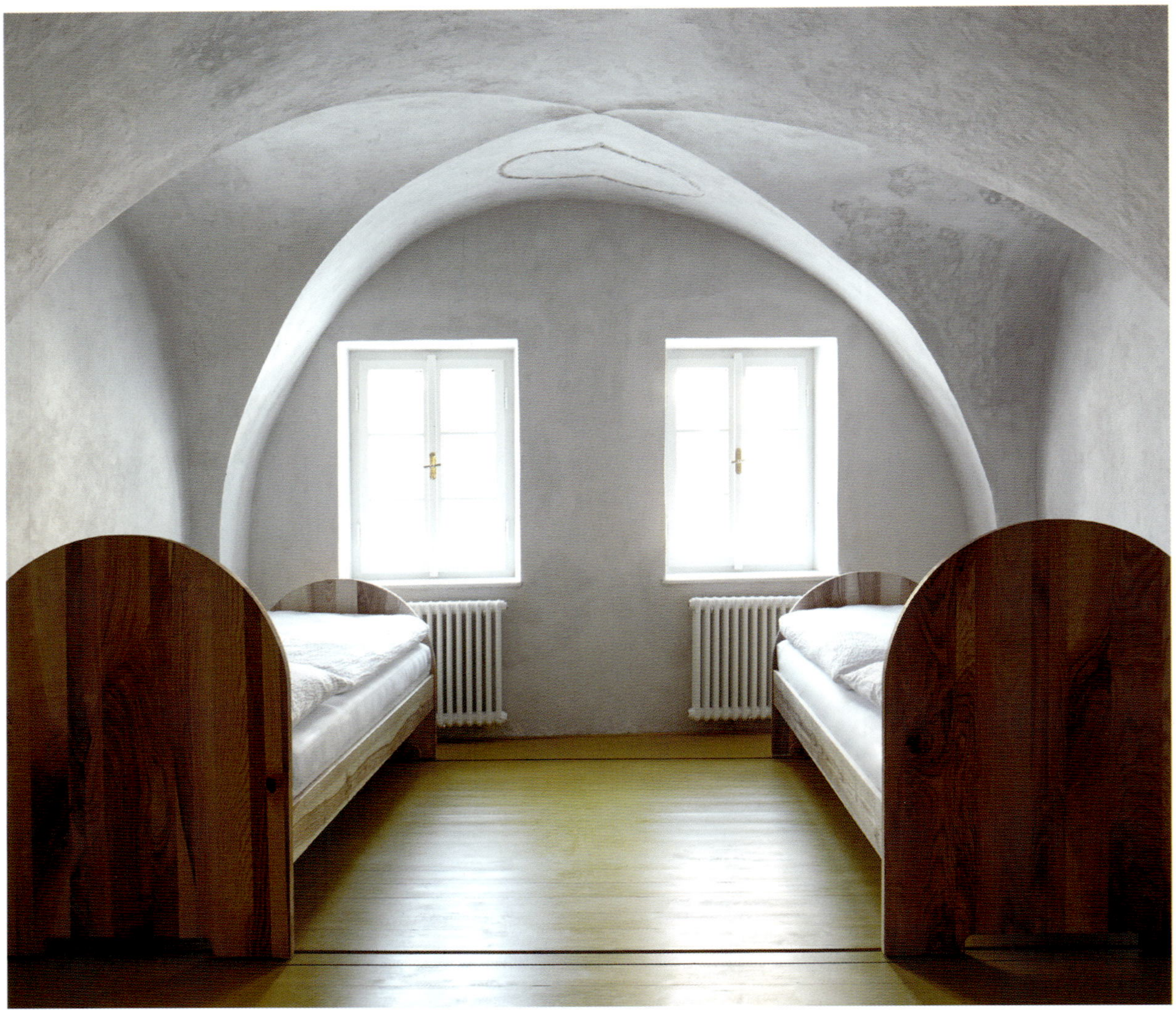

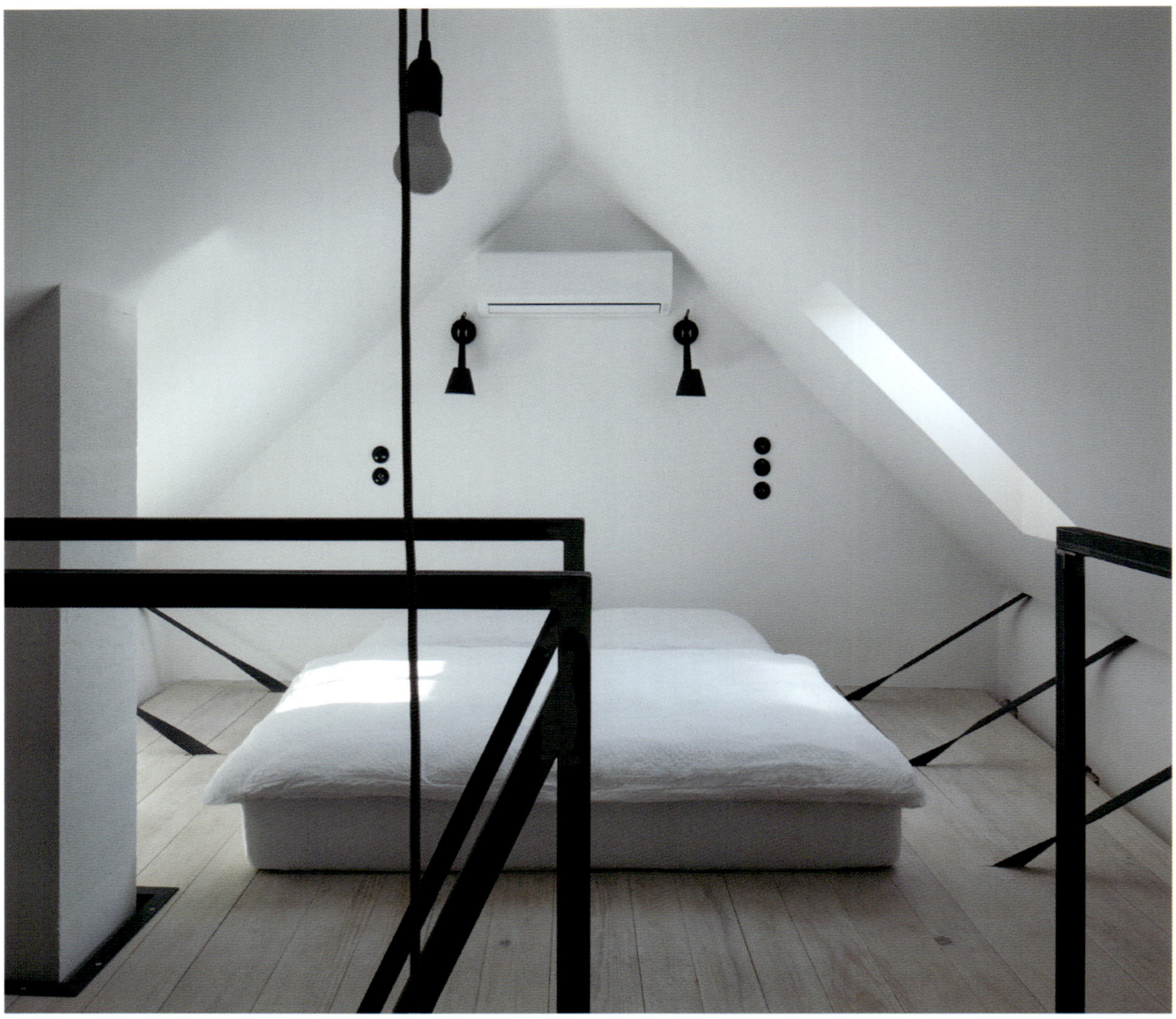

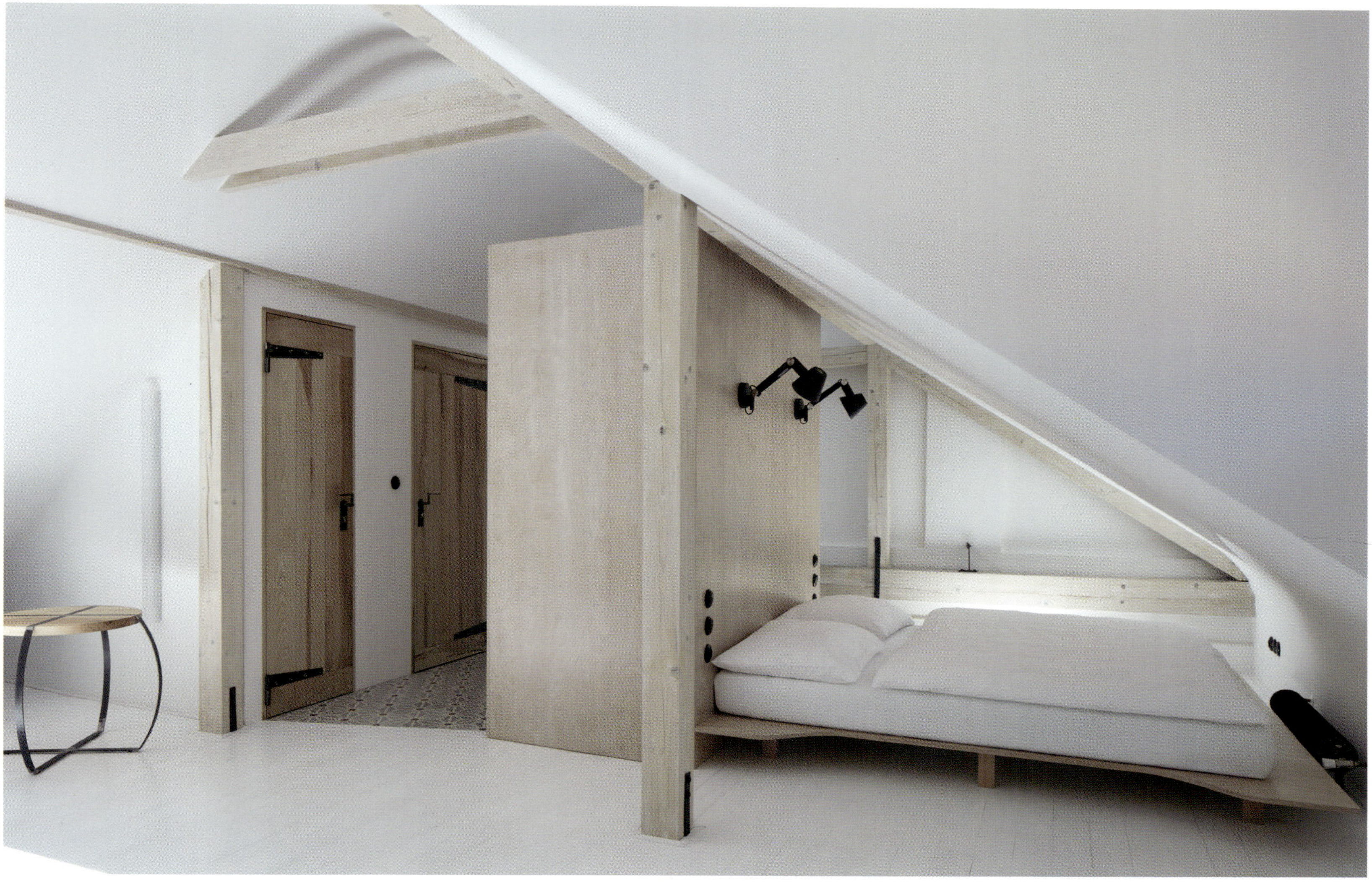

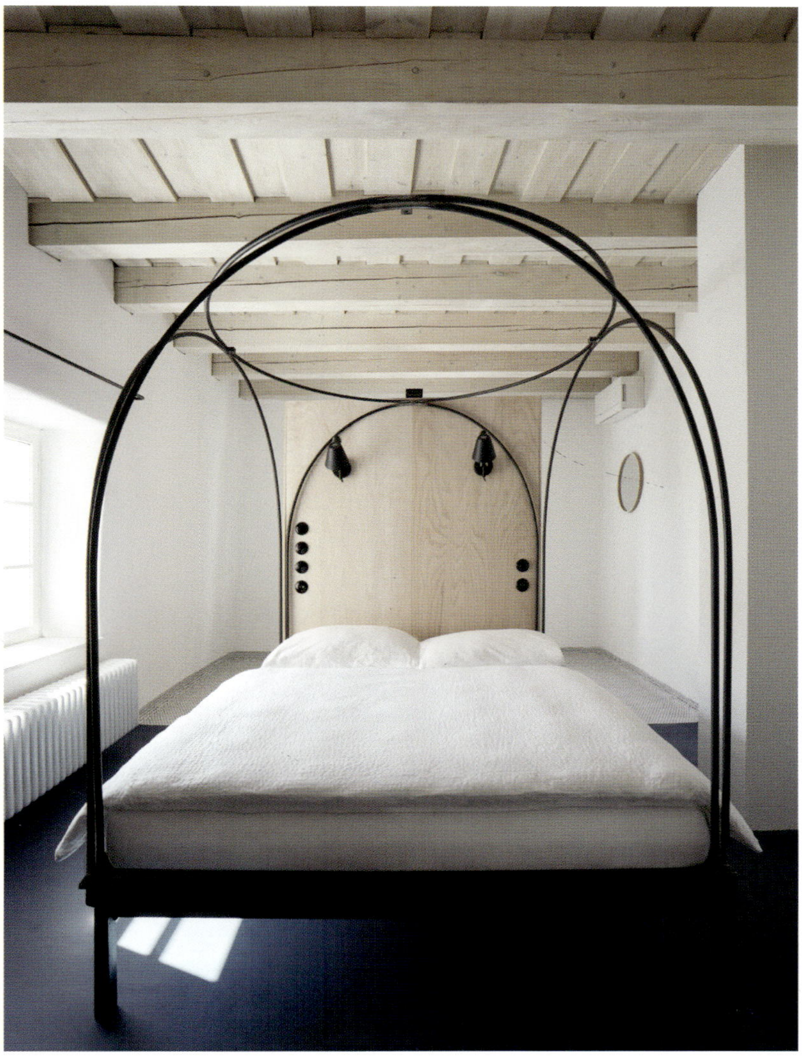

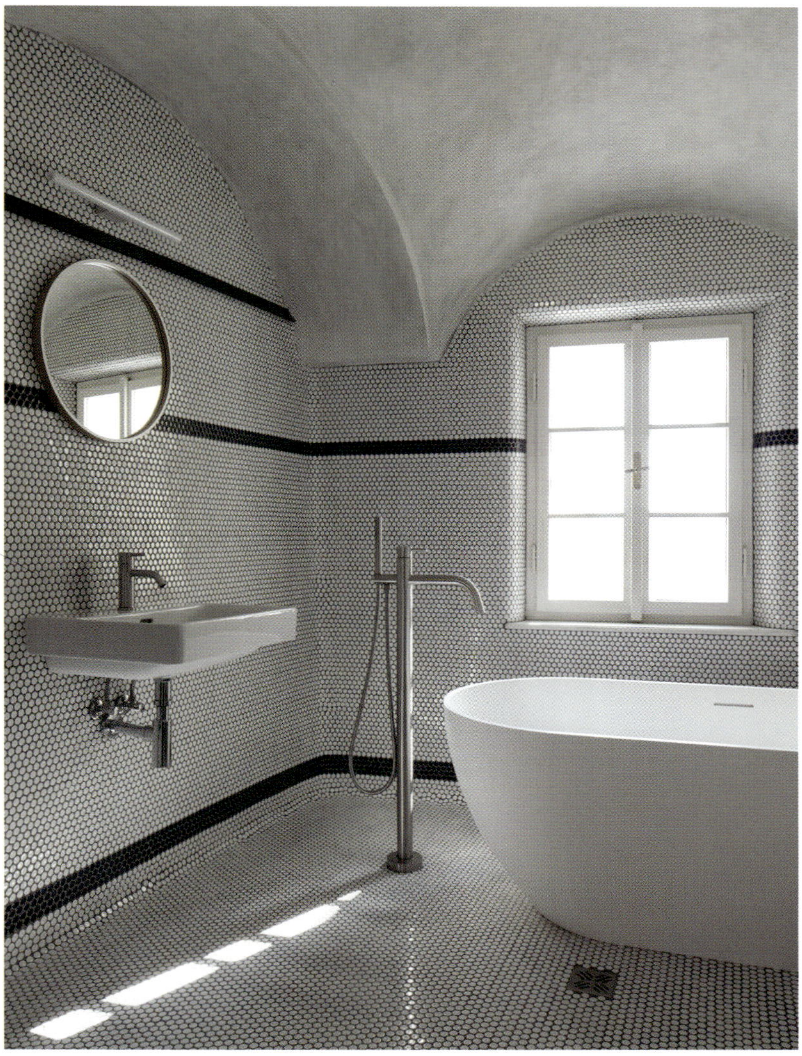

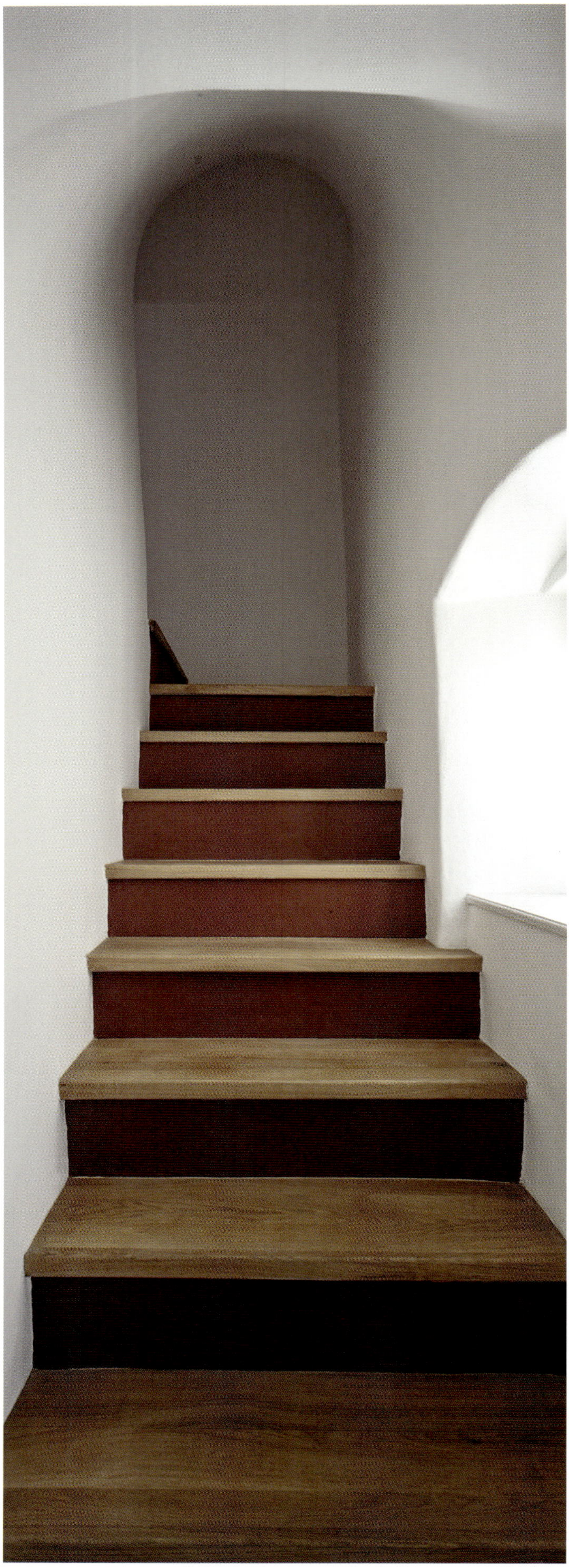

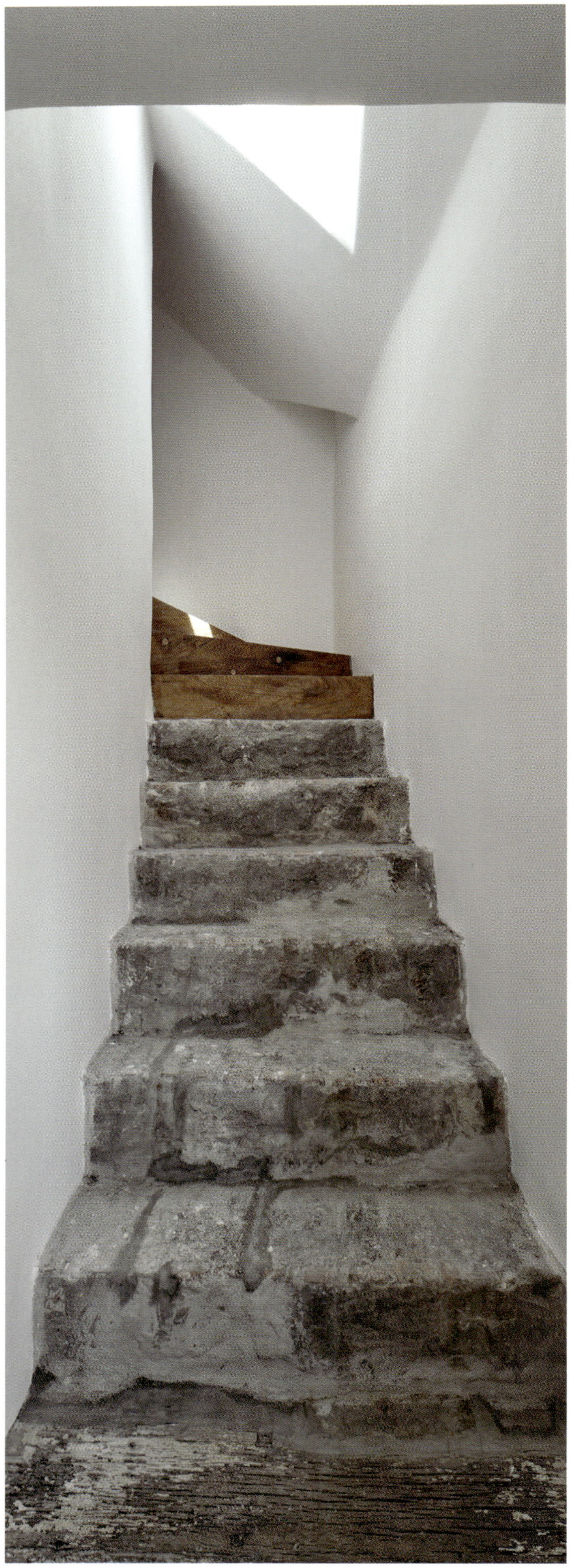

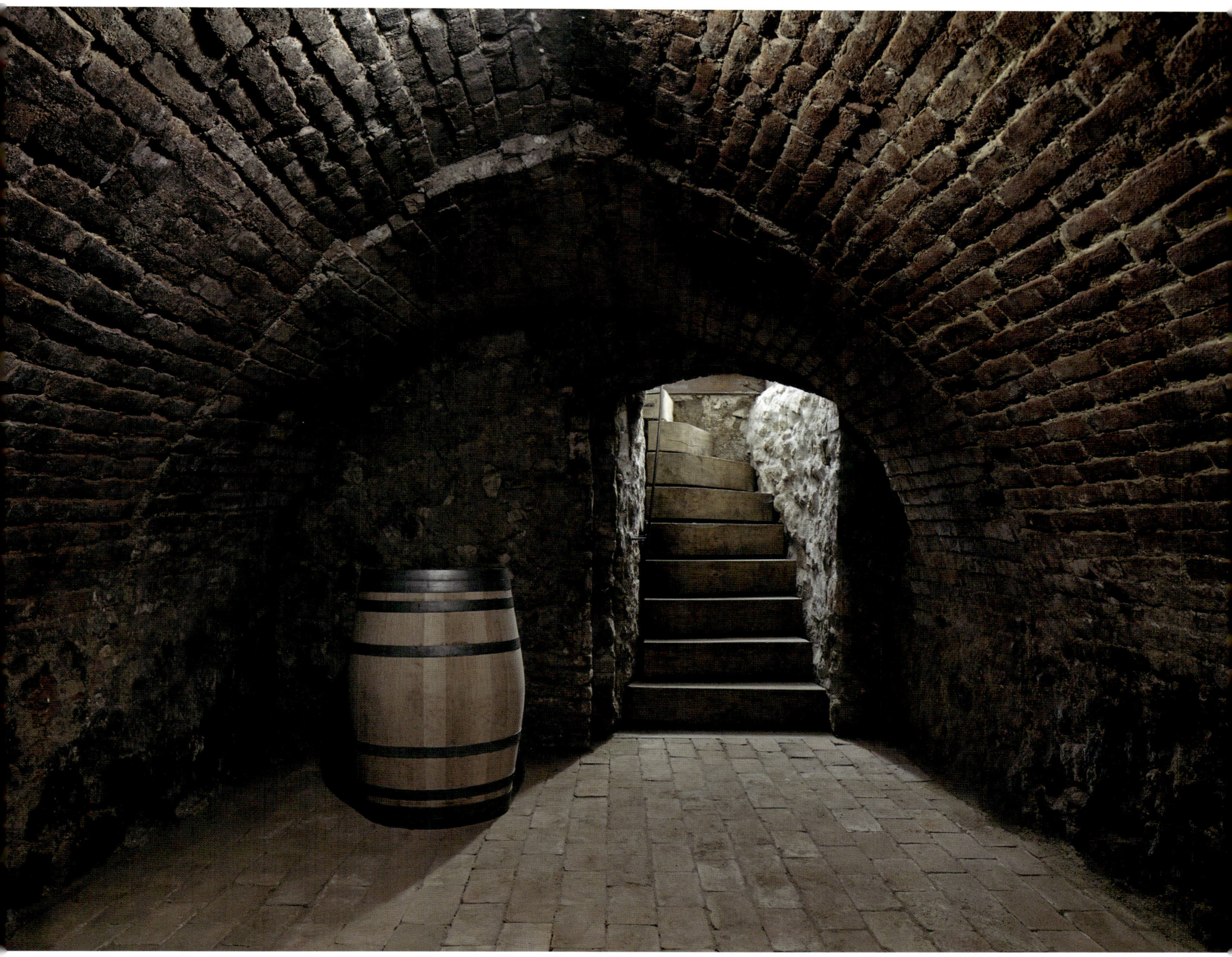

An ancient wine cellar discovered beneath the house was restored to its original function. We are suddenly transported into the past by the structure of its vaulted ceiling and by the original materials—brick, stone and natural tuff—that have been painstakingly restored.

Unter dem Haus wurde ein alter Weinkeller entdeckt, und die Architekten beschlossen, diesen zu restaurieren und seine ursprüngliche Verwendung wiederherzustellen. Sowohl das Tragwerk mit Gewölbedecke als auch die sorgfältig restaurierten Originalmaterialien – Ziegel, Stein und Naturtuffstein – versetzen uns für einen Moment in die Vergangenheit.

Une ancienne cave a été découverte en dessous de la maison ; elle a été restaurée pour lui redonner son usage d'origine. Tant sa structure, avec le plafond voûté, que les matériaux d'origine, la brique, la pierre et le tuf naturel, ont été soigneusement récupérés pour nous transporter un moment dans le passé.

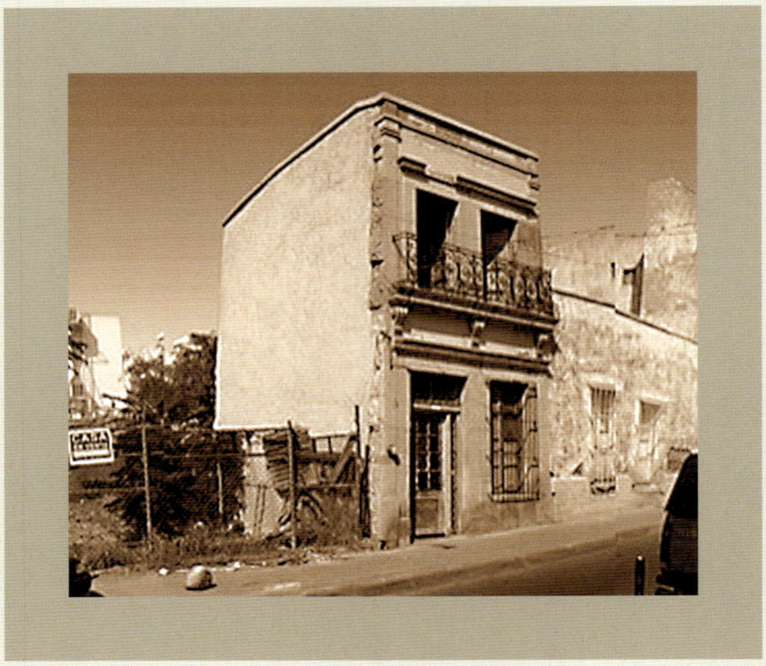

C2A HOUSE

LABOR STUDIO

306 m² | 3,300 sq. ft.

Chihuahua City, Mexico

Photos © **Rafael Gamo**

> Maximize the flow of circulation through the entire house by means of interlocked spaces

> Devise a layout where exterior spaces are just as important as interior ones

> Den Fluss innerhalb des gesamten Hauses durch verbundene Räume verstärken

> Ein Konzept, bei dem die Außenbereiche genauso wichtig wie die Innenräume sind

> Optimiser la fluidité de circulation à travers l'habitation entière par le biais d'espaces interconnectés

> Inventer une configuration dans laquelle les espaces extérieurs sont aussi importants que les intérieurs

The project began with the restoration of an old building dating from the early 20th century in a deteriorated urban environment. This led to a study focused on the refurbishment of derelict building structures and the exploration of the possibilities of urban regeneration.
The neighboring property was added as an extension to the existing old building. This extension was conceived as a series of articulated volumes and a staircase that not only connects the different floor levels of the extension, including a new roof terrace with fantastic views, but also acts as a link between the old and new constructions. All living spaces are interconnected to enhance visual continuity and opened to the outdoors wherever possible to maximize a sense of space.

Das Projekt begann mit der Restaurierung eines alten Gebäudes vom Anfang des 20. Jahrhunderts in einem heruntergekommenen Stadtviertel. Die Architekten prüften die Renovierungsmöglichkeiten für die verkommene Gebäudestruktur und die Neugestaltung des Stadtgebietes.
Das Nachbargrundstück war als Anbau zu diesem alten Gebäude hinzugekommen. Dieser Anbau besteht aus mehreren miteinander verbundenen Räumen und einem Treppenhaus, das nicht nur die einzelnen Stockwerke - einschließlich der neuen Dachterrasse mit fantastischem Ausblick -, sondern auch Alt- und Neubau miteinander verbindet. Um ein optisch fließendes Konzept zu schaffen, sind alle Wohnräume miteinander verbunden und wo immer möglich nach außen hin offen, was zusätzlichen Platz schafft.

Ce projet a débuté avec la rénovation d'un vieux bâtiment du début du XXe siècle dans un environnement urbain dégradé. Cela a mené à une étude sur la rénovation de structures délabrées et sur l'exploration des possibilités de la régénération urbaine.
La propriété voisine a été ajoutée en tant qu'extension à l'ancien bâtiment existant. Celle-ci a été conçue comme une série de volumes articulés ainsi qu'un escalier qui non seulement relie les différents niveaux à l'extension, mais sert également de lien entre les constructions anciennes et nouvelles. Tous les espaces à vivre sont reliés entre eux pour souligner la continuité visuelle et ouverts sur l'extérieur pour autant que possible pour optimiser le sentiment d'espace.

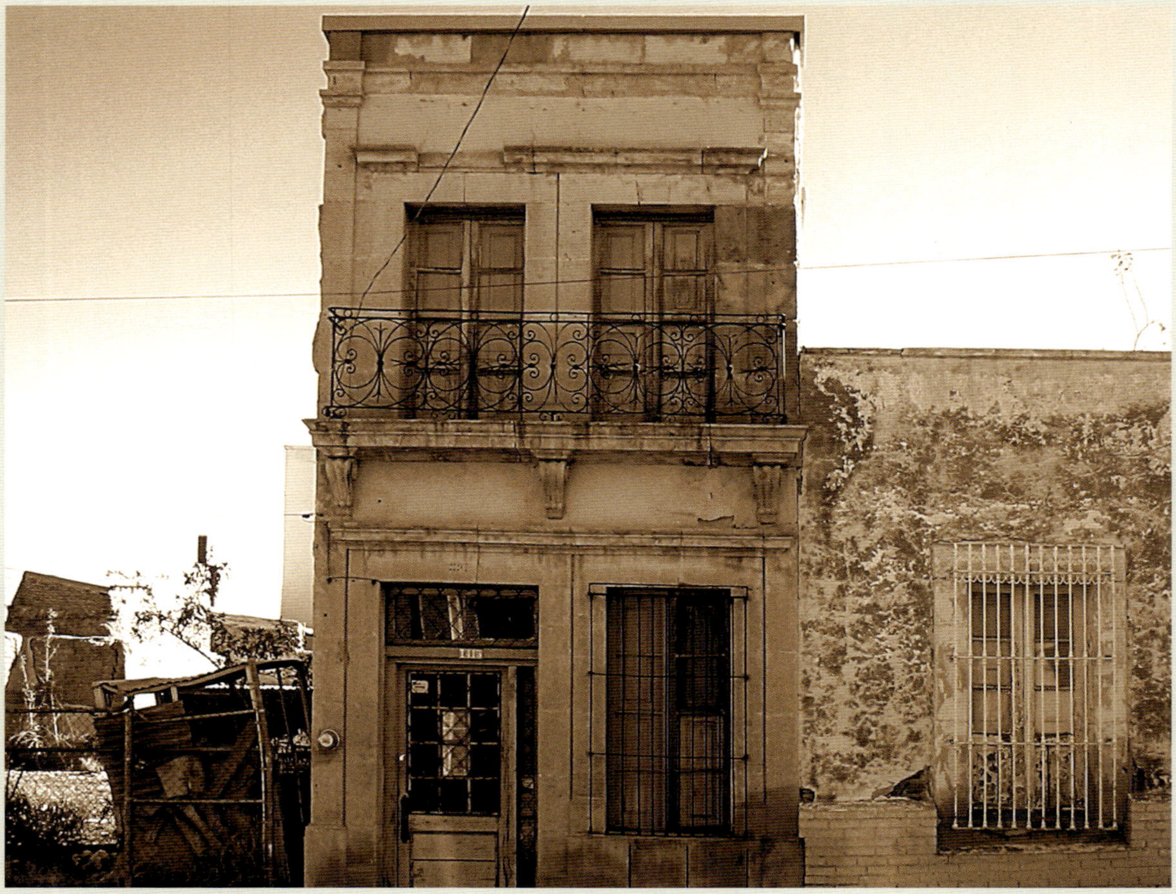

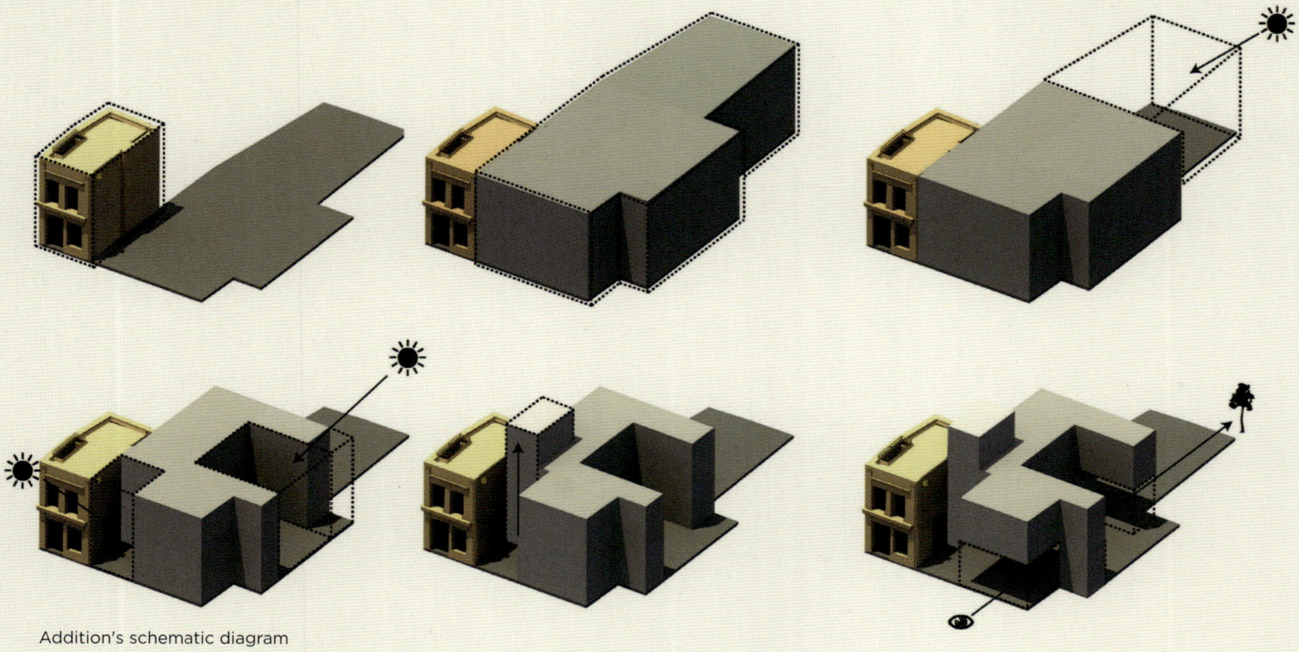

Addition's schematic diagram

The staircase is a key element of the design on two levels: formally, it connects the existing building with the addition; conceptually, it makes a clear separation between two different architecture styles: the old, massive brick building and the modern, almost-transparent addition.

Das Treppenhaus ist ein entscheidendes Element für das Design auf zwei Ebenen. Einerseits verbindet es Alt- und Neubau; gleichzeitig trennt es jedoch auch zwei völlig unterschiedliche Architekturstile: den alten massiven Ziegelbau und den modernen, nahezu transparenten Neubau.

La cage d'escalier est une élément clé du design à deux niveaux : au niveau formel, il relie le bâtiment d'origine à l'annexe ; conceptuellement, il établit une séparation claire entre deux différents styles d'architecture : la vieille maison massive et l'annexe moderne, presque transparente.

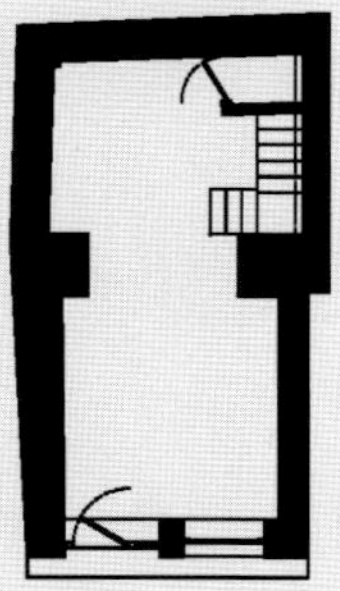

Existing ground floor plan

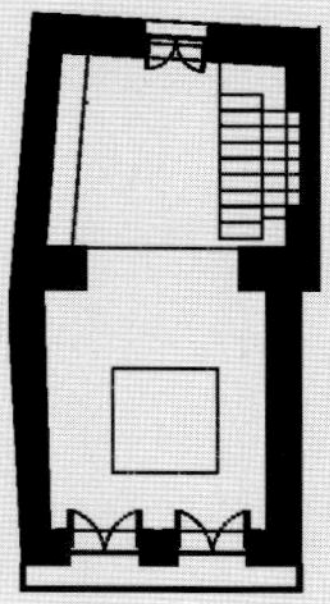

Existing second floor plan

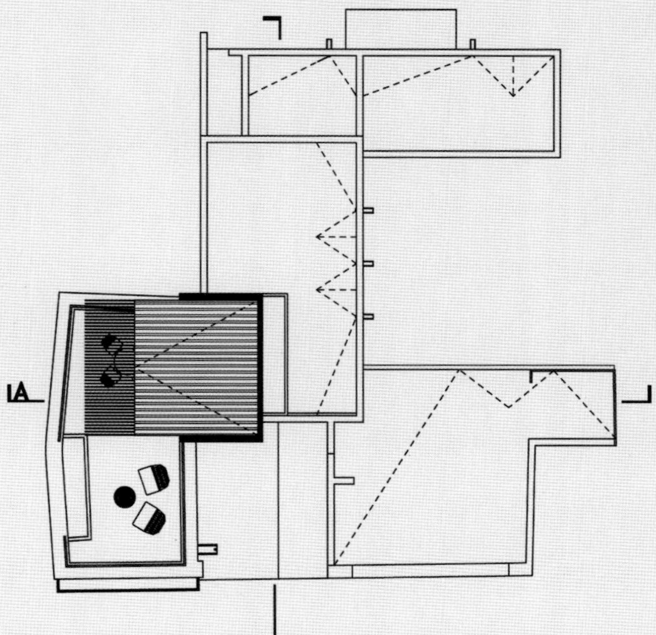

New roof plan

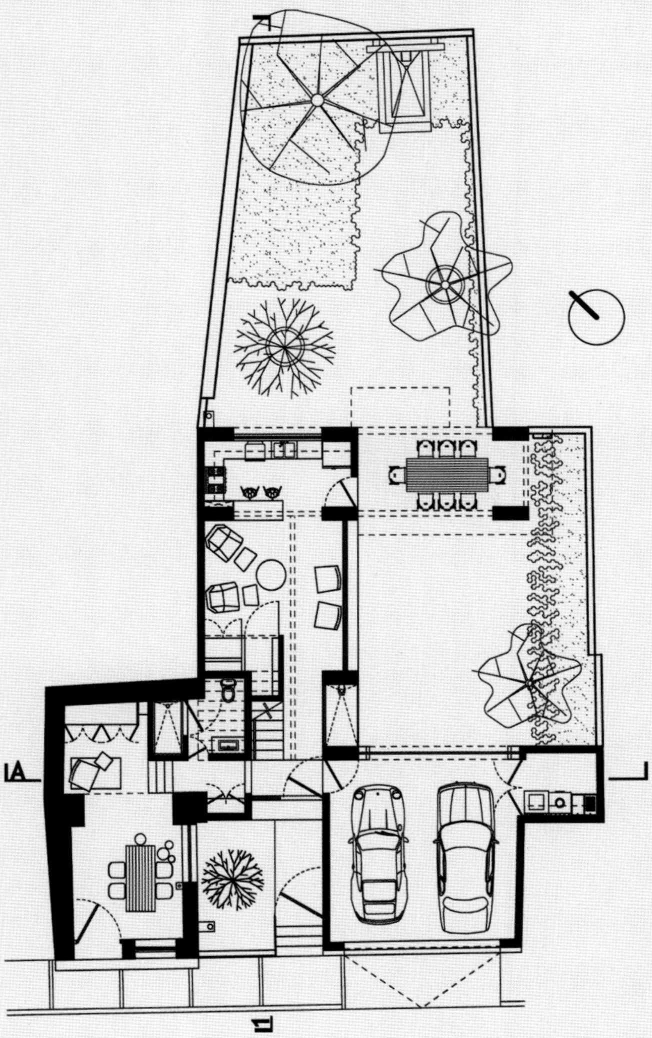

New ground floor plan

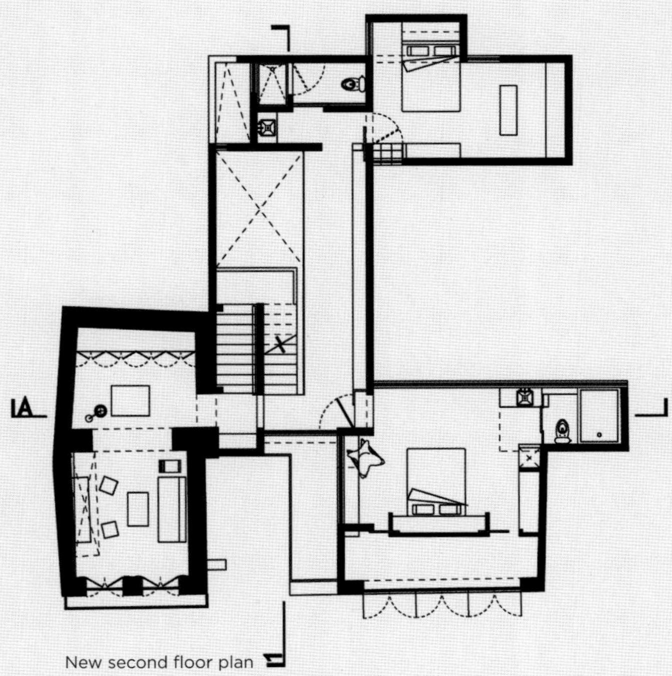

New second floor plan

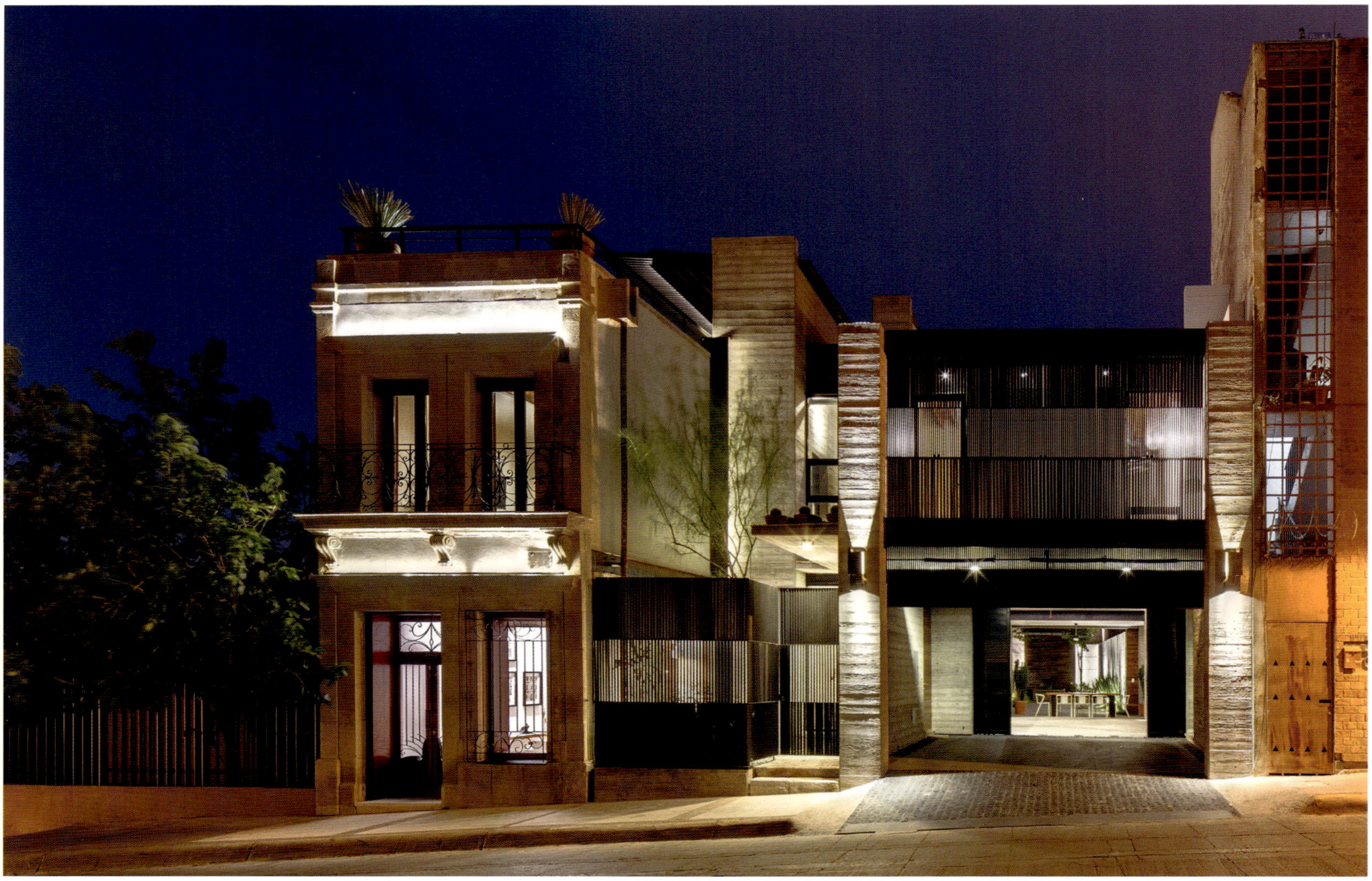

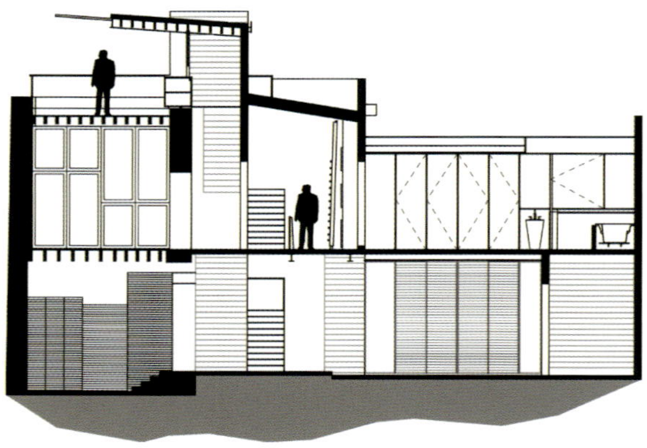

Section A

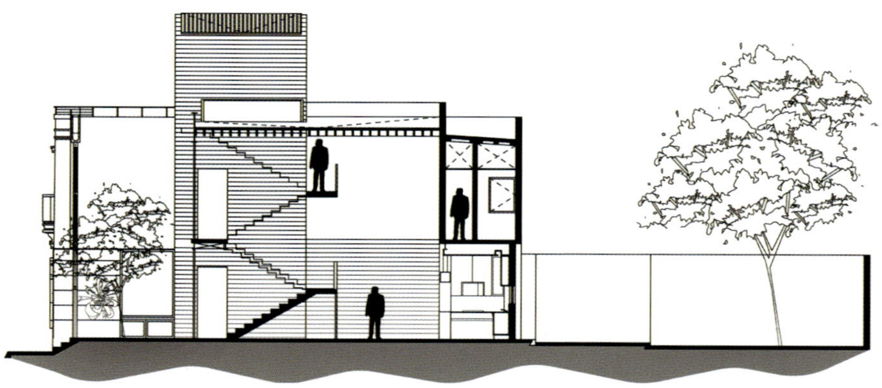

Section 1

The design of the house is a complex composition of interlocking volumes that display a balance of solid and void spaces. The distinction is better appreciated at night, when lights inside the house are turned on, revealing a mosaic of opaque and see-through surfaces.

Für die Hausplanung wurden Räume in komplexer Weise verbunden, um den perfekten Ausgleich aus fest und fließend zu erzielen. Wenn nachts das Licht im Haus angeht, ist das Mosaik aus halbtransparenten und transparenten Flächen noch deutlicher zu sehen.

La conception de la maison est une composition complexe de volumes reliés entre eux qui témoignent d'un équilibre entre les espaces pleins et vides. La distinction est particulièrement appréciable la nuit, lorsque les lumières de l'intérieur de la maison sont allumées, révélant une mosaïque de surfaces opaques et transparentes.

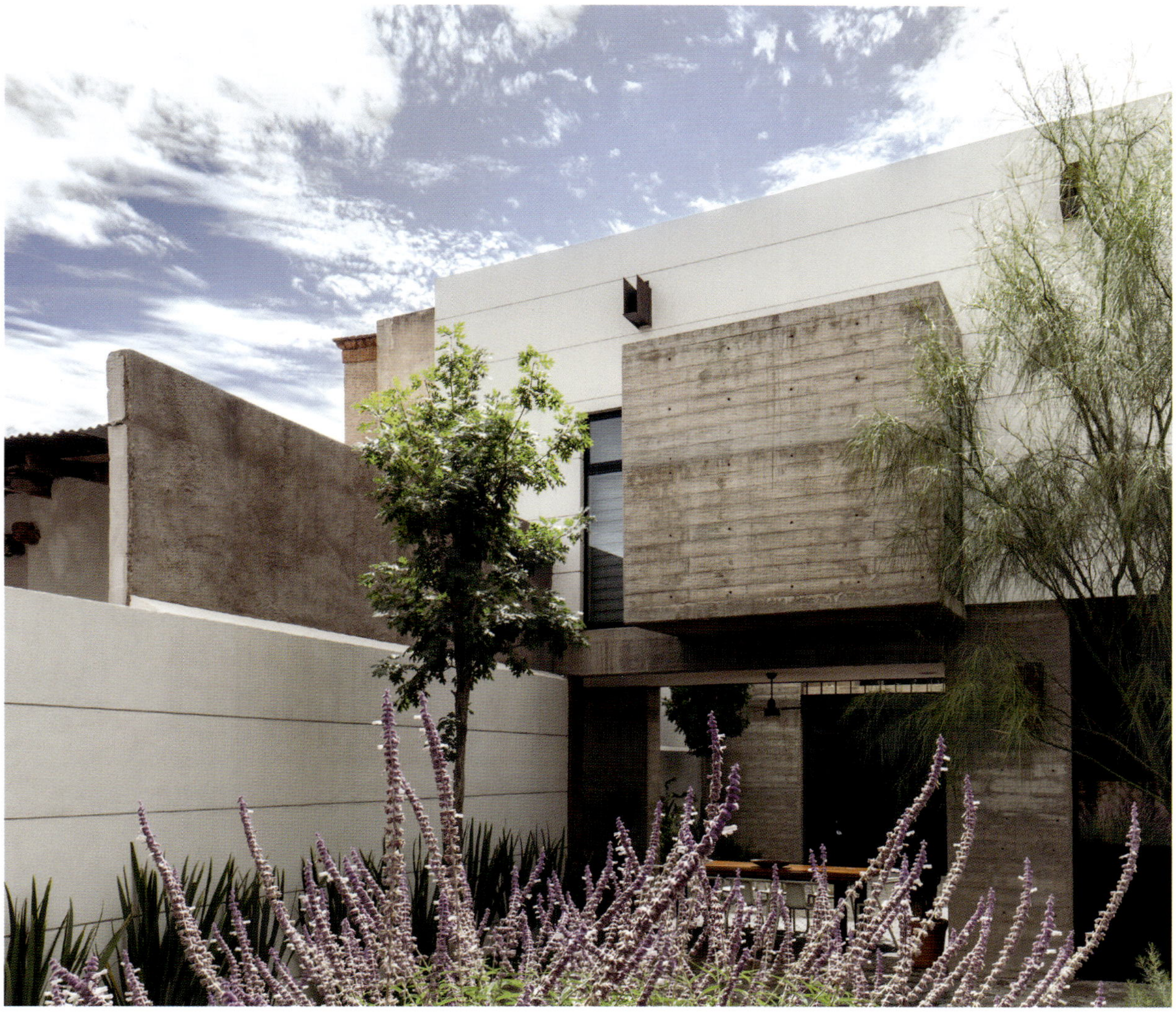

The solid volumes enclose interior spaces, protected from the outside. In contrast, voids make room for passageways and staircases, which act as intermediary spaces that link the interior with the exterior, or for courtyards, as spaces in their own right.

Die undurchlässigen Bereiche beherbergen vor dem Äußeren geschützte Innenräume. Die transparenten Bereiche bestehen aus Durchgangsräumen und Treppenhäusern, die Innenräume mit den Außenbereichen – wie den Innenhöfen – verbinden.

Les volumes compacts enferment les espaces intérieurs, protégés par l'extérieur. En contraste, les vides donnent de la place aux passages et aux escaliers, qui agissent comme espaces intermédiaires qui relient l'intérieur avec l'extérieur ou, dans le cas des cours, comme espaces à part entière.

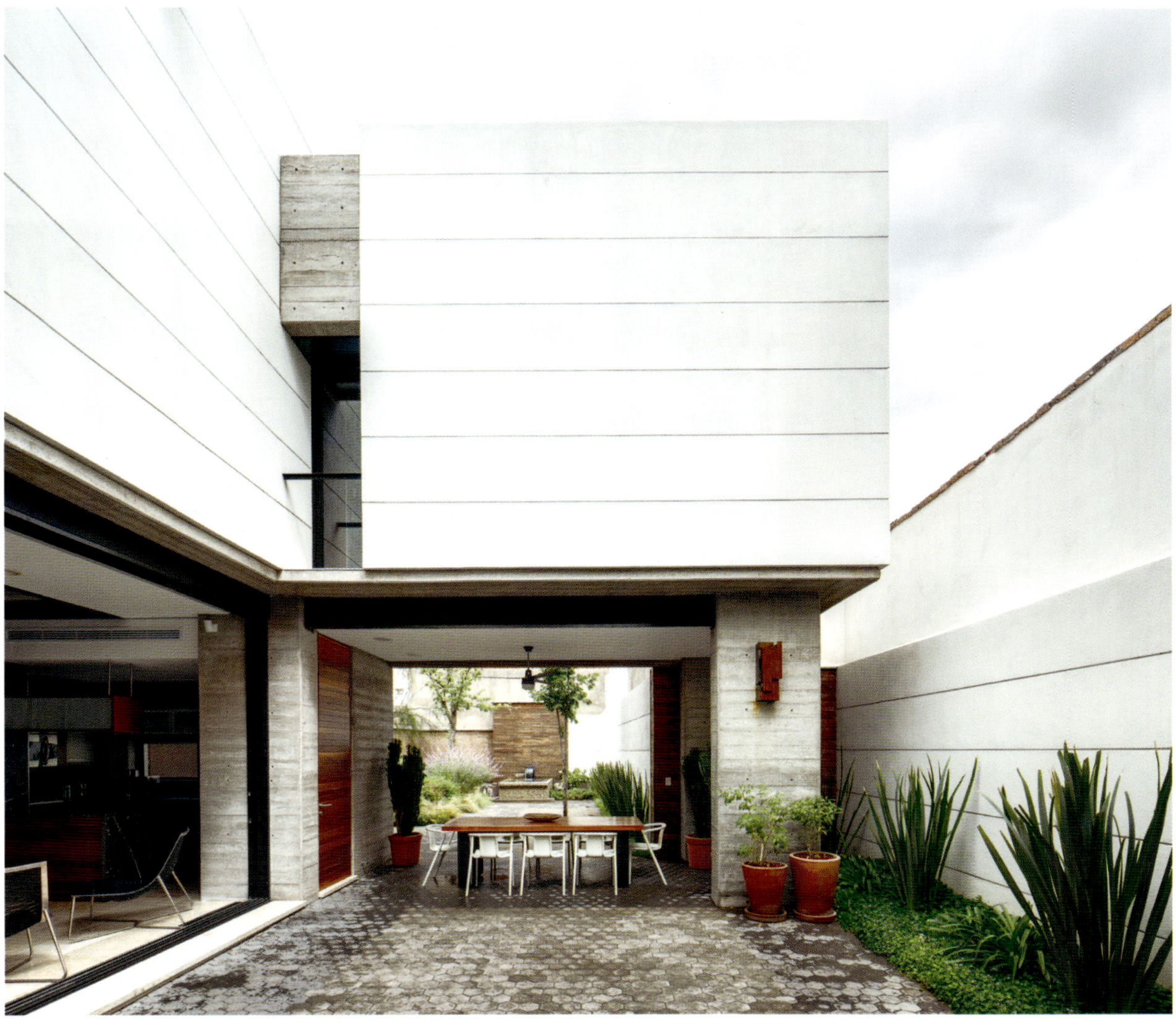

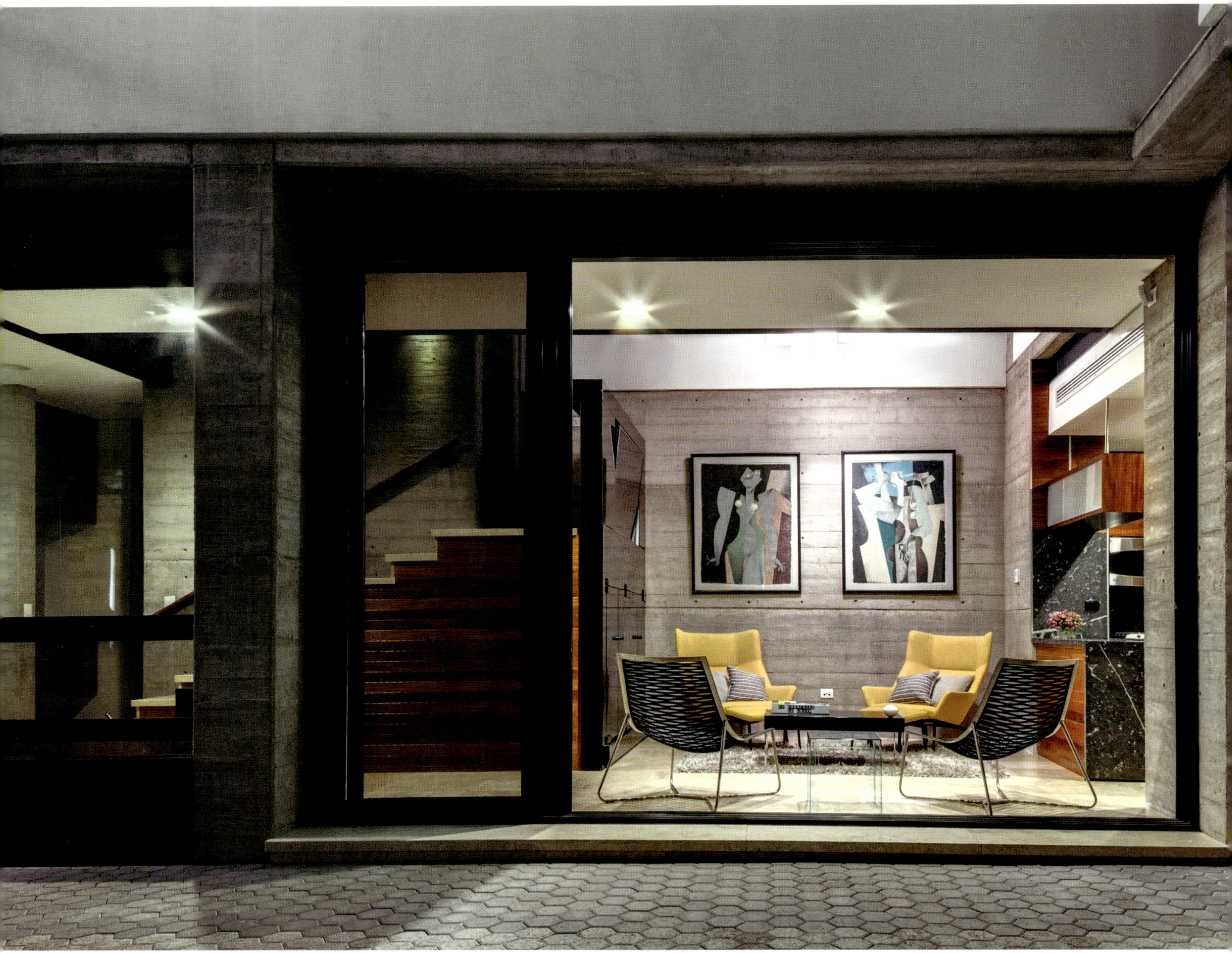

Parts of the house are generously glassed in. The goal was not as much to let light in as to display the interior. By doing so, the interior becomes as much a part of the exterior as the interior is of the exterior.

Manche Hausbereiche sind großzügig verglast. Es ging nicht so sehr um das einfallende Licht, sondern vielmehr darum, das Innere sichtbar zu machen. Hierdurch wird das Innere ein Teil des Äußeren, ebenso wie das Äußere ein Teil des Inneren wird.

Certaines parties de la maison sont généreusement vitrées. L'objectif n'était pas tant de faire entrer la lumière que d'exposer l'intérieur. Ce faisant, l'intérieur fait autant partie de l'extérieur que l'extérieur de l'intérieur.

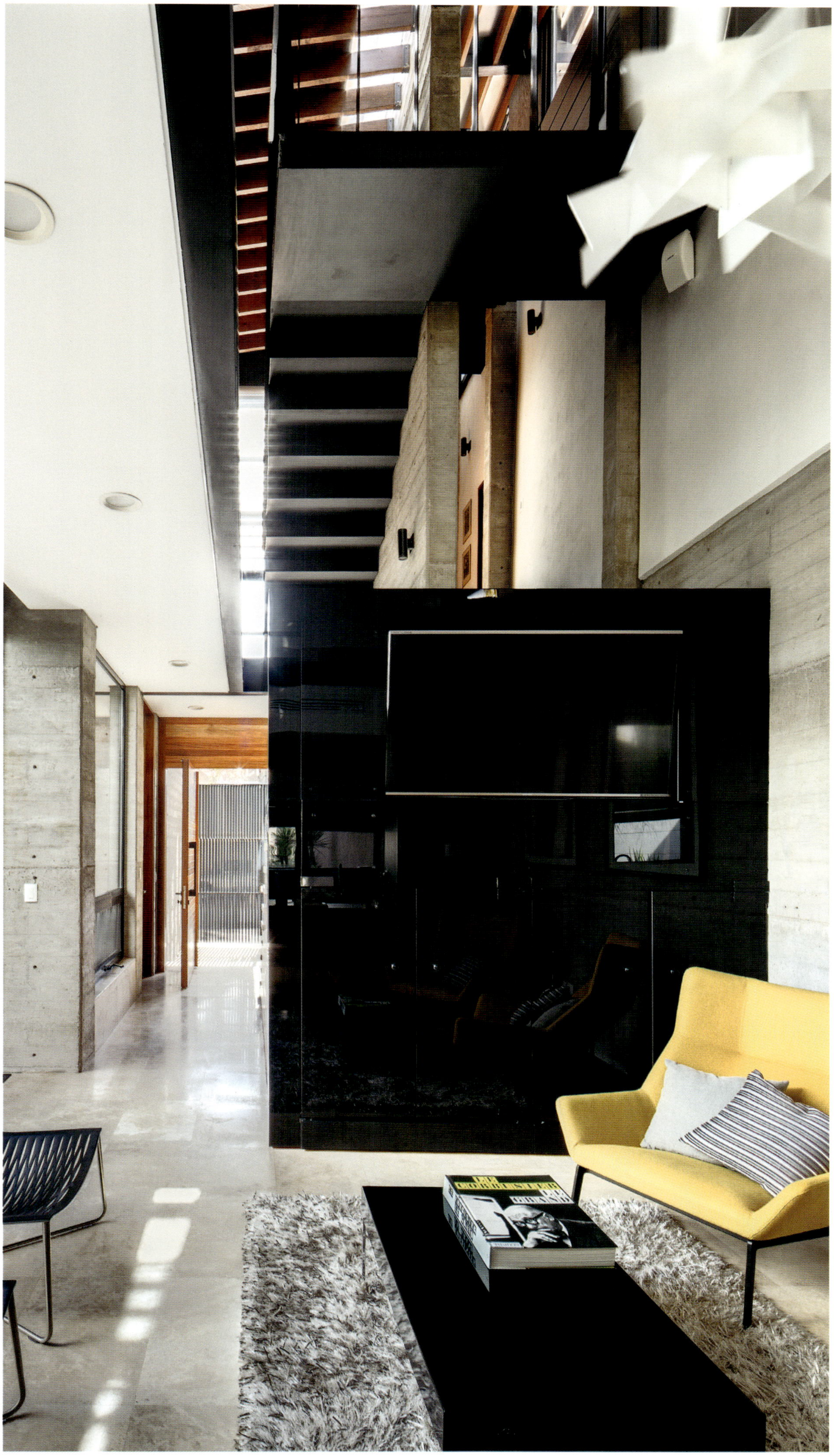

The metal staircase is devised as an object inserted into a void in the interior of the house. This concept is made all the more clear with a slender design detached from the building structure.

Das Metalltreppenhaus wurde in einen transparenten Hausbereich integriert. Das schlanke Design der Gebäudestruktur bringt dieses Konzept noch deutlicher zum Vorschein.

L'escalier en métal est pensé comme un objet inséré dans un vide de l'intérieur de la maison. Ce concept est rendu encore plus clair par un design dépouillé détaché de la structure du bâtiment.

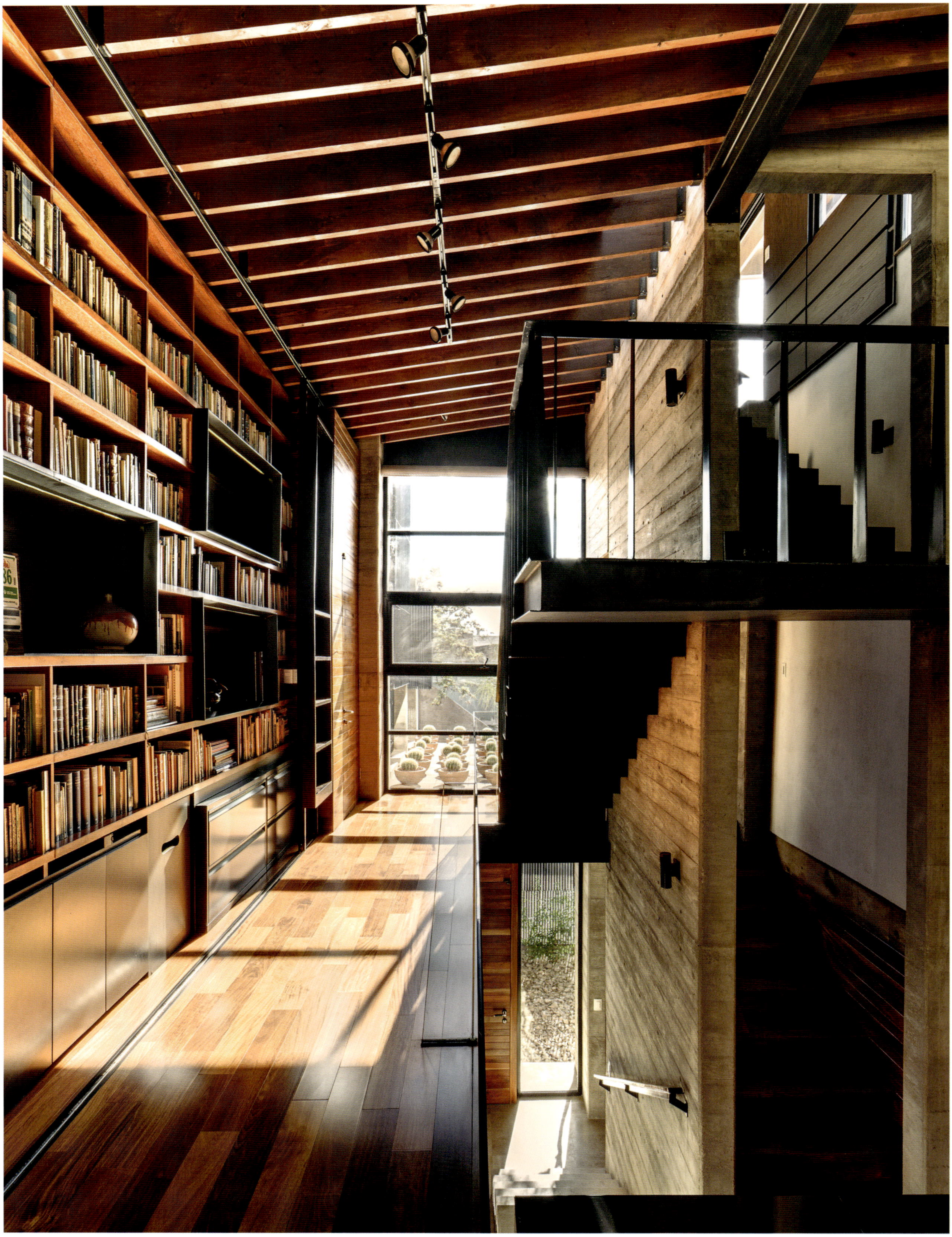

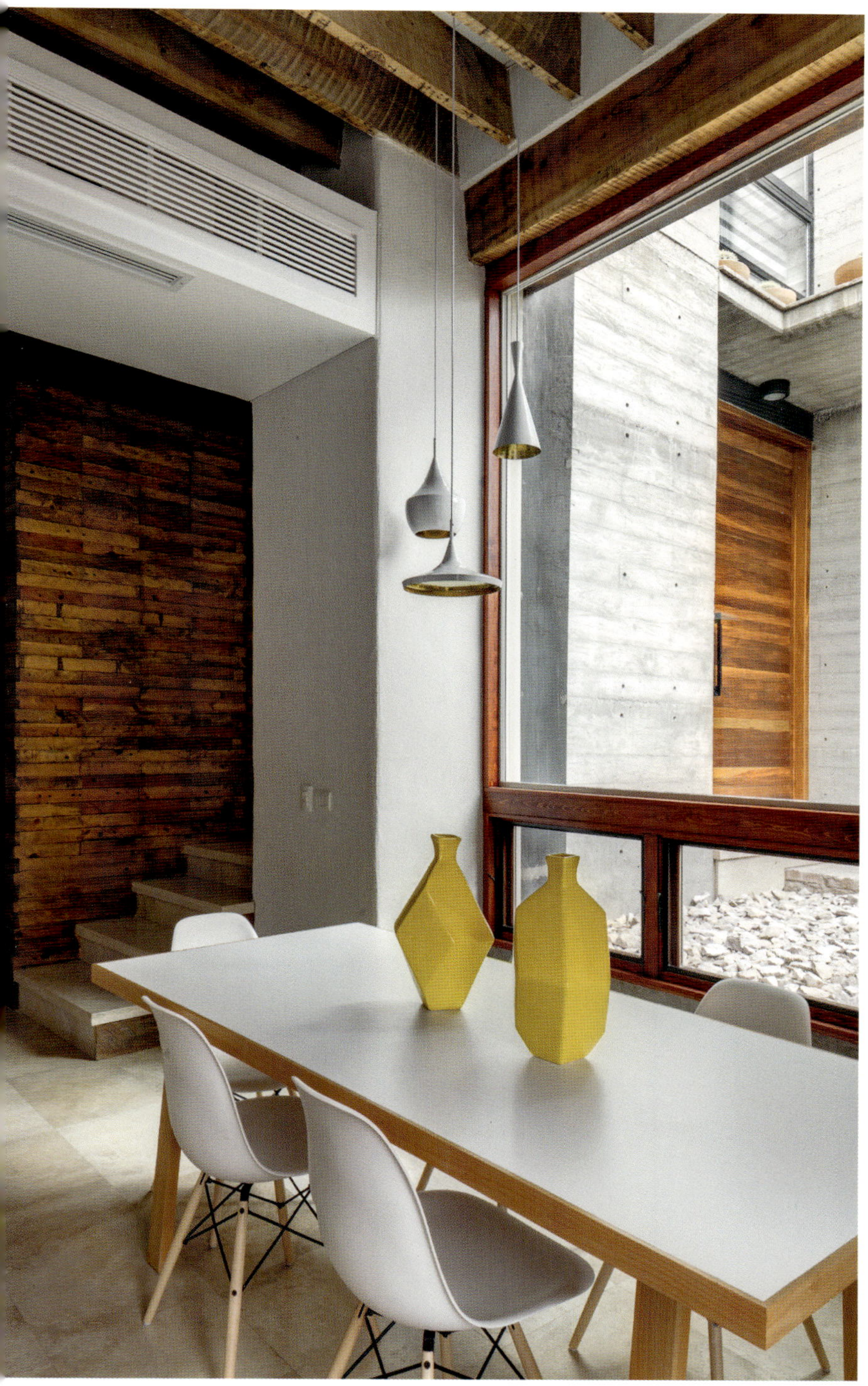

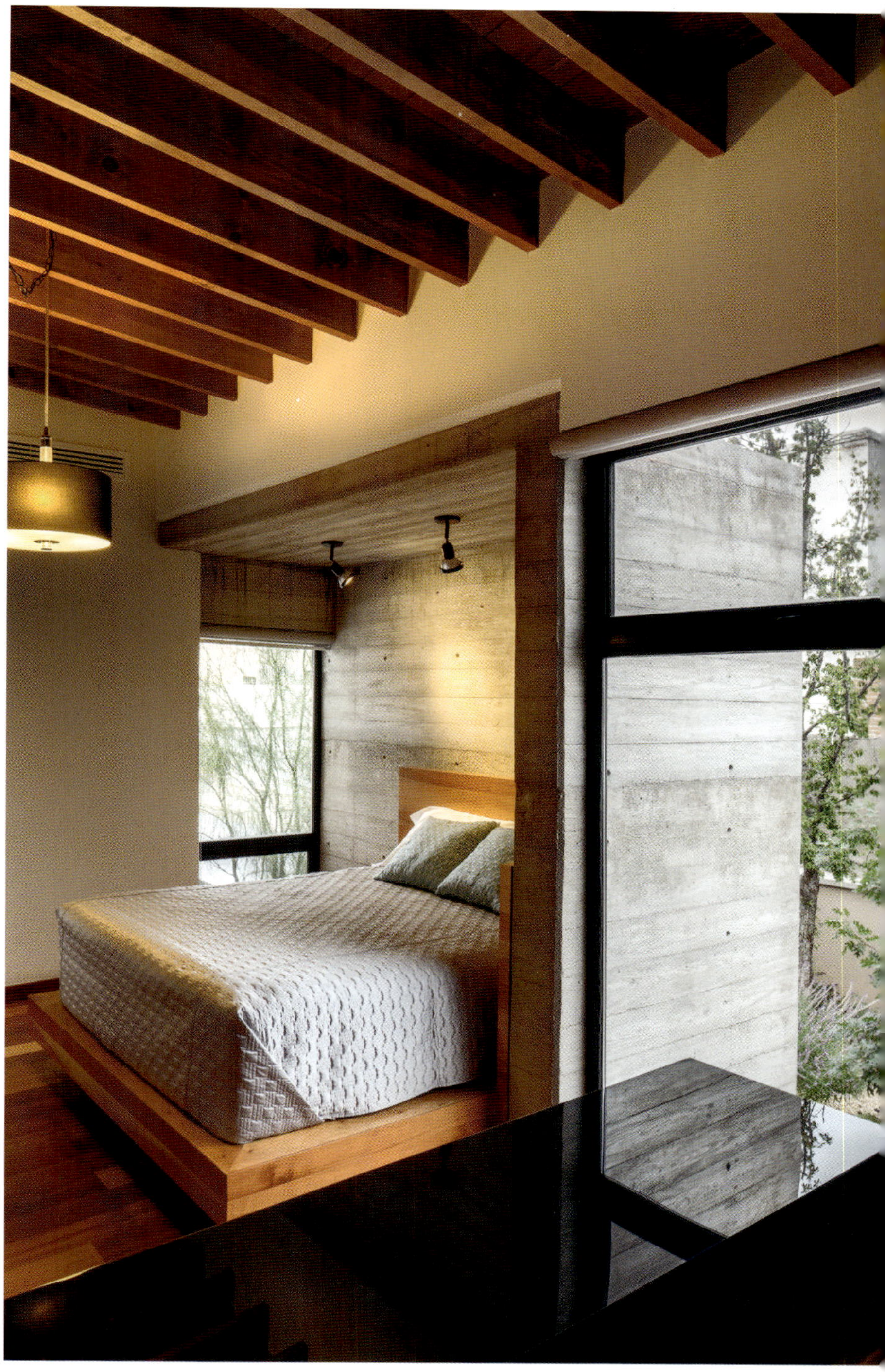

The fenestration is an integral part of the house design, contributing to its strong geometric configuration. Windows, doors, and skylights are parts of the building envelope that accentuate the openness of the house interior toward the exterior.

Die Fenstergestaltung ist ein integraler Bestandteil des Hausdesigns und trägt zu seiner stark geometrischen Ausrichtung bei. Fenster, Türen und Dachfenster sind Teil der Gebäudeumhüllung, die die offene Verbindung des Innenraums mit dem Außenbereich noch deutlicher in Szene setzt.

L'appareillage de fenêtres fait partie intégrante du design de cette habitation, contribuant à sa forte configuration géométrique. Les fenêtres, portes et fenêtres de toit font partie de l'enveloppe de la construction accentuant l'ouverture de l'intérieur de la maison vers l'extérieur.

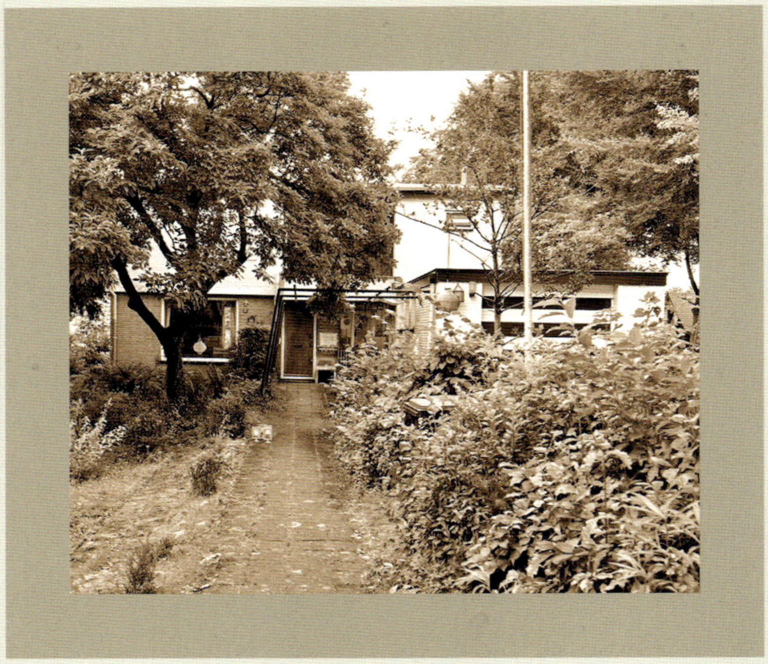

PATIO HOUSE

BLOOT ARCHITECTURE

273 m² | 2,938 sq. ft.

Velp, The Netherlands

Photos © **Ossip van Duivenbode**

> Restore and expand the old dilapidated villa

> Reduce the number of rooms and make them larger

> Create light-filled, open spaces

> Neben der Sanierung die alte, verfallene Villa vergrößern

> Die Zahl der Zimmer verringern und die Zimmer geräumiger machen

> Helle und offene Räume schaffen

> Outre réhabiliter, agrandir l'ancienne villa en ruines

> Réduire le nombre de pièces et les agrandir

> Créer des espaces lumineux et ouverts

This project involved restoring and expanding a decaying villa, built in the 1950s and situated in an incomparable setting: the nature preserve of Veluwezoom National Park.
In the restoration, the large quantity of cramped spaces in the original house was reduced to a small number of spacious and well-lit rooms. An added concrete extension with an atrium-like patio gives the home its name.
The concrete beam along the facade of the original house continues to define the residence's character. Running parallel to the beam is the lower portion of the new addition's ceiling. Since the original beam was only 7.5 feet high, the new construction had to be sunk partially into the ground to create additional height. Besides affording high visual interest, this discrepancy in level also provides a subtle contrast between the different spaces.
Throughout the residence, special emphasis is placed on the visual and physical connections across spaces and with the surrounding setting.

Dieses Projekt ist das Ergebnis der Sanierung und Erweiterung einer heruntergekommenen Villa, die in den 1950er Jahren erbaut wurde und sich in einer wunderschönen Umgebung befindet, dem Veluwezoom Nationalpark, einem Naturschutzgebiet.
Bei der Renovierung wurden die vielen kleinen Zimmer des ursprünglichen Hauses auf eine geringe Anzahl von geräumigen und lichtdurchfluteten Räumen reduziert. Darüber hinaus wurde dem Haus ein Betonanbau mit einem einem Atrium ähnlichen Innenhof hinzugefügt, der dem Projekt seinen Namen gab.
Der Betonträger der Fassade des ursprünglichen Hauses definiert weiterhin die Merkmale des Hauses. Parallel zu diesem Balken befindet sich der untere Teil der neuen Betonbedachung des Anbaus. Da der ursprüngliche Balken nur 2,3 Meter über dem Boden lag, wurde der Anbau teilweise in den Boden eingelassen, um mehr Höhe zu gewinnen. Dieser Höhenunterschied schafft nicht nur einen visuellen Fixpunkt, sondern auch eine subtile Abgrenzung zwischen den verschiedenen Räumen.
Im gesamten Haus wurde besonderer Wert auf die visuellen und physischen Verbindungen zwischen den Räumen und der Umgebung gelegt.

Ce projet est le résultat de la réhabilitation et de l'agrandissement d'une villa en ruines, construite dans les années 50 et située dans un cadre idéal, le Parc national Veluwezoom, une réserve naturelle.
Avec les travaux de rénovation, de nombreuses petites chambres de la maison d'origine ont été réduites à un petit nombre de pièces spacieuses et remplies de lumière. En outre, une extension en béton a été ajoutée à la maison avec un patio semblable à une cour et a donné le nom au projet.
La poutre en béton de la façade de la maison d'origine continue de définir les caractéristiques de l'habitation. Parallèlement à cette poutre se trouve la partie inférieure de la nouvelle toiture en béton de l'extension. Comme la poutre d'origine se trouvait à quelque 2,3 mètres du sol, la poutre supplémentaire a été partiellement enfoncée dans le sol afin de créer plus de hauteur. Cette différence de niveau, en plus de procurer un grand intérêt visuel, présente aussi une subtile distinction entre les divers espaces.
Toute la maison met l'accent sur les connexions visuelles et physiques entre les espaces et le cadre qui l'entoure.

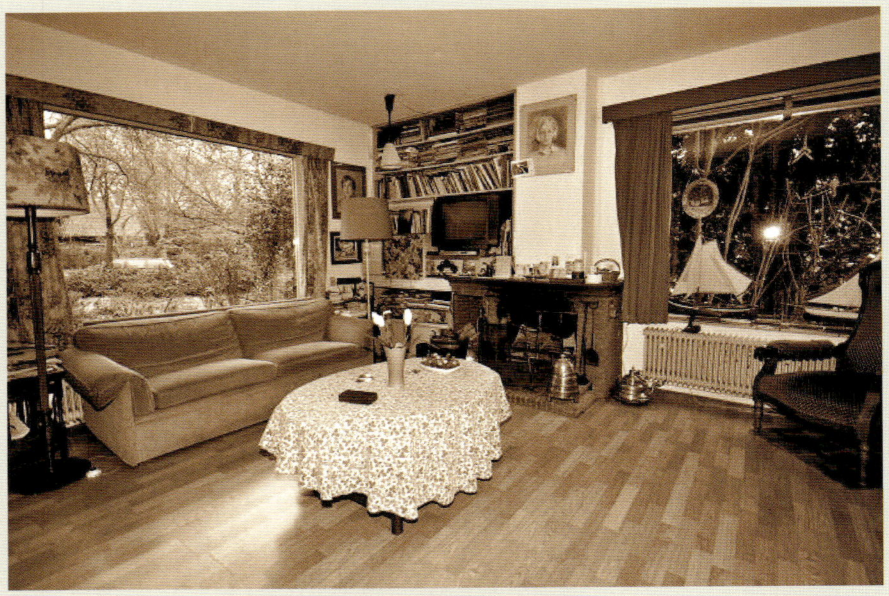

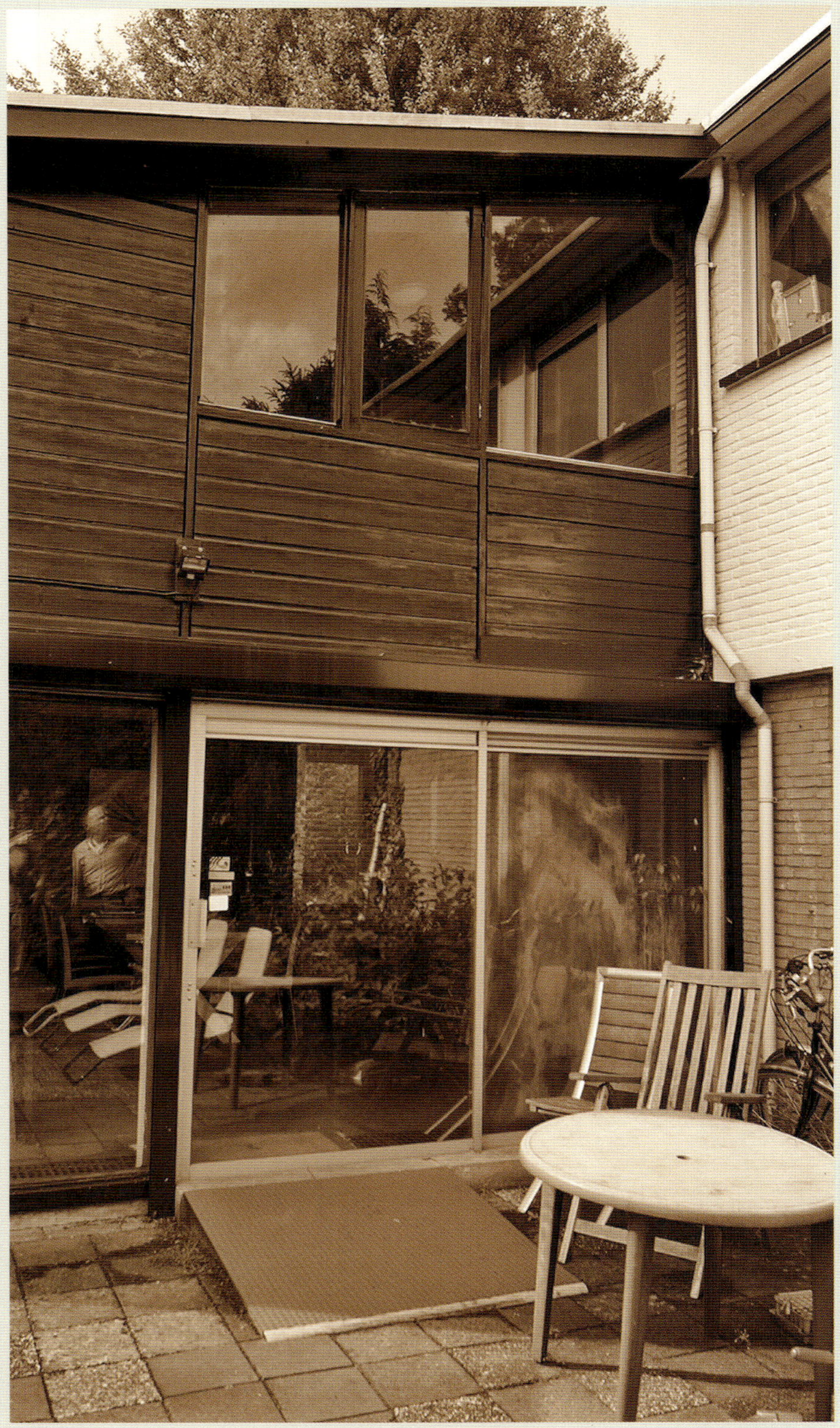

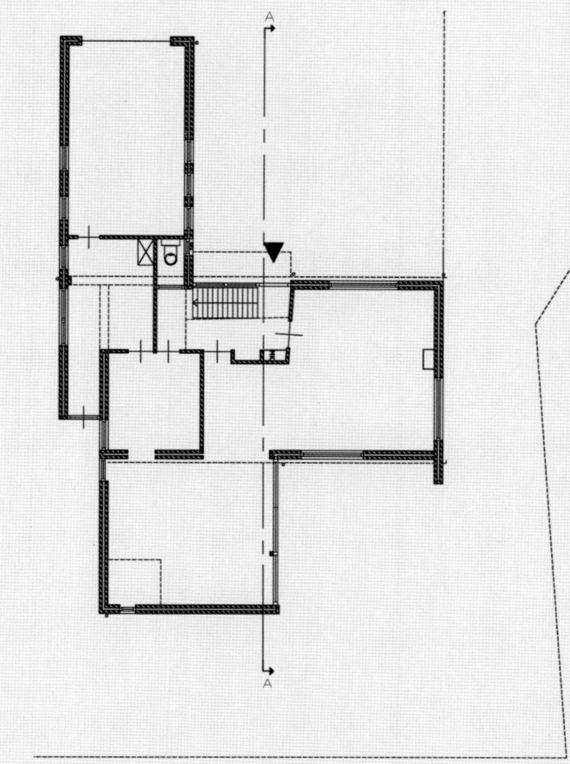

Existing ground floor plan

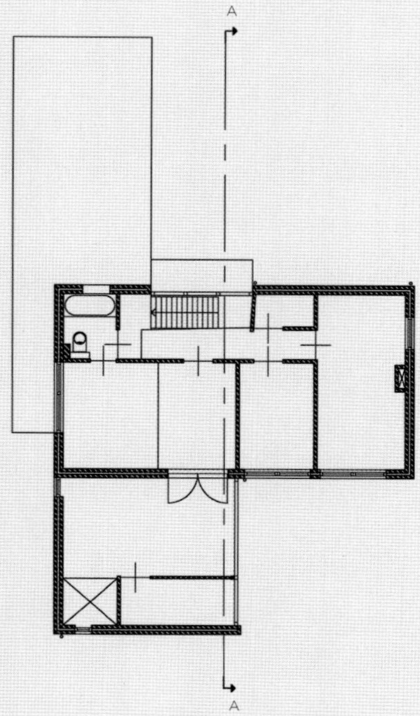

Existing first floor plan

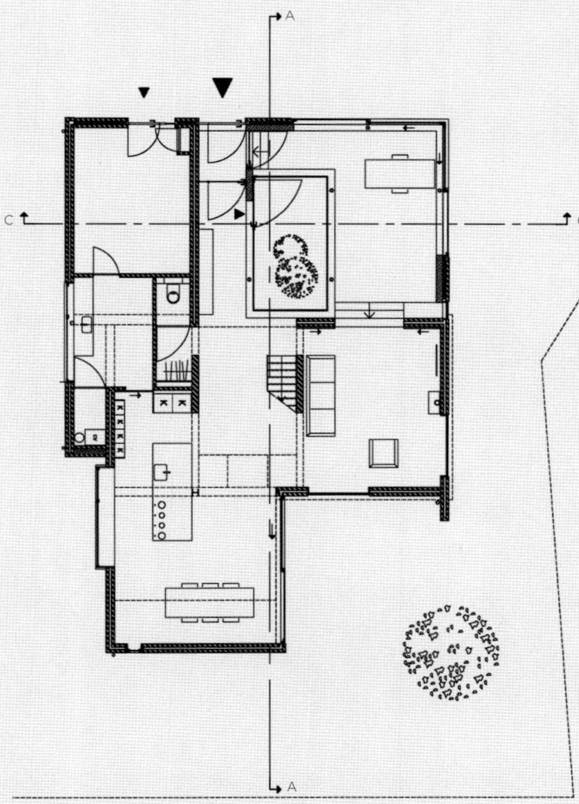

New ground floor plan

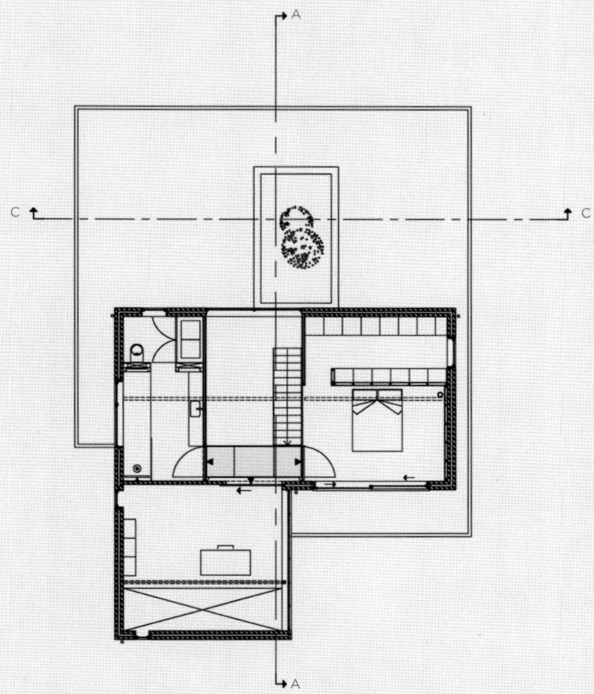

New first floor plan

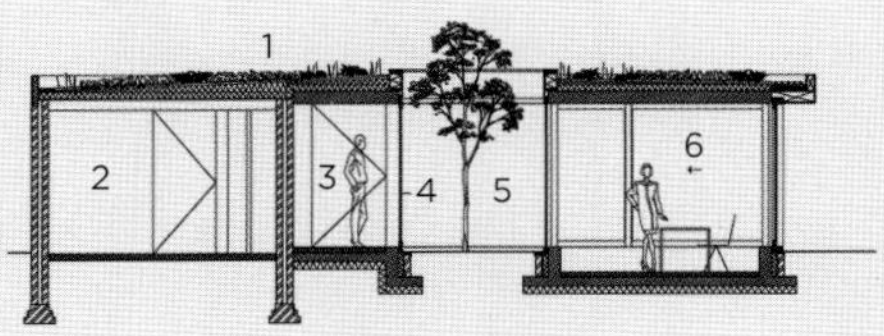

Section CC

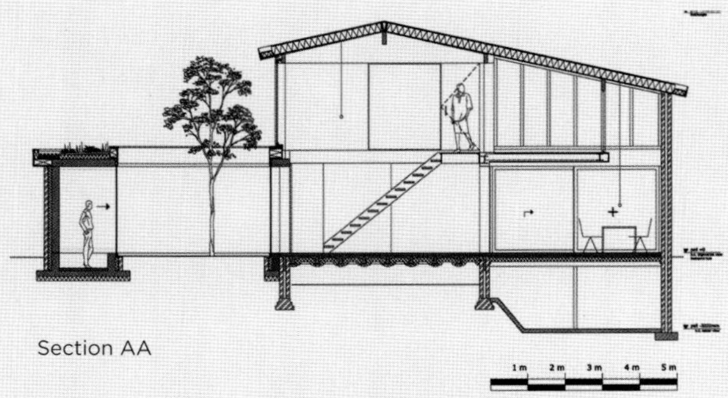

Section AA

1. Green roof
2. Garage (existing structure)
3. Corridor
4. Door
5. Patio
6. Workspace

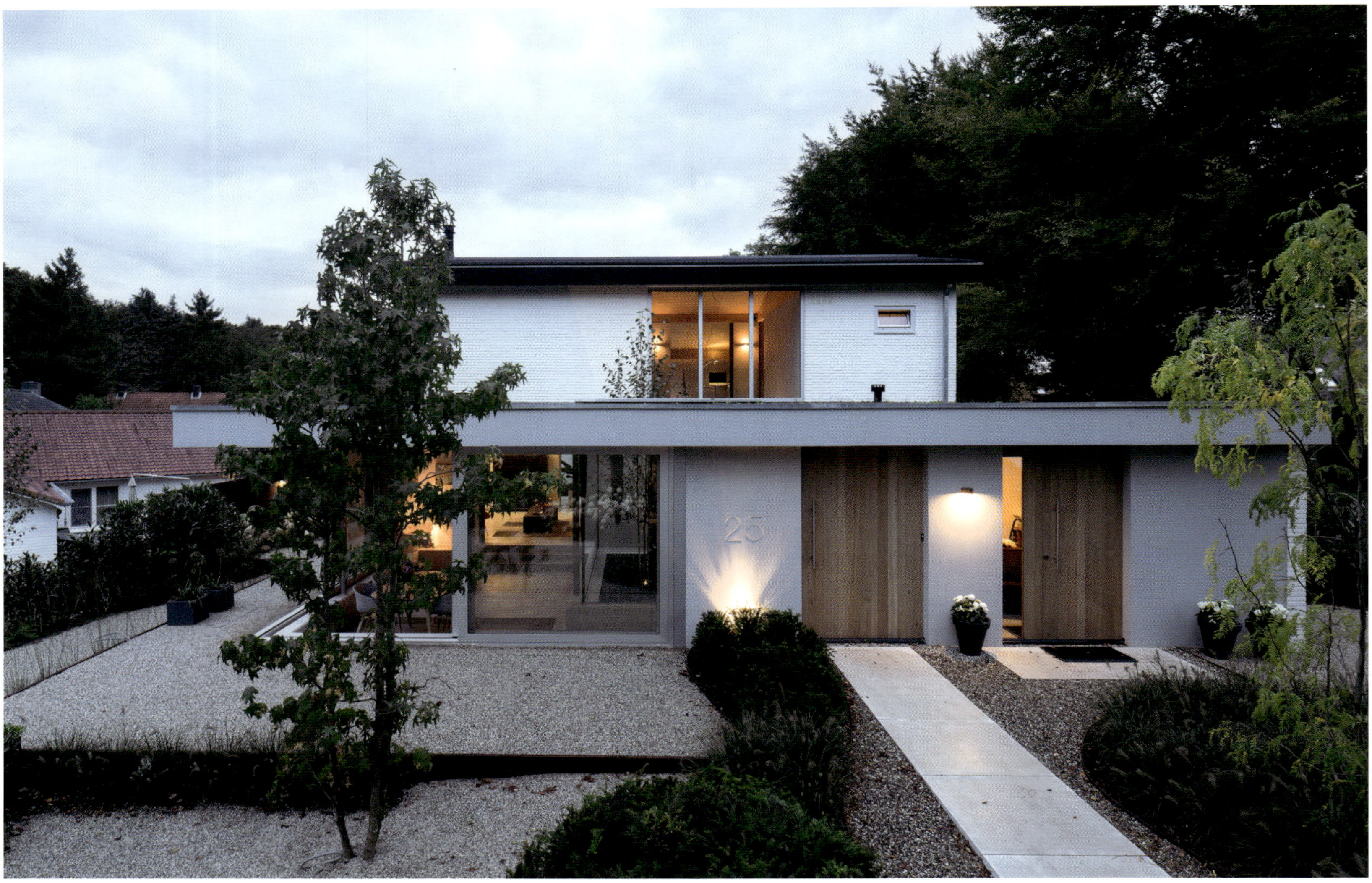
25

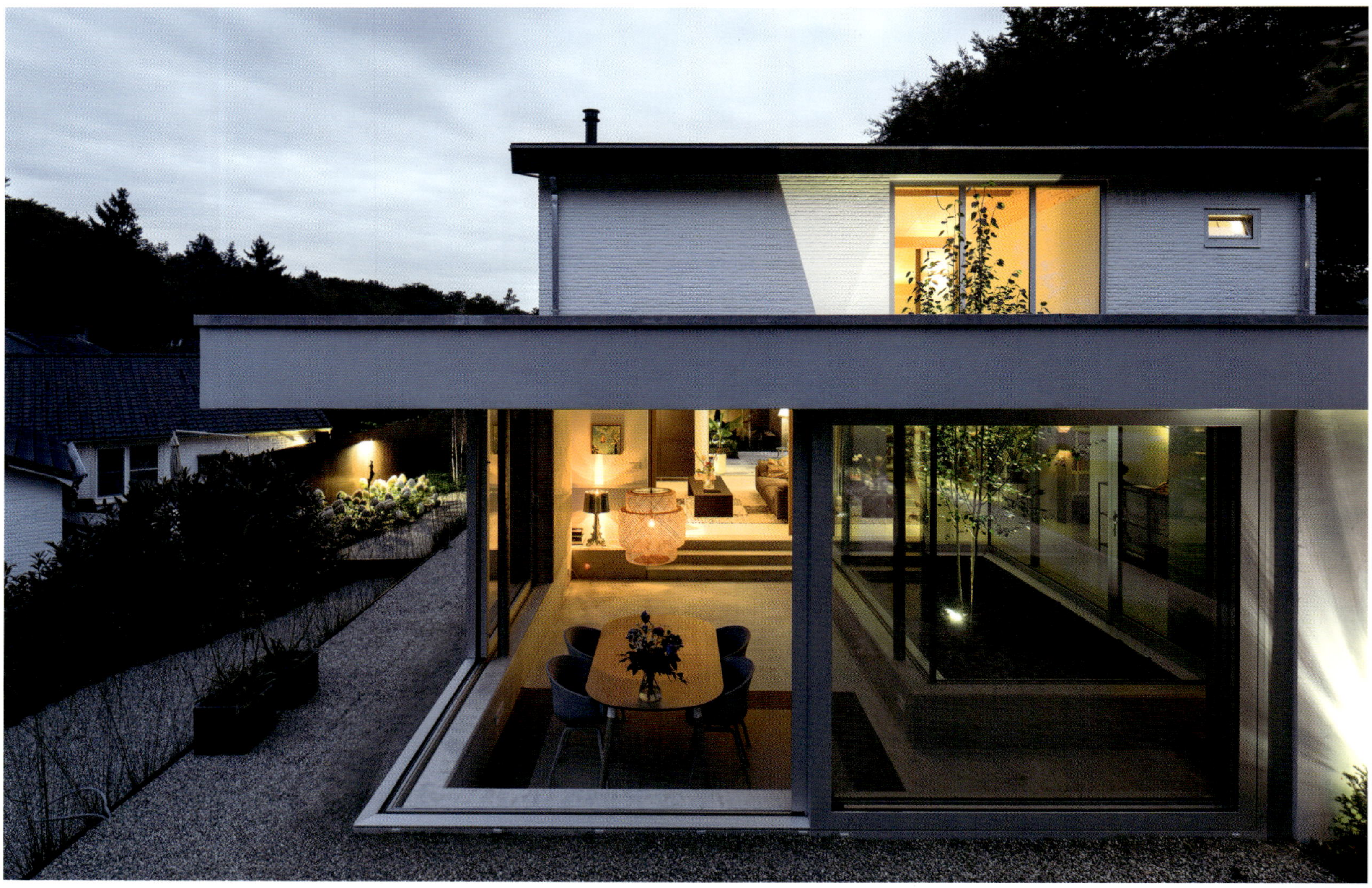

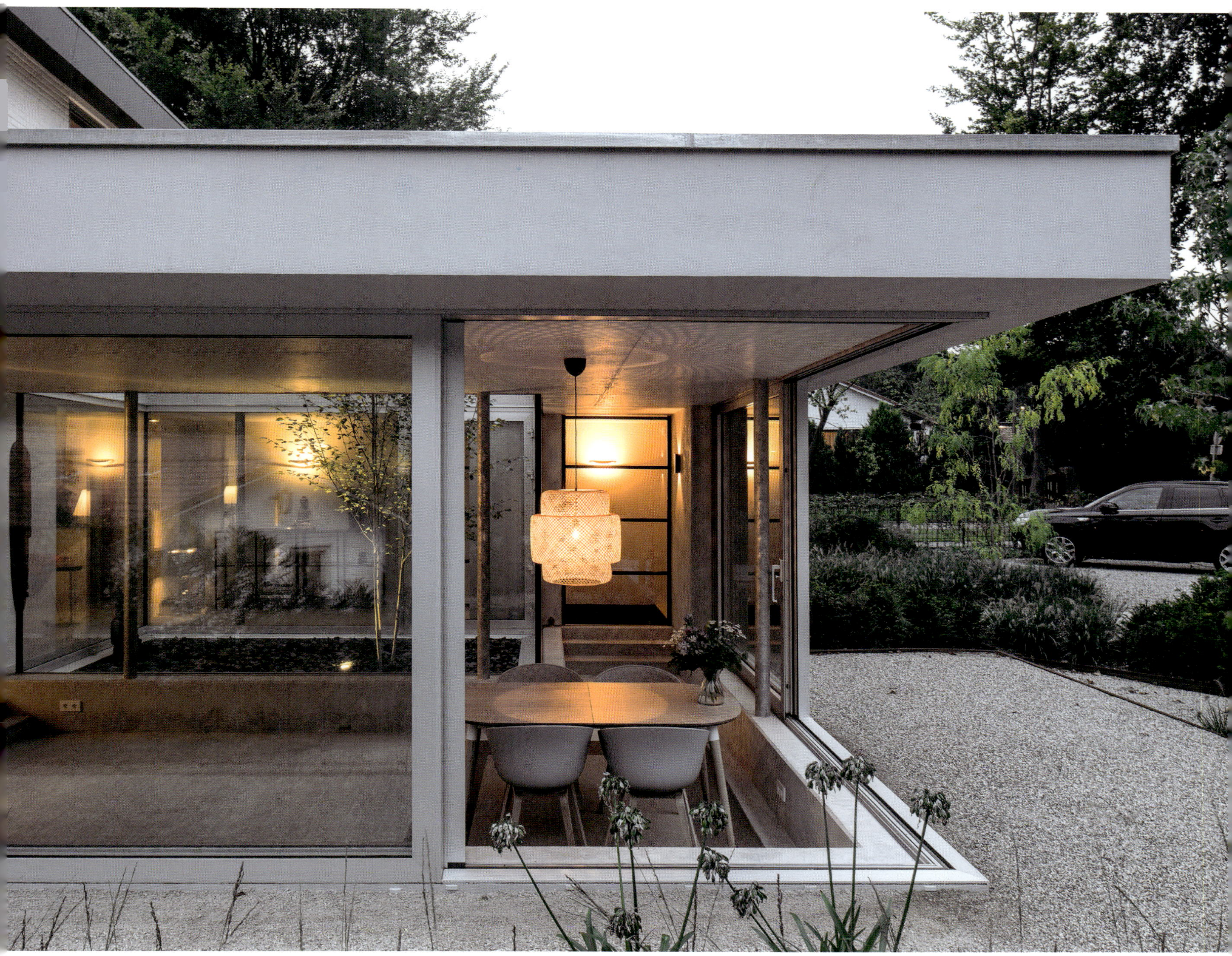

Sunken into the grassy area, the addition blends naturally with the surroundings. Because of the uneven levels, it is possible to sit on the extension's low concrete wall and experience an amusing sensation of being simultaneously inside and outside the structure.

Der Anbau ist im Garten eingelassen und fügt sich auf natürliche Weise in die Umgebung ein. Der Hang ermöglicht es den Bewohnern, auf der niedrigen Betonmauer des Anbaus zu sitzen und das angenehme Gefühl zu genießen, gleichzeitig drinnen und draußen zu sein.

L'extension se trouve engloutie dans le jardin et se fond naturellement au cadre. Le dénivellement permet de s'asseoir sur le muret en béton de l'extension créant une sensation amusante d'être à la fois à l'intérieur et à l'extérieur.

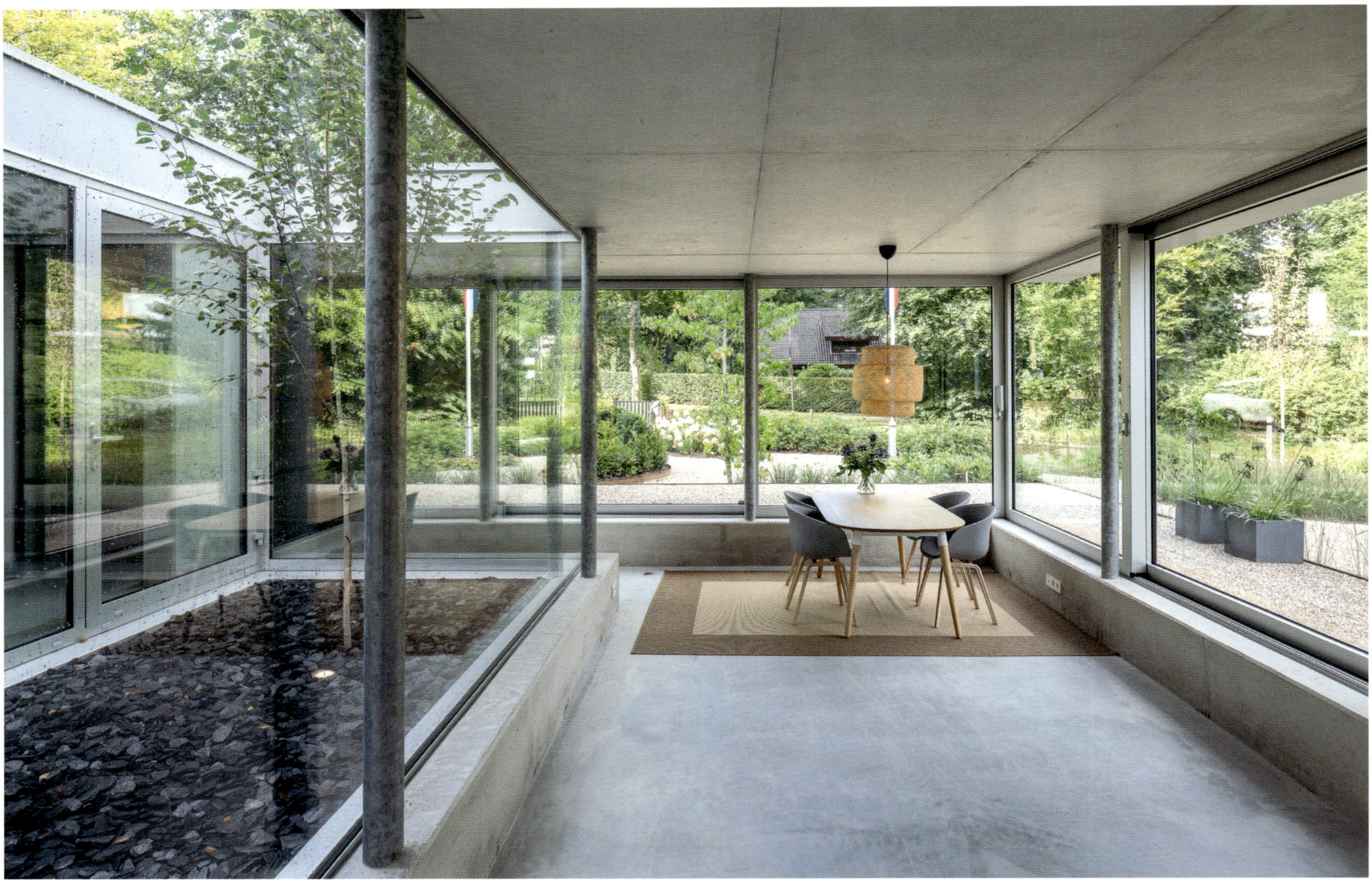

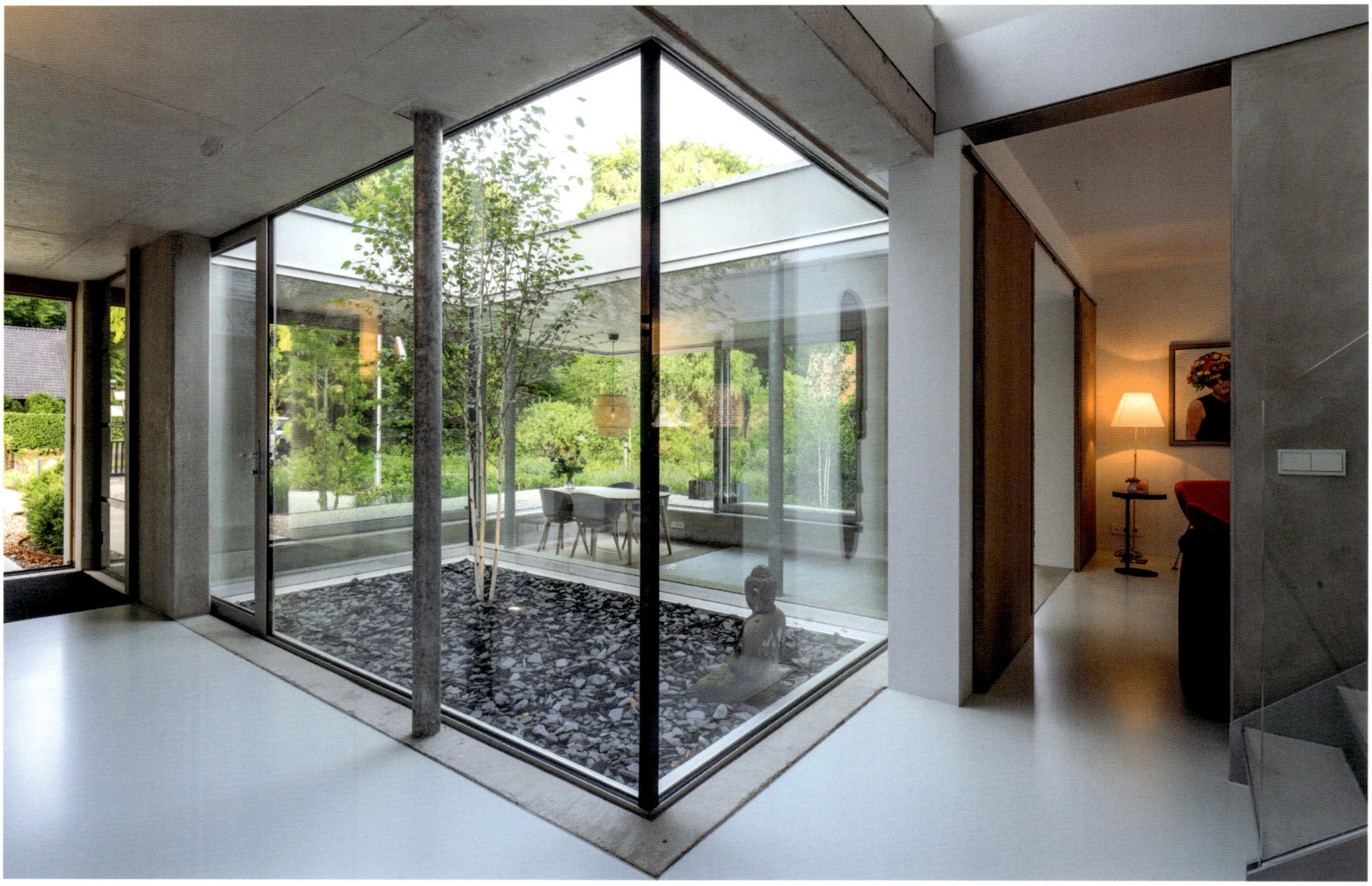

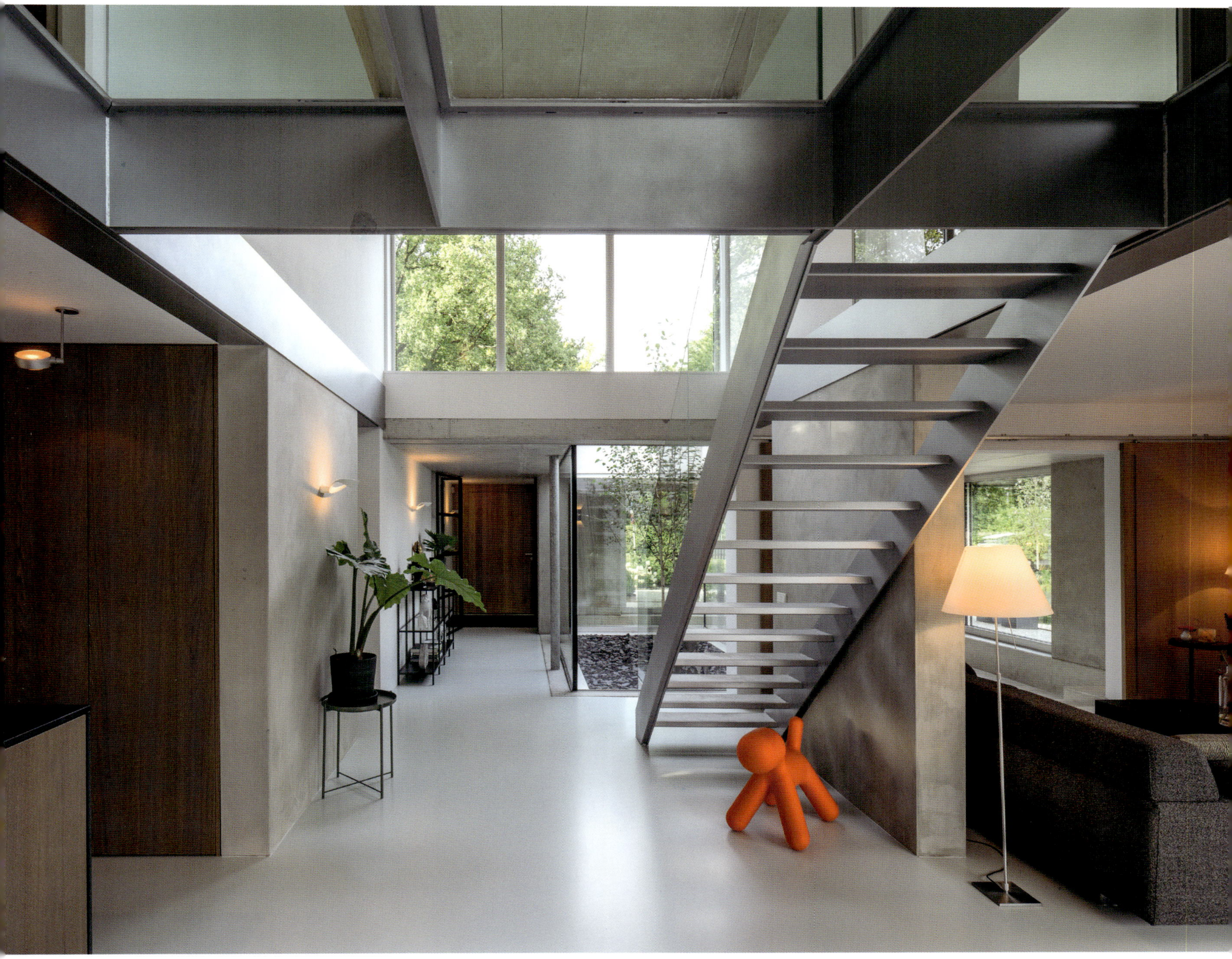

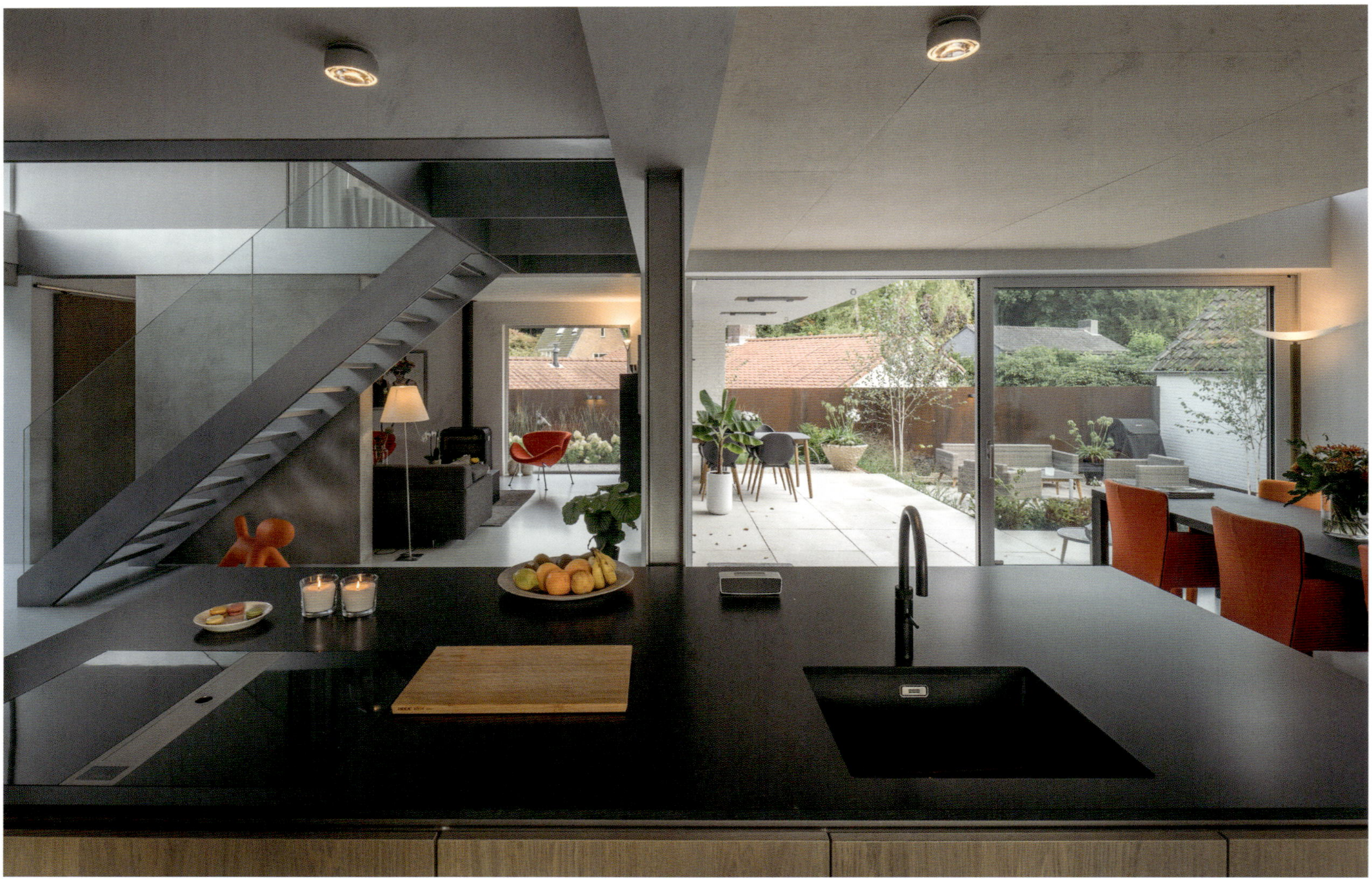

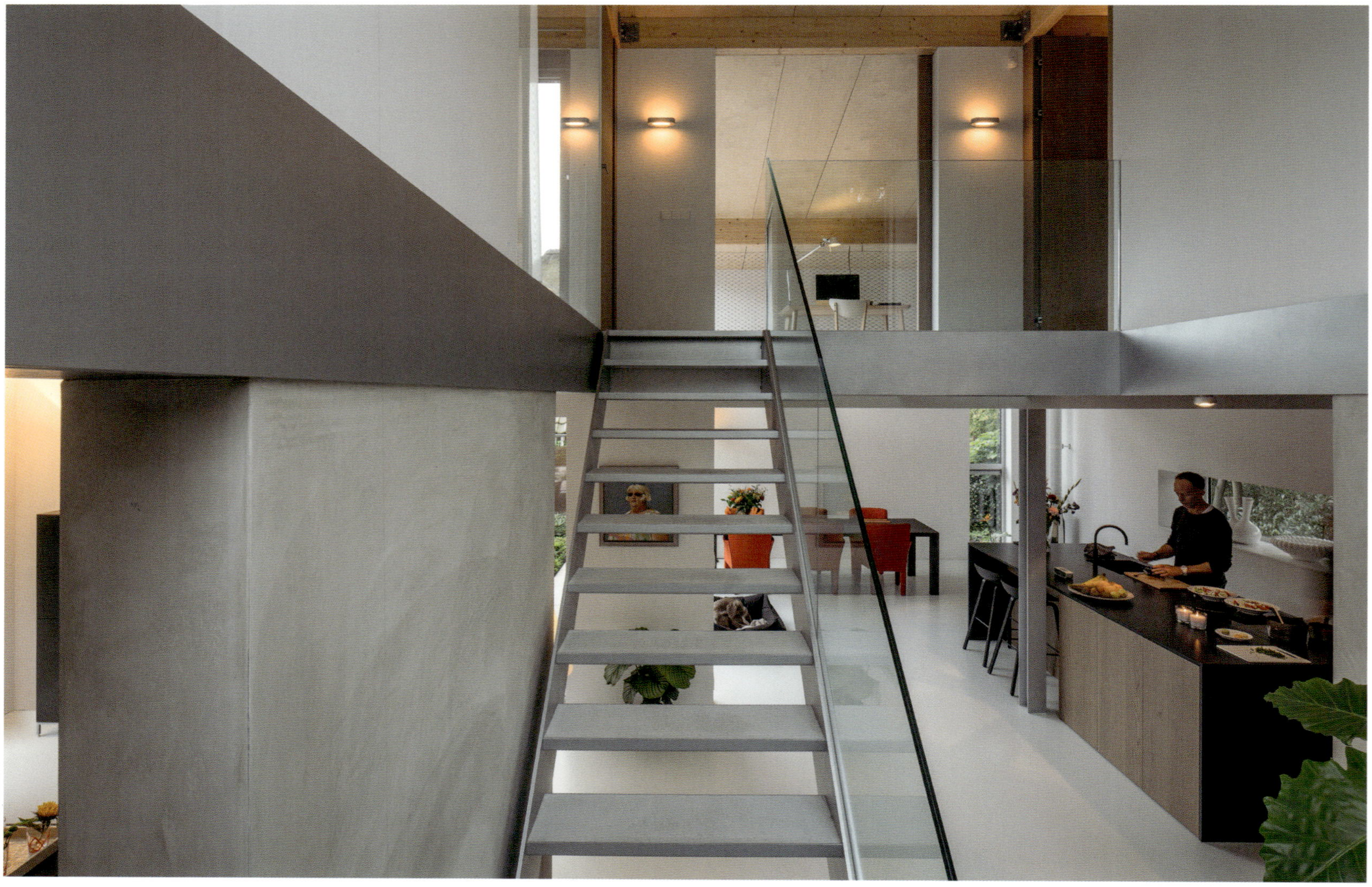

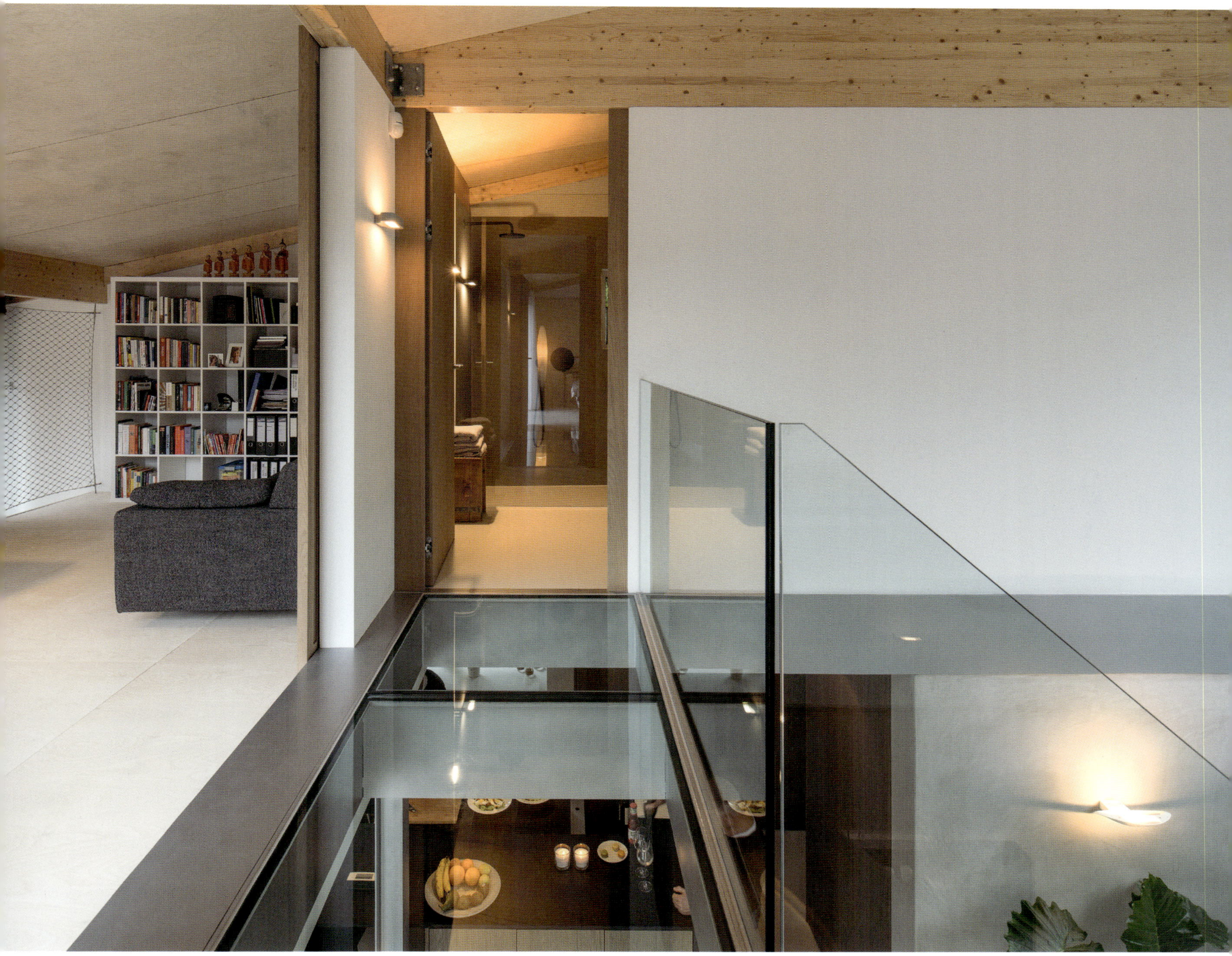

The sparing partition use, patio, large picture windows, and hallways allow natural light to stream into the residence to reveal the sight lines of the various interior and exterior spaces; this effect makes the spaces flow gently into one another.

Möglichst wenige Zwischenwände, Innenhof, Panoramafenster und Korridore sorgen dafür, dass Tageslicht ins Haus kommt und zeigen die Blickachsen der verschiedenen Innen- und Außenräume. Dadurch gehen die Räume fließend ineinander über.

La cour, l'utilisation limitée des cloisons, les baies vitrées plus grandes et les couloirs permettent à la lumière naturelle d'entrer dans la maison et de mettre en relief les lignes de vision des divers espaces intérieurs et extérieurs ; ceci fait que les espaces s'échappent doucement les uns après les autres.

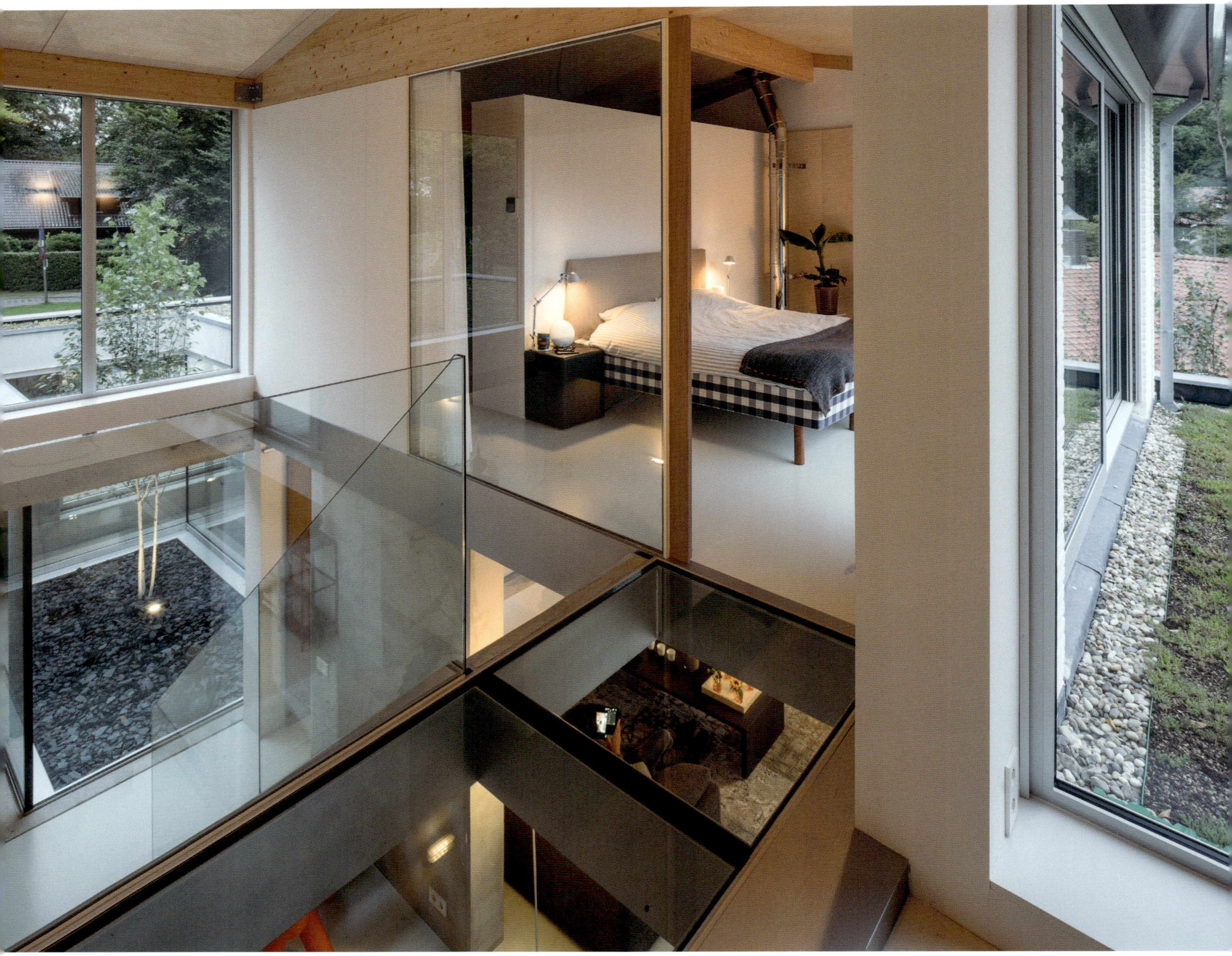

Although the different living spaces are openly interconnected, the separate rooms each retain their own intimate atmosphere.

Obgleich die verschiedenen Wohnräume in offener Verbindung miteinander stehen, behalten die separaten Räume ihre eigene intime Atmosphäre.

Même si les divers espaces habitables sont ouverts entre eux, les chambres séparées conservent leur propre intimité.

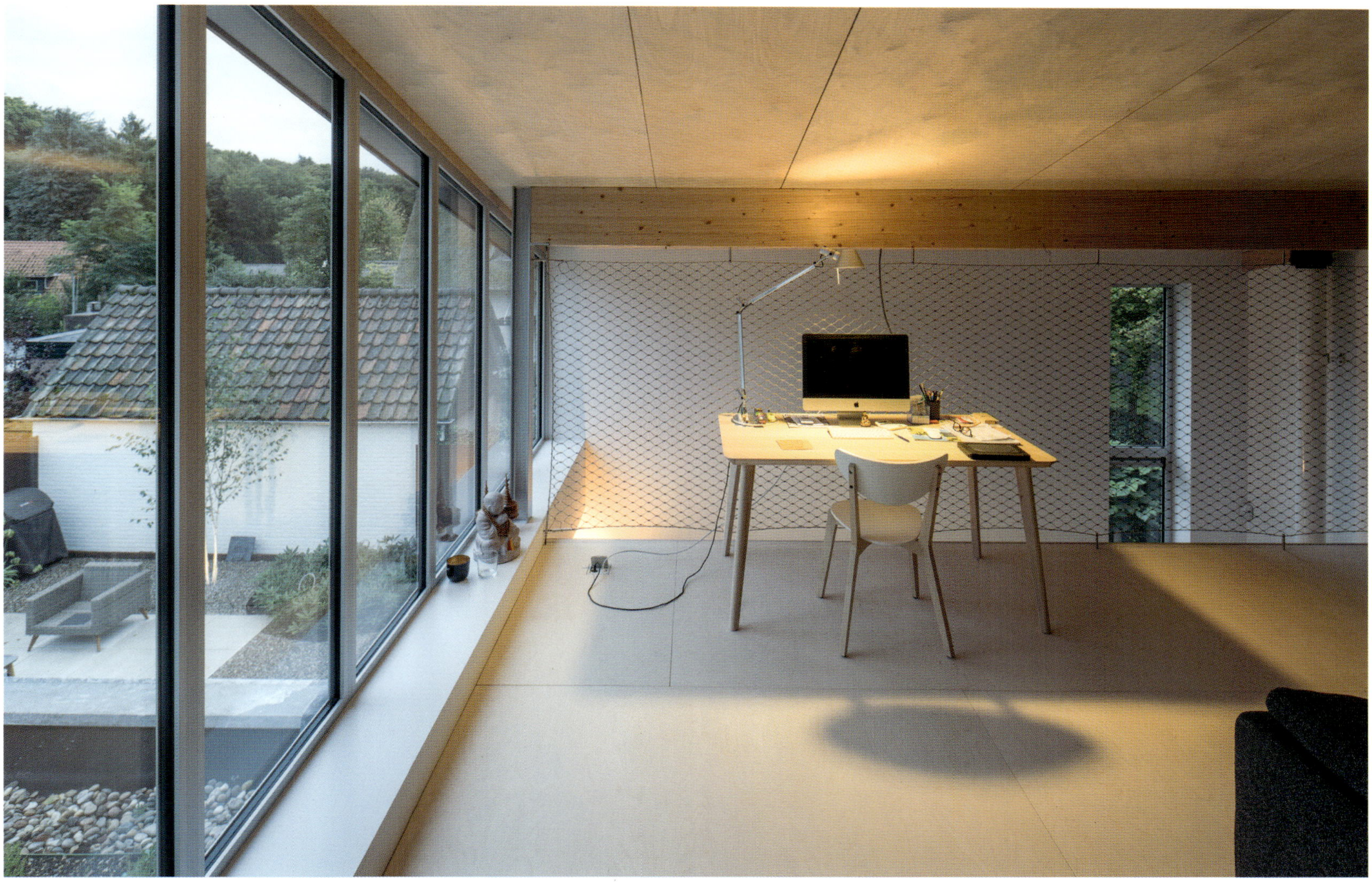

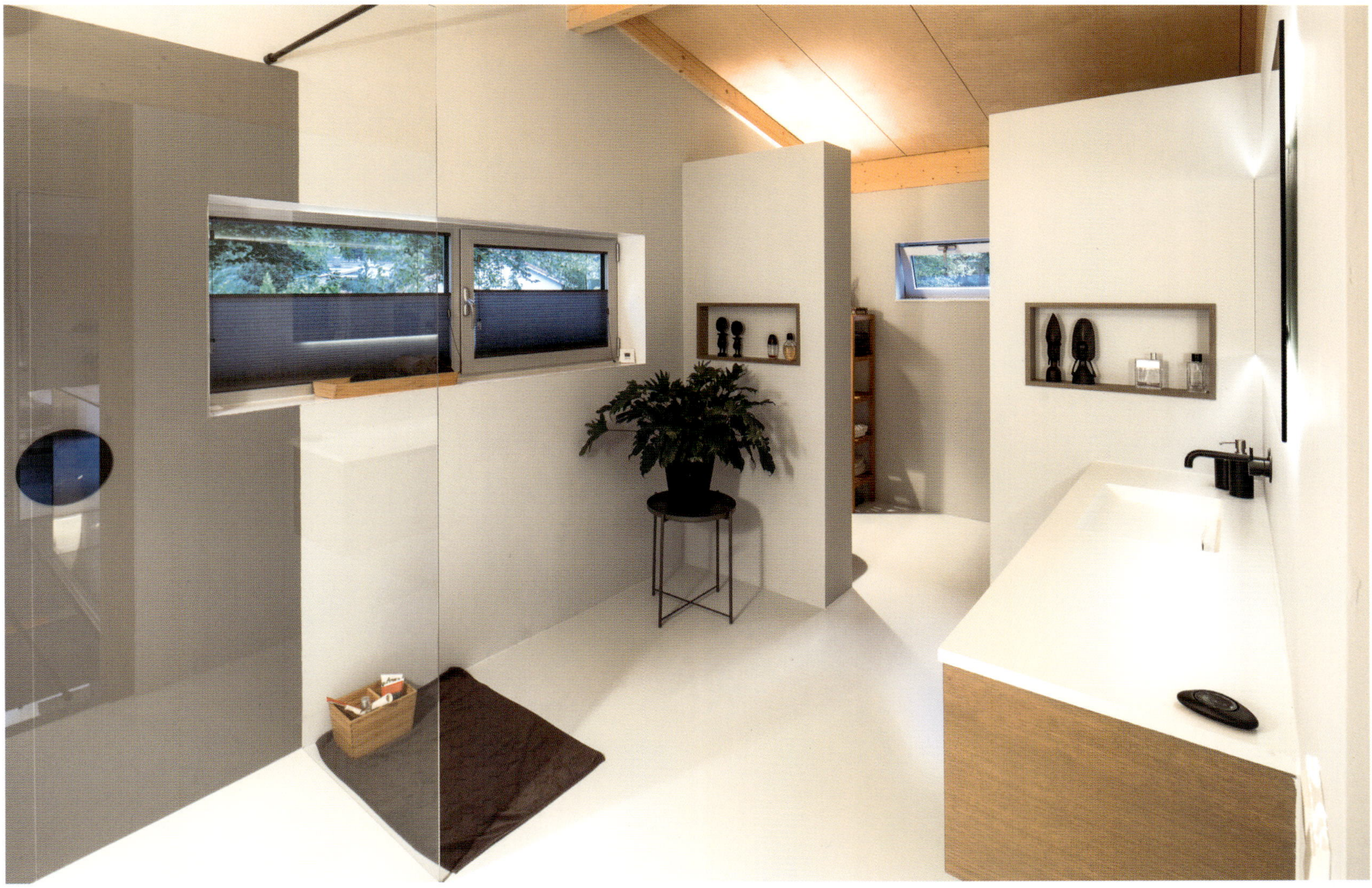

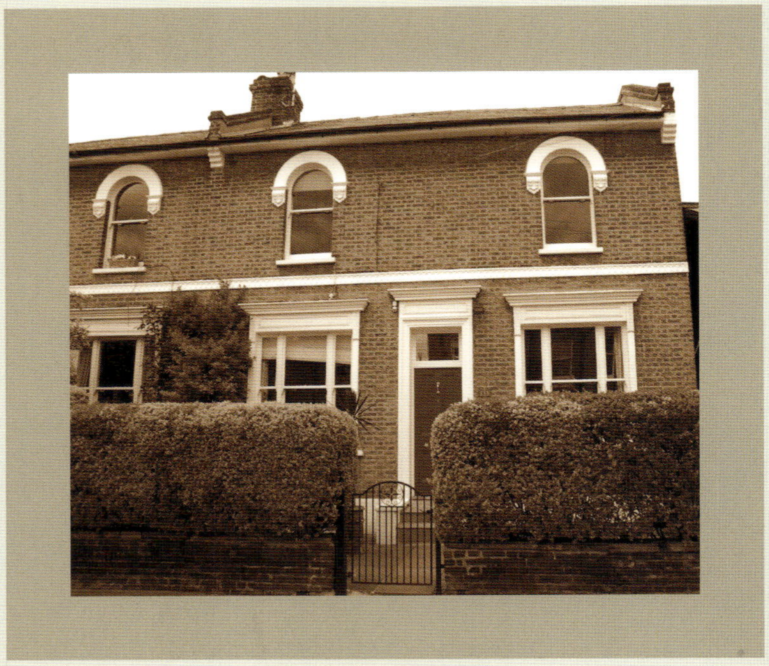

BRACKENBURY HOUSE

NEIL DUSHEIKO ARCHITECTS

180 m^2 | 1,940 sq. ft.

London, United Kingdom

Photos © **Tim Crocker, Agnese Sanvito**

> Expand the residence

> Open up the ground-floor layout as much as possible

> Link the spaces visually

> Achieve maximum connection with outside areas

> Permit the entry of natural light to the greatest possible extent

> Vergrößern des Hauses

> Maximale Öffnung des Raumes im Erdgeschoss und visuelle Verbindung der Bereiche

> Maximale Verbindung mit dem Außenbereich

> Ermöglichen des maximalen Lichteinfalls von außen

> Agrandir la maison

> Ouvrir au maximum le plan au rez-de-chaussée

> Connecter visuellement les espaces

> Connexion maximale avec l'extérieur

> Obtenir la luminosité maximale naturelle

This project involves the remodelling and expansion of a Victorian row house for a young family. The objectives were clear: achieve open, well-lit and visually connected spaces and connect these to the outside; expand the residence to adapt it to the family's needs; use a palette of natural materials to give the home a contemporary style. Furthermore, values of sustainability and energy savings were to be kept very much in mind in tackling this project.
The design adds a new basement beneath the existing house, illuminated throughout by large skylights and featuring an in-home movie theater, game room, and guest bedroom; and a rear extension, expanding the salon and kitchen.
All the levels were opened up, with the original rooms of the Victorian house giving way to an open ground-floor interior and high-ceilinged loft spaces in the bedrooms on the upper floor. A large skylight visually connects the ground floor and the basement, allowing the basement to receive light from above. The kitchen and salon open onto a south-facing patio, achieving in this way a complete integration with the outside area.
Following the renovation, the house gives off a sense of calm and warmth produced by extensive use of natural materials combined with polished concrete and an abundance of natural light.

Dieses Projekt bestand im Umbau und der Erweiterung eines viktorianischen Reihenhauses für eine junge Familie. Die Ziele des Projekts waren klar: Erschaffen offener, lichtdurchfluteter und visuell verbundener Räume wie auch eine Verbindung hin zum Außenbereich, Vergrößern des Gebäudes, um es an die Bedürfnisse der Familie anzupassen und Verwendung einer Palette natürlicher Materialien, um den Zimmern ein modernes Aussehen zu verleihen. Auf der anderen Seite war zu Beginn des Umbaus ebenso wichtig, dass auf Nachhaltigkeit geachtet wurde und Energie eingespart werden soll.
Der Entwurf sieht ein neues Souterrain unterhalb des bestehenden Hauses vor, in dem ein Kinoraum, ein Spielzimmer und ein Zimmer für Gäste liegen werden, die durch große Dachfenster Licht erhalten, sowie eine rückwärtige Erweiterung, in der ein vergrößerter Wohnbereich und eine Küche untergebracht sind.
Jedes der Stockwerke wurde offen gestaltet, damit die ursprünglichen Räume des viktorianischen Hauses nun ein unverbaut gestaltetes Geschoss im Erdgeschoss bilden und in den Schlafzimmern im oberen Stockwerk eine Art Loft-Charakter entsteht. Ein großes Dachfenster eint dieses Geschoss visuell mit dem Souterrain und dem Erdgeschoss, wodurch Tageslicht aus dem darüberliegenden Stockwerk ins Untergeschoss fällt. Die Küche und das Wohnzimmer gehen auf einen nach Süden ausgerichteten Hof hinaus und verbinden so Innen- und Außenbereich perfekt miteinander.
Nach dem Umbau strahlt dieses Haus durch die umfangreiche Verwendung von natürlichen Materialien in Kombination mit dem polierten Zement und den erhöhten Lichteinfall ein Gefühl von Ruhe und Wärme aus.

Ce projet comprend le réaménagement et l'agrandissement d'une maison victorienne mitoyenne pour une jeune famille. Le projet a pour objectif clair d'obtenir des espaces ouverts, lumineux et visuellement connectés, ainsi qu'une connexion avec l'extérieur ; agrandir la maison pour l'adapter aux besoins du client ; utiliser une palette de matériaux naturels pour lui donner un style contemporain. Par ailleurs, au lancement des travaux, il a fallu prendre en considération les critères de durabilité et le gain d'énergie.
La nouvelle conception a permis d'offrir un nouveau sous-sol dans la maison existante, fournissant une salle de cinéma à la maison, une salle de jeux et une chambre d'amis entièrement éclairée par de grandes verrières ; une extension à l'arrière, fournissant ainsi un espace agrandi au salon et à la cuisine.
Tous les niveaux ont été ouverts afin de permettre aux pièces d'origine de la maison victorienne d'offrir un espace ouvert au rez-de-chaussée et des espaces surélevés de type *loft* dans les chambres à l'étage supérieur. Une grande verrière relie visuellement le sous-sol et le rez-de-chaussée permettant au sous-sol de jouir de la lumière du jour provenant d'en haut. La cuisine et le salon donnent sur une cour orientée sud, entièrement intégrés à l'extérieur.
Après avoir réalisé les travaux, la maison irradie de sensation d'apaisement et de chaleur grâce à des matériaux naturels combinés à du béton poli et à l'abondante lumière naturelle.

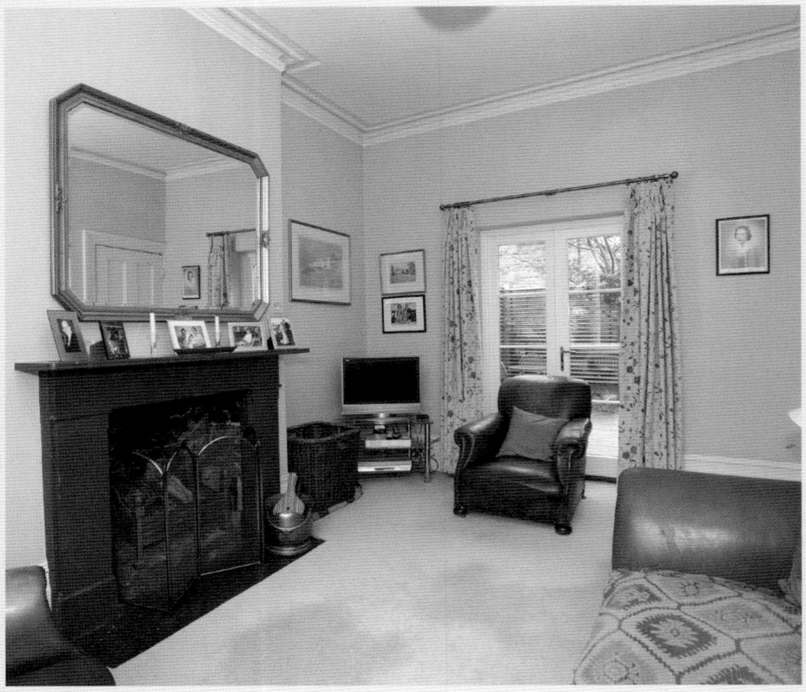

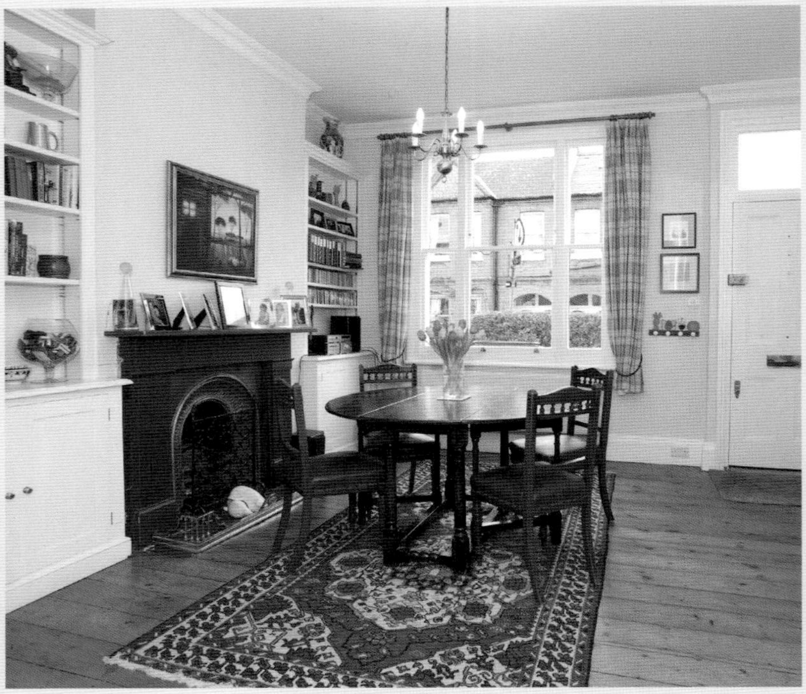

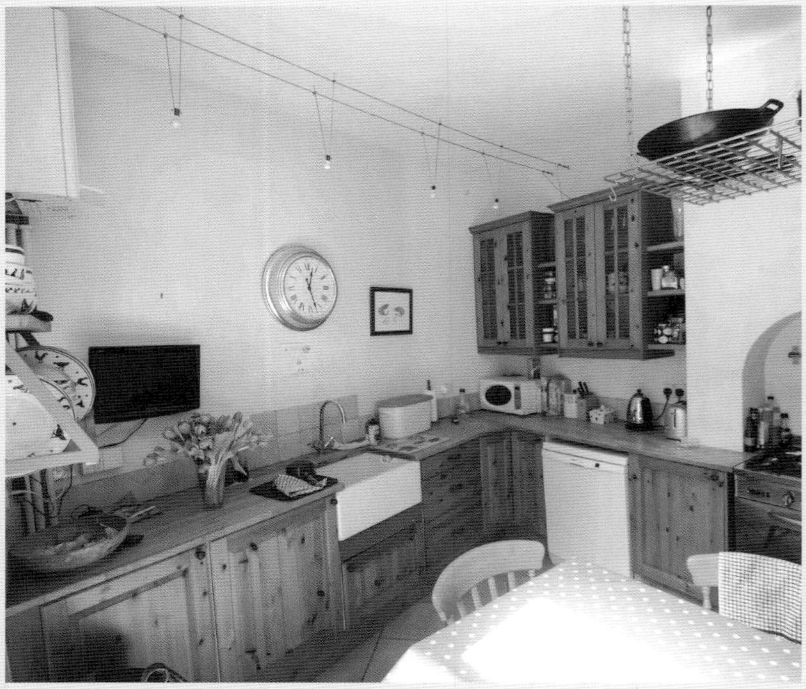

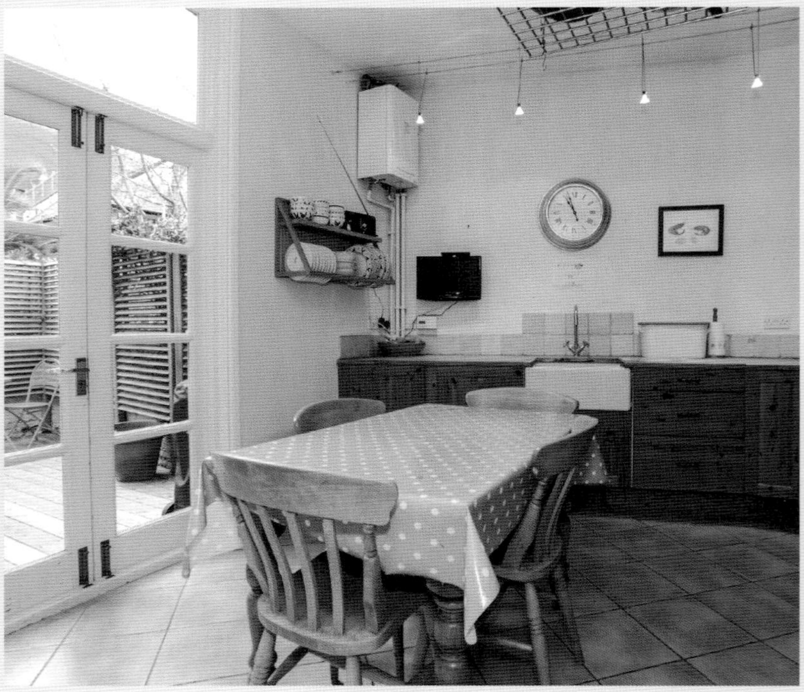

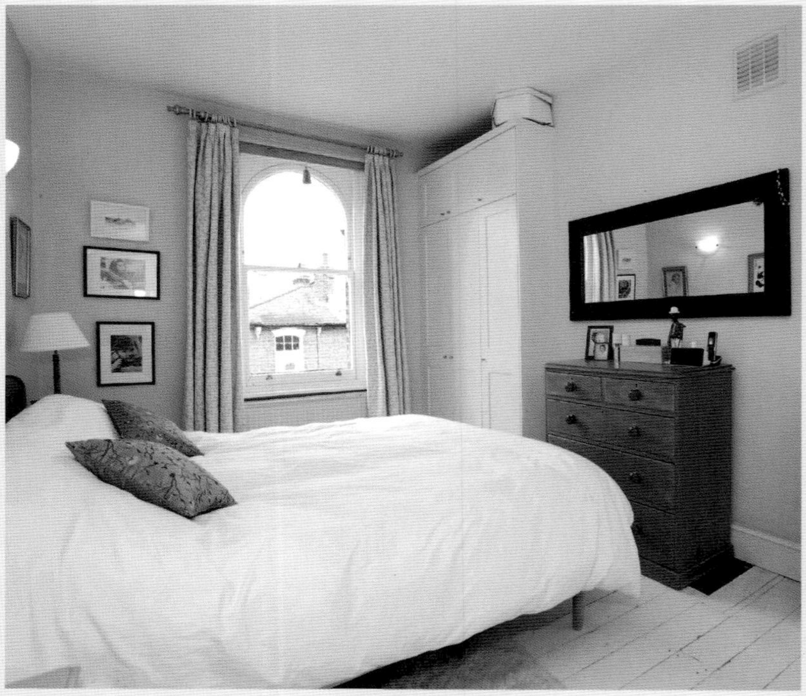

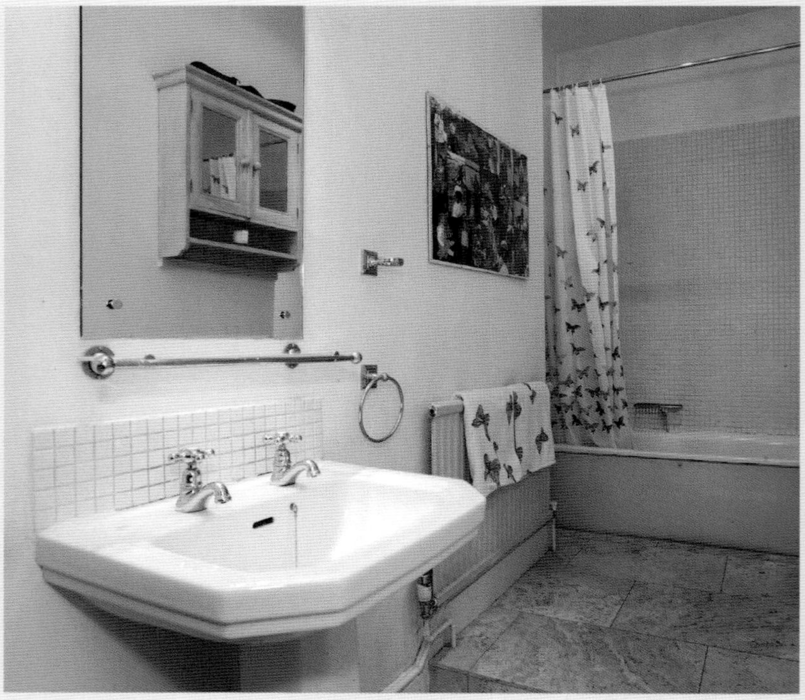

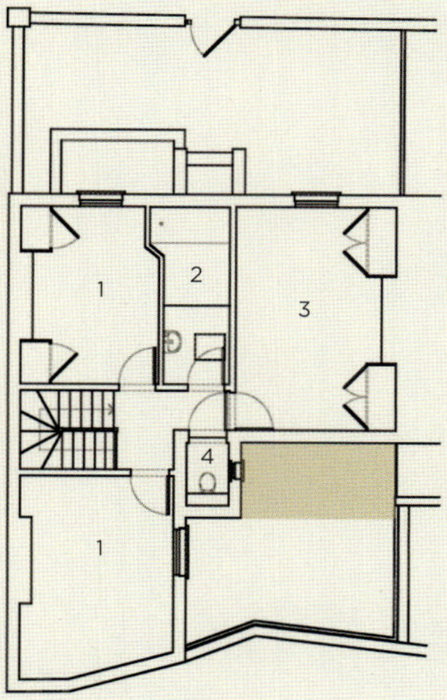

Existing first floor plan

1. Bedroom
2. Bathroom
3. Master bedroom
4. Toilet

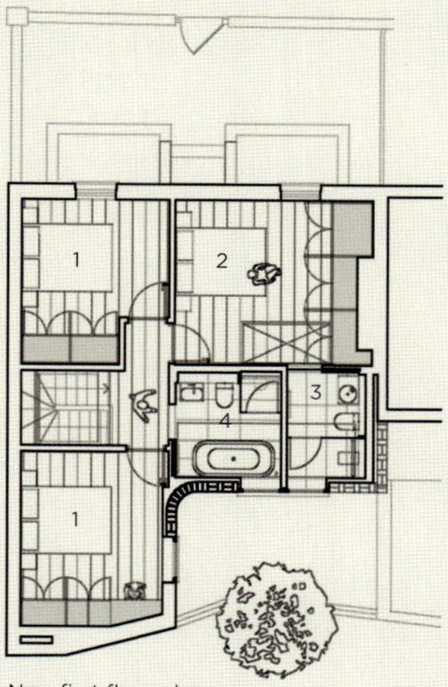

New first floor plan

1. Bedroom
2. Master bedroom
3. En suite
4. Bathroom

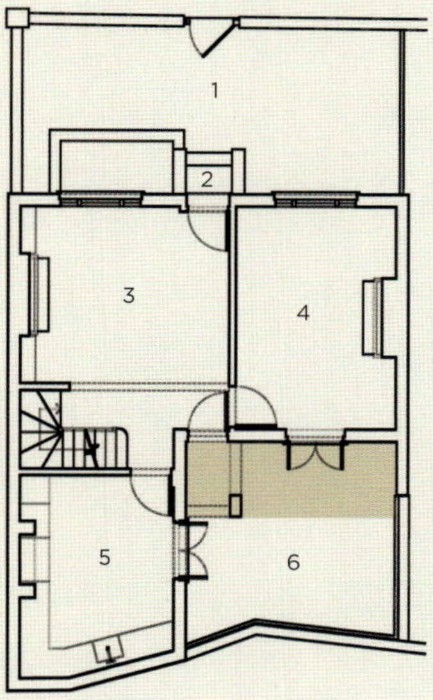

Existing ground floor plan

1. Front garden
2. Entrance
3. Dining room
4. Reception room
5. Kitchen
6. Rear garden

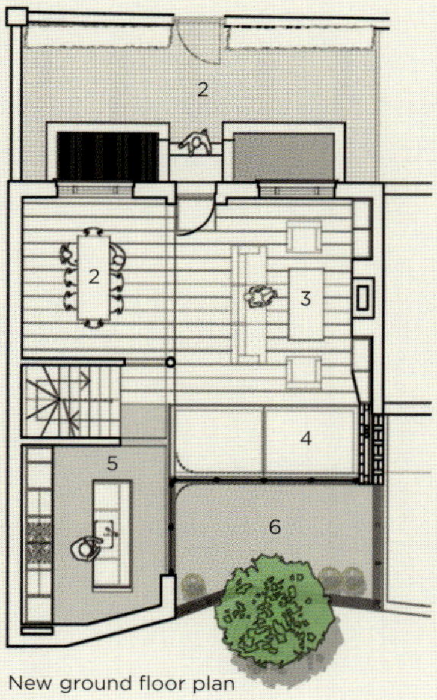

New ground floor plan

1. Front garden
2. Dining
3. Living
4. Glass floor
5. Kitchen
6. Rear garden

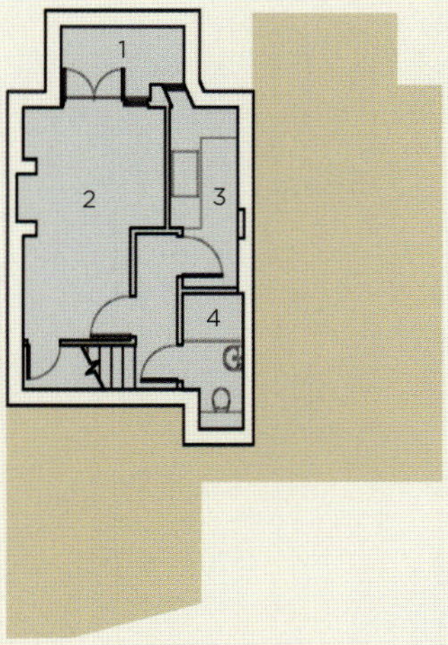

Existing basement plan

1. Light well
2. Bedroom
3. Utility
4. Shower

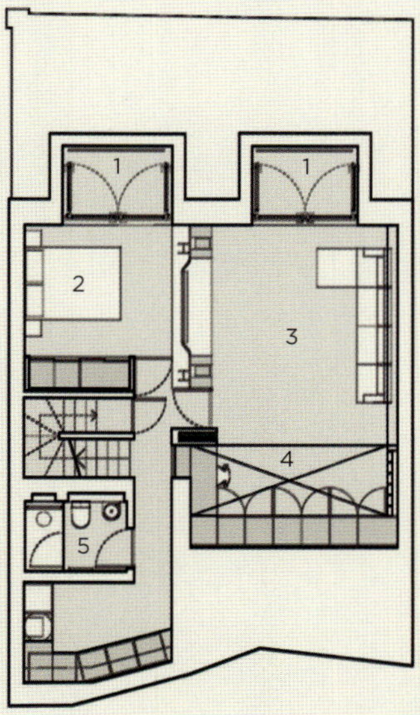

New basement plan

1. Light well
2. Guest bedroom
3. Movie theater
4. Playroom
5. Bathroom

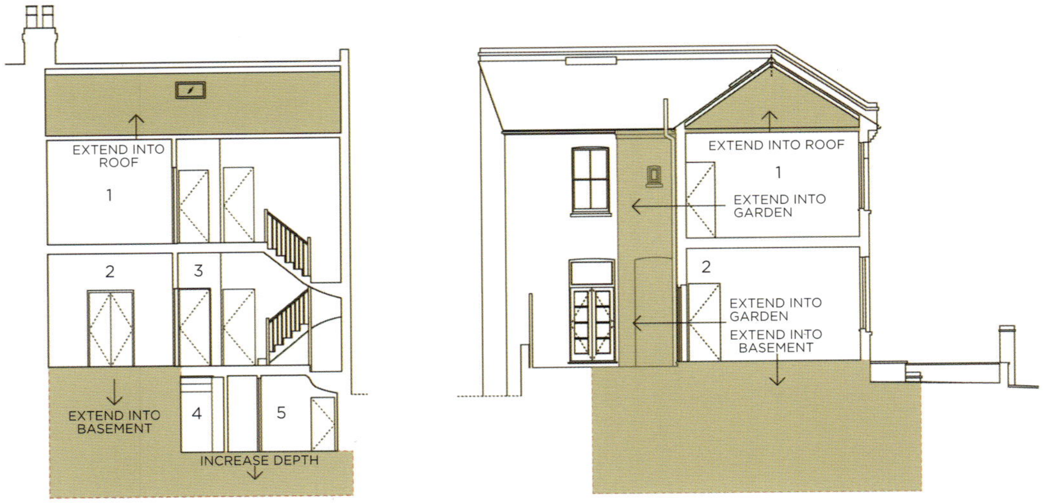

Areas of extension

1. Master bedroom
2. Reception room
3. Dining room
4. Shower
5. Bedroom

Existing sections

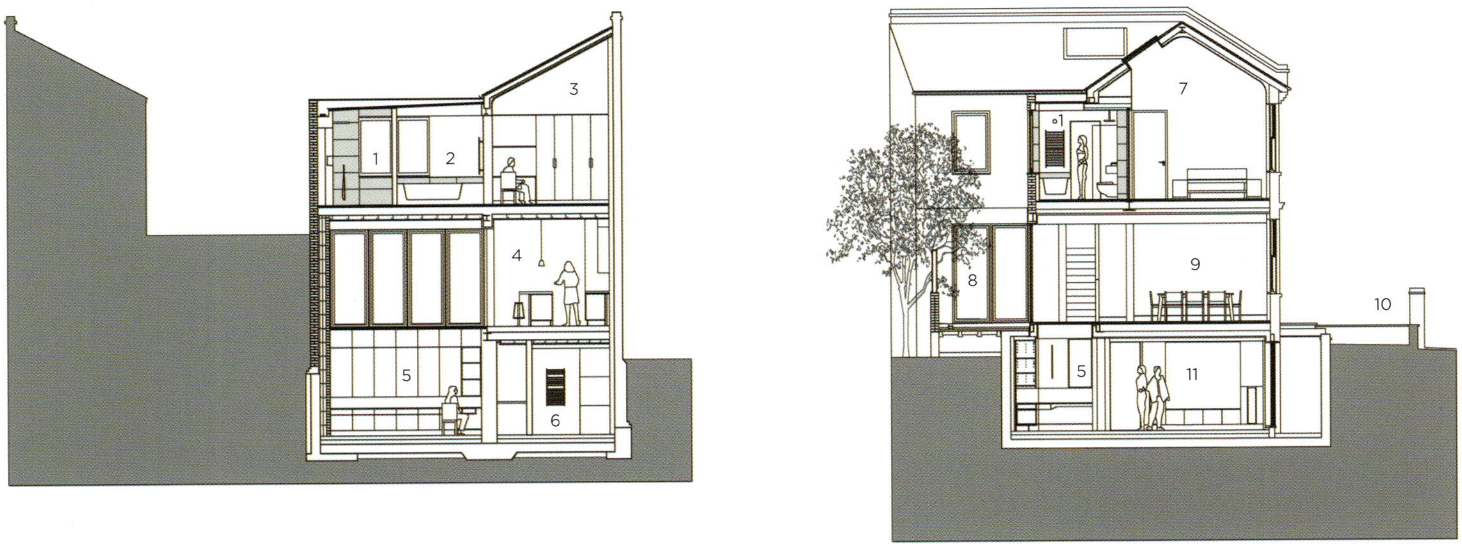

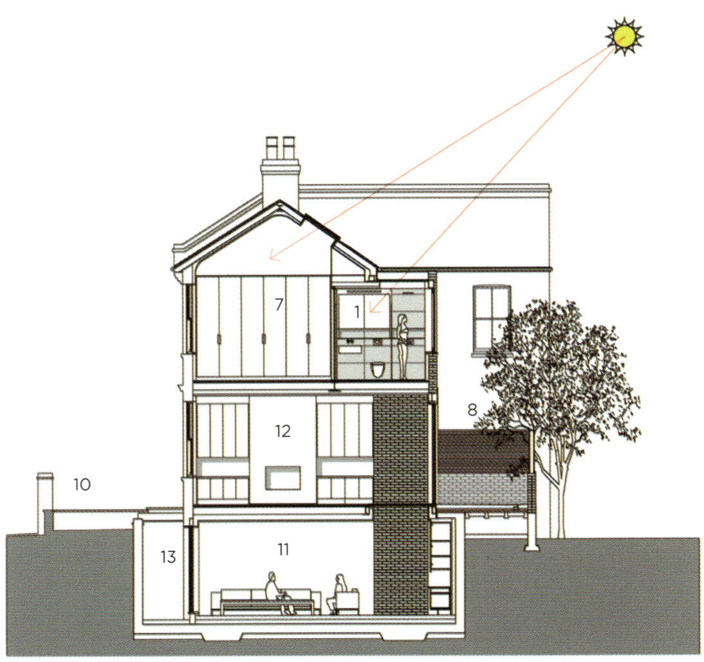

1. En suite bathroom
2. Bathroom
3. Bedroom
4. Kitchen
5. Playroom
6. Bathroom
7. Master bedroom
8. Rear garden
9. Dining
10. Front garden
11. Movie theater
12. Living
13. Light well

New sections

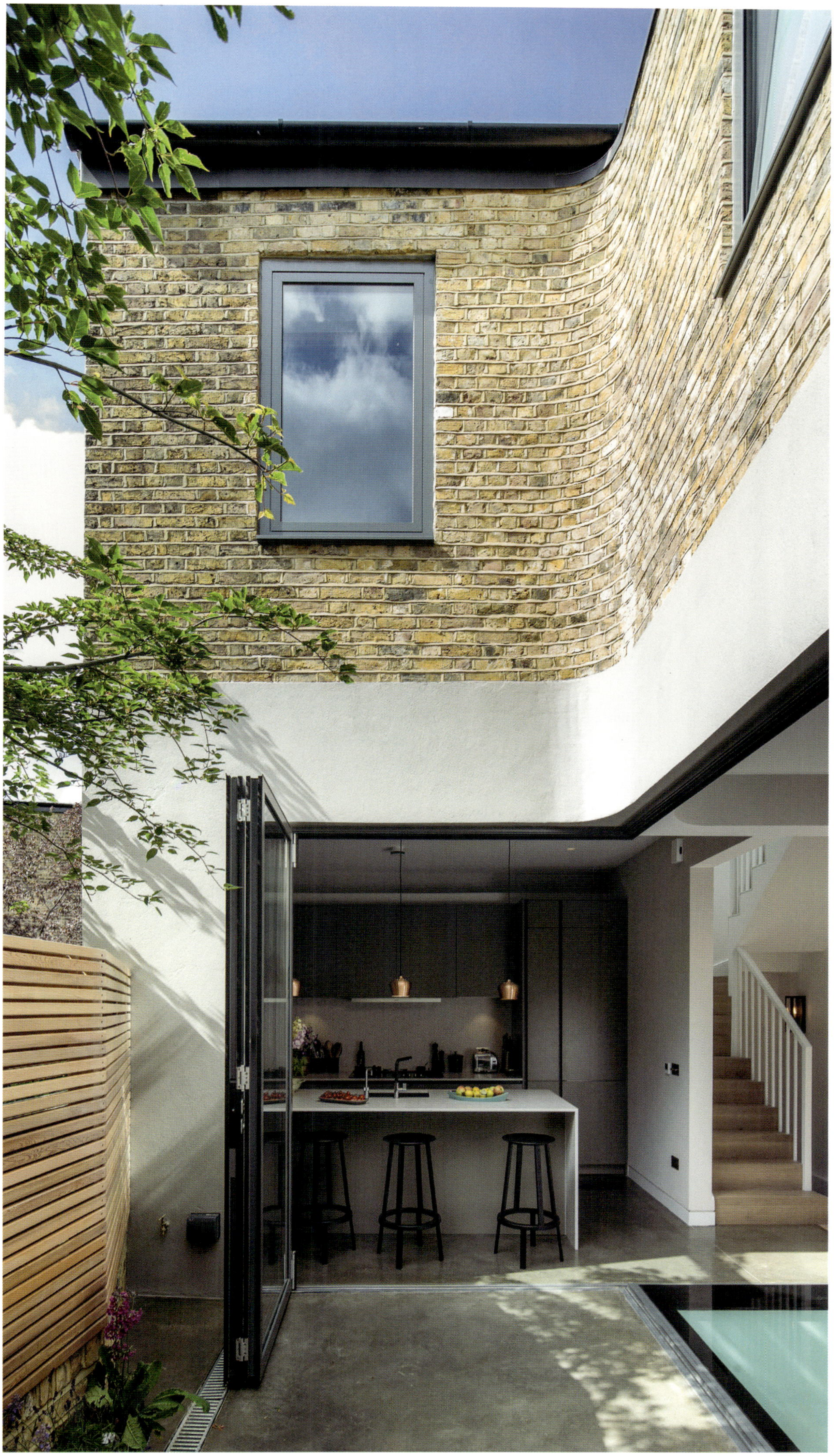

The new extension at the rear of the house is joined to the old facade by a curved wal,made using bricks from the original house. Below it, the facade is completely glazed with a set of folding doors.

Der neue Anbau am rückwärtigen Teil wird mit der alten Fassade durch eine über Eck verlaufende und über dem Boden hängende Wand mit Hilfe eines Falttürelements, das vollständig aus Glas besteht, verbunden. Für dieses Bauelement wurden die Ziegel des Ursprungshauses verwendet.

La nouvelle extension à l'arrière de la maison communique avec l'ancienne façade par un mur courbe suspendu au sol sur un ensemble de portes repliables entièrement vitrées. Des briques de la maison d'origine ont été utilisées pour sa construction.

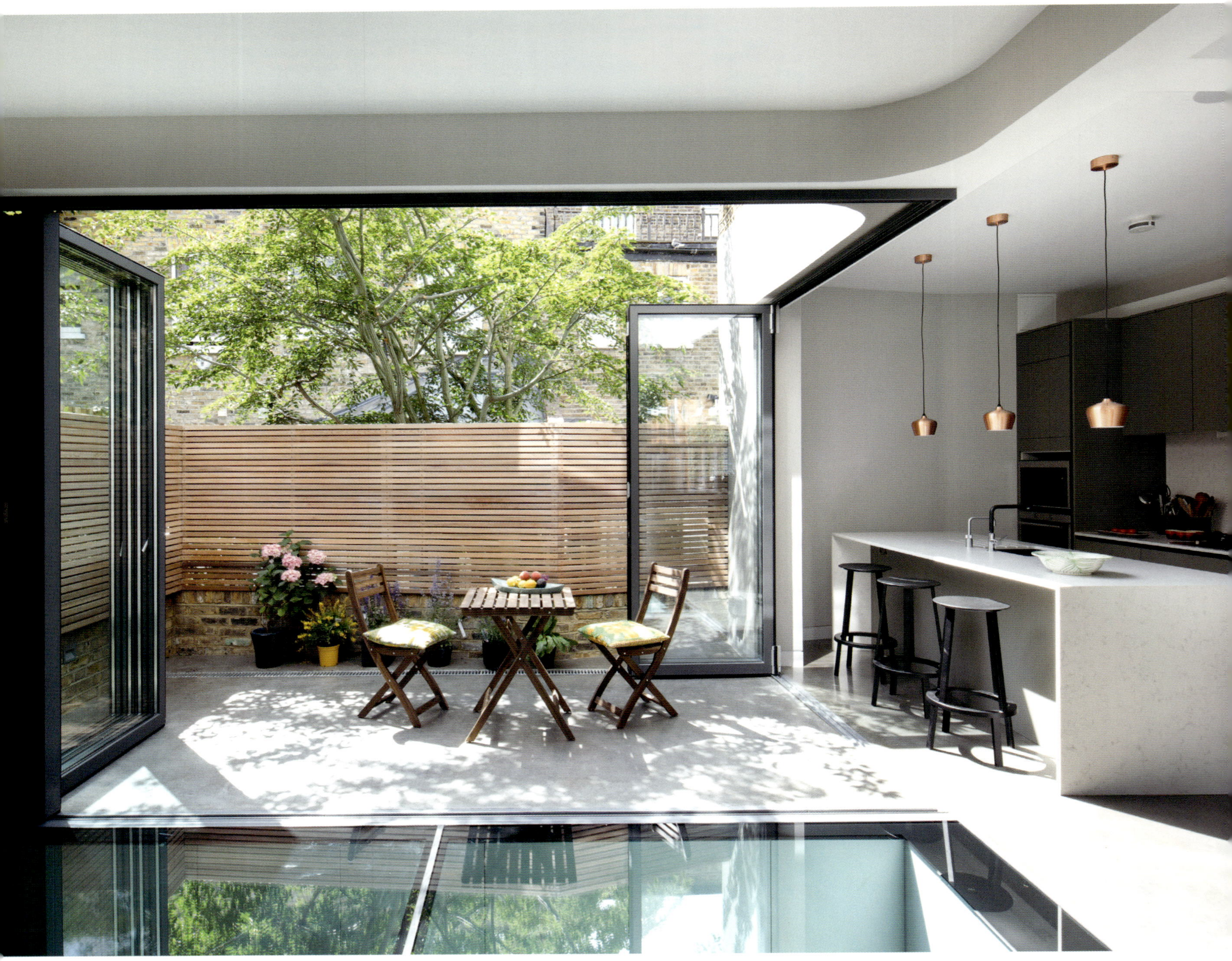

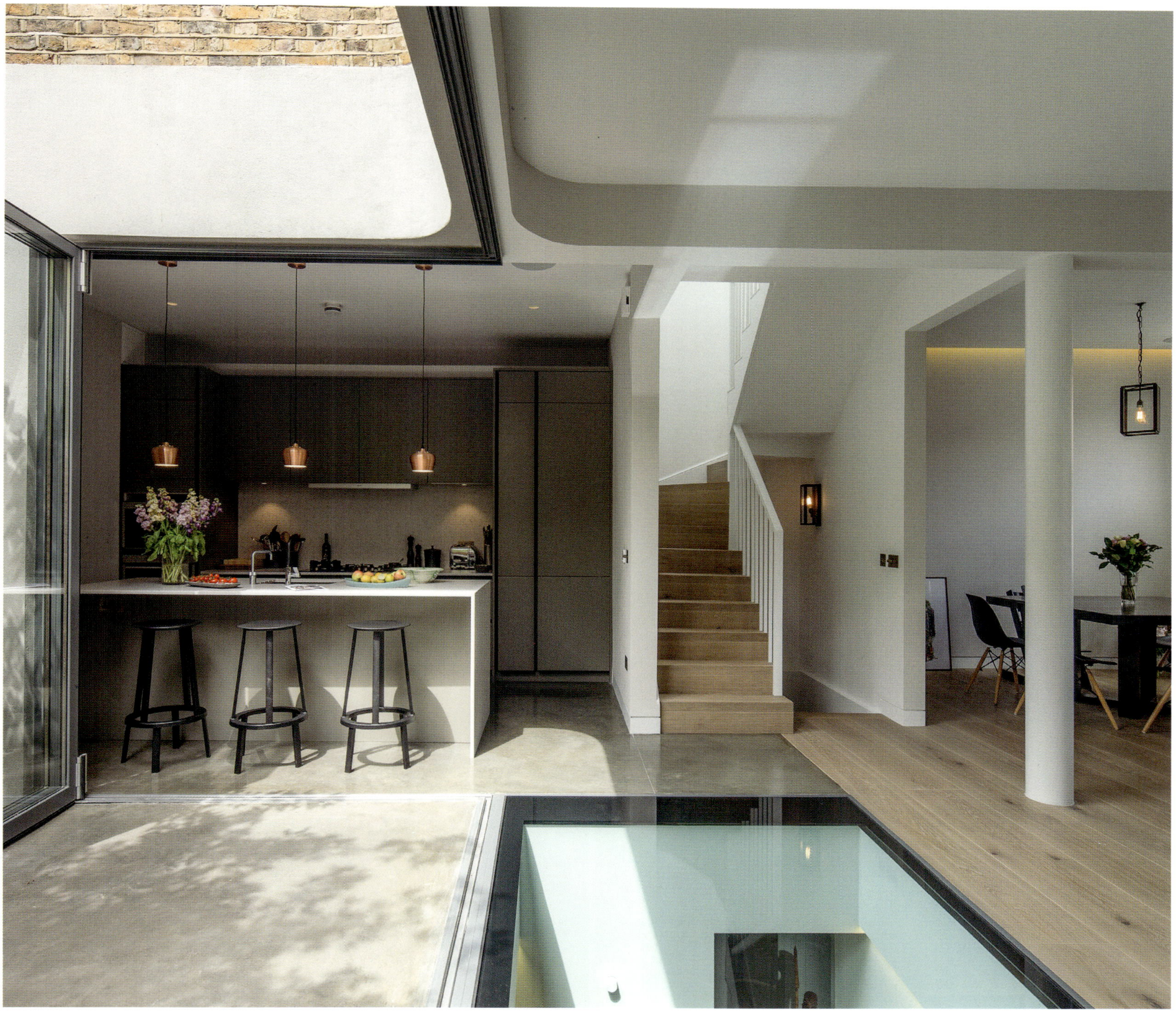

The kitchen and living room open onto a south-facing patio which completely connects the two spaces when the folding glass panels are opened. The polished concrete floor unifies the kitchen and patio in a single space just as the oak wood creates continuity between the dining and living rooms.

Die Küche und das Wohnzimmer öffnen sich zu einem nach Süden ausgerichteten Hof, der mit dem Außenbereich durch einige Falttüren aus Glas vollständig verbunden ist. Der Boden aus poliertem Zement vereint Küche und Wohnzimmer ebenso zu einem einzigen Raum wie das verwendete Eichenholz eine Kontinuität zwischen Ess- und Wohnzimmer herstellt.

La cuisine et le séjour donnent sur la cour orientée sud, entièrement connectés à l'extérieur dès l'ouverture des portes vitrées repliables. Le sol en béton poli réunit la cuisine et la cour en un seul espace, tandis que le bois de chêne crée une continuité entre la salle à manger et le séjour.

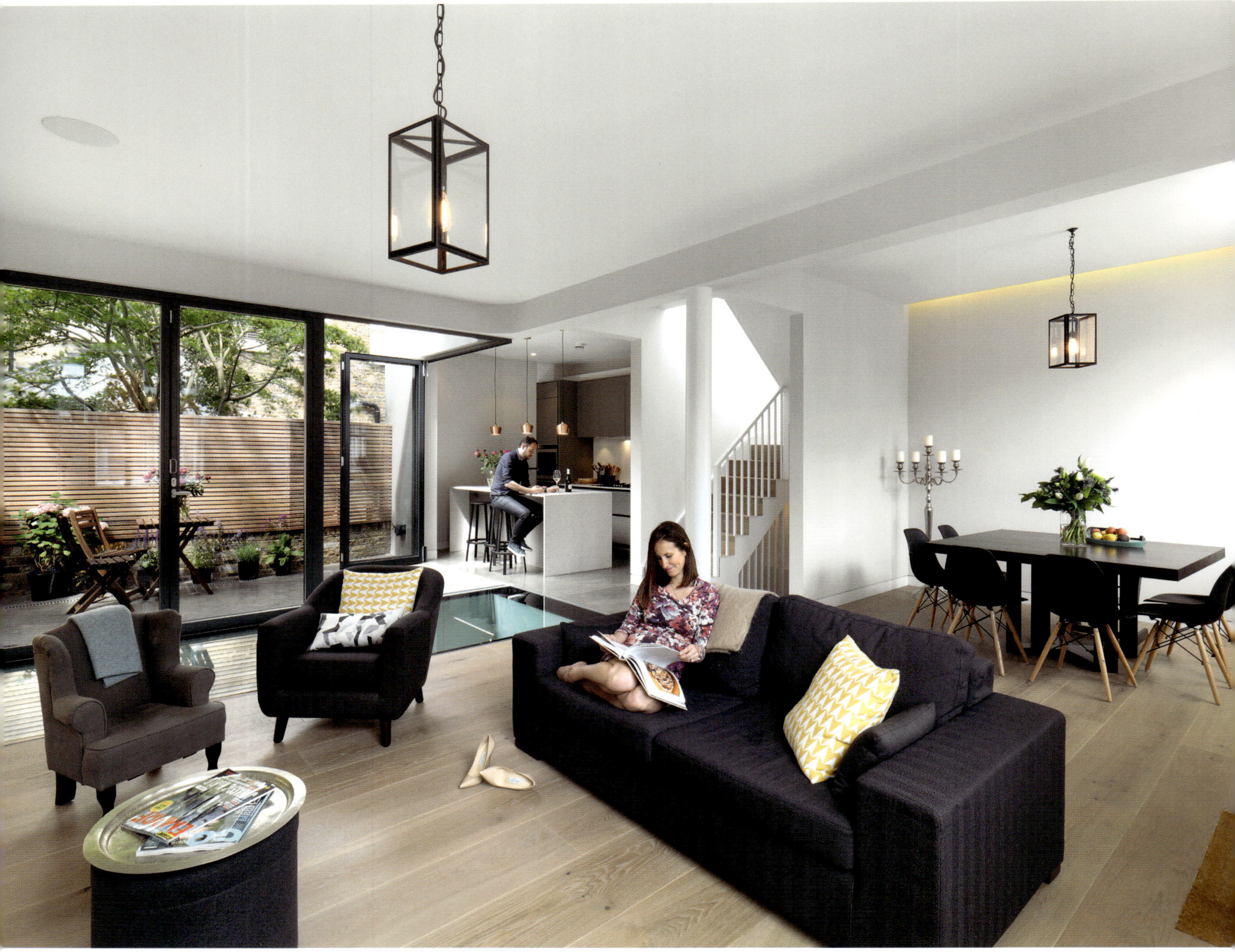

A tranquil interior atmosphere has been created through the use of a unified palette of carefully selected materials, where repurposed historical elements are juxtaposed with modern industrial elements in perfect equilibrium.

Durch die Nutzung einer einheitlichen Palette sorgfältig ausgewählter Materialien erschuf man eine ruhige Atmosphäre im Innenbereich, in dem die erneut verwendeten historischen Elemente modernen Industrie-Elementen in einem perfekten Gleichgewicht gegenübergestellt wurden.

Une palette unifiée de matériaux soigneusement sélectionnés créée une ambiance intérieure tranquille, où les éléments historiques réutilisés se juxtaposent aux éléments industriels modernes dans un équilibre parfait.

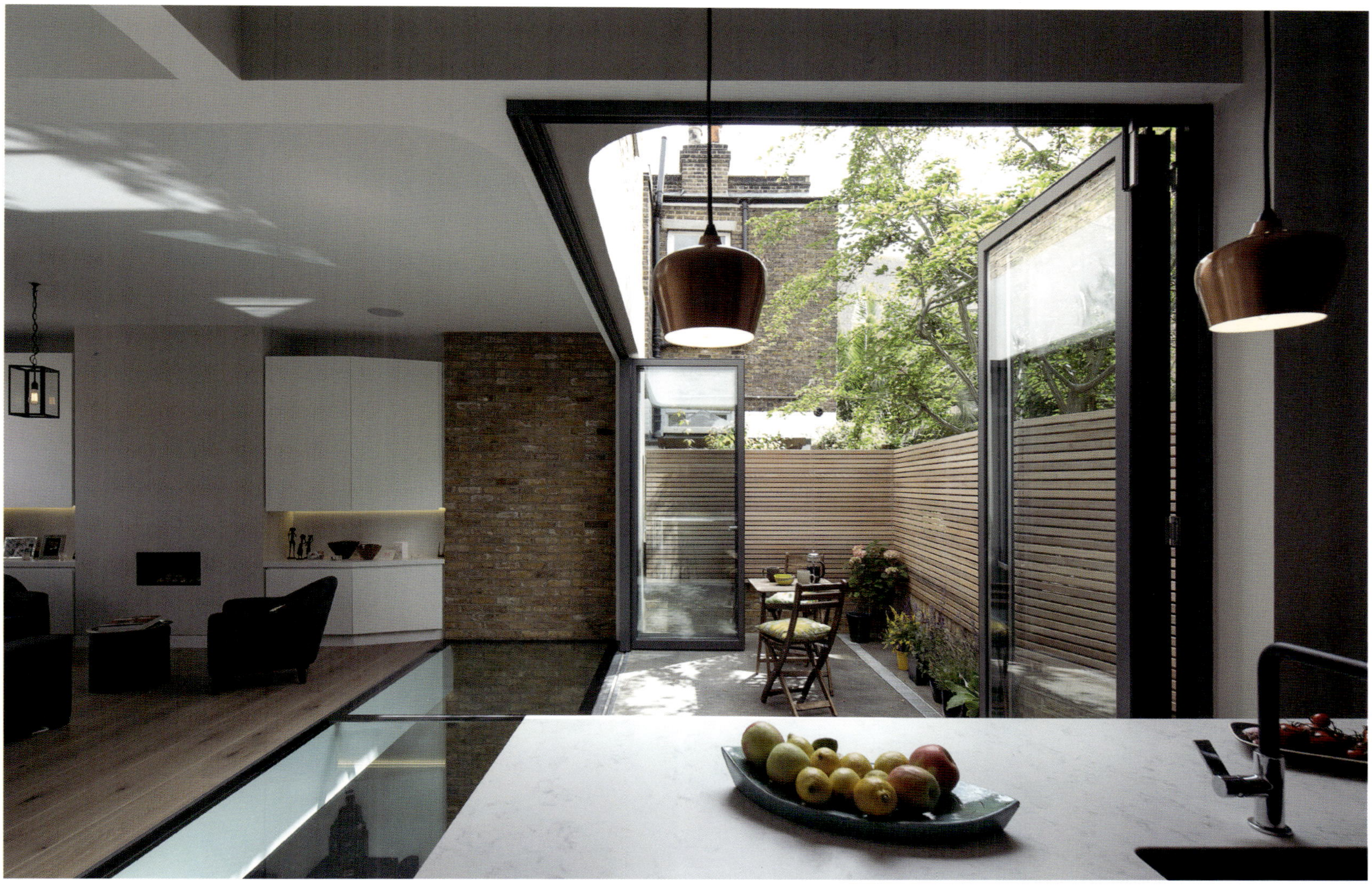

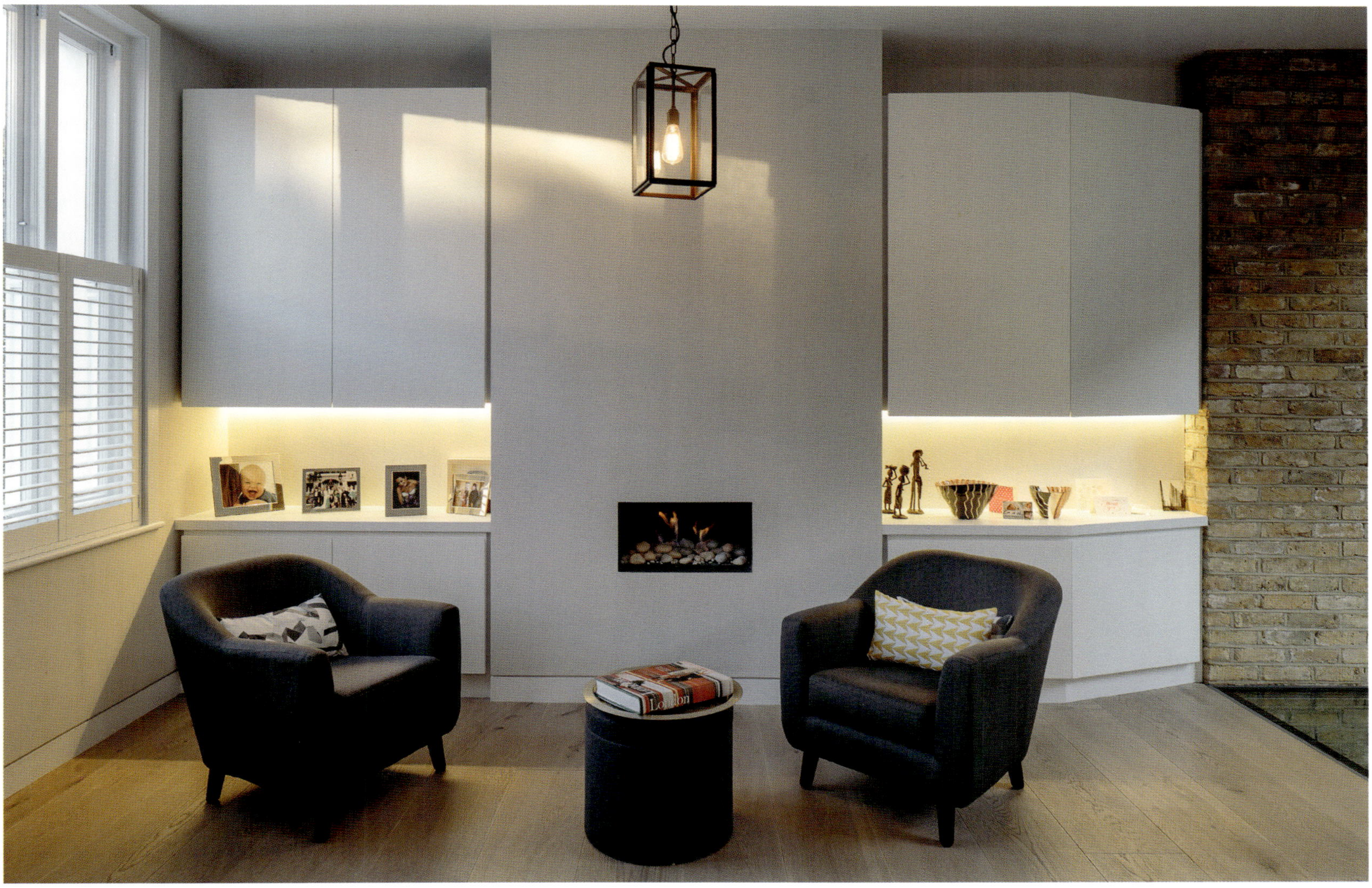

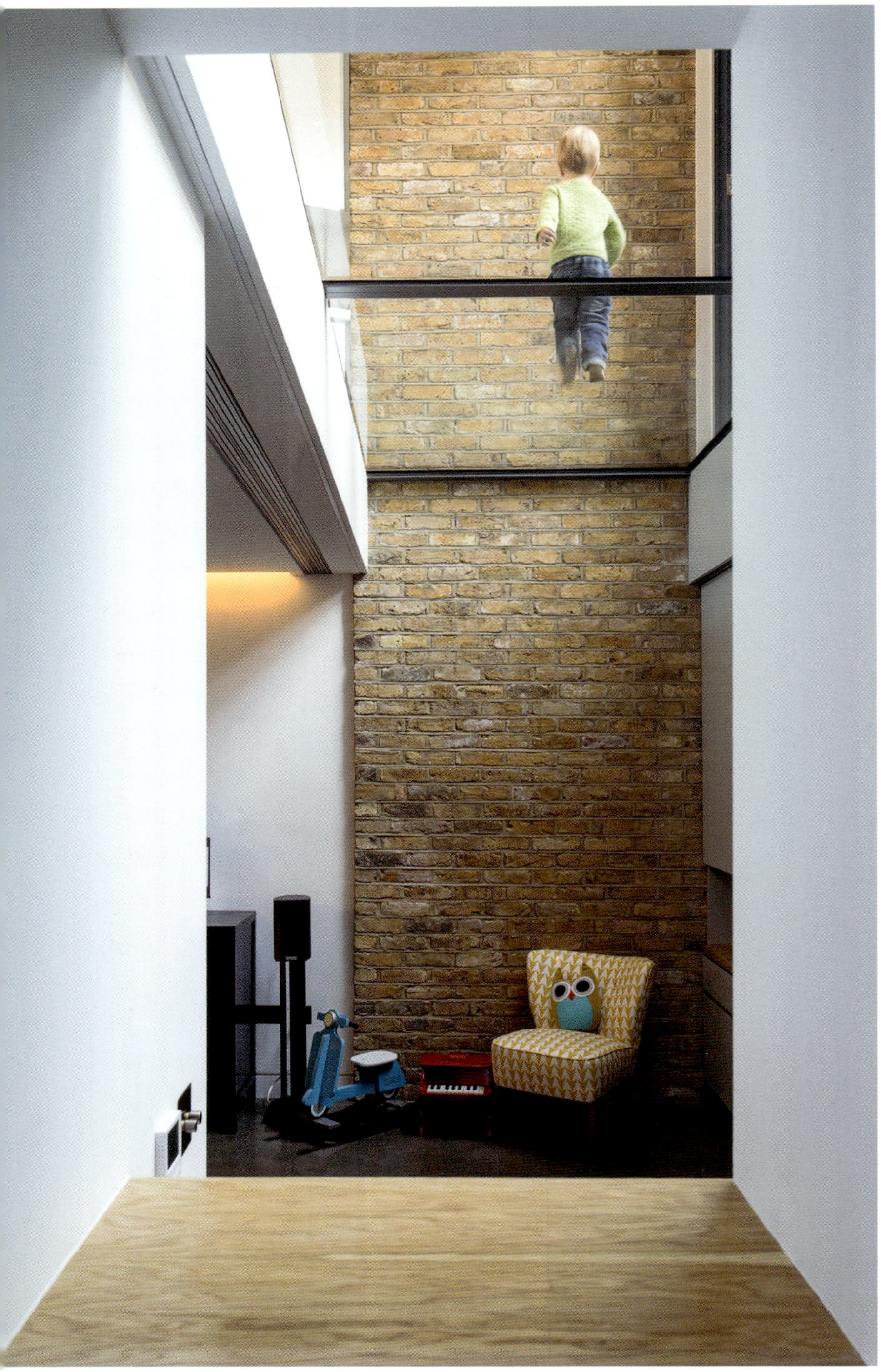

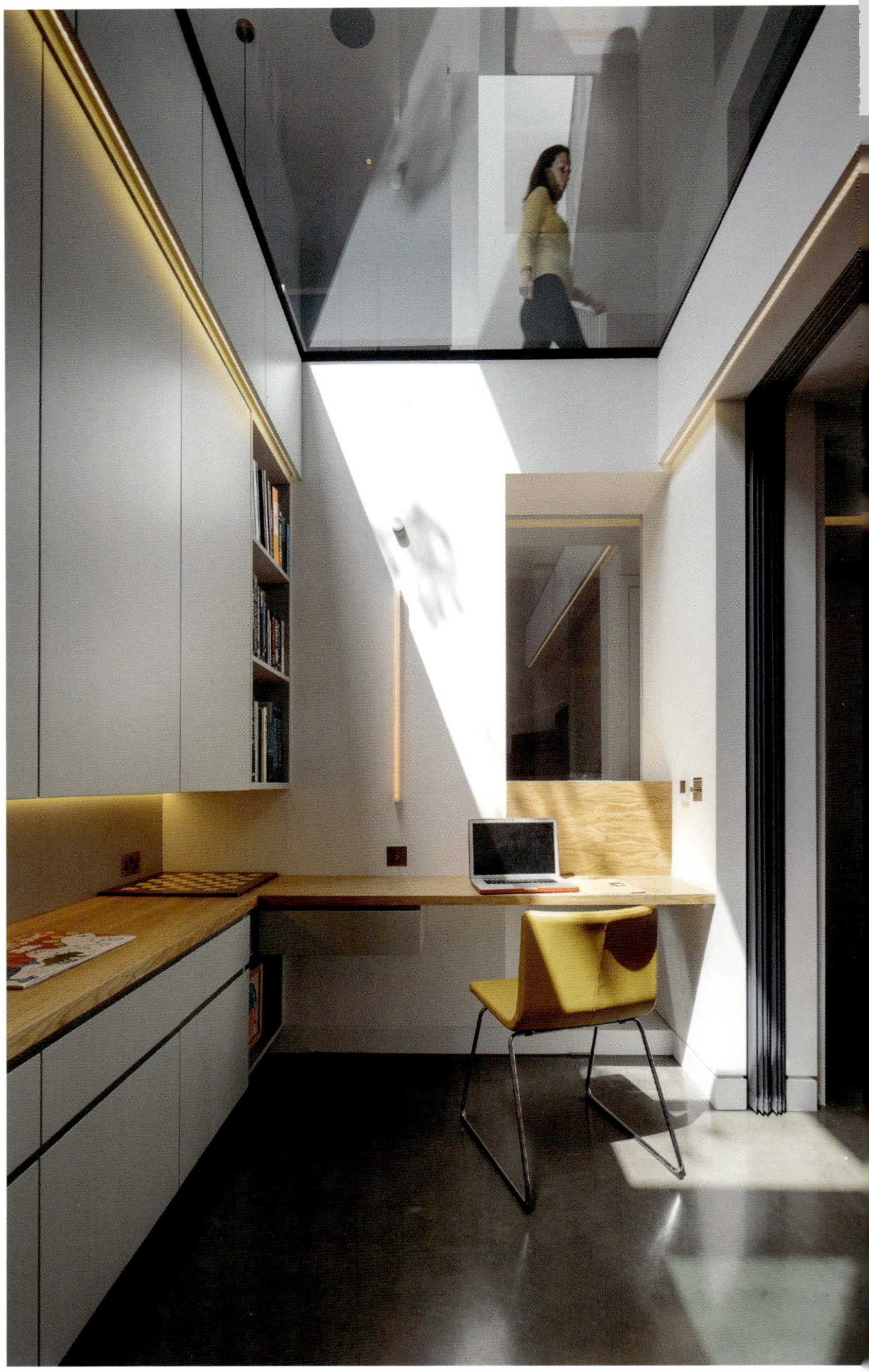

Daylight penetrates into the basement through a skylight that connects it visually with the ground level. The polished concrete floor creates appealing reflections that constantly adjust to the changing light through the course of the day.

Das Licht fällt in das Souterrain durch ein Dachfenster hinein, das diesen Bereich visuell mit dem Erdgeschoss verbindet. Der Boden aus poliertem Zement sorgt für ein interessantes Spiel der Reflektionen, da sich der Lichteinfall im Lauf des Tages verändert.

La lumière pénètre le sous-sol par le biais d'une verrière qui réunit visuellement le rez-de-chaussée. Le sol en béton poli offre un jeu intéressant de reflets au fur et à mesure que la lumière naturelle se déplace au fil de la journée.

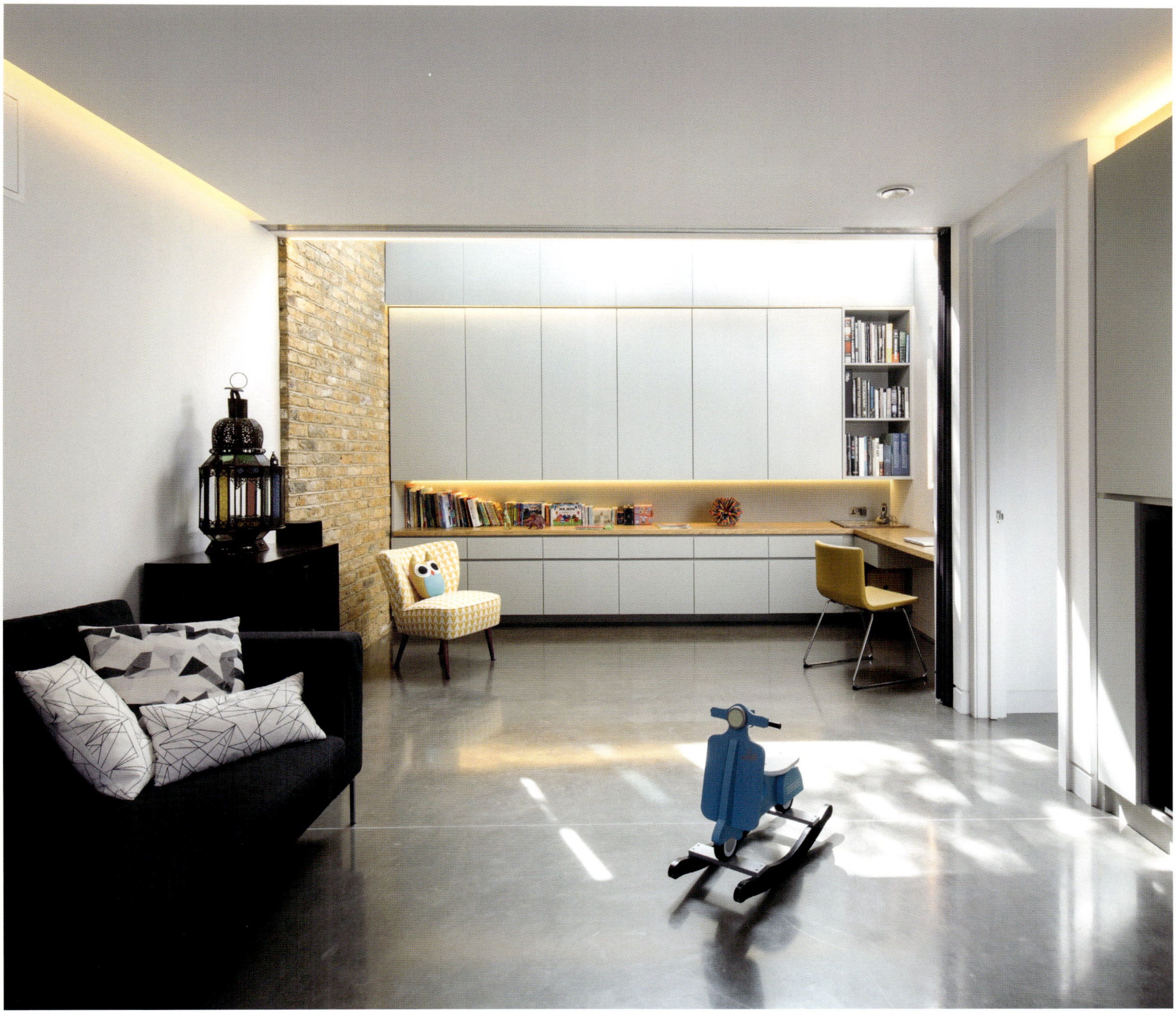

An innovative design solution was found to make the space into a light-filled game room that could also be used as a sophisticated movie theater.

Hier wurde nach einer Lösung mit einem innovativen Design für den Außenbereich vor einem Spielzimmer gesucht, in das viel Licht hereinfällt und das ebenso als ausgeklügelter Kinoraum genutzt werden kann.

Pour que l'espace devienne une salle de jeux remplie de lumière avec la possibilité d'être utilisée comme une salle de cinéma sophistiquée, il a fallu rechercher une solution de conception innovante.

The bedrooms open laterally and vertically to create ample loft spaces. Two south-facing skylights in the bathrooms provide both light and ventilation while reducing the need for—and therefore cost of—artificial lighting and ventilation.

Die Schlafzimmer können seitlich und vertikal geöffnet werden, wodurch sich große Räume im Loft-Stil ergeben. In den Badezimmern sind nach Süden ausgerichtete Oberlichter eingelassen, durch die Licht und Luft einfallen, wodurch gleichzeitig der Heizbedarf während des Tages reduziert und Stromkosten eingespart werden.

Les chambres ont été ouvertes sur les côtés et à la verticale afin de créer de grands espaces de type *loft*. Deux lucarnes orientées sud ont été créées dans les salles de bains afin de donner de la lumière et aérer les pièces tout en réduisant la nécessité de chauffer pendant la journée, supposant ainsi un gain d'énergie.

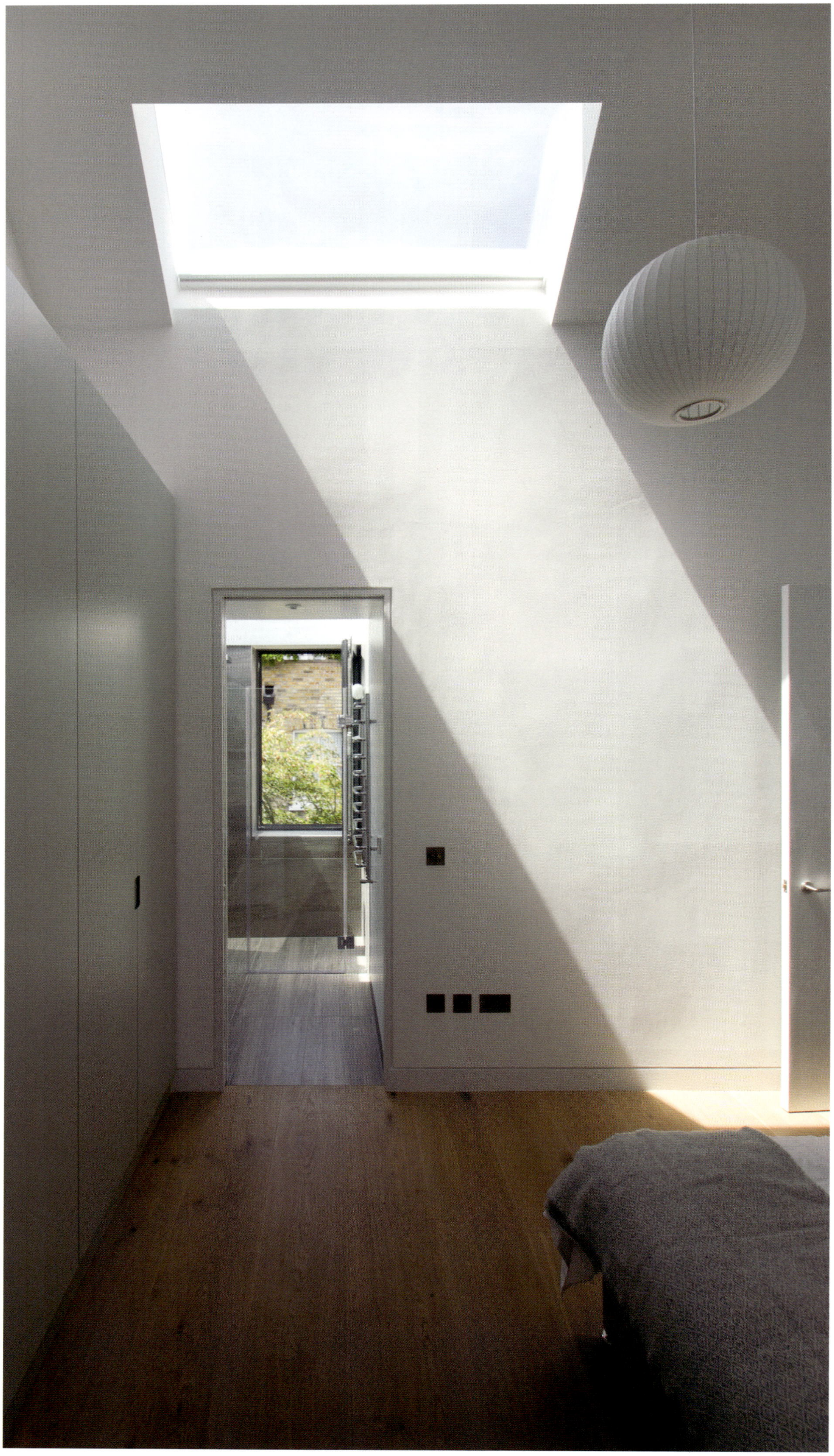

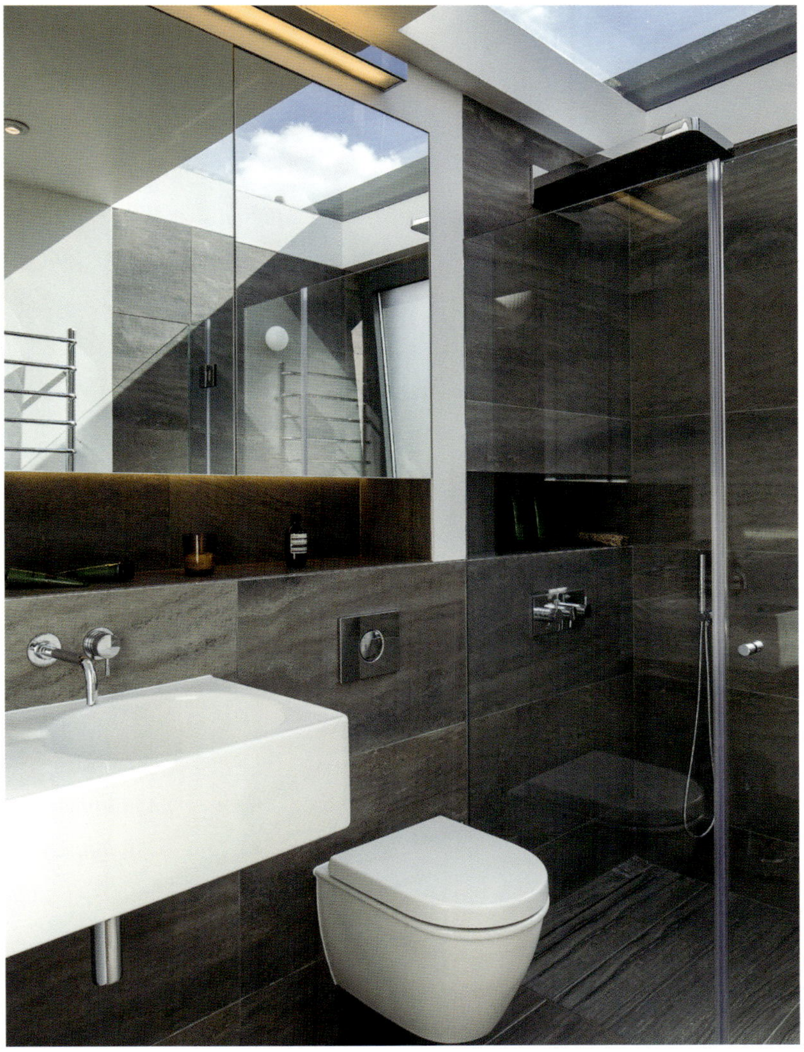

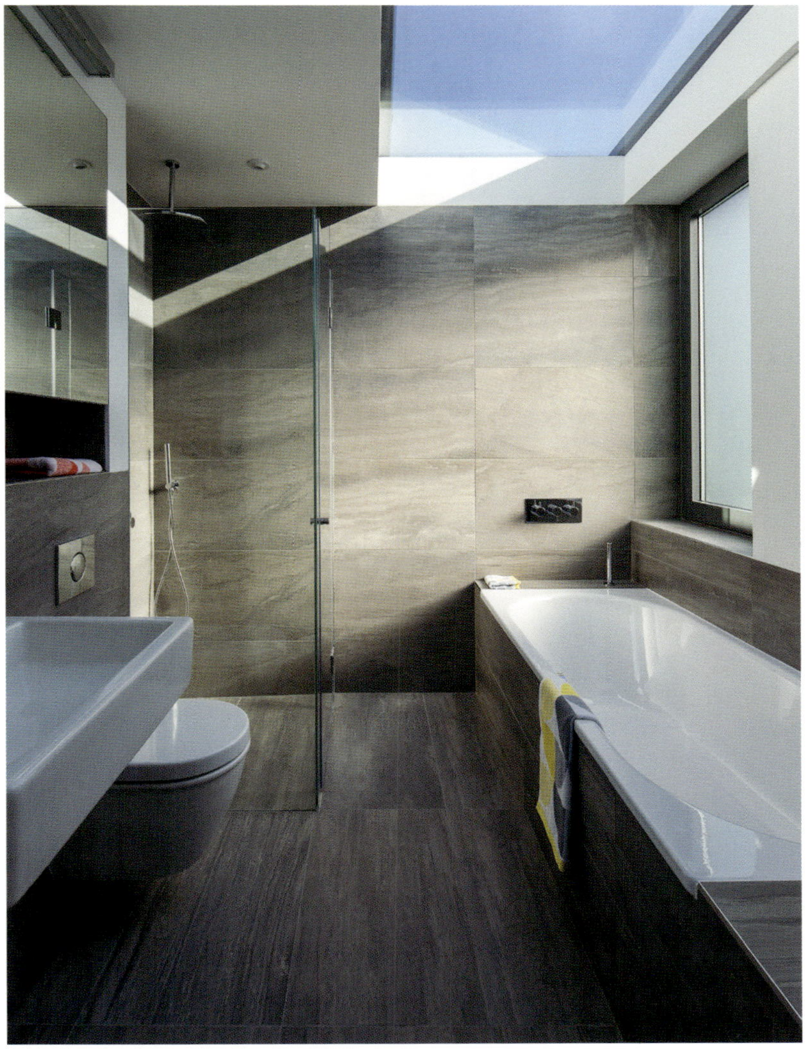

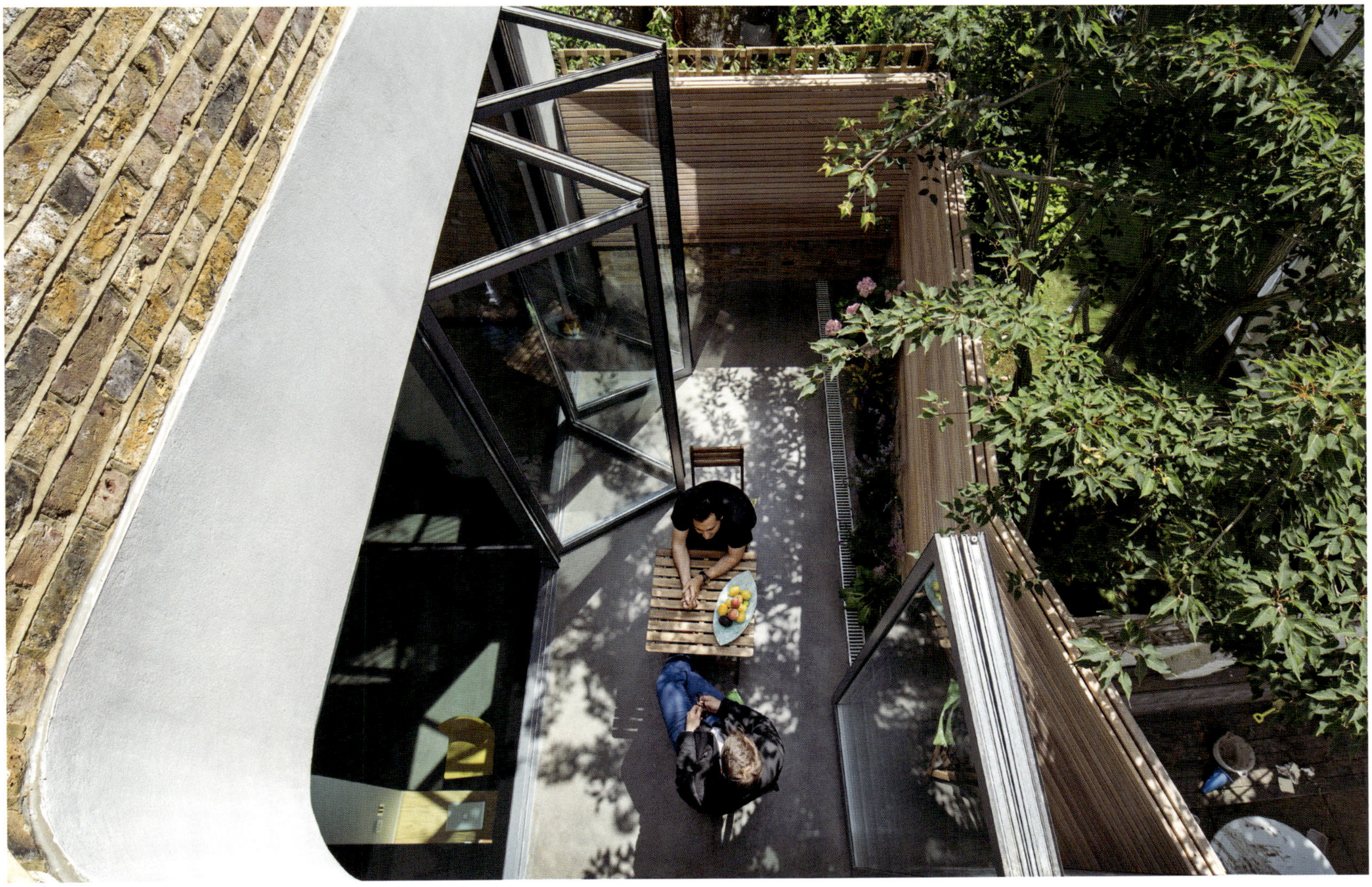

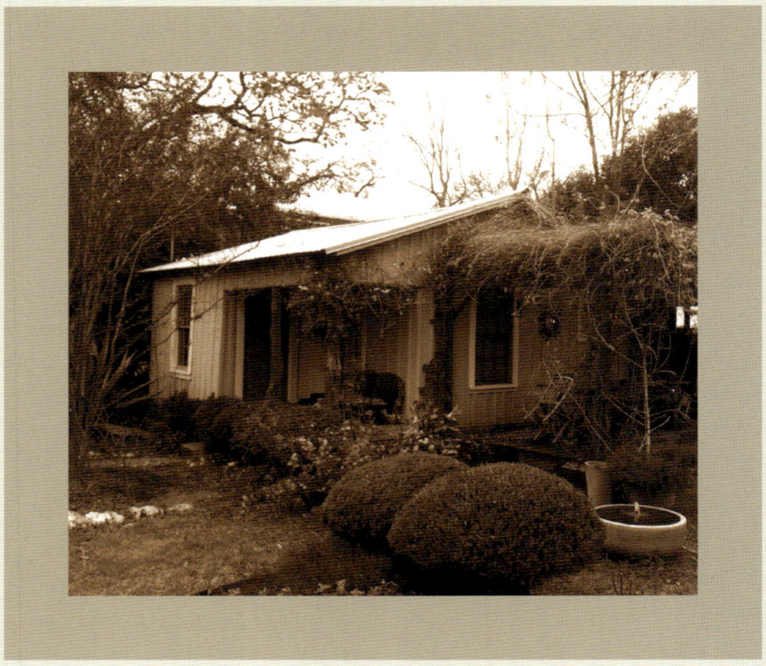

CLARKSVILLE COTTAGE ADDITION AND RENOVATION

ELEMENT 5 ARCHITECTURE

205 m² | 2,207 sq. ft.

Austin, Texas, United States

Photos © **Andrea Calo**

> Expand the residence to include a home office and area to receive visitors

> Preserve some of the residence's original elements

> Erweiterung des Hauses für ein Büro und um Gäste zu empfangen

> Erhalten einiger Elemente des ursprünglichen Hauses

> Agrandir la maison pour créer un bureau et davantage d'espaces pour accueillir des invités

> Conserver le cachet d'origine de la maison

In addressing the project to rehabilitate and expand this small country house in Clarksville, there were several very well-defined assumptions: the owner worked from home, enjoyed gardening, and liked to receive visitors. On the other hand, it was necessary to consider the building restrictions in force in the neighborhood and the city as well as the owner's wish to preserve certain elements from the original house.

The lower level is an open loft-type area that contains the kitchen, dining room, and living room. A large new covered side porch was created for receiving visitors and enjoying the garden view. A small part of the original house and its front porch have been preserved intact to serve as the entrance to the residence. The first floor includes the main living and study areas. Both spaces open onto a balcony that looks out at undeveloped land to the south of the street. The attic serves as a multipurpose space for visitors and work.

Without doubt, these interventions addressed the requirements of the client, who was able to gain much-needed living, gardening, and work space while retaining the original feeling of the Clarksville cottage.

Für die Sanierung und Erweiterung dieses kleinen Landhauses in Clarksville gab es sehr genaue Vorüberlegungen bzw. Ausgangspunkte: Der Besitzer arbeitet von zu Hause aus, er liebt die Gartenarbeit und empfängt gerne Gäste. Auf der anderen Seite mussten die baulichen Einschränkungen des Viertels und der Stadt wie auch der Wunsch des Eigentümers, einige Elemente des ursprünglichen Hauses beizubehalten, berücksichtigt werden.

Das Erdgeschoss ist offen und im Loft-Stil gestaltet: Hier sind die Küche, das Esszimmer und das Wohnzimmer untergebracht. Es führt auf eine neue, seitlich angebaute und überdachte Terrasse hinaus, um dort Besucher zu empfangen und den Garten zu betrachten. Ein kleiner Teil des ursprünglichen Hauses mit seiner Veranda wurde vollständig beibehalten und dient nun als Eingang in das Gebäude. Im ersten Stock liegen das Hauptschlafzimmer und der Studiobereich. Beide gehen auf einen Balkon mit seitlichem Ausblick auf die Landschaft südlich der Straße hinaus. Der Dachboden soll vielseitig nutzbar sein, mögliche Verwendungen sind ein Bereich für Gäste und zum Arbeiten.

Hier wurden die Wünsche des Besitzers komplett umgesetzt, der gerne mehr Raum hätte, den er für sein Zuhause, den Garten und die Anforderungen seines Arbeitsplatzes benötigt, aber gleichzeitig auch den ursprünglichen Charme des alten Häuschens in Clarksville beibehalten will.

Au moment d'analyser le projet de réhabilitation et d'extension de cette petite maison de campagne Clarksville, l'architecte est parti de principes bien définis : le propriétaire travaille depuis chez lui, il est passionné de jardinage et aime recevoir ses amis. Il fallait notamment prendre en considération les restrictions de construction propres du quartier et de la ville, ainsi que le souhait du propriétaire de conserver certains éléments d'origine de la maison.

Le rez-de-chaussée est un espace ouvert de type *loft* qui accueille la cuisine, la salle à manger et le séjour. Elle donne sur un nouveau porche spacieux latéral couvert afin de recevoir des invités tout en admirant le jardin. Seule une infime partie de la maison d'origine et son porche devant sont restés intacts afin de servir d'entrée à la maison. Au premier étage se trouvent la chambre parentale et un espace de travail. Les deux pièces donnent sur un balcon avec des vues sur un terrain non viabilisé du côté sud de la rue. Le dernier étage est destiné à devenir un espace polyvalent pour recevoir des invités et travailler.

Les souhaits du client ont donc été exaucés, ce qui lui a permis de gagner l'espace dont il avait besoin pour la maison, le jardin et les besoins de travail, ainsi que conserver la sensation originelle de l'ancienne cabane de Clarksville.

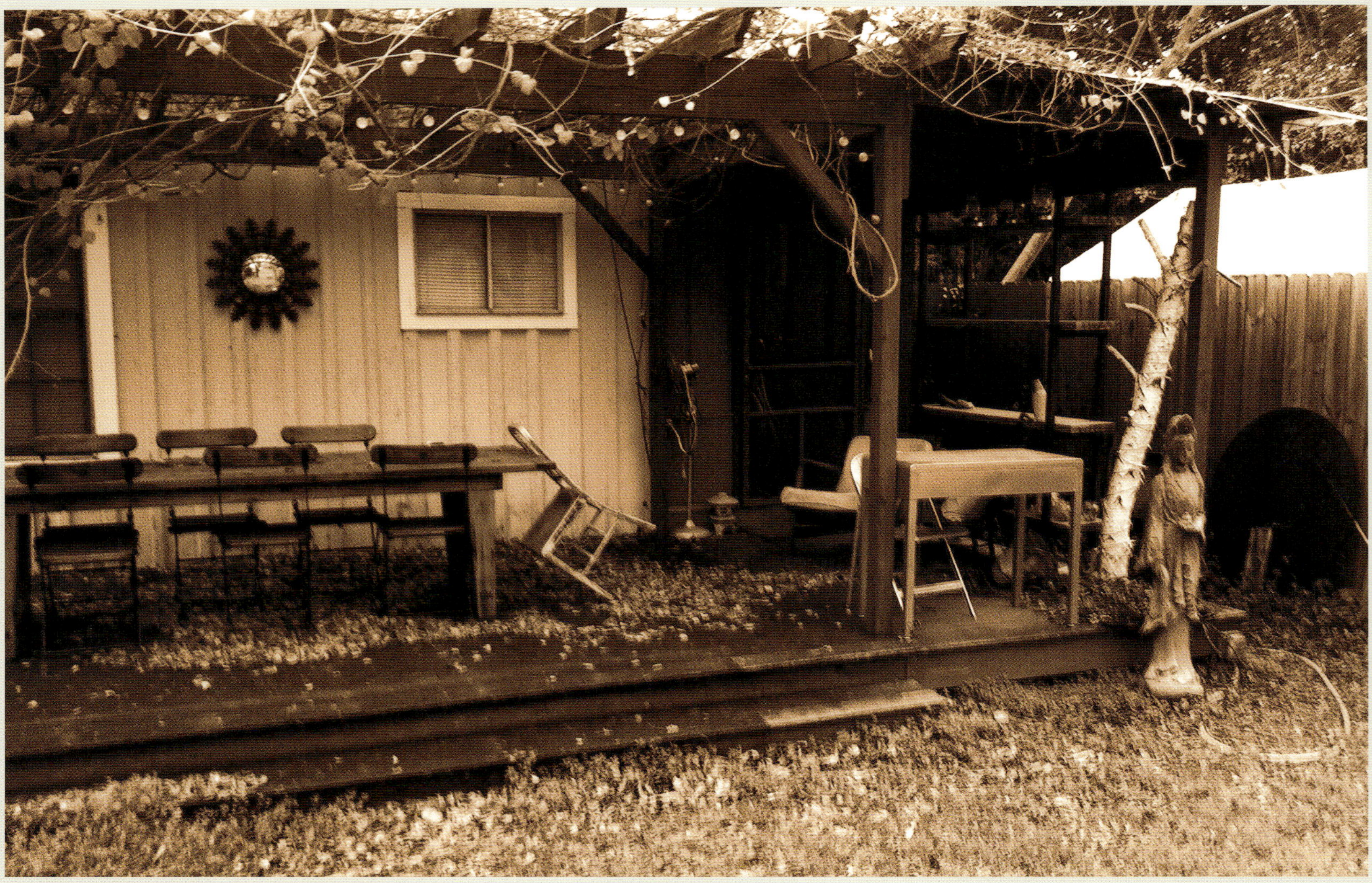

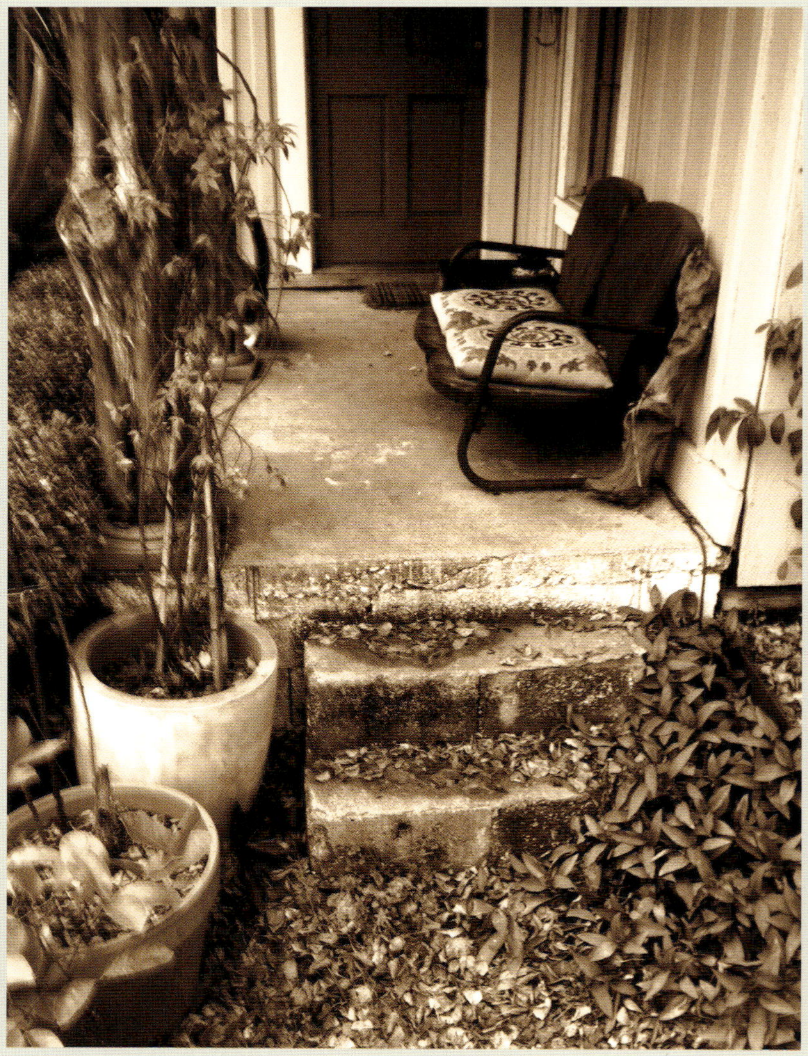

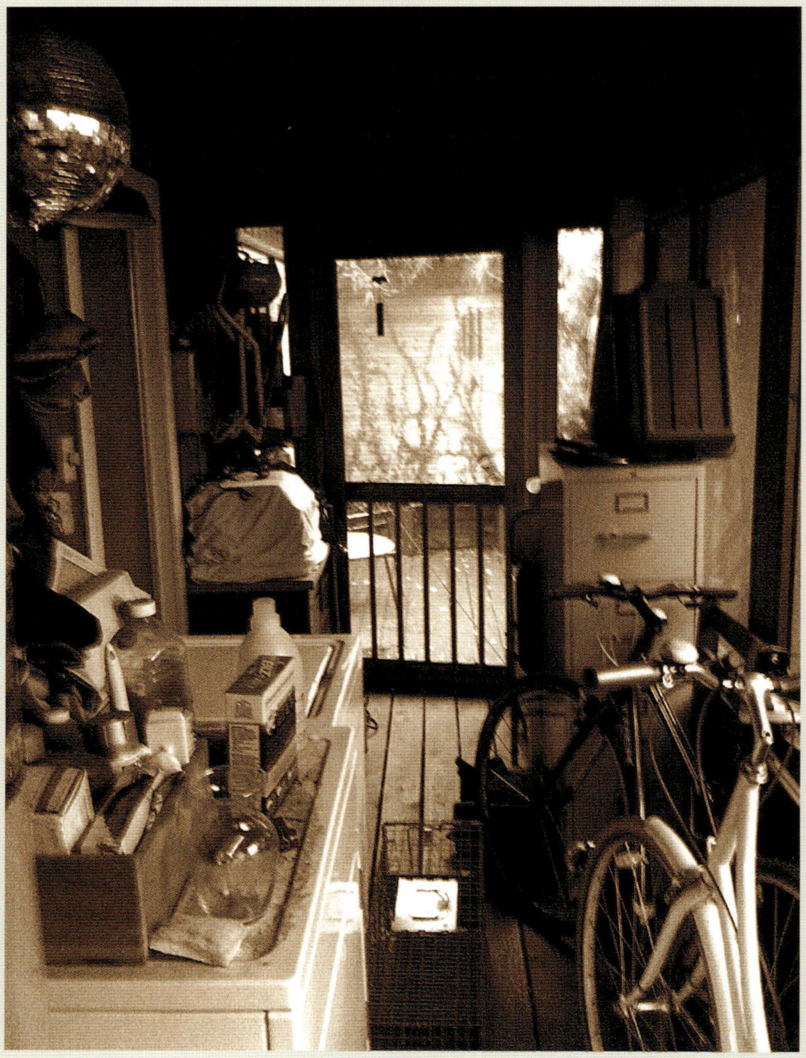

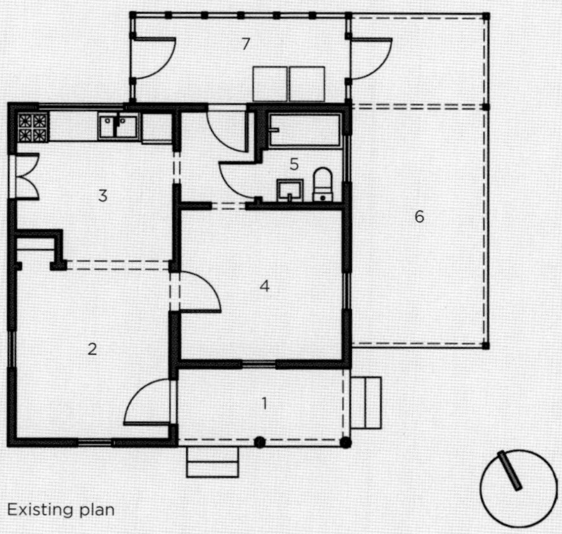

Existing plan

1. Front porch
2. Dining / living
3. Kitchen
4. Bedroom
5. Bathroom
6. Wood deck / pergola
7. Screen porch

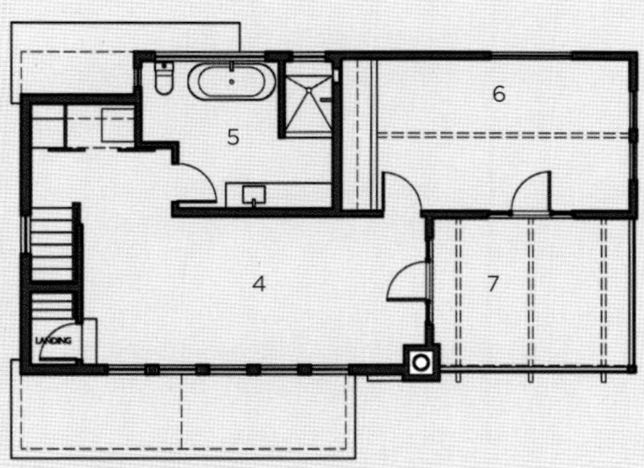

New first floor plan

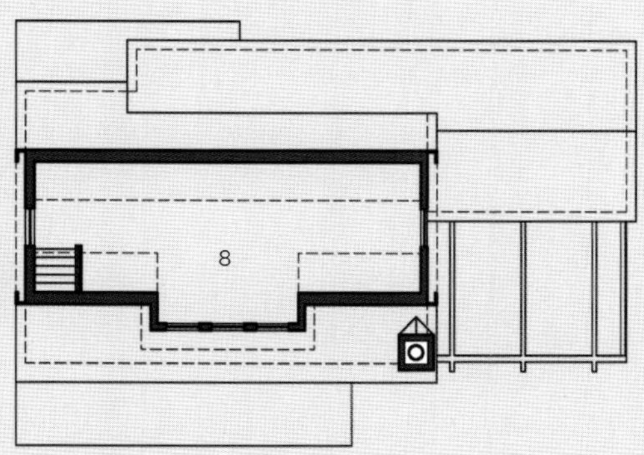

New attic plan

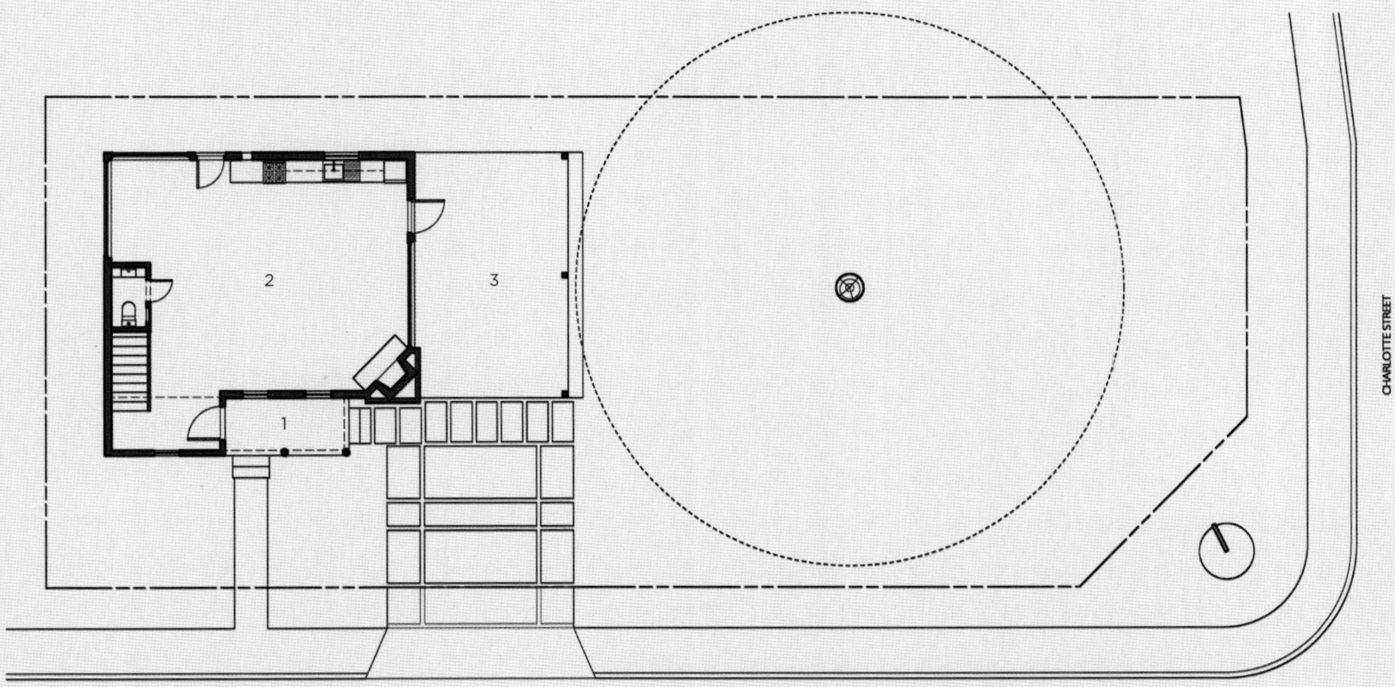

New ground floor plan

1. Front porch
2. Dining / kitchen / living
3. Side porch
4. Studio
5. Bath
6. Bedroom
7. Balcony
8. Attic

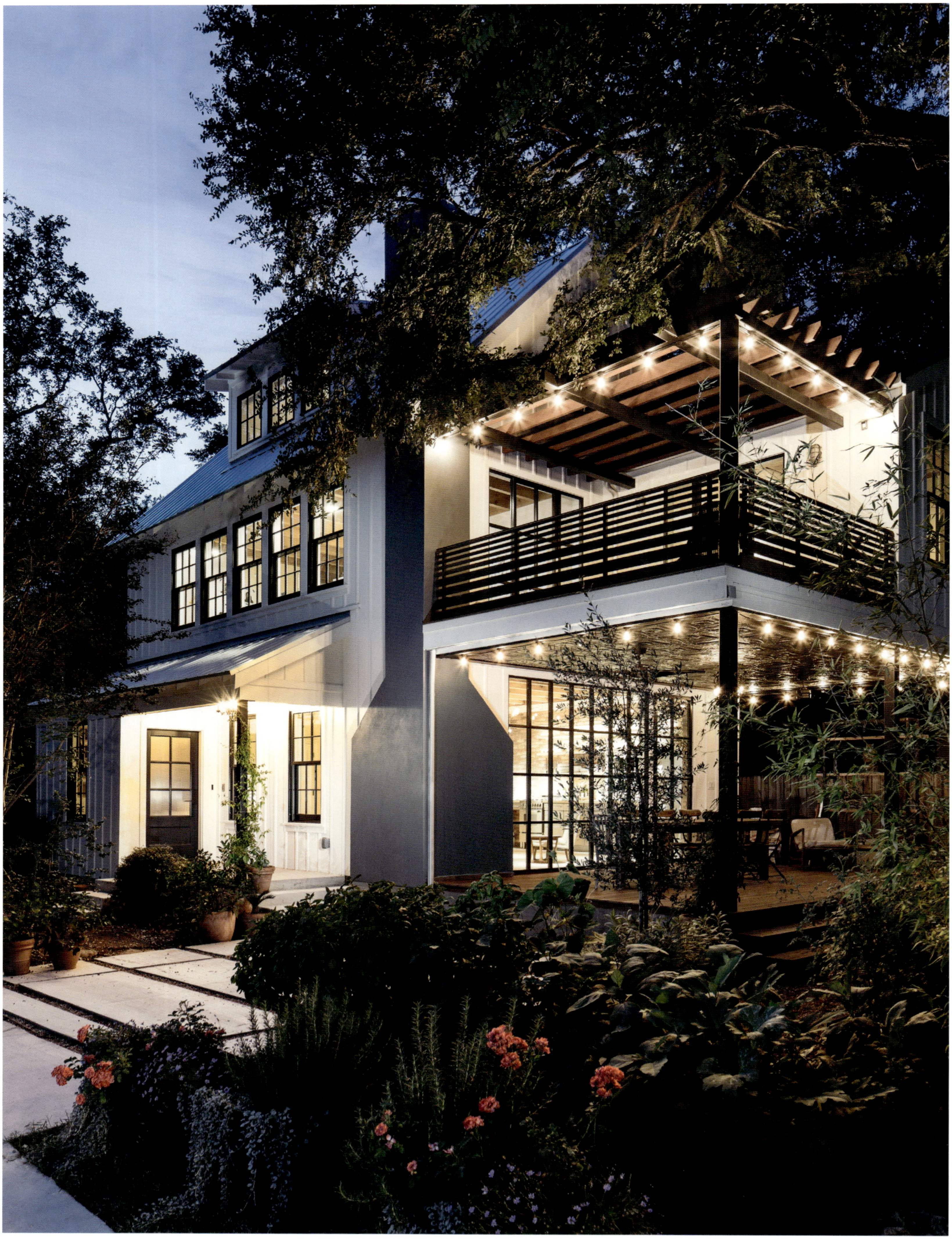

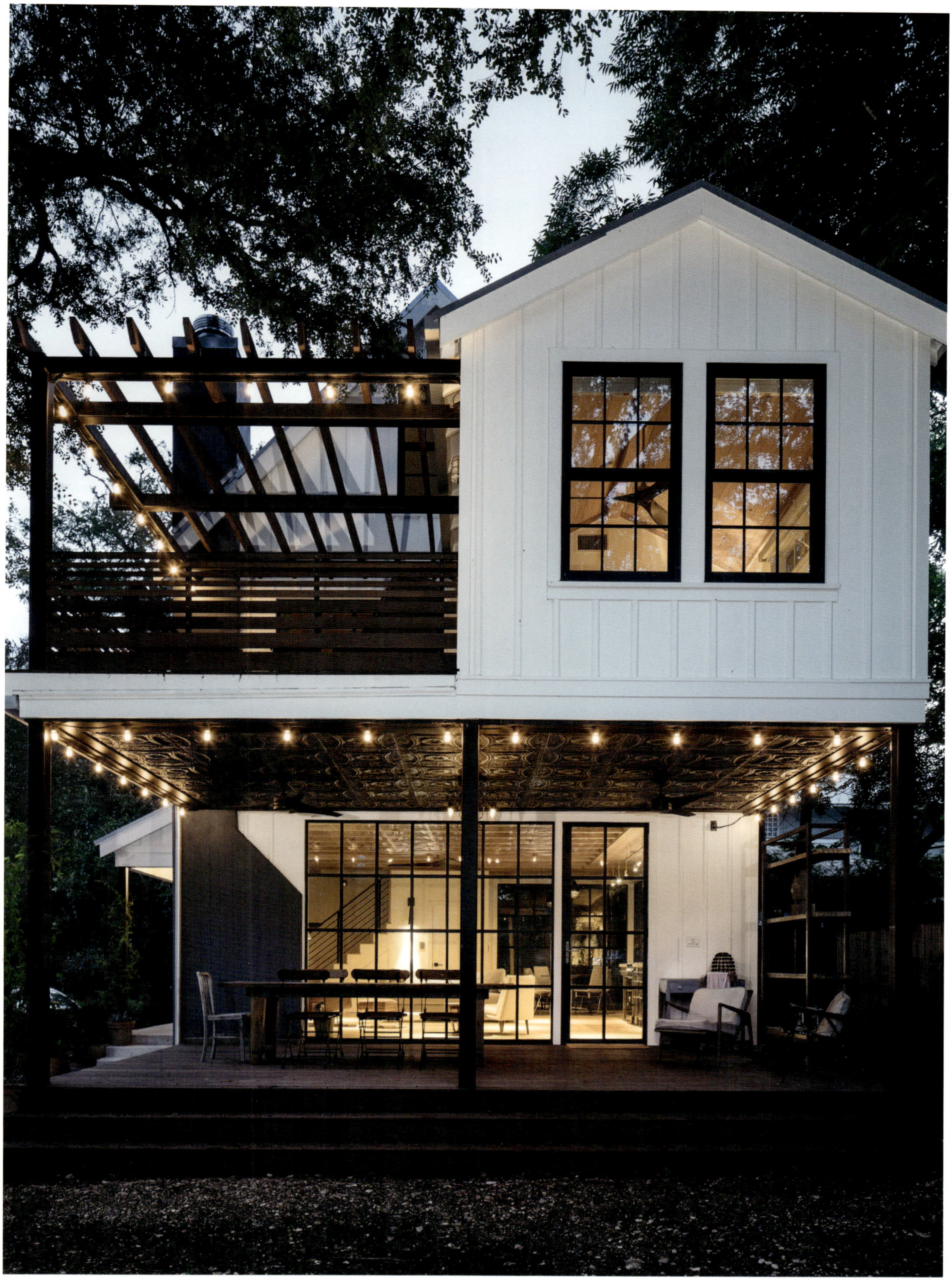

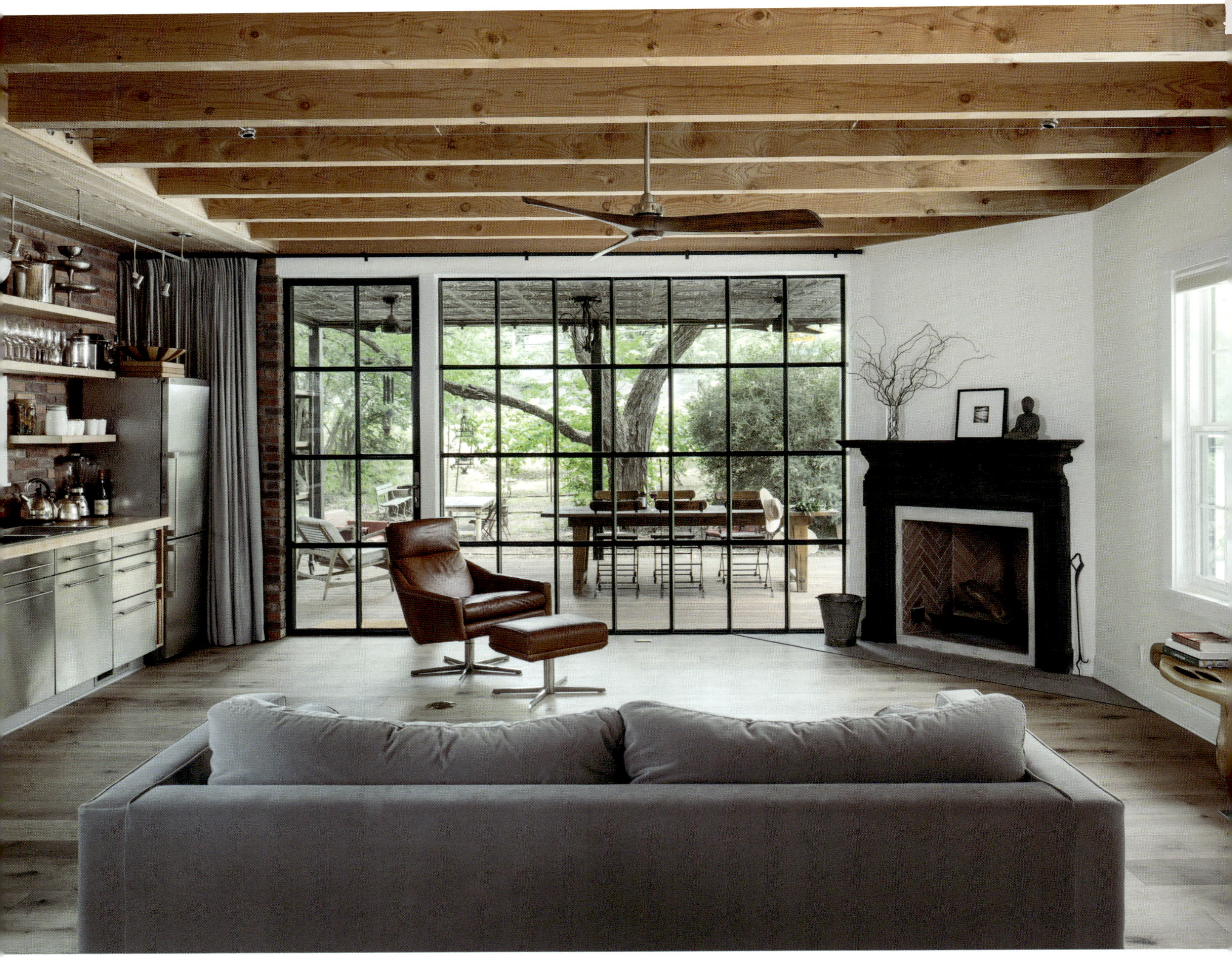

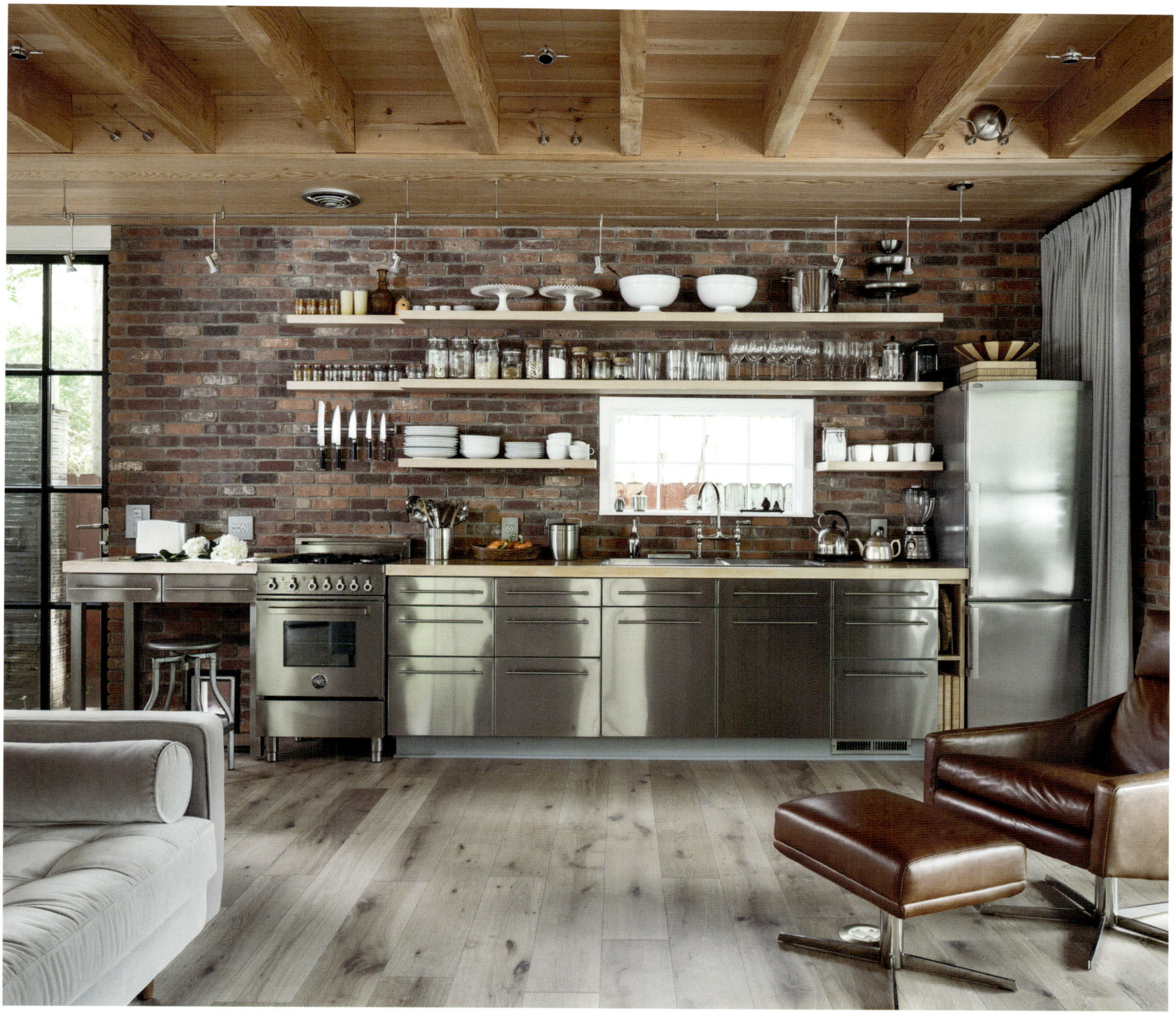

A brick wall forms the backdrop to the kitchen, defines the space and adds personality. The stainless-steel furnishings and appliances add an industrial touch that contrasts with the rustic aspect of the wood ceiling.

Eine Ziegelwand dient als Hintergrund der Küche, definiert diesen Raum und verleiht ihm gleichzeitig eine gewisse Persönlichkeit. Die Möbel aus Edelstahl sorgen für einen leicht industriellen Touch, der im Kontrast zu dem Landhausstil der Holzdecke steht.

Le mur de brique comme toile de fond de la cuisine définit l'espace tout en lui donnant du cachet. Les meubles en acier inoxydable ajoutent une touche industrielle en contraste avec l'aspect rustique du plafond en bois.

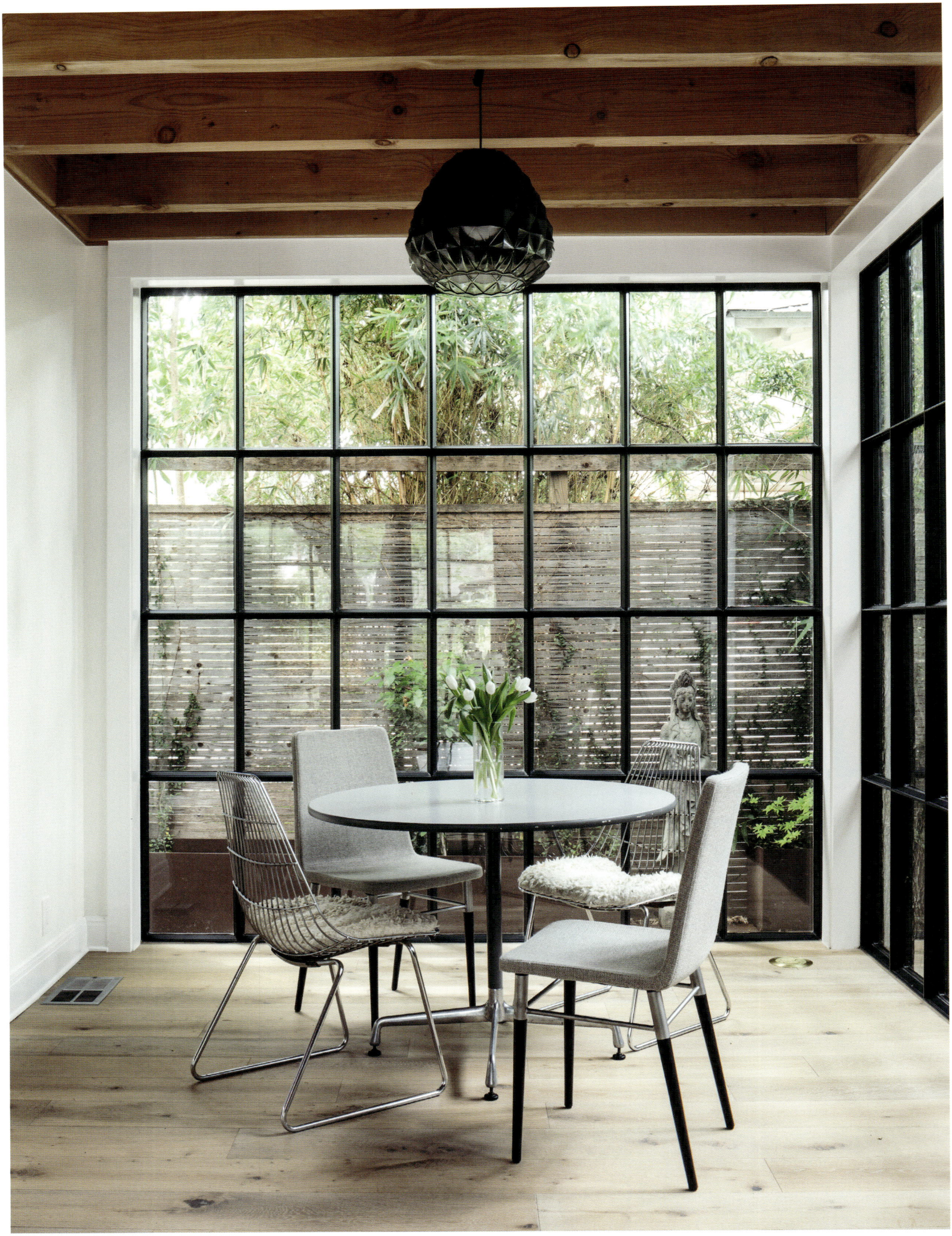

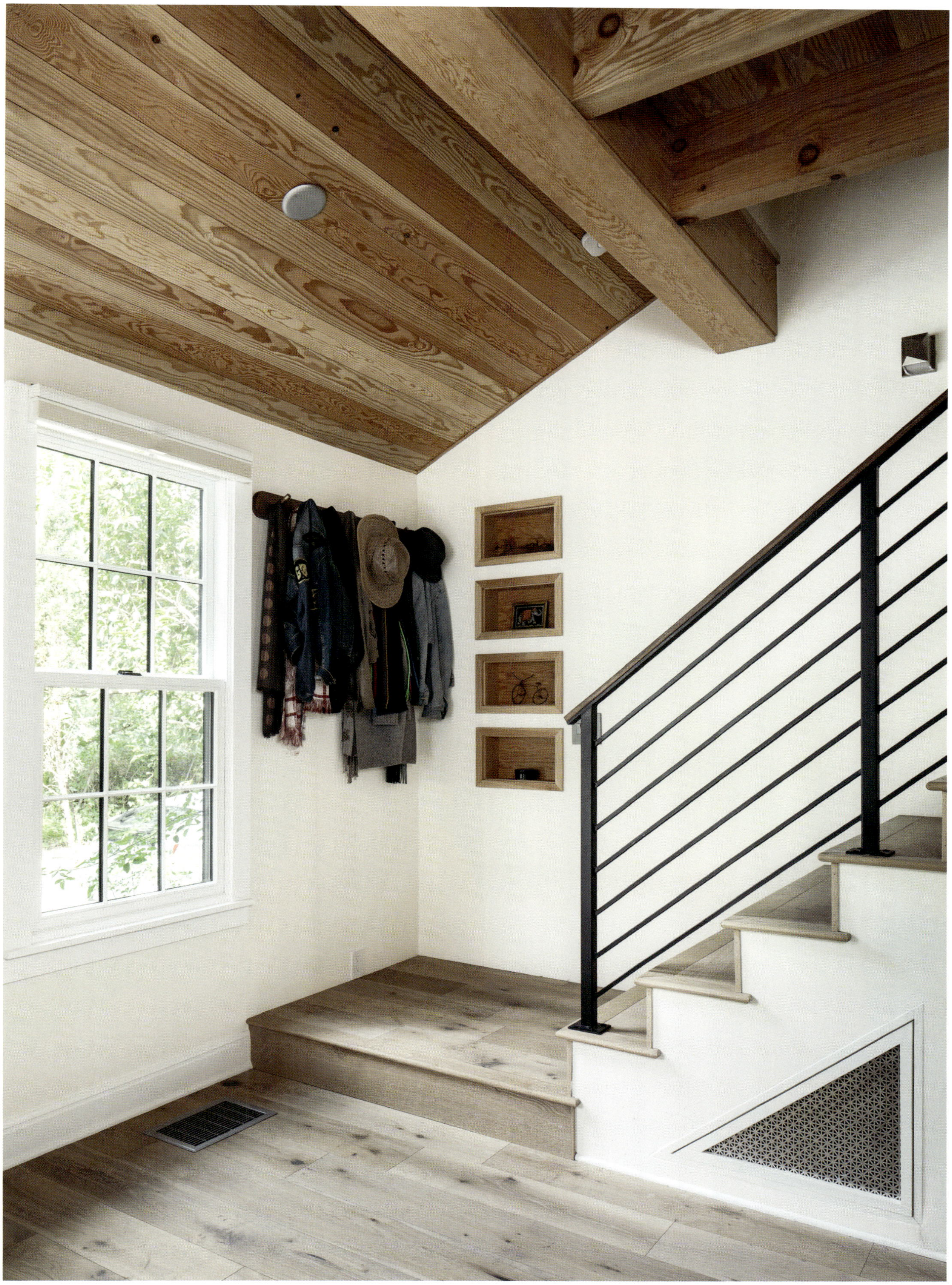

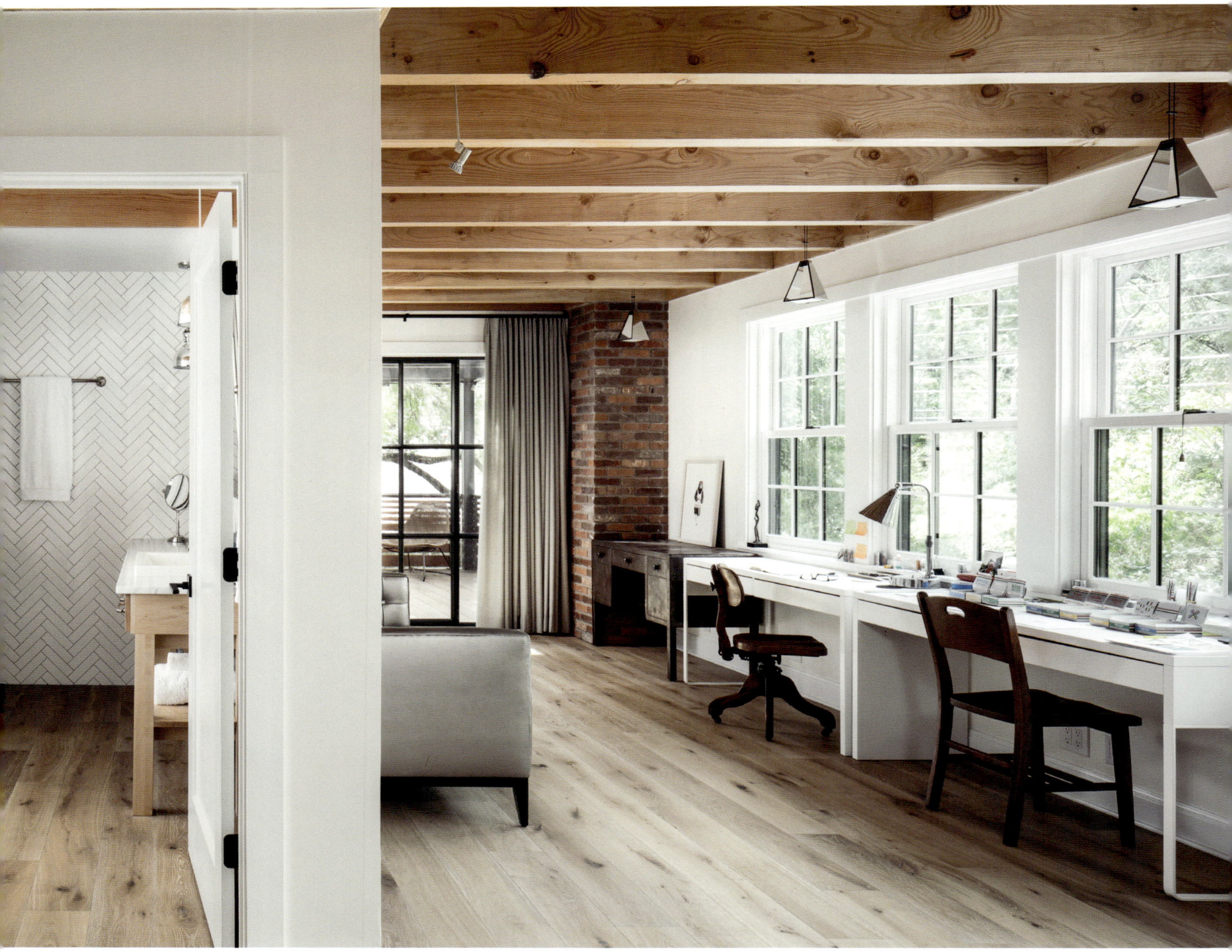

Making maximum use of natural light and further capitalizing on the space, the office areas have been situated along the wall next to the windows. The brick column echoes the wall that frames the kitchen.

Um das natürliche Licht so gut wie möglich zu nutzen und mehr Platz aus diesem Zimmer herauszuholen, wurden die Tische unter die Fenster geschoben. Die Säule aus Ziegeln ist ein Echo der Wand, die die Küche einrahmt.

Pour profiter au maximum de la lumière naturelle et tirer profit de l'espace, des bureaux ont été placés le long du mur à proximité des fenêtres. La colonne de brique rappelle le mur de la cuisine.

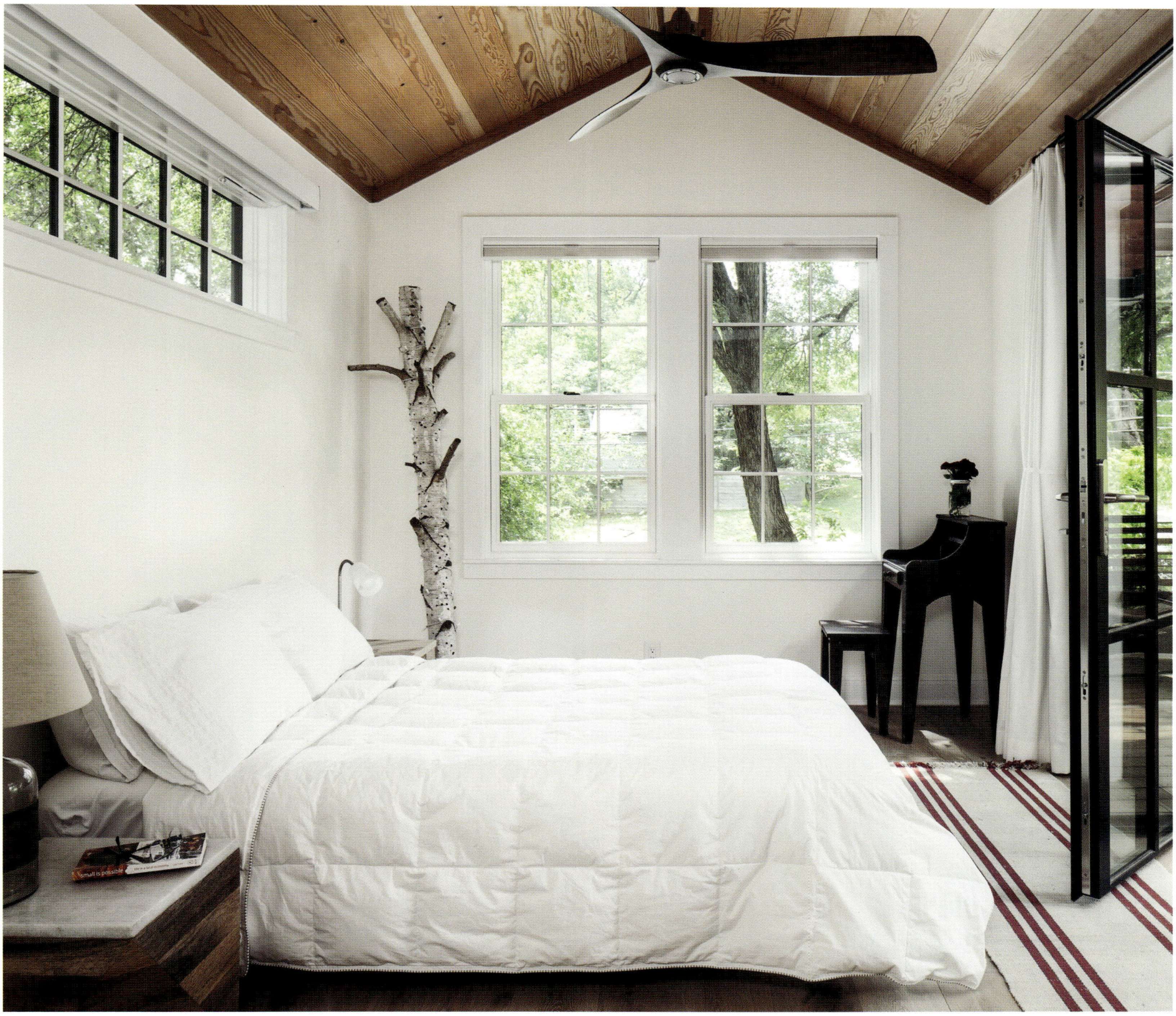

Employed like a work of art, the landscape floats through the bedroom windows and fills the space with color and life, contrasting with the pure whiteness that dominates the space.

Dieser Raum wirkt wie ein Kunstwerk: Die Landschaft, die durch die Fenster des Zimmers zu sehen ist, erfüllt ihn mit Leben und Farbe, was in einem Gegensatz steht zu dem makellosen Weiß, das im Raum selbst vorherrscht.

Comme s'il s'agissait d'une œuvre d'art, le paysage qui se défile au travers des fenêtres de la chambre la remplit de couleur et de vie, en contraste avec le blanc immaculé qui prédomine dans l'espace.

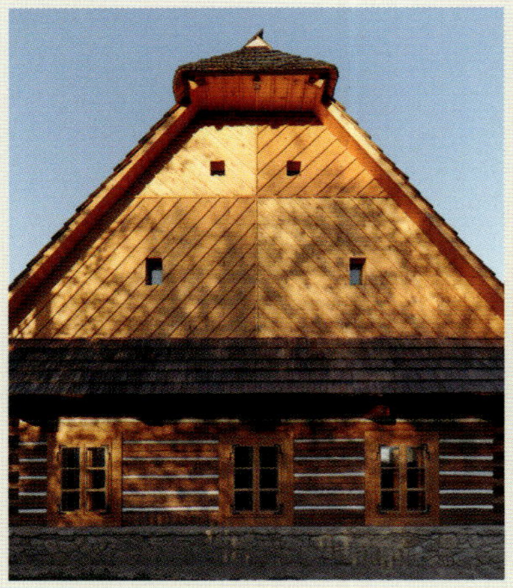

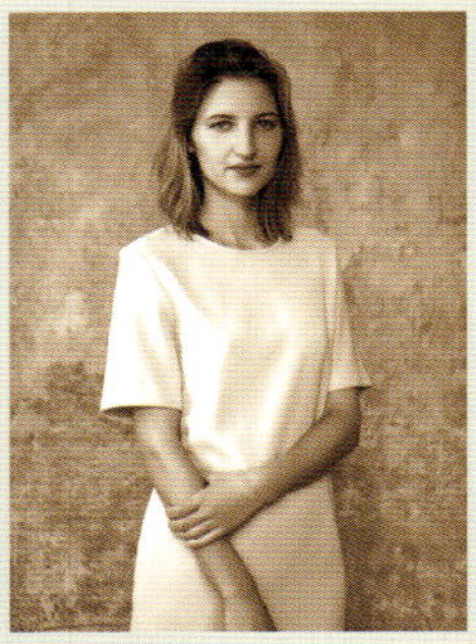

Lenka Míková
Czech Republic
www.lenkamikova.com

TWO HOUSES, DEERS, AND TREES

PAGE 8 > 19

Credits

Principal architect: Lenka Míková

Materials

Cabin structure: massive spruce timbers
Cabin roof: larch shingle
Wooden cladding in the interior (black "chimneys," ceilings, etc.): spruce planks with toning oil
Cabin floor on the ground floor: old brick tiles
Cabin floor on the first floor: massive spruce planks
Barn floor on the ground floor: brushed concrete (almost resembling terrazzo)
Barn floor on the first floor: massive oak planks

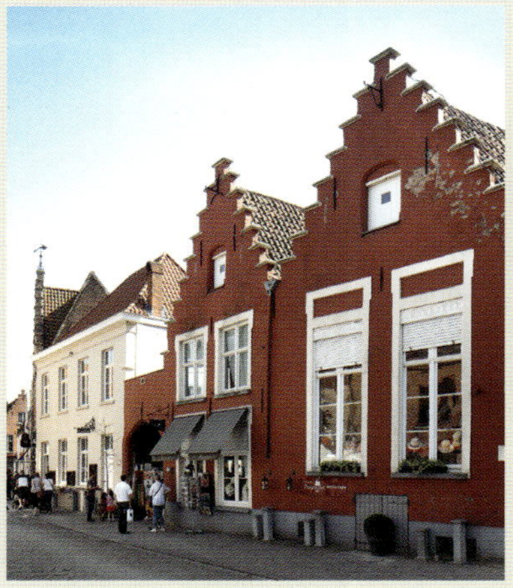

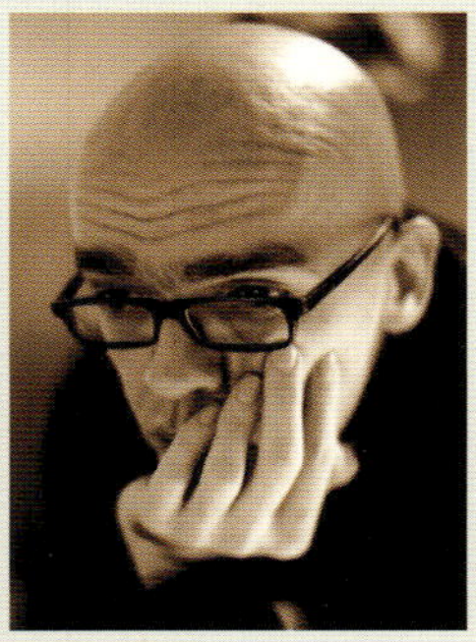

atelier tom vanhee
Belgium
www.ateliertomvanhee.be

PROTECTED 17TH-CENTURY HOUSES

PAGE 20 > 31

Credits

Engineer for the study of stability: Studiebureau Geert Rotsaert bvba

Materials and Suppliers

Roof covering: VMZINC
Parquet floor: Huys Concept NV
Roof panels beneath roofing tiles: Celit 4D
Insulation between old walls and new walls, in former farmhouse: Isover Multimax 30
Terrace floor: Ipe wood
Windows: steel. ODS Janssen
Roof: EPDM Resitrix
Stairs: steel
Balcony: galvanized steel
LED line: Selectron slimline 7mm
Promatect H-platen for fire resistance in the floor

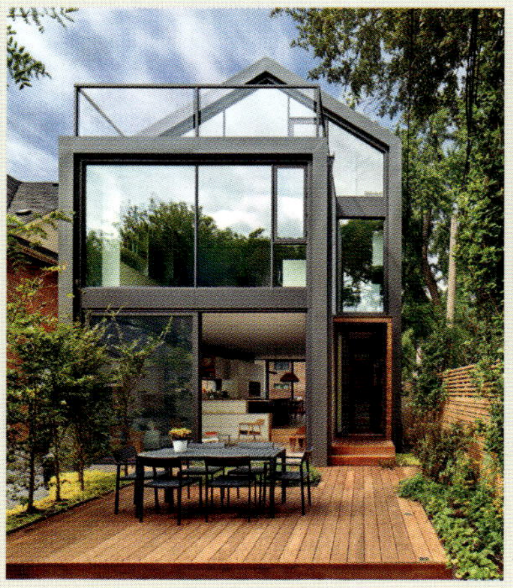

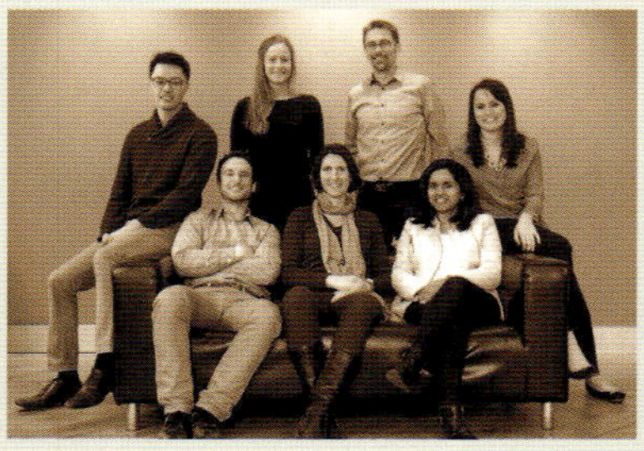

DUBBELDAM Architecture + Design
Canada
www.dubbeldam.ca

SKYGARDEN HOUSE

PAGE 32 > 43

Credits

Project team: Heather Dubbeldam, Principal Architect; Oliver Dang; Jacob JeBailey; Suzanna MacDonald; Amber Baechler
Landscape designer: Evergreen
Structural engineer: David Olivas
Windows: Eliud Chávez

Appliances and Materials

Flooring: Admonter Oak white by Moncer
Millwork: Lakeland Interiors, Kobi's Cabinets, and Gibson Greenwood
Stone: "Marengo" by Silestoneat kitchen counter and backsplash; "White Zeus" by Silestone at kitchen island counter; "Glacier white" by Corian at basement bathroom, en suite bathroom, and third floor bathroom
Tile: Architecture series, "Dark grey" by Stone Tile at vestibule and rear entrance; SRN Carrara by Saltillo Tiles at powder room; EVP Steel Gray by Saltillo Tile at basement bathroom floor and walls; "Edge smoke" by Stone Tile at basement bathroom shower floor; "Ageless white" by Stone Tile at laundry room; Architecture series "Medium grey" by Stone Tile at en suite bathroom; "Ageless white" by Stone Tile at third-floor bathroom floor; "Edge black" by Stone Tile at third-floor bathroom walls and shower floor
Windows: custom windows and Bigfoot sliding rear doors by Just Aluminum & Glass; window shades by Solarfective; skylights by Velux

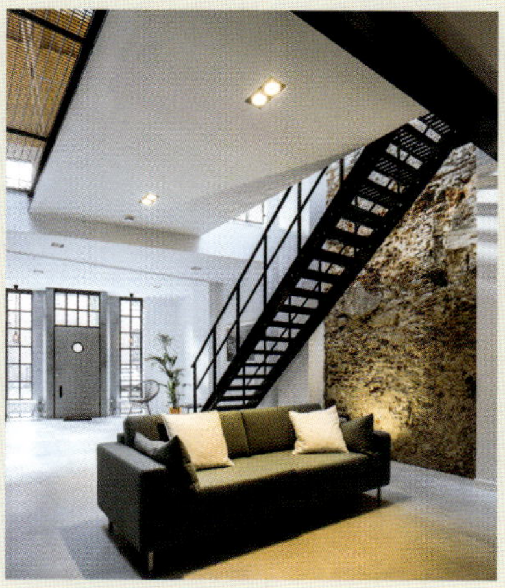

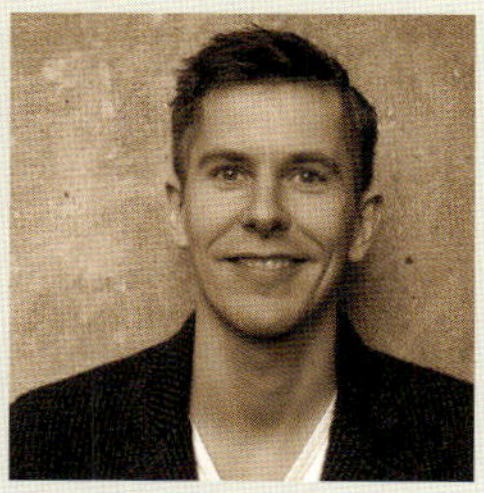

EVA
The Netherlands

www.e-v-a.net

LOFT 64

PAGE 44 > 55

Credits

Architect: Jeroen Makkink
Building contractor: Bouwcomfort Schijndel
Structural engineer: Martijn Bettonvil

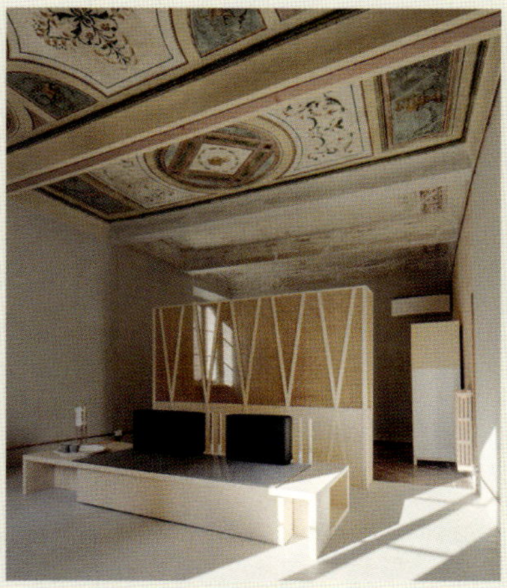

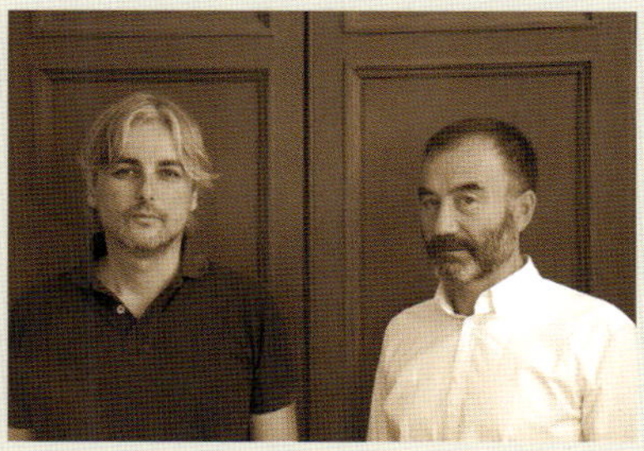

Archiplan Studio
Italy

www.archiplanstudio.com

BROLETTO UNO

PAGE 56 > 69

Credits

Architects: Diego Cisi, Stefano Gorni Silvestrini
Project team: Diego Cisi, Stefano Gorni Silvestrini, Jacopo Rettondini, Christian Tezza architects

Materials

Bedroom and bathroom floor: Resin
Sink: brushed steel and plywood
Bedroom screen: ashwood, cane, plywood
Bench: Frank wood

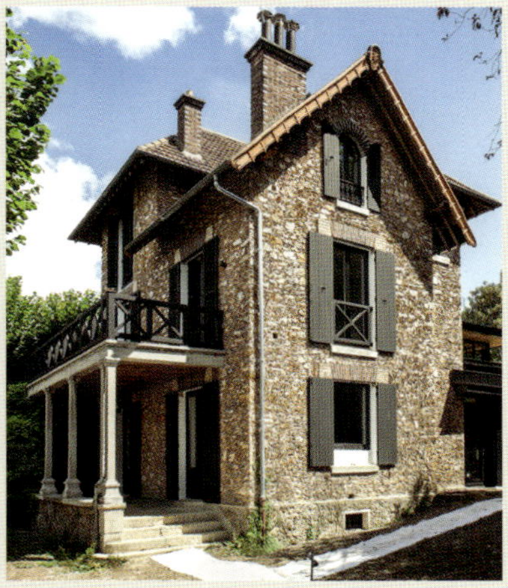

Atelier Lame Architects
France

www.atelierlame.com

SINGLE HOUSE IN HAUTS-DE-SEINE

PAGE 70 > 81

Credits

Architects: Angel Menendez and Alexandre Lahyani

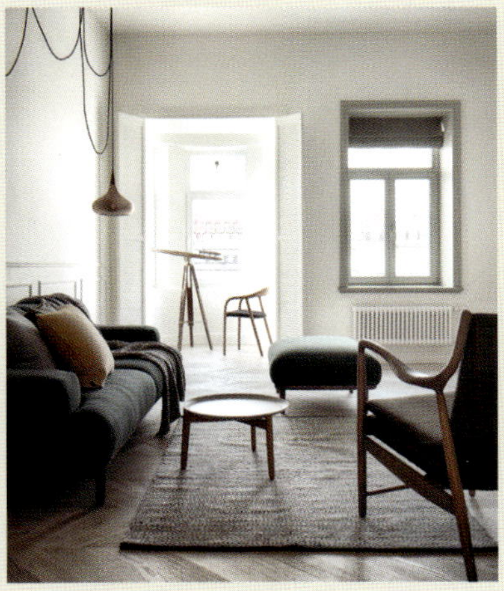

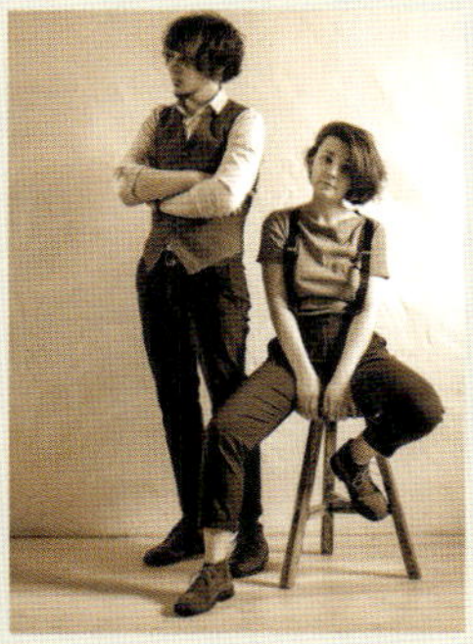

INT2architecture
Russia

www.int2architecture.ru

INTERIOR KG

PAGE 82 > 93

Credits

Architects: Alexander Malinin and Anastasia Sheveleva

Appliances and Sanitary ware

Kitchen appliances: Bosch, Elica
Custom wood fireplace: Grilli Caminetti, finishing - birch plywood
Ethanol fireplace: DP Design Elegante
Taps: Daniel
Bathtubs: Clou Inbe
Toilets: Roca
Sinks: Nero Ceramica
Kitchen sink: Bianco
Radiators: Instal Projekt

Finishing materials

Windows and window sills: Sokolka, oak.
Flooring: parquet T&G - Coswick: chevron, oak. Kitchen - American walnut.
Paint: DULUX BINDO 3 and 7
Cement tiles: Mocais Del Sur
Ceramic granite: Viva Ceramica
Doors: Jeld-Wen, pinewood
Invisible doors: UNION Chameleon
Moldings, plinth: Ultrawood
Cornice, ceiling rose: Gypsum

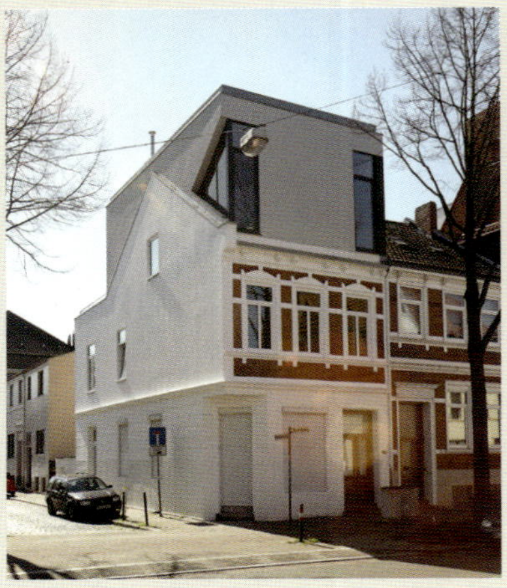

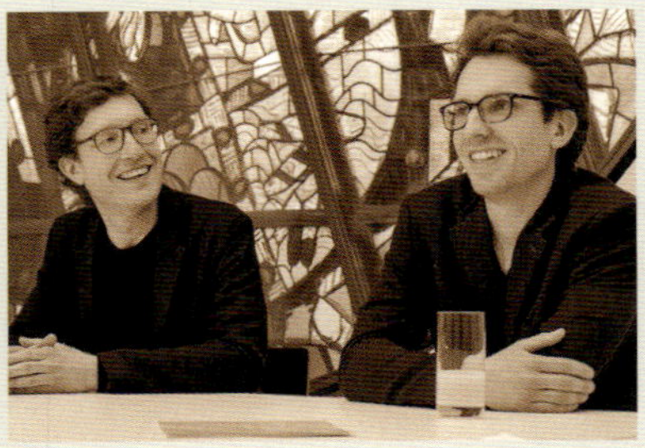

Wirth Architekten
Germany
www.wirth-architekten.com

HOUSE CHAPEAU

PAGE 94 > 101

Credits

Project team: Jan Wirth, Benjamin Wirth
Copyright: JUNG.DE Foto Markus Eichelmann

Materials

Concrete, gas concrete

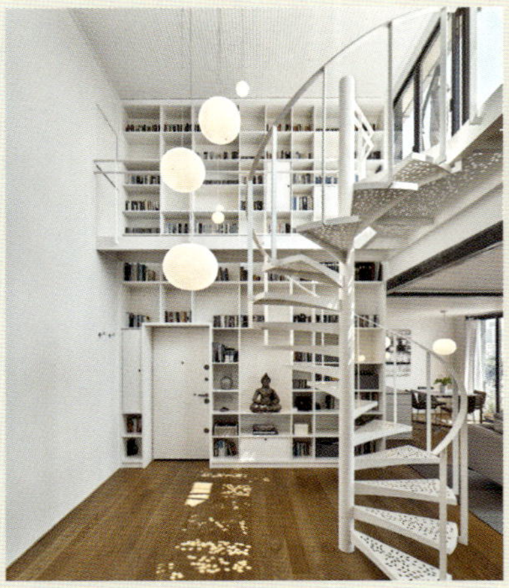

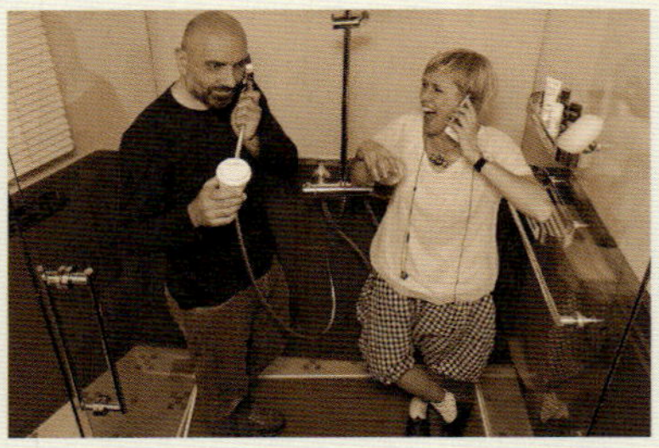

Ofist
Turkey
www.ofist.com

WHITE HOUSE

PAGE 102 > 111

Credits

Design Team: Ofist - Yasemin Arpac / Sebahattin Emir

Materials and Suppliers

Woodworks: Tayfur Somer
Ironworks: Sen Metal
Paintworks: Ali Aksu
Plumbing: Simtes
Electrical works: Ceysa Elektrik
Stoneworks: Ismail Ekmekci
Fireplace: Retas Somine (custom made)
Parquet: Parkes
Marbles: Silver Shadow by Tureks
Tap fittings and sink: Vitra / Artema
Toilet: Starck 3 by Duravit
Lighting elements: Globall by Flos

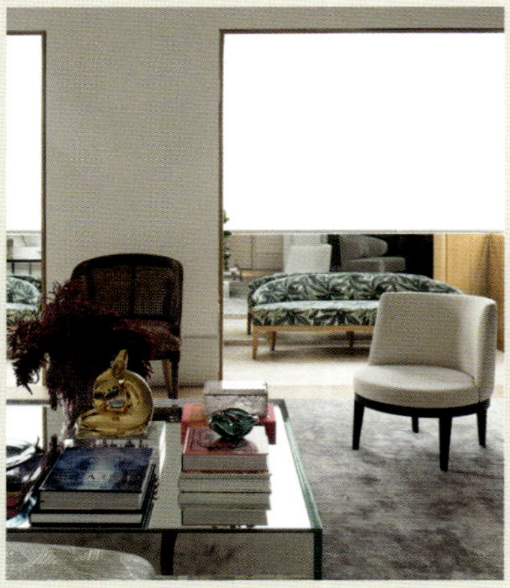

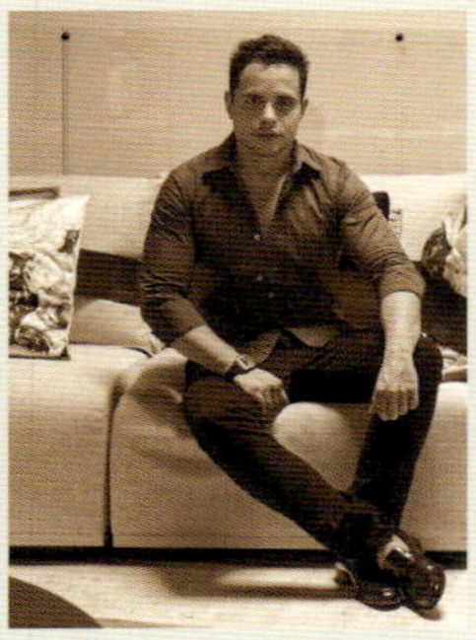

Diego Revollo
Brazil
www.diegorevollo.com.br

BORDÔ APARTMENT

PAGE 112 > 121

Materials

Interior flooring: Tauarí wood
Terrace flooring: oakwood
Panelling: Grigio gray wood

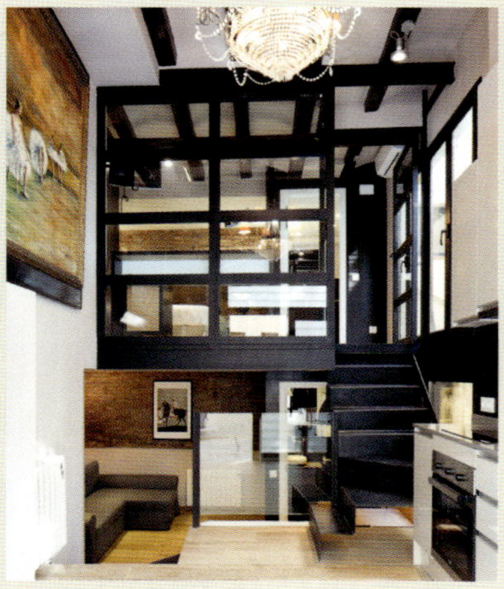

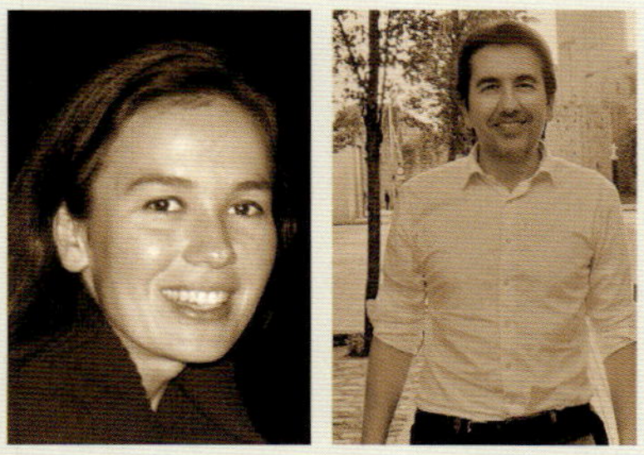

Estudio Atmosfera
Spain
www.atmosferari.com

LOFT CIUTAT VELLA

PAGE 122 > 132

Credits

Architect: Xavier Flores Puig
Works Manager: Eduardo Mateus
Artistic Direction: Cristina Mateus
Technical direction: Juan Manuel García Cerana, Jorge Gustavo Reghenaz
Photos: www.nicolasfotografia.com

Materials and Suppliers

Tiles: Baldosas Ferrolan (Stylnul Merbau roble and Argenta Kursaal RavenLapat Rc)
Kitchen cabinetry: TPC Cocinas
Countertop: Silestone
Kitchen appliances: BEKO
Wooden doors: Maderas San Pascual and Leroy Merlin
Bath cabinetry: Vidre Bany, laminated acacia Wood (Ambient One)
Bathroom fixtures and fittings:
Faucets: Prodelec
Toilet: Prodeloec (SFA SANITOP) Sanitarios Masià (Meridian-N, Debba)
Bath Screen: Novellini

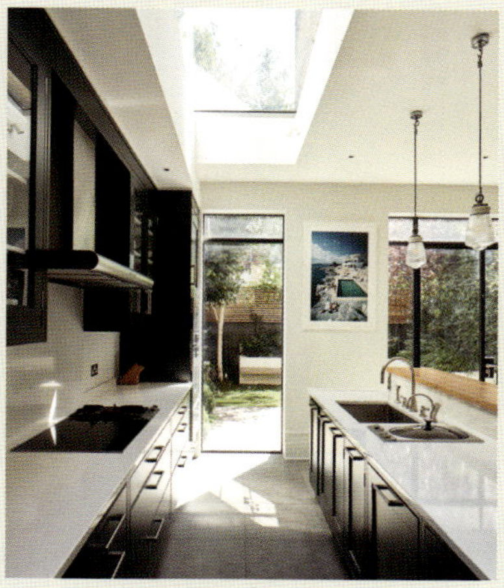

Robert Hirschfield Architects
United Kingdom

www.roberthirschfield.com

CONTEMPORARY CLASSIC

PAGE 132 > 141

Credits

Lead architects: Robert Hirschfield Architects
Structural engineer: Conisbee
Main contractor: Stem & Agate

Materials and Suppliers

Kitchen and woodwork: Woodstock Furniture
Glazing specialist: Lightfoot Windows

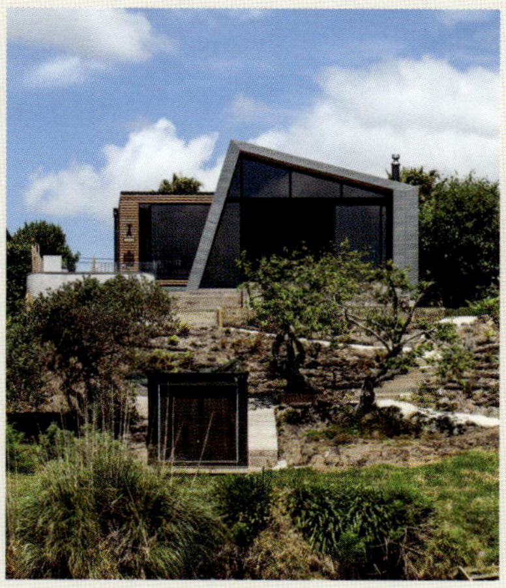

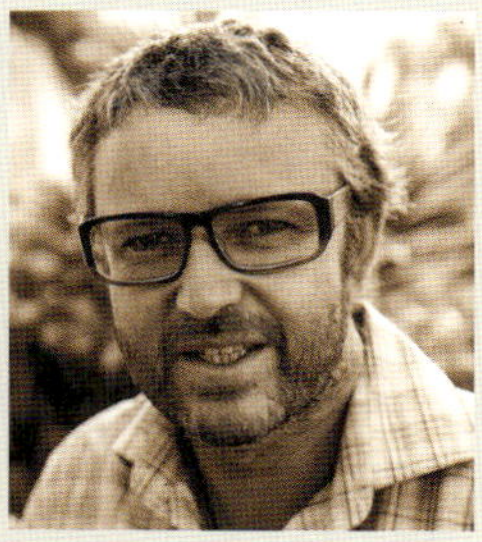

Dorrington Atcheson Architects
New Zealand

www.daa.co.nz

WINSOMERE CRESCENT

PAGE 142 > 151

Credits

Directors: Tim Dorrington and Sam Atcheson

Materials and Suppliers

Roof: zinc and membrane roofing
Cladding: zinc cladding, slatted cedar screens, existing brick–both bagged and solid plastered
Floor: Matai timber strip flooring
Hilton Solution, dyed nylon carpet from Irvine Floorcoverings, New York, cement tiles from Heritage Tiles
White railway tiles from Heritage Tiles, cork flooring from Cork Concepts
Other: Vitex and oak screens
media room with stone composite bar and solid oak-battened cellar

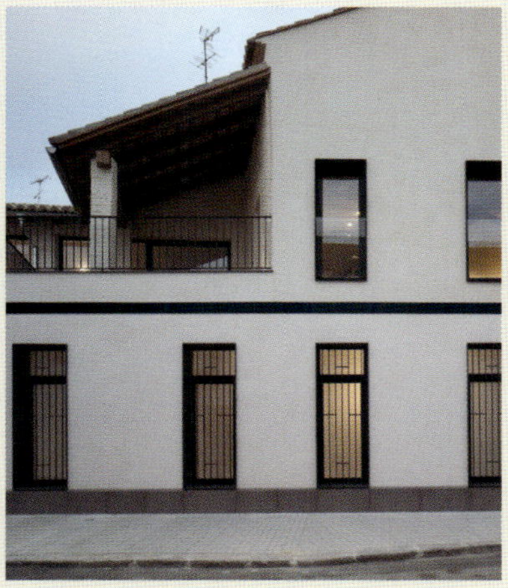

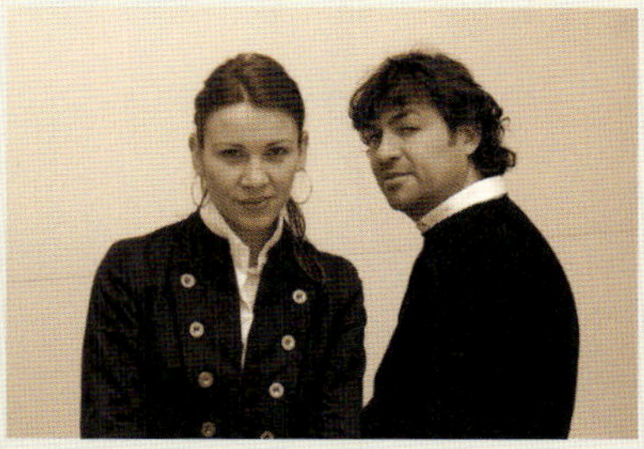

Studio Montañana
Spain

www.studiomontanyana.com

REFURBISHMENT OF A TRADITIONAL RURAL ARCHITECTURE RESIDENCE

PAGE 152 > 163

Credits

Project design, interior architecture direction, and design: Studio Montañana
Collaborating architect: Elías Macías
Builder: Vicente Ibáñez Construcciones

Materials and Suppliers

Joinery and wood rehabilitation: Carpintería Luis Boix

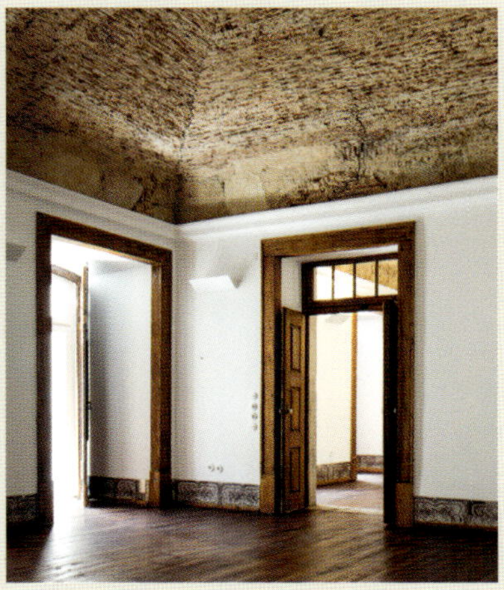

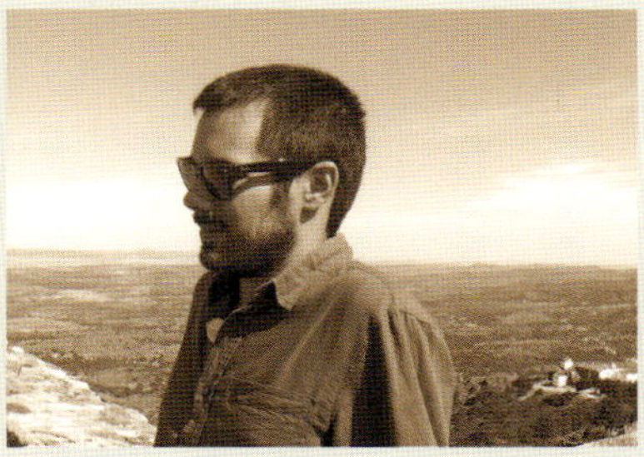

Raul Serra
Portugal

www.commerzn.com

APARTMENT IN CHIADO

PAGE 164 > 173

Credits

Architecture Project: Raul Serra
Contractor: Commerzn Lda
Manager, control, and inspection: Commerzn Lda
Engineering: Entrelogica Lda

Materials and Suppliers

Toilets: NIC Design
Faucets: CEA Design (Serie MILO 360)
Sinks: Exactistone
Joinery: NINI Lda
Kitchen: Bulthaup (Modelo B2)
PVC windows: Schüco
Outlets and switches: Berker (serie R Classic)
Lighting: Tromilux
AC and water heater: Daikin
Ventilation: France Air (Silens' Air)
Paint: CIN
Treatments and waterproofing: Labo

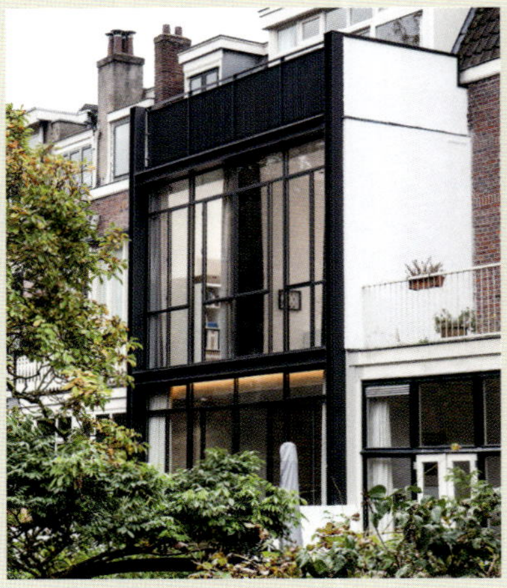

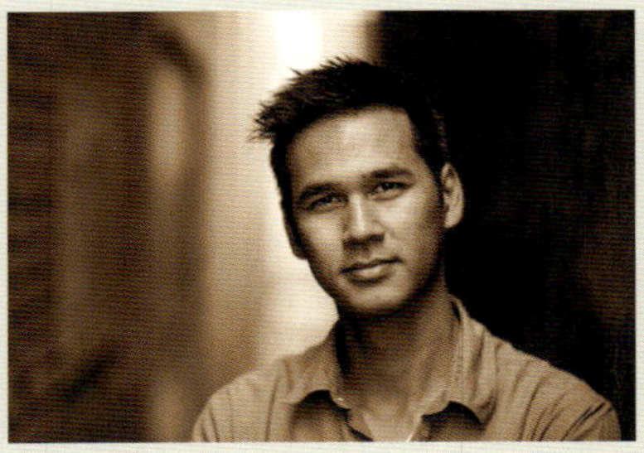

Lab-S
The Netherlands
www.lab-s.nl

RENOVATION AND EXTENSION OF A 30'S ROW HOUSE

PAGE 174 > 181

Credits

Architect: Sjoerd Schaapveld
Structural Engineer: Remco Luijendijk, www.rlca.nl
Builder: Somniare, www.somniare.nl
Steel window frames: Janisol Arte By Jansen (ODS geveltechniek)

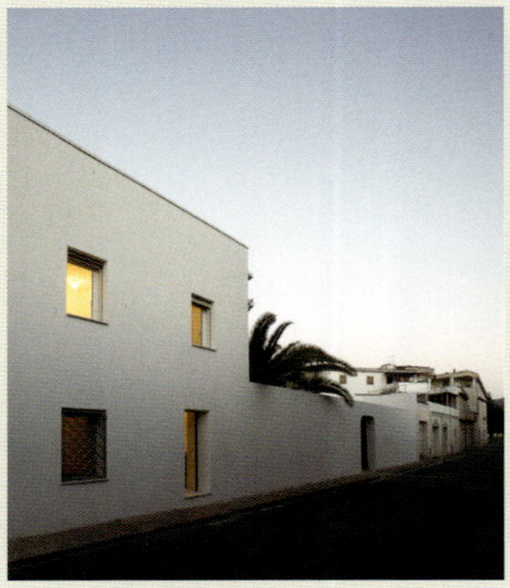

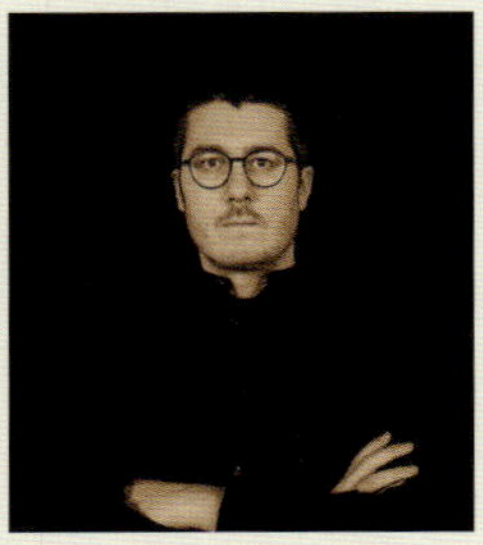

Matteo Foresti
Sweden
www.matteoforesti.com

VILLA RENOVATION CC

PAGE 182 > 193

Credits
Architect: Matteo Foresti
Structural Engineer: Michele Casanova - Gmcstudio
Project manager: Massimiliano Meloni
Builder: Alfredo Murtas - Rcccostruzioni

Materials

Interior and exterior walls: white plaster
Ground floor interior flooring: stone, Carrara marble, matt finishing
First floor interior flooring: oak wood, matte white finishing
Ground floor exteriors: stone, gray porphyr tiles
Kitchen countertop: Okite, colour white

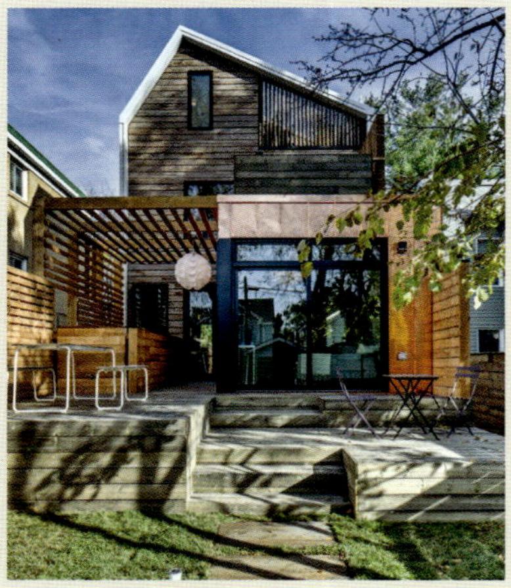

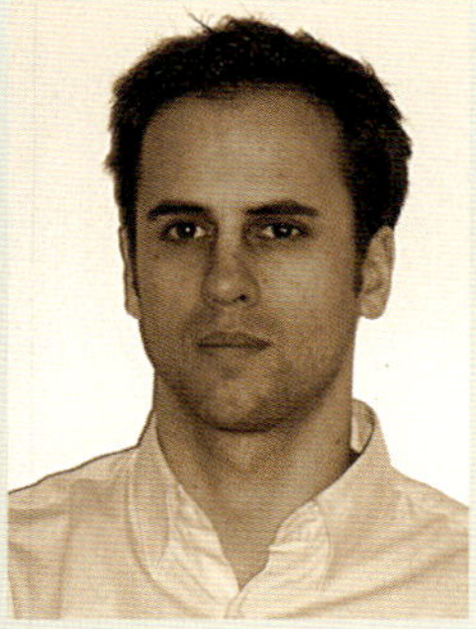

baukultur/ca
Canada
www.baukultur.ca

46H

PAGE 194 > 205

Credits

Project team: Felix Leicher, Lead Architect
Civil engineer: Engineering Link
General contractor: Sasha Lerkhbaum / TIPEQ
HVAC design: BEC Consulting
Kitchen manufacturer: Mooza Wood Arts
Staging: Modern Staging Modern Spaces

Materials and Suppliers

Doors: solid-white doors with black hinges and hardware
Faucets: Hansgrohe
Flooring: white-washed and brushed solid-white oak planks
Front and rear: wood siding with thermally modified larch wood
Front porch: exterior MDF and detailing in black-stained rhombus facade
Kitchen cabinets: super matte white and black with walnut and copper detailing
Kitchen countertop: white quartz
Rear addition: standing-seam copper cladding
Sidewalls: white metal siding
Tiles: Céragrès Canada
Windows: black fiberglass windows and patio doors, double-pane glazing

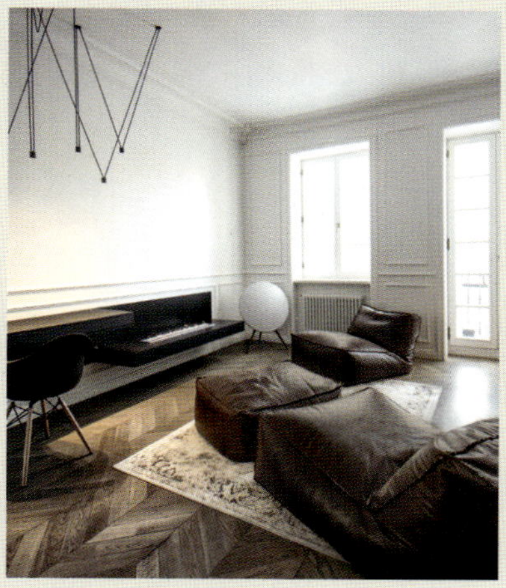

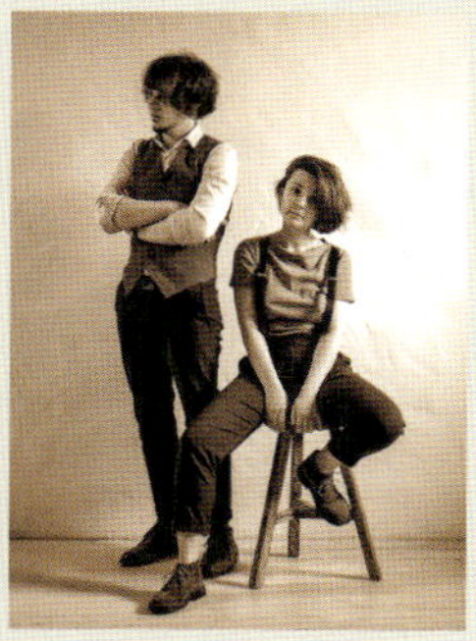

INT2architecture
Russia

www.int2architecture.ru

INTERIOR AM

PAGE 206 > 213

Credits

Architects: Alexander Malinin and Anastasia Sheveleva

Materials and Suppliers

Pendant light above the bar: axo light (AX20)
Pendant light above the desk: Vibia (Match)
Bar chair: Kristalia (BCN)
Mirror (round): Gubi (ADNET CIRCULAIRE)
Posters: Ruben Ireland
Kitchen, desk, and ethanol fireplace stand, cabinet under the sink: Giulia Novars

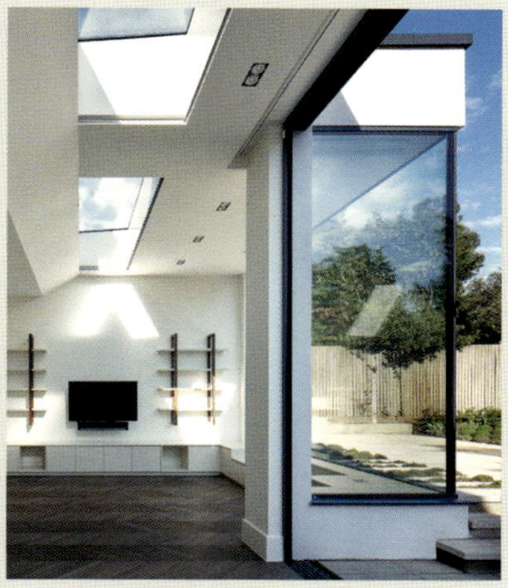

Robert Hirschfield Architects
United Kingdom

www.roberthirschfield.com

OPEN HOUSE

PAGE 214 > 223

Credits

Lead architects: Robert Hirschfield Architects
Structural engineer: Conisbee
Quantity surveyor: Trogal Griffin Associates
Main contractor: Vital Building Services
Designer, manufacturer: Fowler & Co

Materials and Suppliers

Woodwork: Dot Bespoke
Kitchen designer: Bulthaup
Glazing specialist: Culmax

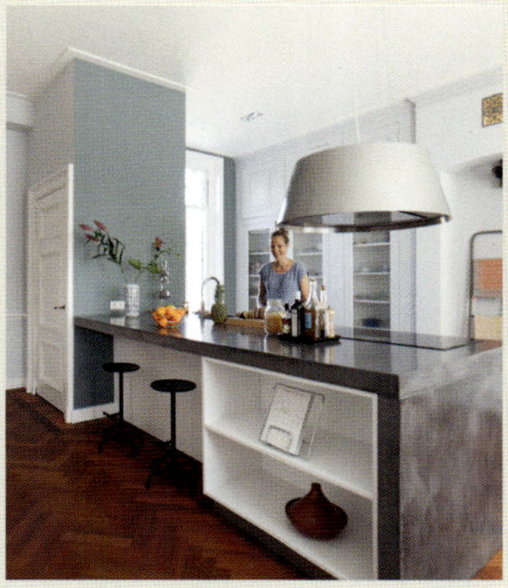

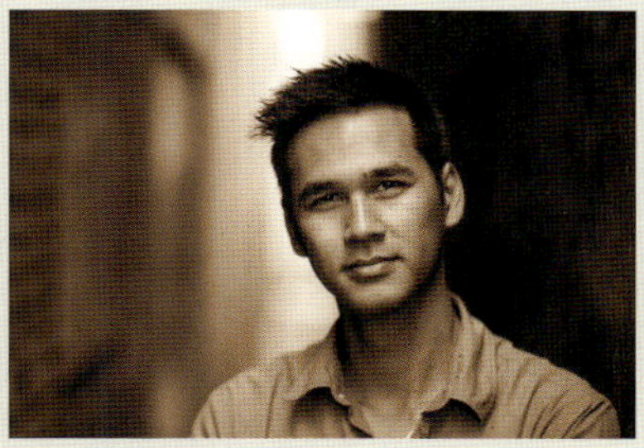

Lab-S
The Netherlands

www.lab-s.nl

CREATING A NEW HOME IN A NATIONAL MONUMENT IN UTRECHT

PAGE 224 > 232

Credits

Architect: Sjoerd Schaapveld
Builder: Westor, www.westor.nl

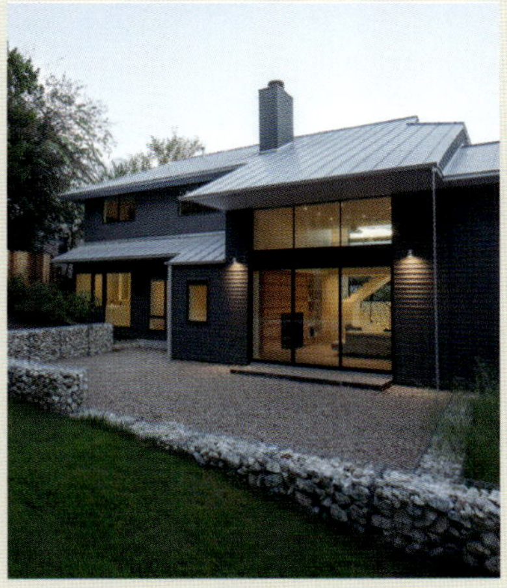

Arbib Hughey Design
United States

www.arbibhughey.com

WINTER PARK

PAGE 232 > 241

Credits

Principals: Ben Arbib and Ed Hughey, AIA
Builder: Alex Pettitt; Spring Builders, LLC
www.springbuilders.net
Engineer: Tats Kiguchi, P.E., S.E.; Leap! Structures
www.leapstructures.com

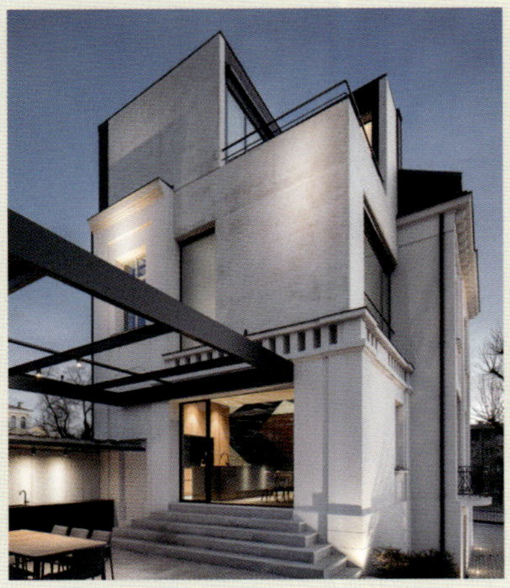

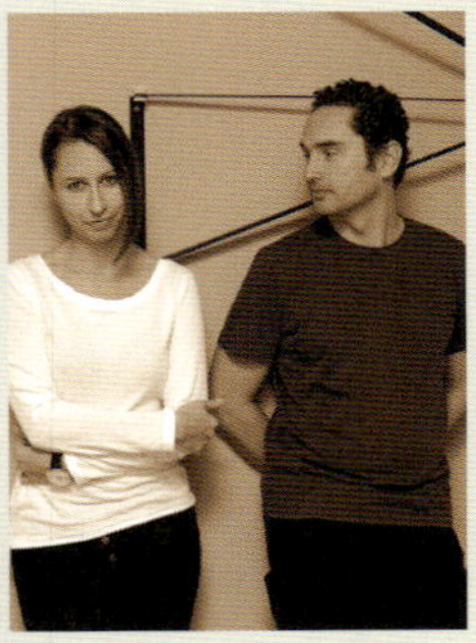

I/O architects
Bulgaria

www.ioarchitects.com

WHITE CONCRETE HOUSE

PAGE 242 > 253

Credits

Design team: Georgi Katov, Viara Jeliazkova, Rositsa Hristova
Structural Engineering: NeoDesk, Petar Chernev

Materials and Suppliers

Sanitary ware: Agape
Sofa: Alivar (Swing)
Table: Artisan (Latus)
Light switches and sockets: Berker (serie R Classic)
Cooktop extractor: Bora (BHU)
Thermal insulation: Foamglass
Steel window frames: Jansen (Arte)
Lamps: Jielde (Loft)
Kitchen cabinets: Key Sbabo (KU45)
Armchair: Mooi (Zio)
Bathroom taps: Zucchetti (Pan)

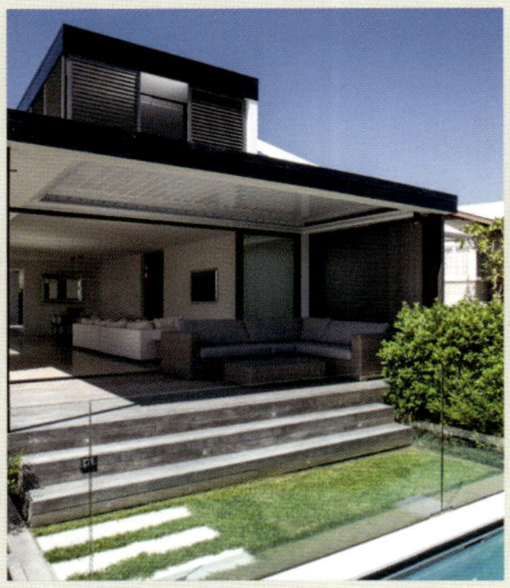

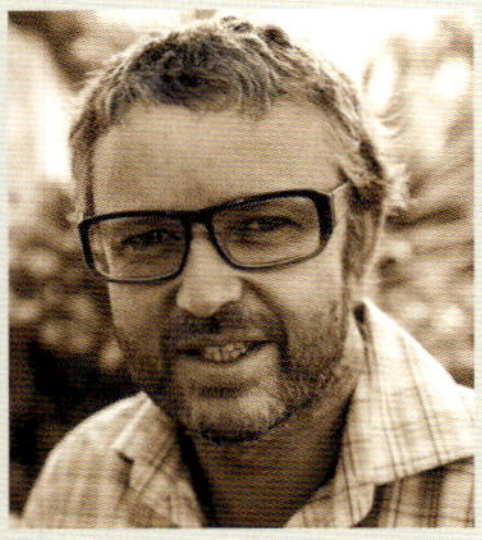

Dorrington Atcheson Architects
New Zealand

www.daa.co.nz

MARINE PARADE 2

PAGE 254 > 265

Credits

Directors: Tim Dorrington and Sam Atcheson
Builder: Boyd Cox Construction Ltd.

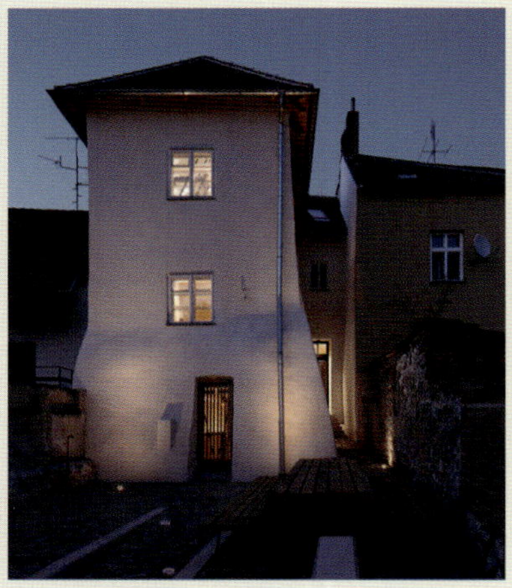

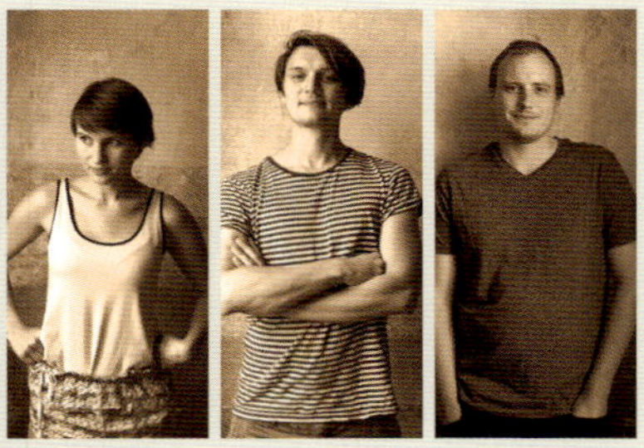

ORA
Czech Republic

www.o-r-a.cz

ŠTAJNHAUS

PAGE 266 > 279

Credits

Architect: ORA - Jan Hora, Barbora Hora, Jan Veisser

Materials and Suppliers

Lights: Wever Ducré (RAY mini 2.0, BOX, TUBE)
Sanitation: Laufen Pro
Plumbing: Kludi Bozz (mainly)
Heating: ISAN atol

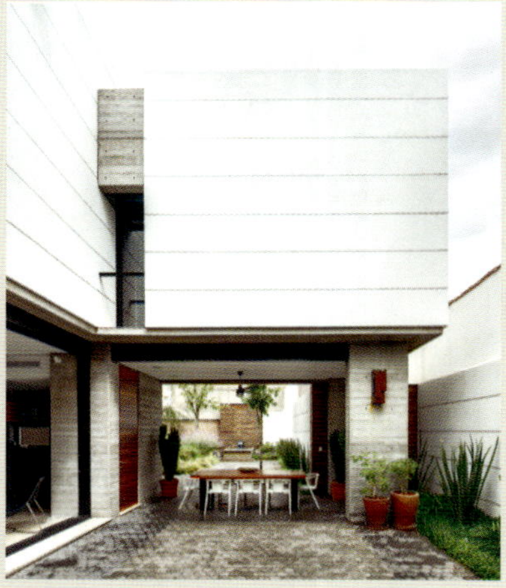

Landscape Architecture Border
Paisaje Arquitectura Frontera
LABor

LABor Studio
Mexico

www.laborstudio.com

C2A HOUSE

PAGE 280 > 289

Credits

Project team: Víctor Mendoza, Diana Ordoque, Pavel Rentería, Marysol Enríquez, Fernanda Arriola, Ilse Esparza
General contractor: Mario Reyes / LABor Studio
Interior designer: Claudia Garza / LABor Studio
Landscape designer: Evergreen
Structural engineer: David Olivas
Windows: Eliud Chávez

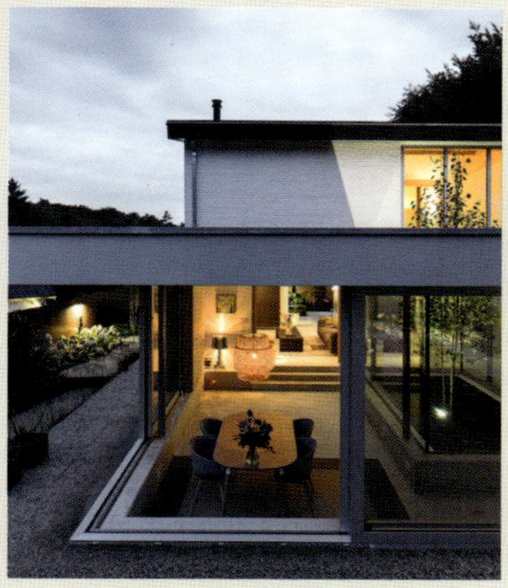

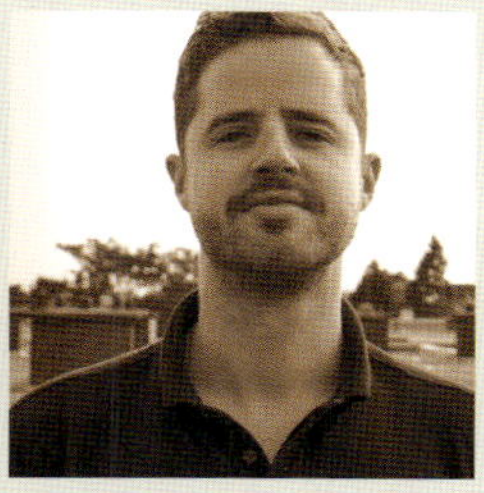

Bloot Architecture
The Netherlands
www.bloota.nl

PATIO HOUSE

PAGE 290 > 301

Credits

Lead Architect: Tjeerd Bloothoofd
Contractor: Jager B.V.
Constructor: Janssen Constructie Bouwadvies; Joop Janssen
Building physics: Bouwkundig Bureau Rhombus

Materials and Suppliers

Aluminum window frames: Aluprof
Hinges (hidden): Tectus
Sliding rails: Henderson

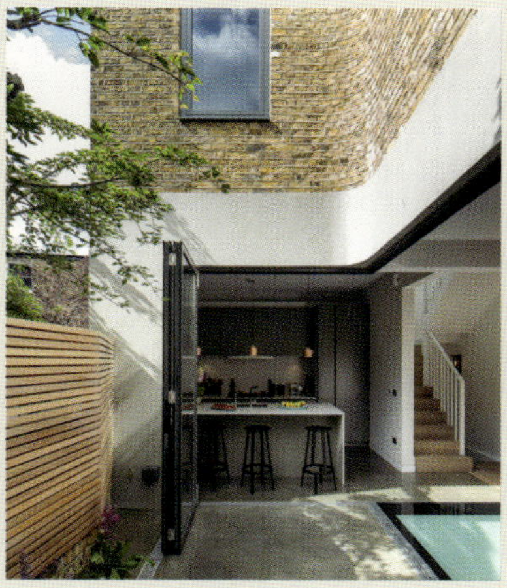

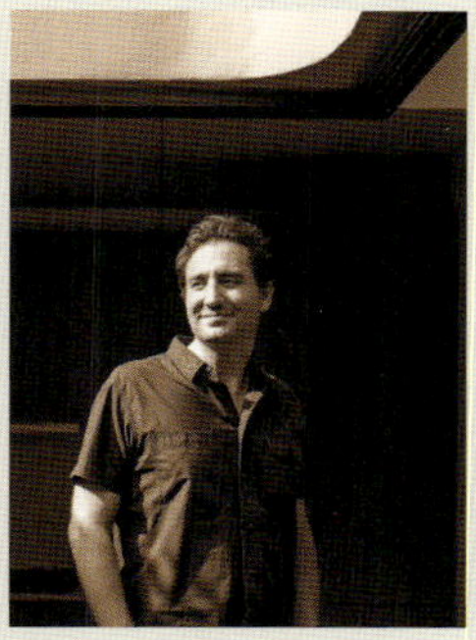

Neil Dusheiko Architects
United Kingdom
www.neildusheiko.com

BRACKENBURY HOUSE

PAGE 302 > 315

Credits

Engineer: Fothergills
www.fothergill.uk.com
Basement works: Structural London
www.structurallondon.com
Party wall: Marc Newton
www.mnasurveyors.co.uk
Quantity surveyor: Geoff Tyler / Vincent and Partners

Materials and Suppliers

Concrete floor: Lazenby
Timber floor: Parkwood Interiors
Kitchen: Schmidt Kitchens
Plumbing fixtures: Just add water
Glazing: EKS
Colorful furniture: Flock / Jenny Wingfield
Lighting: Heals
Tiles: Pentagon Tiles
M&E: Nuaire
Pocket doors: Portman
Ironmongery: SDS
Woodwork: Hoktiff
Brass switches: Sparks
Heating: Timoleon
Blinds: Interiors of Chiswick
Security: Banhams

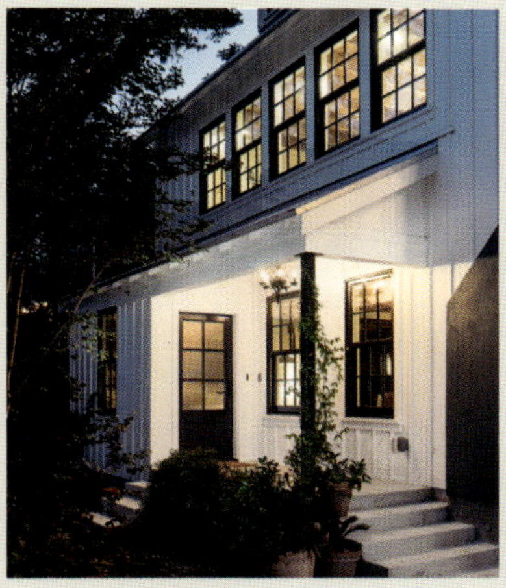

Element 5 Architecture
United States
www.element5architecture.com

CLARKSVILLE COTTAGE ADDITION AND RENOVATION

PAGE 316 > 327

Credits

Principal: Richard Hughes
Builder: Larry Anderson Construction

Second printing

Original texts by Macarena Abascal Valdenebro,
Francesc Zamora Mola
Copyediting by Macarena Abascal Valdenebro
German translations by Thinking Abroad
French translation by Thinking Abroad
English translation by James Buschman
Copyediting by Thinking Abroad

Editorial coordination by Regine Freyberg
Art direction by Mireia Casanovas Soley
Design production by Claudia Martínez Alonso
Layout by Cristina Simó Perales
Production by Nele Jansen
Color separation by Robin Alexander Hopp

ISBN 978-3-96171-131-4

Library of Congress Number: 2018904690

Printed in the Czech Republic by PBtisk a.s.

Bibliographic information published by the Deutsche Nationalbibliothek:
The Deutsche Nationalbibliothek lists this publication in the Deutsche Nationalbibliografie; detailed bibliographic data are available on the Internet at dnb.dnb.de.

MIX
Paper from responsible sources
FSC® C004378

Published by teNeues Publishing Group

teNeues Verlag GmbH
Werner-von-Siemens-Straße 1
86159 Augsburg, Germany

Düsseldorf Office
Waldenburger Straße 13
41564 Kaarst, Germany
e-mail: books@teneues.com

Augsburg/München Office
Werner-von-Siemens-Straße 1
86159 Augsburg, Germany
e-mail: bbarlet@teneues.com

Berlin Office
Lietzenburger Straße 53
10719 Berlin, Germany
e-mail: ajasper@teneues.com

Press department Stefan Becht
Phone: +49-152-2874-9508 /
+49-6321-97067-99
e-mail: sbecht@teneues.com

teNeues Publishing Company
350 Seventh Avenue, Suite 301
New York, NY 10001, USA
Phone: +1-212-627-9090
Fax: +1-212-627-9511

www.teneues.com

teNeues Publishing Group
Augsburg / München
Berlin
Düsseldorf
London
New York

teNeues